P9-CFP-252

An Illustrated History of the

R·A·F

An Illustrated History Of The

R·A·F

Roy Conyers Nesbit

COOMBE
BOOKS

Author's Acknowledgements

The photographs, captions and text of this book are the product of a considerable amount of detailed research, and I am extremely grateful for the assistance given to me by officials and staff of the following organisations:

Aeroplane Monthly, Cheam
Imperial War Museum, London
Ministry of Defence, Air Historical Branch, London
Royal Air Force Museum, Hendon
Public Record Office, Kew

I am also indebted to the following for supplying photographs:

Flight Officer Felicity Ashbee, WAAF; Aviation Bookshop; Aeroplane Monthly; Ministry of Defence, Air Historical Branch; Jeremy Flack, Aviation Photographs International; Royal Air Force Museum, Hendon;
The late Wg Cdr Frederic E. Burton OBE, DFC, RAF;
Mr T. Malcolm English; The Keystone Collection;
Flt Lt Maurice A. Pocock, RAFVR;
The late Flt Lt Antony M. Puckle, MBE, RAFVR;
Flt Lt Ken Reeves, RAF; Herr Hans Schliephake;
The late Wg Cdr Arthur H. Simmonds, DFC, RAF;
Vintage Magazine Co., London.

My thanks are also due, for help in research and in checking captions or narrative, to:

Sqn Ldr Dudley Cowderoy, RAFVR;
Sqn Ldr Norman Hearn-Phillips, AFC, DFM, RAF;
Capt Clive Leach, RAFVR; Mr Harry M Moyle, RAFVR;
Mr Philip N Owen, RAF; Mr Roger Hayward

Designed by
Stonecastle Graphics Ltd.

Paintings by
Frank Wootton P.P.G.Av.A.

Editorial
Gill Waugh and Jane Adams

Commissioning Editor
Andrew Preston

Commissioning Assistant
Laura Potts

Production
Ruth Arthur, David Proffit,
Sally Connolly and Karen Staff

Director of Production
Gerald Hughes

2404 The Illustrated History of the RAF
This edition published in 1999 by Coombe Books
An imprint of Quadrillion Publishing Ltd,
Godalming, Surrey, GU7 1XW, UK

Printed and bound in China
ISBN 0 86283 814 2

ADER'S BUS Co
RUNNING

CONTENTS

CHAPTER 1

WAITING FOR WINGS

"What is the use of a balloon?" was a question put to Benjamin Franklin, when he was American plenipotentiary to France in the early 1780s. "What is the use of a new-born infant?" replied the great statesman and scientist.

For centuries, scientists and philosophers had been obsessed with the flapping of birds' wings as a means of ascending into the air but, since this method had proved disastrous for man, the balloon offered an alternative. When the first manned and free flight was made, in a hot-air balloon in Paris on 21 November 1783, the military possibilities became apparent to many observers. In 1785, a successful crossing of the Channel was made in a hydrogen balloon and in the same year two British officers travelled about twenty miles from London and landed unharmed in Essex.

The first balloon corps was formed in France in 1793, and was subsequently employed on military operations. In the early nineteenth century the British scientist Sir George Cayley set out the aerodynamic principles for heavier-than-air machines, using gliders for experiments. But in the absence of a compact means of propulsion in that period, developments continued to be concentrated on balloons. Captive observation balloons were used in the American Civil War of 1861-5, and free-flying balloons were used in the siege of Paris in 1870. In the British army, balloon sections accompanied expeditions to Bechuanaland in 1884 and to the Sudan in 1885. A permanent balloon section was formed within the Corps of Royal Engineers in 1890. This carried out reconnaissance duties during the South African War ten years later, to the fury of the Boers, who looked on such technical superiority as unfair.

After the South African War, the activities of the Balloon Factory, which had been opened at Farnborough in Hampshire in 1894, were scaled down. Meanwhile, experiments in France had resulted in the development of an electrically propelled airship in 1884. This was non-rigid, but semi-rigid airships followed in that country. In Germany, it was Graf von Zeppelin who developed the fully rigid and steerable airship powered by internal combustion engines. By 1909, Zeppelins had become established as passenger carriers and were also used in military and naval exercises.

In an attempt to keep up with the pace of developments abroad, technicians at Farnborough completed in September 1907 the army airship *Nulli Secundus,* constructed from a balloon covered with a net from which was suspended a gondola. Powered by a 40-h.p. engine, it flew on 5 October on a journey of three and a half hours to London and then landed at Crystal Palace. The flight caused much excitement, particularly since the Kaiser was staying in Buckingham Palace as a guest of King Edward VII.

In Britain, non-rigid and therefore collapsible airships were termed B-limps, giving rise to the somewhat derogatory name which then entered the English language. *Nulli Secundus* was followed by the semi-rigid *Nulli Secundus II,* and then by *Beta* and *Gamma.* Although these British airships suffered from engine troubles, they were responsible for the formation of a nucleus of aircrews and ground crews. Two more airships were ordered, a non-rigid and a semi-rigid, both from France.

Below: *The British Army Dirigible No. 1 was named* Nulli Secundus *('Second to None') and first ascended from Farnborough on 10 September 1907. It had a length of 122 feet, a diameter of 26 feet, and a capacity of 50,000 cubic feet. The engine was French, a 50 h.p. Antoinette. The airship made only one long-distance flight in its original form, from Farnborough to London and then to Crystal Palace on 5 October 1907. It was destroyed in a storm five days later.*

Source: RAF Museum 331113

FOREWORD

At the beginning of September, 1940, I joined 616 (South Yorkshire) Squadron at Coltishall in Norfolk. They had just arrived from Kenley, near Croydon, and in eight days had lost five pilots, killed or missing, with five others wounded and in hospital, and had been 'taken out of the line' to regain their strength. These were bad times for the Squadron, Fighter Command, and England, because the Germans, having conquered Europe in six weeks with *Blitzkrieg*, their new and terrifying style of air-ground warfare, were using the same strategy against these Islands – their intention being to take out Fighter Command and gain air superiority so that their *panzers* could cross the Channel unopposed; and during those fine autumn days they nearly succeeded because we were losing one hundred and twenty five experienced pilots each week who could only be replaced by sixty-five inexperienced pilots like me.

One would have thought, therefore, that with Fighter Command wasting away morale might have been a little shaken. On the contrary, it was superb, and this was well-illustrated to me when one evening all off duty ranks were recalled to the airfield.

Once there, we found Alert No 1, 'invasion imminent and probable within twelve hours', had been declared and our defences were to be brought to the highest state of readiness. The officer's mess was crowded, confused and noisy – that is until Squadron Leader Douglas Bader stumped in and demanded to know what all the flap was about. On being told, he said: 'So the bastards are coming. Bloody good show! Think of all those juicy targets on those nice flat beaches. What shooting!' And he made a rude sound with his lips which was meant to resemble a ripple of machine-gun fire. This was my first encounter with the already legendary Douglas Bader. His spirited and spontaneous riposte serves as a good example of how high morale was, even though the odds were stacked against us.

This book has been written in an easily accessible and informative style which charts the development of the Royal Air Force from the days of experimental balloons and kites, to the modern sophistication of today's advanced technology. It is superbly illustrated with photographs, diagrams and posters, many previously unpublished. These factors combine to produce what I consider to be a vivid and fascinating portrait of the Royal Air Force, surely a fitting tribute to the men and women with whom I served, and to those who today maintain its traditions of enthusiasm, high spirits and comradeship.

Johnnie Johnson.

AIR VICE-MARSHAL J. E. JOHNSON, CB, CBE, DSO, DFC, DL

However, events were taking place which overshadowed the development of airships. On 17 December 1903, near Kitty Hawk beach in North Carolina, the brothers Wilbur and Orville Wright made a powered flight in their biplane *Flyer*, after seven years of research and development. Strangely, this success met at first with indifference in the U.S., where the government dismissed the brothers as charlatans. The Wright brothers continued experimenting and offered their patents and machines to the British, but these were refused by the War Office in 1906 and by the Admiralty in 1907. A French syndicate, far less sceptical, thereupon purchased the inventions and, with the active assistance of Wilbur Wright, took the lead in aeronautical progress. In Britain, development was left to the private enterprise of such pioneers as Robert Blackburn, F. Handley Page, A.V. Roe, Horace and Oswald Short, and T.O.M. Sopwith. Military aeronautical expenditure by the British government amounted to no more than £13,750. Then, on 25 July 1909, Louis Blériot took off in his monoplane from Les Boraques near Calais and, thirty-seven minutes later, landed on a hilltop near Dover. The significance of this flight was not lost on the British government and its military authorities. At the same time, the Press also created public interest in flying.

The military airfield of Larkhill in Wiltshire was opened, while Hendon became the civilian airfield for London. In March 1910, the Royal Aero Club issued its first pilot's certificate. In April of the following year, the War Office formed an Air Battalion at Farnborough, consisting of two companies. No. 1 for balloons, kites and airships, and

Above: *The first Zeppelin, LZ-1* (Luftschiff Zeppelin Nummer 1*), was assembled in a floating hangar on the Bodensee (Lake Constance) and launched on 2 July 1900.*

Source: Air Historical Branch (RAF), MoD, private collection no PRM3478

No. 2 for aeroplanes. Based largely on French designs and adapted French machines, four categories of aircraft were designated. These were the S.E. (Santos Experimental, after Santos-Dumont, the first man to fly an aeroplane in France), the B.E. (Blériot Experimental), the F.E. (Farman Experimental, after the brothers Henri and Maurice Farman), and the R.E. (Reconnaissance Experimental).

Britain still lagged well behind France. In 1911, over 200 aircraft could be seen during army manoeuvres in France, whereas the British army and navy could muster only twelve, with three airships. It was also known that Germany possessed a fleet of thirty Zeppelins. Public alarm at this state of affairs led to a consideration within the Committee of Imperial Defénce, which recommended the setting up of a new service to be known as the Flying Corps, with a military wing and a naval wing, as well as a central flying school. King George V, who had succeeded King Edward VII, granted the royal warrant for the Royal Flying Corps, which came into being on 13 April 1912. A flying badge and the motto *Per Ardua ad Astra* were also approved. The factory at Farnborough became the Royal Aircraft Factory. Fortunately, Britain possessed the technical expertise and industrial strength to begin catching up with her continental rivals, following these far-seeing arrangements.

The Admiralty was determined that no independent service should have control over affairs which it considered were within its authority, and the naval wing began to operate separately from the military wing. The Central Flying School at Upavon in Wiltshire began training military crews, while the naval wing opened a school at Eastchurch in Kent. On 1 July 1914, the Royal Naval Air Service was formed, and the Royal Flying Corps continued solely as an army air force.

Flying training in the RFC took place in Farman, Avro, B.E.2 and B.E.8 biplanes, with engines ranging from 50-h.p. to 80-h.p. All the engines were French. Trainees were recruited from all branches of the army, not solely from the Royal Engineers. Aerobatics were forbidden, and a pilot usually logged about twenty-five hours before being awarded his wings.

At Farnborough, the Royal Aircraft Factory opted for stability in aircraft as its main criterion. In this period, it was envisaged that the primary military role of the aeroplane would be an extension of that of the balloon, observation of enemy dispositions and artillery spotting. Early monoplanes proved difficult to fly and crashed more frequently than biplanes, although they were faster and sometimes more agile. Thus development was concentrated on biplanes, resulting in serious disadvantages to the RFC within the next few years. The engines in these biplanes were usually of the pusher variety, and the observer sat in the nose, from where he had an excellent view. The pilot sat behind the observer and behind him was the engine. Fewer early experiments were made with tractor engines in aircraft. Little consideration was given to armament or to bombing enemy troops.

Above: *The army airship HMA* Beta, *84 feet long and powered by a single 25 h.p. engine, made her first experimental flights in June 1908. In a reconstructed form with a 33 h.p. engine, she flew from Farnborough to London and back on 3 June 1910. Subsequently, she took part in army manoeuvres and became part of the RFC's Military Wing. This photograph was taken in 1914.*

Source: Air Historical Branch (RAF), MoD, private collection.

Left: *HMA* Delta *entered service with No. 1 (Airship) Squadron of the RFC in November 1912, joining the other two airships* Beta *and* Gamma. *The airships of the RFC were turned over to the RNAS when it was formed on 1 July 1914.*

Source: Air Historical Branch (RAF), MoD, private collection 176/5/45

The naval wing, or RNAS, did not look solely to the Royal Aircraft Factory for its aircraft. It turned instead of private industry, with the result in the early years that its aircraft were often superior to those of the RFC. Its policy tended towards aggression, in addition to employing aircraft for observation. Experiments took place with flying aircraft off ships, developing seaplanes, dropping 100-lb bombs and even torpedoes. It also set up a string of ten air bases around the British coasts, for one of the traditional roles of the Royal Navy was the defence of the British Isles.

On 1 September 1913, a separate Directorate of Military Aeronautics was established under Brigadier-General David Henderson, reporting directly to the Secretary of State instead of the War Office. The following year, £1,000,000 was allocated to the RFC, enabling orders to be placed throughout the infant aircraft industry and not solely with the Royal Aircraft Factory. By then, six RFC squadrons had been formed or were coming into being. With the approach of war, privately owned aircraft were requisitioned and lodged in the aircraft park at Farnborough, which was a maintenance and supply depot.

Seven days after the declaration of war on 4 August 1914, four squadrons of the RFC, with a collection of sixty-three aircraft which included Blériots, B.E.2s, B.E.8s, Farmans, Sopwith Tabloids and Avro 504s were either flown to France or taken by sea. Brigadier-General Henderson accompanied them as their commander. The RNAS, which mustered seventy-one aircraft and seven airships, set up a small wing at Dunkirk and also began patrolling the North Sea from British bases. These two air forces were not fully prepared for war, but they did not lack fighting spirit or enterprise.

Above: *The RFC's observation balloons were operated from winches, principally to direct artillery fire. Guide ropes were paid out as the balloon ascended.*

Air Historical Branch (RAF), MoD, private collection no 94

Above: *This tractor monoplane was a Blériot XI, similar to the machine in which Louis Blériot crossed the Channel on 25 July 1909, but fitted with a more powerful Gnome rotary engine instead of the original Anzani 35 h.p. The RFC first received deliveries of these machines in 1912. In the early months of the war, the Blériot XI was one of the most widely used reconnaissance aircraft. It was unarmed, apart from rifles and revolvers carried by the pilot. The photograph of this machine, painted with the RFC's roundels, was taken after the outbreak of the First World War.*

Source: RAF Museum P742

Left: *The Voisin pusher biplane first appeared early in 1914 and was ordered for the RFC and the RNAS. Although intended solely for reconnaissance, later versions were fitted with a machine gun in the observer's position and were also used for daylight bombing. It was from one of these machines that the first enemy aircraft was shot down from the air, by a French crew of the* Aviation Militaire *on 5 October 1914.*

Source: RAF Museum PO17685

Above: *The Royal Aircraft Factory R.E.5 was the first 'reconnaissance experimental' aircraft put into production for the RFC and RNAS. It was a large two-seater, unarmed and built for stability. Several of these machines were sent to France with the RFC soon after the outbreak of war, but their career was short-lived.*

Source: Air Historical Branch (MoD), Ref: H.429

Below: *The Royal Aircraft Factory B.E.2 was first delivered to the RFC in February 1913. It was a two-seater general-purpose aircraft, with the pilot in the rear cockpit. There was no defensive armament but it could carry up to 100lb of bombs. The type became obsolete by 1915. This photograph of B.E.2 serial 272, 3 Squadron, was taken at Larkhill in Wiltshire in 1913.*

Source: Air Historical Branch (RAF), MoD, H.1903

Above: *Pilots of B Flight, 3 Squadron, at Larkhill in Wiltshire in 1913. Their names were recorded as, from left to right, Carroll, Turner, Martin, Dibble, Newby, Aylen and Webb.*

Source: Air Historical Branch (RAF), MoD, H.1902

Right: *Three RFC squadrons were equipped with the Royal Aircraft Factory B.E.2 before the outbreak of the First World War. B.E. stood for 'Blériot Experimental', indicating a two-seat tractor biplane. It was unarmed, one of the main objectives being to design a general-purpose aircraft with very stable characteristics, primarily for reconnaissance and bombing. This photograph is of a B.E.2b, which had redesigned cockpits with better controls, produced in the early years of the war.*

Source: Air Historical Branch (RAF), MoD, 2884

Above: *The Royal Aircraft Factory B.E.2c was built for stability in the early summer of 1914, in the belief that the main use of aircraft would be reconnaissance. Although a safe aircraft to fly, it was slow and unmanoeuvrable and with a ceiling of only 10,000 feet. A few arrived in France late in the same year and in all about 1,300 were built. It was outclassed by the new Fokker monoplanes in 1915, when it earned the unhappy name of 'Fokker fodder'. After withdrawal from the Western Front, however, it did achieve some success as a night-fighter and as a trainer, remaining in service for the remainder of the war.*

Source: Air Historical Branch (MoD), Ref: H.1803

Above: *The Sopwith Tabloid was originally designed in 1913 as a two-seat biplane but during April 1914 a single-seat version was produced for the RFC and the RNAS. It was not fitted with armament when the First World War broke out, being used for scouting over the Western Front and from HMS* Ark Royal, *although it was later equipped with a Lewis gun and even carried a small bomb load. Tabloids also served in the Dardanelles, but the type was withdrawn in 1915. This photograph of serial 1207 of the RNAS was taken at Great Yarmouth.*

Source: RAF Museum P5092

CHAPTER 2

THE FIRST WAR IN THE AIR

When the first motley squadrons of the RFC arrived at the Western Front, on 13 August 1914, they were stationed at Mauberge, on the river Sambre near the Belgian border. As the war progressed, the soldiers of the British Expeditionary Force were somewhat surprised to find that a different breed of men had joined them. The RFC aircrews – the officers in particular – did not conform to the general pattern of men in the old-established army regiments. Most army officers in those days were of the same type, educated at public school before passing through Sandhurst or Woolwich. But the RFC newcomers came from all parts of the British Empire and all walks of life. They wore strange badges, talked about forms of warfare which were unfamiliar to regular regimental officers, and did not treat military traditions or customs with due reverence. They were young, high-spirited and full of initiative. Doubtless some regimental officers were sceptical about the value of these RFC men but early in the war, their worth became apparent.

In spite of coming under fire from British and French as well as German lines, reconnaissance aircraft of the RFC brought back accurate information of the attacking German forces in the retreat from Mons and the battle of the Marne. After the B.E.F. succeeded in repulsing these attacks, the Germans and the British dug in and the long and terrible years of trench warfare began. The contributions being made by British aircraft to the prosecution of the war were, however, recognized by the War Office. When in early 1915 it was proposed to increase the number of RFC squadrons to fifty, with corresponding increases for the RNAS, the Secretary of State for War, Lord Kitchener, ordered the numbers to be doubled.

The first RFC aircraft to be lost was an Avro 504, brought down over enemy lines on 22 August. However, it became evident at this stage that the main danger for the RFC came from "friendly" fire, resulting from the difficulty of the troops in identifying them. The Union Jack was painted on British aircraft, and then the red, white and blue roundel was designed as an easily visible symbol which remains on RAF aircraft to this day. Aerial combats were infrequent at this stage, since no regular armanent was carried. However, to guard against the possibility, aircrews armed themselves with service revolvers, rifles and duck guns, as well as grenades to drop on enemy troops. In twin-seater aircraft, it was usually the observer who fired the gun. On 25 August, an enemy aircraft was brought down but the German crew managed to escape.

Aerial photography assumed great importance and, when the fronts stabilized, it became necessary to make longer flights over enemy territory to reconnoitre trenches, supply routes and ammunition dumps. Simple box cameras were replaced by cameras in which the plates changed automatically. Wireless telegraphy also progressed rapidly, with a more compact and lighter set developed for the observer. Before long, most squadrons were equipped with a wireless flight. Hangars with wooden frames and canvas covers became standard equipment, to protect the flimsy aircraft from the worst vagaries of the weather.

The RNAS began its policy of aggression soon after the war began. On 8 October 1914, a Sopwith Tabloid based at Dunkirk flew to Düsseldorf and dropped two 20-lb

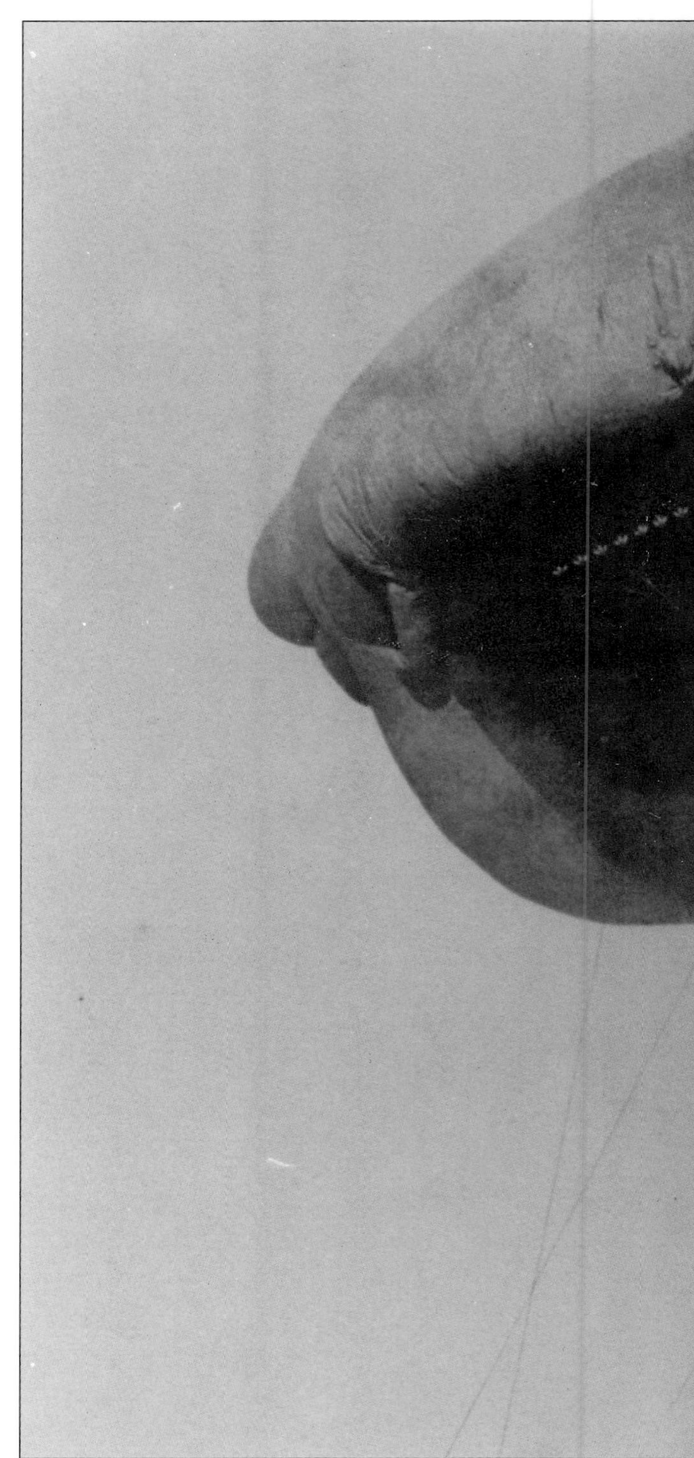

bombs on a Zeppelin shed, destroying an army Zeppelin. In November, three Avro 504s, each carrying four 20-lb bombs, took off from Belfort in southern France and bombed the Zeppelin sheds at Lake Constance. No Zeppelins were destroyed but one Avro failed to return. The RNAS also carried out long and exhausting anti-submarine patrols from its bases. Before flying boats came into service in 1916, these were accomplished partly by seaplanes and partly by airships. Coastal SS (Sea Scout) airships were introduced in the spring of 1915, capable of staying in the air for about eighteen hours. These were followed by larger C (Coastal) airships late in the same year, with an endurance of about twenty-four hours. Some seaplanes were carried by warships, being lowered into the water when the seas were too rough. Seaplanes hunted for Zeppelins as well as U-boats, and sometimes encountered enemy seaplanes. The German aircraft were faster and more agile than the British, but RNAS seaplanes were well-armed and gave good accounts of themselves. In 1916 a few twin-engined Curtiss flying boats arrived from America, and proved to have far better performances than the RNAS machines. The design was adapted by the British at Felixstowe and gave rise to the highly successful 'F' series which continued for the next ten years.

In response to the need of the RNAS for longer ranges, the more powerful engines were allocated to this branch of the services. In December 1914, the RNAS issued a specification for a 'bloody paralyser of an aeroplane' capable of carrying a minimum of six 112-lb bombs at a speed not less than 75 m.p.h, for the purpose of bombing Germany.

Below left: *A German observation balloon, numbered 371 on the wicker basket, with an officer looking through field glasses.*

Source: Air Historical Branch (RAF), MoD, private collection PRM 2841

Below: *The smoke trail from an enemy observation balloon after being hit. Since there were no parachutes in the early years of the First World War, balloons filled with hydrogen could be unpleasant death traps.*

Source: Air Historical Branch (RAF), MoD, private collection 96

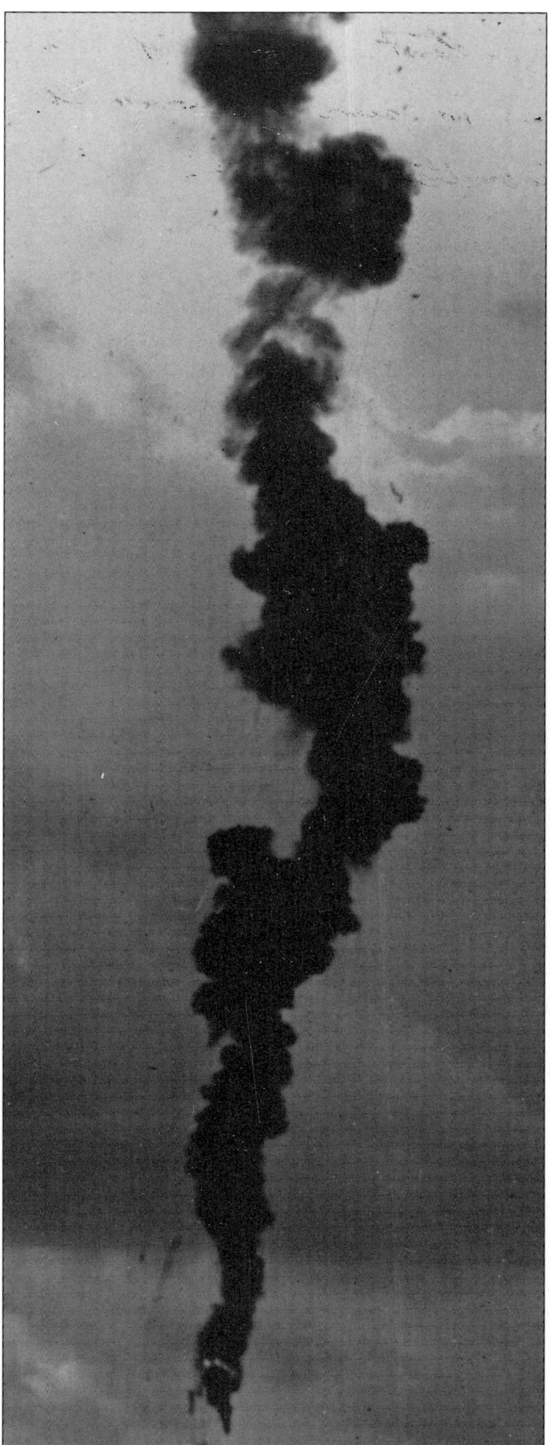

This entered service with the RNAS in France in November 1916 in the form of the Handley Page 0/100, and was followed by even heavier bombers.

One of the important arrivals on the Western Front was Lieutenant-Colonel Hugh Trenchard, who took over command of the RFC's First Wing in November 1914. Trenchard's army service had taken place mainly in Africa, but he had qualified as a pilot in 1912, when he was thirty-nine years old, by paying £75 for flying lessons at the Sopwith School at Brooklands. He had commanded the Military Wing at Farnborough after Sir David Henderson's departure for France, when he became responsible for the organization backing the expansion of the RFC for the next few months. Trenchard's progress was rapid, for when Henderson left to take up a new post in the War Office in August 1915, he was promoted to brigadier-general and given command of the RFC in France. He was the man who later became known as 'the father of the Royal Air Force'.

For the first year of the war, the RFC achieved some dominance over the Western Front. It expanded rapidly, although not as quickly as the armies it served. Squadrons were grouped into wings, and wings were formed into brigades, each supporting a British army and served by an aircraft park. Bombing attacks took place regularly over enemy territory, although only light loads were carried. Some pusher aircraft were fitted with a Lewis machine gun mounted in the front cockpit for the observer, while some scout (or fighter) tractor aircraft carried a similar gun fitted on the top plane, to be fired by the pilot over the propeller. But in June 1915 a new menace appeared in the form of the Fokker E Type monoplane, with a single Spandau machine gun synchronized to fire through the propeller arc.

It is sometimes believed that aerial combat in the First World War was a form of knightly combat, with the opposing aircraft roughly equal in armament and performance, differing mainly in the skill and determination of their pilots. Although this was partly true, a very large number of the combats took place when superior aircraft, often in packs, dived down to attack poorly defended and isolated reconnaissance aircraft. The agile fighters manoeuvred to shoot their opponents in the back or in the underbelly. Damaged aircraft often caught fire and, since there were no parachutes in the early days of the war, the occupants suffered unpleasant deaths. If a pilot succeeded in landing a damaged aircraft within his own lines, the attacking aircraft often shot it up on the ground. The chivalrous wave of the hand to an enemy did take place, but usually when a fighter had run out of ammunition and was forced to return to base. The men in the baskets of observation balloons faced similarly agonizing deaths if attacked by fighters, for they were protected by only a rifle and protective ground fire. Even here, 'dirty tricks' were practised, for decoy balloons were sometimes flown, containing explosives detonated from the ground and capable of blowing up an attacking aircraft.

The main victim of the agile Fokker monoplane was the Royal Aircraft Factory B.E.2c, which was stable and easy to fly but poorly-armed as well as slow and cumbersome. It earned the unhappy name of 'Fokker fodder', before its withdrawal from the Western Front and the beginning of a new life as a night-fighter at home. The Fokker dominated the skies soon after the battle of the Somme began on 19 August 1916. This scourge was partly ended in the spring of the following year with the introduction of the Nieuport Scout, a tractor aircraft with an overwing machine gun, and two pusher aircraft designed by Geoffrey de Havilland, the Airco D.H.2 and the Royal Aircraft Factory F.E.2b, which were sufficiently well-armed to give good accounts of themselves.

The pendulum of success over the Western Front swung to and fro for the remainder of the war. One problem for designers was speed and agility versus weight of machine guns and ammunition, but this was overcome when more powerful engines were produced. A problem for the aircrews was that of gun stoppage and engine failure, particularly at higher altitudes where icing occurred. The Germans began to regain ascendancy in September 1916 with the appearance of large formations of Halberstadt D.IIs and Albatros D.Is. The former was armed with a single gun firing through the propeller arc, but the latter aircraft was the first to be fitted with two guns. One of the pilots who began to gain a reputation at this stage was 'The Red Baron', *Rittmeister* Manfred von Richthofen. Before he was shot down and killed in a Fokker Triplane on 21 April 1918, he became the top-scoring fighter pilot of the war, with eighty victories to his credit. By April 1917, the average effective service of an RFC aircrew member was reduced to no more than two months in the front line. Losses were heavy partly because most operations took place over enemy lines, whereas the German aircraft seldom ventured over Allied territory. The aircrews also faced the problem of the prevailing westerly wind, which retarded their return journeys, especially if aircraft were damaged. RNAS squadrons were pulled in to support the RFC, while training was expanded to cater for an estimated 17,000 pilots in 1917 and 1918, together with their supporting aircrews and ground crews.

The British did not achieve final superiority against the German massed formations until the introduction of the Royal Aircraft Factory S.E.5a in March 1917 and the Sopwith Camel in the following July. These two aircraft proved more than a match for most

Above: *A section of the German line on the Western Front, showing deep trenches, mine craters and shell-pitted ground.*

Source: Air Historical Branch (RAF), MoD, private collection no 29

Above right: *The Farman MF.11 was designed by Maurice Farman in 1914 to replace his MF.7, a type which had appeared in 1913. The predecessor, which was unarmed, had long and curved outriggers with a front elevator and was nicknamed 'Longhorn' by the RFC. The MF.11, as in this photograph, had no front elevator while the observer in the rear cockpit was equipped with a machine gun; it was nicknamed 'Shorthorn' and served on the Western Front and in the Middle East until generally replaced in the autumn of 1915.*

Source: Air Historical Branch (RAF), MoD, H.1854

Above: *An important sector of the German Hindenburg line, showing an elaborate system of well-constructed trenches. The photograph was taken by an RAF reconnaissance aircraft from about 8,000 feet.*
Source: Air Historical Branch (RAF), MoD, private collection no 160

German aircraft and even managed to hold their own against the Fokker D.VII, which was considered to be the finest German fighter of the war after its appearance in April 1918.

While these events were taking place on the main fighting front, English civilians received their first taste of war for centuries. A minor bombing attack was made against Dover by a German seaplane in December 1914, but Zeppelin attacks began on 19 January 1915, when Folkestone was bombed. A Zeppelin attack took place against London at the end of the following May, then against Hull and the Tyneside, causing death and damage. There were more attacks against London and the Midlands. The sight of these monstrous apparitions overhead and the shattered buildings caused panic and even riots among a people who had hitherto believed that wars were fought on foreign soil. Substantial defences had to be built up, if only to restore public morale, and resources were diverted away from the Western Front with the creation of seven defensive RFC squadrons to supplement the RNAS units.

The Zeppelins were not invariably successful and several were brought down by anti-aircraft fire or fighters. The first to be destroyed by an aircraft was on 7 June 1915, when Flight Sub-Lieutenant R.A.J. Warneford of the RNAS dropped six 25-lb bombs on *LZ.37* over Belgium, an act for which he received the Victoria Cross. Zeppelins were soon compelled to switch to night bombing, a task which proved extremely difficult for them with their slow airspeeds in the uncertain British weather.

A new menace appeared over the coasts of the eastern counties in the late spring of 1917, in the shape of Gotha G.IV twin-engined bombers. Although these machines carried a much smaller load than the Zeppelins, the bombs were delivered with far greater accuracy and caused considerable damage and casualties. On 13 June 1917, fourteen of these bombers raided London in daylight, killing or injuring nearly 600 people. Further raids followed, and only one bomber was shot down. The public outrage that followed these raids led to a decision to increase the number of RFC squadrons from about 100 to 200, but this was not practicable. The anti-aircraft defences around London were strengthened, but the Germans switched to night attacks and reinforced their bombing strength with Gotha G.Vs and even a few Zeppelin (Staaken) four-engined 'Giant' aeroplanes. It was not until early 1918 that the balloons, searchlights, anti-aircraft guns and Sopwith Camel night-fighters were able to deal satisfactorily with these attacks. On 19 May 1918, the defences accounted for seven out of nineteen bombers, and the raids petered out with the pressure of events on other fronts.

There were further strains on the resources of the RFC and RNAS, in the eastern Mediterranean and the Middle East, where the forces of the British Empire were in conflict with both Bulgaria and Turkey, who had allied themselves to the Central Powers. There were basically three campaigns, in support of the armies.

When the British and ANZAC forces landed in Gallipoli, on 24 April 1915, they were accompanied by the Eastchurch Wing and the Dunkirk Wing of the RNAS. But the enterprise failed, in spite of the sacrifices and bravery of the attacking troops. Evacuations were completed by 8 January 1916, and the unhappy campaign came to an end.

Meanwhile, Serbia had been conquered by Austria and Bulgaria in November 1915. In response, British and French troops occupied Salonika the following month, where they were joined by a re-equipped Serbian army in May 1916. To provide reconnaissance for these armies, B.E.2cs and B.E.12s were sent over from Egypt but, as on the Western Front, they soon found themselves outclassed by Halberstadt D.II fighters which were escorting German bombers. Sopwith 1½-Strutters of the RNAS, together with D.H.2s of the RFC, helped to restore the situation, but the German supremacy was not broken until the arrival of S.E.5as at the end of 1917. The British aircraft made a significant contribution to the final defeat of the Bulgarian armies, which suffered the highest losses of any during the war, in terms of percentages.

The third campaign took place in Palestine and Mesopotamia against Turkish armies. In the spring of 1916 the Turks advanced along the Sinai Peninsula with the intention of occupying the Suez Canal, but their progress was faithfully reported by a handful of B.E.2cs of the RFC, and the attacks were defeated. The Turks retreated, but in early 1917 the Germans sent Halberstadt D.II and D.III fighters into the area, as well as Rumpler C.I reconnaissance aircraft. Yet again, the British were temporarily outclassed, although reconnaissance flights and map photography continued. The arrival of a number of Bristol Fighters in August 1917 helped to restore the situation, especially in destroying German reconnaissance aircraft, and complete superiority was achieved when S.E.5as arrived two months later. In September 1918, two retreating Turkish armies were caught in defiles and subjected to low-level bombing and machine gun attacks by aircraft, resulting in an appalling slaughter of the soldiers, who had little defence. The rout continued and the armies were destroyed as fighting units. Turkey had no option but to surrender at the end of the following month.

One of the consequences of the German bombing attacks against Britain was the formation of a strategic bombing force to operate over Germany, primarily against industrial targets. In October 1917, the 41st Wing was set up in France, consisting initially of Handley Page 0/100s, D.H.4s and F.E.2bs, to continue the attacks hitherto carried out mainly by RNAS aircraft. The targets included the Ruhr, Cologne, the Saar and Stuttgart. The wing increased in size and effectiveness, and in February 1918 became the VIIIth Brigade. In time, this brigade evolved into an even more important formation.

The RFC and the RNAS had grown to such an extent, with further expansion proposed, that problems developed in organization. Both the War Office and Admiralty believed that their influence should be paramount in air matters, but the prime minister, David Lloyd George, decided to invite an impartial observer to report on the matter. His choice was the eminent South African, Lieutenant-General Jan Smuts. In his report of August 1917, Smuts recommended the setting up of an independent service with an Air Ministry and an air staff. This report was approved by the War Cabinet and a bill was passed through Parliament, but the work of preparing the new organization was complex and was not until 1 April 1918 that the Royal Air Force came into being. Major-General Sir Hugh Trenchard was appointed as the first Chief of Air Staff.

Much grim fighting awaited the new RAF for the seven months that remained in the war. The Germans had opened a major offensive on the Western Front in March, following the withdrawal of armies from the Eastern Front after the armistice with Russia. Their air force was greatly outnumbered by the combined forces of the British and French, to which were added the squadrons of the American Expeditionary Force which had arrived in France during June of the previous year. Nevertheless, there were many air battles, when formations of German fighters attacked escorted reconnaissance aircraft and bombers. In June, the VIIIth Brigade was renamed the Independent Bombing Force and continued long-range strategic bombing; although these attacks were light by later standards, they set a pattern which governed much of the RAF's thinking in the future. By July, the last German offensive petered out. A few RAF squadrons were sent to Italy to support the armies which were engaged with Austrian forces.

The Allies went over to a general offensive in September on both the Western Front and the Italian Front. By now, it was apparent that the German and Austrian resources were exhausted and their defences were crumbling. Austria accepted terms on 3 November and the armistice with Germany was signed on 11 November 1918. The carnage of the war at last came to an end.

Above: *The Bristol Scout was designed before the First World War but not delivered in quantity to the RFC and the RNAS until early 1915. It was capable of the excellent speed of 95 m.p.h. but only small arms were carried. Machine guns were fitted later to a few Scout Cs while others carried darts for dropping on Zeppelins. The Scout D, delivered in November 1915, had provision for a machine gun. Almost every RFC squadron had a few Scout Ds on strength, but most of these were withdrawn by mid-1916 and continued as trainers. The Scout D in this photograph, serial 5575, was flown by James McCudden.*

Source: Air Historical Branch (RAF), MoD, H.1910

Above right: *The Caudron G.III was unusual in that it was a tractor and not a pusher aircraft, used widely in the early years of the First World War. The RFC used the machine, armed with a forward-firing machine gun and small bombs, for ground-strafing operations as well as for observation, while the RNAS employed it for coastal patrols. After withdrawal from front-line duties, it was very successful as a trainer. This photograph of serial 4293, still with its French serial C567, was taken at Brooklands.*

Source: RAF Museum P9457

Right: *The Vickers F.B.5 entered service with the RFC's 11 Squadron during February 1915. Nicknamed the 'Gunbus', it was fitted with a machine gun in the nose, operated by the observer. By the time the squadron arrived in France five months later, it was outclassed by the new Fokker E.1 monoplane with a machine gun synchronized to fire through the propeller.*

Source: Air Historical Branch (RAF), MoD, H.1805

C567

Left: *The prototype of the Royal Aircraft Factory F.E.2b appeared in August 1913, but this two-seat aircraft with a pusher propeller was not produced in quantity until early 1915. The machine was equipped with two Lewis guns, one forward and one backward-firing. F.E.2bs were successful over the Western Front against Fokker monoplanes until the autumn of 1916, but were outclassed when Albatros D.1s began to appear. Many F.E.2bs were transferred to the night bombing role and continued until the end of the war.*

Source: Air Historical Branch (RAF), MoD, H.989

Above: *A faithful replica of an Airco D.H.2, registration GBH7, photographed at Mildenhall in Suffolk on 23 May 1987.*

RAF Museum colour slide PO52159

PUBLIC WARNING

The public are advised to familiarise themselves with the appearance of British and German Airships and Aeroplanes, so that they may not be alarmed by British aircraft, and may take shelter if German aircraft appear. **Should hostile aircraft be seen,** take shelter **immediately** in the nearest available house, preferably in the basement, and remain there until the aircraft have left the vicinity: do not stand about in crowds **and do not touch unexploded bombs.**

In the event of **HOSTILE** aircraft being seen in country districts, the nearest Naval, Military or Police Authorities should, if possible, be advised immediately by Telephone of the TIME OF APPEARANCE, the DIRECTION OF FLIGHT, **and whether the aircraft is an Airship or an Aeroplane.**

GERMAN AIRSHIPS | **BRITISH** AIRSHIPS

Note specially the shape of the Airships and the position of the passenger cars

ZEPPELIN
PARSEVAL
SCHUTTE – LANZ
H.M.A. ASTRA TORRES
H.M.A. BETA
H.M.A. ETA
H.M.A. PARSEVAL

Note specially the sloped-back wings of the German Aeroplanes

AEROPLANES

STAHLTAUBE MONOPLANE
RUMPLER TAUBE MONOPLANE
BRISTOL BIPLANE

AEROPLANES

PRICE TWOPENCE

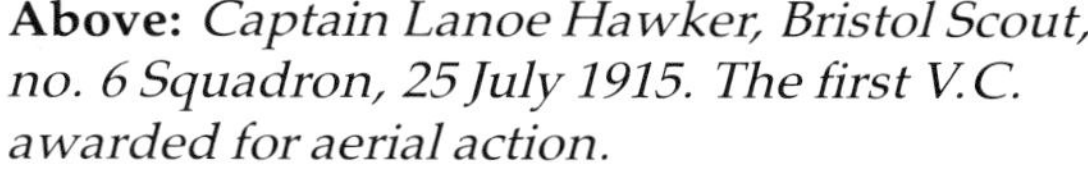

Above: *Captain Lanoe Hawker, Bristol Scout, no. 6 Squadron, 25 July 1915. The first V.C. awarded for aerial action.*

Source: courtesy of Frank Wootton, P.P.G.Av.A.

Right: *The raids by Zeppelins over south-east England in 1915 caused little damage but created such alarm among the civilian population that the sight of any aircraft overhead could cause panic. This poster was displayed to help the public recognize the difference between hostile and friendly aircraft.*

Source: RAF Museum P100174

Left: *The Morane-Saulnier Type L first appeared in 1913 and was ordered for the RFC and RNAS, with the military designation MS.3, as well as for the* Aviation Militaire*. Originally unarmed, it was later equipped with a forward-firing machine gun, with deflector plates fitted to the propeller blades. On 7 June 1915, Flt Sub-Lt R.A.J. Warneford of 1 Squadron RNAS, based at Dunkirk, destroyed the first Zeppelin from the air in one of these machines. He dropped six 20 lb Hale bombs on the army Zeppelin* LZ.37*, which fell in flames on a convent in Belgium.*

Source: RAF Museum P4988

Right: *The Nieuport 11 was ordered at the outbreak of war by the* Aviation Militaire *and entered service with the French in the summer of 1915, who referred to it as the* Bébé*. It was also ordered by the RNAS and was employed both in France and the Dardanelles, being known as the Nieuport Scout. The RFC received deliveries in France during March 1916; armed with a Lewis gun on the upper wing, it helped to overcome the menace of the Fokker monoplanes. The Nieuport Scout in the photograph was serial 3993 of the RNAS.*

Source: RAF Museum PO18140

Left: *The Airco D.H.1, designed by Geoffrey de Havilland, was a two-seat fighter and reconnaissance aircraft with a pusher propeller and dual controls. The observer sat in the front seat and was equipped with a forward-firing machine gun. D.H.1s began to appear in 1915, being employed by the RFC, mainly for home defence and later for training. This photograph is of a D.H.1A.*

Source: Air Historical Branch (RAF), MoD, H.1787

Right: *The* SS.40 *was one of a series of non-rigid airships supplied to the RNAS from May 1915 onwards. It carried a crew of two in a gondola consisting of a fuselage from an Armstrong Whitworth F.K.3 and had an endurance of about sixteen hours at an airspeed of 40 m.p.h. The main function of these 'Sea Scouts' was to carry out anti-submarine patrols in the English Channel and the Irish Sea. This photograph was taken at Kingsnorth in Kent.*

Source: Air Historical Branch (RAF), MoD, private collection 1802K

Above: *A Short 184 seaplane was the first aircraft to sink a ship by torpedo, a Turkish merchant vessel near the Dardanelles on 12 August 1915. However, the Short 184 was used primarily on more routine but vital work by the RNAS from the summer of 1915 onwards, anti-submarine patrols and reconnaissance, in home waters, the Mediterranean and the Far East. A land-based version was also employed for bombing. Short 184s continued in front-line service until April 1917.*

Source: Air Historical Branch (RAF), MoD, H.1022

Left: *Franco-British Aviation was a company which built a series of small flying boats with pusher engines, for training and for patrol purposes. This photograph shows a Type B two-seater, serial N2737, on a beaching trolley. It was built at Gosport and supplied to the RNAS in 1915.*

Source: RAF Museum P4995

Right: *The Airco D.H.2 was a single-seat fighter with a pusher propeller, designed by Geoffrey de Havilland and first delivered in quantity to 24 Squadron in January 1916. When this squadron went to France a month later, it was the first to be equipped entirely with single-seat fighters. The machine was fitted with a Lewis gun and met with some success the threat of the Fokker fighters which were appearing over the Western Front. D.H.2s also served in Palestine and Macedonia, but most were withdrawn in 1917 and continued as trainers.*

Source: Air Historical Branch (RAF), MoD, H.88

Left: *The Voisin L.A. Type 5 appeared late in 1915, a derivation of the earlier Types 3 and 4, both of which were supplied to the RFC and the RNAS. It was a two-seater light bomber with a pusher engine, with provision for a 37mm cannon in the nose for ground strafing, known by the French as the* Avion Canon. *This photograph of a Voisin L.A. Type 5 of 2 Wing, RNAS, was taken on the island of Imbroz, near the Dardanelles, in 1915.*

Source: RAF Museum P532

Above: *The C (Coastal) Type airship entered service with the RNAS in late 1915. Powered by two engines, usually amounting to 300 h.p., it carried a crew of five, one of whom manned a machine gun, and had an endurance of about twenty-four hours. This photograph of C.2 was taken at RNAS Mullion, in Cornwall.*

Source: RAF Museum P3149

Right: *The Vickers F.B.5 first appeared with the RFC's 11 Squadron on the Western Front in February 1915, where it was dubbed the 'Gunbus'. The observer sat in the nose, equipped with a .303 inch Lewis gun, while the machine was powered with a 'pusher' engine.*

Source: Keystone Collection

Right: *A painting used as a crewroom poster showing the unpleasant fate of the crew of an R.E.7, who were so intent on pursuing an Albatross D.III that they failed to spot two Fokker monoplanes swooping down on them. These German monoplanes, fitted with machine guns synchronized to fire through the propellers, accounted for numerous British aircraft when they first appeared over the Western Front in the autumn of 1915.*
Source: RAF Museum

Above: *The Royal Aircraft Factory R.E.7 was designed specifically to carry the new 336 lb bomb developed by the same factory. The first machines, armed with a single machine gun in the front cockpit, first entered service with the RFC's 21 Squadron in France during January 1916.*

Source: Air Historical Branch (RAF), MoD, H.992

Right: *The two-seater Breguet Type 5 was ordered from France by the RNAS while others were built in Britain. Entering service in early 1916, it could carry 661 lb of bombs for a distance of about 375 miles, and was employed in the Aegean as well as France. In late 1916, it was transferred to night bombing operations.*

Source: RAF Museum PO13635

Left: *The Martinsyde G.100 Elephant performed the role of escort to bombers, although it was capable of carrying up to 224 lb of bombs itself. It was a single-seater, with a forward-firing gun mounted over the propeller and provision for a second gun on a bracket over the pilot's left shoulder. In practice, it performed best as a ground attack aircraft, serving from early 1916 on the Western Front and in Mesopotamia and Palestine. This photograph shows the prototype, serial 4735.*

Source: Air Historical Branch (MoD), Ref: H.247

Left: *The Royal Aircraft Factory B.E.2 series ended with the B.E.2e, which entered service in July 1916. Unfortunately, the insistence on a general-purpose aircraft with stable flying characteristics produced a succession of slow and unwieldy machines which were easy prey for the agile German fighters. Hundreds of these aircraft were shot down over the Western Front, even when machine guns were introduced into the observer's cockpit. They were also employed in the Middle East and Macedonia, but most survivors ended the war as trainers. An F.E.2b, serial A836, can be seen in the background of this photograph of a B.E.2e.*

Source: Air Historical Branch (RAF), MoD, H.979

Below: *The Sopwith 1½-Strutter was designed as a multi-purpose two-seat aircraft and first entered service with the RNAS in France during April 1916. It was employed by both the RNAS and RFC, and performed the roles of bomber, reconnaissance, fighter, anti-shipping and carrier aircraft. It was the first British aircraft equipped with a Vickers machine gun which was efficiently synchronised to fire through the propeller. The 1½-Strutter in this photograph, serial A6901, was converted to a single-seater. In the summer of 1917, 1½-Strutters were replaced on the Western Front, and employed at home as trainers or as single-seat night-fighters.*

Source: Air Historical Branch (RAF), MoD, H.1802

Above: *On 31 March 1916, Zeppelin* L.15 *of the German navy was damaged by anti-aircraft fire and by aerial darts dropped from a B.E.2c flown by a New Zealander, Second Lieutenant Alfred de B. Brandon, who took off from Hainault in Essex. She came down in the Thames Estuary. One of her crew was killed and seventeen were taken prisoner.*

Source: Air Historical Branch (RAF), MoD, private collection no 834

Right: *The Royal Aircraft Factory B.E.12 was intended to combat the Fokker monoplanes which were destroying the B.E.2 series over the Western Front. It was provided with a more powerful engine than its predecessors and was converted into a single-seater with a single forward-firing machine gun. It remained unmanoeuvrable, however, and was withdrawn as a fighter soon after its appearance in France during August 1916. Some B.E.12s were converted into light bombers while others served in home defence and in the Middle East.*

Source: Air Historical Branch (RAF), MoD, H.987

Right below: *The Armstrong Whitworth F.K.3, a two-seater bomber and reconnaissance aircraft known as the 'Little Ack' served only with 47 Squadron, in Macedonia, from April 1916 to March 1918. Its successor, the more powerful F.K.8 known as the 'Big Ack', arrived in the Western Front during January 1917; it was more widely used and operated with some success as a light bomber. This photograph is of an F.K.3.*

Source: Air Historical Branch (RAF), MoD, H.761

Above: *An observation balloon ascending with the aid of guide ropes and a motor winch, in order to spot the positions of the Turks.*

Source: Air Historical Branch (RAF), MoD, private collection no 114

Right: *The Nieuport 17 was a more powerful version of the earlier Nieuport 11, with a larger wing span. It entered service with the RNAS and RFC in the summer of 1916 and proved extremely popular among fighter pilots, who praised its agility and rate of climb. At first armed with an overwing Lewis gun, a synchronized Vickers was fitted to later machines. The machine in this photograph was serial A6648 of the RFC's 29 Squadron.*

Source: RAF Museum PO19392

Above: *The Royal Aircraft Factory F.E.8, equipped with a single machine gun in the front cockpit, arrived at the Western Front in August 1916, at a time when pusher aircraft were out-classed by German fighters. On one occasion, 9 March 1917, five of a formation of nine were destroyed by Albatros D.IIIs. Shortly afterwards, F.E.8s were withdrawn and replaced by tractor aircraft.*

Source: Air Historical Branch (MoD), Ref: H.1801

Above: *The Spad Type VII was built mainly in France, although about 100 were also manufactured in Britain. It entered service with the RFC in France in October 1916, at a time when German machines had gained superiority over the British pusher types. With a synchronized forward-firing gun and a fast turn of speed, it helped swing the balance back in favour of the Allies. In this photograph of Spad VII serial A9132, a Royal Aircraft Factory R.E.8 serial A4537 can be seen in the background.*

Source: RAF Museum P33525

Right: *On the night of 22/23 September 1916, twelve German naval Zeppelins attacked targets in London and the Midlands. Two were shot down.* L.32 *crashed in flames near Billericay in Essex and the crew was killed.* L.33 *was damaged by anti-aircraft fire and by Lieutenant Alfred de B. Brandon. It landed in a field near West Mersea in Essex and was set on fire by its crew of twenty-two, all of whom were taken prisoner. The remains of the frame of* L.33 *are shown in this photograph.*

Source: Air Historical Branch (RAF), private collection No 88

Above: *The Sopwith Pup was supplied at first to the RNAS in the autumn of 1916 and towards the end of the same year, in greater quantity, to the RFC. It was a very manoeuvrable and rugged single-seat fighter, normally fitted with a synchronized Vickers machine gun. The performance on the Western Front proved successful, while other Pups flew from aircraft carriers and cruisers. It was withdrawn from front-line service in early 1918 and became very popular as a trainer.*

Source: Air Historical Branch (RAF), MoD, H.296

Left: *The remains of the gondola of the Zeppelin* L.33. *This crash-landing provided useful technical information for the British. This class of Zeppelin had a length of about 650 feet and, powered by six engines, could reach a height of 17,000 feet at an airspeed of 62 m.p.h. The design of the rigid airships* R.33 *and* R.34, *which entered service with the RAF in 1919, was based on* L.33.

Source: Air Historical Branch (RAF), private collection No 89

Above: *The Armstrong Whitworth F.K.8 was a scaled-up version of the F.K.3, employed as a day and night bomber as well as on ground attack and reconnaissance. First delivered to the RFC towards the end of 1916, it arrived in France the following January and also saw service in Palestine and Macedonia. After the First World War, it served with 47 Squadron in support of the White Russian forces.*

Source: RAF Museum P922

Above: *A replica of a Sopwith Pup*

Source: T. Malcolm English colour slide

Left: *The Royal Aircraft Factory R.E.8 was intended to provide a better-armed alternative to the B.E.2 series, being equipped with a Lewis gun firing through the propeller as well as a Lewis gun mounted in the rear cockpit. However, R.E.8s were almost as slow and unmanoeuvrable as their predecessors, and proved no match for agile German fighters. First delivered to the Western Front in November 1916 and known as 'Harry Tates' after the music hall comedian, they plodded through anti-aircraft fire on army co-operation work and were also employed as night bombers. More R.E.8s served in France than any other British two-seater.*

Source: Air Historical Branch (RAF), MoD, H.1855

Above: *A replica of a Bristol F.2B Fighter, serial D8096.*

Source: T. Malcolm English colour slide

Below: *The Handley Page 0/100, a four-seater heavy bomber with folding wings, was designed specifically for the long-range bombing of Germany. It first went into service with the RNAS in France during November 1916. Carrying up to 2,000 lb of bombs, the machine was used at first for daylight sea patrols and then for night bombing. An S.E.5 also appears in this photograph.*

Source: Air Historical Branch (RAF), MoD, H.1455

Left: *The Vickers F.B.19 Mark II, a single seater scout fitted with a single machine gun synchronized with the propeller, appeared in France at the end of 1916 but was not accepted by the RFC. A few were sent to the Middle East and others served on home defence or as trainers.*

Source: RAF Museum PO14079

Right: *The Bristol F.2A Fighter first arrived in France in December 1916 and, although losses were heavy initially, began to achieve considerable success with improvements in tactics. The F.2B, a modified version, was produced in far greater numbers and eventually served with many squadrons on the Western Front as well as with home defence squadrons and two more in Palestine. A tough and reliable reconnaissance fighter, it was known by RAF crews as the 'Biff' and acquired a fearsome reputation with German pilots, who were sometimes reluctant to tackle the machine. Before the end of the First World War, 3,100 Bristol Fighters had been accepted by the RFC and RAF. It then continued in service with the post-war RAF, at home until 1926 and overseas until 1932, being known as the 'Brisfit'. This photograph shows a Bristol F.2B of 208 Squadron in 1925, based at Ismailia in 1925.*

Source: RAF Museum P1414

Left: *Aircrews of the RFC photographed in France, in front of a Bristol Fighter.*

Source: Keystone Collection

Right: *The Airco D.H.4 was designed by Geoffrey de Havilland as a fast day bomber, but it was also employed on many other tasks. It was armed with a forward-firing gun, as well as a single gun on a ring in the observer's position, and could carry about 450 lb of bombs. D.H.4s were delivered to the RNAS and the RFC in France in March 1917, and were also employed in the Mediterranean and the Middle East. Over 1,400 D.H.4s were built in Britain, but in addition nearly 4,900 were manufactured in the United States, where it was named the 'Liberty Plane'. This photograph of D.H.4 serial B9480 was taken at Manston in Kent in September 1917.*

Source: RAF Museum P735

Right: *One objective of every fighter pilot was to fire at the vulnerable under-belly of an enemy aircraft. A crewroom poster showed this desirable state of affairs, with the pilot of a Nieuport 11 scoring hits with his Lewis gun on an unlucky German two-seater of an indeterminate type.*

Source: RAF Museum

Below: *This crewroom poster showed the folly of a pilot of what appeared to be an S.E.5a, who attempted an exuberant loop after shooting down an Albatros D.III. He was evidently unaware that there was structural damage to his tail, presumably caused by enemy fire.*

Source: RAF Museum

Above: *The Royal Aircraft Factory S.E.5 appeared on the Western Front in March 1917 and rapidly established a reputation as a fast and tough single-engined fighter, with good altitude performance. It was also heavily armed for its day, with a synchronized Vickers gun on the port side and a Lewis gun mounted on the upper wing. It remained in service until the end of the war, in the Middle East as well as in France. This photograph of an S.E.5a of 111 Squadron, based at Ramleh in Palestine, was taken in 1918.*

Source: Air Historical Branch (RAF), MoD, H.1875

Below: *The Airco D.H.6 was designed solely as a primary trainer for the RFC and began to appear in early 1917. It proved safe and reliable, remaining as the standard trainer until the arrival of the Avro 504 late in the same year. Some D.H.6s were employed on anti-submarine work around coastal waters by the RNAS, carrying a bomb load of up to 100 lb, while others served on home defence.*

Source: Air Historical Branch (RAF), MoD, H.982

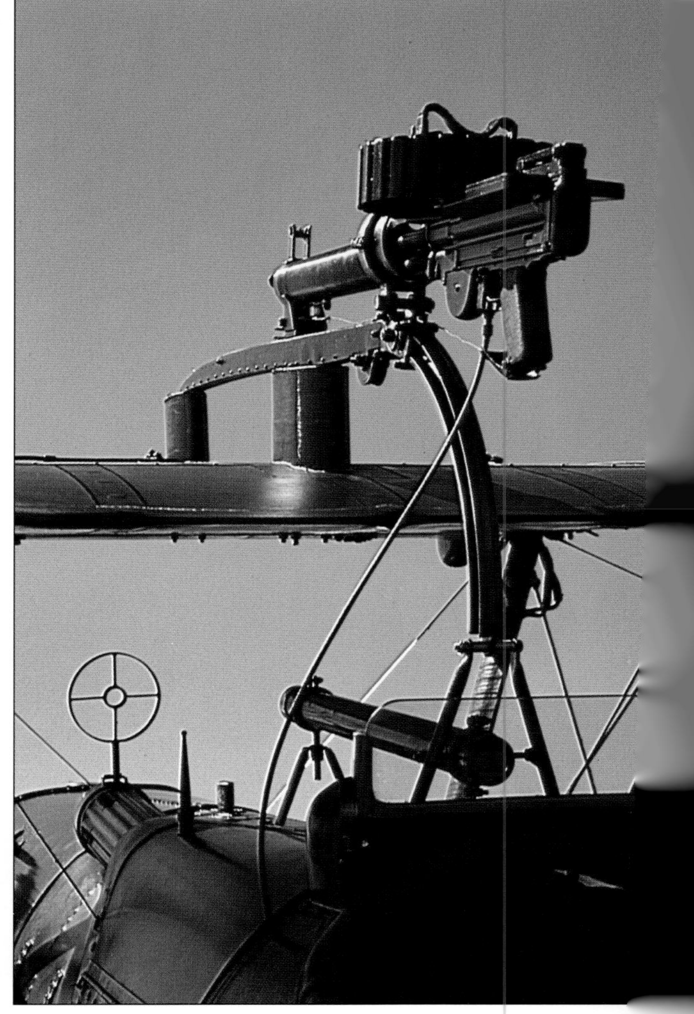

Above: *The Short 320 was the last of seaplanes used for anti-submarine and reconnaissance work in the First World War. As with similar aircraft, it could also be used for torpedo bombing. Short 320s came into service from August 1918 onwards and equipped four RAF squadrons, continuing until October 1919. This photograph is of serial N1361, on a beaching trolley.*

Source: Air Historical Branch (RAF), MoD, H.1024

Left: *The Farman F.40 was designed jointly by the brothers Maurice and Henri, and entered service early in 1916. It was used for reconnaissance and bombing but, armed only with a single machine gun, was found to be too vulnerable for daylight work and was switched to night bombing before withdrawal from front-line squadrons in 1917. This photograph of an RNAS Farman F.40 was taken in 1917.*

Source: RAF Museum PO12317

Left: *The drum-fed machine gun and sight on the centre-section of a Royal Aircraft Factory S.E.5a.*

Source: T. Malcolm English colour slide

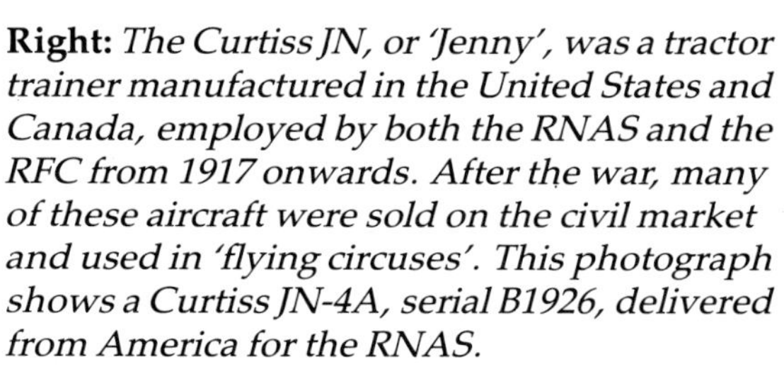

Right: *The Curtiss JN, or 'Jenny', was a tractor trainer manufactured in the United States and Canada, employed by both the RNAS and the RFC from 1917 onwards. After the war, many of these aircraft were sold on the civil market and used in 'flying circuses'. This photograph shows a Curtiss JN-4A, serial B1926, delivered from America for the RNAS.*

Source: RAF Museum P7289

Above: *The Handley Page 0/400 followed the 0/100 as the standard heavy bomber of the First World War. It was fitted with fuel tanks in the fuselage instead of the engine nacelles and with successively more powerful engines. Over 650 were built, the first becoming operational as day bombers in France during April 1917. By the following October, the squadrons were switched to night bombing over Germany. The 0/400 continued in service until 1920.*

Source: RAF Museum P4840

Below: *The Sopwith Triplane was developed from the earlier Sopwith Pup, deliveries beginning to squadrons on the Western Front towards the end of 1916. Like the Pup, it was fitted with a synchronized machine gun, although a few are known to have been fitted with two. With its extraordinary agility and rate of climb, the Triplane fighter caused some alarm among German pilots. It continued in front-line service until the summer of 1917, when replaced by the Sopwith Camel.*

Source: Air Historical Branch (RAF), MoD, H.1950

Above: *The largest bomb manufactured by the Royal Aircraft Factory by 1918 was this formidable 1,650 pounder.*

Source: Air Historical Branch (MoD), Ref: H.504

Above: *Perhaps the best-known of British fighters in the First World War, the Sopwith Camel was first delivered to the Western Front in July 1917. It was not an easy aircraft to fly but, once mastered, RAF pilots found that they could out-turn most German fighters. The Camel was credited with destroying more enemy aircraft than any other Allied fighter. It is estimated that, by the end of the war, over 2,500 Camels were on charge with RAF squadrons, but these did not remain long in service after the war, being replaced by the Sopwith Snipe.*

Source: Keystone Collection

Right: *Another view of the Sopwith Camel.*

Source: Air Historical Branch (MoD), Ref: H.1806

Above: *A replica of a Sopwith Triplane.*

Source: T. Malcolm English colour slide

Left: *The Airco D.H.5, a single-seat fighter with the upper wing staggered backwards to give the pilot a better view and a Vickers machine gun synchronized with the propeller, first entered service in France during May 1917. Its performance proved inadequate at higher altitudes, however, and it was employed mainly for strafing until withdrawn in January 1918.*

Source: Air Historical Branch (RAF), MoD, H.91

Above: *The Airco D.H.9A was a refined version of the D.H.9, with a more reliable engine and a larger wing area. It was delivered to RAF squadrons in France from June 1918 onwards, where it served in the Independent Bombing Force in raids over Germany. It also served with the Allied forces which landed in Murmansk in the same summer. Known as the 'Ninak', it had a remarkably long and successful career in the RAF, until 1931. The photograph shows serial J7013.*

Source: Air Historical Branch, private collection John Stroud: Ref: H.806

Below: *The Airco D.H.9, designed as a two-seat aircraft intended to replace the D.H.4 and undertake day bombing over Germany, began to appear in December 1917. It was armed with a forward-firing Vickers gun and a Lewis gun in the rear cockpit, and could carry up to 500 lb of bombs. The machine suffered from frequent engine failures, but served in France and the Middle East, as well as the Russian theatre, until the end of the war. This photograph was taken at a training unit.*

Source: Air Historical Branch (RAF), MoD, H.1856

Right: *The Fairey Campania seaplane was the first aircraft to be designed for flying off an aircraft carrier, being named after the liner HMS* Campania, *which was refitted as a warship. Take-off from the deck was achieved by using a trolley gear, which was then jettisoned. Campanias were delivered to the RNAS from November 1917 and eventually equipped three RAF squadrons. They were withdrawn in the summer of 1919.*

Source: Air Historical Branch (RAF), MoD, H.43

Below: *The Felixstowe F.2A was first delivered to RNAS squadrons in November 1917. Known as the 'F-boat', it was the first of a series of large and highly successful flying boats. During the remainder of the First World War, 'F-boats' were employed on anti-submarine patrols and escort duties. They could carry up to 460 lb of bombs and had an endurance of about six hours. With a crew of four and an armament of up to seven machine guns, they gave good accounts of themselves in encounters with German seaplanes. They were also credited with shooting down at least two Zeppelins. This photograph of an F.2A named 'Saturn', serial N4438 of 267 Squadron, was taken in Malta in 1922.*

Source: Air Historical Branch (RAF), MoD, H.1336

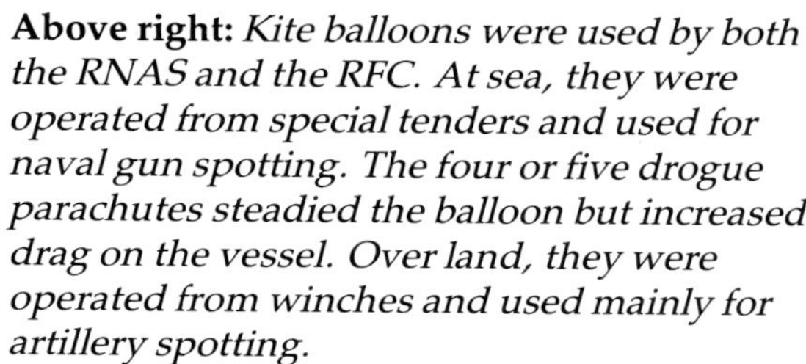

Above right: *Kite balloons were used by both the RNAS and the RFC. At sea, they were operated from special tenders and used for naval gun spotting. The four or five drogue parachutes steadied the balloon but increased drag on the vessel. Over land, they were operated from winches and used mainly for artillery spotting.*

Source: Air Historical Branch (RAF), private collection no 813

Right: *Pilots of 80 Squadron, photographed in January 1918, when the squadron was equipped with Sopwith Camels and setting off for the Western Front.*

Source: Air Historical Branch (RAF), MoD, H.1857

Right: *Monoplanes of the RFC suffered so many crashes before the First World War that there was much prejudice against the prototype Bristol M.1A monoplane when it first flew, even though it reached 132 m.p.h. Only a handful of M.1Bs were built, one of which is shown in this photograph. One hundred and twenty-five M.1Cs were ordered; none of these flew on the Western Front but a few reached the Middle East and Macedonia, while others were used as trainers at home.*

Source: Air Historical Branch (RAF), MoD, H.999

Above: *Captain James T.B. McCudden of 56 Squadron earned the first Victoria Cross awarded to the RAF, gazetted on 2 April 1918. He was also one of the most famous and highly decorated pilots of the First World War, being additionally awarded the DSO and bar, the MC and bar, the MM and the Croix de Guerre. When he lost his life in a flying accident, in July 1918, he had been credited with the destruction of fifty-seven enemy aircraft.*

Source: Air Historical Branch (RAF), MoD, H.1874.

Right: *"Knights of the Air" – Captain James T.B. McCudden, V.C. in aerial battle with the Red Baron, 1918.*

Source: courtesy of Frank Wootton, P.P.G.Av.A.

Left: *The Avro 504 served with both the RFC and the RNAS in the early months of the war, but is best remembered for its remarkable success as a trainer. The first variation for this purpose was the 504J which first appeared in the autumn of 1916. It proved highly reliable as well as fully aerobatic. This 504J was photographed at Abu Sueir in Egypt in 1918.*

Source: RAF Museum PO22214

Below: *The Blackburn Kangaroo was delivered to 246 Squadron at Seaton Carew in Durham during May 1918. This was the only squadron to fly the new four-man bomber which, with an endurance of about eight hours, was engaged on anti-submarine patrols in the North Sea. Before the Armistice, Kangaroos sank one U-boat and damaged several more. The squadron was disbanded in April 1919.*

Source: Air Historical Branch (RAF), MoD, H.1852

Right: *The Sopwith T.1 Cuckoo was the first of the RAF's landplane torpedo bombers, first delivered in June 1918. It had fold-back wings and served on board carriers, but was too late for active service. Cuckoos remained in service until April 1932 with 210 Squadron at Gosport.*

Source: Air Historical Branch (RAF), MoD, H.966

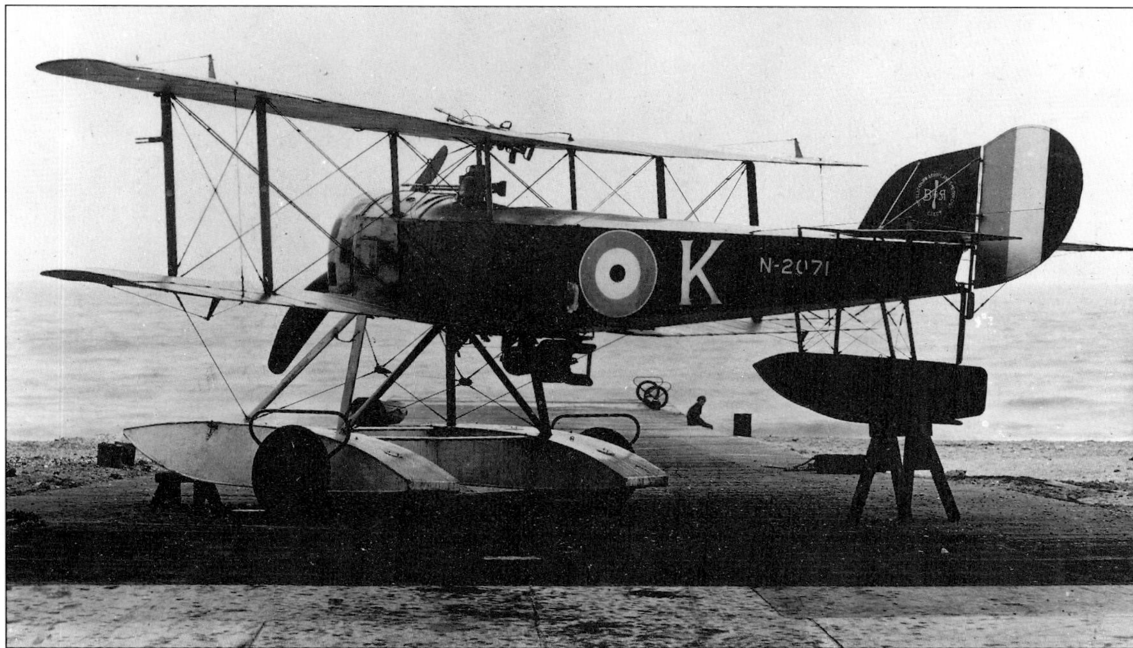

Left: *The Sopwith Baby floatplane served with the RNAS from early 1917 onwards, from bases round the British coast and from seaplane carriers in home waters and in the Mediterranean. Armed with a single machine gun on the upper wing, or a synchronized gun firing through the propeller, they operated on fighter patrols or carried a bomb load of up to 130 lb. Some were converted to landplanes. Most were withdrawn in the summer of 1918.*

Source: Air Historical Branch (RAF), MoD, H.993

Below: *In the summer of 1918 the Felixstowe F.3 followed the F.2A. It was a slightly larger flying boat and was employed in the Mediterranean as well as in home waters. The performance proved less satisfactory than that of the F.2A, however, and it was withdrawn in 1921 whereas its predecessor continued until August 1923.*

Source: Air Historical Branch (RAF), MoD, H.1029

Below: *The formation of the Royal Air Force on 1 April 1918, from the amalgamation of the Royal Flying Corps and the Royal Naval Air Service, offered future recruits an attractive alternative to life in the trenches or at sea.*

Source: RAF Museum POO205

Right: *A Sopwith F.5.1 Dolphin, serial D5261, of the RFC, photographed in 1918. The first of these single-engined fighters were delivered to 19 Squadron at Sainte Marie Cappel in France in January 1918. Later, three more squadrons were equipped with Dolphins which, equipped with two Lewis guns and four 25 lb bombs, were often used for ground attack. They remained in service until 1919, when most remaining aircraft were scrapped.*

Source: Air Historical Branch (RAF), MoD, H.1874

Above: *A replica of an Avro 504K, serial 3404.*
Source: T. Malcolm English colour slide

Left: *The Sopwith Snipe was designed to succeed the Sopwith Camel as Britain's premier single-engined fighter, with improved performance and better vision. The first deliveries were made to 43 Squadron in September 1918, and several squadrons flew Snipes before the Armistice on 11 November. This photograph of Sopwith 7F.1 Snipe, serial E8179, was taken in 1918.*
Source: Air Historical Branch (RAF), MoD, H.1945

Left: *The Handley Page V/1500 was the first four-engined bomber in the RAF as well as the largest British aircraft to be produced in the First World War. It was also the first of the RAF's strategic bombers, having a radius of action of 600 miles and being capable of bombing Berlin from bases in England. It arrived too late to fly operationally and was considered too expensive for peacetime service, preference being given to the smaller Vickers Vimy. However, between December 1918 and January 1919 a V/1500 made the first successful flight from England to India, even though the final landing at Karachi was made on only two engines.*

Source: RAF Museum P4842

Right: *The Sopwith TF.2 Salamander was developed as a ground attack aircraft towards the end of the war, TF standing for 'trench fighter'. It carried two Vickers machine guns synchronized to fire through the propeller, while armour-plating protected the pilot. Only thirty-seven aircraft were delivered to the RAF by the time of the Armistice, the majority of those on order being cancelled.*

Source: Air Historical Branch (RAF), MoD, H.1012

Left: *After the war, the Sopwith Snipe served with thirteen home-based squadron as well as four overseas squadrons, continuing in service until August 1926.*

Source: Aviation Bookshop

Right: *The Martinsyde Buzzard F.4 was first delivered to the RAF towards the end of the First World War, too late to fly operationally. It was a fast fighter with two Vickers machine guns synchronized to fire through the propeller, but further production was cancelled with the Sopwith Snipe as the RAF's standard fighter after the war. This photograph is of serial D4261.*

Source: RAF Museum P4914

Below: *The British Aerial Transport Bantam, nicknamed the 'Bat', was a fast and highly manoeuvrable fighter armed with twin Vickers machine guns, but by the time various problems with engines were overcome, the First World War was over. The machine in this photograph, serial B9945, was one of three prototypes.*

Source: Air Historical Branch (RAF), MoD, H.814

Below: *The Vickers Cow-gun fighter was designed to a specification for an all-metal monoplane capable of firing a quick-firing 37 mm gun manufactured by the Coventry Ordnance Works, in order to fire shells into the underbellies of enemy aircraft. Although this prototype, serial J9566, proved stable, interest was not sustained and the aircraft did not go into production.*

Source: Air Historical Branch (RAF), MoD, H.1819

CHAPTER 3

TRENCHARD IN THE TWENTIES

In November 1918, the strength of the RAF amounted to about 27,500 officers and 264,000 other ranks. There were also about 25,000 women of the Women's Royal Air Force, which had been formed on 1 April 1918 from volunteers who had served with the air units of the Women's Royal Naval Service and the Women's Auxiliary Army Corps. There were over 22,500 aircraft, including 3,300 in the front lines, and about 100 airships.

This enormous force could not be sustained and most squadrons were rapidly wound down and disbanded. Men and women were demobilized, and even Sir Hugh Trenchard lost his job. Thousands of aircraft were scrapped or, if possible, sold and converted to civilian roles. The Independent Bombing Force was disbanded. Outstanding contracts with manufacturers were cancelled, and many companies in the aero industry faced closure or liquidation. The portion of the RAF which remained in Britain was divided into a Southern Area, a Northern Area and a Coastal Area, the last corresponding to the old RNAS.

There is little doubt that, with hindsight, these measures were far too drastic. On the other hand, the participants in the holocaust of the previous four years were sickened with their experiences, together with the appalling loss of life and the maiming of an even greater number of men. It was genuinely believed that it had been a 'war to end wars'. There seemed little point in maintaining a third armed service, and for a while there existed the strong possibility of breaking up the RAF and bringing some of its units back into the control of the army and navy. Only one matter raised the RAF in public esteem, the setting up of an air mail service from Hendon to the British soldiers in the Army of Occupation in Germany.

After the Armistice, some units of the RAF remained in North Russia, having been despatched to Murmansk in the summer of 1918 together with the Allied forces which had landed there after the collapse of the Russian forces, to prevent the use of the base by German U-boats. When the White Russians began their attemps to wrest control of the country from the communists, these Allied forces were reinforced and began a drive towards Moscow in their support. But, under pressure of public opinion, the Allied troops and aircraft were withdrawn and the White Russians were defeated by the Red Army.

It was Winston Churchill who was largely responsible for the salvation of the RAF, after his appointment as Secretary of State for War and Air in January 1919. Although Churchill detested air warfare and particularly the bombing of civilians, he was far-seeing enough to invite Trenchard back to his old position as Chief of Air Staff.

Trenchard was a single-minded commander, highly determined and with a strong sense of purpose. Although he knew that the RAF was in danger of being broken up, or at least losing some of its squadrons to the army and the navy, he led a devoted team which set about putting the whole structure on a permanent basis. In April 1920 he opened the RAF College at Cranwell in Lincolnshire, where suitable cadets underwent a highly professional training before qualifying as officers. Two months later, in a measure designed both to improve morale within the service and to impress civilians, he set up

Below: *The Felixstowe F.5 flying boat followed the F.3 in 1919, having a slightly larger wing span and a longer range. It continued in service until 1925. This photograph is of serial N4838, believed to have been on the strength of 230 Squadron at Calshot.*

Source: Air Historical Branch (RAF), MoD, H.1780

Right: *The de Havilland 10 Amiens, a four-seat day bomber capable of carrying 900 lb of bombs, entered squadron service slightly too late to see action in the First World War and did not remain in the RAF beyond 1919. This machine was photographed while serving with 216 Squadron in Egypt.*

Source: Air Historical Branch (RAF), MoD, H.749

the RAF Central Band at Uxbridge in Middlesex. This band soon established a high reputation for the quality of its performances. Trenchard realized that public interest and approval was essential to the survival of the RAF and, in a remarkably astute exercise in public relations, opened the first RAF Pageant at Hendon on 3 July 1920.

This opening was well-timed, for interest in flying had been re-awakened by the achievement of Alcock and Brown, who had made the first direct crossing of the Atlantic from west to east on 14-15 June of the previous year, in a modified Vickers Vimy bomber. This was followed a few weeks later by the RAF airship *R.34*, which crossed the Atlantic from east to west and then back again. In November, a four-man team flew from England in another Vimy and arrived in Australia less than thirty days later. Thousands flocked to the first RAF pageant and were duly impressed and thrilled by the displays of aerobatics, mock bombing and formation flying. This pageant became a popular annual event and served the additional purpose of attracting youngsters into the flying and technical branches of the RAF.

However, it was the events overseas which finally established the RAF in its permanent form as a third branch of the armed forces. For some years, RAF squadrons had been active on the North West Frontier of India and in Egypt. During this period a dissident known as 'The Mad Mullah' had been so active that some areas of Somaliland had passed to his control. All the efforts by the army to dislodge him and his followers had proved both expensive and unsuccessful. In January 1920 Trenchard sent out a squadron of D.H.9s which promptly bombed the Mullah's forts and camps, putting the tribesmen to flight. A small force of the Camel Corps then occupied the positions and peace was established throughout Somaliland, for a relatively trifling expenditure.

The lesson of this short campaign was not lost on the British government. In February 1921, Churchill took over as Secretary of State for Air and the Colonies, an apparently strange combination. He authorised Trenchard's scheme for the 'air control' of Iraq, a country previously under the control of Turkey but mandated to Britain, which had set up an Arab government preparatory to complete independence. Some powerful tribes disputed the authority of this new government, but they were duly suppressed by the RAF's bombing of villages, after preliminary warnings had been given. Troops were flown in by the RAF to support threatened British garrisons, while columns of armoured cars worked in co-operation with these tactics. An uneasy peace was established in the country, once again at a fraction of the cost of normal army operations. The results were considered so satisfactory that, shortly afterwards, Palestine also came under the control of the RAF. The squadrons in Iraq added to their laurels in 1928 when the Vickers Victorias based at Habbaniya evacuated over 500 British civilians who were threatened

Above: *In 1919 the Australian government offered £A10,000 for the first Australian airmen to fly within thirty days in a British aircraft to Australia. The brothers Lt Keith M. Smith and Capt Ross Smith, together with two mechanics, took off in a Vimy bomber on 12 November 1919 from Hounslow in Middlesex and arrived at Port Darwin on 10 December. Both the Smith brothers were knighted.*
Left to right: Sgt W.H. Spiers, Lt K.M. Smith, Capt R. Smith, Sgt J.M. Bennett.

Source: Keystone Collection

Left: *The* R.34 *was one of two RAF airships, each with a length of 643 feet and powered by five engines, which entered service in 1919. She was based at Pulham in Norfolk, as shown in this photograph, and became notable for the first transatlantic flight made by a lighter-than-air craft. She left East Fortune in East Lothian in the early morning of 2 July 1919 and arrived over Mineola airfield, near New York, four days later. On 10 July, she took off again and arrived at Pulham after a flight of 75 hours. Unfortunately she was damaged beyond repair after hitting a hill on 28 January 1921, although there were no casualties.*

Source: Keystone Collection

by rebel tribesman in Kabul in Afghanistan. In a period of two months, the civilians were successfully flown over mountains 10,000 feet high, without casualties. In the same year, the RAF's Aden Command was set up, controlling a vast area of southern Arabia.

At home, Trenchard was not successful in retaining full control of naval aviation. Squadrons had been allocated to army and naval co-operation, but a hybrid arrangement had developed between the crews of the naval squadrons, whereby the air observers were naval officers but the pilots remained in the RAF. Such a situation could not continue when the first flush-deck carrier, HMS *Eagle*, was commissioned in 1923. On 1 April 1924, the Fleet Air Arm of the RAF was formed. In spite of this title, control passed partially to the Admiralty.

On the other hand, an expansion of RAF squadrons took place. Trenchard did nothing to calm the fears of a public which remembered with dismay the series of German bombing attacks of a few years before. In fact, he coined the grim phrase "the bomber will always get through", a prediction which became deeply impressed in the public consciousness. In March 1922 *The Times* reported that the French Air Force possessed a front-line force of about 600 aircraft, whereas the RAF's defences amounted to less than forty aircraft. In those days, France was considered a potential enemy and there was considerable public alarm. In June of the following year, the Cabinet authorised the creation of an Air Defence of Great Britain, consisting of fifty-two squadrons, although several years were to pass before this force was completed. It was divided into four sections. There were the Fighting Areas and the Bombing Areas. There were the Special Reserve squadrons, composed of a mixture of regular airmen and local volunteers. Lastly, there was the Auxiliary Air Force, consisting of squadrons which depended on 'weekend fliers' in local areas, such as 600 (City of London) Squadron, 601 (County of London) Squadron, 602 (City of Glasgow) Squadron and 603 (City of Edinburgh) Squadron. These four auxiliary squadrons were formed in 1925 and were followed by others.

Another measure put into force by Trenchard in 1924 was the creation of the short-service commission, a system by which suitable applicants were trained and then commissioned for a limited number of years, with the possibility of a permanent commission at the end of that period. Another scheme was the establishment of an apprentice scheme at Halton in Buckinghamshire, where youngsters underwent a rigorous technical training. These became known as 'Trenchard's Brats', a term which the entrants adopted with pride. Some graduated into the flying branch and achieved great distinction in later years. Even nowadays, a 'Halton Brat' is highly regarded in the RAF. In 1925, Trenchard began to form the University Air Squadrons, initially at Oxford and Cambridge, but eventually almost every university boasted its own Air Squadron. Another measure was the creation of the Aeroplane and Armament Experimental Establishment at Martlesham Heath in Suffolk, later to move to Boscombe Down in Wiltshire. The RAF Benevolent Fund also had its origins in the Trenchard era.

On the other hand, financial stringency prevented the design and manufacture of RAF aircraft from progressing at the same rate as during the First World War. At the end of the twenties, many aircraft were little more than improved versions of wartime

Above: *The Vickers Vimy came into service in 1919, too late to see service in the First World War. It was a heavy bomber which could carry nearly 2,500 lb of bombs and was originally intended to attack targets in Germany. However, eight RAF squadrons were equipped with the machine, which remained on squadron strength until 1926. It was in a Vimy, but not a standard RAF machine, that Captain John Alcock and Lieutenant Arthur Whitten Brown made the first direct flight across the Atlantic, from St John's in Newfoundland to Clifton in Ireland, on 14-15 June 1919. This photograph shows the take-off from St John's.*

Source: Keystone Collection

Right: *The Vickers Vimy which made the record flight to Australia in 1919.*

Source: Keystone Collection

Above: *A recruitment poster for the WRAF, which was formed at the same time as the RAF, on 1 April 1918.*

Source: Vintage Magazine Co. colour slide

Above: *The Avro 504K served for many years after the war as the RAF's standard trainer. Over 10,000 Avro 504s of various marks were built, a few carrying on until the beginning of the Second World War. This photograph of a 504K was taken in 1920.*

Source: Air Historical Branch (RAF), MoD, H.1444

Right: *In 1921, Queen Alexandra, the widow of King Edward VII, attended the RAF pageant at Hendon. The eldest daughter of King Christian IX of Denmark, Queen Alexandra died in 1925 at the age of 80.*

Source: Keystone Collection

Right: *The Fairey IIID entered service in late 1920 and could be used as either a floatplane or a landplane, being easily convertible from one configuration to the other. It could be used as a bomber or for reconnaissance. The floatplane version was employed by the Fleet Air Arm as well as by the RAF. Four landplane Fairey IIIDs made the RAF's first formation flight from Egypt to Capetown, in March/April 1926, and then flew back to England.*

Source: Aviation Bookshop

aircraft – wooden and fabric biplanes. Exceptions were, however, the sleek and fast monoplane seaplanes designed by Reginald J. Mitchell, with which the RAF began to win the Schneider Trophies in 1927. These were the forerunners of the splendid Spitfire of a decade later. The same period saw the end of the RAF's ventures with airships, with the tragic destruction of *R.101* in France on 5 October 1930.

In 1927, Trenchard became the first Marshal of the Royal Air Force. Two years later, it was time for him to retire. But the RAF could not bear to part with him, and decreed that holders of their highest rank should *never* retire but stay on the active list for the rest of their lives. Thus Trenchard remained nominally in this position until he died on 10 February 1956, even though he became commissioner for the Metropolitan Police and served as a director of various companies.

The author was one of a handful of bomber crew members who were addressed by Marshal of the Royal Air Force Lord Trenchard at an RAF station in the spring of 1941. It was not a good period of the war for Britain, which was still fighting without allies other than the Commonwealth. Trenchard was sixty-eight years of age, dressed in his uniform and wearing his cap. He looked very old to his young listeners, with an iron-grey moustache and a tired face. His words of encouragement fell somewhat flat for, although his reports and memoranda were models of clarity and incisiveness, his voice was so gruff and inarticulate that he was known as 'Boom' Trenchard. But there was an air of fatherliness and kindness about him. He probably knew, better than anyone, that many of the young men in front of him would not survive the war.

Left: *A mock bombing attack by Bristol Fighters on an 'enemy village' during the Hendon Air Display of 1921.*

Source: Keystone Collection

Below: *The Vickers Vernon was the first of the RAF's troop carriers. It entered service with 45 Squadron in March 1922 and with 70 Squadron the following November, both based at Hinaidi in Iraq. These two squadrons employed their Vernons with great effect in that country, carrying troops to trouble spots, evacuating sick and wounded, and carrying mail to and from Baghdad. Vernons were replaced by Vickers Victorias in 1927.*

Source: Air Historical Branch (MoD), Ref: H-337

Left: *Hendon aerodrome photographed from 800 feet on 20 March 1932.*

Source: RAF Museum P7578

Below: *Troops with a Vickers Victoria or Valentia transport aircraft, on manoeuvres in Egypt. Two squadrons were equipped with these machines, both based at Hinaidi in Iraq.*

Source: Keystone Collection

Bottom: *One of the first replacements for the First World War fighters was the Armstrong Whitworth Siskin III, which came into service in 1924. Only two squadrons were equipped with the machine, which was replaced with the Siskin IIIA in 1927.*

Source: RAF Museum PO12151

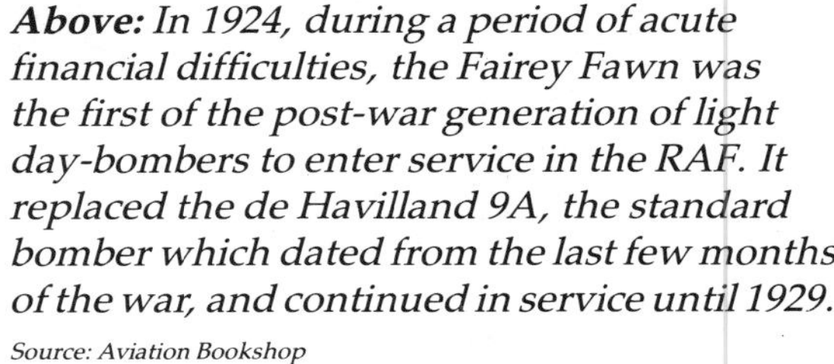

Above left: *The Hawker Woodcock was delivered to the RAF in May 1925, being allocated the role of a night-fighter. It was fitted with lights under the wings. Only two squadrons were equipped with the machine, which continued in service until 1928.*

Source: Aviation Bookshop

Above: *In 1924, during a period of acute financial difficulties, the Fairey Fawn was the first of the post-war generation of light day-bombers to enter service in the RAF. It replaced the de Havilland 9A, the standard bomber which dated from the last few months of the war, and continued in service until 1929.*

Source: Aviation Bookshop

Left: *The Supermarine Southampton was one of the longest-serving flying boats in the RAF. It first entered service in August 1925 and continued until 1936. Designed by Reginald J. Mitchell, it set the pattern for flying boats until the introduction of the Short Sunderland. In October 1927 four Southamptons of the Far East Flight set off for Singapore, Australia and the China Sea, returning to Singapore without serious problems. This was a remarkable technical achievement for the era. This photograph is of a Southampton of 201 Squadron, based at Calshot, flying over The Needles, Isle of Wight.*

Source; RAF Museum P1010 25

Right: *The Gloster Grebe was one of the first of the post-war generation of RAF fighters, first coming into service in October 1923. In 1926 two Grebes were launched from the airship R33, as an experiment. The machine continued in first-line service until 1929.*

Source: RAF Museum P4493

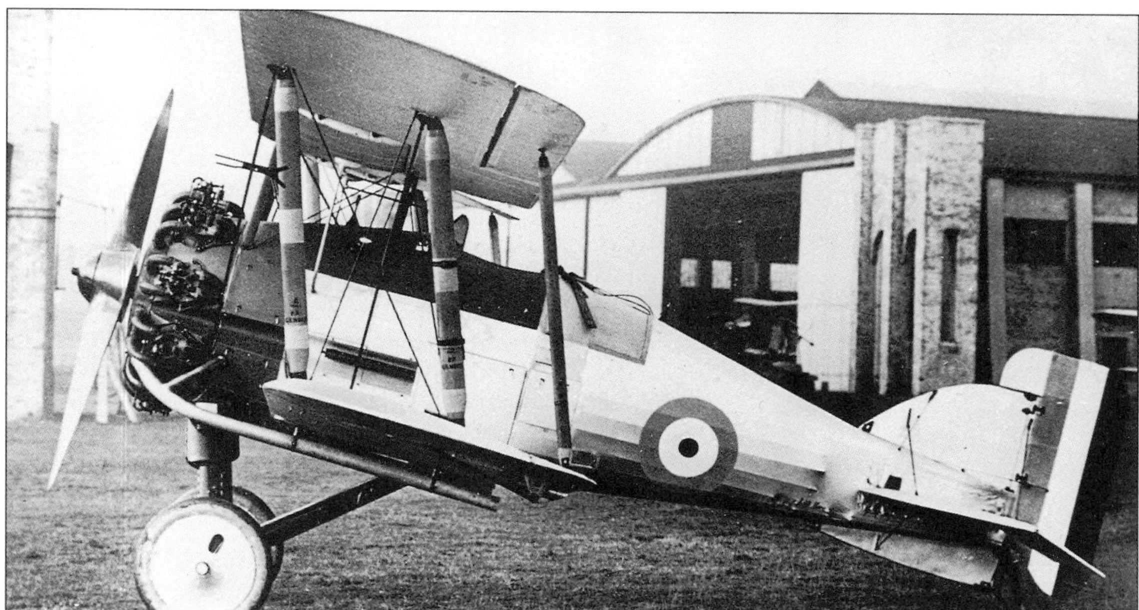

Above: *The Handley Page Hyderabad, a heavy night-bomber, entered service with 99 Squadron at Bircham Newton in Norfolk during December 1925, and eventually equipped three other RAF squadrons. It was the RAF's last heavy bomber of wooden construction, and was withdrawn from front-line service at the end of 1930. This photograph shows a formation of Hyderabads of 99 Squadron.*

Source: Air Historical Branch (RAF), MoD, H.1198

Left: *The Gloster Gamecock was a highly aerobatic fighter, introduced into the RAF in March 1926, although only production for the RAF numbered only 91. One of these machines was flown by Pilot Officer Douglas Bader at the RAF air display at Hendon in 1931. The machine went out of service in 1933.*

Source: Aviation Bookshop

Right: *Together with the Gloster Grebe, the Armstrong Whitworth Siskin III began to replace the wartime generation of fighters which had remained as standard equipment for five years. It came into service in May 1924 and, in a time of financial stringency, equipped only two squadrons. Siskins were finally withdrawn in November 1931.*

Source: Air Historical Branch (MoD), Ref: H.12

Right: *The Armstrong Whitworth Atlas was the first RAF aircraft designed specifically for the role of army co-operation. It first entered service in October 1927, replacing the adapted Bristol Fighter which had been employed on this capacity hitherto. Fitted with dual controls, it was also employed as an advanced trainer. The machines in this photograph, dated 1932, were on the strength of the Oxford University Air Squadron.*

Source: RAF Museum P101666

Left: *The Fairey Fox day-bomber was first delivered to 12 Squadron in June 1926 and proved over 50 m.p.h. faster than the Fairey Fawn which it superseded. It was also faster than any RAF fighter at the time. However, owing to national financial constraints, no other squadron was supplied with the machine, which remained in service with 12 Squadron until 1931.*

Source: Aviation Bookshop

Right: *The Vickers Virginia, known with affection as the 'Ginny', saw service as a heavy night-bomber in the RAF with a series of marks from 1924 to 1937. Even after withdrawal from front-line service, some machines continued as parachute trainers, and a few carried on in varied capacities right up to 1941. Although the four-man crew were accommodated in open cockpits and the machine trundled along at less than 100 m.p.h., the Virginia was well-liked for its dependable and robust qualities. This photograph is of a Mark X, the last of the series, part of the Parachute Test Section at Henlow in Bedfordshire.*

Source: RAF Museum P101427

Above: *The Avro 504N, or 'Lynx-Avro' was the post-war version of the Avro 504K trainer, fitted with a Lynx radial in 1927. Fully aerobatic, it was used with great success in flying schools until 1933, when replaced with Avro Tutors. This photograph shows an Avro 504N of the Cambridge University Air Squadron.*

Source: RAF Museum P100773

Right: *The Fairey IIIF entered service in late 1927 and proved a reliable day-bomber at home and a general-purpose aircraft in the Middle East. There was also a seaplane version, which continued at Malta until August 1935.*

Source: Aviation Bookshop

Left: *Manston aerodrome photographed from 3,000 feet, showing Vickers Virginias in the foreground.*
Source: RAF Museum P4331

Right: *The eleventh Schneider Trophy was held in the Solent in September 1929, following the RAF's win at Venice two years before. In preparation the RAF formed a High Speed Flight and entered two Supermarine S.6 seaplanes as well as two Gloster VI Seaplanes. Fl Off H.R.D. Waghorn came in first place in Supermarine N247 (pictured here) at an average speed of 328.63 m.p.h.*
Source: Keystone Collection

Below: *An airman adjusting the fusing mechanism of a Royal Aircraft Factory 520 lb bomb beneath a Vickers Virginia, photographed in 1928 when the RAF was engaged in air raid manoeuvres over London.*
Source: Keystone Collection

Below: *In 1927, the RAF entered a team for the first time in the Schneider Trophy. This contest was an international event, first held in 1913 by Jacques Schneider, a patron of French aviation. The three machines entered by the RAF were Supermarine S.5 seaplanes, designed by Reginald J. Mitchell, who later designed the Spitfire. The contest was held in Venice and was won on 27 September 1927 by Flt Lt N. Webster in N220 at an average speed of 281.65 m.p.h. Second place was won by N219 (photographed here at Calshot in Hampshire after a test flight) flown by Flt Lt O.E. Worsley at an average speed of 273.07 m.p.h.*

Source: Keystone Collection

Left: *The RAF team for the eleventh Schneider Trophy in 1929 consisted of (left to right) Fl Off H.R.D. Waghorn, Fl Off T.H. Moon, Flt Lt D'Arcy Greig, Sqdn Ldr A.H. Orlebar, Flt Lt G.H. Stainforth and Fl Off R.L.R. Atcherley.*

Source: Keystone Collection

Below: *The* R.101*, 777 feet long, over the town of Bedford in October 1929, after leaving Cardington on one of her test flights. She suffered from several technical problems, including engine defects.*

Source: Keystone Collection

Left: *From 1928 most Vimys were refitted with radial engines and employed at Flying Training Schools. Some were used for training parachutists, at Henlow in Bedfordshire. This photograph was taken at the Henlow Air Pageant in June 1931.*

Source: Keystone Collection

Below: *The twelfth Schneider Trophy was held in the Solent in September 1931. The two main entries by the RAF were Supermarine S.6B seaplanes. First place went to Flt Lt J.N. Boothman in S1595 (pictured here after a test flight, with Fl Lt F.W. Long being carried ashore) who achieved an average speed of 340.08 m.p.h. This gave the RAF its third successive win in the Schneider Trophy, and thus, they retained the trophy in perpetuity.*

Source: Keystone Collection

Bottom: *The pilot being brought ashore.*

Source: Keystone Collection

Left: *The remains of the* R.101 *after her crash at 02.08 hours on 5 October 1930, near Beauvais in France, while on her journey from Cardington to India. The airship burnt out and there were only six survivors from the fifty-four on board. Among those who lost their lives were the Air Minister, Lord Thompson, and the Director of Civil Aviation, Sir Sefton Brancker. In this photograph, the French firemen are holding up the Royal Air Force ensign.*

Source: Keystone Collection

Above: *The Handley Page Hinaidi was a heavy night-bomber, the successor to the Handley-Page Hyderabad. It first came into service in October 1929, and four RAF squadrons were equipped with the Hinaidi before the Handley Page Heyford arrived in 1933.*

Source: RAF Museum PO15337

Left: *The Westland Wapiti is best remembered for its active service on the North-West Frontier of India and in Iraq, where it was employed as a day-bomber on army co-operation. First delivered in July 1928, it remained in service until 1939. Several Auxiliary Air Force squadrons at home were also equipped with the machine. It proved to be strong and reliable, as well as fully aerobatic. This photograph shows Wapiti IIAs of 604 Squadron in 1931, when the squadron was based at Hendon.*

Source: RAF Museum P101174

Above: *Lord Trenchard, Marshal of the Royal Air Force, speaking after he had opened the town headquarters of 604 (County of Middlesex) Squadron at Hampstead on 7 April 1934. The squadron was part of the Auxiliary Air Force, based at Hendon and equipped with Westland Wapiti IIA day bombers.*

Source: Keystone Collection

Right: *The Hawker Horsley was employed both as a day-bomber and as a torpedo-bomber. Although only 128 Horsleys were manufactured for the RAF, they began as all-wooden construction, then of wood and metal, and finally as all-metal. The machine entered service in 1927 and continued to 1935.*

Source: Aviation Bookshop

CHAPTER 4

PRELUDE TO WAR

Left: *The Boulton Paul Sidestrand was a medium day bomber, first delivered to 101 Squadron at Bircham Newton in Norfolk in March 1929. It was a remarkably manoeuvrable aircraft for a twin-engined machine and could also fly on one engine. Only 101 Squadron was equipped with this machine, which was replaced with the Overstrand in January 1935.*

Source: RAF Museum P9812

Trenchard's place as Chief of Staff was taken over by one of his lieutenants, Sir John Salmond, but this period of tenure was quite short and uneventful. In 1933, Sir Edward Ellington was appointed to the position. Although Ellington was a self-effacing commander who was not considered to have the charisma of Trenchard, he proved to be a first-class staff officer who presided over a technical revolution which shaped the RAF of the Second World War.

These were the years which saw the rise of dictatorships and international aggression, in which air forces played prominent and unpleasant roles. In 1932, the Japanese began the bombing of China from the air, and the world saw films of the horrifying effect on a defenceless civilian population, especially in Shanghai. Mussolini had assumed the Fascist dictatorship of Italy in 1922, after his 'march on Rome', but this caused little public disquiet in Britain until it was realized that Germany was developing its own version of this political philosophy with the rise of the National Socialist Party. In 1933, when Adolf Hitler was appointed Chancellor, the industrial strength and military prowess of Germany were feared far more than any threat from Italy.

The conditions of the Treaty of Peace with Germany, signed at Versailles in June 1919, had reduced that country's military forces to an army of 100,000 with a small navy, for defensive purposes, and completely prohibited any air force. However, in the post-war years it became apparent that aircrews in Germany were receiving military training under the guise of civilians, allegedly for sporting purposes, while others were being trained in other countries, including Russia. Moreover, German aircraft designers were able to exercise their skills in Sweden, Switzerland and Italy, while their home industry had produced civil aircraft for the German airline *Lufthansa* which were readily adaptable to military use. The Junkers Ju52 and the Heinkel He111 became examples of such conversions.

Although the danger of a resurgent Germany with a National Socialist philosophy, which included the dangerously explosive concept of the right to territorial expansion in Europe under the name of *Lebensraum*, was startlingly apparent to some observers in Britain, the overwhelming mass of people still refused to believe that another European war was possible. Improved standards of living and the conquest of unemployment, together with a widespread belief in pacifism, dominated the thoughts of many British people. Advocates of re-armament and a stronger air force were not popular, although at the same time there was a fascination with flying. The long-distance records established by such pilots as Charles A. Lindbergh, Amelia Earhart, Amy Johnson and Charles Kingsford Smith were headline news and greeted with wild acclaim bordering on worship of the achievers.

In 1934, only forty-two of the fifty-two RAF squadrons ordered in 1923 had been established, with a first-line strength of 488 aircraft. However, in that year the government decided to embark on another expansion programme, against opposition in Parliament and some censure in the Press. The RAF was to increase as rapidly as possible to seventy-five squadrons, and to a hundred and twenty-eight squadrons within five years. This programme was dominated by the theory of the 'knock-out

Below: *The Bristol Bulldog was one of the most successful RAF fighters in the inter-war period, first entering service in May 1929. It was fast, extremely strong, fully aerobatic and, by comparison with its predecessors, took off quickly and had a high rate of climb. Over 300 aircraft were eventually supplied until, in 1937, the fighter was replaced with Gloster Gauntlets and Gladiators or Hawker Demons.*

Source: RAF Museum P3599

K
1085
K-1085

Right: *A restored Hawker Hart, registration G-ABMR, repainted as J9941 of 57 Squadron, which was equipped with Harts from October 1931 to May 1936.*

Source: RAF Museum colour slide P36021

Left: *The air displays at Hendon had become popular events by the 1930s, and most of the RAF's aircraft could be seen at these. This poster, representing a Hawker Hart, appeared in 1931.*

Source: RAF Museum (Crown copyright) P00512

Below: *The Hawker Hart, a light day-bomber, was the progenitor of a series of derivatives which served in the RAF in the inter-war period. First delivered in January 1930, it outpaced every RAF fighter in its day. It had a tendency to swing to the left on take-off but this was followed by a steep rate of climb and an excellent performance in aerobatics. The streamlined and elegant shape included a tapered nose which gave the pilot a splendid view. It was still in service in 1939 and continued on active operations in India until 1942. Other Harts continued as trainers in the early war years.*

Source: Keystone Collection

blow', for it was believed that air bombardment alone could win a war and that Britain should be equipped with a force capable of getting in the first major attacks. Additional fighter squadrons were to be formed, but primarily as a defensive force to appease a population which feared the type of air attacks they saw in cinemas and newspaper photographs.

At this stage, the RAF was still equipped mainly with biplanes in its bomber, fighter and coastal squadrons, mostly of wood or metal frames covered with fabric, resulting from the continuation of the belief that these were safer to fly than monoplanes. This thinking had not prevailed among civilian airliner companies, with the incongruous situation that some civil aircraft were faster than those of the RAF. However, the situation was changing, with the development of military monoplanes such as the Avro Anson reconnaissance aircraft, the Vickers Wellesley and Wellington bombers, the Armstrong Whitworth Whitley heavy bomber, the Handley Page Hampden medium bomber, the army co-operation Westland Lysander, and the Short Sunderland flying boat. In addition, the team headed by Sir Edward Ellington put out three far-seeing specifications which heralded further technical advances.

The first was Air Ministry Spec. F.5/34, issued in November 1934 but revised the following year after a design conference. This called for a fighter to replace the four-gun Gloster Gauntlet and Gladiator biplanes which were in production. It was to have a much better speed, rate of climb and ceiling, as well as the ability to carry eight machine guns. Two private companies responded to this specification. These were Hawker, with Sydney Camm as chief engineer, and Supermarine, with Reginald J. Mitchell as chief designer. Both design teams worked in close collaboration with RAF officers, fortunately at a time when two other technical developments came to fruition. These were the Merlin engine designed by Rolls Royce and the .303 inch Browning machine gun perfected by the Armament Research Department of the Air Ministry. The various strands came together in the prototypes of the Hawker Hurricane, which eventually entered service in December 1937, and the Supermarine Spitfire, which was delivered to RAF squadrons from June of the following year.

The second specification was B.12/36 of July 1936, which resulted in the Short Stirling, the first four-engined bomber to serve in the RAF, from August 1940 onwards. The third specification was P.13/36 of September 1936, which called for an all-metal medium/heavy bomber with a mid-wing and twin engines. This resulted in the Avro Manchester, a bomber which entered service in November 1940 and proved unsuccessful but earned its place in RAF history as the progenitor of the famous four-engined Lancaster. The other bomber which resulted from this specification was the very successful Handley Page Halifax, originally designed as a twin-engined aircraft but modified to take four engines, which also entered squadron service in November 1940. Another important development took place in this period, almost by accident. The

belief that 'the bomber will always get through' had led to the setting up in January 1935 of a Aeronautical Research Committee consisting of a number of eminent scientists, charged with the function of finding ways to repel an air attack. One of the possibilities examined was the notion of a 'death ray' which would destroy approaching aircraft. The scientists consulted R.A. Watson-Watt of the Radio Department of the National Physical Laboratory, who pointed out that, although the death ray idea was nonsense, approaching aircraft re-radiated radio signals. From this, the concept of Radio Direction Finding (RDF) was born, later to be shortened to 'radar'. The instruments led eventually to the setting up of twenty 'Chain Home' (CH) radar stations around the coasts of Britain, and to the invention of the 'Identification Friend or Foe' (IFF) equipment carried in all operational RAF aircraft. By the time war broke out, it was possible to detect approaching enemy aircraft from distances up to 100 miles from British shores, with considerable accuracy.

Meanwhile, the march of the dictators continued. Hitler assumed complete power in Germany in 1934 and in February of the following year the *Luftwaffe* was reborn, in defiance of the Treaty of Versailles. With Hermann Goering, a renowned pilot of the First World War, as its commander-in-chief, it possessed over 1,800 aircraft (of which about 580 were first-line) and 20,000 personnel. Moreover, it was set on an accelerated pace of expansion. Factories which had hitherto manufactured products which were apparently unwarlike were suddenly able to make machine guns, while other companies such as Henschel and Blohm und Voss found that they were capable of manufacturing military aircraft, especially trainers.

Italy attacked Abyssinia on 3 October 1935, bombing villages and eventually even using poison gas, a weapon banned by the League of Nations. The world was shocked by films and photographs showing these attacks against villagers. Economic sanctions were instigated against Italy as an alternative to military intervention, but these proved ineffectual. The RAF moved squadrons to Egypt, Somaliland and Malta, while Ellington even offered to bomb northern Italy from bases in southern France, but no military action was taken.

In the same year, the Saar was returned to Germany, following a plebiscite. In March 1936, Hitler began the remilitarisation of the Rhineland, and made no secret of his territorial ambitions in Europe. In July of that year, General Francisco Franco brought troops from Morocco to Spain in an attempt to overturn the government and impose a Fascist dictatorship on the country. He achieved this objective after almost three years of cruel civil war, assisted by contingents of aircraft from Italy and Germany. Once again, films of attacks against civilian populations were shown around the world. For the first time, the effectiveness of German aircraft such as the Heinkel He111, the Dornier Do17, the Junkers Ju52 and the Messerschmitt Bf109, became apparent to the RAF.

In 1936, the RAF at home was divided into five sections: the Western Area, consisting of heavy bombers; the Central Area, with light bombers and general-purpose aircraft; the Fighting Area, with single-engined fighters; the Inland Area, with army co-operation squadrons; and the Coastal Area, with flying boats and a squadron of torpedo bombers. Overseas, there were five commands: the Middle East, the Mediterranean, India, Aden and the Far East. In May of that year, important structural alterations began at home, dividing the RAF according to function. A Training Command was set up, while the operational sections were grouped into Bomber Command, Fighter Command and Coastal Command, each responsible to the Chief of Air Staff via the Air Council. These Commands controlled regional Groups, which administered their own stations, which in turn administered squadrons. This was the structure of the RAF which fought the Second World War.

At the same time as the expansion programme got under way, the RAF was authorised to increase the number of its aerodromes from fifty-two to a hundred and thirty-eight. Many of these new aerodromes were built in East Anglia, Lincolnshire and Yorkshire, facing Germany. Bomber squadrons which had formed the Western Area, with France as a potential enemy, were transferred to these new aerodromes.

Another measure organized in 1936 was the creation of the Royal Air Force Volunteer Reserve, a form of 'Citizen Air Force' which was the RAF's equivalent of the Territorial Army. Young men were invited from April 1937 onwards to learn to train as pilots, observers or wireless operators in their spare time. The scheme proved extremely popular, so much so that by the time war broke out the RAFVR stood at over 10,000 men in these three aircrew categories, the majority being pilots.

On 1 September 1937, Sir Cyril Newhall took over from Sir Edward Ellington as Chief of Air Staff. In that year, the Air Estimates rose to £137.6 million, compared with only £16.8 million in 1933. The new Chief of Air Staff presided over the continued expansion, at a time when the international situation became even more threatening.

In July 1937 the Japanese had begun their attempted conquest of the whole of China, causing appalling casualties with a series of bombing attacks designed to spread terror among civilians. This war was still continuing when the Japanese attacked Pearl Harbour on 7 December 1941. In February 1938 Germany annexed Austria, with the apparent enthusiasm of the majority of the Austrian population. Neville Chamberlain, the prime minister of a coalition government, flew out to Munich and returned with a piece of paper signed by Hitler, Mussolini, Daladier and himself, purporting to

Above: *The Fairey Gordon entered service in the RAF in England in April 1931, and was employed as a light day-bomber. It remained in front-line service, both at home and in the Middle East until 1938. Several aircraft were lost on operations during the insurrections in Palestine. The machine continued as a drogue-tower and armament trainer in the early months of the Second World War.*

Source: Aviation Bookshop

Below left: *The Hawker Fury I became one of the most admired of the RAF's standard fighters after it entered service in May 1931. It was the first RAF fighter to attain a maximum speed of over 200 m.p.h. with a full warload. The sleek and elegant lines exemplified its high manoeuvrability and instant response at the controls, which were demonstrated by formation flying at air shows. An improved version, the Fury II, was introduced in December 1936, but by the Second World War the Fury was rendered obsolete with the arrival of the monoplane Hurricane.*

Source: Aviation Bookshop

Below: *The cockpit of a Hawker Fury. Within a few years, the flying panels of most operational aircraft in the RAF were standardised to present six instruments in a set pattern: airspeed indicator, artificial horizon, rate of climb, altimeter, gyroscope, and turn and bank.*

Source: Air Historical Branch (RAF), MoD, H.1985

Right: *The Hawker Demon was a two-seat fighter, a variant of the Hawker Hart day-bomber, originally called the Hart Fighter. It began service in March 1931 and eleven home-based squadrons were eventually equipped with the machine, as well as seven overseas. Later Demons were fitted with a Fraser-Nash folding metal cupola, to protect the gunner from the slip-stream. The machine was taken out of service in 1939.*

Source: Aviation Bookshop

Right: *Yet another variation of the Hawker Hart was the Hawker Audax. It first went into service from February 1932 with army co-operation squadrons but perhaps became better known as an advanced trainer with Service Flying Training Schools. As a front-line aircraft at home, it was replaced in 1938 but it continued as a trainer until the early years of the Second World War. Overseas, it saw action with 237 (Rhodesian) Squadron in East Africa and also during the investment of RAF Habbaniya in Iraq in May 1941.*

Source: Aviation Bookshop

guarantee 'peace for our time'. Very few people were convinced, but the RAF breathed a sigh of relief, for its expansion programme had not yet reached fulfilment.

The worst fears were realized when Hitler annexed Bohemia and Moravia from Czechoslovakia in March 1939, and forced Lithuania to cede the region of Memel in the same month. Italy occupied Albania in April, and entered into the 'Axis' pact with Germany. Germany began a propaganda campaign against Poland. Not even the most blinkered observer could have any doubts about the approach of war when Britain and France 'guaranteed' the Polish frontiers. Then Germany signed a non-aggression pact with Russia, giving Germany a free hand on Poland's western frontier.

The expansion of the RAF continued apace. In November 1938, a Balloon Command was formed, with barrages around most major cities, and its own squadrons. On 24 May 1939, the future of the Fleet Air Arm was settled when this air arm, which had been somewhat neglected in the programme, was returned in its entirety to the Admiralty. A week later, the Women's Royal Air Force was established, and those volunteers who had trained in the Auxiliary Territorial Service for service with the RAF were transferred to this new body.

The German invasion of Poland began on 1 September and, when Hitler failed to respond to the British and French ultimatum, war was declared two days later.

Left: *Over 1,000 de Havilland Tiger Moths were delivered to the RAF before the Second World War, the first consignments arriving in February 1932. The Tiger was the last biplane ab initio* trainer employed by the RAF in the UK and continued until 1947, by which time about 8,800 had been built. Although the open cockpits could be cold and draughty, the trainer was robust and easy to fly. It was regarded with great affection by most RAF pilots of the era. This photograph was taken at 32 Elementary Flying Training School at Swift Current, Bowden, Alberta. In Canada, many Tigers were fitted with canopies as protection against the bitterly cold winters.*

Source: RAF Museum PO16608

Right: *The Avro Tutor succeeded the Avro 504N and was first delivered to the Central Flying School in 1932, becoming standard as an* ab initio *trainer in RAF flying schools until 1939. This photograph shows an Avro Tutor of the Cambridge University Air Squadron.*

Source: RAF Museum P3773

Left: *The Vickers Vildebeest was first delivered to the RAF in 1932 and continued in service until 1942. On the outbreak of the Second World War, it was the only torpedo bomber available to Coastal Command and the maritime squadrons overseas. The home-based squadrons were re-equipped with the Bristol Beaufort in 1940. This photograph shows Vildebeest IVs, from the last batch of seventeen delivered to the RAF in 1937. Torpedoes were suspended in a nose-down attitude, so that they would enter the sea at the correct angle when dropped from the operating height of eighty feet.*

Source: Keystone Collection

Above: *The Westland Wallace was similar to the Westland Wapiti, but fitted with a more powerful engine and a lengthened fuselage. It first entered service in January 1933 and eventually four squadrons were equipped with this general-purpose aircraft. The Westland Wallace II, as in this photograph of serial K6085, was fitted with an even more powerful engine and an enclosed canopy for both seats. After withdrawal from front-line service, Wallaces continued as target-towers until final retirement in 1943.*

Source: Air Historical Branch (MoD), Ref: H.1989

Above: *'Stunt flying' was of great interest to the air-minded public of the 1930s, with perhaps the opportunity to go up in an aircraft for a short flight at 5/- a time. Many young men who joined the RAF in the Second World War had their first taste of flying at Hendon.*

Source: RAF Museum (Crown copyright) P00404

Left: *The Handley Page Heyford, with its fuselage attached to the upper wing and its equally distinctive 'dustbin' ventral turret, was the last of the RAF's biplane heavy bombers. The first Heyfords were delivered to the RAF in late 1933, and the aircraft continued in front-line service until 1937, when most gave way to the Vickers Wellington. Some machines then continued as trainers and test vehicles, the last being withdrawn in July 1941. In this photograph, a Heyford I with its dustbin retracted is being 'attacked' by a Hawker Demon.*

Source: RAF Museum P105338

Left: *The World's Long-distance Record for Aviation was a prize which the Air Ministry wished to gain for Great Britain in the late 1920s, and two long-range monoplanes were specially designed by Fairey for this purpose. They could carry up to 1,000 gallons of fuel, giving them a range of over 5,000 miles. Unfortunately the first, serial J9479, crashed in 1929 in Tunisia, killing the crew of two. The second, serial K1991, flew on 27-28 October 1931 from Cranwell to Abu Sueir in Egypt; this photograph was taken in Heliopolis. On 6 February 1933, it took off from Cranwell and reached Walvis Bay in S.W. Africa after 57 hours 25 minutes, a distance of 5,309 miles, thus gaining the record for Great Britain.*

Source: RAF Museum P1540

Right: *A view of the amphibian Walrus, flying low over Southampton Water in May 1936. The wheels are folded up into the wings.*

Source: Keystone Collection

Above: *Only 209 Squadron, based at Mount Batten in Devonshire, was equipped with the Blackburn Iris, from February 1930 to June 1934. In this period, the Iris was the largest aircraft in service in the RAF and flew on a number of V.I.P. flights, to Iceland, Gibraltar and Egypt. The last Iris to be manufactured was fitted with a 37 mm C.O.W. gun in an enlarged front cockpit. The Iris flying boats were eventually replaced with Blackburn Perths.*

Source: Air Historical Branch (MoD), Ref: H.2056

Left: *The Blackburn Perth entered service in January 1934, as the fastest RAF flying boat of its period. Only four were built, serving with 209 Squadron at Mount Batten in Devon until January 1936.*

Source: RAF Museum P101403

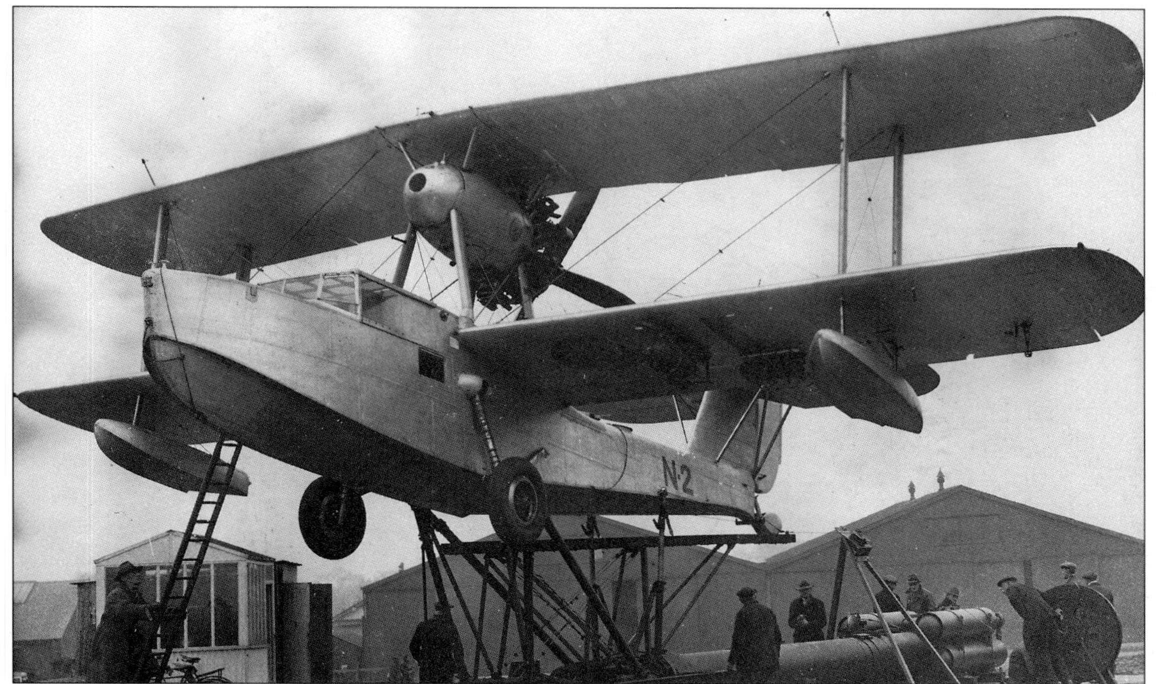

Left: *The Supermarine Walrus, originally known as the Seagull V, came into RAF service in 1934. It was an amphibian aircraft with a pusher engine, used by both the Fleet Air Arm and the RAF. Although it had an ungainly appearance and only a slow cruising speed, it was regarded with enormous affection by RAF airmen, who referred to it somewhat disrespectfully as the 'Shagbat'; according to RAF legend, this was a mythical Egyptian bird which could fly in ever-decreasing circles until it finally disappeared. The Walrus achieved renown during World War Two as an air-sea rescue aircraft at home, in the Mediterranean and the Indian Ocean. Many heroic and life-saving deeds were performed by the aircrews who flew this machine, which remained in service until the end of the war, being built by Saro as well as Supermarine.*

Source: Keystone Collection

Left: *The Short Singapore III first entered service in January 1935. The four engines of the flying boat were of the 'push-pull' variety, in tandem. Thirty-seven were built for the RAF, equipping six squadrons at home and two overseas. Some Singapores remained with the RAF at the outbreak of the Second World War, both at home and abroad, but these were soon replaced by Sunderlands.*

Source: Keystone Collection

Below: *The Supermarine Scapa was a development on the highly reliable Southampton flying boat, first entering service in May 1935 with 202 Squadron at Kalafrana in Malta. Scapas were employed on anti-submarine patrols during the Spanish Civil War, to protect shipping. Only fourteen were built for the RAF, continuing in service until December 1938. This photograph is of serial K4191 of 204 Squadron, refuelling from a depot ship.*

Source: Air Historical Branch (MoD), Ref: H.332

Above: *The Boulton Paul Overstrand, a medium bomber which was delivered to 101 Squadron in 1935 and remained in front-line service until 1938. It was the first RAF bomber to be fitted with the new power-operated turret, in the nose, with a single Lewis gun. In the Second World War, it saw active service for a few months as a gunnery trainer.*

Source: Keystone Collection

Above: *The first power-operated turret in the RAF, in the nose of the Boulton Paul Overstrand, fitted with a single .303 inch Lewis gun.*

Source: Keystone Collection

Below: *The Vickers Valentia was developed from the Vickers Victoria troop carrier. It first entered service in September 1935, with 216 Squadron at Heliopolis in Egypt. Most Valentias flew in the Middle East and India, until phased out in 1941. This photograph was taken in Egypt, with the pyramids in the background.*

Source: Keystone Collection

Above: *The Gloster Gauntlet was the fastest fighter in the RAF from 1935 to 1937, fourteen squadrons being equipped with the machine. Unlike the Gladiator which followed it, the cockpit was open. The machine was obsolescent at the outbreak of the Second World War but four Gauntlets operated against the Italians in the autumn of 1940.*

Source: Aviation Bookshop

Right: *A Hawker Audax flying over the Pyramids of Giza. The aircraft was probably from 208 Squadron, which was based nearby at Heliopolis from April to December 1936.*

Source: Keystone Collection

Above: *A Lewis Mark III .303 inch machine gun with a ring sight, in the gunner's cockpit of a Hawker Audax. The foresight was a Norman Vane Sight, which turned with the slipstream and compensated for the motion of the gunner's aircraft, although it was still necessary to make allowances for deflection caused by the manoeuvres of the enemy aircraft.*

Source: Keystone Collection

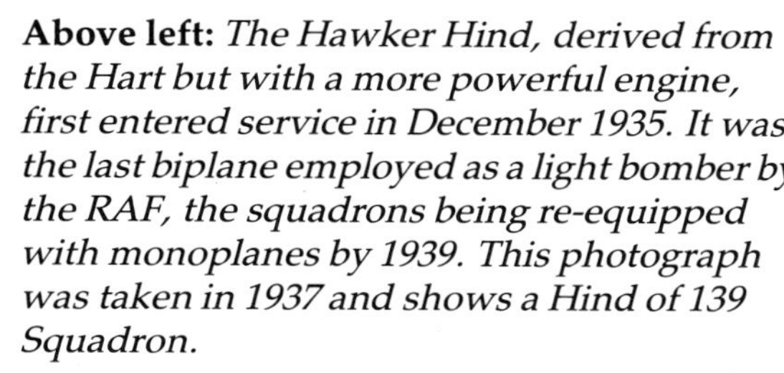

Above left: *The Hawker Hind, derived from the Hart but with a more powerful engine, first entered service in December 1935. It was the last biplane employed as a light bomber by the RAF, the squadrons being re-equipped with monoplanes by 1939. This photograph was taken in 1937 and shows a Hind of 139 Squadron.*

Source: Keystone Collection

Above: *A Hawker Hart of 603 (City of Edinburgh) Squadron, which was equipped with the machine from February 1934 to February 1938.*

Source: RAF Museum P101457

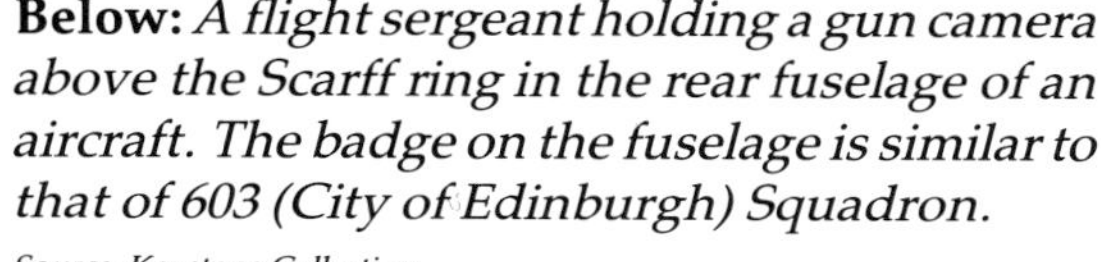

Below: *A flight sergeant holding a gun camera above the Scarff ring in the rear fuselage of an aircraft. The badge on the fuselage is similar to that of 603 (City of Edinburgh) Squadron.*

Source: Keystone Collection

On 16 January 1936, a standard frame for unit badges for the RAF was devised, with the King's Crown above and a scroll beneath. Squadrons and other units were able to submit specimens to an Inspector of Royal Air Force Badges. Several were approved within the next few months, and these were published in 1936 and 1937.

No. 2 (Army Co-operation) Squadron, equipped with Hawker Audaxes and based at Hawkinge in Kent.

RAF Museum colour slide PO30006

No. 4 (Army Co-operation) Squadron, equipped with Hawker Audaxes and based at Farnborough in Hampshire. Motto: To see into the Future.

RAF Museum colour slide PO30011

No. 12 (Bomber) Squadron, equipped with Hawker Hinds and based at Andover in Hampshire.

RAF Museum colour slide PO30028

No. 15 (Bomber) Squadron, equipped with Hawker Hinds and based at Abingdon in Berkshire.

RAF Museum colour slide PO30033

No. 18 (Bomber) Squadron, equipped with Hawker Hinds and based at Upper Heyford in Oxfordshire. Motto: With Courage and Faith.

RAF Museum colour slide PO30039

No. 22 (Torpedo Bomber) Squadron, equipped with Vickers Vildebeests and based at Hal Far in Malta. Motto: Valiant and Brave.

RAF Museum colour slide PO30044

No. 33 (Bomber) Squadron, equipped with Hawker Harts and based at Mersa Matruh in Egypt.

RAF Museum colour slide PO30056

No. 40 (Bomber) Squadron, equipped with Hawker Hinds and based at Abingdon in Berkshire. Motto: To Drive the Enemy from the Sky.

RAF Museum colour slide PO30067

No. 41 (Fighter) Squadron, equipped with Hawker Demons and based at Catterick in Yorkshire.

RAF Museum colour slide PO30070

No. 74 (Fighter) Squadron, equipped with Hawker Demons and based at Hornchurch in Essex.

RAF Museum colour slide PO30104

No. 201 (Flying Boat) Squadron, equipped with Short Southamptons and Saro Londons, and based at Calshot in Hampshire. Motto: Here and Everywhere.

RAF Museum colour slide PO30173

No. 203 (Flying Boat) Squadron, equipped with Short Singapores and based at Basra in Iraq. Motto: West and East.

RAF Museum colour slide PO30175

No. 207 (Bomber) Squadron, equipped with Fairey Gordons and based at Gebeit in the Sudan. Motto: Always Prepared

RAF Museum colour slide PO30179

No. 230 (Flying Boat) Squadron, equipped with Short Singapores and based at Seletar in Singapore. Motto: (Malay) We Seek Far.

RAF Museum colour slide PO30198

No. 604 (County of Middlesex) Squadron, equipped with Hawker Demons and based at Hendon in Middlesex. Motto: If You Want Peace, Prepare For War.

RAF Museum colour slide PO30245

Right: *The Avro Anson was originally ordered by the RAF for coastal reconnaissance duties and came into service in March 1936. It was one of the first aircraft in the RAF with a retractable undercarriage, although this was wound up with a handle which required 122 turns. The Anson entered the war with twelve squadrons of Coastal Command, engaged mainly on reconnaissance and convoy escort duties, but was gradually replaced with more modern machines such as the Hudson and the Beaufort. However, the Anson continued as a standard twin-engined trainer for pilots, navigators, wireless operators and air gunners, remaining in service until 1968. A highly reliable and well-liked machine, it deserved its nickname of 'Faithful Annie'.*

Source: Keystone Collection

Above: *Wheeling in an Avro Anson after a flight.*

Source: Keystone Collection

Left: *The Saro London entered service with the RAF in April 1936 and flew operationally until mid 1941. At the end of 1937, five Londons of 204 Squadron, fitted with long-range tanks, cruised from England to New South Wales and returned the following May.*

Source: RAF Museum P101501

Below: *The RAF gained the World's Altitude Record on two occasions with the Bristol Type138A, serial K4879, constructed of wood to meet an Air Ministry specification. In September 1936 it flew from Farnborough to reach the record height of 49,967 feet. This record was beaten by Italy the following May, but regained for the RAF on 30 June 1937 when the Type 138A reached 53,937 feet.*

Source: RAF Museum PO12644

Above: *The Fairey Hendon in this photograph entered service with 38 Squadron in November 1936. It was a heavy night-bomber, but only fourteen machines were built. The machine was replaced by the new Wellington bomber in July 1939.*

Source: Aviation Bookshop

Below: *The Saro Cloud was an amphibian flying boat, used for training pilots and navigators. It entered service in August 1933 at Calshot in Hampshire and was retired in 1936. Only sixteen of this aircraft were produced.*

Source: Keystone Collection

Right: *The Handley Page Harrow came into service in January 1937 as one of the first monoplane heavy bombers to replace the RAF's biplanes. It could carry 3,000 lb of bombs but was already out-dated by the outbreak of the Second World War, by which time the squadrons had converted to Wellingtons. Apart from some work in aerial minelaying and as a troop transport, the Harrow did not see operational service. This photograph was taken in November 1936 and shows the first Harrow, at Radlett aerodrome in Hertfordshire on the occasion of its christening by the Mayoress of Harrow.*

Source: Keystone Collection

Left: *The last of the RAF's biplane fighters was the Gloster Gladiator, which first entered service in February 1937 and equipped more than thirty squadrons. It proved easy to fly and was highly manoeuvrable, being quite formidable with four Browning guns. Most Gladiators were superseded by monoplane fighters by the outbreak of the Second World War, but some went to France as part of the Advanced Air Striking Force, while others operated in Norway during the German invasion of that country. The Gladiator is perhaps best remembered for the heroic defence of Malta and for operations in Africa against the* Regia Aeronautica, *before being outclassed by German fighters. This photograph of serial L7619 of 33 Squadron was taken in Ismailia in Egypt.*

Source: RAF Museum P8548

Right: *The Armstrong Whitworth Whitley, first delivered to the RAF in March 1937, formed part of the heavy bomber force in the early years of the Second World War. Its appearance was rather ungainly and it required firm handling, but the construction was rugged enough to absorb a lot of punishment. It was the first bomber to be equipped with a power-operated turret containing four Browning machine guns, as well as the first to fly over Berlin, on a leaflet raid of 1/2 October 1939. The last operational flight was on the night of 29/30 April 1942. These three Whitleys of 102 Squadron were photographed in 1940.*

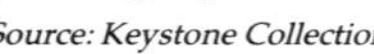
Source: Keystone Collection

Above: *The Supermarine Stranraer entered service with 228 Squadron in April 1937, four Coastal Command squadrons being eventually equipped with this flying boat. Stranraers were steadily replaced with Sunderlands and Catalinas, being finally withdrawn from squadron service in April 1941, although some continued as trainers. This photograph shows serial K7295 of 240 Squadron, taking off.*

Source: RAF Museum P7375

Right: *When the Fairey Battle monoplane entered service with the RAF in May 1937, it was hailed a worthy successor to biplane light bombers. In the event, it proved seriously under-powered and under-armed. Although obsolescent by the outbreak of the Second World War, several squadrons equipped with the machine were sent to France in 1939. When the Wehrmacht attacked through the Low Countries in May 1940, these Battles went into action, unescorted and in daylight; in spite of the astonishing bravery of the crews, they suffered very heavy losses. Most Fairey Battles were retired from front-line service by the end of 1940 and were used as trainers for bomb aimers and air gunners.*

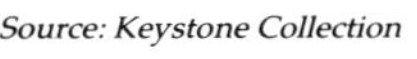

Source: Keystone Collection

Left: *The Hawker Hector entered service in May 1937 as a replacement for the Hawker Audax, in the role of army co-operation. Most Hectors were replaced by Westland Lysanders by the outbreak of the Second World War, but several went into action during the German invasion of France in May 1940. Thereafter, the remaining aircraft were used primarily as glider towers.*

Source: Aviation Bookshop

Right: *The Blenheim I first appeared in RAF squadrons in 1937, as a fast monoplane bomber. However, by the outbreak of the Second World War, the home bomber force of Blenheim Is had been largely replaced by Blenheim IVs, and many aircraft had been converted into night-fighters. Overseas, the Blenheim I saw operational service in Greece and the Western Desert. This photograph shows a Blenheim I of 90 Squadron, which was a training squadron for Bomber Command from May 1937 to April 1940.*

Source: RAF Museum P1680

Right: *In September 1937 the first monoplane trainer entered service with the RAF. This was the Miles Magister, made of wood and fully aerobatic. Known inevitably as the 'Maggie', it was a successful* ab initio *trainer which equipped Elementary Flying Training Schools until the end of the war.*

Source: RAF Museum PO14437

Below: Feldmarshall *von Blomberg visiting RAF Andover in Hampshire, in 1937. The aircraft is a Harrow Mark I.*

Source: Keystone Collection

Right: *The Airspeed Oxford, first introduced in November 1937, was the first twin-engined monoplane to be used as an advanced trainer by the RAF. The Oxford I was fitted with a dorsal turret, since the aircraft was designed as a trainer for pilots, navigators, wireless operators and air gunners. In the event, however, the machine was employed primarily for training pilots at Service Flying Training Schools, and the Oxford II was built without a turret. A later version, with Wasp engines instead of Cheetah's, was the Oxford V. By the end of the Second World War, over 8,500 Oxfords had been produced, these being employed in Britain, Canada, Australia, New Zealand, Southern Rhodesia and Egypt. After the war, the Oxford continued in service until 1954.*

Source: RAF Museum PO16741

Above: *The guns of a Hawker Hurricane in action at night, against the butts.*

Source: Keystone Collection

Above right: *The prototype Hawker Hurricane, serial K5083, designed by Sydney Camm. It was ordered on 21 February 1935 and made its first flight on 6 November 1935.*

Source: Air Historical Branch, MoD. Ref: H.1848

Left: *The possibility of air attacks against British cities necessitated a rapid expansion of Balloon Command. A recruiting drive was begun with the aid of posters.*

Source: RAF Museum (Crown copyright)

Left: *In December 1937 the new Hawker Hurricane I entered service with 111 Squadron at Northolt, inaugurating a new era of eight-gun monoplane fighters which could fly faster than 300 m.p.h. The following May, a Hurricane of this squadron flew from Edinburgh to Northolt at an average speed of 408 m.p.h. This was a remarkable achievement at the time, although the aircraft was helped by a strong tail wind. Hurricanes bore the brunt of the war in France and, during the Battle of Britain, shot down eighty per cent of all aircraft claimed by the RAF. Although less elegant than the Spitfire, it was a tough and reliable aircraft which gave splendid service in all the RAF's theatres of war.*

Source: Keystone Collection

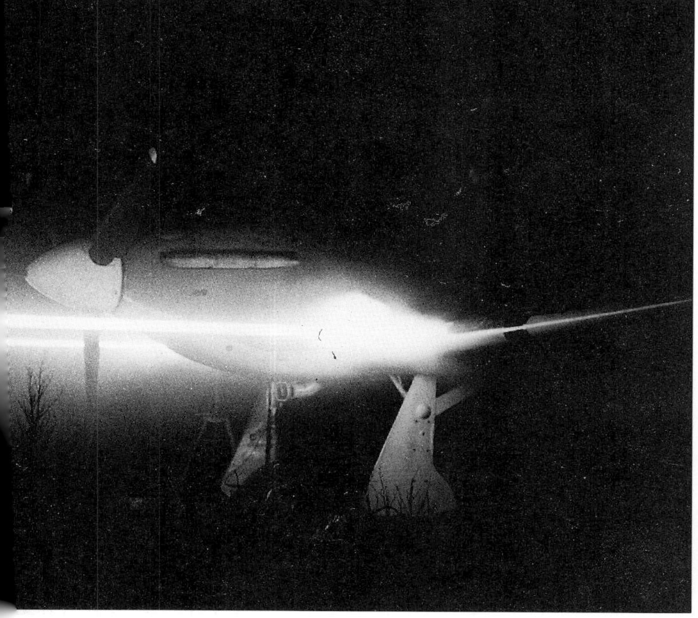

Right: *One of the most remarkable aircraft to enter RAF service before the Second World War was the Vickers Wellington. The first production model flew in December 1937, and Wellingtons then formed the mainstay of Bomber Command's force until the arrival of four-engined bombers. The metal lattice work of the airframe gave the aircraft the ability to withstand considerable punishment from enemy fire. Wellingtons continued in service throughout the war, being employed not only with Bomber Command but on weather reconnaissance, on anti-submarine patrols, as transport aircraft and even as torpedo bombers. Well-liked by RAF crews, it was nicknamed the 'Wimpy' after the character J. Wellington Wimpy in the Popeye cartoons. The aircraft in this photograph is a Wellington I, crossing the toll bridge over the river Wey, in Surrey, between the Weybridge factory and Brooklands aerodrome.*

Source: Keystone Collection

Left: *The Westland Lysander, nicknamed 'The Lizzie', entered service in the RAF in May 1938. It was the first high-wing monoplane specially designed for army co-operation. Four Lysander squadrons were sent to France in 1939, where they fought gallantly and also helped cover the evacuation from Dunkirk. The aircraft also gave excellent service in the Western Desert, Greece, Palestine and India. After retirement from army co-operation in 1941, Lysanders continued in roles such as air-sea rescue, target tugs, liaison as well as landing and retrieving Allied secret agents in Occupied Europe. It had an excellent downward field of vision together with the ability to land on strips of no more than 150 yards in length. This photograph shows the prototype Lysander, serial K6127, which made its first flight on 15 June 1936.*

Source: Keystone Collection

Above: *The prototype Supermarine Spitfire, serial K5054, which made its maiden flight in March 1936, probably on the 6th, at Eastleigh in Hampshire. It was fitted with a fine pitch propeller for the first flight and the undercarriage was locked down.*

Source: Air Historical Branch, MoD. Ref: H.1835

Left: *In June 1938, the Short Sunderland I was the first monoplane to replace the biplane flying boats with which the RAF had been equipped since the First World War. It was derived from the Imperial Airways flying boat and, equipped with nose and tail turrets as well as beam guns, became known to German airmen as 'the flying porcupine'. This splendid aircraft gave noble service in Coastal Command as well as in maritime squadrons abroad. Sunderlands of various marks continued in RAF service for twenty years.*

Source: Keystone Collection

Left: *Two volunteers, from British Columbia and Vancouver Island in Canada, en route to the RAF Reception Depot at West Drayton in Middlesex, photographed on 24 August 1938.*

Source: Keystone Collection

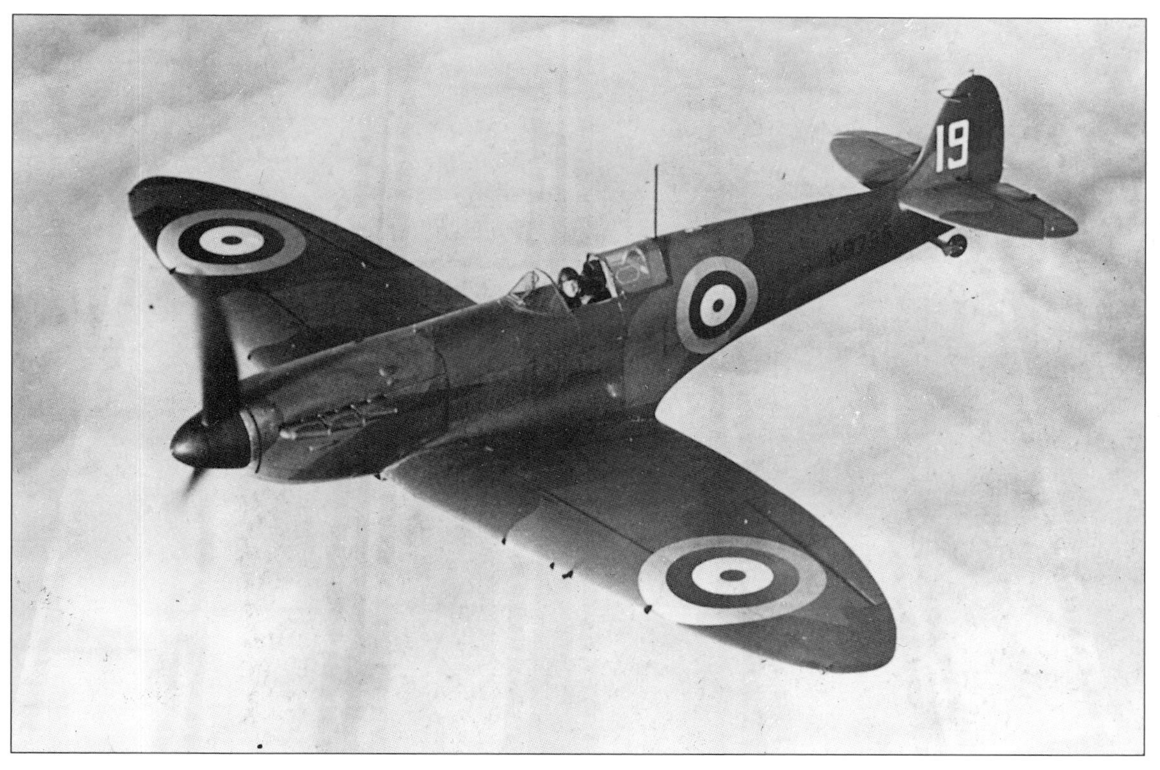

Left: *The legendary Spitfire, designed by R.J.Mitchell, entered service with the RAF in June 1938. Its performance, ease of handling, and elegant appearance delighted those pilots who were fortunate enough to fly the splendid machine. This photograph shows a Spitfire I, serial K9759, of 19 Squadron at Duxford in Cambridgeshire. This was the first squadron to be supplied with the new machine. By September 1939, nine RAF squadrons were fully equipped with Spitfire Is.*

Source: Keystone Collection

Right: *The Handley Page Hampden I was first delivered to 49 Squadron in September 1938 and became one of Bomber Command's premier trio of aircraft on the outbreak of the Second World War, the others being the Armstrong Whitworth Whitley and the Vickers Wellington. In spite of poor armament and cramped crew accommodation, the Hampden was not unpopular with aircrews, who named it the 'Flying Suitcase'. Its merits were a good field of vision, ease of handling, excellent manoeuvrability and long range. The Hampden was the last of the twin-engined monoplane bombers in Bomber Command, and continued on night operations until September 1942. This photograph of Serial L4033 was taken in 1939.*

Source: RAF Museum P5628

Left: *A Vickers Wellesley, flying over Eritrea. This was the first RAF aircraft to introduce the geodetic 'basket-weave' construction, in advance of the Vickers Wellington. The machine became well-known for its long-distance performance; in November 1938, three Wellesleys flew non-stop from Egypt to Australia. After the outbreak of war, it was employed as a light bomber or on reconnaissance work in the Middle East, becoming obsolete in August 1943.*

Source: Keystone Collection

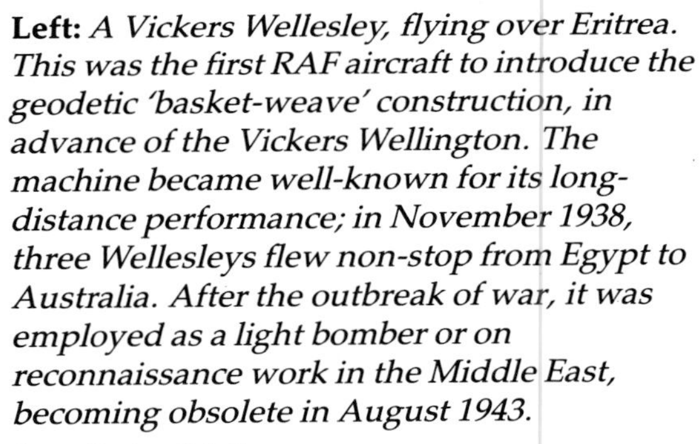

Right: *The de Havilland Dominie was the military version of the civilian Rapide and first entered service with the RAF in September 1939 as a trainer for wireless operators. Also used for communication duties, it continued in service throughout the war.*

Source: RAF Museum PO15259

Left: *The North American Harvard proved one of the most successful trainer aircraft in the RAF. After the first deliveries from the US in December 1938, Harvards remained in service for sixteen years, mainly in RAF Service Flying Training Schools throughout the Commonwealth. It was nick-named 'the yellow peril', since the first aircraft were painted in that colour and the Pratt & Whitney Wasp engine gave out a rasping sound. However, the machine performed well in aerobatics while the array of instruments in the front cockpit provided excellent instruction for the pupil pilot before graduating on to operational machines. This photograph shows one of the earliest machines, a Harvard I.*

Source: Keystone Collection

Right: *Vickers Wellesley Is of 45 Squadron, at Helwan in Egypt in November 1938.*

Source: Keystone Collection

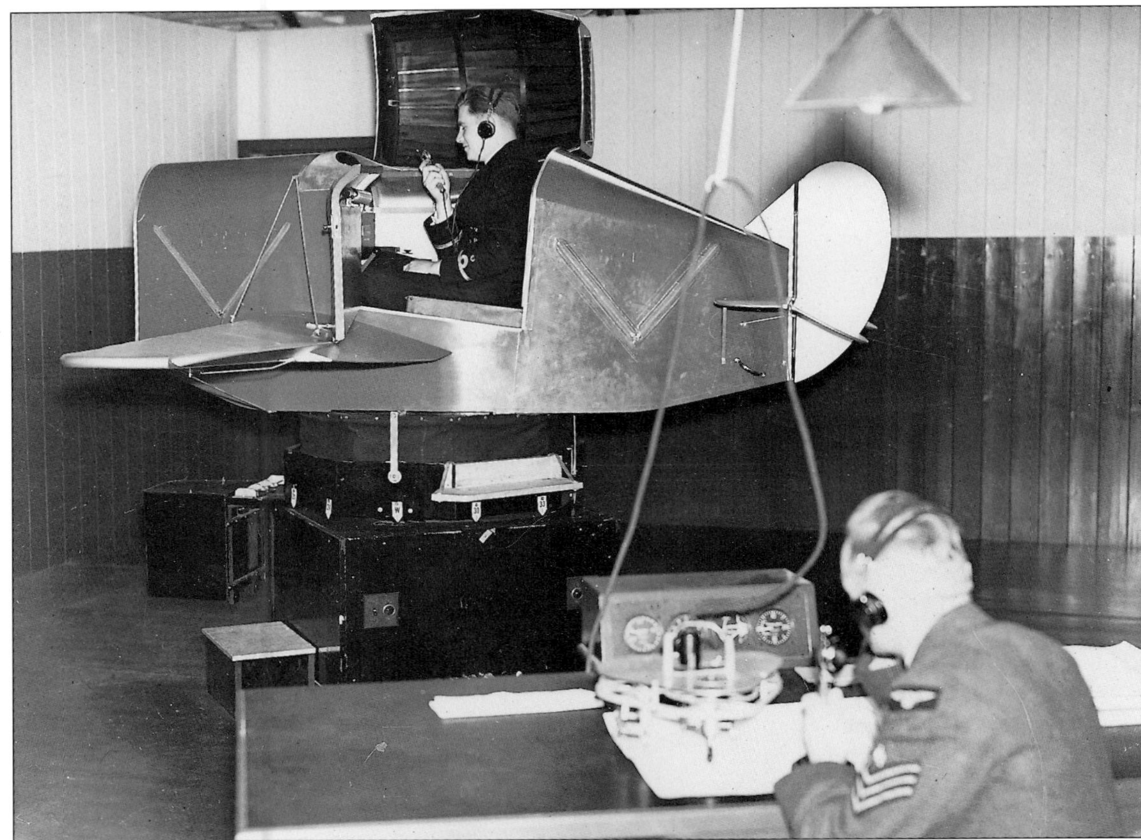

Right: *Soldiers of the Royal Ulster Rifles disembarking on 14 August 1939 from a Bristol Bombay at RAF Yatesbury, for manoeuvres on Salisbury Plain, after transport from the Isle of Wight.*

Source: Keystone Collection .

Above: *The defence of RAF aerodromes against air attack was practised by the army, with temporary machine gun posts dotted around the perimeters during exercises.*

Source: Keystone Collection

Above: *Introduced shortly before the Second World War, the Link Trainer proved an effective and inexpensive means of teaching instrument flying to pilots, even after they had earned their wings. The hood could be closed, so that the trainee flew 'blind'. This photograph, taken on 31 October 1938 at No 1 Flying Training School, Netheravon, Wiltshire, shows a Fleet Air Arm pilot receiving instruction from an RAF flight sergeant.*

Source: Keystone Collection

Right: *On 16 April 1939 the Rt Hon Winston Churchill, who had been gazetted as an air commodore, arrived by air on a visit to 615 Squadron at Kenley in Surrey. At the time, the squadron was part of the Auxiliary Air Force, equipped with Gloster Gauntlet IIs; these were replaced with Gloster Gladiator Is the following month.*

Source: Keystone Collection

Far right: *The Hawker Demon, which entered service at the end of 1931, was the first two-seat fighter in the RAF since the First World War, serving at home and in the Middle East. Demons continued as trainers after 1939. In this photograph, which was taken in August 1940, the trainee is holding his parachute pack above what appears to be a Vickers K machine gun, apparently fitted with a camera gun. On foot, a wireless operator is carrying an amunition drum.*

Source: Keystone Collection

CHAPTER 5

THE PHONEY WAR

The first eight months of the Second World War were so inactive on the Western Front that they earned the name of 'The Phoney War' in America and *la drôle de guerre* in France. However, these terms did not apply to the operations of every squadron in the RAF, nor to the activities of the Royal Navy's warships or Britain's merchant vessels.

In September 1939, the first-line strength of the home (or Metropolitan) RAF was 1,476 aircraft, while there were 435 more aircraft overseas. The total strength of the RAF's regular personnel was 118,000, with 68,000 reservists. Britain's intelligence concerning the strength of the Luftwaffe was accurate. Germany possessed about 3,600 first-line aircraft, with 500,000 personnel. In addition there were 500,000 personnel in Germany's anti-aircraft defences, which came under the control of the *Luftwaffe*.

Although Germany was temporarily occupied with her drive through Poland, and was joined on 17 September by Russian troops attacking from the east, it became obvious to Britain's War Cabinet that the RAF was not capable of executing the 'knock-out blow' so favoured by strategists. The French Air Force possessed only a negligible number of heavy bombers. Any air attack by the Allies on German soil would invite a massive retaliation from the *Luftwaffe*, which became fully available when Poland capitulated on 27 September. That unfortunate country was partitioned and occupied by her two giant invaders.

Bomber Command, commanded by Air Chief Marshal Sir Ludlow Hewitt, mustered only thirty-three squadrons at the outbreak of war, the aircraft consisting of Armstrong Whitworth Whitleys, Vickers Wellingtons, Handley Page Hampdens, Bristol Blenheim Is and IVs, and Fairey Battles. Of these, ten squadrons of Battles of 1 Group had flown out to France on 2 September as part of the Advanced Air Striking Force, commanded from January 1940 by Air Marshal Sir Arthur Barratt. They were joined by five squadrons of Blenheims, four of Hurricanes, and five of Westland Lysanders for army co-operation.

Of the Bomber Command aircraft remaining in Britain, the seven squadrons of Blenheims in 2 Group had too short a range to bomb deep into Germany from Britain. Only the squadrons of 3, 4 and 5 Groups possessed medium or heavy bombers capable of such a bombing offensive. The War Cabinet came to the conclusion that the only military attacks to be made by Bomber Command should be against naval warships at sea. Over land, orders were given to confine flights to leaflet-dropping. The Whitley squadrons were chosen for this task, supported occasionally by Wellington squadrons. These began immediately, operating at night. The leaflets told the German people the truth, although this was not apparent at the time: the war could only end in disaster for them and would cost the lives of many of their citizens and the ruination of their country. But this propaganda had little, if any, effect on people who had been thoroughly indoctrinated with the Nazi philosophy and who knew that the *Wehrmacht* was sweeping victoriously across Poland. In any event, the punishments which awaited those who dared to challenge the state were so hideous that those who agreed with the propaganda were forced to keep their thoughts to themselves.

However, the leaflet flights, known as 'Nickel', did demonstrate to the Germans that the RAF was capable of flying over their territory, even as far as Berlin, Prague and Vienna. The operations were also beneficial to the RAF in terms of reconnaissance, intelligence and experience, but one enemy proved to be the winter weather. Losses were heavy, about six per cent on average per numbers of sorties, a level which later in the war was considered unacceptable for any sustained period.

Towards the end of the Phoney War, the efforts of these heavy bomber squadrons were directed towards minelaying at night. The magnetic mine, code-named 'cucumber' weighed about 2,000-lb and lay on the sea-bed, waiting to be activated by the steel hull of a vessel passing over it. The results of these rather undramatic operations were shown, both during and after the war, to have been very effective.

The attacks against warships began the day after war was declared, with a daylight strike by ten Blenheim IVs against the German pocket battleship *Admiral von Scheer* and the cruiser *Emden* off Wilhelmshaven. It was an extremely gallant attack, but fruitless. Two 500-lb bombs bounced off the armoured deck of the battleship and did not explode. Five Blenheims failed to return, one of which crashed on the fo'c'sle of *Emden* and caused some damage. At almost the same time, fourteen Wellingtons attacked naval vessels off Brunsbüttel. No damage was caused and two aircraft were lost.

At the beginning of the war, the RAF set great store by its power-operated turrets, which were fitted with twin Browning guns in many bombers. It was believed that if squadrons of bombers such as Wellingtons flew in close formation in daylight,

Below: *There was never any shortage of volunteers for RAF aircrew in the Second World War, as can be seen from this photograph of men waiting in the early morning of 17 June 1940 for the opening of a recruiting bureau in Cannon Street, City of London. All RAF aircrew were volunteers, none being conscripted into this branch of the armed services.*

Source: Keystone Collection

Above left: *Three volunteers signing up as RAF aircrew, in December 1941.*

Source: Keystone Collection

combined fire from the front and rear turrets would render them almost invulnerable from enemy fighter attack, although anti-aircraft fire could cause casualties. This belief was proved incorrect during a series of further attacks. On 26 September, a sortie by eleven Hampdens resulted in the loss of five aircraft. On 13 December, twelve Wellingtons took off on an attack against warships and five were shot down, while another crashed near home. It was still believed that most of the losses resulted from anti-aircraft fire. However, five days later, twenty-two Wellingtons took off on an attack against warships, which were found so close to the shore that bombing was not possible, for fear of causing civilian casualties. The Germans could not understand the tactics of the RAF, which appeared suicidal. Their fighters brought down ten Wellingtons, for the loss of four of their number. Two more Wellingtons 'ditched' nearer home and three crash-landed in England. After this tragedy, Bomber Command recognized that long-distance fighter escorts were essential for daylight bombing against German targets, but these were not available at this stage of the war.

Another bombing operation, which was proposed but not carried out, was an air attack against the Russian oil wells and refineries in the Caucasus. This was the period when Germany and Russia were in an uneasy alliance. Germany, which had almost no natural supplies of oil and depended largely on synthetic production, had access to these Russian deposits with which to wage war. The Supreme War Council, consisting of the Prime Ministers of Britain and France, together with senior members of their Cabinets, ordered an examination of the possibility of destroying the Russian installations at Batum, Grozny and Baku. It was intended to use a combined force from the RAF and the French Air Force, from bases in Syria and Iraq. Two reconnaissance and photographic flights were made over Russia, on 30 March and 5 April 1940, by an RAF

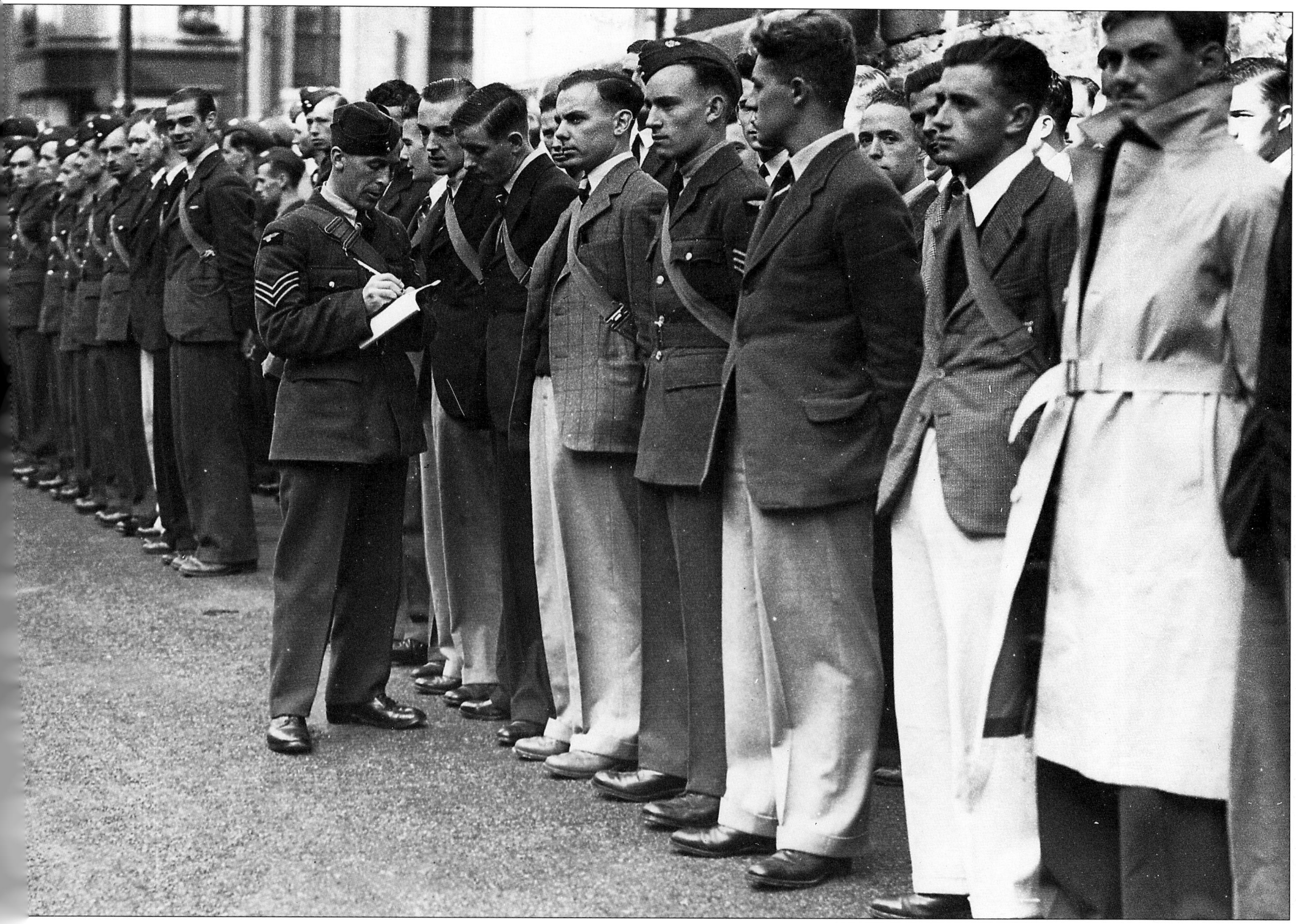

Above: *Civilian and RAF volunteers for pilot and navigator training reporting for duty on 6 October 1939. The next move was then to Initial Training Wing for drill and ground instruction.*

Source: Keystone Collection

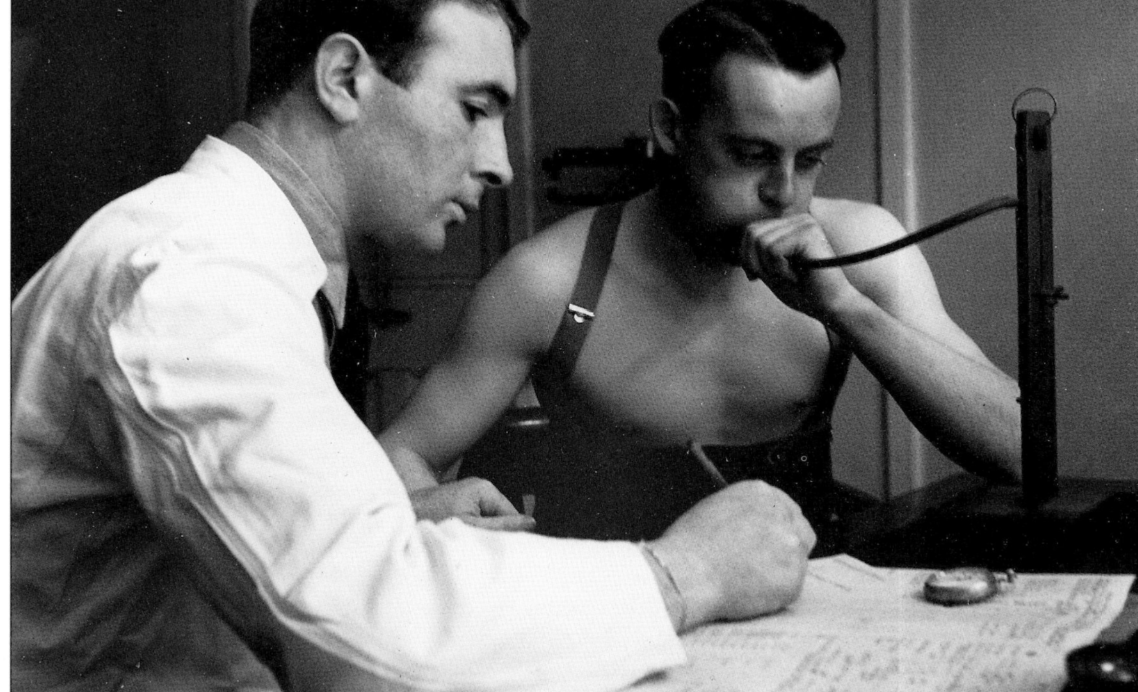

Right: *A volunteer for pilot or observer under medical examination, blowing into a 'U-tube manometer' while his pulse rate is monitored. Medical requirements were stringent and many applicants were rejected for quite minor physical defects, to their dismay.*

Source: Keystone Collection

Left: *One of the proudest occasions for trainees was the issue of their full flying kit. This was photographed in July 1940.*

Source: Keystone Collection

crew in a 'civilian' Lockheed 14 airliner, from Habbaniya in Iraq. Although dressed in civilian clothes, the men were serving officers and airmen of the RAF's Photographic Development Unit at Heston. It was estimated that the bombing attacks would begin at the end of the following June, the force consisting of four squadrons of Bomber Command's Blenheim IVs and one squadron of Wellesleys already based in the Middle East, together with five squadrons of Marylands of the French Air Force. Both the British and the French were highly optimistic about the results which these attacks would achieve. This plan, which is likely to have brought Russia into military alliance with Germany against Britain and France, was shelved following the attack of the *Wehrmacht* in the west in May 1940.

Coastal Command entered the war with three groups, in the west and east of England, and in Scotland, under the command of Air Chief Marshal Sir Frederick Bowhill. Its collection of aircraft consisted of Avro Ansons, Lockheed Hudsons from America, antiquated Vickers Vildebeest torpedo bombers, together with the flying boat squadrons of Short Sunderlands, Saro Londons and Supermarine Stranraers. Their main duty was reconnaissance over the North Sea, a task which had been begun on 24 August 1939. In addition, the aircraft performed the role of escorts for Atlantic convoys, when within range of the British coast. U-boats were sometimes found and attacked, but the bombs carried at the time proved of little use. Depth charges were rapidly developed for use by aircraft.

Another function was to explode the magnetic mines laid by the Germans around the British coasts, which began to account for many ships in home waters. This was accomplished by fitting Wellingtons with enormous rings containing a magnetic coil operated by an engine within the fuselage, and then flying low over the sea. This process, known as 'degaussing', soon achieved remarkable results.

Although Coastal Command was known as 'the Cinderella of the RAF', since it received lower priority than the other two operational Commands, it carried out its work with considerable efficiency. It was a Hudson which scored the RAF's first aerial victory of the war, by shooting down a Do18 flying boat over Jutland on 8 October 1939. Together with the Royal Navy, the aircraft of Coastal Command established an effective economic blockade of Germany's North Sea coastline in the first eight months of the war.

The work of Fighter Command, commanded by Air Chief Marshal Sir Hugh Dowding, was largely confined to building up its strength in the early months of the war. It was estimated that fifty-three squadrons were needed for the air defence of Great

Above: *New RAF cadets marching to a Receiving Centre in London to collect their kit, on 15 September 1942, before undergoing training as either pilots or navigators.*

Source: Keystone Collection

RESERVED MEN!
CHANGE YOUR
OVERALLS FOR
FLYING KIT
YOU ARE FREE TO FLY WITH THE
RAF

Right: *Men in reserved occupations could obtain release by volunteering for RAF aircrew, as can be seen from this poster. All aircrew members were volunteers, even if they had been first conscripted into the armed forces.*

Source: RAF Museum (Crown copyright) P00774

Left: *Before the U.S.A. entered the war, General Henry H. 'Hap' Arnold devised a scheme whereby his country undertook to train 8,000 RAF pilots each year. The first group of 550 cadets set sail for the U.S.A. in June 1941, and were divided among six civilian training schools in the Southern States. This photograph of one of the first groups of British cadets, wearing the olive-green overalls of the U.S. Army Air Corps, was taken at the Southern Aviation School at Camden, South Carolina.*

Source: Keystone Collection

Left: *A pupil pilot entering a Harvard trainer, in September 1940.*

Source: Keystone Collection

Left: *Volunteers to fly with the RAF arrived from all parts of the Commonwealth. These two pilots were part of a batch from the Indian Air Force which arrived in England during October 1940.*

Source: Keystone Collection

Right: *All aircrew were expected to understand the mechanism of RAF machine guns, such as the standard Browning .303 inch being shown here to a group of trainee air gunners. Air gunners, as well as pilots and navigators in 1940, were taught how to strip down and reassemble the gun, as well as how to identify and clear stoppages.*

Source: Keystone Collection

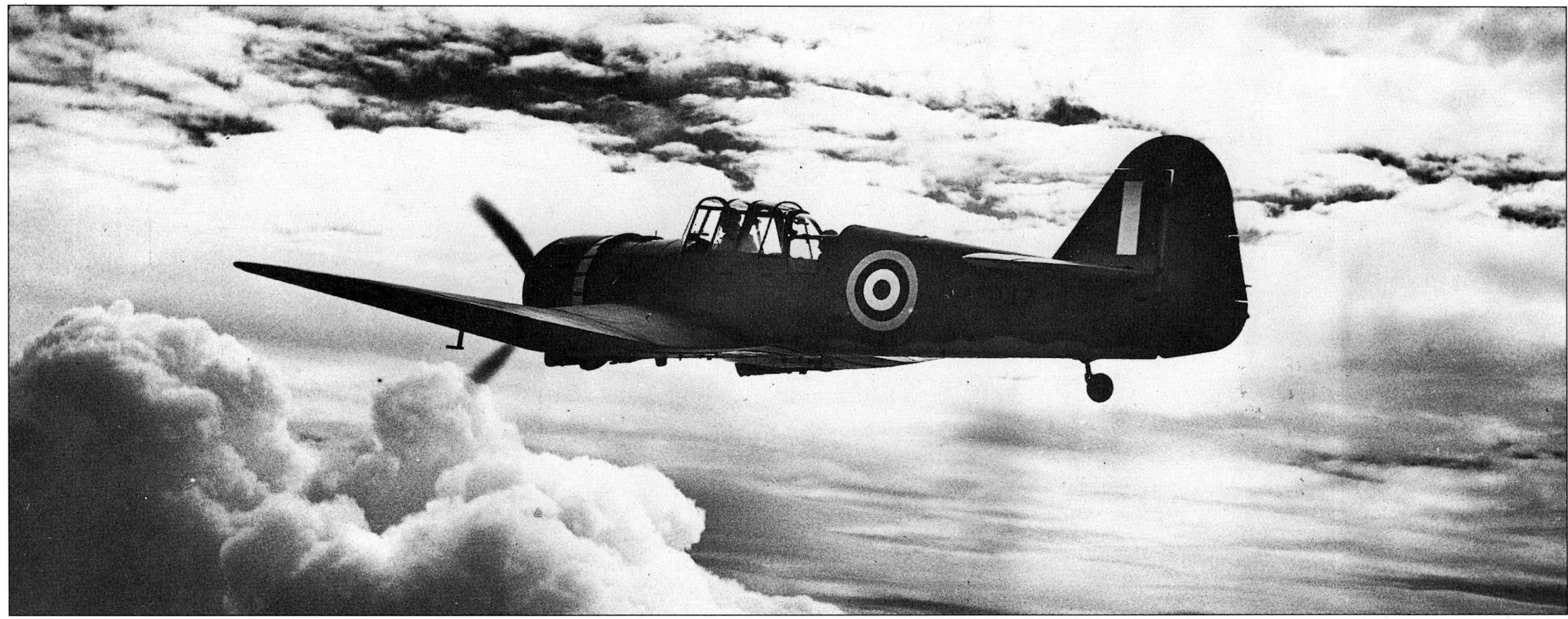

Above: *The Miles Master II, which came into service in November 1939. This high-speed trainer, in which the pupil pilot could also practice low-level bombing and forward-firing gunnery, saw service mainly in Advanced Flying Units.*

Source: Keystone Collection

Britain, but only thirty-five had been formed in September 1939, within three Groups. These were equipped with Hawker Hurricanes, Supermarine Spitfires, and Gloster Gladiator biplanes. Dowding was the most vociferous as well as the most successful of the commanders in demanding new squadrons and aircraft, although some of these new squadrons were equipped temporarily with Blenheims and Battles, since the output of Hurricans and Spitfires could not meet the demand.

In one major respect, the RAF had reason to be thankful for the Phoney War, for it provided a breathing space in which training could be accelerated. The number of technical schools was doubled. Operational Training Units were created, even at the expense of pulling experienced aircrews away from operational squadrons to act as instructors. Above all, the Empire Air Training Scheme was formed, with Canada, Australia and New Zealand agreeing in December 1939 to set up Elementary Flying Training Schools, Service Flying Training Schools, Air Observer Schools, Bombing and Gunnery Schools and Air Navigation Schools, partly staffed with RAF instructors. Southern Rhodesia set up a training group, largely staffed and run by the RAF, while South Africa also provided facilities. By mid 1942, when this scheme was at full flow, it was producing as many as 11,000 pilots and 17,000 other aircrew each year. The first school was opened in Canada on 29 April 1940, but by then the *Wehrmacht* had attacked Norway.

Left: *Air gunnery involved hitting a flying object from a moving platform. One method of training in the ground was the 'hareplane', which trundled electrically round a track. This gave the trainees some experience of handling a power-operated turret on the move while twisting the handlebar grips up and down and from side to side. Aircrew cadets wore white flashes in their forage caps to indicate their trainee status.*

Source: Keystone Collection

Below: *Air gunners received training in power-operated turrets, such as that fitted to the Avro Anson. This photograph shows the men carrying their parachute packs while one trainee has a Browning .303 inch machine gun over his shoulder. This gun had a rate of fire of 1,150 rounds per minute. Training took place against drogues towed by other aircraft, the numbers of holes being counted later for assessment purposes.*

Source: Keystone Collection

Right: *Another method of training air gunners consisted of aiming at a low-flying aircraft from turrets mounted on the ground. The aircraft acting as 'target practice' was a Miles Martinet.*

Source: Keystone Collection

Below: *The Miles Martinet T.T.1 was designed as a target-tug and served in the RAF from 1942 to 1948. It was an adaptation of the Miles Master, with a longer nose to compensate for shift to aft of the centre of gravity. After the war, some Martinets were built as pilotless and radio-controlled targets.*

Source: RAF Museum colour slide P100482

Right: *On the ground, trainee air gunners practised range and 'deflection firing' with the reflector sight against scale models of German aircraft such as the Bf110 and Bf109. The models were manoeuvred by other trainees. This photograph shows a group of Lysander airmen of the RCAF training with a Vickers gun.*

Source: Keystone Collection

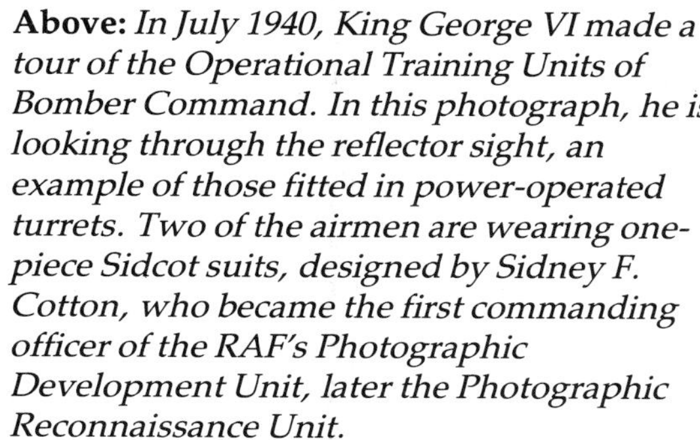

Above: *In July 1940, King George VI made a tour of the Operational Training Units of Bomber Command. In this photograph, he is looking through the reflector sight, an example of those fitted in power-operated turrets. Two of the airmen are wearing one-piece Sidcot suits, designed by Sidney F. Cotton, who became the first commanding officer of the RAF's Photographic Development Unit, later the Photographic Reconnaissance Unit.*

Source: Keystone Collection

Top right: *When this photograph was taken, on 13 December 1941, air navigators were called air observers. They were trained in navigation, bombing and gunnery, being expected to perform all these functions on sorties. At Operational Training Units such as this, navigation exercises were carried out on the ground as well as in the air. The instrument by the right hand of the officer instructor is a 'course and speed calculator' for solving the 'triangle of velocities' caused by wind speed and direction. On the other side of the screen, another instructor is giving imaginary tracks and other information to the trainee, who is making calculations and entering them in his log.*

Source: Keystone Collection

Right: *The RAF trained its own despatch riders, drawn from volunteers among the ground personnel. After passing their course, the despatch riders were posted to RAF units at home and abroad.*

Source: Keystone Collection

Left: *These practice bombs weighed 11½ lb and exploded with a small puff of smoke, enabling the results to be plotted by observers on the ground. The bomb aimer was then assessed at the end of his training. The photograph was taken on 13 March 1940.*

Source: Keystone Collection

Above: *There was a school for RAF firemen, who were then posted to all aerodromes. This fire tender was capable of 65 m.p.h. and carried a 300 gallon tank which produced 3,000 gallons of air foam per minute. There were four air foam projectors and two gas jets.*

Source: Keystone Collection

Above: *The RAF School of Cookery trained cooks, butchers, messing advisers and caterers. Six leading civilian chefs were on the training staff in 1941, and the dishes were specified in an Air Ministry diet sheet. Morning parade included an inspection of hands and nails.*

Source: Keystone Collection

Top left: *By 1942, the RAF had set up its own pig farm in central London and, in addition to the meat, was able to turn out 6,000 lb of pork sausages per week.*

Source: Keystone Collection

Right: *The crew of six in the fire tender included one man in an asbestos suit.*

Source: Keystone Collection

Above: *The Percival Proctor I, a military version of the Vega Gull, entered service with the RAF in 1939 as a three-seat communications aircraft. Later marks were also employed as radio trainers. This photograph is of a Proctor Mark IV, serial LA589, a prototype of the last mark which saw service in the RAF; it was taken on 10 August 1943.*

Source: RAF Museum colour slide P100507

Right: *Boy entrants were admitted into the RAF, principally as trainee fitters and riggers. They were known as 'brats', a term which carried high status when they progressed in their career.*

Source: Keystone Collection

Left: *The WAAF formed its own band in 1939.*

Source: Keystone Collection

Below: *WAAF armourers under training, practising the installation of Browning .303 inch machine guns in a Spitfire.*

Source: Keystone Collection

Right: *Another trade in which airwomen were engaged was that of radio operator.*
Source: Keystone Collection

Right: *WAAF parachute packers were often responsible for the highly-important task of ensuring that the packs and harnesses of aircrew were in good order. Each aircrew member collected his own pack and usually kept it in a locker in the crew room, but it was checked from time to time. The straps on the harnesses were adjustable.*
Source: Keystone Collection

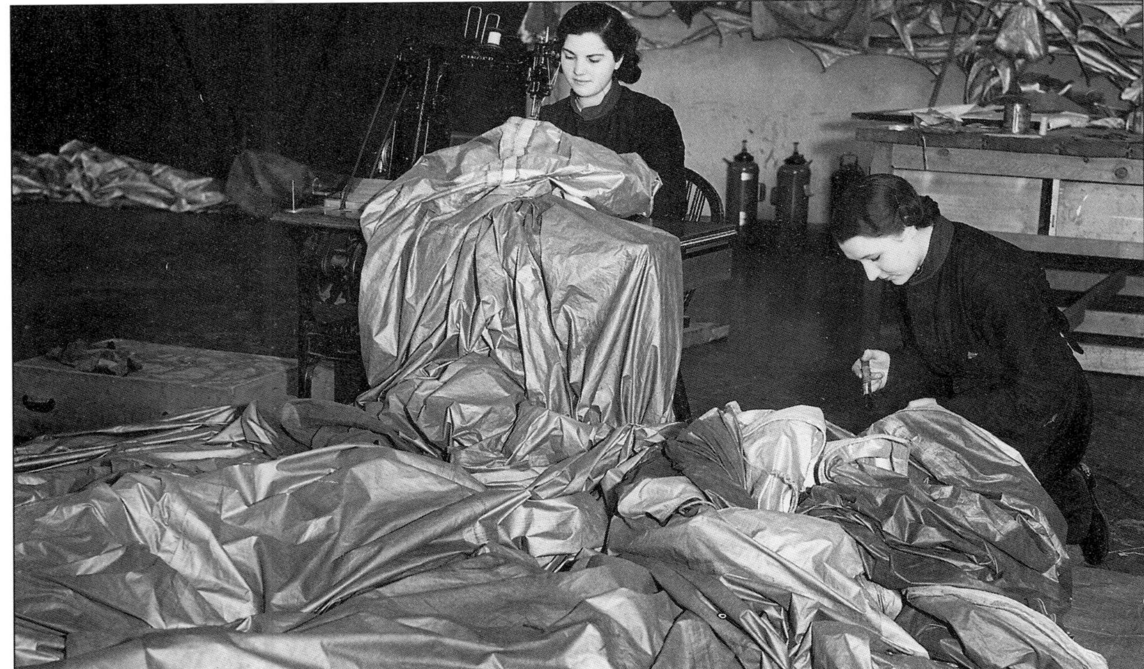

Left: *Another trade which was fulfilled by the WAAF was that of 'fabric worker, balloon'. Balloons were subject to considerable wear and tear from the weather, particularly from electrical storms.*

Source: Keystone Collection

Right: *These standard 'low zone' balloons protected cities and towns, usually flown at an altitude of about 5,000 feet.*

Source: Keystone Collection

Below: *WAAF balloon operators studying the construction of balloons from a model.*

Source: Keystone Collection

Left: *A WAAF instrument mechanic working on the automatic pilot, called 'George', in a Lancaster bomber.*

Source: Keystone Collection

Right: *Three volunteers for the WAAF signing up at Kingsway in London as motor transport drivers, in January 1941. This was one of the most popular trades open to women.*

Source: Keystone Collection

Above: *A WAAF motor transport mechanic greasing the wheels of a lorry.*

Source: Keystone Collection

Left: *One of the positions open to the WAAF was flight mechanic (airframe), which involved the skills of acetylene welding and paint-spraying.*

Source: Keystone Collection

Right: *Selected WAAF underwent training as flight mechanics, for both engineering and airframes.*

Source: Keystone Collection

Right: *Two WAAF flight mechanics working on an aircraft.*

Source: Keystone Collection

Below: *Some of the ladies of No 5 Ferry Pilots Pool Women's Section, in full flying kit.*

Source: Keystone Collection

Right: *Although not part of the RAF, the men and women of the Air Transport Auxiliary provided invaluable and sometimes dangerous help by delivering new aircraft to aerodromes. The officer commanding No 5 Ferry Pilots Pool Women's Section, based at Hatfield in Berkshire, was Miss Pauline Gower (centre), the 27 year old daughter of Sir Robert Gower, M.P.*

Source: Keystone Collection

Below: *Two fighter pilots on standby during the Phoney War while away the time in the crew room by playing chess, while another is dozing with a bull terrier. Black appears to be winning on the chess board, which is placed on two parachute boxes.*

Source: Keystone Collection

Above: *Morse code was taught to all RAF aircrew trainees, although a higher standard of efficiency was expected from wireless operators. These trainees were between 16 and 18 years of age, some of them civilians underage for aircrew.*

Source: Keystone Collection

Above: *Loading packets of propaganda leaflets into an Armstrong Whitworth Whitley bomber, in February 1940. Dropping such leaflets over Germany was one of the main occupations of Bomber Command during the Phoney War.*

Source: Keystone Collection

Right: *The leaflets were usually dropped down the flare chute of the aircraft.*

Source: Keystone Collection

Left: *RAF flight mechanics at work on the Rolls-Royce Merlin engines of an Armstrong Whitworth Whitley Mark V. Earlier Whitleys, the Marks I, II and III, were powered by Tiger radials.*

Source: Keystone Collection

Left: *A Whitley bomber crew reporting to the intelligence officer in the operations room after an operational flight. In the early part of the Second World War, RAFVR officers were allowed to wear VR insignia on their uniforms, but this privilege was later withdrawn, to their indignation.*

Source: Keystone Collection

Below: *The wireless operator in a Wellington Mark I passes a message to the second pilot. This photograph is dated May 1940 and the wireless operator has the rank of leading aircraftman. In autumn of that year, all airmen who had qualified as aircrew were upgraded to the minimum rank of sergeant.*

Source: Keystone Collection

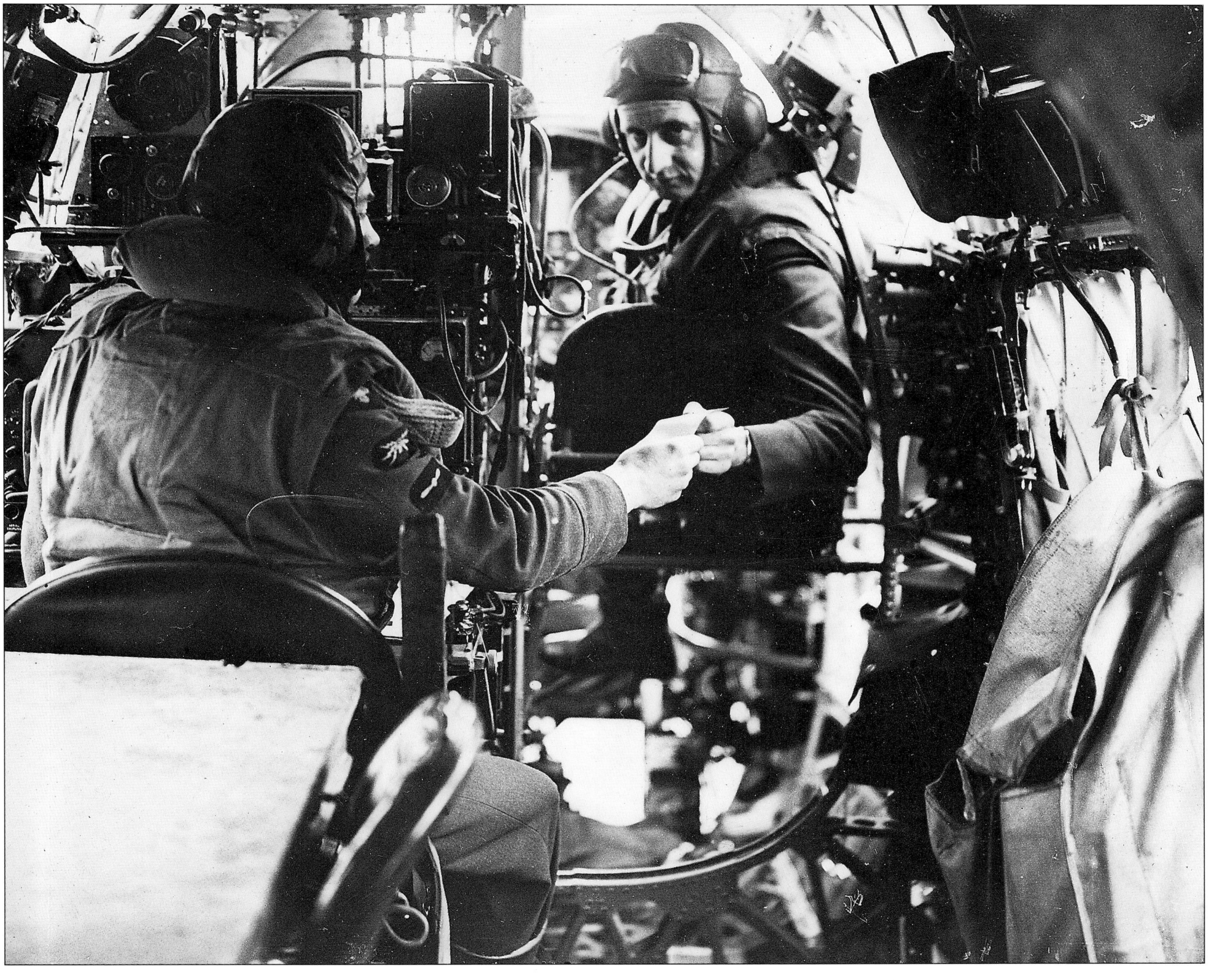

CHAPTER 6

THE BATTLES OF NORWAY, FRANCE AND BRITAIN

When Russia attacked Finland in November 1939, the assault was resisted with extraordinary valour by the forces of that small country, until she was finally forced to agree to terms of surrender on 13 March 1940. At the time, the Supreme War Cabinet gave serious thoughts to backing the Finns by occupying part of northern Norway and Sweden, to allow the passage of 'volunteer brigades' to come to their aid. There was an additional purpose in such a project. Some two-thirds of Germany's consumption of iron ore was mined in Sweden, and much of this passed through the Norwegian port of Narvik before being shipped to Germany. When the Baltic was frozen over, this was the only route. Denial of this source would limit severely Germany's capacity for waging war, and would also pre-empt any plans which the Russians might have for occupying the region.

It is known that these considerations weighed heavily on Hitler's mind when, in December 1939, he ordered his forces to make plans to secure control of Denmark and Norway. The operation, code-named *Weserübung*, began on 9 April 1940, although the expedition set sail for Norway three days earlier. Some naval units were spotted by the RAF and attacked by a squadron of Blenheims on 7 April. By this time, the British government had warned Norway and Sweden that it intended to lay mines off their coasts. Bomber Command began these operations on the night of 7/8 April, while the Royal Navy also laid mines off Norway.

The German naval forces were favoured by low cloud and poor visibility, escaping further detection from the air. However, the Norwegian government was sufficiently alerted to order general mobilisation. The German vessels entering Oslo fjord and Kristiansand met stiff opposition, although there was less resistance elsewhere. On 9 April, 600 German bombers and 600 air transports appeared in the skies over Norway. Paratroops and ground forces seized control of almost every airfield and port in the country. At the same time, the *Wehrmacht* entered Denmark, shortening the German lines of communication, while the British were faced with the problem of operating over a distance of 600 miles or more.

Some German warships were spotted on their return journeys, and twelve Wellingtons attacked two cruisers off Bergen, inflicting minor damage. One of these vessels, the *Königsberg*, was sunk by a dive-bombing attack by Blackburn Skuas of the Fleet Air Arm on 10 April, operating from the Orkneys. A further attack on warships, by twelve Hampdens of Bomber Command, resulted in the loss of half this number by German fighters. Thereafter, the efforts of Bomber Command were concentrated on night attacks against Norwegian airfields, particularly Stavanger/Sola, which was within easy range.

One of the responses of the Supreme War Cabinet to the German invasion was the

Below: *Bristol Blenheims in low level flight over Holland.*

Source: courtesy of Frank Wootton, P.P.G.Av.A.

Left: *The aircrew and ground crew of a Bristol Blenheim IV of 21 Squadron, which was equipped with these machines from September 1939 to July 1942.*

Source: Keystone Collection

Left: *The Blenheim IV began to replace the Blenheim I in RAF service during 1938, the main difference being a longer nose to accommodate the navigator/bomb aimer. Later modifications were armour-plating, an extra gun in the dorsal turret and armour plating. Blenheim IVs were employed on daylight attacks, usually without fighter escort, and suffered very heavy casualties. They continued with Bomber Command until August 1942, and served overseas in Singapore and the Western Desert. This photograph shows a Blenheim IV of 53 Squadron which, after heavy losses in the German invasion of France, was transferred to Coastal Command in July 1940. It was then engaged on equally dangerous sorties, against shipping and ports.*

Source: RAF Museum PO19544

despatch of a combined force to northern Norway. The first contingent put ashore at Namsos on 14 April, with the intention of recapturing Trondheim. This was followed by a landing at Aandalsnes, with a third in the north near Narvik. Although these troops linked up with Norwegians who were putting up a desperate defence, they were harried from the air by German aircraft. There was a severe shortage of anti-aircraft guns, and the Germans inflicted considerable damage, particularly at Namsos.

Meanwhile, the RAF continued to bomb airfields and to lay mines in the approaches to German ports. The Allied expeditionary force received continued support from FAA aircraft but, in the absence of landing grounds from which to operate, the RAF was unable to provide direct assistance. A single squadron of Gladiators left on 23 April on board the carrier HMS *Glorious* and attempted to operate from the frozen waters of Lake Lesjaskog, inland from Aandalsnes. Most of the engines refused to start and, when the *Luftwaffe* attacked, the machines were soon destroyed. Most of the pilots were transported safely back to Britain.

More German troops were transported northwards, and the Allied military situation in the two southerly areas of Aandalsnes and Namsos became hopeless. Evacuation began on 2 May, leaving the contingent near Narvik. An RAF survey team was sent out to this remaining area and chose a landing ground at Bardufoss, north of Narvik, as a suitable spot for aircraft. The two short landing strips were extended by Trojan efforts, including assistance from about 1,000 Norwegian volunteers. The re-equipped Gladiator squadron returned to Norway on the carrier HMS *Furious*, arriving on 21 May. Two days later, a Hurricane squadron arrived on HMS *Glorious*.

By then, the *Wehrmacht* had attacked through the Low Countries, and the Allied effort in Norway could not be sustained. The pilots of both squadrons fought effectively against continual *Luftwaffe* attacks. Narvik was captured by the Allied troops and the port installations were destroyed, before the final evacuation from Norway. The airfield at Bardufoss was demolished and the RAF aircraft made successful landings on HMS *Glorious*. Tragically, this carrier was sunk on the return journey, together with her two destroyer escorts, by the battleships *Scharnhorst* and *Gneisenau*. Only a handful of men survived.

On 10 May 1940 the German assault in the west began with *Panzer* divisions crossing the frontiers of the Low Countries, with the support of dive-bombing attacks by Ju87s. Bombers attacked airfields and transports dropped paratroops in key positions, while other troops landed in gliders.

The direction of these attacks, out-flanking the defensive Maginot line along France's border with Germany, had been anticipated by the Anglo-French forces, who immediately advanced into Belgium. At the same time, the RAF's Advanced Air Striking Force in France went into action. Five squadrons of Lysanders and four of Hurricanes supported the British troops. Ten squadrons of Battles and Blenheims bombed the advancing Germany columns in Belgium, escorted by two squadrons of Hurricanes. In the northern sector, seven squadrons of Blenheims of Bomber Command attacked in daylight, while two squadrons of Whitleys delivered night attacks. The RAF had intended to bomb marshalling yards and oil refineries in the Ruhr, but the French insisted that all attacks should be made in the vicinity of the front line.

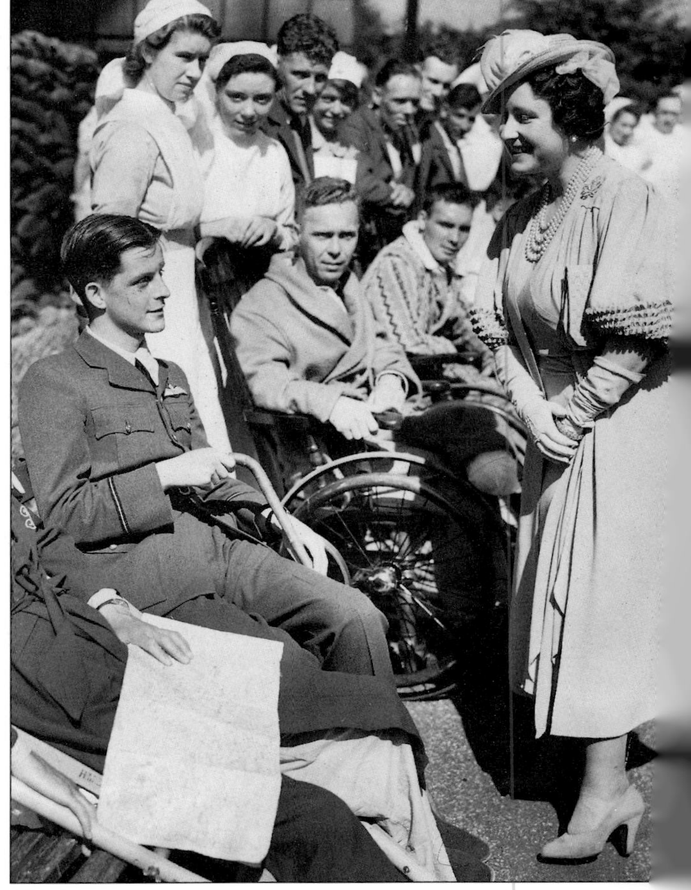

Above: *Soon after the evacuation from Dunkirk, Queen Elizabeth visited Wellhouse Hospital at Barnet in London, to talk to some of the wounded.*

Source: Keystone Collection

Three more Hurricane squadrons were sent to France, bringing the total number of fighter squadrons up to ten. Other squadrons operated from England, including mixed formations of Spitfires and Boulton Paul Defiants. An enormous toll was taken of the *Luftwaffe*, particularly Bf110s and He111s, although the RAF was heavily outnumbered. Even a few Gladiators, which remained with some of the Hurricane squadrons in France, acquitted themselves well in combats.

The employment of medium bombers proved disastrous, however. The new chief of Bomber Command, Air Chief Marshal Sir Charles Portal, voiced strong objections to sending out his Blenheims in daylight, and events soon proved that he was correct. The squadrons of Battles and Blenheims in France fared even worse than Bomber Command. Their targets were bridges and armoured spearheads, and they were met with hails of gunfire and swarms of fighters. Hurricanes could provide only partial support. Within three days, the number of RAF bombers in France was reduced from 135 to 72, while some of the surviving aircraft were damaged. In spite of the heroism of the crews, the results achieved were small.

The *Panzers* broke through the French lines and, on 14 May, were attacked once more by the remaining Battles and Blenheims. Seventy-one took off and forty did not return. Twenty-eight Blenheims of Bomber Command lost seven of their number on the same day. This further sacrifice was not entirely in vain, for there is evidence that the attacks contributed to a slowing down of the German advance.

In Holland, the Dutch forces put up a fierce resistance, but their air force was destroyed within three days. Rotterdam was subjected to an intense bombardment by Ju87s, which destroyed 20,000 buildings and killed almost 1,000 civilians. On 14 May, the Dutch capitulated. At last, the British War Cabinet, with Winston Churchill at the head of a new coalition government, gave permission for the RAF to bomb the Ruhr, and the first attacks began on the night of 15/16 May.

Meanwhile, four more Hurricane squadrons flew out to France, and six more operated alternatively from the congested French airfields, while continuing to be based in England. These were all that could be spared, with the need to protect Britain from air attack. The squadrons fought well and inflicted losses, but they were hampered by the lack of an effective radar system in France. The losses of medium bombers continued. On 17 May a squadron of twelve Blenheims from England was caught by Bf109s and all save one were shot down.

It seemed that nothing could stop the remorseless advance of the *Panzers*. As the Allied troops fell back, the RAF aircraft flew back to prepared grass airstrips, their equipment being transported in lorries. On 19 May, almost all the serviceable aircraft flew to England, from where they could operate equally effectively with the shortened lines of communication. The Hurricane squadrons, originally amounting to 261 aircraft, left behind 195 of their number, either destroyed in combat or too badly damaged to be flown home. About a quarter of the RAF's modern fighters had been lost, but operations over northern France continued at the rate of about 200 sorties a day.

The Germans entered Boulogne on 24 May, and Belgium capitulated three days later. By then, the remaining British Expeditionary Force and some French contingents were hemmed in at Dunkirk, and the Royal Navy began its miraculous evacuation. Heavily out-numbered, RAF fighters covered the beaches from first to last light, although resources were so short that only up to four squadrons could be present at any one time. Meanwhile, RAF bombers pounded enemy batteries and troops. Inevitably, most of these encounters took place out of sight of the troops, resulting in bitterness among soldiers who believed that the RAF was doing little to protect them from the Ju87 dive-bombers. In fact, if the RAF aircraft flew too close to the beaches and naval vessels, they were almost invariably fired on by their own side. The flotilla of 'little ships' began to arrive at Dunkirk on 30 May. French as well as British troops were taken off, and by 4 June the evacuation was as complete as human endeavour could achieve. Over 335,000 men reached England.

The remaining French troops to the south faced an impossible task. The Germans broke through their lines at will, and on 10 June Italy invaded Southern France through the Alps. Thereupon, Whitleys of Bomber Command gave Turin and Genoa a small taste of things to come, after refuelling in the Channel Islands. Some elements of the British forces remained in France and evacuations were arranged from ports on the north and west coasts, protected by detachments of RAF fighters. A major disaster took place on 17 June when German bombers sank the liner *Lancastria* in the port of St Nazaire, with the loss of over 3,000 lives.

On 22 June, France accepted terms for an armistice, and hostilities ceased three days later. During May and June, the RAF had lost 959 aircraft, but had played a major part in the destruction of 1,284 enemy aircraft.

The defeats in Norway and France did not create a feeling of hopelessness in Britain, even though the country was fighting alone against a military giant. Instead, its people

Above: *After the fall of France in June 1940, merchant convoys sailing around the British coasts came under intense attacks from German aircraft. To help protect the convoys, the RAF's Balloon Command formed the Mobile Balloon Barrage Flotilla. RAF personnel served on the balloon barrage vessels, often in conditions of great danger. In this photograph, a vessel is leaving Southampton, bound for the Thames Estuary. It is flying a 'low zone' balloon, which would be raised to about 2,000 feet during an attack. The balloon is painted with an anti-dazzle band, with chevrons on the nose representing each convoy successfully completed.*

Source: the late Flight Lieutenant A. Puckle, MBE

were imbued with a sense of resolve and even cheerfulness, later known as the 'Dunkirk spirit'. Political and social differences were forgotten as everyone bent themselves to the task of increasing military strength and effectiveness. It was obvious that the might of the *Wehrmacht* would shortly fall on Britain, and that somehow the country must be prepared for an onslaught, at first from the air. The prospect of ultimate defeat was barely considered.

It was fortunate that the RAF's radar system was already largely established and that Fighter Command still retained much of its strength. The radar system was rapidly extended to the west and north, to cover the whole of Britain's southern and eastern coastlines, while the efficient network of Observer Corps posts covering the entire country was similarly expanded. Aircraft production remained a major priority, under the direction of Lord Beaverbrook of the Ministry of Aircraft Production, and this was already rising. At the expense of other military production, Beaverbrook continued the expansion, from 256 fighters in April 1940 to 476 the following August.

Meanwhile, the Germans consolidated their gains in Europe and Hitler looked for signs that Britain was prepared to reach a settlement with Germany, for his immediate military ambitions lay to the east rather than to the west. It was not until mid July when he decided that, if Britain wished to remain obstinate, plans must be prepared for her invasion. The prelude would be a massive air attack, to begin on 10 August, under the code-name of *Unternehmen Adlerangriff* (Operation 'Attack of the Eagles'). The code-name for the eventual invasion of Britain was *Seelöwe* (Sealion).

These few weeks of respite proved a godsend to the RAF, which was able to make good the losses suffered in the Battle of France and indeed to increase the number of its fighter squadrons. The fighter groups were increased from three to four. When the Battle of Britain opened, Dowding had over 700 operational aircraft at his disposal. Although these faced some 1,000 fighters, 1,000 long-range bombers and 250 dive-bombers, within three German air fleets, the situation was a great deal better than had been feared.

After France fell, German aircraft were active over England, although not in any great strength, bombing airfields and coastal convoys in daylight, and laying mines at night. In general, the losses were roughly equal on both sides when they encountered Hurricanes or Spitfires. However, Bf109s proved their superiority over Defiants when not accompanied by single-seat fighters; in a short encounter on 19 July, nine of the RAF turret fighters lost six of their number.

In this period, the RAF was able to improve its system of air-sea rescue, forming the squadrons of reconnaissance aircraft and high-speed launches which were to prove so efficient in the coming months. At the same time, both Bomber Command and Coastal Command were active, bombing airfields and shipping, and causing extensive fires in enemy ports. Heavy bombers raided German aircraft manufacturing industries at night, but these attacks achieved little, other than demonstrating to the Germans that the RAF was still a potent force.

Unfavourable weather prevented *Reichsmarschall* Hermann Goering from opening his main offensive until 12 August. It began with a series of attacks against radar stations and airfields. Damage was inflicted, although almost all stations were quickly back in action. On the next day, the attacks were directed solely at airfields. During the same night, German bombers raided aircraft factories, without much result. It was evident that the initial purpose of the *Luftwaffe* was to knock out the RAF, and indeed the German high command believed that they were doing this, for their crews brought back grossly exaggerated reports of the number of fighters they had shot down, roughly treble the true figures. At the same time, German propaganda announced only about half the true losses of the *Luftwaffe* to the public. The British government gave out figures of German losses which, after the war, were shown to be over twice the true numbers, although the announcements of RAF losses were accurate.

The next couple of days were much quieter, both by day and night, for Goering was waiting for clearer weather before launching a massive attack by all three of his air fleets, *Luftflotte 3* in Western France, *Luftflotte 2* in Northern France, Belgium and Holland, and *Luftflotte 5* in Norway and Denmark, thus spreading the RAF's defences as thinly as possible. The day of 15 August proved suitable, and again the main targets were airfields. In north-east England, formations of He111s and Bf110s attacked outside the range of escorting Bf109s, and their losses were so severe that they never attempted further daylight attacks in that area; the RAF suffered no losses at all. In the south and south-east of England, the air combats were less one-sided, but overall on the day the enemy lost fifty-five aircraft while the RAF lost thirty-four. Damage to installations was negligible.

The battles continued with over 1,700 German aircraft over England on 16 August. There was a respite during the next day, but the *Luftwaffe* achieved some success on 18 August, when they caused damage to airfields and radar stations; but they lost forty-nine aircraft against the RAF's twenty-seven. Since 8 August, Fighter Command had

Above: *The RAF held out great hopes for the Boulton Paul Defiant when it entered service with 264 Squadron in December 1939. It was believed that the turret, with four machine guns and rotating through 360 degrees, would account for many enemy aircraft. These hopes seemed to be justified when the Defiant proved quite successful during the German invasion of the Low Countries, but the German pilots soon realized that the Defiant was not very fast or manoeuvrable and that the turret cut out automatically in the forward position. Two Defiants squadrons were almost wiped out by Bf109s during the Battle of Britain and the survivors were withdrawn for duties as nightfighters. This photograph is of Defiant Mark I, serial N3313, of 264 Squadron.*

Source: RAF Museum PO17822

Above: *The Observer Corps was formed in 1924 and the resulting groups became an integral part of the defence of Great Britain during the Second World War. RAF radar located enemy aircraft approaching British shores, but thereafter the aircraft were tracked by the Observer Corps (later the Royal Observer Corps), working in close liaison with the RAF. This photograph shows one of the group headquarters and the plotting table.*

Source: Keystone Collection

Left: *After the failure of Fairey Battles during the German attack through the Low Countries, many remaining machines were turned over to training. Some became target-towers while others were used for pilot training in dive bombing. This photograph shows a Battle being bombed up with 250 lb general-purpose bombs on 13 September 1940.*

Source: Keystone Collection

Below: *The Filter Room of Fighter Command's headquarters at Bentley Priory in Middlesex, after underground building had been completed on 9 March 1940. WAAF 'plotters' moved arrow-topped counters on the table in response to information about enemy aircraft fed in from the Chain Home (CH) and Chain Home Low (CHL) radar stations sited around the coasts. In the balconies above, RAF and WAAF 'tellers' interpreted these movements, which were then "filtered" and passed on via a controller to operations rooms in sectors and stations of Fighter Command. This Filter Room was known as 'The Hole' to those who worked in it.*

Source: Flight Officer Felicity Ashbee

lost 183 aircraft in combat and thirty on the ground, together with 154 pilots. Of course, some pilots were able to bale out while others were picked up by air-sea rescue. But the losses of Spitfires and Hurricanes exceeded the rate of replacement, and it seemed that the *Luftwaffe* might win the war of attrition unless there was some respite.

There was heavy cloud in the next five days, with only desultory attacks. The mass assaults began again on 24 August and continued until 6 September, normally with over 1,000 sorties per day. The damage to the buildings on some airfields was considerable, but somehow the stations continued to function. This period saw the final withdrawal of the Defiants, however, which lost heavily in every combat. The whittling down of Hurricanes and Spitfires continued to be serious. It is estimated that if the attacks against airfields and the RAF had continued at the same scale, the reserves of fighters would have been exhausted within three weeks. Fortunately for Britain the Germans changed their tactics at a critical time.

Infuriated by Bomber Command raids over Germany and perplexed by the capacity of Fighter Command to put up so many aircraft, Goering ordered his bombers to strike at the British civilian population. Hitler decided that London was to be the main target. On 7 September a great air battle took place when about 300 RAF fighters engaged formations of about 900 German bombers and fighters near the capital, with heavy losses on both sides. Large areas of London's East End were set ablaze.

These attacks continued over the next few days, but the *Luftwaffe* was not able to penetrate to the capital in any great strength and lost heavily. The climax came on 15 September when they lost about fifty aircraft. The RAF claimed to have shot down 187, their greatest exaggeration of the whole campaign. This is the day now commemorated as the Battle of Britain Day, and although it is now widely recognized that double or treble counting of downed German aircraft must have occurred, it was nevertheless a great victory. The *Luftwaffe* continued to attack in daylight until the end of September, when Goering decided to change tactics to night bombing.

Post-war German figures show that the *Luftwaffe* lost over 1,400 aircraft over Britain from 10 July to the end of September, together with many of its best pilots and crews. Although there were greater air battles later in the war, these were losses which could not be sustained at the time. They effectively ended any German invasion plans, which were shelved on 12 October. Morale in Britain rose even higher among the civilian population, and the myth of German invincibility was shattered around the world. In particular, the victory demonstrated to America that Britain was unbowed and, moreover, could provide a platform from which to win the final victory.

Right: *A Westland Lysander being fitted with a canister for supply-dropping.*

Source: Keystone Collection

Left: *Pilots of 32 Squadron on standby in front of their Hurricanes. This squadron flew over northern France during the German Blitzkrieg. In the Battle of Britain it flew from Biggin Hill in Kent from 4 June to 27 August 1940, before moving up to Acklington in Northumberland.*

Source: Keystone Collection

Left: *A further photograph of the pilots of 32 Squadron at Biggin Hill. It is dated July 1940.*

Source: Keystone Collection

Right: *Pilots scramble to their Hurricane Mark Is. These aircraft are part of 111 Squadron, which was the first to receive the new fighter, in December 1937 when at Northolt.*

Source: Keystone Collection

Below: *Hurricanes of 501 Squadron taking off from Gravesend on 14 September 1940, at the height of the Battle of Britain. They had been refuelled and re-armed.*

Source: Keystone Collection

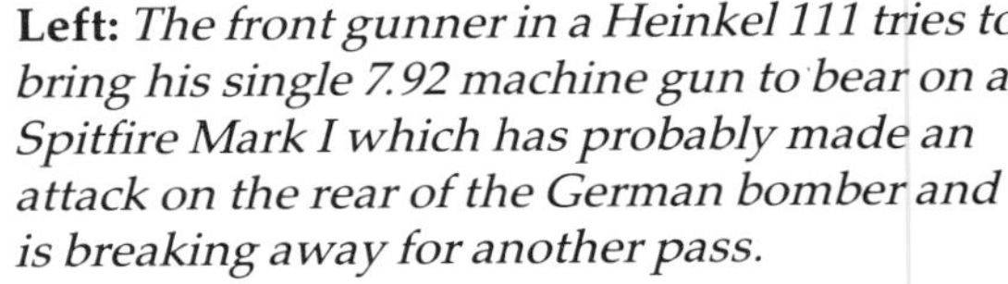

Left: *The front gunner in a Heinkel 111 tries to bring his single 7.92 machine gun to bear on a Spitfire Mark I which has probably made an attack on the rear of the German bomber and is breaking away for another pass.*

Source: Keystone Collection

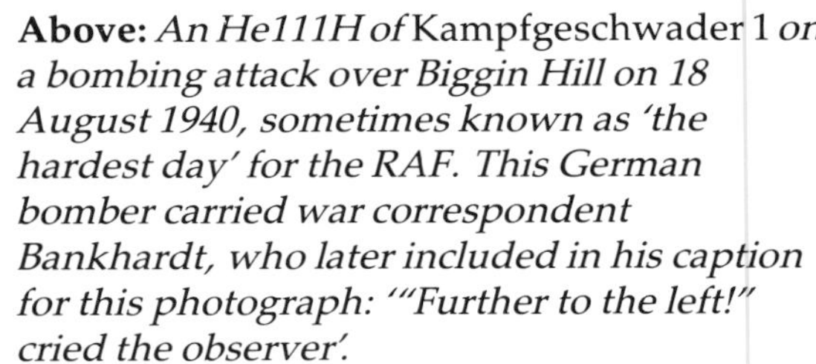

Above: *An He111H of* Kampfgeschwader 1 *on a bombing attack over Biggin Hill on 18 August 1940, sometimes known as 'the hardest day' for the RAF. This German bomber carried war correspondent Bankhardt, who later included in his caption for this photograph: '"Further to the left!" cried the observer'.*

Source: RAF Museum P7002

Left: *On the night of 25/26 August 1940, the RAF made a bombing attack against Berlin, in retaliation for German attacks against London. This was the first occasion the German capital had been bombed since the First World War. Eighty-one heavy bombers of the RAF took part in the attack, which was repeated over the next few nights. This photograph, taken on 31 August 1940, shows some of the crews who participated.*

Source: Keystone Collection

Right: *The Spitfire Fighter Fund raised considerable sums of money during and after the Battle of Britain, from collection centres and boxes. In this poster, the serial number K9795 was taken from the first production batch of Spitfire Is.*

Source: RAF Museum (Crown copyright) P00548

K9795
Support the District
SPITFIRE
FIGHTER FUND
Do it NOW
Hon. Treasurer J. H. OLIVER
WESTMINSTER BANK LTD. GREEN LANE

Drawing by FLIGHT
H.R. MILLAR
ASKING FOR IT
DO NOT LET YOURSELF BE SURPRISED BY THE ENEMY. KEEP A GOOD LOOK-OUT ALL ROUND AT ALL TIMES.
AIR DIAGRAM 1305
FOR OFFICIAL USE ONLY

Left: *One piece of advice given to fighter pilots did not alter in either of the two world wars – keep a good look-out at all times. This crewroom poster showed Bf110s diving down on unwary Hurricane pilots.*

Source: RAF Museum AD1305

Right: *A Messerschmitt Bf109E of* 7/Jagdgeschwader 27, *flown by* Oberleutnant *Karl Fischer, was damaged on 30 September 1940 and the pilot attempted to crash-land in Windsor Great Park. The machine turned on its back, but was later righted, as shown here. Fischer, who was taken prisoner, was lucky to be uninjured.*

Source: Keystone Collection

Above: *A fine photograph of a Hurricane I of 32 Squadron at Biggin Hill, after landing.*

Source: Keystone Collection

Right: *The Hurricane was refuelled immediately, while the pilot left the cockpit to report to the squadron intelligence officer.*

Source: Keystone Collection

Above: *An armourer loading magazines with .303 inch rounds during the Battle of Britain. Both the main fighters, the Hurricane and the Spitfire, carried eight guns firing simultaneously. Each magazine held 300 rounds, enough for bursts of fire of up to four seconds.*

Source: Keystone Collection

Right: *Supermarine Spitfire II, serial P7350, in 266 Squadron markings. Hawker Hurricane IIC, serial LF363, in 242 Squadron markings, banking in the background. These two aircraft form part of the Battle of Britain Memorial Flight.*

Source: Keystone Collection

LE D

THIS OR THIS!

SUPPLY LBS □IN

RAD TEMP

PNEUMATIC PRESSURE 280–300 LBS □"

RADIATOR TEMPERATURE 85° TO 90°

THESE WILL

Drawing by THE AEROPLANE

WILL YOUR GUNS FIRE?

AIR DIAGRAM 1303

FOR OFFICIAL USE ONLY

LESLIE CARR

SUPPLY LBS □IN

RAD TEMP

PNEUMATIC PRESSURE

RADIATOR TEMPERATURE

THESE WON'T

Above left: *This crewroom poster reminded Spitfire pilots that their machine guns would not fire unless their radiator (which was ducted to the guns to prevent freezing) was between 80 and 90 degrees Centigrade, or their pneumatic pressure (which operated the firing mechanism) was between 280 to 300 lb per square inch. The poster showed the fate of an unwise pilot, who had failed to check his instrument dials and was duly shot down by the front gunner of an He111.*

Source: RAF Museum AD1303

Above right: *Two German airmen being escorted from their burning aircraft by British soldiers. The airman on the left is a* Feldwebel, *or sergeant. The airman on the right, smoking a cigarette which might have been given to him by a soldier, is an* Unteroffizier, *or corporal.*

Source: Keystone Collection

Left: *A Dornier Do17 bomber burning out after a crash-landing.*

Source: Keystone Collection

Above left: *On 24 November 1940, Air Marshal Sir W. Sholto Douglas took over Fighter Command from Air Marshal Sir Hugh C. T. Dowding.*

Source: Keystone Collection

Left: *From left to right, Mrs Gabrielle Patterson and Mrs Grace Brown, pilots of the Air Transport Auxiliary, with a Tiger Moth. Mrs Patterson was a qualified instructor. Mrs Brown astonished RAF pilots when she landed at an advanced airfield in France during the German attack, carrying consignments of blood for the wounded. This photograph was taken on 7 October 1940.*

Source: Keystone Collection

Above: *On 14 September 1942, this photograph was taken at the Air Ministry to commemorate some of the pilots who were part of the 'Few' in the Battle of Britain two years before.*

Left to right: Sqdn Ldr A.C. Bartley, DFC, (England)
Wg Cdr D.F.B. Sheen, DFC and bar, (Australia),
Wg Cdr I.R. Gleed, DSO, DFC, (England),
Wg Cdr M. Aitken, DSO, DFC, (Canada),
Wg Cdr A.G. Malan, DSO, DFC, (South Africa),
Sqdn Ldr A.C. Deere, DFC, (New Zealand),
Air Chief Marshal Sir Hugh Dowding, GCB, GCVO, CMG,
Flt Off E.C. Henderson, MM, (Scotland),
Flt Lt R.H. Hillary, (England),
Wg Cdr J.A. Kent, DFC, AFC, (Canada),
Wg Cdr C.F.B. Kingcombe, DFC, (England),
Sqdn Ldr D.H. Watkins, DFC (England), and
Warr Off R.H. Gretton (England).

Source: Keystone Collection

CHAPTER 7

THE TURN OF THE TIDE

The price that had to be paid for the success of the RAF in the Battle of Britain was the nightly bombardment of cities and towns. It was known by British scientists that the Germans possessed a system of identifying targets by flying along a beam, which they called *Knickebein*, and then releasing the bombs when the beam intersected another. The system was sufficiently accurate for the "area bombing" of large towns, but fortunately by the time the *Blitz* on London began, British scientists had found a way of 'bending' the beams so that the bombs would be likely to fall wide of the target.

However, Fighter Command, by then commanded by Air Marshal Sir W. Sholto Douglas, did not at this time possess any specialized night-fighters, but depended instead on Blenheims and obsolescent Defiants. The air interception radar fitted to the Blenheim had a limited range, while the aircraft was slower than many of the attacking bombers. Hurricane and Spitfire squadrons were pressed into service but the usual method of attack was visual, often carried out in the middle of anti-aircraft fire and searchlights. Ground control of night-fighters was inadequate, partly because the 'Chain Home' radar system was directed only towards the sea. Inland tracking depended on the Observer Corps who, although extremely accurate during the day, experienced more difficulties at night. Balloon barrages usually flew at 5,000 feet, while searchlights were ineffective above 12,000 feet and there were insufficient heavy anti-aircraft guns for the upper altitudes.

Thus the early attacks by the *Luftwaffe* over London met with little effective opposition. However, the anti-aircraft defences were soon strengthened and the barrage became tremendous. The racket of the guns was music to the ears of Londoners while the intensity of fire forced the bombers to fly higher, but few bombers were shot down. Great fires were started in the capital, mainly from incendiaries, during the 12,000 sorties which the *Luftwaffe* flew between the nights of 7/8 September and 12/13 November. Over 13,000 civilians were killed, with 20,000 injured. Yet morale held up surprisingly well, and Londoners became proud of their demonstration to the world that they could 'take it'.

The ordeal of London was lessened when Goering decided to switch some of the attacks to other industrial centres. These opened with a raid on Coventry on the night of 14/15 November, intended to demolish aircraft plants and other industrial works. The attack was led by the 'Pathfinder' unit *Kampfgruppe 100*, which used an advanced form of beam known as *'X' Gerät*. Many of the bombs and parachute mines fell on the city centre, killing 380 civilians, injuring 800 others, and destroying numerous buildings and public works. From this beginning, which created a wave of fury in Britain, attacks were launched against other towns and ports, some of which were severely hit. They continued until February 1941, but during this period there was improved jamming of the enemy's navigation system coupled with the use of decoy fires to divert the main bomber streams. The German high command then decided that ports must be given top priority, since Britain's capacity to wage war depended largely on imports reaching the country by sea. At the same time, the U-boat war was intensified.

Up to 12 May 1941, the weight of the onslaught fell on English, Welsh, Scottish and Northern Irish ports, which were badly damaged. But by now the raiders themselves were under attack, for a new Mark IV air interception radar was fitted to the cannon-firing Beaufighter, while the ground control stations directing the aircraft were improved and expanded. Suddenly the bombers began to lose a significant proportion of their number. British propaganda spread 'disinformation' which asserted that RAF pilots had improved their night vision by the diligent eating of carrots, a belief that gained widespread credence.

The bombing attacks began to diminish in June. Although the British public was unaware of the reason at the time, the *Luftwaffe* was withdrawing its units to join in the invasion of Soviet-occupied territory. This was operation 'Barbarossa', Hitler's plan for conquering Russia, which began on 22 June 1941 and led to the greatest series of land battles in history. For nearly four years, Germany's strength bled away in a war against a country which the world believed possessed such a rickety military structure that it would soon collapse.

The British War Cabinet realized that this was the time to turn to the offensive, if only to draw some of the resources of the *Wehrmacht* away from Britain's new military ally. It was obvious that an invasion of German-occupied Europe (the Second Front) was beyond Britain's capacity for the present, but at least Britain possessed a strategic strike force in the form of the RAF's Bomber Command.

Below: *The P-38 Lockheed Lightning. This US long-distance fighter was ordered by the RAF in early 1940 but subsequently rejected after testing.*

Source: Keystone Collection

On 25 October 1940, Air Chief Marshal Sir Charles Portal had taken over as Chief of Air Staff from Sir Cyril Newall, who had steered the RAF through the difficult early months of the war. Portal, who was soon to establish himself as a form of human dynamo in his new post, handed over his position as commander-in-chief of Bomber Command to Air Marshal Sir Richard Peirse. In July 1941, Sir Richard was directed to throw the main weight of his command against the German transportation system and to destroy the morale of the civil population, especially the industrial workers. It was reasoned that such a policy would be of maximum benefit to the Russian forces, who were falling back from the German onslaught.

Although the new C-in-C had forty-nine squadrons at his disposal in July 1941, there were formidable problems in executing the orders. Eight of the squadrons were still equipped with Blenheims, which were not capable of long-distance raids, while two-thirds of the remainder were crewed by men who were not yet fully trained. Of the 1,000 aircraft within the command, only 400 were available, and only a small proportion of these could operate each night. Another major problem was the weather over northern Germany, which was frequently unfavourable during these months. No new navigational aids had yet reached the squadrons. Long flights over Germany could be accomplished only by 'dead reckoning' navigation and any visual observation of landmarks such as rivers, or by positions obtained from sextant observations if the sky was clear enough. More often than not, the precise position of a target could not be found, even when there was a 'bomber's moon'. Similar problems faced the crews on return to England, for the eastern counties were often shrouded in fog and industrial pollution, resulting in numerous crashes when aircraft ran out of fuel or lost their way.

The effects of the bombing campaign over Germany were not impressive, in terms of damage. A post-war examination of the records of Cologne, which was attacked on thirty-three occasions between 1 June 1941 and 28 February 1942, including some 2,000 sorties, revealed that only about one sixth of the high-explosive bombs dropped fell on the city. Certainly some damage to industrial plants was caused, but the loss of production was soon made good. The limited effects of the heavy bomber campaign were appreciated at the time, for in September 1941 interpretation of photographs taken by long-range Spitfires of the Photographic Reconnaissance Unit (PRU) indicated that only one in three of the crews claiming to have scored hits had dropped their loads within five miles of the targets.

However, there is no doubt that the heavy bombing tied up large numbers of German personnel in defence, at the expense of the war effort against the Russians. In November 1941, Bomber Command's attacks against the German heartland were reduced in order to concentrate on the more accessible French ports in which U-boat shelters had been built. These harbours consituted a greater threat to Britain than the industry of the Ruhr, and were also very heavily defended. Moreover, it was known that new navigational instruments were in production for the RAF, as well as new four-engined bombers with enormous carrying capacity, and that these would soon transform the effectiveness of Bomber Command over Germany.

In addition to the night raids, Bomber Command began a series of daylight attacks with increasingly successful results. These were carried out in combination with Fighter Command, which had grown steadily in strength since the end of the Battle of Britain. In December 1940, formations of Spitfires and Hurricanes began cross-Channel raids known as 'Rhubarbs', designed to bring the war to enemy airfields and engage their aircraft in combat. When they escorted bombers, usually Blenheims, the fighters went out in greater strength and the operations were termed 'Circuses'. Their purposes were to cause damage to enemy ports, shipping, power supplies, airfields and transport.

Above: *The Boulton Paul Defiant proved no match for German fighters during the Battle of Britain and many remaining machines were employed as night-fighters. Fitted with air interception radar and painted black, they gave good service until replaced with Beaufighters and Mosquitos. This photograph shows a Defiant of 151 Squadron in this night-fighter role.*

Source: RAF Museum PO19131

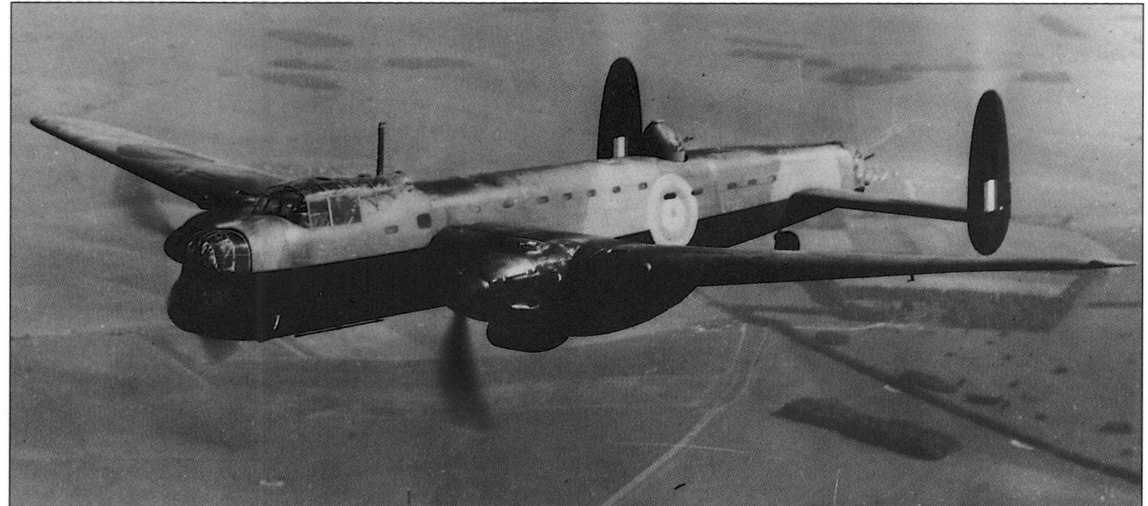

Left: *The twin-engined Avro Manchester entered RAF service in November 1940 and eventually seven Bomber Command squadrons were equipped with the machine. Unhappily, the engines proved to be under-powered and there were many failures. It continued until June 1942 and was then withdrawn. The Manchester is perhaps best remembered as the forerunner of the famous Avro Lancaster.*

Source: RAF Museum P11931

Left: *Canadian airmen cleaning the Browning machine guns of a Handley Page Halifax II Series I, photographed in 1941. These machine guns fired at the rate of 1,200 rounds per minute; this Halifax was fitted with four in the tail, two in the dorsal turret and two in the nose turret.*

Source: Keystone Collection

Following the German advances into Russia, these daylight operations were stepped up. The arrival of the Douglas Boston from America in August 1941 provided Bomber Command with a light bomber which was faster than the Blenheim and also carried a heavier bomb load. From post-war records, it is possible to establish that the RAF lost slightly more aircraft than the *Luftwaffe* in these raids, but damage was caused to the targets. At the same time, Fighter Command carried out 'Intruder' raids over enemy airfields at night, using Blenheims at first but later employing the Douglas Havoc, a version of the Boston. Experienced German pilots were pulled back from the Eastern Front to meet the challenge of the RAF in France and the Low Countries.

Another task, performed by 'special' squadrons of the RAF, was the support of the Special Operations Executive (SOE), an undercover organization set up by Winston Churchill after the fall of France to 'set Europe ablaze' by sabotaging enemy communications and operations. The saboteurs and agents were landed and picked up by Lysanders, which had remarkably short take-off and landing runs, or dropped by parachute from Whitleys. Later in the war, Halifaxes, Hudsons and Wellingtons were also used. These flights were usually carried out in bright moonlight, guided by torch signals from a field, following wireless messages from a resistance group. From Britain, coded messages were sent out on the foreign news bulletins of the BBC, always preceded by the 'V for Victory' signal taken from Beethoven's Fifth Symphony. The clandestine flights were almost invariably successful and grew steadily in number throughout the war. The agents themselves carried out some great feats of sabotage, while their work helped to keep alive the spirit of hope and resistance in the occupied and oppressed countries.

The Commando organization was formed at the same time at the SOE, drawn from volunteers in all branches of the armed services. Under the new Directorate of Combined Operations, in which the RAF played its part, the initial objective was to carry out raids on the coasts of Occupied Europe. One of the achievements of this tough force took place on the night of 27/28 February 1942, after RAF interpreters at Medmenham in Buckinghamshire had identified from PRU photographs an unusual radar apparatus at Bruneval, near Le Havre. This turned out to be a German *Würzburg*, used for controlling anti-aircraft defences and night-fighters. Whitleys dropped paratroops, including some RAF men, near the site. After a stiff fight with German troops, part of the German equipment was dismantled and taken to the coast, where the survivors of the Commando force were picked up by the Royal Navy.

While Britain turned to the offensive, an event took place which expanded the conflict into a global war. On 7 December 1941, the Japanese bombed Pearl Harbor in the Hawaiian Islands, destroying a large proportion of the US Pacific Fleet. The USA was at last in a military alliance with Britain and Russia, bringing its enormous industrial strength as well as its armed forces into the war.

Left: *Polish aircrews formed squadrons with RAF numbers, after training within the RAF. However, the Polish Air Force was a separate force, with its own administration. The Poles proved to be fanatical fighters and achieved an astonishing record in combat. In this photograph three fighter pilots, wearing the Polish silver wings, had been decorated by the Polish premier in exile, General Sikorski. Polish Spitfire squadrons were employed on sweeps over northern France from the end of 1941.*

Source: Keystone Collection

Left: *The first Spitfire with a four-bladed propeller was the Mark VI, which was built with a pressurized cockpit and a Merlin engine rated at high altitude to combat German bombers and reconnaissance aircraft developed for flying at higher levels. Spitfire Mark VIs were first delivered to 616 Squadron at Tangmere in April 1942, and only three squadrons were equipped with this version. This photograph was taken on 10 December 1942.*

Source: Keystone Collection

Left: *Boeing Fortress I, serial AM528, of 90 Squadron. Twenty of these bombers, B-17c's the forerunner of the more famous B-17e's, were flown to Britain in the spring of 1941, but they did not prove successful with Bomber Command. There were many mechanical failures, the armament was inadequate and no long-range fighters were available for daylight raids. A few were sent to the Middle East and the remainder were transferred to Coastal Command for reconnaissance and meteorological work.*

Source: Keystone Collection

Right: *When the first Fortresses arrived for the RAF, servicing was undertaken by RAF ground crews. Here the .50 inch Browning gun in the ball turret of a USAA B-17e Fortress is being demonstrated by a US armourer. The turret is labelled 'Nookie'.*

Source: Keystone Collection

Left: *A view of Spitfire VB serial EN951 of 303 (Polish) Squadron, showing the 'Donald Duck' emblem.*

Source: Keystone Collection

Below: *The Supermarine Spitfire VB, fitted with two 20 mm cannons and four .303 inch machine guns, began to appear in February 1941. The Spitfire VB in this photograph, serial EN951, was one of the machines flown by Squadron Leader J. Zumbach, who commanded 303 (Polish) Squadron from May to December 1942.*

Source: Keystone Collection

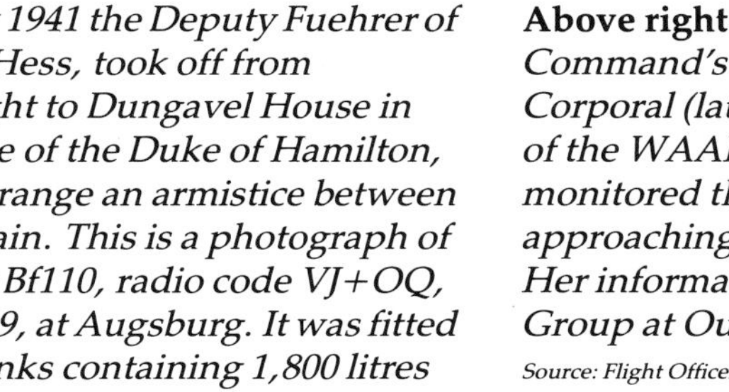

Above: *On 10 May 1941 the Deputy Fuehrer of Germany, Rudolf Hess, took off from Augsburg on a flight to Dungavel House in Scotland, the home of the Duke of Hamilton, in an attempt to arrange an armistice between Germany and Britain. This is a photograph of his Messerschmitt Bf110, radio code VJ+OQ, works number 3869, at Augsburg. It was fitted with large drop-tanks containing 1,800 litres of extra fuel.*

Source: Archive Schliephake

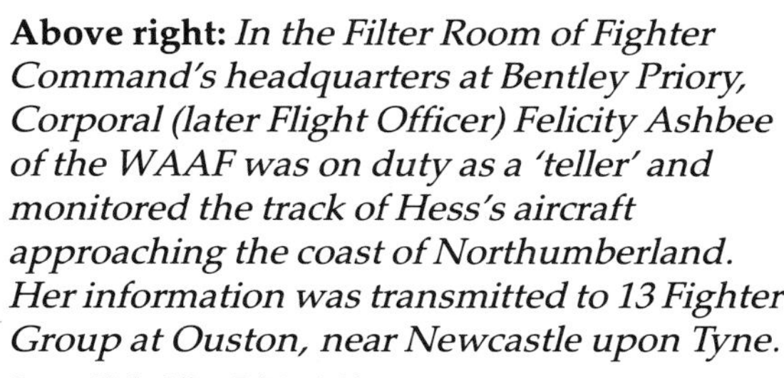

Above right: *In the Filter Room of Fighter Command's headquarters at Bentley Priory, Corporal (later Flight Officer) Felicity Ashbee of the WAAF was on duty as a 'teller' and monitored the track of Hess's aircraft approaching the coast of Northumberland. Her information was transmitted to 13 Fighter Group at Ouston, near Newcastle upon Tyne.*

Source: Flight Officer Felicity Ashbee

Above: *Sergeant Maurice A. Pocock of 72 Squadron, based at Acklington in Northumberland, was sent up in a Spitfire IIa to shoot down the approaching aircraft, which was thought to be another German bomber. But Hess went into a steep dive when he reached the coast and managed to escape.*

Source: Flight Lieutenant Maurice A. Pocock

Above: *A Boulton Paul Defiant, similar to that in this photograph, was sent up by 141 Squadron at Ayr to attack the Messerschmitt, but Hess baled out when the RAF night-fighter was only a few minutes away from him. He landed on Floors Farm, south of Glasgow, and remained in various prisons until his death on 17 August 1987.*

Source: Aeroplane Monthly

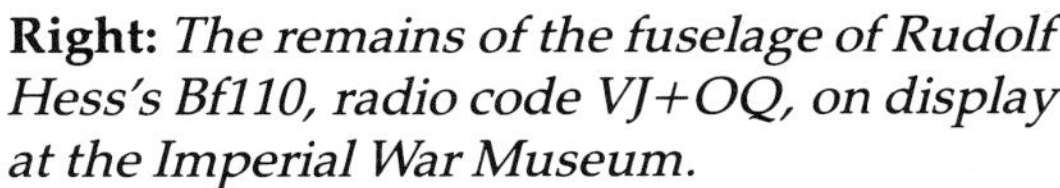

Right: *The remains of the fuselage of Rudolf Hess's Bf110, radio code VJ+OQ, on display at the Imperial War Museum.*

Source: Roy C. Nesbit

Left: *Volunteers from the USA enlisted in the RAF before their country entered the Second World War, forming 'Eagle' Squadrons. The first was 71 Squadron, formed in September 1940 and becoming operational with Hurricanes in February 1941. The second was 121 Squadron, which was equipped with Hurricanes in May 1941. In this photograph, a pilot of 121 Squadron tries his hand at the British game of shove-ha'penny in the crew room.*

Source: Keystone Collection

Below: *As the war progressed, the RAF could look with pride on the cosmopolitan nature of its aircrews. This photograph is of a group of Hurricane pilots from Texas, Australia, Canada, The Punjab, Czechoslovakia, Poland, England, Scotland and Wales. All these men were serving in the same squadron.*

Source: Keystone Collection

Left: *US pilots of the RAF's 121 Squadron, the second Eagle squadron to be formed, photographed on 28 November 1941 while discussing aerobatics.*

Source: Keystone Collection

Right: *The Westland Whirlwind, designed as a long-range escort and night-fighter, was the first single-seat fighter to enter service in the RAF, in June 1940. It had four 20 mm cannon mounted in the nose and could also carry 1,000 lb of bombs. Whirlwinds escorted Blenheims on a daylight raid against Cologne on 18 August 1941, but they were mainly used on low-level sweeps across the Channel. The engines were underpowered and the landing speed was high, and only two RAF squadrons were equipped with the machine, which was withdrawn in November 1943. This example is a Whirlwind of 263 Squadron operating from Filton, near Bristol.*

Source: Keystone Collection

Left: *The four Hispano 20 mm guns in a Westland Whirlwind. Each carried a magazine holding 60 rounds, with a rate of fire of approximately 650 rounds per minute.*

Source: Keystone Collection

Above: *Bombing up a Lockheed Ventura with four 250 lb general-purpose and three 500 lb medium-capacity bombs.*

Source: Keystone Collection

Right: *A Canadian officer fitting his parachute harness over his Mae West lifejacket.*

Source: Keystone Collection

Left: *A photograph showing a contrast in bombs. The sergeant is holding an 11½ lb practice bomb, coloured white, while sitting on a 1,000 lb general-purpose bomb, coloured yellow. This was the largest general-purpose bomb available when this photograph was taken in early 1941. Soon afterwards, high-explosive bombs were coloured green, so that dumps were less visible from the air.*

Source: Keystone Collection

CANADA

Left: *The Bell Airacobra, or P-39D. These US fighters, with their tricycle undercarriages, were delivered to the RAF's 601 Squadron in August 1941, replacing Hawker Hurricanes. The squadron operated with its new aircraft in ground attacks over the French coast, but there were major problems with unserviceability and the Airacobras were taken off operations the following December and eventually replaced with Spitfires.*

Source: Keystone Collection

Right: *The Airacobra was heavily armed, with one 20 mm cannon firing through the propeller boss, two .303 inch machine guns in the nose and four more in the wings. It was considered capable of carrying more ammunition than any other fighter at that time. This photograph, showing ammunition boxes being loaded with 20 mm shells, was taken in October 1941.*

Source: Keystone Collection

Left: *Aircrews of 408 (RCAF) Squadron walking out to their Hampden Is. One of the first Canadian bomber squadrons, 408 Squadron, began operating from Syerston in Nottinghamshire in July 1941.*

Source: Keystone Collection

Left: *After the fall of France in June 1940, those French airmen who managed to escape were at first distributed among RAF squadrons. In November 1941, however, 340 Squadron was formed at Turnhouse as the first Free French unit, equipped with Spitfires. Moving south in April 1942, 540 Squadron began sweeps over northern France, with Spitfire VBs. The Cross of Lorraine can be seen on this Spitfire, photographed in December 1942.*

Source: Keystone Collection

Right: *Many of the Free French airmen took the precaution of covering their faces with their intercom masks when being photographed, in case they were recognised by the Gestapo and reprisals were carried out against their relatives in Occupied France.*

Source: Keystone Collection

Left: *Walt Disney emblems were popular with the Free French.*

Source: Keystone Collection

Below: *Pilots of 609 Squadron enjoying an improvised game of cricket on 30 June 1941. The squadron was based at Biggin Hill in Kent at the time, equipped with Supermarine Spitfire Vs and engaged on offensive sweeps over France.*

Source: Keystone Collection

Above: *In mid-1941 the Hawker Hurricane was modified for fighter-bomber duties. Nicknamed the 'Hurribomber', it carried two 250 lb bombs and later two 500 lb bombs. These aircraft operated over the Channel, from Malta, in the Western Desert and over Burma. This photograph shows a Hurricane IIB fighter-bomber of 402 (RCAF) Squadron, which was equipped with these machines from August 1941 to March 1942 and carried out many daylight raids over France.*

Source: Keystone Collection

Above left: *After its excellent record in the Battle of Britain, the Hawker Hurricane I became almost obsolescent. In April 1941, the Hurricane IIC, fitted with four 20 mm cannons, was supplied to 3 and 257 Squadrons.*

Source: Keystone Collection

Left: *The newly-formed RAF Regiment began to take over responsibility for the defence of aerodromes in early 1942, with officers appointed from both the army and the RAF.*

Source: Keystone Collection

Above: *Many of the recruits for the newly-formed RAF Regiment were volunteers from the army, and wore khaki battledresses with RAF insignia as working dress. RAF uniforms were provided as "best blue".*

Source: Keystone Collection

Below: *The RAF Regiment trained dogs to help guard the lengthy perimeters of aerodromes, seen here with their handlers.*

Source: Keystone Collection

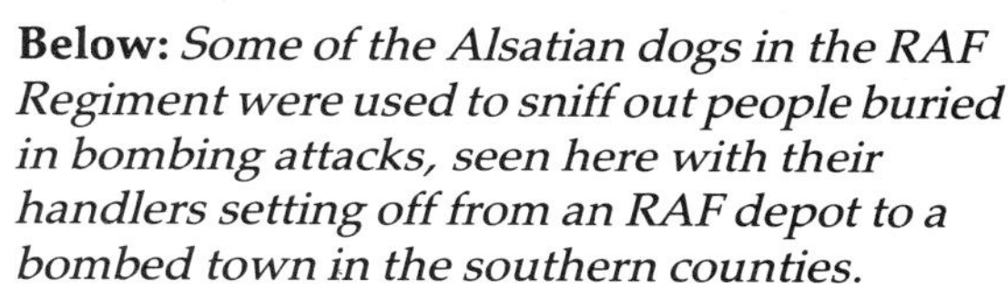

Below: *Some of the Alsatian dogs in the RAF Regiment were used to sniff out people buried in bombing attacks, seen here with their handlers setting off from an RAF depot to a bombed town in the southern counties.*

Source: Keystone Collection

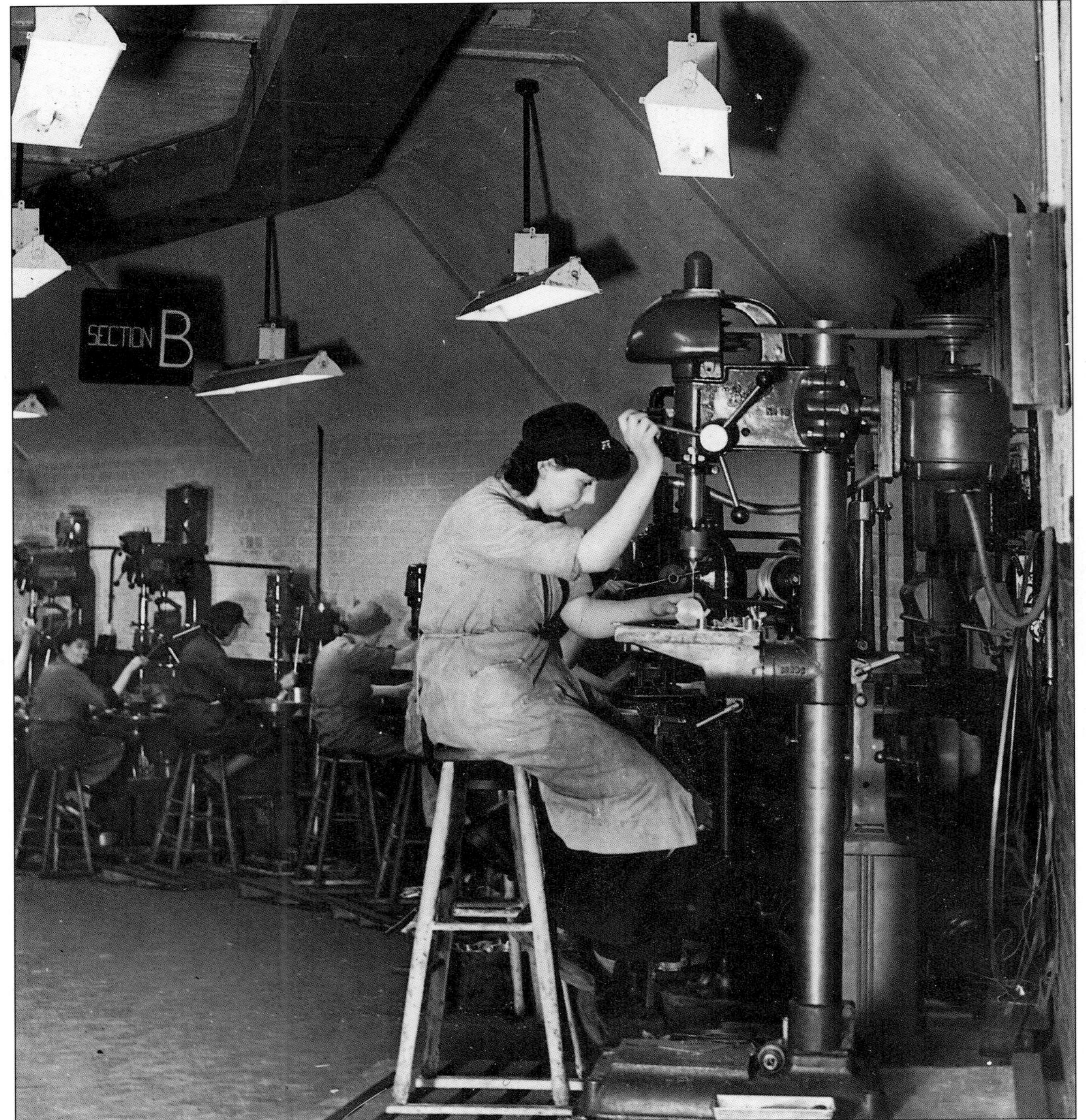

Above: *A store room containing aircraft parts, hollowed out of solid chalk.*

Source: Keystone Collection

Left: *Certain chalk mines and quarries along the banks of the lower Thames, where the product was combined with London clay for the cement industry, were used as underground works for aircraft parts. These factories, fitted with air conditioning and fluorescent lights, were almost immune from air attack. This photograph, showing a section of one of the drilling shops, was taken on 4 March 1942.*

Source: Keystone Collection

Left: *The Director of Recruiting in the RCAF during the Second World War was Air Marshal W.A. "Billy" Bishop, VC, DSO and bar, MC, DFC, Legion of Honour, Croix de Guerre with palm. One of the most famous air aces in the First World War, he had been credited with 72 victories. In September 1942, he visited 411 (RCAF) Squadron at Digby in Lincolnshire, at a time when it was equipped with Spitfire Vbs and engaged on sweeps over the Low Countries and France. Billy Bishop was immensely popular with airmen, as can be seen from this photograph of his visit.*

Source: Keystone Collection

Right: *The ground crews had to put their backs into their work, sometimes quite literally. These men were lifting up the wing of a fighter in order to change the wheel of an undercarriage, on 5 November 1942.*

Source: Keystone Collection

Below: *The North American Mustang I was designed to meet the RAF's specification and entered service in May 1942, on sweeps over the Channel. The performance was good at low altitudes but the Allison engine was under-powered for high-altitude escort of large bomber formations over Germany. This photograph shows a Mustang I of 2 Squadron, which was equipped with the machine until May 1944.*

Source: Keystone Collection

Left: *On 29 September 1942 the three Eagle squadrons, numbers 71, 121 and 133, were transferred to the USAAF and thereafter flew as US fighter squadrons over Europe. This photograph shows a number of the former Eagle pilots after returning from a raid over enemy territory in which they escorted B-17 Fortresses.*

Source: Keystone Collection

Left: *The Lockheed Ventura was similar to the Lockheed Hudson, a military development of a civilian aircraft. It was, however, more heavily armed than the Hudson, with two .50 inch machine guns in the nose as well as six .303 inch guns in three positions. It entered service with Bomber Command in May 1942, being given the unflattering nickname of 'The Pig', and was employed primarily on daylight raids. On 3 May 1943, Sqdn Ldr L.H. Trent of 487 (RNZAF) Squadron was awarded a Victoria Cross following a daylight raid which he led against a power station at Amsterdam, during which the whole formation of eleven Venturas was shot down and he was taken prisoner. The machine was withdrawn from Bomber Command in September 1943 and thereafter served with Coastal Command and the maritime squadrons overseas, on reconnaissance and meteorological flights.*

Source: RAF Museum P4537

Above: *The Douglas Boston III, or DB-7. Eight RAF squadrons were equipped with this fast US day-bomber, four in the UK and four in the Middle East. It was the first RAF machine with a tricycle undercarriage, which required a longer runway. Unusually for an RAF aircraft, all crew members sat in separate compartments, communicating only by intercom. It was the only machine in the RAF in which the pilot was not expected to be the last to bale out; a detachable control column was available in the upper gunner's compartment, in the hope that he could fly straight and level so that the pilot could avoid hitting the very high tailplane after clambering out of his top hatch and diving off the trailing edge of the wing.*

Source: Keystone Collection

Left: *Bombing up the DB-7 Douglas Boston with 500 lb bombs. The aircraft carried a maximum of 2,000 lb.*

Source: Keystone Collection

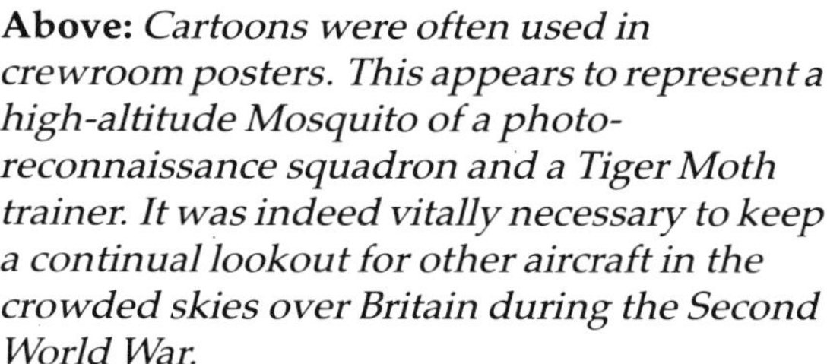

Above: *Cartoons were often used in crewroom posters. This appears to represent a high-altitude Mosquito of a photo-reconnaissance squadron and a Tiger Moth trainer. It was indeed vitally necessary to keep a continual lookout for other aircraft in the crowded skies over Britain during the Second World War.*

Source: RAF Museum (Crown copyright) POO397

Above: *A formation of DB-7 Douglas bombers in flight. The new aircraft was liked by RAF pilots, although the tricycle undercarriage required more runway for landings.*

Source: Keystone Collection

Below: *An aerial view of two Douglas Bostons of 88 Squadron.*

Source: Keystone Collection

Above: *Many crashes during the Second World War occurred on high ground, sometimes on mountains where access by ambulance was impossible. The RAF formed a Mountain Rescue Service which carried out excellent work in saving the lives of injured aircrew. This photograph was taken in Wales in November 1943.*

Source: Keystone Collection

Left: *To commemorate the 25th anniversary of the formation of the RAF, the RAF Regiment took over the guard at Buckingham Palace for a period in 1943.*

Source: Keystone Collection

Left: *In retaliation for the raids by Bomber Command over Germany, Hitler ordered the Luftwaffe to carry out raids over London, which lasted from 21 January 1944 to the beginning of the following March. Many of the German raiders were shot down by RAF night-fighters. This aircraft was a Do217M of 3/Kampfgeschwader 2, shot down on the night of 24/25 February 1944 by a combination of AA fire and cannon fire from a Mosquito of 29 Squadron flown by Sqdn Ldr C. Kirkland, based at Ford in Sussex. Two of the German crew baled out and were captured, but the other two were killed in the crash, at Westcott near Dorking. In this photograph, Kirkland's navigator, Fl Off R.C. Raspin, was displaying a German radio code taken from the fin of the Dornier. All the bombs were still in the aircraft, but did not explode.*

Source: Keystone Collection

Above: *This strange aircraft, named the Libellula, was designed by George Miles, the chief designer of the company which produced the Miles Magister and Master. It was a tandem-winged and twin-engined machine which gave the pilot an excellent view, suitable for landing on aircraft carriers. This photograph was taken in August 1945, but the aircraft did not progress beyond the experimental stage. During the war, queer machines such as this could occasionally be seen by startled RAF crews flying near the experimental station of Boscombe Down in Wiltshire.*

Source: Keystone Collection

Above: *In August 1943, 464 (RAAF) Squadron received de Havilland Mosquito V1s to replace its obsolescent Lockheed Venturas, when based at Sculthorpe in Norfolk. By the end of the year, the squadron was engaged on night intruder missions with these fighter-bombers, and continued in this role until the end of the war.*

Source: Keystone Collection

Left: *The insignia on the aircraft of Sqdn Ldr E. Herbaczewski, Cross of Valour and three bars, DSO, DFC. He commanded 315 (Polish) Squadron from February to August 1944, at a time when it was equipped with North American Mustang IIIs and based at various aerodromes in southern England. Fourteen Polish squadrons flew with the RAF during the Second World War.*

Source: Keystone Collection

CHAPTER 8

REAPING THE WHIRLWIND

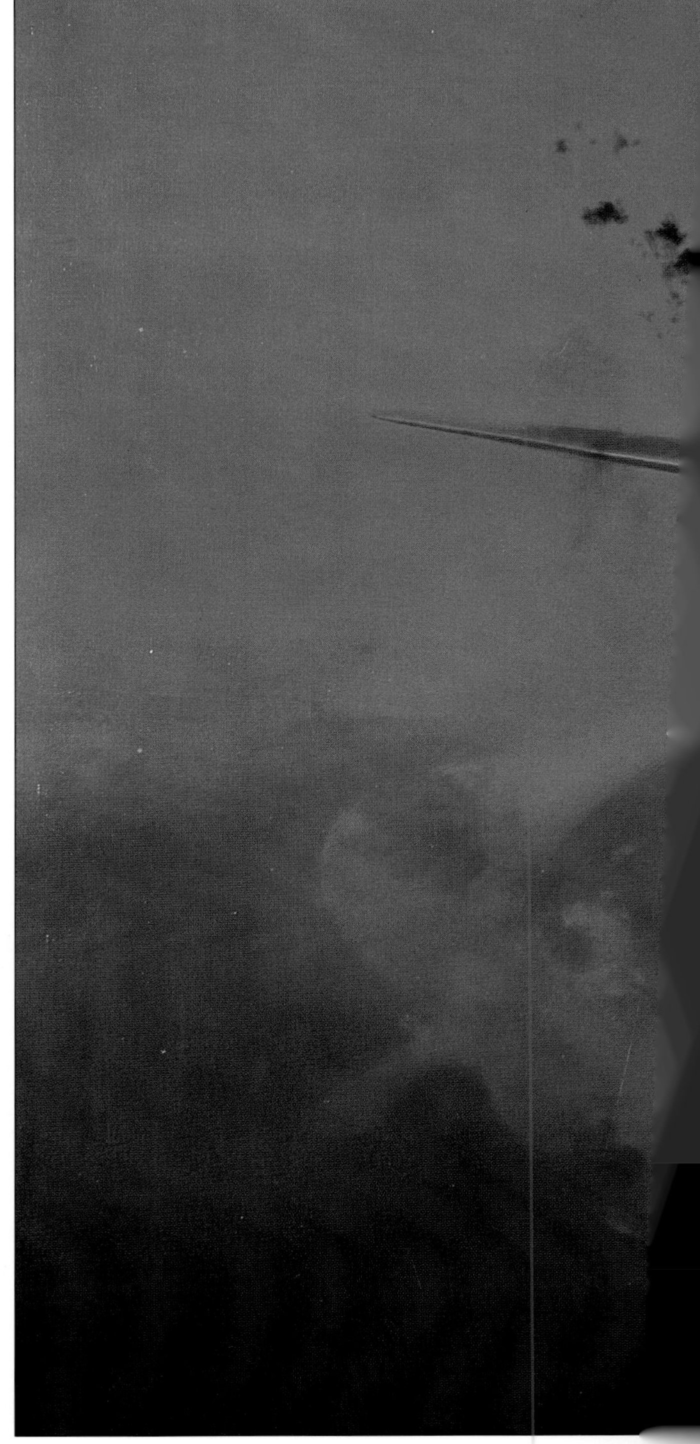

On 14 February 1942, Bomber Command was issued with a new directive. This stressed that the primary object of the bombing campaign was to be 'the morale of the enemy civil population and in particular of the industrial workers'. Eight days later, a new commander-in-chief replaced Sir Richard Peirse. This was Air Marshal Sir Arthur T. Harris, an able and experienced RAF officer with a strong personality and a marked gift for leadership, which was sometimes to display itself in an obstinacy which brought him into dispute with leading members of the Air Staff. Harris remained in this position for the remainder of the war and brought his command up to the massive force which demonstrated to the Germans the grim truth of the biblical message 'They have sown the wind, and they shall reap the whirlwind'.

The directive was issued in the knowledge that a new navigational aid was available to the RAF. This was 'Gee', which came into general service in the following month. Synchronized radio pulses were sent out from three radio stations in Britain, each situated about 100 miles from the next. A receiver fitted in the bomber enabled the navigator to see the time differences between the reception of the various pulses. He then plotted the results on a special Gee map and, with three stations sending out signals could ascertain the point at which the position lines intersected. For a bomber at 20,000 feet, the range was 200 miles, sufficient to reach the Ruhr.

New heavy bombers had been coming into RAF service since 1941. These were the twin-engined Avro Manchester, and the four-engined Handley Page Halifax and Short Stirling. Their increased carrying capacity was such that the old 'heavy' bombers such as the Whitley, the Wellington and the Hampden, were reclassified as 'medium', while the Blenheim became a 'light' bomber. The Manchester was not successful but gave rise to the four-engined Lancaster, the most successful and renowned RAF bomber of the war, which began to enter service at the end of 1941. At almost the same time as the Lancaster, the de Havilland Mosquito began to enter RAF service, gaining fame as the best light bomber of the war.

At the time of assuming his new command, Harris had only about fifty of the new heavy bombers and 250 medium bombers at operational readiness, but the carrying capacity had increased and, above all, they were able to find their targets with a high degree of accuracy. He made his first experiment on the night of 3/4 March 1942, against the Renault factory at Billancourt, near Paris. The heavy bombers equipped with Gee led the bomber stream, and hit the target precisely. Over 220 bombers dropped successfully and caused so much devastation that the plant was unable to return to full production for about three months. After two other successful attacks against industrial targets at Poissy in France, Harris felt the time had come to deal with Germany, principally the Ruhr and the Rhineland.

The first of these attacks took place on 8/9 March, against Essen in the Ruhr, the home of the great Krupps works. The bombers in the first wave were equipped with Gee but the incendiaries dropped were too widespread and the weight of the main force fell on the southern outskirts. Other attacks in the following days also missed the main target. It was obvious that, although Gee was excellent as a navigation aid, it was not so precise that it could be used for aiming bombs at a specific target, especially when industrial haze limited visibility. On the other hand, the contrast between sea and land usually enabled bomb aimers to identify ports from the air, provided they were not covered by low cloud.

The most effective early raid carried out by the new bombing force took place on 28/29 March against the Hanseatic port of Lübeck on the Baltic coast. Although outside the range of Gee, the new instrument provided an aid for the majority of the flight, and the crews were able to pick out the port visually. About 190 aircraft dropped their bombs, and acres of buildings, most of which were of wood, went up in flames. Warehouses, port facilities, a power station and many factories were destroyed. Nearly 6,000 people lost their lives, and some 8,000 buildings were destroyed or badly damaged. The RAF lost five per cent of the attacking bombers, more than was considered sustainable for any length of time; with an operational tour of thirty bombing sorties, these odds were weighted too heavily against any crew's chance of survival. Nevertheless, the Nazi leaders were alarmed at the effect such raids could have on civilian morale, and braced themselves for worse to come.

For the next few weeks, raids against the Ruhr did not produce uniformly accurate results. A particularly gallant attack on 17 April against the M.A.N. Diesel Engine Works at Augsburg by twelve of the new Lancasters, in daylight at low level, resulted in some

Below: *Air Commodore John Searby, D.S.O., D.F.C. Master bomber – Lancaster over Peenemunde, 17 August 1943.*

Source: Courtesy of Frank Wootton, P.P.G. Av A.

Left: *Aircrew were taken out by truck to dispersal areas before taking off on operational sorties. There was the prospect of several hours of extreme danger ahead, in cold and darkness, over enemy territory.*

Source: Keystone Collection

damage for the loss of seven aircraft. The raid created a sensation in Britain and amazement in Germany, but confirmed the view that heavy bombers should not make daylight attacks unless escorted by long-distance fighters. On the night of 23/24 April, however, the Baltic port of Rostock came under attack in clear weather and with the aid of a bright moon. Although more distant than Lübeck, the crews identified the dock area accurately. The bombers went back for the next three nights. About seventy per cent of the centre was destroyed, while severe damage was caused to a factory manufacturing Heinkel aircraft, and to some U-boat building yards. Casualties were heavy and 100,000 people had to be evacuated. Hitler was reported to have been enraged, but the next development was sufficient to bring him to a state of apoplexy.

On the night of 30/31 May, over 1,000 bombers were despatched to Cologne. Preparations for this massive attack had been made for several weeks. To make up the number, which was about four times the maximum quantity despatched on previous raids, crews and aircraft from Bomber Command's flying training group were willingly pressed into service. The first wave of aircraft was equipped with Gee, and the whole attack lasted only ninety minutes. The conflagration from the city was visible for 150 miles on the return journey, and the damage was later confirmed as immense. Over 18,000 buildings were destroyed and 9,500 heavily damaged. Nearly 500 people were killed, 5,000 injured and over 59,000 made homeless. Half the industrial plants in the city were badly damaged, and nearly 500 other businesses destroyed. Forty bombers failed to return, as well as two of the fifty engaged on diversionary work. Operation 'Millenium', as it was called, was counted a success. Even worse was in store for the Third Reich, although raids on this scale were not possible in the next few months except on rare occasions.

At the same time as the intensification of the nightly war against the German cities and towns, the cross-Channel raids in daylight were stepped up. This was the period in which the FW190, the latest German fighter, came into service. In some ways, its performance was superior to the Spitfire V, and the RAF losses mounted. However, the raids succeeded in drawing increased numbers of Luftwaffe units away from the Eastern Front.

At dawn on 19 August, a combined raid on Dieppe took place, with Canadian regiments and Commandos landed by the Royal Navy. The purposes were to experiment with a large-scale landing in preparation for the re-opening of the Second Front on the Continent, and to bring more German fighters into combat over the beachhead at a time when the RAF enjoyed a numerical superiority. The defences proved too strong for the raiding forces, which suffered over 4,000 casualties. There was a great air battle, during which the RAF lost 106 aircraft whereas the *Luftwaffe* lost only forty-eight. It was an expensive experiment, but one in which valuable lessons were learnt and later put into practice.

In July 1942, the first Boeing Fortress B-17s of the US Eighth Air Force reached Britain, and participated in the bombing of Dieppe. The machines were flown over the Atlantic from Gander in Newfoundland to Prestwick in Ayrshire, the first of a flood which would join in the air assault on Germany. It was intended that the Americans, who specialized in precision bombing in daylight with heavily armed aircraft which carried a fairly light bomb load, would join with the RAF in a 'round the clock' bombing of German targets. But this objective proved to be several months ahead.

Above: *A Canadian crew walking out to their Wellington before taking off on a bombing raid.*

Source: Keystone Collection

Right: *The first four-engined bomber to enter service in the RAF was the Short Stirling, in August 1940. However there were a number of technical snags and Stirlings did not begin operating until February 1941. The bomber had an insufficient wingspan and could not achieve an altitude of more than about 12,000 feet for the bombing run, well within the range of light as well as heavy flak. Stirlings suffered heavy casualties but carried on until September 1944, by which time many had been relegated to the role of glider-towing or transport. This photograph is of Stirling I, serial N6103, of 149 (East India) Squadron.*

Source: RAF Museum P10345

In August 1942, Bomber Command formed the Pathfinder Force (PFF), under Gp Capt Don C.T. Bennett. At first, Harris opposed this formation, for he feared that his squadrons would be weakened when their best crews were picked for this work. The idea was to create an elite force to lead the bomber streams with the aid of Gee and then drop flares and markers to illuminate the target for the heavy bombers. However, the new PFF squadrons soon became efficient and, provided the weather was reasonably good, marked their targets accurately on about seventy-five per cent of the raids. This was in spite of German jamming of Gee, which reduced its effective range.

Two months later, Bomber Command was instructed to divert its efforts temporarily to industrial centres in northern Italy, to support the Allied landings in Morocco and the advance of British forces in North Africa. Genoa, Milan and Turin received the full weight of the heavy bombers, to the dismay of the Italian people, many of whom were waging their war with less than fervent enthusiasm.

By February 1943, a conference held by Churchill and Roosevelt, together with their Chiefs of Staff, had included in their decisions a directive to the Allied Air Forces, to the effect that the primary objective was the destruction of German economic and military system, coupled with the undermining of the morale of the German people. In descending order of priority, the targets were to be U-boat construction yards, the aircraft industry, transport, oil plants and other war industries. However, these objectives were left open to wide interpretation by the bomber force commanders, for they were dependent on weather conditions and tactical feasibility.

Left: *The Handley Page Halifax was the first four-engined bomber of the RAF to drop bombs in Germany during the Second World War. It first entered service in December 1940, preceding the Avro Lancaster. The Mark I acquired a poor reputation with aircrews, owing to its inability to maintain sufficient altitude during operations, but various modifications were made and the record of the Halifax in Bomber Command was exceeded only by the Avro Lancaster. Some Halifaxes were allocated to Coastal Command and made a major contribution to the war against U-boats and coastal shipping. Eventually over 6,000 of the various marks were built. This photograph shows a Halifax III of 423 (RCAF) Squadron, taken on charge on 18 November 1943. Unfortunately, it was shot down during a raid on Magdeburg on 21 January 1944 and the entire crew lost their lives.*

Source: RAF Museum PO12020

Two further navigational aids became available to Bomber Command at the end of 1942. One was 'H2S', a device in the aircraft which transmitted a signal to the surface of the earth; this was reflected back and luminised on a small screen with a revolving trace. The early version was not easy to read, but it could show up a town, or more definitely a port. It also operated through cloud and was not subject to jamming. The other aid was 'Oboe', which depended on two transmitters in the Eastern Counties. These sent out a series of pulses which the aircraft amplified and returned. One of the ground stations could tell the navigator whether he was left or right of track, while the other told him when he was at the point of intersection over the target, with a high degree of accuracy. Oboe was used by Pathfinder Mosquitos, dropping target indicators. The early transmitters could handle only one aircraft at a time but a later adaptation, called GH, involved the installation of the system in the aircraft itself, enabling many aircraft to use it simultaneously. However, like Gee, Oboe was subject to range limitation and eventually to jamming.

These new devices enabled Bomber Command to achieve some notable successes in early 1943. Among these was a series of forty-three major raids on the Ruhr, known ironically as 'Happy Valley' by the crews, between March and July, in which heavy damage was inflicted. By March 1943, Bomber Command comprised sixty-five squadrons, including light bombers and the Pathfinder Group. On the night of 16/17 May, the newly-formed 617 Squadron carried out a raid which captured the imagination of the world, the breaching of the Möhne and Eder dams with the special 'bouncing bombs' invented by the designer of the Wellington, Barnes Wallis. The raid caused havoc and temporarily brought to a halt the water supply to millions of people in the Ruhr.

A series of attacks on Hamburg were made towards the end of July, when the 'Window' technique was used. This consisted of the dropping of showers of aluminium strips which clouded the German radar screens, interrupting the control of flak and night-fighters. A great firestorm was created, resulting in devastation on a scale which had not been seen before. A small section of the U.S. Eighth Air Force also attacked the port in daylight, their first operation over German soil. About sixty-one per cent of the living accommodation of Hamburg was demolished, 41,800 people were killed and about 38,000 injured. Many of the remaining population fled from this dreadful holocaust. Manufacture almost came to a halt, including the production of U-boats, and it is estimated that between six to twelve weeks were lost in the various industries.

Right: *This early colour photograph of a Vickers Wellington III, serial Z1572 of 419 (RCAF) Squadron, was taken on 27 May 1942. The squadron was based at Mildenhall in Suffolk at the time.*

Source: RAF Musuem P100692

Above: *Vickers Wellingtons setting course at dusk, over cloud.*

Source: Keystone Collection

Left: *The crew of a Handley Page Hampden I of 83 Squadron, returning from an operational sortie over a German coastal port in October 1940. The squadron was based at Scampton in Lincolnshire at that time.*

Source: Keystone Collection

Right: *As soon as possible after landing from an operational flight, crews were always debriefed by an intelligence officer. Long flights were physically and mentally exhausting, and the strain shows on the faces of some of the men in this photograph, four of whom are wearing sheepskin Irvin jackets. A mug of tea and a cigarette were usually provided at these debriefings.*

Source: Keystone Collection

However, these operations were not an unqualified success in terms of RAF losses. These had been considered acceptable during much of 1942, but they began to rise rapidly in the spring of 1943, when the Germans began to improve their defences under *General der Flieger* Josef Kammhuber. The numbers of radar stations, searchlights and flak guns were increased, forming a 'Kammhuber Line' across the normal paths of the bomber streams from England. A network not unlike the Royal Observer Corps was expanded. The number of night-fighter units was increased, until these comprised nearly 500 aircraft in the summer of 1943. These night-fighters, mostly Bf110s and Ju88s, were equipped in the late autumn of 1942 with the *Lichtenstein Gerät* radar apparatus, which gave excellent results on the screens of the air operators. Some fighters were fitted with the deadly *Schräge Musik* (jazz music), two upward-slanting cannons firing into the blind spots of bombers, similar to the system used in the First World War.

The German night-fighters accounted for the majority of Bomber Command's losses. In the first three major attacks on Berlin at the end of August and the beginning of September 1943, 123 heavy bombers were shot down, eighty of them by night-fighters. In the subsequent attacks against Berlin, from the following November to March 1944, 1,047 RAF bombers were lost. The rate of losses, 5.2 per cent per sortie, was higher than acceptable for an extended campaign. On 30/31 March 1944, there was a catastrophic raid on Nuremberg, when ninety-four bombers were lost from the 795 despatched, a rate of attrition of nearly twenty-one per cent.

The results of raids were assessed by information brought back by the high-flying Mosquitos and Spitfires of the Photographic Reconnaissance Unit, part of Coastal Command. Highly-skilled RAF interpreters assessed the results, with considerable accuracy. In addition, cameras were installed in the bombers, taking a series of films at the same time as the bombs and a flash-bomb containing magnesium powder were released. There was a human tendency for crews to drop their bombs slightly short of the targets when under intense fire, and these night photographs showed any "creep-back", as it was termed. If a crew brought back photographs showing creep-back the sortie was not counted as one of the thirty prescribed for an operational tour.

Although Bomber Command's raids, combined with the daylight attacks of the Eighth Air Force, were steadily flattening German cities, production of war materials in the Third Reich was mounting, under the guidance of Albert Speer, the Minister of Armaments and Munitions. It is probable, however, that production would have increased at a much greater rate if the bombing campaign had not taken place. The morale of the German people did not crack in 1944, contrary to the hopes expressed at the Casablanca Conference. But the damage caused by air attacks on Germany up to this period, although immense, was dwarfed by the air assault launched in the last twelve months of the war in Europe.

Right: *Forty-seven RCAF Squadrons flew with the RAF during the Second World War. This photograph shows the mascot on a Wellington of 405 (RCAF) Squadron in July 1941.*

Source: Keystone Collection

Centre right: *The first heavy bomber squadron of the RCAF was 405 Squadron, formed on 23 April 1941 at Driffield in Yorkshire, equipped with Vickers Wellington IIs. An early example of 'nose art' can be seen here, photographed on 28 July 1941.*

Source: Keystone Collection

Far right: *Twenty-three RAAF squadrons flew with the RAF during the Second World War. The first bomber squadron to be formed in the UK was 458 Squadron, based at Holme-in-Spalding-Moor in Yorkshire in August 1941. This photograph was taken in November 1941, showing a badge on a Vickers Wellington IV.*

Source: Keystone Collection

Left: *Group Captain Hughie I. Edwards was the first Australian airman to win the VC in the Second World War, after he led Blenheims of 105 Squadron in a daylight attack on 4 July 1941 against Bremen. He was also the first man in the war to win the VC, DSO, DFC and bar.*

Source: Keystone Collection

Right: *In October 1941, a Short Stirling I named 'MacRobert's Reply' began operations, following £25,000 donated by Lady MacRobert for the purchase of a bomber. Lady MacRobert had lost three sons, one in a flying accident before the war and two while serving in the RAF.*

Source: Keystone Collection

THUNDER-CLOUD.

STOP ME & BUY ONE

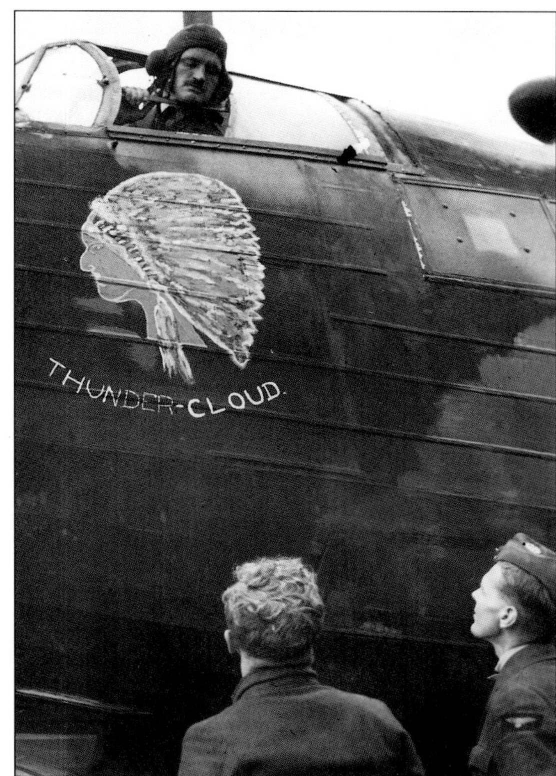

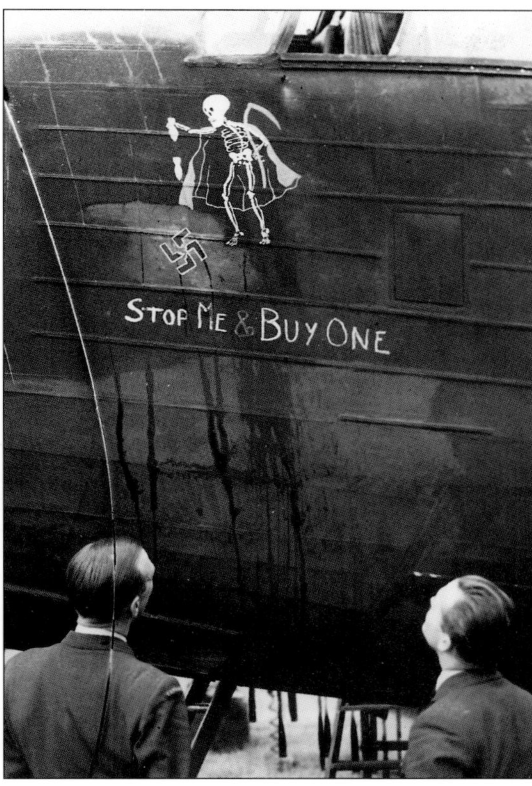

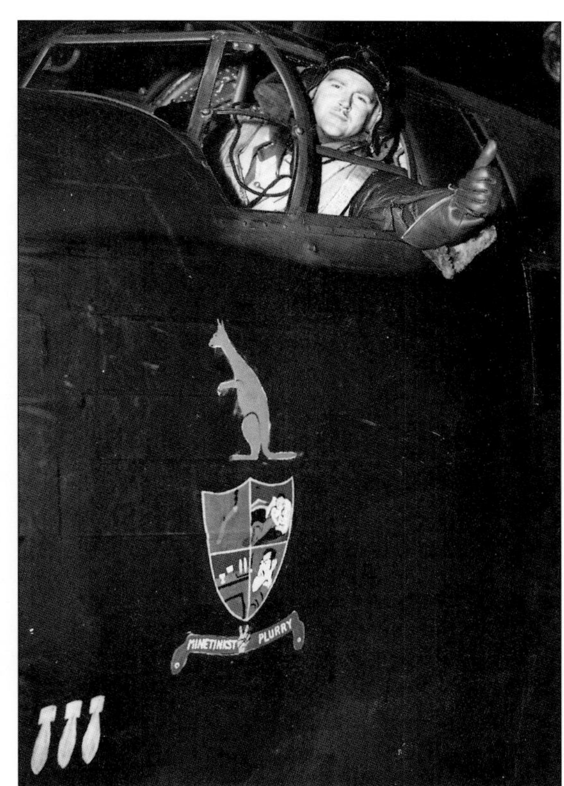

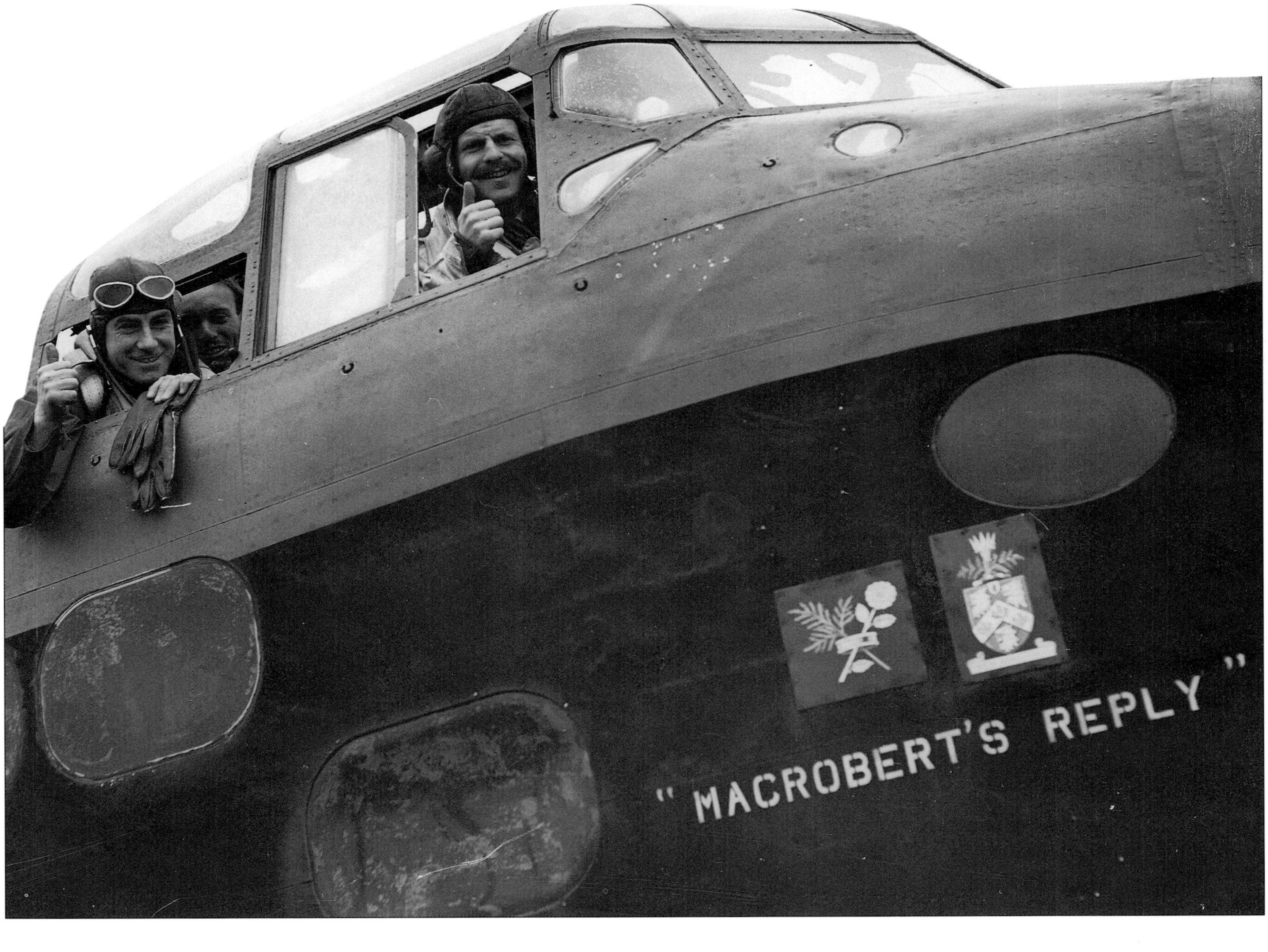
"MACROBERT'S REPLY"

Above: *Air Marshal Sir Arthur T. Harris, who was appointed to the post of Air Officer Commanding-in-Chief, Bomber Command, on 22 February 1942.*

Source: Keystone Collection

Above: *The dispersal bays of Avro Lancasters of 50 Squadron, which was first equipped with these bombers in May 1942 and continued with them until November 1946.*

Source: Keystone Collection

Below: *Flying Officer G. Leonard Cheshire, together with his aircrew and ground crew, in front of Handley Page Halifax 'Offenbach' of 35 Squadron.*

Source: RAF Museum P000688

Above left: *The 'Wings for Victory' campaign was intended to encourage saving and keep down inflation. The squadron letters on the Avro Lancasters in this poster may have been imaginery; the letters VS were not used by any RAF squadron, but the letters VN were those of 50 Squadron, which was equipped with Lancasters from May 1942 onwards.*

Source: RAF Museum (Crown copyright) P00473

Above: *The heavy attack by Bomber Command on the port of Lübeck, on the night of 28/29 March 1942, when over 200 acres were devastated by a mixture of bombs and incendiaries, inspired this poster showing Short Stirlings. At the time, the public was demanding attacks by the RAF in retaliation for the German bombing of British cities.*

Source: RAF Museum (Crown copyright) P00164

Far left: *The assembly line of a factory manufacturing de Havilland Mosquitos.*
Source: Keystone Collection

Left: *Geoffrey de Havilland (right) with the new Mosquito aircraft developed by his company.*
Source: Keystone Collection

ZOOJUIST TERUG VAN DUITSCHLAND!

Hoog de hoofden, Belgische vrienden!

HEBT ge het geronk onzer motoren gehoord toen wij vorigen nacht hoog boven Uwe daken heenvlogen? We hebben aan U gedacht, de Belgen daar beneden . . .

Wij kwamen terug van Duitschland, waar onze bommen een schoonen boel schepten, dien de Moffen nu kunnen opklaren.

Wij dachten dat gij het heerlijk vinden zoudt, te vernemen dat wij bij hen de hel hebben losgelaten, vermits zij van Uw leven ook een hel hebben gemaakt.

En wij gaan daarmee voort, gestadig. Wij betalen het hun volledig terug.

Moed houden! Met vereende krachten krijgen wij den Mof er wel onder!

De jongens van de R.A.F. groeten U!

BOMBER COMMAND — Royal Air Force

Aan onze vrienden:
Gelieve aan te plakken

Above right: *As Bomber Command aircraft flew over Belgium, leaflets were dropped to encourage the people in the occupied country. This leaflet was in French and Flemish, and read:*

JUST BACK FROM GERMANY!
COURAGE, BELGIAN FRIENDS!
Did you hear the drone of our engines as we flew high over your roofs the other night? We thought of you Belgians down there.... We were on our way back from Germany where our bombs left a nice mess for the Boche to clear up.
We thought you would like to know that we gave them a night of hell because they're giving you a life of hell. And now, night after night, we'll continue to pay them back in their own coin!
Courage! Together we're going to beat the Boche!
Greetings from the boys of the R.A.F. BOMBER COMMAND - Royal Air Force

On the picture of the Stirling was a box with the message
To our friends:
Please paste this up in public.
Source: RAF Museum (Crown copyright)

Right: *Avro Lancaster letter N of 50 Squadron in flight.*
Source: Keystone Collection

Left: *The de Havilland Mosquito must be classed as one of the most superb aircraft built in Britain. Constructed of wood, originally as a private venture, the bomber version of the 'Mossie' had no defensive armament but relied on altitude and speed for protection. The Mosquito IV, which carried a bomb load of 2,000 lb, first entered service in November 1941. The Mosquito XVI, with more powerful engines, entered service in December 1943 and could carry the surprisingly large load of 4,000 lb. This photograph is of serial numbers DZ353 and DZ367 of 105 Squadron, which first received Mark IVs in November 1941.*
Source: RAF Museum P9547

Right: *Detail of the assembly of a de Havilland Mosquito, which was sometimes known as 'the wooden wonder'.*
Source: Keystone Collection

Left: *About 6,500 Lancasters were manufactured during the Second World War.*

Source: Keystone Collection

Below: *The Avro Lancaster justified its reputation as the finest heavy bomber employed by the RAF during the Second World War. Developed from the unsuccessful Avro Manchester, it proved easy to fly, highly reliable and capable of absorbing considerable punishment. The first Lancasters entered service in December 1941 and, before the end of the war, fifty-six squadrons of Bomber Command were equipped with these machines. In 1945, Lancasters carried the enormous 'Grand Slam', a bomb of 22,000 lbs. This photographs shows a Lancaster I, serial R5868, of 467 (RAAF) Squadron, one of the original heavy bomber squadrons, being loaded with a 4,000 lb 'cookie' and 5000 lb medium-capacity bombs. This aircraft completed 144 operations and survived the war.*

Source: Keystone Collection

Above: *The 200 foot gap in the Moehne dam after the attack by Lancasters of 617 Squadron on the night of 16/17 May 1943. Nineteen Lancasters, led by Wg Cdr Guy Gibson, attacked the Moehne, Eder, Sorpe, Lister and Schwelme dams, breaching the Moehne and Eder but losing eight aircraft. This photograph was discovered in German archives after the war.*

Source: Keystone Collection

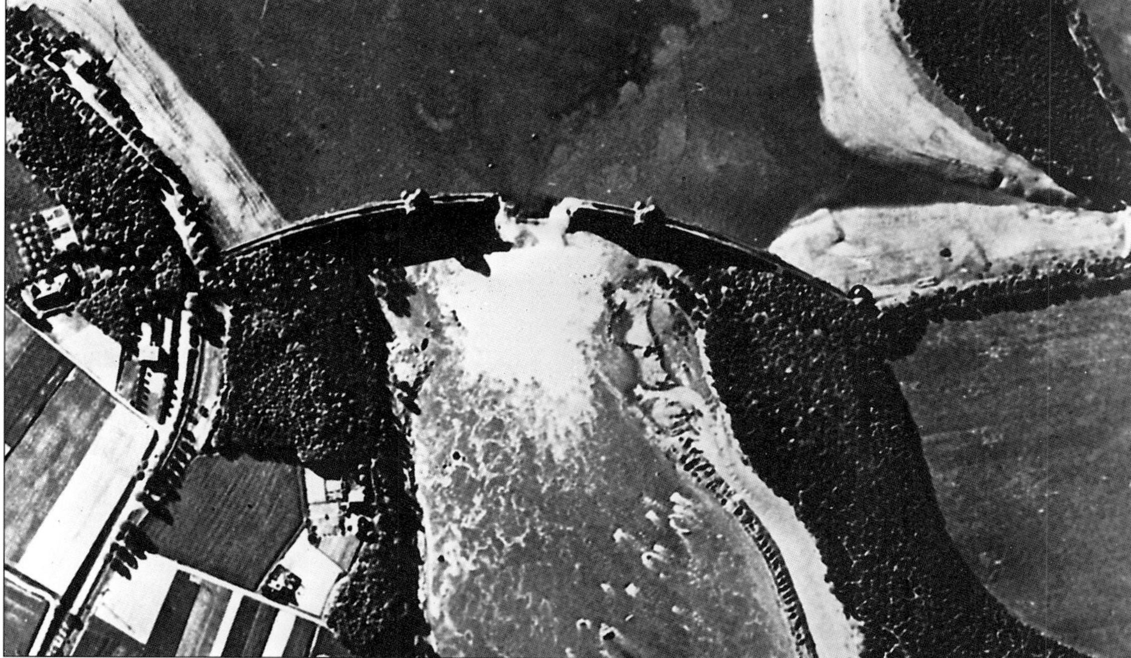

Right: *The breached Moehne dam on 17 May 1943, the morning after the attack by 617 Squadron, photographed by Flying Officer F.D. Fray in a Spitfire PR XI of 542 Squadron. Wg Cdr Guy Gibson described the water during the attack "like stirred porridge in the moonlight, rushing through a great breach". The dam served the needs of over four million people in the Ruhr and was not fully repaired until August 1944.*

Source: Keystone Collection

Left: *A Lancaster being fitted with a 4,000 lb blast bomb, called a 'block-buster' or a 'cookie'. The bomb exploded a few feet above the ground, causing a lateral blast, and was often dropped in combination with showers of incendiaries, to cause maximum destruction of buildings.*

Source: Keystone Collection

Left: *Wg Cdr Guy Gibson (with pipe) photographed a few days after returning from a raid on Berlin in January 1943.*

Source: Keystone Collection

Left: *Wg Cdr Guy Gibson (centre), after his investiture with the Victoria Cross at Buckingham Palace in June 1943, together with the Australian airmen who took part in the raid. Gibson lost his life during a raid on München-Gladbach on 19 September 1944, by which time he had been awarded the VC, the DSO and bar, and the DFC and bar.*

Source: Keystone Collection

Below: *A fully-laden Avro Lancaster taking off at dusk on a bombing mission.*

Source: Keystone Collection

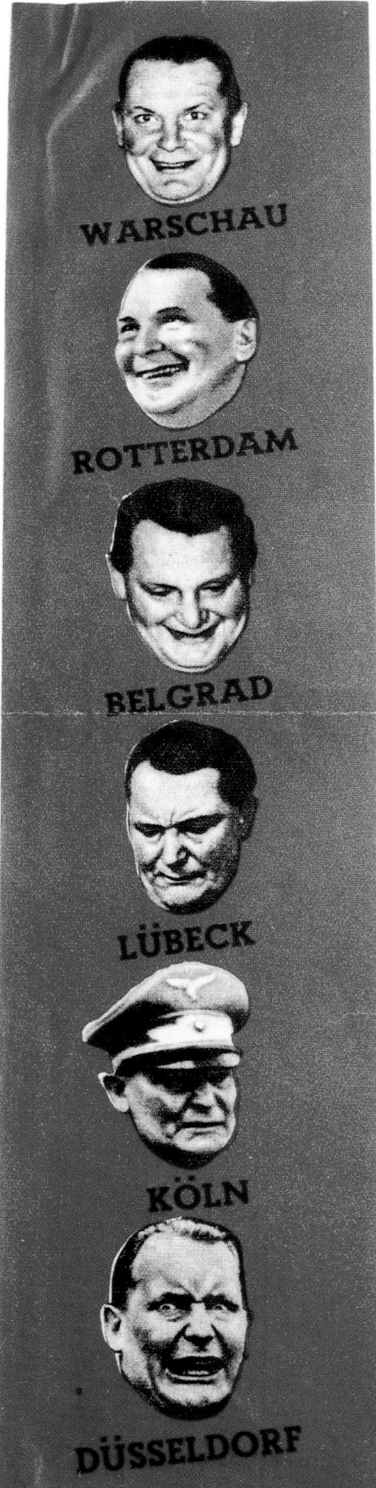

Above: *Bomber Command continued to drop propaganda leaflets over Germany when the major bombing attacks began against German cities. This leaflet showed Hermann Goering looking cheerful when he ordered the German bombing attacks against Warsaw, Rotterdam and Belgrade, but increasingly miserable when the RAF attacked Lübeck, Rostock and Cologne. The leaflet pointed out "Who said: Above all, I shall see to it that the enemy will not be able to drop any bombs?"*

Source: RAF Museum (Crown copyright)

BATTLE OF GERMANY

JOIN AN AIR CREW

HOLMES

Above: *The continuing destruction of German cities by Bomber Command was portrayed in this recruiting poster showing Avro Lancasters.*

Source: RAF Museum (Crown copyright) P00545

Left: *A 'cookie', or 'blockbuster', 4,000 lb blast bomb being loaded on a de Havilland Mosquito. The bomb bay of this light bomber, originally intended to carry only 2,000 lb, was modified to accommodate the extra size. A Mosquito of 692 Squadron first dropped one of these bombs over Düsseldorf on the night of 23/24 February 1944.*

Source: Keystone Collection

Right: *As the war progressed, the bombs carried by Lancasters became larger. The new 8,000 lb high-capacity bomb was first dropped on 10 February 1942. This photograph was released by the censor in September 1943.*

Source: Keystone Collection

Left: *This Lancaster force-landed in October 1943 after a raid over Germany. One engine had burnt out, the undercarriage was smashed and the propellers twisted. In this photograph it is being hoisted by self-propelled cranes on to bogies, to move it to the side of the aerodrome. Damaged aircraft such as this were dismantled and transported in parts to repair depots, where they were repaired and reassembled.*

Source: Keystone Collection

Left: *Canadian aircrews in a Mosquito squadron relaxing over cards in their crew room.*

Source: Keystone Collection

Right: *The 'Grand Slam' bomb of 22,000 lb. The first of these bombs was dropped on 14 March 1945 by an Avro Lancaster Mark I (Special) of 617 Squadron on the viaduct at Bielefeld in Germany. In all, 41 of these bombs were dropped before the end of the war. This photograph was taken in June 1946 at an exhibition in Oxford Street, showing the contrast with a cadet of the Air Training Corps. The bomb was 25 ft 5 in long and had a charge/weight ratio of 42 per cent.*

Source: Keystone Collection

Below: *A plaque in the Officers' Mess of 9 Squadron on 11 January 1944, at a time when the squadron was based at Bardney in Lincolnshire and equipped with Avro Lancaster Is and IIIs. The squadron motto was* Per noctum volamus *(Through the night we fly).*

Source: Keystone Collection

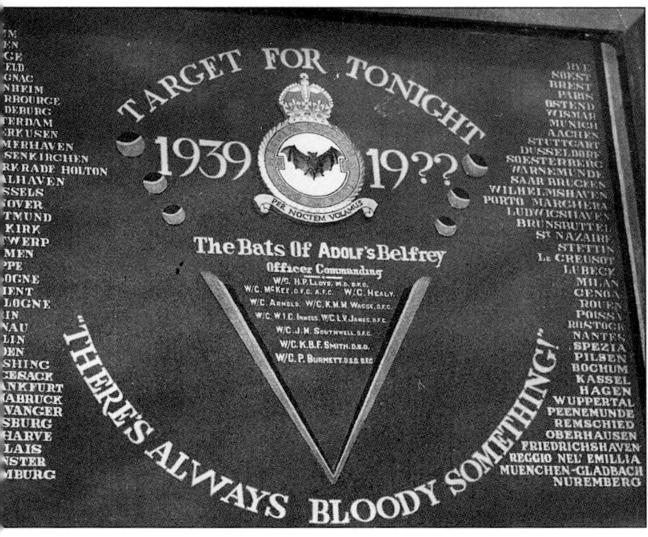

CHAPTER 9

THE ATLANTIC AND HOME WATERS

The tasks faced by Coastal Command after the German occupation of Norway, Denmark, the Low Countries and France were herculean. A coastline extending from the Arctic Circle to the Franco-Spanish border was suddenly and unexpectedly controlled by the enemy. Even ignoring long inlets and large islands, the length was 16,500 miles. In July 1940, Germany was able to ply captured enemy merchant ships along much of this coastline, almost with impunity. Moreover, U-boat shelters were built in Norwegian and French ports, giving this deadly branch of the *Kriegsmarine* improved access to arctic waters, the North Sea and the Atlantic. Together with the Royal Navy and the Fleet Air Arm, Coastal Command shared responsibility for asserting Allied control over these seas.

The U-boats found their major pickings in the Western Approaches to England, following the convoys by day and then closing in after nightfall to make their attacks, when protection from escort vessels and from the air was very limited. Other attacks were made by Focke-Wulf FW 200's, the military version of a civil airliner, which carried out very long-range work in collaboration with U-boats. Shorter-range work was carried by He111s and Do17s. In the last seven months of 1940, sinkings of British and Allied shipping rose to the appalling total of 4,500,000 tons, about 1,200 vessels, reducing essential imports by a fifth. At the outbreak of war, Britain had possessed about 21,000,000 tons of merchant shipping, including 3,000 deep-sea vessels and 1,000 coastal vessels. Since replacement during these seven months amounted to only 500,000 tons, it was evident that Britain could not last out for long, unless the U-boat menace could be overcome.

In January 1941, Coastal Command consisted of twenty-three operational squadrons within five groups, including a squadron of the Photographic Reconnaissance Unit and a squadron in Gibraltar. The principal land-based aircraft were Ansons, Hudsons, Wellingtons, and the new Bristol Beaufort torpedo bombers. The most important flying boat was the Sunderland, but there were still a few Supermarine Stranraers, while very long-range Consolidated Catalinas had been ordered from America. Some of the squadrons were based in Iceland, for the British had forestalled a German invasion by landing in that country in May 1940.

An expansion programme forecast an increase of fifteen squadrons in the command by the following June. In April 1941, it was decided that Coastal Command should come under the Admiralty's operational control, while remaining part of the RAF. In practice, the outcome was simply an improved liaison, for Coastal Command continued to conduct its day-to-day operations without interference, while conferring with the Admiralty on broad issues.

Although bad weather in the first two months of 1941 reduced the activities of German U-boats and aircraft, over 530,000 tons of shipping were sunk in March and 644,000 tons in April. There was a further threat from German surface vessels, the battleships *Scharnhorst* and *Gneisenau*, the pocket-battleship *Admiral von Scheer*, and the cruiser *Hipper*, all of which had broken out into the Atlantic and were sinking merchant ships. The resources of Coastal Command were so stretched that three

Left: *A Sunderland Mark III of Coastal Command. This type was fitted with a dorsal turret instead of beam guns, as well as a faired main step which reduced air drag by about ten per cent.*

Source: RAF Museum P020896

Below: *A Short Sunderland Mark I on a slipway.*

Source: Keystone Collection

squadrons of Blenheims were transferred to it, one from Bomber Command, one from Army Co-operation, and one from Fighter Command. In addition, a Swordfish squadron was temporarily transferred from the Fleet Air Arm. These additional squadrons took part in patrols and anti-shipping attacks over the North Sea, relieving other squadrons for duties elsewhere.

The turning point in the war against British merchant shipping came with improved tactics by naval escort vessels, the cracking of the German signal code, and the installation of new equipment in the growing number of aircraft. Also, fighters catapulted from auxiliary escort vessels gave cover to convoys and began to account for enemy bombers. During March 1941, the Royal Navy escort vessels sank five U-boats, in which three of the most experienced German commanders were lost. From the beginning of the war, the *Kreigsmarine* had lost thirty-seven U-boats, while thirty-two were still operational, and a further eighty-one were undergoing training and trials. Up to this time, the RAF had sunk no U-boats, although aircraft had shared in sinkings with the escort vessels and damaged several others.

The new equipment was an improved mark of 'Air to Surface Vessel' (ASV) radar, installed at first in Sunderlands. This consisted of a transmitter and receiving system, sending out a series of pulses which were reflected back and displayed on a screen. Ships on the surface showed up as blips along a central line, indicating the distance away and whether they were to the left or right of the aircraft's heading. Serviceability of this ASV Mark II was not perfect at first, but results were achieved. U-boats needed to come to the surface for periods during each day in order to recharge their batteries as well as to change their foul air. It was extremely unnerving to suddenly find themselves the target of an aircraft armed with depth charges and machine guns.

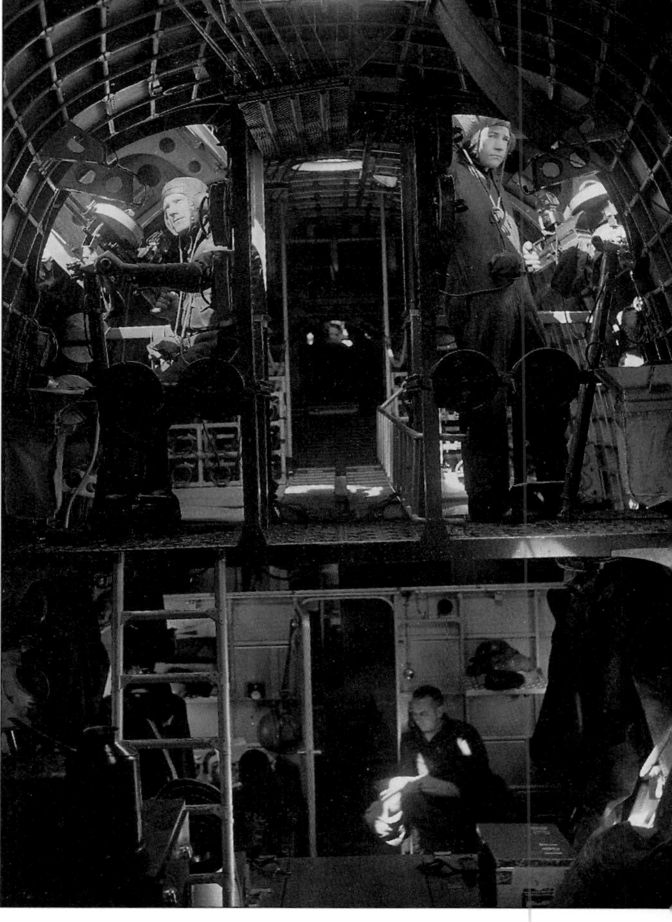

Above: *The interior of a Short Sunderland I, showing the two beam gunners and the accommodation on the deck below. In some of the Sunderland Mark IIs, the beam guns were replaced by a dorsal turret, and this became standard in the later Mark III. This photograph is dated 16 June 1941.*

Source: Keystone Collection

On 8 May 1941, a destroyer escort brought *U-110* to the surface with depth charges, and the Germans abandoned her. Their explosive charges failed and British sailors boarded the vessel, discovering code books as well as a secret 'Enigma' coding machine. From this time, the Government Code and Cipher School at Bletchley Park in Buckinghamshire knew almost as much about the movements of U-boats in home waters as the Germans themselves, as well as the times of sailing and cargoes of German coastal convoys.

Later in May 1941, the U-boats were forced to cease operating in the Western Approaches, and to turn their attention to the central and southern Atlantic, outside the range of aircraft based in Britain and Iceland. Even then, they were harried off the West African coast by Sunderlands and Hudsons based near Freetown in Sierra Leone. Sinkings of Allied ships dropped dramatically to an average of 125,000 tons per month during June, July and August. The period which the U-boat commanders called 'the happy time' was over.

On 6 April 1941, *Gneisenau* was badly damaged by a torpedo dropped in a dawn attack by a solitary Beaufort, while in the roads of Brest, before the defences blew the aircraft out of the sky. On 13 June, the pocket-battleship *Lützow* off Norway was damaged by a torpedo from another Beaufort. On 27 May, the immensely powerful battleship *Bismarck* was sunk in the Atlantic by the Royal Navy and carrier-borne Fairey Swordfish of the FAA. Part of her journey from the Baltic, together with the accompanying cruiser *Prinz Eugen*, had been monitored by reconnaissance aircraft of Coastal Command and the FAA, enabling British warships to close in when the enemy formation reached the waters north of Iceland and then pursue the battleship. The threat from German surface vessels diminished, while Bomber Command continued to pound the harbours in which they and the U-boats were sheltering.

In June 1941, Air Chief Marshal Sir Frederick Bowhill left Coastal Command to form the RAF's new Ferry Command. He left behind a force of increasing effectiveness, which was taken over by Air Chief Marshal Sir Philip de la Ferté, who was familiar with the command, for he had been its chief in 1936-7. He was to remain in this post until February 1943, when Air Marshal Sir John Slessor took over.

On 27 August 1941, a Hudson based in Iceland attacked *U-570* with depth charges. The U-boat was forced to the surface and the crew waved a white shirt when treated to bursts of machine gun fire. Relays of aircraft circled the unlucky vessel until a destroyer arrived and towed her to Iceland, enabling details of her construction to be studied.

The merchant shipping losses began to mount again in September 1941, with U-boats operating outside the range of Coastal Command's aircraft. It was proposed that some of Bomber Command's heavier aircraft, such as the Halifax, should be transferred to Coastal Command, but this move was fiercely opposed by Sir Arthur Harris. Instead, an increased bombardment of the U-boat shelters in ports on the west coast of France took place, including Brest, Lorient, St Nazaire, La Pallice and Bordeaux. But so thick were the concrete roofs that almost no damage was caused to the pens, although the general port facilities were shattered.

Hitler became impatient with the role of his surface warships as targets for Bomber Command in Brest and ordered their return to German waters. He believed that the

Allies would attempt another landing in Norway and that his battleships and cruisers should be available to help repel such a move. On the foggy night of 11/12 February 1942, the battleships *Scharnhorst* and *Gneisenau*, together with the cruiser *Prinz Eugen* and a flotilla of destroyers, torpedo boats and E-boats, slipped out of the roads at Brest and began their 'Channel Dash' at high speed to the Strait of Dover, protected by relays of night-fighters and day fighters. Astonishingly, by mischances which included the failure of the ASV Mark IIs in patrolling aircraft, they reached the Strait in daylight before the FAA and Coastal Command began to make their torpedo attacks. In spite of the heroism of the crews and heavy casualties, none of these were successful. Bomber Command also flew 242 sorties over the low cloud and lost fifteen aircraft, without result. The German fleet reached its destination, although both battleships were damaged when they struck magnetic mines dropped previously by the RAF. Hitler was jubilant, but the exercise availed nothing. A few days later, *Prinz Eugen* was torpedoed by a British submarine and saw no more service. Bomber Command put *Gneisenau* permanently out of action at Kiel on the night of 27/28 February. *Scharnhorst* was sunk by the Royal Navy in a battle off the North Cape of Norway in December 1943.

In 1942, two important branches of Coastal Command were expanded. One was the Photographic Reconnaissance Unit, which had consisted of high-level and unarmed Spitfires. To these were added Mosquitos, increasing the range of PRU activities. By October 1942, five separate squadrons formed part of PRU, with over 1,000 men and women in specialized sections of the Central Interpretation Unit at Medmenham, engaged on the work of examining about 5,500 reports annually, together with almost 1,500,000 photographs. A great deal of Allied intelligence derived from this source. The other development was air-sea rescue which, in October 1941, was passed to the control of Coastal Command. During 1942, seven squadrons operated round British coasts, in co-operation with the squadrons of high-speed launches, and over 1,000 airmen were recovered from the sea.

Coastal Command also provided protection for Allied convoys on the arctic route to Murmansk, which were menaced by the presence of the battleship *Tirpitz*, sister-ship of *Bismarck*, in Trondheim fjord, as well as by other warships. Catalinas were involved in the recapture of Spitsbergen during the summer of 1942 and then, together with two squadrons of torpedo-carrying Hampdens and a flight of PRU Spitfires, flew to North Russia the following September. After providing protection for a convoy, the Catalinas flew back to the Shetlands, but the other aircraft were left behind as presents for the Russian Air Force. Detachments of PRU Spitfires also flew to North Russia in September 1943 and March 1944.

In early 1942, the U-boats found a new hunting ground off the eastern coasts of America, following the entry of that country into the war. In May, 109 ships totalling 531,000 tons were sunk in those waters, before the Americans organized convoys and patrols. Meanwhile, Coastal Command had been developing the Leigh Light, a dazzling searchlight invented by Sqdn Ldr H. de V. Leigh. These were first fitted under Wellingtons and switched before the attack, after homing with the aid of ASV on

Left: *The navigator in a Short Sunderland, sitting in the seat of the first pilot and signalling with an Aldis lamp to a convoy. All navigators were trained to proficiency with Morse code.*

Source: Keystone Collection

surfaced U-boats. Targets were found at night in the Bay of Biscay and 'kills' were made from July 1942 onwards. At the same time, new Bristol Beaufighters of Coastal Command patrolled the Bay of Biscay during daylight, scoring successes against German bombers.

By August 1942, U-boats were gathering in 'Wolf packs' in the central Atlantic, in the gaps outside the range of aircraft. This new menace was countered by the gradual introduction of small aircraft carriers in the convoys and by the employment of very long-range Halifaxes and Consolidated B-24 Liberators, mainly based in Northern Ireland and Iceland. In January 1943, Coastal Command aircraft were equipped with the new ASV Mark III, which was similar to Bomber Command's H2S navigational aid. Sinkings of U-boats mounted and, somewhat in desperation, *Grossadmiral* Karl Dönitz, who commanded the *Kriegsmarine*, ordered them to group together on the surface and fight it out with attacking aircraft. They did so during the summer of 1943, and casualties were heavy on both sides, but the effectiveness of the U-boats diminished. By the end of the war, Coastal Command had sunk, or shared in the sinking, of no less than 213 U-boats and had badly damaged 120 more. Casualties of the men in this branch of the German armed forces amounted to over seventy per cent during the war.

Another role carried out by aircraft of Coastal Command was the assault on the enemy's coastal traffic. At first, these attacks were usually made in daylight by single aircraft on 'Rover' patrols, making use of cloud cover. The aircraft involved were Blenheims, Hudsons and torpedo-carrying Beauforts. At night, magnetic mines were dropped in the approaches to enemy ports. One of the main purposes of these attacks was the interruption of the trade in iron ore between Sweden and Germany, amounted to some 10,000,000 tons per year, which was highly profitable to Sweden and helped sustain the war economy of the Third Reich. On the return journey, the vessels carried coal and coke to the Norwegian industries, as well as supplies for the German occupation forces. These convoys were heavily defenced by flak-ships and fighter escorts.

These anti-shipping attacks were by far the most dangerous of all the RAF's activities. In November 1942, it was calculated that the chance of survival of an operational tour in a torpedo bomber squadron was below eighteen per cent, compared with sixty-six per cent in Sunderlands and over seventy-seven per cent in Catalinas. The equivalent figures in the other commands were forty-three per cent in fighters and forty-four per cent in medium and heavy bombers.

In the spring of 1942, the Beaufort squadrons were sent out to the Mediterranean, to attack the Axis ships carrying supplies to North Africa. Their place was taken by Hampdens coverted into torpedo bombers, while Hudsons continued low-level bombing attacks on shipping. By the following June, Coastal Command was losing one aircraft in four on low-level attacks and was forced to order crews to attack only at

Above: *The Sunderland V was fitted with Pratt & Whitney Twin Wasp engines instead of the Bristol Pegasus XVIII and entered RAF service in February 1945. Painted 'Coastal white', it remained in service until May 1949. This photograph shows the crew of a Sunderland V of 10 (RAAF) Squadron, which was equipped with this mark of the flying boat from May 1944 to June 1945, while based at Mount Batten in Devonshire. The RAAF uniforms, which were dark blue, can be distinguished on some of the crew members, with the letters RB on the Sunderland.*

Source: Keystone Collection

Right: *The Bristol Beaufort was employed as a low-level bomber and torpedo bomber by Coastal Command and the maritime air forces overseas, first entering service in November 1939. The targets were enemy warships and merchant ships, but Beauforts also bombed ports and laid mines outside entrances. Fl Off Kenneth Campbell of 22 Squadron was awarded a posthumous VC for a dawn torpedo attack on the German battleship* Gneisenau *at Brest on 6 April 1941. In statistical terms of losses, the operations carried out by Beauforts were the most dangerous of all RAF activities during the Second World War. This photograph was taken in 1941 and shows a Beaufort I, serial L9878, flying over St Eval in Cornwall. The author flew in this aircraft on a number of operational sorties.*

Source: RAF Museum colour slide P100079

Left: *The Consolidated Catalina, otherwise the PBY-5 of the US Navy, began to arrive in Coastal Command early in 1941. Slow but highly reliable, it could stay in the air for about 27 hours when fitted with extra fuel tanks. RAF Catalinas served in the North Atlantic, the Arctic, the Mediterranean, the Indian Ocean and the Far East. Detachments were also sent to North Russia to protect the arctic convoys. This photograph of a Catalina armed with four 250 lb depth charges was taken at moorings in Iceland.*

Source: Aeroplane Monthly

medium level, resulting in a decrease in effectiveness. A post-war analysis of the period from January 1940 to March 1943 revealed that the RAF sank only 107 enemy vessels, totalling 155,076 tons, by direct attack in European waters. It lost 648 aircraft in the process, giving an average of 239 tons sunk per aircraft lost. On the other hand, aerial mines sank 369 vessels totalling 361,821 tons for the loss of 329 aircraft, giving an average of 980 tons per aircraft lost.

This unhappy state of affairs was transformed in early 1943 by the use of the Beaufighter as an anti-shipping aircraft, with some aircraft in the role of torpedo bombers while others carried cannons and machine guns to suppress the flak ships. Special 'Strike Wings' were formed, each consisting of two or three squadrons, and their combined attacks in daylight were protected by Spitfires. The Germans suddenly began to lose heavily, while the Swedes became less enthusiastic about using their ships on the 'gold run', as they called this trade. In April 1943 the rocket projectile arrived, eight of these being fitted under the wings of a Beaufighter. Rockets were aimed at the sea in front of the target and the warheads were capable of sinking any merchant ship or escort vessel if they struck below the waterline.

By June 1944, other Strike Wings were formed from Mosquito squadrons, initially operating over the west coast of France. Some of the Mosquitos carried cannons and rockets while others were fitted with anti-tank guns of 57 mm calibre, firing six-pounder shells. These squadrons accounted for U-boats as well as warships and merchant vessels. Before the end of the war the Strike Wings, consisting of nine squadrons of Beaufighters and Mosquitos, almost obliterated the German coastal traffic, sinking over 300,000 tons and badly damaging another 118,000 tons.

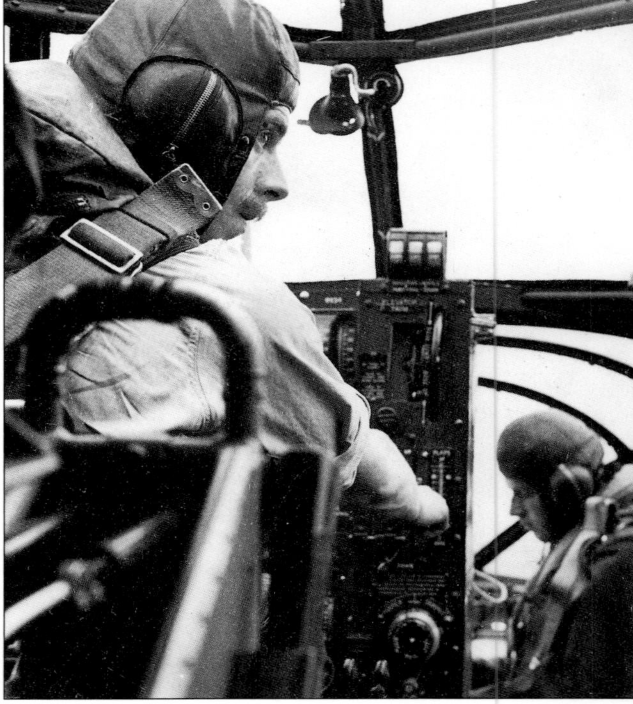

Above: *The pilot of a Bristol Beaufort, with the navigator at his chart table in the nose of the torpedo bomber.*

Source: Keystone Collection

Left: *The author's crew in front of Beaufort I of 217 Squadron, photographed in July 1941 at St Eval in Cornwall. Left to right: Sgt 'Davy' Davies, wireless operator: Fl Off John 'Percy' Percival, pilot: Sgt Ken Reeves, gunner: Plt Off Roy Nesbit, navigator. The crew survived their tour, but Percival was killed later in the war, while Reeves survived a very bad crash. The fate of Davies is unknown, and the author was not harmed.*

Source: Flt Lt K. Reeves

Left: *A Mark XII torpedo of 1,610 lb, with a contact warhead, being loaded into the bomb bay of a Bristol Beaufort. The bomb doors could be only partially closed when the torpedo was in place.*

Source: Keystone Collection

Above: *The Blackburn Botha was designed as a torpedo bomber for Coastal Command and was delivered to 608 Squadron in June 1940. However, it proved to be underpowered and was withdrawn five months later. Thereafter it was employed as an operational trainer, in numerous schools and units, but it was not at all popular with aircrews. It was declared obsolete in August 1943.*

Source: Aviation Bookshop

Below: *A crewroom poster showing views, dimensions, speeds and ceilings of German flying boats and floatplanes.*

Source: RAF Museum AD1359

GERMAN AIRCRAFT

SHEET 4

BLOHM & VOSS Ha 138 (3-JUMO 205)
FUNCTION: RECONNAISSANCE
SPAN: 88' 7" LENGTH: 65' 4"
MAXIMUM SPEED: 190 m.p.h. CRUISING " : 170 m.p.h.

BLOHM & VOSS Ha 139 (4-JUMO 205)
FUNCTION: COASTAL-RECONNAISSANCE
SPAN: 80' 7" LENGTH: 64'
MAXIMUM SPEED: 215 m.p.h. CRUISING " : 190 m.p.h.

BLOHM & VOSS Ha 140 (2-B.M.W. 132)
FUNCTION: TORPEDO-RECONNAISSANCE
SPAN: 69' LENGTH: 57' 9"
MAXIMUM SPEED: 200 m.p.h. CRUISING " : 180 m.p.h.

DORNIER Do 18 (2-JUMO 205 or B.M.W. 132)
FUNCTION: RECONNAISSANCE
SPAN: 77' 8" LENGTH: 63' 2"
MAXIMUM SPEED: 155 m.p.h. CRUISING " : 135 m.p.h.

DORNIER Do 24 (3-B.M.W. 132)
FUNCTION: RECONNAISSANCE
SPAN: 88' 6" LENGTH: 72'
MAXIMUM SPEED: 210 m.p.h. CRUISING " : 170 m.p.h.

DORNIER Do 26 (4-JUMO 205)
FUNCTION: RECONNAISSANCE
SPAN: 98' 6" LENGTH: 80' 6"
MAXIMUM SPEED: 210 m.p.h. CRUISING " : 185 m.p.h.

HEINKEL He 59 (2-B.M.W.)
FUNCTION: GENERAL PURPOSE FLOAT PLANE
SPAN: 77' 6" LENGTH: 56' 6"
MAXIMUM SPEED: 135 m.p.h. CRUISING " : 120 m.p.h.

HEINKEL He 114 (BRAMO 323)
FUNCTION: COASTAL-RECONNAISSANCE
SPAN: 44' 7" LENGTH: 39'
MAXIMUM SPEED: 210 m.p.h. CRUISING " : 185 m.p.h.

HEINKEL He 115 (2 B.M.W. 132)
FUNCTION: TORPEDO-RECONNAISSANCE
SPAN: 73' LENGTH: 56' 8"
MAXIMUM SPEED: 220 m.p.h. CRUISING " : 185 m.p.h.

OFFICIAL USE ONLY
AIR DIAGRAM 1359 4·41

Above: *A soldier of the Royal Corps of Signals with a pigeon named "Beachcomer" which brought news of the Dieppe landings of 19 August 1942. Pigeons were used in the RAF, particularly by Coastal Command, being carried in wicker baskets. Flying at a speed of about 50 m.p.h., they could carry news of aircrews in dinghies after 'ditching' in the sea.*

Source: Keystone Collection

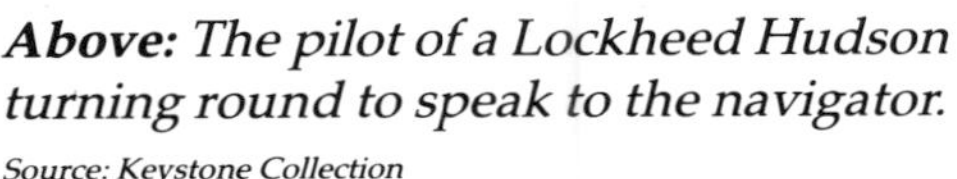

Above: *The pilot of a Lockheed Hudson turning round to speak to the navigator.*

Source: Keystone Collection

Above: *The Lockheed Hudson, a military version of the Lockheed 14-WF62 Super Electra airliner, was the first American-built aircraft to serve on operational duties with the RAF during the Second World War. In May 1939, Hudsons began to replace the Avro Ansons of Coastal Command as reconnaissance and anti-submarine aircraft. Three Hudsons of 224 Squadron scored the RAF's first aerial victory of the war when they shot down a Do18 flying boat on 8 October 1939. After the fall of France, Hudsons were also employed on anti-shipping strikes, a role for which they were not entirely suitable. This photograph shows a Hudson of 320 (Royal Netherlands Air Force) Squadron. Three Dutch squadrons served with the RAF during the war, many of the personnel being former members of the Royal Netherlands Air Service.*

Source: RAF Museum P8143

Right: *Three of the crew of a Lockheed Hudson of 206 Squadron, based at St Eval in Cornwall, playing a game of draughts in front of their aircraft. This Coastal Command squadron was at St Eval during July and August 1941, engaged on bombing the German battleships* Scharnhorst *and* Gneisenau *in the French port of Brest.*

Source: Keystone Collection

Right: *The wireless operator of a Lockheed Hudson operating an F24 camera from the port side.*

Source: Keystone Collection

Below: *WAAF instrument repairers with the aerial cameras on which they worked. The P14 camera on the left was the forerunner of the standard F24 which took a series of 5 inch by 5 inch exposures from a magazine and could be either cranked manually or operated automatically when installed in a fixed position. The G28 gun cameras, centre and left, were based on the Vickers machine gun and produced negatives of about 2½ inch by 2½ inch from a roll film.*

Source: Keystone Collection

Above: *'Tea Wagons' were much appreciated by aircrews and ground crews alike. This was one of four allocated to Coastal Command from a batch of fifty donated to Britain by the British War Relief Society of America. The photograph was taken on 10 December 1941, four days after America entered the war, and shows a lieutenant of the USNAF finishing a design on the wagon.*

Source: Keystone Collection

Left: *An air gunner of 206 Squadron, carrying two Vickers .303 machine guns.*

Source: Keystone Collection

Left: *The mascot of 407 (RCAF) Squadron was named "Squadron Leader Bill", photographed at Bircham Newton on 24 July 1941. The squadron was formed as an anti-shipping squadron in May 1941 and equipped with Lockheed Hudsons. It carried out a series of successful attacks against German shipping off the Dutch coast until October 1942, and then concentrated on anti-submarine patrols from Cornwall. Eventually, forty-five RCAF squadrons flew alongside the RAF in Europe and the Mediterranean, apart from those Canadians who served in the RAF itself.*

Source: Keystone Collection

Right: *The only RAF squadron to be equipped with Northrop N3P-Bs was 330 (Norwegian) Squadron, which flew these US seaplanes from Iceland on reconnaissance work from June 1941 to May 1943. Five Norwegian squadrons served with distinction as part of the RAF during the Second World War.*
Source: RAF Museum PO17844

Above: *An Armstrong Whitworth Whitley V, serial Z6640, of 1484 Flight at Driffield in Yorkshire, where it was used for target-towing, bombing and gunnery. This machine had served with 78 Squadron at Croft in Yorkshire, which was re-equipped with Handley Page Halifaxes during March 1942.*
Source: RAF Museum P788

Left: *A magnetic mine being transported to the bomb bay of a Handley Page Hampden in November 1942.*
Source: Keystone Collection

Left: *A magnetic mine being loaded on the Handley Page Hampden. These mines, each of 2,000 lb, descended with the aid of their parachutes and rested on the sea bed, where they were activated by metal in the hulls of vessels passing overhead. They were code-named 'cucumbers', while the operation was 'gardening'. Although the operations were less dramatic than direct attacks on enemy vessels during daylight, the results were often more effective since RAF losses were lower. The mines were dropped by both Coastal and Bomber Command.*

Source: Keystone Collection

Left: *On 26 April 1942, 455 (RAAF) Squadron was transferred from Bomber Command to Coastal Command, together with its Handley Page Hampden Is. The squadron then trained in torpedo bombing and operated mainly along the Norwegian coast. This colour photograph of a Hampden T.B.1, serial AT137, of 455 Squadron was taken in 1942.*

Source: RAF Museum colour slide P100325

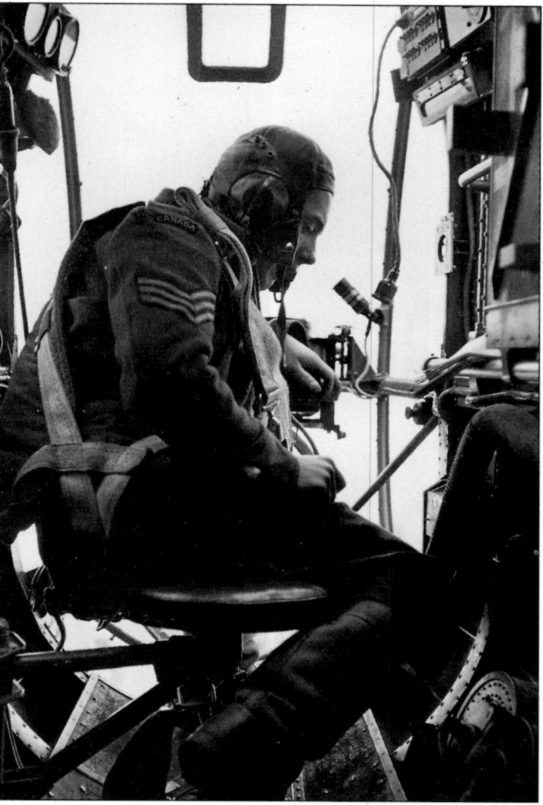

Right: *A Canadian navigator in the nose of a Handley Page Hampden, showing bomb release switches (top right) and ammunition pans (bottom right) for the forward-firing Vickers K gun.*

Source: Keystone Collection

Left and above: *On 12 June 1942, Flight Lieutenant Ken Gatward and his navigator Sergeant George Fern flew in a Beaufighter IC of 236 Squadron, Coastal Command, on a daring daylight raid over Paris. The intention was to attack a German parade in the Champs Elysées, but on arrival there were no troops in sight. Instead, they dropped a tricolour over the Arc de Triomphe, then roared down the Champs Elysées at roof-top height and attacked with cannon fire the headquarters of the* Kriegsmarine *in the Place de la Concorde, where they dropped another tricolour. The episode caused astonishment in France, and the RAF dropped showers of these leaflets soon after the event.*

Source: RAF Museum (Crown copyright)

Above: *A Westland Lysander dropping dinghies into the sea.*

Source: Keystone Collection

Right: *An airman practising in an 'H-type' dinghy while wearing his 'Mae West' lifejacket, and obviously enjoying the experience. This round dinghy was stowed in the wing of most RAF bomber aircraft, and inflated automatically when a handle was pulled. It had a drogue and paddles, but only minor progress could be made against wind and currents. Most survivors simply drifted until help appeared.*

Source: Keystone Collection

Left: *A Supermarine Walrus amphibian flying boat has cruised to the rescue, and a crew member is pulling in the dinghy with a boathook. Although these photographs merely show practice, they are representative of many genuine rescues of downed airmen.*

Source: Keystone Collection

Left: *The airborne lifeboat was carried under the fuselage of an aircraft and dropped by a cluster of five parachutes near survivors in the sea. It was designed so that it could not capsize. The equipment consisted of an engine which gave a range of about eighty miles, together with wireless, sails, food and water. The Vickers Warwick was often used on this type of air-sea rescue work. This photograph was taken in October 1944 and shows a Warwick with the black and white 'invasion stripes'.*

Source: Keystone Collection

Above: *The Leigh Light was first devised in 1940 by Sqdn Ldr H. de V. Leigh, who had been a pilot in the First World War. It consisted of a searchlight which gave out a brilliant beam, used to illuminate a U-boat at night in the final stage of attack after initial detection by air-to-surface vessel radar. It did not come into operation until June 1942 but proved immediately successful. This photograph, taken in October 1944, shows a test being made by an RAF B-24 Liberator.*

Source: Keystone Collection

Left: *The amphibian Supermarine Sea Otter was designed as a replacement for the Walrus and served as air/sea rescue aircraft with Coastal command from April 1944 as well as in Burma and the Far East. This photograph is of the prototype, serial K8854, which first flew in September 1938.*

Source: RAF Museum P806

Left: *Air-Sea Rescue proved its worth during the Battle of Britain, when Westland Lysanders and Walruses worked effectively with high-speed launches in rescuing 'ditched' airmen. In August 1941, the U.K. rescue services came under the direction of Coastal Command. If weather permitted, high-speed launches remained in positions near flight paths, waiting for 'crash calls' over the W/T or R/T before speeding to the rescue. Hundreds of airmen were rescued by these RAF marine craft from the seas around Britain and from the Mediterranean.*

Source: RAF Museum colour slide P100747

Below: *The Vickers Warwick 1, a larger version of the Vickers Wellington, served in Coastal Command squadrons at home and maritime squadrons abroad as an air-sea rescue aircraft, from November 1944. Another version, the Warwick III, served as a transport aircraft. The Warwick V was modified with a longer nose and radome, as well as a Leigh Light under the roundel, for anti-submarine duties. This photograph of a Warwick V, serial PN811, of 179 Squadron, was taken on 15 December 1945. Warwicks did not continue in service beyond 1946.*

Source: RAF Museum colour slide P100687

Right: *The ability of the de Havilland Mosquito to fly at high altitudes and at high speeds for long distances proved a godsend to the RAF's photographic reconnaissance squadrons. The machines were stripped of armament and all possible equipment, being fitted with extra fuel tanks which gave ranges of about 3,500 miles. They carried out magnificent work in all theatres of war. This photograph of Mosquito XVI, serial NS502, of 544 Squadron was taken in 1944.*

Source: RAF Museum PO16733

Above: *The German U-boat pens built on the west coast of France, at Brest, Lorient, St Nazaire, La Pallice and Bordeaux, proved resistant to much of the Allied bombing. However, one well-aimed bomb penetrated the concrete roof of one of the pens in Brest. This photograph was taken on 23 September 1944, shortly after the German garrison capitulated.*

Source: Keystone Collection

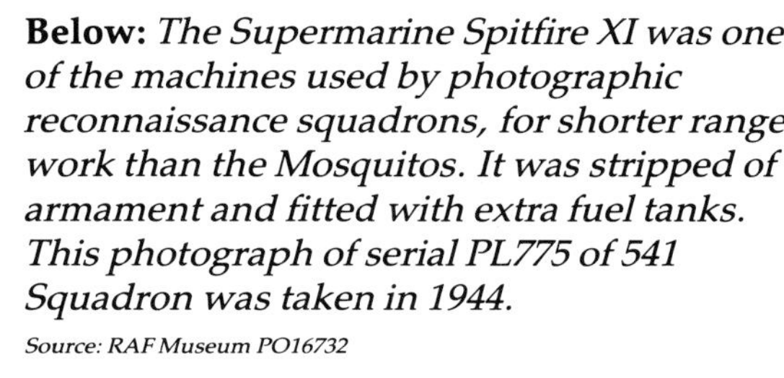

Below: *The Supermarine Spitfire XI was one of the machines used by photographic reconnaissance squadrons, for shorter range work than the Mosquitos. It was stripped of armament and fitted with extra fuel tanks. This photograph of serial PL775 of 541 Squadron was taken in 1944.*

Source: RAF Museum PO16732

Left: *The rocket-firing Bristol Beaufighter TFX, specially designed for Coastal Command, was one of the most effective aircraft used by the Strike Wings. It carried eight rockets as well as four 20 mm cannons and was flown with devastating effect against German coastal shipping. This Beaufighter was on the strength of 455 (RAAF) Squadron, based at Langham in Norfolk from April to October 1944, operating in partnership with 489 (RNZAF) Squadron along the Dutch and German coasts.*

Source: RAF Museum PO19119

Left: *The pilot's cockpit of a Strike Wing Beaufighter with the reflector gunsight locked into a central position.*

Source: British Aerospace

Below: *The Strike Wings of Coastal Command employed the de Havilland Mosquito VI as a fighter-bomber from early June 1944 to the end of the war. This photograph shows serial RF610 of 248 Squadron, one of the first squadrons to be equipped with the machine.*

Source: RAF Museum PO21827

Above: *An attack on 2 May 1945 by Mosquitos of the Banff Strike Wing on U-boats in the Kattegat.*

Source: The late Wg Cdr F.E. Burton, OBE, DFC.

Above: *An attack by the Banff Strike Wing, consisting of Beaufighter TFXs of 144 and 404 Squadrons and Mosquito VIs of 235 Squadron, off Stong Fjord in Norway on 19 September 1944. Two merchant ships were sunk,* Lynx *of 1,367 tons and* Tyrifjord *of 3,080 tons.*

Source: RAF Museum PO21837

Below: *The Danish freighter* Java *in Nakskov harbour in Denmark, under attack by rocket-firing TFXs of the Dallachy Strike Wing on 3 May 1945. These rockets had 25 lb solid-shot warheads designed to penetrate below the waterline. The* Java *sank and the two freighters behind her were damaged.*

Source: The late Wg Cdr F.E. Burton, OBE, DFC.

CHAPTER 10

NORTH AFRICA, MALTA AND ITALY

At the outbreak of the war with Germany, nineteen RAF squadrons were stationed in what may be loosely termed the Middle East and the Mediterranean. Fourteen of these were based in Egypt and the Sudan, one in Palestine, one in Iraq, three in Aden and one in Malta. They were commanded by Air Chief Marshal Sir William Mitchell, who handed over to Air Chief Marshal Sir Arthur Longmore in May 1940, shortly before Italy entered the war. By this date, the aircraft, numbering some 300, were an extraordinarily assorted collection. There were Blenheims, Lysanders, Gladiators, Battles, Wellesleys and Sunderlands, but also a miscellany of obsolete bombers, transports and biplane fighters. Against these were ranged about 500 Italian machines in Libya, East Africa and the Dodecanese. These were roughly equal to the RAF aircraft in performance, but to their numerical superiority was added ease of reinforcement from Italy, where their home strength was about 1,200.

The RAF went on to the offensive immediately, operating over Libya, but resources were too limited for large-scale attacks and there was a major difficulty with reinforcement. Long-range aircraft could fly from Cornwall to Gibraltar and then via Malta to Egypt, but fighters were usually crated and sent by sea, and the route through the Mediterranean was subject to attack. To overcome this problem, an air route was devised from the Gold Coast port of Takoradi, where the crated aircraft were assembled and fitted with long-range tanks, to Nigeria and then across French Chad to the Sudan. RAF ferry pilots flew the aircraft on this route, which served well until the Axis was finally cleared out of Africa.

The geographical position of Malta was to prove one of the most decisive factors of the war in the Mediterranean, but when Italy entered the war the only operational aircraft on the island were four FAA Gladiators, apart from five Swordfish target-towers. One of the Gladiators was damaged, and the remaining three, nicknamed Faith, Hope and Charity, constituted the only defence of Malta against the *Regia Aeronautica* until a few Swordfish and Hurricanes arrived at the end of June. These were followed by more Hurricanes in August and November. Three Marylands arrived in September, and a squadron of Wellingtons in November. With these scanty forces, the RAF in Malta went on to the offensive, primarily against the Italian forces in Libya.

In the Western Desert, as the vast area of Libya was called, the British scored considerable successes at first. In November, two Wellington squadrons arrived in Egypt from the U.K., as well as a squadron of Hurricanes via Takoradi. Another Hurricane and three Blenheim squadrons were switched to the front from the defence of Egypt and the Canal Zone. The British began to attack on 9 November and by early February had chased the Italians all the way past Benghazi to El Agheila on the Gulf of Sirte, taking 130,000 prisoners. Both the ground and air forces were then weakened by the withdrawal of some of their strength to the defence of Greece. In February 1941 the *Deutsches Afrika Korps* arrived in the Western Desert and, headed by the dynamic *General* Erwin Rommel, began to fight in a way which outwitted its opponents. The co-ordination of *Panzers*, artillery, infantry and aircraft sent the British reeling back across the desert. By April 1941, the British were back behind the Egyptian border, leaving only some well-defended positions around the port of Tobruk.

Strong Italian forces were concentrated in Abyssinia, Eritrea and Italian Somaliland, heavily outnumbering British forces on the ground but roughly equal in the air. The Italians overran part of British Somaliland, but their success was short-lived. British ground forces were supported by RAF squadrons based in the Sudan, Aden and Kenya, and the Italians were subjected to some very effective bombing attacks. British reinforcements arrived by sea in January 1941 and a three-pronged invasion began from the Sudan, British Somaliland and Kenya. Four Italian destroyers off Eritrea were sunk by the RAF and the FAA, while two others were scuttled. In the south, the invading forces were supported by squadrons of the South African Air Force (SAAF). On 6 April, the British entered Addis Ababa, and a mopping-up began, which lasted until the last Italian troops capitulated in the following November.

In other areas, the British met with disaster. Mussolini's invasion of Greece on 28 October 1940 resulted in a request from the Greek government to support the Royal Hellenic Air Force, which numbered only seventy-five aircraft. Three Blenheim and three Gladiator squadrons were sent to ill-prepared bases near Athens, from where they were engaged in bombing enemy airfields and repelling air attacks, with considerable success. But the humiliating reverses which the Italian forces suffered at the hands of the Greek army drove Hitler to despair. In any event, he had planned to move southwards into the Aegean, having entered Romania in October 1940 and Bulgaria in March 1941. On 6 April 1941, the *Wehrmacht* invaded Yugoslavia and Greece. By then,

Below: *The more seriously wounded prisoners were repatriated to their own countries. Here, a sergeant observer of the RAF who had lost a leg is arriving at Lisbon on 22 April 1943, after repatriation from Italy. He is being attended by Portuguese medical orderlies.*

Source: Keystone Collection

four Commonwealth divisions had arrived in Greece, while two more Blenheim squadrons were on their way, together with three squadrons equipped with a mixture of Gladiators, Hurricanes and Lysanders. Two temporary detachments of Wellingtons followed. But nothing could stop the massive assault of the *Wehrmacht*, which included twenty-seven divisions and 1,200 aircraft. The German forces swept into Yugoslavia and Greece, crushing the determined opposition. After nine days of fighting against impossible odds, only forty-six RAF aircraft remained serviceable, while the Royal Yugoslav and Royal Hellenic Air Forces were all but wiped out. On 20 April, the surviving aircraft were withdrawn to Crete, while the surviving Commonwealth troops sailed for that island, covered by the remnants of the RAF to the best of their ability.

Worse was to follow when *General* Kurt Student's airborne troops began to descend on Crete on 20 May. The *Luftwaffe* mustered about 650 aircraft for the attack, as well as over 700 air transports and gliders to carry an invading force of 15,000 men. Although the defending troops were numerically superior, they had left most of their equipment behind in Greece. The only air cover that could be provided was twenty-four aircraft of the RAF and the FAA, consisting of Hurricanes, Gladiators and Fulmars. The island was outside the range of fighters in Egypt. Nevertheless, the outcome of the battle hung in the balance for several days. At the expense of enormous casualties, the Germans finally overcame the defenders. The Royal Navy evacuated half the survivors, at the cost of three cruisers and six destroyers sunk.

These setbacks threatened to undermine the position of Iraq, where Britain was responsible for internal security, and in Syria, where there was a possibility that the controlling French Vichy government might be forced to make available airfields for the *Luftwaffe*. A German presence in these countries would constitute a serious threat to Britain's oil supplies in the Middle East. In Iraq, the pro-British government was ousted at the end of 1941 by Rashid Ali, who supported the Axis. At the end of the following month, about 9,000 Iraqi troops laid siege to the RAF base at Habbaniya, near Baghdad, subjecting the camp to artillery fire. The RAF and local levies put up a defence which was classed as a minor epic of the Second World War. Wellington bombers from Shaibah on the Persian Gulf bombed the Iraqi positions, while Gladiators and Audaxes from the RAF Flying School at Habbiniya delivered strafing attacks. After several days the Iraqis decided they had had enough and retired to Baghdad, where they were defeated by a British column at the end of May. The previous government in Iraq was restored. The British then turned their attention to Syria, advancing into that country with the support of about sixty RAF and FAA aircraft. The Vichy French forces resisted fiercely, supported by about a hundred aircraft, but capitulated on 14 July.

The battle lines in the Mediterranean were thus more clearly drawn. The British 8th Army faced the Axis forces in the Western Desert, where Rommel threatened Egypt, the Suez Canal and eventually India, while Malta provided a strategic base from which the RAF and FAA could attack enemy positions and supply lines. On 1 June 1941, Air Marshal Sir Arthur Tedder took over the RAF's Middle East Command, and a few weeks later the *Luftwaffe* began withdrawing some of its strength for the invasion of Russia. By the following November, the RAF and FAA numbered about 660 aircraft in the Western Desert with another 120 in Malta. These included Blenheims, Wellingtons, Marylands, Hurricanes, Tomahawks, Swordfish, Albacores, Beauforts and Beaufighters. The *Luftwaffe* mustered 180 aircraft in Greece, while *Fliegerführer Afrika* supported Rommel with 240 aircraft in Libya. The *Regia Aeronautica* in Libya possessed about 300 aircraft. Although outnumbered, the rate of serviceability of the RAF was higher than that of its opponents, and it was more capable of moving bases rapidly.

The 8th Army opened the 'Crusader' offensive on 18 November, following a fierce bombardment of the enemy's airfields and land transport by the RAF, including low-level attacks by cannon-firing Beaufighters and continued assaults on sea supplies from the air and by British submarines. The British had an advantage which Rommel would have considered incredible had he known. Using a captured 'Enigma' coding machine, they were decrypting regularly the messages which the Germans were passing to their forces in North Africa. They knew the state of the *Afrika Korps* and the dates of sailing of almost all Axis convoys, as well as the contents of their cargoes. PRU aircraft based at Malta knew where to hunt for the convoys and the RAF was able to concentrate its few anti-shipping aircraft at critical times. In November, fourteen of the twenty-two supply vessels sent from Italy were sunk. The Axis forces fell back to Agedabia and Tobruk was relieved by the 8th Army. But in December two large convoys, heavily escorted by most of the Italian Fleet, succeeded in reaching North Africa. In the following month, 400 German aircraft arrived in Sicily, under the command of *Generalfeldmarschall* Albert Kesselring. Rommel went over to the offensive and by 6 February the 8th Army had retreated as far as Gazala.

Meanwhile, Malta underwent the protracted agony of an intense bombardment, and, in spite of the arrival of a handful of Spitfires, only six serviceable fighters and a handful of bombers remained by the end of March 1942. Forty-seven Spitfires were

Above: *One of the most unusual fighter aces of the war was George Frederick Beurling, known as "Screwball" from his frequent use of the name and his craving for combat. He was a Canadian of Anglo-Swedish parentage, and qualified as a pilot when too young to hold a licence. He tried unsuccessfully to join various air forces, but then worked his passage to England in 1941 , where he enlisted in the RAF and became a sergeant pilot. After flying Spitfires with 41 Squadron he was posted to Malta, where he came the top-scoring Spitfire pilot during the siege of the island. He later flew Spitfires with 412 (RCAF) Squadron in the 2nd Tactical Air Force. By the end of the war, his score was 31 1/3 aircraft destroyed and he had been awarded a DSO, DFC, DFM and bar. He lost his life in 1948 in an air crash, while ferrying a North American B-25 Mitchell to Israel.*

Source: Keystone Collection

Right: *A German airman posing on a Bristol Blenheim IV of 11 Squadron, letter V serial T2177, captured after the Germans conquered Greece in April 1941.*

Source: Keystone Collection

Above: *Three Hawker Hurricane IIB fighter-bombers of 1 (SAAF) Squadron, photographed in May 1941 while flying over the Sudan from Amriya in Egypt. This South African squadron had been equipped with Hurricanes during the previous month. It eventually moved up to the Western Desert and began ground attacks against the Axis forces. Twenty-eight SAAF squadrons flew with the RAF, mainly in the Mediterranean theatre of war.*

Source: Keystone Collection

flown to the island on 20 April from the US carrier *Wasp* but most of these were destroyed by air attack on the following day. The Axis had plans to invade Malta in its weakened state, but these were abandoned owing to pressure of events in Russia and the need to defend Germany from attacks by Bomber Command. However, supplies streamed across the Mediterranean for the Axis forces, while the Allied forces were supplied from the route round the Cape of Good Hope and via Takoradi.

In the Western Desert, Rommel struck again, on 26 May. This time, he met with enormous success, capturing Tobruk, taking 45,000 prisoners and capturing 1,500,000 gallons of precious fuel. With its remarkably efficient organization, the RAF fell back in good order to prepared airfields, while the 8th Army took up new positions at El Alamein.

There was then a period of stalemate on the ground, while the RAF shot up Axis road convoys and bombed airfields and ports. Fighters intercepted Ju52 air transports flying between Libya and Crete. U.S. bomber and fighter squadrons began to arrive in Egypt, to serve alongside the RAF. By October, the RAF and FAA in the Middle East controlled ninety-six operational squadrons, including thirteen American, thirteen South African, five Australian, one Rhodesian, one Canadian, two Greek, one French and one Yugoslav. At the same time, Malta began to receive air reinforcements, including Spitfires, as well as some sea-borne supplies. In June, the Beaufort squadrons in the U.K. flew out to the island and immediately began to attack, escorted by Beaufighters and guided by the PRU squadron. Torpedo-carrying Wellingtons from Malta and Egypt also joined in these attacks, using ASV at night. By August the Axis convoys began to suffer heavy losses, both from aircraft and submarines. Although the anti-shipping squadrons lost many aircraft, the attacks continued, while RAF medium bombers pounded the enemy ports. Once again, Rommel began to run short of fuel and military supplies in his advanced positions.

When the British opened their bombardment at El Alamein on the evening of 23 October 1942, they were supported by about 1,200 first-line aircraft based in Egypt and Palestine and another 300 in Malta, whereas only about 690 Axis aircraft supported Rommel in Africa. The bombing and strafing attacks from the air and the weight of armour contributed to the Allied victory, but perhaps the decisive factor was the almost complete destruction of the Axis vessels attempting to reach North Africa, which were attacked from both Malta and Egypt. With only a couple of days fuel in hand, Rommel was forced into a fighting retreat, still in good order in spite of severe losses, all the way along the North African coast to Tunisia.

On 7 November, the landings of Anglo-American forces at Oran and Algiers, under the code-name of operation 'Torch', transformed the military situation in North Africa. The RAF provided cover for these landings, primarily from Gibraltar, where the runway of the airfield had been lengthened, and then flew to forward bases in Algeria in support of the ground forces. The Axis responded by occupying Vichy France and setting up bases in Tunisia. Supplies for the Axis began to pour across the 100 miles of sea which

LIBYA

Help them finish the job

Left: *This poster shows a Spitfire shooting down a Heinkel He111.*

Source: Vintage Magazine Co. colour slide

Below: *An attack on 6 October 1942 by four long-range Bristol Beaufighters on 252 Squadron on the Axis camp at Gazala in Libya, in which it was estimated that fifty casualties were caused to enemy troops. The Beaufighters were returning from an attack against the Italian seaplane base at Bomba.*

Source: Keystone Collection

separate Tunisia and Sicily, while *Fliegerkorps II* increased its transport aircraft from 250 to about 750. Spitfires, Beauforts, Beaufighters and FAA Albacores from Malta kept up constant attacks against these sea and air supply routes, shooting down many Ju52s and sinking many ships, while bombers from Libya and Malta began to lay waste to the ports in Sicily and Tunisia. Nevertheless, the *Panzerarmee Afrika* put up a fierce and skilful defence until the last remnants surrendered on 14 May, bringing the total of prisoners taken in Tunisia to 250,000.

Air Chief Marshal Sir Arthur Tedder had been appointed on 17 February 1943 as C-in-C of the new Mediterranean Air Command, controlling the whole of the Allied air activities in that vast area. The next task of the Allies was the invasion of Sicily, under the code-name of operation 'Husky', preparatory to an invasion of the Italian mainland. This operation began with sustained air attacks on the enemy airfields in Sicily, Sardinia and southern Italy, as well as ports and industrial targets. On 10 July, airborne troops were landed in the south of Sicily by Waco and Hadrian gliders towed by Dakotas, Halifaxes and Albemarles, while others parachuted in. At dawn on the same day, troops

Right: *The Martin Baltimore, a development of the Martin Maryland, was produced in the USA to meet a British specification for a light bomber. It first entered service with the RAF in January 1942. Baltimores were used exclusively in the Mediterranean theatre of war, by nine RAF squadrons as well as two RAAF and three SAAF squadrons. The original Wright engines gave some trouble in the desert, but later Pratt & Whitney engines stood up well to these conditions. Although the machine was heavy and crew conditions were cramped, the Baltimore was strongly constructed and could take a fair amount of punishment. This photograph shows a formation of 55 Squadron, which was equipped with these aircraft from May 1942 to October 1944.*

Source: RAF Museum PO14682

Left: *Curtiss Kittyhawks, designated P-40D onwards by the USAAF, served only in the Mediterranean when delivered to the RAF from late 1941 onwards. With a more powerful engine and heavier armament than the Tomahawk, they were employed as interceptors and fighter-bombers until the end of the war in Europe. This photograph shows a Kittyhawk Mark III, or P-40M, serial FR452, of 112 Squadron, which adopted the famous shark's head motif.*

Source: RAF Museum P10159

from convoys amounting to about 2,000 vessels landed on the southern tip of the island, under constant air cover. The Germans resisted fiercely, although their air support was noticeably weaker. Within hours, RAF fighters landed on Sicilian airfields. On 25 July, the dictator Mussolini was arrested and imprisoned by the Fascist Grand Council, although he was later rescued by German paratroops and taken to Germany, where he formed a puppet 'government'. The Allies steadily advanced through Sicily and drove out the last of the defenders on 17 August, capturing many Italian prisoners. The wreckage of some 1,100 enemy aircraft was left on Sicilian airfields.

Elements of the British 8th Army crossed the Strait of Messina on 3 September and landed on the "toe" of Italy. On 8 September, the terms of an armistice arranged between the Allies and the Italian government were announced, the day before divisions of the U.S. Fifth Army landed at Salerno in Campania. By then, the *Luftwaffe* in Italy had been almost neutralised by air attacks and air combats, but the invaders on the beach-head met with determined opposition from German *Panzers*. The weight of the Allied air force fell upon the German counter-attacks, while airborne troops were dropped behind enemy lines. By 15 September, the Allies were more firmly established and began to advance. On 1 October, the vital port of Naples was captured, enabling all-important military supplies to be landed.

In the Aegean, however, the Allies met with a reverse. Their objective was the capture of the Italian Dodecanese Islands, as a prelude to an invasion of Greece. The enterprise bypassed the island of Rhodes, which was strongly held by the Germans. On 13 September, British troops landed on the island of Kos, followed by paratroops dropped from Dakotas. The island of Leros and Samos were also occupied, without opposition from the Italian garrisons. Spitfires of the SAAF landed at Kos, and the airfield was protected by units of the RAF Regiment. However, the *Luftwaffe* withdrew units from other areas and, with its short lines of communication, began to bomb and strafe the British positions. The RAF responded by bombing the enemy airfields near Athens and on Crete and Rhodes, but on 3 October German troops landed by sea and air on Kos, over-running the island. Leros received the same treatment on 12 November and Samos fell ten days later. It was generally agreed that the Allied venture had been unwise, since insufficient resources had been allocated and distances were too great for the RAF to provide adequate air cover.

The Allied troops continued the hard slog up the peninsula of Italy, against skilful and determined opposition from the *Wehrmacht* and hampered by the unexpectedly bad weather which restricted the activities of the air force. Another important capture, on 28 September, was the group of airfields around Foggia in Apulia. This made possible the strategic bombing of the oil fields of Romania as well the industrial areas of Czechoslovakia, Austria and southern Germany, a task which was carried out by the U.S. Fifteenth Air Force and the RAF's 205 Group. The bases were also ideal for the sorties of the Balkan Air Force, an organization which was formed in June 1944 to support the guerilla war being waged by the Yugoslav Partisan Army.

Another development which became possible after the *Luftwaffe* had been almost eliminated from the skies was the 'Cab Rank' system of army co-operation, whereby fighter-bombers patrolled over army positions, waiting to be called upon to attack specific targets with bombs or cannon. The Allies advanced steadily, if slowly, and entered Rome on 4 June 1944.

Right: *The Curtiss Tomahawk was the RAF's name for the P-40A and the P-40B of the USAAF. These pursuit aircraft were first delivered to the UK at the end of 1940, where they were employed mainly on reconnaissance. When they arrived in the Western Desert during the following July, however, they soon proved successful as ground attack aircraft and as interceptors of Axis supply aircraft. This photograph shows Tomahawks of 414 (RCAF) Squadron in April 1942, when the squadron was based at Croydon, with a IIB in the lead and on its port, and a IIA on its starboard.*

Source: RAF Museum P9548

Above: *Curtiss Tomahawk IIs of 3 (RAAF) Squadron, taking off in January 1942. At the time, the squadron was based at LG110 in the Western Desert and engaged on escorting bombers on daylight raids, on low-level ground attack, and on escorting Allied shipping to and from Tobruk.*

Source: Keystone Collection

Left: *El Aouina aerodrome near Tunis suffered intensive attacks by Allied aircraft during the final stages of the campaign in North Africa. By the time the Axis was cleared out of Africa, in May 1943, the aerodrome was a graveyard for destroyed Axis aircraft.*

Source: Keystone Collection

Right: *The crew of an RAF aircraft, probably a Wellington, being debriefed after return from an attack against the port of Tunis in December 1942.*

Source: Keystone Collection

Left: *The Martin Marauder, or B-26 in the USAAF, was employed by only two RAF squadrons, both operating in the Mediterranean. It first arrived in April 1942 and was employed on maritime reconnaissance as well as bombing and mine-laying.*

Source: Aeroplane Monthly

Below: *The Armstrong Whitworth Albemarle was originally built as a reconnaissance bomber but by the time production lines were flowing it was already superseded by more advanced machines. Albemarles entered service in November 1942 as transport aircraft. Others were used as glider-tugs in the invasion of Sicily in July 1943. They also took part in the Normandy invasion and at Arnhem. This photograph of serial P1372 was taken in March 1942.*

Source: RAF Museum P6155

Left: *Posters encouraging young ladies of 18 to 40 years to join the WAAF were displayed in Egypt. This invited volunteers to seek information from centres in Cairo and Alexandria.*

Source: RAF Museum (Crown copyright) P00543

Left: *The Douglas Dakota, a military version of the DC-3 airliner, first entered service with the RAF in the Mediterranean during March 1943. Normally unarmed, Dakotas were used as transports in every theatre of war and earned their place in the affections of RAF aircrews as highly reliable and faithful workhorses. These Dakota IIIs of 267 Squadron at Bari in Italy during 1944 were lined up with little fear of air attck.*

Source: RAF Museum P1691

Left: *Wrecked Ju52 transports in Libya, photographed in January 1943 during the advance of the 8th Army after the Battle of El Alamein. The aircraft in the background is a Lockheed Hudson VI of the RAF, used for transport purposes over the Western Desert.*

Source: Keystone Collection

Below: *This photograph was taken early in 1943 at Malta and shows a march past of soldiers at Luqa aerodrome prior to the invasion of Sicily the following July. Inside the blast pen, to the top left of centre, is a Beaufort torpedo bomber of 39 Squadron. These blast pens were usually made of limestone blocks salvaged from the building destroyed by enemy bombing of the island.*

Source: Keystone Collection

Left: *A Spitfire being refuelled at Taranto in October 1943, shortly after the Allied invasion of the Italian mainland.*

Source: Keystone Collection

Right: *Taylorcraft Austers, designed in the USA but built under licence in England, were supplied to the RAF for 'air observation post' duties. These duties included artillery spotting, reconnaissance and communication. This photograph was taken in February 1944, near the front in northern Italy, and shows an Auster used in co-operation with New Zealander gunners of the 8th Army.*

Source: Keystone Collection

Right: *The German* Kreigsmarine *employed heavily defended barges of over 200 tons for supply purposes in the Mediterranean. Known as F-boats, they were regularly attacked by Beaufighters with cannons and bombs. In this photograph, which was taken in January 1944 south of Kalino in the Dodecanese, the bombs can be seen falling away from the racks of a Beaufighter while cannon and flak shells are splashing in the sea.*

Source: Keystone Collection

Left: *Two Martin Baltimore bombers of the RAF silhouetted against the snow-covered Apennine Mountains in central Italy, photographed in March 1944 while on their way to bomb targets in the north.*

Source: Keystone Collection

Right: *DC-3 Dakotas were employed in transporting supplies to the front line in Italy. Mount Vesuvius, near Naples, is in the background of the Dakota taking off in this photograph.*

Source: Keystone Collection

CHAPTER 11

D-DAY TO VE-DAY

The planning for the Anglo-American assault on Hitler's 'western wall' began in April 1943 and continued for over a year. After considerable discussion it was agreed that the supreme commander should be an American, General Dwight Eisenhower, who had led the successful expedition to North Africa, while his deputy should be an Englishman, Air Chief Marshal Sir Arthur Tedder, the former chief of the Mediterranean Air Command. The choice of an RAF officer for this post was a recognition of the important part which the air forces would play in the enterprise, which was code-named operation 'Overlord'. Eisenhower and Tedder presided over Supreme Headquarters, Allied Expeditionary Force (SHAEF). The naval forces were commanded by Admiral Sir Bertram Ramsay, the land forces by the victor of the Western Desert, General Sir Bernard Montgomery, and the air forces by Air Chief Marshal Sir Trafford Leigh-Mallory.

On 15 November 1943, Leigh-Mallory controlled the 2nd Tactical Air Force, the U.S. Ninth Air Force (which was also tactical), and the Air Defence of Great Britain (as Fighter Command was renamed). Bomber Command, under Air-Chief Marshal Sir Arthur Harris, and the U.S. Strategic Forces in Europe, under General Carl Spaatz, were not under his control; instead, both reported directly to the Combined Chiefs of Staff.

The preliminary objective of the air forces was the destruction of the French transportation system. With the agreement of the Chiefs of Staff, Tedder issued on 15 April 1944 a list of targets for the heavy bombers to attack. Lancasters and Halifaxes of Bomber Command began destroying marshalling yards and railways centres at night, and U.S. B-24 Liberators and B-17 Flying Fortresses joined in with daylight attacks, escorted by fighters. The Spitfires, Typhoons and Mustangs of the 2nd Tactical Air Force, under Air Marshal Sir Arthur Coningham, has been reinforced with the Bostons and Mosquitos of Bomber Command's 2 Group, and also shared in these attacks. To these massive operations was added the sabotage carried out by the French Resistance. By June, thousands of photographs taken by the reconnaissance squadrons showed that the French railway system had been seriously damaged. Allied aircraft losses had been relatively slight.

As the day for the landings drew near, rocket-firing fighter-bombers were directed against the chain of radar stations constructed by the enemy along the coasts of north-west France and the Low Countries, while larger W/T stations were put out of action by Bomber Command. Road and rail bridges leading to the invasion area were also destroyed, and major airfields and maintenance depots also came under low-level strafing as well as heavy bombing. Lastly, the coastal batteries were subjected to bombing attacks, both within and outside the areas where the invasion forces intended to land. Meanwhile, Coastal Command and the FAA carried out patrols over both ends of the Channel, hunting and sinking U-boats as well as any surface vessels which dared put out to sea.

In the late evening of 5 June the first Albermarles of Leigh-Mallory's Allied Expeditionary Air Force took off with airborne soldiers of the Parachute Regiment, heading for dropping zones behind the German lines. Dakotas, Stirlings and Halifaxes

followed, dropping paratroops or towing gliders carrying troops, guns, jeeps and motor cycles. At the same time as the great invasion armada sailed to the beaches of Normandy, spoof flights were made by Lancasters and Stirlings of Bomber Command, dropping 'Window' aluminium strips to confuse the German radar, and circling ships which emitted signals designed to indicate that large convoys were approaching other areas. The radar stations had been conveniently left functioning in these coastal areas. Other Halifaxes and Stirlings dropped dummy paratroops and firecrackers which simulated the noise of gunfire. The main force of Bomber Command was directed at the coastal batteries where the landings were to take place. These batteries were also shelled from the sea.

By dawn the first landing parties were ashore and fighting their way over the beaches. In the skies above, no fewer than 171 squadrons provided cover for the invading forces and naval vessels, co-ordinated from three specially fitted 'fighter direction' ships. The *Luftwaffe*, already reduced on this front to barely 500 aircraft, was overwhelmed. On the flanks of the invasion fleet, Coastal Command successfully kept the seas clear of the *Kriegsmarine*. More towed gliders arrived, heavily escorted by fighters, bearing reinforcements and supplies. By the end of D-Day, 6 June, the beachheads were secure.

Air cover continued from English bases, with Typhoons, Spitfires and Mustangs shooting up enemy columns approaching the combat area and knocking out hundreds

Below: *Ground crew servicing the engines of a Short Stirling.*

Source: Keystone Collection

of trucks and armoured fighting vehicles. On 7 June, the RAF's Servicing Commando and Construction Wings began setting up airstrips in France. These were used as refuelling depots at first but were soon expanded into air bases. Bomber Command continued to pound the remnants of the railway system, while fighter-bombers ensured that the Germans could move only in the hours of darkness. Within three weeks, thirty-one Allied squadrons were operating in France, using the 'Cab Rank' system which had been developed in Italy. Further behind the lines, fighters as well as Mosquitos pounced on columns trying to reach the battle area. The German commander, *Feldmarschall* Erwin Rommel, was wounded in one of these attacks, and was later forced to commit suicide when accused of complicity in the plot to kill Hitler of 20 July. Coastal Command continued to defend the approaches to the Allied convoys and within four days after D-Day attacked twenty-five U-boats, while its Strike Wings scored numerous successes against German coastal convoys off the Low Countries, Norway and western France.

The German air fleet in the area, *Luftflotte 3*, was so reduced that its activities became limited to defensive patrols, while its units continued to suffer heavy casualties. However, the defending German ground forces did not break under the colossal attack, and Bomber Command was directed to attack their positions on the battlefield itself. On the evening of 7 July, 457 bombers dropped their loads on targets north of Caen, before an infantry attack. Ten days later, 1,919 RAF and U.S. bombers delivered an even heavier attack, but the tenacious Germans somehow held out amid the heaps of rubble. Four similar attacks were made before they were dislodged. Nevertheless, the remaining *Panzers* contrived to make a determined counter-attack, designed to cut off American forces from their beach-heads, until they were decimated by waves of RAF Typhoons and the assault came to a halt. On 9 August, American armoured divisions broke through and began to sweep round the rear of the German positions, towards Paris and Belgium. The encircled Germans tried to extricate themselves but were harried remorselessly by marauding aircraft. Their commander, *Feldmarschall* Günther von Kluge, committed suicide after being dismissed by Hitler. Paris was liberated on 25 August, and British forces entered Brussels on 3 September.

Before the opening of this Second Front, it was known from reconnaissance photographs and intelligence sources that Germany possessed special weapons designed to bombard England. The centre of development was Peenemünde, on the Baltic coast, where activities were kept under constant surveillance by PRU Mosquitos. Bomber Command set back the progress of the German scientists with an accurate attack by 597 aircraft on the night of 17/18 August 1943, but a ramp with an object similar to a jet aircraft was identified the following October by the Central Photographic Interpretation Unit. In the following months, seventy-two similar ramps were identified in northern France. These sites came under continuous attacks by fighter-bombers as well as medium and heavy bombers, and about two-thirds of them were destroyed before May 1944. But others began to spring up, faster than they could be destroyed. In May, a prototype flying bomb crashed in Sweden and the details were passed to British Intelligence, and the threat of this indiscriminate weapon to British civilians became fully understood.

The first flying bomb, the V.I 'doodlebug', arrived over England on 12 June 1944. By the end of the month, over 2,000 had been despatched against London. At first, the air forces were fully occupied in supporting the invasion force and only a few aircraft could be diverted from this all-important task to attack the launching sites. But masses of balloons were deployed to the south-east of London together with lines of anti-aircraft guns. Areas in which fighters of the Air Defence of Great Britain patrolled were designated. The bombs usually flew at altitudes up to 4,000 feet, but with speeds of up to 400 m.p.h. they were difficult to catch. However, accurate interceptions were made with the help of radar and the Royal Observers Corps. Anti-aircraft guns also shot down a large number, but about half the V.Is reached the London area. As soon as they could be spared, heavy and light bombers began to knock out the sites in France, and by 5 September the advancing Allied armies had overrun most of these. Thereafter, flying bombs were launched at night from Heinkel 111s flying over the North Sea, but these aircraft suffered severely from the attentions of RAF Mosquito night-fighters and achieved very limited results. New launching sites were built in Holland, and some V.Is continued to be despatched until March 1945. Over 4,000 of these bombs were destroyed by British defences, but the remainder killed more than 6,000 people in England.

On 8 September 1944, the first V.2 rocket arrived, at Chiswick. The Germans had experimented with these at Blizna, west of Warsaw, and the site was not identified until PRU brought back photographs in March 1944. Polish agents discovered some important details and one man was picked up by an RAF Dakota and flown to Italy. It was revealed that the V.2 had a range of about 200 miles. Rockets which lifted off vertically and then flew through the sound barrier, controlled by radio, could not be pursued by aircraft. However, rocket sites were identified in northern France and heavily bombed. Then it was realized that others were being launched from Holland,

Below: *It was considered that the North American Mustang III, the RAF equivalent of the P-51 B or C, was the fighter which finally established Allied air supremacy in the skies over Germany. The combination of the Packard Merlin engine and the superbly aerodynamic airframe gave the aircraft a performance at long range which was more than a match for any German piston-engined fighter in 1944. Mustang IIIs were first delivered to the RAF in December 1943. This photograph is of serial FB353 of 315 (Polish) Squadron, which was first equipped with Mustang IIIs in March 1944 when based at Heston.*

Source: RAF Museum PO17036

Right: *The Central School of Aircraft Recognition was set up to teach instructors in the Allied air forces, including the RAF, RCAF, RAAF, RNZAF, RAF Regiment, Royal Observer Corps, the US Eighth Air Force and the US Ninth Air Force. This photograph, in which an RAF sergeant is demonstrating an He111, is dated 4 April 1944.*

Source: Keystone Collection

and these sites were attacked by Spitfire fighter-bombers. The rockets continued intermittently and with no great accuracy, but they resulted in 2,855 deaths before the last fell on 27 March 1945.

As the Allied armies swept through France and into Belgium and Holland, the Germans continued to hold out in a few ports which Hitler called 'Fortresses'. These were eliminated in turn by Bomber Command. Le Havre, Boulogne and Calais surrendered in September, but other ports such as Dunkirk and Brest still held out, while the invasion armies had more important business elsewhere. On 17 September, Albemarles, Stirlings, Halifaxes and Dakotas of the RAF's Transport Command carried airborne soldiers to the town of Arnhem in Holland, behind the Rhine and the German lines. Other lifts took place over the next two days, against intense light and heavy flak. Thereafter, supply drops were attempted but, in spite of heavy losses, only a small proportion fell in the area occupied by British troops, who were overwhelmed.

Another enterprise in which the RAF was involved, with far more success, was the reduction of Hitler's 'fortress' of the island of Walcheren, in the estuary of the Scheldt. In this instance, Bomber Command breached the dyke holding back the North Sea, on the afternoon of 3 October, and the waters rushed in. Other inundations were caused in the south and north-east, while German batteries were attacked by fighter-bombers and heavy bombers. The island was finally overrun by the infantry on 8 November, after tough and difficult fighting. In the course of these battles, Leigh-Mallory was posted to command the Allied Air Forces in the Far East, but unhappily was killed en route when his aircraft crashed. His command in Europe was absorbed into SHAEF.

On 16 December, the Germans delivered their last major offensive of the war, against the American forces in the Ardennes. With the advantage of fog and low cloud which restricted flying for over a week, the *Panzers* advanced rapidly. Then the weather lifted and both Bomber Command and the U.S. heavy bombers were able to bring their weight on to the attackers. The 2nd Tactical Air Force also went out in strength. One of the German aircraft shot down was a new jet fighter, the twin-engined Messerschmitt 262, with a speed of over 500 m.p.h. On 1 January 1945, the *Luftwaffe* made a last desperate effort against Allied air strength, sending over 800 aircraft on low-level attacks against airfields. They succeeded in destroying 144 aircraft on the ground, damaging many more, but also lost heavily from their remaining units.

By now, the enemy was in retreat on all fronts. On the night of 14/15 August 1944, the USAAF had dropped paratroops in the south of France, having taken off from Corsica, an island which the Allies had occupied at the end of the previous September. These were followed by over 400 gliders and a sea-borne invasion force. The U.S. troops encountered only slight opposition on the beaches before racing northwards, to join up with their victorious counterparts from England on 12 September. Meanwhile, the U.S. Fifteenth Air Force and the Wellingtons and Liberators of the RAF's 205 Group continued their long-distance strategic attacks from the airfields around Foggia. The RAF also scored notable successes during 1944 by mining the Danube and thus interrupting Germany's oil supplies from Romania. These sorties continued until the Red Army captured the oilfields at the end of August.

The Allied advance up the Italian peninsula was slowed by the withdrawal of American troops for the invasion of southern France. It was also hampered by mud from continuous rain and by the stubborn and skilful defence of the German troops, who had little support from the air. The Allied air forces gave these troops little respite, and attacks were delivered with mounting intensity and concentration. By April 1945, the Germans had fallen back to the river Po and were beginning to crack under the intense bombardment. On 28 April, the former dictator Mussolini was captured and shot by Italian partisans.

Meanwhile, Bomber Command's assault on Germany mounted in intensity. With the liberation of most of France and Belgium, the ground control stations for 'Gee' and 'GH' navigational aids were moved much closer to enemy territory. In addition to night bombing, attacks could also be made in daylight, escorted by long-range Mustangs of the 2nd Tactical Air Force or home-based fighters of Fighter Command, as the Air Defence of Great Britain was named once again. The Ruhr was one of the main objectives, but most major German towns were gradually obliterated by the RAF and the USAAF. Of the total tonnage of bombs used in raids on Germany throughout the war, the greater part was dropped after 1 July 1944, causing enormous destruction. Apart from towns, oil installations and transport facilities came under attack. The battleship *Tirpitz* was sunk in Tromsö in Norway on 12 November 1944 by Lancasters operating from Lossiemouth. It was obvious even to the most determined Nazis that the end was near, but the *Wehrmacht* still fought on.

On 22 February 1945, the whole of the Allied air forces, numbering nearly 9,000 aircraft, began a concentrated effort to wipe out Germany's remaining transport. A month later, the Allied forces crossed the Rhine at Wesel, while airborne troops parachuted in or landed by glider. Allied armies then broke through all along the German frontier and raced through the country. The First U.S. Army linked up with the Red Army at the Elbe on 23 April, while the Second British Army reached Lübeck on 2 May. Hitler killed himself in his Berlin bunker on 30 April. His successor, *Grossadmiral* Karl Dönitz, surrendered unconditionally on 7 May and VE-Day was celebrated on the following day. Meanwhile, the war with Japan continued.

Right: *Mosquito night-fighters, designated Mark IIs, began to replace Bristol Beaufighters and Douglas Havocs in 1942, and served in all the RAF's theatres of war. Other improvements in air interception radar followed. This photograph shows a Mosquito XIII of 604 Squadron, with a radome in the nose and aerials on the wings. This squadron was equipped with Mosquito XIIIs from April 1944 to the end of the war.*

Source: Keystone Collection

Below: *Although the RAF Regiment was formed originally to protect airfields, its scope was widened later into attack roles, such as capturing enemy airfields. The Regiment was then equipped with armoured fighting vehicles. This photograph of Morris 'Type E' armoured cars, which were fitted with Boys anti-tank rifles and Bren guns, was taken in England in April 1944.*

Source: Keystone Collection

Above: *A photograph taken on D-Day, 6 June 1944, showing Short Stirlings towing Airspeed Horsa gliders across the English Channel for the airborne landings.*

Source: Keystone Collection

Left: *The devastating effect of the Allied bombing attacks against the French transport system is shown by this photograph of rolling stock at the town of Vire in Lower Normandy, at the base of the Cherbourg Peninsula. The Allies occupied the town on 7 August 1944.*

Source: Keystone Collection

Above: *As the Allies advanced in France and the Low Countries, they left behind centres of resistance which Germans described as 'fortresses'. One of these was Calais, seen here under attack by Halifaxes on 25 September 1944. The Germans surrended a few days later.*

Source: Keystone Collection

Above: *A bomb dump containing American semi-armour piercing bombs of 1,000 lb, used by fighter-bombers of the 2nd Tactical Air Force to pulverise installations in the German enclave of Boulogne. Each bomb had two protective rings which were removed before being fitted to the aircraft. The photograph was taken two days before the German garrison surrendered on 26 September 1944.*

Source: Keystone Collection

Left: *Special RAF squadrons were formed to supply resistance forces in France. A Stirling of 138 Squadron is shown here dropping containers to the Armée Blanche, the Belgian Resistance Movement.*

Source: Keystone Collection

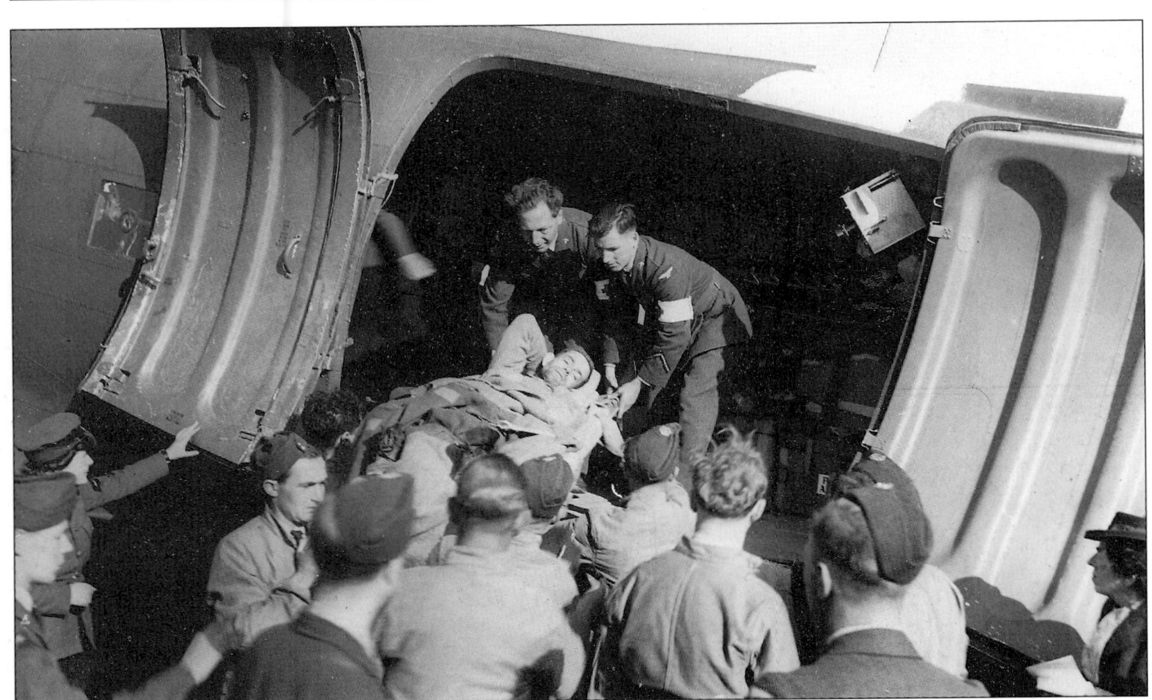

Left: *DC-3 Dakotas were used to carry casualties from Normandy to England. Three WAAF flew operationally in this aircraft on 14 June 1944, to tend the wounded, and were the first servicewomen to land in France after D-Day.*

Source: Keystone Collection

Left: *Airmen attaching the tubes and stabilising fins of rocket projectiles to 60 lb warheads containing high explosive, for use against armoured fighting vehicles and ground troops. Typhoon fighter-bombers of the 2nd Tactical Air Force used these weapons. The other type of warhead, not shown here, was the 25 lb solid-shot used for sinking ships. This was photographed in France, about a week after the D-Day landings.*

Source: Keystone Collection

Below: *The Hawker Typhoon was fitted with four 20 mm cannons and could also carry eight rockets with 60 lb warheads.*

Source: Keystone Collection

Above: *This attack by rocket-firing Typhoons of the 2nd Tactical Air Force, against Carpiquet aerodrome, near Caen in Normandy, was photographed by the RAF Film Unit on 4 July 1944.*

Source: Keystone Collection

Left: *As an alternative to carrying eight 60 lb rockets, the Typhoon had provision for two 500 lb bombs under the wings. It was the only Allied fighter-bomber which could carry such a load. In this form, it was sometimes known as a 'Bombphoon'. This photograph of airmen rolling a 500 lb medium-capacity bomb near a Typhoon of 193 Squadron, was taken in Holland in December 1944.*

Source: Keystone Collection

Left: *Loading 1,000 lb medium-capacity bombs under a Hawker Typhoon of 175 Squadron, which was based in Belgium in September 1944.*

Source: Keystone Collection

Right: *The Hawker Tempest V was developed from the Hawker Typhoon, being faster and with a longer range. It was known as a 'Tiffy with the bugs removed', being responsive and with an excellent combat vision. The first machines were delivered to the RAF in January 1944, and the Tempest squadrons became celebrated for success against V1 flying bombs, destroying 632 in all. Later, Tempest Squadrons formed part of the 2nd Tactical Air Force in Europe, achieving much success in air combat and in the ground-attack role.*

Source: Aviation Bookshop

Left: *One of the most celebrated of the fighter pilots in the 2nd Tactical Air Force was Gp Capt J.E. "Johnny" Johnson, DSO and two bars, DFC and bar. He was the RAF's top British scorer, with thirty-eight confirmed victories. Here he is the central figure, in a reunion of 83 Group held on 29 March 1946.*

Source: Keystone Collection

Below: *The RAF set up Construction Wings and Servicing Commandos in order to provide airfields for the 2nd Tactical Air Force as the Allies advanced. Runways were sometimes made of steel wire netting, similar to those constructed in England, as shown in this photograph.*

Source: Keystone Collection

Right: *Pegging down the portable runway, which was known as the Sommerfield Track.*

Source: Keystone Collection

Left: *The North American Mitchell, designated B-25 by the USAAF, entered service with the RAF in September 1942 and eventually equipped six squadrons of Bomber Command and the 2nd Tactical Air Force. The RAF pilots liked flying this light day-bomber, which proved fast, highly manoeuvrable and easy to handle, in spite of its unfamiliar tricycle undercarriage. The Mitchell remained in RAF service until the end of the war. This photograph shows a bombing attack by a Mitchell of 98 Squadron.*

Source: RAF Museum P7449

Right: *The General Aircraft Hotspur was the standard training glider used in the Second World War. RAF instructors trained NCOs of the army's Glider Regiment at five schools, after which the pilots earned their wings.*

Source: Keystone Collection

Above: *The Hotspur was towed by Hawker biplanes or Miles Master monoplanes, and was able to glide for up to 80 miles if released from 20,000 feet. About 1,000 were built, but the machine was not used operationally.*

Source: Keystone Collection

Above: *The Airspeed Horsa was the standard operational glider used for carrying troops of the Airborne Divisions of the British Army during World War Two. Horsas landed in Sicily during June 1943, in Normandy during June 1944, and at Arnhem in September 1944. They were usually towed by Stirlings, Halifaxes, Dakotas and Albemarles of the RAF's Transport Command. This photograph was taken half an hour after the paratroops had jumped from Dakotas over Arnhem on 17 September 1944. They are clearing the bushes of any enemy opposition while a Horsa comes in to land.*

Source: Keystone Collection

Right: *The mass of gliders at Arnhem after the landings. Over 500 Horsas landed on 17 and 18 September 1944, as well as twenty-eight General Aircraft Hamilcars carrying vehicles.*

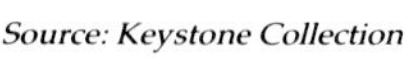

Source: Keystone Collection

Left: *An army pilot in a Hotspur glider.*
Source: Keystone Collection

Above: *The Westland Welkin was intended as a high-altitude fighter for the RAF. It had a service ceiling of 44,000 feet but, although sixty-seven were built, it was never used operationally.*
Source: Keystone Collection

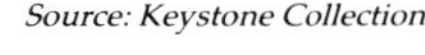

Below: *A B-25 Mitchell of the RAF in a camouflaged hangar captured from the Germans during the final stages of the war.*
Source: Keystone Collection

Right: *Fl Officer David S.A. "Lumme" Lord (right) photographed in the Middle East. On 19 September 1944 he was a pilot of a Dakota of 271 Squadron over Arnhem when his starboard engine was hit twice by flak and set on fire. Nevertheless he continued to fly over the dropping zone until most of the containers had been pushed out. He then ordered his crew to bale out while he remained at the controls. There was only one survivor from his crew. Fl Lt David Lord, who had already been gazetted with the DFC, was awarded a posthumous Victoria Cross.*

Source: Keystone Collection

Below: *A B-25 Mitchell of 180 Squadron, based at Melsbroek in Belgium, being repaired on 14 December 1944. In the background is a camouflaged building used by the Germans as a workshop, and an RAF 'Queen Mary' low-loader.*

Source: Keystone Collection

Above: *Several German aircraft which crash-landed in Britain were restored to flying condition. These were air tested by 1426 (Enemy Aircraft) Flight and the results were sent to the Air Ministry and the Royal Aircraft Establishment for analysis. Flying the machines over England could be dangerous and they were given RAF markings. At first, the Flight was based at Duxford in Cambridgeshire but it was transferred to Collyweston in Northamptonshire on 24 March 1943. This photograph, taken on 7 March 1944, shows (left to right) a Ju88, a Bf110, a Bf109G, an FW190 and an Hs129.*

Source: Keystone Collection

Left: *The Ju88 at Collyweston, with RAF markings.*

Source: Keystone Collection

Above right: *Four of the pilots at Collyweston, with a Bf110 in the background.*

Source: Keystone Collection

Left: *The Hs129 at Collyweston, still with German markings, undergoing examination.*

Source: Keystone Collection

Right: *On 14 April 1944, the RAF's Gunnery Research Unit arrived at Collyweston from Exeter. A collection of German aerial guns can be seen in this photograph, with a poster of a Do217E-2 in the background.*

Source: Keystone Collection

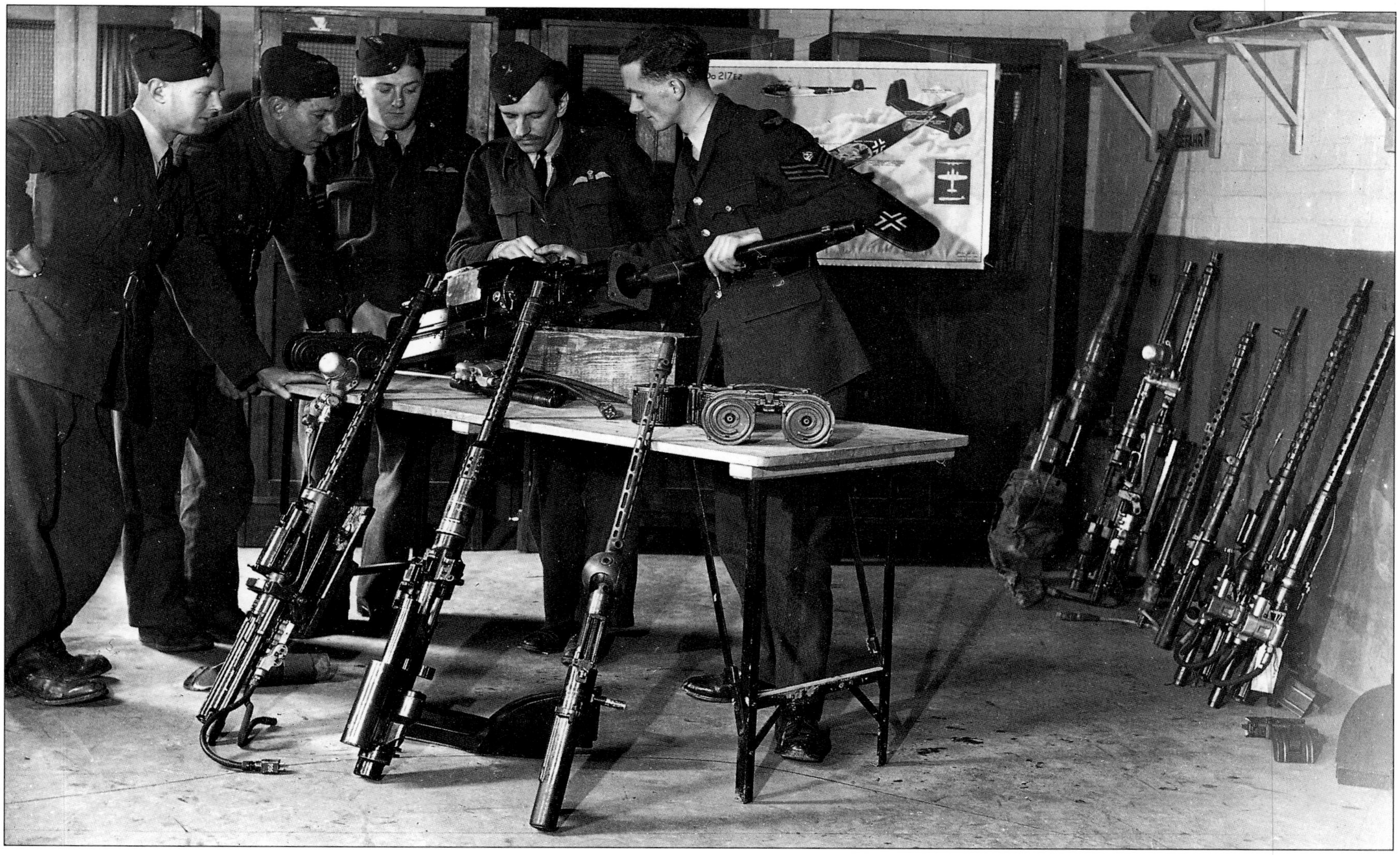

Left: *Pilots of 439 (RCAF) Squadron building their own dispersal huts in January 1945. The squadron was equipped with Typhoon IBs as part of the 2nd Tactical Air Force, based at the forward aerodrome B.78 Eindhoven in Holland.*

Source: Keystone Collection

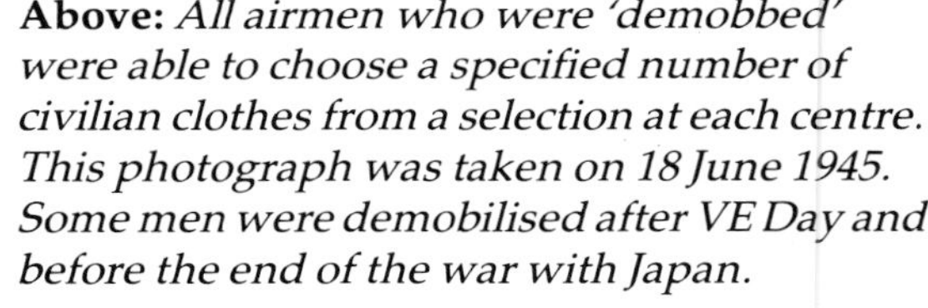

Above: *All airmen who were 'demobbed' were able to choose a specified number of civilian clothes from a selection at each centre. This photograph was taken on 18 June 1945. Some men were demobilised after VE Day and before the end of the war with Japan.*

Source: Keystone Collection

Left: *The first helicopter to enter service in the RAF was the Sikorsky Hoverfly I, in May 1945. This photograph was taken at the Helicopter Training Flight at Andover in Hampshire. Only 529 Squadron, based at Henley-on-Thames, was equipped with this machine, but the squadron was disbanded in October 1945.*

Source: RAF Museum PO21609

Right: *Part of the celebration in Whitehall, London, during VE Day on 8 May 1945.*

Source: Keystone Collection

Below: *The 'nose art' on the Handley Page Halifax III 'Friday the 13th', which made 118 operational flights. In addition to the ominous message "As ye sow, so shall ye reap", the art included paintings of the VC, DSO and DFC won by members of the aircrews who flew in the machine. This bomber formed part of an exhibition "Britain's Aircraft" on a bombed site in Oxford Street, London, during June 1945.*

Source: Keystone Collection

Above: *The devastation at Magdeburg, on the river Elbe, photographed in April 1945, shortly before the end of the war. The cathedral had largely escaped the worst of the blast bombs and incendiaries.*

Source: Keystone Collection

Above left: *The view from Cologne Cathedral towards the wrecked Hohenzollern Bridge over the Rhine.*

Source: Keystone Collection

Left: *The ruined heart of Essen in the Ruhr, showing a path cleared through the rubble. This was photographed shortly after the end of the war.*

Source: Keystone Collection

Top right: *The remains of the railway station at Potsdam, to the south-west of Berlin. This photograph was taken on 24 July 1945, during the Potsdam Conference in which one of the matters discussed by the USA, Britain and Russia was the future of defeated Germany.*

Source: Keystone Collection

Right: *The march past of the RAF in Brussels on 8 July 1945 on the occasion of leaving Belgium. The RAF had been presented with a flag, carried by the flight lieutenant in front of the parade. The salute was taken by Air Marshal Sir Arthur Coningham, who commanded the 2nd Tactical Air Force, and the Burgomaster of Brussels.*

Source: Keystone Collection

CHAPTER 12

THE FORGOTTEN AIR WAR

Below: *Brewster Buffaloes were rejected as a first-line fighters in the UK during the autumn of 1940 and diverted to two RAF, two RAAF and one RNZAF squadrons at Singapore. The first consignment was delivered to 67 Squadron at Kallang in Singapore in March 1941. Unfortunately, the US fighters were no match for the Japanese Zeros and suffered heavy losses, although the pilots had claimed thirty enemy aircraft destroyed by the time Singapore fell on 15 February 1942.*

Source: Keystone Collection

One of the greatest disasters ever to befall British arms stemmed from the failure of the government to recognise the capacity of the Japanese to wage war against a western power. On 8 December 1941, when the Japanese landed at Kota Bahru on the north-east coast of Malaya, the defending Commonwealth forces were woefully ill-equipped. The troops had no tanks, very few anti-tank weapons, and little training in jungle warfare. They had minimal support from the Malayan or Chinese population. The RAF was hopelessly outnumbered and outclassed. Air Chief Marshal Sir Robert Brooke-Popham, the C-in-C Far East, had been presented with an impossible task. His meagre air forces consisted of only 362 aircraft, mostly outdated, of which about two-thirds were serviceable. Of these, two squadrons were equipped with obsolete Vildebeest torpedo bombers, four with Blenheims, two with Hudsons, four with Brewster Buffalo fighters, and one with Catalinas. These included squadrons of the RAAF and RNZAF, but there were insufficient pilots and some had not been trained on operational machines. There were four airfields in Singapore, but most of those in the Malayan archipelago were poorly constructed and ill-defended, while servicing facilities were inadequate. The radar system was extremely patchy, most of the stations being still under construction.

The invading Japanese included battle-hardened troops who had been imbued with a fanatical desire to die in the service of their country. They were lightly equipped for jungle warfare, but well-trained and supported by numerous land-based aircraft. Of their aircraft, the Mitsubishi A6M2 Zero outclassed every Allied fighter in the Far East or Pacific and was far superior to the Buffalo. There were two Japanese Air Forces, one subordinate to the army and the other to the navy. Both performed a formidably aggressive role. The pilots were skilled and their commanders had studied the tactics used in Europe, particularly those of their allies in the *Luftwaffe*, on which their command structure and air formations were largely based. Later in the war, there was no shortage of volunteer suicide pilots, who were known as *Tokkatai* in the Army Air Force and *Kamikaze* in the Navy Air Force. There was, however, no long-range strategic bombing force.

On the day of the landings, a badly cripped Beaufort of PRU (the only machine of this type to serve in South-East Asia) flew into the small airfield of Kota Bahru, carrying photographs of a Japanese landing further north at Singora and Patani in Siam, as well as revealing the presence of about sixty Japanese aircraft on the airfield. Kota Bahru was invested by the invaders and overrun the following day, shortly after the remaining RAF aircraft were evacuated. On the night before, Singapore had undergone its first bombing attack. The city was not fully blacked out and thus presented an excellent target. Next, the airfields in Malaya were attacked continuously by bombers escorted by fighters, resulting in the destruction of aircraft and numerous casualties. Although the number of RAF aircraft in northern Malaya was reduced to about fifty, the enemy airfield at Singora was attacked and some Japanese aircraft destroyed. But the majority of the surviving RAF bombers soon succumbed to further attacks on their airfields.

Japanese bombers and torpedo aircraft then scored a resounding success by sinking

Above: *A Brewster Buffalo I of 71 Squadron, the first Eagle Squadron manned by US personnel. Buffaloes were received in October 1940, at a time when the squadron was based at Church Fenton in Yorkshire, but these were used only for training before being shipped out to the Far East.*

Source: RAF Museum P5253

the two British battleships *Prince of Wales* and *Repulse*, which had steamed up the east coast of Malaya to intercept the invasion fleet, without the benefit of long-range fighter escort, which was not available. After this disaster, the Japanese controlled the seas as well as the air. The British troops and the RAF had no option but to pull back, destroying installations as best they could, while the few surviving Buffalos tried to support rearguard actions. The Malayan Volunteer Air Force, flying light aircraft, helped with liaison work, reconnaissance and jungle rescue.

Meanwhile, Hong Kong and Borneo were captured by the Japanese, neither having any air support. Brooke-Popham was replaced by Lieutenant General Sir Henry Roydes Pownall, but the new C-in-C was similarly unable to perform a miracle. Reinforcements arrived in Singapore in the form of fifty-one Hurricanes in crates, while twenty-four pilots were either flown in or arrived by sea. Apart from these, only seventy-five twin-engined aircraft and twenty-eight fighters remained in service. The Hurricanes achieved successes by shooting down a number of bombers over Singapore but the escorting Zeros were faster and more agile at the low levels in which most combats took place. Twenty-two bombers of the Netherlands Indies Army Air Corps also arrived in Singapore.

The Vildebeests lost five out of nine aircraft during a torpedo attack on a further Japanese landing on the east coast of Malaya. By the beginning of February 1942, the last of the exhausted troops were back over the causeway connecting Singapore with the mainland.

It soon became apparent that the island could not hold out against the continual shelling and air bombardment. Only twenty-one of the Hurricanes remained serviceable, while there were six Buffalos left. Apart from a token force, evacuation of the remaining RAF to the Dutch island of Sumatra was ordered. The operation lasted for a fortnight, employing a motley selection of shipping for the ground personnel. On 15 February the remaining troops on Singapore under Lieutenant General A.E. Percival, surrendered. They numbered 70,000, and over half these later died as a result of the brutish and cruel treatment to which they were subjected as prisoners-of-war.

Only forty-eight RAF aircraft were present in Sumatra and many of these were in poor condition. They supported the Dutch and British forces by carrying out reconnaissance flights and bombing raids, but there was little they could do to prevent another Japanese invasion. On 14 February, enemy paratroops descended on the fighter airfield of Palembang, where they soon overpowered the defences. A secret airfield had been built in the jungle, and the remaining RAF aircraft operated from there, attacking with considerable success a Japanese invasion fleet. But the military situation on the island became hopeless and another withdrawal was ordered, to Java, which was completed on 18 February. By then, eighteen Hurricanes remained serviceable, with twelve Hudsons and six Blenheims. The situation there became untenable after an entire fleet, commanded by the Dutch, was sunk in an engagement in the Java Sea on 27 February. The Japanese landed on Java on 1 March and the handful of surviving aircraft were flown to Australia. The RAF aircrews and ground personnel were evacuated by ship, so far as possible. Some reached Australia, while a few even arrived in Ceylon, after many privations.

The Japanese plans for further conquest were carried out with remorseless purpose, seeking and exploiting the weaknesses of their opponents. The occupation of Burma was of great importance to Japan, for it would cut the supply route of the western powers to China, where their armies were still engaged in bitter fighting. This 'Burma Road' was protected by an American Volunteer Group, consisting of three squadrons of Curtiss P-40s (known to the RAF as Tomahawks) based at Kunming. The RAF was represented by 221 Group, with headquarters in Rangoon, where they were joined by the Americans. Unlike Malaya, there were a number of well-constructed airfields in Burma, with good runways and accommodation for personnel, as well as positions for ground defences. Unfortunately, by Christmas 1941, when the Japanese Air Force began to attack Rangoon, only a handful of RAF aircraft occupied these bases, supported by liaison aircraft of the Burmese Volunteer Air Force. The only fighters were a few Buffalos, while there were almost no anti-aircraft guns together with a patchy system of observer posts. The officer commanding the RAF in Burma was the energetic and resourceful Air Vice-Marshal D.F. Stevenson.

Against this little force, the Japanese were able to pit about 400 bombers and long-range fighters, based in Siam. However, the aggressive tactics of the Anglo-American fighters proved surprisingly effective, for they gained altitude and then went into steep dives in order to tear into the enemy formations. After suffering many losses over Rangoon, the Japanese drew off for a few weeks, and in this period about thirty Hurricanes and a squadron of Blenheims arrived in Burma. Stevenson immediately sent these into the attack, the bombers against Bangkok and the fighters against advanced airfields, achieving considerable success until the operations were hampered by shortage of spares. The Japanese came back with increased force, but failed to achieve air superiority.

However, the limited air operations were unable to do more than postpone the advance of the Japanese army. Rangoon was finally evacuated on 7 March, but not before British sappers had wrecked and set on fire the oil installations in the area. The army withdrew northwards, following the trail of panic-striken refugees who had fled the city, while the remnants of the air force flew to the island of Akyab, from where they attacked Mingaladon, the airfield at Rangoon, and destroyed many Japanese aircraft. But the Japanese delivered mass air attacks on Akyab and wiped out the remainder of the RAF and American fighters. The only possible course of action for the RAF was retreat to India, behind the range of mountains which separate the two countries, and attempt to build up strength. From here, the remaining Blenheims gave what support they could to the retreating army and the refugees, but the Japanese Air Force was able to attack with impunity town after town in Burma. A few Dakotas dropped supplies to the army and took out the sick and wounded, while Lysanders were converted into light bombers. By May 1942, the remnants of the army reached Imphal in Manipur, and Burma had fallen to the enemy. The Japanese were within air striking range of Calcutta.

Ceylon was threatened with the Japanese Fleet, but this strategically important island was protected by the British Far Eastern Fleet and reinforced with four squadrons of Hurricanes. On 5 April, Japanese aircraft flew from carriers to bomb Colombo and the airfield at Ratmalana; several were shot down for the loss of fifteen Hurricanes and four FAA Fulmars. But on the same day, Japanese dive bombers sank the cruisers HMS

Above: *The Chindits led by Brigadier Charles Orde Wingate were supplied by C-47 Dakotas during their excursions behind Japanese lines in Burma during February to June 1943.*

Source: Keystone Collection

Above: *The Curtiss Mohawk IV, the American P-36A, served with the RAF solely in the Burma theatre of war, being first delivered to 5 Squadron at Dum Dum in India in December 1941. The fighter continued with some success on this front with three RAF squadrons, continuing until January 1944. The Mohawk in this photograph was serial AR645.*

Source: RAF Museum PO19168

Right: *One of the effective aircraft in the Burma campaign was the Vultee Vengeance dive bomber, flown by four RAF squadrons and supplied under Lend-Lease by the USA. Later Vengeances were employed in the U.K. as target-towers. This photograph of a Vengeance II, serial AN609, was taken in November 1942.*

Source: RAF Museum P9245

Right: *Indian paratroops lining up to enter a Douglas Dakota, for their first flight in an aircraft, with a Lockheed Hudson in the background. The photograph was taken in early November 1943.*

Source: Keystone Collection

Left: *Two of Wingate's Chindits brought out from a landing strip in Burma in July 1943. According to publicity at the time, they were examining a grenade which had fallen out of a pack and which they had found rolling about on the floor of the fuselage.*

Source: Keystone Collection

Cornwall and HMS *Dorsetshire* in the Indian Ocean. On 9 April, Trincomalee was bombed, while the aircraft carrier HMS *Hermes* was also sunk by dive bombers. However, after these successes, the Japanese fleet withdrew to the Pacific, where its presence was urgently required.

The Japanese Air Force, with many commitments in the Pacific, did not begin attacks against Calcutta until December 1942. Although only a few bombs were dropped, all at night, about a million and a half Indians fled the city in panic. During the next month, a flight of Beaufighter night-fighters arrived and soon shot down five of the raiders. The Japanese did not persist, and the mollified citizens returned to their normal dwellings.

With the Burma Road cut, an alternative method of carrying troops and military equipment to China was found by the USAAF, by flying from airfields near Calcutta across the Patkai mountains to Kunming. RAF Dakotas also flew on this hazardous route which, beset by towering clouds and great mountain peaks, became known as the 'Hump Run'. General Sir Archibald Wavell took over command of the British army in India while the RAF was commanded by Air Chief Marshal Sir Richard Peirse. One of Wavell's main tasks was to convince his troops that the Japanese were not invincible, while Peirse built up his squadrons, which by December 1942 amounted to 1,443 aircraft. These included three operational groups, two in India and one in Ceylon, equipped with Hurricanes, Blenheims, Hudsons, Vultee Vengeances, Catalinas, Lysanders, Dakotas, Wellingtons and Beauforts. It was intended to increase the number of squadrons to eighty-three, after the Axis forces had been cleared out of North Africa.

In December, Wavell opened an offensive, with the limited objective of seizing the island of Akyab. The troops moved down the coast unopposed as far as the port of Indin, which they reached on 27 December, while the RAF and USAAF carried out bombing attacks against Japanese positions and transports further south. Eventually, the troops met stiff resistance and did not reach their objective. At same time, a force trained to operate behind the Japanese lines, known as the Chindits and led by Brigadier Orde Wingate, set off for a long-range penetration into the interior of Burma. These columns, which depended wholly on supplies dropped from the air, cut railway lines, destroyed bridges, and caused confusion among the Japanese forces. The operations came to an end with the monsoon which began in June 1943, having attained limited results, but the ground forces now knew that they could beat the enemy, provided they could be supported by air supplies. The immediate need was to build up the air transport squadrons. This expansion took place at such a pace that by January 1944 it was possible to transport whole divisions by air. By this time, no fewer than 275 airfields had been built, and South East Asia Command had been created, under Lord Louis Mountbatten, controlling the whole of the RAF in north-east India as well as the U.S. Tenth Army Air Force and including a Tactical Air Force, a Strategic Air Force and a Photographic Reconnaissance Force.

By early 1944, there were forty-eight RAF and seventeen USAAF squadrons in the new command. The Japanese possessed about 370 aircraft in Burma, and the first task of the Allies was to obliterate these. Spitfire VIIIs proved more than a match for the Japanese Oscars, and air supremacy over northern Burma was established. Beaufighters and Hurricanes shot up Japanese transport while Vengeances dive-bombed installations and Liberators carried out long-distance bombing attacks. The 14th Army, under General Sir William Slim, penetrated once more down the Arakan coast towards Akyab. When in February 1944 their headquarters and advanced troops were surrounded in a village named Sinzweya – known as the 'Admin Box' – they were successfully supplied from the air and fought their way out. A Japanese counter-attack was destroyed with the help of air support.

Above left: *B-24 Liberator bombers were ferried from the USA via Canada, Britain and Africa to India or Ceylon, from where they were employed on long-distance raids against Japanese positions in south-east Asia. This Liberator was snowbound at Montreal in April 1944, but a blower removed the foreground snow and trenches were cut for the wheels. An hour after the photograph was taken, the aircraft was on its way.*

Source: Keystone Collection

Above: *A Douglas Dakota III, serial FL512, at Myitikyina airstrip in northern Burma. The largest air base in northern Burma, Myitikyina was recaptured from the Japanese on 17 May 1944 and Dakotas immediately flew in troops and supplies.*

Source: RAF Museum P3506

Right: *The desperate attempts by Blenheims of 221 Group to halt the Japanese invasion of Burma in early 1942 were somewhat imaginatively portrayed in this poster.*

Source: RAF Museum (Crown copyright) P00167

Left: *A Hurricane fighter-bomber attacking a bridge on the road from Tiddim to Kalemyo in Burma during the retreat of the Japanese Fifteenth Army in the monsoon period of 1944.*

Source: Keystone Collection

Below left: *In April 1945, the RAF continued to make daylight attacks against the infamous railway which the Japanese had built with forced labour between Bangkok in Thailand and Moulmein in Burma. The main problem was the distance, involving over seventeen hours of flight. On the bombing attack shown in this photograph, the crews saw prisoners waving to them from the railway sidings.*

Source: Keystone Collection

Left: *The Republic Thunderbolt, named the P-47 by the USAAF, was employed by the RAF exclusively in South East Asia, where it replaced the Hurricane fighter/bomber from May 1944 onwards. With eight .50 inch forward-firing guns and provision for 2,000 lb of bombs, this tough aircraft knocked out numerous Japanese ground positions in low-level attacks. Sixteen RAF squadrons were equipped with Thunderbolts, which continued in service until December 1946.*

Source: Aeroplane Monthly

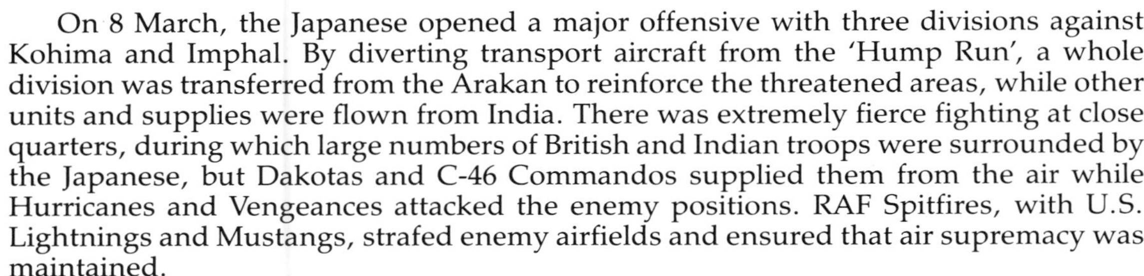

On 8 March, the Japanese opened a major offensive with three divisions against Kohima and Imphal. By diverting transport aircraft from the 'Hump Run', a whole division was transferred from the Arakan to reinforce the threatened areas, while other units and supplies were flown from India. There was extremely fierce fighting at close quarters, during which large numbers of British and Indian troops were surrounded by the Japanese, but Dakotas and C-46 Commandos supplied them from the air while Hurricanes and Vengeances attacked the enemy positions. RAF Spitfires, with U.S. Lightnings and Mustangs, strafed enemy airfields and ensured that air supremacy was maintained.

Meanwhile, over 9,000 Chindits were flown in troop carriers or towed in gliders to positions well behind the Japanese front, while other Chindits set off on foot. The columns were accompanied by RAF officers equipped with R/T and W/T sets, entrusted with the tasks of guiding the supply aircraft and directing the tactical fighter-bombers. At the same time, a Chinese division under the U.S. General J.W. Stilwell pushed southwards, supplied from the air, to capture the vital airfield of Myitkyina, even further east. By the end of May 1944, the Japanese around Imphal and Kohima began to weaken, and a retreat turned into a rout, harried from the air. In the three months before mid May, the Japanese had lost 30,000 men in northern Burma. They were being outclassed and outfought.

More Liberators arrived, while Hurricanes were replaced with Thunderbolts and Vengeances with Mosquitos. The Japanese had been reduced to no more than 125 aircraft. In November 1944, Air Chief Marshal Sir Richard Pierse's successor, Air Chief Marshal Sir Trafford Leigh-Mallory, was killed en route to take up his new command. The post was filled temporarily by Air Marshal Sir Guy Garrod until Air Marshal Sir Keith Park arrived in February 1945. The Japanese supply lines came under continual attack, including the railway line from Bangkok to Moulmein, built at the cost of thousands of lives of Allied prisoners of war. The photographic squadrons carried out extensive operations, including a survey of fifty-seven per cent of the entire area of Burma, which had never been adequately mapped. Japanese U-boats were hunted, while coastal and river shipping came under low-level attack.

In January 1945, the Japanese withdrew from Akyab, and the island was used by the Allies for an amphibious assault on the mainland. At the same time the armies broke through from the north, closely supported by the air forces, and began to sweep down the central plain of Burma. The liquid fire bomb of napalm was first used in these attacks. By April, the Japanese were in full retreat and within a few weeks had evacuated Rangoon, which was occupied by the 14th Army without a fight. From this time, the war became a form of massacre, with the tattered and starving remnants of the Japanese army ruthlessly cut down as they attempted to retreat to Siam.

After the end of the campaign in Burma, the next stage was the preparation for an invasion of Malaya, under the code-name of operation 'Zipper'. But this was not necessary. On 6 August 1945 the first atomic bomb fell on Hiroshima and three days later the second was dropped on Nagasaki. On 14 August the Japanese surrendered unconditionally and the Second World War was at an end.

Above: *Wing Commander R.R.S. Tuck, DSO, DFC and two bars, who achieved fame flying Hawker Hurricanes in 257 Squadron during the Battle of Britain, carrying the RAF Ensign into Westminster Abbey on 13 September 1946, during a rehearsal for the Battle of Britain ceremony the following day.*

Source: Keystone Collection

Far left: *On 15 September 1945, a great flypast took place over London to commemorate the end of the Second World War. This photograph shows 'The Few', those who flew in the Battle of Britain, led by Group Captain Douglas Bader, over St. Paul's.*
Source: Keystone Collection

Left: *Group Captain Douglas Bader, the celebrated air ace who lost his legs before the Second World War, climbing into a Spitfire to lead the flypast of 15 September 1945.*
Source: Keystone Collection

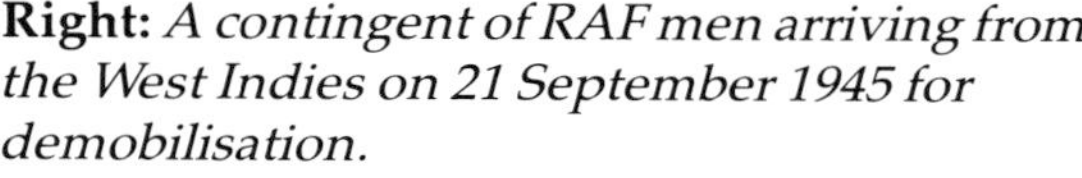

Right: *A contingent of RAF men arriving from the West Indies on 21 September 1945 for demobilisation.*
Source: Keystone Collection

Right: *A contingent from the RAF Regiment marching along Parliament Street as part of the Victory Parade of 8 June 1946.*
Source: Keystone Collection

Above: *In November 1947, Gp Capt Douglas Bader unveiled a new engine named 'Fighter Pilot' for Southern Railway. Also present were Wg Cdr W.G. Clouston and the former commander of Fighter Command's 11 Group during the Battle of Britain, Air Chief Marshal Sir Keith Park.*
Source: Keystone Collection

CHAPTER 13

THE COLD WAR

Above: *The Gloster Meteor F.4 first entered service in November 1947 and eventually twenty-one RAF squadrons were equipped with the machine. This photograph is of Meteor F.4, serial EE521.*

Source: RAF Museum colour slide P100283

The enormous size of the air force with which Britain had ended the Second World War was obviously impractical for the years of peace which everyone hoped would stretch ahead. Many squadrons were disbanded while large numbers of aircraft in service or on the production lines were scrapped. In any event, the economy of the country was in a parlous state and the political climate was averse to spending on defence. By 1948/9, the budget for the RAF had been reduced to only £173 million.

Air Chief Marshal Sir Arthur Tedder, who had taken over as Chief of Air Staff from Marshal of the Royal Air Force Lord Portal in January 1946, was well aware that the United States was continuing with atomic research and that the Soviet Union would soon develop similar weapons. Conventional defence of the U.K. had lost much of its meaning in the knowledge that the use of atomic bombs in another war could result in the annihilation of the entire population. The government had to make up its mind whether Britain should develop its own nuclear capability or stand on the sidelines of world events.

In October 1947, the government announced that it intended to fund atomic research and that the RAF would be the carrier of the resulting weapons. In the same year, the Air Staff put forward 'Plan E', which proposed fifty-one fighter squadrons, forty-one bomber squadrons, thirteen maritime squadrons, forty-two transport squadrons and a reserve of twelve squadrons. These totalled about 1,500 aircraft, but a cutback of about 240 aircraft resulted from a limit on the air estimates, falling mainly on Transport Command.

But whatever the plan, the reality depended partly on the availability of trained men, and almost all the experienced wartime entrants had disappeared into civilian life. Moreover, many of the aircraft were outmoded and remained suitable only for some of the commitments outside Europe. Although Britain possessed excellent aeronautical designers, the U.S. had forged well into the lead with aircraft production. The RAF was still mainly equipped with piston-engined aircraft, although some jet aircraft such as the Gloster Meteor and the de Havilland Vampire had entered service. The piston-engined Avro Lincoln was being produced to replace the Lancaster, but a strategic jet bomber was required for nuclear weapons. In 1948 the RAF at home consisted of eighty squadrons, with twenty more in the Royal Auxiliary Air Force. Overseas, there were thirty-three squadrons. Meanwhile, although events in the Middle and Far East were looking ominous, it was in Europe that the RAF was suddenly needed.

On 24 June 1948, six months after the breakdown of a Four-Power Conference on the future of Germany, the Soviet Union closed all road and rail communications with West Berlin, thus denying access to the British, American and French sectors of the former capital. This move had been anticipated by the West, and both the RAF and the USAF were prepared to mount an airlift designed to keep their garrisons supplied. Dakotas immediately began ferrying supplies into Gatow in the British sector and Tempelhof in the American sector of the city. However, the British and American governments then decided that their air forces should supply the needs of the entire civilian population of

West Berlin, numbering over two million people, as a bargaining counter with the Russians. Such a colossal task seemed impossible of achievement, for the required load was 4,000 to 5,000 short tons per day, but both air forces rose magnificently to the occasion.

By 29 July, the entire Dakota fleet of the RAF's Transport Command, numbering sixty-four aircraft, had arrived at the base of Wunstorf, near Hanover, in the British zone of occupied Germany. Two days later, the RAF's fleet of fifty-six Avro Yorks also arrived. Ten Sunderlands of Coastal Command flew to Hamburg, from where they could carry loads to Havel Lake in Berlin, a small but impressive contribution. The Americans were able to muster an even larger transport force of C-47 Dakotas and Douglas C-54 Skymasters at their bases of Wiesbaden and Rhein/Main in their zone of Germany. Operation 'Plain Fare', as it was called, was under way.

Congestion in the airports in West Berlin and in the occupied zones of Germany presented a major problem. There was also the limitation of only three permitted air corridors, each twenty miles wide. The northern corridor was used by the British, the southern by the Americans, and the central by returning aircraft. The four-engined C-54 Skymasters could carry about ten tons, the Yorks about eight and a half tons, and the Dakotas about three and a half tons. In order to increase carrying capacity, the Americans soon withdrew their Dakotas and brought in more Skymasters. The RAF Dakotas moved to Lübeck, to relieve congestion at Wunstorf.

Below: *The Avro Lincoln was intended to succeed the Avro Lancaster but did not arrive in the RAF until August 1945, too late to serve in the war. It was armed with 20 mm cannons and .50 inch machine guns, and could carry 14,000 lb of bombs. It flew on operations against terrorists in Malaya and Kenya, and continued in RAF service until 1963. This photograph shows a Lincoln of 7 Squadron, which was equipped with the machine from August 1949 to December 1955.*

Source: RAF Museum P11922

During July, the combined air forces carried an average of 2,226 short tons a day to West Berlin, of which the RAF contribution was forty-two per cent. The average daily tonnage rose to 3,839 tons in August and 4,641 tons in September. This increased tonnage was mainly carried by the USAF, with the advantage of the larger payload of the C-54 Skymasters. However, in September, British charter aircraft carried an additional 177 tons a day, and continued until the end of the operation.

The main cargo in terms of weight was coal, which was urgently required with the onset of winter. Of course, foodstuffs were also required, and these were dehydrated where possible, in order to save space. An airfield in the British zone, Fassberg, was opened in August for the American C-54 Skymasters. The average tonnage carried in October rose to 4,760 per day, but there was dip to 3,786 tons in November, owing to fog. The new Handley Page Hastings began to join in during that month, but the RAF's contribution did not increase; instead, improved facilities were provided for USAF aircraft in the British zone. In December, the new airport of Tegel was opened in the French sector of Berlin, having been built since the beginning of the operation. Another air base for the American C-54 Skymasters was opened at Celle in the British sector. The tonnage then rose steadily from 4,563 tons in December to 5,546 tons in January, 6,327 tons in March and 8,091 tons in May. In January, Air Chief Marshal Sir John Slessor took over from Lord Tedder as Chief of Air Staff, to preside over the RAF's contribution to this success.

The capacity of the USAF and RAF amazed the Russians, who were losing face in the eyes of the world and particularly the delighted West Berliners. They lifted their blockade on 12 May 1949, after 'Plain Fare' had been in operation for over ten months. However, the airlift continued for another four months, to build up a stockpile in case the Russians decided to renew their interference. The operation demonstrated that the run down of the RAF had been allowed to go too far, but that the personnel were capable of rising to an emergency, given reasonable backing. The close collaboration of the RAF and the USAF was also a contributory factor in the formation of the North Atlantic Treaty Organization, which came into being on 24 August 1949. Four weeks later, the Federal Republic of Germany was also established, marking a new solidarity among western nations against the Communist bloc.

These events gave impetus to the establishment of a strategic deterrent. By 1949, Bomber Command had been reduced to only about 150 aircraft, Lincolns and Mosquitos, but during the following year was reinforced by Boeing B-29 Superfortresses, which were called Washingtons by the RAF. Canberras began to enter service in 1951, but this otherwise excellent tactical bomber could not carry an atomic bomb. The RAF was awaiting its V-bombers, as these were called. The first of these, the four-jet Vickers Valiant, began to arrive in 1955, and eventually equipped ten squadrons. Meanwhile, the Blue Danube plutonium bomb had been developed by British scientists and tested in the Monte Bello Islands, off Western Australia, in October 1952. The first of these bombs became available to the RAF in November 1953, ten months after Air Chief Marshal Sir William Dickson took over as Chief of Air Staff. Ten airfields were enlarged in England for the new V-bombers, and a dispersal system in other airfields was also arranged, to give the bombers protection against a 'first strike'. The crews underwent intensive training in high-level operations, in collaboration with the USAF.

In 1956, the year in which Air Chief Marshal Sir Dermot Boyle took over as Chief of Air Staff, the delta-winged Avro Vulcan V-bomber arrived, and the first squadron became operational with these the following year. The third of the V-bomber trio, the Handley Page Victor entered squadron service in 1958. In the same year, sixty Thor intermediate-range missiles from the U.S.A. were installed on dispersed sites, operated by the RAF in conjunction with the Americans. Defence of airfields was provided by Bloodhound ground-to-air missiles, together with an efficient guidance system. By 1959, those V-bombers at readiness were capable of flying clear within three minutes and then setting off in retaliation. An early warning station was completed in 1963 at Fylingdales in Yorkshire, by which time the nuclear deterrent force consisted of fifteen squadrons, equipped with the more powerful hydrogen bombs. During this period there were two further appointments as Chief of Air Staff, Air Chief Marshal Sir Thomas Pike on 1 January 1960 and Air Chief Marshal Sir Charles Elworthy on 1 September 1963.

As a counter to the surface-to-air missiles which the Soviet Union was known to have developed, the V-bombers were equipped in 1963 with the Blue Steel 'stand-off' missile, capable of being launched a hundred miles from the target. As an additional counter to enemy radar and defensive missiles, the Vulcan and Victor crews trained in low-level approaches, climbing up at the last moment to launch their missiles. In the same year, the RAF's V-bomber force came under the authority of NATO for nuclear strikes, while retaining its conventional bombing capacity for any national needs. However, a change of policy followed the introduction of Polaris missiles launched from submarines, and in this year the RAF began to wind down its nuclear strike force. In 1964, the British Aircraft Corporation TSR 2, a tactical strike and reconnaissance bomber

Above: *The Gloster Meteor was the first jet aircraft to enter service in the RAF, in July 1944, and the only Allied jet aircraft to fly operationally in the Second World War. Its main role was to intercept V.1. flying bombs, thirteen of which were destroyed. In 1945, a Meteor achieved the record speed of 606 m.p.h. This photograph of a Meteor F.3 of 74 Squadron was taken at Colerne in Wiltshire on 30 August 1945.*

Source: Keystone Collection

Below: *The Boeing B-29 Superfortress was named the Washington by the RAF when supplied from the USAF in 1950. It was gradually replaced by the English Electric Canberra, but continued with the RAF until 1958. This photograph shows a Washington with engines prepared for storage.*

Source: Aviation Bookshop

Above: *The first production batch of de Havilland Vampires, one of which is shown in this photograph, entered 247 Squadron in April 1946, too late for war service. The new jet fighter-bomber gained a high reputation for its aerobatic qualities as well as reliability and ease of access for servicing. The first RAF jet crossing of the Atlantic was made by six Vampires of 54 Squadron in July 1948. Although several overseas squadrons were equipped with the Vampire, only those in Malaya and Singapore flew operationally, on anti-terrorist strikes. Other Vampires served as night-fighters. As trainers, a few continued in RAF service until 1969.*

Source: RAF Museum PO12562

which had been under development for five years, was cancelled. Some of the V-bombers were retained for reconnaissance purposes and as conventional bombers, while others entered a new life as in-flight tankers and receivers.

In common with Bomber Command, Fighter Command was wound down rapidly after the end of the Second World War. By early 1947, it consisted of under 200 aircraft, mainly Meteors, Vampires, Hornets and Mosquitos, together with a small but efficient Control and Reporting system. In parallel with Bomber Command, an expansion programme began when operation 'Plain Fare' emphasised the seriousness of the Cold War, and by 1952 the number of aircraft had doubled, while there were about 160 additional Meteors and Vampires in the Royal Auxiliary Air Force. These aircraft could not match the Russian MiGs, however, and in 1952 the swept-wing North American Sabre entered service as a stop-gap jet until modern British jet fighters came off the production lines. These arrived two years later in the form of the Supermarine Swift and the Hawker Hunter, both swept-wing and subsonic in level flight. The Hunter proved the more successful and became the RAF's standard single-seat fighter until 1960. The two-seat Gloster Javelin, also subsonic, entered service in 1956; this was the first RAF fighter to carry an air-to-air missile, the heat-seeking Firestreak, as standard armament. By the end of that year, Fighter Command numbered 600 aircraft in thirty-five squadrons.

After this expansion, military thinking favoured the use of surface-to-air missiles for defence of the U.K., together with the introduction of a supersonic fighter, the English Electric Lightning, armed with air-to-air missiles. Moreover, it was believed that there was no defence against the new Russian surface-to-surface intercontinental missiles and that fighters were consequently losing much of their relevance for the defence of the U.K.

The Lightning, capable of achieving twice the speed of sound, came into service in 1960. Five years later Fighter Command was reduced to only sixty aircraft, all Lightnings and Javelins, fitted with the more powerful Red Top air-to-air missile. At this time, however, incursions by Russian reconnaissance aircraft in air space around the British Isles caused some alarm. The early warning system was improved by the employment of Avro Shackletons, while the number of fighter aircraft was gradually increased to seventy-six by 1975. One new aircraft was the McDonnell Douglas Phantom, which arrived in squadron service in 1968, replacing some of the ageing Lightnings. In April of the same year Fighter Command was combined with Bomber Command to form the RAF's new Strike Command. Air Chief Marshal Sir John Grandy took over as Chief of Air Staff in April 1967, followed by Air Chief Marshal Sir Denis Spotswood in April 1971, Air Chief Marshal Sir Andrew Humphrey in April 1974 and Air Chief Marshal Sir Neil Cameron in January 1976.

In addition to commitments at home, the RAF continued as a potent force in West Germany. In July 1945 the 2nd Tactical Air Force was renamed the British Air Forces of Occupation (BAFO), consisting of thirty-four front-line squadrons. In common with the RAF practise everywhere, these squadrons were rapidly wound down, until only ten remained at the end of 1947. With the beginning of the Cold War in 1948 and the formation of NATO the following year, these squadrons were moved to bases along the eastern frontier and an expansion began. By 1951, there were sixteen squadrons in BAFO, equipped with Vampires and Meteors, under the control of NATO. By the following year there were two divisions, the 2nd Allied Tactical Air Force (2ATAF) and the 4th Allied Tactical Air Force (4ATAF), the former consisting mainly of RAF squadrons.

The 2ATAF grew rapidly to twenty-five squadrons, in which Venoms replaced the Vampires, and Sabre squadrons were formed. In 1954 four squadrons of Canberras arrived, 'on loan' from Bomber Command. Over the next few years Javelins replaced the Vampires, and Hunters began to replace the Sabres. In 1958 the number of front-line squadrons was reduced to eighteen, with economic problems at home and the advent of the V-bomber nuclear deterrent. By the end of 1962, there were only twelve RAF squadrons in Germany. In 1965, Wessex helicopters replaced the Whirlwinds which had arrived two years earlier, while Lightnings equipped two squadrons as replacements for the Javelins. Phantoms began to take over reconnaissance duties from Canberras in 1970, and the Harriers and Buccaneers first arrived in that year, replacing Hunters. By 1972, there were four squadrons of Phantoms, three of Harriers, two of Buccaneers, two of Lightnings and one of Wessex helicopters. Jaguars began to replace the Phantom squadrons in 1975, and in turn the Phantoms were sent to the Lightning squadrons.

Above: *A poster inviting donations for the RAF Benevolent Fund, the best known of all the RAF charities, sponsored by Rolls Royce.*

Source: Vintage Magazine Co. colour slide

Right: *The Vickers Valiant was the RAF's first four-jet bomber and entered squadron service in April 1955. Its introduction gave rise to the V-bomber force, Britain's strategic nuclear deterrent. Valiants dropped bombs on Egypt during the Suez Crisis and also dropped Britain's atom and hydrogen bombs during nuclear trials in the Pacific. They continued as front-line aircraft for ten years and then some were adapted to the role of in-flight refuelling tankers. Valiants were withdrawn from service in May 1965. This photograph of serial WB215, the second prototype, was taken on 23 September 1953.*

Source: RAF Museum colour slide P100635

Left: *When the English Electric Canberra B.2 first entered service in May 1951, with 101 Squadron, it marked the beginning of jet bombers in the RAF. With its sleek lines and speeds in excess of 500 m.p.h., the aircraft proved one of the most durable and versatile bombers in aeronautical history. It flew on bombing attacks against terrorists in Malaya and against Egyptian aerodromes during the Suez crisis. Later variations of the Canberra were phased out as front-line bombers at the end of 1961, but until recently others were employed for photographic reconnaissance and jamming enemy radar. Some are still in service as trainers. Ironically, Canberras were employed by the Argentine Air Force in the Falklands War. This photograph, of two Canberras of 61 Squadron and one of 109 Squadron, was taken in July 1955.*

Source: RAF Museum colour slide P100257

Right: *The Handley Page Hastings became the standard long-range transport in the RAF after 47 Squadron was first equipped with the machine at Dishforth in Yorkshire in September 1948. It operated throughout the Berlin airlift, and continued in first-line service until 1967. This photograph, of the prototype Hastings C.1, was taken on 23 May 1946.*

Source: RAF Museum colour slide P100326

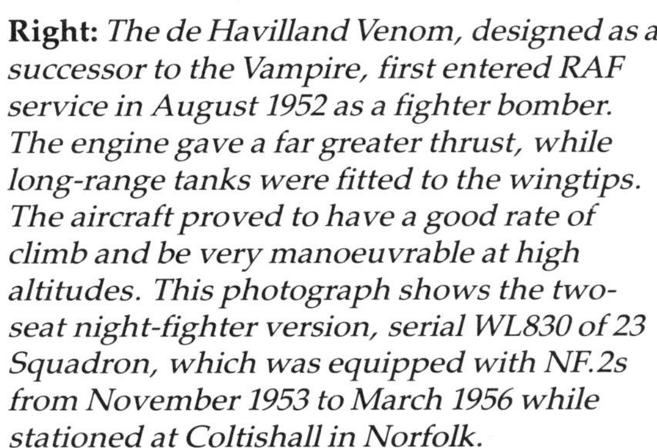

Right: *The de Havilland Venom, designed as a successor to the Vampire, first entered RAF service in August 1952 as a fighter bomber. The engine gave a far greater thrust, while long-range tanks were fitted to the wingtips. The aircraft proved to have a good rate of climb and be very manoeuvrable at high altitudes. This photograph shows the two-seat night-fighter version, serial WL830 of 23 Squadron, which was equipped with NF.2s from November 1953 to March 1956 while stationed at Coltishall in Norfolk.*

Source: RAF Museum P019078

Below: *The Avro York flew in Transport Command, most of the handful built during the Second World War serving as VIP aircraft. It was a development of the Avro Lancaster, but the fuselage was deeper and wider to give double the cubic capacity. After the war, large-scale production resulted in Yorks being delivered to six RAF squadrons. They came into prominence during the Berlin airlift, from 1 July 1948 to 12 May 1949, when they made 29,000 flights to the beleagured city. It was a slow aircraft, but regarded as docile and reliable. The last York was withdrawn from service in 1957. This photograph, of a York of 511 Squadron, serial MW102, was taken at Northolt.*

Source: Keystone Collection

Opposite: *The Avro Vulcan B.1, serial VX777, was the second prototype and made its maiden flight on 3 September 1953. The Vulcan was the first large bomber in the world with the delta-wing. It entered service in Bomber Command in July 1956 as part of the 'V' Class of long-range bombers. Range was extended in 1959 by in-flight refuelling from Valiant tanker aircraft.*

Source: Aviation Bookshop

Below: *The Avro Vulcan, the first large strike aircraft in the world designed with the delta wing, or V-bomber, entered service with the RAF's Bomber Command squadrons in July 1957. The B.1 version could carry a bomb load of 21,000 lb and proved easy to handle and maintain. The B.2 version followed in 1960, as shown in this photograph. This was larger, more powerful and capable of flying for about 4,600 miles without refuelling. Vulcans remained in service until the end of 1982.*

Source: RAF Museum PO21342

Above: *The prototype Vulcan B.1, serial VX770, photographed in September 1952.*

Source: RAF Museum P100457

Left: *The Handley Page Victor B.1 followed the Vickers Valiant and the Avro Vulcan as the last of the trio of V-bombers. This graceful four-jet aircraft first entered squadron service in April 1958 and continued until 1964 when the B.2 began to replace the earlier version. The Victor B.2 carried the Blue Steel air-to-surface nuclear missile, which had a range of 200 miles. Victors were phased out of the bomber role in 1968 but continued as in-flight refuelling tankers. This photograph of a Victor B.1, serial ZA918, was taken in January 1957.*

Source: RAF Museum P100354

Left: The Times *marked the air display of 7-13 September 1953 at Farnborough with a special 'Survey of British Aviation'. Their poster showed the prototype Avro Vulcan bomber, serial VX770.*

Source: RAF Museum P100163

Below: *The larger missile in this photograph, taken at Farnborough, was the air-to-surface Blue Steel, manufactured by Hawker Siddeley Dynamics. Carrying a thermo-nuclear warhead for a range of about 200 miles, it became the main strategic weapon of Britain's V-bombers from February 1963. It continued until 1970. The smaller missile was the air-to-air Firestreak of British Aerospace Dynamics, which first came into service with Fighter Command in 1958. It had a high-explosive warhead and a range of about five miles.*

Source: RAF Museum P36046

Right: *The first Handley Page Victor B.1 with under-wing fuel tanks and facilities for in-flight refuelling was serial XA930.*

Source: RAF Museum P100359

Right: *The Beagle Basset C.C.1 was a communications aircraft, adapted from the executive jet Beagle B.206 and first supplied to the RAF in 1965 for the transport of V-bomber crews. The twenty which were supplied suffered from some technical problems and the last was withdrawn in May 1974.*

Source: RAF Museum PO21677

Below: *The Douglas Thor was a surface-to-surface missile with a nuclear warhead and a range of 1,725 miles. The length was 65 feet and the speed at burn-out was up to Mach 15. It entered RAF service in August 1958 and eventually twenty squadrons of Bomber Command were each equipped with three of these missiles. They were withdrawn in 1963.*

Source: RAF Museum PO15249

Right: *The Supermarine Spitfire F.21 was one of the later versions powered by the Rolls Royce Griffon instead of the Merlin, entering service in January 1945. This photograph shows a Spitfire F.21 of 602 (City of Glasgow) Squadron, squadron letters RAI, which was equipped with these fighters from April 1947 to May 1951.*

Source: RAF Museum P7202

Below: *The North American Sabre was supplied to the RAF from the beginning of 1953 as a stop-gap before the arrival of swept-wing fighters manufactured in Britain. Squadrons in Germany and in the UK were equipped with Sabres, which gave good service until superseded by Hawker Hunters by the summer of 1956. This photograph is of Sabre serial XD727 of 92 Squadron, based at Linton-on-Ouse in Yorkshire.*

Source: Aeroplane Monthly

Above: *The* Evening News *marked the air display of 7-13 September 1953 at Farnborough with a series which included combat stories from Battle of Britain pilots. Their poster showed a Hurricane I of 87 Squadron.*

Source: RAF Museum PIC75/15/14

Left: *The Bloodhound surface-to-air missile was first deployed in 1958 to protect V-bomber and Thor surface-to-surface missile bases. It was fitted with a proximity-fuse nuclear warhead and was directed to the target by radar. Fifteen Air Defence Missile Squadrons of Fighter Command were equipped with the Bloodhound Mark 1, in groups of sixteen. The Bloodhound Mark 2 was introduced in 1964, using continuous-wave radar instead of pulse radar, and is still part of Strike Command's defence system. This photograph shows Bloodhound Mark 2s of B Flight, 25 Squadron.*

Source: T. Malcolm English

Above: *The Hawker Hunter F.6 entered service in October 1956 and became the RAF's standard single-seat interceptor, capable of Mach 0.95 at 36,000 feet. It was beloved by pilots for its superb handling capabilities as well as its elegant appearance. The formation flying and aerobatics of 111 Squadron's* Black Arrows *and 92 Squadron's* Blue Diamonds *were regarded as breathtaking by spectators. The Hunter F.6 was phased out at the end of 1962.*

Source: RAF Museum colour slide P36033

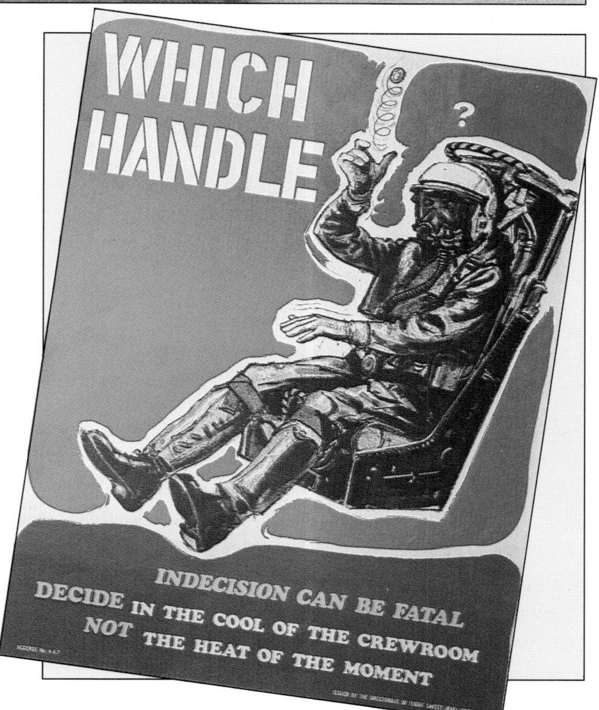

Right: *An unfortunate pilot in a state of indecision as to which handle to pull to operate his ejector seat, shown on a crewroom poster in 1967.*

Source: RAF Museum (Crown copyright) P00409

Left: *The Supermarine Swift F.1 was the RAF's first swept-wing fighter to enter frontline squadron service, in February 1953. It was built in case the Hawker Hunter proved unsatisfactory but in fact it was the Swift which was outclassed. On 25 September 1953, however, the prototype Swift F.4 established a World Air Speed Record by flying to North Africa at 737 m.p.h., photographed here at Idris in Libya.*

Source: RAF Museum P3510

Above: *Some Supermarine Swift F.1s were employed in the fighter-reconnaissance role, and proved satisfactory at low-level tactical work. This photograph of Swift F.R.5, serial XD922, of 2 Squadron, was taken at Geilenkirchen in West Germany. Swift F.R.5s remained in service until March 1961.*

Source: RAF Museum P10086

Right: *The Hawker Hunter F.G.A.9 was a development of the F.6, fitted with extra drop-tanks and weapon points beneath the wings for the ground attack role. It entered squadron service in September 1961 and continued until December 1971, although some continued as trainers until June 1976. This photograph is of an F.G.A.9 of 79 Squadron.*

Source: RAF Museum P3475

Left and below: *The Gloster Javelin was the first delta-winged twin-jet fighter as well as the largest fighter employed in the RAF. It was introduced to the RAF in February 1956, as a high performance aircraft capable of flying at great altitude. Extra radar made it highly suitable for night fighter interception. However, the machine had its faults, one of which was poor recovery from stalls, which was probably responsible for several accidents. There were nine marks, and the aircraft continued in service until April 1968. In these photographs, WT827 was the third prototype which first flew on 7 March 1953, while XH966 was Javelin FAW 8 which first flew on 9 May 1958.*

Source: Aviation Bookshop

Right: *When the British Aircraft Corporation Lightning was delivered to the RAF in December 1959, it marked the beginning of single-seat fighters which exceeded the speed of sound in level flight. The Lightning could reach Mach 2, whereas the machine it began to replace, the Hawker Hunter, reached Mach 0.95. It also contained sophisticated guidance systems, and at the time was regarded by the RAF pilots as the finest interceptor in the world. This photograph, of a Lightning F.6 of 5 Squadron, shows the machine about to land and carrying the Red Top air-to-air missiles, which have a speed of Mach 3, and a range of seven miles.*

Source: RAF Museum colour slide PO18668

Left: A Red Top air-to-air missile being fitted to a Lightning F.6 of 5 Squadron.

Source: T. Malcolm English

Right: *The McDonnell Douglas Phantom F.G.1 entered service with 43 Squadron in February 1969 as an interceptor. The F.G.R.2 followed in May 1969 in the reconnaissance and ground attack role, and eventually fourteen RAF squadrons were equipped with this version. Although it is heavier and less manoeuvrable than most aircraft in the same role, it is considered easy to fly and can carry up to eight tons of weaponry. It is also equipped with excellent radar systems. This photograph, of an F.G.R.2 serial XV407 of 41 Squadron, shows the aircraft fitted with four Raytheon Sparrow air-to-air missiles; these have a range of twenty miles and reach the speed of Mach Four. It is also carrying four BL755 cluster bombs, each of 600 lb and carrying 147 small bomblets. The squadron badge on the tail is a 'double armed cross'.*

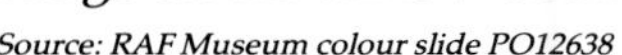

Source: RAF Museum colour slide PO12638

Left: *The Hawker Siddeley Buccaneer I first entered service with the Fleet Air Arm as a strike aircraft designed to fly at less than 200 feet, beneath radar screens. When aircraft carriers were phased out in 1968, however, existing contracts for Fleet Air Arm Buccaneers were added to those intended for the RAF. The first aircraft began to arrive in the RAF in October 1969 and replaced Canberras as low-level strike aircraft with advanced instrumentation and guidance systems, capable of flying close to Mach 0.85 while retaining excellent manoeuvrability. This photograph of Buccaneer XK490, Fleet Air Arm, was taken in September 1959.*

Source: RAF Museum colour slide P100414

Right: *The first aircraft capable of vertical take-off and landing in the RAF, or any of the world's air forces, was the British Aerospace Harrier G.R.1, originally manufactured by Hawker Siddeley. It was delivered to 1 Squadron in July 1969. Although sub-sonic, the Harrier has proved one of the most remarkable and successful ground-attack aircraft. The Harrier G.R.3, with a more powerful engine, a lengthened nose and more advanced systems for naviation and ground attack, updated the G.R.1. This photograph shows Harrier G.R.1s, serials WV746 and WV753, of 1 Squadron.*

Source: RAF Museum colour slide PO18654

Left: *A Hawker Siddeley Harrier G.R.3 of 4 Squadron.*

Source: T. Malcolm English

CHAPTER 14

MARITIME AND TRANSPORT

By the end of 1946, Coastal Command had been whittled down to a front-line strength of no more than fifty aircraft within eight squadrons, together with a meteorological squadron and two long-distance photographic reconnaissance squadrons. The command was divided into 18 Group with headquarters in Scotland and 19 Group with headquarters in Devon, together with RAF Northern Ireland and the Central Photographic Establishment at Benson in Oxfordshire. Of its commitments, meteorological reconnaissance over the Atlantic was considered of major importance for weather forecasting; this task was carried out by Halifaxes until Hastings arrived in 1950. The photographic squadrons, equipped with Spitfires, Mosquitos and Lancasters, were frequently engaged on air survey work. The anti-submarine squadrons, numbering six, were equipped with Sunderlands and Lancasters, armed for the most part with the equipment of the Second World War. This was in a period when it was known that the Soviet Union was already engaged on a massive expansion of her submarine fleet and surface warships.

Coastal Command was allowed to expand after the Cold War began in 1948. The first Avro Shackletons arrived in 1951, giving the anti-submarine squadrons a much longer range. Production of these was inadequate, however, and Lockheed Neptunes were imported as stopgaps. Three years later, Coastal Command consisted of thirteen squadrons, equipped with Shackletons, Neptunes and Sunderlands. An important development was the introduction of the Mark 30 homing torpedo. These were used in conjunction with sonobuoys, which detected underwater noises and transmitted their direction by radio. When two or more sonobuoys were dropped in the vicinity of a submarine, the aircrew could work out an accurate position and the homing torpedoes gave them an excellent chance of a 'kill'. Armed with this strike capability, Coastal Command operated in conjunction with NATO. In 1955, Whirlwind helicopters arrived for search and rescue operations, beginning a new phase of this highly-regarded RAF activity around the coasts and in the mountain areas of the U.K.

The contraction of the RAF in the second half of the 1950s affected Coastal Command somewhat less than the other commands, since the expansion of the Russian Navy was continuing at such a pace. However, the Neptune and Sunderland squadrons were disbanded in 1956 and 1957. More problems arose with the advent of Soviet nuclear submarines in the early 1960s, since these were capable of much higher speeds and were also able to travel underwater at greater depths for many days. Improved radar and navigational equipment was installed in the Shackletons, while some squadrons were transferred to more northerly airfields, in order to detect Soviet submarines and surface vessels moving into the North Atlantic.

A replacement for the Shackleton was found with the introduction in late 1970 of the Hawker Siddeley Nimrod, an adaption of the de Havilland Comet airliner. With the arrival of this aircraft, the front-line squadrons were reduced to only four, together with two helicopter squadrons equipped with Whirlwinds. However, in October 1969, a Buccaneer squadron of the RAF's new Strike Command was converted to the maritime

strike role. A month later, Coastal Command itself was absorbed into Strike Command, becoming 18 Group with headquarters at Northwood in Greater London.

Transport Command had experienced an enormous increase during the last years of the Second World War, growing to a force of 1,200 aircraft in 1945, little more than two years after its formation in March 1943. It was poised for further work in carrying troops to the Far East when the atom bombs dropped on Japan put an end to the war. The main task then was the repatriation of prisoners of war and the return to the U.K. of servicemen for demobilisation. Thereafter, Transport Command maintained a regular but small air service with British bases overseas; in this period, sea transport was the more normal method employed by the armed forces. As with all other RAF commands, Transport Command also faced the problem of insufficient trained aircrews and ground personnel as well as the lack of new aircraft.

The Dakotas, which had formed the mainstay of Transport Command during the war, had been supplied under Lend-Lease and were due for return to the U.S.A. As a temporary measure, Britain purchased some of these and renewed the leases of others. In addition, Avro Yorks were produced in greater numbers, a few having been used primarily for V.I.P. work in the final years of the war. Other than these, Transport Command relied on a mixture of converted heavy bombers which were not ideal for its tasks.

In Germany, much of the work of Transport Command was taken over by British European Airways, although Dakotas continued to supply freight and to carry

Below: *The Bristol Brigand was intended as a successor to the Bristol Beaufighter T.F.X. torpedo-bomber of Coastal Command. The prototype, serial MX988, first flew on 4 December 1944, but production aircraft were too late to serve in the Second World War.*

Source: RAF Museum P5273

passengers to the occupying British forces. Other Dakotas served on routes to Austria, the Balkans and Malta. The Yorks were employed on long-distance routes to the Far East, via the Middle East and India or Ceylon. In the absence of full radar coverage as aids for navigation, some stretches of these routes could be difficult in poor weather.

Some training with airborne forces were also carried out, but these were severely limited as a result of defence cuts. When the Cold War began, with the airlift to Berlin from June 1948, the whole of Transport Command's resources were transferred to Europe for over a year and the overseas routes were temporarily abandoned. Even when they were resumed, the command was whittled down drastically while available finance went into expansion of the other commands. By 1951, only fifty aircraft remained, mainly Yorks, Hastings and the new Vickers Valettas.

When the Korean War broke out in June 1950, Transport Command's tasks were increased with the need to extend the Far East route to Japan from Singapore, in order to carry the British troops who served in this theatre. At the same time, political troubles in the Middle East placed extra burdens on the command in transporting troops and supplies. Training with paratroops also increased, as did 'mercy missions' such as carrying relief supplies to Greece after a volcano erupted.

Somewhat paradoxically, it was the withdrawal of British forces around the world which determined an expansion of Transport Command, for it became necessary to carry a small but highly mobile force at speed to trouble spots in the Commonwealth when the need arose. Moreover, it was realized somewhat belatedly that it was more economical to transport troops by air than on lengthy sea journeys. The need to expand the command also coincided with the completion of re-equipment in other commands, releasing finance for the creation of a modern fleet of strategic and tactical air transports. This began in early 1956 with the arrival of de Havilland Comets for long-range work and Blackburn Beverleys for shorter ranges. Three years later, Bristol Britannias entered service, giving Transport Command the impressive total of ten Comets and twenty-three Britannias as a strategic force, within four squadrons. These were kept fully employed, not only on the regular routes but also on carrying troops to such trouble spots as Cyprus, the Middle East and Borneo. In 1966, ten Shorts Belfasts arrived to give the command the benefit of a long-range strategic freighter, and in the following year fourteen Vickers VC10s provided another addition to the long-range passenger and freight service.

Below: *The Avro Shackleton was designed to replace Avro Lancasters, Consolidated Liberators and Boeing Fortresses in the anti-submarine role, but entered RAF service in April 1951 as a long-range maritime reconnaissance aircraft. Eleven Coastal Command squadrons were equipped with this reliable machine, as well as three maritime squadrons serving overseas. The marine reconnaissance version continued until 1972 but an 'airborne early warning' Shackleton was developed in 1971 and 8 Squadron will remain equipped with these machines until the arrival of the Boeing E-3 Sentry. This photograph of Avro Shackleton M.R.1 serial VW135, one of the prototypes, was taken on 18 April 1950.*

Source: RAF Museum colour slide P100447

By the middle of the 1960s there were five squadrons in the shorter-range tactical force, equipped with Beverleys, Hastings and the new Armstrong Whitworth Argosy. For short-range work in the 1960s, there were five helicopter squadrons, equipped with Scottish Aviation Pioneers and Sycamore and Whirlwind helicopters. Westland Wessex helicopters arrived in 1964. These performed army co-operation duties in the U.K. but were sometimes detached for duties in Germany and Borneo. The tactical squadrons trained in paratroop work and in the air lifting of heavy equipment for the army, as part of a NATO force. Two squadrons of Hunters were transferred from Fighter Command, to give striking power to the tactical group.

In August 1967, Transport Command was renamed Air Support Command. In this new role, which included a more aggressive element, it was augmented in 1969 by a squadron of Harriers and two squadrons of Phantoms. Another Phantom squadron was added in 1972. Meanwhile, the shorter-range tactical squadrons were re-equipped with the arrival of Hawker Siddeley Andovers in 1966 and the very important introduction of Lockheed C-130 Hercules transports a year later. These gradually replaced the remaining Argosies, Hastings and Beverleys. Two Westland Puma helicopter squadrons were added in 1971, while the Whirlwinds were withdrawn.

In September 1972, Air Support Command was absorbed by Strike Command. Three years later, the two support groups within this overall structure reached a peak of twenty-one squadrons with 227 aircraft, including sixty aircraft in the offensive role and fifty-two helicopters. By this time, the RAF's need for scheduled services to small garrisons in the world had diminished, while its participation in NATO was increasing. Troops were flown on a regular basis to and from Germany, as well as Gibraltar and Cyprus. Training exercises involved the air transport of large contingents of paratroops to Denmark, Germany and Turkey.

In 1976, the transport support groups were assigned to NATO, serving its Allied Command Europe Mobile Force as well as the home-based United Kingdom Mobile Force. At the same time, there was an increased need to transport troops and military supplies to Northern Ireland. Many of the long-distance strategic squadrons were wound down and disbanded, beginning with the Comet and Britannia squadrons in 1975 and the Belfast squadron in the following year. The Hunters and some of the Hercules also disappeared, while a Puma squadron was transferred and the two air support groups in Strike Command were combined into one. Following other reductions, the number of aircraft in the transport element fell to 145 in that year.

Above: *The Hawker Siddeley Nimrod, a maritime reconnaissance aircraft derived from the famous Comet airliner, entered service with maritime squadrons of Strike Command from October 1970, replacing Avro Shackletons. Equipped with Sidewinder missiles, they took part in the Falklands War, but their primary role remains anti-submarine with Harpoon air-to-surface missiles and sophisticated radar equipment. The early-warning development of the Nimrod was cancelled in December 1986, but the reliable maritime version remains in service. This photograph of a Nimrod M.R.2, serial XV250, of 42 Squadron, was taken in September 1986.*

Source: RAF Museum colour slide PO51748

Above: *The flight deck of a Hawker Siddeley Nimrod.*

Source: T. Malcolm English

Above: *The first production Bristol Brigand T.F.1 was serial RH742, as shown in this photograph. The machine was armed with a Mark XVII torpedo and eight rockets with 25 lb solid-shot warheads. However, the Brigand did not serve in the role of a torpedo-bomber, partly because it was realized that this form of attack against surface vessels armed with radar-controlled anti-aircraft guns had become suicidal. Instead, the Brigand entered RAF service in early 1949 as the last piston-engined light bomber in the RAF. From early 1950 to late 1952, Brigands of 45 and 84 Squadrons flew operationally with bombs and rockets against terrorists in the Malayan jungle.*

Source: BAC via Roger Hayward

Right: *From January 1952 onwards, Lockheed Neptune M.R.1s were delivered to four Coastal Command squadrons, as a stop-gap until Avro Shackletons arrived. The aircraft was armed with two .50 inch machine guns in a mid-upper turret, with twin 20 mm cannons in a nose and a tail turret, and it could also carry rockets and bombs. Four Neptunes were converted to operate as early warning aircraft. All these maritime reconnaissance aircraft were phased out by March 1957.*

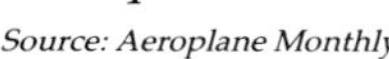
Source: Aeroplane Monthly

Above: *The RAF's premier operational aerodrome off the north Cornish coast is St. Mawgan, photographed here in 1960. Established in 1943 and used principally by ferrying aircraft, it fell into disuse in 1946 but was reopened in 1951. Nowadays, it is the home of 42 Squadron and 236 Operational Conversion Unit, both equipped with Hawker Siddeley Nimrods.*

Source: RAF Museum PO17587

Right: *The Vickers Valetta C.1, a military version of the Viking airliner, entered RAF squadron service in May 1949, being employed as a troop or freight carrier and for casevac operations. Valettas were active in Malaya during the anti-terriorist war, mainly dropping supplies to troops. A later Valetta version, the T.3, was used for navigation training. Valettas continued in service until April 1966. This photograph of serial VL263, the second Valetta C.1 to enter RAF service, was taken over Southampton docks on 2 February 1949.*

Source: RAF Museum P100628

Above: *The de Havilland Comet Series 2 was the RAF's military version of BOAC's turbojet airliner. First delivered to Transport Command in July 1956, Comets brought Australia within thirty hours flying time of the U.K. All were given the names of star constellations, the Comet 2 in this photograph being serial XK695 'Pegasus' of 216 Squadron. The stretched version, Comet Series 4, was delivered to the Transport Command from February 1962. Comet 2s were withdrawn in April 1967 and Comet 4s in June 1975.*

Source: RAF Museum colour slide P100421

Below: *The Blackburn Beverley was the first RAF transport aircraft designed to off-load equipment through "clam shell" rear-loading doors. It was also the largest aircraft to enter service with the RAF when first delivered to 47 Squadron at Abingdon in March 1956. As a medium-range aircraft capable of carrying very large loads, it continued in service with Transport Command until 1968. This photograph, of Beverley C.1 serial XB283 of 47 Squadron, was taken in November 1956.*

Source: RAF Museum colour slide P100238

Above: *The first turboprop transport aircraft introduced into the RAF was the military version of the Bristol Britannia airliner, which arrived at 99 Squadron in June 1959. Twenty-three Britannias in all were delivered, and all were given the names of stars. This Britannia, XL639 Atria, saw service with both 99 and 511 Squadrons, the two Transport Command (later Air Support Command) squadrons equipped with the machine until January 1976.*

Source: RAF Museum colour slide PO18660

Left: *The Short Belfast, first delivered to 53 Squadron of the RAF's Transport Command in January 1966, was designed specifically as a strategic freighter, the payload being 22,000 lb over a range of 3,600 miles. They were withdrawn from service at the end of 1976. The ten which served in the RAF were given names from the Bible or from Greek and Roman mythology. The Belfast Mark I in this photograph was serial XR368 'Theseus'.*

Source: RAF Musuem colour slide PO18672

Above: *The British Aerospace VC10, a military version of a civil airliner, began to enter service with the RAF's Transport Command in 1966. It proved capable of carrying 150 troops and their kit for nearly 3,700 miles. All the VC10s in the RAF were named after holders of the Victoria Cross; the aircraft in this photograph, serial XR806, was named after Flight Sergeant George Thompson, a wireless operator in a Lancaster of 9 Squadron, who was awarded a posthumous Victoria Cross after a raid over Germany on 1 January 1945. The VC10 remains in service with 10 Squadron, based at Brize Norton in Oxfordshire.*

Source: RAF Museum PO22051

Below: *The Andover C.1, a military version of the turboprop Avro 748 civil transport, first entered service in December 1965 with 46 Squadron at Abingdon in Berkshire. Andovers served as multi-purpose transports with four RAF squadrons. They are still in service with 115 Squadron at Benson in Oxfordshire, engaged on radar calibration. This photograph, of Andover C.1, serial XS596, of 115 Squadron, was taken at Alconbury in Huntingdonshire in August 1982.*

Source: RAF Museum PO18081

Above: *The Scottish Aviation Twin Pioneer C.C.1 was the military version of the civil transport and entered RAF service in 1958. Like its predecessor, the single-engined Pioneer, it was capable of short take-off and landing. Six squadrons were equipped with the machine, which was nicknamed 'The Twin Pin'. The last Twin Pioneers continued in squadron service until December 1968. This photograph, of serial XM286, was taken on 22 July 1958.*

Source: RAF Museum P100534

Left: *The Lockheed Hercules C.1 is the RAF's equivalent of the USAF's C-130E turbo-prop transport. With the shrinking of Britain's overseas territories, it became necessary to acquire a long-range aircraft to transport troops and supplies over great distances; and the Hercules supplied this need, first entering RAF squadron service in August 1967. It is able to carry almost 100 passengers and their kit over a range of nearly 5,000 miles, and at the same time is easy to handle and service. Sixteen modified aircraft, known as Hercules C.1Ks, entered service as flight refuellers from May 1982, during the Falklands War. In addition, twenty-six Hercules were 'stretched' from 1980 onwards, designated Hercules C.3s.*

Source: RAF Museum PO15217

CHAPTER 15

ON WORLD SERVICE

The commitments of the RAF in the Far East did not end after Japan surrendered on 14 August 1945. The existence of the atom bombs had been such a well-kept secret that South East Asia Command was prepared for the war continuing for at least another year. One immediate task of the RAF was to help in the repatriation of thousands of debilitated Allied prisoners of war and internees, and this was completed by the following December. At the end of the war, the RAF component of SEAC numbered seventy-three squadrons, but of course many of the wartime entrants among the servicemen were either due for demobilisation or their release dates were coming up. The area allocated to it included Siam, Malaya, French Indo-China south of the 16th parallel, Borneo, Java, Sumatra, Hong Kong, the Dutch East Indies and the Celebes, in addition to the old area of India, Burma and Ceylon. Some of these areas were expected to resist the reimposition of colonial rule, and the RAF was faced with some difficult and delicate tasks at the same time as it was being run down.

Small RAF contingents were sent to Siam but soon withdrawn when the government resumed control. Similarly, two squadrons sent to Indo-China were withdrawn when the French Air Force took over in January 1946. In Java, however, a British division was involved in fighting with extremists, supported by RAF Spitfires, Mosquitos, Thunderbolts and Dakotas. These operations continued until November 1946, when the Dutch resumed responsibility for their colonial possessions until these achieved independence. The RAF's Air Command Far East was created in the same month.

In India, the remaining RAF squadrons were withdrawn soon after the country was partioned and gained its independence in August 1947, both India and Pakistan remaining in the Commonwealth. In Burma, the Dakota squadrons were progressively reduced and the remainder finally withdrawn when the country gained independence and left the Commonwealth in January 1948. In Ceylon, the RAF was able to retain a staging post after the country became independent within the Commonwealth in February 1948.

In Malaya, there was an emergency which began in 1948 and lasted for several years. In China, an RAF Sunderland was involved in the 'Yangste incident'. The frigate HMS *Amethyst* was damaged by Chinese gunfire on the river in April 1949 and, before the warship made its escape, the flying boat made several attempts to transfer medical supplies and a doctor. Following this, three RAF Sunderland squadrons as well as two Auster flights operated in the Korean War, which lasted from June 1950 to July 1953. The Sunderlands helped in the blockade of the Korean coastline, while the Austers were used in army co-operation.

The RAF contribution to the anti-guerrilla war in the Malayan jungle began with detailed reconnaissance of much of the country by Mosquitos and Spitfires, enabling maps to be constructed. Transport was provided by Dakotas, while Beaufighters, Tempests and Harvards strafed terrorist camps and Lincolns made bombing attacks. Meteors, Hornets and Valettas also arrived, and Sunderlands maintained coastal patrols. Dragonfly, Sycamore and Whirlwind helicopters proved their worth, as did the

Scottish Aviation Pioneer in liaison work, while Austers marked targets and carried out reconnaissance. The terrorists began to surrender in 1956, but the emergency did not end until July 1960, almost a year after Malaya achieved independence within the Commonwealth.

Although some of the squadrons were then withdrawn or disbanded, many were retained under the South East Asia Treaty Organization, based in Malaya. When in December 1962 a new emergency arose in the Sultanate of Brunei and the colony of Sarawak in Borneo, these squadrons were well placed to deal with the jungle warfare, although the terrain was even more difficult and the climate far wetter and more humid. Using tactics similar to those learned in Malaya, the rebellions were suppressed. Then Britain came into conflict with Indonesian guerrillas who infiltrated across the borders of these countries and even made a few landings on the west coast of Malaya itself. These conflicts ended in August 1966, after modern aircraft such as Hunters and Belvedere helicopters had arrived in the area. By then, a rapid run down of FEAF was possible, and by October 1971 the last RAF squadron had left the Far East.

In the Mediterranean and Middle East, the RAF had been whittled down to fifteen squadrons by 1947, but still covered an area which included Malta, Cyprus, Palestine, Iraq, the canal zone of Egypt, Bahrain, Sharjah, Oman, Aden, Kenya and Somaliland. By 1949, the command was split in two, the Middle East Air Force and the air component of the British Forces Arabian Peninsula.

Below: *The de Havilland Hornet was designed as a successor to the Mosquito fighter, faster and with a longer range. Originally intended for the war in the Pacific, the first batch was slightly too late for the Second World War. However, Hornets flew operationally in rocket attacks against terrorists in the Malayan jungle during 1951. The last as well as the fastest piston-engined fighters in front-line service in the RAF, they were finally withdrawn in 1955. This Hornet, of 33 Squadron, was being serviced at Tengah in Singapore on 6 October 1951.*

Source: Keystone Collection

Once again, the RAF faced many problems as these countries progressed to independence, in an area which included vital air links as well as major oil fields. One of its first tasks immediately after the war was patrolling with Wellingtons, Warwicks and Spitfires, hunting ships bringing illegal immigrants into Palestine, while the RAF Regiment was involved with the internal security in that country. Some aircraft were destroyed in attacks on airfields. When the British forces pulled out of Palestine in May 1948, the general reconnaissance Lancasters were sent to Malta and the Spitfires to Cyprus.

Unrest in Kenya had been simmering for several years among the Kikuyu tribe, but it flared up into widespread violence in 1952 and by October a state of emergency was declared against the Mau Mau, as they called themselves. Army reinforcements were flown in by Hastings transports, while Harvards of the Rhodesian Air Training Group operated over the terrain, after being fitted with guns and bomb racks. Lincolns and Meteors were brought down from the Canal Zone. In 1955 many of the terrorists surrendered and the RAF was able to withdraw in June of that year.

Trouble arose in the Arabian Gulf during 1952, with an incursion by Saudi Arabians into an Omani village on the border with Abu Dhabi, threatening the important Buraimi Oasis. The RAF regiment, together with Vampires, Lancaster G.R.3s, Valettas and Ansons, blockaded the Saudi positions until they withdrew. However, the Saudis gave support to an 'Omani Liberation Army' formed in 1957 in the rocky interior of Oman, and the RAF gave support to the Sultan's forces and the British SAS by attacking these positions with bombing from Shackletons and rockets from Venoms. The conflict continued until ground forces overcame the rebels' positions in January 1959.

From 1952 onwards, the British withdrew from the Canal Zone, and by December 1954 the Middle East Air Force was established in Cyprus. On that island, however, Britain faced open hostility from April 1955 onwards, when elements of the Greek population began a guerrilla campaign with the objective of union with Greece. Shackletons from Malta were engaged on surveillance patrols to prevent smuggling of arms, while Sycamore helicopters worked with the army in trying to drive the terrorists from their mountain hideouts.

Above: *The first helicopter built in Britain to enter service with the RAF was the Westland Dragonfly, in 1950. It was, however, designed by Sikorsky in the U.S.A. In February 1953, Dragonflies were supplied to 194 Squadron at Sembawang in Malaya and employed on casevac and communications work in the jungle during anti-terrorist operations. 194 Squadron was the RAF's first to be equipped entirely with helicopters, and it continued to use Dragonflies until February 1956. This photograph, of Dragonfly serial WF321, was taken in February 1950.*

Source: RAF Museum P6121

Left: *The Scottish Aviation Pioneer C.C.1 was a high-wing monoplane with seating for the pilot and four passengers, first delivered to the RAF in August 1953. With a short take-off run of only seventy-five yards and even shorter landing run, it proved ideal for liaison work in rough or jungle territories. Forty Pioneers were delivered to seven RAF squadrons, based at home, in Libya, Aden, Cyprus, Malaya and Borneo. It was finally withdrawn in January 1970.*

Source: RAF Museum P9823

While these operations were continuing, the RAF participated in the Anglo-French venture code-named operation 'Musketeer', intended to prevent Egypt taking over control of the Suez Canal. Seven squadrons of Canberra bombers and two of Hunters flew from the U.K. to Cyprus, where three squadrons of Venoms were available, while four squadrons of Valiants and four of Canberras flew to Malta. From the end of October, numerous attacks were made against Egyptian airfields and many aircraft were destroyed on the ground. These were followed by attacks on tanks and communications, and on 4 November Valettas and Hastings dropped 600 paratroops near Port Said. The paratroops were reinforced by a seaborne landing, while Sycamores and Whirlwinds ferried Commandos ashore. A ceasefire was arranged for 6 November, and the last base of the troops was handed over to a United Nations force on 20 December.

In Iraq, unrest continued intermittently after the end of the Second World War and the remaining RAF squadrons were withdrawn to Cyprus from May 1955, closing down finally at Habbaniya in May 1959. In Jordan there was also hostility to the remaining British forces, and the RAF elements withdrew in May 1957. However, Jordan called for help in the following year, when stability was threatened following violence in neighbouring Lebanon. In July 1958 U.S. Marines landed in Lebanon, while Beverleys, Hastings and Valettas ferried British paratroops to Jordan, where they remained until the following month. Yet another problem arose in 1961 when Iraq threatened to annex Kuwait and the RAF flew Commandos to the State in July, discouraging these intentions. In Aden, violent unrest intensified in 1963. In January of the following year the rebels were attacked by Hunters and Shackletons, while Belvederes and Twin Pioneers supplied the ground troops. The rebellion continued until 1968, however, when Britain left Aden.

Air Forces Gulf was then based at Bahrain and a fairly quiet period followed while the Gulf States developed their own air forces, enabling the RAF to withdraw completely from the Gulf at the end of 1971. The last RAF units left Malta in 1979. The Near East Air Force was disbanded in 1976, leaving airfields in Cyprus under the RAF's Strike Command, which at present house a squadron of the RAF Regiment and a squadron of Wessex helicopters.

Right: *The Westland Wessex began service with the RAF in January 1964 as a troop carrier and for casevac operations, but from May 1976 also began search and rescue operations overland and in coastal waters. It is also employed in Northern Ireland on anti-terrorist work. This photograph shows Wessex H.C.2, serial XS675, of 22 Squadron at Finningley in Yorkshire in September 1986.*

Source: RAF Museum colour slide PO51770

Below: *The Westland Sea King H.A.R.3 helicopter was introduced into 202 Squadron in December 1977 for search and rescue operations. It has a longer range and a greater carrying capacity than the Westland Wessex, and many dramatic rescues have been achieved by the crews of this squadron, which is still equipped with the Sea Kings. In the Falklands, 86 Squadron has also been equipped with Sea Kings since April 1986.*

Source: RAF Museum colour slide PO51757

Below right: *Boeing Vertol Chinooks were introduced into 18 Squadron in August 1981, in response to the RAF's need for heavy-lift helicopters. Three squadrons and one flight are now equipped with these helicopters. Fitted with twin rotors, the Chinook is capable of lifting a huge payload of about 22,000 lb. This photograph of serial ZA707, 7 Squadron, was taken at Finningley in Yorkshire on 29 August 1986.*

Source: RAF Museum colour slide PO51803

Below: *The Westland Whirlwind H.A.R.4 was first delivered to the RAF in September 1954, a "tropicalised" version being employed in Malaya during the anti-terrorist campaign. The following February, H.A.R.2s were delivered to Coastal Command for search and rescue operations. These were followed in November 1961 by the H.A.R.10, fitted with a turbine engine instead of a piston engine; these also operated in Borneo, Cyprus and Germany. This photograph shows Whirlwind H.A.R.10, serial XP353, of 22 Squadron at Manston, which was equipped with these machines until November 1981.*

Source: RAF Museum PO13203

Left: *The first helicopter with twin engines and twin rotors to enter RAF service was the Westland Belvedere H.C.1, in September 1961. It was employed as a troop and freight carrier, and on casevac operations. Belvederes operated in Tanzania, in South Arabia and in Borneo, before being retired in 1969. This photograph, of Belvedere serial XG455 in service with 72 Squadron at Odiham in Hampshire, was taken in February 1967.*

Source: RAF Museum P2075

Left: *This Bristol Sycamore H.R.12, serial WV781, was first delivered to the RAF at St Mawgan in Cornwall on 19 February 1952, being the first British-designed helicopter to enter service in the RAF. At home, Sycamores were employed on search-and-rescue operations, but overseas they operated in Malaya, Borneo and Cyprus. They continued in RAF service until August 1972.*

Source: RAF Museum P8870

Right: *The Westland/Aérospatiale Puma was built both in France and in Britain for the RAF, first entering service in June 1971. Pumas are used for troop carrying, transport duties, casevac and as gunships, and have served in Germany, Northern Ireland and Cyprus, as well as in Rhodesia during the 1980 general election after the end of the guerilla war. They remain in service with two RAF squadrons. This photograph is of Puma serial XW220, 230 Squadron.*

Source: RAF Museum P721

Below: *The Hunting Percival Pembroke, derived from a civil feeder-liner, began to replace the venerable Avro Anson as a communications aircraft at the end of 1953. The capacious cabin included eight passenger seats, while reversible pitch airscrews shortened the landing run. Of the fifty-six ordered, six were modified for photo-reconnaissance with 81 Squadron in Malaya, arriving in January 1956. Pembrokes continued in RAF service until 1988.*

Source: RAF Museum PO19515

CHAPTER 16

THE FALKLANDS WAR

When the conflict with the Argentine began in April 1982, Britain's overseas commitments were largely concentrated in Europe, organized as part of NATO to meet any aggression from the Soviet Union. Indeed, it is probably true to say that the majority of British people were barely aware of the existence of the Falkland Islands and their dependency of South Georgia before they became headline news when seized by armed forces of the Argentine.

The decision to form a South Atlantic Task force with the objective of returning the islands to British rule, which the inhabitants had enjoyed for over 200 years, created unusual problems in logistics. The islands were about 8,000 miles from Britain, whereas the Argentine possessed three air bases (with runways of over 7,000 feet) within 600 miles of the combat area.

The first vessels of the Task Force left Portsmouth on 5 April, and the burden of recapturing the islands rested with the Royal Navy, the Royal Marines and the British Army, as well as the RAF. For air support, the Fleet Air Arm provided its Sea Harriers together with its helicopters, which included Sea Kings, Lynxes, Wasps and Wessexes. The Royal Marines Commando Brigade and the Army Air Corps provided Scout and Gazelle helicopters. The contribution of the RAF was numerically smaller but consisted of Vulcans, Nimrods, Hercules, VC10s, Victors, Harriers and Chinook helicopters. The RAF's Chief of Staff was Air Chief Marshal Sir Michael Beetham, who had taken over from Marshal of the Royal Air Force Sir Neil Cameron in March 1977. The ultimate success of the enterprise, which was named operation 'Corporate', depended on the skilful co-operation of all these branches of the armed services as well as the courage of those involved.

Fortunately, the RAF was able to use as a staging post the U.S. air base of Wideawake on the British colonial possession of Ascension Island. This island is situated about halfway to the Falklands, leaving a distance of about 3,900 miles to the targets. The tasks of the RAF included the establishment of an air bridge to Ascension Island and the protection of that tiny island from a possible landing by forces of the Argentine. Its other duties were the provision of anti-submarine and air cover for the Task Force, search and rescue operations, and the maintenance of a threat against airfields on the Argentine mainland in order to tie up enemy aircraft in defence. However, the only aircraft the RAF could use in close support of the navy and army during the reoccupation of the Falklands were its Harriers and helicopters, which could be accommodated in aircraft carriers or container ships. There was, moreover, a worrying defect with the lack of any 'Airborne Early Warning' aircraft such as the U.S. Boeing Sentry.

By comparison with the RAF, nevertheless, the equipment of the Argentine Air Force was not well-balanced, even though it was one of the most powerful in South America. There were only seven transport aircraft, C-130 Hercules, with two more in the tanker role. The long-range bomber fleet contained only six Canberra B.62s, with two Canberra trainers. The shorter-range bomber fleet consisted of about sixty Douglas A-4P Skyhawks, small but powerful single-engined jets which could be effective in anti-shipping strikes in spite of their age. There were about sixty IA.58 Pucarás, twin-

engined turboprop aircraft which were designed primarily for ground attack and were intended for counter-insurgency in their homeland. The jet fighter element, which could also carry out ground attack and anti-shipping operations, consisted of about twenty Dassault-Breguet Mirage IIIEAs, capable of flying at Mach 2, as well as twenty-six Daggers (the Israeli version of the Mirage 5). Among the helicopters, there were three Boeing-Vertol Chinooks, six Bell Hueys and three Aérospatiale Pumas.

The Argentine Navy also had an air arm, based partly on its aircraft carrier *Veinticinco de Mayo*. The aircraft carried included twelve Douglas A-4Q Skyhawks, six piston-engined Grumman S-2Es, several Sikorsky Sea King and three Puma helicopters, three Lockheed Neptunes for maritime reconnaissance, and ten Aermacchi MB.339s used as jet trainers or for attack. Perhaps most threatening of all, there were five Dassault-Breguet Super Etendard supersonic jets, armed with the deadly Exocet sea-skimming missiles. However, the aircraft carrier could not venture out of home waters, since the Royal Navy's nuclear-powered submarines would have soon made short work of it.

The Argentine Army possessed three Aeritalia G.222s, twin-engined turboprop transports which performed a similar role to that of the Hercules. Its helicopter force included two Boeing Vertol Chinooks, nine Agusta A.109s, seven Bell Jet Rangers, twenty Hueys and twelve Pumas.

Other than grass airstrips, there was only one airfield on the Falkland Islands, the

Below: *The aircraft carrier HMS* Hermes, *23,900 tons, approaching the Falkland Islands, with Harrier G.R.3s of 1 Squadron (RAF) and Sea Harrier F.R.S.1s of the Fleet Air Arm on her deck.*

Source: RAF Museum PO21362

4,200 ft strip at Port Stanley, built on rock with a tarmac surface. This could take the transports, the Pucarás and the Aermacchi MB.339s, but it was too short for the Mirages, Daggers, Super Etendards and Skyhawks, unless hydraulic arrester gears could be installed. The Argentine air forces thus faced their own problems in trying to establish superiority when the British attempted their landings.

The RAF had to overcome several difficulties in preparing its aircraft for sea transport. Its Harrier G.R.3 was fitted with the Ferranti FE541 inertial navigation system (in which instruments control the flight path by comparison with stored data), but this equipment was upset by the moving deck of a ship. Ferranti produced a inertial platform which enabled the equipment to be levelled and checked against true north before each Harrier took off, and this was installed on the aircraft carrier HMS *Hermes*. Also, special sealing used by Sea Harriers against salt water corrosion had to be applied to the Harrier G.R.3s.

On 3 May, ten RAF Harriers took off from St Mawgan in Cornwall for Ascension, refuelled en route by Victor K.2 tankers. One of these, probably a spare, turned back to St Mawgan, while another was diverted to West Africa. The other eight arrived safely. Six of these took off to land on the container ship *Atlantic Conveyor*. The other two RAF Harriers remained behind to defend Ascension, where they were joined by the diverted aircraft; these were eventually replaced by the RAF's Phantom F.G.Rs on 24 May. Five more RAF Harriers flew to Ascension at the end of May, and two of these eight Harriers reached HMS *Hermes* off the Falklands before the end of the conflict.

The RAF still possessed three squadrons of Vulcans, including S.R.2s (strategic reconnaissance), B.2s (bombers) and K.2s (tankers). These veteran aircraft were due for retirement, but a Vulcan bomber could still carry twenty-one 1,000 lb 'iron' bombs. Some of the B.2s were refitted with refuelling probes while one was fitted with extra fuel tanks in the bomb bay and equipped with Shrike anti-radar missiles. These B.2s already carried electronic counter-measures which could jam enemy radar. In addition, some of the RAF's Nimrods were fitted with Sidewinder missiles as well as Stingray or Harpoon torpedoes, while some Hercules were converted to the tanker role.

The RAF's operations began when eight Hercules flew to Ascension on 3 April, the day after the Argentine seized the Falklands and two days before the Task Force left Portsmouth. These were followed by streams of other aircraft, until Wideawake air base was dealing with as many as 400 aircraft movements a day, compared with the normal forty per month. Apart from the Hercules, which carried troops, equipment and helicopters, there were Nimrods, Vulcans, VC10s, Sea Kings, Harriers and Phantoms. In the midst of this congestion, priority was given to the RAF's Victor tankers, which played a vital part in enabling attacks to be carried out.

Below: *A British Aerospace Harrier G.R.3 of 1 Squadron landing on the deck of HMS* Hermes.

Source: RAF Museum PO21361

The Task Force arrived at Ascension and then sailed on 16 April for the Falklands, supported by air drops from RAF Hercules while FAA Sea Kings flew anti-submarine patrols from the vessels *Olmeda, Fort Grange* and *Fort Austin*. On the evening of 30 April, two Vulcan bombers left Ascension for an attack on Port Stanley airfield. The main purpose of this operation was to ensure that the Mirages, Daggers, Skyhawks and Super Etendards could not use the runway and would thus be forced to operate at the limits of their ranges from bases on the mainland. One Vulcan turned back with technical trouble but the other was refuelled en route by a series of Victor tankers. Before dawn on the next day it dropped its stick of twenty-one bombs at an angle of about thirty degrees over the runway at Port Stanley. One bomb hit the centre line of the runway, while others damaged parked aircraft and airport buildings. There seemed to be no defensive fire. The attack must have been a very unpleasant shock to the Argentinians, who had optimistically renamed the airfield 'Aeroporto Malvinas'. They were never able to land their fast jets there.

This high-level attack was followed up by a low-level strike at dawn by Sea Harriers of the Task Force, armed with 30 mm Aden cannons and 3,000 lb of bombs, escorted by other Harriers armed with Sidewinder missiles. These met intense ground fire but were not intercepted by enemy aircraft, and all returned safely. The airfield was then bombarded in the afternoon by warships of the Task Force. The Argentine Air Force was stung into action and sent over a number of Mirages. Britain's Harriers had never been involved in air-to-air combat, but on this occasion one of these subsonic aircraft (flown by an RAF pilot, one of seven seconded to the FAA's Sea Harrier force) brought down a supersonic Mirage with an AIM-9L air-to-air missile, while a second Sea Harrier probably destroyed another Mirage. A flight of Canberras then appeared near the Task Force, and one was shot down by a Sea Harrier before the remainder turned back. An Argentine patrol craft was sunk and another badly damaged during the next night by missiles fired by FAA Sea Kings and Lynxes. However, the destroyer HMS *Sheffield* was herself destroyed on the following afternoon by an Exocet missile fired by one of three Super Etendards, which attacked the Task Force from a range of over five miles.

On 4 May, another Vulcan raid was delivered on Stanley airfield, and a Sea Harrier was shot down by ground fire during an attack on Goose Green airfield. Two days later, two more Sea Harriers were lost, it is believed, in a collision in the fog which interrupted air operations for three weeks. On 12 May, several Skyhawks attempted to attack the Task Force; two were shot down and the remainder achieved nothing. Three days later, several Pucarás were destroyed on the ground by FAA Sea Kings, during a landing by SAS troops on Pebble Island, but a Sea King ditched as a result of a bird strike the following day, with the loss of twenty-one men. On 16 May, Sea Harriers destroyed the Argentine support vessel *Rio Carcarania*.

On 18 and 19 May, reinforcements of FAA Sea Harriers as well as the six RAF Harrier G.R.3s were transferred from *Atlantic Conveyor* to the two aircraft carriers HMS *Hermes* and HMS *Invincible*. On 20 May, the RAF Harriers flew from *Hermes* in a devastating attack against fuel dumps near Fox Bay. One of their number was lost the following day to a hand-held Blowpipe ground-to-air missile, during the landings of the ground forces at San Carlos Bay. Two Royal Marine Gazelles were also shot down on that day.

At this point, the Argentine air attacks intensified, the pilots exhibiting determination and courage. They came in low to keep below radar coverage but many were destroyed by Harriers or surface-to-air missiles. Some Aermacchi MB.339s managed to get through and sank the frigate HMS *Ardent* with bombs and rockets, but the British claimed the destruction of nine Mirages or Daggers, five Skyhawks and three Pucarás, without losing any aircraft. However, two Sea Harriers were lost in accidents within the next few days and a third was brought down by a Blowpipe missile. For the most part, the RAF's Harriers were engaged in close support of the advancing ground forces; they carried out this task very effectively, although two more were shot down by ground fire.

On 1 June, a Sea Harrier shot down an Argentine Hercules, probably one of several which were attempting to sink British supply vessels by pushing bombs out of their rear loading ramps. On 8 June, two Sea Harriers accounted for three of a formation of four Skyhawks which approached the Task Force. While these sorties were carried out, the Vulcan B.2 fitted with Shrike missiles operated from Ascension, refuelled by Victor tankers, and attacked enemy radar stations with some success. Other Victors and Nimrods provided photographic reconnaissance of enemy positions, and Nimrods also carried out search-and-rescue missions. The RAF's Hercules transports made parachute supply drops to the fighting troops in the battle zone, while a squadron of the RAF Regiment deployed its surface-to-air Rapier missiles around the beachhead at San Carlos and carried out numerous other tasks such as bomb disposal. On 9 June, an 800 ft airstrip was opened near this beachhead.

The container ship *Atlantic Conveyer* was hit by an Exocet missile. Although the vessel did not sink immediately, three RAF Chinook helicopters were destroyed in the explosion, leaving just one which carried out sterling work for the remainder of the campaign. A final Vulcan raid was made on 11 June. Three days later, the Argentine soldiers were seen to be waving white flags and the fierce campaign was over.

The Ministry of Defence listed the number of Argentine aircraft 'destroyed' or 'probably destroyed' as 117, including twenty-seven Mirages or Daggers, forty-five Skyhawks, twenty-one Pucarás, three Canberras, three MB.339s and one Hercules. The remainder were mostly helicopters. In addition, about thirty other Argentine aircraft were captured. The British lost ten Sea Harriers or RAF Harriers, of which five were in accidents, together with twenty-three helicopters, of which nineteen were in accidents or on board destroyed or damaged ships. No RAF pilots lost their lives. Without doubt, the FAA and the RAF played a major part in securing the British victory in the Falklands.

Above: *Lockheed Hercules C.1s of 30 Squadron, which were employed in the Falklands campaign on supply missions.*
Source: T. Malcolm English

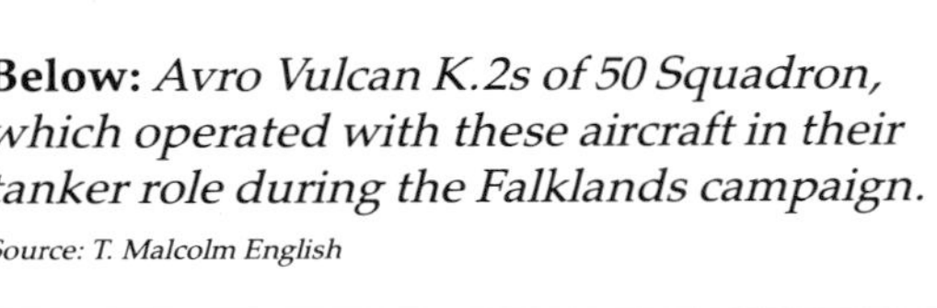

Below: *Avro Vulcan K.2s of 50 Squadron, which operated with these aircraft in their tanker role during the Falklands campaign.*
Source: T. Malcolm English

Above: *British Aerospace Harrier G.R.3s of 1453 Flight at Stanley, formed from a detachment from 1 Squadron in August 1983. They were fitted with Sidewinder air-to-air missiles, with a range of eleven miles at a speed of Mach 3.*

Source: RAF Museum colour slide PO18407

Right: *An Avro Vulcan B.2, similar to those which carried out bombing attacks against Argentine positions at Port Stanley.*

Source: T. Malcolm English

Left: *The Westland/Aérospatiale Gazelle entered service with the RAF in October 1976 and has been employed mainly as a trainer helicopter, although a few serve as communications aircraft with 32 Squadron at Northolt. Most Gazelles were supplied to the Army Air Corps, the Fleet Air Arm, and the Royal Marines. This photograph shows a Gazelle A.H.1 of the Royal Marines in the Falklands during 1982, with a Westland Wessex in the background.*

Source: RAF Museum PO21370

Below: *On 12 October 1982, 1,050 members of the Falklands task force marched through the City of London in a victory parade. These Hawker Siddeley Nimrod M.R.1s, serials XV260, XV247 and XV230, took part in the flypast.*

Source: RAF Museum PO15210

Above: *A British Aerospace Harrier G.R.3 of 1 Squadron, armed with Sidewinder air-to-air missiles, hovering over Stanley aerodrome. Six Pucarás of the Argentine Air Force, all damaged, can be seen in the background.*

Source: RAF Museum PO15209

Left: *Boeing Vertol Chinook H.C.1, serial ZA713, of 18 Squadron, lifting the badly damaged FMA IA 58A Pucará, serial A509, from Stanley aerodrome.*

Source: RAF Museum PO15205

CHAPTER 17

TRAINING AND SUPPORT

After the Second World War, the two training commands, Flying and Technical, were reduced in size even more rapidly than Bomber, Fighter, Coastal and Transport Commands. Meanwhile, Maintenance Command was presented with the formidable task of salvaging immense stocks of equipment and thousands of aircraft which had suddenly become surplus when Japan was forced to surrender, and then disposing of these where possible to industry. Other aircraft, supplied on Lend-Lease, were returned to the U.S.A.

Most of the flying training during the war had taken place with Volunteer Reserve pupils under the Empire Air Training Scheme, which was rapidly wound down while the aircrew members were being steadily demobilised. The remaining provision for training either flying or ground crews was inadequate. Many officers with short-service commissions had served their time during the war and achieved senior ranks, but most of these could be offered regular commissions only at junior ranks. In any event, the RAF required a small but steady flow of younger entrants into the service.

The Royal Air Force College at Cranwell was reopened to provide basic flying training for suitable young men, as well as training entrants into the Administrative Branch and the RAF Regiment. Of course, one of the principal requirements was flying training in jets and very few wartime RAF pilots had experience in these machines of the future. The Gloster Meteor T.7 was introduced in 1948 and remained the only jet trainer for several years.

By 1950, the pattern of pilot training was established with Flying Training School (FTS), Advanced Flying School (AFS) and Operational Conversion Unit (OCU), with the Cranwell cadets joining at the AFS stage after about thirty months of training. Flying instructors were trained at the Central Flying School (CFS) and there was a Central Fighter Establishment (CFE) with flight or squadron commanders. There was also the Empire Air Navigation School and the Empire Test Pilots' School. In 1957 the training of aircrew on fast jets had become so advanced and costly that the Royal Auxiliary Air Force and the Royal Air Force Volunteer Reserve were closed down after a defence review with the object of limiting public expenditure.

As aircraft became more advanced, the RAF's maintenance units were faced with dealing with far more complex technical matters, and it became common for aircraft to be returned to manufacturers for repair. This led to the introduction of specialist working parties from civilian contractors on RAF stations, and a closer liaison grew up between manufacturers and the service. However, the RAF's maintenance units continue to carry out repairs and modifications, and are responsible for the storage of parts and reserves. In September 1973, Maintenance Command was combined with Training Command to form Support Command.

Recruitment into the RAF today is encouraged by sixty-three Careers Information Offices in the U.K. with headquarters at Stanmore in Middlesex. Publicity is provided by organising school and other visits to RAF stations, while recruitment is encouraged by the displays of the Red Arrows aerobatic team, the Falcons free-fall parachute team, the RAF Police Dog display team, the Queen's Colour Squadron of the RAF Regiment,

Left: *The Percival Prentice was introduced into Training Command in November 1947 as one of the successors to the de Havilland Tiger Moth biplane. Unlike its predecessor, the seats were side by side instead of in tandem. It continued as a basic trainer for pilots until 1953, and was also used as a radio trainer and for communications. This photograph of the prototype, serial TV163, was taken on 27 May 1946.*

Source: RAF Museum colour slide P100499

Below: *The Vickers Varsity was produced as a trainer of all RAF crew members, replacing the Wellington T.10 which was used during the war. It entered service in October 1951 and continued until May 1976. This photograph of the prototype Varsity, serial VX828, was taken on 10 September 1949.*

Source: RAF Museum colour slide P100640

and the RAF bands. There are 925 Air Training Corps Squadrons in the U.K., with a membership of about 39,000 cadets, and some thirty per cent of the RAF's entrants originate from that source. The recruitment organisation also arranges presentation teams for the RAF's Engineering, Medical and Nursing Services, which visit schools and universities.

It has always been expensive to train RAF aircrews, but a Harrier pilot now costs about £3 million and a helicopter pilot about £1.6 million. Students arrive in the RAF either from university or by direct entry. The University Air Squadrons (UASs) were threatened with disbandment in the 1960s but sixteen hung on until 1968 when the RAF introduced its university cadet scheme. Nowadays there are seventeen UASs, with the membership standing at about 900. Women have been admitted since 1985. In addition to attracting pilots, they cater for air navigators and the various ground specializations. The entrants are either cadets, bursars or volunteer reservists. Cadets are commissioned as acting pilot officers, while bursars are given the status of officer cadet. The reservists have no commitment to the RAF and are usually young people who simply want to fly but may later apply for a cadetship or a bursarship. The flying members usually spend up to a day each week in flying and one evening a week in ground studies, as well as four weeks a year of flying at an RAF station. The cadets sometimes spend these four weeks at an overseas base. This system is also beneficial to the RAF since it weeds out students who would be unlikely to achieve success in the advanced courses. About forty per cent of fast jet pilots in the RAF today began their service in a University Air Squadron.

The officer training course at RAF College Cranwell admits eight intakes a year. The entrants from university, civilian life, senior NCOs, and Commonwealth or foreign countries number about 1,200 a year, of both sexes. There is quite a tough initial training of eighteen weeks, designed to make each entrant develop his or her identity and qualities of leadership. From this, the entrants go on to basic flying training.

The basic flying training schools, including Cranwell, are being equipped with the new Shorts Tucano, a turboprop trainer which replaces the Jet Provost. Although slower than the aircraft it is replacing, it gives better value for money, since a top speed of about 310 m.p.h. is the maximum required during basic training while an altitude of no more than 20,000 feet is needed at this stage. The aircraft handles like a jet, however, and leads on to the Hawk T.1, the standard jet trainer at Advanced Flying School.

Pilots are 'streamed' according to aptitude. Group 1 includes those suitable for fast jet aircraft, while Group 2 includes multi-engined pilots and Group 3 those who become helicopter pilots. From FTS, the pilots move on to Advanced Flying School and then, if they are destined for fast jets, to a Tactical Weapons Unit (TTU). From there, the next move is to an Operational Conversion Unit, and at last to a squadron. For those pilots (and navigators) who are to join the Tornado G.R.1 squadrons, however, the move from FTS is to the Tri-National Tornado Training Establishment at Cottesmore in Rutland, which includes German and Italian pilots, and thence to the Tornado Weapons Conversion Unit at Honington, before joining a squadron.

The Central Flying School (CFS) trains experienced pilots, at three bases, in the procedures of teaching students how to fly. Graduates from the CFS move on to the other schools and become key members of the RAF's training system. The world-famous Red Arrows aerobatic team is based at CFS at Scampton in Lincolnshire.

All navigators are trained at the Air Navigation School at RAF Finningley, passing through basic navigation training and then moving on to the Tactical Air Navigation System (TANS), a digital computer which takes input from other equipment and displays the aircraft's position. The students practice in a radar navigation ground trainer before air training begins in the Hawker Siddeley Dominie. As with the pilots, the navigators are 'streamed', since they are required in a variety of aircraft such as Tornados, Buccaneers, Phantoms, Nimrods, Hercules, VC.10s and helicopters. Those who are destined for fast jets then train on Jet Provosts at Finningley, while those who are moving on to other groups go back to the Dominie for Advanced Navigation Training. Nowadays, navigators enjoy equal status with pilots on the RAF's ladder of promotion; they can become captains of aircraft and commanding officers of squadrons, stations and groups, although a navigator has yet to occupy the position of Chief of Air Staff. Air Electronics officers and Air Engineers are also trained on Dominies at Finningley.

Helicopter crewmen, including the winchmen, are trained on Gazelles and Wessexes at FTS at Shawbury in Shropshire, and on Chinooks and Pumas at Odiham in Hampshire. The Central Air Traffic Control School is also at Shawbury.

In 1940, the RAF established a Parachute Training School, at Manchester's Ringway airport under the joint direction of the RAF and the army. After various moves, the RAF's school arrived at Brize Norton in Oxfordshire during 1975 and remains at this base today. In 1982, it provided a valuable detachment to the Special Forces which supported the SAS in the Falklands. Training is provided by Hercules transports, which can carry up to ninety fully-laden paratroops of the airborne forces of the Army, Royal Marines or

Above: *The de Havilland Chipmunk was built as a tandem two-seat successor to the Tiger Moth biplane. It first flew in May 1946 and was adopted by the RAF in 1949. Easy to handle and with good aerobatic qualities, it provided* ab initio *training for many RAFVR, National Service and direct-entry pilots until finally withdrawn in 1973. This photograph shows the first production Chipmunk which entered service in the RAF, serial WB549.*

Source: RAF Museum P6589

Right: *The Handley Page Marathon T.11 was a navigation trainer adapted from the civil medium-range airliner, first delivered in December 1953 to the Air Navigation School at Hullavington in Wiltshire. It carried a crew of three and two pupil navigators. Twenty-eight Marathons served in the RAF, the last being retired in June 1958.*

Source: RAF Museum P820

the RAF regiment. Drops sometimes take place at night, from heights of up to 25,000 feet.

Ground subjects are taught at various stations, notably the Schools of Technical Training at Halton and Cosford, expected to combine at Cosford in the near future. Students from these schools can rise to high rank, and some enter the flying branches. In addition there is the Airman's Command School at RAF Hereford which began in September 1980 for potential sergeants and now runs two courses, one for senior and the other for junior NCOs. Over 3,000 students pass through the school each year, which gives three weeks of instruction to the senior students and two weeks to the junior students.

The RAF runs a small school at Mount Batten in Devonshire, which provides an aircrew survival course, a combat survival and rescue officers' course, a survival rescue course for instructors, and a non-temperate climate course which is held in Brunei. The students number about 2,000 a year. Most are from the aircrew branches but others are from the physical education and medical branches or from the RAF Regiment. Apart from this school, instructors from the RAF Regiment itself provide courses to RAF personnel of all grades, covering the subjects of ground operations, ground defence and combat.

Lastly, the RAF reserve forces provide important training facilities. In the mid 1970s, the value of the Royal Auxiliary Air Force and the Royal Air Force Volunteer Reserve was again recognised, so that nowadays there are sixteen R Aux AF and four RAFVR units. These forces carry out regular training exercises and are fully capable of backing up the RAF immediately in critical times. The R Aux AF maintains three maritime headquarters units, seven regiment squadrons, one movements squadron, one aeromedical evacuation squadron and four support forces, numbering over 2,000 men and women. The RAFVR consists of about 180 men and women, providing two intelligence flights, a photographic interpretation flight and a public relations flight. These groups of enthusiastic volunteers are both highly dedicated and cost-effective.

Left: *The second production Chipmunk, serial WB550, delivered to Oxford University Air Squadron at Kidlington, near Oxford, photographed on 29 September 1949. The type was designated T.10 and the total delivered to the RAF was 735, the last being XZ884 on 1 October 1953.*

Source: RAF Museum colour slide P100141

Below: *The Hunting Percival Jet Provost T.1 began to replace the piston-engined Provost in 1955. In this machine, the pupil pilot began basic training on jets, often after only a few hours air experience on piston-engined trainers. This photograph of the prototype Jet Provost, serial XD674, was taken on 25 August 1954.*

Source: RAF Museum colour slide P100113

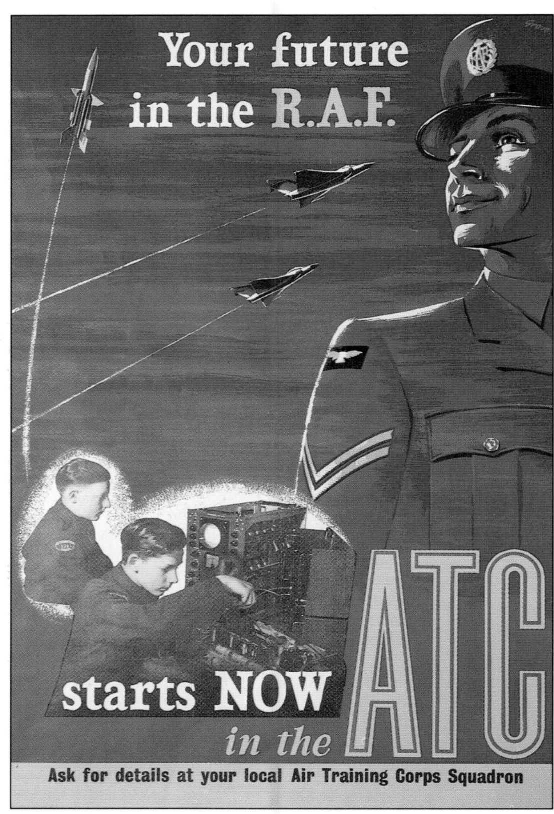

Above: *The Air Training Corps, founded in 1941, has always been highly regarded by the RAF. This poster appeared in about 1959. Nowadays, 925 ATC squadrons encourage boys and girls to take an interest in aviation, their activities including evening lectures, visits to RAF stations and air museums, sports and even gliding.*

Source: RAF Museum (Crown copyright) P00356

Far right: *The British Aircraft Corporation Jet Provosts T.3, T.4 and T.5 followed the T.1 in succession, each with various improvements and developments. Provosts remain in service in the RAF's Flying Training Schools. This photograph is of T.5 serial XW319, 3 F.T.S.*

Source: RAF Museum colour slide PO18685

Left: *The dual-control English Electric Canberra T.4 entered service in 1954. This photograph, taken in September 1952, is of the prototype WN467.*

Source: RAF Museum colour slide P100254

Below: *In 1953, the Hunting Percival Provost began to replace the Percival Prentice as a basic trainer for pilots. It had a higher performance than its predecessor and four Provosts of the Central Flying School, known as* The Sparrows, *gave displays of formation aerobatics. The last machine continued in service until 1969. This photograph of the prototype, serial WE522, was taken on 21 May 1952.*

Source: RAF Museum colour slide P100515

Above: *Gloster Meteor F.7 trainers, photographed at Driffield in Yorkshire in October 1949. The last Gloster Meteor of the RAF was taken out of service in July 1961.*

Source: Keystone Collection

Left: *The Boulton Paul Balliol was originally designed as an advanced trainer with a turboprop engine, as shown in this photograph of the third prototype, serial VL935. However, a decision was made to revert to a piston-engined trainer as a successor to the North American Harvard. In 1952, piston-engined Balliols entered service at 7 Flying Training School at Cottesmore in Rutland. Soon afterwards, another decision was made to concentrate on jet trainers and the Balliol was phased out, until the last flew with the RAF in 1957.*

Source: RAF Museum PO18347

Above: *The Hawker Hunter T.7 was a modified version for dual-control training, entering service with the RAF's Operational Conversion Units from August 1958. Hunters continued in service until June 1976. This photograph is of one of the first T.7s, serial XL586.*

Source: Aviation Bookshop

Below: *A British Aircraft Corporation Lightning T.5, serial XS417, of the Lightning Training Flight.*

Source: RAF Museum PO18669

Above: *A British Aerospace Hawk T.1A of Central Flying School. Although it carries out the role of the RAF's standard advanced trainer, the T.1A is also a back-up aircraft in the U.K. defence system.*

Source: T. Malcolm English

Below: *The Hawker Siddeley Dominie T.1, a military version of the HS.125 executive jet, was the first jet aircraft employed by the RAF as a navigation trainer. It entered service in December 1965 and continues today at Finningley in Yorkshire. This photograph, of Dominie T.1 serial XS735 of 6 Flying Training School, was taken in August 1986 at Fairford in Gloucestershire.*

Source: RAF Museum colour slide PO51344

Left: *The Hawker Siddeley Gnat T.1 replaced de Havilland Vampire T.11s from February 1962 as the RAF's standard advanced trainer for jet fighters and bombers. It had two seats in tandem and was fully aerobatic with drop tanks. In 1964, Gnats of 4 Flying Training School at Valley in Anglesey formed an aerobatic team named the* Yellowjacks, *which was replaced by the* Red Arrows *during the following year. This photograph shows the third production Gnat, serial XM693.*

Source: RAF Museum colour slide P36009

Above: *The Scottish Aviation Bulldog began to replace the de Havilland Chipmunk as the RAF's standard* ab initio *trainer for pilots in April 1973. It is a sturdy piston-engined aircraft with two seats, used for teaching the full range of aerobatics, instrument flying and cross-country navigation. The trainer remains in RAF service. This photograph shows Bulldog T.1 serial XX515 of Central Flying School at Scampton in Lincolnshire.*

Source: RAF Museum colour slide PO18658

Below: *The two-seater trainer British Aerospace Harriers T.2 and T.4 entered service in July 1970.*

Source: RAF Museum colour slide PO18656

Above: *The Hawker Siddeley Gnat continued as the RAF's standard advanced trainer until replaced by the British Aerospace Hawk in 1978.*

Source: RAF Museum PO19098

Right: *The British Aerospace (Hawker Siddeley) Hawk T.1 began to enter service with the RAF in November 1976, superseding the Hawker Siddeley Gnat and the Hunter T.7 as an advanced trainer. Although more powerful and with a longer endurance than its predecessors, it has proved comfortable to fly as well as highly reliable. From November 1979, Hawks have replaced Gnats in the* Red Arrows *aerobatic team.*

Source: RAF Museum P3473

Above: *The Shorts Tucano turboprop trainer was selected as the RAF's successor to the Jet Provost, the decision being based partly on lower operating costs. Unlike its predecessor, it had tandem seating instead of the side-by-side seating employed for many years. The Tucano is now being introduced into the RAF training units.*

Source: RAF Museum PO22149

Below: *The Scottish Aviation Jetstream T.1 replaced the Vickers Varsity and entered Training Command in June 1973 for training pilots in twin-engined turboprops. Jetstreams continue in service at 6 Flying Training School at Finningley in Yorkshire. This photograph, of serial XX499, was taken at Upper Heyford in Oxfordshire.*

Source: RAF Museum PO51596

CHAPTER 18

RAF IN THE NINETIES

Below: *The Sepecat Jaguar, produced from an Anglo-French venture between British Aircraft Corporation and Dassault/Breguet, began to enter squadron service in March 1974. It is a single-seat aircraft, designed primarily for high speed and low-level ground attack, but it is also capable of classic air-to-air combat. Jaguars are now being replaced by Panavia Tornados. This photograph, of Jaguar G.R.1, serial XX119, of 226 Operational Conversion Unit, was taken at Upper Heyford in Oxfordshire in August 1986.*
Source: RAF Museum colour slide PO51609

Although the RAF of today is numerically small, it is equipped with some of the most advanced and costly machines yet devised for the purpose of defence or waging war. By comparison with the RAF at the end of the Second World War in Europe, which possessed an operational strength of 9,200 aircraft and over a million officers and airmen, the RAF in 1990 consisted of only fifty-two squadrons and seven flights equipped with front-line aircraft, with a total force of about 83,200 officers, airmen and airwomen. It shared in a defence budget which formed less than twelve per cent of the U.K.'s public expenditure. Air Chief Marshal Sir Peter Harding took over as Chief of Air Staff in February 1988, while Marshal of the Royal Air Force Sir David Craig was appointed as Chief of the Defence Staff.

Other than in Germany, the RAF's commitments overseas are not normally extensive. There are four flights in the Falklands, consisting of one of Phantoms for air defence, one of Hercules for tanker and reconnaissance, one of Chinook helicopters for air transport, and one of Sea King helicopters for search and rescue. These are supported by a squadron of the RAF Regiment equipped with Rapier missiles. In Belize, a flight of Harriers, a flight of Puma helicopters and half a squadron of the RAF Regiment discourage any territorial ambitions of the country's neighbours. Hong Kong is the home for a squadron of Wessex helicopters which work in close liaison with the army and police, in such tasks as search and rescue, troop lifting, disaster relief, prevention of smuggling and operations concerning illegal immigrants. Another squadron of Wessex helicopters is based at Cyprus, together with a squadron of the RAF Regiment equipped with light armour. Here, the RAF base of Akrotiri remains an important staging post for aircraft flying between Britain and Africa, the Middle East and Far East, while the island is frequently used by the RAF for training exercises.

In Germany, the RAF maintains seven squadrons of Tornado G.R.1s for strike/attack and one of G.R.1As for reconnaissance, together with two squadrons of Harrier G.R.3s for offensive support. The supersonic, two-seat Tornado G.R.1A is one of the RAF's most successful weapons in the constant need for tactical intelligence. It is fitted with the Infra-red Line Scanner (IRLS), with one sensor mounted in a blister under the fuselage and two more mounted sideways. These sensors measure the relative levels of thermal radiation, by both day and night, from horizon to horizon. The system is controlled by a computer and recorded with high resolution on video tapes. Although its two 27 mm cannons have been removed to make way for this equipment, the Tornado retains its offensive capability with a warload of 18,000 lb, which can include a nuclear weapon or laser-guided bombs. Pilots of these aircraft are required to fly at an altitude of about 100 feet at speeds in excess of 700 m.p.h., in all weathers, to avoid radar detection. For air transport in Germany, there is a squadron of Andovers as well as one of Pumas and one of Chinooks. For air defence, there are two squadrons of Phantoms supported by four squadrons of the RAF Regiment with Rapier missiles and one squadron with light armour.

At home, the RAF's Strike Command at High Wycombe in Buckinghamshire consists of three groups. With headquarters at Upavon in Wiltshire, No. 1 Group has

Left: *A Sepecat Jaguar G.R.1 of 54 Squadron, based at Coltishall in Norfolk, with two BAC Lightnings in the background.*

Source: T. Malcolm English

two squadrons of Tornado G.R.1s, three of Jaguar G.R.1s and one of Harriers, for strike/attack, reconnaissance and offensive support. The single-seat Jaguar is equipped with two 30 mm Aden cannons and five weapon stations which can carry up to 1,000 lb of bombs; these can be free-fall, cluster or laser-guided. It also has the Ferranti inertial navigation and attack system, which enables the pilot to navigate and deliver his weapons accurately, even at low level, and displays the aircraft's position to him on a moving map. The single-seat Harrier G.R.5 is coming into service, with a larger wing than its predecessor and capable of carrying double the payload for twice the distance. No. 1 Group also has twelve tanker and transport squadrons, equipped with Hercules, Tristars, VC10s, Victors and Andovers, as well as Chinook, Puma and Wessex helicopters. This air transport force maintains a twenty-four-hour-a-day service on a world basis, like a huge charter company working in constantly changing conditions. For ground defence, the RAF Regiment provides four squadrons with light armour and one field squadron. Three more field squadrons are manned by the R Aux AF.

With headquarters at Bentley Priory in Middlesex, No. 11 Group controls the air defence of the U.K., with five squadrons of Tornado F.3s and two of Phantoms, as well as a squadron of Shackletons for airborne early warning. The group also controls the ballistic early warning system and the aircraft early warning network. Its area extends from the coastal approaches to Norway and Iceland to the south-west approaches and the Scilly Islands. In this region, aircraft of the group sometimes provide a close 'escort service' for uninvited guests in the forms of the Russian Tupolev Tu-20 'Bear' or Tu-16 'Badger', although this type of intrusion has become less threatening with the détente between East and West. For ground defence in the group, the RAF Regiment mans two squadrons with Bloodhound missiles and two with Rapier missiles, while the R Aux AF element of the RAF Regiment provides a field squadron as well as another squadron armed with 35 mm twin-barrelled A.A. guns served by the Skyguard fire control equipment.

No. 18 Group, with headquarters at Northwood in Greater London, provides maritime patrols with four squadrons of Nimrods. Regrettably, the cost of maintaining this elegant aircraft are now so high that the remaining machines are likely to be run down and will disappear within a few years. There is as yet no arrangement for replacements for their role as maritime patrol and air-sea rescue aircraft. Until 1990, this group also maintained a squadron of Canberras for reconnaissance. This aircraft, dubbed the 'Cranberry' by the RAF, still continues its long service which began with its maiden flight in May 1949, but solely with Support Command. Canberra pilots point out that the machine can out-turn the Tornado at 50,000 feet, and they believe that it still has many years of useful life ahead. For strike/attack in the maritime role, No. 18 Group operates two squadrons of Buccaneer S2Bs, armed with either laser-guided bombs or Sea Eagle 'sea-skimming' air-to-surface missiles. For search and rescue, there is a squadron of Sea King helicopters and another of Wessex helicopters. For ground defence, there is a field squadron of the R Aux AF. The group also controls the Queen's Flight at Benson in Oxfordshire, with three BAe 146s and two Wessex helicopters.

Strike Command is in the middle of a major re-equipment programme. The Boeing Sentry will become the RAF's standard 'airborne early warning' aircraft, replacing the faithful Shackleton A.E.W.s of No. 11 Group. It had been intended originally that an A.E.W. version of the Nimrod would perform this role, but after mounting costs and much debate this programme was cancelled in December 1986. The Sentry, which has been in service with the USAAF since 1977 and with NATO since 1983, has an enormous 'rotodome' radar antenna above the fuselage which can detect aircraft flying at low level as well as high level. It operates as a command post for other aircraft and can remain on station for six hours when 1,000 miles from base. The RAF's first Sentry arrived at Waddington in Lincolnshire on 4 July 1990. It is an E-3D version, capable of two methods of air-to-air refuelling. This machine can also be equipped for maritime reconnaissance, and it is possible that Sentries will also replace the Nimrods of No. 18 Group.

Strike Command's new helicopter will be the multi-role EH 101, manufactured by EH Industries, a company formed in 1980 by Westland Helicopters and Augusta. The Royal Navy has ordered fifty EH 101s, to be known as the Merlin, and will use them in all-weather operations from land bases, as well as from large and small vessels and oil rigs. This naval version will be fitted with the latest detection equipment and will also be able to carry four homing torpedoes. The RAF has ordered twenty-five EH 101s to replace its Pumas as support helicopters during the 1990s. The new helicopter will improve the capacity of the RAF in providing mobility for the army, since it is able to transport thirty combat-equipped troops for an estimated distance of over 600 miles with standard fuel tanks. It will doubtless be used for other roles in Strike Command, RAF Germany and bases overseas.

One of the most ambitious projects which will affect the RAF is the European Fighter Aircraft (EFA), being developed by CMM and Dornier in Germany, Aeritalia in Italy, CASA in Spain and British Aerospace in the United Kingdom. Managed by Eurofighter

GmbH in Munich, the outcome will be a supersonic and very agile single-seat fighter, capable of short take-offs and landings, with a combat radius of about 320 miles. It is being designed mainly for the air-to-air role but will be also capable of ground attack. It is expected that large-scale production will begin in 1993. Deliveries of nearly 800 aircraft are expected to begin in 1996, subject to any political rethinking. In the RAF, the EFA will serve with Strike Command, replacing the ageing Phantoms and Jaguars. It will also replace the Phantoms in Germany, where it is believed that it will be more than a match for the equivalent Russian fighters, and will serve in RAF bases around the world. Equipped with the latest developments in avionics and most up-to-date weapons systems, it is designed for a service life of twenty-five years.

The RAF is being equipped with even more sophisticated and specialist weaponry. One of the objectives is to reduce the enemy's ability to bring down RAF aircraft, by the use of such weapons as the Martel anti-radar missile with which the maritime Buccaneers of No. 18 Group are equipped. The RAF has also obtained the Alarm (air-launched anti-radar missile) for a similar use overland. This enables the Tornados to create a corridor in the enemy's defences through which attacking RAF aircraft can penetrate. A forthcoming weapon is the ARD (anti-radiation drone), a slow-speed drone launched from the ground which will suppress the air defence systems of enemy aircraft and enable them to be tackled by the RAF's interceptors. This is expected to be in service shortly.

A weapon which has recently come into service with the RAF's Tornado G.R.1s is the JP233 cluster bomb, a dispenser containing SG357 explosive devices, which produce craters in runways, together with HB876 explosives, which prevent the enemy from effecting repairs for a period. The RAF's anti-tank (or armoured vehicle) weapon is the BL755, which contains 147 bomblets delivered on the principle of shotgun pellets but at very high velocity. An even more effective version of this weapon, designed to penetrate any advanced armour of the future, will enter service in the mid 1990s.

For the purpose of destroying static targets such as bridges, power stations or oil refineries, the RAF has a so-called 'smart' bomb, the laser-guided Paveway. The laser enables the bomb, after the target has been pinpointed by the acquisition system of one aircraft, to be delivered with precise accuracy by another aircraft. A similar bomb, capable of being launched at low level further away from the target, is expected to enter service shortly. This new bomb will be developed further so that it incorporates a seeker capable of recognizing its target. Fitted in its bombs, the RAF has what is regarded as the most effective fuse in the world, the multi-function bomb fuse (MFBF).

The RAF will also procure 'stand-off' weapons, which can be delivered from outside the range of some of the enemy's defences. For fixed targets, the RAF is obtaining for its Tornados the modular stand-off weapon (MSOW), which is being developed by five NATO countries. Another version of this weapon, designed for mobile targets, is also being developed.

Above: *Sepecat Jaguar G.R.1 of 41 Squadron, based at Coltishall in Norfolk.*

Source: T. Malcolm English

Left: *The pilots and Hawk T.1s of the Red Arrows constitute the RAF's premier display team of today, performing precise and intricate manoeuvres with nine aircraft. First formed with Gnats in 1965, the Red Arrows received their Hawks in the winter of 1979/80. The team has become a symbol of both flying skill and high standard of engineering. It has made an enormous contribution to the prestige of the RAF throughout the world. This photograph was taken at Mildenhall in Suffolk on 24 May 1986.*

Source: RAF Museum colour slide PO50519

Although it was hoped that the RAF's formidable array of aircraft and weaponry would never be put to the test in war, world events were to determine otherwise, after Iraq invaded Kuwait on 2 August 1990 and then announced that it had annexed the country. The RAF began to make plans immediately, since Britain was one of the thirty coalition countries intent on implementing the resolutions of the United Nations and removing Iraq from this sovereign state.

The British code-named the entire enterprise operation 'Granby', while to the Americans it was at first operation 'Desert Shield'. A week after the invasion, the RAF sent five Mobile Air Movements Squadron teams to the area by transport aircraft, together with cargo handling equipment. Two of these handling teams were sent to Dhahran in Saudi Arabia, in order to receive a squadron of Tornados, while five were sent to Akrotiri in Cyprus in order to reinforce this staging post. Shortly afterwards, two more teams were sent to Thumrait in Oman, to receive a squadron of Jaguars. Equipment was loaded by these teams at the RAF stations of Coltishall in Norfolk, Wittering in Northamptonshire and Coningsby in Lincolnshire. The pressure on the transport squadrons at Lyneham in Wiltshire was immense, but the work of moving equipment and troops was carried out smoothly. The combat aircraft flew out to the area, together with Victor K2 refuelling tankers.

After international sanctions had been applied to Iraq and all diplomatic efforts had failed, the coalition forces began air operations in the early hours of 16 January 1991, under the American operation 'Desert Storm'. The air attacks had been preceded by intelligence provided by satellite photographs, decrypting of Iraqi communications signals, and reconnaissance by high-flying American TR-1s and Boeing Sentries. Although the RAF's contribution was numerically small by comparison with that of the USAF, the squadrons were allocated one of the most important and dangerous tasks of the campaign – the neutralisation of the enemy's airfields and aircraft. The Alarm anti-radar missiles, which had been undergoing evaluation trials, were almost certainly used by Tornado F-3s and Jaguars to blind enemy defences while the Tornado G.R.1s delivered attacks with JP233 cluster bombs on runways and Paveway 'smart' bombs against aircraft bunkers. Jaguars also joined in attacks with laser-guided bombs, dive-bombing from heights of 15,000 feet. Then Buccaneer S2Bs of No. 18 Group were also sent from Lossiemouth in Morayshire to the Gulf, partly to act as target designators for the Tornados and partly to carry out their own bombing attacks. By 12 February, the RAF had dropped 2,000 of their 1,000 lb bombs on various military targets such as bunkers and bridges, and further consignments of these weapons arrived by sea. Air refuelling for the fighter-bombers was carried out by Victor tankers. The technical superiority of the RAF and USAF over the equipment supplied to the Iraqis by the Russians became startingly apparent.

The Lynx helicopters of Fleet Air Arm, operating from British destroyers, made a valuable contribution to the air war by destroying Iraqi naval vessels with their Sea Skua missiles. It is possible that Nimrod aircraft of No. 18 Group located and identified some of these enemy vessels.

Below: *the Panavia Tornado must be classed as the premier aircraft of today's RAF. First introduced as an operational aircraft in January 1982, it is a swing-wing tactical strike aircraft capable of operating just above ground level with a formidable range of weaponry. The guidance system on board the aircraft enables the crew to penetrate deep into enemy territory in all weathers and deliver their warload with precision. This photograph is of the second prototype Tornado F.2, ZA267, in April 1983.*

Source: RAF Museum colour slide PO15198

Above: *A Tornado F.3 of 11 Squadron, based at Leeming in Yorkshire.*
Source: T. Malcolm English

Below: *A Tornado F.2 of 229 Operational Conversion Unit, based at Coningsby in Lincolnshire.*
Source: T. Malcolm English

Unfortunately, six Tornados were lost during these operations. However, coupled with intense bombing from medium and high level by US bombers, the attacks were so effective that many of the surviving Iraqi aircraft, such as the Su-24s, MiG-29s and Mirages, were forced to flee the country for internment in Iran. Iraq was then bereft of any air cover for her ground forces and was also without reliable intelligence as to the movement of coalition ground forces.

When the ground war began in the early morning of 24 February, under the American operation 'Desert Sabre', the air supremacy of the coalition forces proved a potent factor. Within three days, armoured columns had routed and surrounded the Iraqi forces in Kuwait and southern Iraq. As the enemy columns attempted to withdraw to Baghdad, they were subjected to an accurate and devastating bombardment from the air and the ground, on a scale which the world had never seen before. The RAF's combat aircraft joined in these attacks, with the Jaguars using CRV7 rockets. The Iraqi forces suffered enormous casualties and collapsed. Large numbers of their troops surrendered, while casualties among the coalition forces were amazingly light. With the enemy defeated, the offensive was suspended on 28 February. The Chief of the Defence Staff, Sir David Craig, sent a message to Strike Command at High Wycombe, which included these words:

"Today's suspension of hostilities after one of the most outstanding, successful and impressive campaigns in warfare is a moment for congratulation and thanksgiving. Under your leadership all the forces and staffs of Operation Granby have performed superbly."

Once again, the RAF has served its country with skill and courage, but there is some doubt about its future role. Since April 1975, Strike Command has been allocated to NATO's Supreme Allied Commander Europe (SACEUR), but the political and military developments during 1990 have resulted in a decrease in tension between East and West. It seems possible that this will result in large-scale cuts in military expenditure and the RAF will lose more of its squadrons. There is no doubt, however, that the RAF will continue to maintain and improve its technical superiority as well as to provide such a high mobility that it is able to strike any aggressor in the right place and at the same time, over land, sea and in the air. No matter what the twists and turns of world politics, the RAF, with its excellent standards and distinguished history, will always be ready to serve both NATO and its country.

Left: *The experience of the Falklands War brought into prominence the need for both air refuelling and long-range transport in the RAF. Nine Lockheed Tristar airliners were purchased, all for serveice with 216 Squadron, which was re-formed at Brize Norton in Oxfordshire. The Tristar K.1 is a tanker/freighter, while the K.C.2 is a tanker/passenger aircraft. This photograph of serial ZD948 was taken in 1983, while still in the passenger role and before conversion to the K.1 configuration.*
Source: RAF Museum PO18299

Above: *A Hawker Siddeley Buccaneer S.2 of 208 Squadron, photographed at Lakenheath in Suffolk on 12 July 1986.*
Source: RAF Museum PO52159

Right: *Buccaneer S.2s of 12 Squadron, based at Lossiemouth in Morayshire, on 'escort duties' with a Tupolev Tu-20 (Bear), a Russian maritime and reconnaissance aircraft which had been picked up by RAF radar.*
Source: T. Malcolm English

Left: *The Boeing E.3A Sentry was ordered from the U.S.A. in 1986 as the RAF's new early-warning aircraft, following the Ministry of Defence's decision to cancel the Nimrod A.E.W., which had been under development for several years. It is expected to come into service in 1990, when it will replace the Avro Shackletons which are still performing this role. This photograph of LX-N90456 of NATO's early-warning force was taken at Mildenhall in Suffolk on 24 May 1986.*
Source: RAF Museum PO50719

Right: *A McDonnell Douglas Phantom F.4 of 29 Squadron. This squadron has since been equipped with Panavia Tornado F.3s.*
Source: T. Malcolm English

Below: *Hawker Siddeley Harrier G.R.3s of 3 and 4 Squadrons, in the engineering wing hangar at Gutersloh in West Germany during 1981.*
Source: T. Malcolm English

Above: *McDonnell Douglas Harpoon air-to-surface missile. This sea-skimming anti-shipping weapon has a range of seventy-five miles, and several are carried in the bomb-bays of the RAF's Nimrods.*
Source: Jeremy Flack/Aviation Photographs International

Above: *British Aircraft Corporation Rapier ground-to-air missile, photographed in the Falklands. Since 1972, these missiles have been used by the RAF Regiment in defence of airfields against low-flying attack.*
Source: Jeremy Flack/Aviation Photographs International

Left: *The RAF operators of a Rapier missile.*
Source: Jeremy Flack/Aviation Photographs International

Below: *A British Aerospace BAe 146 C.C.2 of the Queen's Flight. The Queen first flew in one of these VIP aircraft on 2 August 1986. A BAe 146 was employed on the internal flights during her visit to China the following October.*
Source: Jeremy Flack/Aviation Photographs International

Right: *Four sections of Phantoms flying over Buckingham Palace during the 50th anniversary celebrations of the Battle of Britain, on Saturday 15 September 1990.*
Source: Jeremy Flack/Aviation Photographs International

Below: *A mock-up of the European Fighter Aircraft, now being developed by Britain, West Germany, Italy and Spain.*
Source: Jeremy Flack/Aviation Photographs International

Above: *Troops deploying from a Puma HC1 helicopter of the RAF, on manoeuvres at Ras al Gar in Saudi Arabia. Pumas were camouflaged in 'desert sand'. The rotor blades were temporarily removed, and the helicopters were then flown out to the Gulf in transport aircraft.*
Source: Crown copyright (RAF), print from M.A.R.S. Lincs

Below: *A Chinook Mk I helicopter of the RAF, This is the RAF's heavy lift helicopter, of great value in combined operations.*
Source: Crown Copyright (RAF), print from M.A.R.S. Lincs

Above: *Lockheed Tristar multi-role transport/ tanker of 216 Squadron, at Palermo, painted in the washable camouflage colour 'desert sand'. These aircraft were used to carry troops and freight to the Gulf, as well as for air-to-air refuelling. By early Janurary 1991, the RAF and charter aircraft had airlifted about 30,000 British troops to the Gulf.*
Source: Jeremy Flack/Aviation Photographs International

Left: *The short version of the Lockheed Hercules, the C1, being camouflaged in 'desert sand' at Lyneham in Wiltshire. This aircraft has a refuelling probe. Hercules C1s, together with the 'stretched' version, the C3, bore much of the burden in transporting personnel and freight to the Gulf. A Hercules of 47 Squadron was the first RAF aircraft to land at Kuwait airport after the liberation of the country.*
Source: Jeremy Flack/ Aviation Photographs International

Left: *A Tornado F3 of the RAF, with standard European grey camouflage, flying from Dhahran over Saudi Arabia. It is fitted with Sidewinder air-to-air missiles beside the fuel tanks, as well as Sky Flash air-to-air missiles, for longer range, recessed under the fuselage. These fighter aircraft had little opportunity to engage in air-to-air combat, since many of the Iraqi fighters took refuge in Iran, where they were interned.*

Source: Crown Copyright (RAF), print from M.A.R.S. Lincs.

Below: *Two Tornado GR1s of the RAF, camouflaged in 'desert sand', flanked by two Tornado F3 fighters in standard grey camouflage. A laser target designator can be seen beneath the fuselage of each GR1, while the F3s are carrying air-to-air missiles. The photograph was taken from one of the F3s.*

Source: T. Malcolm English

Right: *A Nimrod MR1 of No. 18 Group, flying from Kinloss in Morayshire. A detachment of Nimrod MR2Ps, the version fitted with the more advanced 'Searchwater' electronic equipment, was sent to the Gulf to carry out maritime patrols as well as for the search and rescue of downed airmen. The Nimrod can also carry Sidewinder air-to-air missiles and Harpoon anti-shipping missiles.*

Source: Jeremy Flack/Aviation Photographs International

Below: *A Tornado F3 of the RAF, in standard camouflage, carrying Sidewinder and Sky Flash missiles, flying from Dhahran in Saudi Arabia. Detachments of several Tornado squadrons, both from the UK and from Germany, were sent to the Gulf.*

Source: Crown Copyright (RAF), print from M.A.R.S. Lincs.

Left: *A Jaguar GR1 deployed in the Gulf, with a laser target designator in the nose, 1,000 lb bombs in tandem under the wings, and overwing Sidewinder missiles mounted above the bomb pylons. The devices on the outboard pylons are intended to deceive enemy radar and missiles. These aircraft dived from 15,000 feet to bomb Iraqi positions during the Gulf War.*

Source: Crown Copyright (RAF), print from M.A.R.S. Lincs.

Below: *Two Jaguar GR1s refuelling from a VC10 tanker, with a Tornado GR1 in the foreground, flying near the Gulf war zone. The Tornado and the Jaguars are painted in 'desert sand'. The VC10 is painted in 'hemp', which is now the RAF's standard colour for this type of aircraft.*

Source: Crown Copyright (RAF), print from M.A.R.S. Lincs.

Above: *The Eurofighter will provide the backbone of the RAF interceptor force. It can carry a range of weaponry, including ASRAAM and Sidewinder air-to-air missiles.*
Source: Jeremy Flack/Aviation Photographs International

Left: *Replacement of the aging C-130K Hercules became an RAF priority and 25 of the much-improved C-130Js were ordered as the Hercules C.5 and stretched C.4 (shown).*
Source: Jeremy Flack/Aviation Photographs International

Below: *The Harrier GR.7 has replaced the GR.3 variant in RAF service. With a larger airframe and more powerful engine, it is capable of delivering an improved warload over a greater distance.*
Source: Jeremy Flack/Aviation Photographs International

INDEX TO ILLUSTRATIONS

THE RAF BENEVOLENT FUND'S BATTLE OF BRITAIN 50TH ANNIVERSARY APPEAL

In the summer of 1940, for four fateful months the future of Europe lay in the hands of a few courageous men.

They fought, and they succeeded, against all the odds.

One man in three failed to return.

Of the survivors, many are still alive today.

Between 1939-1945, some 1.75 million personnel served in the Royal Air Force, and the organisations associated with it.

Fifty years later the survivors of these, and their dependants, in need of support from the Royal Air Force Benevolent Fund are peaking in number.

World War II veterans now account for two-thirds of the claims upon the Fund. Their needs will increase over the next decade, placing a huge demand on our resources. That's why in 1990, we launched our *Reach for the Sky* Appeal, with a target of £20 million.

The Fund aims to ensure that no current or former RAF serviceman, or his family, suffers from need or distress as a result of accident, injury or illness. There is no time or monetary limit to the help that we give.

Why We Need £20 Million

We are at a point where we have a considerable and growing deficit of expenditure over income. It is imperative that we rectify the situation very swiftly.

By raising £20 million, we will help overcome the problem not just temporarily, but for the foreseeable future.

With our funds, as well as giving financial help for specific projects of equipment, we also commit ourselves to long-term help and care.

For example, we provide residential accommodation and convalescent homes for partially disabled and elderly former servicemen and their dependants, and serving RAF members and their families.

We provide block grants to institutions which assist us – over £500,000 was awarded to them in 1988;

Housing for widows with dependant children, an independent preparatory boarding school administered by the Fund, for RAF personnels' children, assistance with fees for further education and general welfare, from re-roofing a house to assisting with personal maintenance.

The Fund distributes all donations to the widows of RAF personnel, disabled RAF personnel and children and dependants of serving and former RAF personnel.

Of every £1 of total income, at least 85p goes to those in need. In supporting this Appeal, you'll be in very good company – helping to give an assured and dignified future to those who fought so courageously to give us our freedom.

"Reach for the Sky"
PO Box 1940
Fairford
Gloucestershire
GL7 4NA
England

RAF Benevolent Fund
67 Portland Place
London
W1N 4AR
England

Principles of Foundation Engineering

THE PWS SERIES IN ENGINEERING

Anderson, *Thermodynamics*
Askeland, *The Science and Engineering of Materials*, Third Edition
Baliga, *Power Semiconductor Devices*
Bolluyt, Stewart, and Oladipupo, *Modeling for Design Using SilverScreen*
Borse, *FORTRAN 77 and Numerical Methods for Engineers*, Second Edition
Clements, *68000 Family Assembly Language*
Clements, *Microprocessor Systems Design*, Second Edition
Clements, *Principles of Computer Hardware*, Second Edition
Das, *Principles of Foundation Engineering*, Third Edition
Das, *Principles of Geotechnical Engineering*, Third Edition
Das, *Principles of Soil Dynamics*
Duff and Ross, *Freehand Sketching for Engineering Design*
Fleischer, *Introduction to Engineering Economy*
Gere and Timoshenko, *Mechanics of Materials*, Third Edition
Glover and Sarma, *Power System Analysis and Design*, Second Edition
Janna, *Design of Fluid Thermal Systems*
Janna, *Introduction to Fluid Mechanics*, Third Edition
Kassimali, *Structural Analysis*
Keedy, *Introduction to CAD using CADKEY*, Third Edition
Keedy and Teske, *Engineering Design Graphics Using CADKEY 5&6*
Knight, *The Finite Element Method in Mechanical Design*
Knight, *Finite Element Primer for Mechanical Design*
Logan, *A First Course in the Finite Element Method*, Second Edition
McGill and King, *Engineering Mechanics: Statics*, Third Edition
McGill and King, *Engineering Mechanics: An Introduction to Dynamics*, Third Edition
McGill and King, *Engineering Mechanics: Statics and an Introduction to Dynamics*, Third Edition
Pfeiffer, *Basic Probability Topics Using MATLAB*
Raines, *Software for Mechanics of Materials*
Ray, *Environmental Engineering*
Reed-Hill and Abbaschian, *Physical Metallurgy Principles*, Third Edition
Reynolds, *Unit Operations and Processes in Environmental Engineering*
Schmidt and Wong, *Fundamentals of Surveying*, Third Edition
Segui, *Fundamentals of Structural Steel Design*
Segui, *LRFD Steel Design*
Shen and Kong, *Applied Electromagnetism*, Second Edition
Stewart, Bolluyt and Oladipupo, *Modeling for Design Using AutoCad*
Strum and Kirk, *Contemporary Linear Systems with MATLAB*
Sule, *Manufacturing Facilities*, Second Edition
Uyemura, *VLSI Layout Using L-EDIT*
Vardeman, *Statistics for Engineering Problem Solving*
Weinman, *FORTRAN for Scientists and Engineers*
Weinman, *VAX FORTRAN*, Second Edition
Wempner, *Mechanics of Solids*

PRINCIPLES OF FOUNDATION ENGINEERING

Third Edition

BRAJA M. DAS
California State University, Sacramento

PWS PUBLISHING COMPANY

An International Thomson Publishing Company

Boston · Albany · Bonn · Cincinnati · Detroit · London · Madrid · Melbourne · Mexico City
New York · Paris · San Francisco · Singapore · Tokyo · Toronto · Washington

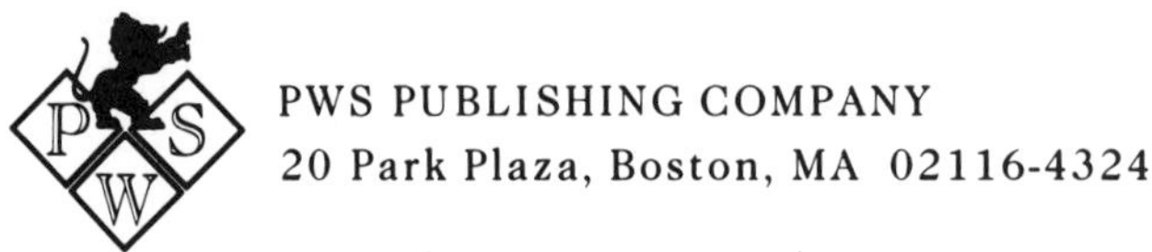

International Thomson Publishing
The trademark ITP is used under license.

For more information, contact:

PWS Publishing Co.
20 Park Plaza
Boston, MA 02116

International Thomson Publishing Europe
Berkshire House I68–I73
High Holborn
London WC1V 7AA
England

Thomas Nelson Australia
102 Dodds Street
South Melbourne, 3205
Victoria, Australia

Nelson Canada
1120 Birchmont Road
Scarborough, Ontario
Canada M1K 5G4

International Thomson Editores
Campos Eliseos 385, Piso 7
Col. Polanco
11560 Mexico D.F., Mexico

International Thomson Publishing GmbH
Königswinterer Strasse 418
53227 Bonn, Germany

International Thomson Publishing Asia
221 Henderson Road
#05–10 Henderson Building
Singapore 0315

International Thomson Publishing Japan
Hirakawacho Kyowa Building, 31
2-2-1 Hirakawacho
Chiyoda Ku, Tokyo 102
Japan

Library of Congress Cataloging-in-Publication Data
Das, Braja M.
Principles of foundation engineering/Braja M. Das.—3rd. ed.
p. cm
Includes bibliographical references.
ISBN 0-534-20646-8
1. Foundations. I. Title.
Library of Congress Catalog Card Number: 94-48565

Sponsoring Editor: Jonathan Plant
Editorial Assistant: Lai Wong
Developmental Editor: Mary Thomas
Production Editor: Kirby Lozyniak
Marketing Manager: Nathan Wilbur
Manufacturing Coordinator: Marcia Locke
Interior Designer: Cynthia Bogue

Interior Illustrator: Santype International, Ltd.
Typesetter: Santype International, Ltd
Cover Printer: Henry N. Sawyer Company, Inc.
Text Printer/Binder: Quebecor Printing/Martinsburg

Printed and bound in the United States of America.
95 96 97 98 99—10 9 8 7 6 5 4 3 2

**In the memory of my father,
and to Janice and Valerie**

CONTENTS

CHAPTER ONE

GEOTECHNICAL PROPERTIES OF SOIL 1

CHAPTER TWO

NATURAL SOIL DEPOSITS AND SOIL EXPLORATION 68

CHAPTER FOUR

MAT FOUNDATIONS 231

CHAPTER FIVE

LATERAL EARTH PRESSURE AND RETAINING WALLS 273

CHAPTER SIX

SHEET PILE WALLS 352

CHAPTER SEVEN

BRACED CUTS 423

CHAPTER EIGHT

PILE FOUNDATIONS 465

CHAPTER NINE

DRILLED-PIER AND CAISSON FOUNDATIONS 578

CHAPTER TEN

FOUNDATIONS ON DIFFICULT SOILS 628

CHAPTER ELEVEN

REINFORCED EARTH STRUCTURES 666

CHAPTER TWELVE

SOIL IMPROVEMENT 723

APPENDIX A

REINFORCED CONCRETE DESIGN 774

APPENDIX B

CONVERSION FACTORS 812

ANSWERS TO EVEN-NUMBERED PROBLEMS 815

INDEX 821

PREFACE

The second edition of *Principles of Foundation Engineering* published in 1990 was primarily intended to be used as a text by undergraduate civil engineering students. It was well received by students and practicing engineers and, consequently, provided the encouragement needed to prepare this third edition.

The format of this edition has not changed greatly. It contains 12 chapters and 2 appendices. Appendix A covers reinforced concrete design of shallow foundations and retaining walls, and Appendix B gives the conversion factors from SI (Système International) units to English units and from English units to SI units. Both English and SI units are used in the text, including those for all empirical equations. The split between English and SI unit use in the solved problems and the end of chapter homework problems is about 50–50.

To bridge theory and practice, some actual case histories have been added in this edition. Sections on natural soil deposits, which were in Chapter 1 of the first and second editions, were moved to Chapter 2, along with the topics on subsoil exploration. In Chapter 3, values of Terzaghi's bearing capacity factors are now presented in tabular rather than graphic form. A section on the dynamic bearing capacity of shallow foundations was added to Chapter 3, along with several recently published design charts for anchored bulkheads. The chapters on reinforced earth structures and soil improvement were expanded to include recently published materials.

Because the text introduces civil engineering students to the fundamental concepts and application of foundation analysis and design, the mathematical derivations of some equations are not presented; instead, just the final forms of those equations are given. However a list of references for further information and study is included in every chapter.

Foundation analysis and design, as my colleagues in the geotechnical engineering area well know, is not just a matter of using theories, equations, and graphs from a textbook. In nature, soil profiles are seldom homogeneous, elastic, and isotropic. The judgment needed to apply properly the theories, equations, and graphs to the evaluation of soils and foundation design cannot be overemphasized or completely taught by any textbook. Field experience must supplement classroom work.

Acknowledgments

The main driving force in the completion of the revised edition of this text is my wife, Janice, who appears to be the inexhaustible source of energy for me. She typed the revision and completed the original graphs and figures.

I wish to acknowledge Paul C. Hassler, formerly of the University of Texas at El Paso, Gerald R. Seeley of Valparaiso University, Ronald B. McPherson of New Mexico State University, and Said Larbi-Cherif, formerly of Navarro and Associates, El Paso, Texas, for their help, support, and encouragement during the preparation of the first edition of the manuscript. In addition, I want to thank Ronald P. Anderson of Tensar Earth Technologies, Inc., and Henry Ng, consulting engineer, El Paso, Texas, for their help in the development of the third edition.

I also wish to acknowledge the following reviewers of the third edition, whose useful comments have helped immensely:

A. G. Altschaeffl
Purdue University

Norman D. Dennis, Jr.
United States Military Academy

Jeffrey C. Evans
Bucknell University

Steven Perkins
Montana State University

Thomas F. Zimmie
Rensselaer Polytechnic Institute

I would also like to thank the following reviewers who gave their feedback to a pre-revision survey:

Eilas Abu-Saba, *North Carolina A&T State University;*
Sherif Aggour, *University of Maryland;*
Joe O. Akinmusuru, *Lawrence Technological University;*
Farshad Amini, *University of DC;*
Glen R. Anderson, *Tulane University;*
Thomas J. Anessi, *The Citadel;*
Reda Bakeer, *Tulane University;*
S. Bang, *South Dakota School of Mines and Technology;*
Charles W. Bartholomew, *Widener University;*
Ronald L. Baus, *University of South Carolina;*
David Bloomquist, *University of Florida;*
Ross W. Boulanger, *University of California–Davis;*
J. Budiman, *Illinois Institute of Technology;*
Dr. Ron Chaney, *Humboldt State University;*
Paul C. Chan, *New Jersey Institute of Technology;*
Dr. Yochia Chen, *Pennsylvania State University–Harrisburg;*
Shi-Cheh Cheng, *Drexel University;*
Paul J. Cosentino, *Florida Institute of Technology;*
Steve Cross, *University of Kansas;*
Dr. James A. Crovetti, *Marquette University;*
Dimitris Dermatas, *Stevens Institute of Technology;*
Andrew Drescher, *University of Minnesota;*
Fouad H. Fouad, *University of Alabama–Birmingham;*

M. A. Gabr, *West Virginia University;*
Ron Gallagher, *University of Toledo;*
Chris A. Gwaltney, *University of Evansville;*
Rachid Hankour, *Tufts University;*
R. D. Holtz, *University of Washington;*
Chongyu Hua, *Bradley University;*
Thomas C. Kinney, *University of Alaska–Fairbanks;*
A. E. Kumbojkar, *University of Miami;*
K. Madhavan, *Christian Brothers University;*
Earl S. McCullogh, *University of Wisconsin–Platteville;*
Blair McDonald, *University of Utah;*
Barry S. Mines, *United States Air Force Academy;*
Anil Misra, *University of Missouri–Kansas City;*
H. C. Moore, *Wentworth Institute of Technology;*
Robert Nicholls, *University of Delaware;*
Frank Pepe, Jr, *The Cooper Union;*
Monte L. Phillips, *University of North Dakota;*
Luis A. Prietor-Portar, *Florida International University;*
V. K. Puri, *Southern Illinois University;*
Dr. Ramsamoaj, *California State University–Fullerton;*
L. N. Reddi, *Kansas State University;*
Oswald Rendon-Herrero, *Mississippi State University;*
Gilbert L. Roderick, *University of Wisconsin–Milwaukee;*
Mary Roth, *Lafayette College;*
Roger K. Seeds, *Louisiana State University;*
Dr. Sunil Sharma, *University of Idaho;*
Thomas C. Sheahan, *Northeastern University;*
Trevor David Smith, *Portland State University;*
R. W. Stephenson, *University of Missouri–Rolla;*
John B. Stevens, *Norwich University;*
Hon H. Su, *California State University—Sacramento;*
Vahin Tanal, *Columbia University;*
George Veyera, *University of Rhode Island;*
Stan Vitton, *University of Alabama;*
Robert Warren, *Point Park College;*
Albert T. Yeung, *Texas A & M University.*

Professor Haskell Monroe, formerly the chancellor of the University of Missouri at Columbia and President of the University of Texas at El Paso, has been my mentor for the past 15 years. His continuous encouragement has made my professional career both rewarding and satisfying. I am most grateful for his generosity.

I extend thanks also to the staff of PWS Publishing Company for their interest and patience during the preparation and production of this text.

As a final note, I welcome suggestions from students and instructors for use in further editions.

Braja M. Das
Sacramento, California

CHAPTER ONE

GEOTECHNICAL PROPERTIES OF SOIL

1.1 INTRODUCTION

The design of foundations of structures such as buildings, bridges, and dams generally requires a knowledge of such factors as (a) the load that will be transmitted by the superstructure to the foundation system, (b) the requirements of the local building code, (c) the behavior and stress-related deformability of soils that will support the foundation system, and (d) the geological conditions of the soil under consideration. To a foundation engineer, the last two factors are extremely important because they concern soil mechanics.

The geotechnical properties of a soil—such as the grain-size distribution, plasticity, compressibility, and shear strength—can be assessed by proper laboratory testing. And, recently, emphasis has been placed on *in situ* determination of strength and deformation properties of soil, because this process avoids the sample disturbances that occur during field exploration. However, under certain circumstances, all of the needed parameters cannot be determined or are not determined because of economic or other reasons. In such cases, the engineer must make certain assumptions regarding the properties of the soil. To assess the accuracy of soil parameters—whether they were determined in the laboratory and the field or were assumed—the engineer must have a good grasp of the basic principles of soil mechanics. At the same time, he or she must realize that the natural soil deposits on which foundations are constructed are not homogeneous in most cases. Thus the engineer must have a thorough understanding of the geology of the area—that is, the origin and nature of soil stratification and also the groundwater conditions. Foundation engineering is a clever combination of soil mechanics, engineering geology, and proper judgment derived from past experience. To a certain extent, it may be called an "art."

When determining which foundation is the most economical, the engineer must consider the superstructure load, the subsoil conditions, and the desired tolerable settlement. In general, foundations of buildings and bridges may be divided into two major categories: (1) *shallow foundations* and (2) *deep foundations. Spread footings, wall footings*, and *mat foundations* are all shallow foundations. In most shallow foundations, the *depth of embedment can be equal to or less than three to four times the width of the foundation. Pile* and *caisson* foundations are deep foundations. They are used when top layers have poor load-bearing capacity and when use of shallow foundations will cause considerable structural damage and/or instability. The problems relating to shallow foundations and mat foundations are considered in Chapters 3 and 4, respectively. Chapter 8 discusses pile foundations, and Chapter 9 examines drilled shafts.

This chapter serves primarily as a review of the basic geotechnical properties of soils. It includes topics such as grain-size distribution, plasticity, soil classification, effective stress, consolidation, and shear strength parameters. It is based on the assumption that you have already been exposed to these concepts in a basic soil mechanics course.

1.2 GRAIN-SIZE DISTRIBUTION

In any soil mass, the sizes of various soil grains vary greatly. To classify a soil properly, you must know its *grain-size distribution*. The grain-size distribution of *coarse-grained* soil is generally determined by means of *sieve analysis*. For a *fine-grained* soil, the grain-size distribution can be obtained by means of *hydrometer analysis*. The fundamental features of these analyses are presented in this section. For detailed descriptions, see any soil mechanics laboratory manual (for example, Das, 1993).

Sieve Analysis

A sieve analysis is conducted by taking a measured amount of dry, well-pulverized soil. The soil is passed through a stack of progressively finer sieves with a pan at the bottom. The amount of soil retained on each sieve is measured, and the cumulative percentage of soil passing through each sieve is determined. This percentage is generally referred to as *percent finer*. Table 1.1 contains a list of U.S. sieve numbers and the corresponding size of their hole openings. These sieves are commonly used for the analysis of soil for classification purposes.

The percent finer for each sieve determined by a sieve analysis is plotted on *semilogarithmic graph paper*, as shown in Figure 1.1. Note that the grain diameter, D, is plotted on the *logarithmic scale*, and the percent finer is plotted on the *arithmetic scale*.

Two parameters can be determined from the grain-size distribution curves of coarse-grained soils: (1) the *uniformity coefficient* (C_u) and (2) the *coefficient of gradation*, or *coefficient of curvature* (C_z). These coefficients are

$$\boxed{C_u = \frac{D_{60}}{D_{10}}} \tag{1.1}$$

TABLE 1.1 U.S. Standard Sieve Sizes

Sieve no.	Opening (mm)
4	4.750
6	3.350
8	2.360
10	2.000
16	1.180
20	0.850
30	0.600
40	0.425
50	0.300
60	0.250
80	0.180
100	0.150
140	0.106
170	0.088
200	0.075
270	0.053

$$C_z = \frac{D_{30}^2}{(D_{60})(D_{10})} \tag{1.2}$$

where D_{10}, D_{30}, and D_{60} are the diameters corresponding to percents finer than 10, 30, and 60%, respectively

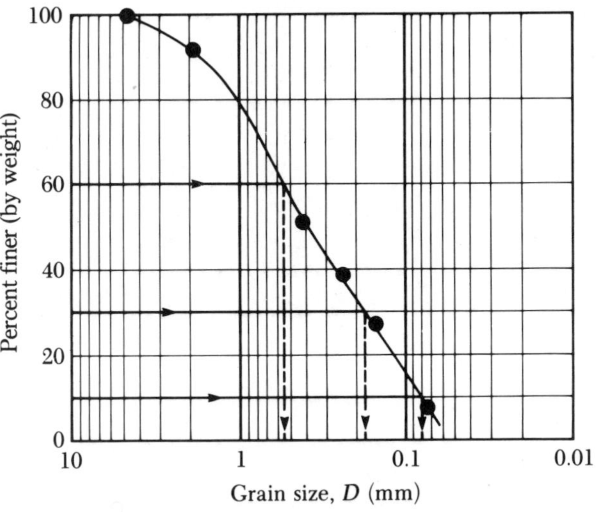

FIGURE 1.1 Grain-size distribution curve of a coarse-grained soil obtained from sieve analysis

For the grain-size distribution curve shown in Figure 1.1, $D_{10} = 0.08$ mm, $D_{30} = 0.17$ mm, and $D_{60} = 0.57$ mm. Thus the values of C_u and C_z are

$$C_u = \frac{0.57}{0.08} = 7.13$$

$$C_z = \frac{0.17^2}{(0.57)(0.08)} = 0.63$$

Parameters C_u and C_z are used in the *Unified Soil Classification System*, which is described later in this chapter.

Hydrometer Analysis

Hydrometer analysis is based on the principle of sedimentation of soil particles in water. This test involves the use of 50 grams of dry, pulverized soil. A *deflocculating* agent is always added to the soil. The most common deflocculating agent used for hydrometer analysis is 125 cc of 4% solution of sodium hexametaphosphate. The soil is allowed to soak for at least 16 hours in the deflocculating agent. After the soaking period, distilled water is added, and the soil-deflocculating agent mixture is thoroughly agitated. The sample is then transferred to a 1000-ml glass cylinder. More distilled water is added to the cylinder to fill it to the 1000-ml mark, and then the mixture is again thoroughly agitated. A hydrometer is placed in the cylinder to measure—usually over a 24-hour period—the specific gravity of the soil–water suspension in the vicinity of its bulb (Figure 1.2). Hydrometers are calibrated to show the amount of soil that is still in

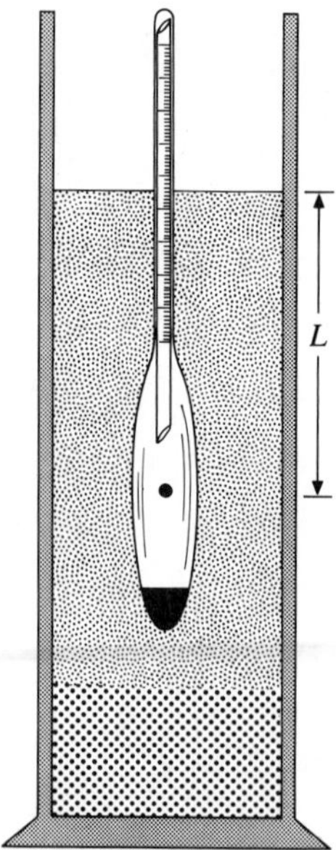

▼ **FIGURE 1.2** Hydrometer analysis

suspension at any given time, t. The largest diameter of the soil particles still in suspension at time t can be determined by Stokes's law:

$$D = \sqrt{\frac{18\eta}{(G_s - 1)\gamma_w}}\sqrt{\frac{L}{t}} \tag{1.3}$$

where D = diameter of the soil particle
G_s = specific gravity of soil solids
η = viscosity of water
γ_w = unit weight of water
L = effective length (that is, length measured from the water surface in the cylinder to the center of gravity of the hydrometer; see Figure 1.2)
t = time

Soil particles having diameters larger than those calculated by Eq. (1.3) would have settled beyond the zone of measurement. In this manner, with hydrometer readings taken at various times, the soil *percent finer* than a given diameter D can be calculated, and a grain-size distribution plot can be prepared. The sieve and hydrometer techniques may be combined for a soil having both coarse-grained and fine-grained soil constituents.

1.3 SIZE LIMITS FOR SOILS

Several organizations have attempted to develop the size limits for *gravel, sand, silt,* and *clay* based on the grain sizes present in soils. Table 1.2 presents the size limits recommended by the American Association of State Highway and Transportation Officials (AASHTO) and the Unified (Corps of Engineers, Department of the Army, and Bureau of Reclamation) Soil Classification systems. Table 1.2 shows that soil particles smaller than 0.002 mm have been classified as *clay*. However, clays by nature are cohesive and can be rolled into a thread when moist. This property is caused by the presence of *clay*

TABLE 1.2 Soil-Separate Size Limits

Classification system	Grain size (mm)
Unified	Gravel: 75 mm to 4.75 mm
	Sand: 4.75 mm to 0.075 mm
	Silt and clay (fines): <0.075 mm
AASHTO	Gravel: 75 mm to 2 mm
	Sand: 2 mm to 0.05 mm
	Silt: 0.05 mm to 0.002 mm
	Clay: <0.002 mm

minerals such as *kaolinite, illite,* and *montmorillonite.* In contrast, some minerals such as *quartz* and *feldspar* may be present in a soil in particle sizes as small as clay minerals. But these particles will not have the cohesive property of clay minerals. Hence they are called *clay-size particles,* not *clay particles.*

1.4 WEIGHT–VOLUME RELATIONSHIPS

In nature, soils are three-phase systems consisting of solid soil particles, water, and air (or gas). To develop the *weight–volume relationships* for a soil, the three phases can be separated as shown in Figure 1.3a. Based on this separation, the volume relationships can be defined in the following manner.

Void ratio, e, is the ratio of the volume of voids to the volume of soil solids in a given soil mass, or written as

$$e \frac{V_v}{V_s} \tag{1.4}$$

where V_v = volume of voids
V_s = volume of soil solids

Porosity, n, is the ratio of the volume of voids to the volume of the soil specimen, or

$$n = \frac{V_v}{V} \tag{1.5}$$

where V = total volume of soil

Moreover,

$$n = \frac{V_v}{V} = \frac{V_v}{V_s + V_v} = \frac{\dfrac{V_v}{V_s}}{\dfrac{V_s}{V_s} + \dfrac{V_v}{V_s}} = \frac{e}{1 + e} \tag{1.6}$$

Degree of saturation, S, is the ratio of the volume of water in the void spaces to the volume of voids, generally expressed as a percentage, or

$$S(\%) = \frac{V_w}{V_v} \times 100 \tag{1.7}$$

where V_w = volume of water

Note that, for saturated soils, the degree of saturation is 100%.

The weight relationships are *moisture content, moist unit weight, dry unit weight,* and *saturated unit weight.* They can be defined as follows:

$$\text{Moisture content} = w(\%) = \frac{W_w}{W_s} \times 100 \tag{1.8}$$

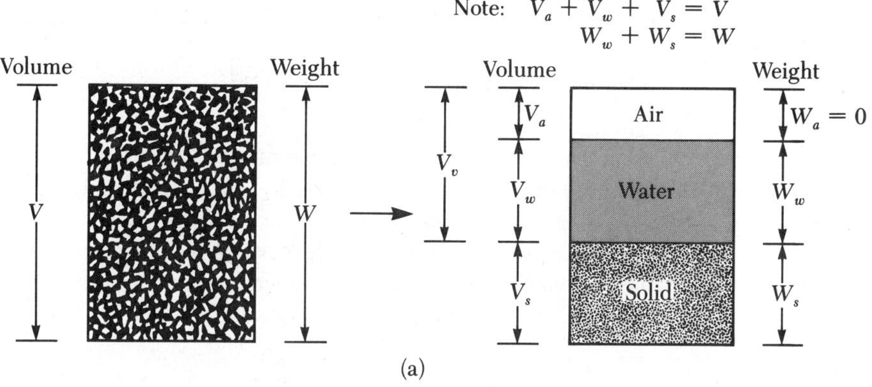

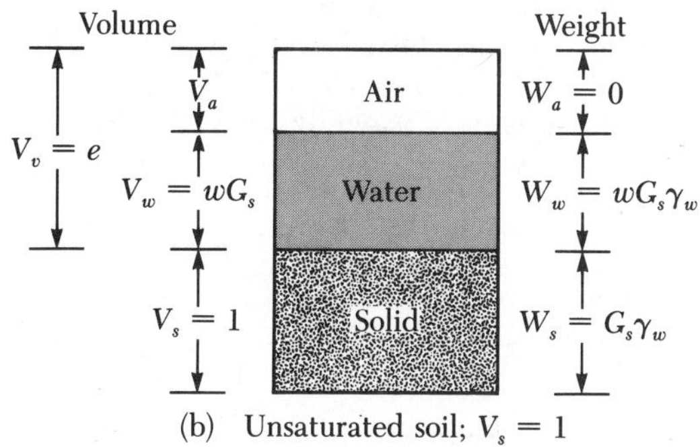

(b) Unsaturated soil; $V_s = 1$

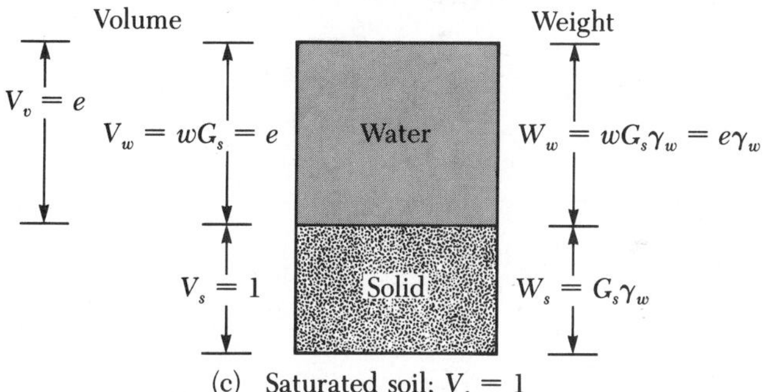

(c) Saturated soil; $V_s = 1$

▼ **FIGURE 1.3** Weight–volume relationships

where W_s = weight of the soil solids
W_w = weight of water

$$\text{Moist unit weight} = \gamma = \frac{W}{V} \tag{1.9}$$

where W = total weight of the soil specimen = $W_s + W_w$

The weight of air, W_a, in the soil mass is assumed to be negligible.

$$\text{Dry unit weight} = \gamma_d = \frac{W_s}{V} \tag{1.10}$$

When a soil mass is completely saturated (that is, all the void volume is occupied by water), the moist unit weight of a soil [Eq. (1.9)] becomes equal to the *saturated unit weight* (γ_{sat}). So $\gamma = \gamma_{sat}$ if $V_v = V_w$.

More useful relations can now be developed by considering a representative soil specimen in which the volume of soil solids is equal to *unity*, as shown in Figure 1.3b. Note that if $V_s = 1$, from Eq. (1.4), $V_v = e$ and the weight of the soil solids is

$$W_w = G_s \gamma_w$$

where G_s = specific gravity of soil solids
γ_w = unit weight of water (9.81 kN/m³, or 62.4 lb/ft³)

Also, from Eq. (1.8), the weight of water $W_w = wW_s$. Thus, for the soil specimen under consideration, $W_w = wW_s = wG_s\gamma_w$. Now, for the general relation for moist unit weight given in Eq. (1.9),

$$\boxed{\gamma = \frac{W}{V} = \frac{W_s + W_w}{V_s + V_v} = \frac{G_s\gamma_w(1 + w)}{1 + e}} \tag{1.11}$$

Similarly, the dry unit weight [Eq. (1.10)] is

$$\boxed{\gamma_d = \frac{W_s}{V} = \frac{W_s}{V_s + V_v} = \frac{G_s\gamma_w}{1 + e}} \tag{1.12}$$

From Eqs. (1.11) and (1.12), note that

$$\gamma_d = \frac{\gamma}{1 + w} \tag{1.13}$$

If a soil specimen is completely saturated as shown in Figure 1.3c,

$$V_v = e$$

Also, for this case

$$V_v = \frac{W_w}{\gamma_w} = \frac{wG_s\gamma_w}{\gamma_w} = wG_s$$

Thus

$$e = wG_s \qquad \text{(for saturated soil } \textit{only}\text{)} \tag{1.14}$$

The saturated unit weight of soil becomes

$$\gamma_{sat} = \frac{W_s + W_w}{V_s + V_v} = \frac{G_s \gamma_w + e\gamma_w}{1 + e} \tag{1.15}$$

Relationships similar to Eqs. (1.11), (1.12), and (1.15) in terms of porosity can also be obtained by considering a representative soil specimen with a unit volume. These relationships are

$$\gamma = G_s \gamma_w (1 - n)(1 + w) \tag{1.16}$$

$$\gamma_d = (1 - n) G_s \gamma_w \tag{1.17}$$

$$\gamma_{sat} = [(1 - n)G_s + n]\gamma_w \tag{1.18}$$

1.5 REPRESENTATIVE VALUES OF G_s, e, AND γ_d FOR NATURAL SOILS

Except for peat and highly organic soils, the general range of the values of specific gravity of soil solids (G_s) found in nature is rather small. Table 1.3 gives some representative values. For practical purposes, a reasonable value can be assumed in lieu of running a test.

▼ TABLE 1.3 Specific Gravities of Some Soils

Soil type	G_s
Quartz sand	2.64–2.66
Silt	2.67–2.73
Clay	2.70–2.9
Chalk	2.60–2.75
Loess	2.65–2.73
Peat	1.30–1.9

Table 1.4 presents some representative values for the void ratio, dry unit weight, and moisture content (in a saturated state) of some naturally occurring soils. Note that in most cohesionless soils the void ratio varies from about 0.4 to 0.8. The dry unit weights in these soils generally fall within a range of about 90–120 lb/ft^3 (14–19 kN/m^3).

TABLE 1.4 Typical Void Ratio, Moisture Content, and Dry Unit Weight for Some Soils

Type of soil	Void ratio e	Natural moisture content in saturated condition (%)	Dry unit weight, γ_d (lb/ft³)	(kN/m³)
Loose uniform sand	0.8	30	92	14.5
Dense uniform sand	0.45	16	115	18
Loose angular-grained silty sand	0.65	25	102	16
Dense angular-grained silty sand	0.4	15	120	19
Stiff clay	0.6	21	108	17
Soft clay	0.9–1.4	30–50	73–92	11.5–14.5
Loess	0.9	25	86	13.5
Soft organic clay	2.5–3.2	90–120	38–51	6–8
Glacial till	0.3	10	134	21

1.6 RELATIVE DENSITY

In *granular soils*, the degree of compaction in the field can be measured according to *relative density*, D_r, which is defined as

$$D_r(\%) = \frac{e_{max} - e}{e_{max} - e_{min}} \times 100 \tag{1.19}$$

where e_{max} = void ratio of the soil in the loosest state
e_{min} = void ratio in the densest state
e = *in situ* void ratio

The values of e_{max} are determined in the laboratory in accordance with the test procedures outlined in the American Society for Testing and Materials, *ASTM Standards* (1992, Test Designation D-4254).

The relative density can also be expressed in terms of dry unit weight, or

$$D_r(\%) = \left\{\frac{\gamma_d - \gamma_{d(min)}}{\gamma_{d(max)} - \gamma_{d(min)}}\right\} \frac{\gamma_{d(max)}}{\gamma_d} \times 100 \tag{1.20}$$

where γ_d = *in situ* dry unit weight
$\gamma_{d(max)}$ = dry unit weight in the *densest* state—that is, when the void ratio is e_{min}
$\gamma_{d(min)}$ = dry unit weight in the *loosest* state—that is, when the void ratio is e_{max}

The denseness of a granular soil is sometimes related to its relative density. Table 1.5 gives a general correlation of the denseness and D_r. For naturally occurring sands, the magnitudes of e_{max} and e_{min} [Eq. (1.19)] may vary widely. The main reasons

TABLE 1.5 Denseness of a Granular Soil

Relative density, D_r (%)	Description
0–20	Very loose
20–40	Loose
40–60	Medium
60–80	Dense
80–100	Very dense

for such wide variations are the uniformity coefficient, C_u, and the roundness of the particles, R. The uniformity coefficient is defined in Eq. (1.1). *Roundness* is defined as

$$R = \frac{\text{minimum radius of the particle edges}}{\text{inscribed radius of the entire particle}} \tag{1.21}$$

Measuring R is difficult, but it can be estimated. Figure 1.4 shows the general range of the magnitude of R with particle roundness. Figure 1.5 shows the variation of e_{max} and e_{min} with the uniformity coefficient for various values of particle roundness (Youd, 1973). This range is applicable to clean sand with normal to moderately skewed particle-size distribution.

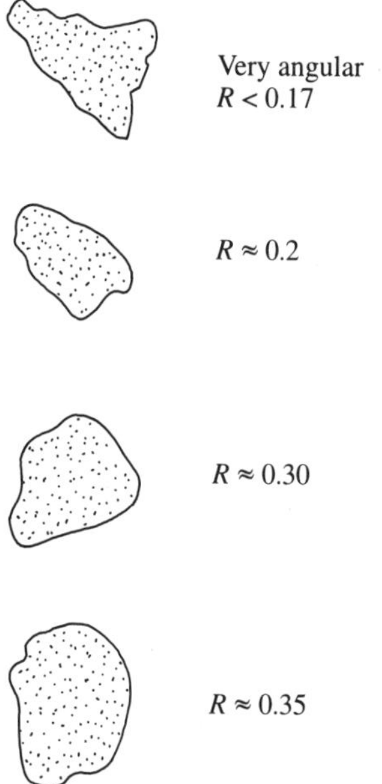

FIGURE 1.4 General range of the magnitude of R

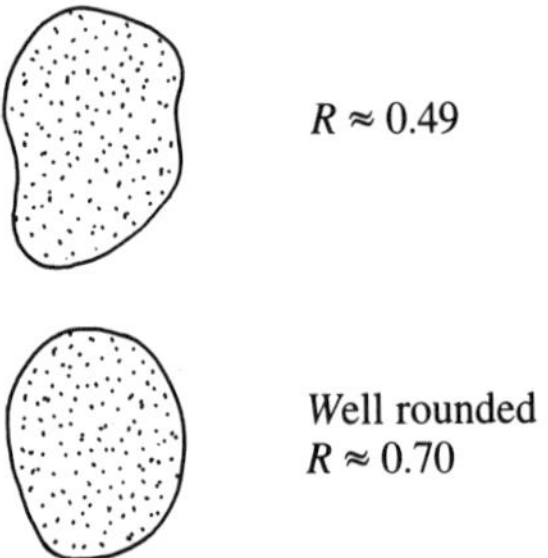

▼ **FIGURE 1.4** (continued)

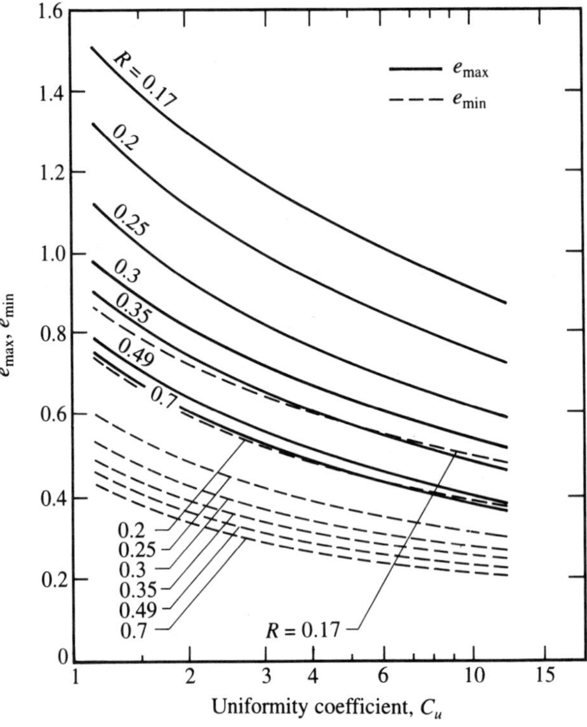

▼ **FIGURE 1.5** Approximate variation of e_{max} and e_{min} with uniformity coefficient (based on Youd, 1973)

▼ EXAMPLE 1.1

For a soil with void ratio = 0.81, moisture content = 21%, and $G_s = 2.68$, calculate the

a. Porosity
b. Degree of saturation
c. Moist unit weight in lb/ft^3
d. Dry unit weight in lb/ft^3

Solution

Part a: Porosity

From Eq. (1.6)

$$n = \frac{e}{1+e} = \frac{0.81}{1+0.81} = \mathbf{0.448}$$

Part b: Degree of Saturation

From Eqs. (1.7) and (1.14)

$$S = \frac{V_w}{V_v} = \frac{wG_s}{e} = \frac{(0.21)(2.68)}{0.81} = 0.695 = \mathbf{69.5\%}$$

Part c: Moist Unit Weight

From Eq. (1.11)

$$\gamma = \frac{G_s \gamma_w (1+w)}{1+e} = \frac{(2.68)(62.4)(1+0.21)}{1+0.81} = \mathbf{111.8\ lb/ft^3}$$

Part d: Dry Unit Weight

From Eq. (1.12)

$$\gamma_d = \frac{G_s \gamma_w}{1+e} = \frac{(2.68)(62.4)}{1+0.81} = \mathbf{92.4\ lb/ft^3}$$ ▼

▼ EXAMPLE 1.2

A representative soil specimen collected in the field weighs 1.8 kN and has a volume of 0.1 m^3. The moisture content as determined in the laboratory is 12.6%. For $G_s = 2.71$, determine the

a. Moist unit weight
b. Dry unit weight
c. Void ratio
d. Porosity
e. Degree of saturation

Solution

Part a: Moist Unit Weight

From Eq. (1.9)

$$\gamma = \frac{W}{V} = \frac{1.8\ \text{kN}}{0.1\ \text{m}^3} = \mathbf{18\ kN/m^3}$$

Part b: Dry Unit Weight

From Eq. (1.13)

$$\gamma_d = \frac{\gamma}{1+w} = \frac{18}{1+\dfrac{12.6}{100}} = \mathbf{15.99\ kN/m^3}$$

Part c: Void Ratio

From Eq. (1.12)

$$\gamma_d = \frac{G_s \gamma_w}{1+e}$$

or

$$e = \frac{G_s \gamma_w}{\gamma_d} - 1 = \frac{(2.71)(9.81)}{15.99} - 1 = \mathbf{0.66}$$

Part d: Porosity

From Eq. (1.6)

$$n = \frac{e}{1+e} = \frac{0.66}{1+0.66} = \mathbf{0.398}$$

Part e: Degree of Saturation

Refer to Figure 1.3b:

$$S = \frac{V_w}{V_v} = \frac{wG_s}{e} = \frac{(0.126)(2.71)}{0.66} \times 100 = \mathbf{51.7\%}$$ ▼

▼ EXAMPLE 1.3

For a granular soil having $\gamma = 108\ \text{lb/ft}^3$, $D_r = 82\%$, $w = 8\%$, and $G_s = 2.65$, if $e_{min} = 0.44$, what would be e_{max}? What would be the dry unit weight in the loosest state?

Solution From Eq. (1.13)

$$\gamma_d = \frac{\gamma}{1+w} = \frac{108}{1+0.08} = \mathbf{100\ lb/ft^3}$$

From Eq. (1.12)

$$\gamma_d = \frac{G_s \gamma_w}{1+e}$$

$$100 = \frac{(2.65)(62.4)}{1+e}$$

$$e = 0.654$$

From Eq. (1.19)

$$D_r = \frac{e_{\max} - e}{e_{\max} - e_{\min}}$$

$$0.82 = \frac{e_{\max} - 0.654}{e_{\max} - 0.44}$$

$$e_{\max} = \mathbf{1.63}$$

$$\gamma_{d(\min)} = \frac{G_s \gamma_w}{1 + e_{\max}} = \frac{(2.65)(62.4)}{1 + 1.63} = \mathbf{62.9\ lb/ft^3}$$ ▼

1.7 ATTERBERG LIMITS

When a clayey soil is mixed with an excessive amount of water, it may flow like a *semiliquid.* If the soil is gradually dried, it will lose moisture. Depending on its moisture content, it will behave like a *plastic, semisolid,* or *solid* material. The moisture content, in percent, at which the soil changes from a liquid to a plastic state is defined as the *liquid limit* (*LL*). Similarly, the moisture contents, in percent, at which the soil changes from a plastic to a semisolid state and from a semisolid to a solid state are defined as the *plastic limit* (*PL*) and the *shrinkage limit* (*SL*), respectively. These limits are referred to as *Atterberg limits* (Figure 1.6).

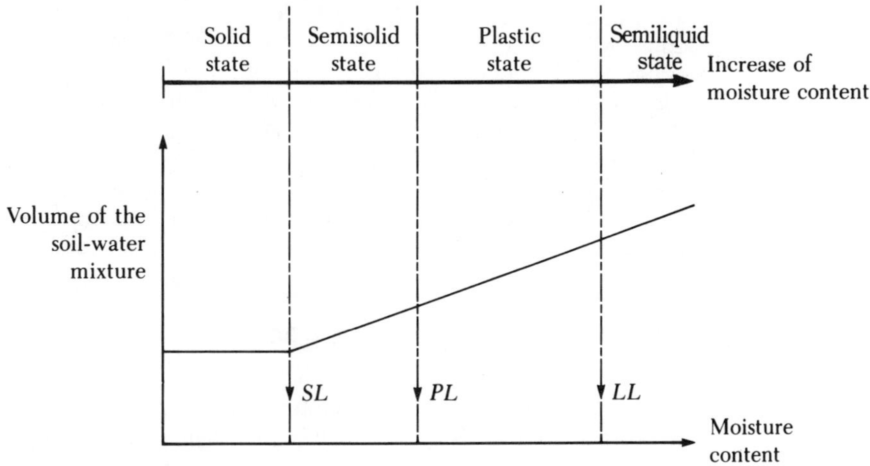

▼ **FIGURE 1.6** Definition of Atterberg limits

- The liquid limit of a soil is determined by Casagrande's liquid device (ASTM Test Designation D-4318) and is defined as the moisture content at which a groove closure of $\frac{1}{2}$ in. (12.7 mm) occurs at 25 blows.
- The *plastic limit* is defined as the moisture content at which the soil crumbles when rolled into a thread of $\frac{1}{8}$ in. (3.18 mm) in diameter (ASTM Test Designation D-4318).

▶ The *shrinkage limit* is defined as the moisture content at which the soil does not undergo further volume change with loss of moisture (ASTM Test Designation D-427). Figure 1.6 shows this limit.

The difference between the liquid limit and the plastic limit of a soil is defined as the *plasticity index* (*PI*), or

$$PI = LL - PL \tag{1.22}$$

Table 1.6 gives some representative values of liquid limit and plastic limit for several clay minerals and soils. However, Atterberg limits for various soils will vary considerably, depending on the soil's origin and the nature and amount of clay minerals in it.

▼ **TABLE 1.6 Typical Liquid and Plastic Limits for Some Clay Minerals and Soils**

Description	Liquid limit	Plastic limit
Kaolinite	35–100	25–35
Illite	50–100	30–60
Montmorillonite	100–800	50–100
Boston Blue clay	40	20
Chicago clay	60	20
Louisiana clay	75	25
London clay	66	27
Cambridge clay	39	21
Montana clay	52	18
Mississippi Gumbo	95	32
Loessial soils in north and northwest China	25–35	15–20

1.8 SOIL CLASSIFICATION SYSTEMS

Soil classification divides soils into groups and subgroups based on common engineering properties such as *grain-size distribution, liquid limit,* and *plastic limit.* The two major classification systems presently in use are (1) the *AASHTO* (*American Association of State Highway and Transportation Officials*) *System* and (2) the *Unified Soil Classification System* (also *ASTM*). The AASHTO classification system is used mainly for classification of highway subgrades. It is not used in foundation construction.

AASHTO System

The AASHTO Soil Classification System was originally proposed by the Highway Research Board's Committee on Classification of Materials for Subgrades and Granular Type Roads (1945). According to the present form of this system, soils can be classified according to eight major groups, A-1 through A-8, based on their grain-size distribution, liquid limit, and plasticity indices. Soils listed in groups A-1, A-2, and A-3 are coarse-grained materials, and those in groups A-4, A-5, A-6, and A-7 are fine-grained materials. Peat, muck, and other highly organic soils are classified under A-8. They are identified by visual inspection.

The AASHTO classification system (for soils A-1 through A-7) is presented in Table 1.7. Note that group A-7 includes two types of soil. For the A-7-5 type, the

TABLE 1.7 AASHTO Soil Classification System

General classification	Granular materials (35% or less of total sample passing no. 200 sieve)						
	A-1			*A-2*			
Group classification	A-1-a	A-1-b	A-3	A-2-4	A-2-5	A-2-6	A-2-7
Sieve analysis (%) passing)							
No. 10 sieve	50 max						
No. 40 sieve	30 max	50 max	51 min				
No. 200 sieve	15 max	25 max	10 max	35 max	35 max	35 max	35 max
For fraction passing No. 40 sieve							
Liquid limit (*LL*)				40 max	41 min	40 max	41 min
Plasticity index (*PI*)	6 max		Nonplastic	10 max	10 max	11 min	11 min
Usual type of material	Stone fragments, gravel, and sand		Fine sand	Silty or clayey gravel and sand			
Subgrade rating	Excellent to good						

General classification	Silt-clay materials (More than 35% of total sample passing no. 200 sieve)			
Group classification	A-4	A-5	A-6	A-7 A-7-5[a] A-7-6[b]
Sieve analysis (% passing)				
No. 10 sieve				
No. 40 sieve				
No. 200 sieve	36 min	36 min	36 min	36 min
For fraction passing No. 40 sieve				
Liquid limit (*LL*)	40 max	41 min	40 max	41 min
Plasticity index (*PI*)	10 max	10 max	11 min	11 min
Usual types of material	Mostly silty soils		Mostly clayey soils	
Subgrade rating	Fair to poor			

[a] If $PI \le LL - 30$, it is A-7-5
[b] If $PI > LL - 30$, it is A-7-6

plasticity index of the soil is less than or equal to the liquid limit minus 30. For the A-7-6 type, the plasticity index is greater than the liquid limit minus 30.

For qualitative evaluation of the desirability of a soil as a highway subgrade material, a number referred to as the *group index* has also been developed. The higher the value of the group index for a given soil, the weaker will be the soil's performance as a subgrade. A group index of 20 or more indicates a very poor subgrade material. The formula for group index, *GI*, is

$$GI = (F_{200} - 35)[0.2 + 0.005(LL - 40)] + 0.01(F_{200} - 15)(PI - 10) \tag{1.23}$$

where F_{200} = percent passing no. 200 sieve, expressed as a whole number
LL = liquid limit
PI = plasticity index

When calculating the group index for a soil belonging to groups A-2-6 or A-2-7, use only the partial group index equation relating to the plasticity index:

$$GI = 0.01(F_{200} - 15)(PI - 10) \tag{1.24}$$

The group index is rounded to the nearest whole number and written next to the soil group in parentheses; for example,

$$\underbrace{\text{A} = 4}_{\text{Soil group}}\ \underbrace{(5)}_{\text{Group index}}$$

Unified System

The Unified Soil Classification System was originally proposed by A. Casagrande in 1942 and was later revised and adopted by the United States Bureau of Reclamation and the Corps of Engineers. This system is presently used in practically all geotechnical work.

In the Unified System, the following symbols are used for identification.

Symbol	*G*	*S*	*M*	*C*	*O*	*Pt*	*H*	*L*	*W*	*P*
Description	Gravel	Sand	Silt	Clay	Organic silts and clay	Peat and highly organic soils	High plasticity	Low plasticity	Well graded	Poorly graded

Table 1.8 and the plasticity chart (Figure 1.7 on page 23) show the procedure for determining the group symbols for various types of soil. When classifying a soil be sure to provide the group name that generally describes the soil, along with the group symbol. Tables 1.9, 1.10, and 1.11, respectively, give the criteria for obtaining the group names for coarse-grained soil, inorganic fine-grained soil, and organic fine-grained soil. These tables are based on ASTM Designation D-2487.

TABLE 1.8 Group Symbols for Soil According to the Unified Classification System [Based on Material Passing 3-in. (75-mm) Sieve]

Major divisions	Criteria	Group symbol
Coarse-grained soil **$R_{200} > 50$**	$F_{200} < 5$, $C_u \geq 4$, $1 \leq C_z \leq 3$	GW
	$F_{200} < 5$, $C_u < 4$, and/or C_z not between 1 and 3	GP
Gravelly soil $R_4 > 0.5R_{200}$	$F_{200} > 12$, $PI < 4$, or Atterberg limits plot below A line (Figure 1.7)	GM
	$F_{200} > 12$, $PI > 7$, and Atterberg limits plot on or above A line (Figure 1.7)	GC
	$F_{200} > 12$, $LL < 50$, $4 \leq PI \leq 7$, and Atterberg limits plot on or above A line	GC-GM[a]
	$5 \leq F_{200} \leq 12$; meets the gradation criteria of GW and the plasticity criteria of GM	GW-GM[a]
	$5 \leq F_{200} \leq 12$; meets the gradation criteria of GW and the plasticity criteria of GC	GW-GC[a]
	$5 \leq F_{200} \leq 12$; meets the gradation criteria of GP and the plasticity criteria of GM	GP-GM[a]
	$5 \leq F_{200} \leq 12$; meets the gradation criteria of GP and the plasticity criteria of GC	GP-GC[a]
Sandy soil $R_4 \leq 0.5R_{200}$	$F_{200} < 5$, $C_u \geq 6$, $1 \leq C_z \leq 3$	SW
	$F_{200} < 5$, $C_u < 6$, and/or C_z not between 1 and 3	SP
	$F_{200} > 12$, $PI < 4$, or Atterberg limits plot below A line (Figure 1.7)	SM
	$F_{200} > 12$, $PI > 7$, and Atterberg limits plot on or above A line (Figure 1.7)	SC
	$F_{200} > 12$, $LL > 50$, $4 \leq PI \leq 7$, and Atterberg limits plot on or above A line (Figure 1.7)	SC-SM[a]
	$5 \leq F_{200} \leq 12$; meets the gradation criteria of SW and the plasticity criteria of SM	SW-SM[a]
	$5 \leq F_{200} \leq 12$; meets the gradation criteria of SW and the plasticity criteria of SC	SW-SC[a]
	$5 \leq F_{200} \leq 12$; meets the gradation criteria of SP and the plasticity criteria of SM	SP-SM[a]
	$5 \leq F_{200} \leq 12$; meets the gradation criteria of SP and the plasticity criteria of SC	SP-SC[a]
Fine-grained soil (inorganic), $R_{200} \leq 50$	$PI < 4$, or Atterberg limits plot below A line (Figure 1.7)	ML
Silty and clayey soil $LL < 50$	$PI > 7$, and Atterberg limits plot on or above A line (Figure 1.7)	CL
	$4 \leq PI \leq 7$, and Atterberg limits plot above A line (Figure 1.7)	CL-ML[a]
	Atterberg limits plot below A line (Figure 1.7)	MH
Silty and clayey soil $LL \geq 50$	Atterberg limits plot on or above A line (Figure 1.7)	CH
Fine-grained soil (organic)		
Organic silt and clay $LL < 50$	$\frac{LL_{\text{not oven dry}}}{LL_{\text{oven dry}}} < 0.75$	OL
Organic silt and clay $LL \geq 50$	$\frac{LL_{\text{not oven dry}}}{LL_{\text{oven dry}}} < 0.75$	OH

Note: F_{200} = percent finer than no. 200 sieve; R_{200} = percent retained on no. 200 sieve; R_4 = percent retained on no. 4 sieve; C_u = uniformity coefficient; C_z = coefficient of gradation; LL = liquid limit; PI = plasticity index; Atterberg limits based on minus no. 40 fraction

[a] Borderline case; dual classification

TABLE 1.9 Group Names for Coarse-Grained Soils (Based on ASTM D-2487)

Group symbol	Criteria: Gravel fraction (%)	Criteria: Sand fraction (%)	Group name
GW		<15	Well-graded gravel
		≥15	Well-graded gravel with sand
GP		<15	Poorly graded gravel
		≥15	Poorly graded gravel with sand
GM		<15	Silty gravel
		≥15	Silty gravel with sand
GC		<15	Clayey gravel
		≥15	Clayey gravel with sand
GC-GM		<15	Silty clayey gravel
		≥15	Silty clayey gravel with sand
GW-GM		<15	Well-graded gravel with silt
		≥15	Well-graded gravel with silt and sand
GW-GC		<15	Well-graded gravel with clay
		≥15	Well-graded gravel with clay and sand
GP-GM		<15	Poorly graded gravel with silt
		≥15	Poorly graded gravel with silt and sand
GP-GC		<15	Poorly graded gravel with clay
		≥15	Poorly graded gravel with clay and sand
SW	<15		Well-graded sand
	≥15		Well-graded sand with gravel
SP	<15		Poorly graded sand
	≥15		Poorly graded sand with gravel
SM	<15		Silty sand
	≥15		Silty sand with gravel
SC	<15		Clayey sand
	≥15		Clayey sand with gravel
SM-SC	<15		Silty clayey sand
	≥15		Silty clayey sand with gravel
SW-SM	<15		Well-graded sand with silt
	≥15		Well-graded sand with silt and gravel
SW-SC	<15		Well-graded sand with clay
	≥15		Well-graded sand with clay and gravel
SP-SM	<15		Poorly graded sand with silt
	≥15		Poorly graded sand with silt and gravel
SP-SC	<15		Poorly graded sand with clay
	≥15		Poorly graded sand with clay and gravel

Note: Sand fraction = percent of soil passing no. 4 sieve but retained on no. 200 sieve = $R_{200} - R_4$; gravel fraction = percent of soil passing 3-in. sieve but retained on no. 4 sieve = R_4

TABLE 1.10 Group Names for Inorganic Fine-Grained Soils (Based on ASTM D-2487)

	Criteria				
		Sand fraction			
Group symbol	R_{200}	*Gravel fraction*	*Gravel fraction*	*Sand fraction*	**Group name**
CL	<15				Lean clay
	15 to 29	≥1			Lean clay with sand
		<1			Lean clay with gravel
	≥30	≥1	<15		Sandy lean clay
		≥1	≥15		Sandy lean clay with gravel
		<1		<15	Gravelly lean clay
		<1		≥15	Gravelly lean clay with sand
ML	<15				Silt
	15 to 29	≥1			Silt with sand
		<1			Silt with gravel
	≥30	≥1	<15		Sandy silt
		≥1	≥15		Sandy silt with gravel
		<1		<15	Gravelly silt
		<1		≥15	Gravelly silt with sand
CL-ML	<15				Silty clay
	15 to 29	≥1			Silty clay with sand
		<1			Silty clay with gravel
	≥30	≥1	<15		Sandy silty clay
		≥1	≥15		Sandy silty clay with gravel
		<1		<15	Gravelly silty clay
		<1		≥15	Gravelly silty clay with sand
CH	<15				Fat clay
	15 to 29	≥1			Fat clay with sand
		<1			Fat clay with gravel
	≥30	≥1	<15		Sandy fat clay
		≥1	≥15		Sandy fat clay with gravel
		<1		<15	Gravelly fat clay
		<1		≥15	Gravelly fat clay with sand
MH	<15				Elastic silt
	15 to 29	≥1			Elastic silt with sand
		<1			Elastic silt with gravel
	≥30	≥1	<15		Sandy elastic silt
		≥1	≥15		Sandy elastic silt with gravel
		<1		<15	Gravelly elastic silt
		<1		≥15	Gravelly elastic silt with sand

Note: R_{200} = percent of soil retained on no. 200 sieve; sand fraction = percent of soil passing no. 4 sieve but retained on no. 200 sieve = $R_{200} - R_4$; gravel fraction = percent of soil passing 3-in. sieve but retained on no. 4 sieve = R_4

TABLE 1.11 Group Names for Organic Fine-Grained Soils (Based on ASTM D-2487)

	Criteria					
Group symbol	*Plasticity*	R_{200}	*Sand fraction* / *Gravel fraction*	*Gravel fraction*	*Sand fraction*	Group name
OL	$PI \geq 4$, and Atterberg limits on or above *A* line	<15				Organic clay
		15 to 29	≥1			Organic clay with sand
			<1			Organic clay with gravel
		≥30	≥1	<15		Sandy organic clay
			≥1	≥15		Sandy organic clay with gravel
			<1		<15	Gravelly organic clay
			<1		≥15	Gravelly organic clay with sand
	$PI < 4$, and Atterberg limits plot below *A* line	<15				Organic silt
		15 to 29	≥1			Organic silt with sand
			<1			Organic silt with gravel
		≥30	≥1	<15		Sandy organic silt
			≥1	≥15		Sandy organic silt with gravel
			<1		<15	Gravelly organic silt
			<1		≥15	Gravelly organic silt with sand
OH	Atterberg limits plot on or above *A* line	<15				Organic clay
		15 to 29	≥1			Organic clay with sand
			<1			Organic clay with gravel
		≥30	≥1	<15		Sandy organic clay
			≥1	≥15		Sandy organic clay with gravel
			<1		<15	Gravelly organic clay
			<1		≥15	Gravelly organic clay with sand
	Atterberg limits plot below *A* line	<15				Organic silt
		15 to 29	≥1			Organic silt with sand
			<1			Organic silt with gravel
		≥30	≥1	<15		Sandy organic silt
			≥1	≥15		Sandy organic silt with gravel
			<1		<15	Gravelly organic silt
			<1		≥15	Gravelly organic silt with sand

Note: R_{200} = percent of soil retained on no. 200 sieve; sand fraction = percent of soil passing no. 4 sieve but retained on no. 200 sieve = $R_{200} - R_4$; gravel fraction = percent of soil pasing 3-in. sieve but retained on no. 4 sieve = R_4

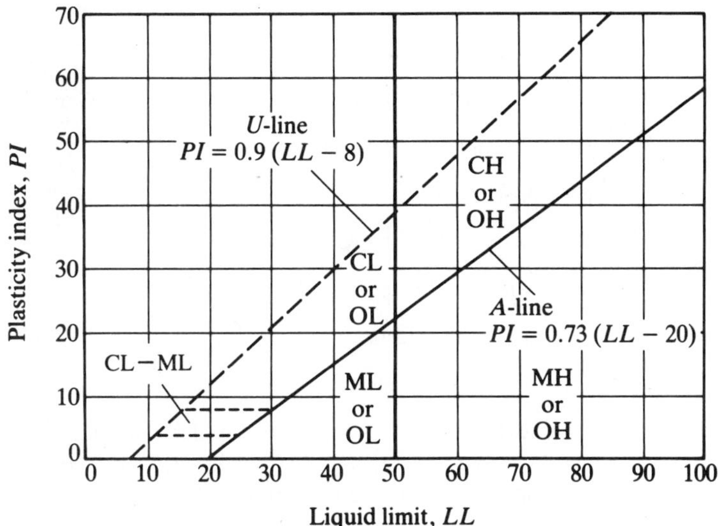

▼ **FIGURE 1.7** Plasticity chart

▼ EXAMPLE 1.4

Classify the following soil by the AASHTO classification system:

Percent passing no. 4 sieve = 82

Percent passing no. 10 sieve = 71

Percent passing no. 40 sieve = 64

Percent passing no. 200 sieve = 41

Liquid limit = 31

Plasticity index = 12

Solution Refer to Table 1.7. More than 35% passes through a no. 200 sieve, so it is a silt-clay material. It could be A-4, A-5, A-6, or A-7. Because $LL = 31$ (that is, less than 40) and $PI = 12$ (that is, greater than 11), this soil falls in group A-6. From Eq. (1.23)

$$GI = (F_{200} - 35)[0.02 + 0.005(LL - 40)] + 0.01(F_{200} - 15)(PI - 10)$$

So

$$GI = (41 - 35)[0.02 + 0.005(31 - 40)] + 0.01(41 - 15)(12 - 10)$$

$$= 0.37 \approx 0$$

Thus the soil is **A-6(0).** ▼

▼ EXAMPLE 1.5

Classify the following soil by the AASHTO classification system.

$$\text{Percent passing no. 4 sieve} = 92$$

$$\text{Percent passing no. 10 sieve} = 87$$

$$\text{Percent passing no. 40 sieve} = 65$$

$$\text{Percent passing no. 200 sieve} = 30$$

$$\text{Liquid limit} = 22$$

$$\text{Plasticity index} = 8$$

Solution Table 1.7 shows that it is a granular material because less than 35% is passing a no. 200 sieve. With $LL = 22$ (that is, less than 40) and $PI = 8$ (that is, less than 10), the soil falls in group A-2-4. From Eq. (1.24)

$$GI = 0.01(F_{200} - 15)(PI - 10) = 0.01(30 - 15)(8 - 10)$$

$$= -0.3 \approx 0$$

The soil is **A-2-4(0).** ▼

▼ EXAMPLE 1.6

Classify the soil described in Example 1.5 according to the Unified Soil Classification System.

Solution For $F_{200} = 30$,

$$R_{200} = 100 - F_{200} = 100 - 30 = 70$$

As $R_{200} > 50$, it is a coarse-grained soil.

$$R_4 = 100 - \text{percent passing no. 4 sieve}$$

$$= 100 - 92 = 8$$

As $R_4 = 8 < 0.5R_{200} = 35$, it is a sandy soil. Now, refer to Table 1.8. Becaue F_{200} is greater than 12, the group symbol would be SM or SC. As the *PI* is greater than 7 and the Atterberg limits plot above the *A* line in Figure 1.7, it is *SC*.

For the group name, refer to Table 1.9. The gravel fraction is less than 15%, so the group name is **clayey sand.** ▼

1.9 PERMEABILITY OF SOIL

The void spaces or pores between soil grains allow water to flow through them. In soil mechanics and foundation engineering, you must know how much water is flowing through a soil in unit time. This knowledge is required to design earth dams, determine the quantity of seepage under hydraulic structures, and dewater before and during the construction of foundations. Darcy (1856) proposed the following equation (Figure 1.8) for calculating the velocity of flow of water through a soil.

$$v = ki \tag{1.25}$$

where v = Darcy velocity (unit: cm/sec)
k = coefficient of permeability of soil (unit: cm/sec)
i = hydraulic gradient

The hydraulic gradient, i, is defined as

$$i = \frac{\Delta h}{L} \tag{1.26}$$

where Δh = piezometric head difference between the sections at AA and BB
L = distance between the sections at AA and BB

(*Note:* Sections AA and BB are perpendicular to the direction of flow.)

Darcy's law [Eq. (1.25)] is valid for a wide range of soil types. However, with materials like clean gravel and open-graded rockfills, Darcy's law breaks down because of the turbulent nature of flow through them.

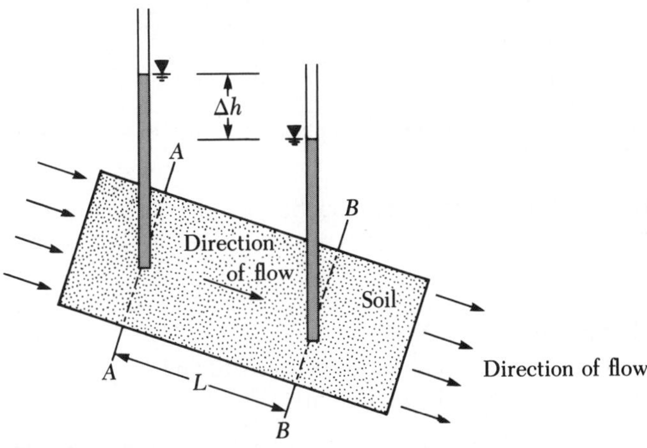

▼ **FIGURE 1.8** Definition of Darcy's law

The value of the coefficient of permeability of soils varies greatly. In the laboratory, it can be determined by means of *constant head* or *falling head* permeability tests. The constant head test is more suitable for granular soils. Table 1.12 provides the general range for the values of k for various soils. In granular soils, the value primarily

TABLE 1.12 Range of the Coefficient of Permeability for Various Soils

Type of soil	Coefficient of permeability, k (cm/sec)
Medium to coarse gravel	Greater than 10^{-1}
Coarse to fine sand	10^{-1} to 10^{-3}
Fine sand, silty sand	10^{-3} to 10^{-5}
Silt, clayey silt, silty clay	10^{-4} to 10^{-6}
Clays	10^{-7} or less

depends on the void ratio. In the past, several equations have been proposed to relate the value of k with the void ratio in the granular soil:

$$\frac{k_1}{k_2} = \frac{e_1^2}{e_2^2} \tag{1.27}$$

$$\frac{k_1}{k_2} = \frac{\left(\dfrac{e_1^2}{1+e_1}\right)}{\left(\dfrac{e_2^2}{1+e_2}\right)} \tag{1.28}$$

$$\frac{k_1}{k_2} = \frac{\left(\dfrac{e_1^3}{1+e_1}\right)}{\left(\dfrac{e_2^3}{1+e_2}\right)} \tag{1.29}$$

where k_1 and k_2 are the coefficients of permeability of a given soil at void ratios e_1 and e_2, respectively

Hazen (1930) proposed an equation for the coefficient of permeability of fairly uniform sand as

$$k = AD_{10}^2 \tag{1.30}$$

where k is in mm/sec
A = a constant that varies between 10 and 15
D_{10} = effective soil size, in mm

For clayey soils in the field, a practical relationship for estimating the coefficient of permeability (Tavenas et al., 1983) is

$$\log k = \log k_0 - \frac{e_0 - e}{C_k} \tag{1.31}$$

where k = coefficient of permeability at a void ratio e
k_0 = *in situ* coefficient of permeability at a void ratio e_0
C_k = permeability change index $\approx 0.5e_0$

For clayey soils, the coefficient of permeability for flow in the vertical and horizontal directions may vary substantially. The coefficient of permeability for flow in the vertical direction (k_v) for *in situ* soils can be estimated from Figure 1.9. For marine and other massive clay deposits

$$\frac{k_h}{k_v} < 1.5 \tag{1.32}$$

where k_h = coefficient of permeability for flow in the horizontal direction

For varved clays, the ratio of k_h/k_v may exceed 10.

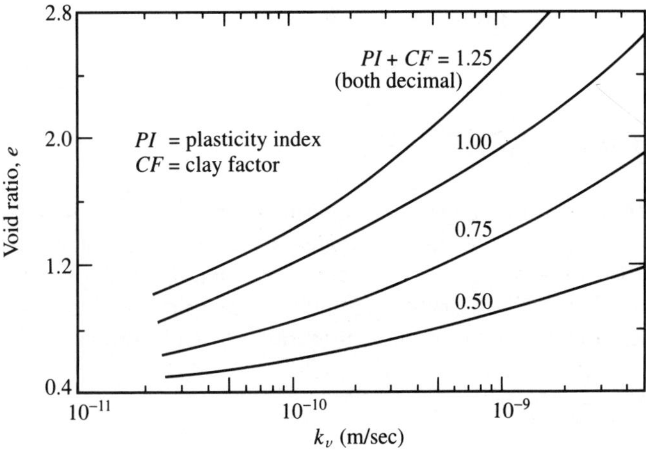

▼ **FIGURE 1.9** Variation of *in situ* k_v for clay soils (after Tavenas et al., 1983)

▼ EXAMPLE 1.7

The coefficient of permeability of a fine sand is 0.012 cm/sec at a void ratio of 0.57. Estimate the permeability coefficient of the sand at a void ratio of 0.72. Use Eqs. (1.27) and (1.29).

Solution From Eq. (1.27)

$$\frac{k_1}{k_2} = \frac{e_1^2}{e_2^2}$$

For $k_1 = 0.012$ cm/sec, $e_1 = 0.57$, and $e_2 = 0.72$

$$\frac{0.012}{k_2} = \frac{(0.57)^2}{(0.72)^2}$$

$$k_2 = \mathbf{0.019\ cm/sec}$$

From Eq. (1.29)

$$\frac{k_1}{k_2} = \frac{\dfrac{e_1^3}{1+e_1}}{\dfrac{e_2^3}{1+e_2}}$$

$$\frac{0.012}{k_2} = \frac{\dfrac{(0.57)^3}{1+0.57}}{\dfrac{(0.76)^3}{1+0.72}} = 0.544$$

$$k_2 = \mathbf{0.022\ cm/sec}$$ ▼

1.10 STEADY STATE SEEPAGE

For most cases of seepage under hydraulic structures, the flow path changes direction and is not uniform over the entire area. In such cases, one of the ways of determining the rate of seepage is by a graphical construction referred to as *flow net*. The flow net is based on Laplace's theory of continuity. According to this theory, for a steady flow condition, the flow at any point A (Figure 1.10) can be represented by the equation

$$k_x \frac{\partial^2 h}{\partial x^2} + k_y \frac{\partial^2 h}{\partial y^2} + k_z \frac{\partial^2 h}{\partial z^2} = 0 \tag{1.33}$$

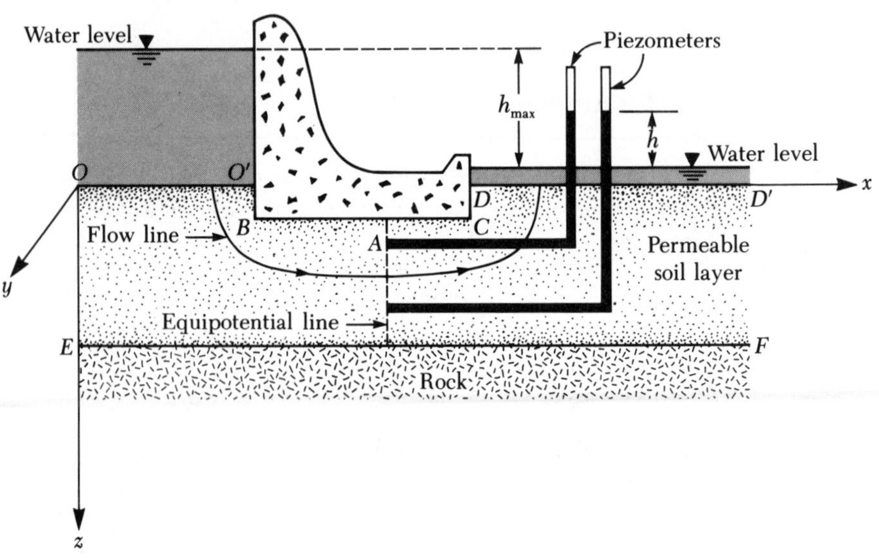

▼ **FIGURE 1.10** Steady state seepage

where k_x, k_y, k_z = coefficient of permeability of the soil in x, y, and z directions, respectively

h = hydraulic head at point A (that is, the head of water that a piezometer placed at A would show with the *datum* as the *downstream water level* as shown in Figure 1.10)

For a two-dimensional flow condition as shown in Figure 1.10

$$\frac{\partial^2 h}{\partial^2 y} = 0$$

So Eq. (1.33) takes the form

$$k_x \frac{\partial^2 h}{\partial x^2} + k_z \frac{\partial^2 h}{\partial z^2} = 0 \quad (1.34)$$

If the soil is isotropic with respect to permeability, $k_x = k_z = k$, and

$$\boxed{\frac{\partial^2 h}{\partial x^2} + \frac{\partial^2 h}{\partial z^2} = 0} \quad (1.35)$$

Equation (1.35), which is referred to as Laplace's equation and is valid for confined flow, represents two orthogonal sets of curves that are known as *flow lines* and *equipotential lines*. A flow net is a combination of numerous equipotential lines and flow lines. A flow line is a path that a water particle would follow in traveling from the upstream side to the downstream side. An equipotential line is a line along which water in piezometers would rise to the same elevation (see Figure 1.10).

In drawing a flow net, you need to establish the *boundary conditions*. For example, in Figure 1.10 the ground surfaces on the upstream (OO') and downstream (DD') sides are equipotential lines. The base of the dam below the ground surface, $O'BCD$, is a flow line. The top of the rock surface, EF, is also a flow line. Once the boundary conditions are established, a number of flow lines and equipotential lines are drawn by trial and error so that all the flow elements in the net have the same length-to-width ratio (L/B). In most cases, the L/B ratio is kept as 1—that is, the flow elements are drawn as curvilinear "squares." This method is illustrated by the flow net shown in Figure 1.11. Note that all flow lines must intersect all equipotential lines at *right angles*.

Once the flow net is drawn, the seepage in unit time per unit length of the structure can be calculated as

$$q = kh_{\max} \frac{N_f}{N_d} n \quad (1.36)$$

where N_f = number of flow channels

N_d = number of drops

n = width-to-length ratio of the flow elements in the flow net (B/L)

$h_{\max}$ = difference in water level between the upstream and downstream sides

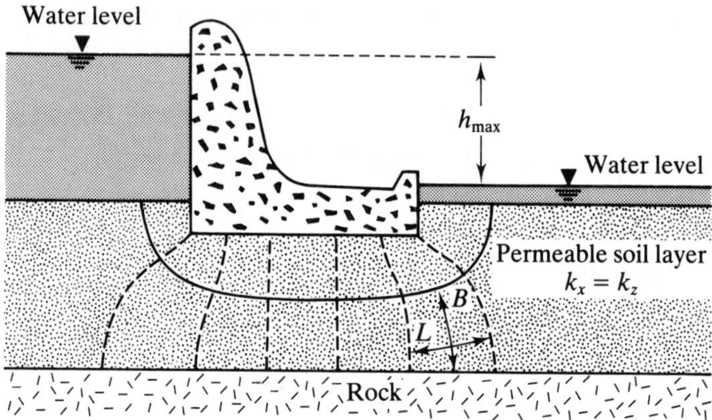

▼ **FIGURE 1.11** Flow net

The space between two consecutive flow lines is defined as a *flow channel,* and the space between two consecutive equipotential lines is called a *drop*. In Figure 1.11, $N_f = 2$, $N_d = 7$, and $n = 1$. When square elements are drawn in a flow net,

$$q = kh_{max}\frac{N_f}{N_d} \tag{1.37}$$

1.11 FILTER DESIGN CRITERIA

In the design of earth structures the engineer often encounters problems caused by the flow of water, such as soil erosion, which may result in structural instability. Erosion is generally prevented by building soil zones that are referred to as *filters* (see Figure 1.12). Two main factors influence the choice of filter material: The grain-size distribution of the filter materials should be such that (a) the soil to be protected is not washed into the filter and (b) excessive hydrostatic pressure head is not created in the soil that has a lower coefficient of permeability.

The preceding conditions can be satisfied if the following requirements are met (Terzaghi and Peck, 1967):

$$\frac{D_{15(F)}}{D_{85(B)}} < 5 \qquad \text{[to satisfy condition (a)]} \tag{1.38}$$

$$\frac{D_{15(F)}}{D_{15(B)}} > 4 \qquad \text{[to satisfy condition (b)]} \tag{1.39}$$

In these relations, the subscripts F and B refer to the *filter* and the *base* material (that is, the soil to be protected). Also D_{15} and D_{85} refer to the diameters through which 15% and 85% of the soil (filter or base, as the case may be) will pass.

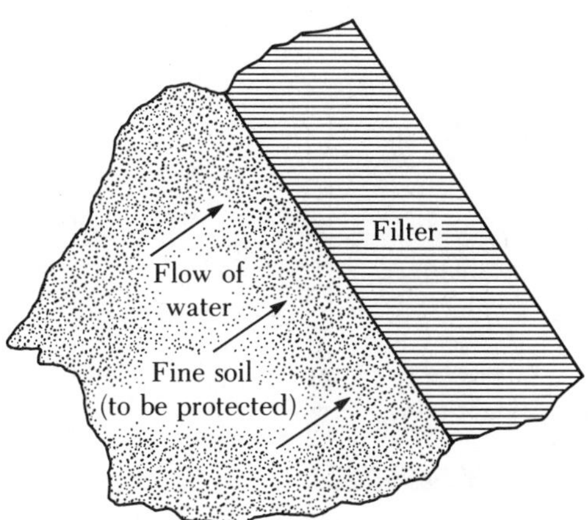

▼ **FIGURE 1.12** Filter design

The U.S. Department of the Navy (1971) provides some additional requirements for filter design to satisfy condition (a):

$$\frac{D_{50(F)}}{D_{50(B)}} < 25 \tag{1.40}$$

$$\frac{D_{15(F)}}{D_{15(B)}} < 20 \tag{1.41}$$

Currently, geotextiles are also used as filter materials (see Chapter 11).

1.12 EFFECTIVE STRESS CONCEPT

Consider the vertical stress at a point A located at a depth $h_1 + h_2$ below the ground surface, as shown in Figure 1.13a. The total vertical stress, σ, at A is

$$\sigma = h_1\gamma + h_2\gamma_{sat} \tag{1.42}$$

where γ and γ_{sat} are unit weights of soil above and below the water table, respectively

The total stress is carried partially by the *pore water* in the void spaces and partially by the *soil solids* at their points of contact. For example, consider a wavy plane AB drawn through point A (see Figure 1.13a) that passes through the points of contact of soil grains. The plan of this section is shown in Figure 1.13b. The small dots in Figure 1.13b represent the areas in which there is solid-to-solid contact. If the sum of these areas equals A', the area filled by water equals $XY - A$. The force carried by the pore water over the area shown in Figure 1.13b then is

$$F_w = (XY - A')u \tag{1.43}$$

where u = pore water pressure $= \gamma_w h_2$ (1.44)

Now let $F_1, F_2, \ldots$ be the forces of the contact points of the soil solids as shown in Figure 1.13a. The sum of the vertical components of these forces over a horizontal area

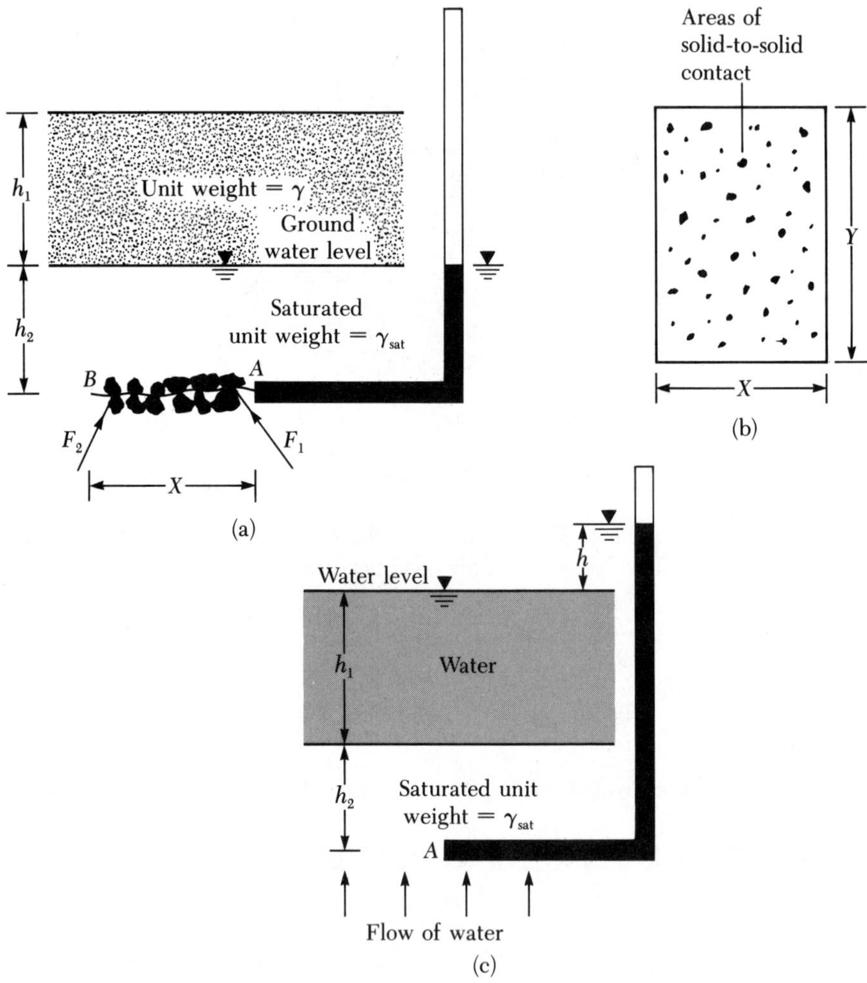

▼ **FIGURE 1.13** Effective stress calculation

XY is

$$F_s = \Sigma F_{1(v)} + F_{2(v)} + \cdots \tag{1.45}$$

where $F_{1(v)}, F_{2(v)}, \ldots$ are vertical components of forces $F_1, F_2, \ldots$, respectively

Based on the principles of statics

$$(\sigma)XY = F_w + F_s$$

or

$$(\sigma)XY = (XY - A')u + F_s$$

So

$$\sigma = (1 - a)u + \sigma' \tag{1.46}$$

where $a = A'/XY$ = fraction of the unit cross-sectional area occupied by solid-to-solid contact

$\sigma' = F_s/(XY)$ = vertical component of forces at solid-to-solid contact points over a unit cross-sectional area

The term σ' in Eq. (1.46) is generally referred to as the *vertical effective stress.* Also, the quantity a in Eq. (1.46) is very small. Thus

$$\boxed{\sigma = u + \sigma'} \tag{1.47}$$

Note that the effective stress is a *derived* quantity. Also, because the effective stress σ' is related to the contact between the soil solids, changes in effective stress will induce volume changes. It is also responsible for producing *frictional resistance* in soils and rocks. For dry soils, $u = 0$; hence $\sigma = \sigma'$.

For the problem under consideration in Figure 1.13a, $u = h_2\gamma_w$ (γ_w = unit weight of water). Thus the effective stress at point A is

$$\sigma' = \sigma - u = (h_1\gamma + h_2\gamma_{sat}) - h_2\gamma_w$$
$$= h_1\gamma + h_2(\gamma_{sat} - \gamma_w) = h_1\gamma + h_2\gamma' \tag{1.48}$$

where γ' = effective or the submerged unit weight of soil
$= \gamma_{sat} - \gamma_w$

From Eq. (1.15)

$$\gamma_{sat} = \frac{G_s\gamma_w + e\gamma_w}{1+e}$$

So

$$\gamma' = \gamma_{sat} - \gamma_w = \frac{G_s\gamma_w + e\gamma_w}{1+e} - \gamma_w = \frac{\gamma_w(G_s - 1)}{1+e} \tag{1.49}$$

For the problem in Figure 1.13a and 1.13b, there was *no seepage of water* in the soil. Figure 1.13c shows a simple condition in a soil profile where there is upward seepage. For this case, at point A

$$\sigma = h_1\gamma_w + h_2\gamma_{sat}$$

$$u = (h_1 + h_2 + h)\gamma_w$$

Thus from Eq. (1.47)

$$\sigma' = \sigma - u = (h_1\gamma_w + h_2\gamma_{sat}) - (h_1 + h_2 + h)\gamma_w$$
$$= h_2(\gamma_{sat} - \gamma_w) - h\gamma_w = h_2\gamma' - h\gamma_w$$

or

$$\sigma' = h_2\left(\gamma' - \frac{h}{h_2}\gamma_w\right) = h_2(\gamma' - i\gamma_w) \tag{1.50}$$

Note in Eq. (1.50) that h/h_2 is the hydraulic gradient, i. If the hydraulic gradient is very high, so that $\gamma' - i\gamma_w$ becomes zero, *the effective stress will become zero*. In other words, there is no contact stress between the soil particles, and the soil structure will break up. This situation is referred to as the *quick condition*, or *failure by heave*. So, for heave,

$$i = i_{cr} = \frac{\gamma'}{\gamma_w} = \frac{G_s - 1}{1 + e} \tag{1.51}$$

where i_{cr} = critical hydraulic gradient.

For most sandy soils, i_{cr} ranges from 0.9 to 1.1, with an average of about 1.

▼ EXAMPLE 1.8

For the soil profile shown in Figure 1.14, determine the total vertical stress, pore water pressure, and effective vertical stress at A, B, and C.

Solution At A:

$$\sigma = \mathbf{0}$$

$$u = \mathbf{0}$$

$$\sigma' = \mathbf{0}$$

At B:

$$\sigma = (\gamma_d)(10) = (110)(10) = \mathbf{1100\ lb/ft^2}$$

$$u = \mathbf{0}$$

$$\sigma' = 1100 - 0 = \mathbf{1100\ lb/ft^2}$$

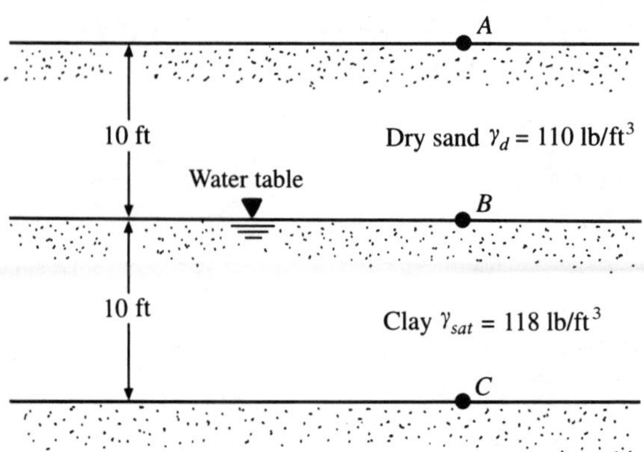

▼ **FIGURE 1.14**

At C:

$$\sigma = (\gamma_d)(10) + (\gamma_{sat})(10) = (110)(10) + (118)(10) = \mathbf{2280\ lb/ft^2}$$

$$u = (\gamma_w)(10) = (62.4)(10) = \mathbf{624\ lb/ft^2}$$

$$\sigma' = \sigma - u = 2280 - 624 = \mathbf{1656\ lb/ft^2}$$ ▼

1.13 CAPILLARY RISE IN SOIL

When a capillary tube is placed in water, the water level in the tube rises (Figure 1.15a). This rise is caused by the *surface tension* effect. According to Figure 1.15a, the pressure at any point A in the capillary tube (with respect to the atmospheric pressure) can be expressed as

$$u = -\gamma_w z' \qquad (\text{for } z' = 0 \text{ to } h_c)$$

and

$$u = 0 \qquad (\text{for } z' \geq h_c)$$

In a given soil mass, the interconnected void spaces can behave like a number of capillary tubes with varying diameters. The surface tension force may cause water in the soil to rise above the water table, as shown in Figure 1.15b. The height of the capillary rise will depend on the diameter of the capillary tubes. The capillary rise will *decrease* with the increase of the tube diameter. Because the capillary tubes in soil have variable diameters, the height of capillary rise will be nonuniform. The pore water pressure at any point in the zone of capillary rise in soil can be approximated as

$$u = -S\gamma_w z' \tag{1.52}$$

where S = degree of saturation of soil [Eq. (1.7)]
z' = distance measured above the water table

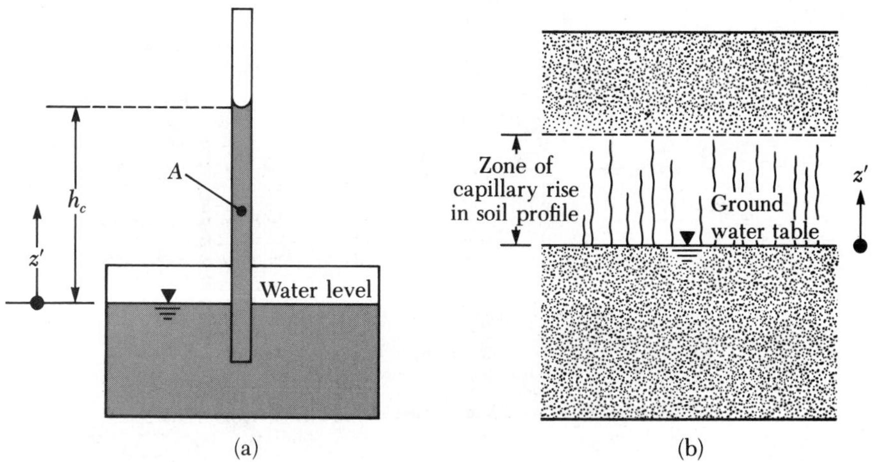

▼ **FIGURE 1.15** Capillary rise

1.14 CONSOLIDATION

In the field when the stress on a saturated clay layer is increased—for example, by the construction of a foundation—the pore water pressure in the clay will increase. Because the coefficients of permeability of clays are very small, some time will be required for the excess pore water pressure to dissipate and the stress increase to be transferred to the soil skeleton gradually. According to Figure 1.16, if Δp is a surcharge at the ground surface over a very large area, the increase of total stress, $\Delta\sigma$, at any depth of the clay layer will be equal to Δp, or

$$\Delta\sigma = \Delta p$$

However, at time $t = 0$ (i.e., immediately after the stress application), the excess pore water pressure at any depth, Δu, will equal Δp, or

$$\Delta u = \Delta h_i \gamma_w = \Delta p \qquad \text{(at time } t = 0\text{)}$$

Hence the increase of effective stress at time $t = 0$ will be

$$\Delta\sigma' = \Delta\sigma - \Delta u = 0$$

Theoretically, at time $t = \infty$, when all the excess pore water pressure in the clay layer has dissipated as a result of drainage into the sand layers,

$$\Delta u = 0 \qquad \text{(at time } t = \infty\text{)}$$

Then the increase of effective stress in the clay layer is

$$\Delta\sigma' = \Delta\sigma - \Delta u = \Delta p - 0 = \Delta p$$

This gradual increase in the effective stress in the clay layer will cause settlement over a period of time and is referred to as *consolidation*.

Laboratory tests on undisturbed saturated clay specimens can be conducted (ASTM Test Designation D-2435) to determine the consolidation settlement caused by

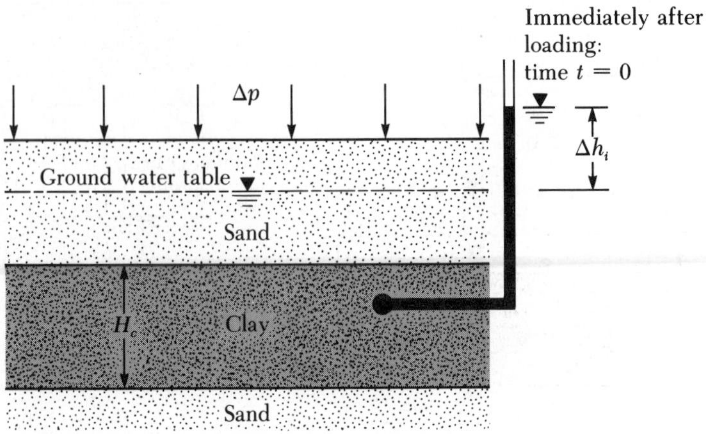

▼ **FIGURE 1.16** Principles of consolidation

various incremental loadings. The test specimens are usually 2.5 in. (63.5 mm) in diameter and 1 in. (25.4 mm) in height. Specimens are placed inside a ring, with one porous stone at the top and one at the bottom of the specimen (Figure 1.17a). Load on the specimen is then applied so that the total stress is equal to p. Settlement readings for the specimen are taken for 24 hours. After that, the load on the specimen is doubled and settlement readings are taken. At all times during the test the specimen is kept under water. This procedure is continued until the desired limit of stress on the clay specimen is reached.

Based on the laboratory tests, a graph can be plotted showing the variation of the void ratio e at the *end* of consolidation against the corresponding stress p (semilogarithmic graph: e on the arithmetic wcale and p on the log scale). The nature of variation of e against log p for a clay specimen is shown in Figure 1.17b. After the

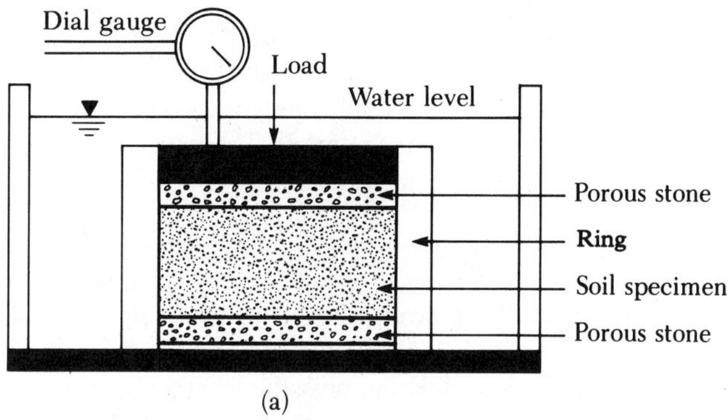

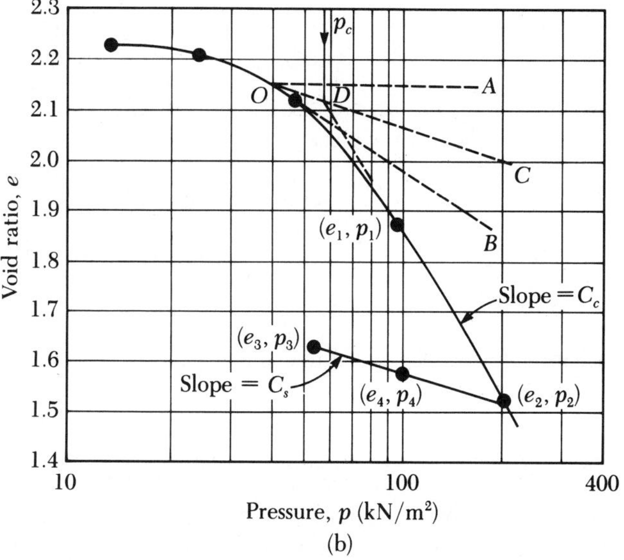

▼ **FIGURE 1.17** (a) Schematic diagram of consolidation test arrangement; (b) e–log p curve for a soft clay from East St. Louis, Illinois

desired consolidation pressure has been reached, the specimen can be gradually unloaded, which will result in the swelling of the specimen. Figure 1.17b also shows the variation of the void ratio during the unloading period.

From the e–log p curve shown in Figure 1.17b, three parameters necessary for calculating settlement in the field can be determined.

1. The *preconsolidation pressure*, p_c, is the *maximum past effective overburden pressure* to which the soil specimen has been subjected. It can be determined by using a simple graphical procedure as proposed by Casagrande (1936). This procedure for determining the preconsolidation pressure, with reference to Figure 1.17b, involves five steps:
   a. Determine the point O on the e–log p curve that has the sharpest curvature (that is, the smallest radius of curvature).
   b. Draw a horizontal line OA.
   c. Draw a line OB that is tangent to the e–log p curve at O.
   d. Draw a line OC that bisects the angle AOB.
   e. Produce the straight line portion of the e–log p curve backward to intersect OC. This is point D. The pressure that corresponds to point p is the preconsolidation pressure, p_c.

Natural soil deposits can be *normally consolidated* or *overconsolidated* (or *preconsolidated*). If the present effective overburden pressure $p = p_o$ is equal to the preconsolidated pressure p_c, the soil is *normally consolidated*. However, if $p_o < p_c$, the soil is *overconsolidated*.

Preconsolidation pressure (p_c) has been correlated with the index parameters by several investigators. Stas and Kulhawy (1984) suggested that

$$\frac{p_c}{\sigma_a} = 10^{(1.11 - 1.62LI)} \tag{1.53a}$$

where σ_a = atmospheric stress in derived unit
LI = liquidity index

The liquidity index of a soil is defined as

$$LI = \frac{w - PL}{LL - PL} \tag{1.53b}$$

where w = *in situ* moisture content
LL = liquid limit
PL = plastic limit

The U.S. Department of the Navy (1982) also provided generalized relationships between p_c, LI, and the sensitivity of clayey soils (S_t). This relationship was also recommended by Kulhawy and Mayne (1990). The definition of sensitivity is given in Section 1.17. Figure 1.18 shows the relationship.

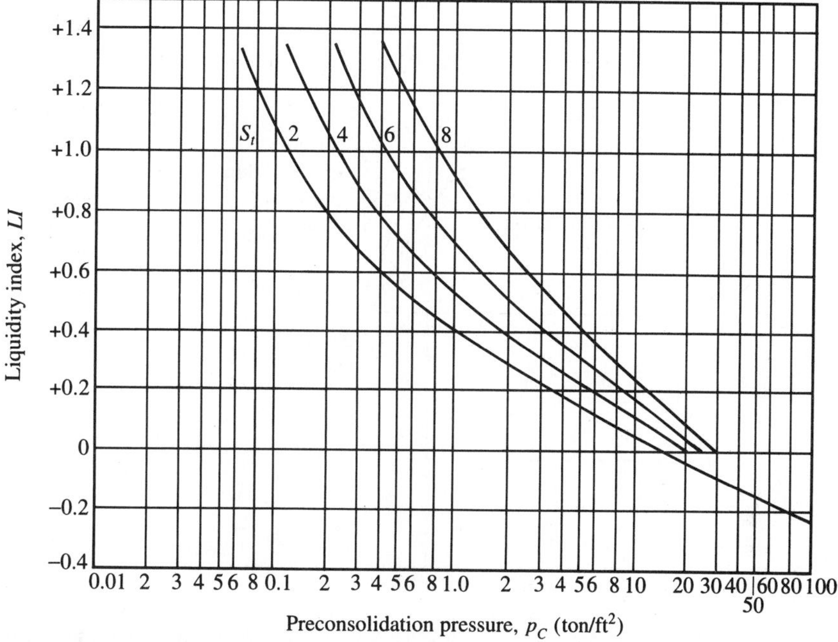

FIGURE 1.18 Variation of p_c with LI (after U.S. Department of the Navy, 1982)

2. The *compression index*, C_c, is the slope of the straight-line portion (latter part of the loading curve), or

$$C_c = \frac{e_1 - e_2}{\log p_2 - \log p_1} = \frac{e_1 - e_2}{\log\left(\frac{p_2}{p_1}\right)} \tag{1.54}$$

where e_1 and e_2 are the void ratios at the end of consolidation under stresses p_1 and p_2, respectively

The *compression index*, as determined from the laboratory e–log p curve, will be somewhat different from that encountered in the field. The primary reason is that the soil remolds to some degree during the field exploration. The nature of variation of the e–log p curve in the field for a normally consolidated clay is shown in Figure 1.19. It is generally referred to as the *virgin compression curve*. The virgin curve approximately intersects the laboratory curve at a void ratio of $0.42e_o$ (Terzaghi and Peck, 1967). Note that e_o is the void ratio of the clay in the field. Knowing the values of e_o and p_c, you can easily construct the virgin curve and calculate the compression index of the virgin curve by using Eq. (1.54).

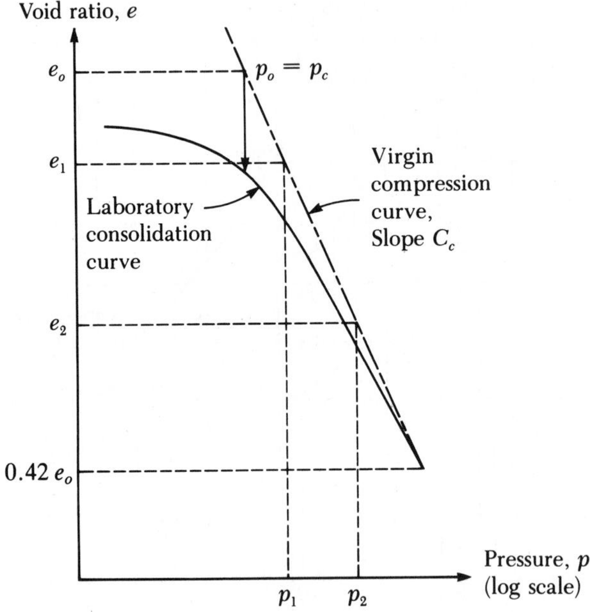

▼ **FIGURE 1.19** Construction of virgin compression curve for normally consolidated clay

The value of C_c can vary widely depending on the soil. Skempton (1944) has given an empirical correlation for the compression index in which

$$C_c = 0.009(LL - 10) \tag{1.55}$$

where LL = liquid limit

Besides Skempton, other investigators have proposed correlations for the compression index. Some of these correlations are summarized in Table 1.13.

3. The *swelling index*, C_s, is the slope of the unloading portion of the e–log p curve. In Figure 1.17b, it can be defined as

$$C_s = \frac{e_3 - e_4}{\log\left(\dfrac{p_4}{p_3}\right)} \tag{1.56}$$

In most cases the value of the swelling index (C_s) is $\frac{1}{4}$ to $\frac{1}{5}$ of the compression index. Following are some representative values of C_s/C_c for natural soil deposits.

Description of soil	C_s/C_c
Boston Blue clay	0.24–0.33
Chicago clay	0.15–0.3
New Orleans clay	0.15–0.28
St. Lawrence clay	0.05–0.1

▼ TABLE 1.13 Correlations for Compression Index

Reference	Correlation
Azzouz, Krizek, and Corotis (1976)	$C_c = 0.01w_n$ (Chicago clay) $C_c = 0.208e_o + 0.0083$ (Chicago clay) $C_c = 0.0115w_n$ (organic soils, peat) $C_c = 0.0046(LL - 9)$ (Brazilian clay)
Rendon-Herrero (1980)	$C_c = 0.141G_s^{1.2}\left(\frac{1+e_o}{G_s}\right)^{2.38}$
Nagaraj and Murty (1985)	$C_c = 0.2343\left(\frac{LL}{100}\right)G_s$
Wroth and Wood (1978)	$C_c = 0.5G_s\left(\frac{PI}{100}\right)$
Leroueil, Tavenas, and LeBihan (1983)	

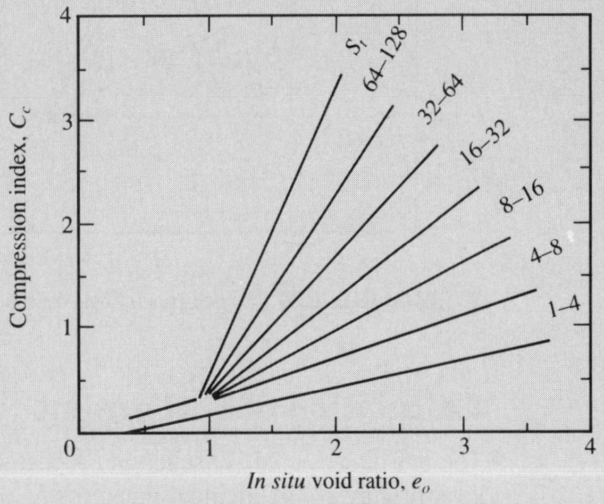

Note: G_s = specific gravity of soil solids
LL = liquid limit
PI = plasticity index
S_t = sensitivity
w_n = natural moisture content

The swelling index determination is important in the estimation of consolidation settlement of *overconsolidated clays*. In the field, depending on the pressure increase, an overconsolidated clay will follow and e–log p path abc, as shown in Figure 1.20. Note that point a, with coordinates of p_o and e_o, corresponds to the field conditions before any pressure increase. Point b corresponds to the preconsolidation pressure (p_c) of the clay. Line ab is approximately parallel to the laboratory unloading curve cd (Schmertmann, 1953). Hence, if you know e_o, p_o, p_c, C_c, and C_s, you can easily construct the field consolidation curve.

Nagaraj and Murthy (1985) expressed the swelling index as

$$C_s = 0.0463\left(\frac{LL}{100}\right)G_s \tag{1.57}$$

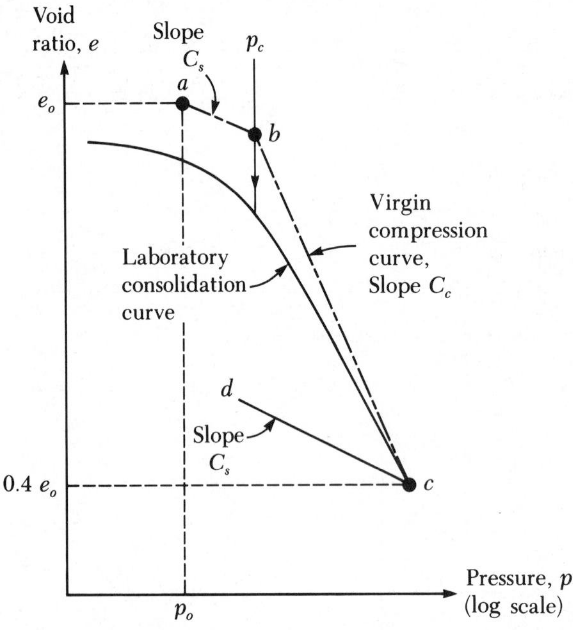

▼ **FIGURE 1.20** Construction of field consolidation curve for overconsolidated clay

Calculation of Settlement

The one-dimensional consolidation settlement (caused by an additional load) of a clay layer (Figure 1.21a) having a thickness H_c may be calculated as

$$S = \frac{\Delta e}{1 + e_o} H_c \tag{1.58}$$

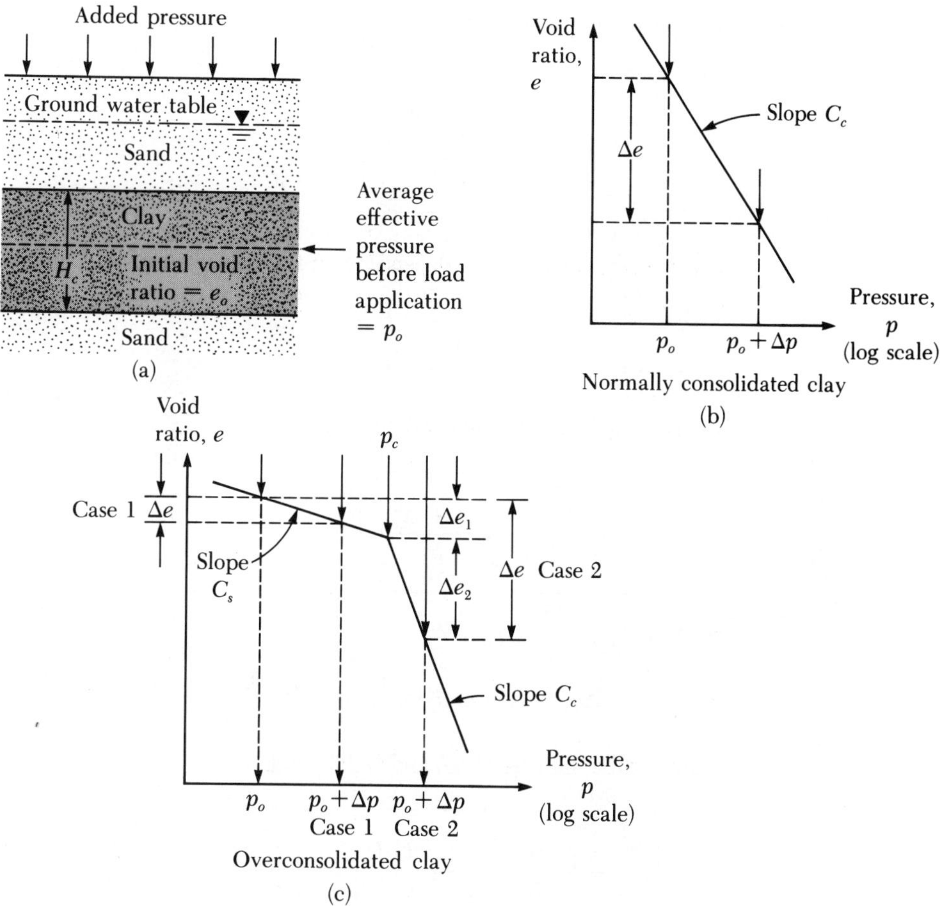

▼ **FIGURE 1.21** One-dimensional settlement calculation: (b) is for Eq. (1.59); (c) is for Eqs. (1.62) and (1.64)

where S = settlement
Δe = total change of void ratio caused by the additional load application
e_o = the void ratio of the clay before the application of load

Note that

$$\frac{\Delta e}{1 + e_o} = \mathcal{E}_v = \text{vertical strain}$$

For normally consolidated clay, the field e–log p curve will be like the one shown in Figure 1.21b. If p_o = initial average effective overburden pressure on the clay layer and Δp = average pressure increase on the clay layer caused by the added load, the change of void ratio caused by the load increase is

$$\Delta e = C_c \log \frac{p_o + \Delta p}{p_o} \tag{1.59}$$

Now, combining Eqs. (1.58) and (1.59) yields

$$S = \frac{C_c H_c}{1 + e_o} \log \frac{p_o + \Delta p}{p_o} \tag{1.60}$$

For overconsolidated clay, the field e–log p curve will be like the one shown in Figure 1.21c. In this case, depending on the value of Δp, two conditions may arise. First, if $p_o + \Delta p < p_c$,

$$\Delta e = C_s \log \frac{p_o + \Delta p}{p_o} \tag{1.61}$$

Combining Eqs. (1.58) and (1.61) gives

$$S = \frac{H_c C_s}{1 + e_o} \log \frac{p_o + \Delta p}{p_o} \tag{1.62}$$

Second, if $p_o < p_c < p_o + \Delta p$

$$\Delta e = \Delta e_1 + \Delta e_2 = C_s \log \frac{p_c}{p_o} + C_c \log \frac{p_o + \Delta p}{p_o} \tag{1.63}$$

Now, combining Eqs. (1.58) and (1.63) yields

$$S = \frac{C_s H_c}{1 + e_o} \log \frac{p_c}{p_o} + \frac{C_c H_c}{1 + e_o} \log \frac{p_o + \Delta p}{p_c} \tag{1.64}$$

Average Degree of Consolidation

Earlier in this section (see Figure 1.16) we showed that consolidation is the result of gradual dissipation of the excess pore water pressure from a clay layer. Pore water pressure dissipation, in turn, increases the effective stress, which induces settlement. Hence, to estimate the degree of consolidation of a clay layer at some time t after the load application, you need to know the rate of dissipation of the excess pore water pressure.

Figure 1.22a shows a clay layer of thickness H_c that has highly permeable sand layers at its top and bottom. Here, the excess pore water pressure at any point A at any time t after the load application is $\Delta u = (\Delta h)\gamma_w$. For a vertical drainage condition (that is, in the direction of z only) from the clay layer, Terzaghi derived the following differential equation:

$$\frac{\partial(\Delta u)}{\partial t} = C_v \frac{\partial^2(\Delta u)}{\partial z^2} \tag{1.65}$$

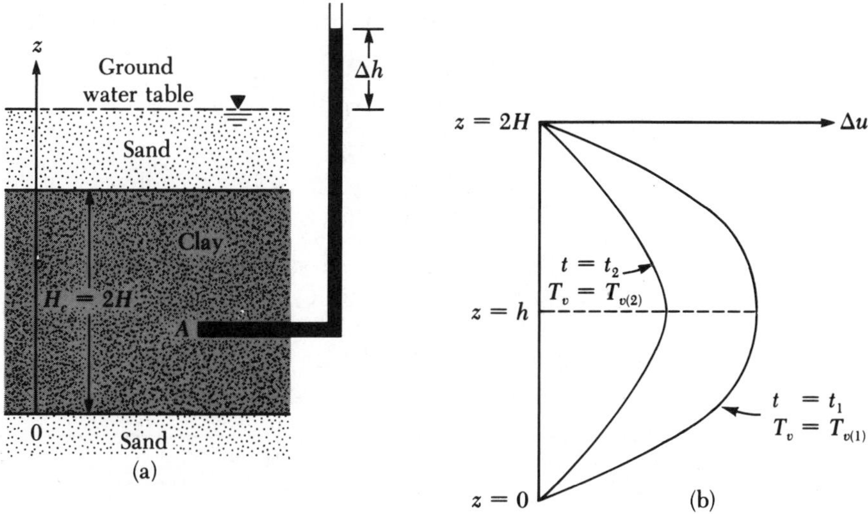

▼ **FIGURE 1.22** (a) Derivation of Eq. (1.67); (b) nature of variation of Δu with time

where C_v = coefficient of consolidation

$$C_v = \frac{k}{m_v \gamma_w} = \frac{k}{\dfrac{\Delta e}{\Delta p(1 + e_{av})} \gamma_w} \tag{1.66}$$

where k = coefficient of permeability of the clay
Δe = total change of void ratio caused by a stress increase of Δp
e_{av} = average void ratio during consolidation
m_v = volume coefficient of compressibility = $\Delta e/[\Delta p(1 + e_{av})]$

Equation (1.65) can be solved to obtain Δu as a function of time t with the following boundary conditions.

1. Because highly permeable sand layers are located at $z = 0$ and $z = H_c$, the excess pore water pressure developed in the clay at those points will be immediately dissipated. Hence

   $\Delta u = 0$ at $z = 0$

   $\Delta u = 0$ at $z = H_c = 2H$

   where H = length of maximum drainage path (due to two-way drainage condition—that is, at the top and bottom of the clay)

2. At time $t = 0$

   $\Delta u = \Delta u_o$ = initial excess pore water pressure after the load application

With the preceding boundary conditions, Eq. (1.65) yields

$$\Delta u = \sum_{m=0}^{m=\infty} \left[\frac{2(\Delta u_o)}{M} \sin\left(\frac{Mz}{H}\right) \right] e^{-M^2 T_v} \tag{1.67}$$

where $M = [(2m + 1)\pi]/2$

m = an integer = 1, 2, ...

T_v = nondimensional time factor = $(C_v t)/H^2$ (1.68)

Determining the field value of C_v is difficult. Figure 1.23 provides a first-order determination of C_v using the liquid limit (U.S. Department of the Navy, 1971). The value of Δu for various depths (that is, $z = 0$ to $z = 2H$) at any given time t (thus T_v) can be calculated from Eq. (1.67). The nature of this variation of Δu is shown in Figure 1.22b.

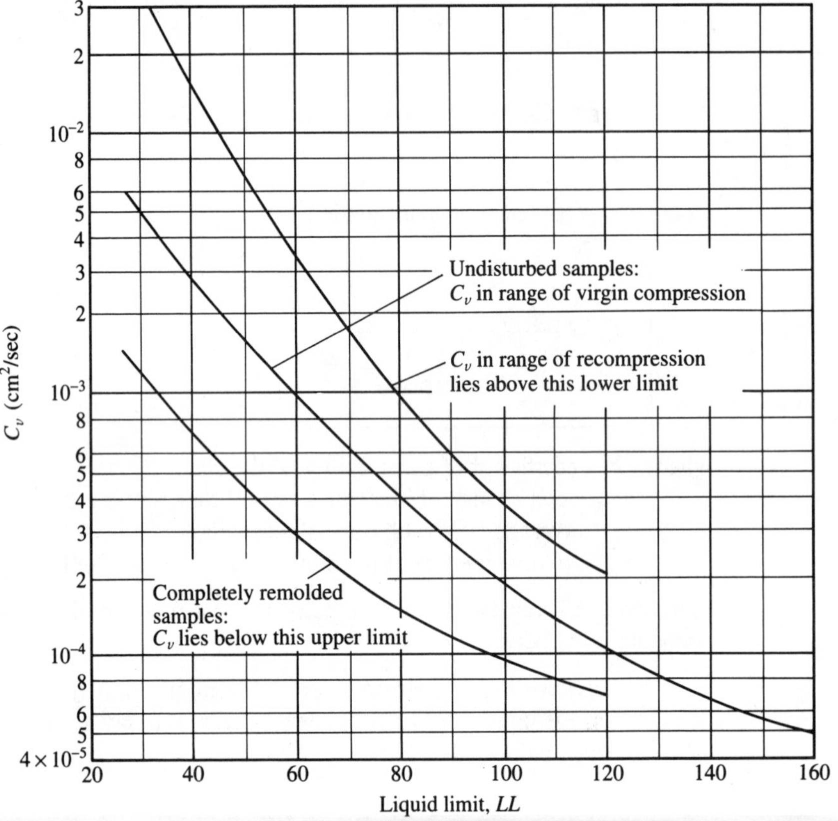

▼ **FIGURE 1.23** Range of C_v (after U.S. Department of the Navy, 1971)

The *average degree of consolidation* of clay layer can be defined as

$$U = \frac{S_t}{S_{\max}} \tag{1.69}$$

where U = average degree of consolidation
S_t = settlement of a clay layer at time t after the load application
S_{max} = maximum consolidation settlement that the clay will undergo under a given loading

If the initial pore water pressure (Δu_o) distribution is constant with depth as shown in Figure 1.24a, the average degree of consolidation can also be expressed as

$$U = \frac{S_t}{S_{max}} = \frac{\int_0^{2H} (\Delta u_0) dz - \int_0^{2H} (\Delta u) dz}{\int_0^{2H} (\Delta u_0) dz} \tag{1.70}$$

or

$$U = \frac{(\Delta u_0) 2H - \int_0^{2H} (\Delta u) dz}{(\Delta u_o) 2H} = 1 - \frac{\int_0^{2H} (\Delta u) dz}{2H(\Delta u_o)} \tag{1.71}$$

Now, combining Eqs. (1.67) and (1.71), we obtain

$$U = \frac{S_t}{S_{max}} = 1 - \sum_{m=0}^{m=\infty} \left(\frac{2}{M^2}\right) e^{-M^2 T_v} \tag{1.72}$$

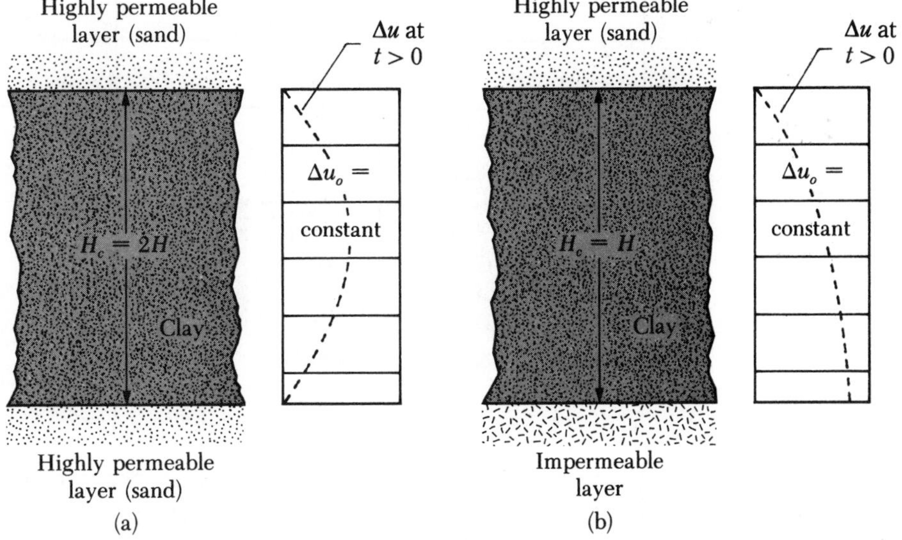

▼ **FIGURE 1.24** Drainage condition for consolidation: (a) two-way drainage; (b) one-way drainage

The variation of U with T_v can be calculated from Eq. (1.72) and is plotted in Figure 1.25. Note that Eq. (1.72) and thus Figure 1.25 are also valid when an impermeable layer is located at the bottom of the clay layer (Figure 1.24b). In that case, excess pore water pressure dissipation can take place in one direction only. The length of the *maximum drainage path* then is equal to $H = H_c$.

The variation of T_v with U shown in Figure 1.25 can also be approximated by

$$T_v = \frac{\pi}{4}\left(\frac{U\%}{100}\right)^2 \qquad \text{(for } U = 0\text{–}60\%\text{)} \tag{1.73}$$

and

$$T_v = 1.781 - 0.933 \log (100 - U\%) \qquad \text{(for } U > 60\%\text{)} \tag{1.74}$$

Sivaram and Swamee (1977) have also developed an empirical relationship between T_v and U that is valid for U varying from 0 to 100%. It is of the form

$$T_v = \frac{\left(\frac{\pi}{4}\right)\left(\frac{U\%}{100}\right)^2}{\left[1 - \left(\frac{U\%}{100}\right)^{5.6}\right]^{0.357}} \tag{1.75}$$

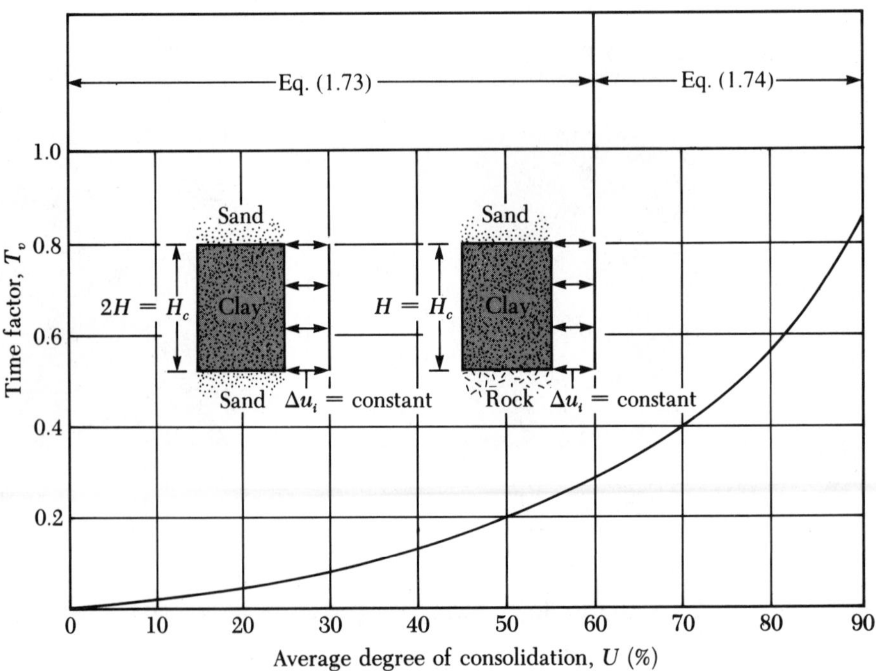

FIGURE 1.25 Plot of time factor against average degree of consolidation (Δu_o = constant)

▼ EXAMPLE 1.9

A laboratory consolidation test on a normally consolidated clay showed the following.

Load, p (kN/m^2)	Void ratio at the end of consolidation, e
140	0.92
212	0.86

The specimen tested was 25.4 mm in thickness and drained on both sides. The time required for the specimen to reach 50% consolidation was 4.5 min.

A similar clay layer in the field, 2.8 m thick and drained on both sides, is subjected to similar average pressure increase (that is, $p_o = 140$ kN/m^2 and $p_o + \Delta p = 212$ kN/m^2). Determine the

a. Expected maximum consolidation settlement in the field
b. Length of time required for the total settlement in the field to reach 40 mm

Solution

Part a

For normally consolidated clay [Eq. (1.54)]

$$C_c = \frac{e_1 - e_2}{\log\left(\frac{p_2}{p_1}\right)} = \frac{0.92 - 0.86}{\log\left(\frac{212}{140}\right)} = 0.333$$

From Eq. (1.60)

$$S = \frac{C_c H_c}{1 + e_o} \log \frac{p_o + \Delta p}{p_o} = \frac{(0.333)(2.8)}{1 + 0.92} \log \frac{212}{140} = 0.0875 \text{ m} = \mathbf{87.5\ mm}$$

Part b

From Eq. (1.69) the average degree of consolidation is

$$U = \frac{S_t}{S_{max}} = \frac{40}{87.5}(100) = 45.7\%$$

The coefficient of consolidation, C_v, can be calculated from the laboratory test. From Eq. (1.68)

$$T_v = \frac{C_v t}{H^2}$$

For 50% consolidation (Figure 1.25), $T_v = 0.197$, $t = 4.5$ min, and $H = H_c/2 = 12.7$ mm. So

$$C_v = T_{50}\frac{H^2}{t} = \frac{(0.197)(12.7)^2}{4.5} = 7.061 \text{ mm}^2/\text{min}$$

Again, for field consolidation, $U = 45.7\%$. From Eq. (1.73)

$$T_v = \frac{\pi}{4}\left(\frac{U\%}{100}\right)^2 = \frac{\pi}{4}\left(\frac{47.5}{100}\right)^2 = 0.177$$

But

$$T_v = \frac{C_v t}{H^2}$$

or

$$t = \frac{T_v H^2}{C_v} = \frac{0.177\left(\frac{2.8 \times 1000}{2}\right)^2}{7.061} = 49132 \text{ min} = \mathbf{34.1\ days}$$ ▼

1.15 SHEAR STRENGTH

The shear strength, s, of a soil, in terms of effective stress, is

$$\boxed{s = c + \sigma' \tan\phi} \tag{1.76}$$

where σ' = effective normal stress on plane of shearing
c = cohesion, or apparent cohesion
ϕ = angle of friction

Equation (1.76) is referred to as the *Mohr–Coulomb failure criteria.* The value of c for sands and normally consolidated clays is equal to zero. For overconsolidated clays, $c > 0$.

For most day-to-day work, the shear strength parameters of a soil (that is, c and ϕ) are determined by two standard laboratory tests. They are (a) the *direct shear test* and (b) the *triaxial test.*

Direct Shear Test

Dry sand can be conveniently tested by direct shear tests. The sand is placed in a shear box that is split into two halves (Figure 1.26a). A normal load is first applied to the

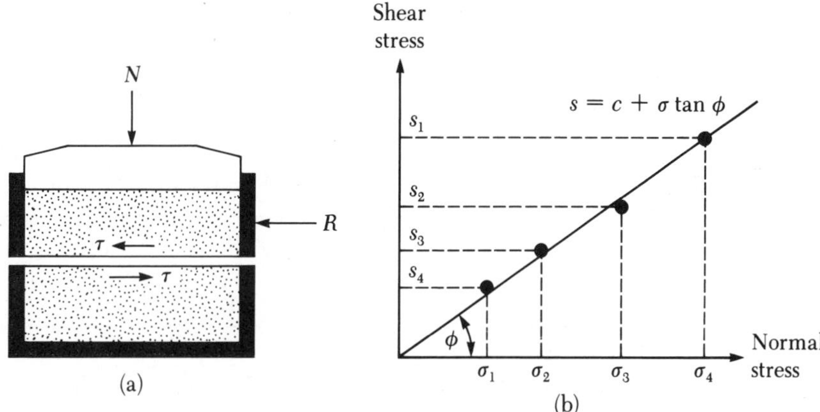

FIGURE 1.26 Direct shear test in sand: (a) schematic diagram of test equipment; (b) plot of test results to obtain the friction angle, ϕ

specimen. Then a shear force is applied to the two halves of the shear box to cause failure in the sand. The normal and shear stresses at failure are

$$\sigma' = \frac{N}{A}$$

$$s = \frac{R}{A}$$

where A = area of the failure plane in soil—that is, the area of cross section of the shear box

Several tests of this type can be conducted by varying the normal load. The angle of friction of the sand can be determined by plotting a graph of s against σ', as shown in Figure 1.26b, or

$$\boxed{\phi = \tan^{-1}\left(\frac{s}{\sigma'}\right)} \tag{1.77}$$

For sands the angle of friction usually ranges from 26° to 45°, increasing with the relative density of compaction. The approximate range of the relative density of compaction and the corresponding range of the angle of friction for various coarse-grained soils is shown in Figure 1.27.

Triaxial Tests

Triaxial compression tests can be conducted on sands and clays. Figure 1.28a shows a schematic diagram of the triaxial test arrangement. Essentially, it consists of placing a soil specimen confined by a rubber membrane in a lucite chamber. An all-around confining pressure (σ_3) is applied to the specimen by means of the chamber fluid (generally

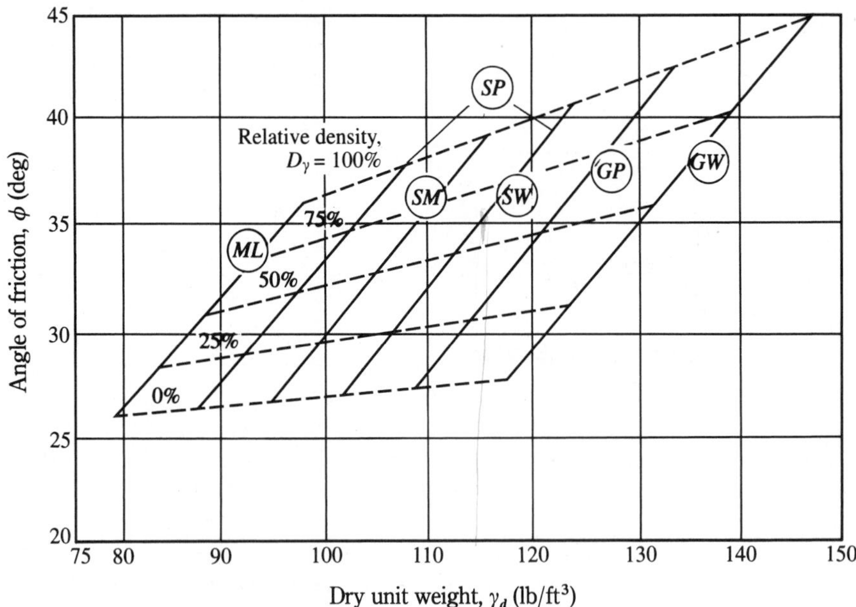

▼ **FIGURE 1.27** Range of relative density of compaction and corresponding range of angle of friction for coarse-grained soil (after U.S. Department of the Navy, 1971)

water or glycerin). An added stress ($\Delta\sigma$) can also be applied to the specimen in the axial direction to cause failure ($\Delta\sigma = \Delta\sigma_f$ at failure). Drainage from the specimen can be allowed or stopped, depending on the test condition. For clays, three main types of tests can be conducted with triaxial equipment:

1. Consolidated-drained test (CD test)
2. Consolidated-undrained test (CU test)
3. Unconsolidated-undrained test (UU test)

Table 1.14 summarizes these three tests.

For *consolidated-drained tests*, at failure,

Major principal effective stress $= \sigma_3 + \Delta\sigma_f = \sigma_1 = \sigma'_1$

Minor principal effective stress $= \sigma_3 = \sigma'_3$

Changing σ_3 allows several tests of this type to be conducted on various clay specimens. The shear strength parameters (c and ϕ) can now be determined by plotting Mohr's circle at failure, as shown in Figure 1.28b, and drawing a common tangent to the Mohr's circles. This is the *Mohr–Coulomb failure envelope*. (*Note:* For normally consolidated clay, $c \approx 0$.) At failure

$$\sigma'_1 = \sigma'_3 \tan^2\left(45 + \frac{\phi}{2}\right) + 2c \tan\left(45 + \frac{\phi}{2}\right) \tag{1.78}$$

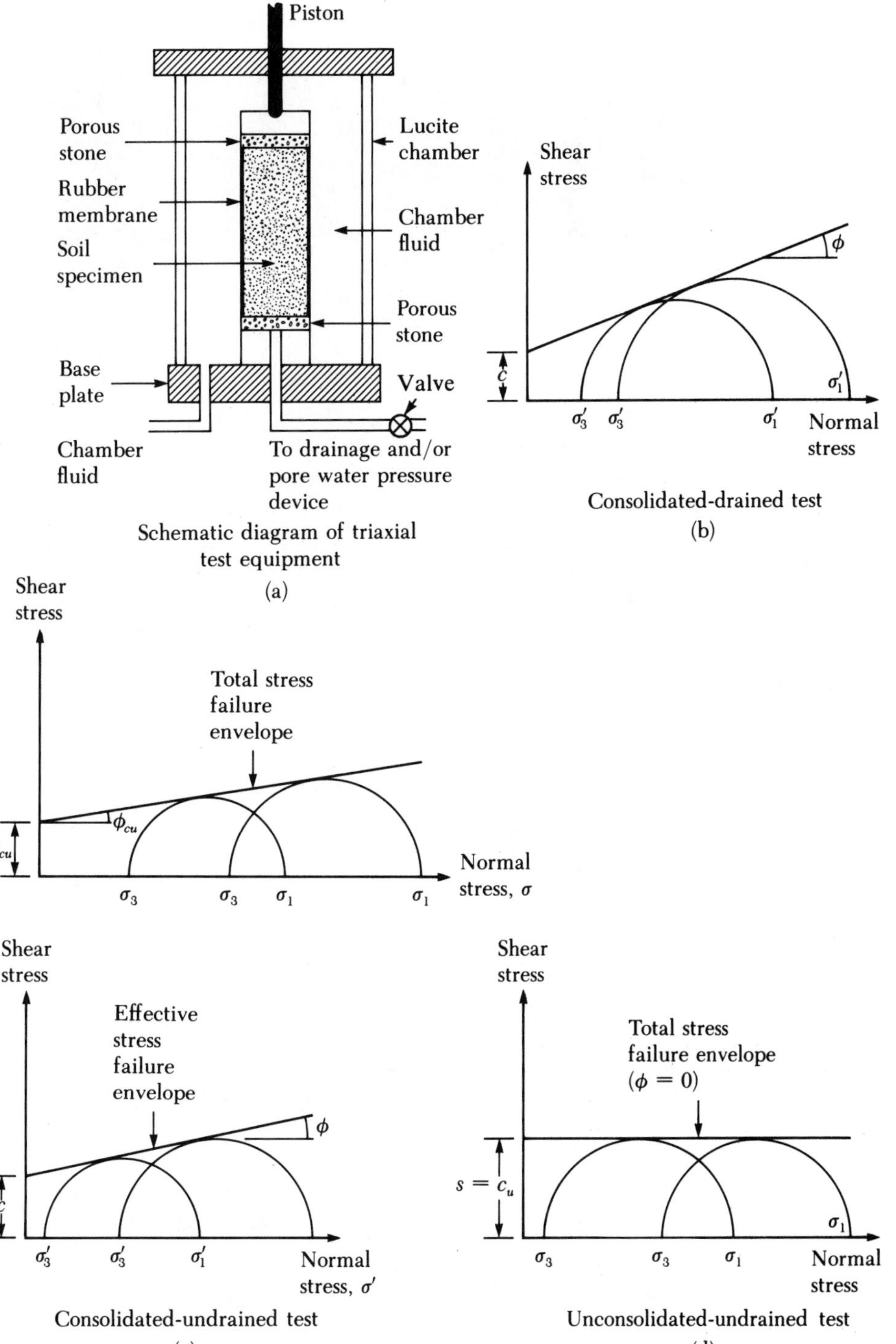

FIGURE 1.28 Triaxial test

TABLE 1.14 Summary of Triaxial Tests on Saturated Clays

Test type	Step 1	Step 2
Consolidated-drained	Apply chamber pressure, σ_3. Allow complete drainage, so pore water pressure ($u = u_a$) developed is zero.	Apply axial stress, $\Delta\sigma$, slowly. Allow drainage, so pore water pressure ($u = u_d$) developed through application of $\Delta\sigma$ is zero. At failure, $\Delta\sigma = \Delta\sigma_f$; total pore water pressure $u_f = u_a + u_d = 0$.
Consolidated-undrained	Apply chamber pressure, σ_3. Allow complete drainage, so pore water pressure ($u = u_a$) developed is zero	Apply axial stress, $\Delta\sigma$. Do not allow drainage ($u = u_d \neq 0$). At failure, $\Delta\sigma = \Delta_f$; pore water pressure $u = u_f = u_a + u_d = 0 + u_{d(f)}$.
Unconsolidated-undrained	Apply chamber pressure, σ_3. Do not allow drainage, so pore water pressure ($u = u_a$) developed through application of σ_3 is not zero.	Apply axial stress, $\Delta\sigma$. Do not allow drainage ($u = u_d \neq 0$). At failure $\Delta\sigma = \Delta\sigma_f$; pore water pressure $u = u_f = u_a + u_{d(f)}$.

For *consolidated-undrained* tests, at failure,

$$\text{Major principal total stress} = \sigma_3 + \Delta\sigma_f = \sigma_1$$

$$\text{Minor principal total stress} = \sigma_3$$

$$\text{Major principal effective stress} = (\sigma_3 + \Delta\sigma_f) - u_f = \sigma_1'$$

$$\text{Minor principal effective stress} = \sigma_3 - u_f = \sigma_3'$$

Changing σ_3 permits multiple tests of this type to be conducted on several soil specimens. The total stress Mohr's circles at failure can now be plotted, as shown in Figure 1.28c, and then a common tangent can be drawn to define the *failure envelope*. This *total stress failure envelope* is defined by the equation

$$s = c_{cu} + \sigma \tan \phi_{cu} \tag{1.79}$$

where c_{cu} and ϕ_{cu} are the *consolidated-undrained cohesion* and *angle of friction*, respectively (*note:* $c_{cu} \approx 0$ for normally consolidated clays)

Similarly, effective stress Mohr's circles at failure can be drawn to determine the *effective stress failure envelopes* (Figure 1.28c). They follow the relation expressed in Eq. (1.76).

Kenney (1959) has given a correlation between the friction angle, ϕ, and the plasticity index, *PI*, of normally consolidated clays based on the observations of more than 60 soils. This correlation is shown in Figure 1.29. Based on the average plot, the value of ϕ generally decreases from about 37–38° with a plasticity index of about 10, to about 25° with a plasticity index of about 100. The consolidated undrained friction angle (ϕ_{cu}) of normally consolidated saturated clays generally ranges from 5° to 20°.

For *unconsolidated-undrained* triaxial tests

Major principal total stress $= \sigma_3 + \Delta\sigma_f = \sigma_1$

Minor principal total stress $= \sigma_3$

The total stress Mohr's circle at failure can now be drawn, as shown in Figure 1.28d. For saturated clays, the value of $\sigma_1 - \sigma_3 = \Delta\sigma_f$ is a constant, irrespective of the chamber confining pressure, σ_3 (also shown in Figure 1.28d). The tangent to these Mohr's circles will be a horizontal line, called the $\phi = 0$ condition. The shear stress for this condition is

$$\boxed{s = c_u = \frac{\Delta\sigma_f}{2}} \tag{1.80}$$

where c_u = undrained cohesion (or undrained shear strength)

The pore pressure developed in the soil specimen during the unconsolidated-undrained triaxial test is

$$u = u_a + u_d \tag{1.81}$$

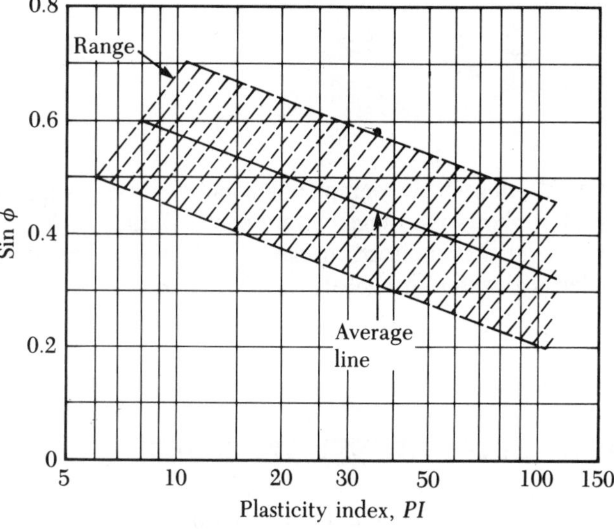

▼ **FIGURE 1.29** Variation of sin ϕ with the plasticity index of several clays (redrawn after Kenney, 1959)

The pore pressure u_a is the contribution of the hydrostatic chamber pressure, σ_3. Hence

$$u_a = B\sigma_3 \tag{1.82}$$

where B = Skempton's pore pressure parameter

Similarly, the pore pressure u_d is the result of added axial stress, $\Delta\sigma$, so

$$u_d = A\ \Delta\sigma \tag{1.83}$$

where A = Skempton's pore pressure parameter

However

$$\Delta\sigma = \sigma_1 - \sigma_3 \tag{1.84}$$

Combining Eqs. (1.81), (1.82), (1.83), and (1.84) gives

$$u = u_a + u_d = B\sigma_3 + A(\sigma_1 - \sigma_3) \tag{1.85}$$

The pore water pressure parameter B in soft saturated soils is 1, so

$$\boxed{u = \sigma_3 + A(\sigma_1 - \sigma_3)} \tag{1.86}$$

The value of the pore water pressure parameter A at failure will vary with the type of soil. Following is a general range of the values of A at failure for various types of clayey soil encountered in nature.

Type of soil	*A at failure*
Sandy clays	0.5–0.7
Normally consolidated clays	0.5–1
Overconsolidated clays	−0.5–0

Figure 1.30 shows a photograph of laboratory triaxial equipment.

Figure 1.31 shows the range of variation between c_u/σ_a (σ_a = atmospheric stress) and liquidity index for undisturbed clayey soils of low sensitivity. The definition of liquidity index is given in Eq. (1.53a).

1.16 UNCONFINED COMPRESSION TEST

The *unconfined compression test* (Figure 1.32a) is a special type of unconsolidated-undrained triaxial test in which the confining pressure $\sigma_3 = 0$, as shown in Figure 1.32b. In this test an axial stress, $\Delta\sigma$, is applied to the specimen to cause failure

▼ **FIGURE 1.30** Triaxial test equipment

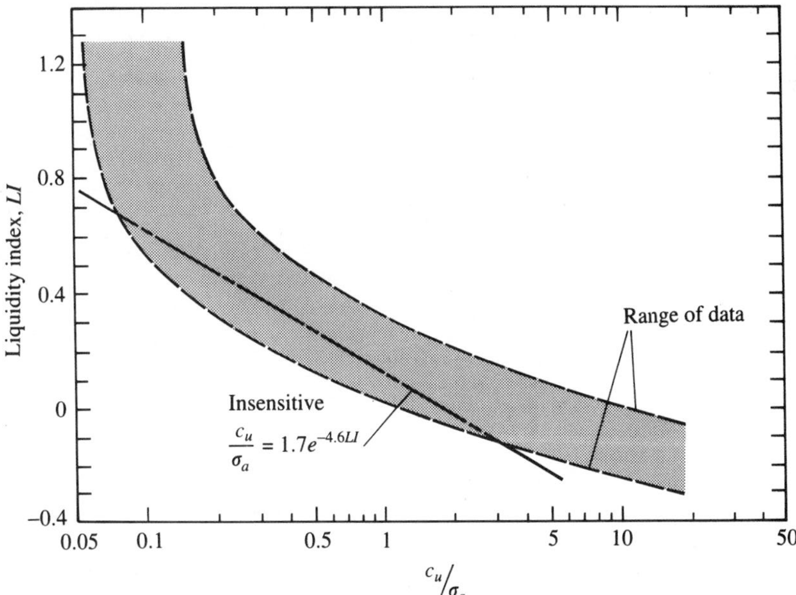

▼ **FIGURE 1.31** Variation of c_u/σ_a with liquidity index (based on Wood, 1983; Kulhawy and Mayne, 1990)

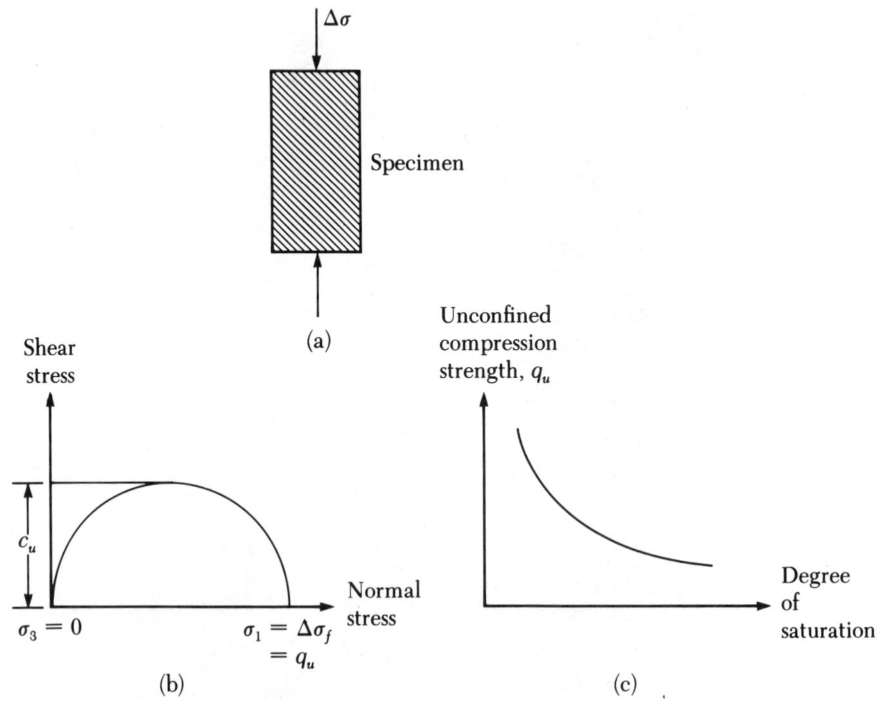

▼ **FIGURE 1.32** Unconfined compression test: (a) soil specimen; (b) Mohr's circle for the test; (c) variation of q_u with the degree of saturation

is, $\Delta\sigma = \Delta\sigma_f$). The corresponding Mohr's circle is shown in Figure 1.32b. Note that, for this case,

Major principal total stress $= \Delta\sigma_f = q_u$

Minor principal total stress $= 0$

The axial stress at failure, $\Delta\sigma_f = q_u$, is generally referred to as the *unconfined compression strength*. The shear strength of saturated clays under this condition ($\phi = 0$), from Eq. (1.76), is

$$s = c_u = \frac{q_u}{2} \tag{1.87}$$

The unconfined compression strength can be used as an indicator for the consistency of clays.

Unconfined compression tests are sometimes conducted on unsaturated soils. With the void ratio of a soil specimen remaining constant, the unconfined compression strength rapidly decreases with the degree of saturation (Figure 1.32c).

Figure 1.33 shows an unconfined compression test in progress.

▼ **FIGURE 1.33** Unconfined compression test in progress (courtesy of Soiltest, Inc., Lake Bluff, Illinois)

The undrained cohesion, c_u, is an important parameter in the design of foundations. For normally consolidated clay deposits (Figure 1.34), the magnitude of c_u increases almost linearly with the increase of effective overburden pressure, p. Skempton (1957) correlated c_u with p in the form

$$\frac{c_u}{p} = 0.11 + 0.0037(PI) \qquad \text{(normally consolidated clay)} \tag{1.88}$$

where PI = plasticity index

The variation of c_u/p with overconsolidation ratio, $OCR = p/p_c$ (p_c = preconsolidation pressure) for some natural clays is shown in Figure 1.35. Based on these observations, we can say that

$$\left(\frac{c_u}{p}\right)_{\text{overconsolidated}} = \alpha\left(\frac{c_u}{p}\right)_{\text{normally consolidated}} \tag{1.89}$$

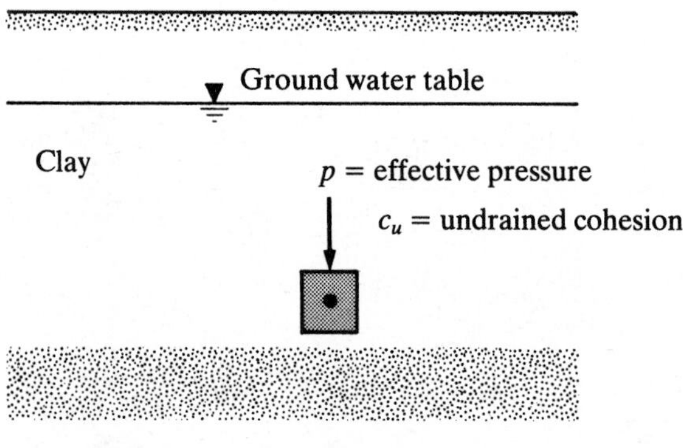

▼ **FIGURE 1.34** Clay deposit

Figure 1.36 shows the range of variation of α with *OCR* based on the experimental results depicted in Figure 1.35. For initial estimation purposes, the value of α from the average plot of Figure 1.35 may be used in Eq. (1.89).

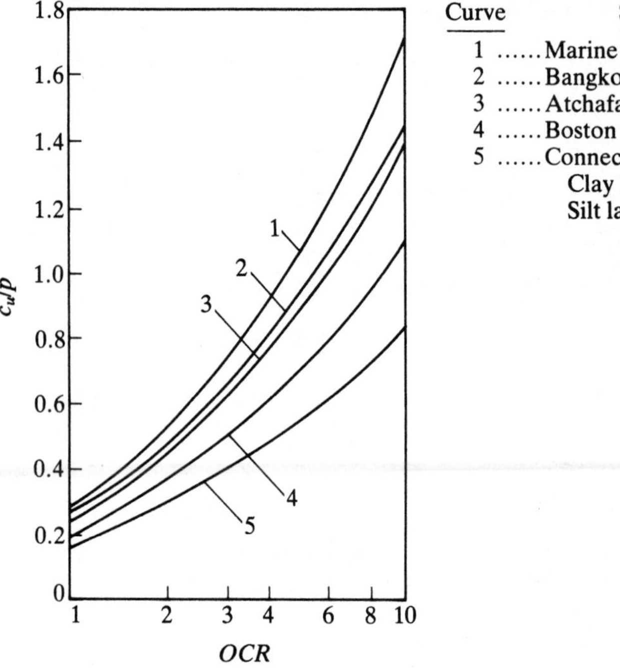

▼ **FIGURE 1.35** Variation of c_u/p with *OCR* for five clay soils (after Ladd and Foot, 1974)

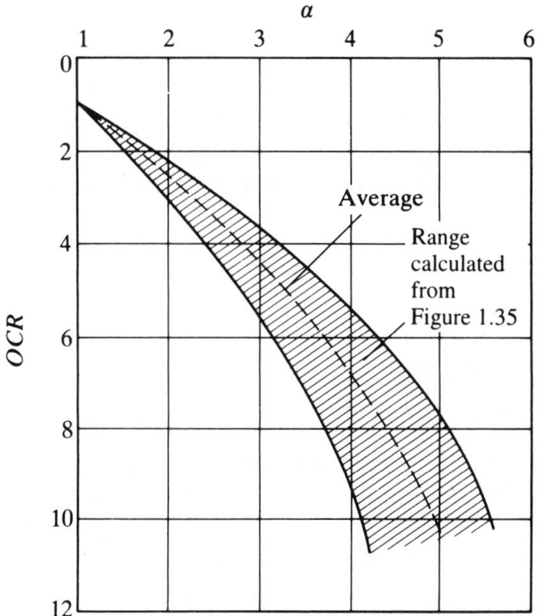

▼ **FIGURE 1.36** Variation of α with *OCR* [Eq. (1.89)] based on the results shown in Figure 1.35

▼ EXAMPLE 1.10

At a point in a saturated overconsolidated clay deposit, $p = 2300$ lb/ft². The plasticity index of the clay is 24, and the overconsolidation ratio, *OCR*, is 2.5. Estimate the undrained cohesion, c_u.

Solution

From Eq. (1.88) for normally consolidated clay,

$$\frac{c_u}{p} = 0.11 + 0.0037(PI) = 0.11 + 0.0037(24)$$

$$= 0.199$$

For $OCR = 2.5$, the value of α from Figure 1.36 is about 1.9. From Eq. (1.89)

$$\left(\frac{c_u}{p}\right)_{\text{overconsolidated}} = \alpha\left(\frac{c_u}{p}\right)_{\text{normally consolidated}}$$

$$= (1.9)(0.199) = 0.378$$

So

$$c_u = (0.378)(p) = (0.378)(2300) = \mathbf{869.4\ lb/ft^2}$$ ▼

1.17 SENSITIVITY

For many naturally deposited clay soils, the unconfined compression strength is much less when the soils are tested after remolding without any change in the moisture content. This property of clay soil is called *sensitivity*. The degree of sensitivity is the ratio of the unconfined compression strength in an undisturbed state to that in a remolded state, or

$$S_t = \frac{q_{u(\text{undisturbed})}}{q_{u(\text{remolded})}} \tag{1.90}$$

The sensitivity ratio of most clays ranges from about 1 to 8; however, highly flocculent marine clay deposits may have sensitivity ratios ranging from about 10 to 80. Some clays turn to viscous liquids upon remolding, and these clays are referred to as "quick" clays. The loss of strength of clay soils from remolding is caused primarily by the destruction of the clay particle structure that was developed during the original process of sedimentation.

PROBLEMS

1.1 For a natural sand, $D_{60} = 0.8$ mm, $D_{30} = 0.3$ mm, and $D_{10} = 0.15$ mm. Calculate:

a. The uniformity coefficient
b. The coefficient of gradation

1.2 A moist soil has a void ratio of 0.65, the moisture content of the soil is 14%, and $G_s = 2.7$. Determine:

a. Porosity
b. Degree of saturation (%)
c. Dry unit weight (kN/m^3)

1.3 For the soil described in Problem 1.2:

a. What would be the saturated unit weight in kN/m^3?
b. How much water, in kN/m^3, needs to be added to the soil for complete saturation?
c. What would be the moist unit weight in kN/m^3 when the degree of saturation is 70%?

1.4 The moist unit weight of a soil is 119.5 lb/ft^3. For a moisture content of 12% and $G_s =$ 2.65, calculate:

a. e
b. n
c. S
d. γ_d

1.5 For the soil described in Problem 1.4:

a. What would be the saturated unit weight in lb/ft^3?

b. How much water, in lb/ft^3, needs to be added to the soil for complete saturation?

c. What would be the moist unit weight in lb/ft^3 when the degree of saturation is 80%?

1.6 A saturated soil specimen has $w = 36\%$ and $\gamma_d = 85.43$ lb/ft^3. Determine:

a. Void ratio

b. Porosity

c. Specific gravity of soil solids

d. Saturated unit weight (in lb/ft^3)

1.7 For a soil sample, $V = 3.2$ ft^3, $W = 378$ lb, $w = 12.5\%$, and $G_s = 2.67$. Calculate:

a. e

b. n

c. γ

d. γ_d

e. S

1.8 The laboratory test results of a sand are $e_{max} = 0.91$, $e_{min} = 0.48$, and $G_s = 2.67$. What would be the dry and moist unit weights of this sand when compacted at a moisture content of 10% to a relative density of 65%?

1.9 The laboratory test results of six soils are given in the following table. Classify the soils by the AASHTO soil classification system and give the group indices.

	Sieve analysis—percent passing					
	Soil					
Sieve no.	*A*	*B*	*C*	*D*	*E*	*F*
4	92	100	100	95	100	100
10	48	60	98	90	91	82
40	28	41	82	79	80	74
200	13	33	72	64	30	55
Liquid limit	31	38	56	35	43	35
Plastic limit	26	25	31	26	29	21

1.10 Classify the soils in Problem 1.9 by using the Unified Soil Classification System.

1.11 The permeability of a sand was tested in the laboratory at a void ratio of 0.6 and was determined to be 0.14 cm/sec. Use Eq. (1.27) to estimate the coefficient of permeability of this sand at a void ratio of 0.8.

1.12 A sand has a coefficient of 0.3 cm/sec at a void ratio of 0.65. Estimate the void ratio at which its coefficient of permeability would be 0.15 cm/sec. Use Eq. (1.29).

1.13 The *in situ* coefficient of permeability of a clay is 4.2×10^{-6} cm/sec at a void ratio of 0.92. What would be the coefficient of permeability at a void ratio of 0.72? Use Eq. (1.31).

1.14 A soil profile is shown in Figure P1.14. Determine the total stress, pore water pressure, and effective stress at A, B, C, and D.

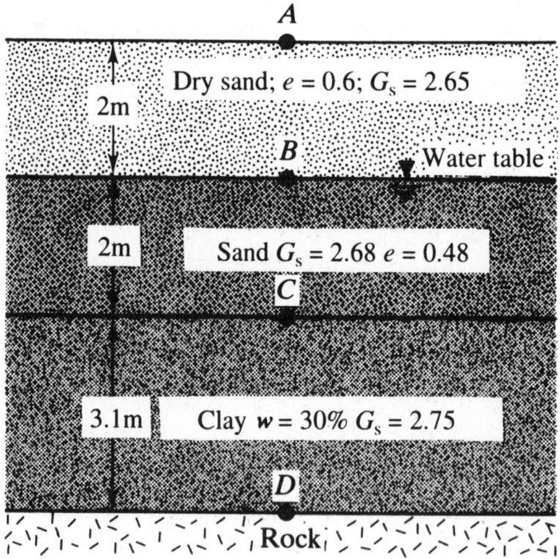

▼ **FIGURE P1.14**

1.15 A sandy soil ($G_s = 2.66$), in its densest and loosest states, has void ratios of 0.42 and 0.97, respectively. Estimate the range of the critical hydraulic gradient in this soil at which quicksand condition might occur.

1.16 A saturated clay deposit in the field has

Liquid limit = 61%

Plastic limit = 21%

Moisture content = 38%

Estimate the preconsolidation pressure, p_c (lb/ft^2). Use Eq. (1.53).

1.17 A normally consolidated clay layer 8.53 ft thick has a void ratio of 1.3, $LL = 41$, and average effective stress on the clay layer = 1720 lb/ft^2. How much consolidation settlement would the clay layer undergo if the average effective stress on the clay layer is increased to 2510 lb/ft^2 as a result of the construction of a foundation?

1.18 Refer to Problem 1.17. Assume that the clay layer is preconsolidated, $p_c = 1980$ lb/ft^2, and $C_s = \frac{1}{4}C_c$. Estimate the consolidation settlement.

1.19 Refer to Figure P1.14. The clay is normally consolidated. A laboratory consolidation test on the clay gave the following results.

Pressure (kN/m^2)	*Void ratio*
100	0.905
200	0.815

a. Calculate the average effective stress on the clay layer.
b. Determine the compression index, C_c.
c. If the average effective stress on the clay layer is increased ($p_0 + \Delta p$) to 115 kN/m^2, what would be the total consolidation settlement?

1.20 Refer to Problem 1.19c. For the clay soil, if $C_v = 5.6$ mm^2/min, how long will it take to reach half the consolidation settlement? (*Note:* The clay layer in the field is drained on one side only.)

1.21 A clay soil specimen, 1 in. thick (drained on top and bottom), was tested in the laboratory. For a given load increment, the time for 50% consolidation was 5 min 20 sec. How long will it take for 50% consolidation of a similar clay layer in the field that is 8.2 ft thick and drained on one side only?

1.22 A direct shear test was conducted on a 2 in. × 2 in. specimen of dry sand, with the following results.

Normal force (lb)	*Shear force at failure (lb)*
33	20.67
55.17	35.8
66.16	40.2

Draw a graph of shear stress at failure vs. normal stress and determine the soil friction angle.

1.23 A consolidated-drained triaxial test on a normally consolidated clay yielded the following results:

All around confining pressure = $\sigma_3 = 20$ lb/in.^{2}

Added axial stress at failure = $\Delta\sigma = 40$ lb/in.^{2}

Determine the shear strength parameters.

1.24 Following are the results of two consolidated-drained triaxial tests on a clay.

Test I: $\sigma_3 = 82.8$ kN/m^2; $\sigma_{1(\text{failure})} = 329.2$ kN/m^2

Test II: $\sigma_3 = 165.6$ kN/m^2; $\sigma_{1(\text{failure})} = 558.6$ kN/m^2

Determine the shear strength parameters—that is, c and ϕ.

1.25 A consolidated-undrained triaxial test was conducted on a saturated normally consolidated clay. Following are the test results.

$\sigma_3 = 13$ lb/in.^{2}

$\sigma_{1(\text{failure})} = 32$ lb/in.^{2}

Pore water pressure at failure = $u_f = 5.5$ lb/in.^{2}
Determine c_u, ϕ_{cu}, c, and ϕ.

1.26 A normally consolidated clay soil has $\phi = 28°$ and $\phi_{cu} = 20°$. If a consolidated-undrained test is conducted on this clay with $\sigma_3 = 21.5$ lb/in.^{2}, what would be the magnitude of the principal stress, σ_1, and the pore water pressure, u, at failure?

1.27 A saturated clay layer has

Saturated unit weight, $\gamma_{sat} = 19.6\ \text{kN/m}^3$

Plasticity index = 21

The water table coincides with the ground surface. If the clay is normally consolidated, estimate the magnitude of c_u (kN/m^2) at a depth of 8 m from the ground surface.

1.28 Assume that the clay layer in Problem 1.27 is overconsolidated and that the $OCR = 2.5$. Estimate the magnitude of c_u (kN/m^2) at a depth of 6.5 m below the ground surface.

REFERENCES

American Society for Testing and Materials (1992). *Annual Book of ASTM Standards*, Vol. 04.08, Philadelphia, Pa.

Azzouz, A. S., Krizek, R. J., and Corotis, R. B. (1976). "Regression Analysis of Soil Compressibility," *Soils and Foundations*, Vol. 16, No. 2, pp. 19–29.

Casagrande, A. (1936). "Determination of the Preconsolidation Load and Its Practical Significance," *Proceedings*, First International Conference on Soil Mechanics and Foundation Engineering, Cambridge, Mass., Vol. 3, pp. 60–64.

Darcy, H. (1856). *Les Fontaines Publiques de la Ville de Dijon*, Paris.

Das, B. M. (1993). *Soil Mechanics Laboratory Manual*, 3rd ed., Engineering Press, San Jose, Calif.

Hazen, A. (1930). "Water Supply," *American Civil Engineers Handbook*, Wiley, New York.

Highway Research Board (1945). *Report of the Committee on Classification of Materials for Subgrades and Granular Type Roads*, Vol. 25, pp. 375–388.

Kenney, T. C. (1959). "Discussion," *Journal of the Soil Mechanics and Foundations Division*, American Society of Civil Engineers, Vol. 85, No. SM3, pp. 67–69.

Kulhawy, F. H., and Mayne, P. W. (1990). *Manual on Estimating Soil Properties for Foundation Design*, Report EL-6800, EPRI.

Ladd, C. C., and Foot, R. (1974). "New Design Procedure for Stability of Soft Clays," *Journal of the Geotechnical Engineering Division*, American Society of Civil Engineers, Vol. 92, No. GT2, pp. 79–103.

Leroueil, S., Tavenas, F., and LeBihan, J. P. (1983). "Propriétés Caractéristiques des Argiles de l'est due Canada," *Canadian Geotechnical Journal*, Vol. 20, No. 4, pp. 681–705.

Nagaraj, T. S., and Murthy, B. R. S. (1985). "Prediction of the Preconsolidation Pressure and Recompression Index of Soils," *Geotechnical Testing Journal*, American Society for Testing and Materials, Vol. 8, No. 4, pp. 199–202.

Rendon-Herrero, O. (1980). "Universal Compression Index Equation," *Journal of the Geotechnical Engineering Division*, American Society of Civil Engineers, Vol. 106, No. GT11, pp. 1178–1200.

Schmertmann, J. H. (1953). "Undisturbed Consolidation Behavior of Clay," *Transactions*, American Society of Civil Engineers, Vol. 120, p. 1201.

Sivaram, B., and Swamee, P. (1977). "A Computational Method for Consolidation Coefficient," *Soils and Foundations*, Tokyo, Japan, Vol. 17, No. 2, pp. 48–52.

Skempton, A. W. (1944). "Notes on the Compressibility of Clays," *Quarterly Journal of Geological Society*, London, Vol. C, pp. 119–135.

Skempton, A. W. (1957). "The Planning and Design of New Hong Kong Airport," *Proceedings*, The Institute of Civil Engineers, London, Vol. 7, pp. 305–307.

Stas, C. V., and Kulhawy, F. H. (1984). *Critical Evaluation of Design Methods for Foundations Under Axial Uplift and Compression Loading*, Report EL-3771, EPRI.

Tavenas, F., Jean, P., Leblond, P., and Leroueil, S. (1983). "The Permeability of Natural Soft Clays. Part II: Permeability Characteristics," *Canadian Geotechnical Journal,* Vol. 20, No. 4, pp. 645–660.

Terzaghi, K., and Peck, R. B. (1967). *Soil Mechanics in Engineering Practice,* Wiley, New York.

U.S. Department of the Navy (1971). "Design Manual—Soil Mechanics, Foundations and Earth Structures," *NAVFAC DM-7,* U.S. Government Printing Office, Washington, D.C.

U.S. Department of the Navy (1982). "Soil Mechanics," *NAVFAC DM7.1,* U.S. Government Printing Office, Washington, D.C.

Wood, D. M. (1983). "Index Properties and Critical State Soil Mechanics," *Proceedings,* Symposium on Recent Developments in Laboratory and Field Tests and Analysis of Geotechnical Problems, Bangkok, pp. 301–309.

Wroth, C. P., and Wood, D. M. (1978). "The Correlation of Index Properties with Some Basic Engineering Properties of Soils," *Canadian Geotechnical Journal,* Vol. 15, No. 2, pp. 137–145.

Youd, T. L. (1973). "Factors Controlling Maximum and Minimum Densities of Sands," *Special Technical Publication No. 523,* American Society for Testing amd Materials, pp. 98–122.

CHAPTER TWO

NATURAL SOIL DEPOSITS AND SOIL EXPLORATION

2.1 INTRODUCTION

To design a foundation that will adequately support a structure, an engineer must understand the type of soil deposits that will support the foundation. Moreover, foundation engineers must remember that soil at any site frequently is nonhomogeneous—that is, the soil profile may vary. Soil mechanics theories involve idealized conditions, so the application of these theories to foundation engineering problems involves judicious evaluation of site conditions and soil parameters. To do so requires some knowledge of the geological process by which the soil deposit at the site was formed, supplemented by subsurface exploration. Good professional judgment constitutes an essential part of geotechnical engineering—and it comes only with practice.

This chapter is divided into two parts. The first is a general overview of natural soil deposits generally encountered, and the second describes the general principles of subsoil exploration.

NATURAL SOIL DEPOSITS

2.2 SOIL ORIGIN

Most of the soils that cover the earth are formed by the weathering of various rocks. There are two general types of weathering: (1) mechanical weathering and (2) chemical weathering.

Mechanical weathering is the process by which rocks are broken into smaller and smaller pieces by physical forces. These physical forces may be running water, wind, ocean waves, glacier ice, frost action, and expansion and contraction caused by gain and loss of heat.

Chemical weathering is the process of chemical decomposition of the original rock. In the case of mechanical weathering, the rock breaks into smaller pieces without a change of chemical composition. However, in chemical weathering, the original material may be changed to something entirely different. For example, the chemical weathering of feldspar can produce clay minerals.

Soil produced by the weathering of rocks can be transported by physical processes to other places. These soil deposits are called *transported soils*. In contrast, some soils stay where they were formed and cover the rock surface from which they derive. These soils are referred to as *residual soils*.

Based on the *transporting agent*, transported soils can be subdivided into three major categories:

1. *Alluvial*, or *fluvial:* deposited by running water
2. *Glacial*: deposited by glacier action
3. *Aeolian:* deposited by wind action

In addition to transported and residual soils, there are *peats* and *organic soils*, which derive from the decomposition of organic materials.

2.3 RESIDUAL SOIL

Residual soil deposits are common in the tropics, Hawaii, and the southeastern United States. The nature of a residual soil deposit will generally depend on the parent rock. When hard rocks such as granite and gneiss undergo weathering, most of the materials are likely to remain in place. These soil deposits generally have a top layer of clayey or silty clay material below which are silty and/or sandy soil layers. They are generally underlain by a partially weathered rock and then sound bedrock. The depth of the sound bedrock may vary widely, even within a distance of a few meters. Figure 2.1 shows the log of a boring in a residual soil deposit derived from the weathering of granite.

In contrast to hard rocks, some chemical rocks, such as limestone, are made up chiefly of calcite ($CaCo_3$) mineral. Chalk and dolomite have large concentrations of dolomite minerals [$CaMg(Co_3)_2$]. These rocks have large amounts of soluble materials, some of which are removed by ground water, leaving behind the insoluble fraction of the rock. Residual soils that derive from chemical rocks possess a gradual transition zone to the bedrock, as shown in Figure 2.1. The residual soils derived from the weathering of limestonelike rocks are mostly gray in color. Although uniform in kind, the depth of weathering may vary greatly. The residual soils immediately above the bedrock may be normally consolidated. Large foundations with heavy loads may be susceptible to large consolidation settlements on these soils.

2.4 ALLUVIAL DEPOSITS

Alluvial soil deposits derive from the action of streams and rivers. They can be divided into two major categories: (1) *braided-stream deposits* and (2) deposits caused by the *meandering belt of streams*.

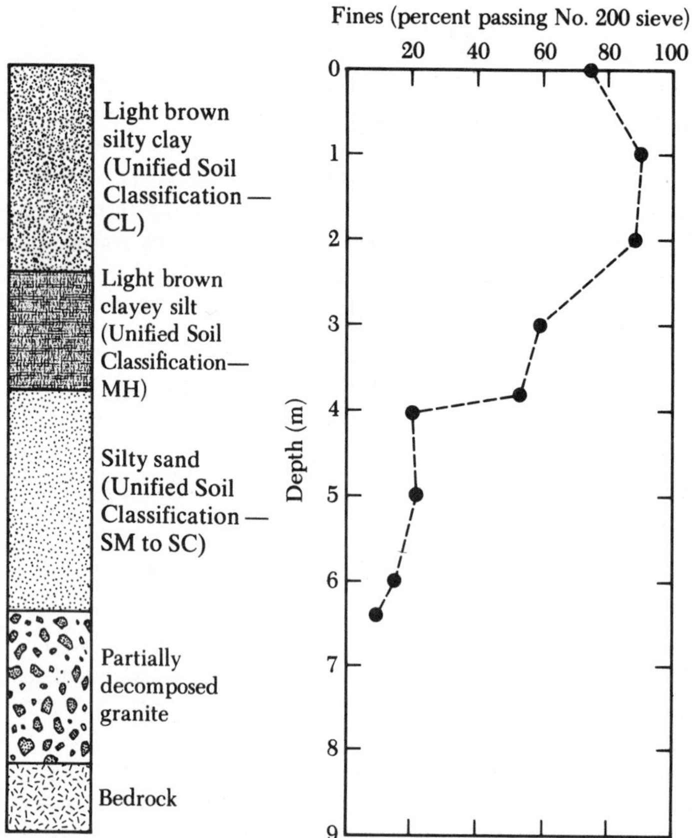

▼ **FIGURE 2.1** Boring log for a residual soil derived from granite

Deposits from Braided Streams

Braided streams are high-gradient, rapidly flowing streams. They are highly erosive and carry large amounts of sediment. Because of the high bed load, a minor change in the velocity of flow will cause deposit of sediments. By this process, these streams may build up a complex tangle of converging and diverging channels separated by sandbars and islands.

The deposits formed from braided streams are very irregular in stratification and have a wide range of grain sizes. Figure 2.2 shows a cross section of such a deposit. These deposits share several characteristics.

1. The grain sizes usually range from gravel to silt. Clay-size particles are generally *not* found in these deposits.
2. Although grain size varies widely, the soil in a given pocket or lens is rather uniform.
3. At any given depth, the void ratio and unit weight may vary over a wide range within a lateral distance of only a few meters. This variation can be

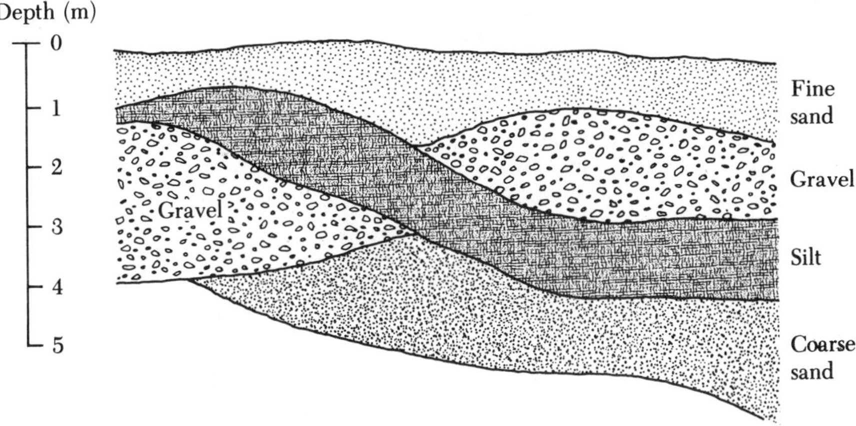

▼ **FIGURE 2.2** Cross section of a braided-stream deposit

observed during soil exploration for construction of a foundation for a structure. The standard penetration resistance (N value) at a given depth obtained from various bore holes will be highly irregular and variable.

Alluvial deposits are present in several parts of the western United States, such as Southern California, Utah, and the basin and range sections of Nevada. Also, a large amount of sediment originally derived from the Rocky Mountain range was carried eastward to form the alluvial deposits of the Great Plains. On a smaller scale, this type of natural soil deposit, left by braided streams, can be encountered locally.

Meander Belt Deposits

The term *meander* is derived from the Greek word *maiandros*, which means "bends." Mature streams in a valley curve back and forth. The valley floor in which a river meanders is referred to as the *meander belt.* In a meandering river, the soil from the bank is continually eroded from the points where it is concave in shape and deposited at points where the bank is convex in shape, as shown in Figure 2.3. These deposits are called *point bar deposits,* and they usually consist of sand and silt-size particles. Sometimes, during the process of erosion and deposition, the river abandons a meander and cuts a shorter path. The abandoned meander, when filled with water, is called an *oxbow lake* (see Figure 2.3).

During floods, rivers overflow low-lying areas. The sand and silt-size particles carried by the river are deposited along the banks to form ridges known as *natural levees* (Figure 2.4). Finer soil particles consisting of silts and clays are carried by the water farther onto the flood plains. These particles settle at different rates to form what is referred to as *backswamp deposits* (Figure 2.4). These clays may be highly plastic. Table 2.1 gives the properties of soil deposits found in natural levees, point bars, abandoned channels, backswamps, and swamps in the Mississippi alluvial valley.

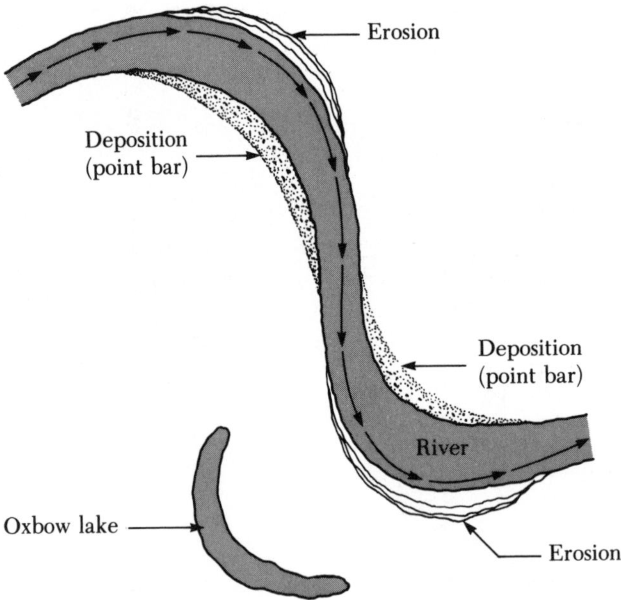

▼ **FIGURE 2.3** Formation of point bar deposits and oxbow lake in a meandering stream

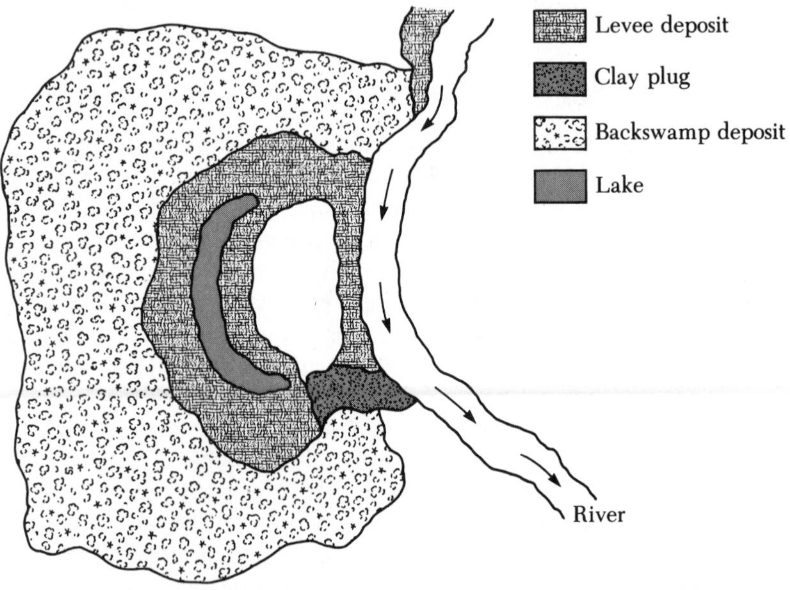

▼ **FIGURE 2.4** Levee and backswamp deposit

▼ **TABLE 2.1 Properties of Deposits within the Mississippi Alluvial Valley**[a]

Environment	Soil texture	Natural water content (%)	Liquid limit	Plasticity index	Shear strength: Cohesion[b] (kN/m^2)	Shear strength: Angle of friction (deg)
Natural levees	Clay (CL)	25–35	35–45	15–25	17–57	0
	Silt (ML)	15–35	NP[c]–35	NP–5	9–33	10–35
Point bar	Silt (ML) and silty sand (SM)	25–45	30–55	10–25	0–41	25–35
Abandoned channel	Clay (CL, CH)	30–95	30–100	10–65	14–57	0
Backswamps	Clay (CH)	25–70	40–115	25–100	19–120	0
Swamp	Organic clay (OH)	100–265	135–300	100–165	—	—

[a] After Kolb and Shockley (1959)
[b] Rounded off
[c] NP = nonplastic

2.5 GLACIAL DEPOSITS

During the Pleistocene Ice Age, glaciers covered large areas of the earth. The glaciers advanced and retreated with time. During their advance, the glaciers carried large amounts of sand, silt, clay, gravel, and boulders. *Drift* is a general term usually applied to the deposits laid down by glaciers. Unstratified deposits laid down by glaciers when they melt are referred to as *till*. The physical characteristics of till may vary from glacier to glacier.

The land forms that developed from the deposits of till are called *moraines*. A *terminal moraine* (Figure 2.5) is a ridge of till that marks the maximum limit of a

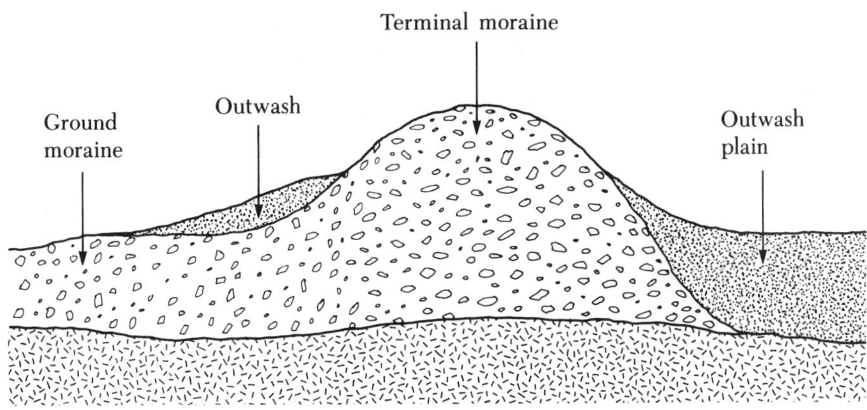

▼ **FIGURE 2.5** Terminal moraine, ground moraine, and outwash plain

glacier's advance. *Recessional moraines* are ridges of till developed behind the terminal moraine at varying distances apart. They are the result of temporary stabilization of the glacier during the recessional period. The till deposited by the glacier between the moraines is referred to as *ground moraine* (Figure 2.5). Ground moraines constitute large areas in the central United States and are called *till plains*.

The sand, silt, and gravel that are carried by the melting water from the front of a glacier are called *outwash*. In a pattern similar to the braided-stream deposits, the melted water deposits the outwash, forming *outwash plains* (Figure 2.5). They are usually called *glaciofluvial deposits*.

The range of grain sizes present in a till varies greatly. Figure 2.6 compares the grain-size distribution of *glacial till* and *dune sand* (see Section 2.6). The amount of clay-size fractions present and the plasticity indices of tills also vary widely. Field exploration may also reveal erratic values of standard penetration resistances.

Glacial water also carries with it silts and clays. The water finds its way to many basins and forms lakes. The silt particles initially tend to settle to the bottom of the lake when the water is still. During the winter, when the top of the lake freezes, the suspended clay particles gradually settle to the bottom. During the summer, the snow on the lake melts. The supply of freshwater, loaded with sediments, repeats the process. As a result, the lacustrine soil formed from such a deposit has alternate layers of silt and clay. This soil is called *varved clay*. The varves are usually a few millimeters thick; however, in some instances they can be 50–100 mm (2–4 in.) thick. Varved clays can be found in the Northeast and the Pacific Northwest of the United States. They are mostly normally consolidated and may be sensitive. The coefficient of permeability in the vertical direction is usually several times smaller than that in the horizontal direction. The load-bearing capacity of these deposits is quite low, and significant settlement of structures with shallow foundations may be anticipated.

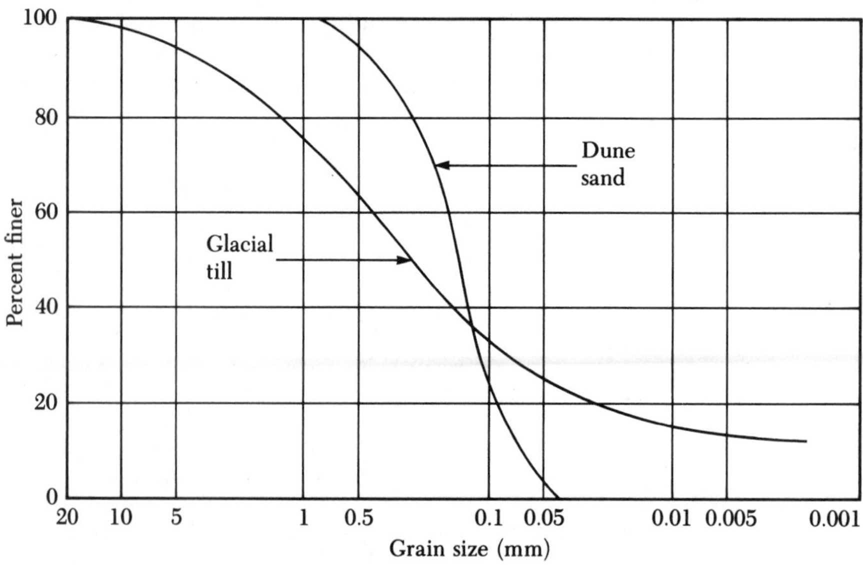

FIGURE 2.6 Comparison of the grain-size distribution between glacial till and dune sand

2.6 AEOLIAN SOIL DEPOSITS

Wind is also a major transporting agent leading to formation of soil deposits. When large areas of sand lie exposed, wind can blow it away and redeposit it somewhere else. Deposits of windblown sand generally take the shape of *dunes* (Figure 2.7). As dunes

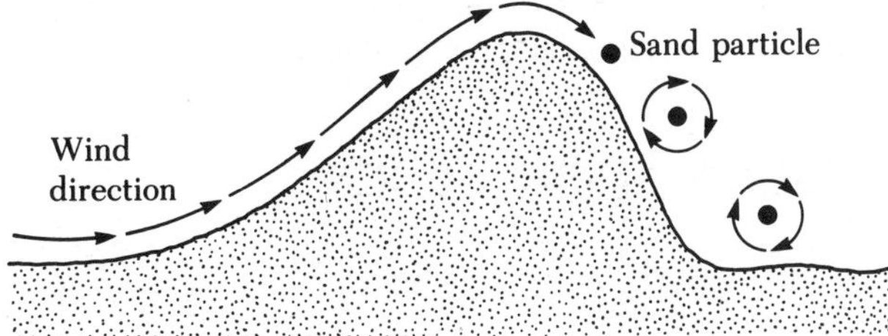

▼ **FIGURE 2.7** Sand dune

are formed, the sand is blown over the crest by the wind. Beyond the crest, the sand particles roll down the slope. This process tends to form a *compact sand deposit* on the *windward side* and a rather *loose deposit* on the *leeward side*. Dunes exist along the southern and eastern shores of Lake Michigan, the Atlantic Coast, the southern coast of California, and at various places along the coasts of Oregon and Washington. Sand dunes can also be found in the alluvial and rocky plains of the western United States. Following are some of the typical properties of *dune sand*.

1. The grain-size distribution of the sand at any particular location is surprisingly uniform. This uniformity can be attributed to the sorting action of the wind.
2. The general grain size decreases with the distance from the source because the wind carries the small particles farther than the large ones.
3. The relative density of sand deposited on the windward side of dunes may be as high as 50–65% and may decrease to about 0–15% on the leeward side.

Loess is an aeolian deposit consisting of silt and silt-size particles. The grain-size distribution of loess is rather uniform. The cohesion of loess is generally derived from a clay coating over the silt-size particles, which contributes to a stable soil structure in an unsaturated state. The cohesion may also be the result of the precipitation of chemicals leached by rainwater. Loess is a *collapsing* soil, because when the soil becomes saturated, it loses its binding strength between the soil particles. Special precautions need to be taken for construction of foundations over loessial deposits. There are extensive deposits of loess in the United States—mostly in the midwestern states of Iowa, Missouri, Illinois, and Nebraska and for some distance along the Mississippi River in Tennessee and Mississippi.

2.7 ORGANIC SOIL

Organic soils are usually found in low-lying areas where the water table is near or above the ground surface. The presence of a high water table helps in the growth of aquatic plants that, when decomposed, from organic soil. This type of soil deposit is usually encountered in coastal areas and in glaciated regions. Organic soils show the following characteristics.

1. The natural moisture content may range from 200% to 300%.
2. They are highly compressible.
3. Laboratory tests have shown that, under loads, a large amount of settlement is derived from secondary consolidation.

2.8 SOME LOCAL TERMS FOR SOILS

Soils are sometimes referred to by local terms. Following are a few of these terms with a brief description of each.

1. *Caliche:* a Spanish word derived from the Latin word *calix*, meaning *lime*. It is found mostly in the desert southwest of the United States. It is a mixture of sand, silt, and gravel bonded together by *calcareous deposits*. The calcareous deposits are brought to the surface by a net upward migration of water. The water evaporates in the high local temperature. Because of the sparse rainfall, the carbonates are not washed out of the top layer of soil.
2. *Gumbo:* a highly plastic, clayey soil.
3. *Adobe:* a highly plastic, clayey soil found in the southwestern United States.
4. *Terra Rossa:* residual soil deposits that are red in color and derive from limestone and dolomite.
5. *Muck:* organic soil with a vey high moisture content.
6. *Muskeg:* organic soil deposit.
7. *Saprolite:* residual soil deposit derived from mostly insoluble rock.
8. *Loam:* a mixture of soil grains of various sizes, such as sand, silt, and clay.
9. *Laterite:* characterized by the accumulation of iron oxide (Fe_2O_3) and aluminum oxide (Al_2O_3) near the surface, and the leaching of silica. Lateritic soils in Central America contain about 80–90% of clay and silt-size particles. In the United States, lateritic soils are present in the southeastern states of Alabama, Georgia, and the Carolinas.

Figure 2.8 (pages 78–79) shows the general nature of the various soil deposits encountered in the United States.

SUBSURFACE EXPLORATION

2.9 PURPOSE OF SOIL EXPLORATION

The process of identifying the layers of deposits that underlie a proposed structure and their physical characteristics is generally referred to as *subsurface exploration.* The purpose of subsurface exploration is to obtain information that will aid the geotechnical engineer in

1. Selecting the type and depth of foundation suitable for a given structure.
2. Evaluating the load-bearing capacity of the foundation.
3. Estimating the probable settlement of a structure.
4. Determining potential foundation problems (for example, expansive soil, collapsible soil, sanitary landfill, and so on).
5. Determining the location of water table.
6. Predicting lateral earth pressure for structures such as retaining walls, sheet pile bulkheads, and braced cuts.
7. Establishing construction methods for changing subsoil conditions.

Subsurface exploration may also be necessary when additions and alterations to existing structures are contemplated.

2.10 SUBSURFACE EXPLORATION PROGRAM

Subsurface exploration comprises several steps, including collection of preliminary information, reconnaissance, and site investigation.

Collection of Preliminary Information

This step includes obtaining information regarding the type of structure to be built and its general use. For the construction of buildings, the approximate column loads and their spacing and the local building-code and basement requirements should be known. The construction of bridges requires determining span length and the loading on piers and abutments.

A general idea of the topography and the type of soil to be encountered near and around the proposed site can be obtained from the following sources.

1. United States Geological Survey maps.
2. State government geological survey maps.
3. United States Department of Agriculture's Soil Conservation Service county soil reports.
4. Agronomy maps published by the agriculture departments of various states.
5. The hydrological information published by the United States Corps of Engineers. These include the records of stream flow, high flood levels, tidal records, and so on.
6. Highway department soils manuals published by several states.

The information collected from these sources can be extremely helpful in planning a site investigation. In some cases, substantial savings may be realized by anticipating problems that may be encountered later in the exploration program.

Glacial Soils

Young and old drift, including associated sands and gravel

Lacustrine deposits, predominantly silts and clays

Loessial Soils

Silts and very fine sands

Soils of the Coastal Plain

Sand-clay; interbedded and mixed sands, gravels, clays, and silts; gravel and sand; or sand

Clay

Soils of the Filled Valleys and Great Plains Outwash Mantle

Predominantly sands and gravels with silts; sandy clays and clays

Residual Soils

All types

Recent Alluvium

Predominantly silts and clays

Nonsoil areas

▼ **FIGURE 2.8** Soil deposits of the United States (adapted from *Foundation Engineering*, Second Edition, by R. B. Peck, W. E. Hanson, and T. H. Thornburn. Copyright 1974 by John Wiley and Sons. Reprinted by permission.)

Reconnaissance

The engineer should always make a visual inspection of the site. Its purpose is to obtain information about

1. The general topography of the site, possible existence of drainage ditches, abandoned dumps of debris, or other materials. Also, evidence of creep of slopes and deep, wide shrinkage cracks at regularly spaced intervals may be indicative of expansive soils.
2. Soil stratification from deep cuts, such as those made for construction of nearby highways and railroads.
3. Type of vegetation at the site, which may indicate the nature of the soil. For example, a mesquite cover in central Texas may indicate the existence of expansive clays that can cause possible foundation problems.
4. High-water marks on nearby buildings and bridge abutments.
5. Ground water levels, which can be determined by checking nearby wells.
6. Types of construction nearby and existence of any cracks in walls or other problems.

The nature of stratification and physical properties of the soil nearby can also be obtained from any available soil-exploration reports for existing structures.

Site Investigation

The site investigation phase of the exploration program consists of planning, making test boreholes, and collecting soil samples at desired intervals for subsequent observation and laboratory tests. The approximate required minimum depth of the borings should be predetermined. The depth can be changed during the drilling operation, depending on the subsoil encountered. To determine the approximate minimum depth of

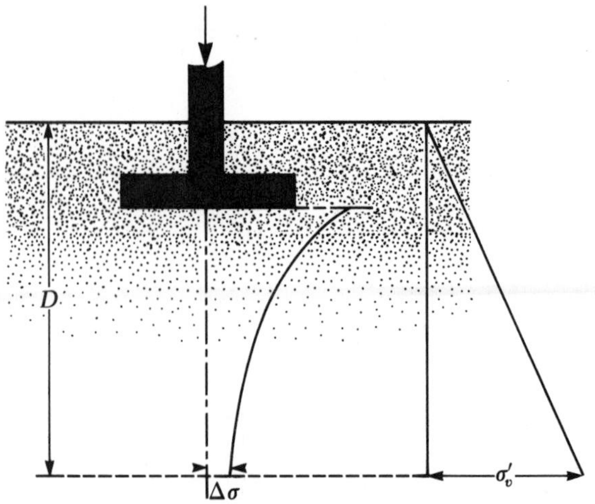

▼ **FIGURE 2.9** Determination of the minimum depth of boring

boring, engineers may use the rules established by the American Society of Civil Engineers (1972):

1. Determine the net increase of stress, $\Delta\sigma$, under a foundation with a depth as shown in Figure 2.9. (The general equations for estimating stress increase are given in Chapter 3.)
2. Estimate the variation of the vertical effective stress, σ'_v, with depth.
3. Determine the depth, $D = D_1$, at which the stress increase $\Delta\sigma$ is equal to $(\frac{1}{10})q$ (q = estimated net stress on the foundation).
4. Determine the depth, $D = D_2$, at which $\Delta\sigma/\sigma'_v = 0.05$.
5. Unless bedrock is encountered, the smaller of the two depths, D_1 and D_2, just determined is the approximate minimum depth of boring required.

If the preceding rules are used, the depths of boring for a building with a width of 30.5 m (100 ft) will be approximately the following, according to Sowers and Sowers (1970).

No. of stories	*Boring depth*
1	3.5 m (11 ft)
2	6 m (20 ft)
3	10 m (33 ft)
4	16 m (53 ft)
5	24 m (79 ft)

For hospitals and office buildings, they also use the following rule to determine boring depth.

$$D_b = 3S^{0.7} \quad \text{(for light steel or narrow concrete buildings)} \tag{2.1a}$$

and

$$D_b = 6S^{0.7} \quad \text{(for heavy steel or wide concrete buildings)} \tag{2.1b}$$

where D_b = depth of boring, in meters
S = number of stories

In English units, the preceding equations take the form

$$D_b\ (\text{ft}) = 10S^{0.7} \quad \text{(for light steel or narrow concrete buildings)} \tag{2.2a}$$

and

$$D_b\ (\text{ft}) = 20S^{0.7} \quad \text{(for heavy steel or wide concrete buildings)} \tag{2.2b}$$

When deep excavations are anticipated, the depth of boring should be at least 1.5 times the depth of excavation.

Sometimes subsoil conditions require that the foundation load be transmitted to bedrock. The minimum depth of core boring into the bedrock is about 3 m (10 ft). If the bedrock is irregular or weathered, the core borings may have to be deeper.

There are no hard and fast rules for borehole spacing. Table 2.2 gives some general guidelines. Spacing can be increased or decreased, depending on the subsoil condition. If various soil strata are more or less uniform and predictable, fewer boreholes are needed than in nonhomogeneous soil strata.

▼ TABLE 2.2 Approximate Spacing of Boreholes

Type of project	Spacing	
	(m)	*(ft)*
Multistory building	10–30	30–100
One-store industrial plants	20–60	60–200
Highways	250–500	800–1600
Residential subdivision	250–500	800–1600
Dams and dikes	40–80	130–260

The engineer should also take into account the ultimate cost of the structure when making decisions regarding the extent of field exploration. The exploration cost generally should be 0.1–0.5% of the cost of the structure. Soil borings can be made by several methods, including auger boring, wash boring, percussion drilling, and rotary drilling.

2.11 EXPLORATORY BORINGS IN THE FIELD

Auger boring is the simplest method of making exploratory boreholes. Figure 2.10 shows two types of hand auger—the *post hole auger* and the *helical auger*. Hand augers cannot be used for advancing holes to depths exceeding 3–5 m (10–16 ft). However, they can be used for soil exploration work for some highways and small structures. *Portable power-driven helical augers* (76.2 mm to 304.8 mm in diameter) are available for making deeper boreholes. The soil samples obtained from such borings are highly disturbed. In some noncohesive soils or soils having low cohesion, the walls of the boreholes will not stand unsupported. In such circumstances, a metal pipe is used as a *casing* to prevent the soil from caving in.

When power is available, *continuous-flight augers* are probably the most common method used for advancing a borehole. The power for drilling is delivered by truck- or tractor-mounted drilling rigs. Boreholes up to about 60–70 m (200–230 ft) can be easily made by this method. Continuous-flight augers are available in sections of about 1–2 m

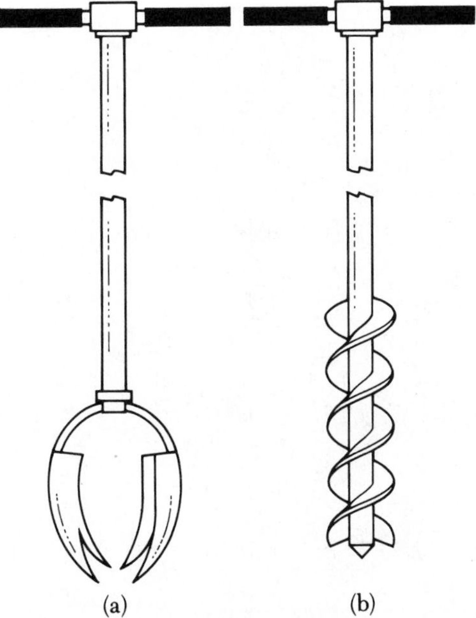

▼ **FIGURE 2.10** Hand tools: (a) post hole auger; (b) helical auger

(3–6 ft) with either a solid or hollow stem. Some of the commonly used solid stem augers have outside diameters of 66.68 mm ($2\frac{5}{8}$ in.), 82.55 mm ($3\frac{1}{4}$ in.), 101.6 mm (4 in.), and 114.3 mm ($4\frac{1}{2}$ in.). Common hollow stem augers commercially available have dimensions of 63.5 mm ID and 158.75 mm OD (2.5 in. × 6.25 in.), 69.85 mm ID and 177.8 OD (2.75 in. × 7 in.), 76.2 mm ID and 203.2 OD (3 in. × 8 in.), and 82.55 mm ID and 228.6 mm OD (3.25 in. × 9 in.).

The tip of the auger is attached to a cutter head (Figure 2.11, page 84). During the drilling operation (Figure 2.12, page 85), section after section of auger can be added and the hole extended downward. The flights of the augers bring the loose soil from the bottom of the hole to the surface. The driller can detect changes in soil type by noting changes in the speed and sound of drilling. When solid stem augers are used, the auger must be withdrawn at regular intervals to obtain soil samples and also to conduct other operations such as standard penetration tests. Hollow stem augers have a distinct advantage over solid stem augers in that they do not have to be removed frequently for sampling or other tests. As shown schematically in Figure 2.13 (page 86), the outside of the hollow stem auger acts as a casing. A removable plug is attached to the bottom of the auger by means of a center rod. During the drilling, the plug can be pulled out with the auger in place, and soil sampling and standard penetration tests can be performed. When hollow stem augers are used in sandy soils below the water table, the sand may be pushed several feet into the stem of the auger by excess hydrostatic pressure immediately after removal of the plug. Under such conditions, the plug should not be used. Instead, water inside the hollow stem should be maintained at a higher level than the water table.

▼ **FIGURE 2.11** Carbide-tipped cutting head on auger flight attached with bolt (courtesy of William B. Ellis, El Paso Engineering and Testing, Inc., El Paso, Texas)

Wash boring is another method of advancing boreholes. In this method, a casing about 2–3 m (6–10 ft) long is driven into the ground. The soil inside the casing is then removed by means of a chopping bit attached to a drilling rod. Water is forced through the drilling rod, and exits at a very high velocity through the holes at the bottom of the chopping bit (Figure 2.14, page 86). The water and the chopped soil particles rise in the drill hole and overflow at the top of the casing through a T connection. The washwater is collected in a container. The casing can be extended with additional pieces as the borehole progresses; however, that is not required if the borehole will stay open and not cave in.

Rotary drilling is a procedure by which rapidly rotating drilling bits attached to the bottom of drilling rods cut and grind the soil and advance the borehole. There are

▼ **FIGURE 2.12** Drilling with continuous-flight augers (courtesy of Danny R. Anderson, Danny R. Anderson Consultants, El Paso, Texas)

several types of drilling bit. Rotary drilling can be used in sand, clay, and rocks (unless badly fissured). Water, or *drilling mud*, is forced down the drilling rods to the bits, and the return flow forces the cuttings to the surface. Boreholes with diameters of 50.8–203.2 mm (2–8 in.) can be easily made by this technique. The drilling mud is a slurry of water and bentonite. Generally, it used when the soil encountered is likely to cave in. When soil samples are needed, the drilling rod is raised and the drilling bit is replaced by a sampler.

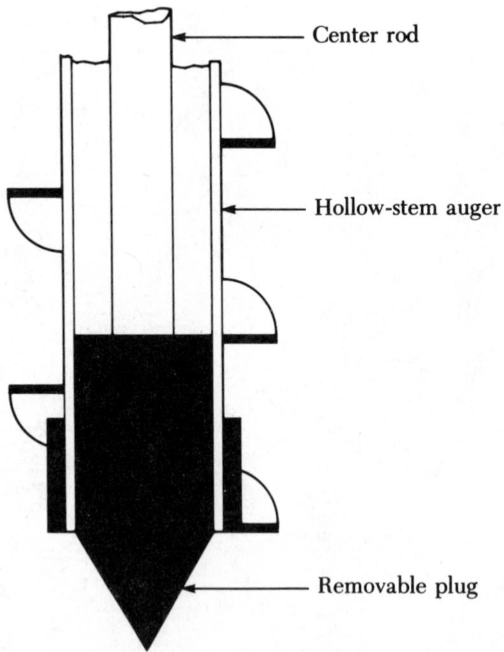

▼ **FIGURE 2.13**
Schematic diagram of the hollow stem auger with removable plug

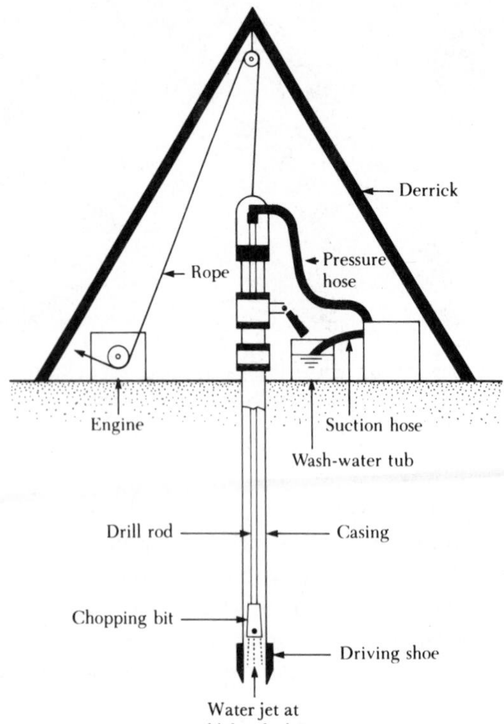

▼ **FIGURE 2.14**
Wash boring

Percussion drilling is an alternative method of advancing a borehole, particularly through hard soil and rock. A heavy drilling bit is raised and lowered to chop the hard soil. The chopped soil particles are brought up by circulation of water. Percussion drilling may require casing.

2.12 PROCEDURES FOR SAMPLING SOIL

Two types of soil samples can be obtained during subsurface exploration: *disturbed* and *undisturbed*. Disturbed but representative samples can generally be used for the following types of laboratory test.

1. Grain-size analysis
2. Determination of liquid and plastic limits
3. Specific gravity of soil solids
4. Organic content determination
5. Classification of soil

Disturbed soil samples, however, cannot be used for consolidation, permeability, or shear strength tests. Undisturbed soil samples must be obtained for these types of laboratory tests.

Split-Spoon Sampling

Split-spoon samplers can be used in the field to obtain soil samples that are generally disturbed but still representative. A section of a *standard split-spoon sampler* is shown in Figure 2.15a. It consists of a tool-steel driving shoe, a steel tube that is split longitudinally in half, and a coupling at the top. The coupling connects the sampler to the drill rod. The standard split tube has an inside diameter of 34.9 mm ($1\frac{3}{8}$ in.) and an outside diameter of 50.8 mm (2 in.); however, samplers having inside and outside diameters up to 63.5 mm ($2\frac{1}{2}$ in.) and 76.2 mm (3 in.), respectively, are also avaliable. When a borehole is extended to a predetermined depth, the drill tools are removed and the sampler is lowered to the bottom of the borehole. The sampler is driven into the soil by hammer blows to the top of the drill rod. The standard weight of the hammer is 622.72 N (140 lb), and for each blow the hammer drops a distance of 0.762 m (30 in.). The number of blows required for spoon penetration of three 152.4-mm (6-in.) intervals are recorded. The number of blows required for the last two intervals are added to give the *standard penetration number* at that depth. This number is generally referred to as the *N value* (American Society for Testing and Materials, 1992, Designation D-1586-84). The sampler is then withdrawn, and the shoe and coupling are removed. The soil sample recovered from the tube is then placed in a glass bottle and transported to the laboratory.

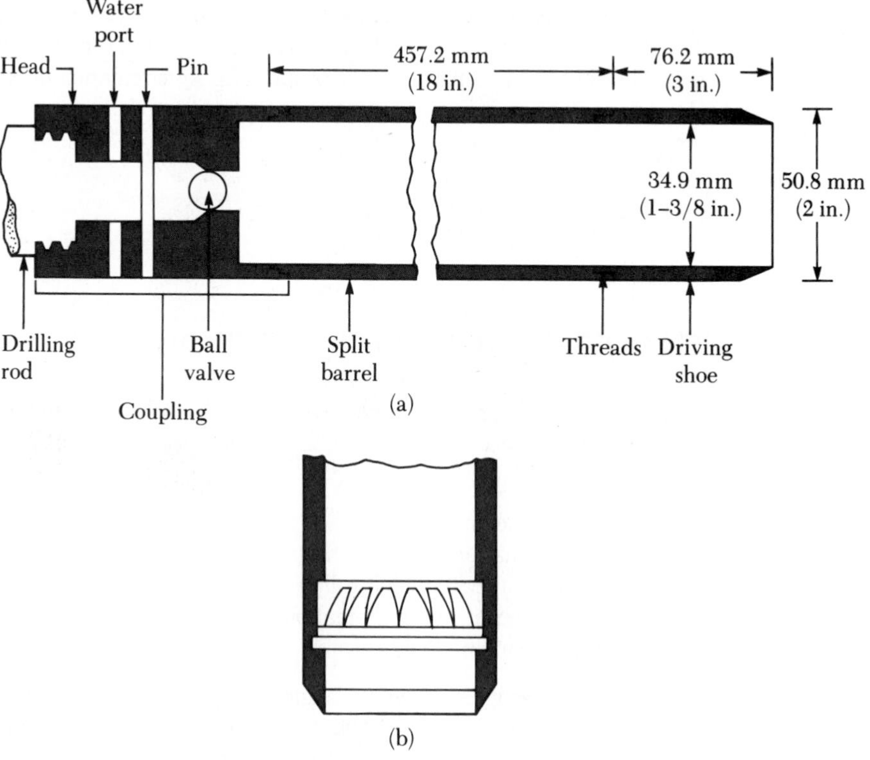

▼ **FIGURE 2.15** (a) Standard split-spoon sampler; (b) spring core catcher

The degree of disturbance for a soil sample is usually expressed as

$$A_R(\%) = \frac{D_o^2 - D_i^2}{D_i^2}(100) \tag{2.3}$$

where A_R = area ratio
D_o = outside diameter of the sampling tube
D_i = inside diameter of the sampling tube

When the area ratio is 10% or less, the sample generally is considered to be undisturbed. For a standard split-spoon sampler

$$A_R(\%) = \frac{(50.8)^2 - (34.93)^2}{(34.93)^2}(100) = 111.5\%$$

Hence these samples are highly disturbed. Split-spoon samples generally are taken at intervals of about 1.53 m (5 ft).

When the material encountered in the field is sand (particularly fine sand below the water table), sample recovery by a split-spoon sampler may be difficult. In that case, a device such as a *spring core catcher* may have to be placed inside the split spoon (Figure 2.15b).

Besides obtaining soil samples, standard penetration tests provide several useful correlations. For example, the consistency of clayey soils can often be estimated from the standard penetration number, N, as shown in Table 2.3. However, correlations for clays require tests to verify that the relationships are valid for the clay deposit being examined.

TABLE 2.3 Consistency of Clays and Approximate Correlation to the Standard Penetration Number, N

Standard penetration number, N	Consistency	Unconfined compression strength, q_u (kN/m^2)
0–2	Very soft	0–25
2–5	Soft	25–50
5–10	Medium stiff	50–100
10–20	Stiff	100–200
20–30	Very stiff	200–400
>30	Hard	>400

The literature contains many correlations between the standard penetration number and the undrained shear strength of clay, c_u. Based on the results of undrained triaxial tests conducted on insensitive clays, Stroud (1974) suggested that

$$c_u = KN \tag{2.4}$$

where K = constant = 3.5–6.5 kN/m^2 (0.507–0.942 lb/in^2)

The average value of K is about 4.4 kN/m^2 (0.638 lb/in^2).

Hara et al. (1971) also suggested that

$$c_u(\text{kN/m}^2) = 29N^{0.72} \tag{2.5}$$

The overconsolidation ratio, OCR, of a natural clay deposit can also be correlated with the standard penetration number. Based on the regression analysis of 110 data points, Mayne and Kemper (1988) obtained the relationship

$$OCR = 0.193\left(\frac{N}{\sigma'_v}\right)^{0.689} \tag{2.6}$$

where σ'_v = effective vertical stress in MN/m^2

In granular soils, the N value is affected by the effective overburden pressure, σ'_v. For that reason, the N value obtained from field exploration under different effective overburden pressures should be changed to correspond to a standard value of σ'_v. That is,

$$N_{cor} = C_N N_F \tag{2.7}$$

where N_{cor} = corrected N value to a standard value of σ'_v [95.6 kN/m² (1 ton/ft²)]
C_N = correction factor
N_F = N value obtained from the field

Several authors, such as Bazaraa (1967); Peck and Bazaraa (1969); Peck et al. (1974); Tang (1962); Seed (1976, 1979); and Tokimatsu and Yoshimi (1983), have proposed empirical relationships for C_N. However, the simplest relationship is that proposed by Liao and Whitman (1986), which gives as good a result as any other. This relationship is

$$C_N = \sqrt{\frac{1}{\sigma'_v}} \tag{2.8}$$

where σ'_v is in (U.S.) ton/ft²

In SI units

$$C_N = 9.78\sqrt{\frac{1}{\sigma'_v\ (\text{kN/m}^2)}} \tag{2.9}$$

In Eqs. (2.8) and (2.9), the standard value of σ'_v is 95.6 kN/m² (1 ton/ft²).

Although Eqs. (2.8) and (2.9) are simple, unusually high values of C_N are obtained at low values of σ'_v. Skempton (1986) also proposed a simple relationship for the correction factor:

$$C_N = \frac{2}{1 + \sigma'_v} \tag{2.10}$$

where σ'_v is in (U.S.) ton/ft²

Figure 2.16 compares the curves obtained from Eqs. (2.8) and (2.10).

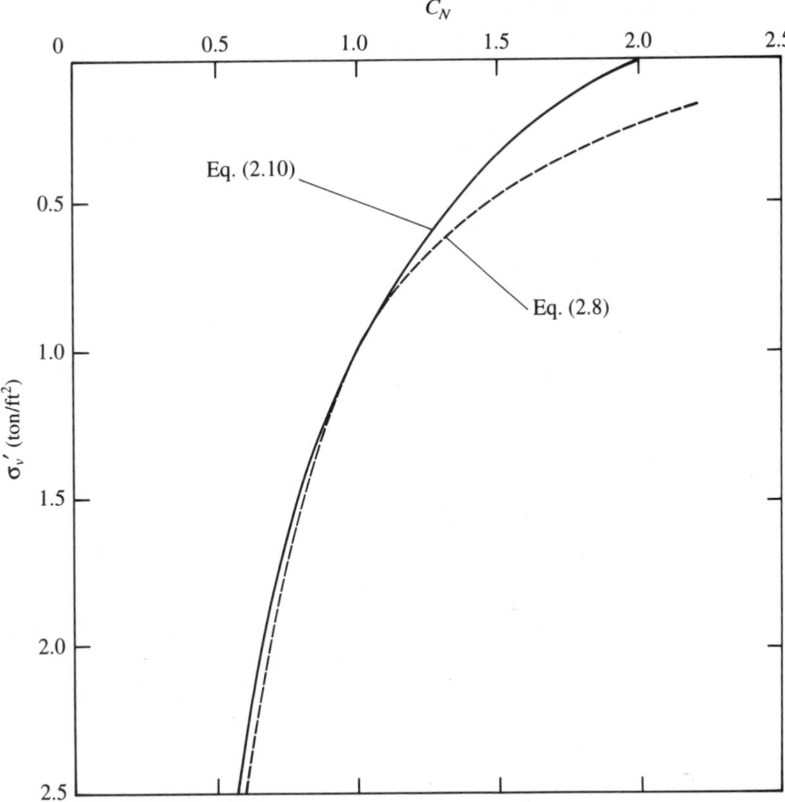

▼ **FIGURE 2.16** Comparison of Eqs. (2.8) and (2.10)

An approximate relationship between the standard penetration number and the relative density of sand is given in Table 2.4. However, these values are approximate, primarily because the effective overburden pressure and the stress history of the soil

▼ **TABLE 2.4 Relation between *N* Values, Relative Density, and Angle of Friction in Sands**

Standard penetration number, *N*	Approximate relative density, D_r (%)	Approximate angle of friction of soil, ϕ (deg)
0–5	0–5	26–30
5–10	5–30	28–35
10–30	30–60	35–42
30–50	60–95	38–46

significantly influence the N values of sand. An extensive study conducted by Marcuson and Bieganousky (1977) produced the empirical relationship

$$D_r(\%) = 11.7 + 0.76(222N_F + 1600 - 53\sigma'_v - 50C_u^2)^{0.5} \tag{2.11}$$

where D_r = relative density
N_F = standard penetration number in the field
σ'_v = effective overburden pressure (lb/in^2)
C_u = uniformity coefficient of the sand

When the standard penetration resistance values are used in the preceding correlations to estimate soil parameters, the following qualifications should be noted.

1. The equations are approximate.
2. Because the soil is not homogeneous, the N values obtained from a given borehole vary widely.
3. In soil deposits that contain large boulders and gravel, standard penetration numbers may be erratic and unreliable.

Although approximate, with correct interpretation the standard penetration test provides a good evaluation of soil properties. The primary sources of errors in standard penetration tests are inadequate cleaning of the borehole, careless measurement of the blow count, eccentric hammer strikes on the drill rod, and inadequate maintenance of water head in the borehole.

Scraper Bucket

When soil deposits are sand mixed with pebbles, obtaining samples by split spoon with a spring core catcher may not be possible because the pebbles may prevent the springs from closing. In such cases, a scraper bucket may be used to obtain disturbed representative samples (Figure 2.17a). The scraper bucket has a driving point and can be attached to a drilling rod. The sampler is driven down into the soil and rotated, and the scrapings from the side fall into the bucket.

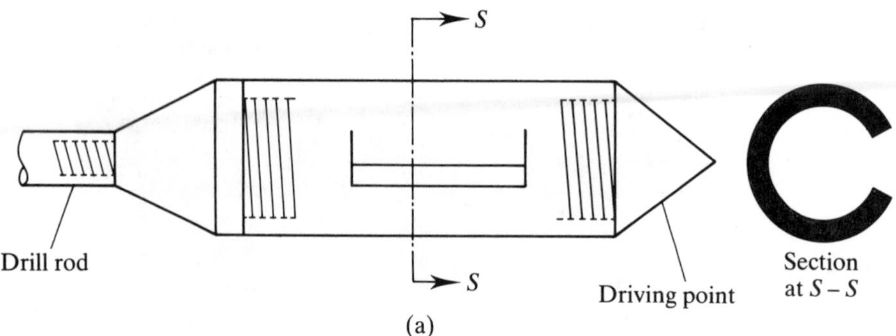

FIGURE 2.17 Sampling devices: (a) scraper bucket; (b) thin wall tube; (c) and (d) piston sampler

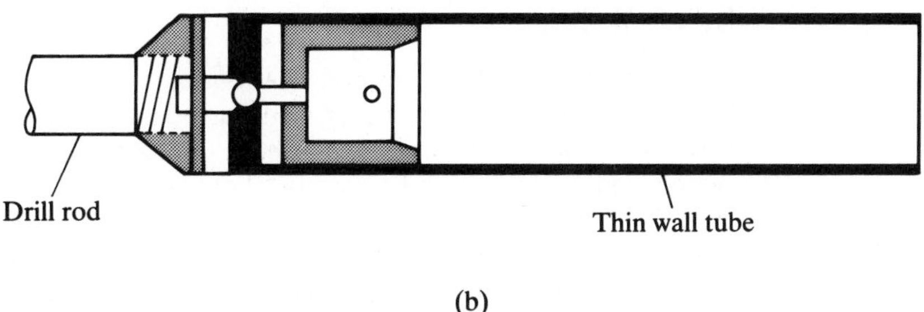

(b)

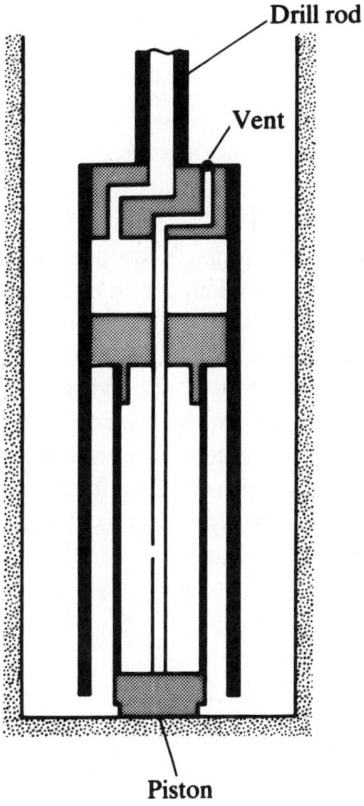

(c)

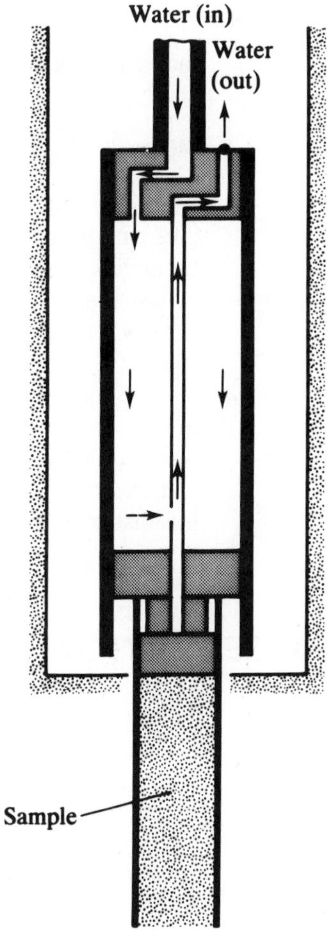

(d)

▼ **FIGURE 2.17** (Continued)

Thin Wall Tube

Thin wall tubes are sometimes referred to as *Shelby tubes*. They are made of seamless steel and are commonly used to obtain undisturbed clayey soils. The commonly used thin wall tube samplers have outside diameters of 50.8 mm (2 in.) and 76.2 mm (3 in.). The bottom end of the tube is sharpened. The tubes can be attached to drilling rods (Figure 2.17b). The drilling rod with the sampler attached is lowered to the bottom of the borehole and the sampler is pushed into the soil. The soil sample inside the tube is then pulled out. The two ends of the sampler are sealed, and it is sent to the laboratory for testing.

Samples obtained in this manner may be used for consolidation or shear tests. A thin wall tube with a 50.8-mm (2-in.) outside diameter has an inside diameter of about 47.63 mm ($1\frac{7}{8}$ in.). The area ratio is

$$A_R(\%) = \frac{D_o^2 - D_i^2}{D_o^2}(100) = \frac{(50.8)^2 - (47.63)^2}{(47.63)^2}(100) = 13.75\%$$

Increasing the diameters of samples increases the cost of obtaining them.

Piston Sampler

When undisturbed soil samples are very soft or larger than 76.2 mm (3 in.) in diameter, they tend to fall out of the sampler. Piston samplers are particularly useful under such conditions. There are several types of piston sampler; however, the sampler proposed by Osterberg (1952) is the most useful (see Figure 2.17c and d). It consists of a thin wall tube with a piston. Initially, the piston closes the end of the thin wall tube. The sampler is lowered to the bottom of the borehole (Figure 2.17c), and the thin wall tube is pushed into the soil hydraulically, past the piston. Then the pressure is released through a hole in the piston rod (Figure 2.17d). To a large extent, the presence of the piston prevents distortion in the sample by not letting the soil squeeze into the sampling tube very fast and by not admitting excess soil. Consequently, samples obtained in this manner are less disturbed than those obtained by Shelby tubes.

2.13 OBSERVATION OF WATER TABLES

The presence of a water table near a foundation significantly affects a foundation's load-bearing capacity and settlement, among other things. The water level will change seasonally. In many cases, establishing the highest and lowest possible levels of water during the life of a project may become necessary.

If water is encountered in a borehole during a field exploration, that fact should be recorded. In soils with high coefficients of permeability, the level of water in a borehole will stabilize about 24 hours after completion of the boring. The depth of the water table can then be recorded by lowering a chain or tape into the borehole.

In highly impermeable layers, the water level in a borehole may not stabilize for several weeks. In such cases, if accurate water level measurements are required, a *piezometer* can be used. A piezometer basically consists of a porous stone or a perforated pipe with a plastic standpipe attached to it Figure 2.18 shows the general placement of a piezometer in a borehole.

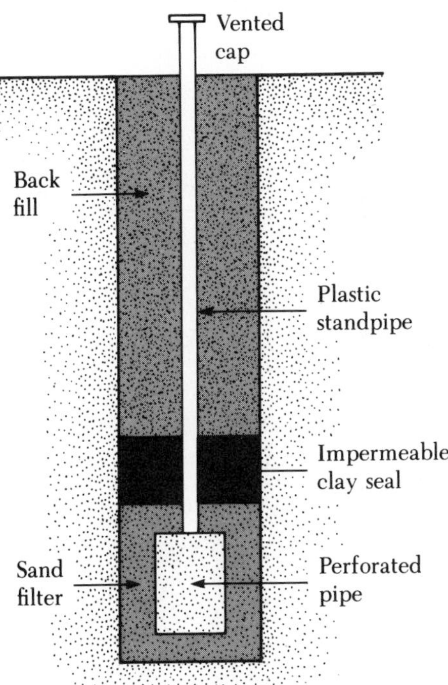

▼ **FIGURE 2.18** Casagrande-type porous stone piezometer

For silty soils, Hvorslev (1949) proposed a technique to determine the water level (see Figure 2.19). This technique involves the following steps.

1. Bail water out of the borehole to a level below the estimated water table.
2. Observe the water levels in the borehole at times

   $t = 0$

   $t = t_1$

   $t = t_2$

   $t = t_3$

   Note that $t_1 - 0 = t_1 - t_2 = t_2 - t_3 = \Delta t$.
3. Calculate Δh_1, Δh_2, and Δh_3 (see Figure 2.19).

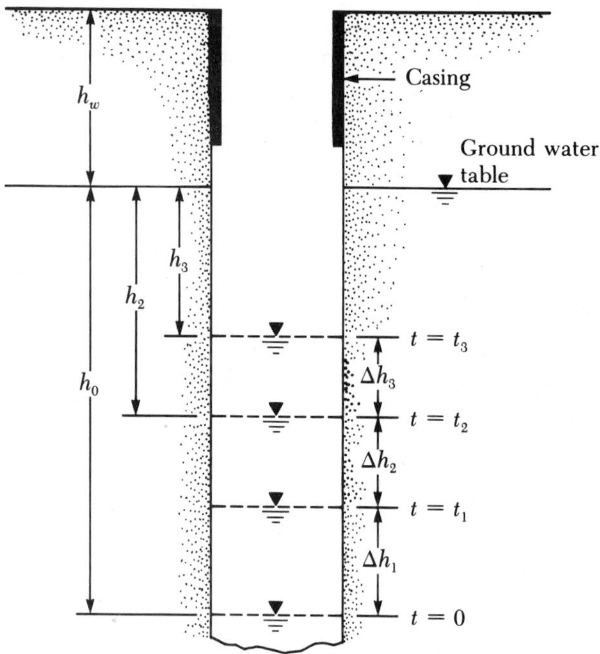

▼ **FIGURE 2.19** Determination of water levels [Eq. (2.12)]

4. Calculate

$$h_0 = \frac{\Delta h_1^2}{\Delta h_1 - \Delta h_2} \tag{2.12a}$$

$$h_2 = \frac{\Delta h_2^2}{\Delta h_1 - \Delta h_2} \tag{2.12b}$$

$$h_3 = \frac{\Delta h_3^2}{\Delta h_2 - \Delta h_3} \tag{2.12c}$$

5. Plot h_0, h_2, and h_3 above the water levels observed at times $t = 0, t_2$, and t_3, respectively, to determine the final water level in the borehole.

▼ EXAMPLE 2.1

Refer to Figure 2.19. For a borehole, $h_w + h_0 = 9.5$ m

$$\Delta t = 24 \text{ hr}$$

$$\Delta h_1 = 0.9 \text{ m}$$

$$\Delta h_2 = 0.70 \text{ m}$$

$$\Delta h_3 = 0.54 \text{ m}$$

Make the necessary calculations and locate the water level.

Solution Using Eq. (2.12),

$$h_0 = \frac{\Delta h_1^2}{\Delta h_1 - \Delta h_2} = \frac{0.9^2}{0.9 - 0.70} = 4.05 \text{ m}$$

$$h_2 = \frac{\Delta h_2^2}{\Delta h_1 - \Delta h_2} = \frac{0.7^2}{0.9 - 0.7} = 2.45 \text{ m}$$

$$h_3 = \frac{\Delta h_3^2}{\Delta h_2 - \Delta h_3} = \frac{0.54^2}{0.7 - 0.54} = 1.82 \text{ m}$$ ▼

Figure 2.20 shows a plot of the preceding calculations and the estimated water levels. Note that $h_w = 5.5$ m.

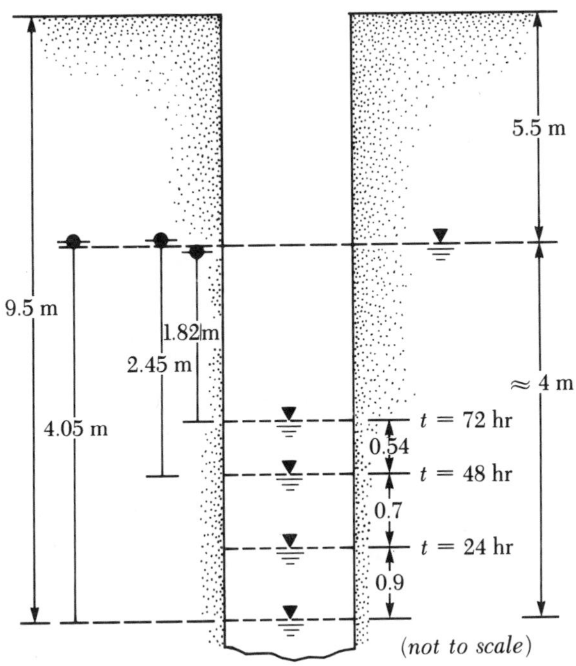

▼ **FIGURE 2.20**

2.14 VANE SHEAR TEST

The *vane shear test* (ASTM D-2573) may be used during the drilling operation to determine the *in situ* undrained shear strength (c_u) of clay soils—particularly soft clays. The vane shear apparatus consists of four blades on the end of a rod, as shown in Figure 2.21. The height, H, of the vane is twice the diameter, D. The vane can be either rectangular or tapered (see Figure 2.21). The dimensions of vanes used in the field are given in Table 2.5. The vanes of the apparatus are pushed into the soil at the

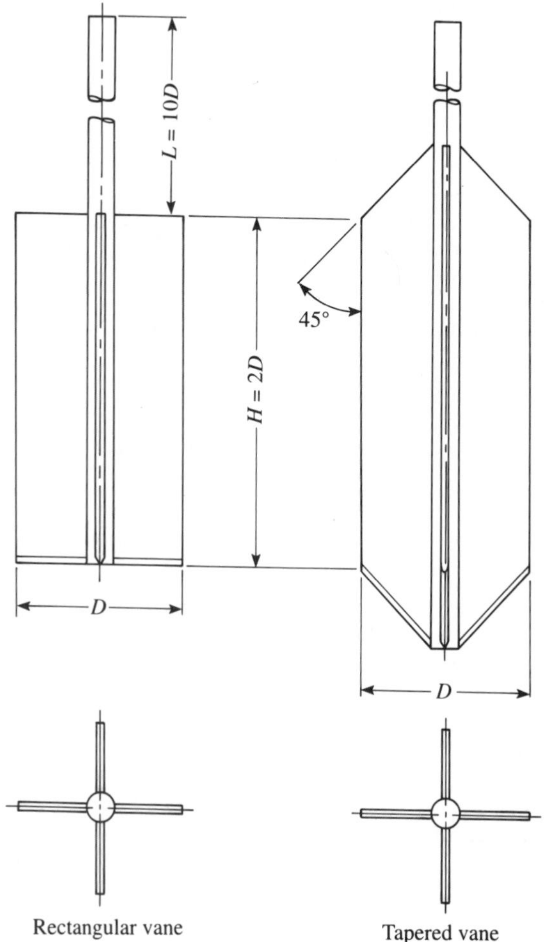

Rectangular vane

Tapered vane

▼ **FIGURE 2.21** Geometry of field vane (after ASTM, 1992)

▼ **TABLE 2.5 Recommended Dimensions of Field Vanes[a] (After ASTM, 1992)**

Casing size	Diameter, D mm (in.)	Height, H mm (in.)	Thickness of blade, mm (in.)	Diameter of rod mm (in.)
AX	38.1 (1½)	76.2 (3)	1.6 (1/16)	12.7 (½)
BX	50.8 (2)	101.6 (4)	1.6 (1/16)	12.7 (½)
NX	63.5 (2½)	127.0 (5)	3.2 (⅛)	12.7 (½)
4 in. (101.6 mm)[b]	92.1 (3⅝)	184.1 (7¼)	3.2 (⅛)	12.7 (½)

[a] Selection of vane size is directly related to the consistency of the soil being tested; that is, the softer the soil, the larger the vane diameter should be.

[b] Inside diameter.

bottom of a borehole without disturbing the soil appreciably. Torque is applied at the top of the rod to rotate the vanes at a standard rate of 0.1°/sec. This rotation will induce failure in a soil of cylindrical shape surrounding the vanes. The maximum torque, T, applied to cause failure is measured. Note that

$$T = f(c_u, H, \text{ and } D) \tag{2.13}$$

or

$$c_u = \frac{T}{K} \tag{2.14}$$

where T is in N · m, and c_u is in kN/m^2
K = a constant with a magnitude depending on the dimension and shape of the vane

$$\boxed{K = \left(\frac{\pi}{10^6}\right)\left(\frac{D^2H}{2}\right)\left(1 + \frac{D}{3H}\right)} \tag{2.15}$$

where D = diameter of vane in cm
H = measured height of vane in cm

If $H/D = 2$, Eq. (2.15) yields

$$K = 366 \times 10^{-8} \underset{\text{(cm)}}{\underset{\uparrow}{D^3}} \tag{2.16}$$

In English units, if c_u and T in Eq. (2.14) are expressed in lb/ft^2 and lb-ft, respectively,

$$\boxed{K = \left(\frac{\pi}{1728}\right)\left(\frac{D^2H}{2}\right)\left(1 + \frac{D}{3H}\right)} \tag{2.17}$$

If $H/D = 2$, Eq. (2.17) yields

$$K = 0.0021 \underset{\text{(in.)}}{\underset{\uparrow}{D^3}} \tag{2.18}$$

Field vane shear tests are moderately rapid and economical and are used extensively in field soil-exploration programs. The test gives good results in soft and medium-stiff clays, and it is also an excellent test to determine the properties of sensitive clays.

Sources of significant error in the field vane shear test are poor calibration of torque measurement and damaged vanes. Other errors may be introduced if the rate of vane rotation is not properly controlled.

2.15 CORRELATIONS FOR FIELD VANE SHEAR STRENGTH

Bjerrum (1972) recommended that, for actual design purposes, the field vane shear values should be corrected as follows:

$$c_{u(\text{corrected})} = \lambda c_{u(\text{field})} \tag{2.19}$$

where λ = correction factor

The magnitude of this correction factor varies with the plasticity indices of soils and is shown in Figure 2.22a. More recently, Aas et al. (1986) gave the variation of λ as a function of $c_{u(\text{field})}$ and σ'_v (that is, present effective overburden pressure). Their proposal is shown in Figure 2.22b.

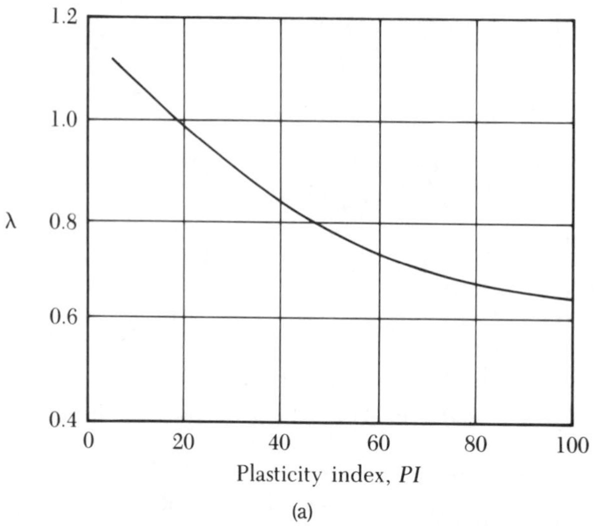

(a)

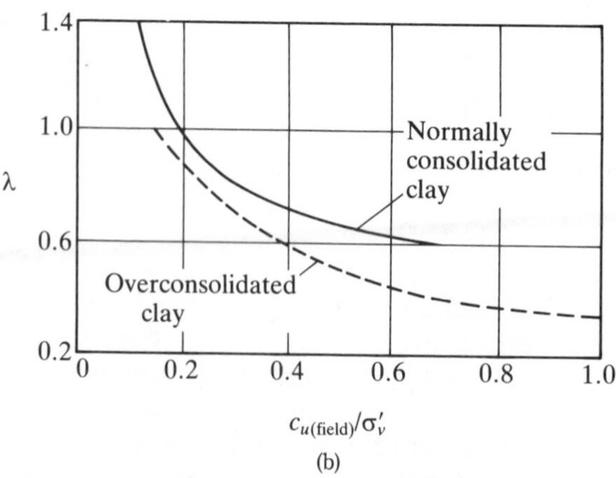

(b)

▼ **FIGURE 2.22** Correction factor, λ [Eq. (2.19)]

The field vane shear strength can also be correlated to preconsolidation pressure and the overconsolidation ratio of the clay. Using 343 data points, Mayne and Mitchell (1988) derived the following empirical relationship for estimation of the preconsolidation pressure of a natural clay deposit.

$$p_c = 7.04[c_{u(\text{field})}]^{0.83} \tag{2.20}$$

where p_c = preconsolidation pressure (kN/m²)
$c_{u(\text{field})}$ = field vane shear strength (kN/m²)

Figure 2.23 shows the plot of the data points from which they derived the relationship. They also showed that the overconsolidation ratio (OCR) can be correlated to $c_{u(\text{field})}$ as

$$OCR = \beta \frac{c_{u(\text{field})}}{\sigma'_v} \tag{2.21}$$

where σ'_v = effective overburden pressure

$$\beta = 22(PI)^{-0.48} \tag{2.22}$$

where PI = plasticity index

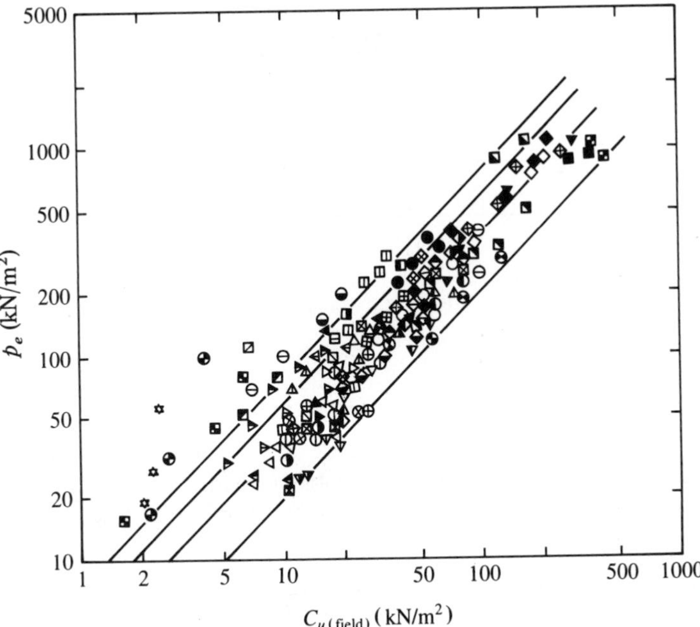

▼ **FIGURE 2.23** Variation of preconsolidation pressure with field vane shear strength (after Mayne and Mitchell, 1988)

Figure 2.24 shows the variation of β with plasticity index.

Other correlations for β presented in the literature are

Hansbo (1957)

$$\beta = \frac{222}{w(\%)} \tag{2.23}$$

Larsson (1980)

$$\beta = \frac{1}{0.08 + 0.0055(PI)} \tag{2.24}$$

Figure 2.25 compares the actual and predicted values of OCR obtained from Eqs. (2.21) and (2.22) for six different sites.

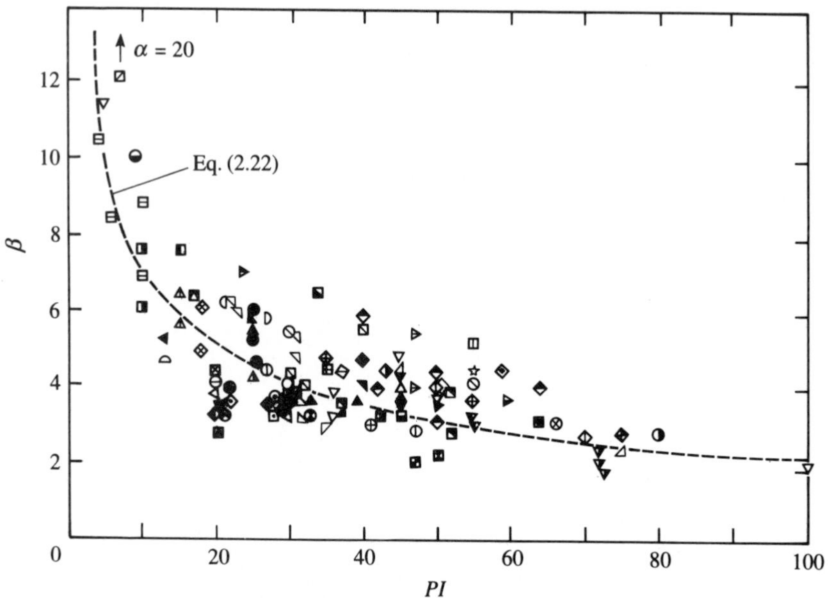

▼ **FIGURE 2.24** Variation of β with plasticity index (after Mayne and Mitchell, 1988)

▼ EXAMPLE 2.2

The magnitude of $c_{u(\text{field})}$ at a depth of 21 ft below the ground surface in a saturated clay soil is 820 lb/ft^2. The water table coincides with the ground surface. For a saturated unit weight of the clay, $\gamma_{sat} = 123$ lb/ft^3 and $PI = 21$, estimate the overconsolidation ratio.

Solution Effective unit weight of clay

$$\gamma' = \gamma_{sat} - \gamma_w = 123 - 62.4 = 60.6 \text{ lb/ft}^3$$

$$\sigma'_v = \gamma'(21) = (60.6)(21) = 1272.6 \text{ lb/ft}^2$$

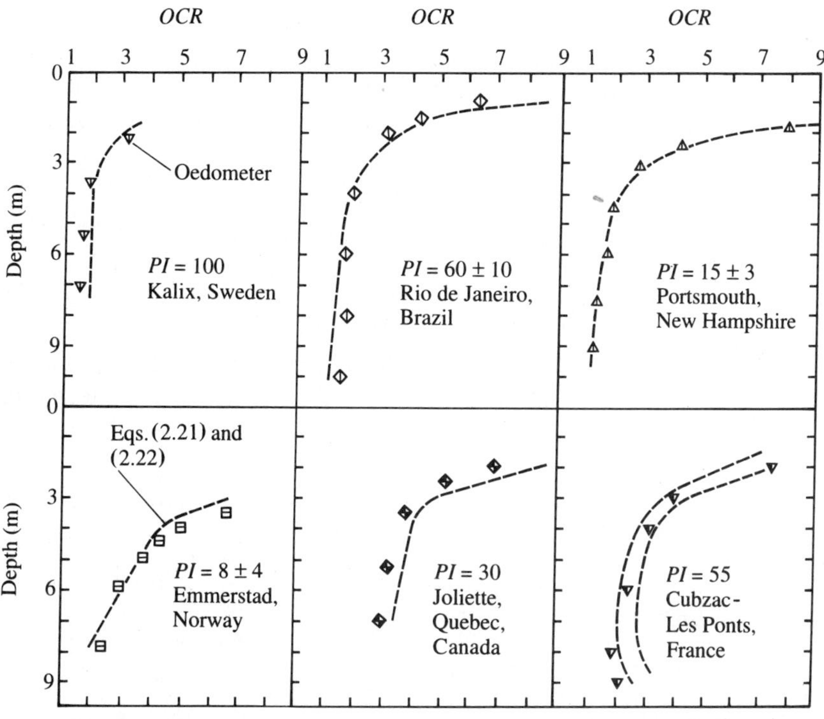

▼ **FIGURE 2.25** Measured *OCR* profiles at six sites from oedometer tests (individual points) and estimated profiles from field vane test data (dashed lines) (after Mayne and Mitchell, 1988)

From Eq. (2.22)

$$\beta = 22(21)^{-0.48} = 5.1$$

From Eq. (2.21)

$$OCR = \beta\left[\frac{c_{u(\text{field})}}{\sigma'_v}\right] = 5.1\left(\frac{820}{1272.6}\right) = \mathbf{3.29} \qquad \blacktriangledown$$

2.16 CONE PENETRATION TEST

The cone penetration test (CPT), originally known as the Dutch cone penetration test, is a versatile sounding method that can be used to determine the materials in a soil profile and estimate their engineering properties. This test is also called the static penetration test, and no boreholes are necessary to perform it. In the original version, a 60° cone with a base area of 10 cm^2 was pushed into the ground at a steady rate of about 20 mm/sec, and the resistance to penetration (called the point resistance) was measured.

The cone penetrometers in use at present measure (a) the *cone resistance* (q_c) to penetration developed by the cone, which is equal to the vertical force applied to the cone divided by its horizontally projected area, and (b) the *frictional resistance* (f_c), which is the resistance measured by a sleeve located above the cone with the local soil surrounding it. The frictional resistance is equal to the vertical force applied to the sleeve divided by its surface area—actually, the sum of friction and adhesion.

Generally, two types of penetrometers are used to measure q_c and f_c:

a. *Mechanical friction-cone penetrometer* (Figure 2.26). In this case the penetrometer tip is connected to an inner set of rods. The tip is first advanced about 40 mm giving the cone resistance. With further thrusting, the tip engages the friction sleeve. As the inner rod advances, the rod force is equal to the sum of the vertical force on the cone and sleeve. Subtracting the force on the cone gives the side resistance.

b. *Electric friction-cone penetrometer* (Figure 2.27). In this case the tip is attached to a string of steel rods. The tip is pushed into the ground at the rate of

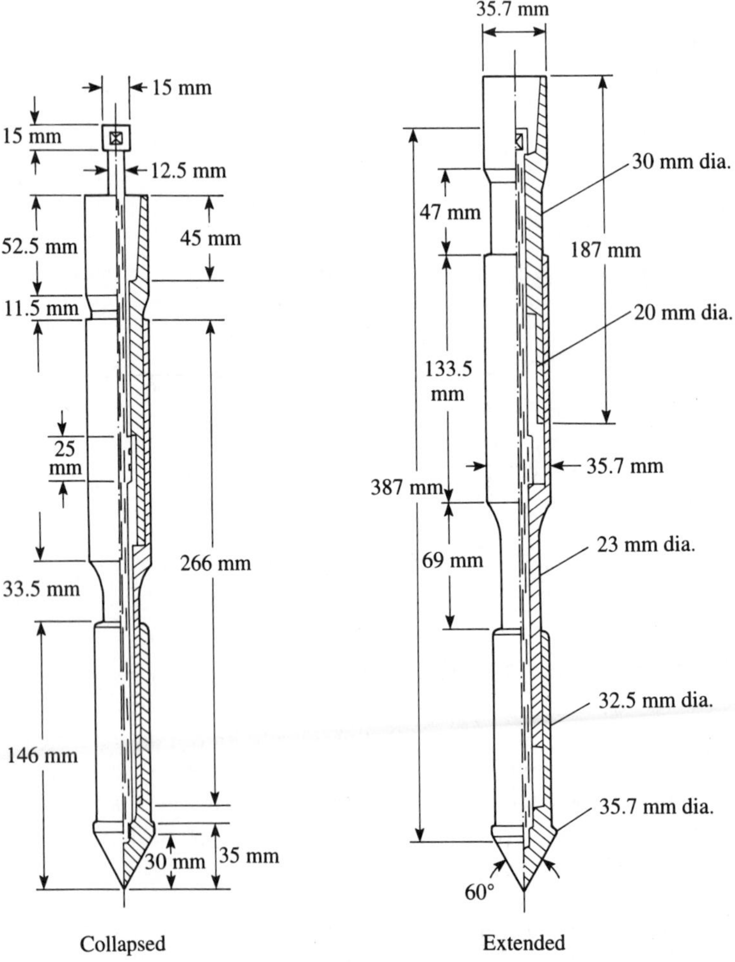

▼ **FIGURE 2.26** Mechanical friction-cone penetrometer (after ASTM, 1992)

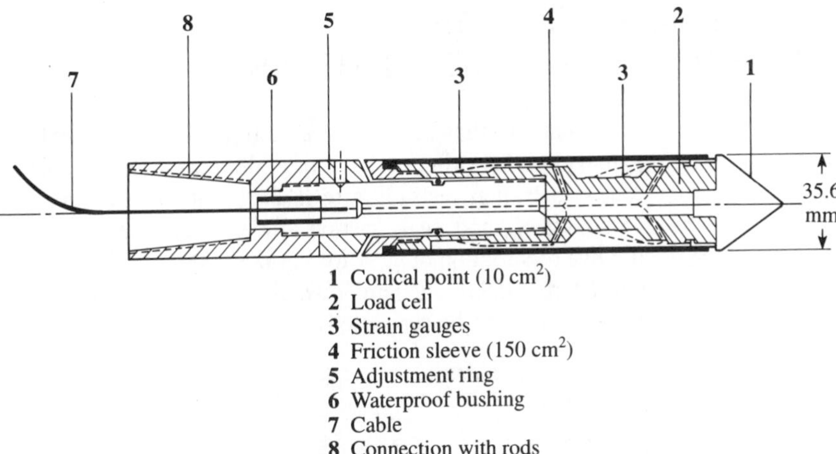

▼ **FIGURE 2.27** Electric friction-cone penetrometer (after ASTM, 1992)

20 mm/sec. Wires from the transducers are threaded through the center of the rods and continuously give the cone and side resistances.

Figure 2.28 shows the results of penetrometer tests in a soil profile with friction measurement by a mechanical friction-cone penetrometer and an electric friction-cone penetrometer.

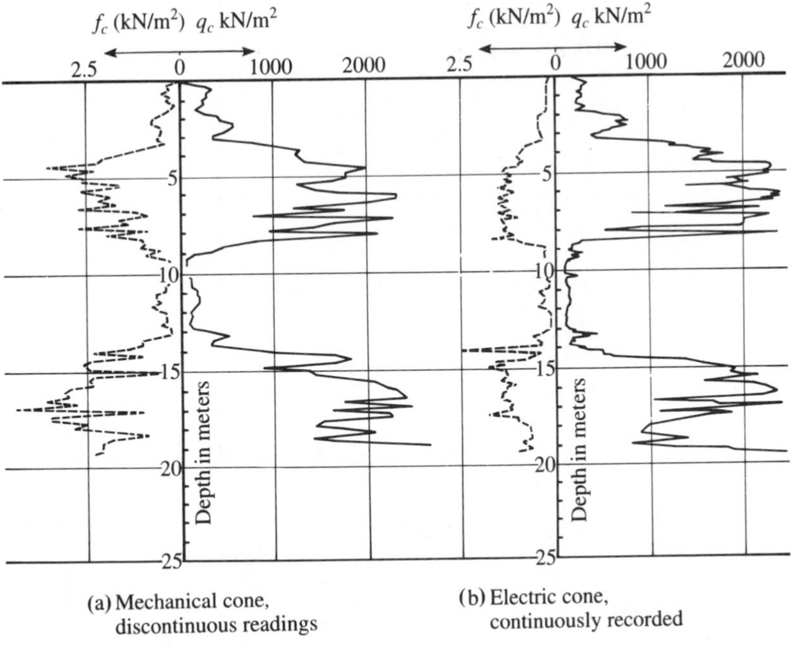

▼ **FIGURE 2.28** Penetrometer tests with friction measurement (after Ruiter, 1971)

2.17 CORRELATIONS FOR CONE PENETRATION TEST RESULTS

Several correlations that are useful in estimating the properties of soils encountered during an exploration program have been developed for the point resistance q_c obtained from cone penetration tests. Figure 2.29 shows the variation of q_c with the vertical effective stress, σ'_v, and peak friction angle, ϕ, in quartz sand. Figure 2.30 shows the general range of variation of q_c/N for various types of soil.

Lancellotta (1983) and Jamilkawski et al. (1985) showed that the relative density of sand, D_r, and q_c can be correlated as

$$D_r(\%) = A + B \log_{10}\left(\frac{q_c}{\sqrt{\sigma'_v}}\right) \tag{2.25}$$

where A, B = constants
σ'_v = vertical effective stress

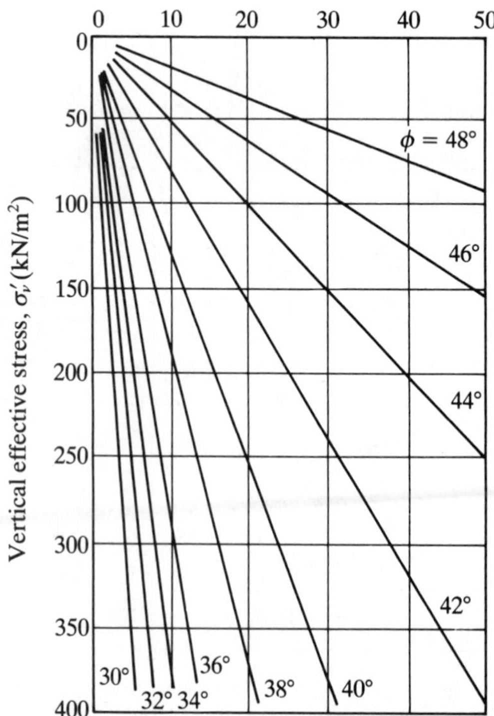

▼ **FIGURE 2.29** Variation of q_c with σ'_v and ϕ in quartz sand (after Robertson and Campanella, 1983)

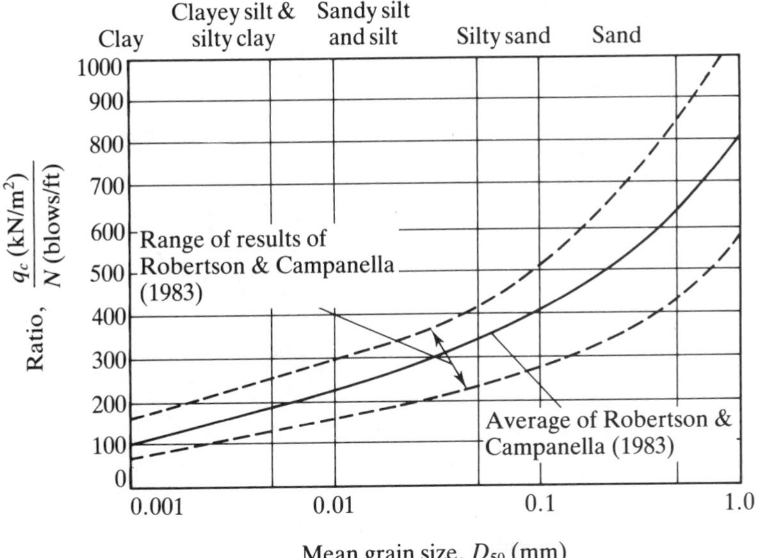

▼ **FIGURE 2.30** General range of variation of q_c/N for various types of soil (after Robertson and Campanella, 1983)

The values of A and B are

A	B	Unit of q_c and σ'_v
−98	66	metric ton/m^2

Figure 2.31 shows the correlations obtained for several sands.

According to Mayne and Kemper (1988), in clayey soil the undrained cohesion c_u, preconsolidation pressure p_c, and the overconsolidation ratio can be correlated as

$$\left(\frac{c_u}{\sigma'_v}\right) = \left(\frac{q_c - \sigma_v}{\sigma'_v}\right)\frac{1}{N_K} \tag{2.26}$$

where N_K = bearing capacity factor ($N_K = 15$ for electric cone, and $N_K = 20$ for mechanical cone)

σ_v = *total* vertical stress

σ'_v = effective vertical stress

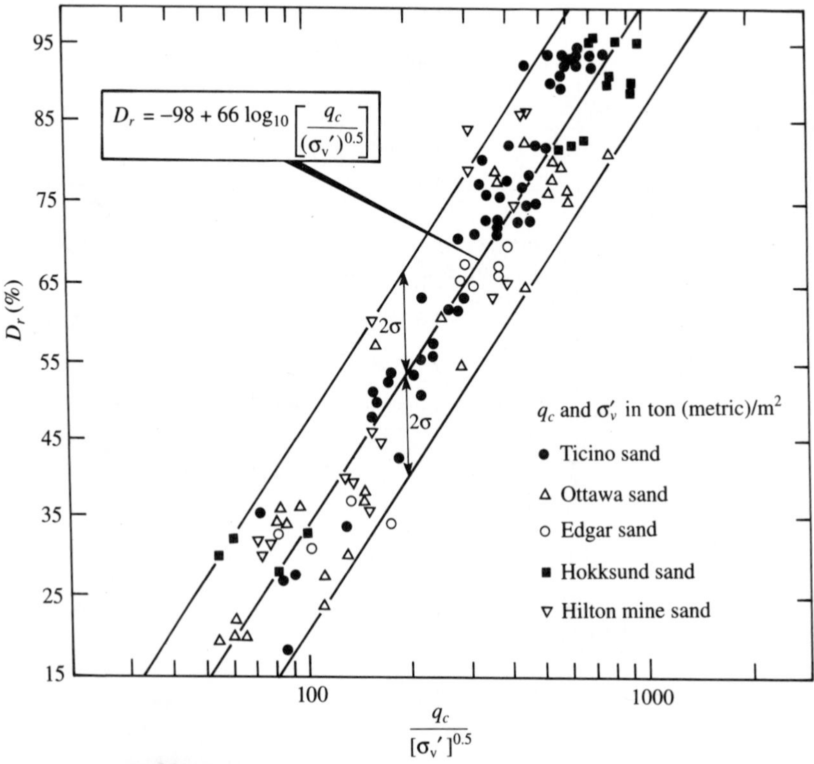

▼ **FIGURE 2.31** Relationship between D_r and q_c (based on Lancellotta, 1983, and Jamilkawski et al., 1985)

Consistent units of c_u, σ_v, σ_v', and q_c should be used with Eq. (2.26):

$$p_c = 0.243(q_c)^{0.96} \quad (p_c \text{ in MN/m}^2,\ q_c \text{ in MN/m}^2) \tag{2.27}$$

and

$$OCR = 0.37\left(\frac{q_c - \sigma_v}{\sigma_v'}\right)^{1.01} \tag{2.28}$$

where σ_v and σ_v' = total and effective stress, respectively.

2.18 CORING OF ROCKS

When a rock layer is encountered during a drilling operation, rock coring may be necessary. For coring of rocks, a *core barrel* is attached to a drilling rod. A *coring bit* is attached to the bottom of the core barrel (Figure 2.32). The cutting elements may be diamond, tungsten, carbide, and so on. Table 2.6 summarizes the various types of core barrel and their sizes, as well as the compatible drill rods commonly used for foundation exploration.

The coring is advanced by rotary drilling. Water is circulated through the drilling rod during coring, and the cutting is washed out.

Two types of core barrel are available: the *single-tube core barrel* (Figure 2.32a) and the *double-tube core barrel* (Figure 2.32b). Rock cores obtained by single-tube core barrels can be highly disturbed and fractured because of torsion. Rock cores smaller than the BX size tend to fracture during the coring process.

When the core samples are recovered, the depth of recovery should be properly recorded for further evaluation in the laboratory. Based on the length of the rock core

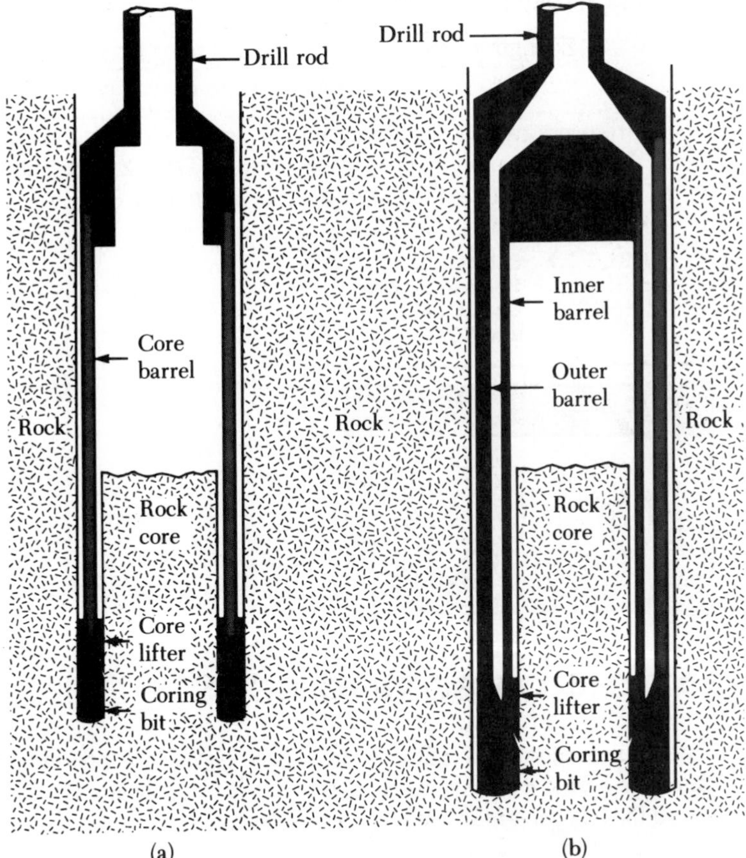

▼ **FIGURE 2.32** Rock coring: (a) single-tube core barrel; (b) double-tube core barrel

▼ **TABLE 2.6 Standard Size and Designation of Casing, Core Barrel, and Compatible Drill Rod**

Casing and core barrel designation	Outside diameter of core barrel bit (mm)	Outside diameter of core barrel bit (in.)	Drill rod designation	Outside diameter of drill rod (mm)	Outside diameter of drill rod (in.)	Diameter of borehole (mm)	Diameter of borehole (in.)	Diameter of core sample (mm)	Diameter of core sample (in.)
EX	36.51	$1\frac{7}{16}$	E	33.34	$1\frac{5}{16}$	38.1	$1\frac{1}{2}$	22.23	$\frac{7}{8}$
AX	47.63	$1\frac{7}{8}$	A	41.28	$1\frac{5}{8}$	50.8	2	28.58	$1\frac{1}{8}$
BX	58.74	$2\frac{5}{16}$	B	47.63	$1\frac{7}{8}$	63.5	$2\frac{1}{2}$	41.28	$1\frac{5}{8}$
NX	74.61	$2\frac{15}{16}$	N	60.33	$2\frac{3}{8}$	76.2	3	53.98	$2\frac{1}{8}$

recovered from each run, the following quantities may be calculated for a general evaluation of the rock quality encountered.

$$\text{Recovery ratio} = \frac{\text{length of core recovered}}{\text{theoretical length of rock cored}} \tag{2.29}$$

Rock quality designation (RQD) =

$$\frac{\Sigma \text{ length of recovered pieces equal to or larger than 101.6 m (4 in.)}}{\text{theoretical length of rock cored}} \tag{2.30}$$

A recovery ratio of 1 will indicate the presence of intact rock; for highly fractured rocks, the recovery ratio may be 0.5 or smaller. Table 2.7 presents the general relationship (Deere, 1963) between the *RQD* and the *in situ* rock quality.

▼ **TABLE 2.7 Relation Between *in situ* Rock Quality and *RQD***

RQD	Rock quality
0–0.25	Very poor
0.25–0.5	Poor
0.5–0.75	Fair
0.75–0.9	Good
0.9–1	Excellent

2.19 PREPARATION OF BORING LOGS

The detailed information gathered from each borehole is presented in a graphical form called the *boring log*. As a borehole is advanced downward, the driller generally should record the following information in a standard log.

1. Name and address of the drilling company
2. Driller's name

3. Job description and number
4. Number and type of boring and boring location
5. Date of boring
6. Subsurface stratification, which can be obtained by visual observation of the soil brought out by auger, split-spoon sampler, and thin wall Shelby tube sampler.
7. Elevation of water table and date observed, use of casing and mud losses, and so on
8. Standard penetration resistance and the depth of *SPT*
9. Number, type, and depth of soil sample collected
10. In case of rock coring, type of core barrel used should be recorded. For each run, the actual length of coring, length of core recovery, and the *RQD* should also be carefully noted.

This information should never be left to memory, because that often results in erroneous boring logs.

After completion of the necessary laboratory tests, the geotechnical engineer prepares a finished log that includes notes from the driller's field log and the results of tests conducted in the laboratory. Figure 2.33 shows a typical boring log. These logs have to be attached to the final soil-exploration report submitted to the client. Note that Figure 2.33 also lists the classifications of the soils in the left-hand column, along with the description of each soil (based on the Unified Soil Classification System).

2.20 DETERMINATION OF COEFFICIENT OF PERMEABILITY IN THE FIELD

Several types of field test are now available to determine the coefficient of permeability of soil. Two fairly easy test procedures described by the U.S. Bureau of Reclamation (1974) are the *open end test* and the *packer test.*

Open End Test

The first step in the open end test (Figure 2.34) is to advance a borehole to the desired depth. A casing is then driven to extend to the bottom of the borehole. Water is supplied at a constant rate from the top of the casing, and it escapes at the bottom of the borehole. The water level in the casing must remain constant. Once the steady state of water supply is established, the coefficient of permeability can be determined as

$$k = \frac{Q}{5.5rH} \tag{2.31}$$

where k = coefficient of permeability
Q = constant rate of supply of water to the borehole
r = inside radius of the casing
H = differential head of water

Any system of consistent units may be used in Eq. (2.31).

Boring Log

Name of the Project Two-story apartment building

Location Johnson & Olive St. Date of Boring March 2, 1982

Boring No. 3 Type of Boring Hollow stem auger Ground Elevation 60.8 m

Soil description	Depth (m)	Soil sample type and number	N	w_n (%)	Comments
Light brown clay (fill)					
Silty sand (SM)	1 2	SS-1	9	8.2	
°G.W.T. 3.5 m Light gray silty clay (ML)	3	SS-2	12	17.6	$LL = 38$ $PI = 11$
	4 5	ST-1		20.4	$LL = 36$ $q_u = 112\ \text{kN/m}^2$
	6	SS-3	11	20.6	
Sand with some gravel (SP)	7				
End of boring @ 8 m	8	SS-4	27	9	

N = standard penetration number (below/304.8 mm)
w_n = natural moisture content
LL = liquid limit; PI = plasticity index
q_u = unconfined compression strength
SS = split-spoon sample; ST = Shelby tube sample

°Ground water table observed after one week of drilling

▼ **FIGURE 2.33** A typical boring log

The head, H, has been defined in Figure 2.34. Note that for pressure tests (Figure 2.34c and d) the value of H is given as

$$H = H_{(\text{gravity})} + H_{(\text{pressure})} \tag{2.32}$$

The pressure head, $H_{(\text{pressure})}$, given in Eq. (2.32) is expressed in meters (or feet) of water ($1\ \text{kN/m}^2 = 0.102\ \text{m}$; $1\ \text{lb/in}^2 = 2.308\ \text{ft}$).

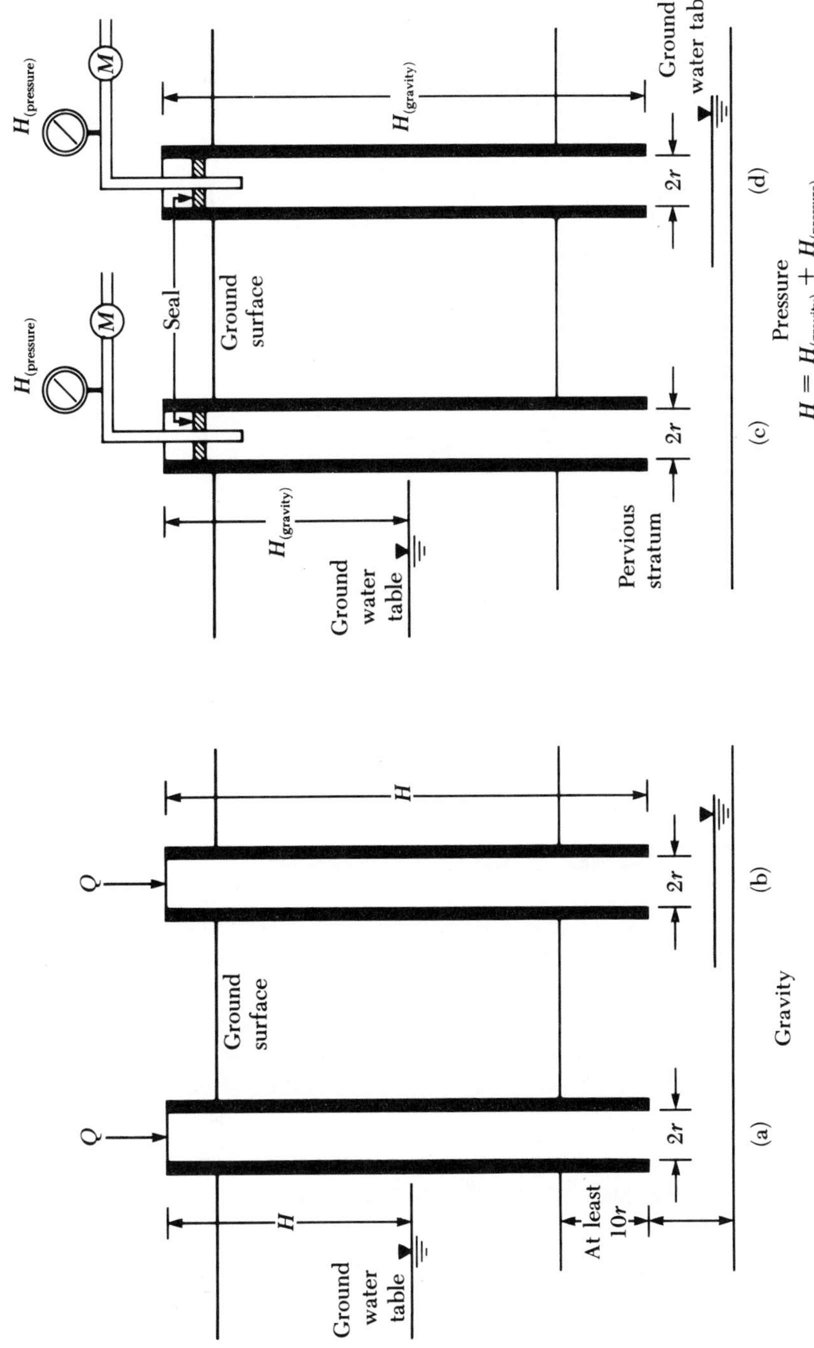

▶ **FIGURE 2.34** Coefficient of permeability—open end test (redrawn after U.S. Bureau of Reclamation, 1974)

Packer Test

The packer test (Figure 2.35) can be conducted in a portion of the borehole during drilling or after drilling has been completed. Water to the portion of the borehole under test is supplied under constant pressure. The coefficient of permeability can be determined from

$$k = \frac{Q}{2\pi LH}\log_e\left(\frac{L}{r}\right) \qquad \text{(for } L \geq 10r\text{)} \tag{2.33}$$

$$k = \frac{Q}{2\pi LH}\sinh^{-1}\frac{L}{2r} \qquad \text{(for } 10r > L \geq r\text{)} \tag{2.34}$$

where k = coefficient of permeability
Q = constant rate of flow into the hole
L = length of portion of the hole under test
r = radius of the hole
H = differential pressure head

Note that the differential pressure head is the sum of the gravity head $[H_{\text{(gravity)}}]$ and the pressure head $[H_{\text{(pressure)}}]$.

The packer test is used primarily to determine the permeability of rock. However, as mentioned previously, it can also be used for soils.

2.21 GEOPHYSICAL EXPLORATION

Several types of geophysical exploration techniques permit rapid evaluation of subsoil characteristics. They allow rapid coverage of large areas and are less expensive than conventional exploration by drilling. However, in many cases, definitive interpretation of the results is difficult. For that reason, these techniques should be used for preliminary work only. Here, we discuss three types of geophysical exploration technique: seismic refraction survey, cross-hole seismic survey, and resistivity survey.

Seismic Refraction Survey

Seismic refraction surveys are useful in obtaining preliminary information about the thickness of the layering of various soils and the depth to rock or hard soil at a site. Refraction surveys are conducted by impacting the surface, as at point A in Figure 2.36a, and observing the first arrival of the disturbance (stress waves) at several other points (e.g., B, C, D, . . .). The impact can be created by a hammer blow or by a small explosive charge. The first arrival of disturbance waves at various points can be recorded by geophones.

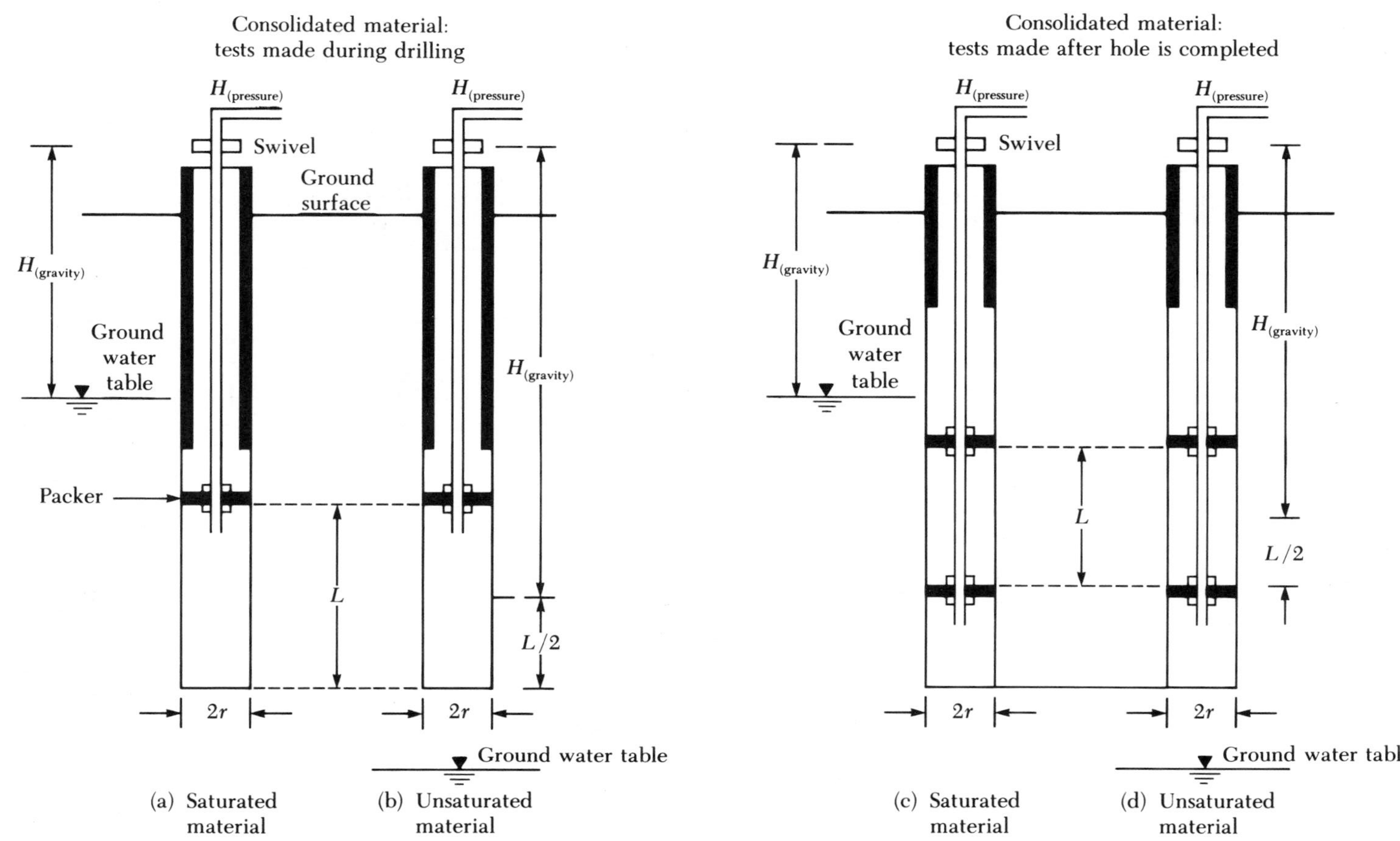

▼ **FIGURE 2.35** Coefficient of permeability determination—packer test (redrawn after U.S. Bureau of Reclamation, 1974)

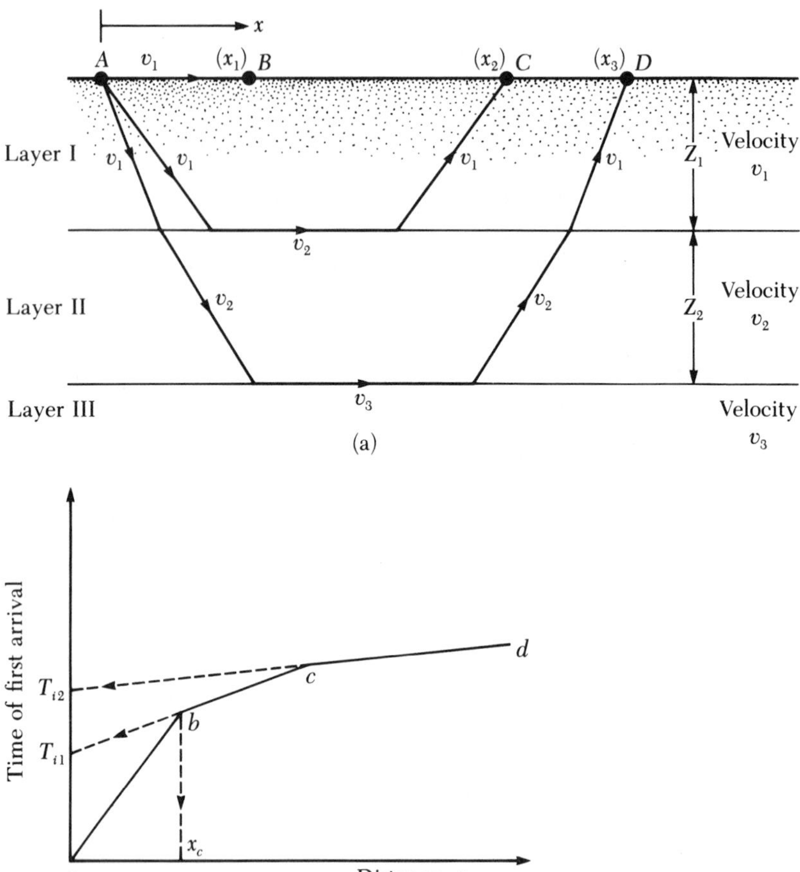

▼ **FIGURE 2.36** Seismic refraction survey

The impact on the ground surface creates two types of *stress wave*: *P waves* (or *plane waves*) and *S waves* (or *shear waves*). The *P* waves travel faster than *S* waves; hence the first arrival of disturbance waves will be related to the velocities of the *P* waves in various layers. The velocity of *P* waves in a medium is

$$v = \frac{E}{\left(\frac{\gamma}{g}\right)} \sqrt{\frac{(1-\mu)}{(1-2\mu)(1+\mu)}} \tag{2.35}$$

where E = modulus of elasticity of the medium
γ = unit weight of the medium
g = acceleration due to gravity
μ = Poisson's ratio

To determine the velocity, v, of P waves in various layers and the thicknesses of those layers, use the following procedure.

1. Obtain the times of first arrival, t_1, t_2, t_3, . . . , at various distances, x_1, x_2, x_3, . . . , from the point of impact.
2. Plot a graph of time, t, against distance, x. The graph will look like the one shown in Figure 2.36b.
3. Determine the slopes of the lines ab, bc, cd, . . .

$$\text{Slope of } ab = \frac{1}{v_1}$$

$$\text{Slope of } bc = \frac{1}{v_2}$$

$$\text{Slope of } cd = \frac{1}{v_3}$$

where v_1, v_2, v_3, . . . are the P-wave velocities in layers I, II, III, . . . , respectively (Figure 2.36a)

4. Determine the thickness of the top layer as

$$Z_1 = \frac{1}{2}\sqrt{\frac{v_2 - v_1}{v_2 + v_1}}\, x_c \tag{2.36}$$

The value of x_c can be obtained from the plot, as shown in Figure 2.36b.

5. Determine the thickness of the second layer, Z_2, shown in Figure 2.36a, as

$$Z_2 = \frac{1}{2}\left[T_{i2} - 2Z_1 \frac{\sqrt{v_3^2 - v_1^2}}{v_3 v_1}\right] \frac{v_3 v_2}{\sqrt{v_3^2 - v_2^2}} \tag{2.37}$$

where T_{i2} is the time intercept of the line cd in Figure 2.36b extended backward.

For detailed derivatives of these equations and other related information, refer to Dobrin (1960) and Das (1983).

Knowing the velocities of P waves in various layers indicates the types of soil or rock that are present below the ground surface. The range of the P-wave velocity that is generally encountered in various types of soil and rock at shallow depths is given in Table 2.8.

In analyzing the results of a refraction survey, two limitations need to be kept in mind:

1. The basic equations for the refraction survey—that is, Eqs. (2.36) and (2.37)—are based on the assumption that the P-wave velocity $v_1 < v_2 < v_3 < \cdots$.
2. When a soil is saturated below the water table, the P-wave velocity may be deceptive. Through water P waves can travel with a velocity of about 1500 m/sec (5000 ft/sec). For dry, loose soils, the velocity may be well below 1500 m/sec. However, in a saturated condition, the waves will travel through

TABLE 2.8 Range of P-Wave Velocity in Various Soils and Rocks

Type of soil or rock	P-wave velocity	
	m/sec	*ft/sec*
Soil		
Sand, dry silt, and fine-grained top soil	200– 1,000	650– 3,300
Alluvium	500– 2,000	1,650– 6,600
Compacted clays, clayey gravel, and dense clayey sand	1,000– 2,500	3,300– 8,200
Loess	250– 750	800– 2,450
Rock		
Slate and shale	2,500– 5,000	8,200–16,400
Sandstone	1,500– 5,000	4,900–16,400
Granite	4,000– 6,000	13,100–19,700
Sound limestone	5,000–10,000	16,400–32,800

water present in the void spaces with a velocity of about 1500 m/sec (5000 ft/sec). If the presence of ground water has not been detected, the P-wave velocity may be erroneously interpreted to indicate a stronger material (e.g., sandstone) than actually present *in situ*. In general, geophysical interpretations should always be verified by the results obtained from borings.

EXAMPLE 2.3

The results of a refraction survey at a site are given in the following table. Determine the P-wave velocities and the thickness of the material encountered.

Distance from the source of disturbance (m)	*Time of first arrival (sec × 10^3)*
2.5	11.2
5	23.3
7.5	33.5
10	42.4
15	50.9
20	57.2
25	64.4
30	68.6
35	71.1
40	72.1
50	75.5

Solution

Velocity

In Figure 2.37, the times of first arrival are plotted against the distance from the source of disturbance. The plot has three straight-line segments. The velocity of the top three layers can now be calculated as follows:

$$\text{Slope of segment } 0a = \frac{1}{v_1} = \frac{\text{time}}{\text{distance}} = \frac{23 \times 10^{-3}}{5.25}$$

or

$$v_1 = \frac{5.25 \times 10^3}{23} = \mathbf{228\ m/sec\ (top\ layer)}$$

$$\text{Slope of segment } ab = \frac{1}{v_2} = \frac{13.5 \times 10^{-3}}{11}$$

or

$$v_2 = \frac{11 \times 10^3}{13.5} = \mathbf{814.8\ m/sec\ (middle\ layer)}$$

$$\text{Slope of segment } bc = \frac{1}{v_3} = \frac{14.75 \times 10^{-3}}{3.5}$$

or

$$v_3 = \mathbf{4214\ m/sec\ (third\ layer)}$$

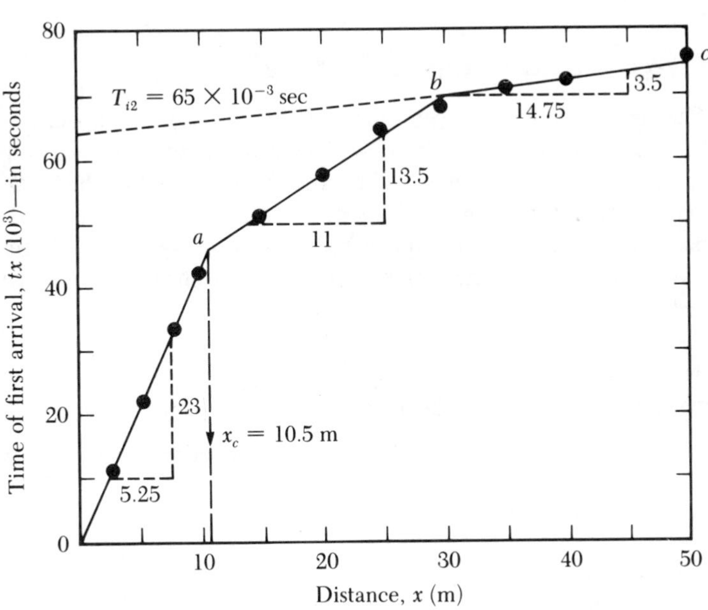

▼ **FIGURE 2.37**

Comparing the velocities obtained here with those given in Table 2.8 indicates that the third layer is a *rock layer.*

Thickness of Layers

From Figure 2.37, $x_c = 10.5$ m, so

$$Z_1 = \frac{1}{2}\sqrt{\frac{v_2 - v_1}{v_2 + v_1}}\, x_c \qquad \text{[Eq. (2.36)]}$$

Thus

$$Z_1 = \frac{1}{2}\sqrt{\frac{814.8 - 228}{814.8 + 228}} \times 10.5 = \mathbf{3.94\ m}$$

Again, from Eq. (2.37)

$$Z_2 = \frac{1}{2}\left[T_{i2} - \frac{2Z_1\sqrt{v_3^2 - v_1^2}}{(v_3 v_1)}\right]\frac{(v_3)(v_2)}{\sqrt{v_3^2 - v_2^2}}$$

The value of T_{i2} (from Figure 2.37) is 65×10^{-3} sec. Hence

$$Z_2 = \frac{1}{2}\left[65 \times 10^{-3} - \frac{2(3.94)\sqrt{(4214)^2 - (228)^2}}{(4214)(228)}\right]\frac{(4214)(814.8)}{\sqrt{(4214)^2 - (814.8)^2}}$$

$$= \frac{1}{2}(0.065 - 0.0345)830.47 = \mathbf{12.66\ m}$$

The rock layer lies at a depth of $Z_1 + Z_2 = 3.94 + 12.66 =$ **16.60 m measured from the ground surface.** ▼

Cross-Hole Seismic Survey

The velocity of shear waves created as the result of an impact to a given soil layer can be effectively determined by *cross-hole seismic survey* (Stokoe and Woods, 1972). The principle of this technique is illustrated in Figure 2.38, which shows two holes drilled into the ground at distance L apart. A vertical impulse is created at the bottom of one borehole by means of an impulse rod. The shear waves thus generated are recorded by a vertically sensitive transducer. The velocity of shear waves, v_s, can be calculated as

$$v_s = \frac{L}{t} \tag{2.38}$$

where t = travel time of shear waves.

The shear modulus of the soil at the depth of the test can be determined from v_s as

$$v_s = \sqrt{\frac{G}{(\gamma/g)}}$$

$$G = \frac{v_s^2\gamma}{g} \tag{2.39}$$

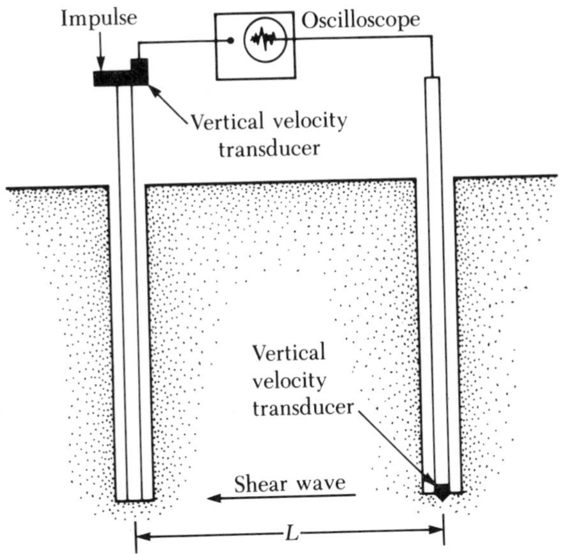

▼ **FIGURE 2.38** Cross-hole method of seismic survey

where G = shear modulus of soil
γ = soil unit weight
g = acceleration due to gravity

The values of shear modulus are useful in the design of foundations to support vibrating machinery and the like.

Resistivity Survey

Another geophysical method for subsoil exploration is the *electrical resistivity survey*. The electrical resistivity, ρ, of any conducting material having a length L and an area of cross section A can be defined as

$$\rho = \frac{RA}{L} \tag{2.40}$$

where R = electrical resistance

The unit of resistivity is generally expressed as *ohm · centimeter* or *ohm · meter*. The resistivity of various soils depends primarily on the moisture content and also on the concentration of dissolved ions. Saturated clays have a very low resistivity; in contrast, dry soils and rocks have a high resistivity. The range of resistivity generally encountered in various soils and rocks is given in Table 2.9.

The most common procedure for measuring electrical resistivity of a soil profile makes use of four electrodes that are driven into the ground and spaced equally along a straight line. It is generally referred to as the *Wenner method* (Figure 2.39a). The two outside electrodes are used to send an electrical current, I, (usually a DC current with nonpolarizing potential electrodes) into the ground. The electrical current is typically in

TABLE 2.9 Representative Values of Resistivity

Material	Resistivity (ohm · m)
Sand	500–1500
Clays, saturated silt	0– 100
Clayey sand	200– 500
Gravel	1500–4000
Weathered rock	1500–2500
Sound rock	>5000

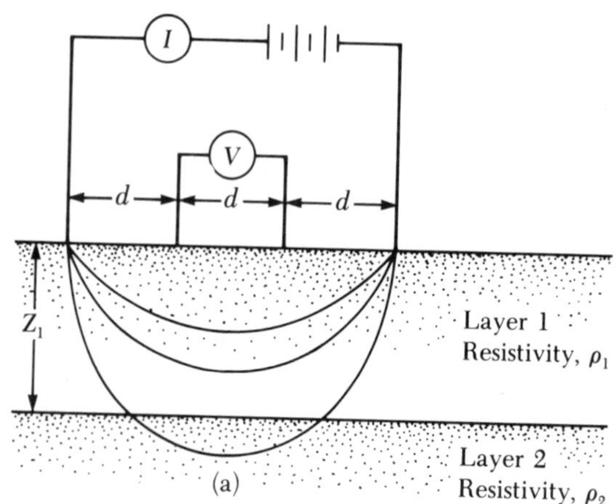

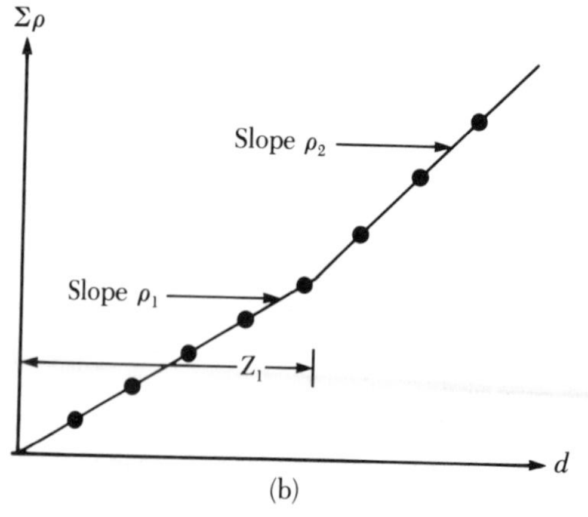

FIGURE 2.39 Electrical resistivity survey: (a) Wenner method; (b) empirical method for determination of resistivity and thickness of each layer

the range of 50–100 milliamperes. The voltage drop, V, is measured between the two inside electrodes. If the soil profile is homogeneous, its electrical resistivity is

$$\rho = \frac{2\pi d V}{I} \tag{2.41}$$

In most cases, the soil profile may consist of various layers with different resistivities and Eq. (2.41) will yield the *apparent resistivity*. To obtain the *actual resistivity* of various layers and their thicknesses, an empirical method may be used. It involves conducting tests at various electrode spacings (i.e., d is changed). The sum of the apparent resistivities, $\Sigma\rho$, is plotted against the spacing d, as shown in Figure 2.39b. The plot thus obtained has relatively straight segments. The slopes of these straight segments give the resistivity of individual layers. The thicknesses of various layers can be estimated as shown in Figure 2.39b.

The resistivity survey is particularly useful in locating gravel deposits within a fine-grained soil.

2.22 SOIL-EXPLORATION REPORT

At the end of all soil-exploration programs, the soil and/or rock specimens collected in the field are subject to visual observation and appropriate laboratory testing (the basic soil tests were described in Chapter 1). After all the required information has been compiled, a soil-exploration report is prepared for the use of the design office and for reference during future construction work. Although the details and sequence of information in the report may vary to some degree, depending on the structure under consideration and the person compiling the report, each report should include the following items.

1. The scope of the investigation.
2. A description of the proposed structure for which the subsoil exploration has been conducted.
3. A description of the location of the site. It should include structure(s) nearby, drainage conditions of the site, nature of vegetation on the site and surrounding it, and any other feature(s) unique to the site.
4. Geological setting of the site.
5. Details of the field exploration—that is, number of borings, depths of borings, type of boring, and so on.
6. General description of the subsoil conditions as determined from soil specimens and from related laboratory tests, standard penetration resistance and cone penetration resistance, and so on.
7. Water-table conditions.
8. Foundation recommendations. These should include the type of foundation recommended, allowable bearing pressure, and any special construction procedure that may be needed. Alternative foundation design procedures should also be discussed in this portion of the report.
9. Conclusions and limitations of the investigations.

The following graphical presentations should be attached to the report.

1. Site location map
2. A plan view of the location of the borings with respect to the proposed structures and those existing nearby
3. Boring logs
4. Laboratory test results
5. Other special graphical presentations

The exploration reports should be well planned and documented. They will help in answering questions and solving foundation problems that may arise later during design and construction.

PROBLEMS

2.1 The inside and outside diameters of a Shelby tube are 3.375 in. and 3.5 in., respectively. Determine the area ratio.

2.2 A Shelby tube has an outside diameter of 2 in. and an inside diameter of 1.875 in. What is its area ratio?

2.3 A soil profile is shown in Figure P2.3 along with the standard penetration numbers in the clay layers. Use Eqs. (2.5) and (2.6) to determine and plot the variations of c_u and OCR with depth.

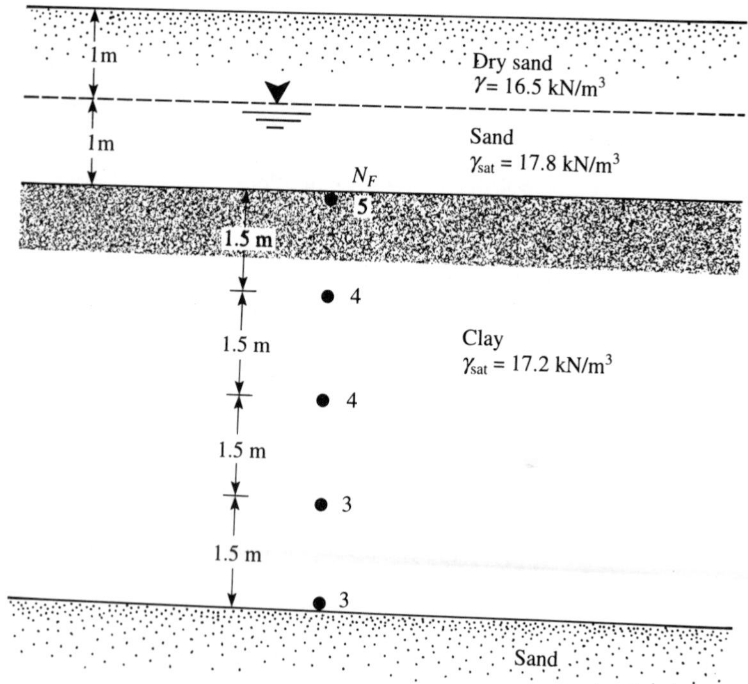

▼ **FIGURE P2.3**

2.4 A boring log in a sandy soil is shown in Figure P2.4. Determine:

a. The corrected standard penetration number from Eq. (2.8).

b. Seed et al. (1975) suggested that

$$C_N = 1 - 1.25 \log\left(\frac{\sigma'_v}{\sigma'_1}\right)$$

where $\sigma'_1 = 1$ ton (U.S.)/ft^2 and σ'_v = effective overburden pressure in ton/ft^2
Use this equation to determine the variation of the standard penetration numbers.

c. Compare the results of parts (a) and (b).

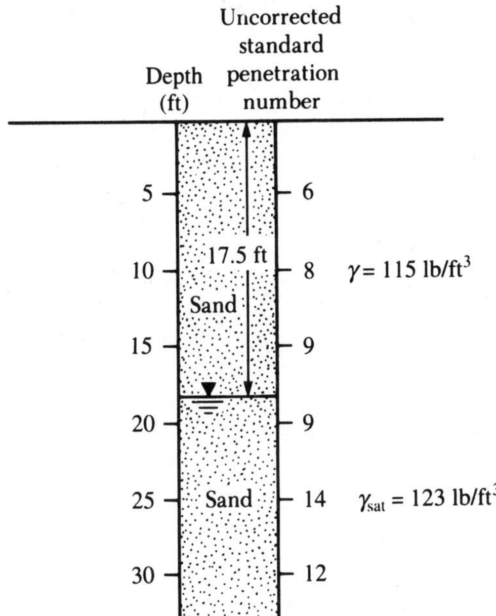

▼ **FIGURE P2.4**

2.5 For the sand deposit described in Problem 2.4, assume that the uniformity coefficient, C_u, is 3.2. Estimate the variation of the relative density of sand with depth. Choose a value of the relative density and an angle of friction of sand for designing a shallow foundation having a width of 5 ft.

2.6 Following are the standard penetration numbers determined from a sandy soil deposit in the field.

Depth (ft)	*Unit weight of soil (lb/ft³)*	N_F
10	106	7
15	106	9
20	106	11
25	118	16
30	118	18
35	118	20
40	118	22

Note: The water table was located at a depth of 43 ft.

Use the following equations to determine the variation of the corrected standard penetration numbers.

a. Equation (2.10)

b. The equation of Seed et al. (1975) given in part (b) of Problem 2.4

c. The equation proposed by Peck et al. (1974):

$$C_N = 0.77 \log\left(\frac{20}{\sigma'_v}\right) \qquad (\text{for } \sigma'_v \geq 0.25 \text{ ton/ft}^2)$$

d. Plot graphs for the variation of N with depth from the results obtained in parts (a), (b), and (c).

2.7 For the soil profile described in Problem 2.6,

a. estimate the variation of relative density with depth up to 25 ft. Use $C_u = 4.5$.

b. Laboratory tests of the soil show that

$$\phi \approx 30 + 0.15D_r$$

where ϕ = soil friction angle

D_r = relative density in percent

Estimate a friction angle for designing a shallow foundation measuring 6 ft × 6 ft in plan.

2.8 Refer to Figure 2.19. The borehole is in a silty soil: $h_w + h_0 = 12.24$ m, $t_1 = 24$ hr, $t_2 = 48$ hr, $\Delta h_1 = 1.2$ m, $\Delta h_2 = 0.86$ m, and $\Delta h_3 = 0.6$ m. Determine h_w (the depth to the water table).

2.9 Repeat Problem 2.8 for

$h_w + h_0 = 42$ ft

$t_1 = 24$ hr $\quad \Delta h_1 = 6$ ft

$t_2 = 48$ hr $\quad \Delta h_2 = 4.8$ ft

$t_3 = 72$ hr $\quad \Delta h_3 = 3.8$ ft

2.10 A soil profile is shown in Figure P2.10. Vane shear tests were conducted in the clay layer underlying the sand. The vane dimensions were 63.5 mm (D) × 127.0 mm (H). For the test at A, if the torque to cause failure is 0.042 N · m, estimate the undrained cohesion (c_u) of the clay at that depth.

2.11 Refer to Problem 2.10. If the plasticity index of the clay is 60, estimate the

a. corrected value of c_u for design purposes. Refer to Figure 2.22a.

b. overconsolidation ratio (OCR). Use Eqs. (2.21) and (2.22).

2.12 **a.** A vane shear test was conducted in a saturated clay. The height and diameter of the vane were 4 in. and 2 in., respectively. During the test the maximum torque applied was 12.4 lb-ft. Determine the undrained shear strength of the clay.

b. The clay soil described in part (a) has a liquid limit of 64 and a plastic limit of 29. What would be the corrected undrained shear strength of this clay for design purposes? Use Figure 2.22a.

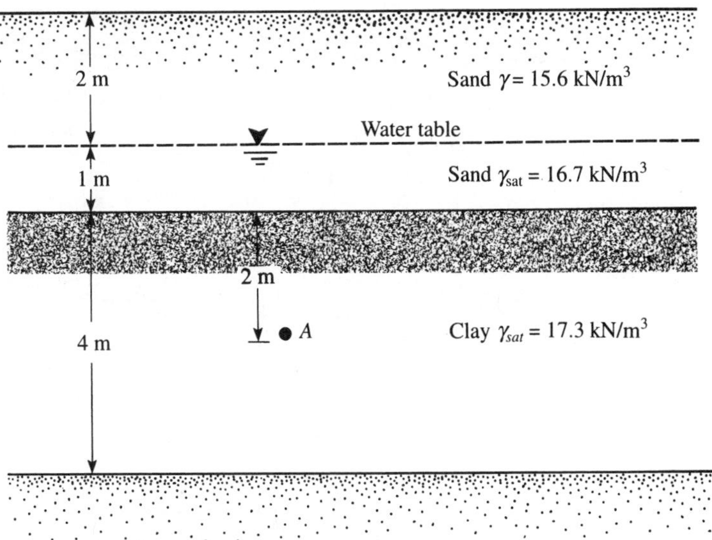

▼ **FIGURE P2.10**

2.13 In a homogeneous deposit of dry sand, a cone penetration test was conducted and the following results were obtained.

Depth (m)	*Point resistance of cone, q_c (kN/m²)*
3	2.7
5	4.8
8	7.4
10	10.1
15	14.5

Assume that the average unit weight of sand is 16.8 kN/m³. Estimate the soil friction angle for design of a shallow foundation.

2.14 Use the cone penetration results given in Problem 2.13 and Eq. (2.25). Estimate an average relative density for the sand.

2.15 Refer to the soil profile shown in Figure P2.15. If the cone penetration resistance (q_c) at A as determined by an electric friction-cone penetrometer is 0.6 MN/m², determine:

a. The undrained cohesion, c_u

b. The overconsolidation ratio, OCR

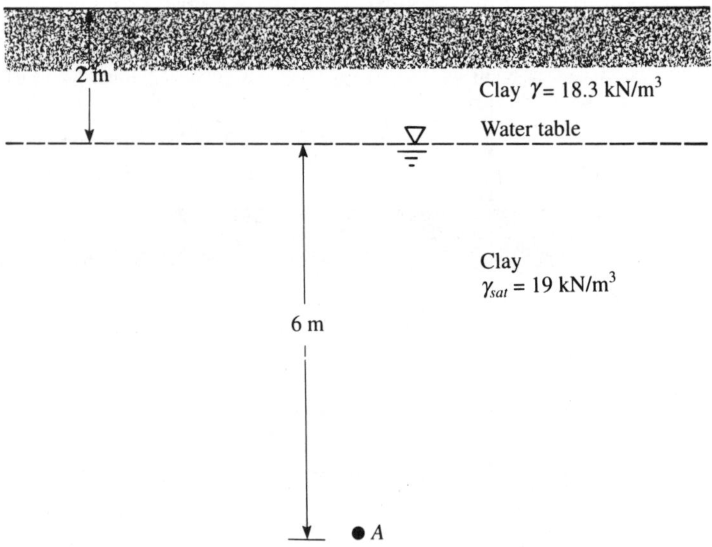

▼ **FIGURE P2.15**

2.16 During a field exploration, coring of rock was required. The core barrel was advanced 5 ft during the coring. The length of the core recovered was 3.2 ft. What was the recovery ratio?

2.17 An open end permeability test was conducted in a borehole (refer to Figure 2.34a). The inside diameter of the casing was 2 in. The differential head of water was 23.4 ft. To maintain a constant head of 23.4 ft, a constant water supply rate of 4.8×10^{-2} ft³/min was required. Calculate the coefficient of permeability of soil.

2.18 The *P*-wave velocity in a soil is 1900 m/sec. Assuming Poisson's ratio to be 0.32, calculate the modulus of elasticity of the soil. Assume that the unit weight of soil is 18 kN/m³.

2.19 The results of a refraction survey (Figure 2.36a) at a site are given in the following table. Determine the thickness and the *P*-wave velocity of the materials encountered.

Distance from the source of disturbance (m)	*Time of first arrival of P waves (sec × 10³)*
2.5	5.08
5.0	10.16
7.5	15.24
10.0	17.01
15.0	20.02
20.0	24.2
25.0	27.1
30.0	28.0
40.0	31.1
50.0	33.9

2.20 Repeat Problem 2.19 for the following data.

Distance from the source of disturbance (ft)	*Time of first arrival of P waves (sec × 10^3)*
25	49.08
50	81.96
75	122.8
100	148.2
150	174.2
200	202.8
250	228.6
300	256.7

REFERENCES

Aas, G., Lacasse, S., Lunne, I., and Høeg, K. (1986). "Use of In Situ Tests for Foundation Design in Clay," *Proceedings, In Situ '86*, American Society of Civil Engineers, pp. 1–30.

American Society for Testing and Materials (1992). *Annual Book of ASTM Standards*, Vol. 04.08, Philadelphia.

American Society of Civil Engineers (1972). "Subsurface Investigation for Design and Construction of Foundations of Buildings," *Journal of the Soil Mechanics and Foundations Division*, American Society of Civil Engineers, Vol. 98, No. SM5, pp. 481–490.

Bazaraa, A. R. (1967). *Use of Standard Penetration Test for Estimating Settlements of Shallow Foundations on Sand*, Ph.D. Thesis, University of Illinois, Urbana.

Bjerrum, L. (1972). "Embankments on Soft Ground," *Proceedings of the Specialty Conference*, American Society of Civil Engineers, Vol. 2, pp. 1–54.

Das, B. M. (1983). *Fundamentals of Soil Dynamics*, Elsevier Science Publishing Co., New York.

Deere, D. U. (1963). "Technical Description of Rock Cores for Engineering Purposes," *Felsmechanik und Ingenieurgeologie*, Vol. 1, No. 1, pp. 16–22.

Dobrin, M. B. (1960). *Introduction to Geophysical Prospecting*, McGraw-Hill, New York.

Hansbo, S. (1957). *A New Approach to the Determination of the Shear Strength of Clay by the Fall Cone Test*, Swedish Geotechnical Institute, Report No. 114.

Hara, A., Ohata, T., and Niwa, M. (1971). "Shear Modulus and Shear Strength of Cohesive Soils," *Soils and Foundations*, Vol. 14, No. 3, pp. 1–12.

Hvorslev, M. J. (1949). *Subsurface Exploration and Sampling of Soils for Civil Engineering Purposes*, Waterways Experiment Station, Vicksburg, Miss.

Jamilkowaski, M., Ladd, C. C., Germaine, J. T., and Lancellotta, R. (1985). "New Developments in Field and Laboratory Testing of Soils," *Proceedings*, 11th International Conference on Soil Mechanics and Foundation Engineering, Vol. 1, pp. 57–153.

Kolb, C. R., and Shockley, W. B. (1959). "Mississippi Valley Geology: Its Engineering Significance," *Proceedings*, American Society of Civil Engineers, Vol. 124, pp. 633–656.

Lancellotta, R. (1983). *Analisi di Affidabilità in Ingegneria Geotecnica*, Atti Istituto Sciencza Costruzioni, No. 625, Politecnico di Torino.

Larsson, R. (1980). "Undrained Shear Strength in Stability Calculation of Embankments and Foundations on Clay," *Canadian Geotechnical Journal*, Vol. 17, pp. 591–602.

Liao, S. S. C., and Whitman, R. V. (1986). "Overburden Correction Factors for SPT in Sand,"

Journal of Geotechnical Engineering, American Society of Civil Engineers, Vol. 112, No. 3, pp. 373–377.

Marcuson, W. F. III, and Bieganousky, W. A. (1977). "SPT and Relative Density in Coarse Sands," *Journal of Geotechnical Engineering Division*, American Society of Civil Engineers, Vol. 103, No. 11, pp. 1295–1309.

Mayne, P. W., and Mitchell, J. K. (1988). "Profiling of Overconsolidation Ratio in Clays by Field Vane," *Canadian Geotechnical Journal*, Vol. 25, No. 1, pp. 150–158. pp. 139–147.

Mane, P. W., and Mitchell, J. K. (1988). "Profiling of Overconsolidation Ratio in Clays by Field Vane," *Canadian Geotechnical Journal*, Vol. 25, No. 1, pp. 150–158.

Osterberg, J. O. (1952). "New Piston-Type Soil Sampler," *Engineering News-Record*, April 24.

Peck, R. B., and Bazaraa, A. S. (1969). "Discussion on Settlement of Spread Footings on Sand," *Journal of the Soil Mechanics and Foundations Division*, American Society of Civil Engineers, Vol. 95, No. SM3, pp. 905–909.

Peck, R. B., Hanson, W. E., and Thornburn, T. H. (1974). *Foundation Engineering*, 2nd ed., Wiley, New York.

Robertson, P. K., and Campanella, R. G. (1983). "Interpretation of Cone Penetration Tests. Part I: Sand," *Canadian Geotechnical Journal*, Vol. 20, No. 4, pp. 718–733.

Ruiter, J. (1971). "Electric Penetrometer for Site Investigations," *Journal of the Soil Mechanics and Foundations Division*, American Society of Civil Engineers, Vol. 97, No. 2, pp. 457–472.

Seed, H. B. (1976). "Evaluation of Soil Liquefaction Effects on Level Ground During Earthquakes," *ASCE Specialty Session Preprint 2752*, American Society of Civil Engineers' National Convention, pp. 1–105.

Seed, H. B. (1979). "Soil Liquefaction and Cyclic Mobility Evaluation for Level Ground During Earthquakes," *Journal of Geotechnical Engineering*, American Society of Civil Engineers, Vol. 111, No. 12, pp. 1425–1445.

Seed, H. B., Arango, I., and Chan, C. K. (1975). "Evaluation of Soil Liquefaction Potential During Earthquakes," *Report No. EERC 75-28*, Earthquake Engineering Research Center, University of California, Berkeley.

Skempton, A. W. (1986). "Standard Penetration Test Procedures and the Effect in Sands of Overburden Pressure, Relative Density, Particle Size, Aging and Overconsolidation," *Geotecchnique*, Vol. 36, No. 3, pp. 425–447.

Sowers, G. B., and Sowers, G. F. (1970). *Introductory Soil Mechanics and Foundations*, 3rd ed., Macmillan, New York.

Stokoe, K. H., and Woods, R. D. (1972). "*In Situ* Shear Wave Velocity by Cross-Hole Method," *Journal of Soil Mechanics and Foundations Division*, American Society of Civil Engineers, Vol. 98, No. SM5, pp. 443–460.

Stroud, M. (1974). "SPT in Insensitive Clays," *Proceedings*, European Symposium on Penetration Testing, Vol. 2.2, pp. 367–375.

Tang, W. C. (1962). *Foundation Design*, Prentice-Hall, Englewood Cliffs, N.J.

Tokimatsu, K., and Yoshimi, Y. (1983). "Empirical Correlation of Soil Liquefaction Based on SPT *N*-Value and Fines Content," *Soils and Foundations*, Vol. 23, No. 4, pp. 56–74.

U.S. Bureau of Reclamation (1974). *Design of Small Dams*, 2nd. ed., U.S. Government Printing Office, Washington, D.C.

CHAPTER THREE

SHALLOW FOUNDATIONS

3.1 INTRODUCTION

To perform satisfactorily, shallow foundations must have two main characteristics:

1. The foundation has to be safe against overall shear failure in the soil that supports it.
2. The foundation cannot undergo excessive displacement, that is, settlement. (The term *excessive* is relative, because the degree of settlement allowable for a structure depends on several considerations.) This chapter discusses in detail the evaluation of the safe load-bearing capacity and settlement of shallow foundations.

ULTIMATE BEARING CAPACITY OF SHALLOW FOUNDATIONS

3.2 GENERAL CONCEPT

Consider a strip foundation resting on the surface of a dense sand or stiff cohesive soil, as shown in Figure 3.1a, with a width of B. Now, if load is gradually applied to the foundation, settlement will increase. The variation of the load per unit area on the foundation, q, with the foundation settlement is also shown in Figure 3.1a. At a certain point—when the load per unit area equals q_u—a sudden failure in the soil supporting the foundation will take place, and the failure surface in the soil will extend to the ground surface. This load per unit area, q_u, is usually referred to as the *ultimate bearing capacity of the foundation.* When this type of sudden failure in soil takes place, it is called the *general shear failure*.

If the foundation under consideration rests on sand or clayey soil of medium compaction (Figure 3.1b), an increase of load on the foundation will also be accompanied by an increase of settlement. However, in this case the failure surface in the soil will gradually extend outward from the foundation, as shown by the solid lines in

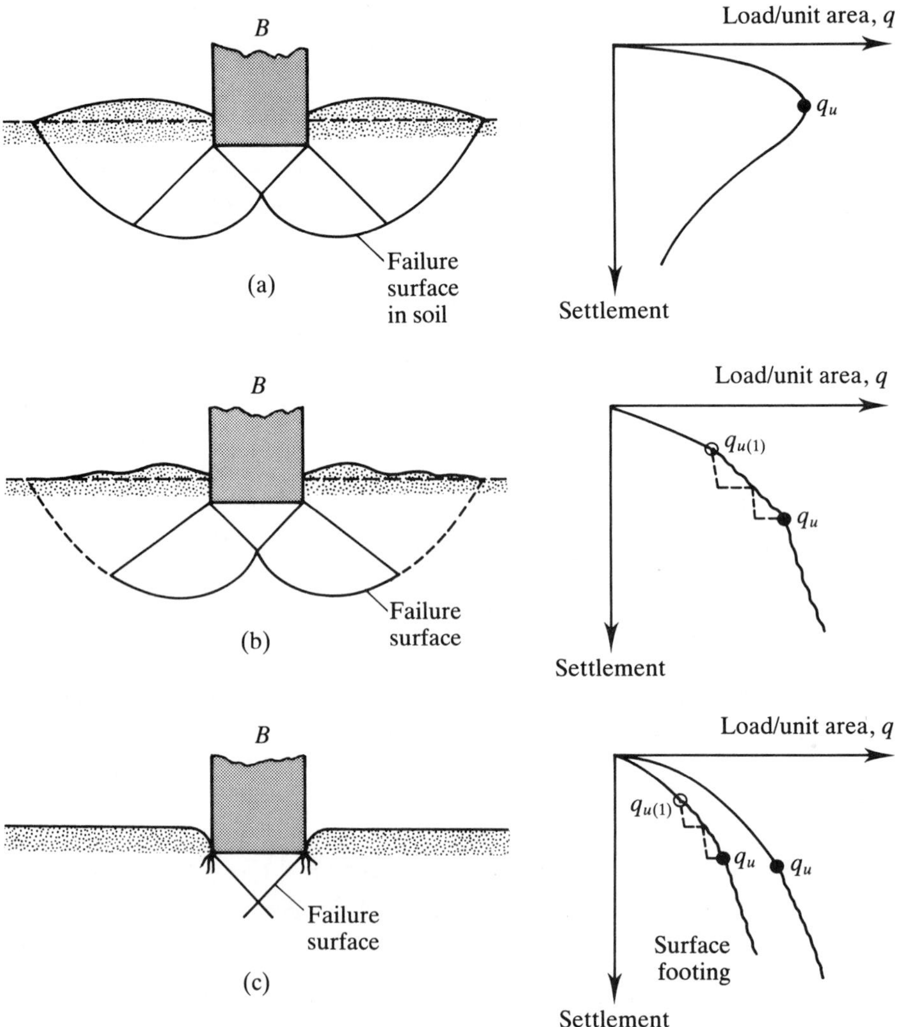

▼ **FIGURE 3.1** Nature of bearing capacity failure in soil: (a) general shear failure; (b) local shear failure; (c) punching shear failure (redrawn after Vesic, 1973)

Figure 3.1b. When the load per unit area on the foundation equals $q_{u(1)}$, the foundation movement will be accompanied by sudden jerks. A considerable movement of the foundation is then required for the failure surface in soil to extend to the ground surface (as shown by the broken lines in Figure 3.1b). The load per unit area at which this happens is the *ultimate bearing capacity*, q_u. Beyond this point, an increase of load will be accompanied by a large increase of foundation settlement. The load per unit area of the foundation, $q_{u(1)}$, is referred to as the *first failure load* (Vesic, 1963). Note that a peak value of q is not realized in this type of failure, which is called the *local shear failure* in soil.

If the foundation is supported by a fairly loose soil, the load–settlement plot will be like the one in Figure 3.1c. In this case, the failure surface in soil will not extend to the ground surface. Beyond the ultimate failure load, q_u, the load–settlement plot will be steep and practically linear. This type of failure in soil is called the ***punching shear failure***.

Based on experimental results, Vesic (1973) proposed a relationship for the mode of bearing capacity failure of foundations resting on sands. Figure 3.2 shows this relationship, which involves the notation

D_r = relative density of sand

D_f = depth of foundation measured from the ground surface

$$B^* = \frac{2BL}{B+L} \tag{3.1}$$

where B = width of foundation
L = length of foundation

(*Note:* L is always greater than B.)

For square foundations, $B = L$; for circular foundations, $B = L$ = diameter. So

$$B^* = B \tag{3.2}$$

For foundations at a shallow depth (that is, small D_f/B^*), the ultimate load may occur at a foundation settlement of 4–10% of B. This condition occurs when general

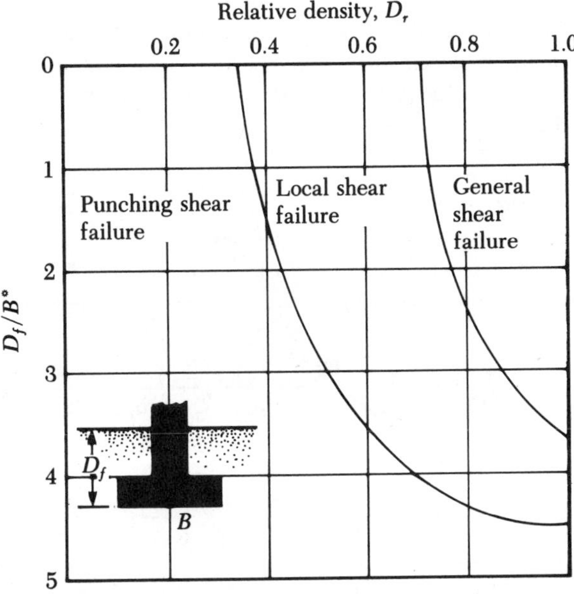

▼ **FIGURE 3.2** Modes of foundation failure in sand (after Vesic, 1973)

shear failure in soil occurs; however, in the case of local or punching shear failure, the ultimate load may occur at settlements of 15–25% of the width of foundation (B).

3.3 TERZAGHI'S BEARING CAPACITY THEORY

Terzaghi (1943) was the first to present a comprehensive theory for the evaluation of the ultimate bearing capacity of rough shallow foundations. According to this theory, a foundation is *shallow* if the depth, D_f (Figure 3.3), of the foundation is less than or equal to the width of the foundation. Later investigators, however, have suggested that foundations with D_f equal to 3–4 times the width of the foundation may be defined as *shallow foundations.*

Terzaghi suggested that for a *continuous,* or *strip, foundation* (that is, the width-to-length ratio of the foundation approaches zero), the failure suface in soil at ultimate load may be assumed to be similar to that shown in Figure 3.3. (Note that this is the case of general shear failure as defined in Figure 3.1a.) The effect of soil above the bottom of the foundation may also be assumed to be replaced by an equivalent surcharge, $q = \gamma D_f$ (where γ = unit weight of soil). The failure zone under the foundation can be separated into three parts (see Figure 3.3):

1. The *triangular zone ACD* immediately under the foundation
2. The *radial shear zones ADF* and *CDE,* with the curves DE and DF being arcs of a logarithmic spiral
3. Two triangular *Rankine passive zones AFH* and *CEG*

The angles CAD and ACD are assumed to be equal to the soil friction angle, ϕ. Note that, with the replacement of the soil above the bottom of the foundation by an equivalent surcharge q, the shear resistance of the soil along the failure surfaces GI and HJ was neglected.

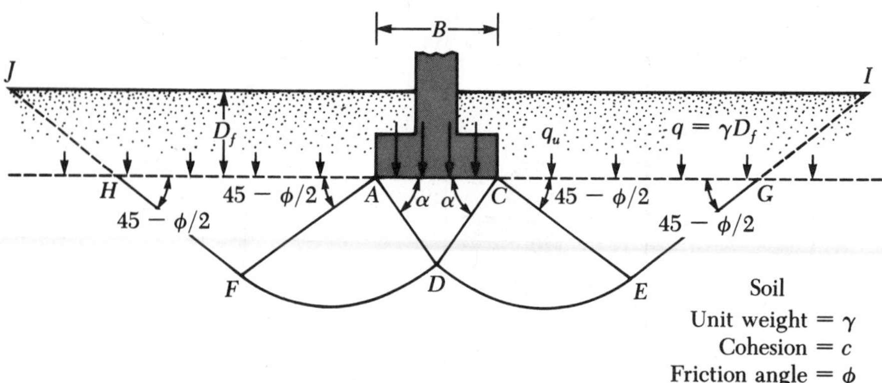

▼ **FIGURE 3.3** Bearing capacity failure in soil under a rough rigid continuous foundation

Using the equilibrium analysis, Terzaghi expressed the ultimate bearing capacity in the form

$$q_u = cN_c + qN_q + \frac{1}{2}\gamma BN_\gamma \qquad \text{(strip foundation)} \tag{3.3}$$

where
c = cohesion of soil
γ = unit weight of soil
$q = \gamma D_f$
N_c, N_q, N_γ = bearing capacity factors that are nondimensional and are only functions of the soil friction angle, ϕ

The bearing capacity factors, N_c, N_q, and N_γ are defined by

$$N_c = \cot\phi\left[\frac{e^{2(3\pi/4-\phi/2)\tan\phi}}{2\cos^2\left(\frac{\pi}{4}+\frac{\phi}{2}\right)}-1\right] \tag{3.4}$$

$$N_q = \frac{e^{2(3\pi/4-\phi/2)\tan\phi}}{2\cos^2\left(45+\frac{\phi}{2}\right)} \tag{3.5}$$

$$N_\gamma = \frac{1}{2}\left(\frac{K_{p\gamma}}{\cos^2\phi}-1\right)\tan\phi \tag{3.6}$$

where $K_{p\gamma}$ = passive pressure coefficient

The variations of the bearing capacity factors defined by Eqs. (3.4), (3.5), and (3.6) are given in Table 3.1.

For estimation of the ultimate bearing capacity of *square* or *circular foundations*, Eq. (3.1) may be modified to

$$q_u = 1.3cN_c + qN_q + 0.4\gamma BN_\gamma \qquad \text{(square foundation)} \tag{3.7}$$

and

$$q_u = 1.3cN_c + qN_q + 0.3\gamma BN_\gamma \qquad \text{(circular foundation)} \tag{3.8}$$

In Eq. (3.7), B equals the dimension of each side of the foundation; in Eq. (3.8), B equals the diameter of the foundation.

TABLE 3.1 Terzaghi's Bearing Capacity Factors—Eqs. (3.4), (3.5), and (3.6)

ϕ	N_c	N_q	N_γ [a]	ϕ	N_c	N_q	N_γ [a]
0	5.70	1.00	0.00	26	27.09	14.21	9.84
1	6.00	1.1	0.01	27	29.24	15.90	11.60
2	6.30	1.22	0.04	28	31.61	17.81	13.70
3	6.62	1.35	0.06	29	34.24	19.98	16.18
4	6.97	1.49	0.10	30	37.16	22.46	19.13
5	7.34	1.64	0.14	31	40.41	25.28	22.65
6	7.73	1.81	0.20	32	44.04	28.52	26.87
7	8.15	2.00	0.27	33	48.09	32.23	31.94
8	8.60	2.21	0.35	34	52.64	36.50	38.04
9	9.09	2.44	0.44	35	57.75	41.44	45.41
10	9.61	2.69	0.56	36	63.53	47.16	54.36
11	10.16	2.98	0.69	37	70.01	53.80	65.27
12	10.76	3.29	0.85	38	77.50	61.55	78.61
13	11.41	3.63	1.04	39	85.97	70.61	95.03
14	12.11	4.02	1.26	40	95.66	81.27	115.31
15	12.86	4.45	1.52	41	106.81	93.85	140.51
16	13.68	4.92	1.82	42	119.67	108.75	171.99
17	14.60	5.45	2.18	43	134.58	126.50	211.56
18	15.12	6.04	2.59	44	151.95	147.74	261.60
19	16.56	6.70	3.07	45	172.28	173.28	325.34
20	17.69	7.44	3.64	46	196.22	204.19	407.11
21	18.92	8.26	4.31	47	224.55	241.80	512.84
22	20.27	9.19	5.09	48	258.28	287.85	650.67
23	21.75	10.23	6.00	49	298.71	344.63	831.99
24	23.36	11.40	7.08	50	347.50	415.14	1072.80
25	25.13	12.72	8.34				

[a] From Kumbhojkar (1993)

For foundations that exhibit the local shear failure mode in soils, Terzaghi suggested modifications to Eqs. (3.3), (3.7), and (3.8) as follows:

$$q_u = \frac{2}{3}cN'_c + qN'_q + \frac{1}{2}\gamma BN'_\gamma \qquad \text{(strip foundation)} \tag{3.9}$$

$$q_u = 0.867cN'_c + qN'_q + 0.4\gamma BN'_\gamma \qquad \text{(square foundation)} \tag{3.10}$$

$$q_u = 0.867cN'_c + qN'_q + 0.3\gamma BN'_\gamma \qquad \text{(circular foundation)} \tag{3.11}$$

N'_c, N'_q, and N'_γ are the *modified bearing capacity factors*. They can be calculated by using the bearing capacity factor equations (for N_c, N_q, and N_γ) by replacing ϕ by $\phi' = \tan^{-1}(\frac{2}{3}\tan\phi)$. The variation of N'_c, N'_q, and N'_γ with the soil friction angle, ϕ, is given in Table 3.2.

TABLE 3.2 Terzaghi's Modified Bearing Capacity Factors, N'_c, N'_q, and N'_γ

ϕ	N'_c	N'_q	N'_γ	ϕ	N'_c	N'_q	N'_γ
0	5.70	1.00	0.00	26	15.53	6.05	2.59
1	5.90	1.07	0.005	27	16.30	6.54	2.88
2	6.10	1.14	0.02	28	17.13	7.07	3.29
3	6.30	1.22	0.04	29	18.03	7.66	3.76
4	6.51	1.30	0.055	30	18.99	8.31	4.39
5	6.74	1.39	0.074	31	20.03	9.03	4.83
6	6.97	1.49	0.10	32	21.16	9.82	5.51
7	7.22	1.59	0.128	33	22.39	10.69	6.32
8	7.47	1.70	0.16	34	23.72	11.67	7.22
9	7.74	1.82	0.20	35	25.18	12.75	8.35
10	8.02	1.94	0.24	36	26.77	13.97	9.41
11	8.32	2.08	0.30	37	28.51	15.32	10.90
12	8.63	2.22	0.35	38	30.43	16.85	12.75
13	8.96	2.38	0.42	39	32.53	18.56	14.71
14	9.31	2.55	0.48	40	34.87	20.50	17.22
15	9.67	2.73	0.57	41	37.45	22.70	19.75
16	10.06	2.92	0.67	42	40.33	25.21	22.50
17	10.47	3.13	0.76	43	43.54	28.06	26.25
18	10.90	3.36	0.88	44	47.13	31.34	30.40
19	11.36	3.61	1.03	45	51.17	35.11	36.00
20	11.85	3.88	1.12	46	55.73	39.48	41.70
21	12.37	4.17	1.35	47	60.91	44.54	49.30
22	12.92	4.48	1.55	48	66.80	50.46	59.25
23	13.51	4.82	1.74	49	73.55	57.41	71.45
24	14.14	5.20	1.97	50	81.31	65.60	85.75
25	14.80	5.60	2.25				

3.4 MODIFICATION OF BEARING CAPACITY EQUATIONS FOR WATER TABLE

Equations (3.3) and (3.7) to (3.11) have been developed for determining the ultimate bearing capacity based on the assumption that the water table is located well below the foundation. However, if the water table is close to the foundation, some modifications of the bearing capacity equations will be necessary, depending on the location of the water table (see Figure 3.4).

Case I: If the water table is located so that $0 \leq D_1 \leq D_f$, the factor q in the bearing capacity equations takes the form

$$q = \text{effective surcharge} = D_1\gamma + D_2(\gamma_{sat} - \gamma_w) \tag{3.12}$$

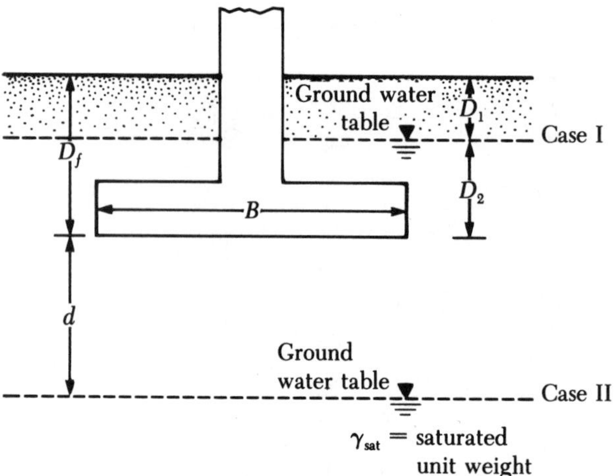

▼ **FIGURE 3.4** Modification of bearing capacity equations for water table

where γ_{sat} = saturated unit weight of soil
γ_w = unit weight of water

Also, the value of γ in the last term of the equations has to be replaced by $\gamma' = \gamma_{sat} - \gamma_w$.

Case II: For a water table located so that $0 \leq d \leq B$,

$$q = \gamma D_f \tag{3.13}$$

The factor γ in the last term of the bearing capacity equations must be replaced by the factor

$$\bar{\gamma} = \gamma' + \frac{d}{B}(\gamma - \gamma') \tag{3.14}$$

The preceding modifications are based on the assumption that there is no seepage force in the soil.

Case III: When the water table is located so that $d \geq B$, the water will have no effect on the ultimate bearing capacity.

3.5 CASE HISTORY: ULTIMATE BEARING CAPACITY IN SATURATED CLAY

Brand, et al. (1972) reported field test results for small foundations on soft Bangkok clay (a deposit of marine clay) in Rangsit, Thailand. The results of the soil exploration are shown in Figure 3.5. Because of the sensitivity of the clay, the laboratory test results for

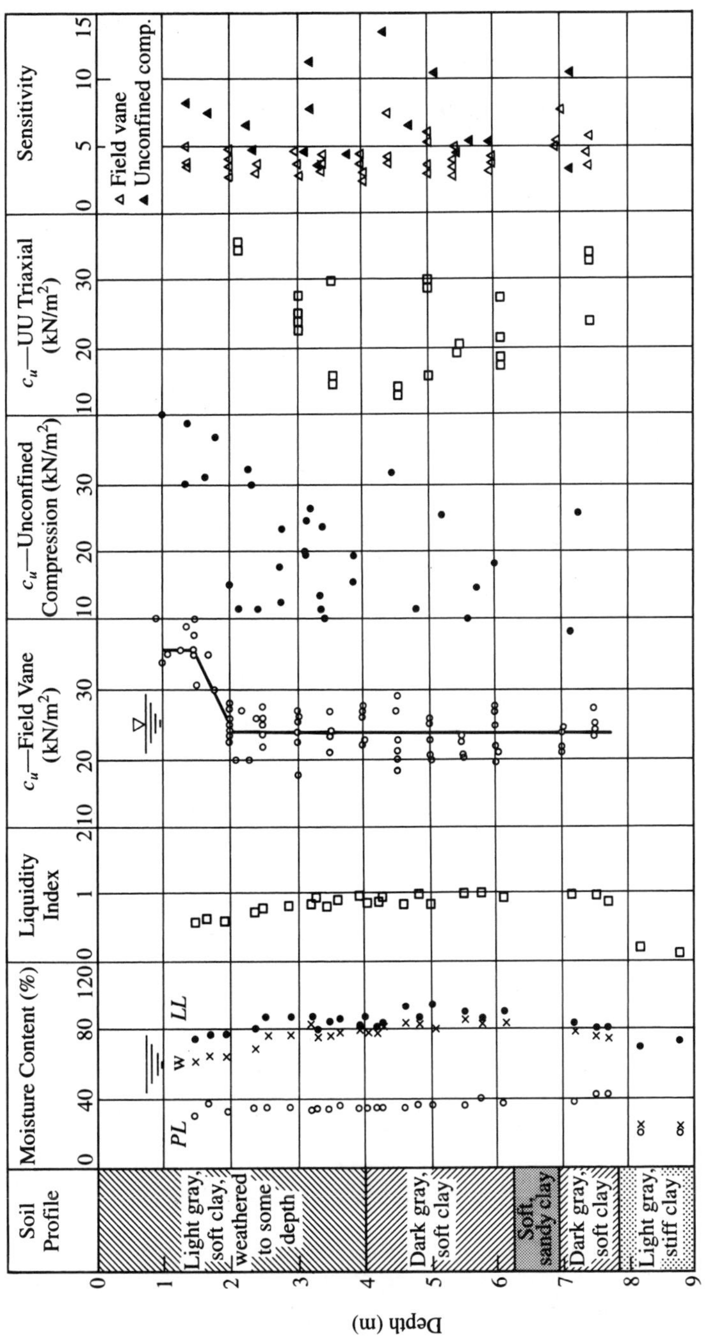

▶ **FIGURE 3.5** Results of soil exploration in soft Bangkok clay at Rangsit, Thailand (redrawn after Brand et al., 1972)

c_u (unconfined compression and unconsolidated undrained triaxial) were rather scattered; however, they obtained better results for the variation of c_u with depth from field vane shear tests. The vane shear test results showed that the average variations of the undrained cohesion were

Depth (m)	c_u (kN/m²)
0–1.5	≈35
1.5–2	Decreasing linearly from 35 to 24
2–8	≈24

Five small square foundations were tested for ultimate bearing capacity. The sizes of the foundations were 0.6 m × 0.6 m, 0.675 m × 0.675 m, 0.75 m × 0.75 m, 0.9 m × 0.9 m, and 1.05 m × 1.05 m. The depth of the bottom of the foundations was 1.5 m measured from the ground surface. The load–settlement plots obtained from the bearing capacity tests are shown in Figure 3.6.

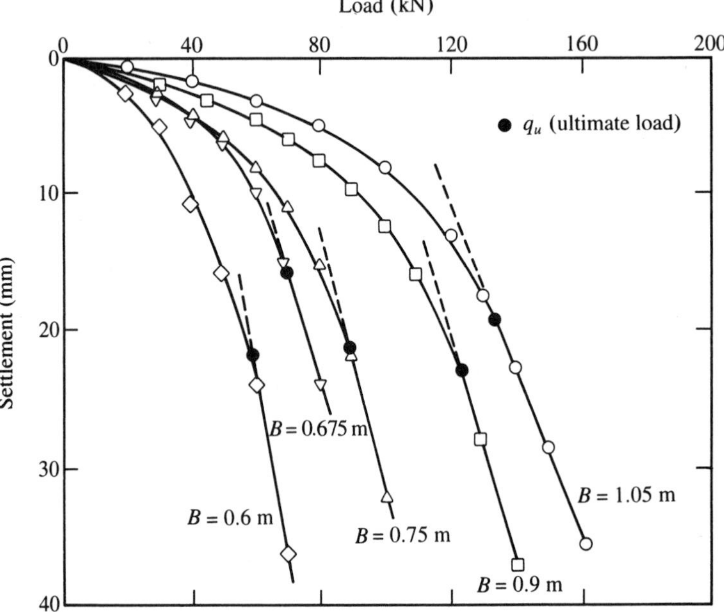

▼ **FIGURE 3.6** Load–settlement plots obtained from bearing capacity tests

Analysis of the Field Test Results

The ultimate loads Q_u, obtained from each test are also shown in Figure 3.6. The ultimate load is defined as the point where the load displacement becomes practically linear. The failure in soil below the foundation is of local shear type. Hence, from Eq. (3.10)

$$q_u = 0.867 c_u N_c' + q N_q' + 0.4 \gamma B N_\gamma'$$

For $\phi = 0$, $c = c_u$ and, from Table 3.2, $N'_c = 5.7$, $N'_q = 1$, and $N'_\gamma = 0$. Thus for $\phi = 0$

$$q_u = 4.49c_u + q \tag{3.15}$$

If we assume that the unit weight of soil is about 18.5 kN/m³, $q \approx D_f\gamma = (1.5)(18.5) = 27.75$ kN/m². We can then assume average values of c_u: for depths of 1.5 m to 2.0 m, $c_u \approx (35 + 24)/2 = 29.5$ kN/m²; for depths greater than 2.0 m, $c_u \approx 24$ kN/m². If we assume that the undrained cohesion of clay at a depth $\leq B$ below the foundation controls the ultimate bearing capacity,

$$c_{u(\text{average})} \approx \frac{(29.5)(2.0 - 1.5) + (24)[B - (2.0 - 1.5)]}{B} \tag{3.16}$$

The $c_{u(\text{average})}$ value obtained for each foundation needs to be corrected in view of Eq. (2.19). Table 3.3 presents the details of other calculations and a comparison of the theoretical and field ultimate bearing capacities.

Note that the ultimate bearing capacities obtained from the field are about 10% higher than those obtained from theory. On reason for such a difference is that the ratio D_f/B for the field tests varies from 1.5 to 2.5. The increase of the bearing capacity due to the depth of embedment has not been accounted for in Eq. (3.16).

TABLE 3.3 Comparison of Theoretical and Field Ultimate Bearing Capacities

B (m)	$c_{u(\text{average})}$[a] (kN/m²)	Plasticity index[b]	Correction factor, λ[c]	$c_{u(\text{corrected})}$[d] (kN/m²)	$q_{u(\text{theory})}$[e] (kN/m²)	$Q_{u(\text{field})}$[f] (kN)	$q_{u(\text{field})}$[g] (kN/m²)
0.6	28.58	40	0.84	24.01	146.4	60	166.6
0.675	28.07	40	0.84	23.58	144.2	71	155.8
0.75	27.67	40	0.84	23.24	142.6	90	160
0.9	27.06	40	0.84	22.73	140.0	124	153
1.05	26.62	40	0.84	22.36	138.2	140	127

[a] Eq. (3.16)
[b] From Figure 3.5
[c] From Figure 2.22
[d] Eq. (2.19)
[e] Eq. (3.15)
[f] Figure 3.6
[g] $Q_{u(\text{field})}/B^2$

EXAMPLE 3.1

A square foundation is 5 ft × 5 ft in plan. The soil supporting the foundation has a friction angle of $\phi = 20°$ and $c = 320$ lb/ft². The unit weight of soil, γ, is 115 lb/ft³. Determine the allowable gross load on the foundation with a factor of safety (FS) of 4. Assume that the depth of the foundation (D_f) is 3 ft and that general shear failure occurs in the soil.

Solution From Eq. (3.7)

$$q_u = 1.3cN_c + qN_q + 0.4\gamma BN_\gamma$$

From Table 3.1, for $\phi = 20°$,

$$N_c = 17.69$$
$$N_q = 7.44$$
$$N_\gamma = 3.64$$

Thus

$$q_u = (1.3)(320)(17.69) + (3 \times 115)(7.44) + (0.4)(115)(5)(3.64)$$
$$= 7359 + 2567 + 2093 = 12{,}019 \text{ lb/ft}^2$$

So, the allowable load per unit area of the foundation is

$$q_{\text{all}} = \frac{q_u}{FS} = \frac{12{,}019}{4} \approx 3005 \text{ lb/ft}^2$$

Thus the total allowable gross load is

$$Q = (3005)B^2 = (3005)(5 \times 5) = 75{,}125 \text{ lb}$$ ▼

3.6 GENERAL BEARING CAPACITY EQUATION

The ultimate bearing capacity equations presented in Eqs. (3.3), (3.7), and (3.8) are for continuous, square, and circular foundations only. They do not address the case of rectangular foundations ($0 < B/L < 1$). Also, the equations do not take into account the shearing resistance along the failure surface in soil above the bottom of the foundation (portion of the failure surface marked as *GI* and *HJ* in Figure 3.3). In addition, the load on the foundation may be inclined. To account for all these shortcomings, Meyerhof (1963) suggested the following form of general bearing capacity equation.

$$q_u = cN_c F_{cs} F_{cd} F_{ci} + qN_q F_{qs} F_{qd} F_{qi} + \frac{1}{2}\gamma B N_\gamma F_{\gamma s} F_{\gamma d} F_{\gamma i} \qquad (3.17)$$

where
c = cohesion
q = effective stress at the level of the bottom of foundation
γ = unit weight of soil
B = width of foundation (= diameter for a circular foundation)
$F_{cs}, F_{qs}, F_{\gamma s}$ = shape factors
$F_{cd}, F_{qd}, F_{\gamma d}$ = depth factors
$F_{ci}, F_{qi}, F_{\gamma i}$ = load inclination factors
N_c, N_q, N_γ = bearing capacity factors

The equations for determining the various factors given in Eq. (3.17) are described briefly in the following sections. Nore that the original equation for ultimate bearing capacity is derived only for the plane-strain case (that is, for continuous foundations). The shape, depth, and load inclination factors are empirical factors based on experimental data.

Bearing Capacity Factors

Based on laboratory and field studies of bearing capacity, the basic nature of the failure surface in soil suggested by Terzaghi now appears to be correct (Vesic, 1973). However, the angle α as shown in Figure 3.3 is closer to $45 + \phi/2$ than to ϕ. If this change is accepted, the values of N_c, N_q, and N_γ for a given soil friction angle will also change from those given in Table 3.1. With $\alpha = 45 + \phi/2$, the relations for N_c and N_q can be derived as

$$N_q = \tan^2\left(45 + \frac{\phi}{2}\right)e^{\pi \tan \phi} \tag{3.18}$$

$$N_c = (N_q - 1)\cot \phi \tag{3.19}$$

The equation for N_c given by Eq. (3.19) was originally derived by Prandtl (1921), and the relation for N_q [Eq. (3.18)] was presented by Reissner (1924). Caquot and Kerisel (1953) and Vesic (1973) gave the relation for N_γ as

$$N_\gamma = 2(N_q + 1)\tan \phi \tag{3.20}$$

Table 3.4 shows the variation of the preceding bearing capacity factors with soil friction angles.

In many texts and reference books, the relationship for N_γ may be different from that in Eq. (3.20). The reason is that there is still some controversy about the variation of N_γ with the soil friction angle, ϕ. *In this text, Eq. (3.20) is used.* Table 3.5 shows other relationships frequently presented in various texts and references. Meyerhof's (1963) bearing capacity factor N_γ is also frequently used in practice. Table 3.6 gives the variation of this N_γ with the soil friction angle ϕ.

Shape, Depth, and Inclination Factors

The relationships for the shape factors, depth factors, and inclination factors *recommended for use* are shown in Table 3.7. Other relationships generally found in many texts and references are shown in Table 3.8.

▼ **TABLE 3.4 Bearing Capacity Factors**[a]

ϕ	N_c	N_q	N_γ	N_q/N_c	$\tan\phi$	ϕ	N_c	N_q	N_γ	N_q/N_c	$\tan\phi$
0	5.14	1.00	0.00	0.20	0.00	26	22.25	11.85	12.54	0.53	0.49
1	5.38	1.09	0.07	0.20	0.02	27	23.94	13.20	14.47	0.55	0.51
2	5.63	1.20	0.15	0.21	0.03	28	25.80	14.72	16.72	0.57	0.53
3	5.90	1.31	0.24	0.22	0.05	29	27.86	16.44	19.34	0.59	0.55
4	6.19	1.43	0.34	0.23	0.07	30	30.14	18.40	22.40	0.61	0.58
5	6.49	1.57	0.45	0.24	0.09	31	32.67	20.63	25.99	0.63	0.60
6	6.81	1.72	0.57	0.25	0.11	32	35.49	23.18	30.22	0.65	0.62
7	7.16	1.88	0.71	0.26	0.12	33	38.64	26.09	35.19	0.68	0.65
8	7.53	2.06	0.86	0.27	0.14	34	42.16	29.44	41.06	0.70	0.67
9	7.92	2.25	1.03	0.28	0.16	35	46.12	33.30	48.03	0.72	0.70
10	8.35	2.47	1.22	0.30	0.18	36	50.59	37.75	56.31	0.75	0.73
11	8.80	2.71	1.44	0.31	0.19	37	55.63	42.92	66.19	0.77	0.75
12	9.28	2.97	1.69	0.32	0.21	38	61.35	48.93	78.03	0.80	0.78
13	9.81	3.26	1.97	0.33	0.23	39	67.87	55.96	92.25	0.82	0.81
14	10.37	3.59	2.29	0.35	0.25	40	75.31	64.20	109.41	0.85	0.84
15	10.98	3.94	2.65	0.36	0.27	41	83.86	73.90	130.22	0.88	0.87
16	11.63	4.34	3.06	0.37	0.29	42	93.71	85.38	155.55	0.91	0.90
17	12.34	4.77	3.53	0.39	0.31	43	105.11	99.02	186.54	0.94	0.93
18	13.10	5.26	4.07	0.40	0.32	44	118.37	115.31	224.64	0.97	0.97
19	13.93	5.80	4.68	0.42	0.34	45	133.88	134.88	271.76	1.01	1.00
20	14.83	6.40	5.39	0.43	0.36	46	152.10	158.51	330.35	1.04	1.04
21	15.82	7.07	6.20	0.45	0.38	47	173.64	187.21	403.67	1.08	1.07
22	16.88	7.82	7.13	0.46	0.40	48	199.26	222.31	496.01	1.12	1.11
23	18.05	8.66	8.20	0.48	0.42	49	229.93	265.51	613.16	1.15	1.15
24	19.32	9.60	9.44	0.50	0.45	50	266.89	319.07	762.89	1.20	1.19
25	20.72	10.66	10.88	0.51	0.47						

[a] After Vesic (1973)

Net Ultimate Bearing Capacity

The net ultimate bearing capacity is defined as the ultimate pressure per unit area of the foundation that can be supported by the soil in excess of the pressure caused by the surrounding soil at the foundation level. If the difference between the unit weight of concrete used in the foundation and the unit weight of soil surrounding is assumed to be negligible,

$$q_{\text{net}(u)} = q_u - q \tag{3.21}$$

where $q_{\text{net}(u)}$ = net ultimate bearing capacity

▼ **TABLE 3.5 Relationships for N_γ Frequently Referred to in Other Texts and References**

Relationship	Source
$N_\gamma = (N_q - 1)\tan(1.4\phi)$ ↑ Eq. (3.18)	Meyerhof (1963)
$N_\gamma = 1.5(N_q - 1)\tan\phi$ ↑ Eq. (3.18)	Hansen (1970)
By numerical methods from theory of plasticity	Lundgren and Mortensen (1953)

ϕ (deg)	N_γ
0	0
5	0.17
10	0.46
15	1.4
25	6.92
30	15.32
35	35.19
40	86.46
45	215.0

▼ **TABLE 3.6 Meyerhof's Bearing Capacity Factor, N_γ**

ϕ	N_γ	ϕ	N_γ	ϕ	N_γ	ϕ	N_γ
0	0.00	27	9.46	14	0.92	41	113.99
1	0.002	28	11.19	15	1.13	43	139.32
2	0.01	29	13.24	16	1.38	44	171.14
3	0.02	30	15.67	17	1.66	44	211.41
4	0.04	31	18.56	18	2.00	45	262.74
5	0.07	32	22.02	19	2.40	46	328.73
6	0.11	33	26.17	20	2.87	47	414.32
7	0.15	34	31.15	21	3.42	48	526.44
8	0.21	35	37.15	22	4.07	49	674.91
9	0.28	36	44.43	23	4.82	50	873.84
10	0.37	37	53.27	24	5.72	51	1143.93
11	0.47	38	64.07	25	6.77	52	1516.05
12	0.60	39	77.33	26	8.00	53	2037.26
13	0.74	40	93.69				

▼ TABLE 3.7 Shape, Depth, and Inclination Factors Recommended for Use

Factor	Relationship	Source
Shape[a]	$F_{cs} = 1 + \frac{B}{L}\frac{N_q}{N_c}$ $F_{qs} = 1 + \frac{B}{L}\tan\phi$ $F_{\gamma s} = 1 - 0.4\frac{B}{L}$ where L = length of the foundation ($L > B$)	De Beer (1970)
Depth[b]	*Condition (a)*: $D_f/B \leq 1$ $F_{cd} = 1 + 0.4\frac{D_f}{B}$ $F_{qd} = 1 + 2\tan\phi(1 - \sin\phi)^2\frac{D_f}{B}$ $F_{\gamma d} = 1$ *Condition (b)*: $D_f/B > 1$ $F_{cd} = 1 + (0.4)\tan^{-1}\left(\frac{D_f}{B}\right)$ $F_{qd} = 1 + 2\tan\phi(1 - \sin\phi)^2\tan^{-1}\left(\frac{D_f}{B}\right)$ $F_{\gamma d} = 1$	Hansen (1970)
Inclination	$F_{ci} = F_{qi} = \left(1 - \frac{\beta^\circ}{90^\circ}\right)^2$ $F_{\gamma i} = \left(1 - \frac{\beta}{\phi}\right)^2$ where β = inclination of the load on the foundation with respect to the vertical	Meyerhof (1963); Hanna and Meyerhof (1981)

[a] These shape factors are empirical relations based on extensive laboratory tests.
[b] The factor $\tan^{-1}(D_f/B)$ is in radians.

General Comments

When the water table is present at or near the foundation, the factors q and γ given in the general bearing capacity equation, Eq. (3.17), will need modifications. The procedure for modifying them is the same as that described in Section 3.4.

For undrained loading conditions ($\phi = 0$ concept) in clayey soils, the general load-bearing capacity equation [Eq. (3.17)] takes the form (vertical load)

$$q_u = cN_c F_{cs} F_{cd} + q \tag{3.22}$$

TABLE 3.8 Shape, Depth, and Inclination Factors Recommended in Other Texts and References

Factor	Relationship	Source
Shape[a]	*For* $\phi = 0$: $F_{cs} = 1 + 0.2\left(\frac{B}{L}\right)$; $F_{qs} = 1$; $F_{\gamma s} = 1$. *For* $\phi \geq 10°$: $F_{cs} = 1 + 0.2\left(\frac{B}{L}\right)\tan^2\left(45 + \frac{\phi}{2}\right)$; $F_{qs} = F_{\gamma s} = 1 + 0.1\left(\frac{B}{L}\right)\tan^2\left(45 + \frac{\phi}{2}\right)$	Meyerhof (1953)
Depth	*For* $\phi = 0$: $F_{cd} = 1 + 0.2\left(\frac{D_f}{B}\right)$; $F_{qd} = F_{\gamma d} = 1$. *For* $\phi \geq 10°$: $F_{cd} = 1 + 0.2\left(\frac{D_f}{B}\right)\tan\left(45 + \frac{\phi}{2}\right)$; $F_{qd} = F_{\gamma d} = 1 + 0.1\left(\frac{D_f}{B}\right)\tan\left(45 + \frac{\phi}{2}\right)$	Meyerhof (1963)
Inclination	$F_{ci} = F_{qi} - \frac{(1 - F_{qi})}{(N_q - 1)}$; $F_{qi} = \left[1 - \frac{(0.5)(Q_u)\sin\beta}{Q_u\cos\beta + BLc\cot\phi}\right]^5$; $F_{\gamma i} = \left[1 - \frac{(0.7)(Q_u)\sin\beta}{Q_u\cos\beta + BLc\cot\phi}\right]^5$	Hansen (1970)

[a] L = length ($\geq B$)

Hence the net ultimate bearing capacity (vertical load) is

$$q_{\text{net}(u)} = q_u - q = cN_c F_{cs} F_{cd} \tag{3.23}$$

Skempton (1951) proposed an equation for the net ultimate bearing capacity for clayey soils ($\phi = 0$ condition), which is similar to Eq. (3.23):

$$q_{\text{net}(u)} = 5c\left(1 + 0.2\frac{D_f}{B}\right)\left(1 + 0.2\frac{B}{L}\right) \tag{3.24}$$

3.7 THE FACTOR OF SAFETY

Calculating the gross allowable load-bearing capacity of shallow foundations requires application of a factor of safety (*FS*) to the gross ultimate bearing capacity, or

$$q_{\text{all}} = \frac{q_u}{FS} \tag{3.25}$$

However, some practicing engineers prefer to use a factor of safety of

$$\text{Net stress increase on soil} = \frac{\text{net ultimate bearing capacity}}{FS} \tag{3.26}$$

Net ultimate bearing capacity has been defined in Eq. (3.21) as

$$q_{\text{net}(u)} = q_u - q$$

Substituting this equation in Eq. (3.26) yields

Net stress increase on soil

= load from the superstructure per unit area of the foundation

$$= q_{\text{all(net)}} = \frac{q_u - q}{FS} \tag{3.27}$$

The factor of safety as defined by Eq. (3.27) may be at least 3 in all cases.

Another type of factor of safety for the bearing capacity of shallow foundations is often used. It is the factor of safety with respect to shear failure (FS_{shear}). In most cases, a value of $FS_{\text{shear}} = 1.4$–1.6 is desirable along with a ***minimum*** factor of safety of 3–4 against gross or net ultimate bearing capacity. The following procedure should be used to calculate the net allowable load for a given FS_{shear}.

1. Let c and ϕ be the cohesion and the angle of friction of soil and let FS_{shear} be the required factor of safety with respect to shear failure. So the developed cohesion and the angle of friction are

$$c_d = \frac{c}{FS_{\text{shear}}} \tag{3.28}$$

$$\phi_d = \tan^{-1}\left(\frac{\tan\phi}{FS_{\text{shear}}}\right) \tag{3.29}$$

2. The gross allowable bearing capacity can now be calculated according to Eqs. (3.3), (3.7), (3.8), or the general bearing capacity equation [Eq. (3.17)], with c_d and ϕ_d as the shear strength parameters of the soil. For example, the gross allowable bearing capacity of a continuous foundation according to Terzaghi's equation is

$$q_{\text{all}} = c_d N_c + qN_q + \frac{1}{2}\gamma B N_\gamma \tag{3.30}$$

where N_c, N_q, and N_γ = bearing capacity factors for friction angle, ϕ_d

3. The net allowable bearing capacity is thus

$$q_{\text{net(all)}} = q_{\text{all}} - q = c_d N_c + q(N_q - 1) + \frac{1}{2}\gamma B N_\gamma \tag{3.31}$$

Irrespective of the procedure by which the factor of safety is applied, the magnitude of FS should depend on the uncertainties and risks involved for the conditions encountered.

▼ EXAMPLE 3.2

A square column foundation to be constructed on a sandy soil has to carry a gross allowable total load of 150 kN. The depth of the foundation will be 0.7 m. The load will be inclined at an angle of 20° to the vertical (Figure 3.7). The standard penetration resistances, N_F, obtained from field exploration are

Depth (m)	N_F
1.5	3
3.0	6
4.5	9
6	10
7.5	10
9	8

Assume that the unit weight of the soil is 18 kN/m³. Determine the width of the foundation, B. Use Eq. (3.17) and a factor of safety of 3.

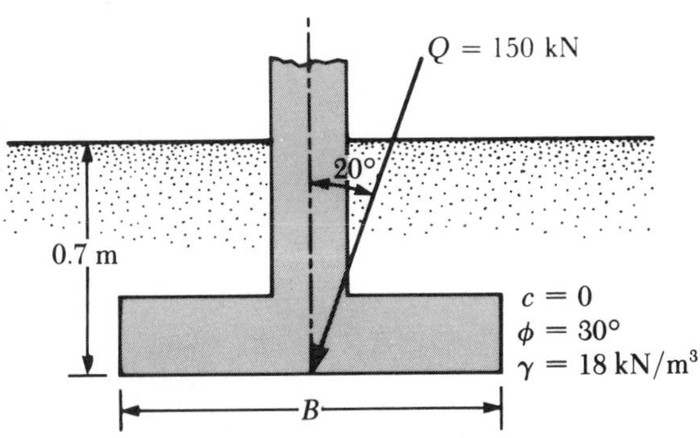

▼ **FIGURE 3.7**

Solution The standard penetration resistances can be corrected by using Eq. (2.9).

Depth (*m*)	*Effective overburden pressure*, σ'_v (kN/m^2)	C_N	N_F	$N = N_F C_N$
1.5	27	1.88	3	≈6
3.0	54	1.33	6	≈8
4.5	81	1.09	9	≈10
6	108	0.94	10	≈9
7.5	135	0.84	10	≈8
9	162	0.77	8	≈6

Note: $\sigma'_v = (\gamma)(\text{depth}) = (18\ \text{kN/m}^3)(\text{depth})$; $C_N = 9.78(1/\sigma'_v)^{0.5}$

The average corrected N value obtained is about 8. Now, referring to Table 2.4, we can conservatively assume the soil friction angle ϕ to be about 30°. With $c = 0$, the ultimate bearing capacity [Eq. (3.17)] becomes

$$q_u = qN_q F_{qs} F_{qd} F_{qi} + \frac{1}{2}\gamma B N_\gamma F_{\gamma s} F_{\gamma d} F_{\gamma i}$$

$$q = (0.7)(18) = 12.6\ \text{kN/m}^2$$

$$\gamma = 18\ \text{kN/m}^3$$

From Table 3.4, for $\phi = 30°$

$$N_q = 18.4$$

$$N_\gamma = 22.4$$

From Table 3.7

$$F_{qs} = 1 + \left(\frac{B}{L}\right)\tan\phi = 1 + 0.577 = 1.577$$

$$F_{\gamma s} = 1 - 0.4\left(\frac{B}{L}\right) = 0.6$$

$$F_{qd} = 1 + 2\tan\phi(1-\sin\phi)^2\frac{D_f}{B} = 1 + \frac{(0.289)(0.7)}{B} = 1 + \frac{0.202}{B}$$

$$F_{\gamma d} = 1$$

$$F_{qi} = \left(1 - \frac{\beta°}{90°}\right)^2 = \left(1 - \frac{20}{90}\right)^2 = 0.605$$

$$F_{\gamma i} = \left(1 - \frac{\beta°}{\phi}\right)^2 = \left(1 - \frac{20}{30}\right)^2 = 0.11$$

Hence

$$q_u = (12.6)(18.4)(1.577)\left(1 + \frac{0.202}{B}\right)(0.605) + (0.5)(18)(B)(22.4)(0.6)(1)(0.11)$$

$$= 212.2 + \frac{44.68}{B} + 13.3B \qquad \text{(a)}$$

Thus

$$q_{\text{all}} = \frac{q_u}{3} = 73.73 + \frac{14.89}{B} + 4.43B \qquad \text{(b)}$$

For Q = total allowable load = $q_{\text{all}} \times B^2$ or

$$q_{\text{all}} = \frac{150}{B^2} \qquad \text{(c)}$$

Equating the right-hand sides of Eqs. (b) and (c) gives

$$\frac{150}{B^2} = 73.73 + \frac{14.89}{B} + 4.43B$$

By trial and error, $B \approx$ **1.3 m** ▼

▼ EXAMPLE 3.3

Refer to Example 3.1. Use the definition of factor of safety given by Eq. (3.27) and $FS = 5$ to determine the net allowable load for the foundation.

Solution From Example 3.1

$$q_u = 12{,}019 \text{ lb/ft}^2$$

$$q = (3)(115) = 345 \text{ lb/ft}^2$$

$$q_{\text{net(all)}} = \frac{12{,}019 - 345}{5} \approx 2335 \text{ lb/ft}^2$$

Hence

$$Q_{\text{net(all)}} = (2335)(5)(5) = \mathbf{58{,}375\ lb}$$ ▼

▼ EXAMPLE 3.4

Refer to Example 3.1. Use Eq. (3.7) and $FS_{\text{shear}} = 1.5$ to determine the net allowable load for the foundation.

Solution For $c = 320$ lb/ft^2 and $\phi = 20°$,

$$c_d = \frac{c}{FS_{\text{shear}}} = \frac{320}{1.5} \approx 213 \text{ lb/ft}^2$$

$$\phi_d = \tan^{-1}\left[\frac{\tan\phi}{FS_{\text{shear}}}\right] = \tan^{-1}\left[\frac{\tan 20}{1.5}\right] = 13.64°$$

From Eq. (3.7),

$$q_{\text{all(net)}} = 1.3c_d N_c + q(N_q - 1) + 0.4\gamma B N_\gamma$$

For $\phi = 13.64°$, the values of the bearing capacity factors from Table 3.1 are

$$N_\gamma \approx 1.2, \qquad N_q \approx 3.8, \qquad \text{and} \qquad N_c \approx 12$$

Hence

$$q_{\text{all(net)}} = 1.3(213)(12) + (345)(3.8 - 1) + (0.4)(115)(5)(1.2) = 4565 \text{ lb/ft}^2$$

and

$$Q_{\text{all(net)}} = (4565)(5)(5) = 114{,}125 \text{ lb} \approx \mathbf{57\ ton}$$

Note: There appears to be a large discrepancy between the results of Examples 3.3 (or 3.1) and 3.4. The use of trial and error shows that, when FS_{shear} is about 1.2, the results are approximately equal. ▼

3.8 ECCENTRICALLY LOADED FOUNDATIONS

In several instances, as with the base of a retaining wall, foundations are subjected to moments in addition to the vertical load, as shown in Figure 3.8a. In such cases, the distribution of pressure by the foundation on the soil is not uniform. The distribution of nominal pressure is

$$q_{\max} = \frac{Q}{BL} + \frac{6M}{B^2 L} \tag{3.32}$$

and

$$q_{\min} = \frac{Q}{BL} - \frac{6M}{B^2 L} \tag{3.33}$$

where Q = total vertical load
M = moment on the foundation

The exact distribution of pressure is difficult to estimate.

The factor of safety for such types of loading against bearing capacity failure can be evaluated by using the procedure suggested by Meyerhof (1953), which is generally referred to as the *effective area* method. The following is Meyerhof's step-by-step procedure for determination of the ultimate load that the soil can support and the factor of safety against bearing capacity failure.

1. Figure 3.8b shows a force system equivalent to that shown in Figure 3.8a. The distance e is the eccentricity, or

$$e = \frac{M}{Q} \tag{3.34}$$

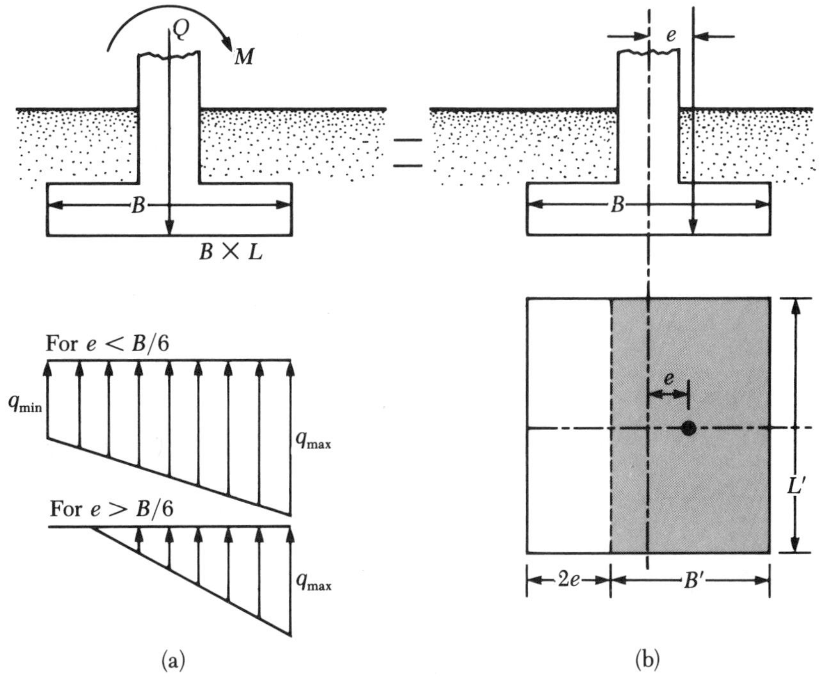

▼ **FIGURE 3.8** Eccentrically loaded foundations

Substituting Eq. (3.34) in Eqs. (3.32) and (3.33) gives

$$q_{max} = \frac{Q}{BL}\left(1 + \frac{6e}{B}\right) \tag{3.35a}$$

and

$$q_{min} = \frac{Q}{BL}\left(1 - \frac{6e}{B}\right) \tag{3.35b}$$

Note that, in these equations, when the eccentricity, e, becomes $B/6$, q_{min} is zero. For $e > B/6$, q_{min} will be negative, which means that tension will develop. Because soil cannot take any tension, there will be a separation between the foundation and the soil underlying it. The nature of the pressure distribution on the soil will be as shown in Figure 3.8a. The value of q_{max} then is

$$q_{max} = \frac{4Q}{3L(B - 2e)} \tag{3.36}$$

2. Determine the effective dimensions of the foundation as

$B' = \text{effective width} = B - 2e$

$L' = \text{effective length} = L$

Note that, if the eccentricity were in the direction of the length of the foundation, the value of L' would be equal to $L - 2e$. The value of B' would equal B. The smaller of the two dimensions (that is, L' and B') is the effective width of the foundation.

3. Use Eq. (3.17) for the ultimate bearing capacity as

$$q'_u = cN_c F_{cs} F_{cd} F_{ci} + qN_q F_{qs} F_{qd} F_{qi} + \frac{1}{2}\gamma B' N_\gamma F_{\gamma s} F_{\gamma d} F_{\gamma i} \tag{3.37}$$

To evaluate F_{cs}, F_{qs}, and $F_{\gamma s}$, use Table 3.7 with *effective length* and *effective width* dimensions instead of L and B, respectively. To determine F_{cd}, F_{qd}, and $F_{\gamma d}$, use Table 3.7 (*do not* replace B with B').

4. The total ultimate load that the foundation can sustain is

$$Q_{\text{ult}} = \overbrace{q'_u(B')(L')}^{A'} \tag{3.38}$$

where A' = effective area

5. The factor of safety against bearing capacity failure is

$$FS = \frac{Q_{\text{ult}}}{Q} \tag{3.39}$$

Note that eccentricity tends to decrease the load-bearing capacity of a foundation. In such cases, placing foundation columns off center, as shown in Figure 3.9, probably is advantageous. Doing so, in effect, produces a centrally loaded foundation with uniformly distributed pressure.

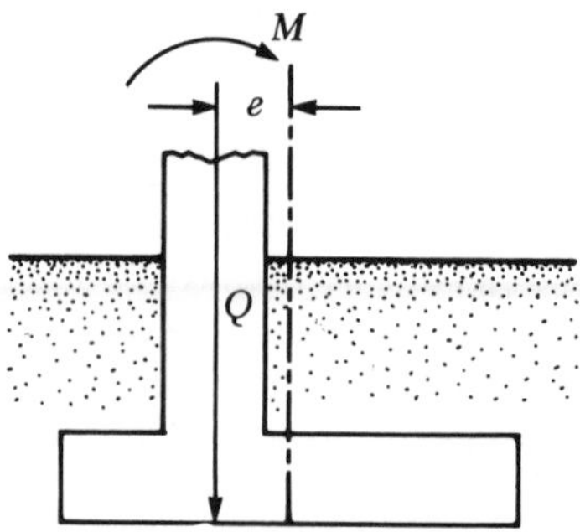

▼ **FIGURE 3.9** Foundation of columns with off-center loading

Foundations with Two-Way Eccentricity

Consider a situation in which a foundation is subjected to a vertical ultimate load Q_{ult} and a moment M as shown in Figure 3.10a and b. For this case, the components of the moment, M, about the x and y axes can be determined as M_x and M_y, respectively (Figure 3.10c). This condition is equivalent to a load Q_{ult} placed eccentrically on the foundation with $x = e_B$ and $y = e_L$ (Figure 3.10d). Note that

$$e_B = \frac{M_y}{Q_{ult}} \tag{3.40}$$

and

$$e_L = \frac{M_x}{Q_{ult}} \tag{3.41}$$

If Q_{ult} is needed, it can be obtained as follows [Eq. (3.38)]:

$$Q_{ult} = q'_u A'$$

where, from Eq. (3.37),

$$q'_u = cN_c F_{cs} F_{cd} F_{ci} + qN_q F_{qs} F_{qd} F_{qi} + \frac{1}{2}\gamma B' N_\gamma F_{\gamma s} F_{\gamma d} F_{\gamma i}$$

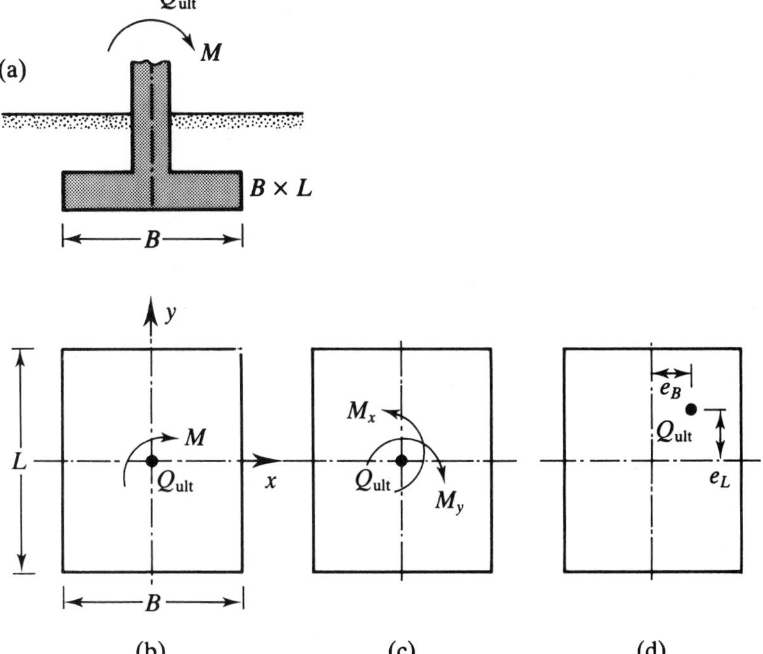

▼ **FIGURE 3.10** Anaysis of foundation with two-way eccentricity

and

$$A' = \text{effective area} = B'L'$$

As before, to evaluate F_{cs}, F_{qs}, and $F_{\gamma s}$ (Table 3.7), use the effective length (L') and effective width (B') dimensions instead of L and B, respectively. To calculate F_{cd}, F_{qd}, and $F_{\gamma d}$, use Table 3.7; however, do not replace B with B'. In determining the effective area (A'), effective width (B'), and effective length (L'), four possible cases may arise (Highter and Anders, 1985).

Case I: $e_L/L \geq \frac{1}{6}$ and $e_B/B \geq \frac{1}{6}$. The effective area for this condition is shown in Figure 3.11, or

$$A' = \frac{1}{2}B_1L_1 \tag{3.42}$$

where $B_1 = B\left(1.5 - \frac{3e_B}{B}\right)$ (3.43a)

$$L_1 = L\left(1.5 - \frac{3e_L}{L}\right) \tag{3.43b}$$

The effective length, L', is the larger of the two dimensions, that is, B_1 or L_1. So, the effective width is

$$B' = \frac{A'}{L'} \tag{3.44}$$

Case II: $e_L/L < 0.5$ and $0 < e_B/B < \frac{1}{6}$. The effective area for this case is shown in Figure 3.12a.

$$A' = \frac{1}{2}(L_1 + L_2)B \tag{3.45}$$

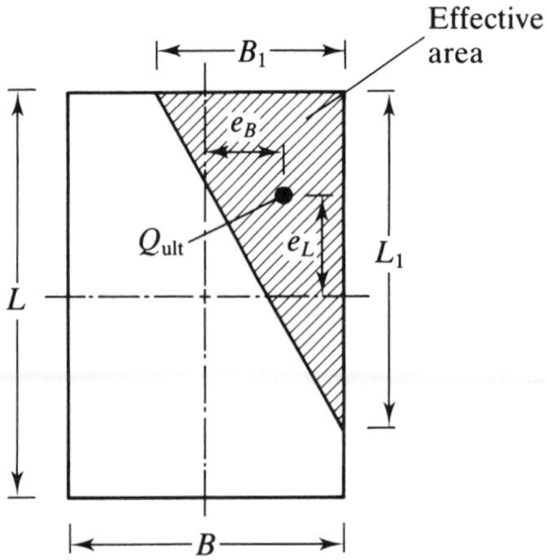

▼ **FIGURE 3.11** Effective area for the case of $e_L/L \geq \frac{1}{6}$ and $e_B/B \geq \frac{1}{6}$

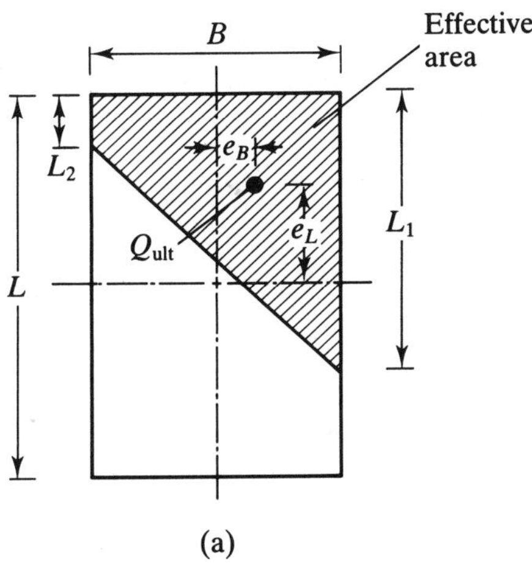

(a)

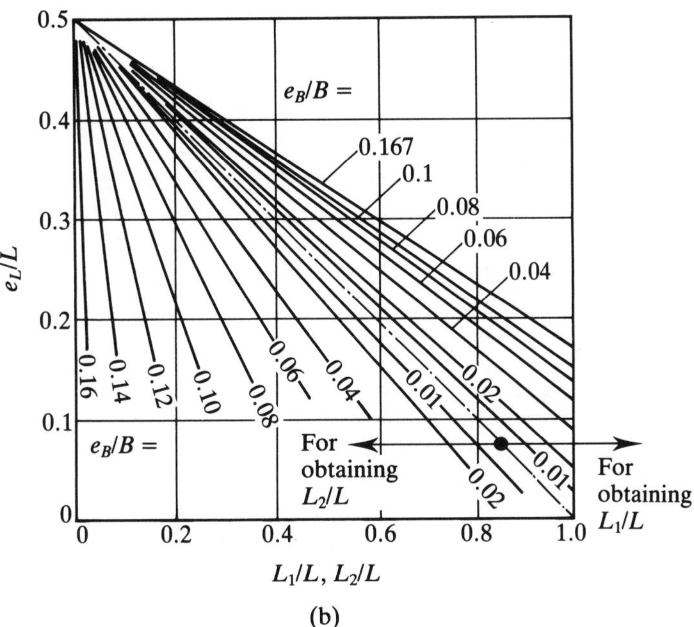

(b)

▼ **FIGURE 3.12** Effective area for the case of $e_L/L < 0.5$ and $0 < e_B/B < \frac{1}{6}$ (after Highter and Anders, 1985)

The magnitudes of L_1 and L_2 can be determined from Figure 3.12b. The effective width is

$$B' = \frac{A'}{L_1 \text{ or } L_2 \quad \text{(whichever is larger)}} \tag{3.46}$$

The effective length is

$$L' = L_1 \text{ or } L_2 \quad \text{(whichever is larger)} \tag{3.47}$$

Case III: $e_L/L < 1/6$ and $0 < e_B/B < 0.5$. The effective area is shown in Figure 3.13a:

$$A' = \frac{1}{2}(B_1 + B_2)L \tag{3.48}$$

The effective width is

$$B' = \frac{A'}{L} \tag{3.49}$$

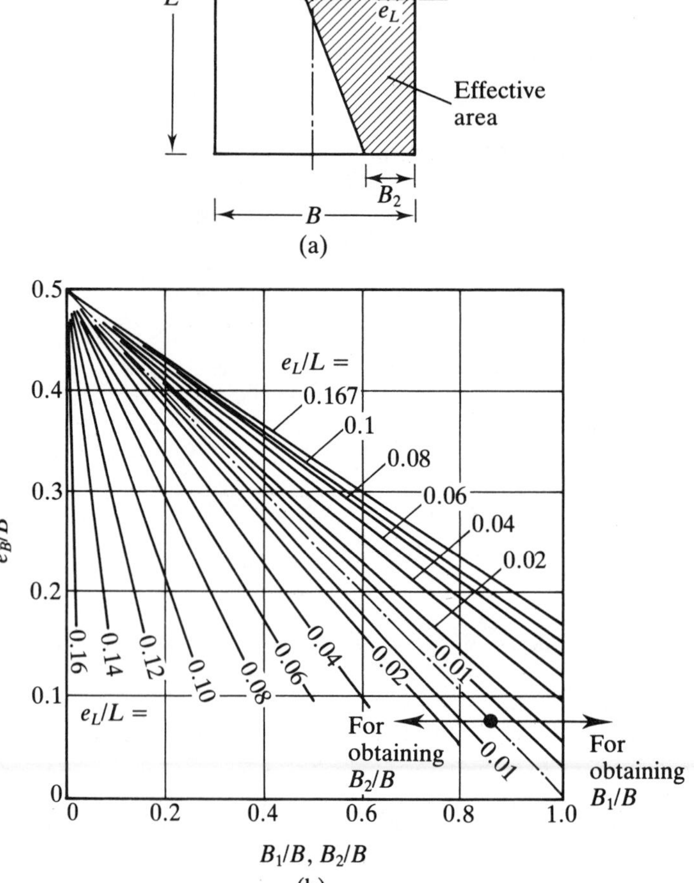

▼ **FIGURE 3.13** Effective area for the case of $e_L/L < 1/6$ and $0 < e_B/B < 0.5$ (after Highter and Anders, 1985)

Effective length is equal to

$$L' = L \tag{3.50}$$

The magnitudes of B_1 and B_2 can be determined from Figure 3.13b.

Case IV: $e_L/L < \frac{1}{6}$ and $e_B/B < \frac{1}{6}$. Figure 3.14a shows the effective area for this case. The ratio B_2/B and thus B_2 can be determined by using the e_L/L curves that slope

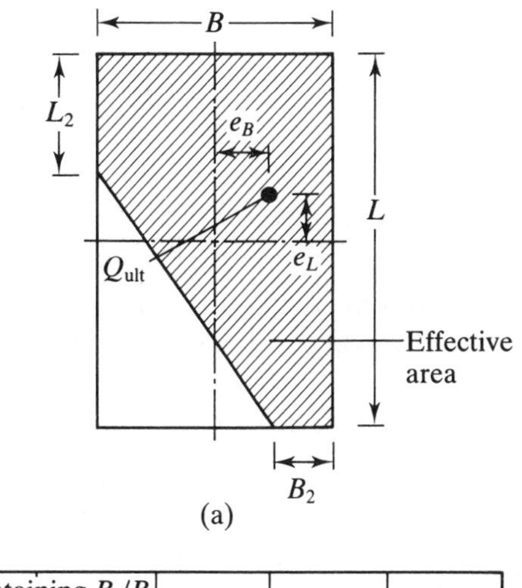

(a)

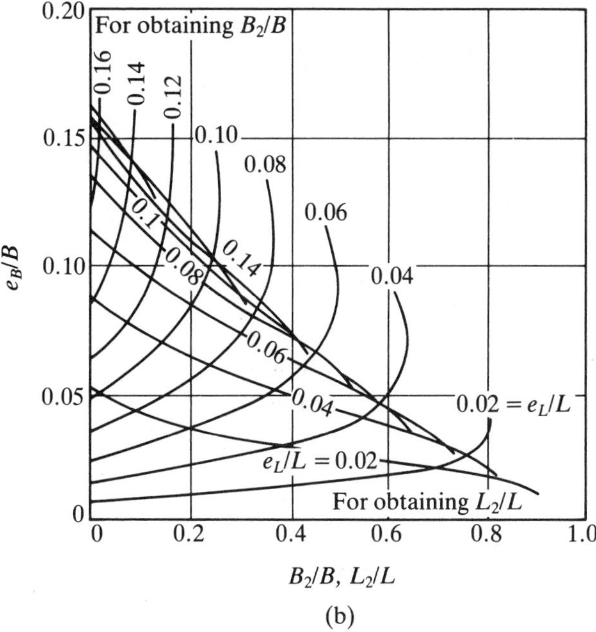

(b)

FIGURE 3.14 Effective area for the case of $e_L/ < \frac{1}{6}$ and $e_B/B < \frac{1}{6}$ (after Highter and Anders, 1985)

upward. Similarly, the ratio L_2/L and thus L_2 can be determined by using the e_L/L curves that slope downward. The effective area is then

$$A' = L_2 B + \frac{1}{2}(B + B_2)(L - L_2) \tag{3.51}$$

The effective width is

$$B' = \frac{A'}{L} \tag{3.52}$$

The effective length is

$$L' = L \tag{3.53}$$

▼ EXAMPLE 3.5

A continuous foundation is shown in Figure 3.15. If the load eccentricity is 0.5 ft, determine the ultimate load, Q_{ult}, per unit length of the foundation.

Solution For $c = 0$, Eq. (3.37) gives

$$q'_u = qN_q F_{qs} F_{qd} F_{qi} + \frac{1}{2}\gamma B' N_\gamma F_{\gamma s} F_{\gamma d} F_{\gamma i}$$

$$q = (110)(4) = 440 \text{ lb/ft}^2$$

For $\phi = 35°$, from Table 3.4, $N_q = 33.3$ and $N_\gamma = 48.03$

$$B' = 6 - (2)(0.5) = 5 \text{ ft}$$

Because it is a strip foundation, B'/L' is zero. Hence $F_{qs} = 1$ and $F_{\gamma s} = 1$, and

$$F_{qi} = F_{\gamma i} = 1$$

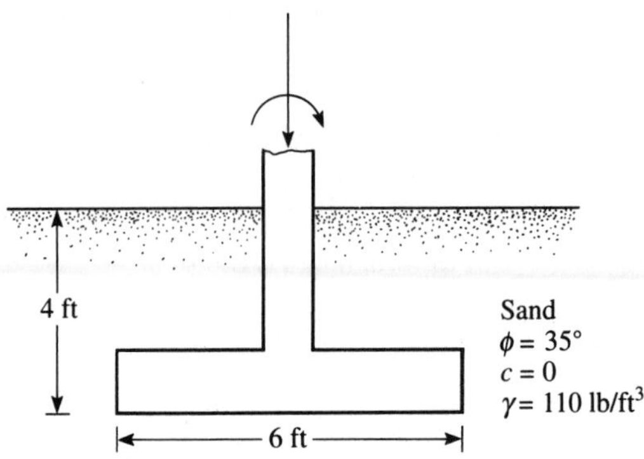

▼ **FIGURE 3.15**

From Table 3.7

$$F_{qd} = 1 + 2\tan\phi(1 - \sin\phi)^2 \frac{D_f}{B} = 1 + 0.255\left(\frac{4}{6}\right) = 1.17$$

$$F_{\gamma d} = 1$$

$$q'_u = (440)(33.3)(1)(1.17)(1) + \left(\frac{1}{2}\right)(110)(5)(48.03)(1)(1)(1) = 30{,}351 \text{ lb/ft}^2$$

Hence

$$Q_{\text{ult}} = (B')(1)(q'_u)(5)(1)(30{,}351) = 151{,}755 \text{ lb/ft} = \mathbf{75.88\ ton/ft}$$ ▼

▼ EXAMPLE 3.6

A square foundation is shown in Figure 3.16, with $e_L = 0.3$ m and $e_B = 0.15$ m. Assume two-way eccentricity and determine the ultimate load, Q_{ult}.

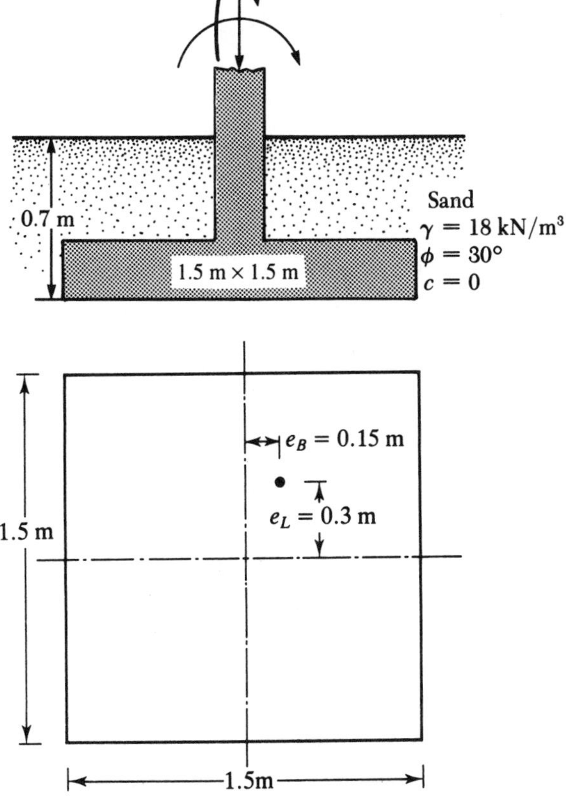

▼ **FIGURE 3.16**

Solution

$$\frac{e_L}{L} = \frac{0.3}{1.5} = 0.2$$

$$\frac{e_B}{B} = \frac{0.15}{1.5} = 0.1$$

This case is similar to that shown in Figure 3.12a. From Figure 3.12b, for $e_L/L = 0.2$ and $e_B/B = 0.1$

$$\frac{L_1}{L} \approx 0.85; \qquad L_1 = (0.85)(1.5) = 1.275 \text{ m}$$

and

$$\frac{L_2}{L} \approx 0.21; \qquad L_2 = (0.21)(1.5) = 0.315 \text{ m}$$

From Eq. (3.45)

$$A' = \frac{1}{2}(L_1 + L_2)B = \frac{1}{2}(1.275 + 0.315)(1.5) = 1.193 \text{ m}^2$$

From Eq. (3.47)

$$L' = L_1 = 1.275 \text{ m}$$

From Eq. (3.46)

$$B' = \frac{A'}{L_1} = \frac{1.193}{1.275} = 0.936 \text{ m}$$

Note, from Eq. (3.37), for $c = 0$

$$q'_u = qN_q F_{qs} F_{qd} F_{qi} + \frac{1}{2}\gamma B' N_\gamma F_{\gamma s} F_{\gamma d} F_{\gamma i}$$

$$q = (0.7)(18) = 12.6 \text{ kN/m}^2$$

For $\phi = 30°$, from Table 3.4, $N_q = 18.4$ and $N_\gamma = 22.4$. Thus

$$F_{qs} = 1 + \left(\frac{B'}{L'}\right)\tan\phi = 1 + \left(\frac{0.936}{1.275}\right)\tan 30° = 1.424$$

$$F_{\gamma s} = 1 - 0.4\left(\frac{B'}{L'}\right) = 1 - 0.4\left(\frac{0.936}{1.275}\right) = 0.706$$

$$F_{qd} = 1 + 2\tan\phi(1 - \sin\phi)^2\frac{D_f}{B} = 1 + \frac{(0.289)(0.7)}{1.5} = 1.135$$

$$F_{\gamma d} = 1$$

So

$$Q_{\text{ult}} = A'q'_u = A'\left(qN_qF_{qs}F_{qd} + \frac{1}{2}\gamma B'N_\gamma F_{\gamma s}F_{\gamma d}\right)$$

$$= (1.193)[(12.6)(18.4)(1.424)(1.135) + (0.5)(18)(0.936)(22.4)(0.706)(1)]$$

$$= \mathbf{605.95\ kN}$$ ▼

3.9 ULTIMATE BEARING CAPACITY FROM SPT AND CPT VALUES

Limited correlations between the *ultimate bearing capacity* of shallow foundations on *sand* and the results of standard penetration tests (SPT) and cone penetration tests (CPT) are available in literature. Using an approximate procedure, Parry (1977) showed that

$$q_u\ (\text{MN/m}^2) = 0.24N_F\left(\frac{D_f + 0.73B}{D_f + 0.75B}\right) \tag{3.54}$$

where N_F = N value obtained from field (standard penetration test) at a depth of 0.75B below the proposed base of the foundation

D_f and B = depth and width of foundation, in meters

For $D_f/B < 1$, Eq. (3.54) may be approximated as

$$q_u(\text{MN/m}^2) = 0.24N_F \tag{3.55}$$

Schmertmann (1978) proposed the following correlations between the ultimate bearing capacity for shallow foundations and the cone penetration resistance, q_c, obtained from CPT tests (for $D_f/B \leq 1.5$).

Foundation on sand

$$q_u\ (\text{kg/cm}^2 \text{ or ton/ft}^2) = 28 - 0.0052(300 - q_c)^{1.5} \quad \text{(for strip foundation)} \tag{3.56}$$

$$q_u\ (\text{kg/cm}^2 \text{ or ton/ft}^2) = 48 - 0.009(300 - q_c)^{1.5} \quad \text{(for square foundation)} \tag{3.57}$$

Foundation on clay

$$q_u\ (\text{kg/cm}^2 \text{ or ton/ft}^2) = 2 + 0.28q_c \quad \text{(for strip foundation)} \tag{3.58}$$

$$q_u\ (\text{kg/cm}^2 \text{ or ton/ft}^2) = 5 + 0.34q_c \quad \text{(for square foundation)} \tag{3.59}$$

The preceding relationships should be considered approximate.

3.10 SEISMIC BEARING CAPACITY AND SETTLEMENT

In some instances shallow foundations may fail during seismic events. Published studies relating to the bearing capacity of shallow foundations in such instances are rare. Recently, however, Richards, et al. (1993) developed a seismic bearing capacity theory that is presented in this section.

Figure 3.17 shows the nature of the failure surface assumed for this analysis. In this figure α_{AE} and α_{PE} are the inclination angles of the failure surface with respect to the horizontal for active and passive pressure conditions based on Coulomb's failure mechanism extended to dynamic earthquake situation. According to this theory, the seismic bearing capacity for a strip foundation may be expressed as

$$q_{uE} = cN_{cE} + qN_{qE} + \frac{1}{2}\gamma BN_{\gamma E} \tag{3.60}$$

where q_{uE} = seismic ultimate bearing capacity

$q = \gamma D_f$

N_{cE}, N_{qE}, and $N_{\gamma E}$ = seismic bearing capacity factors

Equation (3.60) does *not* take depth factors into account. Also,

$$N_{cE}, N_{qE}, \text{ and } N_{\gamma E} = f(\phi, \tan\theta) \tag{3.61}$$

where $\tan\theta = \dfrac{k_h}{1 - k_v}$ (3.62)

k_h = horizontal coefficient of acceleration due to an earthquake

k_v = vertical coefficient of acceleration due to an earthquake

For no earthquake, $k_h = k_v = 0$. Thus Eq. (3.60) becomes

$$q_u = cN_c + qN_q + \frac{1}{2}\gamma BN_\gamma \tag{3.63}$$

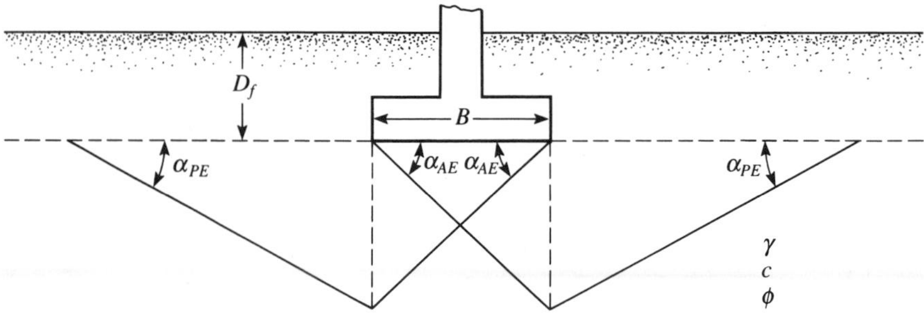

FIGURE 3.17 Failure surface in soil for seismic bearing capacity analysis

Figure 3.18 shows the variations of $N_{\gamma E}/N_\gamma$, N_{qE}/N_q, and N_{cE}/N_c with $\tan\theta$ and the soil friction angle ϕ.

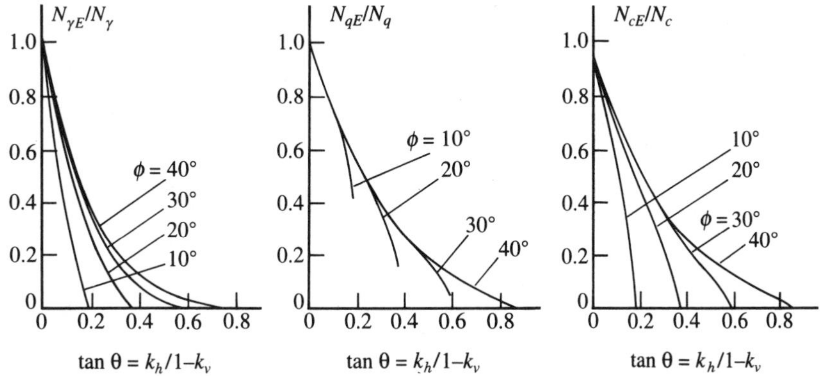

▼ **FIGURE 3.18** Variation of $N_{\gamma E}/N_\gamma$, N_{qE}/N_q, and N_{cE}/N_c (after Richards et al., 1993)

For static conditions, bearing capacity failure can lead to substantial sudden downward movement of the foundation. However, bearing capacity–related settlement in an earthquake takes place when the ratio $k_h/(1 - k_v)$ reaches a critical value $(k_h/1 - k_v)^*$. If $k_v = 0$, then $(k_h/1 - k_v)^*$ becomes equal to k_h^*. Figure 3.19 shows the variation of k_h^* (for $k_v = 0$ and $c = 0$; granular soil) with the static factor of safety (FS) applied to the ultimate bearing capacity [Eq. (3.63)], ϕ, and D_f/B.

The settlement of a strip foundation due to an earthquake (S_{Eq}) can be estimated (Richards et al., 1993) as

$$S_{Eq}\ (\text{m}) = 0.174 \frac{V^2}{Ag} \left| \frac{k_h^*}{A} \right|^{-4} \tan \alpha_{AE} \tag{3.64}$$

where V = peak velocity for the design earthquake (m/sec)
A = acceleration coefficient for the design earthquake
g = acceleration due to gravity (9.81 m/sec^2)

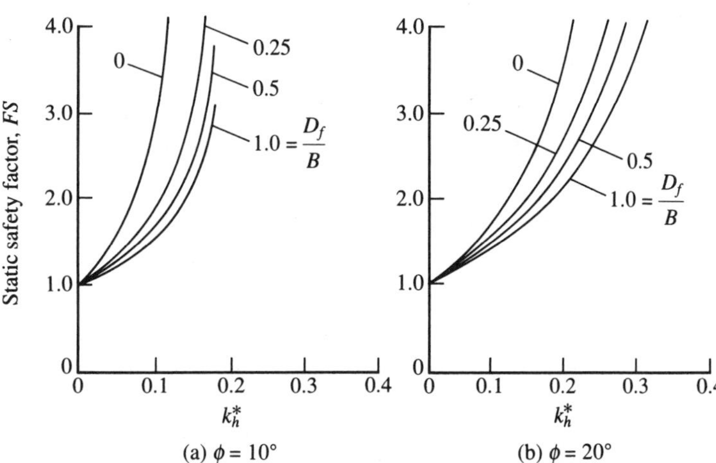

▼ **FIGURE 3.19** Critical acceleration k_h^* for $c = 0$ (after Richards et al., 1993)

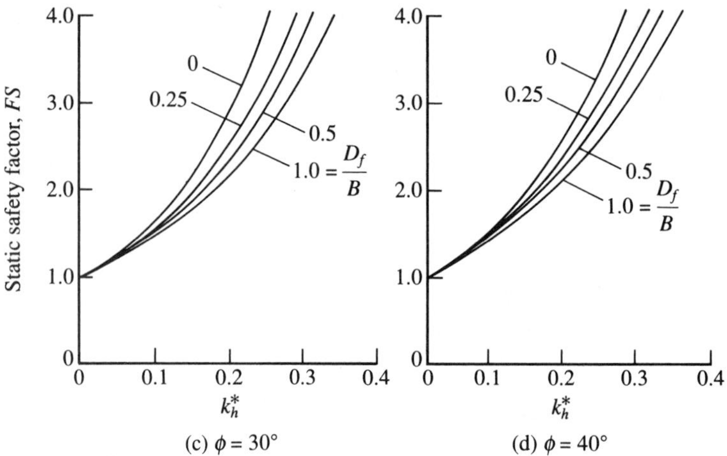

▼ **FIGURE 3.19** (continued)

The values of k_h^* and α_{AE} can be obtained from Figures 3.19 and 3.20, respectively.

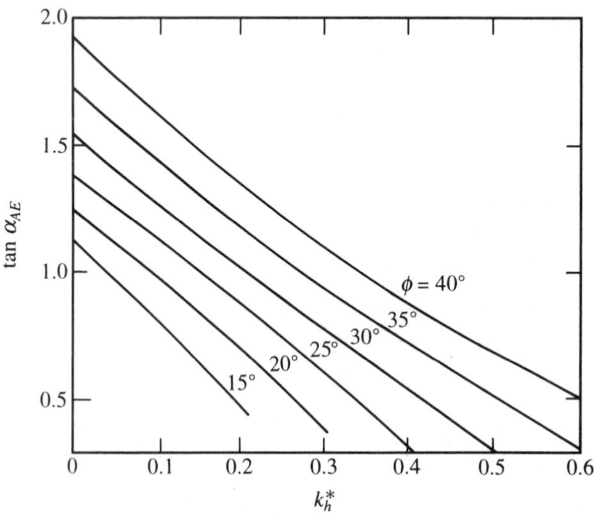

▼ **FIGURE 3.20** Variation of tan α_{AE} with k_h^* and soil friction angle, ϕ (after Richards et al., 1993)

▼ EXAMPLE 3.7

A strip foundation is to be constructed on a sandy soil with $B = 2$ m, $D_f = 1.5$ m, $\gamma = 18$ kN/m^3, $\phi = 30°$, and $FS = 3$. The design earthquake parameters are $V = 0.4$ m/sec and $A = 0.32$. Determine the seismic settlement of the foundation.

Solution For the foundation

$$\frac{D_f}{B} = \frac{1.5}{2} = 0.75$$

From Figure 3.19(c), for $\phi = 30°$, $FS = 3$, and $D_f/B = 0.75$, the value of $k_h^* = 0.26$. Also from Figure 3.20, for $k_h^* = 0.26$ and $\phi = 30°$, the value of $\tan \alpha_{AE} = 0.88$. From Eq. (3.64),

$$S_{\mathrm{Eq}} = 0.174 \frac{V^2}{Ag} \left| \frac{k_h^*}{A} \right|^{-4} \tan \alpha_{AE}$$

$$= 0.174 \frac{(0.4)^2}{(0.32)(9.81)} \left| \frac{0.26}{0.32} \right|^{-4} (0.88) = 0.0179 \text{ m} = \mathbf{17.9\ mm} \qquad ▼$$

3.11 SOME SPECIAL CASES OF ULTIMATE BEARING CAPACITY

The bearing capacity equations presented in the preceding sections involve cases in which the soil supporting the foundation is homogeneous and extends to a considerable depth. Cohesion, angle of friction, and unit weight of soil were assumed to remain constant for the bearing capacity analysis. However, in practice, layered soil profiles are often encountered. In such instances, the failure surface at ultimate load may extend through two or more soil layers. Determination of ultimate bearing capacity in layered soils can be made in only a limited number of cases. This section features the procedure for estimating bearing capacity for layered soils proposed by Meyerhof and Hanna (1978) and Meyerhof (1974).

Foundation on Layered Clay ($\phi = 0$ Condition)

Figure 3.21 shows a shallow foundation on a two-layered clay soil ($\phi = 0$). Soil layer I extends to a depth of H measured below the bottom of the foundation. Soil layer II

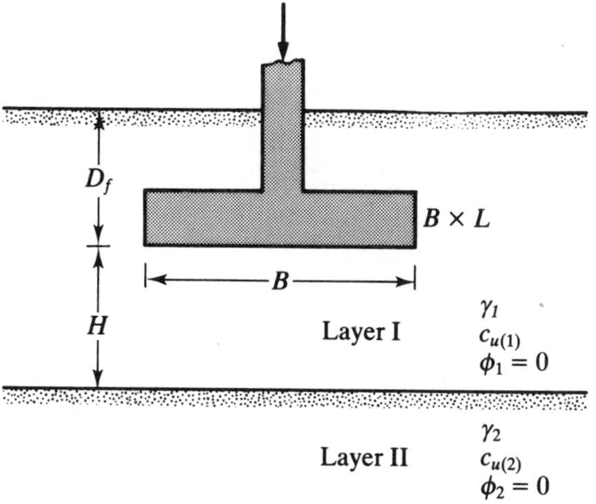

▼ **FIGURE 3.21** Foundation on layered soil

extends downward from that point. The unit weights of the two soil layers, γ_1 and γ_2, will not be too different, so two possible cases may arise.

1. If $c_{u(1)}/c_{u(2)} > 1$, the foundation is on a strong clay layer underlain by a weak clay layer.
2. If $c_{u(1)}/c_{u(2)} < 1$, the foundation is on a weak clay layer underlain by a strong clay layer.

The ultimate bearing capacity theories for each case follow.

Case I: $c_{u(1)}/c_{u(2)} > 1$. If the ratio of H/B is relatively small, failure in the soil under the foundation will take place by punching in the top soil layer followed by a general shear failure in the bottom soil layer, as shown in the left half of Figure 3.22. However, if H/B is relatively large, the failure surface in the soil at ultimate load will be fully contained in the top soil layer, as shown in the right half of Figure 3.22. For such a case (Meyerhof and Hanna, 1978), the ultimate bearing capacity is

$$q_u = \underbrace{\left[1 + 0.2\left(\frac{B}{L}\right)\right]c_{u(2)}N_c}_{\substack{\text{From general shear}\\ \text{failure of bottom}\\ \text{soil layer}}} + \underbrace{\left(1 + \frac{B}{L}\right)\left(\frac{2c_a H}{B}\right) + \gamma_1 D_f}_{\substack{\text{From punching failure}\\ \text{of top soil layer}}}$$

$$\leq \underbrace{\left[1 + 0.2\left(\frac{B}{L}\right)\right]c_{u(1)}N_c + \gamma_1 D_f}_{\substack{\text{From general shear failure}\\ \text{of top soil layer}}} \tag{3.65}$$

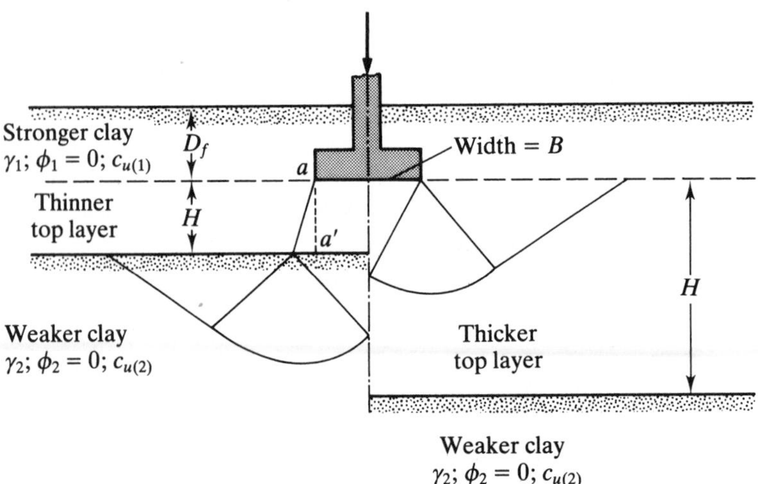

▼ **FIGURE 3.22** Bearing capacity of layered clay—stronger over weaker

where B = width of foundation
L = length of foundation
N_c = 5.14 (bearing capacity factor for $\phi = 0$; Table 3.4)
c_a = adhesion along the interface aa'

Figure 3.23 shows the variation of $c_a/c_{u(1)}$ with $c_{u(2)}/c_{u(1)}$.

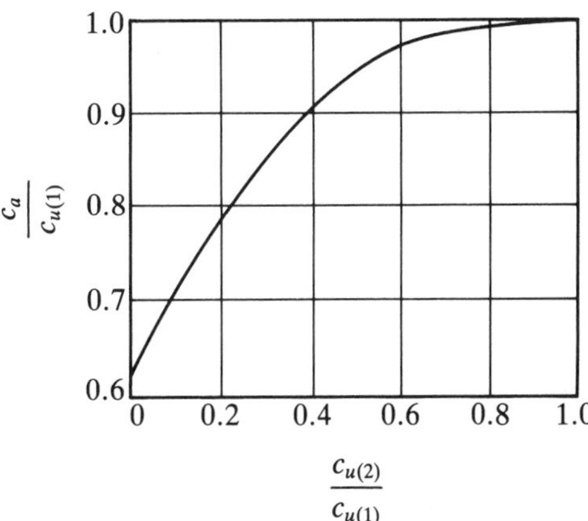

▼ **FIGURE 3.23** Variation of $c_a/c_{u(1)}$ with $c_{u(2)}/c_{u(1)}$ (according to Meyerhof and Hanna, 1978)

Case II: $c_{u(1)}/c_{u(2)} < 1$. The ultimate bearing capacity for this condition (Meyerhof, 1974; Meyerhof and Hanna, 1978) is as follows:

$$q_u = q_t + (q_b - q_t)\left(1 - \frac{H}{H_f}\right)^2 \geq q_t \tag{3.66}$$

where

$$q_t = \left[1 + 0.2\left(\frac{B}{L}\right)\right]c_{u(1)}N_c + \gamma_1 D_f \tag{3.67}$$

$$q_b = \left[1 + 0.2\left(\frac{B}{L}\right)\right]c_{u(2)}N_c + \gamma_2 D_f \tag{3.68}$$

$$H_f \approx B \tag{3.69}$$

Note that $N_c = 5.14$ because $\phi = 0$ (Table 3.4).

In the opinion of some foundation engineers, Eq. (3.66) may be an unconservative relationship. Hence proper judgment should be exercised about using it in designing for field conditions.

Foundations on Dense or Compacted Sand Overlying Soft Clay

In some cases, foundations are constructed on compacted sand layers that overlie soft clay soils. If the thickness of the sand layer uner the foundation is relatively small, the failure surface may extend into the soft clay layer. This is shown in the left half of

Figure 3.24. However, if the sand layer under the foundation is large, the failure surface will lie entirely in the sand layer, as shown in the right half of Figure 3.24. According to Meyerhof (1974), in this case the ultimate bearing capacity of a continuous foundation may be given by

$$q_u = cN_c + \gamma H^2\left(1 + \frac{2D_f}{H}\right)K_s \frac{\tan \phi}{B} + \gamma D_f \tag{3.70}$$

with a maximum of

$$q_u = \frac{1}{2}\gamma B N_\gamma + \gamma D_f N_q \tag{3.71}$$

where ϕ = angle of friction of top sand layer
γ = unit weight of sand
K_s = punching shear resistance coefficient

N_γ and N_q correspond to the angle of friction, ϕ, for sand (Table 3.4). *Note:* for $\phi = 0$, $N_c = 5.14$, as determined from Table 3.4.

For rectangular foundations

$$q_u = \left(1 + 0.2\frac{B}{L}\right)c_u N_c + \left(1 + \frac{B}{L}\right)\gamma H^2\left(1 + \frac{2D_f}{H}\right)K_s \frac{\tan \phi}{B} + \gamma D_f \tag{3.72}$$

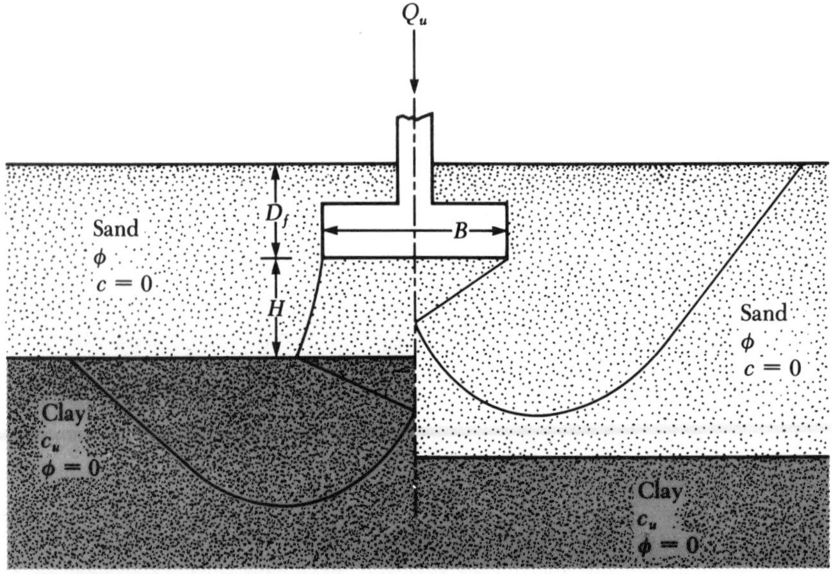

▼ **FIGURE 3.24** Foundation on compacted sand layer overlying soft clay

with a maximum of

$$q_u = \frac{1}{2}\left(1 - 0.4\frac{B}{L}\right)\gamma BN_\gamma + \gamma D_f N_q \tag{3.73}$$

The variation of the punching shear resistance factor, K_s, is given in Figure 3.25. Equations (3.71) and (3.72) are estimates of the values of q_u for continuous and rectangular foundations, respectively, in the upper sand layer. This condition corresponds to that shown in the right half of Figure 3.24.

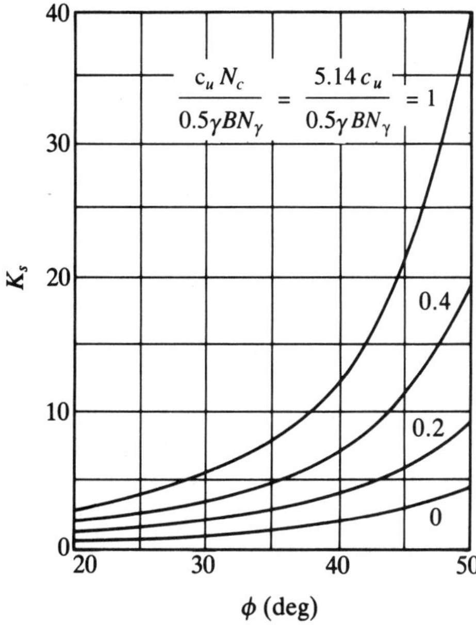

FIGURE 3.25 Variation of K_s with ϕ_1 (according to Meyerhof and Hanna)

EXAMPLE 3.8

Refer to Figure 3.21. A foundation 1.5 m × 1 m is located at a depth, D_f, of 1 m in a clay. A soft clay layer is located at a depth, H, of 1 m measured from the bottom of the foundation. For the top clay layer

Undrained shear strength = 120 kN/m²

Unit weight = 16.8 kN/m³

and for the bottom clay layer

Undrained shear strength = 148 kN/m²

Unit weight = 16.2 kN/m³

Determine the gross allowable load for the foundation with an *FS* of 4.

Solution With $c_{u(1)} = 120\,\text{kN/m}^2$ and $c_{u(2)} = 48\,\text{kN/m}^2$, $c_{u(1)}/c_{u(2)} > 1$ and Eq. (3.65) will apply. So

$$q_u = \left[1 + (0.2)\left(\frac{B}{L}\right)\right] c_{u(2)} N_c + \left(1 + \frac{B}{L}\right)\left(\frac{2c_a H}{B}\right) + \gamma_1 D_f$$

$$\leq \left[1 + (0.2)\left(\frac{B}{L}\right)\right] c_{u(1)} N_c + \gamma_1 D_f$$

where $B = 1$ m $\quad H = 1$ m
$L = 1.5$ m $\quad N_c = 5.14$
$D_f = 1$ m $\quad \gamma_1 = 16.8$ kN/m^3

From Figure 3.23, for $c_{u(2)}/c_{u(1)} = 48/120 = 0.4$, the value of $c_a/c_{u(1)} \approx 0.9$. So

$$c_a = (0.9)(120) = 108 \text{ kN/m}^2$$

and

$$q_u = \left[1 + (0.2)\left(\frac{B}{L}\right)\right] c_{u(2)} N_c + \left(1 + \frac{B}{L}\right)\left(\frac{2c_a H}{B}\right) + \gamma_1 D_f$$

$$= \left[1 + (0.2)\left(\frac{1}{1.5}\right)\right](48)(5.14) + \left[1 + \frac{1}{1.5}\right]\left[\frac{(2)(108)(1)}{1}\right] + (16.8)(1)$$

$$= 279.6 + 360 + 16.8 = 656.4 \text{ kN/m}^2$$

Check:

$$q_u = \left[1 + (0.2)\left(\frac{B}{L}\right)\right] c_{u(1)} N_c + \gamma_1 D_f$$

$$= \left[1 + (0.2)\left(\frac{1}{1.5}\right)\right](120)(5.14) + (16.8)(1)$$

$$= 699 + 16.8 = 715.8 \text{ kN/m}^2$$

Thus $q_u = 656.4$ kN/m^2 (that is, the smaller of the two values calculated above) and

$$q_{\text{all}} = \frac{q_u}{FS} = \frac{656.4}{4} = 164.1 \text{ kN/m}^2$$

The total allowable load is

$$(q_{\text{all}})(1 \times 1.5) = \mathbf{246.15\ kN} \quad \blacktriangledown$$

▼ EXAMPLE 3.9

Refer to Figure 3.24. For sand

$$\gamma = 117 \text{ lb/ft}^3$$

$$\phi = 40^\circ$$

and for clay

$$c_u = 400 \text{ lb/ft}^2$$

For the foundation

$$B = 3 \text{ ft}$$
$$L = 4.5 \text{ ft}$$
$$D_f = 3 \text{ ft}$$
$$H = 4 \text{ ft}$$

Determine the gross ultimate bearing capacity of the foundation.

Solution The foundation is rectangular, so Eqs. (3.72) and (3.73) will apply. For $\phi = 40°$, from Table 3.4, $N_\gamma = 109.41$ and

$$\frac{c_u N_c}{0.5\gamma B N_\gamma} = \frac{(400)(5.14)}{(0.5)(117)(3)(109.41)} = 0.107$$

From Figure 3.25, for $c_u N_c / 0.5\gamma B N_\gamma = 0.107$ and $\phi = 40°$, the value of $K_s \approx 2.5$. Equation (3.72) gives

$$q_u = \left[1 + (0.2)\left(\frac{B}{L}\right)\right] c_u N_c + \left(1 + \frac{B}{L}\right)\gamma H^2\left(1 + \frac{2D_f}{H}\right)K_s \frac{\tan\phi}{B} + \gamma D_f$$

$$= [1 + (0.2)\left(\frac{3}{4.5}\right)\Bigg](400)(5.14) + \left(1 + \frac{3}{4.5}\right)(117)(4)^2$$

$$\times \left[1 + \frac{(2)(3)}{4}\right](2.5)\frac{\tan 40}{3} + (117)(3)$$

$$= 2330 + 5454 + 351 = 8135 \text{ lb/ft}^2$$

Again, from Eq. (3.73)

$$q_u = \frac{1}{2}\left[1 - (0.4)\left(\frac{B}{L}\right)\right]\gamma B N_\gamma + \gamma D_f N_q$$

For $\phi = 40°$, $N_q = 64.20$ (Table 3.4) and

$$q_u = (0.5)\left[1 - (0.4)\left(\frac{3}{4.5}\right)\right](117)(3)(109.41) + (117)(3)(64.20)$$

$$= 14{,}081 + 22{,}534 = 36{,}615 \text{ lb/ft}^2$$

Hence

$$\mathbf{q_u = 8135 \text{ lb/ft}^2}$$ ▼

SETTLEMENT OF SHALLOW FOUNDATIONS

3.12 TYPES OF FOUNDATION SETTLEMENT

Foundation settlement under load can be classified according to two major types: *immediate* (or *elastic*) *settlement*, S_e, and *consolidation settlement*, S_c. Immediate settlement of a foundation takes place during or immediately after the construction of the structure. Consolidation settlement occurs over time. Pore water is extruded from the void spaces of saturated clayey soils. The total settlement of a foundation is the sum of the elastic settlement and the consolidation settlement.

Consolidation settlement comprises two phases: *primary* and *secondary*. The fundamentals of primary consolidation settlement have been explained in detail in Section 1.14. Secondary consolidation settlement occurs after completion of primary consolidation caused by slippage and reorientation of soil particles under sustained load. Primary consolidation settlement is more significant than secondary settlement in inorganic clays and silty clay soils. However, in organic soils, secondary consolidation settlement is more significant.

The settlement of foundations discussed in Section 3.2 for bearing capacity tests was primarily the immediate type. The procedures for calculating foundation settlement are discussed in more detail in the following sections.

3.13 IMMEDIATE SETTLEMENT

Figure 3.26 shows a shallow foundation subjected to a net force per unit area equal to q_o. Let the Poisson's ratio and the modulus of elasticity of the soil supporting it be μ_s and E_s, respectively. Theoretically, if $D_f = 0$, $H = \infty$, and the foundation is perfectly flexible, according to Harr (1966) the settlement may be expressed as

$$S_e = \frac{Bq_o}{E_s}(1 - \mu_s^2)\frac{\alpha}{2} \quad \text{(corner of the flexible foundation)} \tag{3.74}$$

$$S_e = \frac{Bq_o}{E_s}(1 - \mu_s^2)\alpha \quad \text{(center of the flexible foundation)} \tag{3.75}$$

$$\text{where } \alpha = \frac{1}{\pi}\left[\ln\left(\frac{\sqrt{1+m^2}+m}{\sqrt{1+m^2}-m}\right) + m\ln\left(\frac{\sqrt{1+m^2}+1}{\sqrt{1+m^2}-1}\right)\right] \tag{3.76}$$

$$m = L/B \tag{3.77}$$

B = width of foundation
L = length of foundation

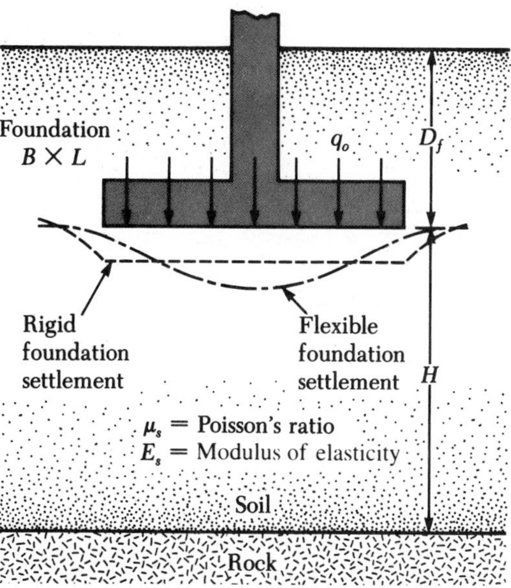

▼ **FIGURE 3.26** Elastic settlement of flexible and rigid foundations

The values of α for various length-to-width (L/B) ratios are shown in Figure 3.27. The average immediate settlement for a flexible foundation also may be expressed as

$$S_e = \frac{Bq_o}{E_s}(1 - \mu_s^2)\alpha_{av} \qquad \text{(average for flexible foundation)} \tag{3.78}$$

Figure 3.27 also shows the values of α_{av} for various L/B ratios of foundation.

However, if the foundation shown in Figure 3.26 is rigid, the immediate settlement will be different and may be expressed as

$$S_e = \frac{Bq_o}{E_s}(1 - \mu_s^2)\alpha_r \qquad \text{(rigid foundation)} \tag{3.79}$$

The values of α_r for various L/B ratios of foundation are shown in Figure 3.27.

The preceding equations for immediate settlement were obtained by integrating the strain at various depths below the foundations for limits of $z = 0$ to $z = \infty$. If an

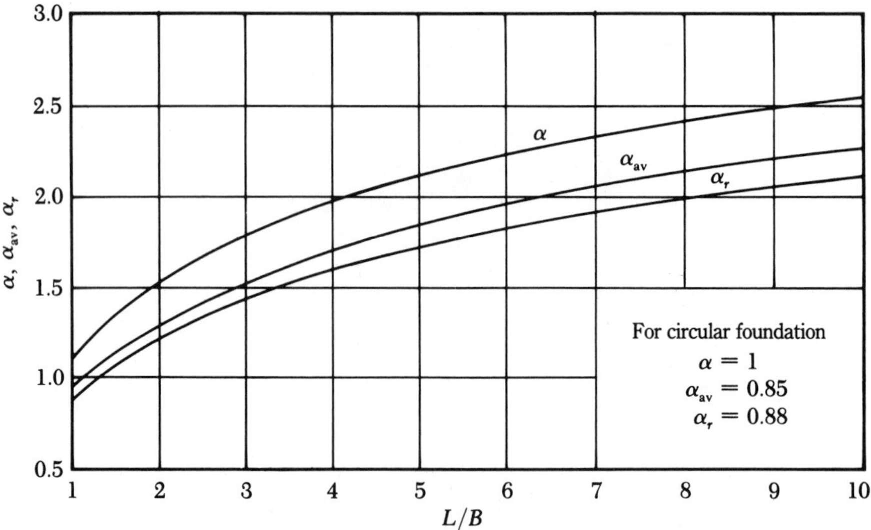

▼ **FIGURE 3.27** Values of α, α_{av}, and α_r—Eqs. (3.74), (3.75), (3.78), (3.79)

incompressible layer of rock is located at a limited depth, the actual settlement may be less than that calculated by the preceding equations. However, if the depth H in Figure 3.26 is greater than about $2B$ to $3B$, the actual settlement would not change considerably. Also note that the deeper the embedment, D_f, the less is the total elastic settlement.

3.14 IMMEDIATE SETTLEMENT OF FOUNDATIONS ON SATURATED CLAY

Janbu et al. (1956) proposed an equation for evaluating the average settlement of flexible foundations on saturated clay soils (Poisson's ratio, $\mu_s = 0.5$). For the notation used in Figure 3.28, this equation is

$$S_e = A_1 A_2 \frac{q_o B}{E_s} \tag{3.80}$$

where A_1 is a function of H/B and L/B and A_2 is a function of D_f/B

Christian and Carrier (1978) modified the values of A_1 and A_2 to some extent, as presented in Figure 3.28.

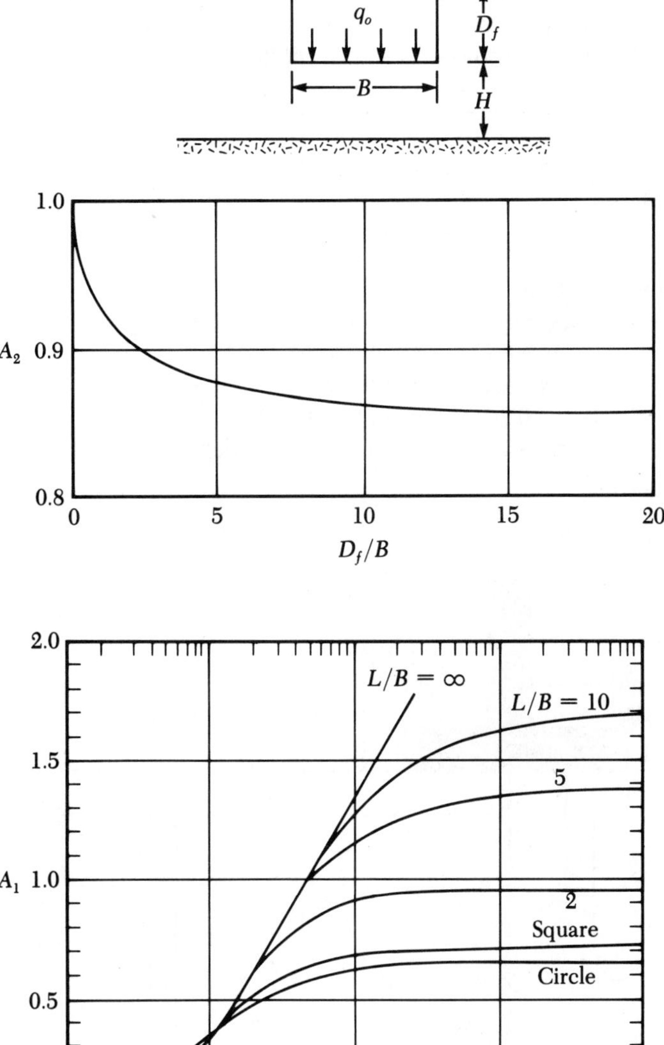

▼ **FIGURE 3.28** Values of A_1 and A_2 for immediate settlement calculation—Eq. (3.80) (after Christian and Carrier, 1978)

3.15 IMMEDIATE SETTLEMENT OF SANDY SOIL: USE OF STRAIN INFLUENCE FACTOR

Immediate settlement of granular soils can also be evaluated by use of a semi-empirical *strain influence factor* (Figure 3.29) proposed by Schmertmann and Hartman (1978). According to this method, the settlement is

$$S_e = C_1 C_2(\bar{q} - q) \sum_{0}^{z2} \frac{I_z}{E_s} \Delta z \tag{3.81}$$

where I_z = strain influence factor
C_1 = a correction factor for the depth of foundation embedment $= 1 - 0.5[q/(\bar{q} - q)]$
C_2 = a correction factor to account for creep in soil $= 1 + 0.2 \log$ (time in years/0.1)
$\bar{q}$ = stress at the level of the foundation
$q = \gamma D_f$

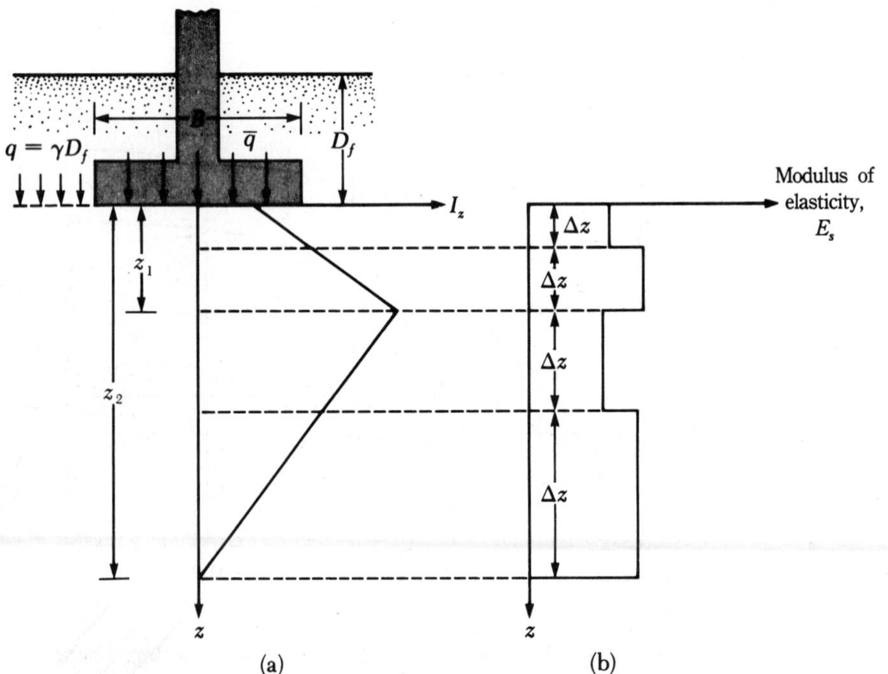

FIGURE 3.29 Elastic settlement calculation by using strain influence factor

The variation of the strain influence factor with depth below the foundation is shown in Figure 3.29a. Note that, for square or circular foundations,

$$I_z = 0.1 \quad \text{at } z = 0$$

$$I_z = 0.5 \quad \text{at } z = z_1 = 0.5B$$

$$I_z = 0 \quad \text{at } z = z_2 = 2B$$

Similarly, for foundations with $L/B \geq 10$,

$$I_z = 0.2 \quad \text{at } z = 0$$

$$I_z = 0.5 \quad \text{at } z = z_1 = B$$

$$I_z = 0 \quad \text{at } z = z_2 = 4B$$

where B = width of the foundation and L = length of the foundation

For values of L/B between 1 and 10, necessary interpolations can be made.

To use Eq. (3.81) first requires evaluation of the approximate variation of the modulus of elasticity with depth (Figure 3.29b). This evaluation can be made by using the standard penetration numbers or cone penetration resistances (Chapter 2). The soil layer can be divided into several layers to a depth of $z = z_2$, and the immediate settlement of each layer can be estimated. The sum of the settlement of all layers equals S_e.

3.16 RANGE OF MATERIAL PARAMETERS FOR COMPUTING IMMEDIATE SETTLEMENT

Sections 3.13–3.15 presented the equations for calculating immediate settlement of foundations. These equations contain the elastic parameters, such as E_s and μ_s. If the laboratory test results for these parameters are not available, certain realistic assumptions have to be made. Table 3.9 shows the approximate range of the elastic parameters for various soils.

TABLE 3.9 Elastic Parameters of Various Soils

Type of soil	Modulus of elasticity, E_s		Poisson's ratio, μ_s
	$lb/in.^2$	MN/m^2	
Loose sand	1,500–3,500	10.35–24.15	0.20–0.40
Medium dense sand	2,500–4,000	17.25–27.60	0.25–0.40
Dense sand	5,000–8,000	34.50–55.20	0.30–0.45
Silty sand	1,500–2,500	10.35–17.25	0.20–0.40
Sand and gravel	10,000–25,000	69.00–172.50	0.15–0.35
Soft clay	600–3,000	4.1–20.7	
Medium clay	3,000–6,000	20.7–41.4	0.20–0.50
Stiff clay	6,000–14,000	41.4–96.6	

Several investigators have correlated the values of the modulus of elasticity, E, with the standard penetration number, N, and the cone penetration resistance, q_c. Mitchell and Gardner (1975) compiled a list of these correlations. Schmertmann (1970) indicated that the modulus of elasticity of sand may be given by

$$E_s\ (\text{kN/m}^2) = 766N \tag{3.82}$$

where N = standard penetration number

In English units

$$E\ (\text{U.S. ton/ft}^2) = 8N \tag{3.83}$$

Similarly

$$E_s = 2q_c \tag{3.84a}$$

where q_c = static cone penetration resistance

Schmertmann and Hartman (1978) further suggested that the following correlations may be used with the strain influence factors described in Section 3.15:

$$E_s = 2.5q_c \quad \text{(for square and circular foundations)} \tag{3.84b}$$

and

$$E_s = 3.5q_c \quad \text{(for strip foundations)} \tag{3.84c}$$

Note: Any consistent set of units may be used in Eq. (3.84a).

The modulus of elasticity of normally consolidated clays may be estimated as

$$E_s = 250c \text{ to } 500c \tag{3.85}$$

and for overconsolidated clays as

$$E_s = 750c \text{ to } 1000c \tag{3.86}$$

where c = undrained cohesion of clay soil

3.17 CASE HISTORY: IMMEDIATE SETTLEMENT

Schmertmann (1970) provided a case history of a rectangular foundation (Belgian bridge pier) having $L = 23$ m and $B = 2.6$ m and being supported by a granular soil deposit. For this foundation we may assume that $L/B \approx 10$ for plotting the strain influence factor diagram. Figure 3.30 shows the details of the foundation along with the approximate variation of the cone penetration resistance, q_c, with depth. For this foundation [Eq. (3.81)] note that

$$\bar{q} = 178.54 \text{ kN/m}^2$$

$$q = 31.39 \text{ kN/m}^2$$

$$C_1 = 1 - 0.5\frac{q}{\bar{q} - q} = 1 - (0.5)\left(\frac{31.39}{178.54 - 31.39}\right) = 0.893$$

$$C_2 = 1 + 0.2 \log\left(\frac{t \text{ yr}}{0.1}\right)$$

For $t = 5$ yr

$$C_2 = 1 + 0.2 \log\left(\frac{5}{0.1}\right) = 1.34$$

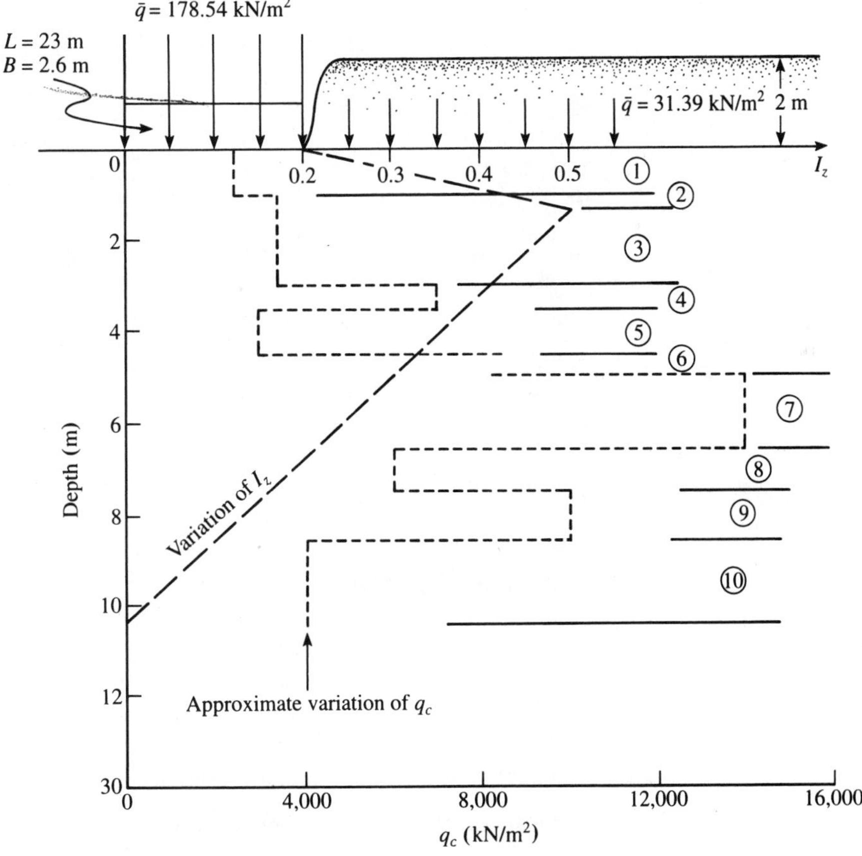

▼ **FIGURE 3.30** Variation of I_z and q_c below the foundation

Table 3.10 shows the calculation of $\sum_0^{z2} (I_z/E_s)\,\Delta z$ in conjunction with Figure 3.30. Hence the immediate settlement is calculated as

$$S = C_1C_2(\bar{q} - q) \sum \frac{I_z}{E_s}\,\Delta z$$

$$= (0.893)(1.34)(178.54 - 31.39)(18.64 \times 10^{-5})$$

$$= 0.0382 \text{ m} \approx 38 \text{ mm}$$

After five years, the actual *maximum* settlement observed for the foundation was about 39 mm. Hence the theoretical and observed values closely agree.

TABLE 3.10 Calculation of $\sum (I_z/E_s)\,\Delta z$

Layer	Δz (m)	q_c (kN/m²)	E_s [a] (kN/m²)	z to the center of the layer (m)	I_z at the center of the layer	$(I_z/E_s)\,\Delta z$ (m²/kN)
1	1	2,450	8,765	0.5	0.315	3.59×10^{-5}
2	0.3	3,430	12,005	1.15	0.465	1.16×10^{-5}
3	1.7	3,430	12,005	2.15	0.453	6.41×10^{5}
4	0.5	6,870	24,045	3.25	0.393	0.81×10^{-5}
5	1.0	2,950	10,325	4.0	0.352	3.40×10^{-5}
6	0.5	8,340	29,190	4.75	0.31	0.53×10^{-5}
7	1.5	14,000	49,000	5.75	0.255	0.78×10^{-5}
8	1	6,000	21,000	7.0	0.187	0.89×10^{-5}
9	1	10,000	35,000	8.0	0.132	0.37×10^{-5}
10	1.9	4,000	14,000	9.45	0.052	0.70×10^{-5}
	$\sum$ 10.4 m = 4B					$\sum 18.64 \times 10^{-5}$

[a] $E_s \approx 3.5q_c$ [Eq. (3.84b)]

3.18 IMMEDIATE SETTLEMENT OF ECCENTRICALLY LOADED FOUNDATIONS

The settlement calculation procedure described in Sections 3.13, 3.14, and 3.15 relate to the settlement of centrally loaded foundations. An eccentrically loaded foundation will undergo vertical settlement and rotation as shown in Figure 3.31. Georgiadis and Butterfield (1988) suggested the following procedure for determining the settlement and rotation of a foundation under such loading conditions.

1. Let the applied total load on the foundation, Q, and the load eccentricity, e, be known and determination of the settlement, S_e, and the rotation angle, t (see Figure 3.31 for notations) be required.

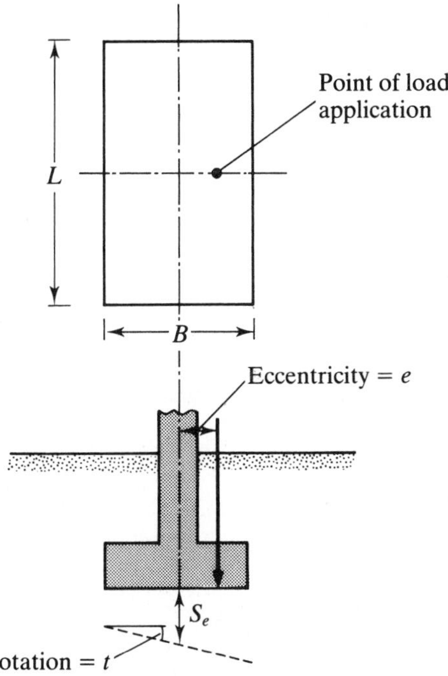

▼ **FIGURE 3.31** Elastic settlement of eccentrically loaded foundation

2. The ultimate load, $Q_{\text{ult}(e)}$, that the foundation can sustain can be evaluated by using Eq. (3.38) [Section 3.8; note the change of notation from Q_{ult} to $Q_{\text{ult}(e)}$].

3. Determine the factor of safety for the eccentrically loaded foundation as

$$FS = \frac{Q_{\text{ult}(e)}}{Q} = F_1 \tag{3.87}$$

4. Determine the ultimate load $Q_{\text{ult}(e=0)}$ for the same foundation with eccentricity $e = 0$ [centrally loaded foundation; Eq. (3.17)].

5. Determine

$$\frac{Q_{\text{ult}(e=0)}}{F_1} = Q_{(e=0)} \tag{3.88}$$

Note that $Q_{(e=0)}$ is the allowable load for the foundation with a factor of safety $FS = F_1$ for central loading condition.

6. For the load $Q_{(e=0)}$ on the foundation, estimate the settlement by using the techniques presented in Sections 3.13–3.15. Let the settlement determined by any one of the methods equal $S_{e(e=0)}$.

7. Now, use the following equations to determine S_e and t:

$$S_e = \underset{\substack{\uparrow \\ \text{Step 6}}}{S_{e(e=0)}}\left[1 - 2\left(\frac{e}{B}\right)\right]^2 \tag{3.89}$$

$$t = \tan^{-1}\left[CS_e\left(\frac{e/B}{\sqrt{BL}}\right)\right] \tag{3.90}$$

where $C = \beta_1\beta_2$ (3.91)

β_1, β_2 = factors dependent on the L/B ratio (Lee, 1963; Whitman and Richart, 1967) (3.92)

Figure 3.32 shows the variation of β_1, β_2, and C. Note that β_1 is related to vertical displacement and that β_2 is related to the rotation of the foundation.

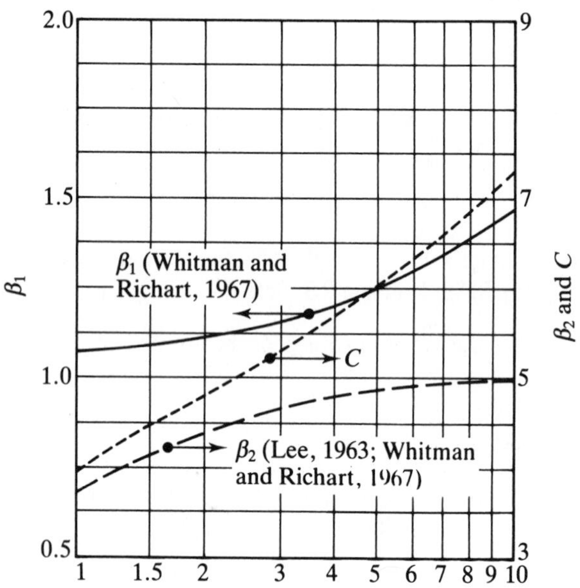

▼ **FIGURE 3.32** Variation of β_1, β_2, and C with L/B

▼ EXAMPLE 3.10

A square foundation is shown in Figure 3.33. It is subjected to a load of 180 kN and a moment of 27 kN · m. Determine the settlement of the foundation (S_e and t) according to the method presented in Section 3.18.

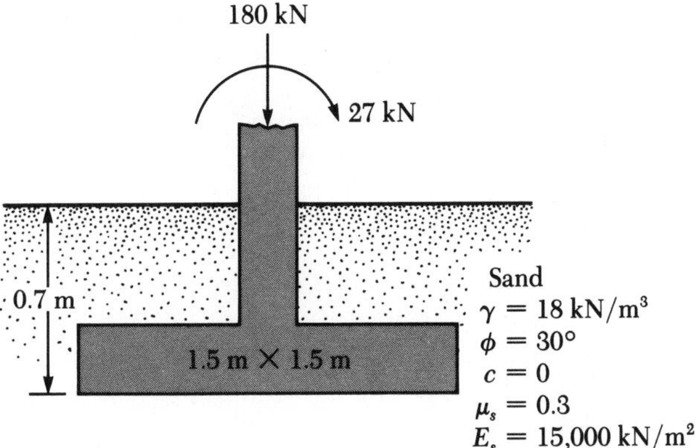

▼ **FIGURE 3.33**

Solution

Step 1

For $Q = 180$ kN and $M = 27$ kN·m, the load eccentricity, $e = M/Q = 27/180 = 0.15$ m.

Step 2: Determine the magnitude of $Q_{\text{ult}(e)}$

With $c = 0$, Eq. (3.37) becomes

$$q'_u = qN_q F_{qs} F_{qd} F_{qi} + \frac{1}{2}\gamma B' N_\gamma F_{\gamma s} F_{\gamma d} F_{\gamma i}$$

$$q = (0.7)(18) = 12.6 \text{ kN/m}^2$$

For $\phi = 30°$, from Table 3.4, $N_q = 18.4$ and $N_\gamma = 22.4$. Then

$$B' = 1.5 - 2(0.15) = 1.2 \text{ m}$$

$$L' = 1.5 \text{ m}$$

From Table 3.7,

$$F_{qs} = 1 + \frac{B'}{L'} \tan \phi = 1 + \left(\frac{1.2}{1.5}\right) \tan 30° = 1.462$$

$$F_{qd} = 1 + 2 \tan \phi (1 - \sin \phi)^2 \frac{D_f}{B} = 1 + \frac{(0.289)(0.7)}{1.5} = 1.135$$

$$F_{\gamma s} = 1 - 0.4\left(\frac{B'}{L'}\right) = 1 - 0.4\left(\frac{1.2}{1.5}\right) = 0.68$$

$$F_{\gamma d} = 1$$

So

$$q'_u = (12.6)(18.4)(1.462)(1.135) + \frac{1}{2}(18)(1.2)(22.4)(0.68)(1)$$

$$= 384.3 + 164.50 = 548.8 \text{ kN/m}^2$$

Hence

$$Q_{\text{ult}(e)} = B'L'(q'_u) = (1.2)(1.5)(548.8)$$

$$Q_{\text{ult}(e)} = 988 \text{ kN}$$

Step 3: Determine factor of safety, F_1

From Eq. (3.87),

$$F_1 = \frac{Q_{\text{ult}(e)}}{Q} = \frac{988 \text{ kN}}{180} = 5.49$$

Step 4: Determine $Q_{\text{ult}(e=0)}$

From Eq. (3.17), because $c = 0$,

$$q_u = qN_q F_{qs} F_{qd} + \frac{1}{2}\gamma B N_\gamma F_{\gamma s} F_{\gamma d}$$

$$q = 12.6 \text{ kN/m}^2$$

From $\phi = 30°$ (from Table 3.4), $N_q = 18.4$ and $N_\gamma = 22.4$.

From Table 3.7

$$F_{qs} = 1 + \frac{B}{L}\tan\phi = 1 + \left(\frac{1.5}{1.5}\right)\tan 30 = 1.577$$

$$F_{dq} = 1 + 2\tan\phi(1 - \sin\phi)^2\frac{D_f}{B} = 1 + \frac{(0.289)(0.7)}{1.5} = 1.135$$

$$F_{\gamma s} = 1 - 0.4\left(\frac{B}{L}\right) = 1 - 0.4\left(\frac{1.5}{1.5}\right) = 0.6$$

$$F_{\gamma d} = 1$$

$$q_u = (12.6)(18.4)(1.577)(1.135) + \frac{1}{2}(18)(1.5)(22.4)(0.6)(1)$$

$$= 414.97 + 181.44 = 596.41 \text{ kN/m}^2$$

So

$$Q_{\text{ult}(e=0)} = (596.41)(1.5 \times 1.5) = 1342 \text{ kN}$$

Step 5: Determine $Q_{(e=0)}$

From Eq. (3.88)

$$Q_{e=0)} = \frac{Q_{\text{ult}(e=0)}}{F_1} = \frac{1342}{5.49} = 244.4 \text{ kN/m}^2$$

Step 6: Determine $S_{e(e=0)}$

From Eq. (3.79)

$$S_{e(e=0)} = \frac{B(Q_{e=0})}{E_s(B \times L)}(1 - \mu_s^2)\alpha_r$$

For $L/B = 1$, $\alpha_r \approx 0.82$ (Figure 3.27), and for $\mu_s = 0.3$ and $E_s = 15{,}000\ \text{kN/m}^2$,

$$S_{e(e=0)} = \frac{(1.5)(244.4)}{(15{,}000)(1.5 \times 1.5)}(1 - 0.3^2)0.82 = 0.0081\ \text{m} = 8.1\ \text{mm}$$

Step 7

From Eq. (3.89)

$$S_e = S_{e(e=0)}\left[1 - 2\left(\frac{e}{B}\right)\right]^2$$

$$= (8.1)[1 - (2)(0.1)]^2 = \mathbf{5.18\ mm}$$

From Eq. (3.90)

$$t = \tan^{-1}\left[CS_e\left(\frac{e/B}{\sqrt{BL}}\right)\right]$$

For $B/L = 1$, $C \approx 3.95$ (from Figure 3.32). So

$$t = \tan^{-1}\left[(3.95)\left(\frac{5.18\ \text{mm}}{1000}\right)\left(\frac{0.1}{\sqrt{(1.5)(1.5)}}\right)\right]$$

$$= \mathbf{0.078\ deg}$$ ▼

3.19 CONSOLIDATION SETTLEMENT

As mentioned before, consolidation settlement occurs over time, and it occurs in saturated clayey soils when they are subjected to increased load caused by foundation construction (Figure 3.34). Based on the one-dimensional consolidation settlement equations given in Chapter 1, we write

$$S_c = \int \varepsilon_v\, dz$$

where ε_v = vertical strain

$$= \frac{\Delta e}{1 + e_o}$$

Δe = change of void ratio

$= f(p_o, p_c, \text{and } \Delta p)$

So

$$S_c = \frac{C_c H_c}{1 + e_o} \log \frac{p_o + \Delta p_{\text{av}}}{p_o} \quad \text{(for normally consolidated clays)} \tag{1.60}$$

$$S_c = \frac{C_s H_c}{1 + e_o} \log \frac{p_o + \Delta p_{\text{av}}}{p_o} \quad \text{(for overconsolidated clays with } p_o + \Delta p_{\text{av}} < p_c\text{)} \tag{1.62}$$

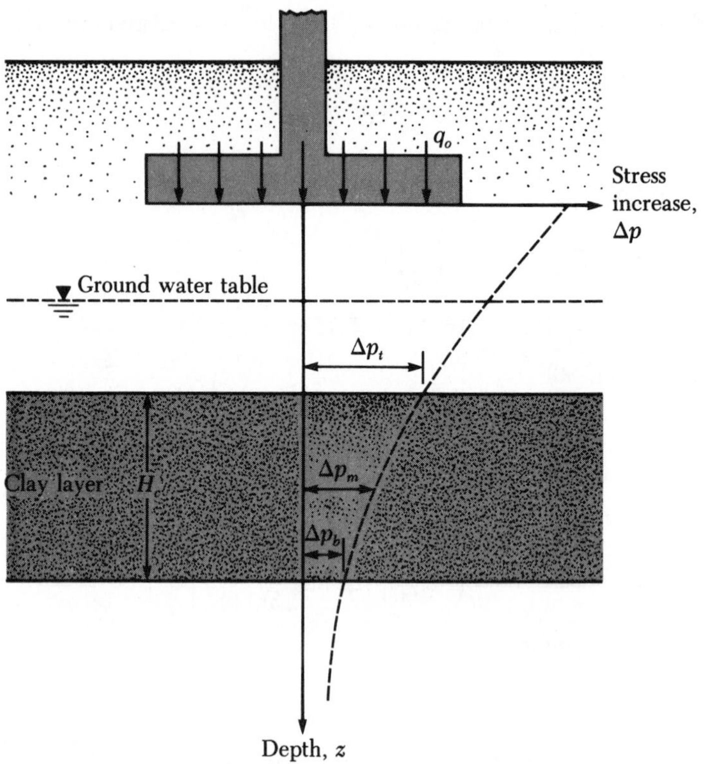

▼ **FIGURE 3.34** Consolidation settlement calculation

$$S_c = \frac{C_s H_c}{1 + e_o} \log \frac{p_c}{p_o} + \frac{C_c H_c}{1 + e_o} \log \frac{p_o + \Delta p_{av}}{p_c}$$

(for overconsolidated clays with $p_o < p_c < p_o + \Delta p_{av}$) (1.64)

where p_o = average effective pressure on the clay layer before the construction of the foundation
Δp_{av} = average increase of pressure on the clay layer caused by the foundation construction
p_c = preconsolidation pressure
e_o = initial void ratio of the clay layer
C_c = compression index
C_s = swelling index
H_c = thickness of the clay layer

The procedures for determining the compression and swelling indexes were discussed in Chapter 1.

Note that the increase of pressure, Δp, on the clay layer is not constant with depth. The magnitude of Δp will decrease with the increase of depth measured from the bottom of the foundation. However, the average increase of pressure may be approximated by

$$\Delta p_{av} = \frac{1}{6}(\Delta p_t + 4\Delta p_m + \Delta p_b) \tag{3.93}$$

where Δp_t, Δp_m, and Δp_b are the pressure increases at the *top*, *middle*, and *bottom* of the clay layer that are caused by the foundation construction.

The method of determining the pressure increase caused by various types of foundation load is discussed in Section 3.21.

3.20 SKEMPTON–BJERRUM MODIFICATION FOR CONSOLIDATION SETTLEMENT

The consolidation settlement calculation presented in the preceding section is based on Eqs. (1.60), (1.62), and (1.64). These equations, as shown in Chapter 1, are based on one-dimensional laboratory consolidation tests. The underlying assumption for these equations is that the increase of pore water pressure, Δu, immediately after the load application equals the increase of stress, Δp, at any depth. For this case

$$S_{c(oed)} = \int \frac{\Delta e}{1 + e_o}\, dz = \int m_v\, \Delta p_{(1)}\, dz \tag{3.94}$$

where $S_{c(oed)}$ = consolidation settlement calculated by using Eqs. (1.60), (1.62), and (1.64)

$\Delta p_{(1)}$ = vertical stress increase (note the change of notation from Δp as given in Section 3.19)

m_v = volume coefficient of compressibility (see Chapter 1)

In the field, however, when load is applied over a limited area on the ground surface, this assumption will not be correct. Consider the case of a circular foundation on a clay layer as shown in Figure 3.35. The vertical and the horizontal stress increases at a point in the clay layer immediately below the center of the foundation are $\Delta p_{(1)}$ and $\Delta p_{(3)}$, respectively. For a saturated clay, the pore water pressure increase at that depth (Chapter 1) is

$$\Delta u = \Delta p_{(3)} + A[\Delta p_{(1)} - \Delta p_{(3)}] \tag{3.95}$$

where A = pore water pressure parameter

For this case

$$S_c = \int m_v\, \Delta u\, dz = \int (m_v)\{\Delta p_{(3)} + A[\Delta p_{(1)} - \Delta p_{(3)}]\}\, dz \tag{3.96}$$

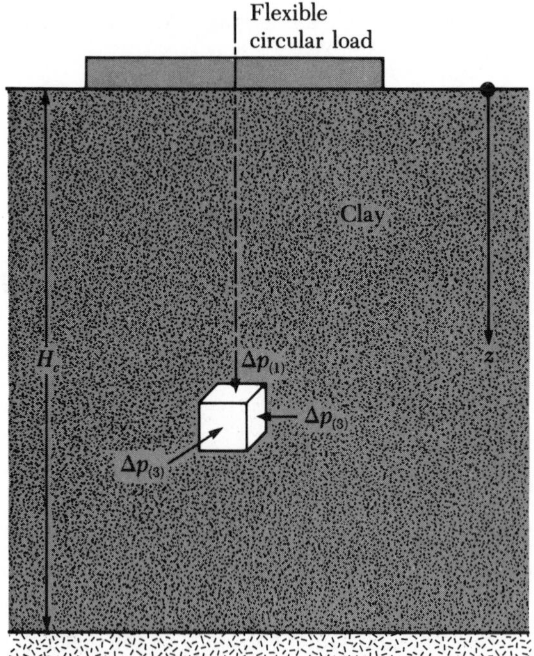

▼ **FIGURE 3.35** Circular foundation on a clay layer

Combining Eqs. (3.94) and (3.96) yields

$$K_{\text{cir}} = \frac{S_c}{S_{c(oed)}} = \frac{\int_0^{H_c} m_v \, \Delta u \, dz}{\int_0^{H_c} m_v \, \Delta p_{(1)} \, dz} = A + (1 - A)\left[\frac{\int_0^{H_c} \Delta p_{(3)} \, dz}{\int_0^{H_c} \Delta p_{(1)} \, dz}\right] \tag{3.97}$$

where K_{cir} = settlement ratio for circular foundations

The settlement ratio for a continuous foundation (K_{str}) can be determined in a manner similar to that for a circular foundation. The variation of K_{cir} and K_{str} with A and H_c/B is given in Figure 3.36. (*Note*: B = diameter of a circular foundation, and B = width of a continuous foundation.)

Following is the procedure for determining consolidation settlement according to Skempton and Bjerrum (1957).

1. Determine the consolidation settlement, $S_{c(oed)}$, using the procedure outlined in Section 3.19. (Note the change of notation from S_c.)
2. Determine the pore water pressure parameter, A.
3. Determine H_c/B.

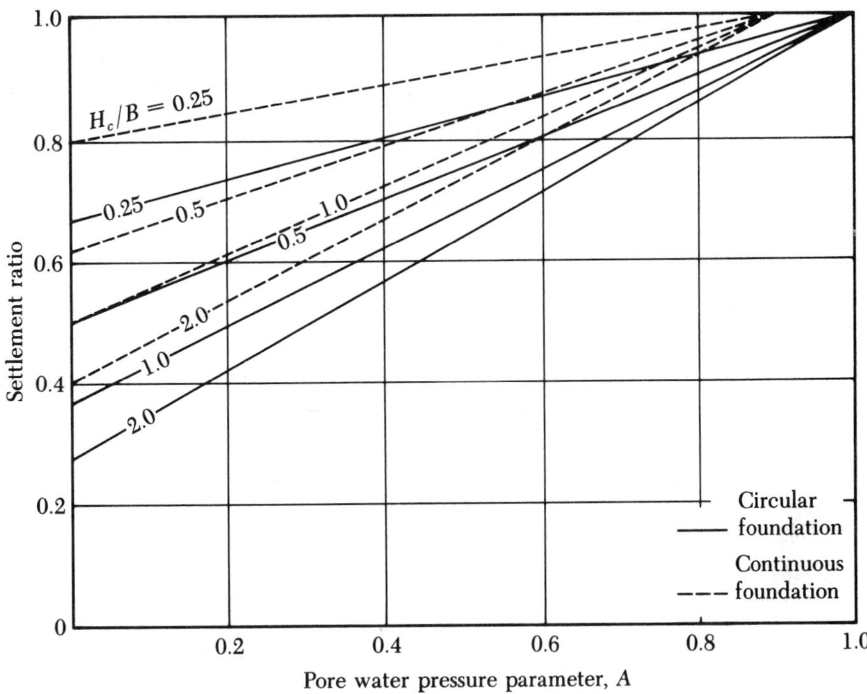

▼ **FIGURE 3.36** Settlement ratios for circular (K_{cir}) and continuous (K_{str}) foundations

4. Obtain the settlement ratio—in this case, from Figure 3.36.
5. Calculate the actual consolidation settlement:

$$S_c = S_{c(oed)} \times \text{settlement ratio} \tag{3.98}$$

This technique is generally referred to as the *Skempton–Bjerrum modification* for consolidation settlement calculation.

3.21 VERTICAL STRESS INCREASE IN A SOIL MASS CAUSED BY FOUNDATION LOAD (FOR CONSOLIDATION SETTLEMENT CALCULATION)

Stress Due to a Concentrated Load

In 1885, Boussinesq developed the mathematical relationships for determining the normal and shear stresses at any point inside *homogeneous, elastic,* and *isotropic* mediums due to a *concentrated point load* located at the surface, as shown in

Figure 3.37. According to his analysis, the *vertical stress increase* (Δp) at point A (Figure 3.37) caused by the point load of magnitude P is

$$\Delta p = \frac{3P}{2\pi z^2\left[1+\left(\frac{r}{z}\right)^2\right]^{5/2}} \tag{3.99}$$

where $r = \sqrt{x^2 + y^2}$

x, y, z = coordinates of the point A

Note that Eq. (3.99) is not a function of the Poisson's ratio of the soil.

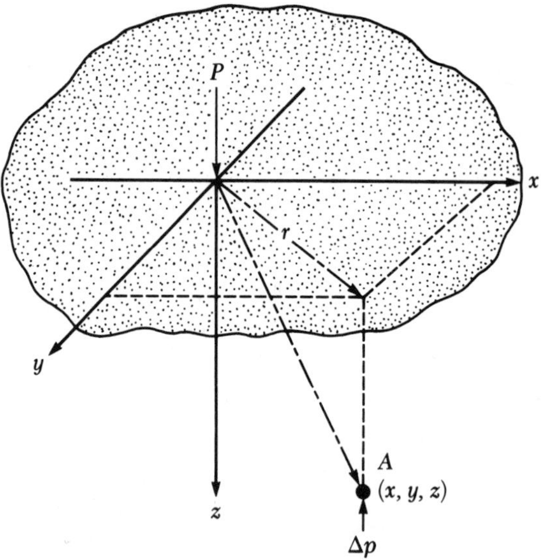

▼ **FIGURE 3.37** Vertical stress at a point, A, caused by a point load on the surface

Stress Due to a Circularly Loaded Area

The Boussinesq equation [Eq. (3.99)] can also be used to determine the vertical stress below the center of a flexible circularly loaded area, as shown in Figure 3.38a. Let the radius of the loaded area be $B/2$, and q_o be the uniformly distributed load per unit area. To determine the stress increase at a point A, located at depth z below the center of the circular area, consider an elemental area on the circle, as shown in Figure 3.38a The load on this elemental area may be considered as a point load and expressed as $q_o r\, d\theta\, dr$. The stress increase at point A caused by this load can be determined from Eq. (3.99):

$$dp = \frac{3(q_o r\, d\theta\, dr)}{2\pi z^2\left[1+\left(\frac{r}{z}\right)^2\right]^{5/2}} \tag{3.100}$$

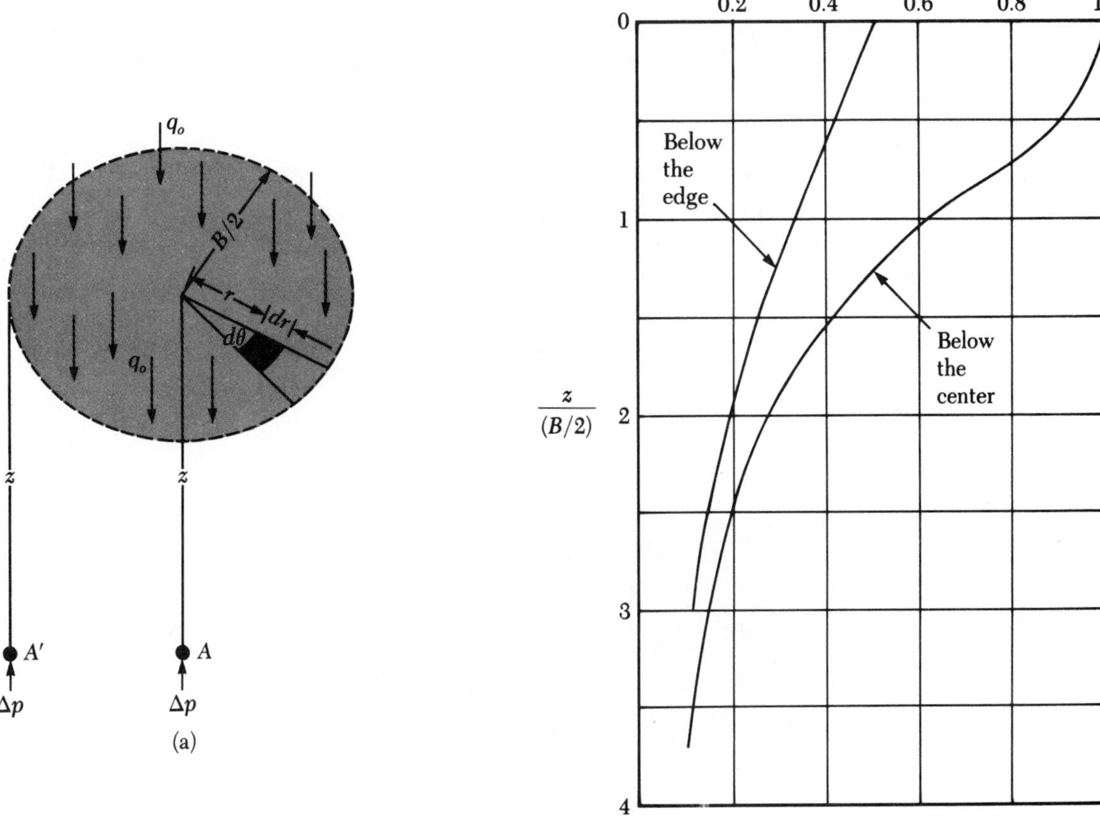

▼ **FIGURE 3.38** Increase of pressure under a uniformly loaded flexible circular area

Thus the total increase of stress caused by the entire loaded area may be obtained by integration of Eq. (3.100), or

$$\Delta p = \int dp = \int_{\theta=0}^{\theta=2\pi} \int_{r=0}^{r=B/2} \frac{3(q_o r\, d\theta\, dr)}{2\pi z^2\left[1+\left(\dfrac{r}{z}\right)^2\right]^{5/2}}$$

$$= q_o\left\{1 - \frac{1}{\left[1+\left(\dfrac{B}{2z}\right)^2\right]^{3/2}}\right\} \tag{3.101}$$

Based on Eq. (3.101), Figure 3.38b shows a plot of $\Delta p/q_o$ against $z/(B/2)$. A similar integration could be performed to obtain the stress increase at point A' (Figure 3.38a), located at depth z below the loaded area. The variation of $\Delta p/q_o$ for point A' is also shown in Figure 3.38b.

Stress Below a Rectangular Area

The integration technique of Boussinesq's equation also allows evaluation of the vertical stress at any point A below a flexible rectangular loaded area (Figure 3.39a). To do that, consider an elementary area $dA = dx\ dy$ on the flexible loaded area. If the load per unit area is q_o, the total load on the elemental area is

$$dP = q_o\ dx\ dy \tag{3.102}$$

This elemental load, dP, may be treated as a point load. The increase of vertical stress at point A caused by dP may be evaluated by using Eq. (3.99). Note, however, the need to substitute $dP = q_o\ dx\ dy$ for P, and $x^2 + y^2$ for r^2, in Eq. (3.99). Thus

$$\text{The stress increase at } A \text{ caused by } dP = \frac{3q_o(dx\ dy)z^3}{2\pi(x^2 + y^2 + z^2)^{5/2}}$$

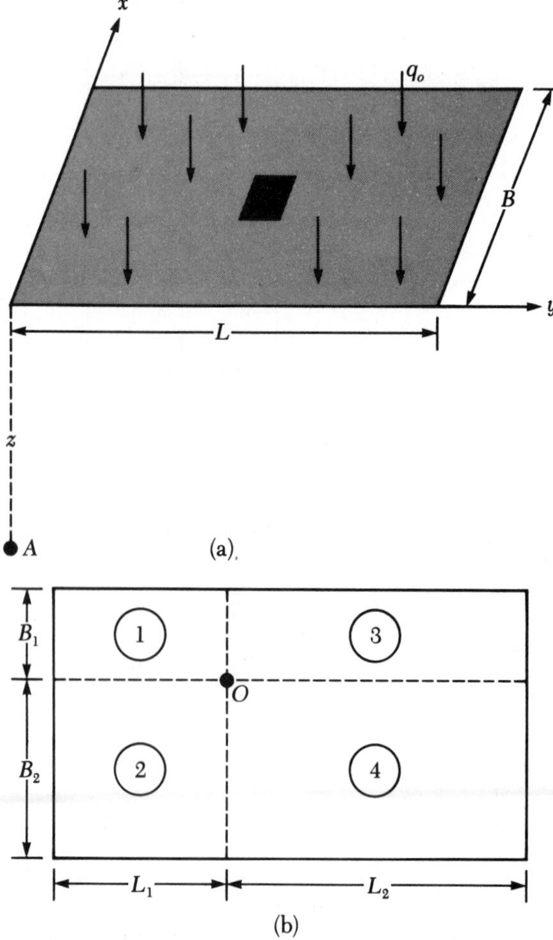

▼ **FIGURE 3.39** Determination of stress below a flexible rectangular loaded area

The total stress increase caused by the entire loaded area at point A may now be obtained by integrating the preceding equation:

$$\Delta p = \int_{y=0}^{L} \int_{x=0}^{B} \frac{3q_o(dx\ dz)z^3}{2\pi(x^2 + y^2 + z^2)^{5/2}} = q_o I \tag{3.103}$$

where Δp = stress increase at A

$$I = \text{influence factor} = \frac{1}{4\pi}\left(\frac{2mn\sqrt{m^2+n^2+1}}{m^2+n^2+m^2n^2+1} \cdot \frac{m^2+n^2+2}{m^2+n^2+1} + \tan^{-1}\frac{2mn\sqrt{m^2+n^2+1}}{m^2+n^2+1-m^2n^2}\right) \tag{3.104}$$

and

$$m = \frac{B}{z} \tag{3.105}$$

$$n = \frac{L}{z} \tag{3.106}$$

The variations of the influence values with m and n are given in Table 3.11. For convenience, they are also plotted in Figure 3.40 (page 198).

The stress increase at any point below a rectangular loaded area can also be found by using Eq. (3.103) in conjunction with Figure 3.39b. To determine the stress at depth z below point O, divide the loaded area into four rectangles. Point O is the corner common to each rectangle. Then use Eq. (3.103) to calculate the increase of stress at depth z below point O caused by each rectangular area. The total stress increase caused by the entire loaded area may now be expressed as

$$\Delta p = q_o(I_1 + I_2 + I_3 + I_4) \tag{3.107}$$

where I_1, I_2, I_3, and I_4 = the influence values of rectangles 1, 2, 3, and 4, respectively

The use of this technique is illustrated in Example 3.11 on page 204. Also, Figure 3.41 shows the variation of $\Delta p/q_o$ below the center of rectangular areas with $L/B = 1, 1.5, 2$, and ∞, as calculated from Table 3.11.

Stress Increase Under a Rectangular Foundation—2 : 1 Method

Foundation engineers often use an approximate method to determine the increase of stress with depth caused by the construction of a foundation. It is referred to as the *2 : 1*

TABLE 3.11 Variation of Influence Value, I [Eq. (3.104)][a]

	n											
m	0.1	0.2	0.3	0.4	0.5	0.6	0.7	0.8	0.9	1.0	1.2	1.4
0.1	0.00470	0.00917	0.01323	0.01678	0.01978	0.02223	0.02420	0.02576	0.02698	0.02794	0.02926	0.03007
0.2	0.00917	0.01790	0.02585	0.03280	0.03866	0.04348	0.04735	0.05042	0.05283	0.05471	0.05733	0.05894
0.3	0.01323	0.02585	0.03735	0.04742	0.05593	0.06294	0.06858	0.07308	0.07661	0.07938	0.08323	0.08561
0.4	0.01678	0.03280	0.04742	0.06024	0.07111	0.08009	0.08734	0.09314	0.09770	0.10129	0.10631	0.10941
0.5	0.01978	0.03866	0.05593	0.07111	0.08403	0.09473	0.10340	0.11035	0.11584	0.12018	0.12626	0.13003
0.6	0.02223	0.04348	0.06294	0.08009	0.09473	0.10688	0.11679	0.12474	0.13105	0.13605	0.14309	0.14749
0.7	0.02420	0.04735	0.06858	0.08734	0.10340	0.11679	0.12772	0.13653	0.14356	0.14914	0.15703	0.16199
0.8	0.02576	0.05042	0.07308	0.09314	0.11035	0.12474	0.13653	0.14607	0.15371	0.15978	0.16843	0.17389
0.9	0.02698	0.05283	0.07661	0.09770	0.11584	0.13105	0.14356	0.15371	0.16185	0.16835	0.17766	0.18357
1.0	0.02794	0.05471	0.07938	0.10129	0.12018	0.13605	0.14914	0.15978	0.16835	0.17522	0.18508	0.19139
1.2	0.02926	0.05733	0.08323	0.10631	0.12626	0.14309	0.15703	0.16843	0.17766	0.18508	0.19584	0.20278
1.4	0.03007	0.05894	0.08561	0.10941	0.13003	0.14749	0.16199	0.17389	0.18357	0.19139	0.20278	0.21020
1.6	0.03058	0.05994	0.08709	0.11135	0.13241	0.15028	0.16515	0.17739	0.18737	0.19546	0.20731	0.21510
1.8	0.03090	0.06058	0.08804	0.11260	0.13395	0.15207	0.16720	0.17967	0.18986	0.19814	0.21032	0.21836
2.0	0.03111	0.06100	0.08867	0.11342	0.13496	0.15326	0.16856	0.18119	0.19152	0.19994	0.21235	0.22058
2.5	0.03138	0.06155	0.08948	0.11450	0.13628	0.15483	0.17036	0.18321	0.19375	0.20236	0.21512	0.22364
3.0	0.03150	0.06178	0.08982	0.11495	0.13684	0.15550	0.17113	0.18407	0.19470	0.20341	0.21633	0.22499
4.0	0.03158	0.06194	0.09007	0.11527	0.13724	0.15598	0.17168	0.18469	0.19540	0.20417	0.21722	0.22600
5.0	0.03160	0.06199	0.09014	0.11537	0.13737	0.15612	0.17185	0.18488	0.19561	0.20440	0.21749	0.22632
6.0	0.03161	0.06201	0.09017	0.11541	0.13741	0.15617	0.17191	0.18496	0.19569	0.20449	0.21760	0.22644
8.0	0.03162	0.06202	0.09018	0.11543	0.13744	0.15621	0.17195	0.18500	0.19574	0.20455	0.21767	0.22652
10.0	0.03162	0.06202	0.09019	0.11544	0.13745	0.15622	0.17196	0.18502	0.19576	0.20457	0.21769	0.22654
∞	0.03162	0.06202	0.09019	0.11544	0.13745	0.15623	0.17197	0.18502	0.19577	0.20458	0.21770	0.22656

[a] After Newmark (1935)

▼ TABLE 3.11 (Continued)

	n										
m	1.6	1.8	2.0	2.5	3.0	4.0	5.0	6.0	8.0	10.0	∞
0.1	0.03058	0.03090	0.03111	0.03138	0.03150	0.03158	0.03160	0.03161	0.03162	0.03162	0.03162
0.2	0.05994	0.06058	0.06100	0.06155	0.06178	0.06194	0.06199	0.06201	0.06202	0.06202	0.06202
0.3	0.08709	0.08804	0.08867	0.08948	0.08982	0.09007	0.09014	0.09017	0.09018	0.09019	0.09019
0.4	0.11135	0.11260	0.11342	0.11450	0.11495	0.11527	0.11537	0.11541	0.11543	0.11544	0.11544
0.5	0.13241	0.13395	0.13496	0.13628	0.13684	0.13724	0.13737	0.13741	0.13744	0.13745	0.13745
0.6	0.15028	0.15207	0.15236	0.15483	0.15550	0.15598	0.15612	0.15617	0.15621	0.15622	0.15623
0.7	0.16515	0.16720	0.16856	0.17036	0.17113	0.17168	0.17185	0.17191	0.17195	0.17196	0.17197
0.8	0.17739	0.17967	0.18119	0.18321	0.18407	0.18469	0.18488	0.18496	0.18500	0.18502	0.18502
0.9	0.18737	0.18986	0.19152	0.19375	0.19470	0.19540	0.19561	0.19569	0.19574	0.19576	0.19577
1.0	0.19546	0.19814	0.19994	0.20236	0.20341	0.20417	0.20440	0.20449	0.20455	0.20457	0.20458
1.2	0.20731	0.21032	0.21235	0.21512	0.21633	0.21722	0.21749	0.21760	0.21767	0.21769	0.21770
1.4	0.21510	0.21836	0.22058	0.22364	0.22499	0.22600	0.22632	0.22644	0.22652	0.22654	0.22656
1.6	0.22025	0.22372	0.22610	0.22940	0.23088	0.23200	0.23236	0.23249	0.23258	0.23261	0.23263
1.8	0.22372	0.22736	0.22986	0.23334	0.23495	0.23617	0.23656	0.23671	0.23681	0.23684	0.23686
2.0	0.22610	0.22986	0.23247	0.23614	0.23782	0.23912	0.23954	0.23970	0.23981	0.23985	0.23987
2.5	0.22940	0.23334	0.23614	0.24010	0.24196	0.24344	0.24392	0.24412	0.24425	0.24429	0.24432
3.0	0.23088	0.23495	0.23782	0.24196	0.24394	0.24554	0.24608	0.24630	0.24646	0.24650	0.24654
4.0	0.23200	0.23617	0.23912	0.24344	0.24554	0.24729	0.24791	0.24817	0.24836	0.24842	0.24846
5.0	0.23236	0.23656	0.23954	0.24392	0.24608	0.24791	0.24857	0.24885	0.24907	0.24914	0.24919
6.0	0.23249	0.23671	0.23970	0.24412	0.24630	0.24817	0.24885	0.24916	0.24939	0.24946	0.24952
8.0	0.23258	0.23681	0.23981	0.24425	0.24646	0.24836	0.24907	0.24939	0.24964	0.24973	0.24980
10.0	0.23261	0.23684	0.23985	0.24429	0.24650	0.24842	0.24914	0.24946	0.24973	0.24981	0.24989
∞	0.23263	0.23686	0.23987	0.24432	0.24654	0.24846	0.24919	0.24952	0.24980	0.24989	0.25000

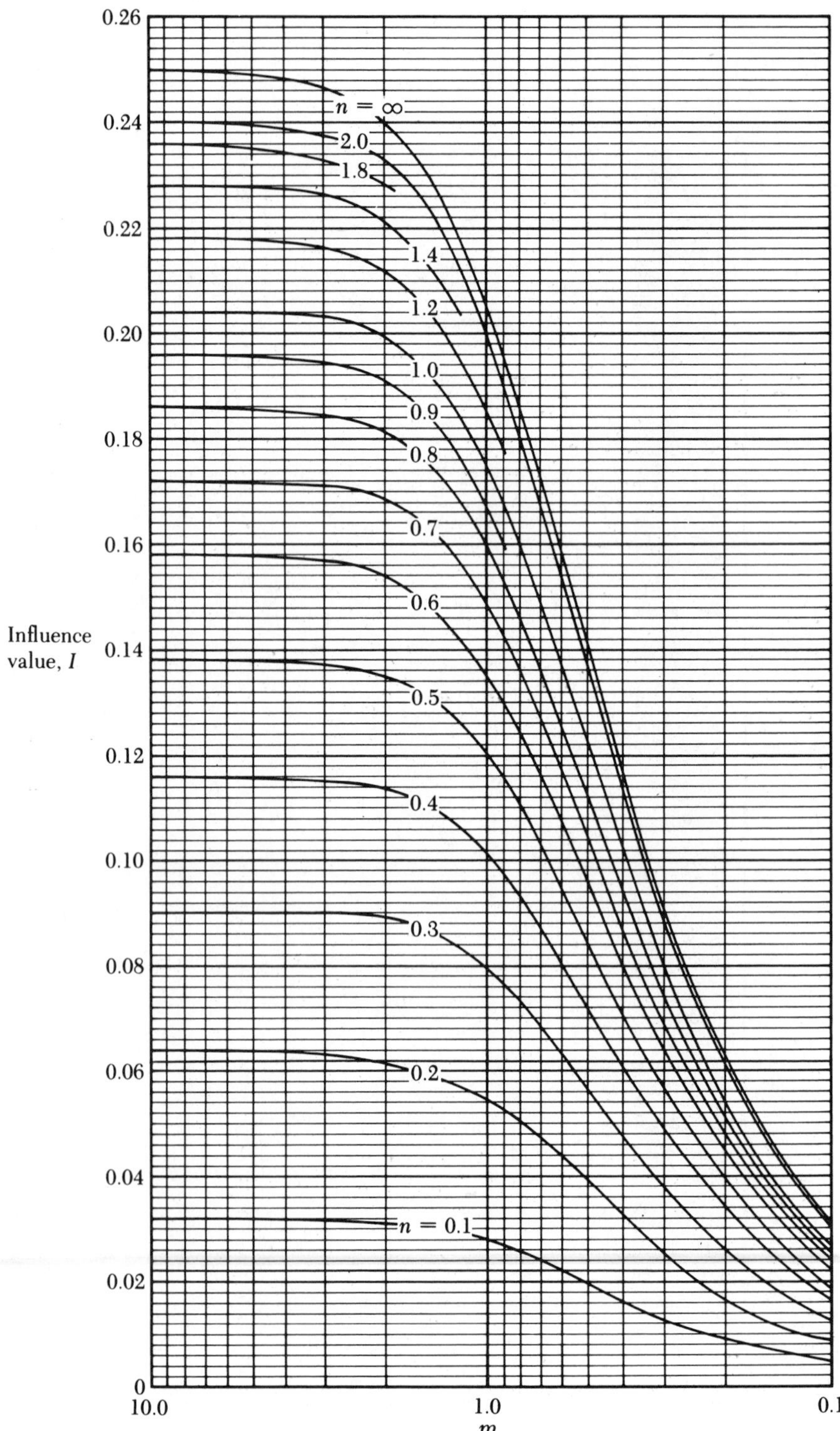

▼ **FIGURE 3.40** Variation of I with m and n—Eqs. (3.103) and (3.104)

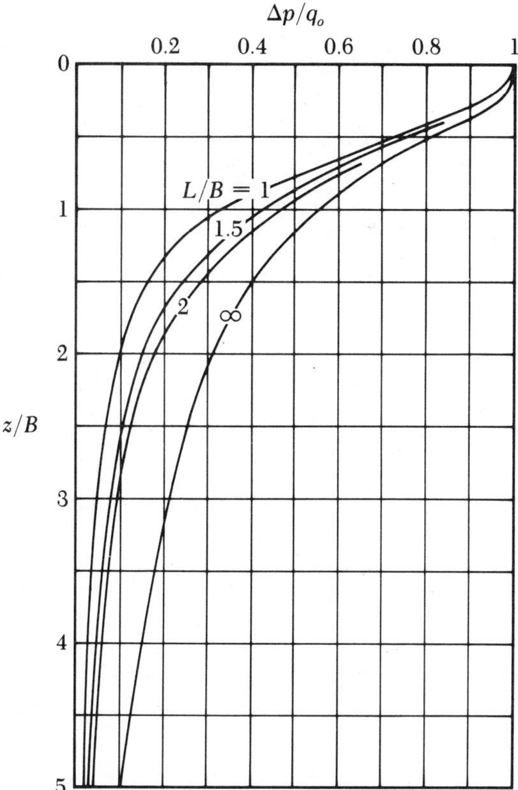

▼ **FIGURE 3.41** Increase of stress under the center of a flexible loaded rectangular area

method (Figure 3.42, page 200). According to this method, the increase of stress at depth z is

$$\Delta p = \frac{q_o \times B \times L}{(B + z)(L + z)} \tag{3.108}$$

Note that Eq. (3.108) is based on the assumption that the stress from the foundation spreads out along lines with a *2 vertical to 1 horizontal slope.*

Stress Increase Under an Embankment

Figure 3.43 shows the cross section of an embankment of height H. For this two-dimensional loading condition the vertical stress increase may be expressed as

$$\Delta p = \frac{q_o}{\pi}\left[\left(\frac{B_1 + B_2}{B_2}\right)(\alpha_1 + \alpha_2) - \frac{B_1}{B_2}(\alpha_2)\right] \tag{3.109}$$

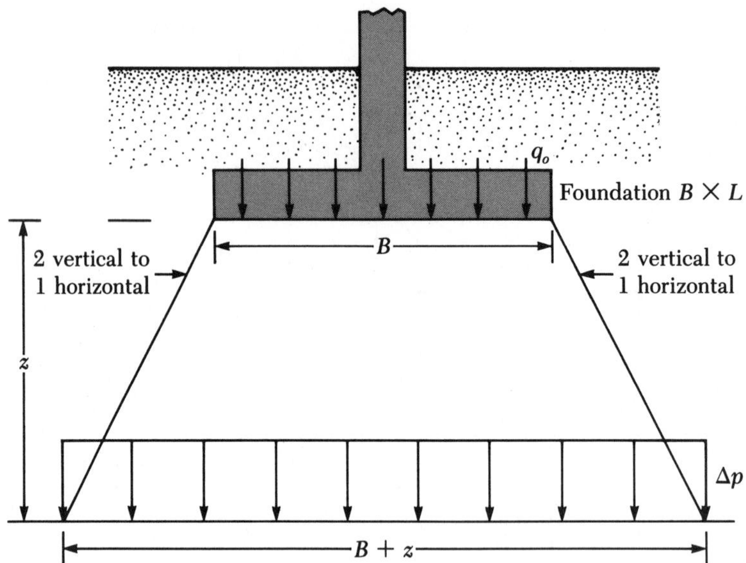

▼ **FIGURE 3.42** 2 : 1 method of finding stress increase under a foundation

where $q = \gamma H$
γ = unit weight of the embankment soil
H = height of the embankment

$$\alpha_1 \text{ (radians)} = \tan^{-1}\left(\frac{B_1 + B_2}{z}\right) - \tan^{-1}\left(\frac{B_1}{z}\right) \tag{3.110}$$

$$\alpha_2 = \tan^{-1}\left(\frac{B_1}{z}\right) \tag{3.111}$$

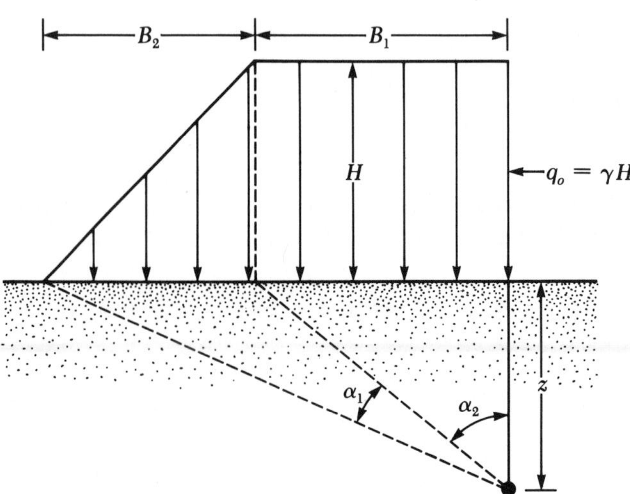

▼ **FIGURE 3.43** Embankment loading

For a detailed derivation of the equation, see Das (1983). A simplified form of Eq. (1.109) is

$$\Delta p = q_o I' \tag{3.112}$$

where I' = a function of B_1/z and B_2/z.

The variation of I' with B_1/z and B_2/z is shown in Figure 3.44. Application of this diagram is shown in Example 3.12 on page 204.

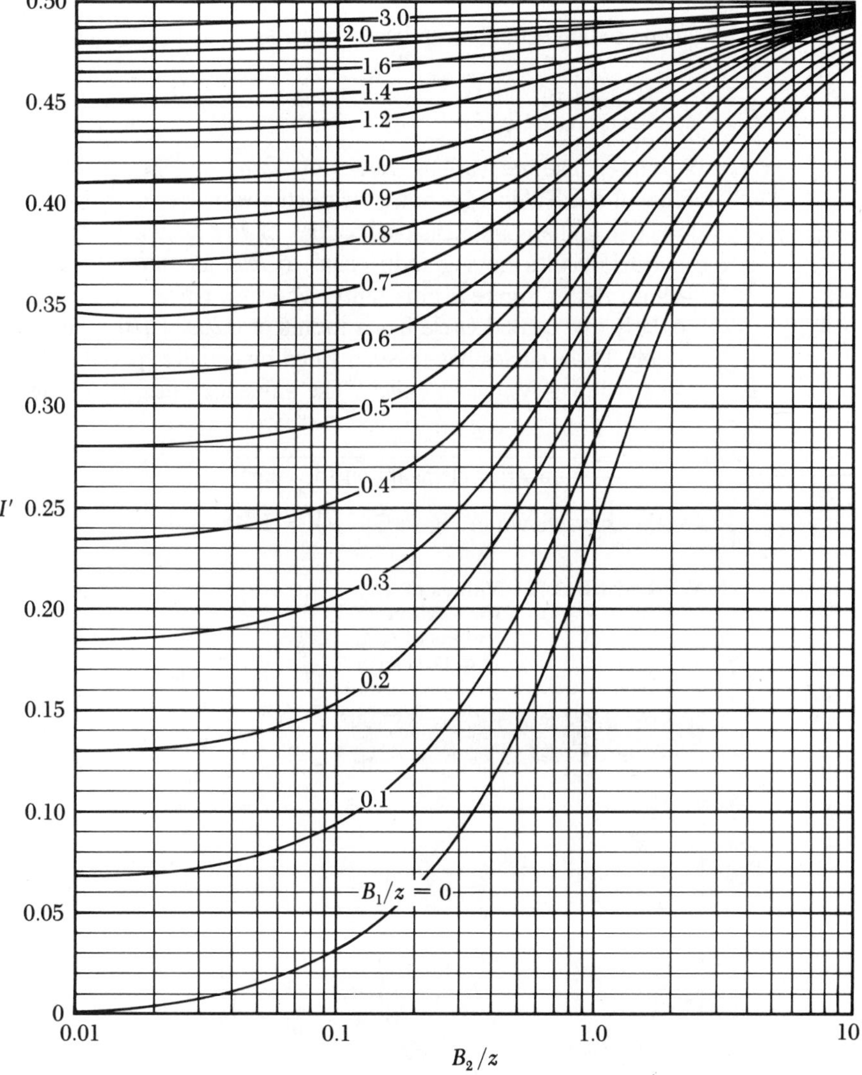

▼ **FIGURE 3.44** Influence value of I' for embankment loading (after Osterberg, 1957)

Stress Increase Due to Any Type of Loading

The increase of vertical stress under any type of flexible loaded area can be easily determined by the use of Newmark's (1942) *influence chart.* The chart, in principle, is based on Eq. (3.101) for the estimation of vertical stress increase under the center of a circularly loaded area. According to Eq. (3.101),

$$\Delta p = q_o\left\{1 - \frac{1}{\left[1 + \left(\frac{B}{2z}\right)^2\right]^{3/2}}\right\}$$

where $B/2$ = radius of the loaded area = R

The preceding equation can be rewritten as

$$\frac{R}{z} = \left[\left(1 - \frac{\Delta p}{q_o}\right)^{-2/3} - 1\right]^{1/2} \tag{3.113}$$

We now substitute various values of $\Delta p/q_o$ into Eq. (3.113) to obtain corresponding values of R/z. Table 3.12 shows the calculated values of R_z for $\Delta p/q_o = 0, 0.1, 0.2, \ldots, 1$.

Using the nondimensional values of R/z shown in Table 3.12, we can draw the concentric circles having radii equal to R/z, as shown in Figure 3.45. Note that the distance AB in Figure 3.45 is unity. The first circle is a point having a radius of zero. Similarly, the second circle has a radius of 0.2698 ($\overline{AB}$). The last circle has a radius of infinity. These circles have been divided by equally spaced radial lines, producing what is referred to as *Newmark's chart.* The influence value, IV, of this chart is

$$IV = \frac{1}{\text{number of elements on the chart}} \tag{3.114}$$

For the chart shown in Figure 3.45, $IV = 1/200 = 0.005$.

TABLE 3.12 **Values of R/z for Various Values of $\Delta p/q_o$ [Eq. (3.113)]**

$\Delta p/q_o$	R/z
0	0
0.1	0.2698
0.2	0.4005
0.3	0.5181
0.4	0.6370
0.5	0.7664
0.6	0.9174
0.7	1.1097
0.8	1.3871
0.9	1.9084
1.0	∞

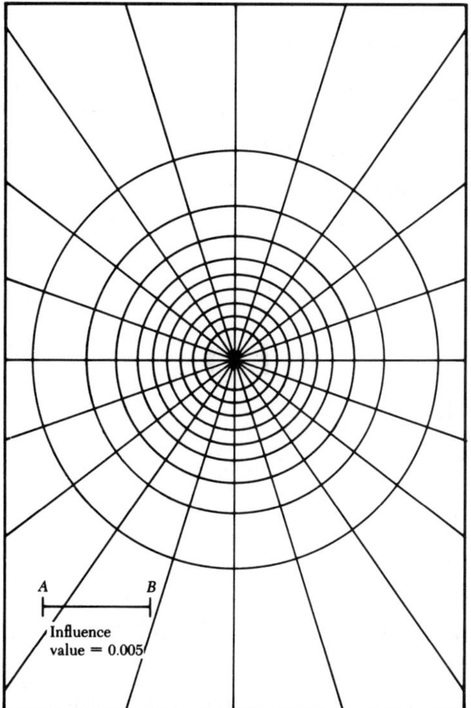

▼ **FIGURE 3.45** Influence chart for vertical pressure calculation (after Newmark, 1942)

Following is a step-by-step procedure for using Newmark's chart to determine vertical stress under a loaded area of any shape.

1. Identify the depth z below the loaded area at which the stress is to be determined.
2. Adopt a scale $z = \overline{AB}$ (that is, unit length according to Newmark's chart).
3. Draw the plan of the loaded area based on the scale adopted in Step 2.
4. Place the plan drawn in Step 3 on the Newmark's chart so that the point under which the stress is to be determined is directly above the center of the chart.
5. Count the number of elements of the chart that fall inside the plan. Let it equal N.
6. Calculate the stress increase as

$$\boxed{\Delta p = (IV)(N)(q_o)} \tag{3.115}$$

where q_o = load per unit area on the loaded area.

▼ EXAMPLE 3.11

A flexible rectangular area, 2.5 m × 5 m, is located on the ground surface and loaded with $q_o = 145\ \text{kN/m}^2$. Determine the stress increase caused by this loading at a depth of 6.25 m below the center of the rectangular area. Use Eq. (3.103).

Solution Refer to Figure 3.39. Hence

$$B_1 = \frac{2.5\ \text{m}}{2} = 1.25\ \text{m}$$

$$L_1 = \frac{5}{2} = 2.5\ \text{m}$$

From Eqs. (3.105) and (3.106)

$$m_1 = \frac{B_1}{z} = \frac{1.25}{6.25} = 0.2$$

$$n_1 = \frac{L_1}{z} = \frac{2.5}{6.25} = 0.4$$

From Table 3.11, for $m_1 = 0.20$ and $n_1 = 0.4$, the value of $I_1 = 0.0328$. Also note that $I_1 = I_2 = I_3 = I_4$. Thus

$$\Delta p = q_o(4I_1) = (145)(4)(0.0328) = \mathbf{19.02\ kN/m^2}$$ ▼

▼ EXAMPLE 3.12

An embankment is shown in Figure 3.46a. Determine the stress increase under the embankment at points A_1 and A_2.

Solution

$$\gamma H = (17.5)(7) = 122.5\ \text{kN/m}^2$$

Stress Increase at A_1

The left side of Figure 3.46b indicates that $B_1 = 2.5$ m and $B_2 = 14$ m. So

$$\frac{B_1}{z} = \frac{2.5}{5} = 0.5$$

$$\frac{B_2}{z} = \frac{14}{5} = 2.8$$

According to Figure 3.44, in this case, $I' = 0.445$. Because the two sides in Figure 3.46b are symmetrical, the value of I' for the right side will also be 0.445. So

$$\Delta p = \Delta p_1 + \Delta p_2 = q_o[I'_{(\text{left side})} + I'_{(\text{right side})}]$$

$$= 122.5[0.445 + 0.445] = \mathbf{109.03\ kN/m^2}$$

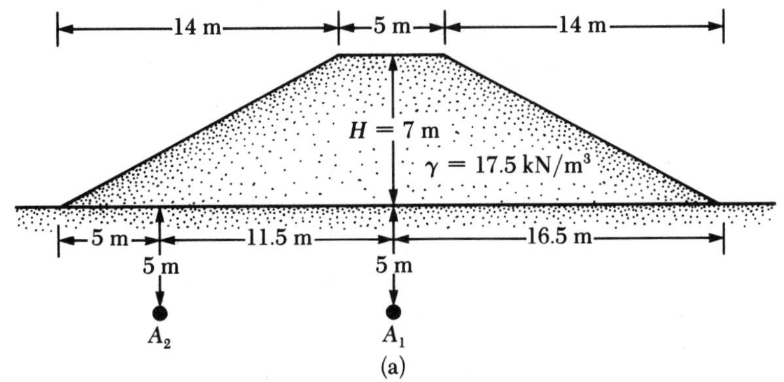
14 m
5 m
14 m
H = 7 m
γ = 17.5 kN/m³
5 m
11.5 m
16.5 m
5 m
5 m
A₂
A₁
(a)

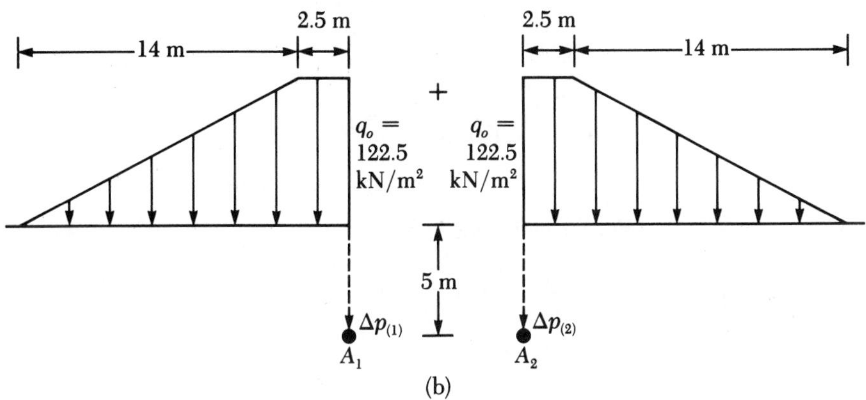
2.5 m
2.5 m
14 m
14 m
+
q₀ =
122.5
kN/m²
q₀ =
122.5
kN/m²
5 m
Δp(1)
A₁
Δp(2)
A₂
(b)

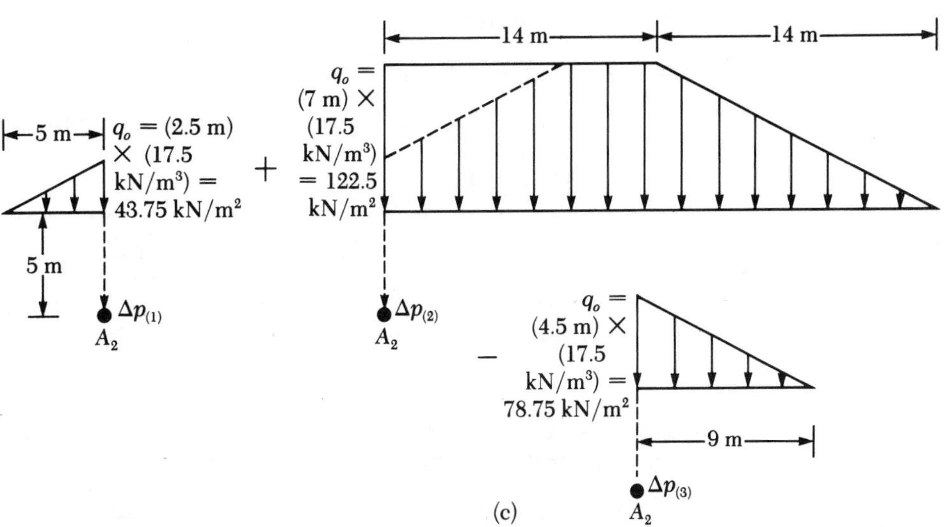
14 m
14 m
5 m
q₀ = (2.5 m)
× (17.5
kN/m³) =
43.75 kN/m²
+
q₀ =
(7 m) ×
(17.5
kN/m³)
= 122.5
kN/m²
5 m
Δp(1)
A₂
Δp(2)
A₂
−
q₀ =
(4.5 m) ×
(17.5
kN/m³) =
78.75 kN/m²
9 m
Δp(3)
A₂
(c)

▼ **FIGURE 3.46**

Stress Increase at A_2

Refer to Figure 3.46c. For the left side, $B_2 = 5$ m and $B_1 = 0$. So

$$\frac{B_2}{z} = \frac{5}{5} = 1$$

$$\frac{B_1}{z} = \frac{0}{5} = 0$$

According to Figure 3.44, for these values of B_2/z and B_1/z, $I' = 0.25$. So

$$\Delta p_1 = 43.75(0.25) = 10.94 \text{ kN/m}^2$$

For the middle section

$$\frac{B_2}{z} = \frac{14}{5} = 2.8$$

$$\frac{B_1}{z} = \frac{14}{5} = 2.8$$

Thus $I' = 0.495$. So

$$\Delta p_2 = 0.495(122.5) = 60.64 \text{ kN/m}^2$$

For the right side

$$\frac{B_2}{z} = \frac{9}{5} = 1.8$$

$$\frac{B_1}{z} = \frac{0}{5} = 0$$

and $I' = 0.335$. So

$$\Delta p_3 = (78.75)(0.335) = 26.38 \text{ kN/m}^2$$

Total stress increase at point A_2 is

$$\Delta p = \Delta p_1 + \Delta p_2 - \Delta p_3 = 10.94 + 60.64 - 26.38 = \mathbf{45.2 \text{ kN/m}^2}$$ ▼

▼ EXAMPLE 3.13

Redo Example 3.11 using the Newmark's chart shown in Figure 3.45.

Solution Here, $z = 6.25$ m, so length $\overline{AB}$ in Figure 3.45 is 6.25 m. With this scale, the plan of the loaded rectangular area can be drawn. Figure 3.47 shows this plan placed over the Newmark's chart with the center of the loaded area above the center of the chart. The reason for this placement is that the stress increase is required at a point immediately below the center of the rectangular area. The number of elements from the influence chart that are inside the plan is about 26. So

$$\Delta p = (IV)(N)(q_o) = (0.005)(26)(145) = \mathbf{18.85 \text{ kN/m}^2}$$

This value of Δp is practically the same as that determined in Example 3.11.

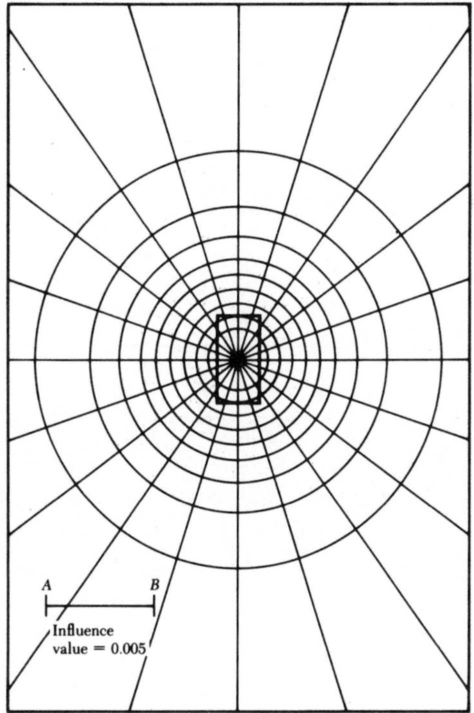

▼ FIGURE 3.47 ▼

▼ EXAMPLE 3.14

A foundation 1 m × 2 m in plan is shown in Figure 3.48. Estimate the total settlement of the foundation.

Solution

Elastic Settlement

The clay layer is located at a depth of 2 m—that is, $2B$ below the foundation. Figure 3.29 shows that the soil at a depth of $z > 2B$ has little influence on elastic settlement. Hence, if Eq. (3.79) is used for the elastic settlement calculation, use of the modulus of elasticity and Poisson's ratio values of the sand layer is reasonable. Thus

$$S_e = \frac{Bq_o}{E_s}(1 - \mu_s^2)\alpha_r$$

Here, $q_o = 150\ \text{kN/m}^2$, $E_s = 10{,}000\ \text{kN/m}^2$, $\mu_s = 0.3$, and $\alpha_r \approx 1.2$ (Figure 3.27). So

$$S_e = \frac{(1)(150)}{10{,}000}(1 - 0.3^2)(1.2) = 0.0163\ \text{m} = \mathbf{16.38\ mm}$$

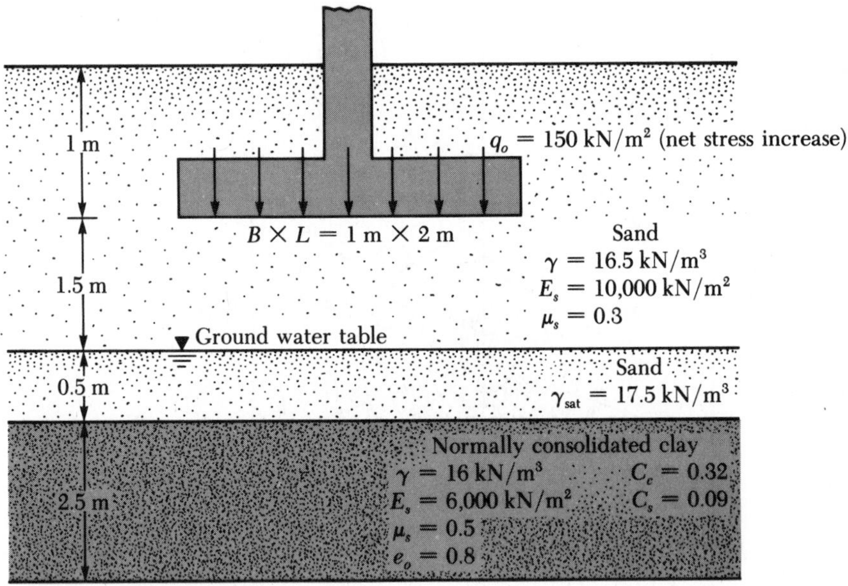

▼ **FIGURE 3.48**

Consolidation Settlement

The clay is normally consolidated. Thus

$$S_c = \frac{C_c H}{1 + e_o} \log \frac{p_o + \Delta p_{av}}{p_o}$$

$$p_o = (2.5)(16.5) + (0.5)(17.5 - 9.81) + 1.25(16 - 9.81)$$

$$= 41.25 + 3.85 + 7.74 = 52.84 \text{ kN/m}^2$$

From Eq. (3.93)

$$\Delta p_{av} = \frac{1}{6}(\Delta p_t + 4\Delta p_m + \Delta p_b)$$

Using the 2 : 1 method

$$\Delta p = \frac{q_o \times B \times L}{(B + z)(L + z)}$$

For the top of the clay layer, $z = 2$ m, so

$$\Delta p_t = \frac{(150)(1)(2)}{(1 + 2)(2 + 2)} = 25 \text{ kN/m}^2$$

Similarly,

$$\Delta p_m = \frac{(150)(1)(2)}{(1 + 3.25)(2 + 3.25)} = 13.45 \text{ kN/m}^2$$

and

$$\Delta p_b = \frac{(150)(1)(2)}{(1 + 4.5)(2 + 4.5)} = 8.39 \text{ kN/m}^2$$

Thus

$$\Delta p_{av} = \frac{1}{6}[25 + 4(13.45) + 8.39] = 14.53 \text{ kN/m}^2$$

So

$$S_c = \frac{(0.32)(2.5)}{1 + 0.8}\log\left(\frac{52.84 + 14.53}{52.84}\right) = 0.0469 \text{ m} = \mathbf{46.90 \text{ mm}}$$

Hence the total settlement $= S = S_e + S_c = 16.38 + 46.90 =$ **63.28 mm**

Note: The total settlement just calculated may exceed the tolerable settlement of the foundation. However, the foundation size may be changed so that it will carry the same total load of 300 kN but cause less settlement. ▼

3.22 CONSOLIDATION SETTLEMENT—GENERAL COMMENTS AND A CASE HISTORY

In predicting the consolidation settlement and the time rate of settlement for actual field conditions, an engineer has to make several simplifying assumptions. They include the compression index, coefficient of consolidation, preconsolidation pressure, drainage conditions, and thickness of the clay layer. Soil layering is not always uniform with ideal properties; hence field performance may deviate from the prediction, requiring adjustments during construction. The following case history on consolidation, as reported by Schnabel (1972), illustrates this reality.

Figure 3.49 shows the subsoil conditions for the construction of a school building in Waldorf, Maryland. Upper Pleistocene sand and gravel soils are underlain by deposits of very loose fine silty sand, soft silty clay, and clayey silt. The softer surface layers are underlain by various layers of stiff to firm silty clay, clayey silt, and sandy silt to a depth of 50 ft. Before construction of the building began, a compacted fill having a thickness of 8–10 ft was placed on the ground surface. This fill initiated the consolidation settlement in the soft silty clay and clayey silt.

To predict the time rate of settlement, based on the laboratory test results, the engineers made the following approximations.

a. The preconsolidation pressure, p_c, was 1600 to 2800 lb/ft^2 *in excess* of the existing overburden pressure.
b. The swell index, C_s, was 0.01 to 0.03.
c. For the more compressive layers $C_v \approx 0.36$ ft^2/day, and for the stiffer soil layers $C_v \approx 3.1$ ft^2/day.

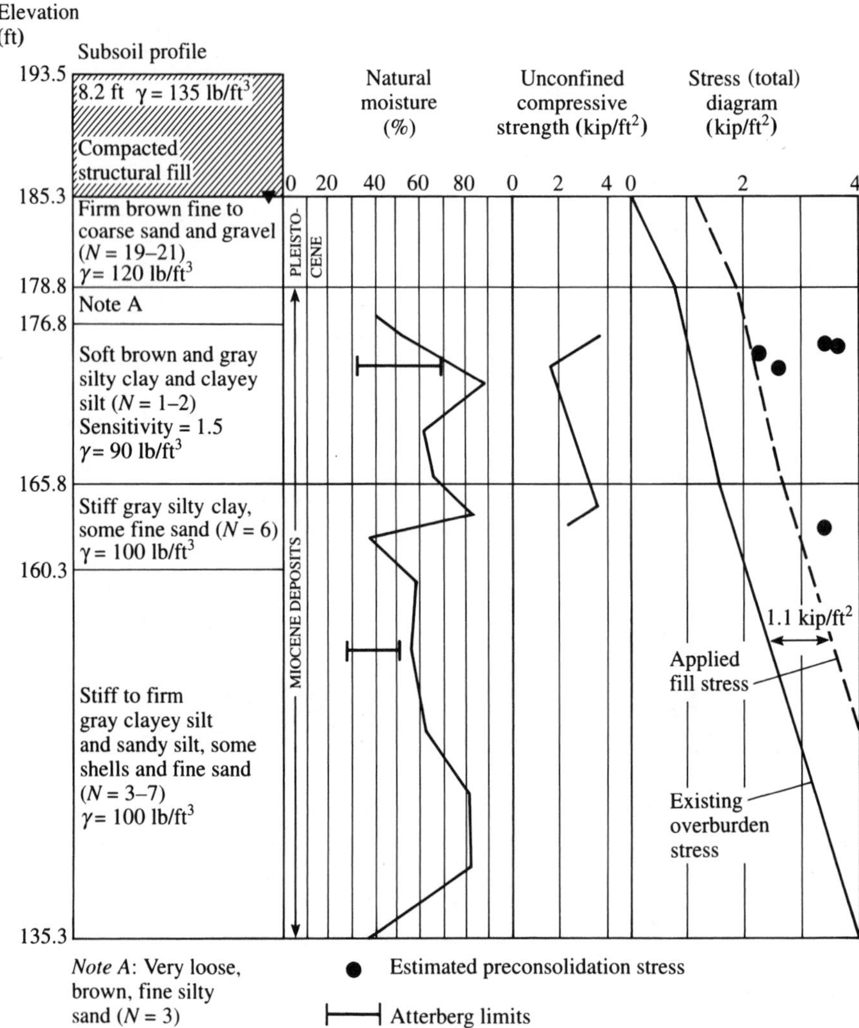

▼ **FIGURE 3.49** Subsoil conditions for the construction of school building (*note:* SPT N values are uncorrected; after Schnabel, 1972)

The total consolidation settlement was estimated to be about 3 in. Under double drainage conditions, 90% settlement was expected to occur in 114 days.

Figure 3.50 shows a comparison of measured and predicted settlement with time, which indicates that

a. $\dfrac{S_{c\text{(observed)}}}{S_{c\text{(estimated)}}} \approx 0.47$

b. 90% of the settlement occurred in about 70 days; hence, $t_{90\text{(observed)}}/t_{90\text{(estimated)}} \approx 0.58$.

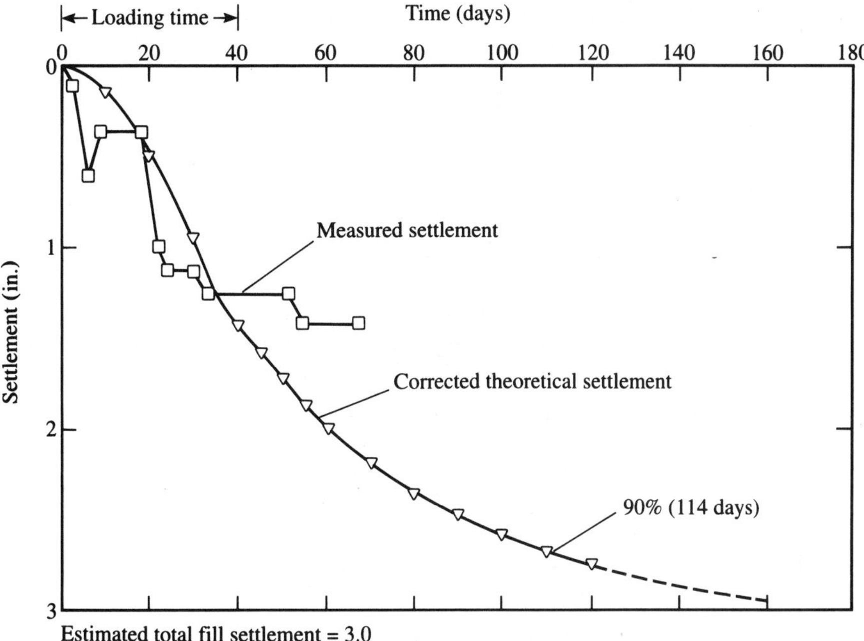

▼ **FIGURE 3.50** Comparison of measured and predicted consolidation settlement with time (after Schnabel, 1972)

The relatively rapid settlement in the field is believed to be due to the presence of a fine sand layer within the Miocene deposits.

3.23 ALLOWABLE BEARING PRESSURE IN SAND BASED ON SETTLEMENT CONSIDERATION

Meyerhof (1956) proposed a correlation for the *net allowable bearing pressure* for foundations with the standard penetration resistance, N. The net pressure was defined in Eq. (3.20) as

$$q_{\text{net(all)}} = q_{\text{all}} - \gamma D_f \tag{3.116}$$

According to Meyerhof's theory, for 1 in. (25.4 mm) of estimated maximum settlement

$$q_{\text{net(all)}}\ (\text{kN/m}^2) = 11.98\ N \qquad (\text{for } B \leq 1.22 \text{ m}) \tag{3.117a}$$

$$q_{\text{net(all)}}\ (\text{kN/m}^2) = 7.99N\left(\frac{3.28B + 1}{3.28B}\right)^2 \qquad (\text{for } B > 1.22 \text{ m}) \tag{3.117b}$$

where N = corrected standard penetration number

Note that in Eqs. (3.117a) and (3.117b) B is in meters.

In English units

$$q_{\text{net(all)}}\ (\text{kip/ft}^2) = \frac{N}{4} \qquad (\text{for } B \le 4 \text{ ft}) \tag{3.118a}$$

and

$$q_{\text{net(all)}}\ (\text{kip/ft}^2) = \frac{N}{6}\left(\frac{B+1}{B}\right)^2 \qquad (\text{for } B > 4 \text{ ft}) \tag{3.118b}$$

Since Meyerhof proposed his original correlation, researchers have observed that its results are rather conservative. Later, Meyerhof (1965) suggested that the net allowable bearing pressure should be increased by about 50%. Bowles (1977) proposed that the modified form of the bearing pressure equations be expressed as

$$q_{\text{net(all)}}\ (\text{kN/m}^2) = 19.16NF_d\left(\frac{S}{25.4}\right) \qquad (\text{for } B \le 1.22 \text{ m}) \tag{3.119a}$$

$$q_{\text{net(all)}}\ (\text{kN/m}^2) = 11.98N\left(\frac{3.28B+1}{3.28B}\right)^2 F_d\left(\frac{S}{25.4}\right) \qquad (\text{for } B > 1.22 \text{ m}) \tag{3.119b}$$

where F_d = depth factor $= 1 + 0.33(D_f/B) \le 1.33$ (3.120)

S = tolerable settlement, in mm

Again, the unit of B is meters.

In English units

$$q_{\text{net(all)}}\ (\text{kip/ft}^2) = \frac{N}{2.5} F_d S \qquad (\text{for } B \le 4 \text{ ft}) \tag{3.121a}$$

$$q_{\text{net(all)}}\ (\text{kip/ft}^2) = \frac{N}{4}\left(\frac{B+1}{B}\right)^2 F_d S \qquad (\text{for } B > 4 \text{ ft}) \tag{3.121b}$$

where F_d is given by Eq. (3.120)

S = tolerable settlement, in in.

The empirical relations just presented may raise some questions. For example, which value of the standard penetration number should be used, and what is the effect of the water table on the net allowable bearing capacity? The design value of N should be determined by taking into account the N values for a depth of $2B$ to $3B$, measured from the bottom of the foundation. Many engineers are also of the opinion that the N value should be reduced somewhat if the water table is close to the foundation. However, the author believes that this reduction is not required because the penetration resistance reflects the location of the water table.

Meyerhof (1956) also prepared empirical relations for the net allowable bearing capacity of foundations based on the cone penetration resistance, q_c:

$$q_{\text{net(all)}} = \frac{q_c}{15} \qquad (\text{for } B \le 1.22 \text{ m and settlement of 25.4 mm}) \tag{3.122}$$

and

$$q_{\text{net(all)}} = \frac{q_c}{25}\left(\frac{3.28B + 1}{3.28B}\right)^2$$

$$\text{(for } B > 1.22 \text{ m and settlement of 25.4 mm)} \qquad (3.123)$$

Note that in Eqs. (3.122) and (3.123) the unit of B is meters, and the units of $q_{\text{net(all)}}$ and q_c are kN/m^2.

In English units

$$q_{\text{net(all)}}\ (\text{lb/ft}^2) = \frac{q_c\ (\text{lb/ft}^2)}{15} \qquad \text{(for } B \leq 4 \text{ ft and settlement of 1 in.)} \qquad (3.124\text{a})$$

and

$$q_{\text{net(all)}}\ (\text{lb/ft}^2) = \frac{q_c\ (\text{lb/ft}^2)}{25}\left(\frac{B + 1}{B}\right)^2$$

$$\text{(for } B > 4 \text{ ft and settlement of 1 in.)} \qquad (3.124\text{b})$$

Note that in Eq. (3.124), the unit of B is feet.

The basic philosophy behind the development of these correlations is that, if the maximum settlement is no more than 1 in. (25.4 mm) for any foundation, the differential settlement would be no more than 0.75 in. (19 mm). These are probably the allowable limits for most building foundation designs.

3.24 ALLOWABLE BEARING CAPACITY CHARTS

Peck et al. (1974) also developed charts of $q_{\text{net(all)}}$ for foundations of varying widths, B, on sand, corrected standard penetration numbers, N, and D_f/B. They are presented in Figure 3.51a, b, and c. These values of $q_{\text{net(all)}}$ correspond to a maximum settlement of 1 in. (25.4 mm). The flat lines in Figure 3.51 are slightly more conservative than Meyerhof's (1965) recommendation and probably should be increased by 50% to agree better with current recommendations.

3.25 FIELD LOAD TEST

The ultimate load-bearing capacity of a foundation, as well as the allowable bearing capacity based on tolerable settlement considerations, can be effectively determined from the field load test. It is generally referred to as the *plate load test* (ASTM, 1982; Test Designation D-1194-72). The plates that are used for tests in the field are usually made of steel and are 25 mm (1 in.) thick and 150 mm to 762 mm (6 in. to 30 in.) in diameter. Occasionally, square plates that are 305 mm × 305 mm (12 in. × 12 in.) are also used.

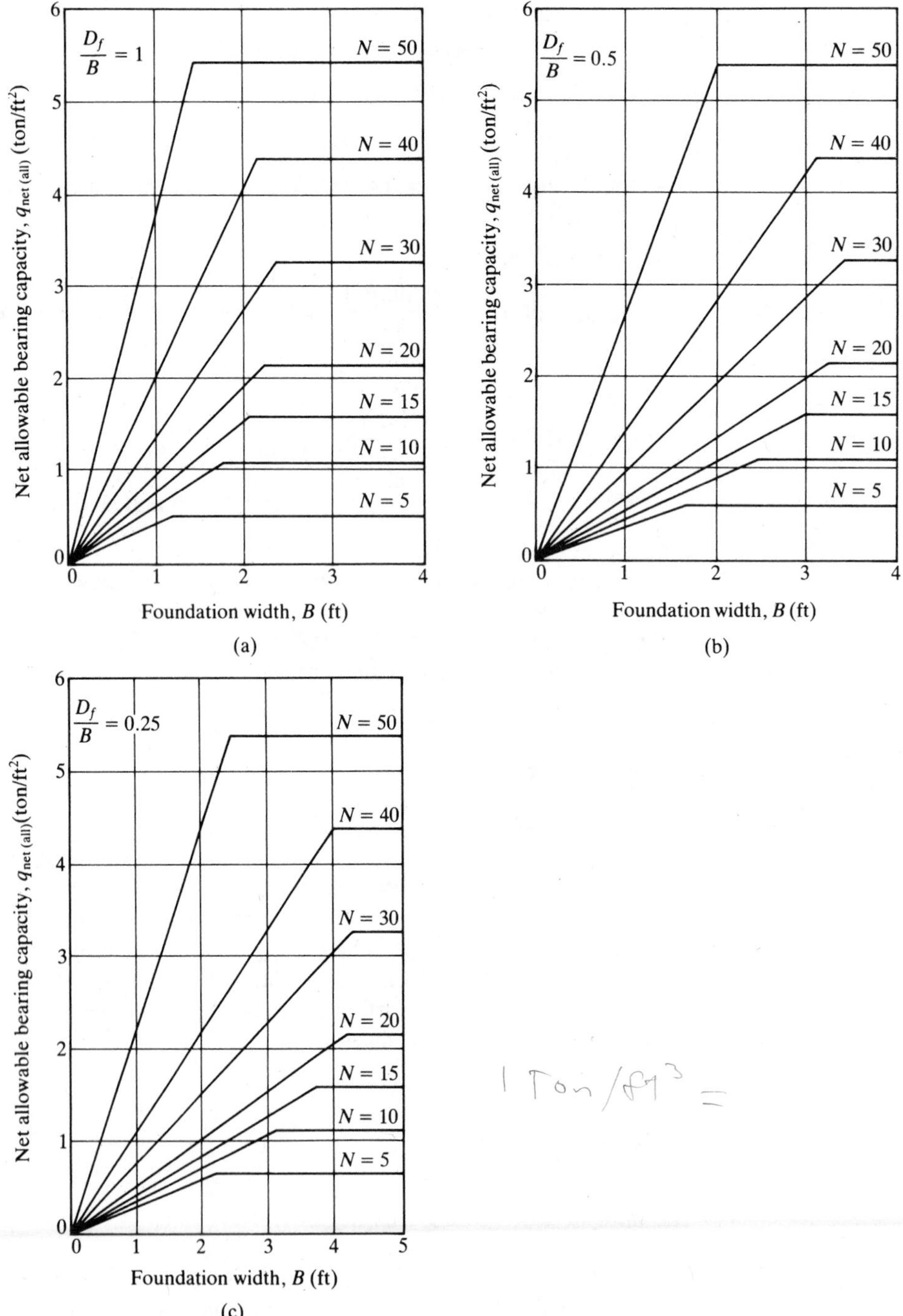

FIGURE 3.51 Correlation of net allowable bearing capacity in sand with standard penetration number for foundation settlements not exceeding 1 in. (25.4 mm) (after Peck et al., 1974)

1 Ton/ft³ =

To conduct a plate load test, a hole is excavated with a minimum diameter $4B$ (B = diameter of the test plate) to a depth of D_f (D_f = depth of the proposed foundation). The plate is placed at the center of the hole. Load is applied to the plate in steps—about one-fourth to one-fifth of the estimated ultimate load—by means of a jack. A schematic diagram of the test arrangement is shown in Figure 3.52a. During each step load application, the settlement of the plate is observed on dial gauges. At least one hour is allowed to elapse between each load application step. The test should be conducted until failure, or at least until the plate has gone through 25 mm (1 in.) of settlement. Figure 3.52b shows the nature of the load–settlement curve obtained from such tests, from which the ultimate load per unit area can be determined.

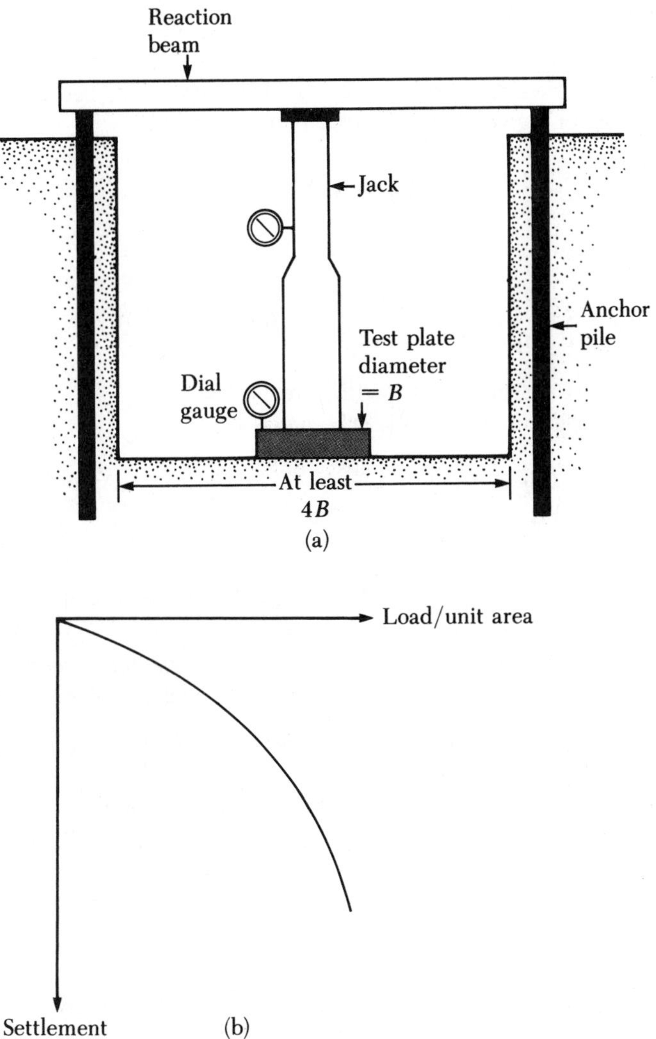

▼ **FIGURE 3.52** Plate load test: (a) test arrangement; (b) nature of load–settlement curve

For tests in clay

$$q_{u(F)} = q_{u(P)} \tag{3.125}$$

where $q_{u(F)}$ = ultimate bearing capacity of the proposed foundation
$q_{u(P)}$ = ultimate bearing capacity of the test plate

Equation (3.125) implies that the ultimate bearing capacity in clay is virtually independent of the size of the plate.

For tests in sandy soils

$$q_{u(F)} = q_{u(P)}\frac{B_F}{B_P} \tag{3.126}$$

where B_F = width of the foundation
B_P = width of the test plate

The allowable bearing capacity of a foundation, based on settlement considerations and for a given intensity of load, q_o, is

$$S_F = S_P\frac{B_F}{B_P} \quad \text{(for clayey soil)} \tag{3.127}$$

and

$$S_F = S_P\left(\frac{B_F}{B_P}\right)^2\left(\frac{3.28B_P + 1}{3.28B_F + 1}\right)^2 \quad \text{(for sandy soil)} \tag{3.128}$$

In Eq. (3.128), the units of B_P and B_F are meters.

In English units, Eq. (3.128) becomes

$$S_F = S_P\left(\frac{B_F}{B_P}\right)^2\left(\frac{B_P + 1}{B_F + 1}\right)^2 \tag{3.129}$$

In Eq. (3.129), B_F and B_P are in feet.

Equations (3.128) and (3.129) are based on the works of Terzaghi and Peck (1967). Example 3.15 illustrates their application.

Housel (1929) proposed a different technique for determining the load-bearing capacity of shallow foundations based on settlement considerations:

1. Requirement is to find the dimensions of a foundation that will carry a load of Q_o with a tolerable settlement of S_{tol}.
2. Conduct two plate load tests with plates of diameters B_1 and B_2.
3. From the load–settlement curves obtained in Step 2, determine the total loads on the plates (Q_1 and Q_2) that correspond to the settlement of S_{tol}.

   For plate no. 1, the total load can be expressed as

$$Q_1 = A_1 m + P_1 n \tag{3.130}$$

Similarly, for plate no. 2

$$Q_2 = A_2 m + P_2 n \tag{3.131}$$

where A_1, A_2 = areas of the plates no. 1 and no. 2, respectively
P_1, P_2 = perimeters of the plates no. 1 and no. 2, respectively
m, n = two constants that correspond to the bearing pressure and perimeter shear, respectively

The values of m and n can be determined by solving Eqs. (3.130) and (3.131).

4. For the foundation to be designed,

$$Q_o = Am + Pn \tag{3.132}$$

where A = area of the foundation
P = perimeter of the foundation

Because Q_o, m, and n are known, Eq. (3.132) can be solved to determine foundation width. An application of this procedure is presented in Example 3.16.

▼ EXAMPLE 3.15

The results of a plate load test in a sandy soil are shown in Figure 3.53. The size of the plate is 0.305 m × 0.305 m. Determine the size of a square column foundation that should carry a load of 2500 kN with a maximum settlement of 25 mm.

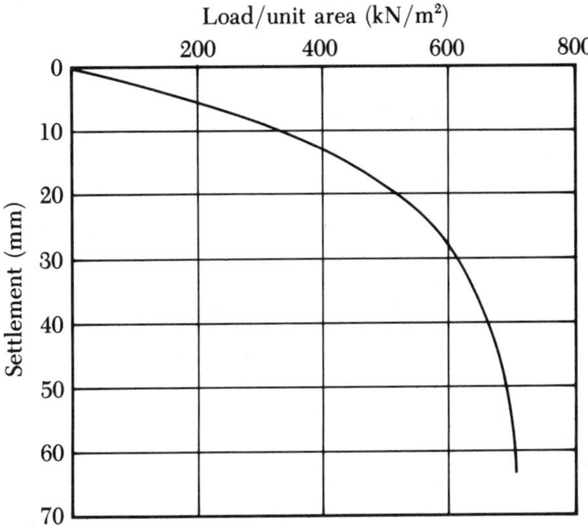

▼ **FIGURE 3.53**

Solution The problem has to be solved by trial and error. Use the following table and Eq. (3.128).

Q_o (kN) (1)	Assume width B_F (m) (2)	$q_o = \frac{Q_o}{B_F^2}$ (kN/m²) (3)	S_P corresponding to q_o in Col. 3 (mm) (4)	S_F from Eq. (3.128) (mm) (5)
2500	4.0	156.25	4.0	13.80
2500	3.0	277.80	8.0	26.35
2500	3.2	244.10	6.8	22.70
2500	3.1	260.10	7.2	23.86

So, a column footing with dimensions of **3.1 m × 3.1 m** will be appropriate. ▼

▼ EXAMPLE 3.16

The results of two plate load tests are given in the following table.

Plate diameter, B (m)	Total load, Q (kN)	Settlement (mm)
0.305	32.2	20
0.610	71.8	20

A square column foundation has to be constructed to carry a total load of 715 kN. The tolerable settlement is 20 mm. Determine the size of the foundation.

Solution Use Eqs. (3.130) and (3.131):

$$32.2 = \frac{\pi}{4}(0.305)^2 m + \pi(0.305)n \tag{a}$$

$$71.8 = \frac{\pi}{4}(0.610)^2 m + \pi(0.610)n \tag{b}$$

From (a) and (b),

$$m = 50.68 \text{ kN/m}^2$$

$$n = 29.75 \text{ kN/m}$$

For the foundation to be designed [Eq. (3.132)],

$$Q_o = Am + Pn$$

or

$$Q_o = B_F^2 m + 4B_F n$$

For $Q_o = 715$ kN,

$$715 = B_F^2(50.68) + 4B_f(29.75)$$

or

$$50.68B_F^2 + 119B_F - 715 = 0$$

$$B_F \approx \mathbf{2.8\ m} \qquad \blacktriangledown$$

3.26 PRESUMPTIVE BEARING CAPACITY

Several building codes (for example, Uniform Building Code, Chicago Building Code, New York City Building Code) specify the allowable bearing capacity of foundations on various types of soil. For minor construction, they often provide fairly acceptable guidelines. However, these bearing capacity values are based primarily on the *visual* classification of near-surface soils. They generally do not take into consideration factors such as the stress history of the soil, water table location, depth of the foundation, and tolerable settlement. So, for large construction projects, the codes' presumptive values should be used only as guides.

3.27 TOLERABLE SETTLEMENT OF BUILDINGS

As has been emphasized in this chapter, settlement analysis is an important part of the design and construction of foundations. Large settlements of various components of a structure may lead to considerable damage and/or may interfere with the proper functioning of the structure. Limited studies have been made to evaluate the conditions for tolerable settlement of various types of structure (for example, Bjerrum, 1963; Burland and Worth, 1974; Grant et al. 1974; Polshin and Tokar, 1957; and Wahls, 1981). Wahls (1981) has provided an excellent review of these studies.

Figure 3.54 gives the parameters for definition of tolerable settlement. Figure 3.54a is for a structure that has undergone settlement without tilt; Figure 3.54b is for a structure that has undergone settlement with tilt.

The parameters are

ρ_i = total vertical displacement at point i

δ_{ij} = differential settlement between points i and j

Δ = relative deflection

ω = tilt

$$\eta_{ij} = \frac{\delta_{ij}}{l_{ij}} - \omega = \text{angular distortion}$$

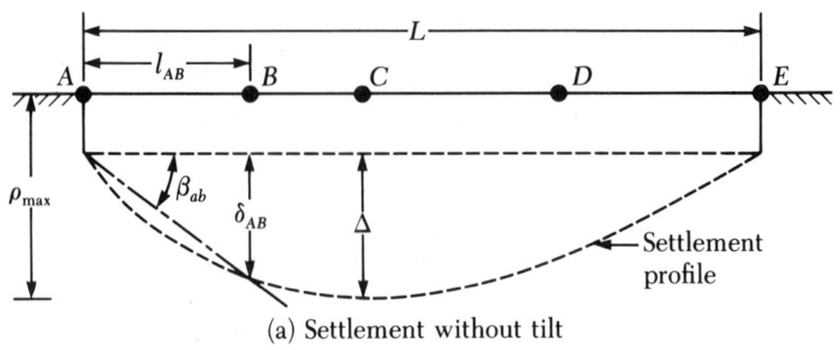

(a) Settlement without tilt

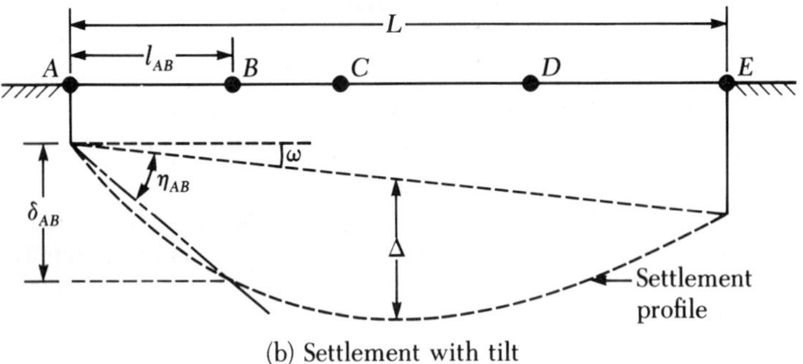

(b) Settlement with tilt

FIGURE 3.54 Parameters for definition of tolerable settlement (redrawn after Wahls, 1981)

$\frac{\Delta}{L}$ = deflection ratio

L = lateral dimension of the structure

Bjerrum (1963) provided the conditions of *limiting* angular distortion, η, for various structures (see Table 3.13).

TABLE 3.13 Limiting Angular Distortion As Recommended by Bjerrum[a]

Category of potential damage	η
Danger to machinery sensitive to settlement	1/750
Danger to frames with diagonals	1/600
Safe limit for no cracking of buildings[b]	1/500
First cracking of panel walls	1/300
Difficulties with overhead cranes	1/300
Tilting of high rigid buildings becomes visible	1/250
Considerable cracking of panel and brick walls	1/150
Danger of structural damage to general buildings	1/150
Safe limit for flexible brick walls, $L/H > 4$[b]	1/150

[a] After Wahls (1981)
[b] Safe limits include a factor of safety.

Polshin and Tokar (1957) presented the settlement criteria of the 1955 U.S.S.R. Building Code. These criteria were based on experience gained from observations of foundation settlement over 25 years. Tables 3.14 and 3.15 present the criteria.

TABLE 3.14 Allowable Settlement Criteria: 1955 U.S.S.R. Building Code[a]

Type of structure	Sand and hard clay	Plastic clay
(a) η		
Civil- and industrial-building column foundations:		
For steel and reinforced concrete structures	0.002	0.002
For end rows of columns with brick cladding	0.007	0.001
For structures where auxiliary strain does not arise during nonuniform settlement of foundations	0.005	0.005
Tilt of smokestacks, towers, silos, and so on	0.004	0.004
Craneways	0.003	0.003
(b) Δ/L		
Plain brick walls:		
For multistory dwellings and civil buildings		
at $L/H \leq 3$	0.0003	0.0004
at $L/H \geq 5$	0.0005	0.0007
For one-story mills	0.0010	0.0010

[a] After Wahls (1981)

TABLE 3.15 Allowable Average Settlement for Different Building Types[a]

Type of building	Allowable average settlement, in. (mm)
Building with plain brick walls	
$L/H \geq 2.5$	3 (80)
$L/H \leq 1.5$	4 (100)
Building with brick walls, reinforced with reinforced concrete or reinforced brick	6 (150)
Framed building	4 (100)
Solid reinforced concrete foundations of smokestacks, silos, towers, and so on	12 (300)

[a] After Wahls (1981)

PROBLEMS

3.1 A continuous foundation is 4.75 ft wide. The design conditions are $D_f = 3.5$ ft, $\gamma = 109.5$ lb/ft^3, $\phi = 26°$, and $c = 585$ lb/ft^2. Use Terzaghi's equation [Eq. (3.3)] to determine the allowable gross vertical load-bearing capacity ($FS = 4$). Assume that general shear failure occurs in the soil.

3.2 A square column foundation is 2 m × 2 m in plan. The design conditions are $D_f = 1.5$ m, $\gamma = 15.9$ kN/m^3, $\phi = 34°$, and $c = 0$. Use Terzaghi's equation to determine the allowable gross vertical load that the column could carry ($FS = 3$). Assume that general shear failure occurs in the soil.

3.3 A square column is 3 m × 3 m in plan. For $D_f = 2$ m, $\gamma = 16.5$ kN/m^3, $\phi = 30°$, and $c = 0$, use Terzaghi's equation to determine the allowable gross vertical load that the column could carry ($FS = 4$). Assume that general shear failure occurs in the soil.

3.4 A gross allowable load of 1882 kN ($FS = 3$) has to be carried by a square foundation, with $D_f = 1.4$ m, $\gamma = 15.9$ kN/m^3, $\phi = 30°$, and $c = 0$. Use Terzaghi's equation to determine the width of the foundation.

3.5 Solve Problem 3.1 with Eq. (3.17).

3.6 Solve Problem 3.2 with Eq. (3.17).

3.7 For the foundation given in Problem 3.3, what will be the gross allowable load-bearing capacity if the load is inclined at an angle 10° to the vertical? Use Eq. (3.17).

3.8 A square foundation ($B \times B$) has to be constructed as shown in Figure P3.8. Assume that $\gamma = 105$ lb/ft^3, $\gamma_{sat} = 118$ lb/ft^3, $D_f = 4$ ft, and $D_1 = 2$ ft. The gross allowable load, Q_{all}, with $FS = 3$ is 150,000 lb. The field standard penetration resistance, N_F, values are as follows:

Depth (ft)	N_F (blow/ft)
5	4
10	6
15	6
20	10
25	5

Determine the size of the footing. Use Eq. (3.17).

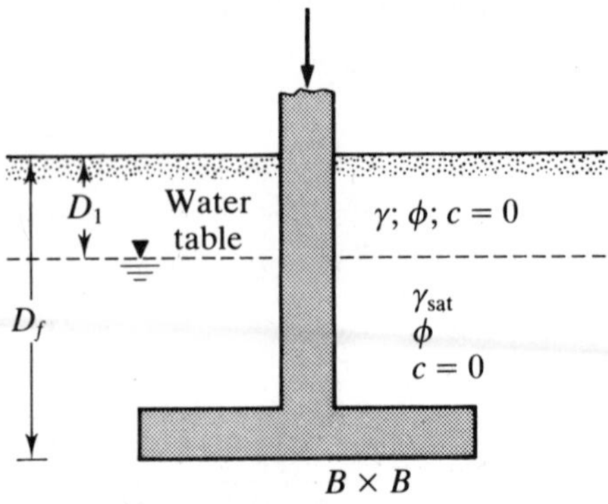

FIGURE P3.8

3.9 A column foundation is 13.0 ft × 6.5 ft in plan. For $D_f = 4.5$ ft, $c = 3200$ lb/ft², $\phi = 0$, and $\gamma = 117$ lb/ft³, what is the net ultimate load that the column could carry?

3.10 For a square foundation that is $B \times B$ in plan, $D_f = 3$ ft, vertical gross allowable load, $Q_{all} = 150{,}000$ lb, $\gamma = 115$ lb/ft³, $\phi = 40°$, $c = 0$; and $FS = 3$. Determine the size of the foundation.

3.11 A square footing is shown in Figure P3.11. Use an *FS* of 6 and determine the size of the footing.

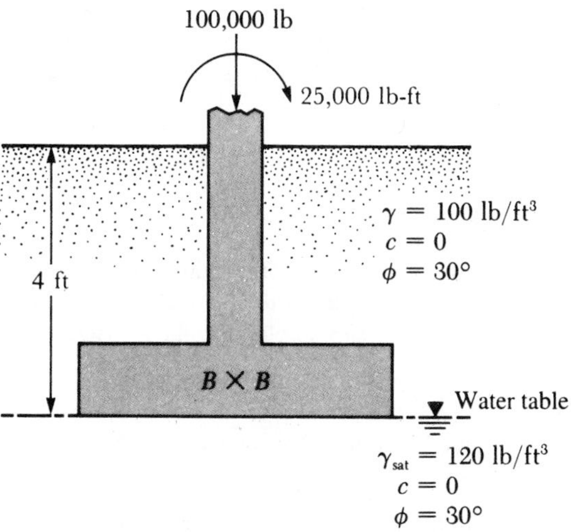

▼ **FIGURE P3.11**

3.12 An eccentrically loaded foundation is shown in Figure P3.12. Use an *FS* of 4 and determine the maximum allowable load that the foundation can carry.

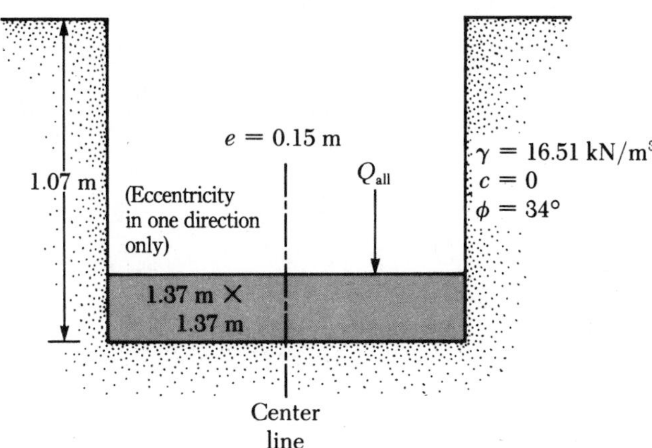

▼ **FIGURE P3.12**

3.13 An eccentrically loaded foundation is shown in Figure P3.13. Determine the ultimate load, Q_u, that the foundation can carry.

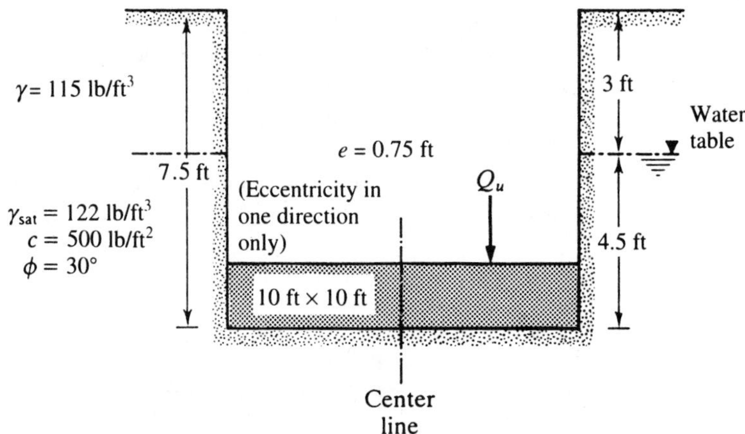

▼ **FIGURE P3.13**

3.14 Refer to Figure 3.10d for a foundation with a two-way eccentricity. The soil conditions are $\gamma = 18$ kN/m^3, $\phi = 35°$, and $c = 0$. The design criteria are $D_f = 1$ m, $B = 1.5$ m, $L = 2$ m, $e_B = 0.3$ m, and $e_L = 0.364$ m. Determine the gross ultimate load that the foundation could carry.

3.15 Repeat Problem 3.14 for $e_L = 0.4$ m and $e_B = 0.19$ m.

3.16 Repeat Problem 3.14 for $e_B = 0.6$ m and $e_L = 0.214$ m.

3.17 Repeat Problem 3.14 for $e_L = 0.286$ m and $e_B = 0.214$ m.

3.18 The variation of the cone penetration resistance in a sand deposit is shown in Figure P3.18. Assume that $\gamma = 18$ kN/m^3.

a. Estimate the soil friction angle.

b. Determine the static ultimate bearing capacity for a continuous foundation with $B = 1.3$ m, $D_f = 1.0$ m. Use Eq. (3.63).

c. Determine the seismic ultimate bearing capacity for the foundation described in part (b). Use $k_h = 0.2$, $k_v = 0$, and Eq. (3.60).

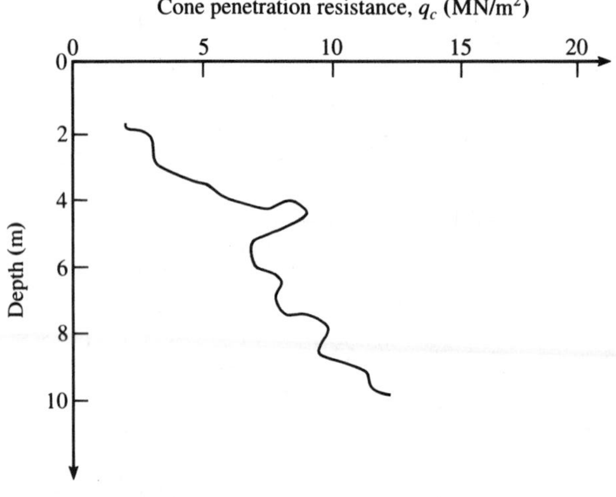

▼ **FIGURE P3.18**

3.19 Assume that the strip foundation described in Problem 3.18(b) is designed with a static $FS = 4$. The design earthquake parameters are $V = 0.35$ m/s and $A = 0.3$. Determine the seismic settlement of the foundation.

3.20 Find the gross ultimate load that the footing shown in Figure P3.20 can carry.

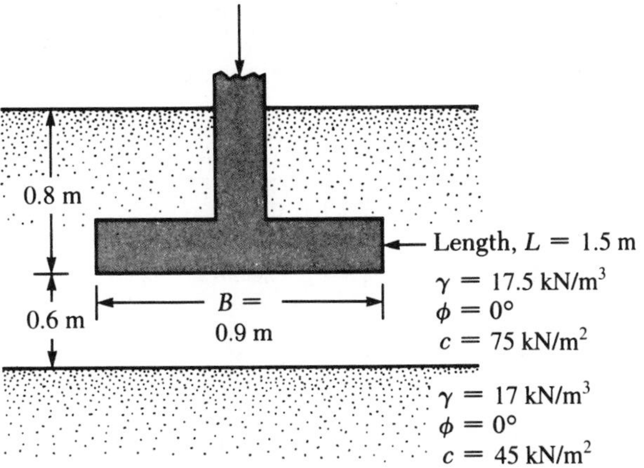

▼ **FIGURE P3.20**

3.21 A continuous foundation is shown in Figure P3.21, along with the field vane shear test results. Estimate the gross allowable bearing capacity for $FS = 3$ and $\gamma \approx 121$ lb/ft³. Use the theory presented in Section 3.11.

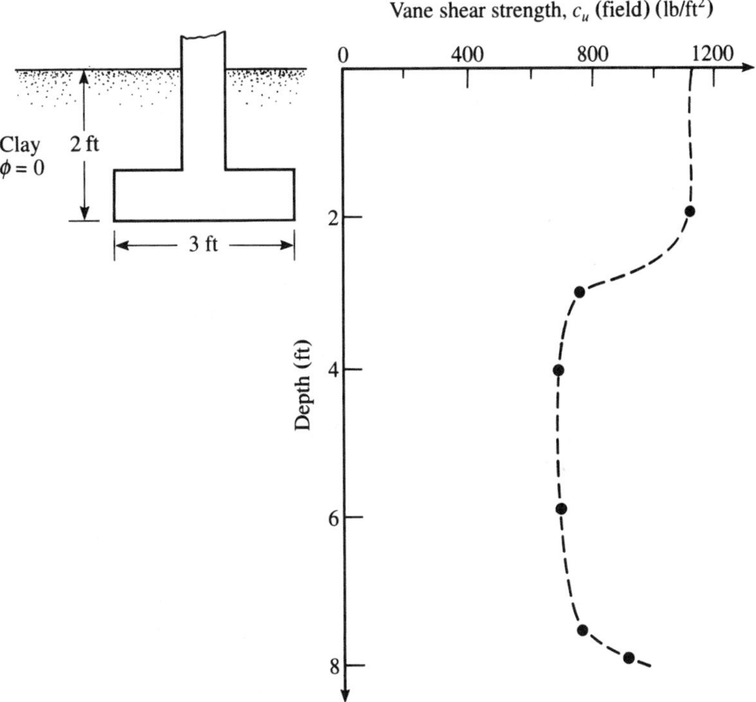

▼ **FIGURE P3.21**

3.22 Refer to Figure 3.24. The foundation is 1 m × 2 m in plan, $D_f = 1$ m, and $H = 1.5$ m. For the sand layer, $\phi = 35°$, $c = 0$, $\gamma = 17.8$ kN/m^3; and for the clay layer, $\phi = 0$, $c = 60$ kN/m^2, $\gamma = 18.2$ kN/m^3. Determine the gross allowable load that the foundation could carry. Use an *FS* of 3 against bearing capacity failure.

3.23 Refer to Figure P3.23. A well-graded sand was compacted on the soft clay, with a relative density of compaction of about 85%. Determine the gross allowable load the foundation could carry with $FS = 4$ against bearing capacity failure. You may use Figure 1.27.

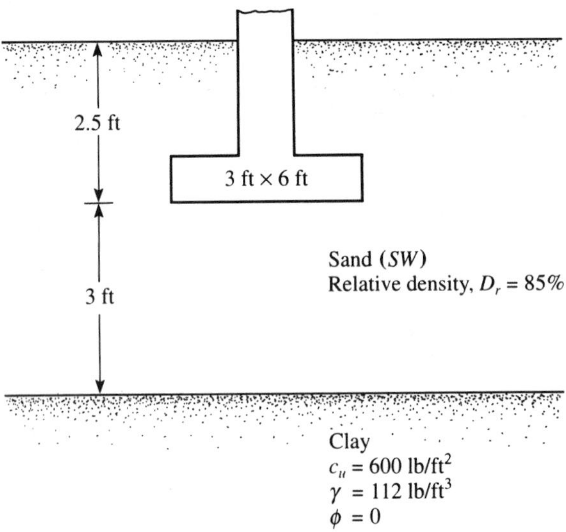

▼ **FIGURE P3.23**

3.24 Refer to Figure 3.26. A foundation that is 10 ft × 6.5 ft in plan is resting on a sand deposit. The net load per unit area at the level of the foundation, q_o, is 3200 lb/ft^2. For the sand, $\mu_s = 0.3$, $E_s = 3200$ lb/in.^{2}, $D_f = 2.95$ ft, and $H = 32$ ft. Assume that the foundation is rigid and determine the elastic settlement that the foundation would undergo. Use Eq. (3.79).

3.25 Repeat Problem 3.24 for foundation criteria of size = 1.8 m × 1.8 m, $q_o = 190$ kN/m^2, $D_f = 1$ m, and $H = 5$ m; and soil conditions of $\mu_s = 0.35$, $E_s = 16{,}500$ kN/m^2, and $\gamma = 16.5$ kN/m^3.

3.26 Solve Problem 3.24 with Eq. (3.81). For the correction factor, C_2, use a time of 5 yr for creep, and for the unit weight of soil, γ, use 110 lb/ft^3.

3.27 Solve Problem 3.25 with Eq. (3.81). For the correction factor, C_2, use a time of 4 yr for creep.

3.28 A flexible circular area is subjected to a uniformly distributed load of 2000 lb/ft^2. The diameter of the loaded area is 11.5 ft. Determine the stress increase in a soil mass at a point 32.8 ft below the center of the loaded area.

3.29 Refer to Figure 3.39b, which shows a flexible rectangular area. The dimensions are $B_1 =$ 3.3 ft, $B_2 = 6.6$ ft, $L_1 = 6.6$ ft, and $L_2 = 9.9$ ft. If the area is subjected to a uniform load of 2250 lb/ft^2, determine the stress increase at a depth of 33 ft immediately below point *O*.

3.30 Use Newmark's chart to solve Problem 3.29.

3.31 Refer to Figure P3.31, in which a square foundation is subjected to a load and a moment. Determine the settlement and the rotation of the foundation.

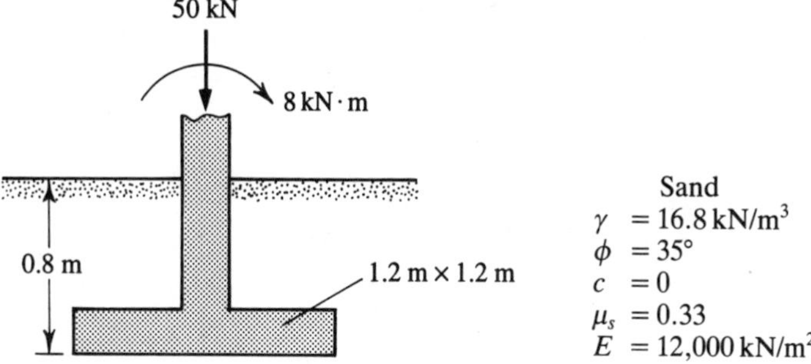

▼ **FIGURE P3.31**

3.32 A square column foundation is shown in Figure P3.32. Determine the average increase of pressure in the clay layer below the center of the foundation

a. by using Figure 3.41.

b. by using the 2 : 1 method (Figure 3.42).

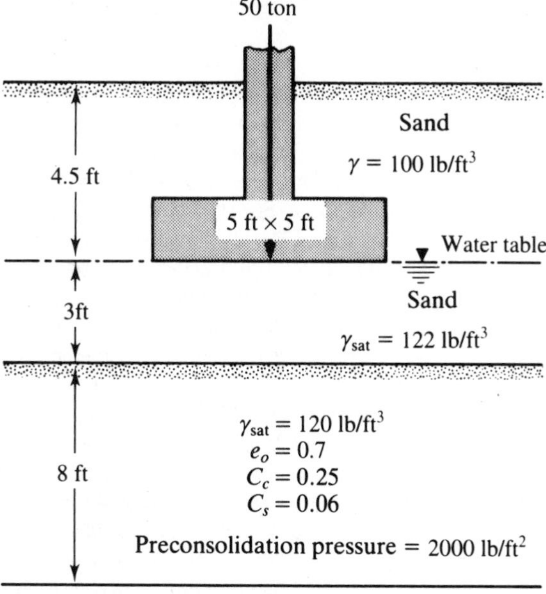

▼ **FIGURE P3.32**

3.33 Solve Problem 3.32 by using Newmark's chart.

3.34 Refer to Figure P3.32. Determine the average increase of stress in the clay layer below the corner of the foundation. Use Newmark's chart.

3.35 Redo Problem 3.34 by using Table 3.11.

3.36 Estimate the consolidation settlement of the clay layer shown in Figure P3.32 from the results of part (a) of Problem 3.32.

3.37 Estimate the consolidation settlement of the clay layer shown in Figure P3.32 from the results of part (b) of Problem 3.32.

3.38 Refer to the soil profile in Problem 2.4. What will be the net allowable bearing capacity of a foundation 5 ft × 5 ft in plan if $D_f = 3$ ft and allowable settlement = 1 in. Use Eq. (3.121).

3.39 Two plate load tests with square plates were conducted in the field. At 1-in. settlement, the results were

Width of plate (in.)	*Load (lb)*
12	8,070
24	25,800

What size of square footing is required to carry a net load of 236,000 at a settlement of 1 in.?

REFERENCES

American Society for Testing and Materials (1982). *Annual Book of ASTM Standards*, Part 19, Philadelphia.

Bjerrum, L. (1963). "Allowable Settlement of Structures," *Proceedings*, European Conference on Soil Mechanics and Foundation Engineering, Wiesbaden, Germany, Vol. III, pp. 135–137.

Bowles, J. E. (1977). *Foundation Analysis and Design*, 2nd ed., McGraw-Hill, New York.

Brand, E. W., Muktabhant, C., and Taechathummarak, A. (1972). "Load Test on Small Foundations in Soft Clay," *Proceedings*, Specialty Conference on Performance of Earth and Earth-Supported Structures, American Society of Civil Engineers, Vol. 1, Part 2, pp. 903–928.

Burland, J. B., and Worth, C. P. (1974). "Allowable and Differential Settlement of Structures Including Damage and Soil-Structure Interaction," *Proceedings*, Conference on Settlement of Structures, Cambridge University, England, pp. 611–654.

Caquot, A., and Kerisel, J. (1953). "Sur le terme de surface dans le calcul des fondations en milieu pulverulent," *Proceedings*, Third International Conference on Soil Mechanics and Foundation Engineering, Zürich, Vol. I, pp. 336–337.

Christian, J. T., and Carrier, W. D. (1978). "Janbu, Bjerrum, and Kjaernsli's Chart Reinterpreted," *Canadian Geotechnical Journal*, Vol. 15, pp. 124–128.

Das, B. M. (1983). *Advanced Soil Mechanics*, McGraw-Hill, New York.

De Beer, E. E. (1970). "Experimental Determination of the Shape Factors and Bearing Capacity Factors of Sand," *Geotechnique*, Vol. 20, No. 4, pp. 387–411.

Georgiadis, M., and Butterfield, R. (1988). "Displacement of Footings on Sand Under Eccentric and Inclined Loads," *Canadian Geotechnical Journal*, Vol. 25, No. 2, pp. 199–212.

Grant, R. J., Christian, J. T., and Vanmarcke, E. H. (1974). "Differential Settlement of Buildings," *Journal of the Geotechnical Engineering Division*, American Society of Civil Engineers, Vol. 100, No. GT9, pp. 973–991.

Hanna, A. M., and Meyerhof, G. G. (1981). "Experimental Evaluation of Bearing Capacity of Footings Subjected to Inclined Loads," *Canadian Geotechnical Journal*, Vol. 18, No. 4, pp. 599–603.

Hansen, J. B. (1970). "A Revised and Extended Formula for Bearing Capacity," Danish Geotechnical Institute, *Bulletin 28*, Copenhagen.

Harr, M. E. (1966). *Fundamentals of Theoretical Soil Mechanics*, McGraw-Hill, New York.

Highter, W. H., and Anders, J. C. (1985). "Dimensioning Footings Subjected to Eccentric Loads," *Journal of Geotechnical Engineering*, American Society of Civil Engineers, Vol. 111, No. GT5, pp. 659–665.

Housel, W. S. (1929). "A Practical Method for the Selection of Foundations Based on Fundamental Research in Soil Mechanics," *Research Bulletin No. 13*, University of Michigan, Ann Arbor.

Janbu, N., Bjerrum, L., and Kjaernsli, B. (1956). "Veiledning ved losning av fundamentering—soppgaver," *Publication No. 16*, Norwegian Geotechnical Institute, pp. 30–32.

Kumbhojkar, A. S. (1993). "Numerical Evaluation of Terzaghi's N_γ," *Journal of Geotechnical Engineering*, American Society of Civil Engineers, Vol. 119, No. 3, pp. 598–607.

Lee, I. K. (1963). "Elastic Settlements of Footing with a Rough Interface," *Proceedings*, Fourth Australia–New Zealand Conference on Soil Mechanics and Foundation Engineering, pp. 225–230.

Lundgren, H., and Mortensen, K. (1953). "Determination by the Theory of Plasticity on the Bearing Capacity of Continuous Footings on Sand," *Proceedings*, Third International Conference on Soil Mechanics and Foundation Engineering, Zürich, Vol. 1, pp. 409–412.

Meyerhof, G. G. (1953). "The Bearing Capacity of Foundations Under Eccentric and Inclined Loads," *Proceedings*, Third International Conference on Soil Mechanics and Foundation Engineering, Zürich, Vol. 1, pp. 440–445.

Meyerhof, G. G. (1956). "Penetration Tests and Bearing Capacity of Cohesionless Soils, *Journal of the Soil Mechanics and Foundations Division*, American Society of Civil Engineers, Vol. 82, No. SM1, pp. 1–19.

Meyerhof, G. G. (1963). "Some Recent Research on the Bearing Capacity of Foundations," *Canadian Geotechnical Journal*, Vol. 1, No. 1, pp. 16–26.

Meyerhof, G. G. (1965). "Shallow Foundations," *Journal of the Soil Mechanics and Foundations Division*, ASCE, Vol. 91, No. SM2, pp. 21–31.

Meyerhof, G. G. (1974). "Ultimate Bearing Capacity of Footings on Sand Layer Overlying Clay," *Canadian Geotechnical Journal*, Vol. 11, No. 2, pp. 224–229.

Meyerhof, G. G., and Hanna, A. M. (1978). "Ultimate Bearing Capacity of Foundations on Layered Soil Under Inclined Load," *Canadian Geotechnical Journal*, Vol. 15, No. 4, pp. 565–572.

Mitchell, J. K., and Gardner, W. S. (1975). "*In Situ* Measurement of Volume Change Characteristics," *Proceedings*, Specialty Conference, Anerican Society of Civil Engineers, Vol. 2, pp. 279–345.

Newmark, N. M. (1935). "Simplified Computation of Vertical Pressure in Elastic Foundation," *Circular 24*, University of Illinois Engineering Experiment Station, Urbana.

Newmark, N. M. (1942). "Influence Charts for Computation of Stresses in Elastic Foundations," *Bulletin No. 338*, University of Illinois Engineering Experiment Station, Urbana.

Osterberg, J. O. (1957). "Influence Values for Vertical Stresses in Semi-Infinite Mass Due to Embankment Loading," *Proceedings*, Fourth International Conference on Soil Mechanics and Foundation Engineering, London, Vol. 1, pp. 393–396.

Parry, R. H. G. (1977). "Estimating Bearing Capacity in Sand from SPT Values," *Journal of the Geotechnical Engineering Division*, American Society of Civil Engineers, Vol. 103, No. 9, pp. 1014–1019.

Peck, R. B., Hanson, W. E., and Thornburn, T. H. (1974). *Foundation Engineering*, 2nd ed., Wiley, New York.

Polshin, D. E., and Tokar, R. A. (1957). "Maximum Allowable Nonuniform Settlement of Structures," *Proceedings*, Fourth International Conference on Soil Mechanics and Foundation Engineering, London, Vol. 1, pp. 402–405.

Prandtl, L. (1921). "Über die Eindringungsfestigkeit (Härte) plastischer Baustoffe und die Festigkeit von Schneiden," *Zeitschrift für angewandte Mathematik und Mechanik*, Vol. 1, No. 1, pp. 15–20.

Reissner, H. (1924). "Zum Erddruckproblem," *Proceedings*, First International Congress of Applied Mechanics, Delft, pp. 295–311.

Richards, R., Jr., Elms, D. G., and Budhu, M. (1993). "Seismic Bearing Capacity and Settlement of Foundations," *Journal of Geotechnical Engineering*, American Society of Civil Engineers, Vol. 119, No. 4, pp. 662–674.

Schmertmann, J. H. (1970). "Static Cone to Compute Settlement Over Sand," *Journal of the Soil Mechanics and Foundations Division*, American Society of Civil Engineers, Vol. 96, No. SM3, pp. 1011–1043.

Schmertmann, J. H. (1978). *Guidelines for Cone Penetrations: Performance and Design*, FHWA-TS-78-209, U.S. Department of Transportation, Washington, D.C.

Schmertmann, J. H., and Hartman, J. P. (1978). "Improved Strain Influence Factor Diagrams," *Journal of the Geotechnical Engineering Division*, American Society of Civil Engineers, Vol. 104, No. GT8, pp. 1131–1135.

Schnabel, J. J. (1972). "Foundation Construction on Compacted Structural Fill in the Washington, D.C., Area," *Proceedings*, Specialty Conference on Performance of Earth and Earth-Supported Structures, American Society of Civil Engineers, Vol. 1, Part 2, pp. 1019–1036.

Skempton, A. W. (1951). "The Bearing Capacity of Clays," *Proceedings*, Building Research Congress, London, pp. 180–189.

Skempton, A. W., and Bjerrum, L. (1957). "A Contribution to Settlement Analysis of Foundations in Clay," *Geotechnique*, London, Vol. 7, p. 178.

Terzaghi, K. (1943). *Theoretical Soil Mechanics*, Wiley, New York.

Terzaghi, K., and Peck, R. B. (1967). *Soil Mechanics in Engineering Practice*, 2nd ed., Wiley, New York.

Vesic, A. S. (1963). "Bearing Capacity of Deep Foundations in Sand," *Highway Research Record No. 39*, National Academy of Sciences, pp. 112–153.

Vesic, A. S. (1973). "Analysis of Ultimate Loads of Shallow Foundations," *Journal of the Soil Mechanics and Foundations Division*, American Society of Civil Engineers, Vol. 99, No. SM1, pp. 45–73.

Wahls, H. E. (1981). "Tolerable Settlement of Buildings," *Journal of the Geotechnical Engineering Division*, American Society of Civil Engineers, Vol. 107, No. GT11, pp, 1489–1504.

Whitman, R. V., and Richart, F. E. (1967). "Design Procedures for Dynamically Loaded Foundations," *Journal of the Soil Mechanics and Foundations Division*, American Society of Civil Engineers, Vol. 93, No. SM6, pp. 169–193.

CHAPTER FOUR

MAT FOUNDATIONS

4.1 INTRODUCTION

Mat foundations are primarily shallow foundations. They are one of four major types of *combined footing* (see Figure 4.1a). A brief overview of combined footings and the methods used to calculate their dimensions follow.

1. *Rectangular Combined Footing:* In several instances, the load to be carried by a column and the soil bearing capacity are such that the standard spread footing design will require extension of the column foundation beyond the property line. In such a case, two or more columns can be supported on a single rectangular foundation, as shown in Figure 4.1b. If the net allowable soil pressure is known, the size of the foundation ($B \times L$) can be determined in the following manner.

   a. Determine the area of the foundation, A:

   $$A = \frac{Q_1 + Q_2}{q_{\text{all(net)}}} \tag{4.1}$$

   where Q_1, Q_2 = column loads
   $q_{\text{all(net)}}$ = net allowable soil bearing capacity

   b. Determine the location of the resultant of the column loads. From Figure 4.1b,

   $$X = \frac{Q_2 L_3}{Q_1 + Q_2} \tag{4.2}$$

   c. For uniform distribution of soil pressure under the foundation, the resultant of the column loads should pass through the centroid of the foundation. Thus

   $$L = 2(L_2 + X) \tag{4.3}$$

   where L = length of the foundation

   d. Once the length L is determined, the value of L_1 can be obtained:

   $$L_1 = L - L_2 - L_3 \tag{4.4}$$

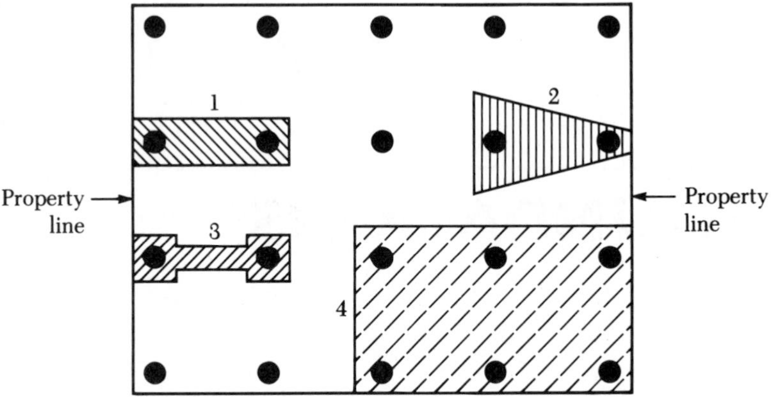

(a)

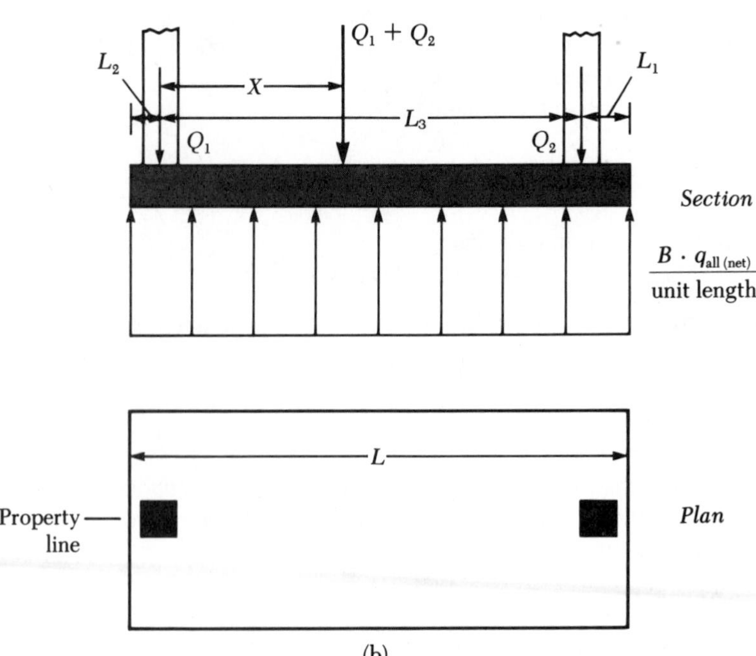

(b)

▼ **FIGURE 4.1** (a) Combined footing; (b) rectangular combined footing; (c) trapezoidal combined footing; (d) cantilever footing

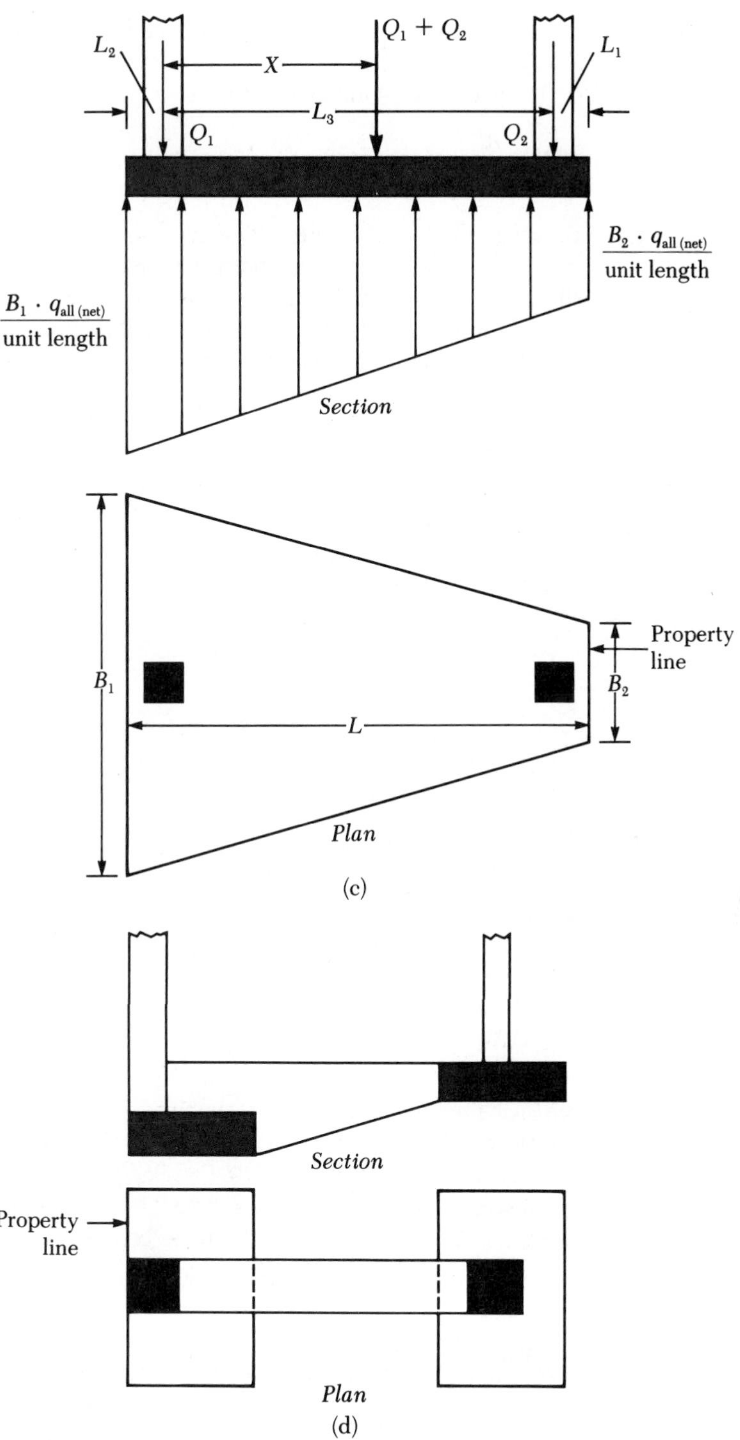

▼ **FIGURE 4.1** (Continued)

Note that the magnitude of L_2 will be known and depends on the location of the property line.

e. The width of the foundation then is

$$B = \frac{A}{L} \tag{4.5}$$

2. *Trapezoidal Combined Footing:* This type of combined footing (Figure 4.1c) is sometimes used as an isolated spread foundation of a column carrying a large load where space is tight. The size of the foundation that will uniformly distribute pressure on the soil can be obtained in the following manner.

a. If the net allowable soil pressure is known, determine the area of the foundation:

$$A = \frac{Q_1 + Q_2}{q_{\text{all(net)}}}$$

From Figure 4.1c,

$$A = \frac{B_1 + B_2}{2} L \tag{4.6}$$

b. Determine the location of the resultant for the column loads:

$$X = \frac{Q_2 L_3}{Q_1 + Q_2}$$

c. From the property of a trapezoid,

$$X + L_2 = \left(\frac{B_1 + 2B_2}{B_1 + B_2}\right)\frac{L}{3} \tag{4.7}$$

With known values of A, L, X, and L_2, solve Eqs. (4.6) and (4.7) to obtain B_1 and B_2. Note that for a trapezoid

$$\frac{L}{3} < X + L_2 < \frac{L}{2}$$

3. *Cantilever Footing:* This type of combined footing construction uses a *strap beam* to connect an eccentrically loaded column foundation to the foundation of an interior column (Figure 4.1d). Cantilever footings may be used in place of trapezoidal or rectangular combined footings when the allowable soil bearing capacity is high and the distances between the columns are large.

4. *Mat Foundation:* This type of foundation, which is sometimes referred to as a *raft foundation,* is a combined footing that may cover the entire area under a structure supporting several columns and walls (Figure 4.1a). Mat foundations are sometimes preferred for soils that have low load-bearing capacities but that will have to support high column and/or wall loads. Under some conditions, spread footings would have to cover more than half the building area, and mat foundations might be more economical.

4.2 COMMON TYPES OF MAT FOUNDATIONS

Several types of mat foundations are used currently. Some of the common types are shown schematically in Figure 4.2 and include:

1. Flat plate (Figure 4.2a). The mat is of uniform thickness.
2. Flat plate thickened under columns (Figure 4.2b).
3. Beams and slab (Figure 4.2c). The beams run both ways, and the columns are located at the intersection of the beams.
4. Slab with basement walls as a part of the mat (Figure 4.2d). The walls act as stiffeners for the mat.

Mats may be supported by piles. The piles help in reducing the settlement of a structure built over highly compressible soil. Where the water table is high, mats are often placed over piles to control buoyancy.

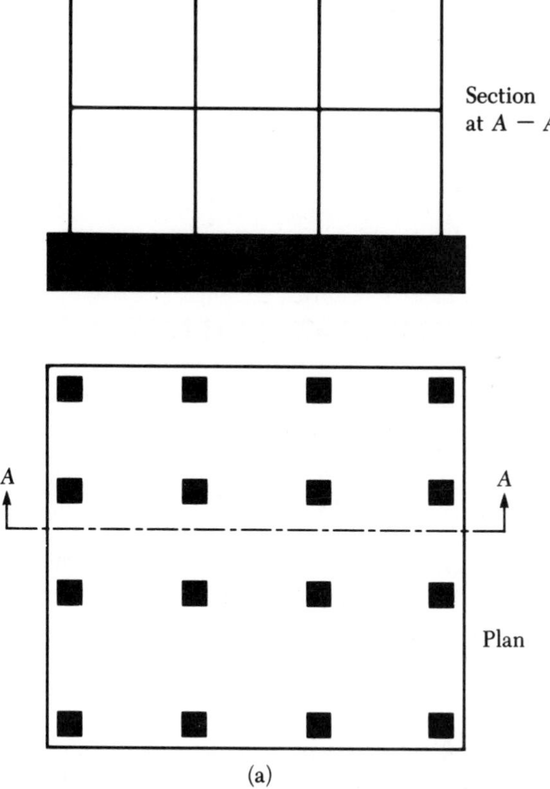

▼ **FIGURE 4.2** Types of mat foundation: (a) flat plate; (b) flat plate thickened under column; (c) beams and slab; and (d) slab with basement wall

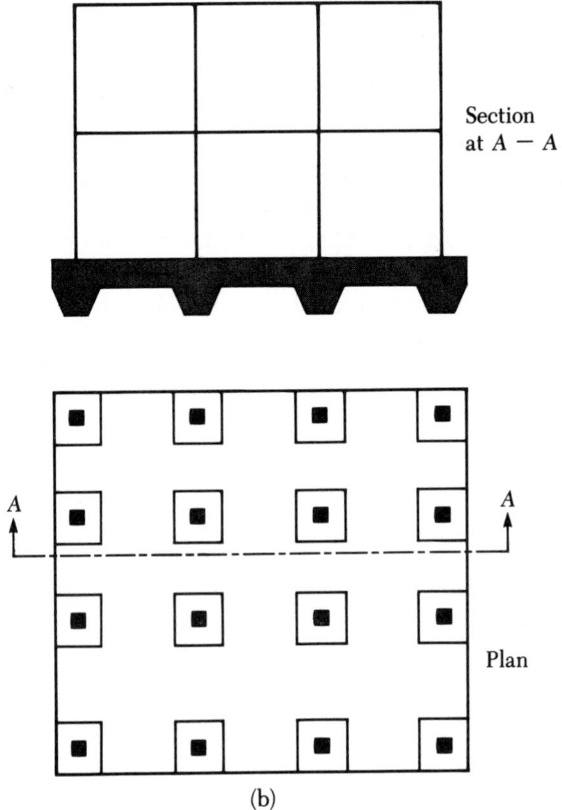

(b)

▼ **FIGURE 4.2** (Continued)

4.3 BEARING CAPACITY OF MAT FOUNDATIONS

The *gross ultimate bearing capacity* of a mat foundation can be determined by the same equation used for shallow foundations (see Section 3.6), or

$$q_u = cN_c F_{cs} F_{cd} F_{ci} + qN_q F_{qs} F_{qd} F_{qi} + \frac{1}{2} \gamma B N_\gamma F_{\gamma s} F_{\gamma d} F_{\gamma i} \tag{3.17}$$

(Chapter 3 gives the proper values of the bearing capacity factors, and the shape, depth, and load inclination factors.) The term B in Eq. (3.17) is the smallest dimension of the mat.

The *net ultimate capacity* is

$$q_{\text{all(net)}} = q_u - q \tag{3.21}$$

A suitable factor of safety should be used to calculate the net *allowable* bearing capacity. For rafts on clay, the factor of safety should not be less than 3 under dead load and maximum live load. However, under the most extreme conditions, the factor of safety should be at least 1.75 to 2. For rafts constructed over sand, a factor of safety of 3

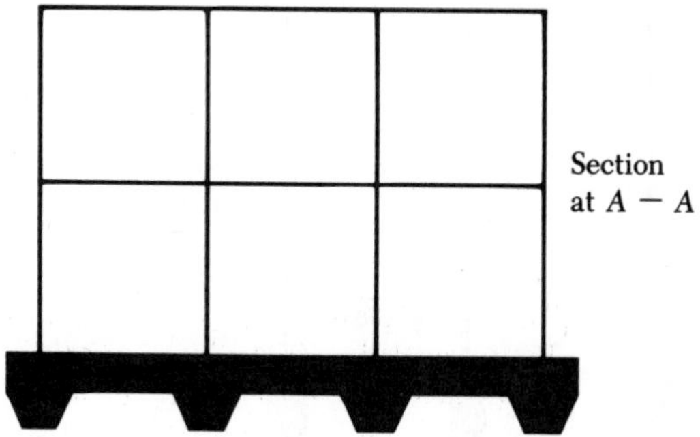

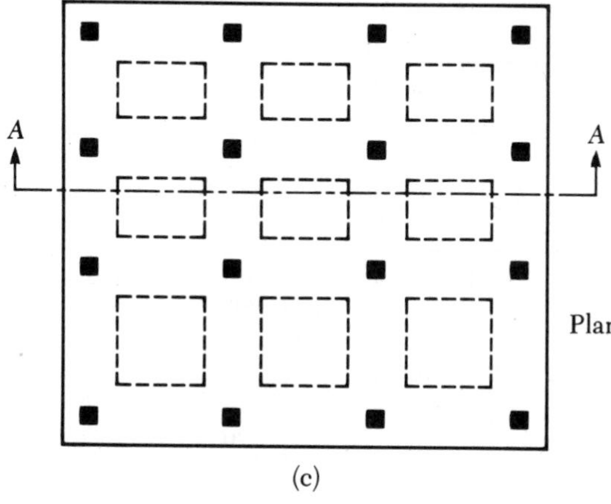

(c)

▼ **FIGURE 4.2** (Continued)

should normally be used. Under most working conditions, the factor of safety against bearing capacity failure of rafts on sand is very large.

For saturated clays with $\phi = 0$ and vertical loading condition, Eq. (3.17) gives

$$q_u = c_u N_c F_{cs} F_{cd} + q \tag{4.8}$$

where c_u = undrained cohesion

(*Note:* $N_c = 5.14$, $N_q = 1$, and $N_\gamma = 0$.)

From Table 3.7, for $\phi = 0$,

$$F_{cs} = 1 + \frac{B}{L}\left(\frac{N_q}{N_c}\right) = 1 + \left(\frac{B}{L}\right)\left(\frac{1}{5.14}\right) = 1 + \frac{0.195B}{L}$$

and

$$F_{cd} = 1 + 0.4\left(\frac{D_f}{B}\right)$$

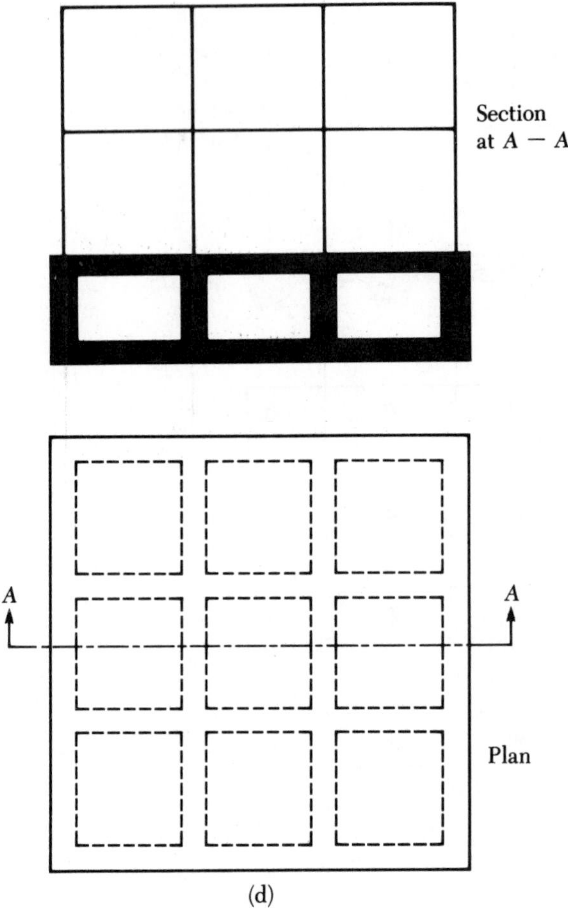

▼ **FIGURE 4.2** (Continued)

Substitution of the preceding shape and depth factors into Eq. (4.8) yields

$$q_u = 5.14c_u\left(\frac{1 + 0.195B}{L}\right)\left(1 + 0.4\frac{D_f}{B}\right) + q \tag{4.9}$$

Hence the net ultimate bearing capacity is

$$q_{u(\mathrm{net})} = q_u - q = 5.14c_u\left(1 + \frac{0.195B}{L}\right)\left(1 + 0.4\frac{D_f}{B}\right) \tag{4.10}$$

For $FS = 3$, the net allowable soil bearing capacity becomes

$$q_{\text{all(net)}} = \frac{q_{u(\text{net})}}{FS} = 1.713c_u\left(1 + \frac{0.195B}{L}\right)\left(1 + 0.4\frac{D_f}{B}\right) \tag{4.11}$$

Figure 4.3 shows a plot of $q_{\text{all(net)}}/c_u$ for various values of L/B and D_f/B, based on Eq. (4.11).

The net allowable bearing capacity for mats constructed over granular soil deposits can be adequately determined from the standard penetration resistance numbers. From Eq. (3.119b), for shallow foundations,

$$q_{\text{all(net)}}\ (\text{kN/m}^2) = 11.98N\left(\frac{3.28B + 1}{3.28B}\right)^2 F_d\left(\frac{s}{25.4}\right)$$

where N = corrected standard penetration resistance
B = width (m)
$F_d = 1 + 0.33(D_f/B) \leq 1.33$
s = settlement, in mm

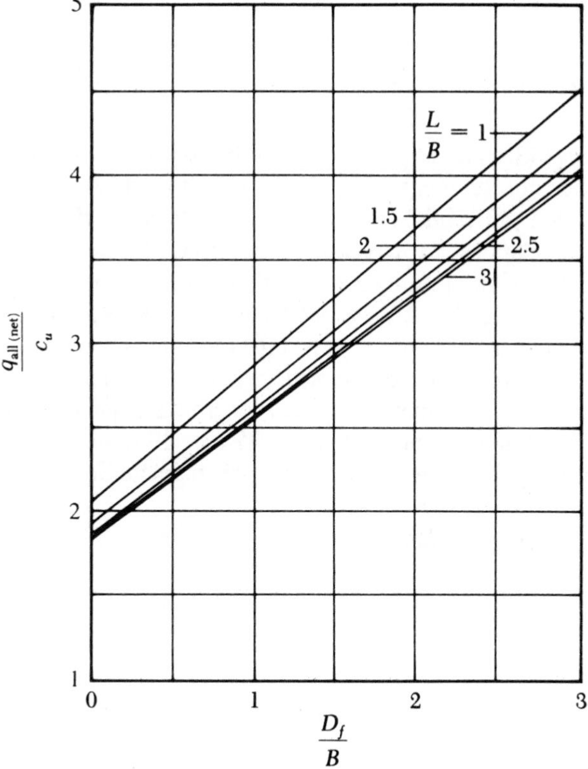

▼ **FIGURE 4.3** Plot of $q_{\text{all(net)}}/c_u$ against D_f/B [Eq. (4.11)] (*note:* factor of safety = 3)

When the width, B, is large, the preceding equation can be approximated (assuming $3.28B + 1 \approx 3.28B$) as

$$q_{\text{all(net)}}\ (\text{kN/m}^2) \approx 11.98NF_d\left(\frac{s}{25.4}\right) = 11.98N\left[1 + 0.33\left(\frac{D_f}{B}\right)\right]\left[\frac{s\ (\text{mm})}{25.4}\right] \leq 15.93N\left[\frac{s\ (\text{mm})}{25.4}\right] \quad (4.12)$$

In English units, Eq. (4.12) may be expressed as

$$q_{\text{all(net)}}\ (\text{kip/ft}^2) = 0.25N\left[1 + 0.33\left(\frac{D_f}{B}\right)\right][s\ (\text{in.})] \leq 0.33N[s\ (\text{in.})] \quad (4.13)$$

Note that Eq. (4.13) could have been derived from Eqs. (3.120) and (3.121b).

Note that the original Eqs. (3.119b) and (3.121b) were for a settlement of 1 in. (25.4 mm) with a differential settlement of about 0.75 in. (19 mm). However, the widths of the raft foundations are larger than the isolated spread footings. As Figure 3.41 shows, the depth of significant stress increase in the soil below a foundation depends on the foundation width. Hence, for a raft foundation, the depth of the zone of influence is likely to be much larger than that of a spread footing. Thus the loose soil pockets under a raft may be more evenly distributed, resulting in a smaller differential settlement. Hence the customary assumption is that, for a maximum raft settlement of 2 in. (50.8 mm), the differential settlement would be 0.75 in. (19 mm). Using this logic and conservatively assuming that F_d equals 1, we can approximate Eqs. (4.12) and (4.13) as

$$q_{\text{all(net)}}\ (\text{kN/m}^2) \approx 23.96N \quad (4.14)$$

and

$$q_{\text{all(net)}}\ (\text{kip/ft}^2) = 0.5N \quad (4.15)$$

The net pressure applied on a foundation (Figure 4.4) may be expressed as

$$q = \frac{Q}{A} - \gamma D_f \quad (4.16)$$

where Q = dead weight of the structure and the live load
A = area of the raft

Hence, in all cases, q should be less than or equal to $q_{\text{all(net)}}$.

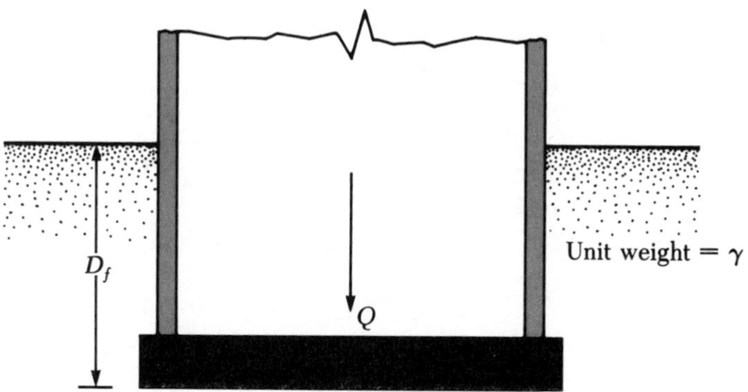

▼ **FIGURE 4.4** Definition of net pressure on soil caused by a mat foundation

▼ EXAMPLE 4.1

Determine the net ultimate bearing capacity of a mat foundation measuring 45 ft × 30 ft on a saturated clay with $c_u = 1950\ \text{lb/ft}^2$, $\phi = 0$, and $D_f = 6.5$ ft.

Solution From Eq. (4.10)

$$q_{u(\text{net})} = 5.14c_u\left[1 + \left(\frac{0.195B}{L}\right)\right]\left[1 + 0.4\left(\frac{D_f}{B}\right)\right]$$

$$= (5.14)(1950)\left[1 + \left(\frac{0.195 \times 30}{45}\right)\right]\left[1 + \left(\frac{0.4 \times 6.5}{30}\right)\right]$$

$$= \mathbf{12{,}307\ lb/ft^2} \quad ▼$$

▼ EXAMPLE 4.2

What will be the net allowable bearing capacity of a mat foundation with dimensions of 45 ft × 30 ft constructed over a sand deposit? Here, $D_f = 6$ ft, allowable settlement = 1 in., and corrected average penetration number $N = 10$.

Solution From Eq. (4.13)

$$q_{\text{all(net)}} = 0.25N\left(1 + \frac{0.33D_f}{B}\right)s \leq 0.33Ns$$

$$q_{\text{all(net)}} = 0.25(10)\left[1 + \frac{0.33(6)}{10}\right](1) \approx \mathbf{3\ kip/ft^2} \quad ▼$$

4.4 DIFFERENTIAL SETTLEMENT OF MATS

The American Concrete Institute Committee 436 (1966) suggested the following method for calculating the differential settlement of mat foundations. According to this method, the rigidity factor (K_r) is calculated as

$$K_r = \frac{E'I_b}{E_s B^3} \tag{4.17}$$

where E' = modulus of elasticity of the material used in the structure
E_s = modulus of elasticity of the soil
B = width of foundation
I_b = moment of inertia of the structure per unit length at right angles to B

The term $E'I_b$ can be expressed as

$$E'I_b = E'\left(I_F + \sum I_{b'} + \sum \frac{ah^3}{12}\right) \tag{4.18}$$

where $E'I_b$ = flexural rigidity of the foundation per unit length at right angles to B
$\Sigma\, E'I_{b'}$ = flexural rigidity of the framed members
$\Sigma\, (E'ah^3/12)$ = flexural rigidity of the shear walls
a = shear wall thickness
h = shear wall height

Based on the value of K_r, the ratio (δ) of the differential settlement to the total settlement can be estimated in the following manner.

1. If $K_r > 0.5$, it can be treated as a rigid mat, and $\delta = 0$.
2. If $K_r = 0.5$, then $\delta \approx 0.1$.
3. If $K_r = 0$, then $\delta = 0.35$ for square mats ($B/L = 1$) and $\delta = 0.5$ for long foundations ($B/L = 0$).

4.5 FIELD SETTLEMENT OBSERVATIONS FOR MAT FOUNDATIONS

Several field settlement observations for mat foundations are currently available in the literature. In this section we compare the observed settlements for some mat foundations constructed over granular soil deposits with those obtained from Eqs. (4.12) and (4.13).

Meyerhof (1965) compiled the observed maximum settlements for mat foundations constructed on sand and gravel, as listed in Table 4.1. In Eq. (4.13), if the depth factor, $1 + 0.33(D_f/B)$, is assumed to be approximately 1,

$$s = \frac{q_{\text{all(net)}}}{0.25N} \tag{4.19}$$

▼ **TABLE 4.1 Observed Maximum Settlement of Mat Foundations on Sand and Gravel**[a]

Case no.	Structure	Reference	B (ft)	N (avg)	$q_{all(net)}$ (kip/ft^2)	Observed maximum settlement, s (in.)
1	T. Edison Sao Paulo, Brazil	Rios and Silva (1948)	60	15	4.8	0.6
2	Banco do Brasil Sao Paulo, Brazil	Rios and Silva (1948); Vargas (1961)	75	18	5.0	1.1
3	Iparanga Sao Paulo, Brazil	Vargas (1948)	30	9	6.4	1.4
4	C.B.I., Esplanada Sao Paulo, Brazil	Vargas (1961)	48	22	8.0	1.1
5	Riscala Sao Paulo, Brazil	Vargas 1948)	13	20	4.8	0.5
6	Thyssen Dusseldorf, Germany	Schultze (1962)	74	25	5.0	0.95
7	Ministry Dusseldorf, Germany	Schultze (1962)	52	20	4.6	0.8
8	Chimney Cologne, Germany	Schultze (1962)	67	10	3.6	0.4

[a] After Meyerhof (1965)

Table 4.2 shows a comparison of the observed maximum settlements in Table 4.1 and the settlements obtained from Eq. (4.19). For the cases considered, the ratio of

▼ **TABLE 4.2 Comparison of Settlements Observed and Calculated**

Case 1[a]	Maximum observed settlement, s (in.)	Calculated settlement, s, [Eq. (4.19)]	$\frac{s_{calculated}}{s_{observed}}$
1	0.6	1.28	2.1
2	1.1	1.11	1.0
3	1.4	2.84	2.03
4	1.1	1.45	1.32
5	0.5	0.96	1.92
6	0.95	0.8	0.84
7	0.8	0.92	1.15
8	0.4	1.44	3.6

[a] Refer to Table 4.1

$s_{calculated}/s_{observed}$ varies from 0.84 to 3.6. Thus calculation of the net allowable bearing capacity with Eq. (4.12) or (4.13) will yield a safe and conservative value.

Stuart and Graham (1975) reported the case history of the 13-story Ashby Institute building of Queens University, Belfast, Ireland, construction of which began in August 1960. It was supported by a mat foundation 180 ft (length) × 65 ft (width). Figure 4.5a shows a schematic diagram of the building cross section. The nature of the subsoil along with the field standard penetration resistance values at the south end of the building are shown in Figure 4.5b. The base of the mat was constructed about 20 ft below the ground surface.

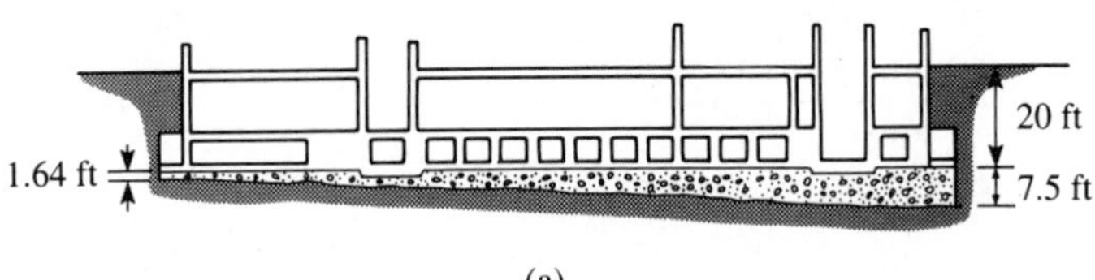

(a)

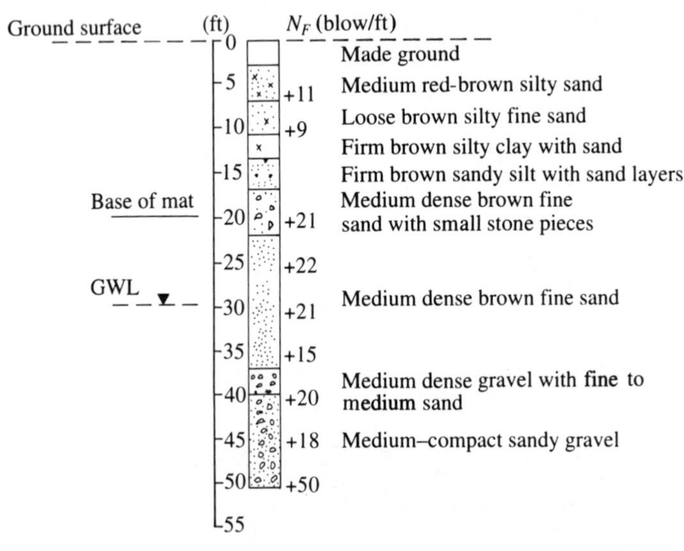

(b)

▼ **FIGURE 4.5** Ashby Institute Building of Queens University, as reported by Stuart and Graham (1975): (a) building cross section; (b) subsoil condition at south end

Equation (2.7) gives the variation of standard penetration number with depth, as shown in Table 4.3. Note that the average N value between the bottom of the mat and a depth of 30 ft ($\approx B/2$) is about 17. The engineers estimated the average net *dead and live load* [Eq. (4.16)] at the level of the mat foundation to be about 3360 lb/ft^2. From

▼ TABLE 4.3 Determination of Corrected Standard Penetration Resistance

Depth below ground surface (ft)	Field standard penetration number, N_F	$\sigma_v'^{a}$ (ton/ft²)	C_N [Eq. (2.8)]	N_{cor} [Eq. (2.7)]
20	21	1.2	0.91	19
25	22	1.5	0.82	18
30	21	1.8	0.75	16
35	15	2.1	0.69	10
40	20	2.4	0.65	13
45	18	2.7	0.61	11
50	50	3.0	0.58	29

[a] σ_v' = depth (γ); γ = 120 lb/ft³ (assumed)

Eq. (4.13)

$$s = \frac{q_{\text{all(net)}}}{0.25N\left[1 + 0.33\left(\frac{D_f}{B}\right)\right]} \tag{4.20}$$

Substituting appropriate values into Eq. (4.20) yields the settlement at the south end of the building:

$$s = \frac{(3360/1000)}{(0.25)(17)[1 + 0.33(20/65)]} = 0.72 \text{ in.}$$

The construction of the building was completed in February 1964. Figure 4.6 shows the variation of the mean settlement of the mat at the south end. In 1972 (eight years after completion of the building) the mean settlement was about 0.55 in. Thus the estimated settlement of 0.72 in. is about 30% higher than that actually observed.

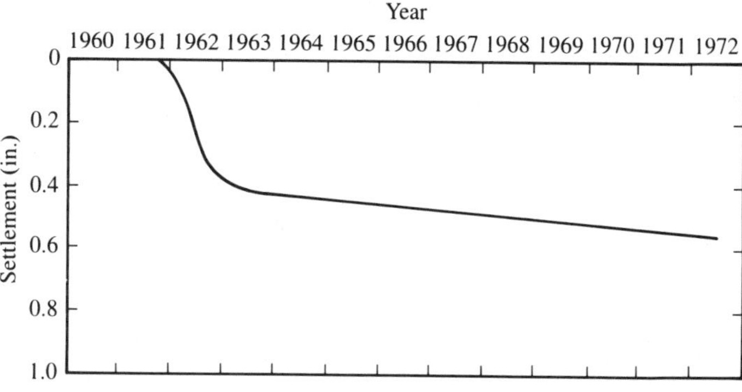

▼ FIGURE 4.6 Mean settlement at the south end of the mat foundation, as reported by Stuart and Graham (1975)

4.6 COMPENSATED FOUNDATIONS

The settlement of a mat foundation can be reduced by decreasing the net pressure increase on soil, which can be done by increasing the depth of embedment, D_f. This increase is particularly important for mats on soft clays, where large consolidation settlements are expected. From Eq. (4.16), the net average applied pressure on soil is

$$q = \frac{Q}{A} - \gamma D_f$$

For no increase of the net soil pressure on soil below a raft foundation, q should be zero. Thus

$$D_f = \frac{Q}{A\gamma} \tag{4.21}$$

This relation for D_f is usually referred to as the depth of a *fully compensated foundation.*

The factor of safety against bearing capacity failure for partially compensated foundations (that is, $D_f < Q/A\gamma$) may be given as

$$FS = \frac{q_{u(\text{net})}}{q} = \frac{q_{u(\text{net})}}{\dfrac{Q}{A} - \gamma D_f} \tag{4.22}$$

For saturated clays, the factor of safety against bearing capacity failure can thus be obtained by substituting Eq. (4.10) into Eq. (4.22):

$$FS = \frac{5.14c_u\left(1 + \dfrac{0.195B}{L}\right)\left(1 + 0.4\dfrac{D_f}{B}\right)}{\dfrac{Q}{A} - \gamma D_f} \tag{4.23}$$

▼ EXAMPLE 4.3

Refer to Figure 4.4. The mat has dimensions of 30 m × 40 m, and the live load and dead load on the mat are 200 MN. The mat is placed over a layer of soft clay having a unit weight of 18.75 kN/m^3. Find D_f for a fully compensated foundation.

Solution From Eq. (4.21)

$$D_f = \frac{Q}{A\gamma} = \frac{200 \times 10^3 \text{ kN}}{(30 \times 40)(18.75)} = \mathbf{8.89\ m}$$ ▼

▼ EXAMPLE 4.4

Refer to Example 4.3. For the clay, $c_u = 12.5$ kN/m². If the required factor of safety against bearing capacity failure is 3, determine the depth of the foundation.

Solution From Eq. (4.23)

$$FS = \frac{5.14c_u\left(1 + \frac{0.195B}{L}\right)\left(1 + 0.4\frac{D_f}{B}\right)}{\frac{Q}{A} - \gamma D_f}$$

Here, $FS = 3$, $c_u = 12.5$ kN/m², $B/L = 30/40 = 0.75$, and $Q/A = (200 \times 10^3)/(30 \times 40) = 166.67$ kN/m². Substituting these values into Eq. (4.23) yields

$$3 = \frac{(5.14)(12.5)[1 + (0.195)(0.75)]\left[1 + 0.4\left(\frac{D_f}{30}\right)\right]}{166.67 - (18.75)D_f}$$

$$500.01 - 56.25D_f = 73.65 + 0.982D_f$$

$$426.36 = 57.23D_f$$

or

$D_f =$ **7.5 m** ▼

▼ EXAMPLE 4.5

Consider a mat foundation 90 ft × 120 ft in plan, as shown in Figure 4.7. The total dead load and live load on the raft is 45×10^3 kip. Estimate the consolidation settlement at the center of the foundation.

Solution For $Q = 45 \times 10^6$ lb, the load per unit area is

$$q = \frac{Q}{A} - \gamma D_f = \frac{45 \times 10^6}{90 \times 120} - (100)(6) \approx 3567 \text{ lb/ft}^2$$

From Eq. (3.93), the average pressure increase on the clay layer below the center of the foundation is

$$\Delta p_{\text{av}} = \frac{1}{6}(\Delta p_t + 4\,\Delta p_m + \Delta p_b)$$

Refer to Figure 3.41 to obtain the values of Δp_t, Δp_m, and Δp_b. At the *top of the clay layer,*

$$\frac{z}{B} = \frac{45}{90} = 0.5$$

$$\frac{L}{B} = \frac{120}{90} = 1.33$$

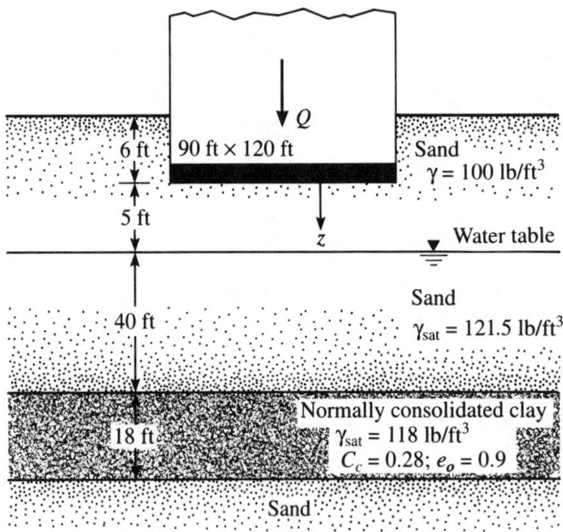

▼ **FIGURE 4.7**

So, for $z/B = 0.5$ and $L/B = 1.33$,

$$\frac{\Delta p_t}{q} = 0.75, \qquad \text{and} \qquad \Delta p_t = (0.75)(3567) = 2567.3 \text{ lb/ft}^2$$

Similarly, for the *middle of the clay layer*,

$$\frac{z}{B} = \frac{54}{90} = 0.6$$

$$\frac{L}{B} = 1.33$$

So $\Delta p_m/q = 0.66$ and $\Delta p_m = 2354.2 \text{ lb/ft}^2$. At the *bottom of the clay layer*,

$$\frac{z}{B} = \frac{63}{90} = 0.7$$

$$\frac{L}{B} = 1.33$$

So, $\Delta p_b/q = 0.58$ and $\Delta p_b = 2069.9 \text{ lb/ft}^2$. Hence

$$\Delta p_{av} = \frac{1}{6}[2567.3 + (4)(2354.2) + 2069.9] = 2342 \text{ lb/ft}^2$$

From Eq. (1.60), the consolidation settlement is

$$S = \frac{C_c H_c}{1 + e_o} \log \frac{p_o + \Delta p_{av}}{p_o}$$

$$p_o = (11)(100) + (40)(121.5 - 62.4) + \frac{18}{2}(118 - 62.4) \approx 3964 \text{ lb/ft}^2$$

$$S = \frac{(0.28)(18 \times 12)}{1.9} \log\left(\frac{3964 + 2342}{3964}\right) = \mathbf{6.4 \text{ in.}}$$

Note: Similar calculations can be made to obtain the settlement at the corner of the mat. In most cases, the differential settlement between the center and the corner of the mat calculated in the preceding manner will be higher than the actual differential settlement. The reason is the stiffness of the superstructure.

The reliability of the settlement calculation will depend on several factors. If the clay is normally consolidated and uniform in thickness, the settlement calculation will yield fairly accurate results. If the compressible soil is erratic in formation and contains several types of soil, the calculation will indicate only the maximum magnitude. ▼

4.7 STRUCTURAL DESIGN OF MAT FOUNDATIONS

The structural design of mat foundations can be carried out by two conventional methods: the conventional rigid method and the approximate flexible method. Finite difference and finite element methods can also be used, but this section covers only the basic concepts of the first two design methods.

Conventional Rigid Method

The *conventional rigid method* of mat foundation design can be explained step by step with reference to Figure 4.8.

1. Figure 4.8a shows mat dimensions of $L \times B$ and column loads of Q_1, Q_2, Q_3, ... Calculate the total column load as

$$Q = Q_1 + Q_2 + Q_3 + \cdots \tag{4.24}$$

2. Determine the pressure on the soil, q, below the mat at points $A, B, C, D, \ldots,$ by using the equation

$$q = \frac{Q}{A} \pm \frac{M_y x}{I_y} \pm \frac{M_x y}{I_x} \tag{4.25}$$

where $A = BL$

$I_x = (1/12)BL^3$ = moment of inertia about the x axis

$I_y = (1/12)LB^3$ = moment of inertia about the y axis

M_x = moment of the column loads about the x axis = Qe_y

M_y = moment of the column loads about the y axis = Qe_x

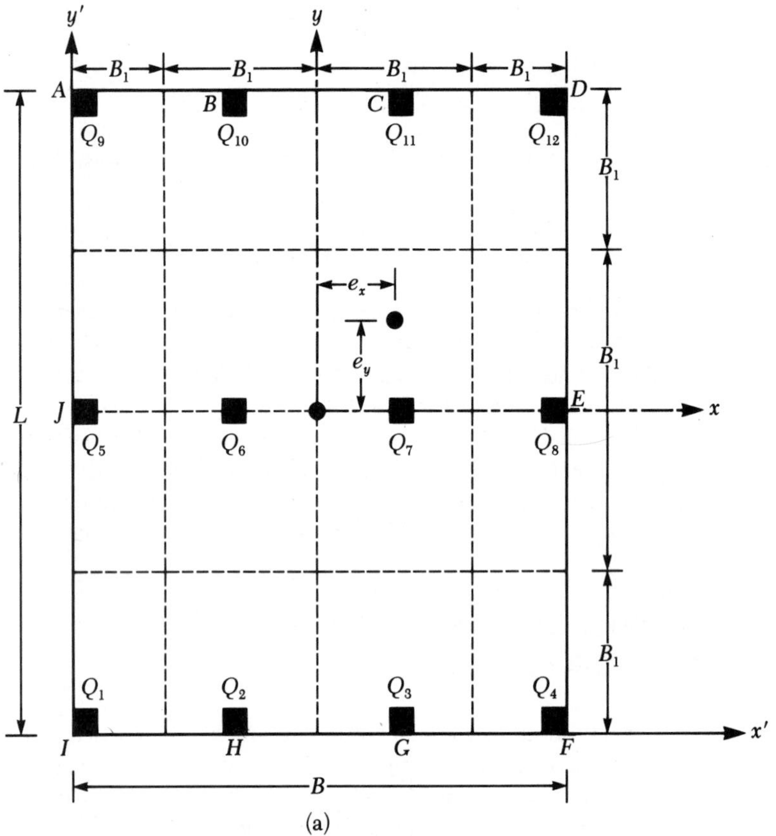

▼ **FIGURE 4.8** Conventional rigid mat foundation design

The load eccentricities, e_x and e_y, in the x and y directions can be determined by using (x', y') coordinates:

$$x' = \frac{Q_1 x'_1 + Q_2 x'_2 + Q_3 x'_3 + \cdots}{Q} \tag{4.26}$$

and

$$e_x = x' - \frac{B}{2} \tag{4.27}$$

Similarly

$$y' = \frac{Q_1 y'_1 + Q_2 y'_2 + Q_3 y'_3 + \cdots}{Q} \tag{4.28}$$

and

$$e_y = y' - \frac{L}{2} \tag{4.29}$$

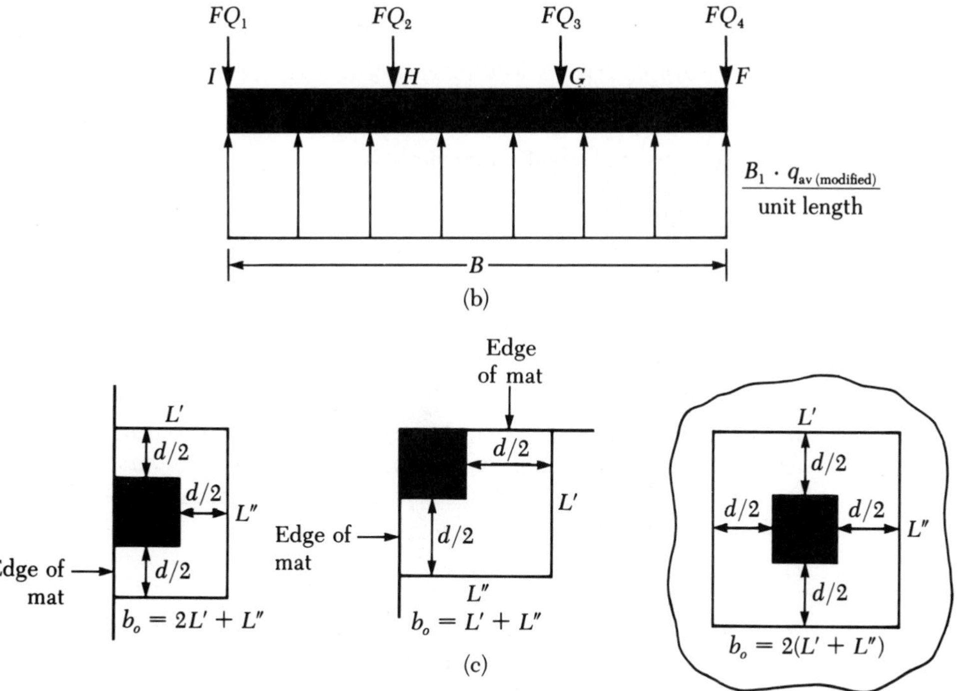

FIGURE 4.8 (Continued)

3. Compare the values of the soil pressures determined in Step 2 with the net allowable soil pressure to determine whether $q \le q_{\text{all(net)}}$.
4. Divide the mat into several strips in x and y directions (see Figure 4.8a). Let the width of any strip be B_1.
5. Draw the shear, V, and the moment, M, diagrams for each individual strip (in the x and y directions). For example, the average soil pressure of the bottom strip in the x direction of Figure 4.8a is

$$q_{av} \approx \frac{q_I + q_F}{2} \tag{4.30}$$

where q_I and q_F = soil pressures at points I and F as determined from Step 2

The total soil reaction is equal to $q_{av}B_1B$. Now obtain the total column load on the strip as $Q_1 + Q_2 + Q_3 + Q_4$. The sum of the column loads on the strip will not equal $q_{av}B_1B$ because the shear between the adjacent strips has not been taken into account. For this reason, the soil reaction and the column loads need to be adjusted, or

$$\text{Average load} = \frac{q_{av}B_1B + (Q_1 + Q_2 + Q_3 + Q_4)}{2} \tag{4.31}$$

Now, the modified average soil reaction becomes

$$q_{\text{av(modified)}} = q_{\text{av}}\left(\frac{\text{average load}}{q_{\text{av}}B_1\text{B}}\right) \quad (4.32)$$

and the column load modification factor is

$$F = \frac{\text{average load}}{Q_1 + Q_2 + Q_3 + Q_4} \quad (4.33)$$

So, the modified column loads are FQ_1, FQ_2, FQ_3, and FQ_4. This modified loading on the strip under consideration is shown in Figure 4.8b. The shear and the moment diagram for this strip can now be drawn. This procedure is repeated for all strips in the x and y directions.

6. Determine the depth of the mat d (refer to Figure A.1 in Appendix A for the definition of d) by checking for diagonal tension shear near various columns. According to ACI Code 318-89 (Section 11.11.2.1, American Concrete Institute, 1989), for the critical section,

$$U = b_o d[\phi(0.34)\sqrt{f'_c}] \quad (4.34)$$

where U = factored column load (MN), or (column load) × (load factor)
ϕ = reduction factor (see Appendix A)
f'_c = compressive strength of concrete at 28 days (MN/m^2)

The units of b_o and d in Eq. (4.34) are in meters. In English units, Eq. (4.34) may be expressed as

$$U = b_o d(4\phi\sqrt{f'_c}) \quad (4.35)$$

where U is in lb, b_o and d are in in., and f'_c is in lb/in^2

The expression for b_o in terms of d, which depends on the location of the column with respect to the plan of the mat, can be obtained from Figure 4.8c.

7. From the moment diagrams of all strips *in one direction* (x or y), obtain the *maximum* positive and negative moments per unit width (i.e., $M' = M/B_1$).
8. Determine the areas of steel per unit width for positive and negative reinforcement in x and y directions from the Appendix Eqs. (A.4) and (A.6):

$$M_u = (M')(\text{load factor}) = \phi A_s f_y\left(d - \frac{a}{2}\right) \quad (A.6)$$

and

$$a = \frac{A_s f_y}{0.85 f'_c b} \quad (A.4)$$

where A_s = area of steel per unit width
f_y = yield stress of reinforcement in tension
M_u = factored moment

Examples 4.6 and 4.7 illustrate the use of the conventional rigid method of mat foundation design.

▼ EXAMPLE 4.6

The plan of a mat foundation with column loads is shown in Figure 4.9. Use Eq. (4.25) to calculate the soil pressures at points *A, B, C, D, E, F, G, H, I, J, K, L, M,* and *N*. The size of the mat is 76 ft × 96 ft, all columns are 24 in. × 24 in. in section, and $q_{\text{all(net)}} = 1.5\ \text{kip/ft}^2$. Verify that the soil pressures are less than the net allowable bearing capacity.

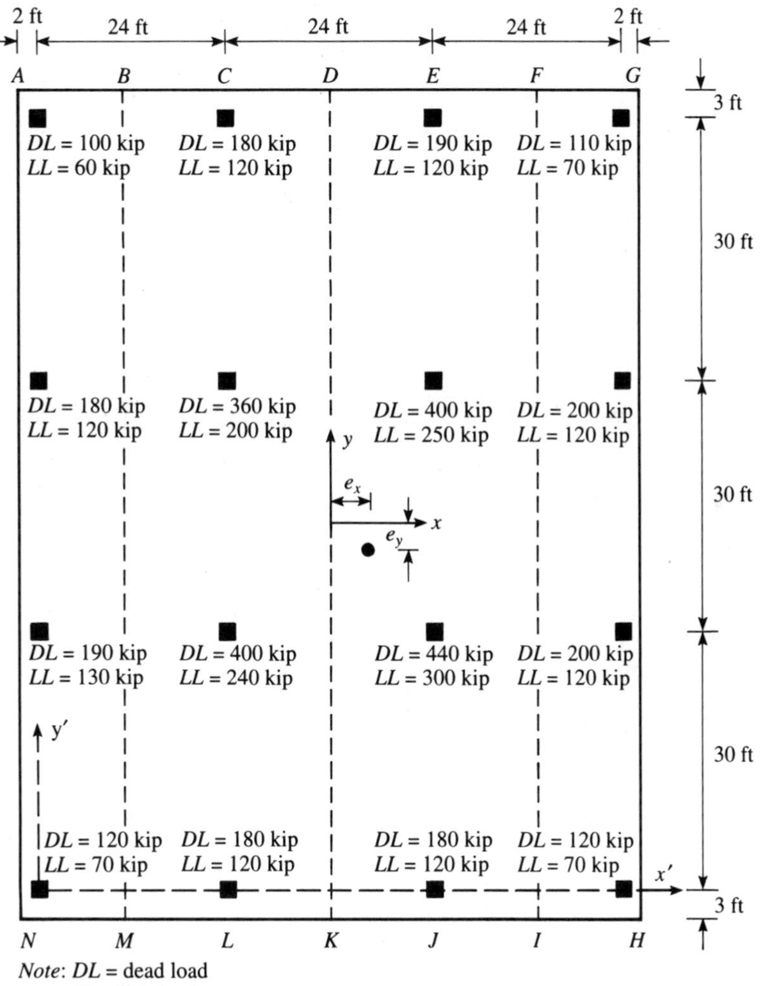

▼ **FIGURE 4.9** Plan of a mat foundation

Solution From Figure 4.9

$$\text{Column dead load } (DL) = 100 + 180 + 190 + 110 + 180 + 360 + 400 + 200 + 190 + 400 + 440 + 200 + 120 + 180 + 180 + 120 = 3550 \text{ kip}$$

$$\text{Column live load } (LL) = 60 + 120 + 120 + 70 + 120 + 200 + 250 + 120 + 130 + 240 + 300 + 120 + 70 + 120 + 120 + 70 = 2230 \text{ kip}$$

So

$$\text{Service load} = 3550 + 2230 = 5780 \text{ kip}$$

$$\text{Factored load} = (1.4)(3550) + (1.7)(2230) = 8761 \text{ kip}$$

The moments of inertia of the foundation are

$$I_x = \frac{1}{12}(76)(96)^3 = 5603 \times 10^3 \text{ ft}^4$$

$$I_y = \frac{1}{12}(96)(76)^3 = 3512 \times 10^3 \text{ ft}^4$$

and

$$\sum M_{y'} = 0$$

So

$$5780x' = (24)(300 + 560 + 640 + 300) + (48)(310 + 650 + 740 + 300) + (72)(180 + 320 + 320 + 190)$$

$$x' = 36.664 \text{ ft}$$

and

$$e_x = 36.664 - 36.0 = 0.664 \text{ ft}$$

Similarly,

$$\sum M_{x'} = 0$$

So

$$5780y' = (30)(320 + 640 + 740 + 320) + (60)(300 + 560 + 650 + 320) + (90)(160 + 300 + 310 + 180)$$

$$y' = 44.273 \text{ ft}$$

and

$$e_y = \frac{90}{2} - 44.273 = -0.727 \text{ ft}$$

The moments caused by eccentricity are

$$M_x = Qe_y = (8761)(0.727) = 6369 \text{ kip-ft}$$

$$M_y = Qe_x = (8761)(0.664) = 5817 \text{ kip-ft}$$

From Eq. (4.25)

$$q = \frac{Q}{A} \pm \frac{M_y x}{I_y} \pm \frac{M_x y}{I_x}$$

$$= \frac{8761}{(76)(96)} \pm \frac{(5817)(x)}{3512 \times 10^3} \pm \frac{(6369)(y)}{5603 \times 10^3}$$

or

$$q = 1.20 \pm 0.0017x \pm 0.0011y \text{ (kip/ft}^2\text{)}$$

Now the following table can be prepared.

Point	$\frac{Q}{A}$ *(kip/ft²)*	*x (ft)*	*±0.0017x (ft)*	*y (ft)*	*±0.0011y (ft)*	*q (kip/ft²)*
A	1.2	−38	−0.065	48	−0.053	**1.082**
B	1.2	−24	−0.041	48	−0.053	**1.106**
C	1.2	−12	−0.020	48	−0.053	**1.127**
D	1.2	0	0.0	48	−0.053	**1.147**
E	1.2	12	0.020	48	−0.053	**1.167**
F	1.2	24	0.041	48	−0.053	**1.188**
G	1.2	38	0.065	48	−0.053	**1.212**
H	1.2	38	0.065	−48	0.053	**1.318**
I	1.2	24	0.041	−48	0.053	**1.294**
J	1.2	12	0.020	−48	0.053	**1.273**
K	1.2	0	0.0	−48	0.053	**1.253**
L	1.2	−12	0.020	−48	0.053	**1.233**
M	1.2	−24	0.041	−48	0.053	**1.212**
N	1.2	−38	0.065	−48	0.053	**1.188**

The soil pressures at all points are less than the given value of $q_{\text{all(net)}} = 1.5$ kip/ft². ▼

▼ EXAMPLE 4.7

Use the results of Example 4.6.

a. Determine the thickness of the slab.
b. Divide the mat into four strips (i.e., *ABMN*, *BCDKLM*, *DEFIJK*, and *FGHI*) and determine the average soil reactions at the ends of each strip.

c. Determine the reinforcement requirements in the y direction for $f'_c = 3000\ \text{lb/in}^2$ and $f_y = 60{,}000\ \text{lb/in}^2$.

Solution

Part a: Determination of Mat Thickness

For the critical perimeter column as shown in Figure 4.10 (ACI 318-89; Section 9.2.1),

$$U = 1.4(DL) + 1.7(LL) = (1.4)(190) + (1.7)(130) = 487 \text{ kip}$$

$$b_o = 2(36 + d/2) + (24 + d) = 96 + 2d \text{ (in.)}$$

From ACI 318-89

$$\phi V_c \geq V_u$$

$$\phi V_c = \phi(4)\sqrt{f'_c}\, b_o d = (0.85)(4)(\sqrt{3000})(96 + 2d)d$$

So

$$\frac{(0.85)(4)(\sqrt{3000})(96 + 2d)d}{1000} \geq 487$$

$$(96 + 2d)d \geq 2615.1$$

$$d \approx 19.4 \text{ in.}$$

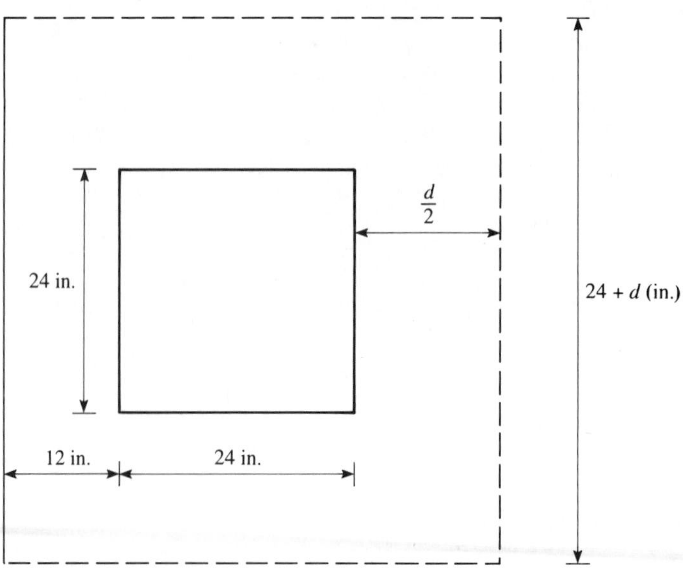

▼ **FIGURE 4.10** Critical perimeter column

For the critical internal column shown in Figure 4.11,

$$b_o = 4(24 + d) = 96 + 4d \text{ (in.)}$$

$$U = (1.4)(440) + (1.7)(300) = 1126 \text{ kip}$$

and

$$\frac{(0.85)(4)(\sqrt{3000})(96 + 4d)d}{1000} \geq 1126$$

$$(96 + 4d)d \geq 6046.4$$

$$d \approx 28.7 \text{ in.}$$

Use $d = 29$ in.

With a minimum cover of 3 in. over the steel reinforcement and 1-in. diameter steel bars, the total slab thickness is

$$h = 29 + 3 + 1 = \mathbf{33 \text{ in.}}$$

Part b: Average Soil Reaction

Refer to Figure 4.9. For strip *ABMN* (width = 14 ft),

$$q_1 = \frac{q_{(\text{at } A)} + q_{(\text{at } B)}}{2} = \frac{1.082 + 1.106}{2} = \mathbf{1.094 \text{ kip/ft}^2}$$

$$q_2 = \frac{q_{(\text{at } M)} + q_{(\text{at } N)}}{2} = \frac{1.212 + 1.188}{2} = \mathbf{1.20 \text{ kip/ft}^2}$$

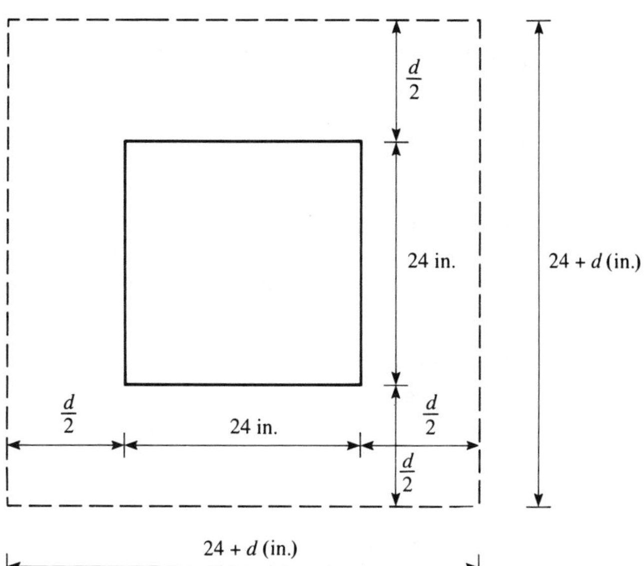

▼ **FIGURE 4.11** Critical internal column

For strip *BCDKLM* (width = 24 ft),

$$q_1 = \frac{1.106 + 1.127 + 1.147}{3} = \mathbf{1.127\ kip/ft^2}$$

$$q_2 = \frac{1.253 + 1.233 + 1.212}{3} = \mathbf{1.233\ kip/ft^2}$$

For strip *DEFIJK* (width = 24 ft),

$$q_1 = \frac{1.147 + 1.167 + 1.188}{3} = \mathbf{1.167\ kip/ft^2}$$

$$q_2 = \frac{1.294 + 1.273 + 1.253}{3} = \mathbf{1.273\ kip/ft^2}$$

For strip *FGHI* (width = 14 ft),

$$q_1 = \frac{1.188 + 1.212}{2} = \mathbf{1.20\ kip/ft^2}$$

$$q_2 = \frac{1.318 + 1.294}{2} = \mathbf{1.306\ kip/ft^2}$$

Check for $\Sigma F_V = 0$:

$$\text{Soil reaction for strip } ABMN = \frac{1}{2}(1.094 + 1.20)(14)(96) = 1541.6 \text{ kip}$$

$$\text{Soil reaction for strip } BCDKLM = \frac{1}{2}(1.127 + 1.233)(24)(96) = 2718.7 \text{ kip}$$

$$\text{Soil reaction for strip } DEFIJK = \frac{1}{2}(1.167 + 1.273)(24)(96) = 2810.9 \text{ kip}$$

$$\text{Soil reaction for strip } FGHJ = \frac{1}{2}(1.20 + 1.306)(14)(96) = \underline{1684.0 \text{ kip}}$$

$$\Sigma\ 8755.2 \text{ kip} \approx \sum \text{Column load} = 8761 \text{ kip—OK}$$

Part c: Reinforcement Requirements

Refer to Figure 4.12 for the design of strip *BCDKLM*. Figure 4.12a shows the load diagram, in which

$$Q_1 = (1.4)(180) + (1.7)(120) = 456 \text{ kip}$$

$$Q_2 = (1.4)(360) + (1.7)(200) = 844 \text{ kip}$$

$$Q_3 = (1.4)(400) + (1.7)(240) = 968 \text{ kip}$$

$$Q_4 = (1.4)(180) + (1.7)(120) = 456 \text{ kip}$$

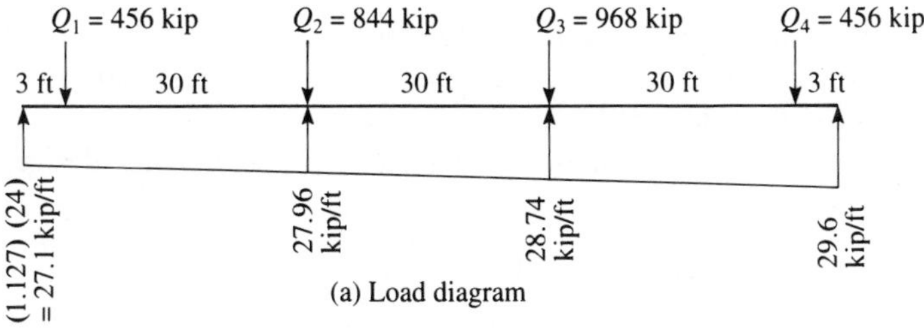

(a) Load diagram

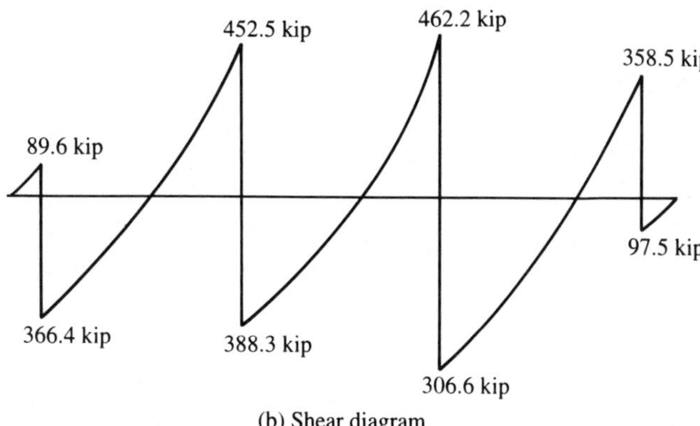

(b) Shear diagram

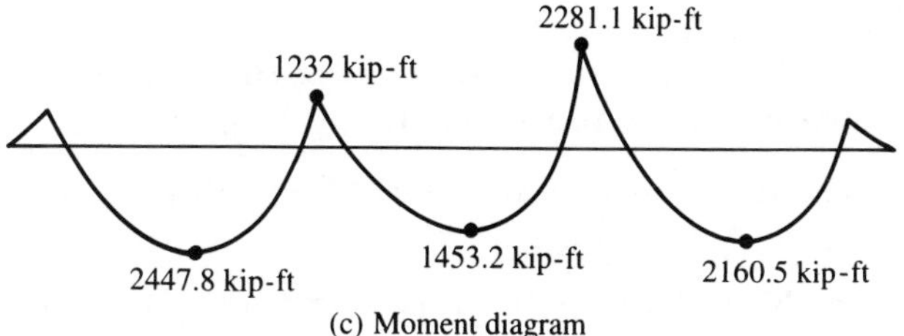

(c) Moment diagram

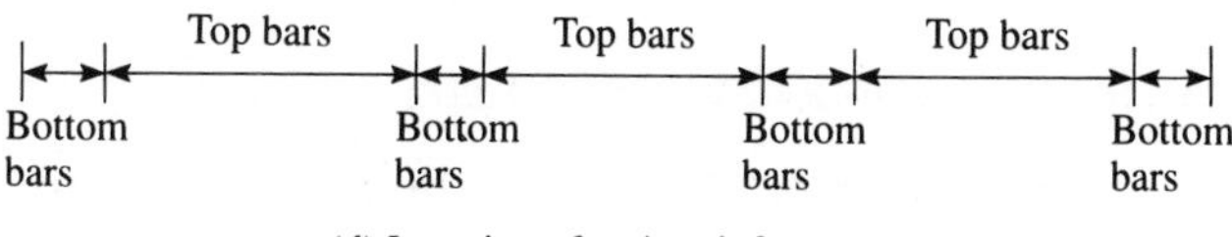

(d) Location of main reinforcement

▼ **FIGURE 4.12**

The shear and moment diagrams are shown in Figures 4.12b and c, respectively. From Figure 4.12c, the maximum positive moment at the bottom of the foundation = 2281.1/24 = 95.05 kip-ft/ft.

Refer to the discussion in Section A.1 (Appendix) for design concepts for a rectangular section in bending:

$$\sum \text{Compressive force, } C = 0.85 f'_c ab$$

$$\sum \text{Tensile force, } T = A_s f_y$$

$$C = T$$

$$(0.85)(3)(12)a = A_s(60)$$

$$A_s = 0.51a$$

From Eq. (A.6),

$$M_u = \phi A_s f_y \left(d - \frac{a}{2}\right)$$

$$(95.05)(12) = (0.9)(0.51a)(60)\left(29 - \frac{a}{2}\right)$$

$$a = 1.47 \text{ in.}$$

Thus

$$A_s = (0.51)(1.47) = 0.75 \text{ in}^2$$

- ▶ Minimum reinforcement, s_{min} (ACI 318-89, Section 10.5) = $200/f_y$ = 200/60,000 = 0.00333
- ▶ Minimum A_s = (0.00333)(12)(29) = 1.16 in^2/ft. Hence use minimum reinforcement with A_s = 1.16 in^2/ft.
- ▶ **Use No. 9 bars at 10 in. center-to-center (A_s = 1.2 in^2/ft) at the bottom of the foundation.**

From Figure 4.12c, the maximum negative moment = 2447.8 kip-ft/24 = 102 kip-ft/ft. By observation, $A_s \leq A_{s(\min)}$.

- ▶ **Use No. 9 bars at 10 in. center-to-center at the top of the foundation.**

Approximate Flexible Method

In the conventional rigid method of design, the mat is assumed to be infinitely rigid. Also, the soil pressure is distributed in a straight line, and the centroid of the soil pressure is concidental with the line of action of the resultant column loads (see Figure 4.13a). In the *approximate flexible method* of design, the soil is assumed to be equivalent to infinitely many elastic springs, as shown in Figure 4.13b. It is sometimes referred to as the *Winkler foundation*. The elastic constant of these assumed springs is referred to as the *coefficient of subgrade reaction, k*.

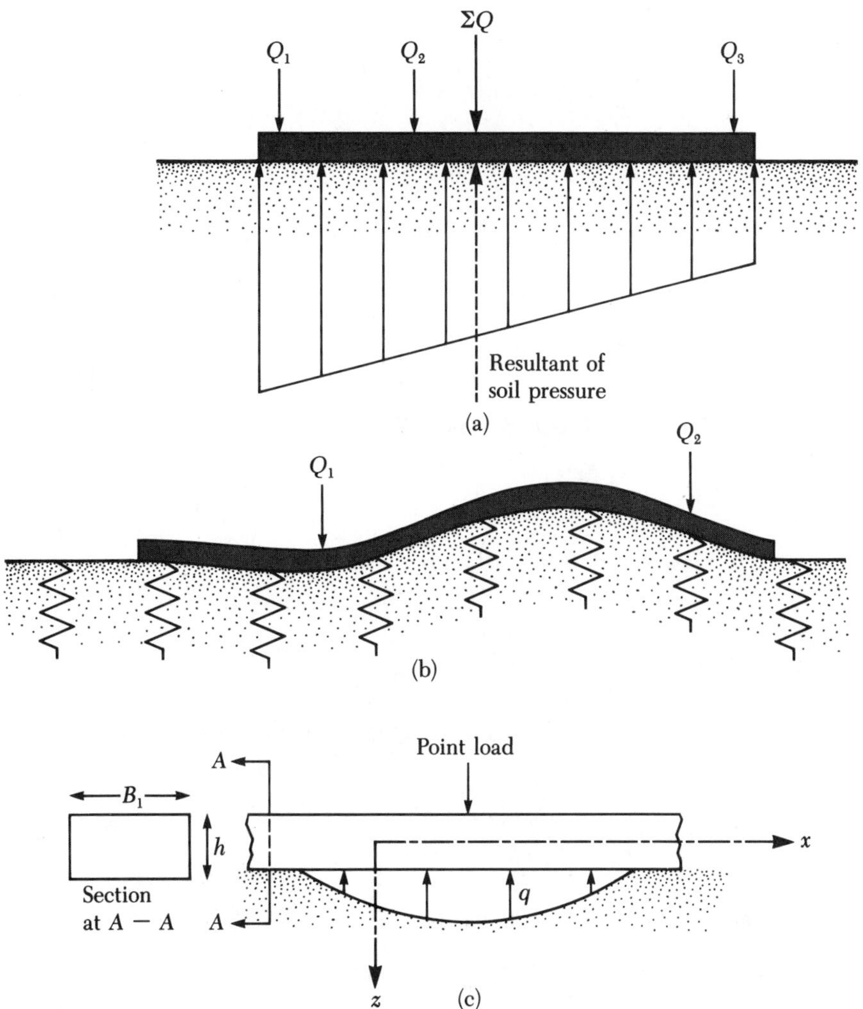

▼ **FIGURE 4.13** (a) Principles of design by conventional rigid method; (b) principles of approximate flexible method; (c) derivation of Eq. (4.40) for beams on elastic foundation

To understand the fundamental concepts behind flexible foundation design, consider a beam of width B_1 having infinite length, as shown in Figure 4.13c. The beam is subjected to a single concentrated load Q. From the fundamentals of mechanics of materials,

$$M = E_F I_F \frac{d^2 z}{dx^2} \tag{4.36}$$

where M = moment at any section
E_F = Modulus of elasticity of foundation material
I_F = moment of inertia of the cross section of the beam = $(1/12)B_1 h^3$ (see Figure 4.13c).

However

$$\frac{dM}{dx} = \text{shear force} = V$$

and

$$\frac{dV}{dx} = q = \text{soil reaction}$$

Hence

$$\frac{d^2M}{dx^2} = q \tag{4.37}$$

Combining Eqs. (4.36) and (4.37) yields

$$E_F I_F \frac{d^4z}{dx^4} = q \tag{4.38}$$

However, the soil reaction is

$$q = -zk'$$

where z = deflection
$k' = kB_1$
k = coefficient of subgrade reaction (kN/m^3 or lb/in^3)

So

$$E_F I_F = \frac{d^4z}{dx^2} = -zkB_1 \tag{4.39}$$

Solution of Eq. (4.39) yields

$$z = e^{-\alpha x}(A' \cos \beta x + A'' \sin \beta x) \tag{4.40}$$

where A' and A'' are constants and

$$\beta = \sqrt[4]{\frac{B_1 k}{4E_F I_F}} \tag{4.41}$$

The unit of the term β as defined by the preceding equation is (length)$^{-1}$. This parameter is very important in determining whether a mat foundation should be designed by conventional rigid method or approximate flexible method. According to the American Concrete Institute Committee 436 (1966), mats should be designed by the conventional rigid method if the spacing of columns in a strip is less than $1.75/\beta$. If the spacing of columns is larger than $1.75/\beta$, the approximate flexible method may be used.

To perform the analysis for the structural design of a flexible mat, you must know the principles of evaluating the *coefficient of subgrade reaction, k*. Before proceeding with the discussion of the approximate flexible design method, let us discuss this coefficient in more detail.

If a foundation of width B (Figure 4.14) is subjected to a load per unit area of q, it will undergo a settlement, Δ. The coefficient of subgrade modulus, k, can be defined as

$$k = \frac{q}{\Delta} \tag{4.42}$$

The unit of k is kN/m^3 (or lb/in^3). The value of the coefficient of subgrade reaction is not a constant for a given soil. It depends on several factors, such as the length, L, and width, B, of the foundation and also the depth of embedment of the foundation. Terzaghi (1955) made a comprehensive study of the parameters affecting the coefficient of subgrade reaction. It indicated that the value of the coefficient of subgrade reaction decreases with the width of the foundation. In the field, load tests can be carried out by means of square plates measuring 1 ft × 1 ft (0.3 m × 0.3 m), and values of k can be calculated. The value of k can be related to large foundations measuring $B \times B$ in the following ways.

Foundations on Sandy Soils

$$k = k_{0.3}\left(\frac{B + 0.3}{2B}\right)^2 \tag{4.43}$$

where $k_{0.3}$ and k = coefficients of subgrade reaction of footings measuring 0.3 m × 0.3 m and B (m) × B (m), respectively (unit is kN/m^3)

In English units, Eq. (4.43) may be expressed as

$$k = k_1\left(\frac{B + 1}{2B}\right)^2 \tag{4.44}$$

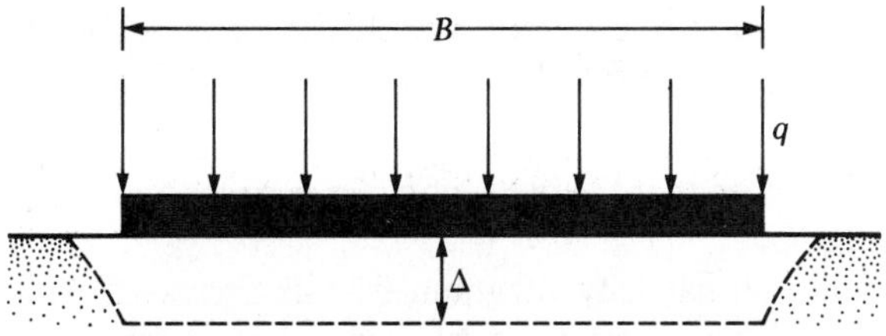

▼ **FIGURE 4.14** Definition of coefficient of subgrade reaction, k

where k_1 and k = coefficients of subgrade reaction of footings measuring 1 ft × 1 ft and B (ft) × B (ft), respectively (unit is lb/in³)

Foundations on Clays

$$k\ (\text{kN/m}^3) = k_{0.3}\ (\text{kN/m}^3)\left[\frac{0.3\ (\text{m})}{B\ (\text{m})}\right] \tag{4.45}$$

The definition of k in Eq. (4.45) is the same as in Eq. (4.43).

In English units,

$$k\ (\text{lb/in}^3) = k_1\ (\text{lb/in}^3)\left[\frac{1\ (\text{ft})}{B\ (\text{ft})}\right] \tag{4.46}$$

The definitions of k and k_1 are the same as in Eq. (4.44).

For rectangular foundations having dimensions of $B \times L$ (for similar soil and q),

$$k = \frac{k_{(B \times B)}\left(1 + 0.5\,\frac{B}{L}\right)}{1.5} \tag{4.47}$$

where k = coefficient of subgrade modulus of the rectangular foundation $(L \times B)$

$k_{(B \times B)}$ = coefficient of subgrade modulus of a square foundation having dimension of $B \times B$

Equation (4.47) indicates that the value of k of a very long foundation with a width B is approximately $0.67k_{(B \times B)}$.

The modulus of elasticity of granular soils increases with depth. Because the settlement of a foundation depends on the modulus of elasticity, the value of k increases as the depth of the foundation increases.

Following are some typical ranges of value for the coefficient of subgrade reaction k_1 for sandy and clayey soils.

Sand (dry or moist)	
Loose:	29–92 lb/in^3 (8–25 MN/m^3)
Medium:	91–460 lb/in^3 (25–125 MN/m^3)
Dense:	460–1380 lb/in^3 (125–375 MN/m^3)
Sand (saturated)	
Loose:	38–55 lb/in^3 (10–15 MN/m^3)
Medium:	128–147 lb/in^3 (35–40 MN/m^3)
Dense:	478–552 lb/in^3 (130–150 MN/m^3)
Clay	
Stiff:	44–92 lb/in^3 (12–25 MN/m^3)
Very stiff:	92–184 lb/in^3 (25–50 MN/m^3)
Hard:	>184 lb/in^3 (>50 MN/m^3)

Scott (1981) proposed that for sandy soils the value of $k_{0.3}$ can be obtained from standard penetration resistance at any given depth, or

$$k_{0.3}\ (\text{MN/m}^3) = 1.8N \tag{4.48}$$

where $N =$ *corrected* standard penetration resistance

In English units,

$$k_1\ (\text{U.S. ton/ft}^3) = 6N \tag{4.49}$$

For long beams, Vesic (1961) proposed an equation for estimating subgrade reaction:

$$k' = Bk = 0.65\sqrt[12]{\frac{E_s B^4}{E_F I_F}}\frac{E_s}{1-\mu^2}$$

or

$$k = 0.65\sqrt[12]{\frac{E_s B^4}{E_F I_F}}\frac{E_s}{B(1-\mu^2)} \tag{4.50}$$

where $E_s =$ modulus of elasticity of soil
$B =$ foundation width
$E_F =$ modulus of elasticity of foundation material
$I_F =$ moment of inertia of the cross section of the foundation
$\mu =$ Poisson's ratio of soil

For most practical purposes, Eq. (4.50) can be approximated as

$$k = \frac{E_s}{B(1-\mu^2)} \tag{4.51}$$

The coefficient of subgrade reaction is also a very useful parameter in the design of rigid highway and airfield pavements. The pavement with a concrete wearing surface is generally referred to as a *rigid pavement*, and the pavement with an asphaltic wearing surface is called a *flexible pavement*. For a surface load acting on a rigid pavement, the maximum tensile stress occurs at the base of the slab. For estimating the magnitude of the maximum horizontal tensile stress developed at the base of the rigid pavement, elastic solutions involving slabs on Winkler foundations are extremely useful. Some of the early work in this area was done by Westergaard (1926, 1939, 1947).

Now that we have discussed the coefficient of subgrade reaction, we will proceed with the discussion of the approximate flexible method of designing mat foundations. This method, as proposed by the American Concrete Institute Committee 436 (1966), is described step by step. The design procedure is based primarily on the theory of plates. Its use allows the effects (that is, moment, shear, and deflection) of a concentrated column load in the area surrounding it to be evaluated. If the zones of influence of two or more columns overlap, superposition can be used to obtain the net moment, shear, and deflection at any point.

1. Assume a thickness, h, for the mat, according to Step 6 as outlined for the conventional rigid method. (*Note:* h is the *total* thickness of the mat.)
2. Determine the flexural ridigity R of the mat:

$$R = \frac{E_F h^3}{12(1 - \mu_F^2)} \tag{4.52}$$

where E_F = modulus of elasticity of foundation material
μ_F = Poisson's ratio of foundation material

3. Determine the radius of effective stiffness:

$$L' = \sqrt[4]{\frac{R}{k}} \tag{4.53}$$

where k = coefficient of subgrade reaction

The zone of influence of any column load will be on the order of 3 to 4 L'.

4. Determine the moment (in polar coordinates at a point) caused by a column load (Figure 4.15a):

$$M_t = \text{tangential moment} = -\frac{Q}{4}\left[A_1 - \frac{(1 - \mu_F)A_2}{\dfrac{r}{L'}}\right] \tag{4.54}$$

$$M_r = \text{radial moment} = -\frac{Q}{4}\left[\mu_F A_1 + \frac{(1 - \mu_F)A_2}{\dfrac{r}{L'}}\right] \tag{4.55}$$

where r = radial distance from the column load
Q = column load
A_1, A_2 = functions of r/L'

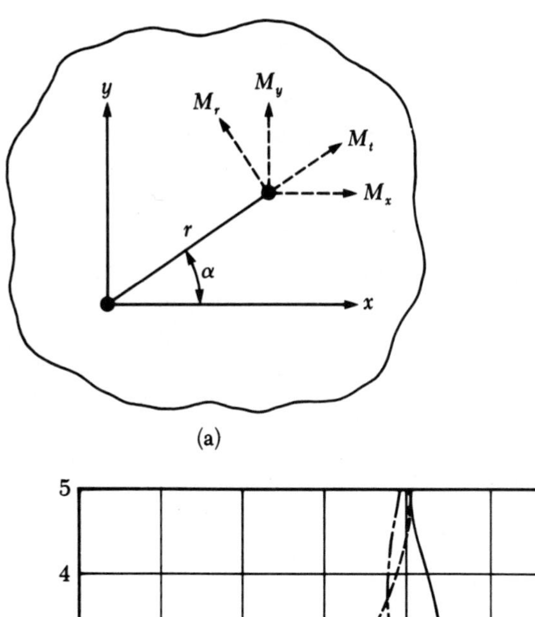

(a)

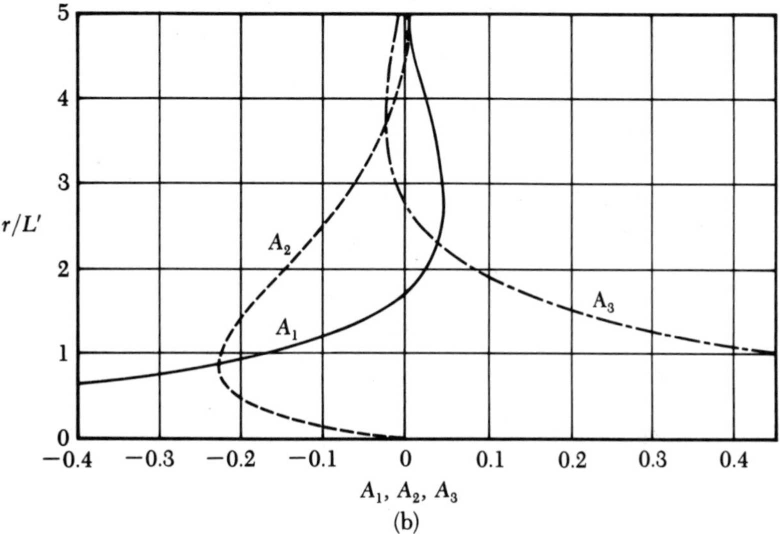

(b)

▼ **FIGURE 4.15** Approximate flexible method of mat design

The variations of A_1 and A_2 with r/L' are shown in Figure 4.15b (for details, see Hetenyi, 1946).

In the cartesian coordinate system (Figure 4.15a),

$$M_x = M_t \sin^2 \alpha + M_r \cos^2 \alpha \tag{4.56}$$

$$M_y = M_t \cos^2 \alpha + M_r \sin^2 \alpha \tag{4.57}$$

5. For the unit width of the mat, determine the shear force, V, caused by a column load:

$$V = -\frac{Q}{4L'} A_3 \tag{4.58}$$

The variation of A_3 with r/L' is shown in Figure 4.15b.

6. If the edge of the mat is located in the zone of influence of a column, determine the moment and shear along the wedge (assume that the mat is continuous). Moment and shear opposite in sign to those determined are applied at the edges to satisfy the known conditions.

▼ EXAMPLE 4.8

From the plate load test (plate dimension 1 ft × 1 ft) in the field, the coefficient of subgrade reaction of a sandy soil was determined to be 80 lb/in³. (a) What will be the value of the coefficient of subgrade reaction on the same soil for a foundation with dimensions of 30 ft × 30 ft? (b) If the full-sized foundation has dimensions of 45 ft × 30 ft, what will be the value of the coefficient of subgrade reaction?

Solution

Part a

From Eq. (4.44),

$$k = k_1\left(\frac{B+1}{2B}\right)^2$$

where $k_1 = 80\ \text{lb/in}^2$
$B = 30$ ft

So

$$k = 80\left[\frac{30+1}{(2)(30)}\right] = \mathbf{21.36\ in^3}$$

Part b

From Eq. (4.47),

$$k = \frac{k_{(B\times B)}\left(1+0.5\dfrac{B}{L}\right)}{1.5}$$

$$k_{(30\ \text{ft}\times 30\ \text{ft})} = 21.36\ \text{lb/in}^3$$

So

$$k = \frac{(21.36)\left(1+0.5\dfrac{30}{45}\right)}{1.5} = \mathbf{19\ lb/in^3}$$ ▼

PROBLEMS

4.1 A mat foundation measuring 45 ft × 30 ft has to be constructed on a saturated clay. For the clay, $c_u = 1950\ \text{lb/ft}^2$ and $\phi = 0$. The depth, D_f, for the mat foundation is 6.5 ft. Determine the net ultimate bearing capacity.

4.2 Repeat Problem 4.1 with the following.

- Mat foundation: $B = 10$ m, $L = 20$ m, and $D_f = 3$ m
- Clay: $\phi = 0$ and $c_u = 100\ \text{kN/m}^2$

4.3 Following are the results of a standard penetration test in the field (sandy soil).

Depth (m)	*Field value of N*
2	8
4	10
6	12
8	9
10	14

Estimate the net allowable bearing capacity of a mat foundation 6 m × 5 m in plan. Here, $D_f = 1.5$ m and allowable settlement = 50.8 mm. Assume that the unit weight of soil, $\gamma = 17.5 \text{ kN/m}^3$.

4.4 Repeat Problem 4.3 for an allowable settlement of 30 mm.

4.5 Consider a mat foundation with dimensions of 60 ft × 40 ft. The combined dead and live load on the mat is 10^7 lb. The mat is to be placed on a clay with $c_u = 850 \text{ lb/ft}^2$ and $\gamma = 112 \text{ lb/ft}^3$. Find the depth, D_f, of the mat for a fully compensated foundation.

4.6 For the mat in Problem 4.5, what will be the depth, D_f, of the mat for $FS = 3$ against bearing capacity failure?

4.7 Repeat Problem 4.6 for an undrained cohesion of the clay of 1250 lb/ft².

4.8 A mat foundation is shown in Figure P4.8. The design considerations are $L = 15$ m, $B = 7.5$ m, $D_f = 3$ m, $Q = 35$ MN, $x_1 = 2.5$ m, $x_2 = 2.75$ m, $x_3 = 4$ m, $p_c = 105 \text{ kN/m}^2$. Calculate the consolidation settlement under the center of the mat.

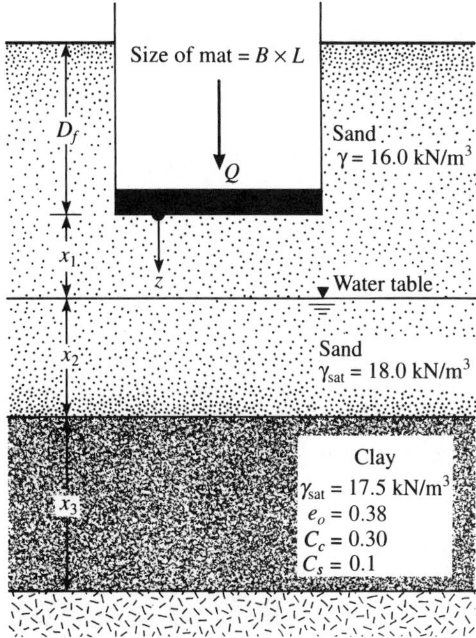

▼ **FIGURE P4.8**

4.9 For the mat foundation in Problem 4.8, estimate the consolidation settlement under the corner of the mat.

4.10 Refer to Figure P4.10. For the mat, Q_1, $Q_3 = 40$ tons, Q_4, Q_5, $Q_6 = 60$ tons, Q_2, $Q_9 =$ 45 tons, and Q_7, $Q_8 = 50$ tons. All columns are 20 in. × 20 in. in cross section. Use the procedure outlined in Section 4.7 to determine the pressure on the soil at *A*, *B*, *C*, *D*, *F*, *G*, and *H*.

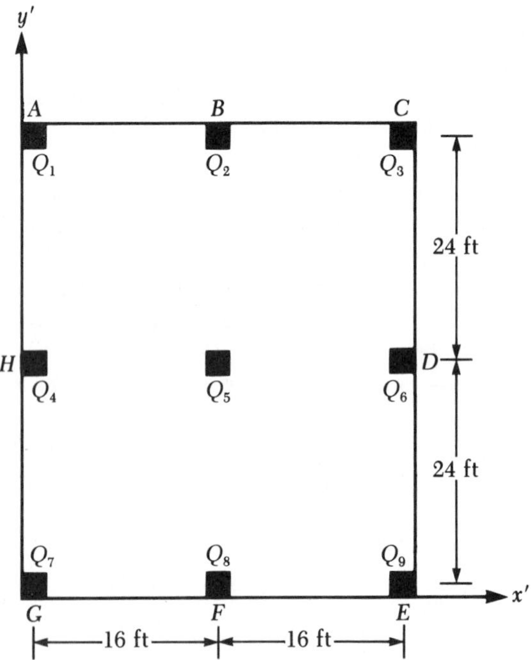

▼ **FIGURE P4.10**

4.11 The plan of a mat foundation with column loads is shown in Figure P4.11. Calculate the soil pressure at points *A*, *B*, *C*, *D*, *E*, and *F*. *Note:* All columns are 0.5 m × 0.5 m in plan.

4.12 Divide the mat shown in Figure P4.11 into three strips, such as *AGHF* ($B_1 = 4.25$ m), *GIJH* ($B_1 = 8$ m), and *ICDJ* ($B_1 = 4.25$ m). Use the results of Problem 4.11 and determine the reinforcement requirements in the *y* direction. Here, $f'_c = 20.7$ MN/m², $f_y = 413.7$ MN/m², and the load factor is 1.7.

4.13 From a plate load test (plate dimension 1 ft × 1 ft) in the field, the coefficient of subgrade reaction of a sandy soil was determined to be 65 lb/in³. What will be the value of subgrade reaction on the same soil for a foundation with dimensions of 30 ft × 30 ft?

4.14 Refer to Problem 4.13. If the full-sized foundation has dimensions of 40 ft × 25 ft, what will be the value of the coefficient of the subgrade reaction?

4.15 The subgrade reaction of a sandy soil obtained from a plate load test (plate dimensions 1 m × 0.7 m) is 22 kN/m². What will be the value of *k* on the same soil for a foundation measuring 4 m × 3 m?

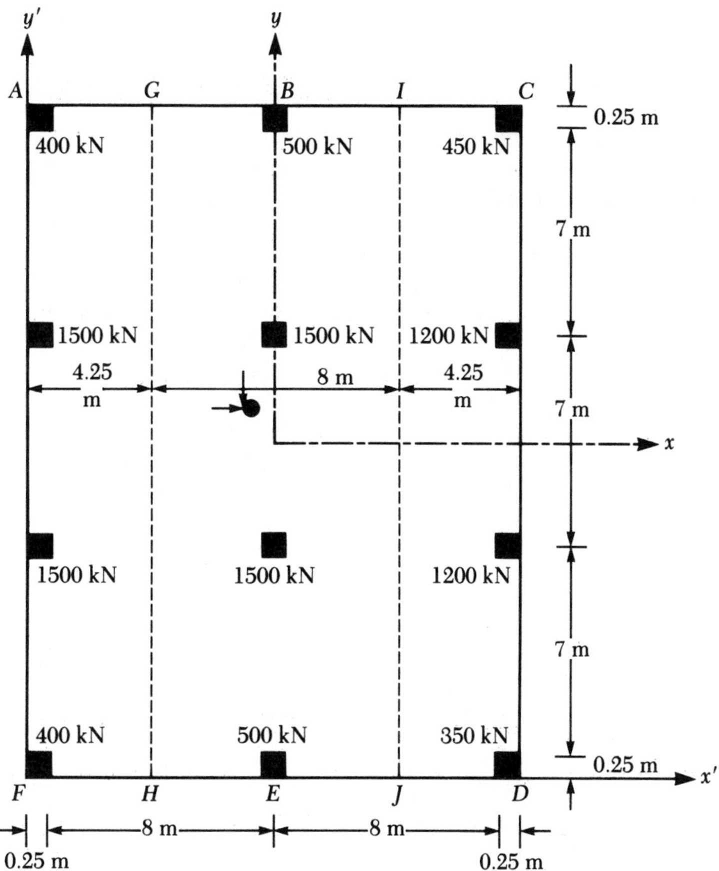

▼ **FIGURE P4.11**

REFERENCES

American Concrete Institute (1989). *ACI Standard Building Code Requirements for Reinforced Concrete*, ACI 318-89, Detroit.

American Concrete Institute Committee 436 (1966). "Suggested Design Procedures for Combined Footings and Mats," *Journal of the American Concrete Institute*, Vol. 63, No. 10, pp. 1041–1077.

Hetenyi, M. (1946). *Beams of Elastic Foundations*, University of Michigan Press, Ann Arbor.

Meyerhof, G. G. (1965). "Shallow Foundations," *Journal of the Soil Mechanics and Foundations Division*, American Society of Civil Engineers, Vol. 91, No. SM2, pp. 21–31.

Rios, L., and Silva, F. P. (1948). "Foundations in Downtown Sao Paulo (Brazil)," *Proceedings*, Second International Conference on Soil Mechanics and Foundation Engineering, Rotterdam, Vol. 4, p. 69.

Schultze, E. (1962). "Probleme bei der Auswertung von Setzungsmessungen," *Proceedings*, Baugrundtagung, Essen, Germany, p. 343.

Scott, R. F. (1981). *Foundation Analysis*, Prentice-Hall, Englewood Cliffs, N.J.

Stuart, J. G., and Graham, J. (1975). "Settlement Performance of a Raft Foundation on Sand," in *Settlement of Structures*, Halsted Press, New York, pp. 62–67.

Terzaghi, K. (1955). "Evaluation of the Coefficient of Subgrade Reactions," *Geotechnique*, Institute of Engineers, London, Vol. 5, No. 4, pp. 197–226.

Vargas, M. (1948). "Building Settlement Observations in Sao Paulo," *Proceedings*, Second International Conference on Soil Mechanics and Foundation Engineering, Rotterdam, Vol. 4, p. 13.

Vargas, M. (1961). "Foundations of Tall Buildings on Sand in Sao Paulo (Brazil)," *Proceedings*, Fifth International Conference on Soil Mechanics and Foundation Engineering, Paris, Vol. 1, p. 841.

Vesic, A. S. (1961). "Bending of Beams Resting on Isotropic Solid," *Journal of the Engineering Mechanics Division*, American Society of Civil Engineers, Vol. 87, No. EM2, pp. 35–53.

Westgaard, H. M. (1926). "Stresses in Concrete Pavements Computed by Theoretical Analysis," *Public Roads*, Vol. 7, No. 12, pp. 23–35.

Westergaard, H. M. (1939). "Stresses in Concrete Runways of Airports," *Proceedings*, Highway Research Board, Vol. 19, pp. 197–205.

Westergaard, H. M. (1947). "New Formulas for Stresses in Concrete Pavements of Airfields," *Proceedings*, American Society of Civil Engineers, Vol. 73, pp. 687–701.

CHAPTER FIVE

LATERAL EARTH PRESSURE AND RETAINING WALLS

5.1 INTRODUCTION

Retaining walls provide lateral support for *vertical* or *near-vertical* slopes of soil. These structures are commonly used in construction projects and may be classified generally as

1. Gravity retaining walls
2. Semigravity retaining walls
3. Cantilever retaining walls
4. Counterfort retaining walls

Gravity retaining walls (Figure 5.1a) are constructed with plain concrete or stone masonry. They depend on their own weight and any soil resting on the masonry for stability. This type of construction is not economical for high walls.

In many cases, a small amount of steel may be used for the construction of gravity walls, thereby minimizing the size of wall sections. Such walls are generally referred to as *semigravity walls* (Figure 5.1b).

Cantilever retaining walls (Figure 5.1c) are made of reinforced concrete that consists of a thin stem and a base slab. This type of wall is economical to a height of about 25 ft (8 m).

Counterfort retaining walls (Figure 5.1d) are similar to cantilever walls. At regular intervals, however, they have thin vertical concrete slabs known as *counterforts* that tie the wall and the base slab together. The purpose of the counterforts is to reduce the shear and the bending moments.

To design retaining walls properly, an engineer must know the basic soil parameters—that is, the *unit weight, angle of friction*, and *cohesion*—for the soil retained behind the wall and the soil below the base slab. Knowing the properties of the soil behind the wall enables the engineer to determine the lateral pressure distribution that has to be designed for.

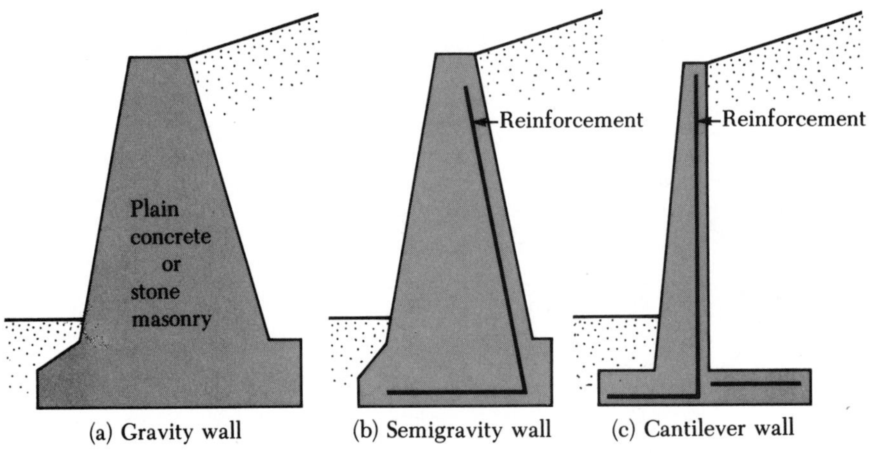

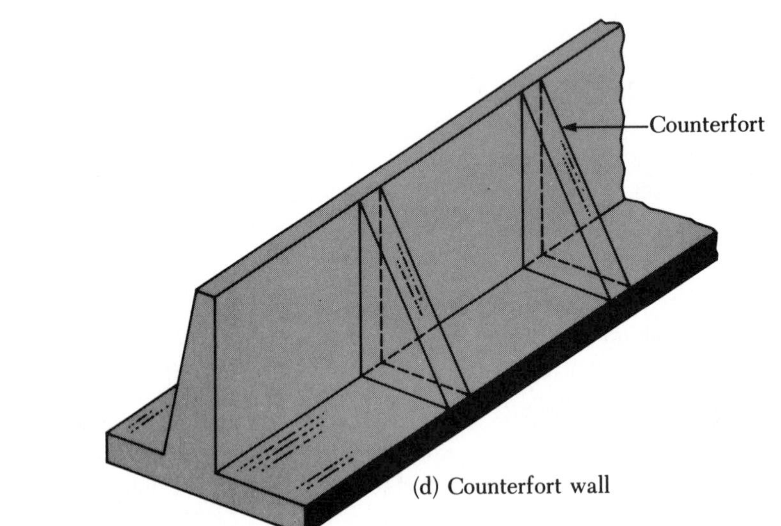

▼ **FIGURE 5.1** Types of retaining wall

There are two phases in the design of a retaining wall. First, with the lateral earth pressure known, the structure as a whole is checked for *stability*. That includes checking for possible *overturning*, *sliding*, and *bearing capacity* failures. Second, each component of the structure is checked for *adequate strength*, and the *steel reinforcement* of each component is determined.

This chapter presents the procedures for determining lateral earth pressure and retaining-wall stability. Checks for adequate strength of each component of the structures are covered in Appendix A.

LATERAL EARTH PRESSURE

5.2 LATERAL EARTH PRESSURE AT REST

Consider a vertical wall of height H, as shown in Figure 5.2, retaining a soil having a unit weight of γ. A uniformly distributed load, q/unit area, is also applied at the ground surface. The shear strength, s, of the soil is

$$s = c + \sigma' \tan \phi$$

where c = cohesion
ϕ = angle of friction
σ' = effective normal stress

At any depth z below the ground surface, the vertical subsurface stress is

$$\sigma_v = q + \gamma z \tag{5.1}$$

If the *wall is not allowed to move at all* either way from the soil mass or into the soil mass (e.g., zero horizontal strain), the lateral pressure at a depth z is

$$\sigma_h = K_o \sigma'_v + u \tag{5.2}$$

where u = pore water pressure
K_o = coefficient of at-rest earth pressure

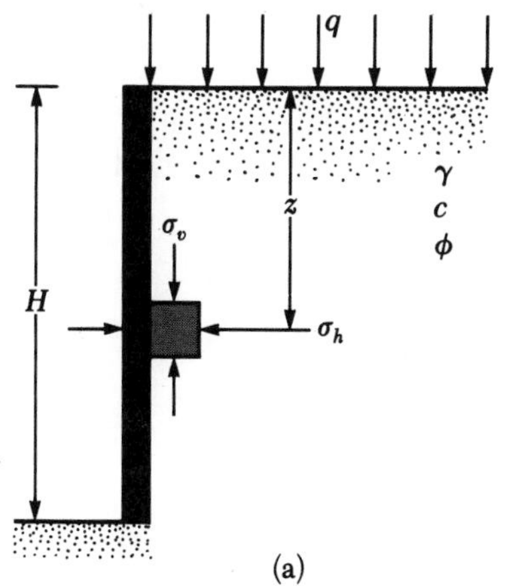

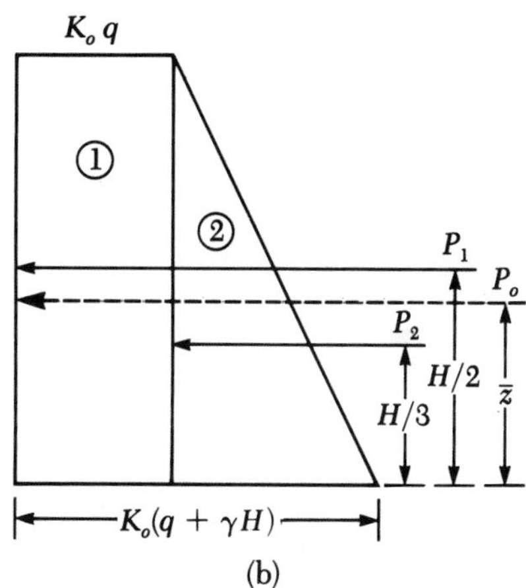

▼ **FIGURE 5.2** At-rest earth pressure

For normally consolidated soil, the relation for K_o (Jaky, 1944) is

$$\boxed{K_o \approx 1 - \sin \phi} \tag{5.3}$$

Equation (5.3) is an empirical approximation.

For normally consolidated clays, the coefficient of earth pressure at rest can be approximated (Brooker and Ireland, 1965) as

$$\boxed{K_o \approx 0.95 - \sin \phi} \tag{5.4}$$

where ϕ = drained friction angle

Based on Brooker and Ireland's (1965) experimental results, the value of K_o for normally consolidated clays may be approximately correlated with the plasticity index (PI):

$$K_o = 0.4 + 0.007(PI) \qquad \text{(for } PI \text{ between 0 and 40)} \tag{5.5}$$

and

$$K_o = 0.64 + 0.001(PI) \qquad \text{(for } PI \text{ between 40 and 80)} \tag{5.6}$$

For overconsolidated clays,

$$\boxed{K_{o(\text{overconsolidated})} \approx K_{o(\text{normally consolidated})}\sqrt{OCR}} \tag{5.7}$$

where OCR = overconsolidation ratio

Mayne and Kulhawy (1982) analyzed the results of 171 different laboratory tested soils. Based on this study, they proposed a general empirical relationship to estimate the magnitude of K_o for sand and clay:

$$K_o = (1 - \sin \phi)\left[\frac{OCR}{OCR_{\max}^{(1-\sin\phi)}} + \frac{3}{4}\left(1 - \frac{OCR}{OCR_{\max}}\right)\right] \tag{5.8}$$

where OCR = present overconsolidation ratio
OCR_{max} = maximum overconsolidation ratio

In Figure 5.3, OCR_{max} is the value of OCR at point B.

With a properly selected value of the at-rest earth pressure coefficient, Eq. (5.2) can be used to determine the variation of lateral earth pressure with depth, z. Figure 5.2b shows the variation of σ_h with depth for the wall shown in Figure 5.2a. Note that if the surcharge $q = 0$ and the pore water pressure $u = 0$, the pressure diagram will

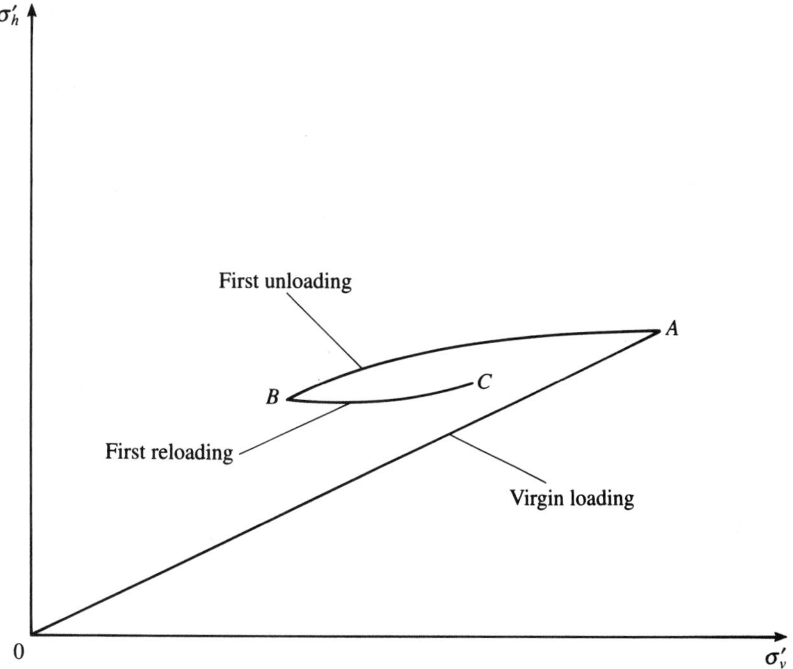

▼ **FIGURE 5.3** Stress history for soil under K_o condition

be a triangle. The total force, P_o, *per unit length* of the wall given in Figure 5.2a can now be obtained from the area of the pressure diagram given in Figure 5.2b as

$$P_o = P_1 + P_2 = qK_oH + \frac{1}{2}\gamma H^2 K_o \tag{5.9}$$

where P_1 = area of rectangle 1
P_2 = area of triangle 2

The location of the line of action of the resultant force, P_o, can be obtained by taking the moment about the bottom of the wall. Thus

$$\bar{z} = \frac{P_1\left(\dfrac{H}{2}\right) + P_2\left(\dfrac{H}{3}\right)}{P_o} \tag{5.10}$$

If the water table is located at depth $z < H$, the at-rest pressure diagram shown in Figure 5.2b will have to be somewhat modified, as shown in Figure 5.4. If the effective unit weight of soil below the water table equals γ' (i.e., $\gamma_{sat} - \gamma_w$),

At $z = 0$, $\sigma'_h = K_o\sigma'_v = K_oq$

At $z = H_1$, $\sigma'_h = K_o\sigma'_v = K_o(q + \gamma H_1)$

At $z = H_2$, $\sigma'_h = K_o\sigma'_v = K_o(q + \gamma H_1 + \gamma' H_2)$

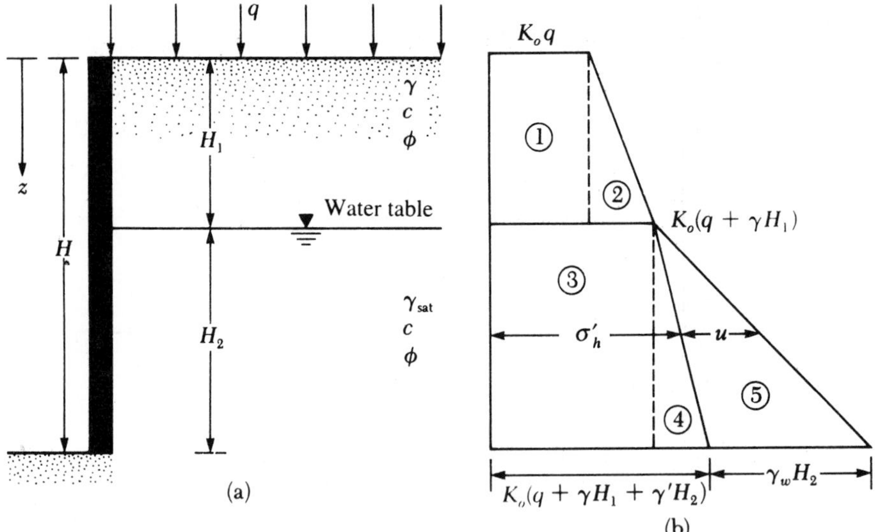

▼ **FIGURE 5.4**

Note that in the preceding equations, σ'_v and σ'_h are effective vertical and horizontal pressures. Determining the total pressure distribution on the wall requires adding the hydrostatic pressure. The hydrostatic pressure, u, is zero from $z = 0$ to $z = H_1$; at $z = H_2$, $u = H_2 \gamma_w$. The variation of σ'_h and u with depth is shown in Figure 5.4b. Hence the total force per unit length of the wall can be determined from the area of the pressure diagram. Thus

$$P_o = A_1 + A_2 + A_3 + A_4 + A_5$$

where A = area of the pressure diagram

So

$$P_o = K_o q H_1 + \frac{1}{2} K_o \gamma H_1^2 + K_o (q + \gamma H_1) H_2 + \frac{1}{2} K_o \gamma' H_2^2 + \frac{1}{2} \gamma_w H_2^2 \quad (5.11)$$

Sherif et al. (1984) showed by several laboratory model tests that Eq. (5.3) gives good results for estimating the lateral earth pressure at rest for loose sands. However, for compacted dense sand, it grossly underestimates the value of K_o. For that reason, they proposed a modified relationship for K_o:

$$K_o = (1 - \sin \phi) + \left(\frac{\gamma_d}{\gamma_{d(\min)}} - 1\right) 5.5 \quad (5.12)$$

where γ_d = *in situ* unit weight of sand
$\gamma_{d(\min)}$ = minimum possible dry unit weight of sand (see Chapter 1)

▼ EXAMPLE 5.1

For the retaining wall shown in Figure 5.5a, determine the lateral earth force at rest per unit length of the wall. Also determine the location of the resultant earth pressure.

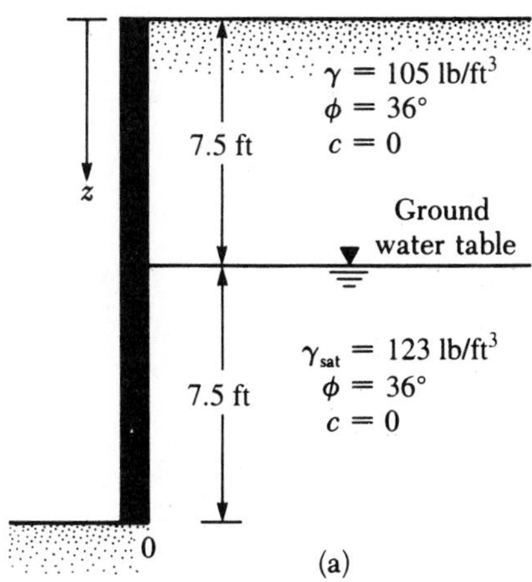

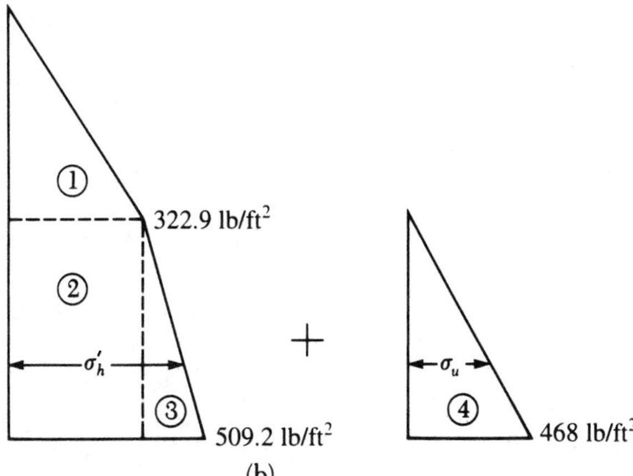

▼ **FIGURE 5.5**

Solution

$$K_o = 1 - \sin \phi = 1 - \sin 36° = 0.41$$

Now the following table can be prepared.

Depth, z (ft)	σ'_v (lb/ft^2)	$\sigma'_h = K_o \sigma'_v$ (lb/ft^2)	u (lb/ft^2)
0	0	0	0
7.5	(105)(7.5) = 787.5	322.9	0
15	(105)(7.5) + (123 − 62.4)(7.5) = 1242	509.2	(62.4)(7.5) = 468

The pressure distribution for the wall is shown in Figure 5.5b.

The total force per unit length of the wall can be determined from the area of the pressure diagram, or

$$P_o = \text{area } 1 + \text{area } 2 + \text{area } 3 + \text{area } 4$$

$$= \frac{1}{2}(7.5)(322.9) + (322.9)(7.5) + \frac{1}{2}(7.5)(509.2 - 322.9) + \frac{1}{3}(7.5)(468)$$

$$= 1210.9 + 2421.8 + 698.6 + 1755 = \mathbf{6086.3\ lb/ft}$$

The location of the center of pressure measured from the bottom of the wall (point O) is

$$\bar{z} = \frac{(\text{area } 1)\left(7.5 + \dfrac{7.5}{3}\right) + (\text{area } 2)\left(\dfrac{7.5}{2}\right) + (\text{area } 3 + \text{area } 4)\left(\dfrac{7.5}{3}\right)}{P_o}$$

$$= \frac{(1210.9)(10) + (2421.8)(3.75) + (698.6 + 1755)(2.5)}{6086.3} = \mathbf{4.49\ ft} \qquad \blacktriangledown$$

5.3 RANKINE ACTIVE EARTH PRESSURE

The lateral earth pressure condition described in Section 5.2 involves walls that do not yield at all. However, if a wall tends to move away from the soil a distance Δx, as shown in Figure 5.6a, the soil pressure on the wall at any depth will decrease. For a wall that is *frictionless*, the horizontal stress, σ_h, at depth z will equal $K_o \sigma_v$ $(=K_o \gamma z)$ when Δx is zero. However, with $\Delta x > 0$, σ_h will be less than $K_o \sigma_v$.

The Mohr's circles corresponding to wall displacements of $\Delta x = 0$ and $\Delta x > 0$ are shown as circles a and b, respectively, in Figure 5.6b. If the displacement of the wall, Δx, continues to increase, the corresponding Mohr's circle eventually will just touch the Mohr–Coulomb failure envelope defined by the equation

$$s = c + \sigma \tan \phi$$

This circle is marked c in Figure 5.6b. It represents the failure condition in the soil mass; the horizontal stress then equals σ_a. This horizontal stress, σ_a, is referred to as the *Rankine active pressure*. The *slip lines* (failure planes) in the soil mass will then make angles of $\pm(45 + \phi/2)$ with the horizontal, as shown in Figure 5.6a.

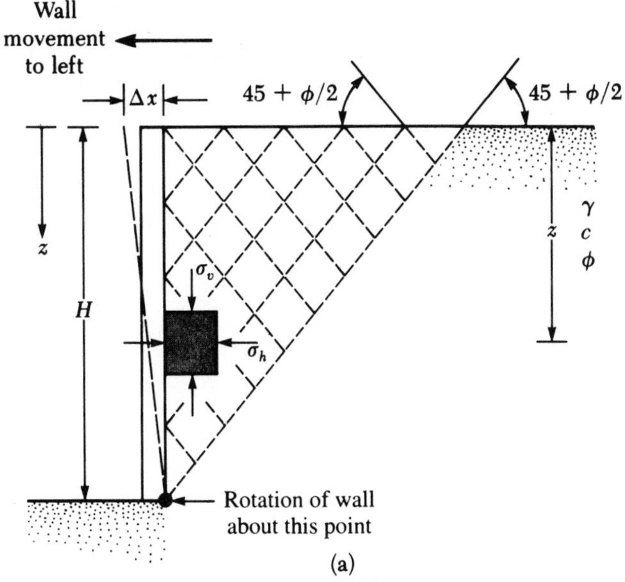

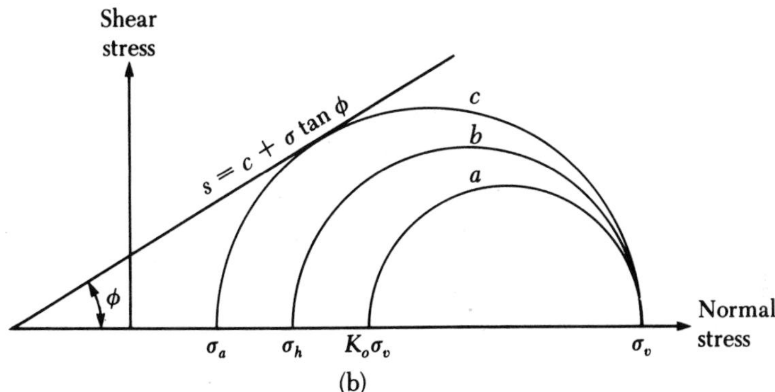

▼ **FIGURE 5.6** Rankine active pressure

Refer back to Eq. (1.78), the equation relating the principal stresses for a Mohr's circle that touches the Mohr–Coulomb failure envelope:

$$\sigma_1 = \sigma_3 \tan^2\left(45 + \frac{\phi}{2}\right) + 2c \tan\left(45 + \frac{\phi}{2}\right)$$

For the Mohr's circle c in Figure 5.6b,

Major principal stress, $\sigma_1 = \sigma_v$

and

Minor principal stress, $\sigma_3 = \sigma_a$

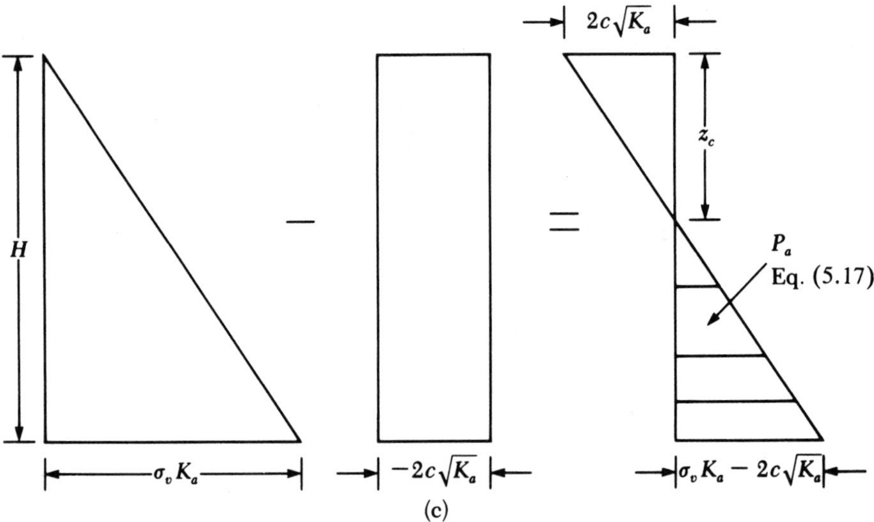

▼ **FIGURE 5.6** (Continued)

Thus

$$\sigma_v = \sigma_a \tan^2\left(45 + \frac{\phi}{2}\right) + 2c \tan\left(45 + \frac{\phi}{2}\right)$$

$$\sigma_a = \frac{\sigma_v}{\tan^2\left(45 + \frac{\phi}{2}\right)} - \frac{2c}{\tan\left(45 + \frac{\phi}{2}\right)}$$

or

$$\sigma_a = \sigma_v \tan^2\left(45 - \frac{\phi}{2}\right) - 2c \tan\left(45 - \frac{\phi}{2}\right) = \sigma_v K_a - 2c\sqrt{K_a} \tag{5.13}$$

where $K_a = \tan^2(45 - \phi/2)$ = Rankine active pressure coefficient (Table 5.1)

The variation of the active pressure with depth for the wall shown in Figure 5.6a is given in Figure 5.6c. Note that $\sigma_v = 0$ at $z = 0$, and $\sigma_v = \gamma H$ at $z = H$. The pressure distribution shows that at $z = 0$ the active pressure equals $-2c\sqrt{K_a}$, indicating tensile stress. This tensile stress decreases with depth and becomes zero at a depth $z = z_c$, or

$$\gamma z_c K_a - 2c\sqrt{K_a} = 0$$

TABLE 5.1 Variation of Rankine K_a

Soil friction angle, ϕ (deg)	$K_a = \tan^2(45 - \phi/2)$
20	0.490
21	0.472
22	0.455
23	0.438
24	0.422
25	0.406
26	0.395
27	0.376
28	0.361
29	0.347
30	0.333
31	0.320
32	0.307
33	0.295
34	0.283
35	0.271
36	0.260
37	0.249
38	0.238
39	0.228
40	0.217
41	0.208
42	0.198
43	0.189
44	0.180
45	0.172

and

$$z_c = \frac{2c}{\gamma\sqrt{K_a}} \tag{5.14}$$

The depth z_c is usually referred to as the *depth of tensile crack*, because the tensile stress in the soil will eventually cause a crack along the soil–wall interface. Thus the total Rankine active force per unit length of the wall before the tensile crack occurs is

$$P_a = \int_0^H \sigma_a \, dz = \int_0^H \gamma z K_a \, dz - \int_0^H 2c\sqrt{K_a} \, dz$$

$$= \frac{1}{2}\gamma H^2 K_a - 2cH\sqrt{K_a} \tag{5.15}$$

After the occurrence of the tensile crack, the force on the wall will be caused only by the pressure distribution between depths $z = z_c$ and $z = H$, as shown by the hatched area in Figure 5.6c. It may be expressed as

$$P_a = \frac{1}{2}(H - z_c)(\gamma H K_a - 2c\sqrt{K_a}) \tag{5.16}$$

or

$$P_a = \frac{1}{2}\left(H - \frac{2c}{\gamma\sqrt{K_a}}\right)(\gamma H K_a - 2c\sqrt{K_a}) \tag{5.17}$$

For calculation purposes in some retaining wall design problems, a cohesive soil backfill is replaced by an assumed granular soil with a triangular Rankine active pressure diagram with $\sigma_a = 0$ at $z = 0$, and $\sigma_a = \sigma_v K_a - 2c\sqrt{K_a}$ at $z = H$ (see Figure 5.7). In such a case, the assumed active force per unit length of the wall is

$$P_a = \frac{1}{2}H(\gamma H K_a - 2c\sqrt{K_a}) = \frac{1}{2}\gamma H^2 K_a - cH\sqrt{K_a} \tag{5.18}$$

However, the active earth pressure condition will be reached only if the wall is allowed to "yield" sufficiently. The amount of outward displacement of the wall necessary is about 0.001H to 0.004H for granular soil backfills and about 0.01H to 0.04H for cohesive soil backfills.

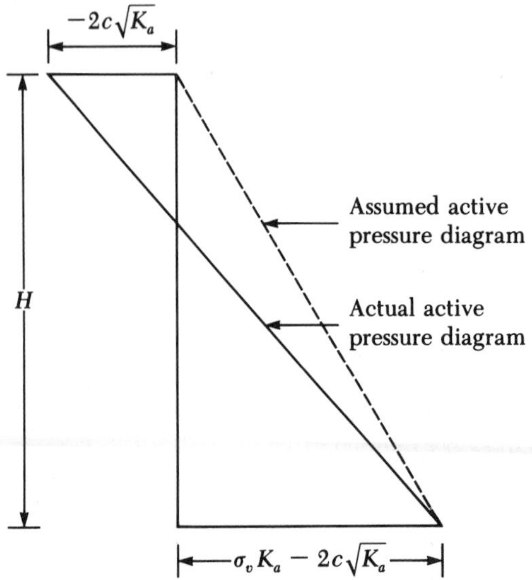

FIGURE 5.7 Assumed active pressure diagram for clay backfill behind a retaining wall

▼ EXAMPLE 5.2

A 6-m high retaining wall is to support a soil with unit weight $\gamma = 17.4\ \text{kN/m}^3$, soil friction angle $\phi = 26°$, and cohesion $c = 14.36\ \text{kN/m}^2$. Determine the Rankine active force per unit length of the wall both before and after the tensile crack occurs, and determine the line of action of the resultant in both cases.

Solution For $\phi = 26°$,

$$K_a = \tan^2\left(45 - \frac{\phi}{2}\right) = \tan^2(45 - 13) = 0.39$$

$$\sqrt{K_a} = 0.625$$

$$\sigma_a = \gamma H K_a - 2c\sqrt{K_a}$$

Refer to Figure 5.6c:

$$\text{At } z = 0,\ \sigma_a = -2c\sqrt{K_a} = -2(14.36)(0.625) = -17.95\ \text{kN/m}^2$$

$$\text{At } z = 6\ \text{m},\ \sigma_a = (17.4)(6)(0.39) - 2(14.36)(0.625)$$

$$= 40.72 - 17.95 = 22.77\ \text{kN/m}^2$$

Active Force Before the Occurrence of Tensile Crack: Eq. (5.15)

$$P_a = \frac{1}{2}\gamma H^2 K_a - 2cH\sqrt{K_a}$$

$$= \frac{1}{2}(6)(40.72) - (6)(17.95) = 122.16 - 107.7 = 14.46\ \text{kN/m}$$

The line of action of the resultant can be determined by taking the moment of the area of the pressure diagrams about the bottom of the wall, or

$$P_a\bar{z} = (122.16)\left(\frac{6}{3}\right) - (107.7)\left(\frac{6}{2}\right)$$

or

$$\bar{z} = \frac{244.32 - 323.1}{14.46} = \mathbf{-5.45\ m}$$

Active Force After the Occurrence of Tensile Crack: Eq. (5.14)

$$z_c = \frac{2c}{\gamma\sqrt{K_a}} = \frac{2(14.36)}{(17.4)(0.625)} = 2.64\ \text{m}$$

Using Eq. (5.16) gives

$$P_a = \frac{1}{2}(H - z_c)(\gamma H K_a - 2c\sqrt{K_a}) = \frac{1}{2}(6 - 2.64)(22.77) = 38.25\ \text{kN/m}$$

Figure 5.6c shows that the force $P_a = 38.25$ kN/m is the area of the hatched triangle. Hence the line of action of the resultant will be located at a height of $\bar{z} = (H - z_c)/3$ above the bottom of the wall, or

$$\bar{z} = \frac{6 - 2.64}{3} = \mathbf{1.12\ m} \quad ▼$$

For most retaining wall construction, a granular backfill is used and $c = 0$. Thus Example 5.2 is an academic problem; however, it illustrates the basic principles of the Rankine active earth pressure equation.

▼ EXAMPLE 5.3

For the retaining wall shown in Figure 5.8a, assume that the wall can yield sufficiently to develop active state. Determine the Rankine active force per unit length of the wall and the location of the resultant line of action.

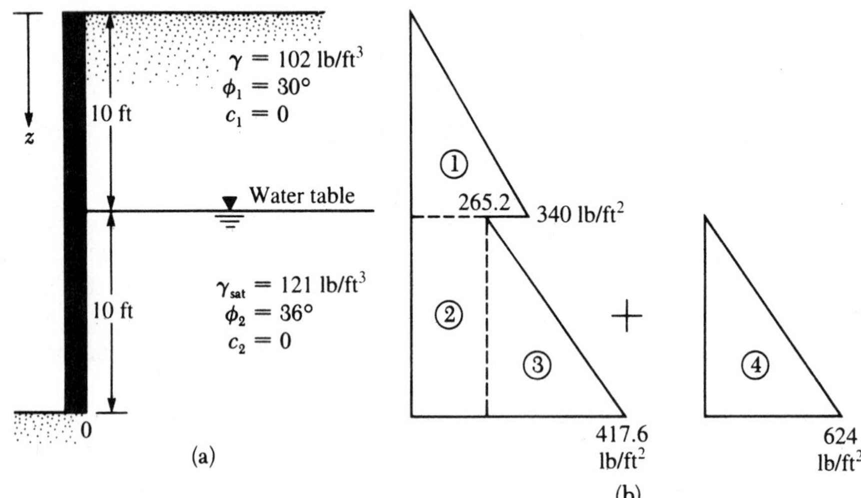

▼ **FIGURE 5.8**

Solution If the cohesion, c, is zero,

$$\sigma_a = \sigma_v K_a$$

For the top soil layer, $\phi_1 = 30°$, so

$$K_{a(1)} = \tan^2\left(45 - \frac{\phi_1}{2}\right) = \tan^2(45 - 15) = \frac{1}{3}$$

Similarly, for the bottom soil layer, $\phi_2 = 36°$, and

$$K_{a(2)} = \tan^2\left(45 - \frac{36}{2}\right) = 0.26$$

Now the following table can be prepared.

Depth, z (*ft*)	σ'_v (*lb/ft²*)	K_a	$\sigma'_a = K_a \sigma'_v$ (*lb/ft²*)	*u* (*lb/ft²*)
0	0	⅓	0	0
10^-	(102)(10) = 1020	⅓	340	0
10^+	1020	0.26	265.2	0
20	(102)(10) + (121 − 62.4)(10) = 1606	0.26	417.6	(62.4)(10) = 624

The pressure distribution diagram is plotted in Figure 5.8b. The force per unit length is

$$P_a = \text{area } 1 + \text{area } 2 + \text{area } 3 + \text{area } 4$$

$$= \frac{1}{2}(10)(340) + (265.2)(10) + \frac{1}{2}(417.6 - 265.2)(10) + \frac{1}{2}(624)(10)$$

$$= 1700 + 2652 + 762 + 3120 = \mathbf{8234\ lb/ft}$$

The distance of the line of action of the resultant from the bottom of the wall, $\bar{z}$, can be determined by taking the moments about the bottom of the wall (point O in Figure 5.8a), or

$$\bar{z} = \frac{(1700)\left(10 + \frac{10}{3}\right) + (2652)\left(\frac{10}{2}\right) + (762 + 3120)\left(\frac{10}{3}\right)}{8234} = \mathbf{5.93\ ft}$$ ▼

5.4 COULOMB'S ACTIVE EARTH PRESSURE

The Rankine active earth pressure calculations discussed in the preceding section were based on the assumption that the wall is frictionless. In 1776, Coulomb proposed a theory to calculate the lateral earth pressure on a retaining wall with granular soil backfill. This theory takes wall friction into consideration.

To apply Coulomb's active earth pressure theory, let us consider a retaining wall with its back face inclined at an angle β with the horizontal, as shown in Figure 5.9a. The backfill is a granular soil that slopes at an angle α with the horizontal. Also, let δ be the angle of friction between the soil and the wall (that is, angle of wall friction).

Under active pressure the wall will move away from the soil mass (to the left in Figure 5.9a). Coulomb assumed that, in such a case, the failure surface in the soil mass would be a plane (e.g., BC_1, BC_2, . . .). So, to find the active force in our example, consider a possible soil failure wedge ABC_1. The forces acting on this wedge, ABC_1 (per unit length at right angles to the cross section shown), are as follows:

1. Weight of the wedge, W.
2. The resultant, R, of the normal and resisting shear forces along the surface, BC_1. The force R will be inclined at an angle ϕ to the normal drawn to the surface BC_1.
3. The active force per unit length of the wall, P_a. The force P_a will be inclined at an angle δ to the normal drawn to the back face of the wall.

For equilibrium purposes, a force triangle can be drawn, as shown in Figure 5.9b. Note that θ_1 is the angle that BC_1 makes with the horizontal. Because the magnitude of W as well as the directions of all three forces are known, the value of P_a can now be determined. Similarly, the active forces of other trial wedges, such as ABC_2, ABC_3, . . . can be determined. The maximum value of P_a thus determined is Coulomb's active force (see top part of Figure 5.9a), which may be expressed as

$$P_a = \frac{1}{2} K_a \gamma H^2 \tag{5.19}$$

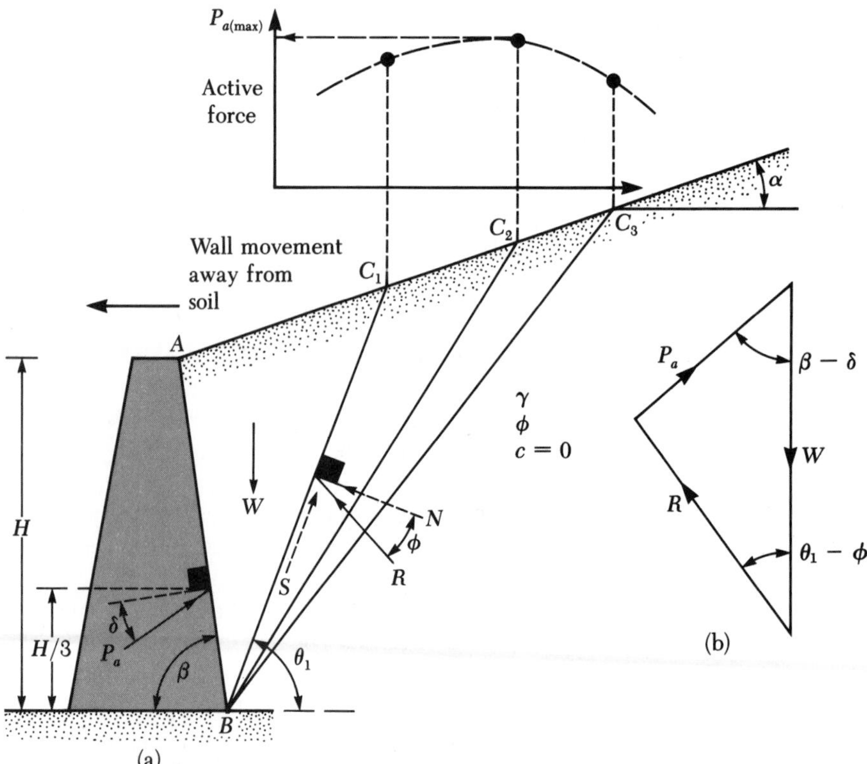

▼ **FIGURE 5.9** Coulomb's active pressure

where

$$K_a = \text{Coulomb's active earth pressure coefficient}$$
$$= \frac{\sin^2(\beta + \phi)}{\sin^2\beta \sin(\beta - \delta)\left[1 + \sqrt{\dfrac{\sin(\phi + \delta)\sin(\phi - \alpha)}{\sin(\beta - \delta)\sin(\alpha + \beta)}}\right]^2} \tag{5.20}$$

and H = height of the wall

The values of the active earth pressure coefficient, K_a, for a vertical retaining wall ($\beta = 90°$) with horizontal backfill ($\alpha = 0°$) are given in Table 5.2. Note that the line of action of the resultant (P_a) will act at a distance of $H/3$ above the base of the wall and will be inclined at an angle δ to the normal drawn to the back of the wall.

▼ TABLE 5.2 Values of K_a [Eq. (5.20)] for $\beta = 90°$, $\alpha = 0°$

	δ (deg)					
ϕ (deg)	0	5	10	15	20	25
28	0.3610	0.3448	0.3330	0.3251	0.3203	0.3186
30	0.3333	0.3189	0.3085	0.3014	0.2973	0.2956
32	0.3073	0.2945	0.2853	0.2791	0.2755	0.2745
34	0.2827	0.2714	0.2633	0.2579	0.2549	0.2542
36	0.2596	0.2497	0.2426	0.2379	0.2354	0.2350
38	0.2379	0.2292	0.2230	0.2190	0.2169	0.2167
40	0.2174	0.2098	0.2045	0.2011	0.1994	0.1995
42	0.1982	0.1916	0.1870	0.1841	0.1828	0.1831

In the actual design of retaining walls, the value of the wall friction angle, δ, is assumed to be between $\phi/2$ and $\frac{2}{3}\phi$. The active earth pressure coefficients for various values of ϕ, α, and β with $\delta = \frac{2}{3}\phi$ are given in Table 5.3. These coefficients are very useful design considerations.

If a uniform surcharge of intensity q is located above the backfill, as shown in Figure 5.10, the active force, P_a, can be calculated as

$$P_a = \frac{1}{2} \underset{\substack{\uparrow \\ \text{Eq. (5.20)}}}{K_a} \gamma_{eq} H^2 \tag{5.21}$$

TABLE 5.3 Values of K_a [Eq. (5.20)] (note: $\delta = \frac{2}{3}\phi$ in all cases)

		β (deg)					
α (deg)	φ (deg)	90	85	80	75	70	65
0	28	0.3213	0.3588	0.4007	0.4481	0.5026	0.5662
	30	0.2973	0.3349	0.3769	0.4245	0.4794	0.5435
	32	0.2750	0.3125	0.3545	0.4023	0.4574	0.5220
	34	0.2543	0.2916	0.3335	0.3813	0.4367	0.5017
	36	0.2349	0.2719	0.3137	0.3615	0.4170	0.4825
	38	0.2168	0.2535	0.2950	0.3428	0.3984	0.4642
	40	0.1999	0.2361	0.2774	0.3250	0.3806	0.4468
	42	0.1840	0.2197	0.2607	0.3081	0.3638	0.4303
5	28	0.3431	0.3845	0.4311	0.4843	0.5461	0.6191
	30	0.3165	0.3578	0.4043	0.4575	0.5194	0.5926
	32	0.2919	0.3329	0.3793	0.4324	0.4943	0.5678
	34	0.2691	0.3097	0.3558	0.4088	0.4707	0.5443
	36	0.2479	0.2881	0.3338	0.3866	0.4484	0.5222
	38	0.2282	0.2679	0.3132	0.3656	0.4273	0.5012
	40	0.2098	0.2489	0.2937	0.3458	0.4074	0.4814
	42	0.1927	0.2311	0.2753	0.3271	0.3885	0.4626
10	28	0.3702	0.4164	0.4686	0.5287	0.5992	0.6834
	30	0.3400	0.3857	0.4376	0.4974	0.5676	0.6516
	32	0.3123	0.3575	0.4089	0.4683	0.5382	0.6220
	34	0.2868	0.3314	0.3822	0.4412	0.5107	0.5942
	36	0.2633	0.3072	0.3574	0.4158	0.4849	0.5682
	38	0.2415	0.2846	0.3342	0.3921	0.4607	0.5438
	40	0.2214	0.2637	0.3125	0.3697	0.4379	0.5208
	42	0.2027	0.2441	0.2921	0.3487	0.4164	0.4990
15	28	0.4065	0.4585	0.5179	0.5869	0.6685	0.7671
	30	0.3707	0.4219	0.4804	0.5484	0.6291	0.7266
	32	0.3384	0.3387	0.4462	0.5134	0.5930	0.6895
	34	0.3091	0.3584	0.4150	0.4811	0.5599	0.6554
	36	0.2823	0.3306	0.3862	0.4514	0.5295	0.6239
	38	0.2578	0.3050	0.3596	0.4238	0.5006	0.5949
	40	0.2353	0.2813	0.3349	0.3981	0.4740	0.5672
	42	0.2146	0.2595	0.3119	0.3740	0.4491	0.5416
20	28	0.4602	0.5205	0.5900	0.6715	0.7690	0.8810
	30	0.4142	0.4728	0.5403	0.6196	0.7144	0.8303
	32	0.3742	0.4311	0.4968	0.5741	0.6667	0.7800
	34	0.3388	0.3941	0.4581	0.5336	0.6241	0.7352
	36	0.3071	0.3609	0.4233	0.4970	0.5857	0.6948
	38	0.2787	0.3308	0.3916	0.4637	0.5587	0.6580
	40	0.2529	0.3035	0.3627	0.4331	0.5185	0.6243
	42	0.2294	0.2784	0.3360	0.4050	0.4889	0.5931

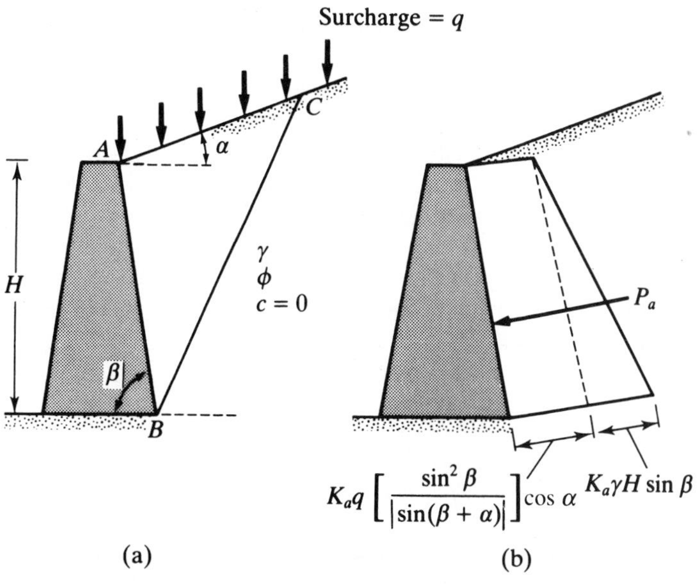

▼ **FIGURE 5.10** Coulomb's active pressure with a surcharge on the backfill

where

$$\gamma_{eq} = \gamma + \left[\frac{\sin\beta}{\sin(\beta+\alpha)}\right]\left(\frac{2q}{H}\right)\cos\alpha \tag{5.22}$$

The derivations of Eqs. (5.21) and (5.22) are contained in other soil mechanics texts (e.g., Das, 1987).

▼ EXAMPLE 5.4

Consider the retaining wall shown in Figure 5.9a. It is 15 ft high, the unit weight of the soil = 105 lb/ft^3, angle of friction of the soil = 36°, the wall friction angle, $\delta = \frac{2}{3}\phi$; the soil cohesion = 0, $\alpha = 0$, and $\beta = 90°$. Calculate the Coulomb's active force per unit length of the wall.

Solution From Eq. (5.19),

$$P_a = \frac{1}{2}\gamma H^2 K_a$$

From Table 5.2, for $\alpha = 0°$, $\beta = 90°$, $\phi = 36°$, and $\delta = \frac{2}{3}\phi = 24°$, $K_a = 0.235$. Hence

$$P_a = \frac{1}{2}(105)(15)^2(0.235) = \mathbf{2776\ lb/ft}$$ ▼

5.5 RANKINE PASSIVE EARTH PRESSURE

Figure 5.11a shows a vertical frictionless retaining wall with a horizontal backfill. At depth z, the vertical pressure on a soil element is $\sigma_v = \gamma z$. Initially, if the wall does not yield at all, the lateral stress at that depth will be $\sigma_h = K_o \sigma_v$. This state of stress is illustrated by the Mohr's circle a in Figure 5.11b. Now, if the wall is pushed into the soil mass by an amount Δx, as shown in Figure 5.11a, the vertical stress at depth z will stay the same; however, the horizontal stress will increase. Thus σ_h will be greater than $K_o \sigma_v$. The state of stress can now be represented by the Mohr's circle b in Figure 5.11b. If the wall moves farther inward (i.e., Δx is increased still more), the stresses at depth z will ultimately reach the state represented by Mohr's circle c (Figure 5.11b). Note that this Mohr's circle touches the Mohr–Coulomb failure envelope, which implies that the

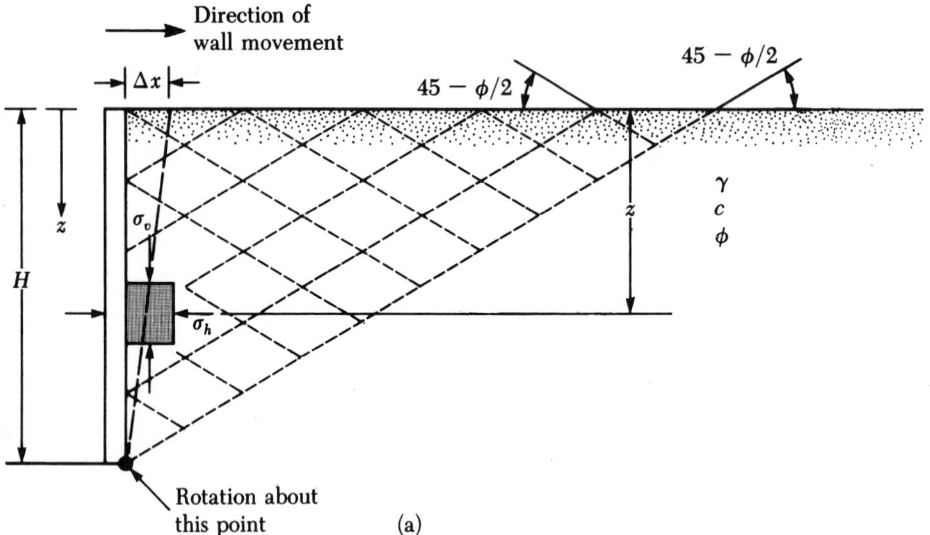

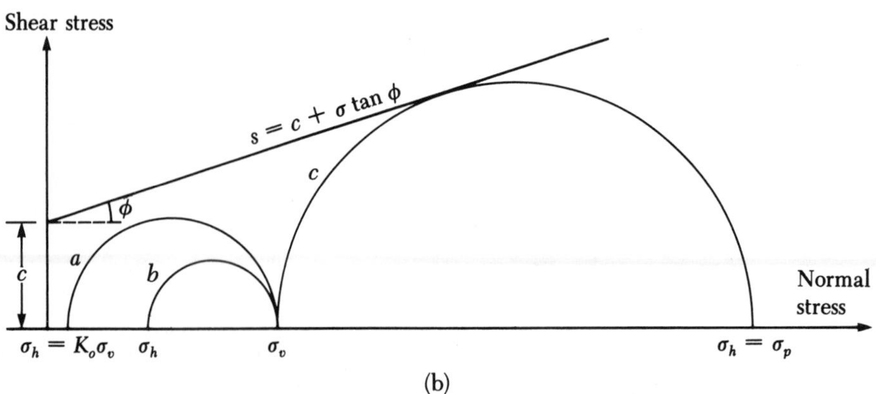

▼ **FIGURE 5.11** Rankine passive pressure

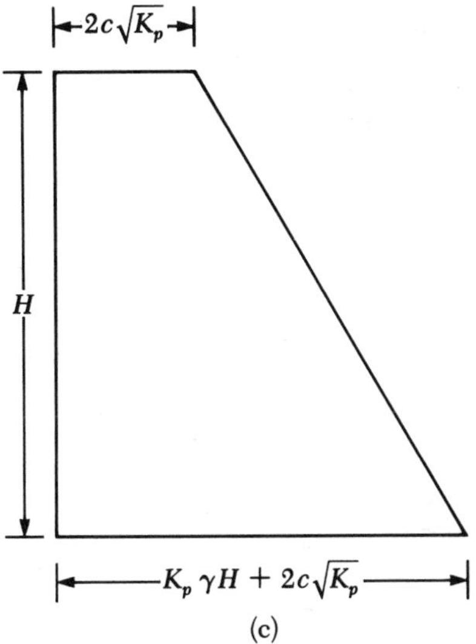

(c)

▼ **FIGURE 5.11** (Continued)

soil behind the wall will fail by being pushed upward. The horizontal stress, σ_h, at this point is referred to as the *Rankine passive pressure*, or $\sigma_h = \sigma_p$.

For Mohr's circle *c* in Figure 5.11b, the major principal stress is σ_p, and the minor principal stress is σ_v. Substituting them into Eq. (1.78) yields

$$\sigma_p = \sigma_v \tan^2\left(45 + \frac{\phi}{2}\right) + 2c \tan\left(45 + \frac{\phi}{2}\right) \tag{5.23}$$

Now, let

$$K_p = \text{Rankine passive earth pressure coefficient} = \tan^2\left(45 + \frac{\phi}{2}\right) \tag{5.24}$$

(see Table 5.4). Hence, from Eq. (5.23),

$$\sigma_p = \sigma_v K_p + 2c\sqrt{K_p} \tag{5.25}$$

▼ **TABLE 5.4 Variation of Rankine K_p**

Soil friction angle, ϕ (deg)	$K_p = \tan^2(45 + \phi/2)$
20	2.040
21	2.117
22	2.198
23	2.283
24	2.371
25	2.464
26	2.561
27	2.663
28	2.770
29	2.882
30	3.000
31	3.124
32	3.255
33	3.392
34	3.537
35	3.690
36	3.852
37	4.023
38	4.204
39	4.395
40	4.599
41	4.815
42	5.045
43	5.289
44	5.550
45	5.828

Equation (5.25) produces Figure 5.11c, the passive pressure diagram for the wall shown in Figure 5.11a. Note that at $z = 0$,

$$\sigma_v = 0 \qquad \text{and} \qquad \sigma_p = 2c\sqrt{K_p}$$

and at $z = H$,

$$\sigma_v = \gamma H \qquad \text{and} \qquad \sigma_p = \gamma H K_p + 2c\sqrt{K_p}$$

The passive force per unit length of the wall can be determined from the area of the pressure diagram, or

$$P_p = \frac{1}{2}\gamma H^2 K_p + 2cH\sqrt{K_p} \tag{5.26}$$

The magnitudes of the wall movements, Δx, required to develop failure under passive conditions are

Soil type	*Wall movement for passive condition, Δx*
Dense sand	$0.005H$
Loose sand	$0.01H$
Stiff clay	$0.01H$
Soft clay	$0.05H$

▼ EXAMPLE 5.5

A 12-ft high wall is shown in Figure 5.12a. Determine the Rankine passive force per unit length of the wall.

Solution For the top layer

$$K_{p(1)} = \tan^2\left(45 + \frac{\phi_1}{2}\right) = \tan^2(45 + 15) = 3$$

From the bottom soil layer

$$K_{p(2)} = \tan^2\left(45 + \frac{\phi_2}{2}\right) = \tan^2(45 + 13) = 2.56$$

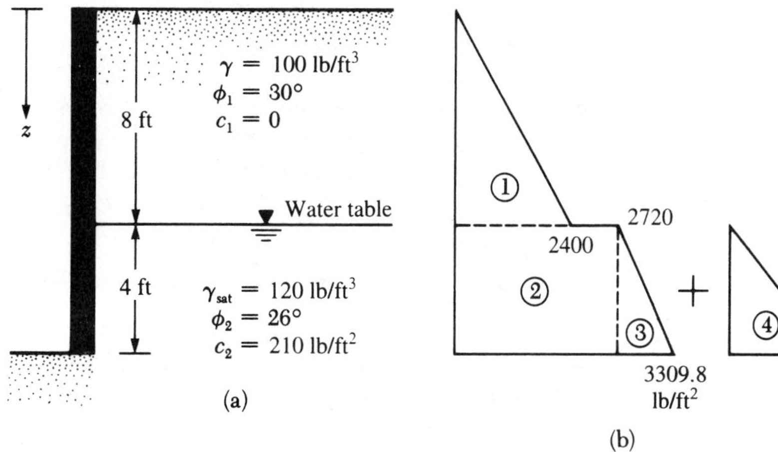

▼ **FIGURE 5.12**

Now the following table can be prepared.

Depth, z (ft)	σ'_v (lb/ft²)	K_p	$\sigma'_v K_p$ (lb/ft²)	c (lb/ft²)	$2c\sqrt{K_p}$ (lb/ft²)	σ_p[a] (lb/ft²)	u (lb/ft²)
0	0	3	0	0	0	0	0
8^-	(100)(8) = 800	3	2400	0	0	2400	0
8^+	800	2.56	2048	210	672	2720	0
12	800 + (120 − 62.4)(4) = 1030.4	2.56	2637.8	210	672	3309.8	(4)(62.4) = 249.6

[a] $\sigma_p = \sigma'_v K_p + 2c\sqrt{K_p}$, where σ'_v = effective vertical stress

The passive pressure diagram is plotted in Figure 5.12b. The passive force per unit length of the wall can be determined from the area of the pressure diagram as follows:

Area no.	Area
1	$(^1/_2)(8)(2400) = 9{,}600$
2	$(2720)(4) = 10{,}880$
3	$(^1/_2)(4)(3309.8 - 2720) = 1{,}179.6$
4	$(^1/_2)(4)(249.6) = \underline{499.2}$
	≈ 22,159 lb/ft

▼

5.6 COULOMB'S PASSIVE EARTH PRESSURE

Coulomb (1776) also presented an analysis for determining the passive earth pressure (i.e., when the wall moves *into* the soil mass) for walls possessing friction (δ = angle of wall friction) and retaining a granular backfill material similar to that discussed in Section 5.4.

To understand the determination of Coulomb's passive force, P_p, consider the wall shown in Figure 5.13a. As in the case of active pressure, Coulomb assumed that the potential failure surface in soil is a plane. For a trial failure wedge of soil, such as ABC_1, the forces per unit length of the wall acting on the wedge are

1. The weight of the wedge, W
2. The resultant, R, of the normal and shear forces on the plane BC_1
3. The passive force, P_p

Figure 5.13b shows the force triangle at equilibrium for the trial wedge ABC_1. From this force triangle, the value of P_p can be determined because the direction of all three forces and the magnitude of one force are known.

Similar force triangles for several trial wedges, such as ABC_1, ABC_2, ABC_3, . . . can be constructed, and the corresponding values of P_p can be determined. The top part

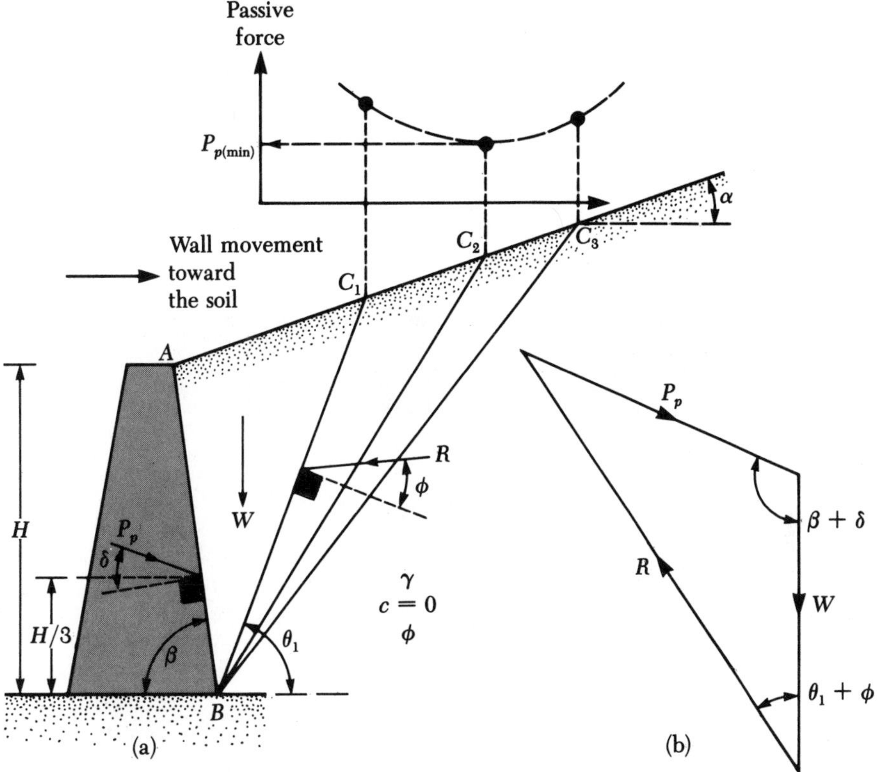

▼ **FIGURE 5.13** Coulomb's passive pressure

of Figure 5.13a shows the nature of variation of the P_p values for different wedges. The *minimum value of* P_p in this diagram is *Coulomb's passive force*. Mathematically, this can be expressed as

$$P_p = \frac{1}{2}\gamma H^2 K_p \tag{5.27}$$

where

$$K_p = \text{Coulomb's passive pressure coefficient}$$

$$= \frac{\sin^2(\beta - \phi)}{\sin^2\beta \sin(\beta + \delta)\left[1 - \sqrt{\dfrac{\sin(\phi + \delta)\sin(\phi + \alpha)}{\sin(\beta + \delta)\sin(\beta + \alpha)}}\right]^2} \tag{5.28}$$

The values of the passive pressure coefficient, K_p, for various values of ϕ and δ are given in Table 5.5 ($\beta = 90°$, $\alpha = 0°$).

Note that the resultant passive force, P_p, will act at a distance of $H/3$ from the bottom of the wall and will be inclined at an angle δ to the normal drawn to the back face of the wall.

TABLE 5.5 Values of K_p [Eq. (5.28)] for $\beta = 90°$ and $\alpha = 0°$

	δ (deg)				
ϕ (deg)	0	5	10	15	20
15	1.698	1.900	2.130	2.405	2.735
20	2.040	2.313	2.636	3.030	3.525
25	2.464	2.830	3.286	3.855	4.597
30	3.000	3.506	4.143	4.977	6.105
35	3.690	4.390	5.310	6.854	8.324
40	4.600	5.590	6.946	8.870	11.772

5.7 RANGE OF WALL FRICTION ANGLE

Retaining walls are generally constructed of masonry or mass concrete. A designer should always have a general idea of the range of the wall friction angle, δ, that may be encountered. Table 5.6 shows the general range of the values of δ for various backfill materials.

TABLE 5.6 General Range of Wall Friction Angles for Masonry or Mass Concrete Walls

Backfill material	Range of δ (deg)
Gravel	27–30
Coarse sand	20–28
Fine sand	15–25
Stiff clay	15–20
Silty clay	12–16

5.8 COMMENTS ON THE FAILURE SURFACE ASSUMPTION FOR COULOMB'S PRESSURE CALCULATIONS

Coulomb's pressure calculation methods for active and passive pressure have been discussed in Sections 5.4 and 5.6. The fundamental assumption for these analyses is the acceptance of *plane failure surfaces*. However, for walls with friction, this assumption does not hold in practice. The nature of *actual* failure surfaces in the soil mass for active and passive pressure is shown in Figure 5.14a and b, respectively (for a vertical wall with a horizontal backfill). Note that the failure surfaces *BC* are curved and that the failure surfaces *CD* are planes.

Although the actual failure surface in soil for the case of active pressure is somewhat different from that assumed in the calculation of the Coulomb pressure, the results are not greatly different. However, in the case of passive pressure, as the value of δ increases, Coulomb's method of calculation gives increasingly erroneous values of P_p.

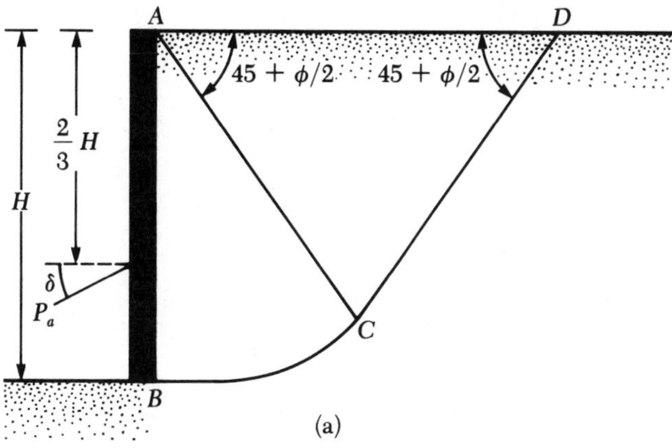

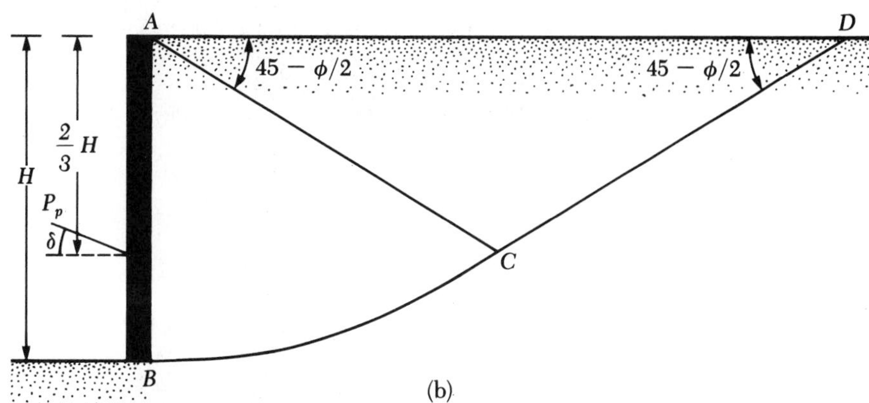

▼ **FIGURE 5.14** Nature of failure surface in soil with wall friction for (a) active pressure case and (b) passive pressure case

This factor of error could lead to an unsafe condition because the values of P_p would become higher than the soil resistance. To remedy this situation, several investigations have been done to calculate the value of P_p using the type of failure surface shown in Figure 5.14b. Some of those investigations are listed in the following table.

Investigator	*Assumption for the curved part, BC (Figure 5.14b)*
1. Packshaw (1969)	Circle
2. Caquot and Kerisel (1948)	Ellipse
3. James and Bransby (1971)	Log spiral
4. Shields and Tolunay (1972, 1973)	Log spiral
5. Terzaghi and Peck (1967)	Log spiral

The details of the calculations involved in the studies listed in the table are beyond the scope of this text. However, the results of Shields and Tolunay's (1973) work appear to be reasonable. They show that

$$P_p = \frac{1}{2}\gamma H^2 K_p \tag{5.29}$$

where K_p = passive pressure coefficient

The values of K_p for a vertical wall with a horizontal granular backfill (that is, $c = 0$) are given in Table 5.7.

TABLE 5.7 Values of K_p [Eq. (5.29)] for a Vertical Wall with Horizontal Cohesionless Soil as Backfill[a]

	ϕ (deg)					
δ (deg)	20	25	30	35	40	45
0	2.04	2.46	3.00	3.69	4.60	5.83
5	2.27	2.78	3.44	4.31	5.46	4.09
10	2.47	3.08	3.86	4.92	6.36	8.43
15	2.64	3.34	4.28	5.53	7.30	9.89
20	2.87	3.61	4.68	6.17	8.30	11.49
25		4.0	5.12	6.85	9.39	13.20
30			5.81	7.61	10.60	15.31
35				8.85	12.00	17.65
40					14.40	20.48
45						25.47

[a] After Shields and Tolunay (1973)

For purposes of comparison, the variation of K_p [Eq. (5.29)] as obtained by using the procedure outlined by Terzaghi and Peck (1967), in which the curved part *BC* in Figure 5.14b is a log spiral, is shown in Figure 5.15.

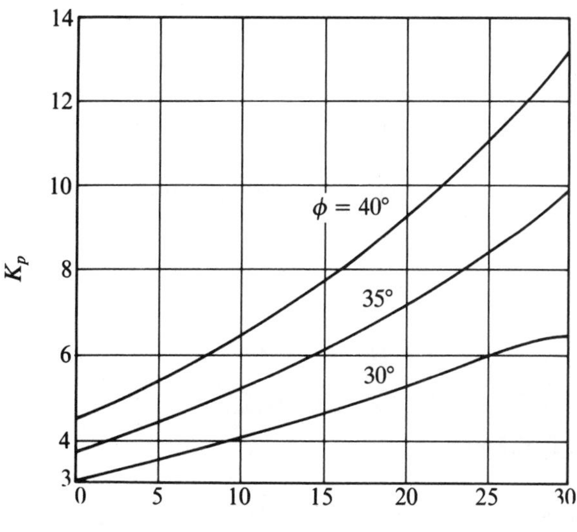

▼ **FIGURE 5.15** Variation of K_p obtained from Terzaghi and Peck's method [vertical backface of wall ($\beta = 90°$) and horizontal granular backfill]

▼ EXAMPLE 5.6

A vertical retaining wall with a horizontal granular backfill has a height of 4 m. The unit weight of backfill, $\gamma = 16.5$ kN/m³, $\phi = 35°$, and $\delta = 10°$. Determine the passive force per unit length of wall using

a. Coulomb's theory
b. Shields and Tolunay's work (Table 5.7)
c. Terzaghi and Peck's work (Figure 5.15)

Solution

Part a

From Eq. (5.27),

$$P_p = \frac{1}{2}\gamma H^2 K_p$$

From Table 5.5 for $\phi = 35°$ and $\delta = 10°$, $K_p = 5.31$. So

$$P_p = \frac{1}{2}(16.5)(4)^2(5.31) = \mathbf{700.9\ kN/m}$$

Part b

From Table 5.7 for $\phi = 35°$ and $\delta = 10°$, $K_p = 4.92$. So

$$P_p = \frac{1}{2}\gamma H^2 K_p = \frac{1}{2}(16.5)(4)^2(4.92) = \mathbf{649.4\ kN/m}$$

Part c

From Figure 5.15 for $\phi = 35°$ and $\delta = 10°$, $K_p \approx 5.2$. So

$$P_p = \frac{1}{2}\gamma H^2 K_p = \frac{1}{2}(16.5)(4)^2(5.2) = \mathbf{686.4\ kN/m}$$

▼

5.9 RANKINE ACTIVE AND PASSIVE EARTH PRESSURE FOR INCLINED GRANULAR BACKFILL

If the backfill of a frictionless retaining wall is a granular soil ($c = 0$) and rises at an angle α with respect to the horizontal (Figure 5.16), the *active earth pressure coefficient*, K_a, may be expressed in the form

$$K_a = \cos\alpha \frac{\cos\alpha - \sqrt{\cos^2\alpha - \cos^2\phi}}{\cos\alpha + \sqrt{\cos^2\alpha - \cos^2\phi}} \tag{5.30}$$

where ϕ = angle of friction of soil

At any depth, z, the *Rankine active pressure* may be expressed as

$$\sigma_a = \gamma z K_a \tag{5.31}$$

Also, the total force per unit length of the wall is

$$P_a = \frac{1}{2}\gamma H^2 K_a \tag{5.32}$$

Note that, in this case, the direction of the resultant force, P_a, is *inclined at an angle α with the horizontal* and intersects the wall at a distance of $H/3$ from the base of the wall. Table 5.8 presents the values of K_a (active earth pressure) for various values of α and ϕ.

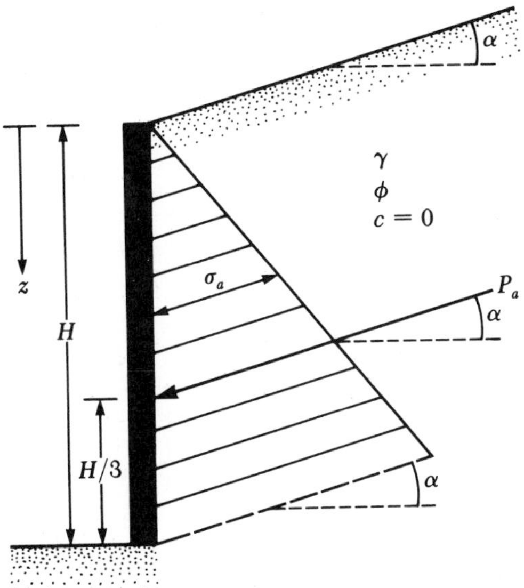

▼ **FIGURE 5.16** Notations for active pressure—Eqs. (5.30), (5.31), (5.32)

▼ **TABLE 5.8 Active Earth Pressure Coefficient, K_a [Eq. (5.30)]**

↓ α (deg)	φ (deg) →						
	28	*30*	*32*	*34*	*36*	*38*	*40*
0	0.361	0.333	0.307	0.283	0.260	0.238	0.217
5	0.366	0.337	0.311	0.286	0.262	0.240	0.219
10	0.380	0.350	0.321	0.294	0.270	0.246	0.225
15	0.409	0.373	0.341	0.311	0.283	0.258	0.235
20	0.461	0.414	0.374	0.338	0.306	0.277	0.250
25	0.573	0.494	0.434	0.385	0.343	0.307	0.275

Note: With $\alpha = \phi$, $K_a = \cos \alpha$. So,

$\alpha = \phi = 28°$, $K_a = 0.883$

$\alpha = \phi = 30°$, $K_a = 0.866$

$\alpha = \phi = 32°$, $K_a = 0.848$

$\alpha = \phi = 34°$, $K_a = 0.829$

$\alpha = \phi = 36°$, $K_a = 0.809$

$\alpha = \phi = 38°$, $K_a = 0.788$

$\alpha = \phi = 40°$, $K_a = 0.866$

Similarly, the *Rankine passive earth pressure* for a wall of height H with a granular sloping backfill is

$$P_p = \frac{1}{2}\gamma H^2 K_p \tag{5.33}$$

where K_p = passive earth pressure coefficient

$$K_p = \cos\alpha \frac{\cos\alpha + \sqrt{\cos^2\alpha - \cos^2\phi}}{\cos\alpha - \sqrt{\cos^2\alpha - \cos^2\phi}} \tag{5.34}$$

As in the case of the active force, the resultant force, P_p, is inclined at an angle α with the horizontal and intersects the wall at a distance of $H/3$ from the bottom of the wall. The values of K_p (passive earth pressure coefficient) for various values of α and ϕ are given in Table 5.9.

TABLE 5.9 Passive Earth Pressure Coefficient, K_p [Eq. (5.34)]

	ϕ (deg) →						
↓ α (deg)	28	30	32	34	36	38	40
0	2.770	3.000	3.255	3.537	3.852	4.204	4.599
5	2.715	2.943	3.196	3.476	3.788	4.136	4.527
10	2.551	2.775	3.022	3.295	3.598	3.937	4.316
15	2.284	2.502	2.740	3.003	3.293	3.615	3.977
20	1.918	2.132	2.362	2.612	2.886	3.189	3.526
25	1.434	1.664	1.894	2.135	2.394	2.676	2.987

Note: With $\alpha = \phi$, $K_p = \cos\alpha$. So

$\alpha = \phi = 28°$, $K_p = 0.883$

$\alpha = \phi = 30°$, $K_p = 0.866$

$\alpha = \phi = 32°$, $K_p = 0.848$

$\alpha = \phi = 34°$, $K_p = 0.829$

$\alpha = \phi = 36°$, $K_p = 0.809$

$\alpha = \phi = 38°$, $K_p = 0.788$

$\alpha = \phi = 40°$, $K_p = 0.766$

5.10 LATERAL EARTH PRESSURE DUE TO SURCHARGE

In several instances, the theory of elasticity is used to determine the lateral earth pressure on retaining structures caused by various types of surcharge loading, such as *line loading* (Figure 5.17a) and *strip loading* (Figure 5.17b).

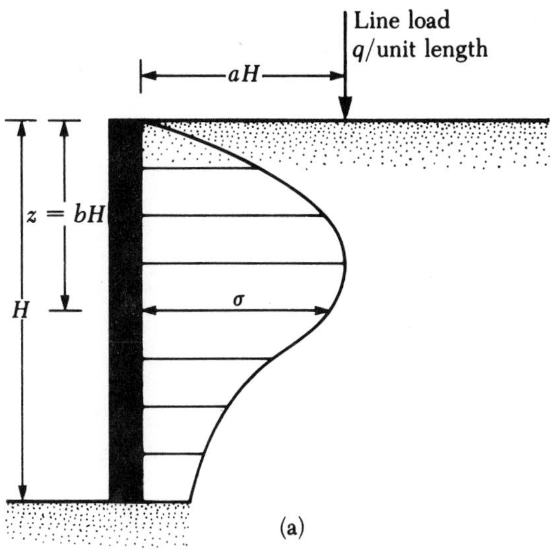

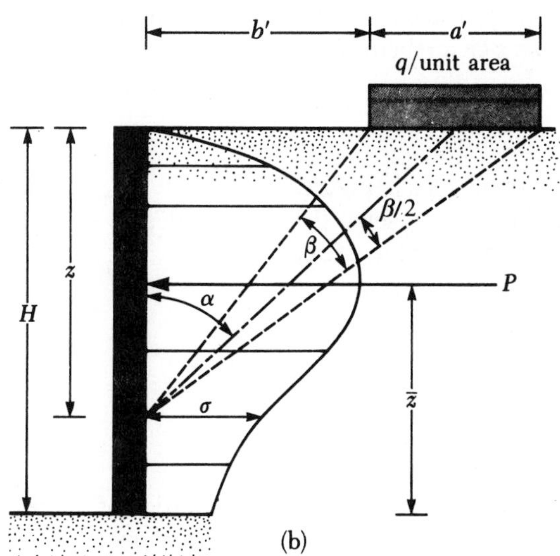

▼ **FIGURE 5.17** Lateral earth pressure caused by (a) line load and (b) strip load

According to the theory of elasticity, the stress at any depth, z, on a retaining structure caused by a line load of intensity q/unit length (Figure 5.17a) may be given as

$$\sigma = \frac{2q}{\pi H} \frac{a^2 b}{(a^2 + b^2)^2} \tag{5.35}$$

where σ = horizontal stress at depth $z = bH$

(See Figure 5.17a for explanations of the terms a and b.)

However, because soil is not a perfectly elastic medium, some deviations from Eq. (5.35) may be expected. The modified forms of this equation generally accepted for use with soils are as follows:

$$\sigma = \frac{4q}{\pi H}\frac{a^2 b}{(a^2 + b^2)^2} \qquad \text{for } a > 0.4 \tag{5.36}$$

and

$$\sigma = \frac{q}{H}\frac{0.203b}{(0.16 + b^2)^2} \qquad \text{for } a \leq 0.4 \tag{5.37}$$

Figure 5.17b shows a strip load with an intensity of q/unit area located at a distance b' from a wall of height H. Based on the theory of elasticity, the horizontal stress, σ, at any depth z on a retaining structure is

$$\sigma = \frac{q}{\pi}(\beta - \sin \beta \cos 2\alpha) \tag{5.38}$$

(The angles α and β are defined in Figure 5.17b.)

However, in the case of soils, the right-hand side of Eq. (5.38) is doubled to account for the yielding soil continuum, or

$$\sigma = \frac{2q}{\pi}(\beta - \sin \beta \cos 2\alpha) \tag{5.39}$$

The total force per unit length (P) and the location of the resultant force, $\bar{z}$, due to the *strip loading only* (Jarquio, 1981) may be expressed as

$$P = \frac{q}{90}[H(\theta_2 - \theta_1)] \tag{5.40}$$

where $\theta_1 = \tan^{-1}\left(\frac{b'}{H}\right)$ (deg) (5.41)

$$\theta_2 = \tan^{-1}\left(\frac{a' + b'}{H}\right) \text{ (deg)} \tag{5.42}$$

$$\bar{z} = H - \frac{H^2(\theta_2 - \theta_1) + (R - Q) - 57.30a'H}{2H(\theta_2 - \theta_1)}$$

$$= \frac{H^2(\theta_2 - \theta_1) - (R - Q) + 57.30a'H}{2H(\theta_2 - \theta_1)} \tag{5.43}$$

and $R = (a' + b')^2(90 - \theta_2)$ (5.44)

$$Q = b'^2(90 - \theta_1) \tag{5.45}$$

▼

▼ EXAMPLE 5.7

Refer to Figure 5.17b. Here, $a' = 2$ m, $b' = 1$ m, $q = 40$ kN/m^2, and $H = 6$ m.

a. Determine the total pressure on the wall caused by the strip loading only.
b. Determine the location of the center of pressure, $\bar{z}$, measured from the bottom of the wall.

Solution

Part a

From Eqs. (5.41) and (5.42),

$$\theta_1 = \tan^{-1}\left(\frac{1}{6}\right) = 9.46°$$

$$\theta_2 = \tan^{-1}\left(\frac{2 + 1}{6}\right) = 26.57°$$

From Eq. (5.40),

$$P = \frac{q}{90}[H(\theta_2 - \theta_1)] = \frac{40}{90}[6(26.57 - 9.46)] = \mathbf{45.63\ kN/m}$$

Part b

Again, from Eq. (5.43),

$$H - \bar{z} = \frac{H^2(\theta_2 - \theta_1) - (R - Q) + 57.30a'H}{2H(\theta_2 - \theta_1)}$$

$$R = (a' + b')^2(90 - \theta_2) = (2 + 1)^2(90 - 26.57) = 570.87$$

$$Q = b'^2(90 - \theta_1) = 1^2(90 - 9.46) = 80.54$$

So

$$H - \bar{z} = \frac{6^2(26.57 - 9.46) - (570.87 - 80.54) + 57.30(2)(6)}{(2)(6)(26.57 - 9.46)}$$

$$= \frac{615.96 - 490.33 + 687.6}{205.32} = 3.96 \text{ m}$$

Hence

$$\bar{z} = H - 3.96 = 6.0 - 3.96 = \mathbf{2.04\ m}$$ ▼

▼ EXAMPLE 5.8

Refer to Figure 5.17a. In this case, $H = 16$ ft, $a = 0.3$, and $q = 1600$ lb/ft. Determine the variation of σ on the face of the wall at $z = 0$, 4, 8, 12, and 16 ft. Plot the variation of σ with depth.

Solution As $a < 0.4$, Eq. (5.371) will be used:

$$\sigma = \frac{q}{H}\frac{0.203b}{(0.16 + b^2)^2}$$

Now the following table can be prepared.

z (ft)	$b = z/H$	σ (lb/ft^2)
0	0	0
4	0.25	102.5
8	0.50	60.4
12	0.75	29.2
16	1.0	15.1

The variation of σ with depth is shown in Figure 5.18.

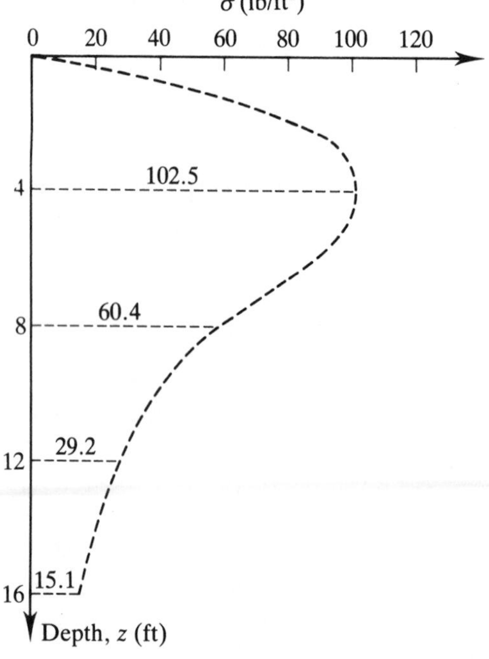

▼ **FIGURE 5.18** ▼

RETAINING-WALL STABILITY

5.11 PROPORTIONING RETAINING WALLS

When designing retaining walls, an engineer must assume some of the dimensions, called *proportioning*, which allows the engineer to check trial sections for stability. If the stability checks yield undesirable results, the sections can be changed and rechecked. Figure 5.19 shows the general proportions of various retaining-wall components that can be used for initial checks.

Note that the top of the stem of any retaining wall should not be less than about 12 in. ($\approx$0.3 m) for proper placement of concrete. The depth, D, to the bottom of the base slab should be a minimum of 2 ft ($\approx$0.6 m). However, the bottom of the base slab should be positioned below the seasonal frost line.

For counterfort retaining walls, the general proportion of the stem and the base slab is the same as for cantilever walls. However, the counterfort slabs may be about 12 in. ($\approx$0.3 m) thick and spaced at center-to-center distances of $0.3H$ to $0.7H$.

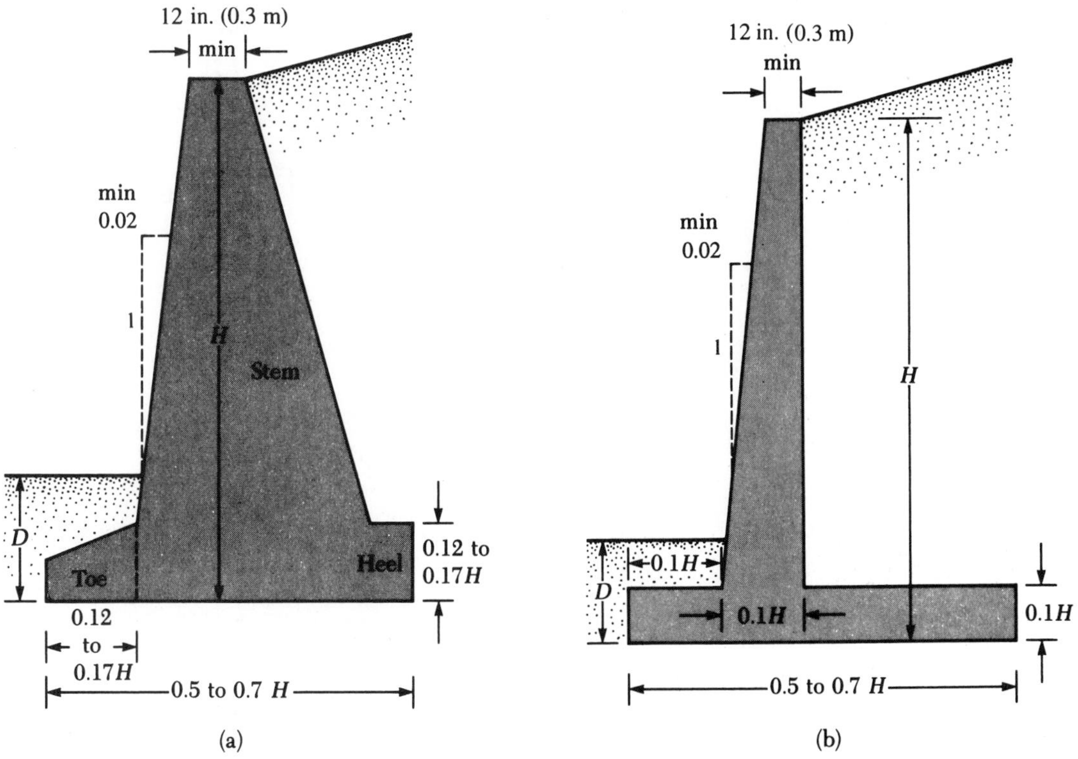

▼ **FIGURE 5.19** Approximate dimensions for various components of retaining wall for initial stability checks: (a) gravity wall; (b) cantilever wall [*note:* minimum dimension of D is 2 ft ($\approx$0.6 m)]

5.12 APPLICATION OF LATERAL EARTH PRESSURE THEORIES TO DESIGN

The preceding sections have presented the fundamental theories for calculating lateral earth pressure. To use these theories in design, an engineer must make several simple assumptions. In the case of cantilever walls, use of the Rankine earth pressure theory for stability checks involves drawing a vertical line AB through point A, as shown in Figure 5.20a (which is located at the edge of the heel of the base slab). The Rankine active condition is assumed to exist along the vertical plane AB. Rankine active earth pressure equations may then be used to calculate the lateral pressure on the face AB. In the analysis of stability for the wall, the force $P_{a(\text{Rankine})}$, the weight of soil above the heel, W_s, and the weight of the concrete, W_c, all should be taken into consideration. The assumption for the development of Rankine active pressure along the soil face AB is theoretically correct if the shear zone bounded by the line AC is not obstructed by the stem of the wall. The angle, η, that the line AC makes with the vertical is

$$\eta = 45 + \frac{\alpha}{2} - \frac{\phi}{2} - \sin^{-1}\left(\frac{\sin \alpha}{\sin \phi}\right) \tag{5.46}$$

For gravity walls, a similar type of analysis may be used, as shown in Figure 5.20b. However, Coulomb's theory also may be used, as shown in Figure 5.20c. If

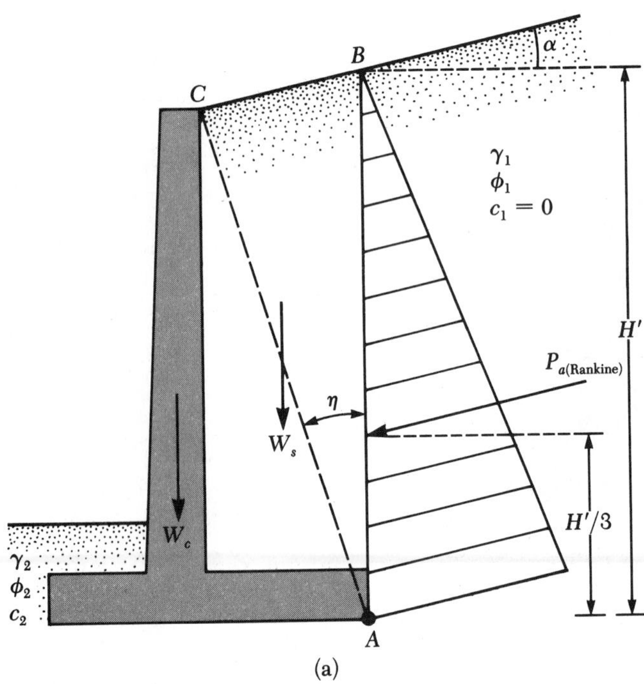

▼ **FIGURE 5.20** Assumption for the determination of lateral earth pressure: (a) cantilever wall; (b) and (c) gravity wall

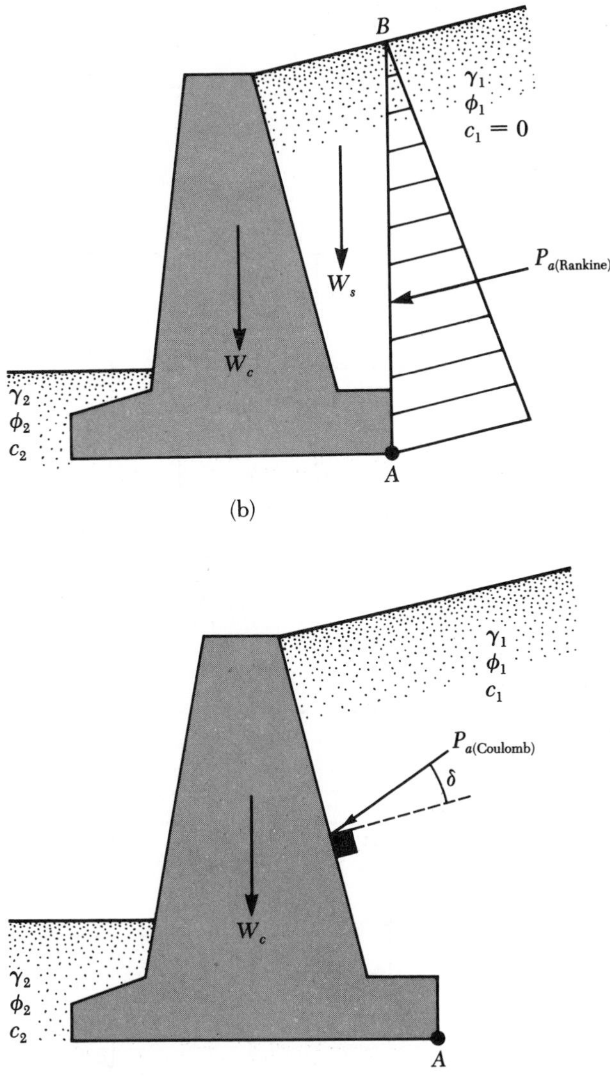

▼ **FIGURE 5.20** (Continued)

Coulomb's active pressure theory is used, the only forces to be considered are $P_{a(\text{Coulomb})}$ and the weight of the wall, W_c.

In the case of ordinary retaining walls, water table problems and hence hydrostatic pressure are not encountered. Facilities for drainage from the soils retained are always provided.

In several instances, for small retaining walls, *semiempirical charts* are used to evaluate lateral earth pressure. Figures 5.21 and 5.22 show two semiempirical charts given by Terzaghi and Peck (1967). Figure 5.21 is for backfills with plane surfaces, and

Figure 5.22 is for backfills that slope upward from the crest of the wall for a limited distance and then become horizontal. Note that $\frac{1}{2}K_v H'^2$ is the vertical component of the active force on plane AB; similarly, $\frac{1}{2}K_h H'^2$ is the horizontal force. The numerals on the curves indicate the types of soil described in Table 5.10.

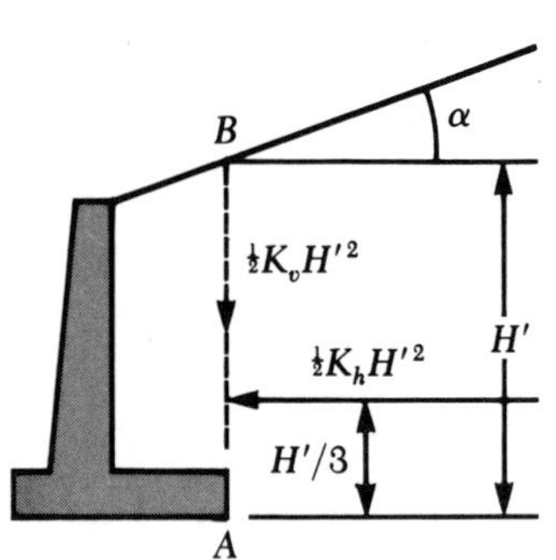

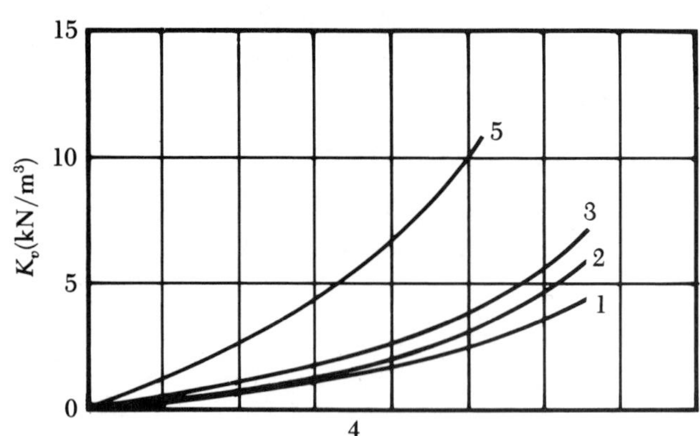

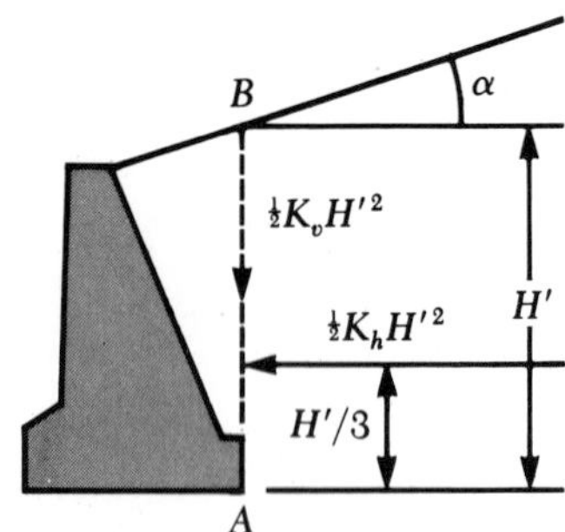

Note: Numerals on curves indicate soil types as described in Table 5.10. For materials, type-5 computations of pressure may be based on value of H' 4 feet less than actual value.

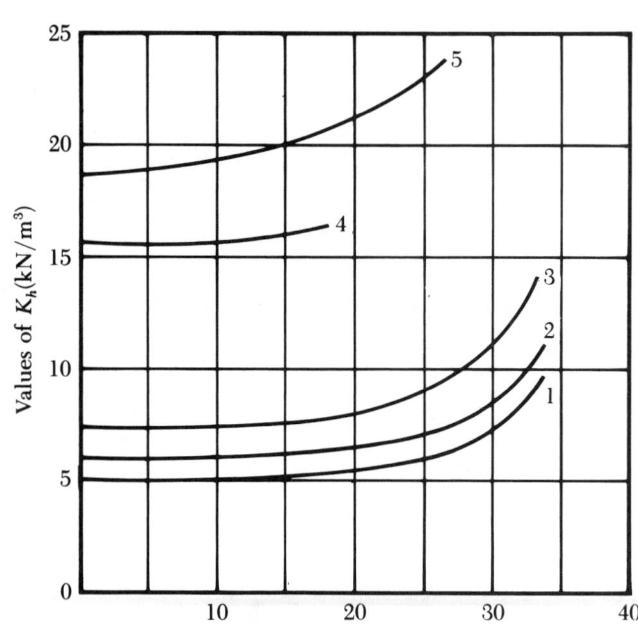

▼ **FIGURE 5.21** Chart for estimating pressure of backfill against retaining walls supporting backfills with plane surface (after *Soil Mechanics in Engineering Practice*, Second Edition, by K. Terzaghi and R. B. Peck. Copyright 1967 by John Wiley and Sons. Reprinted with permission) (*note:* 1 kN/m^3 = 6.361 lb/ft^3)

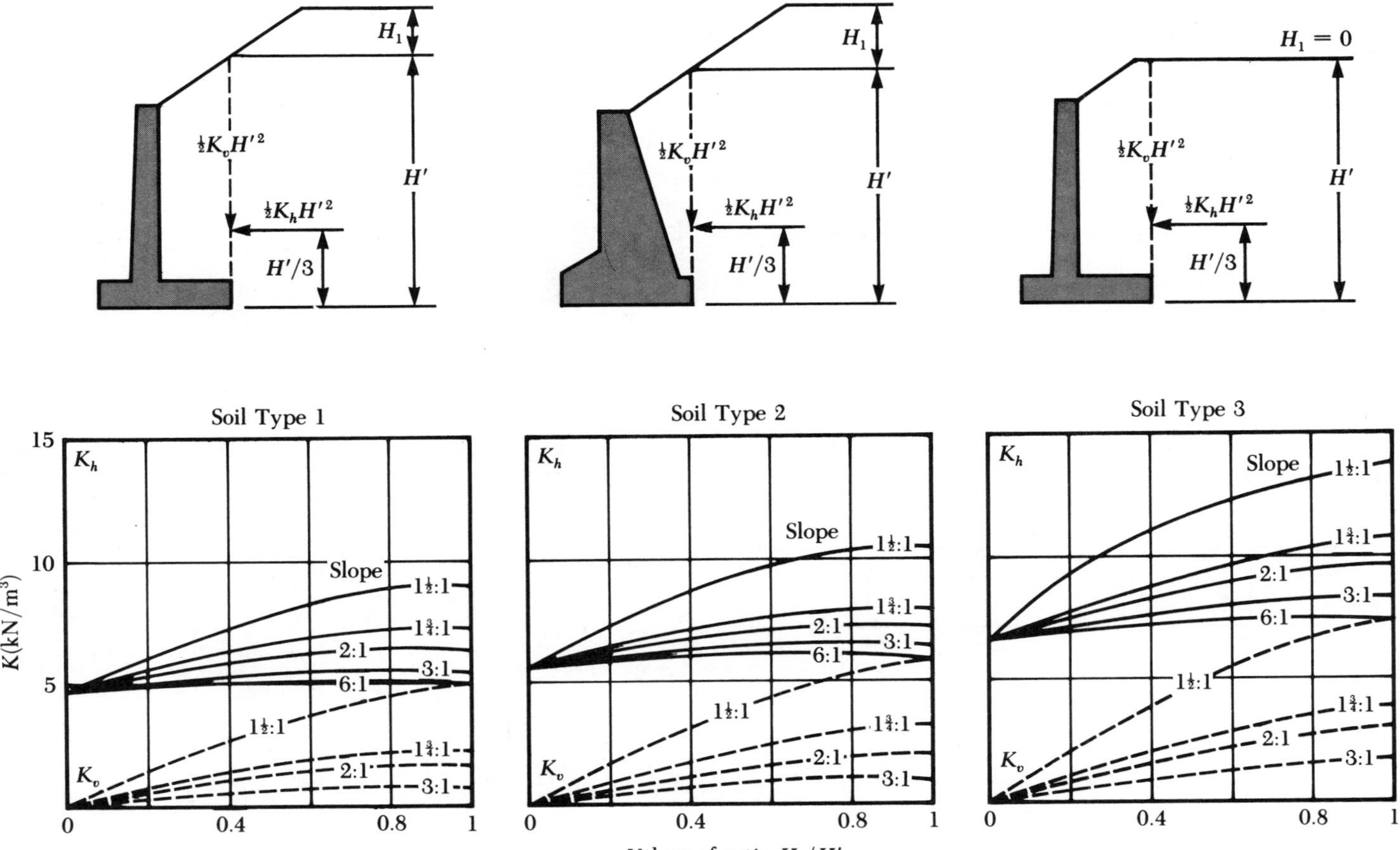

▼ **FIGURE 5.21** (Continued)

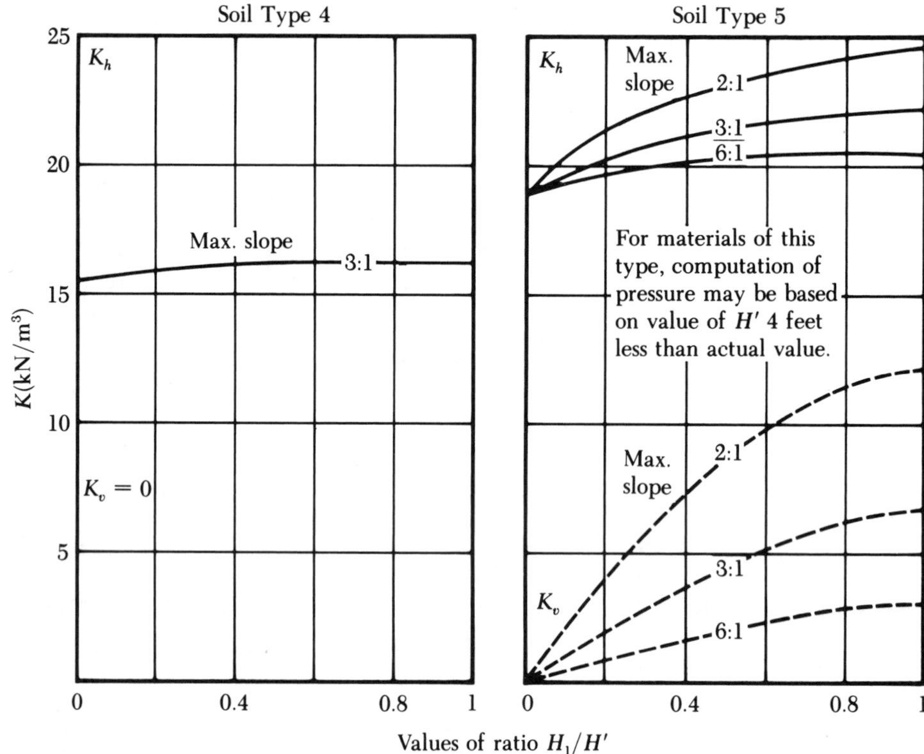

FIGURE 5.22 Chart for estimating pressure of backfill against retaining walls supporting backfills with surface that slopes upward from crest of wall for limited distance and then becoms horizontal (after *Soil Mechanics in Engineering Practice*, Second Edition, by K. Terzaghi and R. B. Peck. Copyright 1967 by John Wiley and Sons. Reprinted with permission) (*note:* 1 kN/m^3 = 6.361 lb/ft^3)

TABLE 5.10 Types of Backfill for Retaining Walls[a]

1. Coarse-grained soil without admixture of fine soil particles, very permeable (clean sand or gravel).
2. Coarse-grained soil of low permeability due to admixture of particles of silt size.
3. Residual soil with stones, fine silty sand, and granular materials with conspicuous clay content.
4. Very soft or soft clay, organic silts, or silty clays.
5. Medium or stiff clay, deposited in chunks and protected in such a way that a negligible amount of water enters the spaces between the chunks during floods or heavy rains. If this condition of protection cannot be satisfied, the clay should not be used as backfill material. With increasing stiffness of the clay, danger to the wall due to infiltration of water increases rapidly.

[a] From *Soil Mechanics in Engineering Practice*, Second Edition, by K. Terzaghi and R. B. Peck. Copyright 1967 by John Wiley and Sons. Reprinted with permission.

5.13 STABILITY CHECKS

To check the stability of a retaining wall, the following steps are necessary:

1. Check for *overturning* about its toe
2. Check for *sliding failure* along its base
3. Check for *bearing capacity failure* of the base
4. Check for *settlement*
5. Check for *overall stability*

This section describes the procedure for checking for overturning and sliding and bearing capacity failure. The principles of investigation for settlement were covered in Chapter 3 and will not be repeated here. Some problems regarding the overall stability of retaining walls are discussed in Section 5.15.

Check for Overturning

Figure 5.23 shows the forces acting on a cantilever and gravity retaining wall, based on the assumption that the Rankine active pressure is acting along a vertical plane AB drawn through the heel. P_p is the Rankine passive pressure; recall that its magnitude is

$$P_p = \frac{1}{2}K_p \gamma_2 D^2 + 2c_2\sqrt{K_p}D \tag{5.26}$$

where γ_2 = unit weight of soil in front of the heel and under the base slab
K_p = Rankine passive earth pressure coefficient $= \tan^2(45 + \phi_2/2)$
c_2, ϕ_2 = cohesion and soil friction angle, respectively

The factor of safety against overturning about the toe—that is, about point C in Figure 5.23—may be expressed as

$$FS_{(\text{overturning})} = \frac{\Sigma M_R}{\Sigma M_O} \tag{5.47}$$

where ΣM_O = sum of the moments of forces tending to overturn about point C
ΣM_R = sum of the moments of forces tending to resist overturning about point C

The overturning moment is

$$\Sigma M_O = P_h\left(\frac{H'}{3}\right) \tag{5.48}$$

where $P_h = P_a \cos\alpha$

For calculation of the resisting moment, ΣM_R (neglecting P_p), a table (such as Table 5.11) can be prepared. The weight of the soil above the heel and the weight of the concrete (or masonry) are both forces that contribute to the resisting moment. Note that

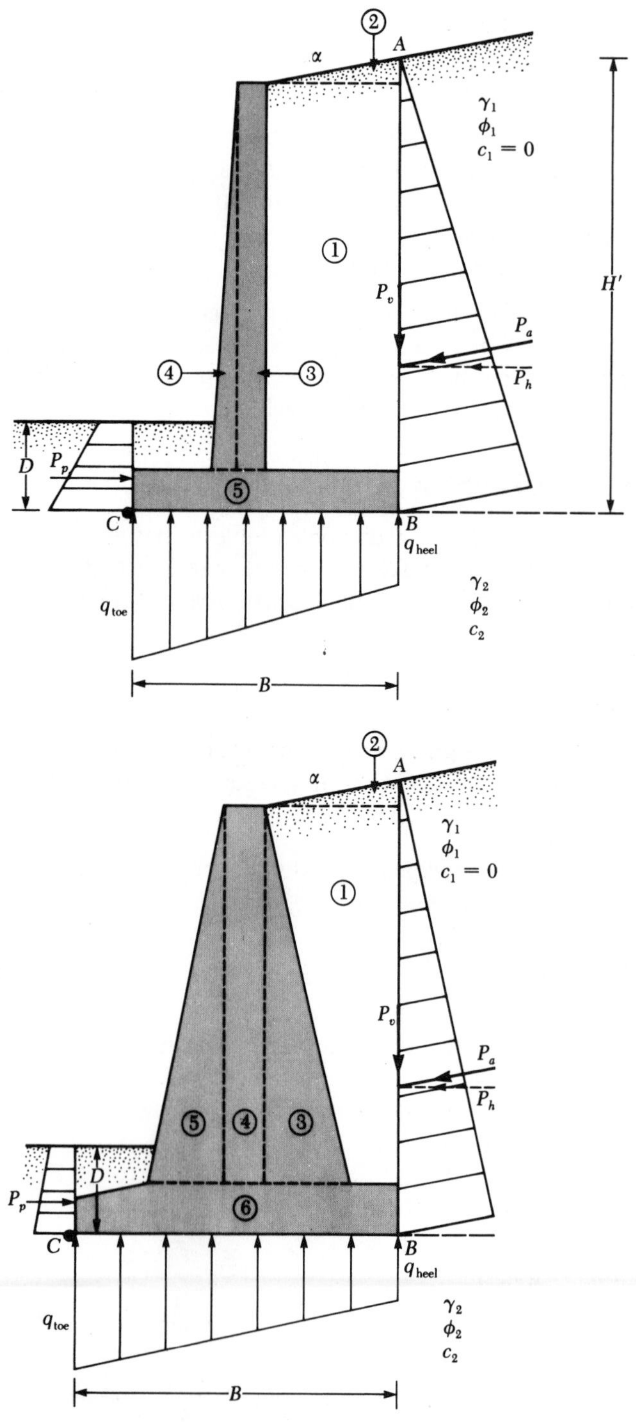

▼ **FIGURE 5.23** Check for overturning; assume that Rankine pressure is valid

▼ **TABLE 5.11 Procedure for Calculation of ΣM_R**

Section (1)	Area (2)	Weight/unit length of wall (3)	Moment arm measured from C (4)	Moment about C (5)
1	A_1	$W_1 = \gamma_1 \times A_1$	X_1	M_1
2	A_2	$W_2 = \gamma_2 \times A_2$	X_2	M_2
3	A_3	$W_2 = \gamma_c \times A_3$	X_3	M_3
4	A_4	$W_2 = \gamma_c \times A_4$	X_4	M_4
5	A_5	$W_2 = \gamma_c \times A_5$	X_5	M_5
6	A_6	$W_2 = \gamma_c \times A_6$	X_6	M_6
		P_v	B	M_v
		$\sum V$		$\sum M_R$

Note: γ_1 = unit weight of backfill
γ_c = unit weight of concrete

the force P_v also contributes to the resisting moment. P_v is the vertical component of the active force P_a, or

$$P_v = P_a \sin \alpha \tag{5.49}$$

The moment of the force P_v about C is

$$M_v = P_v B = P_a \sin \alpha B \tag{5.50}$$

where B = width of the base slab

Once ΣM_R is known, the factor of safety can be calculated as

$$FS_{\text{(overturning)}} = \frac{M_1 + M_2 + M_3 + M_4 + M_5 + M_6 + M_v}{P_a \cos \alpha(H'/3)} \tag{5.51}$$

The usual minimum desirable value of the factor of safety with respect to overturning is 1.5 to 2.

Some designers prefer to determine the factor of safety against overturning with:

$$FS_{\text{(overturning)}} = \frac{M_1 + M_2 + M_3 + M_4 + M_5 + M_6}{P_a \cos \alpha(H'/3) - M_v} \tag{5.52}$$

Check for Sliding Along the Base

The factor of safety against sliding may be expressed by the equation

$$FS_{\text{(sliding)}} = \frac{\Sigma F_{R'}}{\Sigma F_d} \tag{5.53}$$

where $\Sigma F_{R'}$ = sum of the horizontal resisting forces
ΣF_d = sum of the horizontal driving forces

Figure 5.24 indicates that the shear strength of the soil below the base slab may be represented as

$$s = \sigma \tan \phi_2 + c_2$$

Thus the maximum resisting force that can be derived from the soil per unit length of the wall along the bottom of the base slab is

$$R' = s(\text{area of cross section}) = s(B \times 1) = B\sigma \tan \phi_2 + Bc_2$$

However,

$$B\sigma = \text{sum of the vertical force} = \Sigma\ V \text{ (see Table 5.11)}$$

so

$$R' = (\Sigma\ V) \tan \phi_2 + Bc_2$$

Figure 5.24 shows that the passive force P_p is also a horizontal resisting force. The expression for P_p is given in Eq. (5.26). Hence

$$\Sigma\ F_{R'} = (\Sigma\ V) \tan \phi_2 + Bc_2 + P_p \tag{5.54}$$

The only horizontal force that will tend to cause the wall to slide (*driving force*) is the horizontal component of the active force P_a, so

$$\Sigma\ F_d = P_a \cos \alpha \tag{5.55}$$

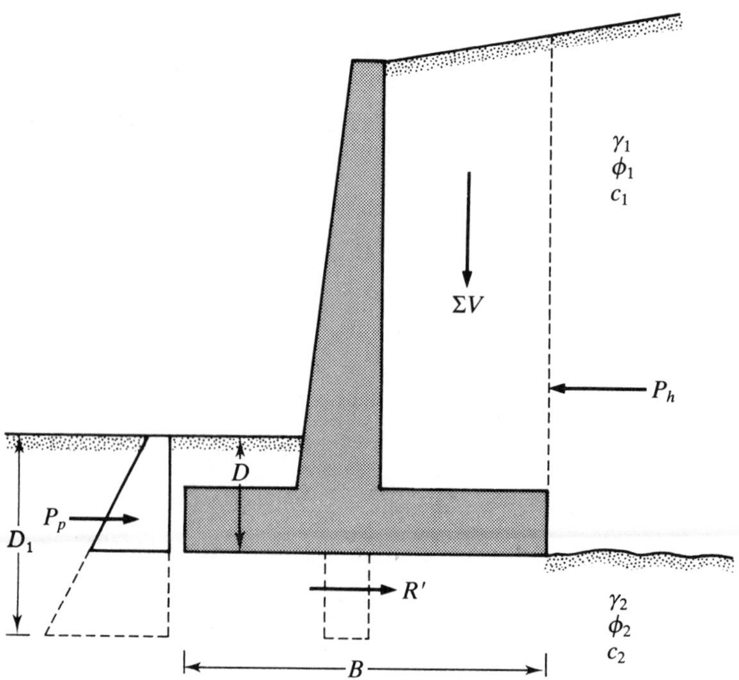

FIGURE 5.24 Check for sliding along the base

Combining Eqs. (5.53), (5.54), and (5.55) yields

$$FS_{(\text{sliding})} = \frac{(\Sigma\ V)\tan\phi_2 + Bc_2 + P_p}{P_a \cos\alpha} \tag{5.56}$$

A minimum factor of safety of 1.5 against sliding is generally required.

In many cases, the passive force P_p is ignored for calculation of the factor of safety with respect to sliding. The friction angle, ϕ_2, is also reduced in several instances for safety. The reduced soil friction angle may be on the order of one-half to two-thirds of the angle ϕ_2. In a similar manner, the cohesion c_2 may be reduced to the value of 0.5 to $0.67c_2$. Thus

$$FS_{(\text{sliding})} = \frac{(\Sigma\ V)\tan(k_1\phi_2) + Bk_2c_2 + P_p}{P_a \cos\alpha} \tag{5.57}$$

where k_1 and k_2 are in the range of $\frac{1}{2}$ to $\frac{2}{3}$

In some instances, certain walls may not yield a desired factor of safety of 1.5. To increase their resistance to sliding, a base key may be used. Base keys are illustrated by broken lines in Figure 5.24. It indicates that the passive force at the toe *without the key* is

$$P_p = \frac{1}{2}\gamma_2 D^2 K_p + 2c_2 D\sqrt{K_p}$$

However, if a key is included, the passive force per unit length of the wall becomes

$$P_p = \frac{1}{2}\gamma_2 D_1^2 K_p + 2c_2 D_1\sqrt{K_p}$$

where $K_p = \tan^2(45 + \phi_2/2)$

Because $D_1 > D$, a key obviously will help increase the passive resistance at the toe and hence the factor of safety against sliding. Usually the base key is constructed below the stem, and some main steel is run into the key.

Another possible way to increase the value of $FS_{(\text{sliding})}$ is to consider reducing the value of P_a [see Eq. (5.57)]. One possible way to do so is to use the method developed by Elman and Terry (1988). The discussion here is limited to the case in which the retaining wall has a horizontal granular backfill (Figure 5.25). In Figure 5.25a, the active force, P_a, is horizontal ($\alpha = 0$) so that

$$P_a \cos\alpha = P_h = P_a$$

and

$$P_a \sin\alpha = P_v = 0$$

However

$$P_a = P_{a(1)} + P_{a(2)} \tag{5.58}$$

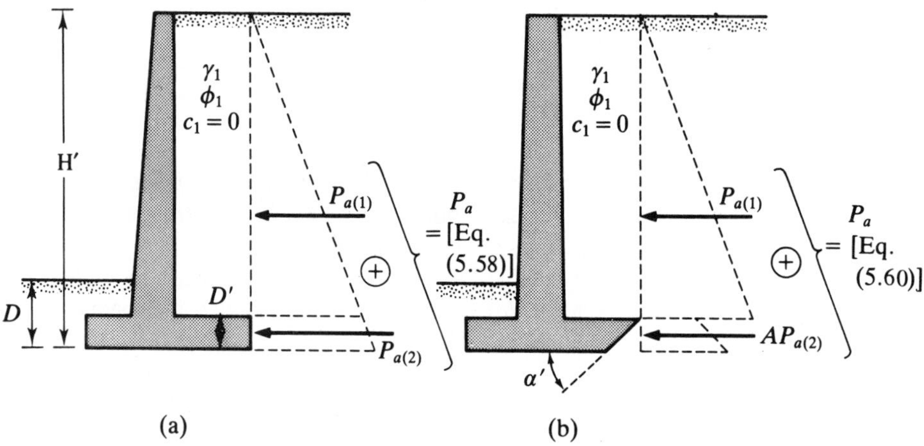

FIGURE 5.25 Retaining wall with sloped heel

The magnitude of $P_{a(2)}$ can be reduced if the heel of the retaining wall is sloped as shown in Figure 5.25b. For this case,

$$P_a = P_{a(1)} + AP_{a(2)} \tag{5.59}$$

The magnitude of A, as shown in Figure 5.26, is valid for $\alpha' = 45°$. However, note that in Figure 5.25a

$$P_{a(1)} = \frac{1}{2}\gamma_1 K_a (H' - D')^2$$

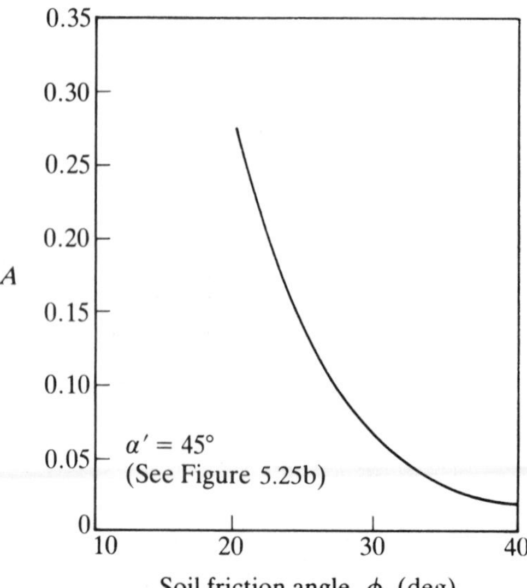

FIGURE 5.26 Variation of A with friction angle of backfill [Eq. (5.60)] (after Elman and Terry, 1988)

and

$$P_a = \frac{1}{2}\gamma_1 K_a H'^2$$

Hence

$$P_{a(2)} = \frac{1}{2}\gamma_1 K_a [H'^2 - (H' - D')^2]$$

So, for the active pressure diagram shown in Figure 5.25b,

$$P_a = \frac{1}{2}\gamma_1 K_a (H' - D')^2 + \frac{A}{2}\gamma_1 K_a [H'^2 - (H' - D')^2] \tag{5.60}$$

Sloping the heel of a retaining wall can thus be extremely helpful in some cases.

Check for Bearing Capacity Failure

The vertical pressure as transmitted to the soil by the base slab of the retaining wall should be checked against the ultimate bearing capacity of the soil. The nature of variation of the vertical pressure transmitted by the base slab into the soil is shown in Figure 5.27. Note that q_{toe} and q_{heel} are the *maximum* and the *minimum* pressures occurring at the ends of the toe and heel sections, respectively. The magnitudes of q_{toe} and q_{heel} can be determined in the following manner.

The sum of the vertical forces acting on the base slab is ΣV (see column 3, Table 5.11), and the horizontal force is $P_a \cos \alpha$. Let R be the resultant force, or

$$\vec{R} = \overrightarrow{\Sigma V} + \overrightarrow{(P_a \cos \alpha)} \tag{5.61}$$

The net moment of these forces about point C (Figure 5.27) is

$$M_{\text{net}} = \Sigma M_R - \Sigma M_O \tag{5.62}$$

Note that the values of ΣM_R and ΣM_O have been previously determined [see column 5, Table 5.11 and Eq. (5.48)]. Let the line of action of the resultant, R, intersect the base slab at E, as shown in Figure 5.27. The distance CE then is

$$\overline{CE} = \bar{X} = \frac{M_{\text{net}}}{\Sigma V} \tag{5.63}$$

Hence the eccentricity of the resultant, R, may be expressed as

$$e = \frac{B}{2} - \overline{CE} \tag{5.64}$$

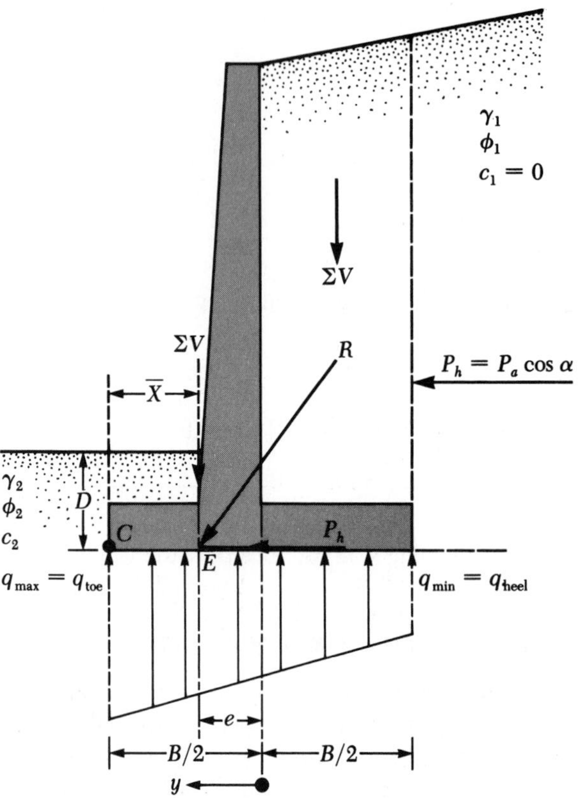

▼ **FIGURE 5.27** Check for bearing capacity failure

The pressure distribution under the base slab may be determined by using the simple principles of mechanics of materials:

$$q = \frac{\Sigma\ V}{A} \pm \frac{M_{\text{net}} y}{I} \tag{5.65}$$

where M_{net} = moment = $(\Sigma\ V)e$

I = moment of inertia per unit length of the base section = $\frac{1}{12}(1)(B^2)$

For maximum and minimum pressures, the value of y in Eq. (5.65) equals $B/2$. Substituting the preceding values into Eq. (5.65) gives

$$q_{\text{max}} = q_{\text{toe}} = \frac{\Sigma\ V}{(B)(1)} + \frac{e(\Sigma\ V)\frac{B}{2}}{\left(\frac{1}{12}\right)(B^3)} = \frac{\Sigma\ V}{B}\left(1 + \frac{6e}{B}\right) \tag{5.66}$$

Similarly,

$$q_{\text{min}} = q_{\text{heel}} = \frac{\Sigma\ V}{B}\left(1 - \frac{6e}{B}\right) \tag{5.67}$$

Note that $\sum V$ includes the soil weight, as shown in Table 5.11, and that, when the value of the eccentricity, e, becomes greater than $B/6$, $q_{\min}$ becomes negative [Eq. (5.67)]. Thus there will be some tensile stress at the end of the heel section. This stress is not desirable because the tensile strength of soil is very small. If the analysis of a design shows that $e > B/6$, the design should be reproportioned and calculations redone.

The relationships for the ultimate bearing capacity of a shallow foundation were discussed in Chapter 3. Recall that

$$q_u = c_2 N_c F_{cd} F_{ci} + qN_q F_{qd} F_{qi} + \frac{1}{2}\gamma_2 B' N_\gamma F_{\gamma d} F_{\gamma i} \tag{5.68}$$

where $q = \gamma_2 D$

$$B' = B - 2e$$

$$F_{cd} = 1 + 0.4\frac{D}{B'}$$

$$F_{qd} = 1 + 2 \tan \phi_2 (1 - \sin \phi_2)^2 \frac{D}{B'}$$

$$F_{\gamma d} = 1$$

$$F_{ci} = F_{qi} = \left(1 - \frac{\psi^\circ}{90^\circ}\right)^2$$

$$F_{\gamma i} = \left(1 - \frac{\psi^\circ}{\phi_2^\circ}\right)^2$$

$$\psi^\circ = \tan^{-1}\left(\frac{P_a \cos \alpha}{\sum V}\right)$$

Note that the shape factors F_{cs}, F_{qs}, and $F_{\gamma s}$ given in Chapter 3 are all equal to 1 because they can be treated as a continuous foundation. For this reason, the shape factors are not shown in Eq. (5.68).

Once the ultimate bearing capacity of the soil has been calculated by using Eq. (5.68), the factor of safety against bearing capacity failure can be determined:

$$FS_{\text{(bearing capacity)}} = \frac{q_u}{q_{\max}} \tag{5.69}$$

Generally, a factor of safety of 3 is required. In Chapter 3 we noted that the ultimate bearing capacity of shallow foundations occurs at a settlement of about 10% of the foundation width. In the case of retaining walls, the width B is large. Hence the ultimate load q_u will occur at a fairly large foundation settlement. A factor of safety of 3 against bearing capacity failure may not ensure, in all cases, that settlement of the structure will be within the tolerable limit. Thus this situation needs further investigation.

▼ EXAMPLE 5.9

The cross section of a cantilever retaining wall is shown in Figure 5.28. Calculate the factors of safety with respect to overturning, sliding, and bearing capacity. Use 150 lb/ft^3 for the unit weight of concrete.

Solution Refer to Figure 5.28. Note that

$$H' = H_1 + H_2 + H_3 = 6 \tan 10° + 18 + 2.75 = 21.81 \text{ ft}$$

$$P_a = \frac{1}{2}\gamma_1 H'^2 K_a$$

For $\phi_1 = 34°$ and $\alpha = 10°$, the value of K_a is 0.294 (Table 5.8), so

$$P_a = \frac{\frac{1}{2}(117)(21.81)^2(0.294)}{1000} = 8.18 \text{ kip/ft}$$

$$P_v = P_a \sin 10° = 1.42 \text{ kip/ft}$$

$$P_h = P_a \cos 10° = 8.06 \text{ kip/ft}$$

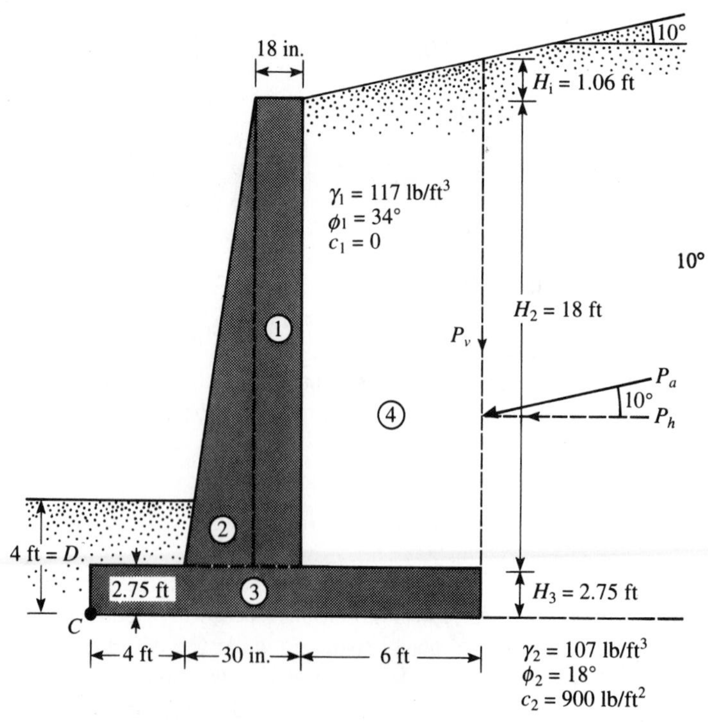

▼ **FIGURE 5.28**

Factor of Safety Against Overturning

The following table can now be prepared for determination of the resisting moment.

Section	Weight (kip/ft)	Moment arm from C (ft)	Moment about C (kip/ft)
1	$(1.5)(18)(0.15) = 4.05$	5.75	23.29
2	$\frac{1}{2}(1.0)(18)(0.15) = 1.35$	$4 + \frac{2}{3}(1) = 4.67$	6.3
3	$(12.5)(2.75)(0.15) = 5.156$	6.25	32.23
4	$\left(\frac{18 + 19.06}{2}\right)(6)(0.117) = 13.01$	$\approx 4 + 2.5 + \frac{6}{2} = 9.5$	123.6
	$P_v = 1.42$	12.5	17.75
	$\Sigma\ V = 24.986$		$\Sigma\ 203.17 = \Sigma\ M_R$

The overturning moment, M_O, is

$$M_O = P_h \frac{H'}{3} = (8.06)\left(\frac{21.81}{3}\right) = 58.6 \text{ kip/ft}$$

So

$$FS_{(\text{overturning})} = \frac{\Sigma\ M_R}{M_O} = \frac{203.17}{58.6} = \mathbf{3.47 > 2\text{—OK}}$$

Factor of Safety Against Sliding

From Eq. (5.57),

$$FS_{(\text{sliding})} = \frac{(\Sigma\ V)\tan(k_1\phi_1) + Bk_2c_2 + P_p}{P_a \cos\alpha}$$

Let $k_1 = k_2 = 2/3$ and $P_p = 0$. So

$$FS_{(\text{sliding})} = \frac{(\Sigma\ V)\tan\left[\frac{2}{3}\phi_2\right] + B\left(\frac{2}{3}c_2\right)}{P_a \cos\alpha}$$

$$= \frac{(24.986)\tan\left[\frac{2}{3}(18)\right] + (12.5)\frac{2}{3}(0.9)}{8.06}$$

$$= \mathbf{1.59 > 1.5\text{—OK}}$$

Factor of Safety Against Bearing Capacity Failure

Combining Eqs. (5.62), (5.63), and (5.64) yields

$$e = \frac{B}{2} - \frac{\Sigma M_R - \Sigma M_o}{\Sigma V} = 6.25 - \frac{203.17 - 58.6}{24.986}$$

$$= 0.464 \text{ ft} < \frac{B}{6} = \frac{6.25}{6} = 1.04 \text{ ft}$$

Again, from Eqs. (5.66) and (5.67),

$$q_{\text{toe}} = \frac{\Sigma V}{B}\left(1 + \frac{6e}{B}\right) = \frac{24.986}{12.5}\left[1 + \frac{(6)(0.464)}{12.5}\right] = 2.44 \text{ kip/ft}^2$$

The ultimate bearing capacity of the soil can be determined from Eq. (5.68):

$$q_u = c_2 N_c F_{cd} F_{ci} + qN_q F_{qd} F_{qi} + \frac{1}{2}\gamma_2 B' N_\gamma F_{\gamma d} F_{\gamma i}$$

From Table 3.4 for $\phi_2 = 18°$, $N_c = 13.1$, $N_q = 5.26$, and $N_\gamma = 4.07$,

$$q = \gamma_2 D = (4)(0.107) = 0.428 \text{ kip/ft}^2$$

$$B' = B - 2e = 12.5 - (2)(0.464) = 11.572 \text{ ft}$$

$$F_{cd} = 1 + 0.4\left(\frac{D}{B'}\right) = 1 + (0.4)\left(\frac{4}{11.572}\right) = 1.138$$

$$F_{qd} = 1 + 2\tan\phi_2(1 - \sin\phi_2)^2\left(\frac{D}{B'}\right) = 1 + (0.31)\left(\frac{4}{11.572}\right) = 1.107$$

$$F_{\gamma d} = 1$$

$$F_{ci} = F_{qi} = \left(1 - \frac{\psi°}{90°}\right)^2$$

$$\psi = \tan^{-1}\left(\frac{P_a \cos\alpha}{\Sigma V}\right) = \left(\frac{8.06}{24.986}\right) = 17.88°$$

So

$$F_{ci} = F_{qi} = \left(1 - \frac{17.88}{90}\right)^2 = 0.642$$

$$F_{\gamma i} = \left(1 - \frac{\psi}{\phi_2}\right)^2 = \left(1 - \frac{17.88}{18}\right)^2 \approx 0$$

Hence

$$q_u = (0.9)(13.1)(1.138)(0.642) + (0.428)(5.26)(1.107)(0.642)$$

$$+ \frac{1}{2}(0.107)(11.572)(4.07)(1)(0)$$

$$= 10.21 \text{ kip/ft}^2$$

So

$$FS_{(\text{bearing capacity})} = \frac{q_u}{q_{\text{toe}}} = \frac{10.21}{2.44} = \mathbf{4.18 > 3—OK}$$ ▼

▼ EXAMPLE 5.10

A concrete gravity retaining wall is shown in Figure 5.29. Determine:

a. The factor of safety against overturning
b. The factor of safety against sliding
c. The pressure on the soil at the toe and heel

(*Note:* Unit weight of concrete $= \gamma_c = 150\ \text{lb/ft}^3$.)

Solution

$$H' = 15 + 2.5 = 17.5\ \text{ft}$$

$$K_a = \tan^2\left(45 - \frac{\phi_1}{2}\right) = \tan^2\left(45 - \frac{30}{2}\right) = \frac{1}{3}$$

$$P_a = \frac{1}{2}\gamma(H')^2K_a = \frac{1}{2}(121)(17.5)^2\left(\frac{1}{3}\right) = 6176\ \text{lb/ft}$$

$$= 6.176\ \text{kip/ft}$$

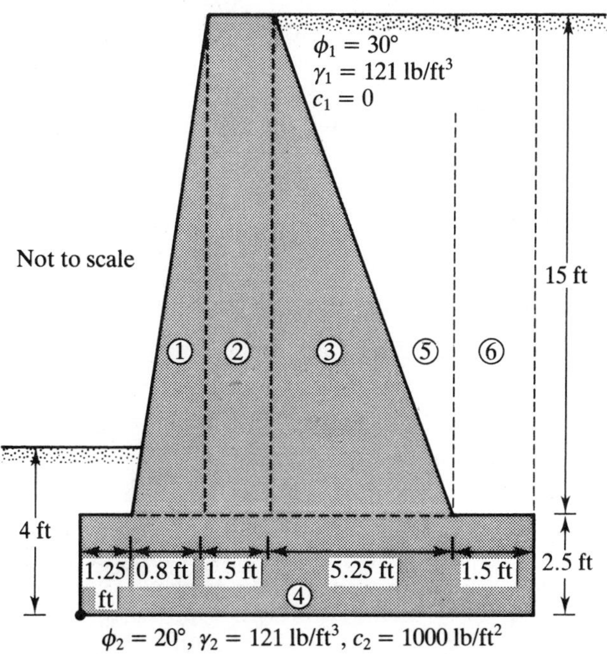

▼ **FIGURE 5.29**

Since $\alpha = 0$

$$P_h = P_a = 6.176 \text{ kip/ft}$$

$$P_v = 0$$

Part a: Factor of Safety Against Overturning

The following table can now be prepared to obtain ΣM_R.

Area (from Figure 5.29)	Weight (kip)	Moment arm from C (ft)	Moment about C (kip/ft)
1	$\frac{1}{2}(0.8)(15)(\gamma_c) = 0.9$	$1.25 + \frac{2}{3}(0.8) = 1.783$	1.605
2	$(1.5)(15)(\gamma_c) = 3.375$	$1.25 + 0.8 + 0.75 = 2.8$	9.45
3	$\frac{1}{2}(5.25)(15)(\gamma_c) = 5.906$	$1.25 + 0.8 + 1.5 + \frac{5.25}{3} = 5.3$	31.30
4	$(10.3)(2.5)(\gamma_c) = 3.863$	$\frac{10.3}{2} = 5.15$	19.89
5	$\frac{1}{2}(5.25)(15)(0.121) = 4.764$	$1.25 + 0.8 + 1.5 + \frac{2}{3}(5.25) = 7.05$	33.59
6	$(1.5)(15)(0.121) = 2.723$	$1.25 + 0.8 + 1.5 + 5.25 + 0.75 = 9.55$	26.0
	21.531		$121.84 = M_R$

The overturning moment

$$M_O = \frac{H'}{3} P_a = \left(\frac{17.5}{3}\right)(6.176) = 36.03 \text{ kip/ft}$$

$$FS_{\text{(overturning)}} = \frac{121.84}{36.03} = \mathbf{3.38}$$

Part b: Factor of Safety Against Sliding

From Eq. (5.57), with $k_1 = k_2 = 2/3$ and assuming that $P_p = 0$,

$$FS_{\text{(sliding)}} = \frac{\Sigma V \tan\left(\frac{2}{3}\right)\phi_2 + B\left(\frac{2}{3}\right)c_2}{P_a}$$

$$= \frac{21.531 \tan\left(\frac{2 \times 20}{3}\right) + 10.3\left(\frac{2}{3}\right)(1.0)}{6.176}$$

$$= \frac{5.1 + 6.87}{6.176} = \mathbf{1.94}$$

Part c: Pressure on the Soil at the Toe and Heel

From Eqs. (5.62), (5.63), and (5.64),

$$e = \frac{B}{2} - \frac{\Sigma M_R - \Sigma M_O}{\Sigma V} = \frac{10.3}{2} - \frac{121.84 - 36.03}{21.531} = 5.15 - 3.99 = 1.16 \text{ ft}$$

$$q_{\text{toe}} = \frac{\Sigma V}{B}\left[1 + \frac{6e}{B}\right] = \frac{21.531}{10.3}\left[1 + \frac{(6)(1.16)}{10.3}\right] = \mathbf{3.5 \ kip/ft^2}$$

$$q_{\text{heel}} = \frac{\Sigma V}{B}\left[1 - \frac{6e}{B}\right] = \frac{21.531}{10.3}\left[1 - \frac{(6)(1.16)}{10.3}\right] = \mathbf{0.678 \ kip/ft^2}$$ ▼

▼ EXAMPLE 5.11

Repeat Example 5.10 and use Coulomb's active pressure for calculation and $\delta = 2\phi/3$.

Solution Refer to Figure 5.30 for the pressure calculation:

$$\delta = \frac{2}{3}\phi = \left(\frac{2}{3}\right)(30) = 20°$$

From Table 5.3, $K_a = 0.4794$ ($\alpha = 0°$, $\beta = 70°$), so

$$P_a = \frac{1}{2}(0.121)(17.5)^2(0.4794) = 8.882 \text{ kip/ft}$$

$$P_h = P_a \cos 40 = (8.882)(\cos 40) = 6.8 \text{ kip/ft}$$

$$P_v = P_a \sin 40 = 5.71 \text{ kip/ft}$$

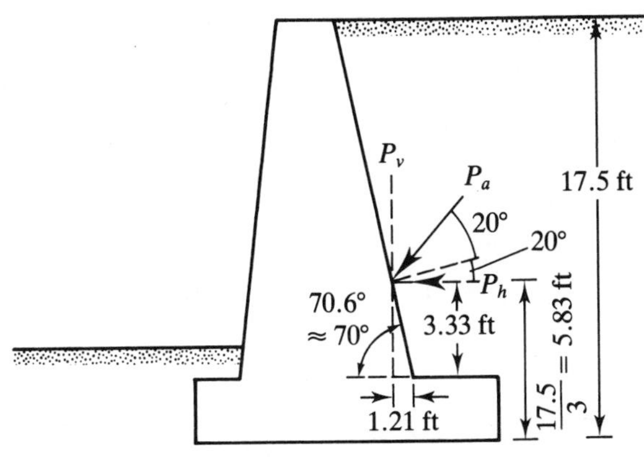

▼ **FIGURE 5.30**

Part a: Factor of Safety Against Overturning

Refer to Figures 5.31 and 5.29.

Area (from Figures 5.29 and 5.31)	*Weight (kip)*	*Moment arm from C (ft)*	*Moment about C (kip/ft)*
1	0.9[a]	1.783[a]	1.605
2	3.375[a]	2.8[a]	9.46
3	5.906[a]	5.3[a]	31.30
4	3.863[a]	5.15[a]	19.89
	$P_v = 5.71$	1.25 + 0.8 + 1.5 + 5.25 − 1.21 = 7.59	43.34
	19.75		105.6

[a] Same as in Example 5.10

The overturning moment is

$$M_O = P_h \frac{H'}{3} = (6.8)\left(\frac{17.5}{3}\right) = 39.67 \text{ kip/ft}$$

Hence

$$FS_{(\text{overturning})} = \frac{105.6}{39.67} = \mathbf{2.66}$$

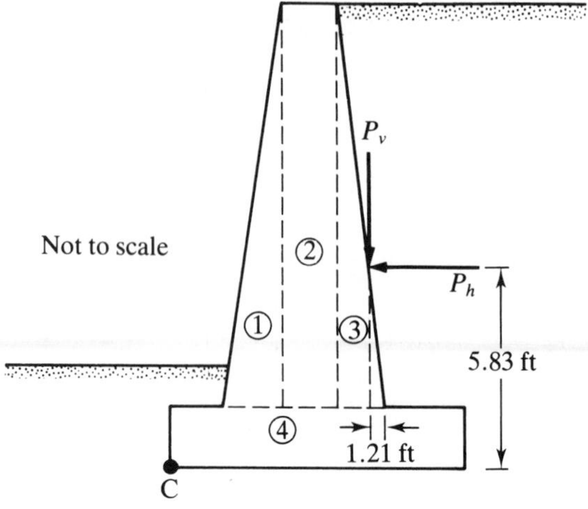

▼ **FIGURE 5.31**

Part b: Factor of Safety Against Sliding

$$FS_{\text{(sliding)}} = \frac{\Sigma V \tan\left(\frac{2}{3}\right)\phi_2 + B\left(\frac{2}{3}\right)c_2}{P_h}$$

$$= \frac{19.75 \tan\left(\frac{2}{3}\right)(20) + 10.3\left(\frac{2}{3}\right)(1.0)}{6.8} = \mathbf{1.7}$$

Part c: Pressure on the Soil at the Toe and Heel

$$e = \frac{B}{2} - \frac{\Sigma M_R - \Sigma M_O}{\Sigma V} = \frac{10.3}{2} - \frac{(105.6 - 39.67)}{19.67} = 1.8 \text{ ft}$$

$$q_{\text{toe}} = \frac{19.75}{10.3}\left[1 + \frac{(6)(1.8)}{10.3}\right] = \mathbf{3.93\ kip/ft^2}$$

$$q_{\text{heel}} = \frac{19.75}{10.3}\left[1 - \frac{(6)(1.8)}{10.3}\right] = \mathbf{-0.093\ kip/ft^2 \approx 0} \qquad \blacktriangledown$$

5.14 OTHER TYPES OF POSSIBLE RETAINING-WALL FAILURE

In addition to the three types of possible failure for retaining walls discussed in Section 5.13, two other types of failure could occur: shallow shear failure and deep shear failure.

Shallow shear failure in soil below the base of a retaining wall takes place along a cylindrical surface *abc* passing through the heel, as shown in Figure 5.32a. The center of the arc of the circle *abc* is located at *O*, which is found by trial and error (corresponds to the minimum factor of safety). This type of failure can occur as the result of excessive induced shear stress along the cylindrical surface in soil. In general, the factor of safety against horizontal sliding is lower than the factor of safety obtained by shallow shear failure. So, if $FS_{\text{(sliding)}}$ is greater than about 1.5, shallow shear failure under the base may not occur.

Deep shear failure can occur along a cylindrical surface *abc*, as shown in Figure 5.32b, as the result of the existence of a weak layer of soil underneath the wall at a depth of about 1.5 times the height of the retaining wall. In such cases, the critical cylindrical failure surface *abc* has to be determined by trial and error with various centers, such as *O* (Figure 5.32b). The failure surface along which the minimum factor of safety is obtained is the *critical surface of sliding*. For the backfill slope with α less than about 10°, the critical failure circle apparently passes through the edge of the heel slab (such as *def* in Figure 5.32b). In this situation, the minimum factor of safety also has to be determined by trial and error by changing the center of the trial circle.

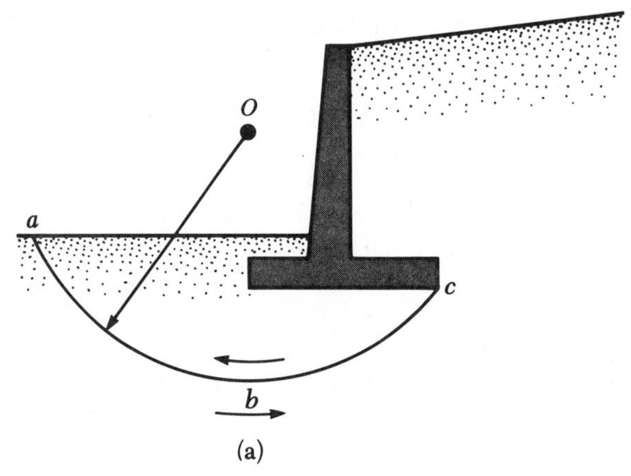

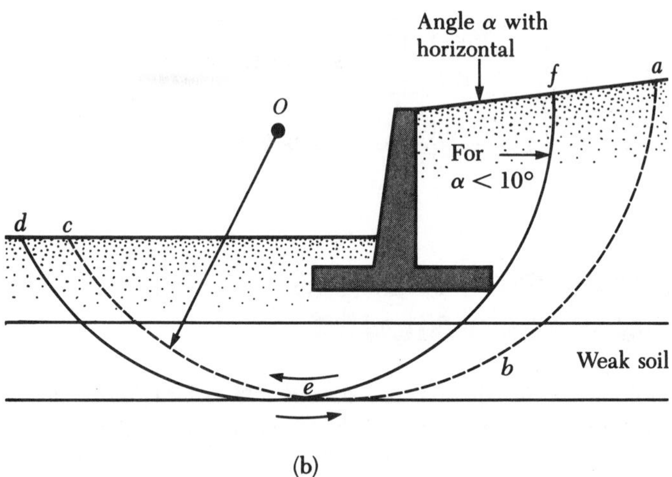

▼ **FIGURE 5.32** (a) Shallow shear failure; (b) deep shear failure

The following is an approximate procedure for determining the factor of safety against deep-seated shear failure for a gently sloping backfill ($\alpha < 10°$) developed by Teng (1962). Refer to Figure 5.33.

1. Draw the retaining wall and the underlying soil layer to a convenient scale.
2. For a trial center O, draw an arc of a circle *abcd*. For all practical purposes, the weight of the soil in the area *abcde* is symmetrical about a vertical line drawn through point O. Let the radius of the trial circle be r.
3. To determine the driving force on the failure surface causing instability (Figure 5.33a), divide the area in the zone *efgh* into several slices. These slices can be treated as rectangles or triangles, as the case may be.
4. Determine the area of each of these slices and then determine the weight W of the soil (and/or concrete) contained inside each slice (per unit length of the wall).

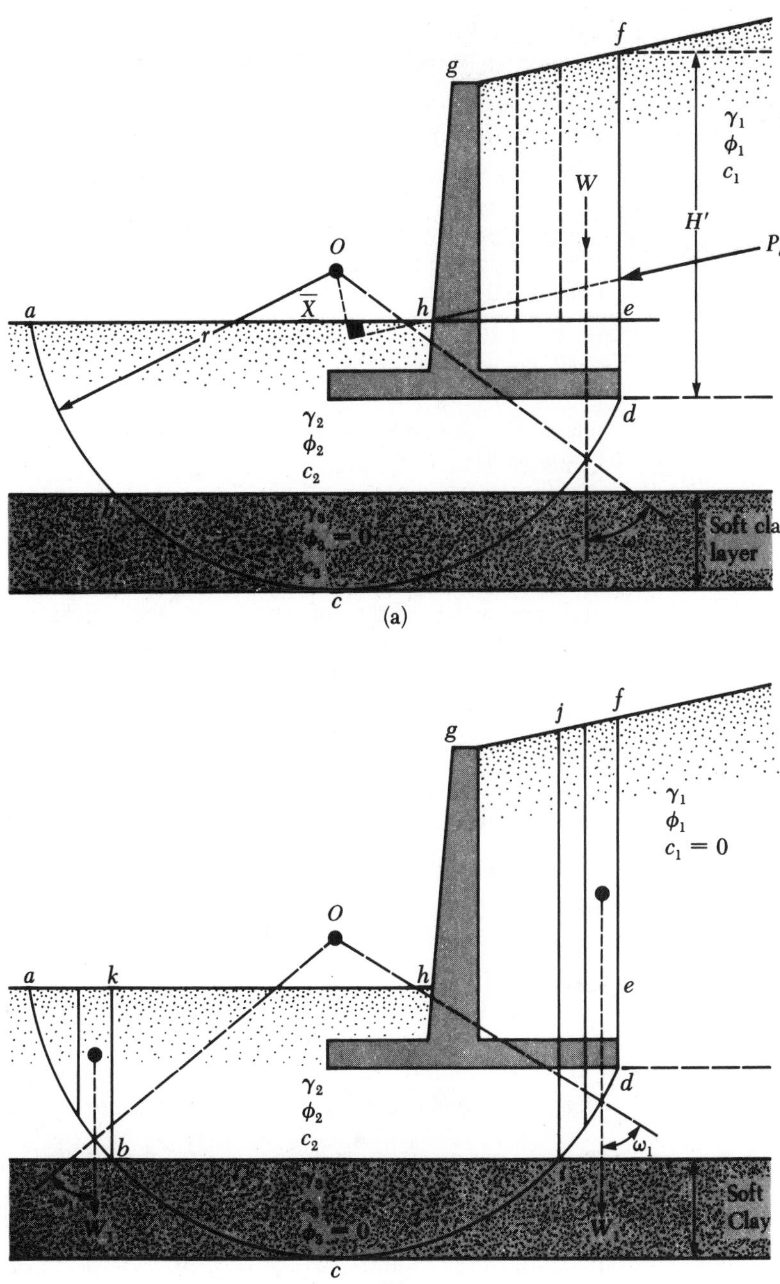

▼ **FIGURE 5.33** Deep shear failure analysis

5. Draw a vertical line through the centroid of each slice, and locate the point of intersection of each vertical line with the trial failure circle.
6. Join point O (that is, the center of the trial circles) with the points of intersection as determined in step 5.
7. Determine the angle, ω, that each vertical line makes with the radial line.
8. Calculate $W \sin \omega$ for each slice.
9. Determine the active force P_a on the face df, $\frac{1}{2}\gamma_1 H'^2 K_a$.
10. Calculate the total driving force:

$$\Sigma (W \sin \omega) + \frac{P_a \bar{X}}{r} \tag{5.70}$$

where $\bar{X}$ = perpendicular distance between the line of action of P_a and the center O

11. To determine the resisting force on the failure surface (Figure 5.33b), divide the area in the zones *abk* and *idefj* into several slices, and determine the weight of each slice, W_1 (per unit length of the wall). Note that points b and i are on top of the soft clay layer; the weight of each slice shown in Figure 5.33b is W_1 in contrast to the weight of each slice W, as shown in Figure 5.33a.
12. Draw a vertical line through the centroid of each slice and locate the point of intersection of each line with the trial failure circle.
13. Join point O with the points of intersection as determined in step 12. Determine the angles, ω_1, that the vertical lines make with the radial lines.
14. For each slice, obtain

$$W_1 \tan \phi_2 \cos \omega_1$$

15. Calculate

$$c_2 l_1 + c_3 l_2 + c_2 l_3$$

where l_1, l_2, and l_3 are the lengths of the arcs *ab*, *bi*, and *id*

16. The maximum resisting force that can be derived along the failure surface is

$$\Sigma (W_1 \tan \phi_2 \cos \omega_1) + c_2 l_1 + c_3 l_2 + c_2 l_3 \tag{5.71}$$

17. Determine the factor of safety against deep shear failure for this trial failure surface:

$$FS_{\text{(deep shear failure)}} = \frac{\Sigma (W_1 \tan \phi_2 \cos \omega_1) + c_2 l_1 + c_3 l_2 + c_2 l_3}{\Sigma (W \sin \omega) + \dfrac{P_a \bar{X}}{r}} \tag{5.72}$$

Several other trial failure surfaces may be drawn, and the factor of safety can be determined in a similar manner. The lowest value of the factor of safety obtained from all trial surfaces is the desired factor of safety.

5.15 COMMENTS RELATING TO STABILITY

When a weak soil layer is located at a shallow depth—that is, within a depth of about 1.5 times the height of the retaining wall—the bearing capacity of the weak layer should be carefully investigated. The possibility of excessive settlement also should be considered. In some cases, the use of lightweight backfill material behind the retaining wall may solve the problem.

In many instances, piles are used to transmit the foundation load to a firmer layer. However, often the thrust of the sliding wedge of soil, in the case of deep shear failure, bends the piles and eventually causes them to fail. Careful attention should be given to this possibility when considering the option of pile foundations for retaining walls. (Pile foundations may be required for bridge abutments to avoid the problem of scouring.)

As illustrated in Examples 5.9, 5.10, and 5.11, the *active earth pressure coefficient* is used to determine the lateral force of the backfill. The active state of the backfill can be established only if the wall yields sufficiently, which does not happen in all cases. The degree of wall yielding will depend on its height and the section modulus. Furthermore, the lateral force of the backfill will depend on several factors, as identified by Casagrande (1973):

a. Effect of temperature
b. Groundwater fluctuation
c. Readjustment of the soil particles due to creep and prolonged rainfall
d. Tidal changes
e. Heavy wave action
f. Traffic vibration
g. Earthquakes

Insufficient wall yielding when combined with other unforeseen factors may generate a larger lateral force on the retaining structure compared to that obtained from the active earth pressure theory. Casagrande (1973) investigated the distribution of lateral earth pressure behind a bridge abutment (in Germany) with a slag backfill, as shown in Figure 5.34. Laboratory tests on the slag backfill gave angles of friction between 37° and 45°, depending on the degree of compaction. For purposes of comparison, the variation of the Rankine active earth pressure with $\phi = 37°$ and $\phi = 45°$ is also shown in Figure 5.34. Comparing the actual and theoretical pressure distribution diagrams indicates:

a. The actual lateral earth pressure distribution may not be triangular.
b. The lateral earth pressure distribution may change with time.
c. The actual active force is greater than the minimum theoretical active force.

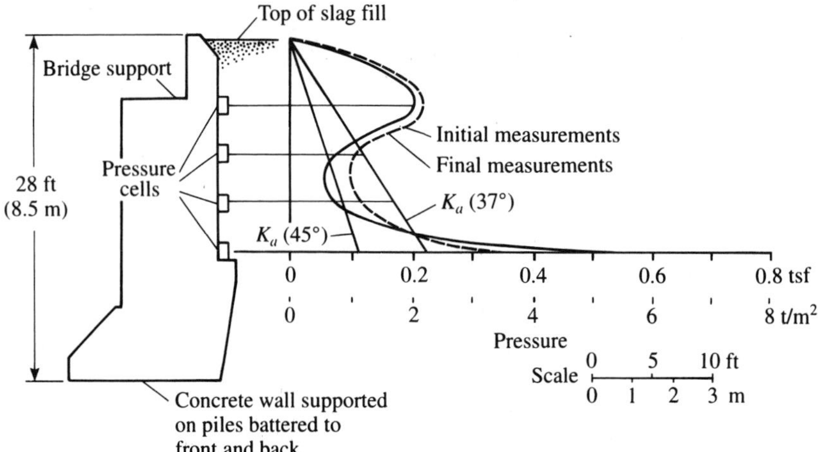

▼ **FIGURE 5.34** Bridge abutment on piles backfilled with granulated slag (after Casagrande, 1973)

The primary reason that many retaining walls designed with theoretical active earth pressure perform satisfactorily is the use of a large factor of safety. Recently, Goh (1993) analyzed the behavior of a retaining wall using the finite element method and proposed the simplified earth pressure distribution shown in Figure 5.35.

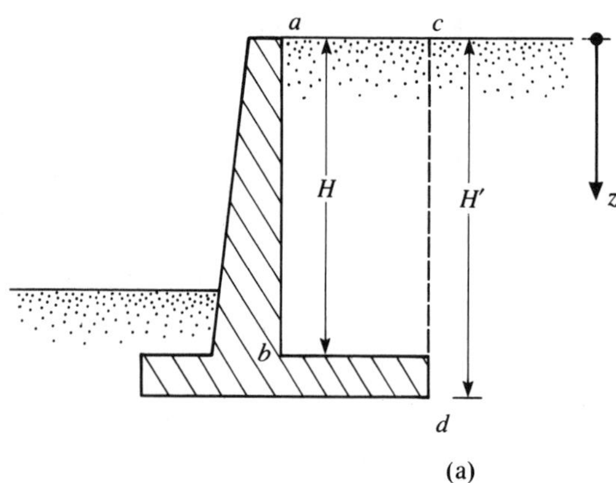

▼ **FIGURE 5.35** Simplified lateral earth pressure (σ_h) profile: (a) retaining wall; (b) pressure distribution behind wall stem; (c) pressure distribution behind virtual wall (after Goh, 1993)

5.16 GRAVITY RETAINING-WALL DESIGN FOR EARTHQUAKE CONDITIONS

Coulomb's active earth pressure theory (see Section 5.4) can be extended to take into account the forces caused by an earthquake. Figure 5.36 shows a condition of active pressure with a granular backfill ($c = 0$). Note that the forces acting on the soil failure

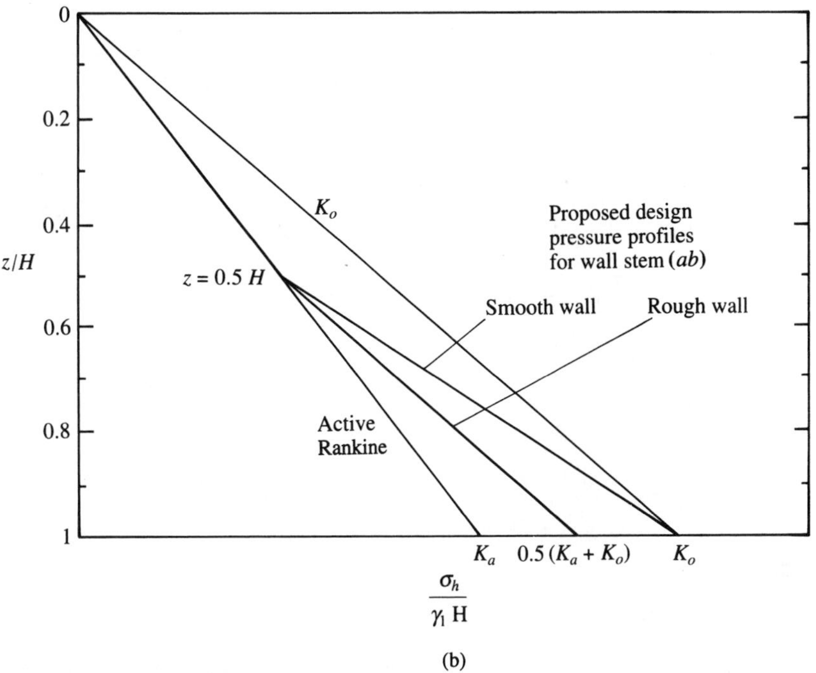

(b)

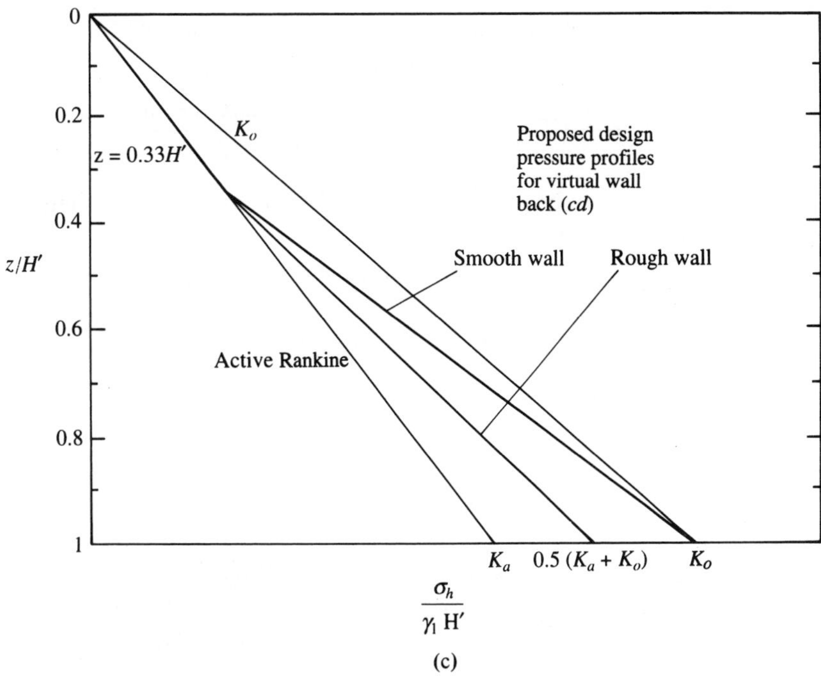

(c)

▼ **FIGURE 5.35** (Continued)

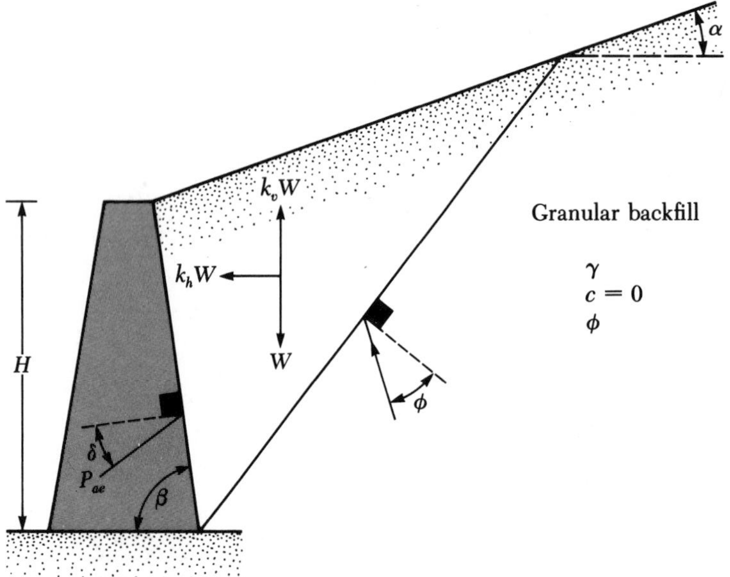

▼ **FIGURE 5.36** Derivation of Eq. (5.75)

wedge in Figure 5.36 are essentially the same as those shown in Figure 5.9a, with the addition of $k_h W$ and $k_v W$ in the horizontal and vertical directions, respectively; k_h and k_v may be defined as

$$k_h = \frac{\text{horizontal earthquake acceleration component}}{\text{acceleration due to gravity, } g} \tag{5.73}$$

$$k_v = \frac{\text{vertical earthquake acceleration component}}{\text{acceleration due to gravity, } g} \tag{5.74}$$

As in Section 5.4, the relation for the active force per unit length of the wall (P_{ae}) can be determined as

$$P_{ae} = \frac{1}{2}\gamma H^2(1 - k_v)K_{ae} \tag{5.75}$$

where

$$K_{ae} = \text{active earth pressure coefficient}$$

$$= \frac{\sin^2(\phi + \beta - \theta')}{\cos\theta' \sin^2\beta \sin(\beta - \theta' - \delta)\left[1 + \sqrt{\dfrac{\sin(\phi + \delta)\sin(\phi - \theta' - \alpha)}{\sin(\beta - \delta - \theta')\sin(\alpha + \beta)}}\right]^2} \tag{5.76}$$

$$\theta' = \tan^{-1}\left[\frac{k_h}{1 - k_v}\right] \tag{5.77}$$

Note that for no earthquake condition

$$k_h = 0, \qquad k_v = 0, \qquad \text{and} \qquad \theta' = 0$$

Hence $K_{ae} = K_a$ [as given by Eq. (5.20)].

The variation of K_{ae} cos δ with k_h for the case of $k_v = 0$, $\beta = 90°$, $\alpha = 0°$, and $\delta = \phi/2$ is shown in Figure 5.37.

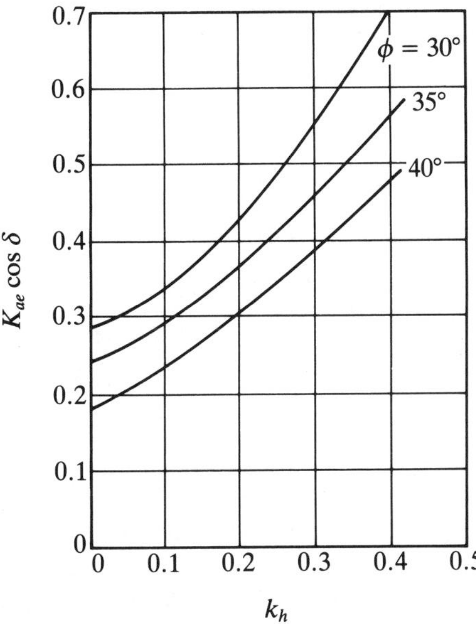

FIGURE 5.37 Variation of K_{ae} cos δ with k_h (*note*: $k_v = 0$, $\beta = 90°$, $\alpha = 0°$, and $\delta = \phi/2$)

Equation (5.75) is usually referred to as the *Mononobe–Okabe* solution. Unlike the case shown in Figure 5.9a the resultant earth pressure in this situation, as calculated by Eq. (5.75), *does not act* at a distance of $H/3$ from the bottom of the wall. The following procedure may be used to obtain the location of the resultant earth pressure.

1. Calculate P_{ae} by using Eq. (5.75).
2. Calculate P_a by using Eq. (5.19).
3. Calculate

$$\Delta P_{ae} = P_{ae} - P_a \tag{5.78}$$

4. Assume that P_a acts at a distance of $H/3$ from the bottom of the wall (Figure 5.38).
5. Assume that ΔP_{ae} acts at a distance of $0.6H$ from the bottom of the wall (Figure 5.38).

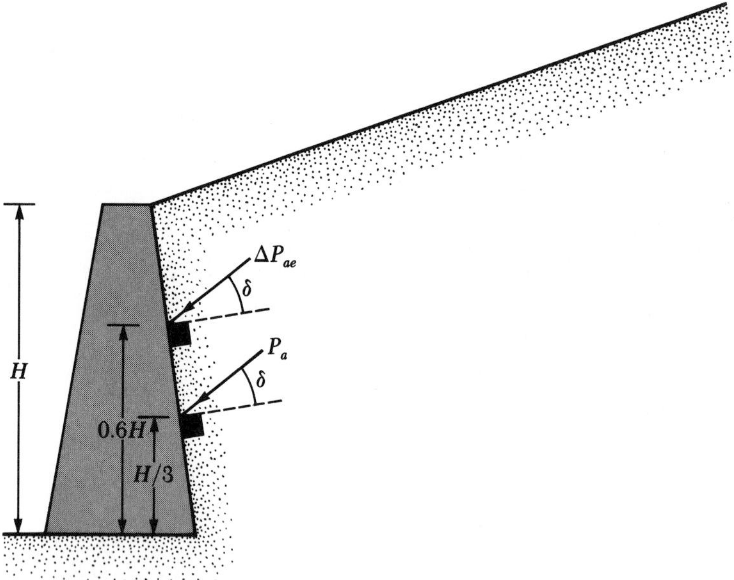

▼ **FIGURE 5.38** Determining the line of action of P_{ae}

6. Calculate the location of the resultant as

$$\bar{z} = \frac{(0.6H)(\Delta P_{ae}) + \left(\frac{H}{3}\right)(P_a)}{P_{ae}} \tag{5.79}$$

Even in mild earthquakes, most retaining walls undergo limited lateral displacement. Richards and Elms (1979) proposed a procedure for designing gravity retaining walls for earthquake conditions that allows limited lateral displacement. This procedure takes into consideration the wall inertia effect. Figure 5.39 shows a retaining wall with various forces acting on it. Note that W_w is equal to the weight of the retaining wall per unit length. Also note that the cohesion, c_2, of the soil on which the retaining wall is resting is assumed to be zero.

Then, considering the equilibrium of the wall,

$$W_w = \left[\frac{1}{2}\gamma_1 H^2(1 - k_v)K_{ae}\right]C_{IE} \tag{5.80}$$

where γ_1 = unit weight of the backfill;

$$C_{IE} = \frac{\sin(\beta - \delta) - \cos(\beta - \delta)\tan\phi_2}{(1 - k_v)(\tan\phi_2 - \tan\theta')} \tag{5.81}$$

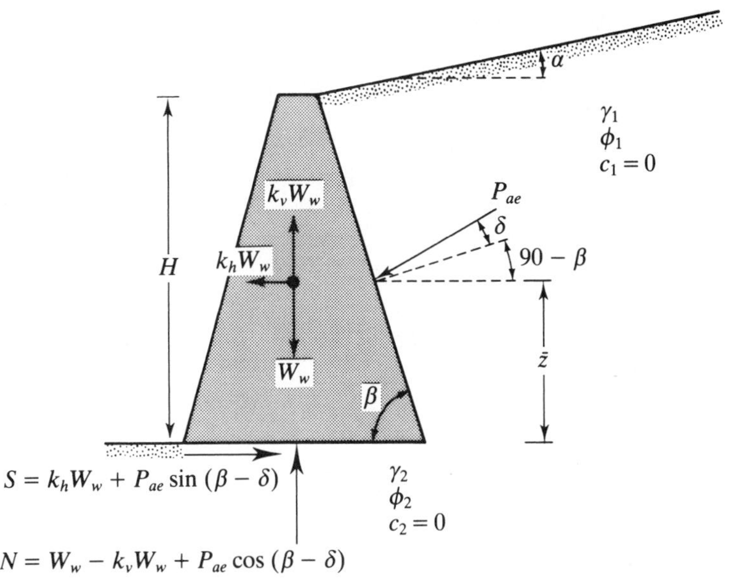

▼ **FIGURE 5.39** Stability of a retaining wall under earthquake forces

and $\theta' = \tan^{-1}\left(\dfrac{k_h}{1 - k_v}\right)$

For a detailed derivation of Eq. (5.81), see Das (1983).

Based on Eqs. (5.80) and (5.81), the following procedure may be used to determine the weight of the retaining wall, W_w, for tolerable displacement that may take place during an earthquake.

1. Determine the tolerable displacement of the wall, Δ.
2. Obtain a design value of k_h from

$$k_h = A_a\left(\frac{0.2A_v^2}{A_a\Delta}\right)^{0.25} \tag{5.82}$$

In Eq. (5.82), A_a and A_v are effective acceleration coefficients and Δ is displacement in inches. The magnitudes of A_a and A_v are given by the Applied Technology Council (1978) for various regions of the United States.

3. Assume that $k_v = 0$, and, with the value of k_h obtained, calculate K_{ae} from Eq. (5.76).
4. Use the value of K_{ae} determined in step 3 to obtain the weight of the wall (W_w).
5. Apply a factor of safety to the value of W_w obtained in step 4.

▼ EXAMPLE 5.12

Refer to Figure 5.40. For $k_v = 0$ and $k_h = 0.3$, determine:

a. P_{ae}
b. The location of the resultant, $\bar{z}$, from the bottom of the wall
c. Weight of the wall for static condition
d. Weight of the wall for zero displacement during an earthquake
e. Weight of the wall for lateral displacement of 1.5 in. during an earthquake

For Part e, assume that $A_a = 0.2$ and $A_v = 0.2$. For Parts c, d, and e, use a factor of safety of 1.5.

Solution

Part a

From Eq. (5.75),

$$P_{ae} = \frac{1}{2}\gamma H^2(1 - k_v)K_{ae}$$

Here, $\gamma = 105$ lb/ft³, $H = 10$ ft, and $k_v = 0$. As $\delta = \phi/2$, we can use Figure 5.37 to determine K_{ae}. For $k_h = 0.3$, $K_{ae} \approx 0.472$. So

$$P_{ae} = \frac{1}{2}(105)(10)^2(1 - 0)(0.472) = \mathbf{2478\ lb/ft}$$

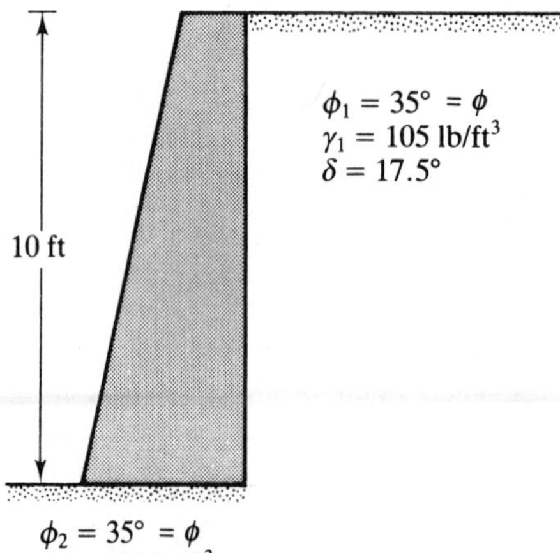

▼ **FIGURE 5.40**

Part b

From Eq. (5.19),

$$P_a = \frac{1}{2}\gamma H^2 K_a$$

From Eq. (5.20) with $\delta = 17.5°$, $\beta = 90°$, and $\alpha = 0°$, $K_a \approx 0.24$. So

$$P_a = \frac{1}{2}(105)(10)^2(0.24) = 1260 \text{ lb/ft}$$

$$\Delta P_{ae} = P_{ae} - P_a = 2478 - 1260 = 1218 \text{ lb/ft}$$

From Eq. (5.79),

$$\bar{z} = \frac{(0.6H)(\Delta P_{ae}) + (H/3)(P_a)}{P_{ae}}$$

$$= \frac{[(0.6)(10)](1218) + (10/3)(1260)}{2478} = \mathbf{4.64\ ft}$$

Part c

For static conditions, $\theta' = 0$ and Eq. (5.81) becomes

$$C_{IE} = \frac{\sin(\beta - \delta) - \cos(\beta - \delta)\tan\phi}{\tan\phi}$$

For $\beta = 90°$, $\delta = 17.5°$, and $\phi = 35°$,

$$C_{IE} = \frac{\sin(90 - 17.5) - \cos(90 - 17.5)\tan 35}{\tan 35}$$

$$= \frac{0.954 - (0.3)(0.7)}{0.7} = 1.06$$

For static conditions, $K_{ae} = K_a$. So

$$W_w = \frac{1}{2}\gamma H^2 K_a C_{IE}$$

For $K_a \approx 0.24$ [Eq. (5.20)],

$$W_w = \frac{1}{2}(105)(10)^2(0.24)(0.16) = 1169 \text{ lb/ft}$$

With a factor of safety of 1.5,

$$W_w = (1169)(1.5) = \mathbf{1753.5\ lb/ft}$$

Part d

For zero displacement, $k_v = 0$,

$$C_{IE} = \frac{\sin(\beta - \delta) - \cos(\beta - \delta)\tan\phi_2}{\tan\phi_2 - \tan\theta'}$$

$$\tan\theta' = \frac{k_h}{1 - k_v} = \frac{0.3}{1 - 0} = 0.3$$

$$C_{IE} = \frac{\sin(90 - 17.5) - \cos(90 - 17.5)\tan 35}{\tan 35 - 0.3}$$

$$= \frac{0.954 - 0.21}{0.7 - 0.3} = 1.86$$

$$W_w = \underbrace{\left[\frac{1}{2}\gamma_1 H^2(1 - k_v)K_{ae}\right]}_{2478\ \text{lb/ft}} C_{IE}$$

$$= (2478)(1.86) = 4609\ \text{lb/ft}$$

With a factor of safety of 1.5, $W_w =$ **6914 lb/ft**

Part e

For a lateral displacement of 1.5 in.,

$$k_h = A_a\left(\frac{0.2A_v^2}{A_a\Delta}\right)^{0.25} = (0.2)\left[\frac{(0.2)(0.2)^2}{(0.2)(1.5)}\right]^{0.25} = 0.081$$

$$\tan\theta' = \frac{k_h}{1 - k_v} = \frac{0.081}{1 - 0} = 0.081$$

$$C_{IE} = \frac{\sin(90 - 17.5) - \cos(90 - 17.5)\tan 35}{\tan 35 - 0.081} = 1.2$$

$$W_w = \frac{1}{2}\gamma_1 H^2 \underset{\substack{\uparrow \\ \approx 0.294\ [\text{Eq. (5.76)}]}}{K_{ae}} C_{IE}$$

$$W_w = \frac{1}{2}(105)(10)^2(0.294)(1.2) = 1852\ \text{lb/ft}$$

With a factor of safety of 1.5, $W_w =$ **2778 lb/ft.** ▼

5.17 DRAINAGE FROM THE BACKFILL OF THE RETAINING WALL

As the result of rainfall or other wet conditions, the backfill material for a retaining wall may become saturated. Saturation will increase the pressure on the wall and may create an unstable condition. For this reason, adequate drainage must be provided by means of *weepholes* and/or *perforated drainage pipes* (see Figure 5.41).

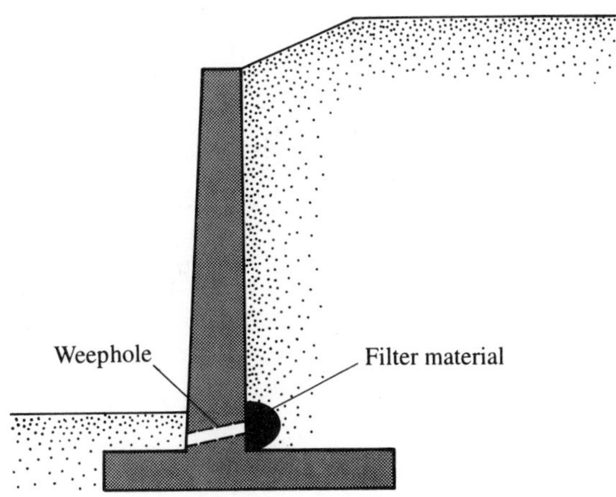

▼ **FIGURE 5.41** Drainage provisions for the backfill of a retaining wall

The *weepholes*, if provided, should have a minimum diameter of about 4 in. (0.1 m) and be adequately spaced. Note that there is always a possibility that the backfill material may be washed into weepholes or drainage pipes and ultimately clog them. Thus a filter material needs to be placed behind the weepholes or around the drainage pipes, as the case may be; geotextiles now serve that purpose. Whenever granular soil is used as a filter, the principles outlined in Section 1.11 should be followed. Example 5.13 gives the procedure for designing a filter.

▼ EXAMPLE 5.13

Figure 5.42 shows the grain-szie distribution of a backfill material. Using the conditions outlined in Section 1.11, determine the range of the grain-size distribution for the filter material.

Solution

From the grain-size distribution curve given in Figure 5.42, the following values can be determined:

$$D_{15(B)} = 0.04 \text{ mm}$$

$$D_{85(B)} = 0.25 \text{ mm}$$

$$D_{50(B)} = 0.13 \text{ mm}$$

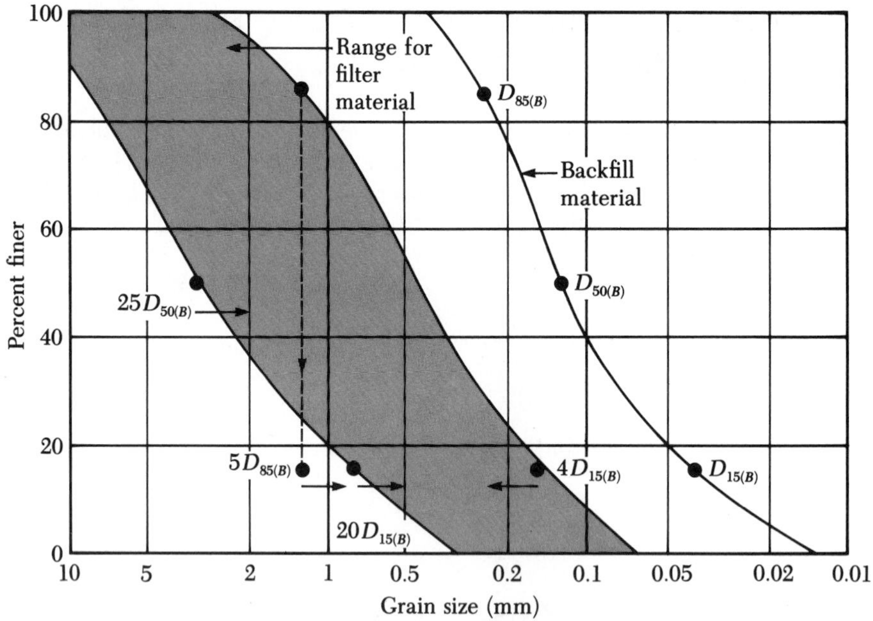

▼ **FIGURE 5.42**

Conditions of Filter

1. $D_{15(F)}$ should be less than $5D_{85(F)}$—that is, $5 \times 0.25 = 1.25$ mm.
2. $D_{15(F)}$ should be greater than $4D_{15(B)}$—that is, $4 \times 0.04 = 0.16$ mm.
3. $D_{50(F)}$ should be less than $25D_{50(B)}$—that is, $25 \times 0.13 = 3.25$ mm.
4. $D_{15(F)}$ should be less than $20D_{15(B)}$—that is, $20 \times 0.04 = 0.8$ mm.

These limiting points are plotted in Figure 5.42. Through these points can be drawn two curves that are similar in nature to the grain-size distribution curve of the backfill material. These curves define the range for the filter material to be used. ▼

5.18 PROVISION OF JOINTS IN RETAINING-WALL CONSTRUCTION

A retaining wall may be constructed with one or more of the following joints.

1. *Construction joints* (Figure 5.43a) are vertical and horizontal joints that are placed between two successive pours of concrete. To increase the shear at the joints, keys may be used. If keys are not used, the surface of the first pour is cleaned and roughened before the next pour of concrete.
2. *Contraction joints* (Figure 5.43b) are vertical joints (grooves) placed in the face of a wall (from the top of the base slab to the top of the wall) that allow the concrete to shrink without noticeable harm. The grooves may be about 0.25 to 0.3 in. ($\approx$6 to 8 mm) wide and 0.5 to 0.6 in. ($\approx$12 to 16 mm) deep.

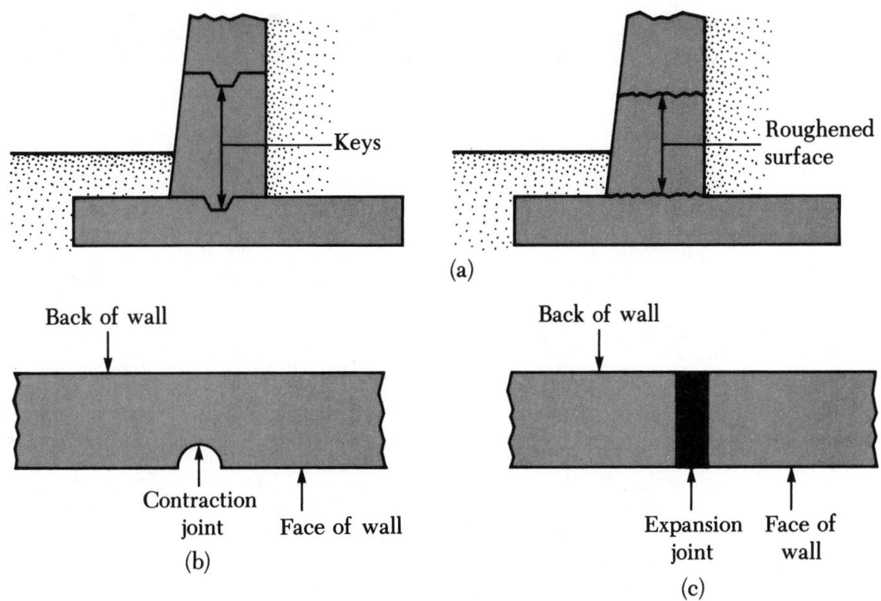

▼ **FIGURE 5.43** (a) Construction joints; (b) contraction joint; (c) expansion joint

3. Expansion joints (Figure 5.43c) allow for the expansion of concrete caused by temperature changes; vertical expansion joints from the base to the top of the wall may also be used. These joints may be filled with flexible joint fillers. In most cases, horizontal reinforcing steel bars running across the stem are continuous through all joints. The steel is greased to allow the concrete to expand.

PROBLEMS

5.1–5.4 Use Eq. (5.3), Figure P5.1, and the following values to determine the at-rest lateral earth pressure per unit length of the wall. Also find the location of the resultant.

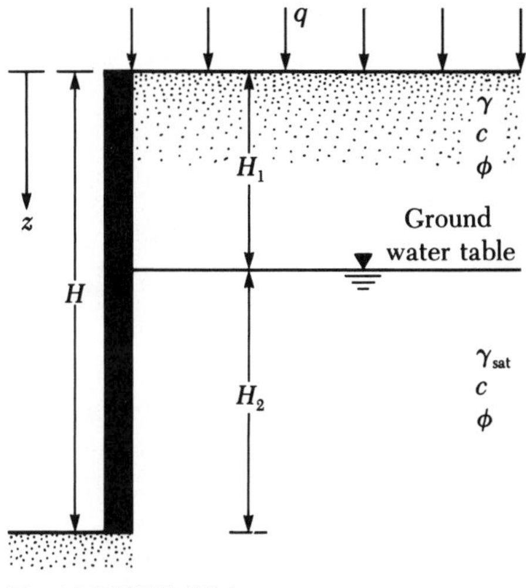

▼ **FIGURE P5.1**

Prob. no.	H	H_1	H_2	γ	γ_{sat}	ϕ	c	q
5.1	15 ft	15 ft	0	112 lb/ft^3	—	34°	0	0
5.2	4 m	4 m	0	17.5 kN/m^3	—	32°	0	10 kN/m^2
5.3	10 ft	4 ft	6 ft	105 lb/ft^3	122 lb/ft^3	30°	0	300 lb/ft^2
5.4	4.5 m	1.5 m	3 m	16 kN/m^3	19.2 kN/m^3	36°	0	0

5.5 Refer to Figure P5.1. Use Eqs. (5.5) and (5.7) and $H = 16$ ft, $H_1 = 16$ ft, $H_2 = 0$, $q = 0$, and $\gamma = 119$ lb/ft^3. The backfill is an overconsolidated clay with a plasticity index of 25. If the overconsolidation ratio is 2.5, determine the at-rest lateral earth force per foot of the wall. Also find the location of the resultant.

5.6 Redo Problem 5.5 for a surcharge, q, of 350 lb/ft^2.

5.7 A retaining wall is 21 ft high with a horizontal saturated clay backfill ($\phi = 0$). The undrained cohesion and the saturated unit weight of the backfill are 630 lb/ft^2 and 113 lb/ft^3, respectively.

a. Determine the Rankine active pressure distribution diagram behind the wall.

b. Determine the depth of the tensile crack, z_c.

c. Estimate the Rankine active force per foot of the wall before and after the occurrence of the tensile crack.

5.8 A vertical retaining wall is 6.5 m high with a horizontal backfill. For the backfill, assume that $\gamma = 16.5$ kN/m^3, $\phi = 28°$, and $c = 20$ kN/m^2. Determine the Rankine active force per unit length of the wall after the occurrence of the tensile crack.

5.9–5.10 Use Figure P5.9 and the following data to determine the Rankine active force per unit length of the wall after the occurrence of the tensile crack.

Prob. no.	H_1	H_2	γ_1	γ_2	ϕ_1	ϕ_2	c_1	c_2
5.9	8 ft	16 ft	110 lb/ft^3	140 lb/ft^3	38°	25°	0	209 lb/ft^2
5.10	8.2 ft	14.8 ft	107 lb/ft^3	125 lb/ft^3	28°	20°	350 lb/ft^2	100 lb/ft^2

5.11 Redo Problem 5.9 for the Rankine passive case.

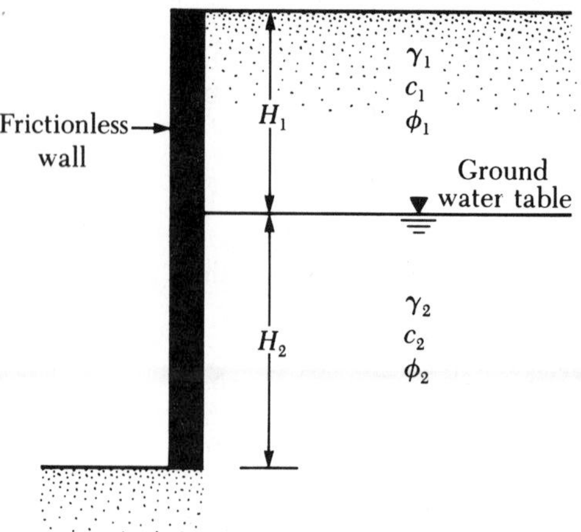

▼ **FIGURE P5.9**

5.12 Redo Problem 5.10 for the Rankine passive case.

5.13 Refer to Problem 5.7.

a. Draw the Rankine passive pressure distribution diagram behind the wall.

b. Estimate the Rankine passive force per foot length of the wall and also the location of the resultant.

5.14 Refer to Figure 5.9a. Here, $H = 5$ m, $\gamma = 18.2$ kN/m^3, $\phi = 30°$, $\delta = 20°$, $c = 0$, $\alpha = 10°$, and $\beta = 85°$. Determine the Coulomb's active force per meter length of the wall and the location and direction of the resultant.

5.15 For the retaining wall in Problem 5.14, determine the Coulomb's passive force per meter length of the wall and the location and direction of the resultant.

5.16 Refer to Figure 5.14b, which shows a vertical retaining wall with a horizontal backfill. Use $H = 13.5$ ft, $\gamma = 105$ lb/ft^3, $\phi = 35°$, and $\delta = 10°$. Based on Shields and Tolunay's work (Table 5.7), what would be the passive force per meter of the wall?

5.17 Refer to Figure 5.16. For the retaining wall, $H = 7.5$ m, $\phi = 32°$, $\alpha = 5°$, $\gamma = 18.2$ kN/m^3, and $c = 0$.

a. Determine the intensity of the Rankine active force at $z = 2$, 4, 6, and 7.5 m.

b. Determine the Rankine active force per meter of the wall and also the location and direction of the resultant.

5.18 Refer to Figure 5.17b. For the retaining wall, $H = 12$ ft, $a' = 3$ ft, $b' = 4.5$ ft, and $q =$ 600 lb/ft^2.

a. Determine the lateral force per unit length of the wall caused by surcharge loading only.

b. Determine the location of the center of pressure, $\bar{z}$.

5.19 For the cantilever retaining wall shown in Figure P5.19, the wall dimensions are $H = 8$ m,

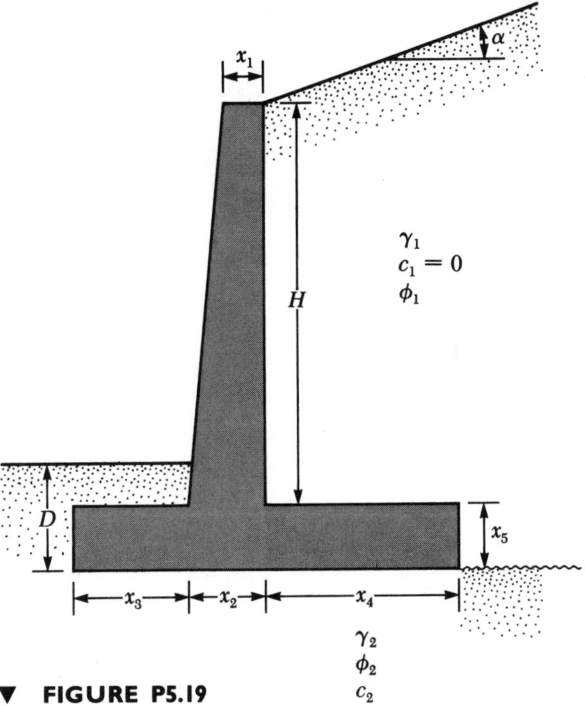

▼ **FIGURE P5.19**

$x_1 = 0.4$ m, $x_2 = 0.6$ m, $x_3 = 1.5$ m, $x_4 = 3.5$ m, $x_5 = 0.96$ m, $D = 1.75$ m, and $\alpha = 10°$; and the soil properties are $\gamma_1 = 16.8$ kN/m^3, $\phi_1 = 32°$, $\gamma_2 = 17.6$ kN/m^3, $\phi_2 = 28°$, and $c_2 = 30$ kN/m^2. Calculate the factors of safety with respect to overturning and sliding and bearing capacity.

5.20 Repeat Problem 5.19 for the wall dimensions $H = 20$ ft, $x_1 = 12$ in., $x_2 = 27$ in., $x_3 = 4.5$ ft, $x_4 = 7.5$ ft, $x_5 = 2.75$ ft, $D = 4$ ft, and $\alpha = 5°$; and the soil properties $\gamma_1 = 117$ lb/ft^3, $\phi_1 = 34°$, $\gamma_2 = 107$ lb/ft^3, $\phi_2 = 18°$, and $c_2 = 1050$ lb/ft^2.

5.21 Repeat Problem 5.19 with wall dimensions of $H = 5.49$ m, $x_1 = 0.46$ m, $x_2 = 0.58$ m, $x_3 = 0.92$ m, $x_4 = 1.55$ m, $x_5 = 0.61$ m, $D = 1.22$ m, and $\alpha = 0°$; and soil properties of $\gamma_1 = 18.08$ kN/m^3, $\phi_1 = 36°$, $\gamma_2 = 19.65$ kN/m^3, $\phi_2 = 15°$, and $c_2 = 44$ kN/m^2.

5.22 The gravity retaining wall shown in Figure P5.22 has wall dimensions of $H = 15$ ft, $x_1 = 1.5$ ft, $x_2 = 0.8$ ft, $x_3 = 5.25$ ft, $x_4 = 1.25$ ft, $x_5 = 1.5$ ft, $x_6 = 2.5$ ft, and $D = 4$ ft; and soil properties of $\gamma_1 = 121$ lb/ft^3, $\phi_1 = 30°$, $\gamma_2 = 121$ lb/ft^3, $\phi_2 = 20°$, and $c_2 = 1000$ lb/ft^2. Calculate the factor of safety with respect to overturning and sliding and bearing capacity. Use Rankine active pressure for the calculation (see Figure 5.20).

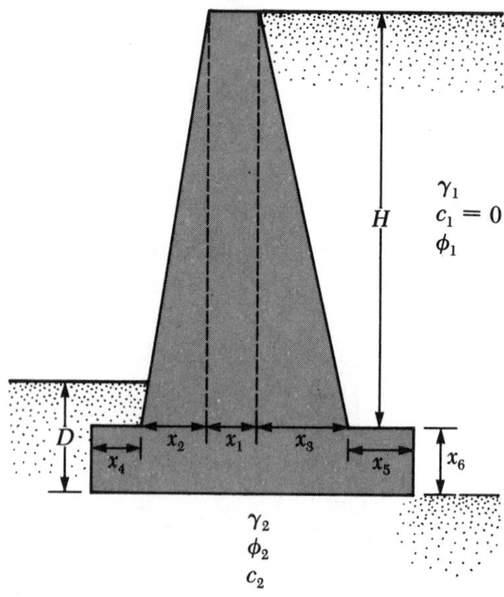

▼ **FIGURE P5.22**

5.23 Repeat Problem 5.22. Use Coulomb's active presure calculation and $\delta = \frac{2}{3}\phi_1$.

5.24 Redo Problem 5.14. Assume that earthquake forces have to be considered, that is, $k_h = 0.3$ and $k_v = 0$. Determine the location of the resultant, P_{ae}.

REFERENCES

Applied Technology Council (1978). "Tentative Provisions for the Development of Seismic Regulations for Buildings," *Publication ATC-3-06.*

Brooker, E. W., and Ireland, H. O. (1965). "Earth Pressure at Rest Related to Stress History," *Canadian Geotechnical Journal*, Vol. 2, No. 1, pp. 1–15.

Caquot, A., and Kerisel, J. (1948). *Tables for Calculation of Pasive Pressure, Active Pressure, and Bearing Capacity of Foundations*, Gauthier-Villars, Paris, France.

Casagrande, L. (1973). "Comments on Conventional Design of Retaining Structure," *Journal of the Soil Mechanics and Foundations Division*, ASCE, Vol. 99, No. SM2, pp. 181–198.

Coulomb, C. A. (1776). *Essai sur une Application des Regles de Maximis et Minimum à quelques Problemes de Statique Relatifs à l'Architecture*, Mem. Acad. Roy. des Sciences, Paris, Vol. 3, p. 38.

Das, B. M. (1983). *Fundamentals of Soil Dynamics*, Elsevier, New York.

Das, B. M. (1987). *Theoretical Foundation Engineering*, Elsevier, Amsterdam.

Elman, M. T., and Terry, C. F. (1988). "Retaining Walls with Sloped Heel," *Journal of Geotechnical Engineering*, American Society of Civil Engineers, Vol. 114, No. GT10, pp. 1194–1199.

Goh, A. T. C. (1993). "Behavior of Cantilever Retaining Walls," *Journal of Geotechnical Engineering*, ASCE, Vol. 119, No. 11, pp. 1751–1770.

Jaky, J. (1944). "The Coefficient of Earth Pressure at Rest," *Journal for the Society of Hungarian Architects and Engineers*, October, pp. 355–358.

James, R. G., and Bransby, P. L. (1971). "A Velocity Field for Some Passive Earth Pressure Problems," *Geotechnique*, London, Vol. 21, No. 1, pp. 61–84.

Jarquio, R. (1981). "Total Lateral Surcharge Pressure Due to Strip Load," *Journal of the Geotechnical Engineering Division*, American Society of Civil Engineers, Vol. 107, No. GT10, pp. 1424–1428.

Mayne, P. W., and Kulhawy, F. H. (1982). "K_o–*OCR* Relationships in Soil," *Journal of the Geotechnical Engineering Division*, ASCE, Vol. 108, No. GT6, pp. 851–872.

Packshaw, S. (1969). "Earth Pressure and Earth Resistance," *A Century of Soil Mechanics*, The Institution of Engineers, London, pp. 409–435.

Richards, R., and Elms, D. G. (1979). "Seismic Behavior of Gravity Retaining Walls," *Journal of the Geotechnical Engineering Division*, American Society of Civil Engineers, Vol. 105, No. GT4, pp. 449–464.

Sherif, M. A., Fang, Y. S., and Sherif, R. I. (1984). "k_a and k_0 Behind Rotating and Non-Yielding Walls." *Journal of Geotechnical Engineering*, American Society of Civil Engineers, Vol. 110, No. GT1, pp. 41–56.

Shields, D. H., and Tolunay, A. Z. (1972). "Passive Pressure Coefficients for Sand by the Terzaghi and Peck Method," *Canadian Geotechnical Journal*, Vol. 9, No. 4.

Shields, D. H., and Tolunay, A. Z. (1973). "Passive Pressure by Method of Slices," *Journal of the Soil Mechanics and Foundations Division*, American Society of Civil Engineers, Vol. 99, No. SM12, pp. 1043–1053.

Teng, W. C. (1962). *Foundation Design*, Prentice-Hall, Englewood Cliffs, N. J.

Terzaghi, K., and Peck, R. B. (1967). *Soil Mechanics in Engineering Practice*, Wiley, New York.

CHAPTER SIX

SHEET PILE WALLS

6.1 INTRODUCTION

Connected or semiconnected sheet piles are often used to build continuous walls for waterfront structures that may range from small waterfront pleasure boat launching facilities to large dock facilities (Figure 6.1a). In contrast to the construction of other types of retaining wall, the building of sheet pile walls does not usually require dewatering of the site. Sheet piles are also used for some temporary structures, such as braced cuts (Figure 6.1b). The principles of sheet pile design used in braced cuts are discussed in Chapter 7.

Several types of sheet pile are commonly used in construction: (a) wooden sheet piles, (b) precast concrete sheet piles, and (c) steel sheet piles. Aluminum sheet piles are also marketed.

Wooden sheet piles are used only for temporary light structures that are above the water table. The most common types are ordinary wooden planks and *Wakefield piles*. The wooden planks are about 2 in. × 12 in. (50 mm × 300 mm) in cross section and are driven edge to edge (Figure 6.2a). Wakefield piles are made by nailing three planks together with the middle plank offset by 2–3 in. (50–75 mm) (Figure 6.2b). Wooden planks can also be milled to form *tongue-and-groove piles*, as shown in Figure 6.2c. Figure 6.2d shows another type of wooden sheet pile that has precut grooves. Metal *splines* are driven into the grooves of the adjacent sheetings to hold them together after they are driven into the ground.

Precast concrete sheet piles are heavy and are designed with reinforcements to withstand the permanent stresses to which the structure will be subjected after construction and also to handle the stresses produced during construction. In cross section, these piles are about 20–32 in. (500–800 mm) wide and 6–10 in. (150–250 mm) thick. Figure 6.2e shows schematic diagrams of the elevation and the cross section of a reinforced concrete sheet pile.

Steel sheet piles in the United States are about 0.4–0.5 in. (10–13 mm) thick. European sections may be thinner and wider. Sheet pile sections may be *Z*, *deep arch*, *low arch*, or *straight web* sections. The interlocks of the sheet pile sections are shaped like a *thumb-and-finger* or a *ball-and-socket* for watertight connections. Figure 6.3a shows schematic diagrams of the thumb-and-finger type of interlocking for straight web sections. The ball-and-socket type of interlocking for *Z* section piles is shown in Figure 6.3b. Table 6.1 shows the properties of the sheet pile sections produced by the U.S. Steel Corporation.

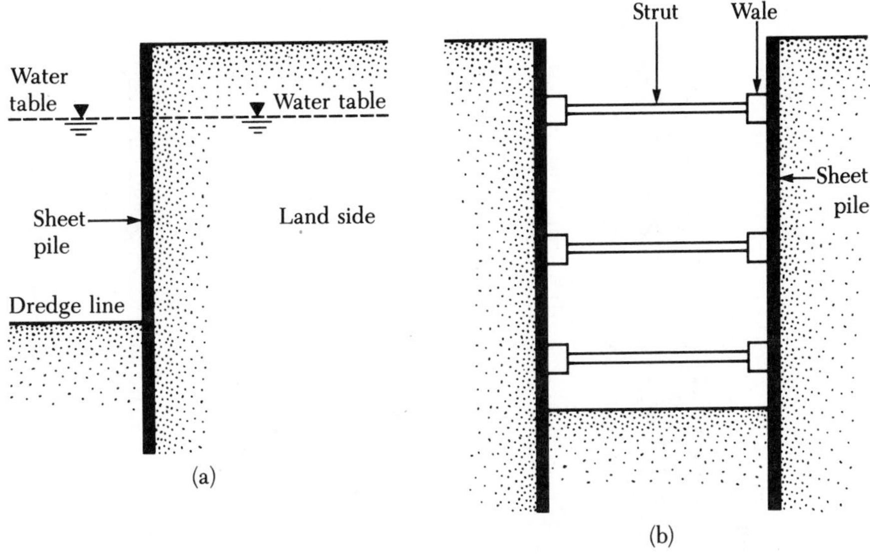

▼ **FIGURE 6.1** Examples of uses of sheet piles: (a) waterfront sheet pile wall; (b) braced cut

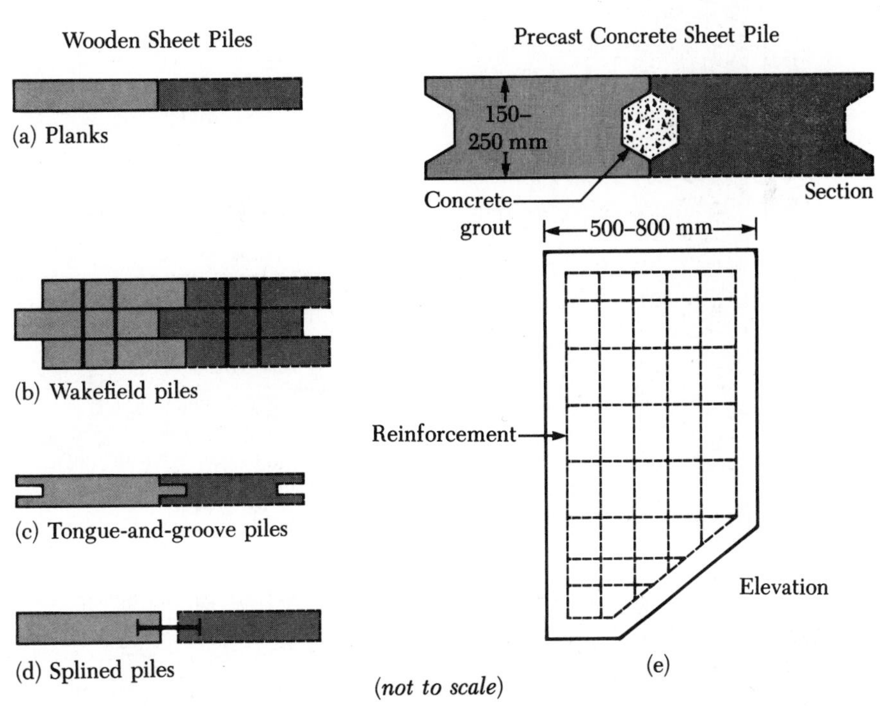

▼ **FIGURE 6.2** Various types of wooden and concrete sheet pile

TABLE 6.1 Properties of Sheet Pile Sections (Produced by the U.S. Steel Corporation)

Section designation	Sketch of section	Driving distance in. (mm)	Section modulus		Moment of inertia		Comments
			in^3/ft of wall	m^3/m of wall $\times 10^5$	in^4/ft of wall	m^4/m of wall $\times 10^6$	
PZ-38	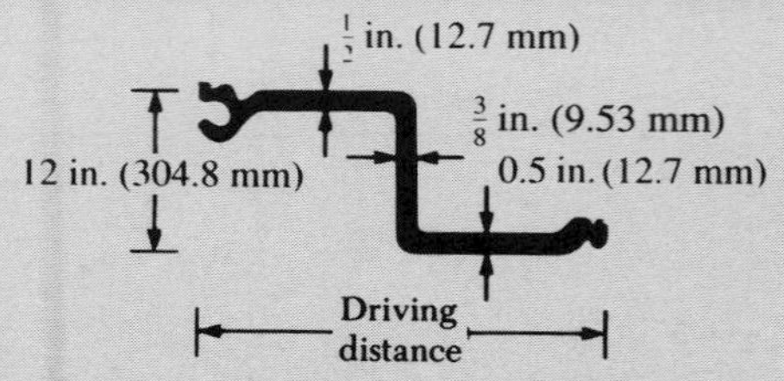 $\frac{1}{2}$ in. (12.7 mm); $\frac{3}{8}$ in. (9.53 mm); 0.5 in. (12.7 mm); 12 in. (304.8 mm); Driving distance	**18** (457.2)	46.8	251.32	280.8	383.29	Interlock with each other and also with PSA-23 or PSA-28
PZ-32	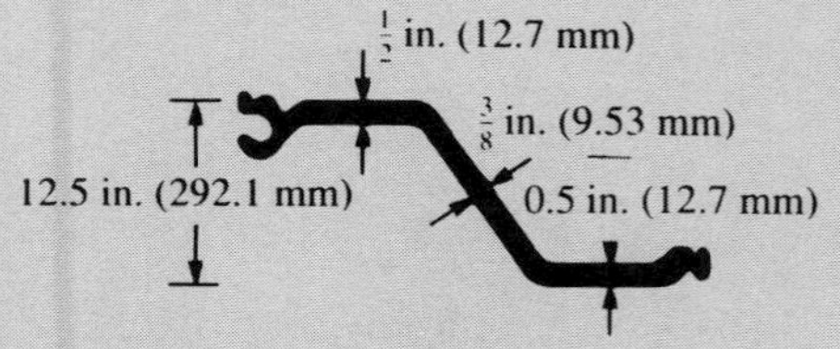 $\frac{1}{2}$ in. (12.7 mm); $\frac{3}{8}$ in. (9.53 mm); 0.5 in. (12.7 mm); 12.5 in. (292.1 mm)	21 (533.4)	38.3	205.67	220.4	300.85	Interlock with each other and also with PSA-23 or PSA-28
PZ-27	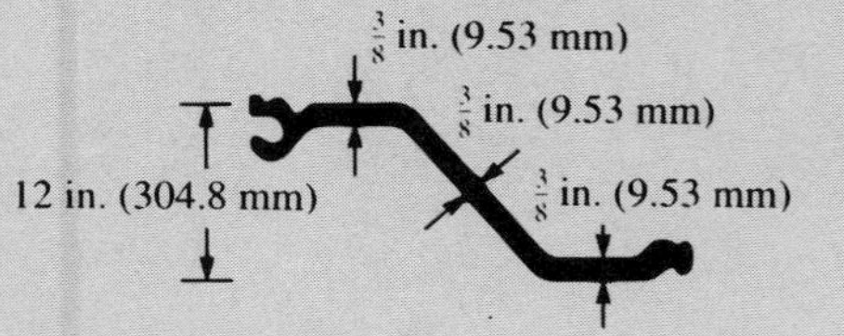 $\frac{3}{8}$ in. (9.53 mm); $\frac{3}{8}$ in. (9.53 mm); $\frac{3}{8}$ in. (9.53 mm); 12 in. (304.8 mm)	18 (457.2)	30.2	162.17	184.2	251.43	Interlock with each other and also with PSA-23 or PSA-28
PDA-27	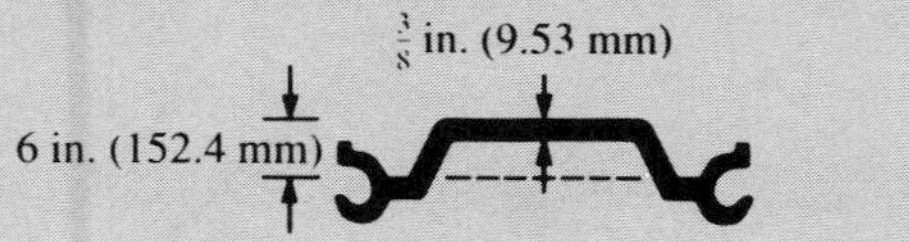 $\frac{3}{8}$ in. (9.53 mm); 6 in. (152.4 mm)	16 (406.4)	10.7	57.46	39.8	54.33	Interlock with each other

▼ **TABLE 6.1 (Continued)**

Section designation	Sketch of section	Driving distance in. (mm)	Section modulus		Moment of inertia		Comments
			in^3*/ft of wall*	*m*^{3}*/m of wall* $\times 10^5$	*in*^{4}*/ft of wall*	*m*^{4}*/m of wall* $\times 10^6$	
PMA-22	$\frac{3}{8}$ in. (9.53 mm); $\frac{3}{4}$ in. (82.55 mm)	19.625 (498.48)	5.4	29.00	13.7	18.70	Interlock with each other
PSA-28	$\frac{1}{2}$ in. (12.7 mm)	16 (406.4)	2.5	13.43	4.5	6.14	Interlock with each other
PSA-23	$\frac{3}{8}$ in. (9.53 mm)	16 (406.4)	2.4	12.89	4.1	5.6	Interlock with each other
PSX-32	$\frac{1}{2}$ in. (12.7 mm)	16.5 (419.1)	2.4	12.89	3.7	5.05	Interlock with each other
PS-32	$\frac{1}{2}$ in. (12.7 mm)	15 (381)	1.9	10.20	2.9	3.96	Interlock with each other
PS-28	$\frac{3}{8}$ in. (9.53 mm)	15 (381)	1.9	10.20	2.8	3.82	Interlock with each other

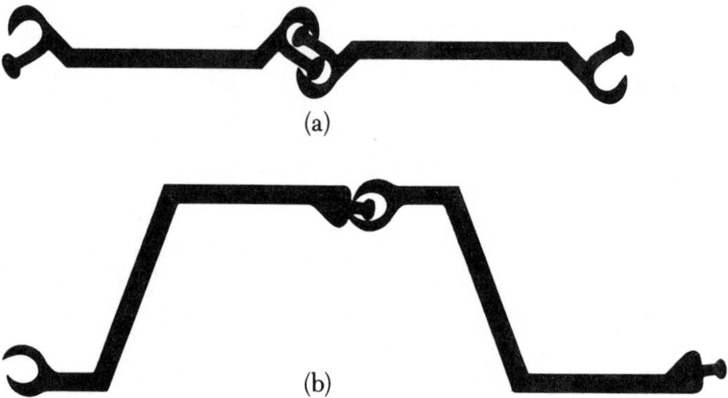

▼ **FIGURE 6.3** Nature of sheet pile connections: (a) thumb-and-finger type; (b) ball-and-socket type

The allowable design flexural stress for the steel sheet piles is as follows:

Type of steel	*Allowable stress* (lb/in^2)
ASTM A-328	25,000 lb/in^2 (170 MN/m^2)
ASTM A-572	30,000 lb/in^2 (210 MN/m^2)
ASTM A-690	30,000 lb/in^2 (210 MN/m^2)

Steel sheet piles are convenient to use because of their resistance to high driving stress developed when being driven into hard soils. They are also lightweight and reusable.

This chapter primarily discusses the design principles for waterfront retaining structures built with sheet piles.

6.2 CONSTRUCTION METHODS FOR SHEET PILE WALLS—GENERAL

Sheet pile walls may be divided into two basic categories: (a) cantilever and (b) anchored. The principles of anchoring sheet pile walls are discussed in more detail in Section 6.14.

In the construction of sheet pile walls, sheet piles may be driven into the ground and then the backfill placed on the land side, or the sheet pile may first be driven into the ground and the soil in front of the sheet pile dredged. In any case, the soil used for backfill behind the sheet pile wall is usually granular. The soil below the dredge line may be sandy or clayey soil. The surface of soil on the water side is referred to as the *mud line* or *dredge line*.

Thus construction methods generally can be divided into two categories (Tsinker, 1983):

1. Backfilled structure
2. Dredged structure

The sequence of construction for a *backfilled structure* is as follows (Figure 6.4):

Step 1. Dredge the *in situ* soil in front and back of the proposed structure.
Step 2. Drive the sheet piles.
Step 3. Backfill up to the level of the anchor and place the anchor system.
Step 4. Backfill up to the top of the wall.

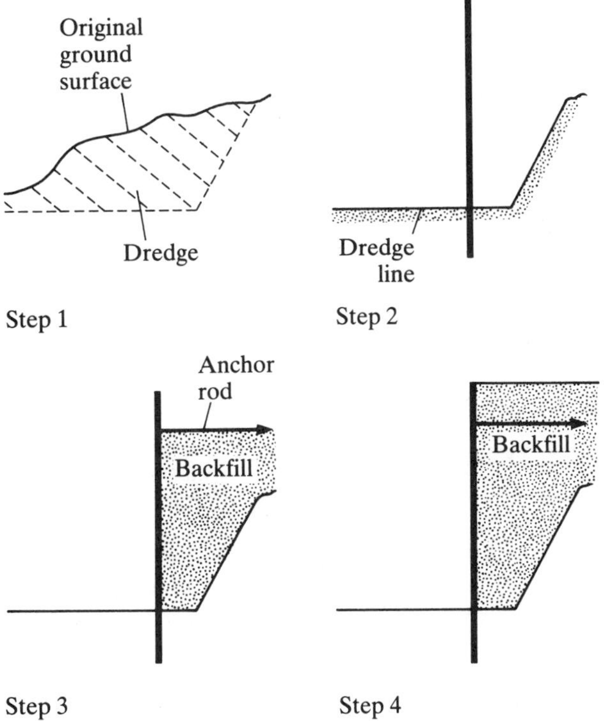

▼ **FIGURE 6.4** Sequence of construction for a backfilled structure

For a cantilever type of wall, only steps 1, 2, and 4 apply.

The sequence of construction for a *dredged structure* is as follows (Figure 6.5):

Step 1. Drive the sheet piles.
Step 2. Backfill up to the anchor level and place the anchor system.
Step 3. Backfill up to the top of the wall.
Step 4. Dredge the front side of the wall.

For cantilever sheet pile walls, step 2 is not required.

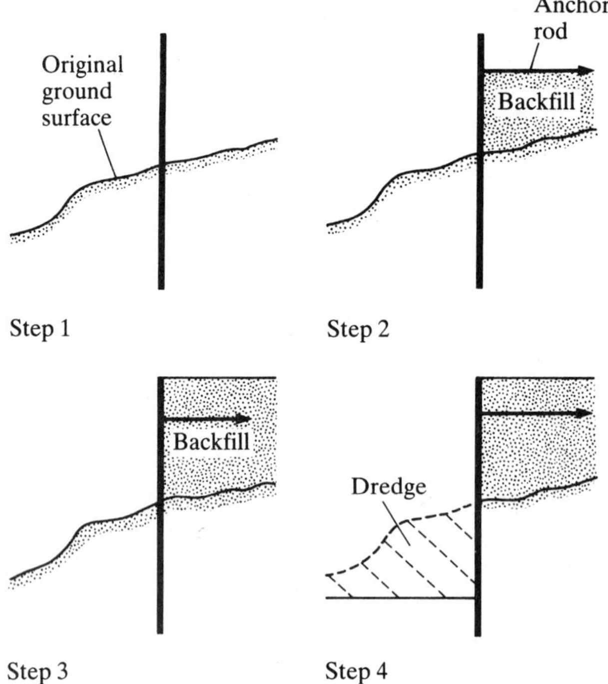

▼ **FIGURE 6.5** Sequence of construction for a dredged structure

CANTILEVER SHEET PILE WALLS

Cantilever sheet pile walls are usually recommended for walls of moderate height—about 20 ft ($\approx$6 m) or less, measured above the dredge line. In such walls, the sheet piles act as a wide cantilever beam above the dredge line. The basic principles for estimating net lateral pressure distribution on a cantilever sheet pile wall can be explained with the aid of Figure 6.6. It shows the nature of lateral yielding of a cantilever wall penetrating a sand layer below the dredge line. The wall rotates about point O. Because the hydrostatic pressures at any depth from both sides of the wall will cancel each other, we consider only the effective lateral soil pressures. In zone A, the lateral pressure is only the active pressure from the land side. In zone B, because of the nature of yielding of the wall, there will be active pressure from the land side and passive pressure from the water side. The condition is reversed in zone C—that is, below the point of rotation, O. The net actual pressure distribution on the wall is like that shown in Figure 6.6b. However, for design purposes, Figure 6.6c shows a simplified version.

Sections 6.3–6.6 present the mathematical formulation of the analysis of cantilever sheet pile walls. Note that, in some waterfront structures, the water level may fluctuate as the result of tidal effects. Care should be taken in determining the water level that will affect the net pressure diagram.

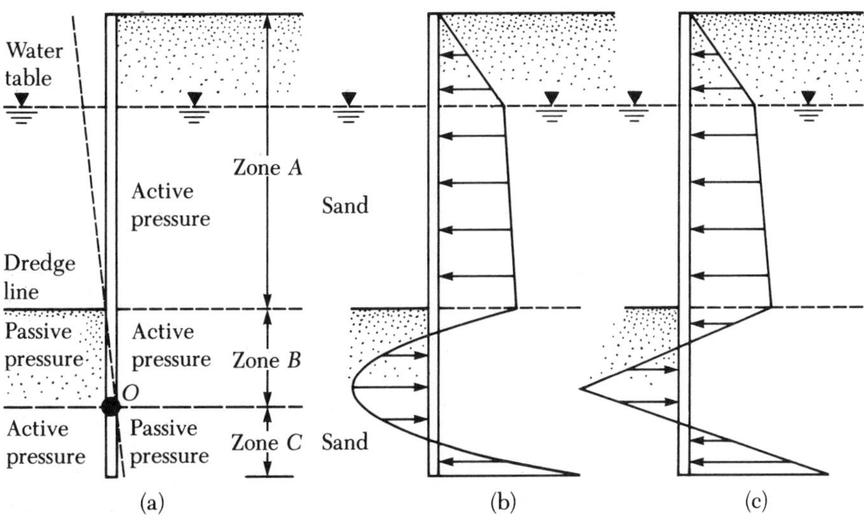

▼ **FIGURE 6.6** Cantilever sheet pile penetrating sand

6.3 CANTILEVER SHEET PILING PENETRATING SANDY SOILS

To develop the relationships for the proper depth of embedment of sheet piles driven into a granular soil, we refer to Figure 6.7a. The soil retained by the sheet piling above the dredge line also is sand. The water table is at depth L_1 below the top of the wall. Let the angle of friction of the sand be ϕ. The intensity of the active pressure at a depth $z = L_1$ is

$$p_1 = \gamma L_1 K_a \tag{6.1}$$

where K_a = Rankine active pressure coefficient = $\tan^2(45 - \phi/2)$
γ = unit weight of soil above the water table

Similarly, the active pressure at depth $z = L_1 + L_2$ (i.e., at the level of the dredge line) is

$$p_2 = (\gamma L_1 + \gamma' L_2) K_a \tag{6.2}$$

where γ' = effective unit weight of soil = $\gamma_{sat} - \gamma_w$

Note that, at the level of the dredge line, the hydrostatic pressures from both sides of the wall are the same magnitude and cancel each other.

To determine the net lateral pressure below the dredge line up to the point of rotation O, as shown in Figure 6.6a, an engineer has to consider the passive pressure acting from the left side (water side) toward the right side (land side) and also the active pressure acting from the right side toward the left side of the wall. For such cases,

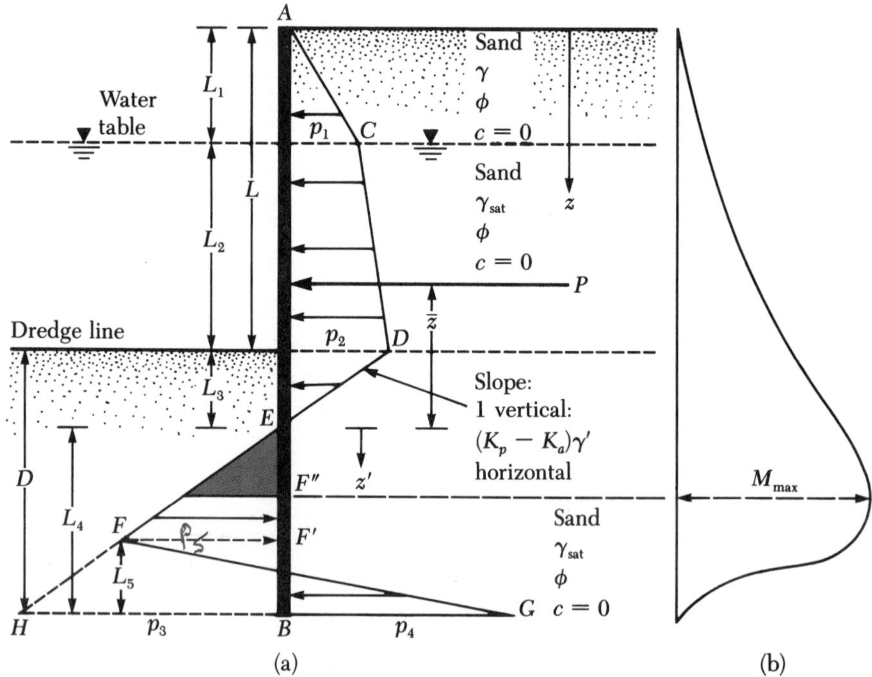

FIGURE 6.7 Cantilever sheet pile penetrating sand: (a) variation of net pressure diagram; (b) variation of moment

ignoring the hydrostatic pressure from both sides of the wall, the active pressure at depth z is

$$p_a = [\gamma L_1 + \gamma' L_2 + \gamma'(z - L_1 - L_2)]K_a \tag{6.3}$$

Also, the passive pressure at depth z is

$$p_p = \gamma'(z - L_1 - L_2)K_p \tag{6.4}$$

where K_p = Rankine passive pressure coefficient = $\tan^2(45 + \phi/2)$

Hence, combining Eqs. (6.3) and (6.4) yields the net lateral pressure:

$$\begin{aligned} p = p_a - p_p &= (\gamma L_1 + \gamma' L_2)K_a - \gamma'(z - L_1 - L_2)(K_p - K_a) \\ &= p_2 - \gamma'(z - L)(K_p - K_a) \end{aligned} \tag{6.5}$$

where $L = L_1 + L_2$

The net pressure, p, equals zero at depth L_3 below the dredge line, so

$$p_2 - \gamma'(z - L)(K_p - K_a) = 0$$

or

$$(z - L) = L_3 = \frac{p_2}{\gamma'(K_p - K_a)} \tag{6.6}$$

Equation (6.6) indicates that the slope of the net pressure distribution line *DEF* is 1 vertical to $(K_p - K_a)\gamma'$ horizontal. So, in the pressure diagram

$$\overline{HB} = p_3 = L_4(K_p - K_a)\gamma' \tag{6.7}$$

At the bottom of the sheet pile, passive pressure, p_p, acts from the right toward the left side and active pressure acts from the left toward the right side of the sheet pile. So, at $z = L + D$,

$$p_p = (\gamma L_1 + \gamma' L_2 + \gamma' D)K_p \tag{6.8}$$

At the same depth

$$p_a = \gamma' D K_a \tag{6.9}$$

Hence the net lateral pressure at the bottom of the sheet pile is

$$\begin{aligned} p_p - p_a = p_4 &= (\gamma L_1 + \gamma' L_2)K_p + \gamma' D(K_p - K_a) \\ &= (\gamma L_1 + \gamma' L_2)K_p + \gamma' L_3(K_p - K_a) + \gamma' L_4(K_p - K_a) \\ &= p_5 + \gamma' L_4(K_p - K_a) \end{aligned} \tag{6.10}$$

where $p_5 = (\gamma L_1 + \gamma' L_2)K_p + \gamma' L_3(K_p - K_a)$ (6.11)

$$D = L_3 + L_4 \tag{6.12}$$

For the stability of the wall, the principles of statics can now be applied:

Σ horizontal forces per unit length of wall = 0

and

Σ moment of the forces per unit length of wall about point $B = 0$

For summation of the horizontal forces,

Area of the pressure diagram *ACDE* − area of *EFHB* + area of *FHBG* = 0

or

$$P - \frac{1}{2}p_3 L_4 + \frac{1}{2}L_5(p_3 + p_4) = 0 \tag{6.13}$$

where P = area of the pressure diagram *ACDE*

Summing the moment of all the forces about point B yields

$$P(L_4 + \bar{z}) - \left(\frac{1}{2}L_4 p_3\right)\left(\frac{L_4}{3}\right) + \frac{1}{2}L_5(p_3 + p_4)\left(\frac{L_5}{3}\right) = 0 \tag{6.14}$$

From Eq. (6.13),

$$L_5 = \frac{p_3 L_4 - 2P}{p_3 + p_4} \tag{6.15}$$

Combining Eqs. (6.7), (6.10), (6,14), and (6.15) and simplifying them further, we obtain the following fourth-degree equation in terms of L_4:

$$L_4^4 + A_1 L_4^3 - A_2 L_4^2 - A_3 L_4 - A_4 = 0 \tag{6.16}$$

where

$$A_1 = \frac{p_5}{\gamma'(K_p - K_a)} \tag{6.17}$$

$$A_2 = \frac{8P}{\gamma'(K_p - K_a)} \tag{6.18}$$

$$A_3 = \frac{6P[2\bar{z}\gamma'(K_p - K_a) + p_5]}{\gamma'^2(K_p - K_a)^2} \tag{6.19}$$

$$A_4 = \frac{P(6\bar{z}p_5 + 4P)}{\gamma'^2(K_p - K_a)^2} \tag{6.20}$$

Step-by-Step Procedure for Obtaining the Pressure Diagram

Based on the preceding theory, the step-by-step procedure for obtaining the pressure diagram for a cantilever sheet pile wall penetrating a granular soil is as follows:

1. Calculate K_a and K_p.
2. Calculate p_1 [Eq. (6.1)] and p_2 [Eq. (6.2)]. *Note:* L_1 and L_2 will be given.
3. Calculate L_3 [Eq. (6.6)].
4. Calculate P.
5. Calculate $\bar{z}$ (that is, the center of pressure for the area *ACDE*) by taking the moment about *E*.
6. Calculate p_5 [Eq. (6.11)].
7. Calculate A_1, A_2, A_3, and A_4 [Eqs. (6.17) to (6.20)].
8. Solve Eq. (6.16) by trial and error to determine L_4.
9. Calculate p_4 [Eq. (6.10)].
10. Calculate p_3 [Eq. (6.7)].
11. Obtain L_5 from Eq. (6.15).
12. Draw the pressure distribution diagram like the one shown in Figure 6.7a.
13. Obtain the theoretical depth [Eq. (6.12)] of penetration as $L_3 + L_4$. The actual depth of penetration is increased by about 20–30%.

Note: Some designers prefer to use a factor of safety on the passive earth pressure coefficient at the beginning. In that case, in step 1

$$K_{p(\text{design})} = \frac{K_p}{FS}$$

where FS = factor of safety (usually between 1.5 to 2)

For this type of analysis, follow steps 1–12 with the value of $K_a = \tan^2(45 - \phi/2)$ and $K_{p(\text{design})}$ (instead of K_p). The actual depth of penetration can now be determined by adding L_3, obtained from step 3, and L_4, obtained from step 8.

Calculation of Maximum Bending Moment

The nature of variation of the moment diagram for a cantilever sheet pile wall is shown in Figure 6.7b. The maximum moment will occur between points E and F'. To obtain the maximum moment (M_{max}) per unit length of the wall requires determining the point of zero shear. For a new axis z' (with origin at point E) for zero shear,

$$P = \frac{1}{2}(z')^2(K_p - K_a)\gamma'$$

or

$$z' = \sqrt{\frac{2P}{(K_p - K_a)\gamma'}} \tag{6.21}$$

Once the point of zero shear force is determined (point F'' in Figure 6.7a), the magnitude of the maximum moment can be obtained as

$$\boxed{M_{\text{max}} = P(\bar{z} + z') - \left[\frac{1}{2}\gamma' z'^2 (K_p - K_a)\right]\left(\frac{1}{3}\right)z'} \tag{6.22}$$

The necessary profile of the sheet piling is then sized according to the allowable flexural stress of the sheet pile material, or

$$\boxed{S = \frac{M_{\text{max}}}{\sigma_{\text{all}}}} \tag{6.23}$$

where S = section modulus of the sheet pile required per unit length of the structure
σ_{all} = allowable flexural stress of the sheet pile.

▼ EXAMPLE 6.1

Figure 6.8 shows a cantilever sheet pile wall penetrating a granular soil. Here, $L_1 = 10$ ft, $L_2 = 20$ ft, $\gamma = 120$ lb/ft³, $\gamma_{sat} = 129.4$ lb/ft³, and $\phi = 40°$.

a. What is the theoretical depth of embedment, D?
b. For a 30% increase in D, what should be the total length of the sheet piles?
c. What should be the minimum section modulus of the sheet piles?

Solution

Part a

The step-by-step procedure given in Section 6.3 will be followed here.

Step 1

$$K_a = \tan^2\left(45 - \frac{\phi}{2}\right) = \tan^2\left(45 - \frac{40}{2}\right) = 0.217$$

$$K_p = \tan^2\left(45 + \frac{\phi}{2}\right) = 4.599$$

Step 2

$$p_1 = \gamma L_1 K_a = (0.12)(10)(0.217) = 0.26 \text{ kip/ft}^2$$

$$p_2 = (\gamma L_1 + \gamma' L_2)K_a = [(0.12)(10) + (0.1294 - 0.0624)(20)]0.217 = 0.551 \text{ kip/ft}^2$$

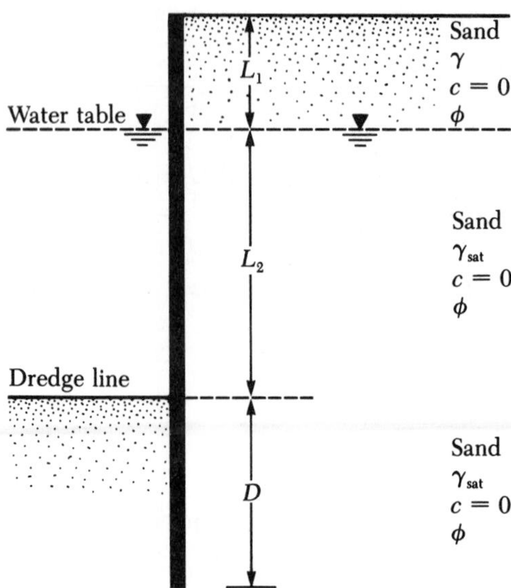

▼ FIGURE 6.8

Step 3

$$L_3 = \frac{p_2}{\gamma'(K_p - K_a)} = \frac{0.551}{(0.1294 - 0.0624)(4.599 - 0.217)} = 1.88 \text{ ft}$$

Step 4

$$P = \frac{1}{2}p_1 L_1 + p_1 L_2 + \frac{1}{2}(p_2 - p_1)L_2 + \frac{1}{2}p_2 L_3$$

$$= \frac{1}{2}(0.26)(10) + (0.26)(20) + \frac{1}{2}(0.551 - 0.26)(20) + \frac{1}{2}(0.551)(1.88)$$

$$= 1.3 + 5.2 + 2.91 + 0.518 = 9.928 \text{ kip/ft}$$

Step 5

Taking the moment about E (see Figure 6.7) yields

$$\bar{z} = \frac{(1.3)\left(\frac{10}{3} + 20 + 1.88\right) + (5.2)\left(1.88 + \frac{20}{2}\right) + (2.91)\left(1.88 + \frac{20}{3}\right) + (0.518)\left(\frac{2}{3}\right)(1.88)}{9.928} = 12.1 \text{ ft}$$

Step 6

$$p_5 = (\gamma L_1 + \gamma' L_2)K_p + \gamma' L_3(K_p - K_a)$$

$$= [(0.12)(10) + (0.1294 - 0.0624)(20)]4.599 + (0.0624)(1.88)(4.599 - 0.217)$$

$$= 12.233 \text{ kip/ft}^2$$

Step 7

$$A_1 = \frac{p_5}{\gamma'(K_p - K_a)} = \frac{12.233}{(0.1294 - 0.0624)(4.382)} = 41.7$$

$$A_2 = \frac{8P}{\gamma'(K_p - K_a)} = \frac{(8)(9.928)}{(0.1294 - 0.0624)(4.382)} = 270.7$$

$$A_3 = \frac{6P[2\bar{z}\gamma'(K_p - K_a) + p_5]}{\gamma'^2(K_p - K_a)^2} = \frac{(6)(9.928)[(2)(12.1)(0.067)(4.382) + 12.233]}{(0.067)^2(4.382)^2} = 13.37$$

$$A_4 = \frac{P(6\bar{z}p_5 + 4P)}{\gamma'^2(K_p - K_a)^2} = \frac{(9.928)[(6)(12.1)(12.233) + (4)(9.928)]}{(0.067)^2(4.382)^2} = 106.95$$

Step 8

From Eq. (6.16),

$$L_4^4 + 41.7L_4^3 - 270.7L_4^2 - 13.37L_4 - 106.95 = 0$$

By trial and error, $L_4 \approx 5.81$ ft and

$$D = 1.88 + 5.81 \approx \mathbf{7.69\ ft}$$

Part b

Total length of the sheet piles = 10 + 20 + (1.3)(7.69) = **40 ft**

Part c

Using Eq. (6.21) gives

$$z' = \sqrt{\frac{2P}{\gamma'(K_p - K_a)}} = \sqrt{\frac{(2)(9.928)}{(0.067)(4.382)}} = 8.23 \text{ ft}$$

From Eq. (6.22),

$$M_{\max} = P(\bar{z} + z') - \left[\frac{1}{2}\gamma' z'^2 (K_p - K_a)\right]\left(\frac{z'}{3}\right)$$

$$= (9.928)(12.1 + 8.23) - \left[\frac{1}{6}(0.067)(8.23)^3(4.382)\right] = 174.7 \text{ kip-ft/ft}$$

$$= 2097 \text{ kip-in./ft}$$

$$S = \frac{2097}{\sigma_{\text{all}}}$$

Let $\sigma_{\text{all}} = 30{,}000 \text{ lb/in}^2 = 30 \text{ kip/in}^2$. Then

$$S = \frac{2097}{30} = \mathbf{69.9\ in^3/ft.}$$ ▼

6.4 SPECIAL CASES FOR CANTILEVER WALL (PENETRATING A SANDY SOIL)

Following are two special cases of the mathematical formulation shown in Section 6.3.

Case I: Sheet Pile Wall in the Absence of Water Table

In the absence of the water table, the net pressure diagram on the cantilever sheet pile wall will be as shown in Figure 6.9, which is a modified version of Figure 6.7. In this case,

$$p_2 = \gamma L K_a \tag{6.24}$$

$$p_3 = L_4(K_p - K_a)\gamma \tag{6.25}$$

$$p_4 = p_5 + \gamma L_4(K_p - K_a) \tag{6.26}$$

$$p_5 = \gamma L K_p + \gamma L_3(K_p - K_a) \tag{6.27}$$

$$L_3 = \frac{p_2}{\gamma(K_p - K_a)} = \frac{LK_a}{(K_p - K_a)} \tag{6.28}$$

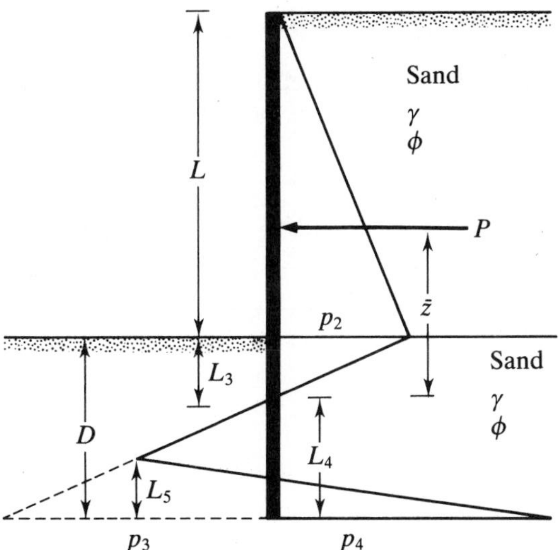

▼ **FIGURE 6.9** Sheet piling penetrating a sandy soil in the absence of the water table

$$P = \frac{1}{2} p_2 L + \frac{1}{2} p_2 L_3 \tag{6.29}$$

$$\bar{z} = L_3 + \frac{L}{3} = \frac{LK_a}{K_p - K_a} + \frac{L}{3} = \frac{L(2K_a + K_p)}{3(K_p - K_a)} \tag{6.30}$$

and Eq. (6.16) transforms to

$$\boxed{L_4^4 + A_1' L_4^3 - A_2' L_4^2 - A_3' L_4 - A_4' = 0} \tag{6.31}$$

where

$$A_1' = \frac{p_5}{\gamma(K_p - K_a)} \tag{6.32}$$

$$A_2' = \frac{8P}{\gamma(K_p - K_a)} \tag{6.33}$$

$$A_3' = \frac{6P[2\bar{z}\gamma(K_p - K_a) + p_5]}{\gamma^2(K_p - K_a)^2} \tag{6.34}$$

$$A_4' = \frac{P(6\bar{z}p_5 + 4P)}{\gamma^2(K_p - K_a)^2} \tag{6.35}$$

Case 2: Free Cantilever Sheet Piling

Figure 6.10 shows a free cantilever sheet pile wall penetrating a sandy soil and subjected to a line load of P per unit length of the wall. For this case,

$$D^4 - \left[\frac{8P}{\gamma(K_p - K_a)}\right]D^2 - \left[\frac{12PL}{\gamma(K_p - K_a)}\right]D - \left[\frac{2P}{\gamma(K_p - K_a)}\right]^2 = 0 \tag{6.36}$$

and

$$L_5 = \frac{\gamma(K_p - K_a)D^2 - 2P}{2D(K_p - K_a)\gamma} \tag{6.37}$$

$$M_{\max} = P(L + z') - \frac{\gamma z'^3(K_p - K_a)}{6} \tag{6.38}$$

$$z' = \sqrt{\frac{2P}{\gamma'(K_p - K_a)}} \tag{6.39}$$

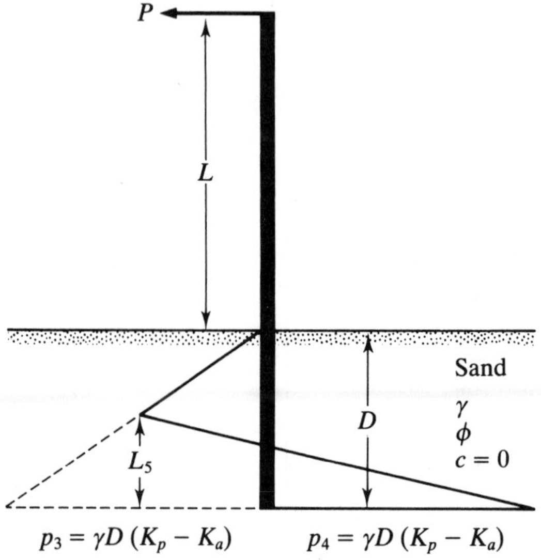

▼ **FIGURE 6.10** Free cantilever sheet piling penetrating a sand layer

▼ EXAMPLE 6.2

Refer to Figure 6.10. For $L = 15$ ft, $\gamma = 110$ lb/ft^3, $\phi = 30°$, and $P = 2000$ lb/ft, determine:

a. The theoretical depth of penetration, D
b. The maximum moment, M_{max} (lb-ft/ft)

Solution

$$K_p = \tan^2\left(45 + \frac{\phi}{2}\right) = \tan^2\left(45 + \frac{30}{2}\right) = 3$$

$$K_a = \tan^2\left(45 - \frac{\phi}{2}\right) = \tan^2\left(45 - \frac{30}{2}\right) = \frac{1}{3}$$

$$K_p - K_a = 3 - 0.333 = 2.667$$

Part a

From Eq. (6.36),

$$D^4 - \left[\frac{8P}{\gamma(K_p - K_a)}\right]D^2 - \left[\frac{12PL}{\gamma(K_p - K_a)}\right]D - \left[\frac{2P}{\gamma(K_p - K_a)}\right]^2 = 0$$

and

$$\frac{8P}{\gamma(K_p - K_a)} = \frac{(8)(2000)}{(110)(2.667)} = 54.54$$

$$\frac{12PL}{\gamma(K_p - K_a)} = \frac{(12)(2000)(15)}{(110)(2.667)} = 1227.1$$

$$\frac{2P}{\gamma(K_p - K_a)} = \frac{(2)(2000)}{(110)(2.667)} = 13.63$$

So

$$D^4 - 54.54D^2 - 1227.1D - (13.63)^2 = 0$$

From the preceding equation, $D \approx$ **13 ft**

Part b

From Eq. (6.39),

$$z' = \sqrt{\frac{2P}{\gamma(K_p - K_a)}} = \sqrt{\frac{(2)(2000)}{(110)(2.667)}} = 3.69 \text{ ft}$$

From Eq. (6.38),

$$M_{max} = P(L + z') - \frac{\gamma z'^3(K_p - K_a)}{6}$$

$$= (2000)(15 + 3.69) - \frac{(110)(3.69)^3(2.667)}{6}$$

$$= 37{,}387 - 2456.65 \approx \mathbf{34{,}923\ lb\text{-}ft/ft}$$ ▼

6.5 CANTILEVER SHEET PILING PENETRATING CLAY

At times, cantilever sheet piles must be driven into a clay layer possessing an undrained cohesion, c ($\phi = 0$ concept). The net pressure diagram will be somewhat different from that shown in Figure 6.7a. Figure 6.11 shows a cantilever sheet pile wall driven into clay with a backfill of granular soil above the level of the dredge line. The water table is at depth L_1 below the top of the wall. As before, Eqs. (6.1) and (6.2) give the intensity of the net pressures p_1 and p_2, and the diagram for pressure distribution

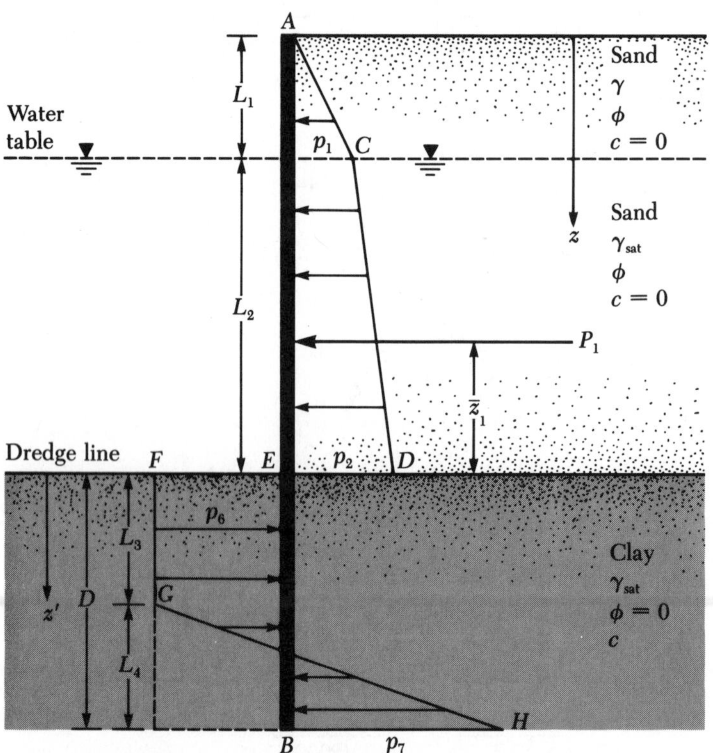

▼ **FIGURE 6.11** Cantilever sheet pile penetrating clay

above the level of the dredge line can be drawn. The diagram for net pressure distribution below the dredge line can now be determined as follows.

At any depth z greater than $L_1 + L_2$ and above the point of rotation (point O in Figure 6.6a), the active pressure, p_a from right to left may be expressed as

$$p_a = [\gamma L_1 + \gamma' L_2 + \gamma_{sat}(z - L_1 - L_2)]K_a - 2c\sqrt{K_a} \tag{6.40}$$

where K_a = Rankine active earth pressure coefficient; with $\phi = 0$, it equals 1

Similarly, the passive pressure, p_p, from left to right may be expressed as

$$p_p = \gamma_{sat}(z - L_1 - L_2)K_p + 2c\sqrt{K_p} \tag{6.41}$$

where K_p = Rankine passive earth pressure coefficient; with $\phi = 0$, K_p equals 1

Thus the net pressure is

$$\begin{aligned} p_6 = p_p - p_a &= [\gamma_{sat}(z - L_1 - L_2) + 2c] \\ &\quad - [\gamma L_1 + \gamma' L_2 + \gamma_{sat}(z - L_1 - L_2)] + 2c \\ &= 4c - (\gamma L_1 + \gamma' L_2) \end{aligned} \tag{6.42}$$

At the bottom of the sheet pile, the passive pressure from right to left is

$$p_p = (\gamma L_1 + \gamma' L_2 + \gamma_{sat} D) + 2c \tag{6.43}$$

Similarly, the active pressure from left to right is

$$p_a = \gamma_{sat} D - 2c \tag{6.44}$$

Hence the net pressure is

$$p_7 = p_p - p_a = 4c + (\gamma L_1 + \gamma' L_2) \tag{6.45}$$

For equilibrium analysis, $\sum F_H = 0$—that is, area of pressure diagram $ACDE$ − area of $EFIB$ + area of $GIH = 0$, or

$$P_1 - [4c - (\gamma L_1 + \gamma' L_2)]D + \frac{1}{2}L_4[4c - (\gamma L_1 + \gamma' L_2) + 4c + (\gamma L_1 + \gamma' L_2)] = 0$$

where P_1 = area of the pressure diagram $ACDE$

Simplifying the preceding equation produces

$$L_4 = \frac{D[4c - (\gamma L_1 + \gamma' L_2)] - P_1}{4c} \tag{6.46}$$

Now, taking the moment about point B, $\sum M_B = 0$, yields

$$P_1(D + \bar{z}_1) - [4c - (\gamma L_1 + \gamma' L_2)]\frac{D^2}{2} + \frac{1}{2}L_4(8c)\left(\frac{L_4}{3}\right) = 0 \tag{6.47}$$

where $\bar{z}_1$ = distance of the center of pressure of the pressure diagram $ACDE$ measured from the level of the dredge line

Combining Eqs. (6.46) and (6.47) yields

$$D^2[4c - (\gamma L_1 + \gamma' L_2)] - 2DP_1 - \frac{P_1(P_1 + 12c\bar{z}_1)}{(\gamma L_1 + \gamma' L_2) + 2c} = 0 \tag{6.48}$$

Equation (6.48) may be solved to obtain D, the theoretical depth of penetration of the clay layer by the sheet pile.

Step-by-Step Procedure to Obtain the Pressure Diagram

1. Calculate $K_a = \tan^2(45 - \phi/2)$ for the granular soil (backfill).
2. Obtain p_1 and p_2 [Eqs. (6.1) and (6.2)].
3. Calculate P_1 and $\bar{z}_1$.
4. Use Eq. (6.48) to obtain the theoretical value of D.
5. Using Eq. (6.46), calculate L_4.
6. Calculate p_6 and p_7 [Eqs. (6.42) and (6.45)].
7. Draw the pressure distribution diagram as shown in Figure 6.11.
8. The actual depth of penetration is

   $$D_{\text{actual}} = 1.4 \text{ to } 1.6(D_{\text{theoretical}})$$

Maximum Bending Moment

According to Figure 6.11, the maximum moment (zero shear) will occur between $L_1 + L_2 < z < L_1 + L_2 + L_3$. Using a new coordinate system z' ($z' = 0$ at dredge line) for zero shear gives

$$P_1 - p_6 z' = 0$$

or

$$z' = \frac{P_1}{p_6} \tag{6.49}$$

The magnitude of the maximum moment may now be obtained:

$$M_{\max} = P_1(z' + \bar{z}_1) - \frac{p_6 z'^2}{2} \tag{6.50}$$

Knowing the maximum bending moment, we determine the section modulus of the sheet pile section from Eq. (6.23).

▼ EXAMPLE 6.3

Refer to Figure 6.12. For the sheet pile wall, determine the

a. Theoretical and actual depth of penetration
b. Minimum size of sheet pile section necessary

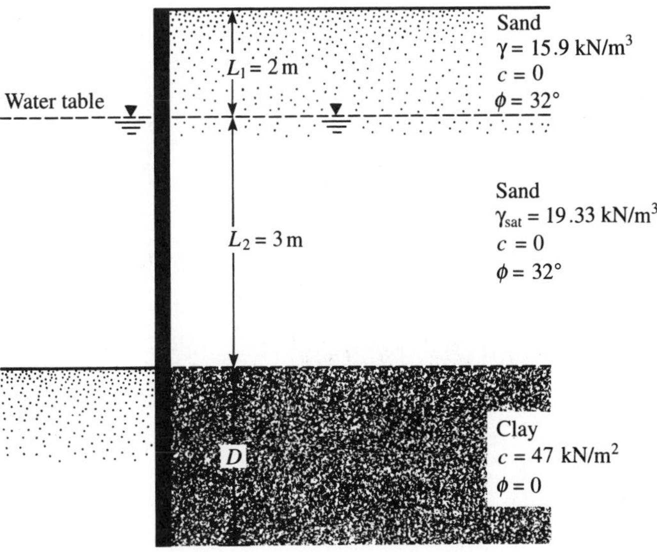

▼ **FIGURE 6.12**

Solution

Part a

Step 1

$$K_a = \tan^2\left(45 - \frac{\phi}{2}\right) = \tan^2\left(45 - \frac{32}{2}\right) = 0.307$$

Step 2

$$p_1 = \gamma L_1 K_a = (15.9)(2)(0.307) = 9.763 \text{ kN/m}^2$$

$$p_2 = (\gamma L_1 + \gamma' L_2)K_a = [(15.9)(2) + (19.33 - 9.81)(3)](0.307) = 18.53 \text{ kN/m}^2$$

Step 3

The net pressure distribution diagram given in Figure 6.11 indicates that

$$P_1 = \frac{1}{2}p_1L_1 + p_1L_2 + \frac{1}{2}(p_2 - p_1)L_2$$

$$= 9.763 + 29.289 + 13.151 = 52.2 \text{ kN/m}$$

$$\bar{z}_1 = \frac{1}{52.2}\left[9.763\left(3 + \frac{2}{3}\right) + 29.289\left(\frac{3}{2}\right) + 13.151\left(\frac{3}{3}\right)\right]$$

$$= 1.78 \text{ m}$$

Step 4

From Eq. (6.48),

$$D^2[4c - (\gamma L_1 + \gamma' L_2)] - 2DP_1 - \frac{P_1(P_1 + 12c\bar{z}_1)}{(\gamma L_1 + \gamma' L_2) + 2c} = 0$$

Substituting proper values yields

$$D^2\{(4)(47) - [(2)(15.9) + (19.33 - 9.81)3]\} - 2D(52.2) - \frac{52.2[52.2 + (12)(47)(1.78)]}{[(15.9)(2) + (19.33 - 9.81)3] + (2)(47)} = 0$$

or

$$127.64D^2 - 104.4D - 357.15 = 0$$

Solving the preceding equation yields $D = 2.13$ m.

Step 5

From Eq. (6.46),

$$L_4 = \frac{D[4c - (\gamma L_1 + \gamma' L_2)] - P_1}{4c}$$

$$4c - (\gamma L_1 + \gamma' L_2) = (4)(47) - [(15.9)(2) + (19.33 - 9.81)3]$$

$$= 127.64 \text{ kN/m}^2$$

So

$$L_4 = \frac{2.13(127.64) - 52.2}{(4)(47)} = 1.17 \text{ m}$$

Step 6

$$p_6 = 4c - (\gamma L_1 + \gamma' L_2) = 127.64 \text{ kN/m}^2$$

$$p_7 = 4c + (\gamma L_1 + \gamma' L_2) = 248.36 \text{ kN/m}^2$$

Step 7

The net pressure distribution diagram can now be drawn, as shown in Figure 6.11.

Step 8

$$D_{\text{actual}} \approx 1.5D_{\text{theoretical}} = 1.5(2.13) \approx \mathbf{3.2\ m}$$

Part b

From Eq. (6.49),

$$z' = \frac{P_1}{p_6} = \frac{52.2}{127.64} \approx 0.41 \text{ m}$$

Again, from Eq. (6.50),

$$M_{\max} = P_1(z' + \bar{z}_1) - \frac{p_6 z'^2}{2}$$

So

$$M_{\max} = 52.2(0.41 + 1.78) - \frac{127.64(0.41)^2}{2}$$

$$= 114.32 - 10.73 = 103.59 \text{ kN} \cdot \text{m}$$

The minimum required section modulus (assuming that $\sigma_{all} = 172.5 \text{ MN/m}^2$)

$$S = \frac{103.59 \text{ kN} \cdot \text{m}}{172.5 \times 10^3 \text{ kN/m}^2} = \mathbf{0.6 \times 10^{-3}\ m^3/m\ of\ the\ wall.}$$ ▼

6.6 SPECIAL CASES FOR CANTILEVER WALL (PENETRATING CLAY)

As in Section 6.4, relationships for special cases for cantilever walls penetrating clay may also be derived.

Case I: Sheet Pile Wall in the Absence of Water Table

Referring to Figure 6.13, we can write

$$p_2 = \gamma L K_a \tag{6.51}$$

$$p_6 = 4c - \gamma L \tag{6.52}$$

$$p_7 = 4c + \gamma L \tag{6.53}$$

$$P_1 = \frac{1}{2} L p_2 = \frac{1}{2} \gamma L^2 K_a \tag{6.54}$$

$$L_4 = \frac{D(4c - \gamma L) - \frac{1}{2}\gamma L^2 K_a}{4c} \tag{6.55}$$

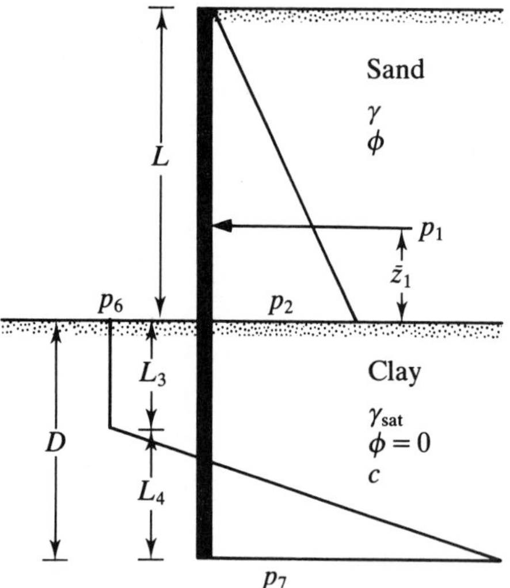

▼ **FIGURE 6.13** Sheet pile wall penetrating clay

The theoretical depth of penetration, D, can be calculated [similar to Eq. (6.48)] as

$$D^2(4c - \gamma L) - 2DP_1 - \frac{P_1(P_1 + 12c\bar{z}_1)}{\gamma L + 2c} = 0 \tag{6.56}$$

$$\text{where } \bar{z}_1 = \frac{L}{3} \tag{6.57}$$

The magnitude of the maximum moment in the wall is

$$M_{\max} = P_1(z' + \bar{z}_1) - \frac{p_6 z'^2}{2} \tag{6.58}$$

$$\text{where } z' = \frac{P_1}{p_6} = \frac{\frac{1}{2}\gamma L^2 K_a}{4c - \gamma L} \tag{6.59}$$

Case 2: Free Cantilever Sheet Pile Wall Penetrating Clay

Figure 6.14 shows a free cantilever sheet pile wall penetrating a clay layer. The wall is being subjected to a line load of P per unit length. For this case,

$$p_6 = p_7 = 4c \tag{6.60}$$

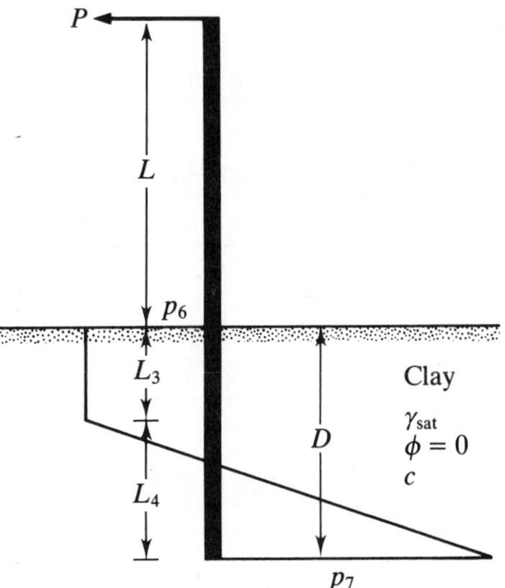

▼ **FIGURE 6.14** Free cantilever sheet piling penetrating clay

The depth of penetration, D, may be obtained from

$$4D^2c - 2PD - \frac{P(P + 12cL)}{2c} = 0 \tag{6.61}$$

Also note that, for pressure diagram construction,

$$L_4 = \frac{4cD - P}{4c} \tag{6.62}$$

The maximum moment in the wall is

$$M_{max} = P(L + z') - \frac{4cz'^2}{2} \tag{6.63}$$

$$\text{where } z' = \frac{P}{4c} \tag{6.64}$$

▼ EXAMPLE 6.4

Refer to the free cantilever sheet pile wall shown in Figure 6.14, for which $P = 32$ kN/m, $L = 3.5$ m, and $c = 12$ kN/m^2. Calculate the theoretical depth of penetration.

Solution From Eq. (6.61),

$$4D^2c - 2PD - \frac{P(P + 12cL)}{2c} = 0$$

$$(4)(D^2)(12) - (2)(32)(D) - \frac{32[32 + (12)(12)(3.5)]}{(2)(12)} = 0$$

$$48D^2 - 64D - 714.7 = 0$$

Hence $D \approx$ **4.6 m.** ▼

ANCHORED SHEET PILE WALLS

When the height of the backfill material behind a cantilever sheet pile wall exceeds about 20 ft ($\approx$6 m), tying the sheet pile wall near the top to anchor plates, anchor walls, or anchor piles becomes more economical. This type of construction is referred to as *anchored sheet pile wall* or an *anchored bulkhead*. Anchors minimize the depth of required penetration by the sheet piles and also reduce the cross-sectional area and weight of the sheet piles needed for construction. However, the tie rods and anchors must be carefully designed.

The two basic methods of constructing anchored sheet pile walls are (a) the *free earth support* method and (b) the *fixed earth support* method. Figure 6.15 shows the assumed nature of deflection of the sheet piles for the two methods.

The free earth support method involves minimum penetration depth. Below the dredge line, no pivot point exists for the static system. The nature of variation of the bending moment with depth for both methods is also shown in Figure 6.15.

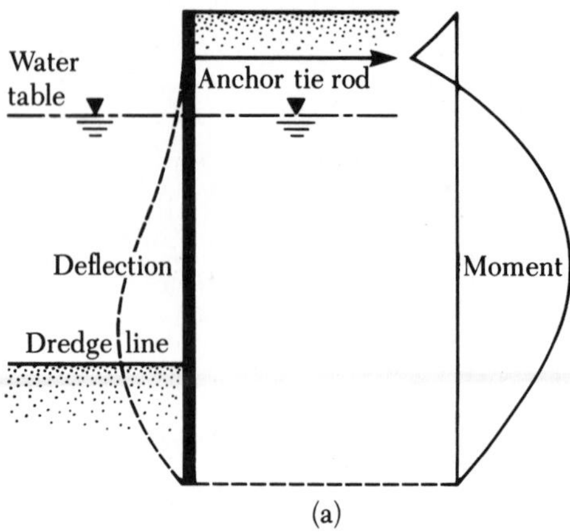

▼ **FIGURE 6.15** Nature of variation of deflection and moment for anchored sheet piles: (a) free earth support method: (b) fixed earth support method

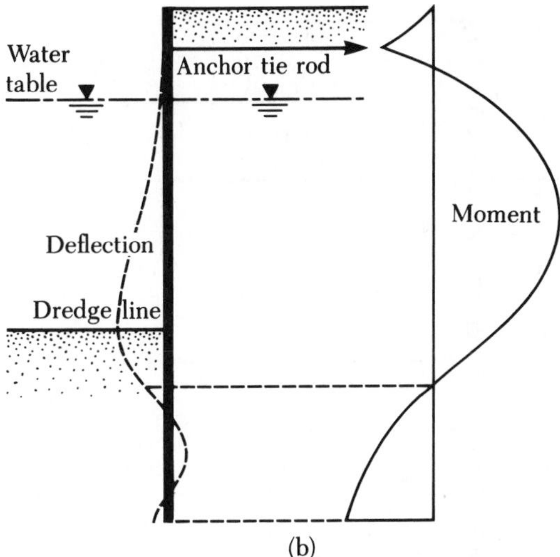

(b)

▼ **FIGURE 6.15** (Continued)

6.7 FREE EARTH SUPPORT METHOD FOR PENETRATION OF SANDY SOIL

Figure 6.16 shows an anchor sheet pile wall with a granular soil backfill; the wall has been driven into a granular soil. The tie rod connecting the sheet pile and the anchor is located at depth l_1 below the top of the sheet pile wall.

The diagram of net pressure distribution above the dredge line is similar to that shown in Figure 6.7. At depth $z = L_1$, $p_1 = \gamma L_1 K_a$; and, at $z = L_1 + L_2$, $p_2 = (\gamma L_1 + \gamma' L_2)K_a$. Below the dredge line, the net pressure will be zero at $z = L_1 + L_2 + L_3$. The relation for L_3 is given by Eq. (6.6), or

$$L_3 = \frac{p_2}{\gamma'(K_p - K_a)}$$

At $z = (L_1 + L_2 + L_3 + L_4)$, the net pressure is given by

$$p_8 = \gamma'(K_p - K_a)L_4 \tag{6.65}$$

Note that the slope of the line *DEF* is 1 vertical to $\gamma'(K_p - K_a)$ horizontal.

For equilibrium of the sheet pile, Σ Horizontal forces = 0, and Σ moment about $O' = 0$. (*Note:* Point O' is located at the level of the tie rod.)

Summing the forces in the horizontal direction (per unit length of the wall) gives

Area of the pressure diagram *ACDE* − area of *EBF* − $F = 0$

where F = tension in the tie rod/unit length of the wall, or

$$P - \frac{1}{2}p_8 L_4 - F = 0$$

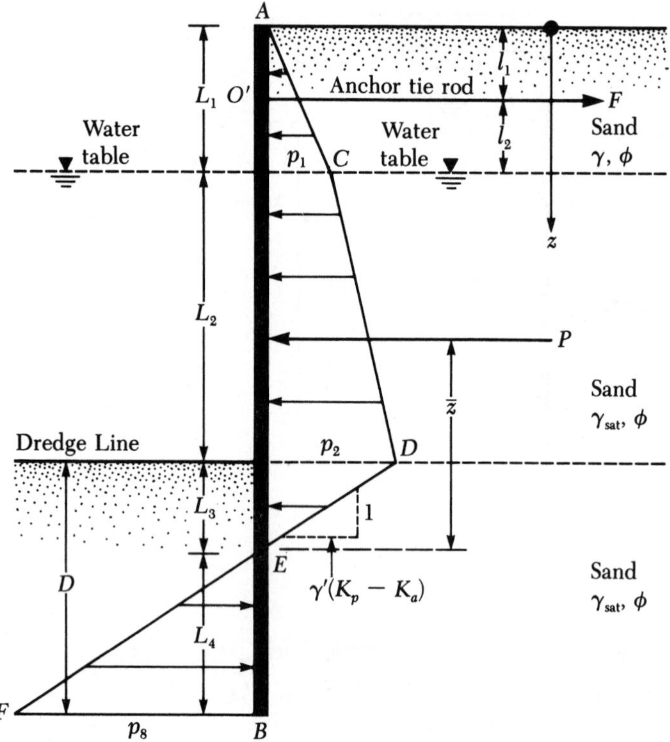

▼ **FIGURE 6.16** Anchored sheet pile wall penetrating sand

or

$$F = P - \frac{1}{2}[(\gamma'(K_p - K_a)]L_4^2 \tag{6.66}$$

where P = area of the pressure diagram $ACDE$

Now, taking the moment about point O' gives

$$-P[(L_1 + L_2 + L_3) - (\bar{z} + l_1)] + \frac{1}{2}[\gamma'(K_p - K_a)]L_4^2\left(l_2 + L_2 + L_3 + \frac{2}{3}L_4\right) = 0$$

or

$$L_4^3 + 1.5L_4^2(l_2 + L_2 + L_3) - \frac{3P[(L_1 + L_2 + L_3) - (\bar{z} + l_1)]}{\gamma'(K_p - K_a)} = 0 \tag{6.67}$$

Equation (6.67) may be solved by trial and error to determine the theoretical depth, L_4:

$$D_{\text{theoretical}} = L_3 + L_4$$

The theoretical depth is increased by about 30–40% for actual construction, or

$$D_{\text{actual}} = 1.3 \text{ to } 1.4 D_{\text{theoretical}} \tag{6.68}$$

The step-by-step procedure in Section 6.3 indicated that a factor of safety can be applied to K_p at the beginning [that is, $K_{p(\text{design})} = K_p/FS$]. If done, there is no need to increase the theoretical depth by 30–40%. This approach is often more conservative.

The maximum theoretical moment to which the sheet pile will be subjected occurs at a depth between $z = L_1$ and $z = L_1 + L_2$. The depth, z, for zero shear and hence maximum moment, may be evaluated from

$$\frac{1}{2}p_1 L_1 - F + p_1(z - L_1) + \frac{1}{2}K_a \gamma'(z - L_1)^2 = 0 \tag{6.69}$$

Once the value of z is determined, the magnitude of the maximum moment is easily obtained. The procedure for determining the holding capacity of anchors is treated in Section 6.14.

▼ EXAMPLE 6.5

Refer to Figure 6.16. Here, $L_1 = 2$ m, $L_2 = 3$ m, $l_1 = l_2 = 1$ m, $c = 0$, $\phi = 32°$, $\gamma =$ 15.9 kN/m^3, and $\gamma_{sat} = 19.33$ kN/m^3.

a. Determine the theoretical and actual depths of penetration
b. Find the anchor force per unit length of the wall
c. Determine M_{max}

Solution

Part a: Depths of Penetration

$$K_a = \tan^2\left(45 - \frac{\phi}{2}\right) = \tan^2\left(45 - \frac{32}{2}\right) = 0.307$$

$$K_p = \tan^2\left(45 + \frac{\phi}{2}\right) = 3.25$$

$$p_1 = \gamma L_1 K_a = (15.9)(2)(0.307) = 9.763 \text{ kN/m}^2$$

$$p_2 = (\gamma L_1 + \gamma' L_2)K_a = [(15.9)(2) + (19.33 - 9.81)3]0.307$$

$$= 18.53 \text{ kN/m}^2$$

$$L_3 = \frac{p_2}{\gamma'(K_p - K_a)} = \frac{18.53}{(19.33 - 9.81)(3.25 - 0.307)} = 0.66 \text{ m}$$

$$P = \frac{1}{2}p_1L_1 + p_1L_2 + \frac{1}{2}(p_2 - p_1)L_2 + \frac{1}{2}p_2L_3$$

$$= \frac{1}{2}(9.763)(2) + (9.763)(3) + \frac{1}{2}(18.53 - 9.763)3 + \frac{1}{2}(18.53)(0.66)$$

$$= 9.763 + 29.289 + 13.151 + 6.115 = 58.32 \text{ kN/m}$$

Taking the moment about E yields

$$\bar{z} = \frac{1}{58.32}\left[9.763\left(0.66 + 3 + \frac{2}{3}\right) + 29.289\left(0.66 + \frac{3}{2}\right) + 13.151\left(0.66 + \frac{3}{3}\right) + 6.115\left(0.66 \times \frac{2}{3}\right)\right] = 2.23 \text{ m}$$

Into Eq. (6.67),

$$L_3^4 + 1.5L_4^2(l_2 + L_2 + L_3) - \frac{3P[(L_1 + L_2 + L_3) - (\bar{z} + l_1)]}{\gamma'(K_p - K_a)} = 0$$

we substitute $l_1 = 1$ m, $l_2 = 1$ m, $K_p = 3.25$, and $K_a = 0.307$ to get

$$L_4^3 + 1.5L_4^2(1 + 3 + 0.66) - \frac{3(58.32)[(2 + 3 + 0.66) - (2.33 + 1)]}{9.52(3.25 - 0.307)} = 0$$

or

$$L_4^3 + 6.99L_4^2 - 14.55 = 0 \quad \text{(a)}$$

The magnitude of L_4 is obtained by trial and error:

Assumed L_4 (m)	*Left-hand side of Eq. (a)*
2.0	+21.41
1.5	+3.55
1.4	+2.89
1.3	−0.54

Hence $L_4 \approx 1.4$ m and

$$D_{\text{theoretical}} = L_3 + L_4 = 0.66 + 1.4 = 2.06 \text{ m}$$

$$D_{\text{actual}} \approx 1.4D_{\text{theory}} = (1.4)(2.06) = 2.88 \text{ m (rounded to } \mathbf{2.9\ m}\text{)}$$

Part b: Anchor Force

From Eq. (6.66),

$$F = P - \frac{1}{2}[\gamma'(K_p - K_a)]L_4^2$$

$$= 58.32 - \frac{1}{2}[9.52(3.25 - 0.307)](1.4)^2 = \mathbf{30.86\ kN/m}$$

Part c: Maximum Moment (M_{max})

From Eq. (6.69) for zero shear,

$$\frac{1}{2}p_1L_1 - F + p_1(z - L_1) + \frac{1}{2}K_a\gamma'(z - L_1)^2 = 0$$

or

$$\frac{1}{2}(9.763)(2) - 30.86 + (9.763)(z - 2) + \frac{1}{2}(0.307)(9.52)(z - 2)^2 = 0$$

Let $z - 2 = x$. So

$$9.763 - 30.86 + 9.763x + 1.461x^2 = 0$$

$$x^2 + 6.682x - 14.44 = 0$$

$$x = 1.72 \text{ m}$$

or

$$z = x + 2 = 1.72 + 2 = 3.72 \text{ m} \qquad (L_1 + L_2 < z < L_1\text{—checks})$$

Taking the moment about the point of zero shear force ($z = 3.72$ m or $x = 1.72$ m) gives

$$M_{max} = -\left(\frac{1}{2}p_1L_1\right)\left[x + \left(\frac{1}{3}\right)(2)\right] + F(x + 1) - (p_1x)\left(\frac{x}{2}\right) - \frac{1}{2}K_a\gamma'(x)^2\left(\frac{x}{3}\right)$$

or

$$M_{max} = -(9.763)(2.387) + (30.86)(2.72) - \frac{9.763(1.72)^2}{2} - \frac{(0.307)(9.52)(1.72)^3}{6}$$

$$= -23.3 + 83.94 - 14.44 - 2.48 = \mathbf{43.72\ kN \cdot m/m.}$$ ▼

6.8 DESIGN CHARTS FOR FREE EARTH SUPPORT METHOD (PENETRATION INTO SANDY SOIL)

Using the free earth support method, Hagerty and Nofal (1992) provided simplified design charts for quick estimation of the depth of penetration, D, anchor force, F, and maximum moment, M_{max}, for anchored sheet pile walls penetrating into sandy soil, as shown in Figure 6.16. They made the following assumptions for their analysis.

a. The soil friction angle, ϕ, above and below the dredge line is the same.
b. The angle of friction between the sheet pile wall and the soil is $\phi/2$.
c. The passive earth pressure below the dredge line has a logarithmic spiral failure surface.
d. For active earth pressure calculation, Coulomb's theory is valid.

The magnitudes of D, F, and M_{max} may be calculated from the following relationships:

$$\boxed{\frac{D}{L_1 + L_2} = (GD)(CDL_1)} \tag{6.70}$$

$$\boxed{\frac{F}{\gamma_a(L_1 + L_2)^2} = (GF)(CFL_1)} \tag{6.71}$$

$$\boxed{\frac{M_{max}}{\gamma_a(L_1 + L_2)^3} = (GM)(CML_1)} \tag{6.72}$$

where γ_a = average unit weight of soil

$$= \frac{\gamma L_1^2 + (\gamma_{sat} - \gamma_w)L_2^2 + 2\gamma L_1 L_2}{(L_1 + L_2)^2} \tag{6.73}$$

GD = generalized nondimensional embedment

$$= \frac{D}{L_1 + L_2} \quad (\text{for } L_1 = 0 \text{ and } L_2 = L_1 + L_2)$$

GF = generalized nondimensional anchor force

$$= \frac{F}{\gamma_a(L_1 + L_2)^2} \quad (\text{for } L_1 = 0 \text{ and } L_2 = L_1 + L_2)$$

GM = generalized nondimensional moment

$$= \frac{M_{max}}{\gamma_a(L_1 + L_2)^3} \quad (\text{for } L_1 = 0 \text{ and } L_2 = L_1 + L_2)$$

CDL_1, CFL_1, CML_1 = correction factors for $L_1 \neq 0$

The variations of GD, GF, GM, CDL_1, CFL_1, and CML_1 are shown in Figures 6.17, 6.18, 6.19, 6.20, 6.21, and 6.22, respectively.

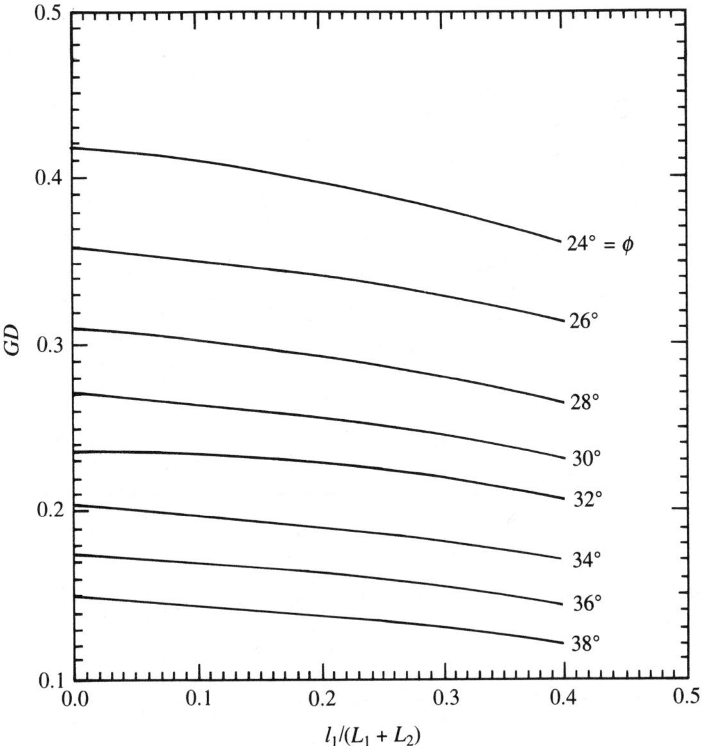

FIGURE 6.17 Variation of GD with $l_1/(L_1 + L_2)$ and ϕ (after Hagerty and Nofal, 1992)

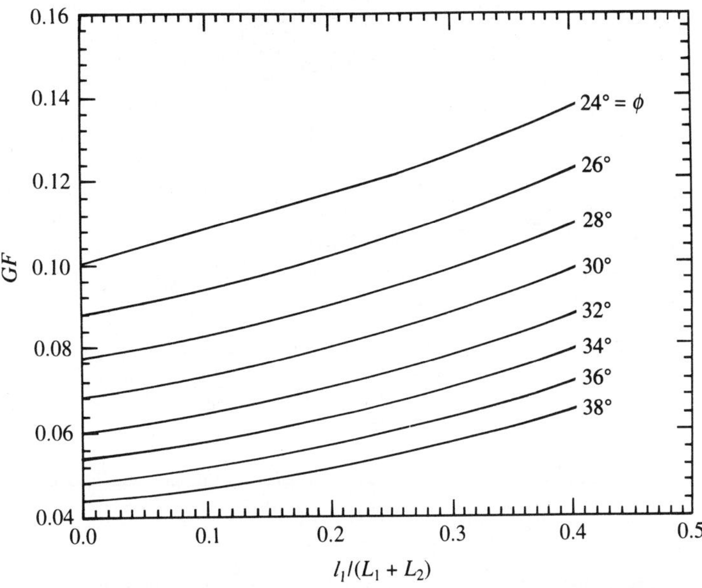

FIGURE 6.18 Variation of GF with $l_1/(L_1 + L_2)$ and ϕ (after Hagerty and Nofal, 1992)

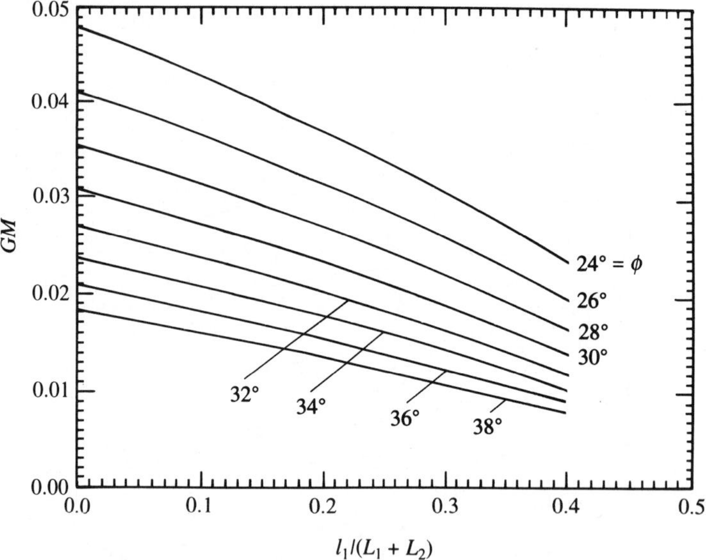

▼ **FIGURE 6.19** Variation of GM with $l_1/(L_1 + L_2)$ and ϕ (after Hagerty and Nofal, 1992)

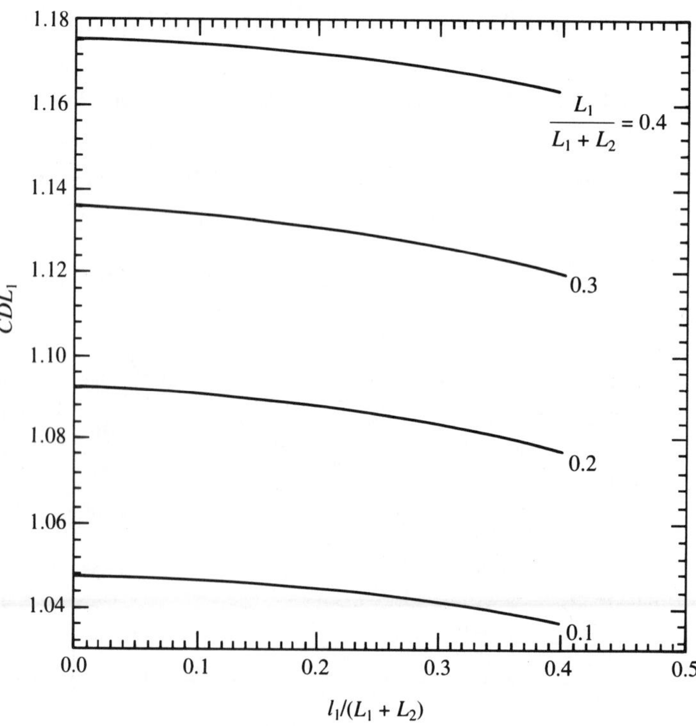

▼ **FIGURE 6.20** Variation of CDL_1 with $L_1/(L_1 + L_2)$ and $l_1/(L_1 + L_2)$ (after Hagerty and Nofal, 1992)

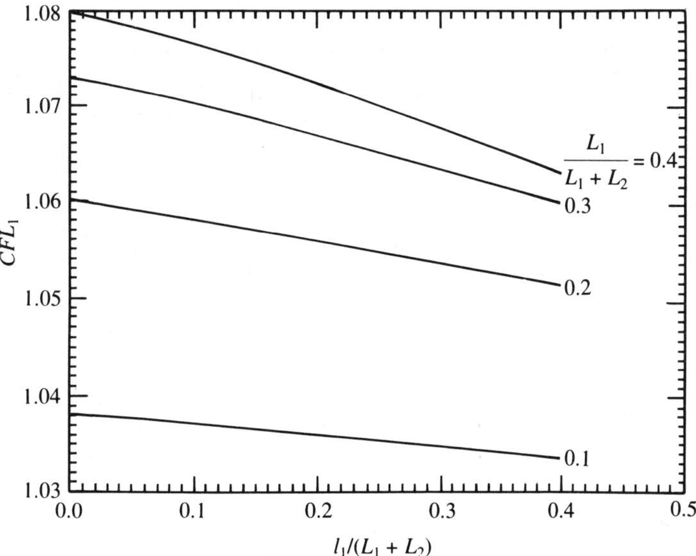

FIGURE 6.21 Variation of CFL_1 with $L_1/(L_1 + L_2)$ and $l_1/(L_1 + L_2)$ (after Hagerty and Nofal, 1992)

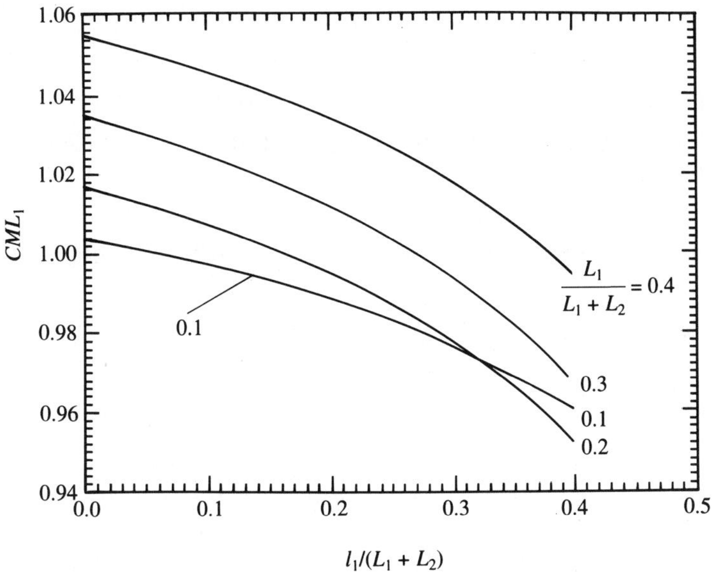

FIGURE 6.22 Variation of CML_1 with $L_1/(L_1 + L_2)$ and $l_1/(L_1 + L_2)$ (after Hagerty and Nofal, 1992)

▼ EXAMPLE 6.6

Use the charts just presented to redo Example 6.5.

Solution

Part a

From Eq. (6.70),

$$\frac{D}{L_1 + L_2} = (GD)(CDL_1)$$

For Problem 6.5,

$$\frac{l_1}{L_1 + L_2} = \frac{1}{2+3} = 0.2$$

From Figure 6.17 for $l_1/(L_1 + L_2) = 0.2$ and $\phi = 32°$, $GD = 0.22$. From Figure 6.20, for

$$\frac{L_1}{L_1 + L_2} = \frac{2}{2+3} = 0.4 \quad \text{and} \quad \frac{l_1}{L_1 + L_2} = 0.2$$

$CDL_1 \approx 1.172$. So

$$D_{\text{theoretical}} = (L_1 + L_2)(GD)(CDL_1) = (5)(0.22)(1.172) \approx 1.3$$

$$D_{\text{actual}} \approx (1.4)(1.3) = 1.82 \approx \mathbf{2\ m}$$

Part b

From Figure 6.18 for $l_1/(L_1 + L_2) = 0.2$ and $\phi = 32°$, $GF \approx 0.074$. Also, from Figure 6.21, for

$$\frac{L_1}{L_1 + L_2} = \frac{2}{2+3} = 0.4, \quad \frac{l_1}{L_1 + L_2} = 0.2, \quad \text{and} \quad \phi = 32°$$

$CFL_1 = 1.073$. From Eq. (6.73),

$$\gamma_a = \frac{\gamma L_1^2 + \gamma' L_2^2 + 2\gamma L_1 L_2}{(L_1 + L_2)^2}$$

$$= \frac{(15.9)(2)^2 + (19.33 - 9.81)(3)^2 + (2)(15.9)(2)(3)}{(2+3)^2} = 13.6 \text{ kN/m}^3$$

Using Eq. (6.71) yields

$$F = \gamma_a (L_1 + L_2)^2 (GF)(CFL_1) = (13.6)(5)^2(0.074)(1.073) \approx \mathbf{27\ kN/m}$$

Part c

From Eq. 6.19, for $l_1/(L_1 + L_2) = 0.2$ and $\phi = 32°$, $GM = 0.021$. Also, from Figure 6.22, for

$$\frac{L_1}{L_1 + L_2} = \frac{2}{2+3} = 0.4, \qquad \frac{l_1}{L_1 + L_2} = 0.2, \qquad \text{and} \qquad \phi = 32°$$

$CML_1 = 1.036$. Hence from Eq. (6.72),

$$M_{max} = \gamma_a (L_1 + L_2)^3 (GM)(CML_1) = (13.6)(5)^3(0.021)(1.036) = \mathbf{36.99\ kN \cdot m/m}$$

Note: The difference between the results in Examples 6.5 and 6.6 is primarily due to the wall friction angle assumed and the method used to calculate passive earth pressure.

▼

6.9 FREE EARTH SUPPORT METHOD FOR PENETRATION OF CLAY

Figure 6.23 shows an anchored sheet pile wall penetrating a clay soil and having a granular soil backfill. The diagram of pressure distribution above the dredge line is similar to that shown in Figure 6.11. From Eq. (6.42), the net pressure distribution below the dredge line (from $z = L_1 + L_2$ to $z = L_1 + L_2 + D$) is

$$p_6 = 4c - (\gamma L_1 + \gamma' L_2)$$

For static equilibrium, the sum of the forces in the horizontal direction is

$$\boxed{P_1 - p_6 D = F} \qquad (6.74)$$

where P_1 = area of the pressure diagram ACD
F = anchor force per unit length of the sheet pile wall

Again, taking the moment about O' produces

$$P_1(L_1 + L_2 - l_1 - \bar{z}_1) - p_6 D\left(l_2 + L_2 + \frac{D}{2}\right) = 0$$

Simplification yields

$$\boxed{p_6 D^2 + 2p_6 D(L_1 + L_2 - l_1) - 2P_1(L_1 + L_2 - l_1 - \bar{z}_1) = 0} \qquad (6.75)$$

Equation (6.75) gives the theoretical depth of penetration, D.

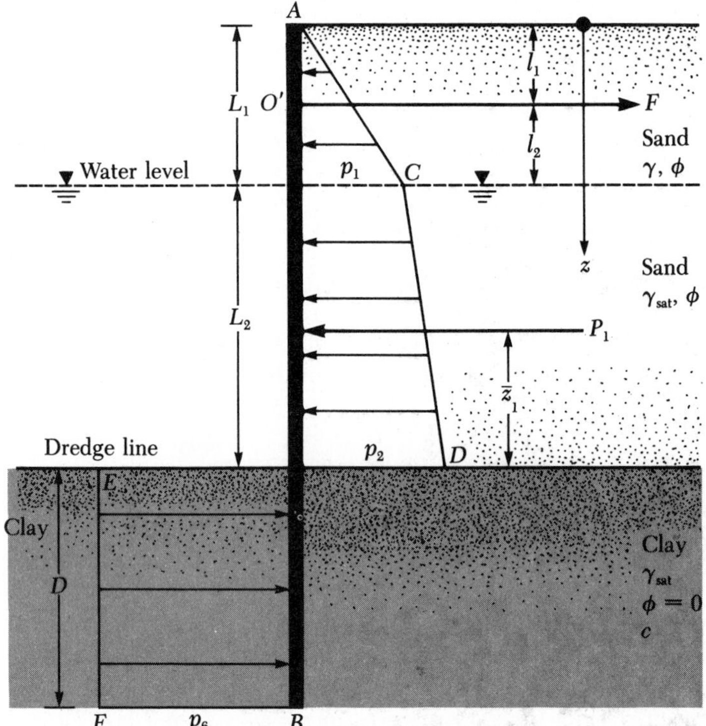

▼ **FIGURE 6.23** Anchored sheet pile wall penetrating clay

As in Section 6.7, the maximum moment in this case occurs at depth $L_1 < z < L_1 + L_2$. The depth of zero shear (and thus the maximum moment) may be determined from Eq. (6.69).

▼ EXAMPLE 6.7

Refer to Figure 6.23, which shows that $L_1 = 10.8$ ft, $L_2 = 21.6$ ft, and $l_1 = 5.4$ ft. Also, $\gamma = 108$ lb/ft^3, $\gamma_{sat} = 127.2$ lb/ft^3, $\phi = 35°$, and $c = 850$ lb/ft^2.

a. Determine the theoretical depth of embedment.
b. Calculate the anchor force per unit length of the sheet pile wall.

Solution

Part a

For $\phi = 35°$,

$$K_a = \tan^2\left(45 - \frac{\phi}{2}\right) = 0.271$$

$$K_p = \tan^2\left(45 + \frac{\phi}{2}\right) = 3.69$$

Refer to the pressure diagram shown in Figure 6.24:

$$p_1 = \gamma L_1 K_a = (0.108)(10.8)(0.271) = 0.316 \text{ kip/ft}^2$$

$$\begin{aligned} p_2 &= (\gamma L_1 + \gamma' L_2)K_a \\ &= [(10.8)(0.108) + (0.0648)(21.6)](0.271) \\ &= (1.1664 + 1.4)(0.271) = 0.695 \text{ kip/ft}^2 \end{aligned}$$

$$\begin{aligned} P_1 &= \text{areas of } 1 + 2 + 3 = 1.706 + 6.826 + 4.093 \\ &= 12.625 \text{ kip/ft} \end{aligned}$$

$$\bar{z}_1 = \frac{(1.706)\left(21.6 + \dfrac{10.8}{3}\right) + (6.826)(10.8) + (4.093)\left(\dfrac{21.6}{3}\right)}{12.625}$$

$$= \frac{42.99 + 73.72 + 29.47}{12.625} = 11.58 \text{ ft}$$

From Eq. (6.75)

$$p_6 D^2 + 2p_6 D(L_1 + L_2 - l_1) - 2P_1(L_1 + L_2 - l_1 - \bar{z}_1) = 0$$

$$\begin{aligned} p_6 &= 4c - (\gamma L_1 + \gamma' L_2) \\ &= 4(0.850) - (1.1664 + 1.4) \approx 0.834 \text{ kip/ft}^2 \end{aligned}$$

So

$$0.834D^2 + (2)(0.834)(D)(27) - (2)(12.625)(15.42) = 0$$

$$D^2 + 54D - 466.85 = 0$$

$$D = \mathbf{7.6 \text{ ft}}$$

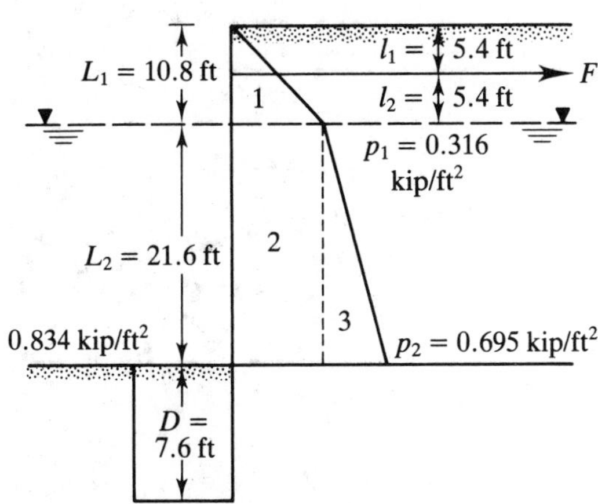

▼ **FIGURE 6.24**

Part b

From Eq. (6.74)

$$F = P_1 - p_6 D = 12.625 - (0.834)(7.6) = \mathbf{6.29\ kip/ft.}$$ ▼

6.10 MOMENT REDUCTION FOR ANCHORED SHEET PILE WALLS

Sheet piles are flexible and hence sheet pile walls yield (i.e., displace laterally), which redistributes the lateral earth pressure. This change tends to reduce the maximum bending moment, M_{max}, as calculated by the procedure outlined in Sections 6.7, 6.8 and 6.9. For thar reason, Rowe (1952, 1957) suggested a procedure to reduce the maximum design moment on the sheet pile walls obtained from the free earth support method. This section discusses the procedure of moment reduction proposed by Rowe.

In Figure 6.25, which is valid for the case of a sheet pile penetrating sand, the following notations are used.

1. H' = total height of pile drive (i.e., $L_1 + L_2 + D_{actual}$)

2. Relative flexibility of file $= \rho = 10.91 \times 10^{-7}\left(\dfrac{H'^4}{EI}\right)$ (6.76)

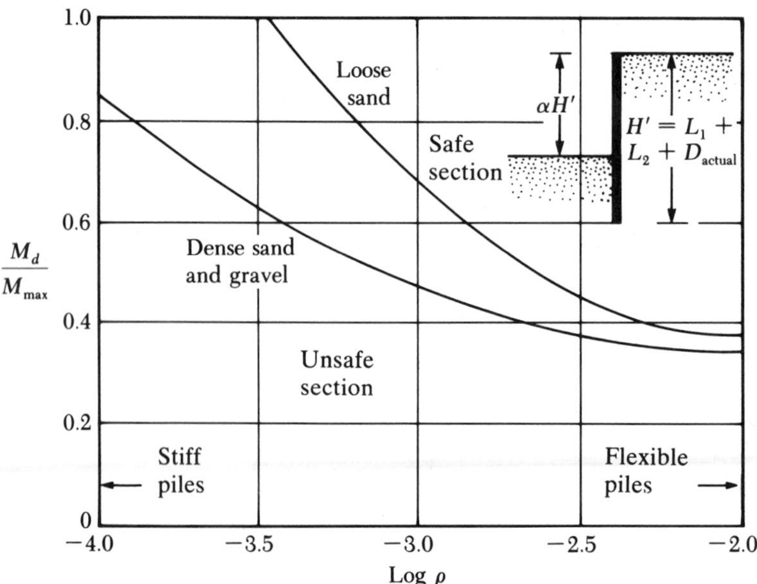

▼ **FIGURE 6.25** Plot of log ρ against M_d/M_{max} for sheet pile walls penetrating sand (after Rowe, 1952)

where H' is in meters
E = modulus of elasticity of the pile material (MN/m^2)
I = moment of inertia of the pile section per foot of the wall (m^4/m of wall)

3. M_d = design moment
4. M_{max} = maximum theoretical moment

In English units, Eq. (6.76) takes the form

$$\rho = \frac{H'^4}{EI} \tag{6.77}$$

where H' is in ft, E is in lb/in^2, and I is in in^4/ft of the wall

The procedure for the use of the moment reduction diagram (Figure 6.25) is as follows:

Step 1. Choose a sheet pile section (such as those given in Table 6.1).
Step 2. Find the section modulus, S, of the selected section (step 1) per unit length of the wall.
Step 3. Determine the moment of inertia of the section (step 1) per unit length of the wall.
Step 4. Obtain H' and calculate ρ [Eq. (6.76) or Eq. (6.77)].
Step 5. Find log ρ.
Step 6. Find the moment capacity of the pile section chosen in step 1 as $M_d = \sigma_{all} S$.
Step 7. Determine M_d/M_{max}. Note that M_{max} is the maximum theoretical moment determined before.
Step 8. Plot log ρ (step 5) and M_d/M_{max} in Figure 6.25.
Step 9. Repeat steps 1–8 for several sections. The points that fall above the curve (loose sand or dense sand, as the case may be) are *safe sections*. Those points that fall below the curve are *unsafe sections*. The cheapest section may now be chosen from those points that fall above the proper curve. Note that the section chosen will have an $M_d < M_{max}$.

For piles penetrating clay soils, the notations in Figure 6.26 are as follows:

1. The stability number is

$$S_n = 1.25 \frac{c}{(\gamma L_1 + \gamma' L_2)} \tag{6.78}$$

where c = undrained cohesion ($\phi = 0$)

For the definition of γ, γ', L_1, and L_2, see Figure 6.23.

2. The nondimensional wall height is

$$\alpha = \frac{L_1 + L_2}{L_1 + L_2 + D_{actual}} \tag{6.79}$$

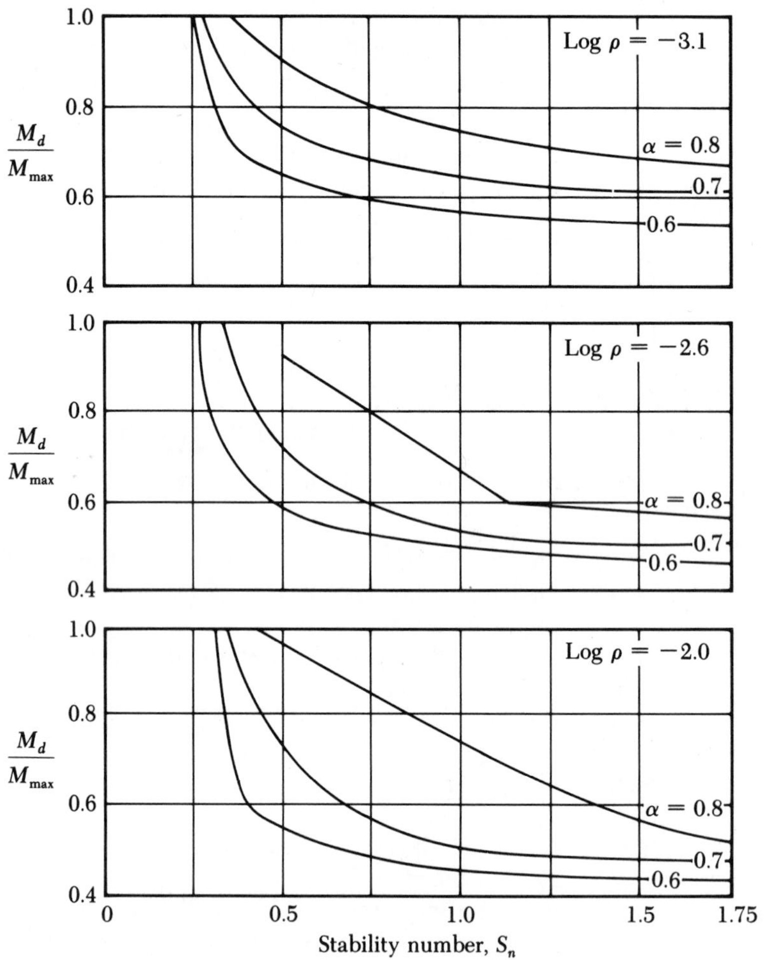

FIGURE 6.26 Plot of M_d/M_{max} against stability number for sheet pile wall penetrating clay (after Rowe, 1957)

3. Flexibility number, ρ [see Eqs. (6.76) or Eq. (6.77)]
4. M_d = design moment
   M_{max} = maximum theoretical moment

The procedure for moment reduction using Figure 6.26 is as follows:

Step 1. Obtain H'.
Step 2. Determine $\alpha = (L_1 + L_2)/H'$.
Step 3. Determine S_n [Eq. (6.78)].
Step 4. For the magnitudes of α and S_n obtained (steps 2 and 3), determine M_d/M_{max} for various values of log ρ from Figure 6.26 and plot M_d/M_{max} against log ρ.
Step 5. Follow steps 1–9 as outlined for the case of moment reduction of sheet pile walls penetrating granular soil.

▼ EXAMPLE 6.8

Refer to Example 6.5, in which $L_1 = 2$ m, $L_2 = 3$ m, and $D_{\text{actual}} = 2.9$ m. Use Rowe's moment reduction diagram (Figure 6.25) and find the most appropriate sheet pile section.

Solution

$$H' = L_1 + L_2 + D_{\text{actual}} = 2 + 3 + 2.9 = 7.9 \text{ m}$$

For moment reduction, the following table can be prepared.

Section (1)	I (m^4/m) (2)	H' (m) (3)	$\rho = \dfrac{10.91 \times 10^{-7} H'^4}{EI}$ (4)	$\log \rho$ (5)	S (m^3/m) (6)	$M_d = S\sigma_{all}$ $(kN \cdot m)$ (7)	$\dfrac{M_d}{M_{max}}$ (8)
PDA-27	54.33×10^{-6}	7.9	0.000378	−3.42	57×10^{-5}	98.32	2.250
PMA-22	18.7×10^{-6}	7.9	0.001098	−2.96	29×10^{-5}	50.02	1.140
PS-32	3.96×10^{-6}	7.9	0.005184	−2.29	10.2×10^{-5}	17.60	0.403
PS-28	3.82×10^{-6}	7.9	0.005370	−2.27	10.2×10^{-5}	17.60	0.403

(1), (2), (6) from Table 6.1
(4) Eq. (6.76), $E = 207 \times 10^3$ MN/m^2
(7) $\sigma_{all} = 172{,}500$ kN/m^2
(8) $M_{max} = 43.72$ kN · m/m

Figure 6.27 shows the calculated values of log ρ and the corresponding values of M_d/M_{max} (the soil is assumed to behave like loose sand). Also shown in Figure 6.27 is the design curve of log ρ plotted against M_d/M_{max}, as given by Rowe (from Figure 6.25). Note that all points plot above the curve, so they are all safe for design use. The point corresponding to **Section PS-28** is on the curve and is the section to be adopted.

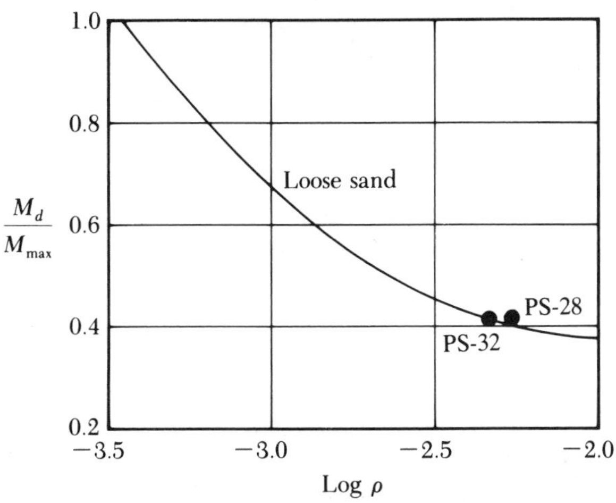

▼ **FIGURE 6.27** ▼

6.11 COMPUTATIONAL PRESSURE DIAGRAM METHOD FOR PENETRATION OF SANDY SOIL

The computational pressure diagram method (CPD method) for sheet pile penetrating a sandy soil is a simplified method of design and an alternative to the free earth method described in Sections 6.7, 6.8, and 6.10 (Nataraj and Hoadley, 1984). In this method, the net pressure diagram shown in Figure 6.16 is replaced by rectangular pressure diagrams, as shown in Figure 6.28. Note that $\bar{p}_a$ is the width of the net active pressure diagram above the dredge line and $\bar{p}_p$ is the width of the net passive pressure diagram below the dredge line. The magnitudes of $\bar{p}_a$ and $\bar{p}_p$ may be expressed as

$$\bar{p}_a = CK_a \gamma_{av} L \tag{6.80}$$

$$\bar{p}_p = RCK_a \gamma_{av} L = R\bar{p}_a \tag{6.81}$$

where γ_{av} = average effective unit weight of sand

$$\approx \frac{\gamma L_1 + \gamma' L_2}{L_1 + L_2} \tag{6.82}$$

C = coefficient

$$R = \text{coefficient} = \frac{L(L - 2l_1)}{D(2L + D - 2l_1)} \tag{6.83}$$

The range of values for C and R is given in Table 6.2.

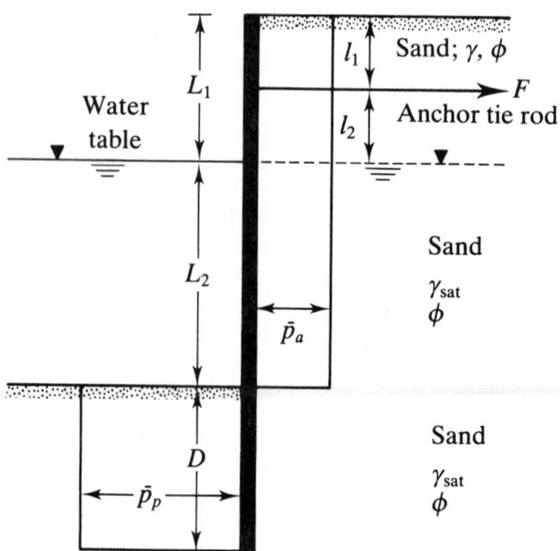

▼ **FIGURE 6.28** Computational pressure diagram method (*note*: $L_1 + L_2 = L$)

TABLE 6.2 Range of Values for C and R [Eqs. (6.80) and (6.81)]

Soil type	C[a]	R
Loose sand	0.8–0.85	0.3–0.5
Medium sand	0.7–0.75	0.55–0.65
Dense sand	0.55–0.65	0.60–0.75

[a] Valid for the case in which there is no surcharge above the granular backfill (i.e., on the right side of the wall as shown in Figure 6.28)

The depth of penetration, D, anchor force per unit length of the wall, F, and maximum moment in the wall, M_{max} are obtained from the following relationships.

Depth of Penetration

$$D^2 + 2DL\left[1 - \left(\frac{l_1}{L}\right)\right] - \left(\frac{L^2}{R}\right)\left[1 - 2\left(\frac{l_1}{L}\right)\right] = 0 \tag{6.84}$$

Anchor Force

$$F = \bar{p}_a(L - RD) \tag{6.85}$$

Maximum Moment

$$M_{max} = 0.5\bar{p}_a L^2\left[\left(1 - \frac{RD}{L}\right)^2 - \left(\frac{2l_1}{L}\right)\left(1 - \frac{RD}{L}\right)\right] \tag{6.86}$$

Note the following qualifications.

1. The magnitude of D obtained from Eq. (6.84) is about 1.25 to 1.5 times the value of $D_{theoretical}$ obtained by the conventional free earth support method (Section 6.7). So

$$\underset{\text{Eq. (6.84)}}{\underset{\uparrow}{D}} \approx \underset{\text{Eq. (6.68)}}{\underset{\uparrow}{D_{actual}}}$$

2. The magnitude of F obtained by using Eq. (6.85) is about 1.2 to 1.6 times the value obtained by using Eq. (6.66). Thus an additional factor of safety for actual design of anchors need not be used.

3. The magnitude of M_{max} obtained from Eq. (6.86) is about 0.6 to 0.75 times the value of M_{max} obtained by the conventional free earth support method. Hence this value of M_{max} can be used as the actual design value, and Rowe's moment reduction may not be applied.

▼ EXAMPLE 6.9

For the anchored sheet pile wall shown in Figure 6.29, determine (a) D, (b) F, and (c) M_{max}. Use the CPD method; assume that $C = 0.68$ and $R = 0.6$.

Solution

Part a

$$\gamma' = \gamma_{sat} - \gamma_w = 122.4 - 62.4 = 60 \text{ lb/ft}^3$$

From Eq. (6.82),

$$\gamma_{av} = \frac{\gamma L_1 + \gamma' L_2}{L_1 + L_2} = \frac{(110)(10) + (60)(20)}{10 + 20} = 76.67 \text{ lb/ft}^3$$

$$K_a = \tan^2\left(45 - \frac{\phi}{2}\right) = \tan^2\left(45 - \frac{35}{2}\right) = 0.271$$

$$\bar{p}_a = CK_a\gamma_{av}L = (0.68)(0.271)(76.67)(30) = 423.9 \text{ lb/ft}^2$$

$$\bar{p}_p = R\bar{p}_a = (0.6)(423.9) = 254.3 \text{ lb/ft}^2$$

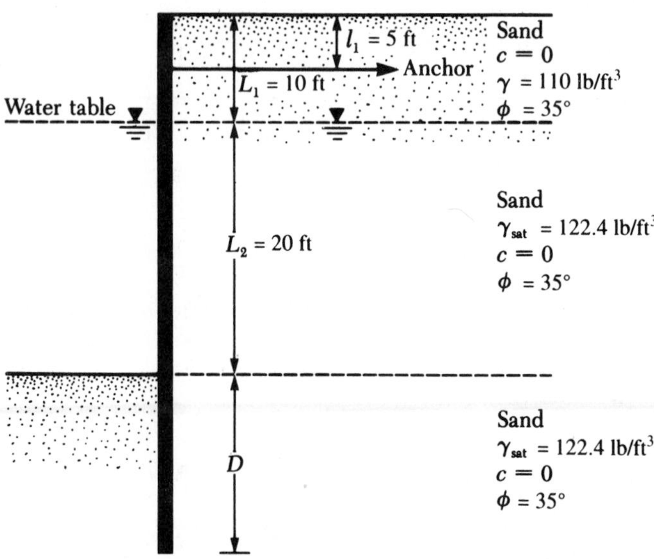

▼ **FIGURE 6.29**

From Eq. (6.84):

$$D^2 + 2DL\left[1-\left(\frac{l_1}{L}\right)\right] - \frac{L^2}{R}\left[1-2\left(\frac{l_1}{L}\right)\right] = 0$$

or

$$D^2 + 2(D)(30)\left[1-\left(\frac{5}{30}\right)\right] - \frac{(30)^2}{0.6}\left[1-2\left(\frac{5}{30}\right)\right] = D^2 + 50D - 1000 = 0$$

Hence $D \approx$ **15.3 ft.**
Check for the assumption of R:

$$R = \frac{L(L-2l_1)}{D(2L+D-2l_1)} = \frac{30[30-(2)(5)]}{15.3[(2)(30)+15.3-(2)(5)]} \approx \mathbf{0.6\text{—OK}}$$

Part b

From Eq. (6.85),

$$F = \bar{p}_a(L - RD) = 423.9[30 - (0.6)(15.3)] = \mathbf{8825\ lb/ft}$$

Part c

From Eq. (6.86),

$$M_{max} = 0.5\bar{p}_a L^2\left[\left(1-\frac{RD}{L}\right)^2 - \left(\frac{2l_1}{L}\right)\left(1-\frac{RD}{L}\right)\right]$$

$$1 - \frac{RD}{L} = 1 - \frac{(0.6)(15.3)}{30} = 0.694$$

So

$$M_{max} = (0.5)(423.9)(30)^2\left[(0.694)^2 - \frac{(2)(5)(0.694)}{30}\right] = \mathbf{88{,}248\ lb\text{-}ft/ft}$$ ▼

6.12 FIXED EARTH SUPPORT METHOD FOR PENETRATION OF SANDY SOIL

When using the fixed earth support method, we assume that the toe of the pile is restrained from rotating, as shown in Figure 6.30a. The net lateral pressure distribution diagram for this condition is also shown in Figure 6.30a. In the fixed earth support solution, the lower portion of the pressure distribution diagram—*HFH′GB*—is replaced by a concentrated force, P'. A simplified solution called the *equivalent beam solution* is generally used to calculate L_4. To understand the equivalent beam solution, refer to point I, which is the point of inflection on the deflected shape of the sheet pile. At this point, the pile may be assumed to be hinged and the bending moment to be zero (Figure 6.30b). The vertical distance between point I and the dredge line is L_5. Blum (1931) presented a mathematical solution between L_5 and $L_1 + L_2$. Figure 6.30d is a plot of $L_5/(L_1 + L_2)$ against the soil friction angle, ϕ.

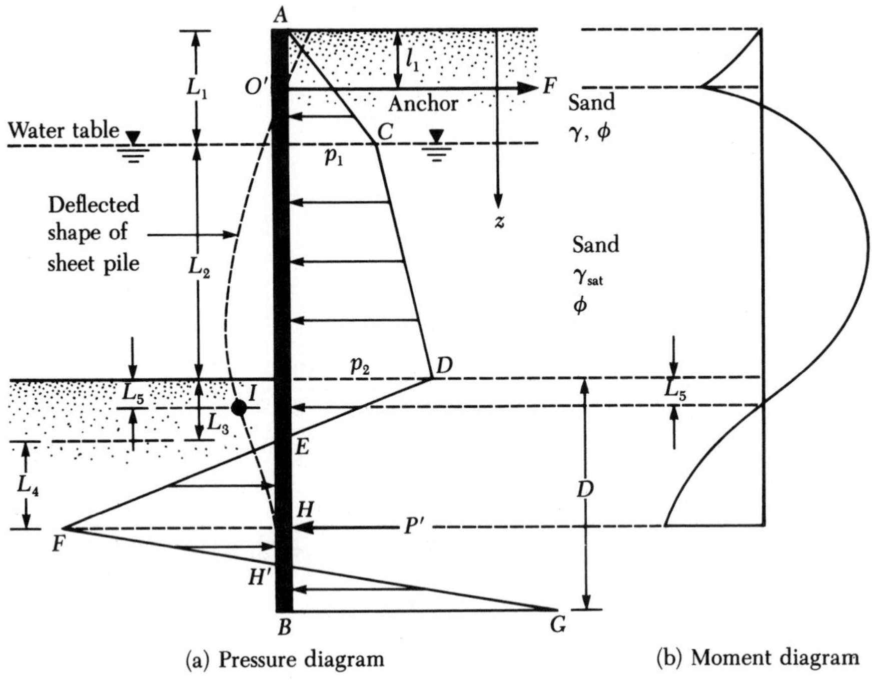

(a) Pressure diagram (b) Moment diagram

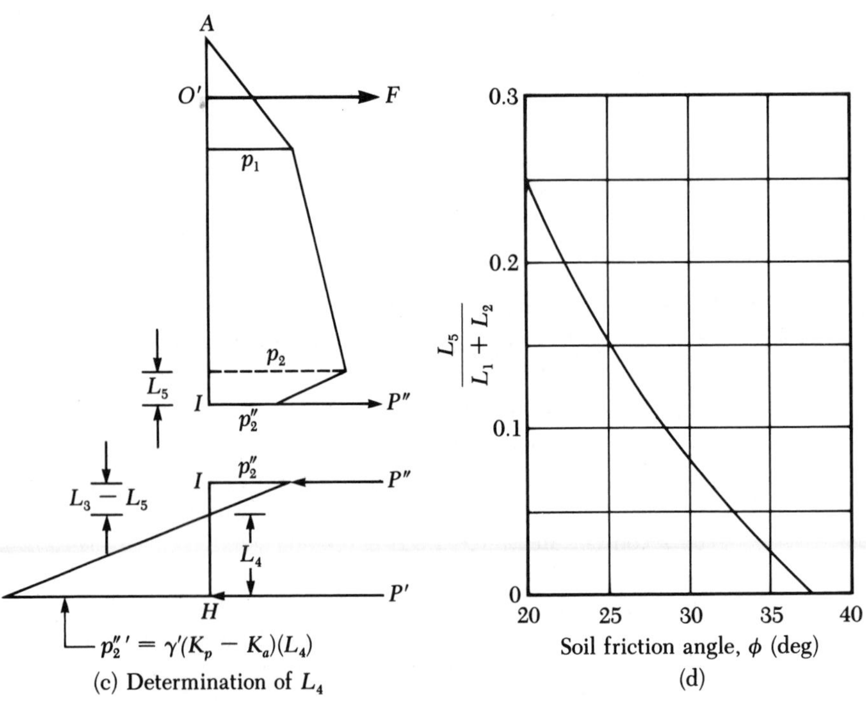

(c) Determination of L_4 (d)

▼ **FIGURE 6.30** Fixed earth support method for penetration of sandy soil

The known values of ϕ and $L_1 + L_2$ are used to obtain the magnitude of L_5. The portion of sheet pile (Figure 6.30c) above point I can now be treated as a beam that resists the net lateral earth pressure via the anchor force F and the shear P''. The shear force P'' can be calculated by taking the moment about O' (i.e., at the anchor level).

Once the magnitude of P'' is known, length L_4 can be obtained by taking the moment about the point H (see the bottom diagram of Figure 6.30c). The depth of penetration, D, now is 1.2 to 1.4 $(L_3 + L_4)$.

Step-by-Step Procedure for Obtaining *D*

The following step-by-step procedure for calculating the depth of embedment of sheet piles is based on the procedure just described.

Step 1. Obtain K_a and K_p.
Step 2. Calculate p_1 and p_2 from Eqs. (6.1) and (6.2), respectively.
Step 3. Calculate L_3 from Eq. (6.6).
Step 4. Determine L_5 from Figure 6.30d.
Step 5. Calculate p_2'' (Figure 6.30c):

$$p_2'' = \frac{p_2(L_3 - L_5)}{L_3} \tag{6.87}$$

Step 6. Draw the pressure distribution for the portion of the sheet pile located above I, as shown in Figure 6.30c.
Step 7. For the diagram drawn in step 6, take the moment about O' to calculate P''.
Step 8. Knowing P'', draw the pressure distribution diagram for the portion of the sheet pile between points I and H, as shown in Figure 6.30c. Note that in this diagram $p_2''' = \gamma'(K_p - K_a)(L_4)$.
Step 9. For the diagram drawn in step 8, take the moment about H to calculate L_4.
Step 10. Calculate $D = 1.2$ to $1.4(L_3 + L_4)$.

6.13 FIELD OBSERVATIONS FOR ANCHORED SHEET PILE WALLS

In the preceding sections, large factors of safety were used for the depth of penetration, D. In most cases designers use smaller magnitudes of soil friction angle, ϕ, thereby ensuring a built-in factor of safety for the active earth pressure. This procedure is followed primarily because of the uncertainties involved in predicting the actual earth pressure a sheet pile wall will be subjected to in the field. In addition, Casagrande (1973) observed that, if the soil behind the sheet pile wall has grain sizes that are predominantly smaller than those of coarse sand, after construction the active earth pressure sometimes increases to an at-rest earth pressure condition. Such an increase causes a large increase in the anchor force, F. The following two case histories are given by Casagrande (1973).

Bulkhead of Pier C—Long Beach Harbor, California (1949)

A typical cross section of the Pier C bulkhead of the Long Beach harbor is shown in Figure 6.31. Except for a rockfill dike which was constructed with 3 in. (76.2 mm) maximum size quarry wastes, the backfill of the sheet pile wall consisted of fine sand.

Figure 6.32a–f shows the lateral earth pressure variation between May 17, 1949, and August 6, 1949 at Station 27 + 30. The fine sand backfill reached the design grade on May 24, 1949. The following general observations are based on Figure 6.32.

1. On May 17 (Figure 6.32a), the backfill was several feet below the design grade. However, the earth pressure was greater on this date than on May 24. This is probably because of the fact that, due to lack of lateral yielding of the wall, the earth pressure was closer to at-rest state than the active state.
2. Due to wall yielding on May 24, the earth pressure reached an active state (Figure 6.32b).
3. Between May 24 and June 3, the anchor resisted further yielding and the lateral earth pressure increased to the at-rest state (Figure 6.32c).
4. Figure 6.32d, e, and f show how the flexibility of sheet piles resulted in a gradual decrease in the lateral earth pressure distribution on the sheet piles.

These observations show that the magnitude of the active earth pressure may vary with time and depends greatly on the flexibility of the sheet piles. Also, the actual variations in the lateral earth pressure diagram may not be identical to those used for design.

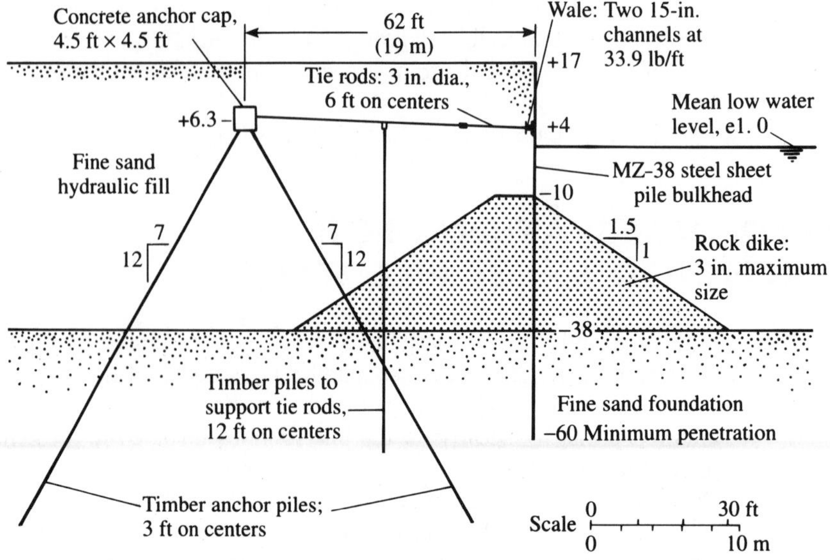

FIGURE 6.31 Pier C bulkhead, Long Beach harbor (after Casagrande, 1973)

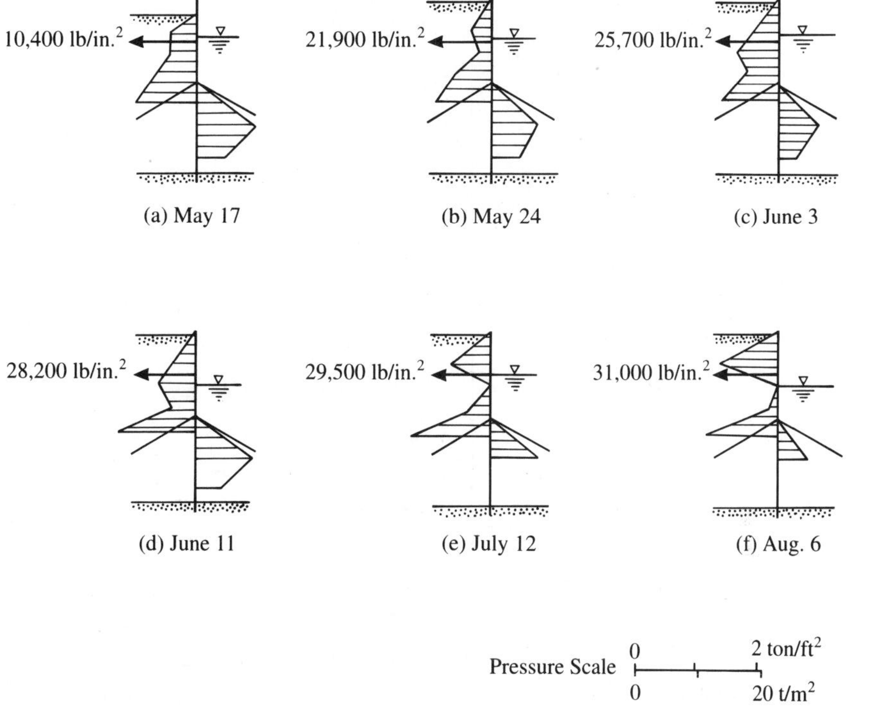

▼ **FIGURE 6.32** Measured stresses at Station 27 + 30 during construction of Pier C bulkhead, Long Beach (after Casagrande, 1973)

Bulkhead—Toledo, Ohio (1961)

A typical cross section of a Toledo bulkhead completed in 1961 is shown in Figure 6.33. The foundation soil was primarily fine to medium sand, but the dredge line did cut into highly overconsolidated clay. Figure 6.33 also shows the actual measured values of stress and bending moment along the sheet pile wall. Casagrande (1973) used the Rankine active earth pressure distribution to calculate the maximum bending moment according to the free earth support method with and without Rowe's moment reduction.

Design method	*Maximum predicted bending moment, M_{max}*
Free earth support method	108 kip-ft/ft
Free earth support method with Rowe's moment reduction	58 kip-ft/ft

Comparisons of these magnitudes of M_{max} with those actually observed show that the field values are substantially larger. The reason probably is that the backfill was primarily fine sand and the measured active earth pressure distribution was larger than that predicted theoretically.

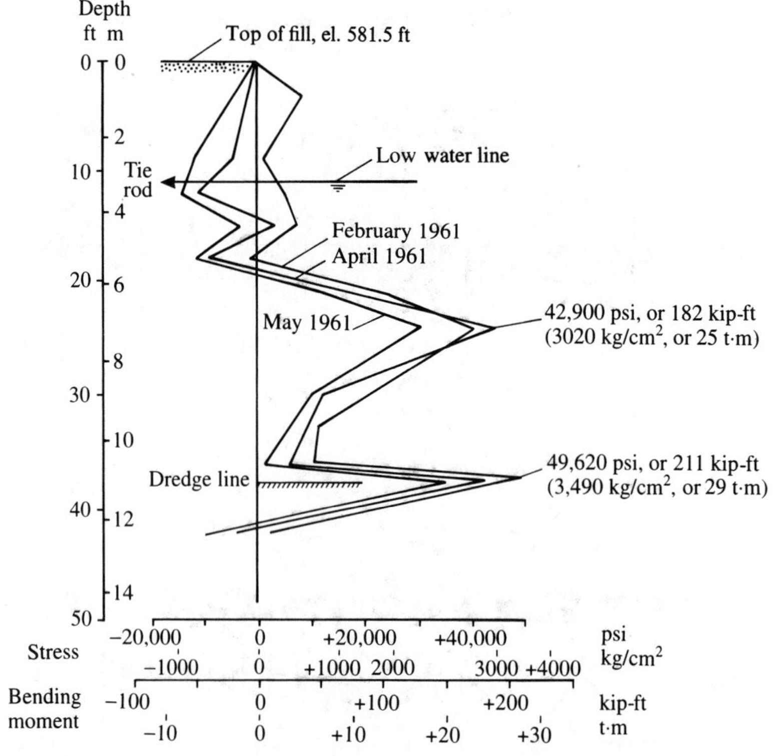

▼ **FIGURE 6.33** Bending moment and stresses from strain gage measurements at test location 3, Toledo bulkhead (after Casagrande, 1973)

6.14 ANCHORS

Sections 6.7–6.13 presented the analysis of anchored sheet pile walls. Those sections also discussed how to obtain the force, F, per unit length of the sheet pile wall that has to be taken by the anchors. This section covers in more detail the various types of anchor generally used and the procedures for evaluating their ultimate holding capacities.

The general types of anchor used in sheet pile walls are

1. Anchor plates and beams (deadman)
2. Tie backs
3. Vertical anchor piles
4. Anchor beams supported by batter (compression and tension) piles

Anchor plates and beams are generally made of cast concrete blocks (Figure 6.34a). The anchors are attached to the sheet pile by *tie rods*. A *wale* is placed at the front or back face of a sheet pile for the purpose of conveniently attaching the tie rod to the wall. To protect the tie rod from corrosion, it is generally coated with paint or asphaltic materials.

In the construction of *tie backs*, bars or cables are placed in predrilled holes (Figure 6.34b) with concrete grout (cables are commonly high-strength, prestressed steel tendons). Figure 6.34c and 6.34d show a vertical anchor pile and an anchor beam with batter piles.

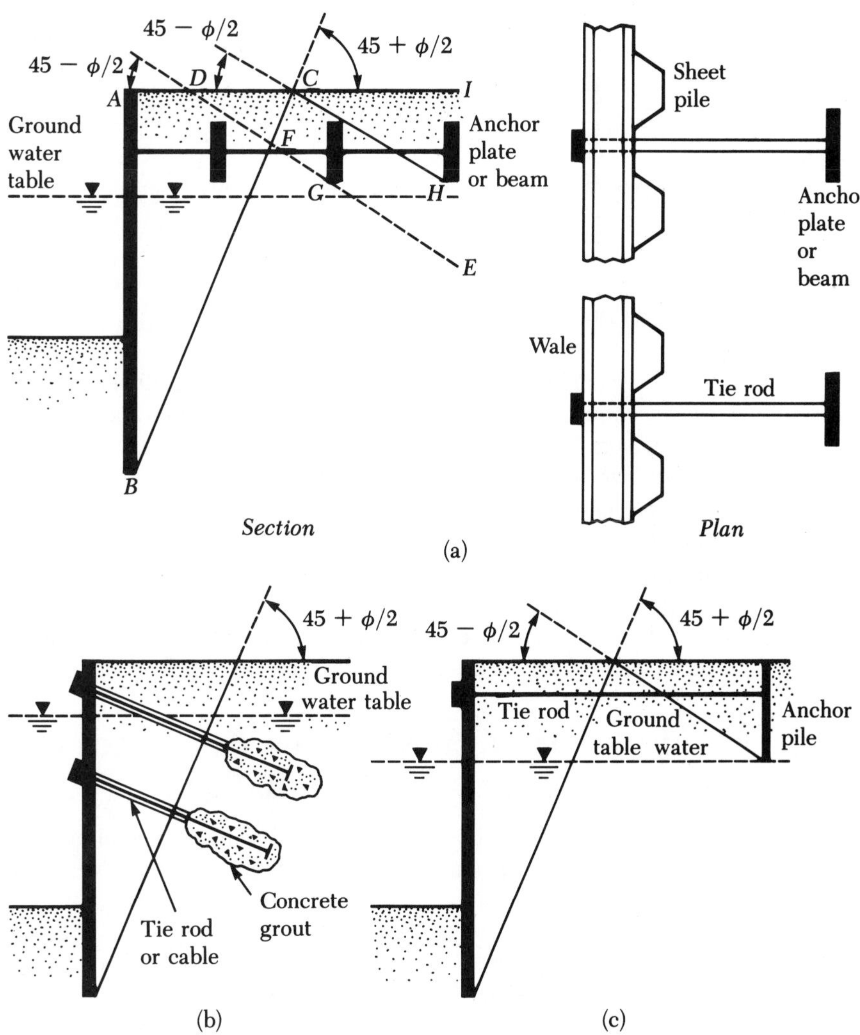

▼ **FIGURE 6.34** Various types of anchoring for sheet pile walls: (a) anchor plate or beam; (b) tie back; (c) vertical anchor pile; (d) anchor beam with batter piles

Placement of Anchors

The resistance offered by anchor plates and beams is derived primarily from the passive force of the soil located in front of them. Figure 6.34a, in which AB is the sheet pile wall, shows the best location for an anchor plate (for maximum efficiency). If the

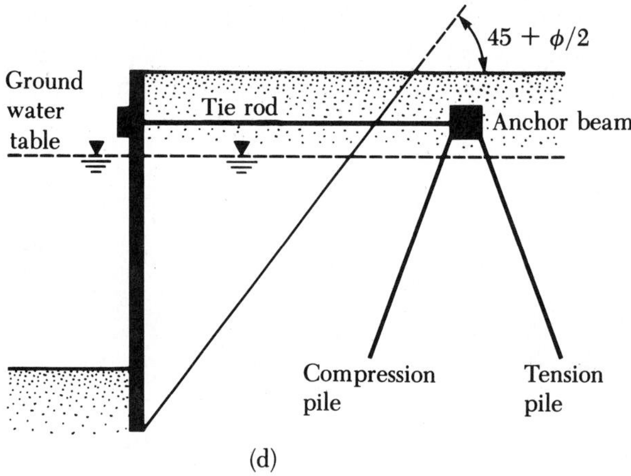

▼ **FIGURE 6.34** (Continued)

anchor is placed inside wedge *ABC*, which is the Rankine active zone, it would not provide any resistance to failure. Alternatively the anchor could be placed in zone *CFEH*. Note that line *DFG* is the slip line for the Rankine passive pressure. If part of the passive wedge is located inside the active wedge *ABC*, full passive resistance of the anchor cannot be realized upon failure of the sheet pile wall. However, if the anchor is placed in zone *ICH*, the Rankine passive zone in front of the anchor slab or plate is located completely outside the Rankine active zone *ABC*. In this case, full passive resistance from the anchor can be realized.

Figure 6.34b, 6.34c, and 6.34d also show the proper locations for placement of tie backs, vertical anchor piles, and anchor beams supported by batter piles.

Calculation of the Ultimate Resistance Offered by Anchor Plates and Beams in Sand

Teng (1962) proposed a method of determining the ultimate resistance of anchor plates or walls in granular soils located at or near the ground surface ($H/h \leq 1.5$ to 2 in Figure 6.35):

$$P_u = B(P_p - P_a) \qquad \text{(for continuous plates or beams—that is, } B/h \approx \infty) \tag{6.88}$$

where P_u = ultimate resistance of anchor
B = length of anchor at right angle to the cross section shown
P_p and P_a = Rankine passive and active force per unit length of anchor

Note that P_p acts in front of the anchor, as shown in Figure 6.35. Also,

$$P_p = \frac{1}{2}\gamma H^2 \tan^2\left(45 + \frac{\phi}{2}\right) \tag{6.89}$$

and

$$P_a = \frac{1}{2}\gamma H^2 \tan^2\left(45 - \frac{\phi}{2}\right) \tag{6.90}$$

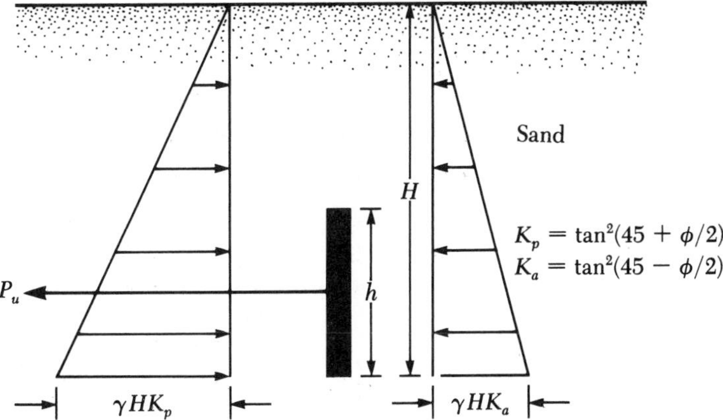

▼ **FIGURE 6.35** Ultimate resistance of anchor plates and beams in sand—Eqs. (6.88) and (6.91)

Equation (6.88) is valid for the plane-strain condition. For all practical cases, $B/h > 5$ may be considered to be plane-strain condition.

For $B/h <$ about 5, considering the three-dimensional failure surface (i.e., accounting for the friction resistance developed at the two ends of an anchor), Teng (1962) gave the following relation for the ultimate anchor resistance:

$$P_u = B(P_p - P_a) + \frac{1}{3}K_O\gamma(\sqrt{K_p} + \sqrt{K_a})H^3 \tan\phi \qquad \left(\text{for}\,\frac{H}{h} \le 1.5 \text{ to } 2\right) \tag{6.91}$$

where K_O = earth pressure coefficient at rest ≈ 0.4

More recently, Ovesen and Stromann (1972) proposed a method for determining the ultimate anchor resistance in sand. The method is described below and is recommended for use as the most rational method available at this time. The calculation is made in three steps.

Step 1. Basic Case Consideration. Determine the depth of embedment, H. Assume that the anchor slab has height H and is continuous (i.e., B = length of anchor slab perpendicular to the cross section = ∞), as shown in Figure 6.36. In Figure 6.36, the following notation is used:

P_p = passive force per unit length of the anchor

P_a = active force per unit length of the anchor

ϕ = soil friction angle

δ = friction angle between the anchor slab and the soil

P'_u = ultimate resistance per unit length of the anchor

W = weight per unit length of the anchor slab

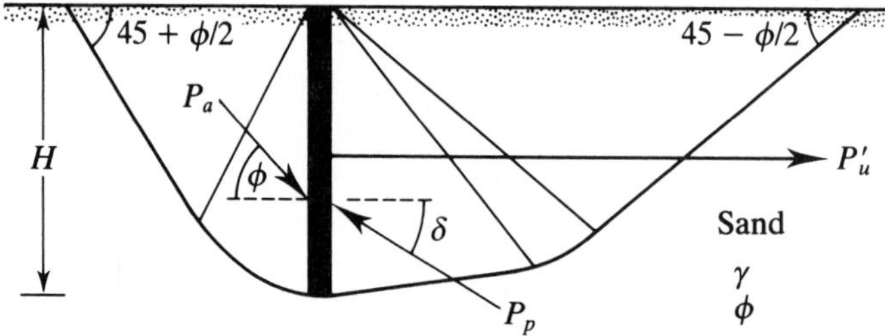

▼ **FIGURE 6.36** Basic case: continuous vertical anchor in granular soil

The magnitude of P'_u is

$$P'_u = \frac{1}{2}\gamma H^2 K_p \cos\delta - P_a \cos\phi = \frac{1}{2}\gamma H^2 K_p \cos\delta - \frac{1}{2}\gamma H^2 K_a \cos\phi$$
$$= \frac{1}{2}\gamma H^2 (K_p \cos\delta - K_a \cos\phi) \qquad (6.92)$$

where K_a = active pressure coefficient with $\delta = \phi$ (see Figure 6.37a)
K_p = passive pressure coefficient

To obtain $K_p \cos\delta$, first calculate $K_p \sin\delta$:

$$K_p \sin\delta = \frac{W + P_a \sin\phi}{\frac{1}{2}\gamma H^2} = \frac{W + \frac{1}{2}\gamma H^2 K_a \sin\phi}{\frac{1}{2}\gamma H^2} \qquad (6.93)$$

Use the magnitude of $K_p \sin\delta$ obtained from Eq. (6.93) to estimate the magnitude of $K_p \cos\delta$ from the plots given in Figure 6.37b.

Step 2. Strip Case. Determine the actual height of the anchor, h, to be constructed. If a continuous anchor (that is, $B = \infty$) of height h is placed in the soil so that its depth of embedment is H, as shown in Figure 6.38, the ultimate resistance per unit length is

$$P'_{us} = \left[\frac{C_{ov} + 1}{C_{ov} + \left(\frac{H}{h}\right)}\right] \underset{\substack{\uparrow \\ \text{Eq. 6.88}}}{P'_u} \qquad (6.94)$$

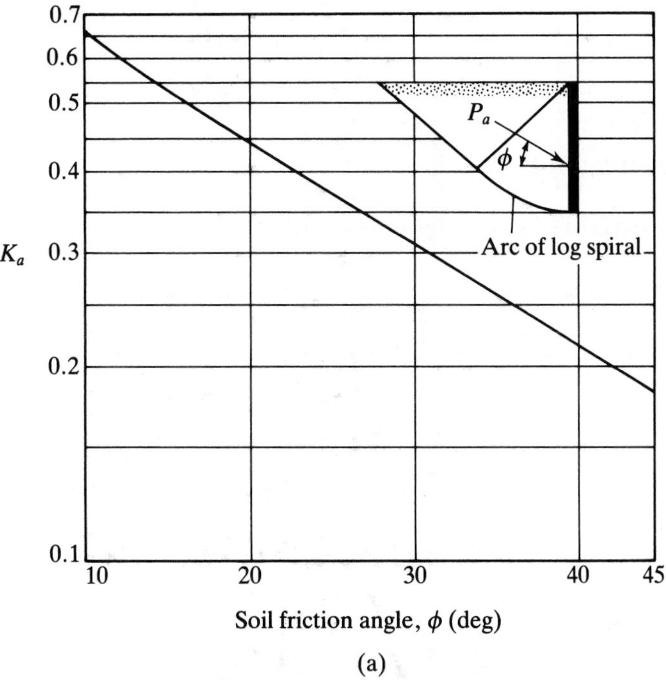

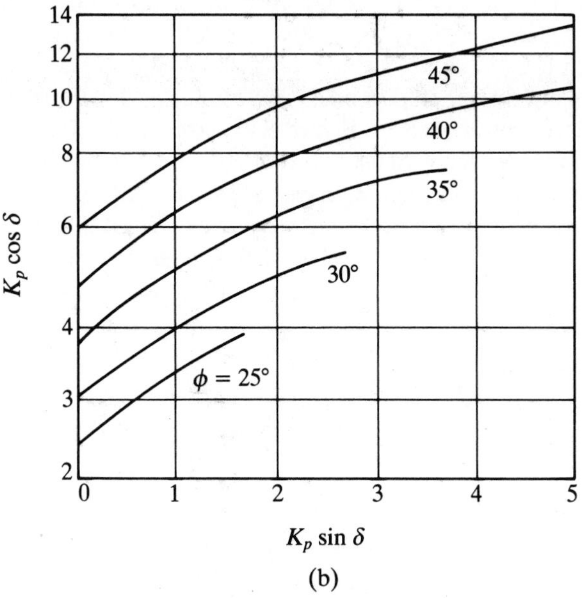

FIGURE 6.37 (a) Variation of K_a (for $\delta = \phi$); (b) variation of $K_p \cos \delta$ with $K_p \sin \delta$ (based on Ovesen and Stromann, 1972)

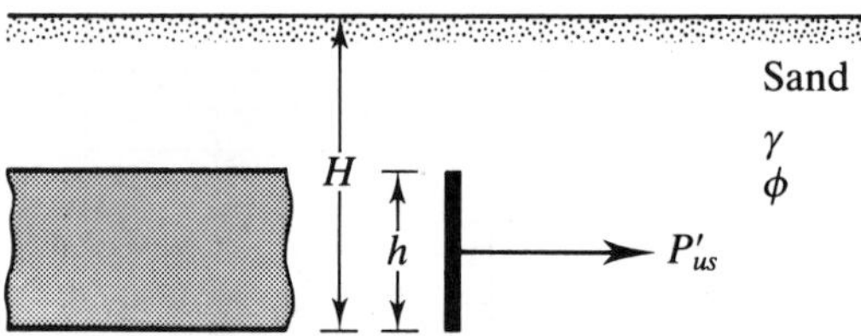

▼ **FIGURE 6.38** Strip case: vertical anchor

where P'_{us} = ultimate resistance for the *strip case*
C_{ov} = 19 for dense sand and 14 for loose sand

Step 3. Actual Case. In practice, the anchor plates are placed in a row with center-to-center spacing, S', as shown in Figure 6.39a. The ultimate resistance of each anchor, P_u, is

$$\boxed{P_u = P'_{us} B_e} \tag{6.95}$$

where B_e = equivalent length

The equivalent length is a function of S', B, H, and h. Figure 6.39b shows a plot of $(B_e - B)/(H + h)$ against $(S' - B)/(H + h)$ for the cases of loose and dense sand. With known values of S', B, H, and h, the value of B_e can be calculated and used in Eq. (6.95) to obtain P_u.

Relatively few studies have been conducted so far to determine the relation of load to displacement of anchors. Figure 6.40 shows an example of nondimensional displacement of anchors for various values of B/h and H/h as obtained by Neeley et al. (1973) experimentally in medium to dense sand. Das (1975) and Das and Seeley (1975) also found essentially similar relations for anchors tested in loose sand. Based on the experimental results, Das and Seeley (1975) presented the following load-displacement relationship for anchors:

$$\bar{P} = \frac{\bar{\Delta}}{0.15 + 0.85\bar{\Delta}} \tag{6.96}$$

$$\text{where } \bar{P} = \frac{\text{load on anchor at horizontal displacement, } \Delta}{\text{ultimate load at horizontal displacement, } \Delta_u} \tag{6.97}$$

$$\bar{\Delta} = \frac{\Delta}{\Delta_u} \tag{6.98}$$

The relationship given by Eq. (6.96) is valid for B/h of 1 to 5 and H/h of 1 to 5.

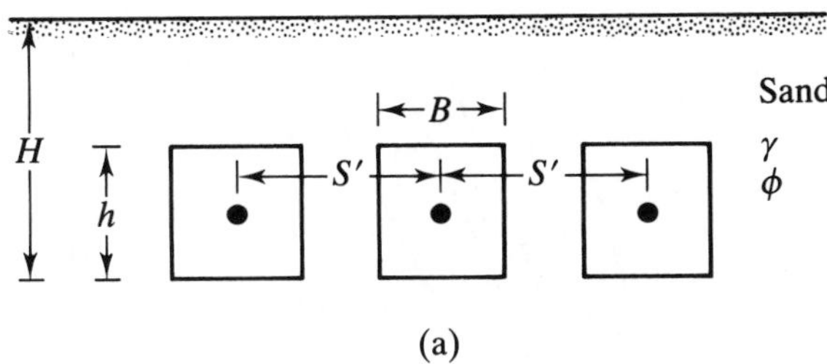

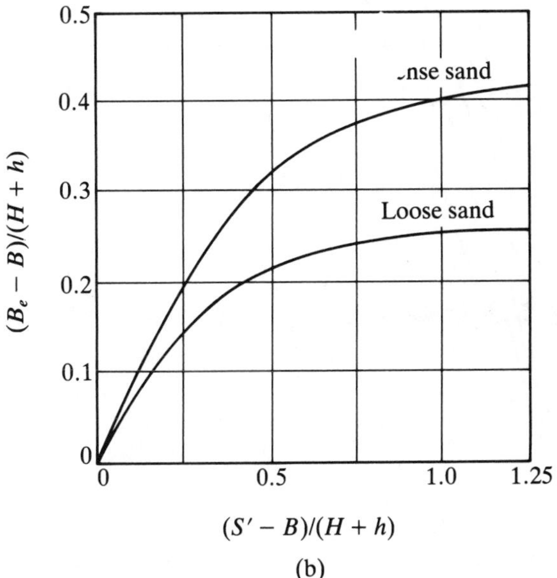

▼ **FIGURE 6.39** (a) Actual case for row of anchors; (b) variation of $(B_e - B)/(H + h)$ with $(S' - B)/(H + h)$ (based on Ovesen and Stromann, 1972)

Ultimate Resistance of Anchor Plates and Beams in Clay ($\phi = 0$ Condition)

Relatively few studies have been conducted on the ultimate resistance of anchor plates and beams in clayey soils ($\phi = 0$). Mackenzie (1955) and Tschebotarioff (1973) identified the nature of the variation of the ultimate resistance of strip anchors and beams as a function of H, h, and c (undrained cohesion based on $\phi = 0$) in a nondimensional form based on laboratory model test results. Das et al., (1985) suggested the following procedure to obtain the ultimate resistance of an anchor embedded in clay.

When an anchor plate having dimensions of $h \times B$ is embedded at depth H, the failure surface in soil at ultimate load may extend to the ground surface, as shown in Figure 6.41a. This condition will arise when the ratio H/h is relatively small. However, for larger values of H/h, local shear failure takes place at ultimate load (Figure 6.41b).

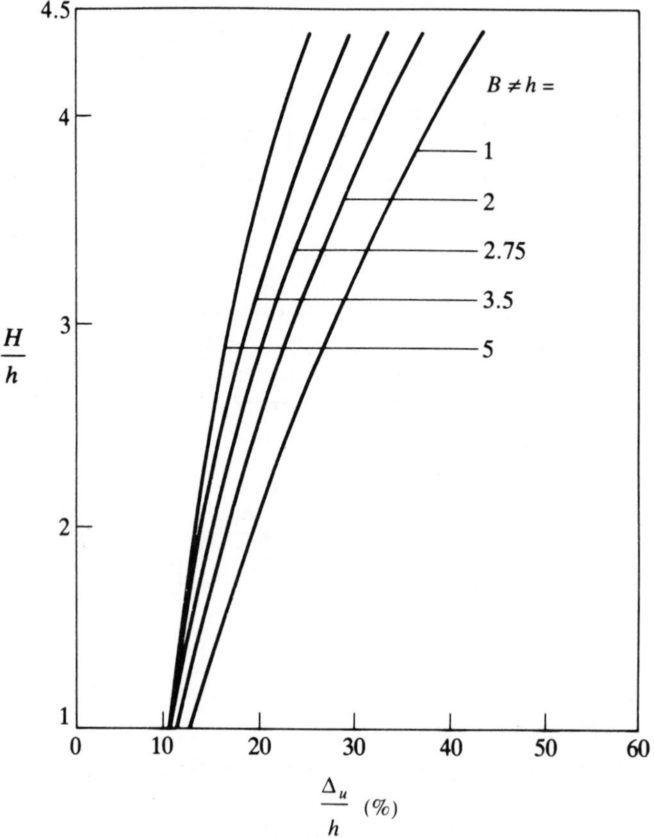

▼ **FIGURE 6.40** Vertical anchor plates or beams: horizontal displacement at ultimate load (redrawn after Neeley et al., 1973)

The critical value of H/h at which general shear failure changes to local shear failure in soil is

$$\left(\frac{H}{h}\right)_{\text{cr-S}} = 4.7 + 2.9 \times 10^{-3} c \leq 7 \qquad \text{(for } \textit{square} \text{ anchors, that is, } B/h = 1\text{)} \tag{6.99}$$

and

$$\left(\frac{H}{h}\right)_{\text{cr-R}} = \left(\frac{H}{h}\right)_{\text{cr-S}} \left[0.9 + 0.1\left(\frac{B}{h}\right)\right] \leq 1.3\left(\frac{H}{h}\right)_{\text{cr-S}} \qquad \text{(for } \textit{rectangular} \text{ anchors, that is, } B/h \geq 1\text{)} \tag{6.100}$$

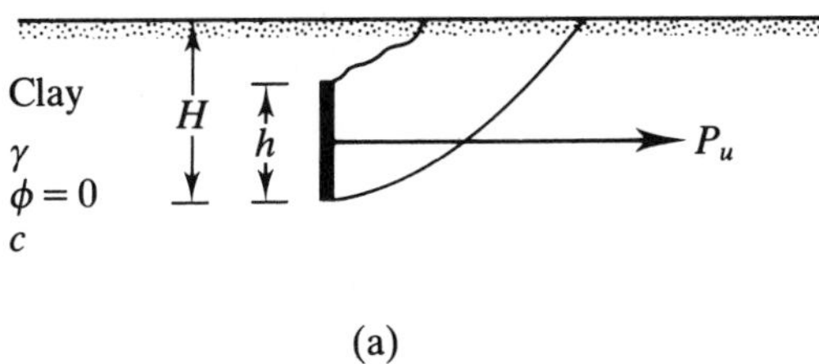

(a)

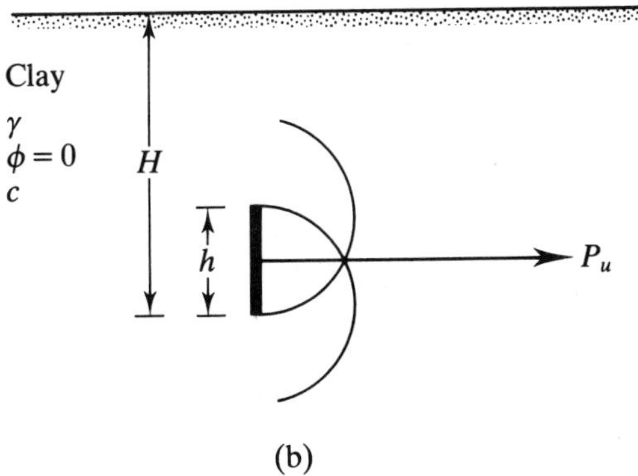

(b)

▼ **FIGURE 6.41** Nature of failure surface in soil around vertical anchor plate: (a) H/h relatively small; (b) $H/h > (H/h)_{cr}$

In Eqs. (6.99) and (6.100), the unit of the undrained cohesion is lb/ft^2.

The ultimate resistance of an anchor plate may be expressed in a nondimensional form as

$$F_c = \frac{P_u}{Bhc} \tag{6.101}$$

where F_c = breakout factor
P_u = ultimate resistance

Figure 6.42 shows the nature of variation of F_c against H/h for an anchor plate embedded in clay. Note that, for $H/h \geq (H/h)_{cr}$, the magnitude of F_c equals that of $F_{c(max)}$, which is a constant. For square anchors ($B = h$), $F_{c(max)} = 9$. So, with $H/h \geq (H/h)_{cr\text{-}S}$,

$$P_u = 9h^2c \qquad \text{(for square anchors)} \tag{6.102}$$

For rectangular anchors with $H/h \geq (H/h)_{cr\text{-}R}$, the ultimate resistance may be given as

$$P_u = 9Bhc\left[0.825 + 0.175\left(\frac{h}{B}\right)\right]$$

or

$$P_u = Bch\left[7.425 + 1.575\left(\frac{h}{B}\right)\right] \tag{6.103}$$

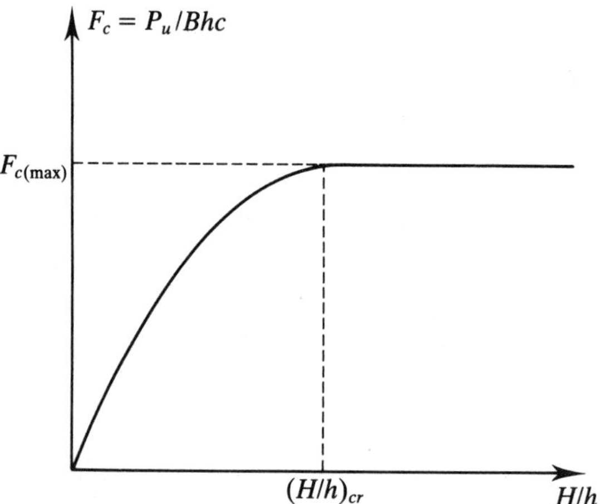

▼ **FIGURE 6.42** Nature of variation of F_c with H/h for vertical anchor in clay

So, for square and rectangular anchors with $H/h \le (H/h)_{cr}$, the ultimate resistance may be calculated from the empirical relationship:

$$\frac{\left[\dfrac{H/h}{(H/h)_{cr}}\right]}{\left[\dfrac{P_u/cBh}{7.425 + 1.575(h/B)}\right]} = 0.41 + 0.59\left[\frac{H/h}{(H/h)_{cr}}\right] \tag{6.104}$$

Factor of Safety for Anchor Plates and Beams

The allowable resistance per anchor plate, P_{all}, may be given as

$$P_{all} = \frac{P_u}{FS} \tag{6.105}$$

where FS = factor of safety

Generally, a factor of safety of 2 is suggested.

Spacing of Anchor Plates

The center-to-center spacing of anchors, S', may be obtained from

$$S' = \frac{P_{all}}{F} \tag{6.106}$$

where F = force per unit length of the sheet pile

Ultimate Resistance of Tie Backs

According to Figure 6.43, the ultimate resistance offered by a tie back in sand is

$$P_u = \pi d l \bar{\sigma}'_v K \tan\phi \tag{6.107}$$

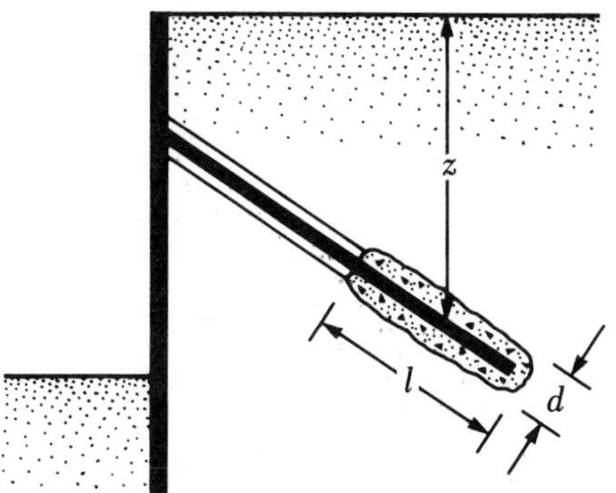

▼ **FIGURE 6.43** Parameters for defining the ultimate resistance of tie backs

where P_u = ultimate resistance
ϕ = angle of friction of soil
$\bar{\sigma}'_v$ = average effective vertical stress ($=\gamma z$ in dry sand)
K = earth pressure coefficient

The magnitude of K can be taken to be equal to the earth pressure coefficient at rest (K_O) if the concrete grout is placed under pressure (Littlejohn, 1970). The lower limit of K can be taken to be equal to the Rankine active earth pressure coefficient.

In clays, the ultimate resistance of tie backs may be approximated as

$$P_u = \pi d l c_a \tag{6.108}$$

where c_a = adhesion

The value of c_a may be approximated as $\frac{2}{3}c_u$ (where c_u = undrained cohesion).

A factor of safety of 1.5–2 may be used over the ultimate resistance to obtain the allowable resistance offered by each tie back.

▼ EXAMPLE 6.10

A row of vertical anchors embedded in sand is shown in Figure 6.44. The anchor plates are made of 6-in. thick concrete. The design parameters are $B = h = 15$ in., $S' = 48$ in., $H = 37.5$ in., $\gamma = 105$ lb/ft^3, $\phi = 35°$, and the unit weight of concrete = 150 lb/ft^3.

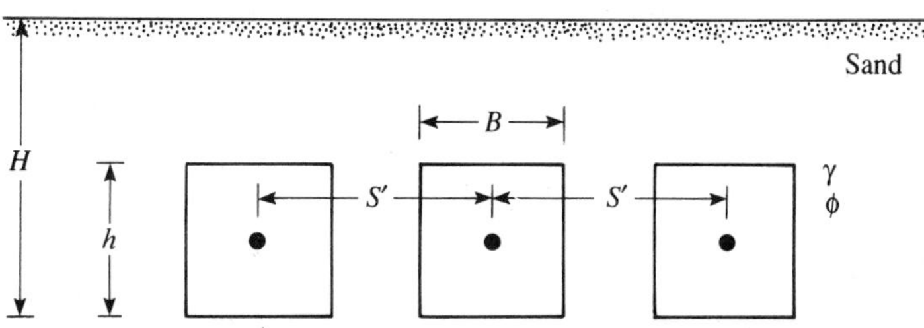

▼ **FIGURE 6.44**

Determine the

a. Ultimate resistance of each anchor plate
b. Anchor resistance for a maximum horizontal displacement of 1.5 in.

Solution

Part a

From Figure 6.37a for $\phi = 35°$, the magnitude of K_a is about 0.26. Also,

$$W = Ht\gamma_{\text{concrete}} = \left(\frac{37.5}{12}\right)\left(\frac{6}{12}\right)(150) = 234.4 \text{ lb/ft}$$

From Eq. (6.93),

$$K_p \sin\delta = \frac{W + \frac{1}{2}\gamma H^2 K_a \sin\phi}{\frac{1}{2}\gamma H^2}$$

$$= \frac{234.4 + \frac{1}{2}(105)\left(\frac{37.5}{12}\right)^2(0.26)(\sin 35)}{\frac{1}{2}(105)\left(\frac{37.5}{12}\right)^2} = 0.606$$

From Figure 6.37b with $\phi = 35°$ and $K_p \sin\delta = 0.606$, the magnitude of $K_p \cos\delta$ is about 4.5. Now, from Eq. (6.92),

$$P'_u = \frac{1}{2}\gamma H^2(K_p \cos\delta - K_a \cos\phi)$$

$$= \frac{1}{2}(105)\left(\frac{37.5}{12}\right)^2[4.5 - (0.26)(\cos 35)] = 2198 \text{ lb/ft}$$

To calculate P'_{us}, we assume the sand to be loose. So, C_{ov} in Eq. (6.94) is 14. Hence

$$P'_{us} = \left[\frac{C_{ov} + 1}{C_{ov} + \left(\frac{H}{h}\right)}\right]P'_u = \left[\frac{14 + 1}{14 + \left(\frac{37.5}{15}\right)}\right](2198) = 1998 \text{ lb/ft}$$

$$\frac{S' - B}{H + h} = \frac{48 - 15}{37.5 + 15} = 0.61$$

For $(S' - B)/(H + h) = 0.61$ and loose sand, Figure 6.39b yields

$$\frac{B_e - B}{H - h} = 0.227$$

So

$$B_e = (0.227)(H + h) + B = \frac{(0.227)(37.5 + 15) + 15}{12} = 2.24 \text{ ft}$$

Hence from Eq. (6.95),

$$P_u = P'_{us} B_e = (1998)(2.24) = \mathbf{4476\ lb}$$

Part b

From Figure 6.40, for $H/h = 2.5$ and $B/h = 1$, $\Delta_u/h = 0.24$. Hence at ultimate load, P_u, the displacement of the anchor will be

$$\Delta_u = 0.24h = 0.24 \times 15 = 3.6 \text{ in.}$$

If $\Delta = 1.5$ in., $\bar{\Delta} = \Delta/\Delta_u = 1.5/3.6 = 0.417$. From Eq. (6.96),

$$\bar{P} = \frac{\bar{\Delta}}{0.15 + 0.85\bar{\Delta}}$$

Hence

$$\bar{P} = \frac{0.417}{0.15 + (0.85)(0.417)} = 0.827$$

Thus

$$P_{\text{at } \Delta = 1.5 \text{ in.}} = 0.827 \times P_u = (0.827)(4476) = \mathbf{3702\ lb.}$$ ▼

▼ EXAMPLE 6.11

For a vertical anchor plate in clay, the design parameters are $B = 5$ ft, $h = 2$ ft, $H = 6$ ft, and $c = 500$ lb/ft². Determine the ultimate resistance of the anchor.

Solution From Eq. (6.99),

$$\left(\frac{H}{h}\right)_{\text{cr-S}} = 4.7 + 2.9 \times 10^{-3} c$$
$$= 4.7 + (2.9 \times 10^{-3})(500) = 6.15$$

Again, from Eq. (6.100),

$$\left(\frac{H}{h}\right)_{\text{cr-R}} = \left(\frac{H}{h}\right)_{\text{cr-S}} \left[0.9 + 0.1\left(\frac{B}{h}\right)\right]$$
$$= (6.15)\left[0.9 + (0.1)\left(\frac{5}{2}\right)\right] = 7.07$$

As $H/h = 6/2 = 3$ is less than $(H/h)_{\text{cr}}$, we use Eq. (6.104) to obtain P_u, from which

$$\frac{\left(\frac{3}{7.07}\right)}{\left[\frac{(P_u/cBh)}{7.425 + 1.575(2/5)}\right]} = 0.41 + (0.59)\left(\frac{3}{7.07}\right)$$

or

$$\frac{0.424}{\left[\frac{(P_u/cBh)}{8.055}\right]} = 0.66$$

So

$$\frac{P_u}{cBh} = \left(\frac{0.424}{0.66}\right)(8.055) = 5.17$$

$$P_u = (5.17)cBh = (5.17)(500)(5)(2) = \mathbf{25{,}850\ lb.}$$ ▼

PROBLEMS

6.1 Figure P6.1 shows a cantilever sheet pile wall penetrating a granular soil. Here, $L_1 = 8$ ft, $L_2 = 15$ ft, $\gamma = 100$ lb/ft^3, $\gamma_{sat} = 110$ lb/ft^3, $\phi = 35°$.

a. What is the theoretical depth of embedment, D?

b. Draw the net pressure distribution diagram.

c. For a 30% increase in D, what should be the total length of the sheet piles?

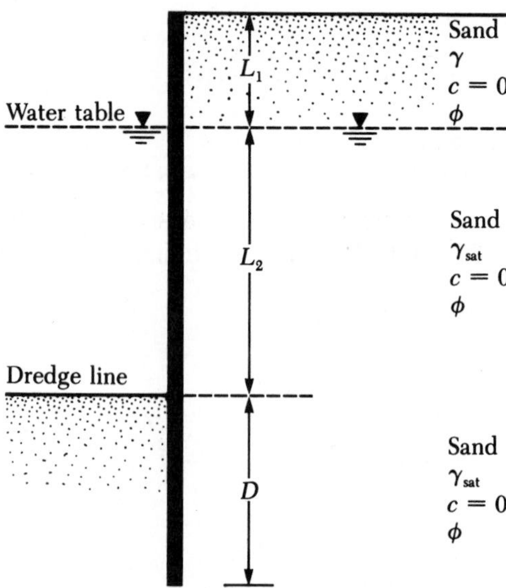

▼ **FIGURE P6.1**

6.2 Redo Problem 6.1, parts (a)–(c) for $L_1 = 3$ m, $L_2 = 6$ m, $\gamma = 17.6$ kN/m^3, $\gamma_{sat} = 18.5$ kN/m^3, and $\phi = 30°$.

6.3 For Problem 6.1, part (b), determine the maximum moment for the sheet pile and then choose the most appropriate sheet pile section.

6.4 For Problem 6.2, determine the theoretical maximum moment for the sheet pile and then choose the most appropriate sheet pile section.

6.5 Redo Problem 6.1, parts (a)–(c), for $L_1 = 10$ ft, $L_2 = 15$ ft, $\gamma = 105$ lb/ft^3, $\gamma_{sat} = 124$ lb/ft^3, and $\phi = 32°$.

6.6 For Problem 6.5, calculate the theoretical maximum moment and choose a sheet pile section.

6.7 Refer to Figure 6.9, for which $L = 10$ ft, $\gamma = 110$ lb/ft^3, and $\phi = 32°$. Calculate the theoretical depth of penetration, D, and the maximum moment.

6.8 Repeat Problem 6.7 for $L = 3$ m, $\gamma = 16.7$ kN/m^3, and $\phi = 30°$.

6.9 Refer to Figure 6.10, which shows a free cantilever sheet pile wall penetrating a sand layer. Determine the theoretical depth of penetration and the maximum moment for $\gamma = 105$ lb/ft^3, $\phi = 38°$, $L = 10$ ft, and $P = 1000$ lb/ft.

6.10 Refer to Figure P6.10, for which $L_1 = 2.4$ m, $L_2 = 4.6$ m, $\gamma = 15.7$ kN/m^3, $\gamma_{sat} = 17.3$ kN/m^3, $c = 29$ kN/m^2, $\phi = 30°$.

a. Find the theoretical depth of penetration, D.
b. Draw the pressure distribution diagram with all dimensions.
c. Increase D by 40%. What length of sheet piles is needed?

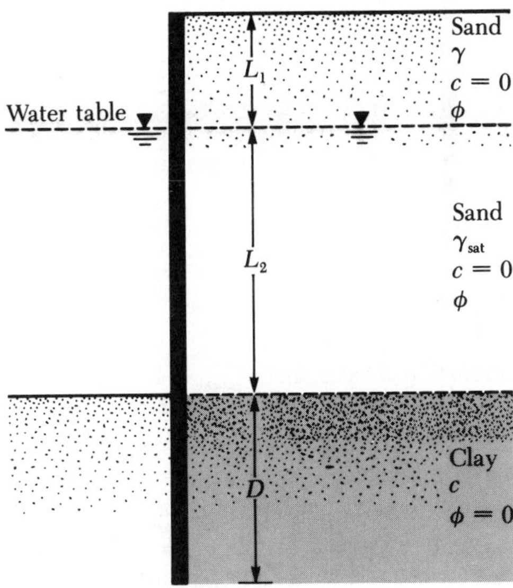

FIGURE P6.10

6.11 Redo Problem 6.7, parts (a)–(c), for $L_1 = 5$ ft, $L_2 = 20$ ft, $\gamma = 108$ lb/ft^3, $\gamma_{sat} = 122.4$ lb/ft^3, $\phi = 36°$, and $c = 800$ lb/ft^2.

6.12 For Problem 6.10, determine the maximum moment and choose a sheet pile section.

6.13 For Problem 6.11, determine the maximum moment and the appropriate section.

6.14 Refer to Figure 6.13, for which $L = 10$ ft, $\gamma = 110$ lb/ft^3, $\phi = 34°$, and $c = 600$ lb/ft^2. Find the theoretical value of D and the maximum moment.

6.15 Refer to Figure 6.14. Here, $L = 3$ m, $P = 6$ kN/m, $c = 35$ kN/m^2, and $\gamma_{sat} = 19.2$ kN/m^3. Find the theoretical value of D and the maximum moment.

6.16 An anchored sheet pile bulkhead is shown in Figure P6.16. The design parameters are $L_1 = 3.05$ m, $L_2 = 6.1$ m, $l_1 = 1.53$ m, $\gamma = 16$ kN/m^3, $\gamma_{sat} = 19.5$ kN/m^3, and $\phi = 30°$. Use the free earth support method to do the following.

a. Calculate the theoretical value of the depth of embedment, D.

b. Draw the pressure distribution diagram.

c. Determine the anchor force per unit length of the wall.

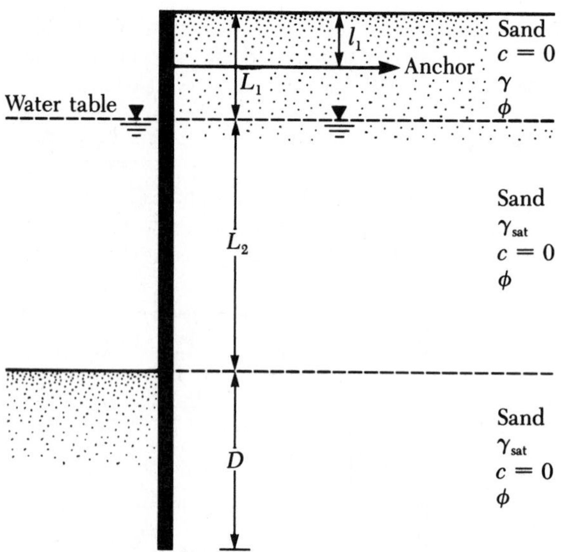

▼ **FIGURE P6.16**

6.17 Refer to Problem 6.16. Assume that $D_{actual} = 1.3D_{theory}$.

a. Determine the theoretical maximum moment.

b. Choose a sheet pile section by using Rowe's moment reduction technique.

6.18 Use the free earth support method and redo Problem 6.16 for $L_1 = 9$ ft, $L_2 = 26$ ft, $l_1 = 5$ ft, $\gamma = 108.5$ lb/ft^3, $\gamma_{sat} = 128.5$ lb/ft^3, and $\phi = 35°$.

6.19 Refer to Problem 6.18. Assume that $D_{actual} = 1.4D_{theory}$ and use Rowe's moment reduction technique method to choose a sheet pile section.

6.20 An anchored sheet pile bulkhead is shown in Figure P6.20, for which $L_1 = 2$ m, $L_2 = 6$ m, $l_1 = 1$ m, $\gamma = 16$ kN/m^3, $\gamma_{sat} = 18.86$ kN/m^3, $\phi = 32°$, and $c = 27$ kN/m^2.

a. Determine the theoretical depth of embedment, D.

b. Calculate the anchor force per unit length of the sheet pile wall. Use the free earth support method.

6.21 Solve Problem 6.20 for $L_1 = 10.8$ ft, $L_2 = 21.6$ ft, $l_1 = 5.4$ ft, $\gamma = 108$ lb/ft^3, $\gamma_{sat} = 127.2$ lb/ft^3, $\phi = 35°$, and $c = 850$ lb/ft^2.

6.22 Solve Problem 6.16, parts (a) and (c), by using the procedure described in Section 6.8.

6.23 Refer to Problem 6.18. For the parameters given, calculate

a. the theoretical depth of embedment.

b. the anchor force per unit length of the wall.

c. the theoretical maximum moment.

Use the procedure described in Section 6.8.

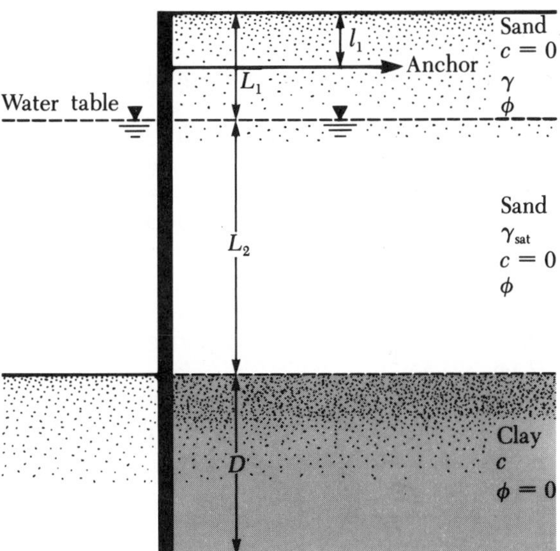

▼ **FIGURE P6.20**

6.24 Refer to Figure P6.16, for which $L_1 = 10$ ft, $L_2 = 20$ ft, $l_1 = 5$ ft, $\gamma = 110$ lb/ft^3, $\gamma_{sat} = 122.4$ lb/ft^3, and $\phi = 35°$. Use the computational diagram method (Section 6.11) to determine D, F, and M_{max}. Assume that $C = 0.68$ and $R = 0.6$.

6.25 Repeat Problem 6.24 for the parameters $L_1 = 8$ ft, $L_2 = 18$ ft, $l_1 = 4$ ft, $\gamma = 105$ lb/ft^3, $\gamma_{sat} = 118$ lb/ft^3, and $\phi = 30°$. Assume that $C = 0.8$ and $R = 0.5$.

6.26 Refer to Figure 6.39a. For the anchor slab in sand, $H = 6$ ft, $h = 2.5$ ft, $B = 3.5$ ft, $S' = 8$ ft, $\phi = 30°$, and $\gamma = 105$ lb/ft^3. Calculate the ultimate holding capacity of each anchor. The anchor plates are made of concrete and have a thickness of 3 in. Use $\gamma_{concrete} = 150$ lb/ft^3.

6.27 A single anchor slab is shown in Figure P6.27. Here, $H = 0.9$ m, $h = 0.3$ m, $\gamma = 17$ kN/m^3, and $\phi = 32°$. Calculate the ultimate holding capacity of the anchor slab if the width B is (a) 0.3 m, (b) 0.6 m, and (c) 0.9 m. (*Note:* center-to-center spacing, $S' = \infty$.)

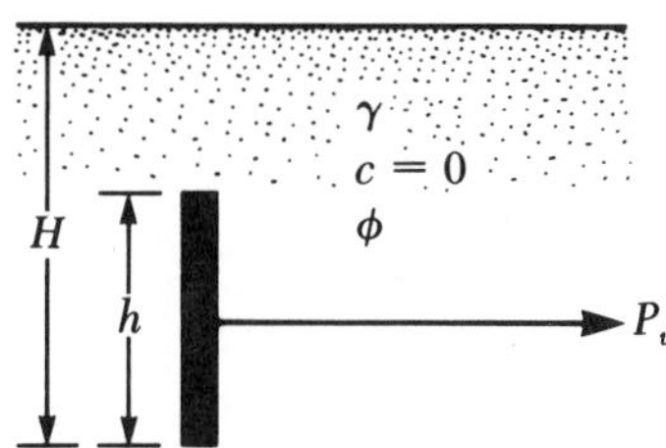

▼ **FIGURE P6.27**

6.28 Refer to Problem 6.27. Estimate the probable horizontal displacement of the anchors at ultimate load. Also estimate the resistance of anchors if the allowable displacement is 20 mm.

6.29 A vertical anchor plate in clay has $B = 3$ ft, $H = 6$ ft, $h = 3$ ft, and $c = 700$ lb/ft^2. Estimate the ultimate resistance of the anchor.

REFERENCES

Blum, H. (1931). *Einspannungsverhältnisse bei Bohlwerken*, W. Ernst und Sohn, Berlin, Germany.

Casagrande, L. (1973). "Comments on Conventional Design of Retaining Structures," *Journal of the Soil Mechanics and Foundations Division*, ASCE, Vol. 99, No. SM2, pp. 181–198.

Das, B. M. (1975). "Pullout Resistance of Vertical Anchors," *Journal of the Geotechnical Engineering Division*, American Society of Civil Engineers, Vol. 101, No. GT1, pp. 87–91.

Das, B. M., and Seeley, G. R. (1975). "Load-Displacement Relationships for Vertical Anchor Plates," *Journal of the Geotechnical Engineering Division*, American Society of Civil Engineers, Vol. 101, No. GT7, pp. 711–715.

Das, B. M., Tarquin, A. J., and Moreno, R. (1985). "Model Tests for Pullout Resistance of Vertical Anchor in Clay," *Journal of Civil Engineering for Practicing and Design Engineers*, Vol. 4, No. 22, pp. 191–209.

Hagerty, D. J., and Nofal, M. M. (1992). "Design Aids: Anchored Bulkheads in Sand," *Canadian Geotechnical Journal*, Vol. 29, No. 5, pp. 789–795.

Littlejohn, G. S. (1970). "Soil Anchors," *Proceedings*, Conference on Ground Engineering, Institute of Civil Engineers, London, pp. 33–44.

Mackenzie, T. R. (1955). *Strength of Deadman Anchors in Clay*, M.S. Thesis, Princeton University, Princeton, N.J.

Nataraj, M. S., and Hoadley, P. G. (1984). "Design of Anchored Bulkheads in Sand," *Journal of Geotechnical Engineering*, American Society of Civil Engineers, Vol. 110, No. GT4, pp. 505–515.

Neeley, W. J., Stuart, J. G., and Graham, J. (1973). "Failure Loads of Vertical Anchor Plates in Sand," *Journal of the Soil Mechanics and Foundations Division*, American Society of Civil Engineers, Vol. 99, No. SM9, pp. 669–685.

Ovesen, N. K., and Stromann, H. (1972). "Design Methods for Vertical Anchor Slabs in Sand," *Proceedings*, Specialty Conference on Performance of Earth and Earth-Supported Structures, American Society of Civil Engineers, Vol. 2.1, pp. 1481–1500.

Rowe, P. W. (1952). "Anchored Sheet Pile Walls," *Proceedings*, Institute of Civil Engineers, Vol. 1, Part 1, pp. 27–70.

Rowe, P. W. (1957). "Sheet Pile Walls in Clay," *Proceedings*, Institute of Civil Engineers, Vol. 7, pp. 654–692.

Teng, W. C. (1962). *Foundation Design*, Prentice-Hall, Englewood Cliffs, N.J.

Tschebotarioff, G. P. (1973). *Foundations, Retaining and Earth Structures*, 2nd ed., McGraw-Hill, New York.

Tsinker, G. P. (1983). "Anchored Sheet Pile Bulkheads: Design Practice," *Journal of Geotechnical Engineering*, American Society of Civil Engineers, Vol. 109, No. GT8, pp. 1021–1038.

CHAPTER SEVEN

BRACED CUTS

7.1 INTRODUCTION

Sometimes construction work requires ground excavations with vertical or near-vertical faces—for example, basements of buildings in developed areas or underground transportation facilities at shallow depths below the ground surface (cut-and-cover type of construction). The vertical faces of the cuts need to be protected by temporary bracing systems to avoid failure that may be accompanied by considerable settlement or by bearing capacity failure of nearby foundations.

Figure 7.1 shows two types of braced cut commonly used in construction work. One type uses the *soldier beam* (Figure 7.1a), which is driven into the ground before excavation and is a vertical steel or timber beam. *Laggings*, which are horizontal timber planks, are placed between soldier beams as the excavation proceeds. When the excavation reaches the desired depth, *wales* and *struts* (horizontal steel beams) are installed. The struts are horizontal compression members. Figure 7.1b shows another type of braced excavation. In this case, interlocking *sheet piles* are driven into the soil before excavation. Wales and struts are inserted immediately after excavation reaches the appropriate depth.

To design braced excavations (i.e., to select wales, struts, sheet piles, and soldier beams), an engineer must estimate the lateral earth pressure to which the braced cuts will be subjected. This topic is discussed in Section 7.2; subsequent sections cover the procedures of analysis and design of braced cuts.

7.2 LATERAL EARTH PRESSURE IN BRACED CUTS

In Chapter 5 you learned that a retaining wall rotates about its bottom (Figure 7.2a). With sufficient yielding of the wall, the lateral earth pressure is approximately equal to that obtained by Rankine's theory or Coulomb's theory. In contrast to retaining walls, braced cuts show a different type of wall yielding (see Figure 7.2b). In this case, deformation of the wall gradually increases with the depth of excavation. The variation of the amount of deformation depends on several factors, such as the type of soil, the depth of excavation, and the workmanship. However, with very little wall

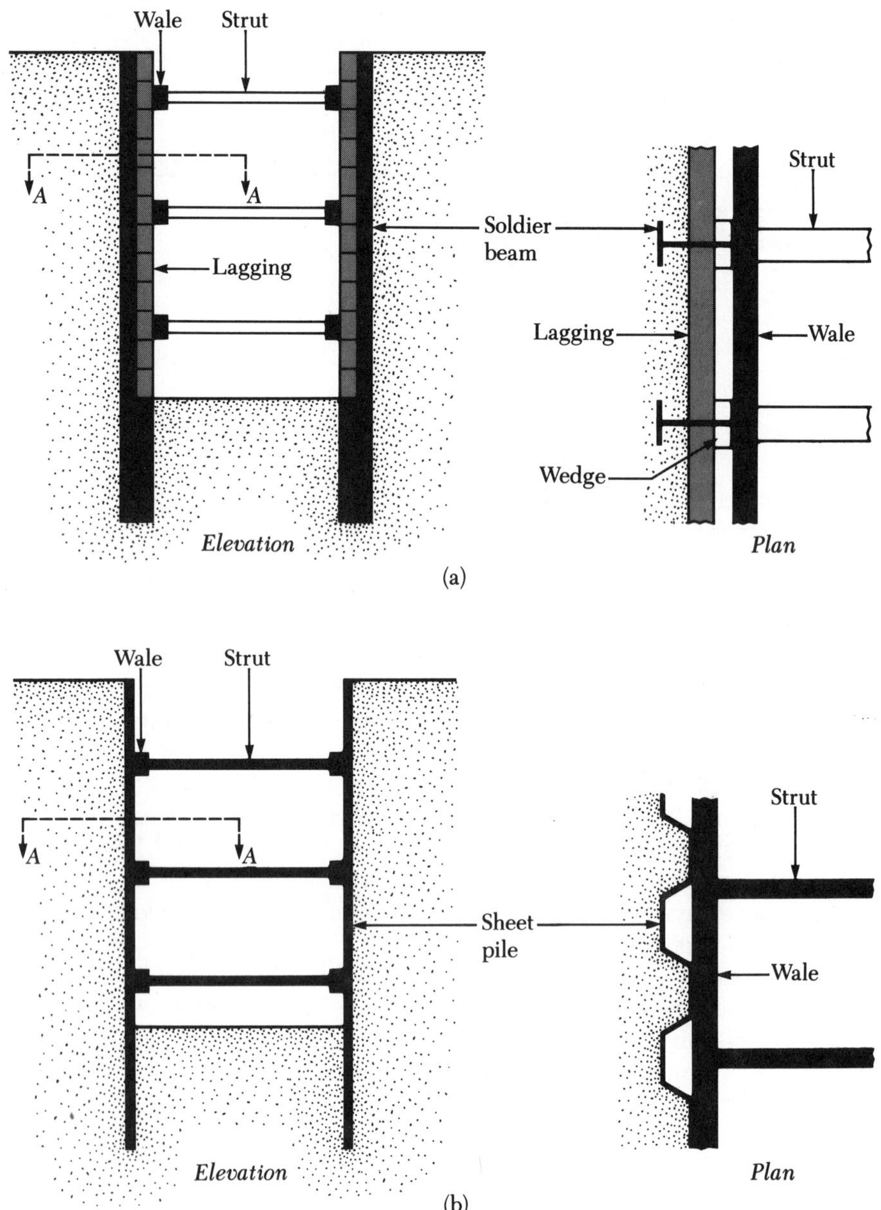

▼ **FIGURE 7.1** Types of braced cut: (a) use of soldier beams; (b) use of sheet piles

yielding at the top of the cut, the lateral earth pressure will be close to the at-rest pressure. At the bottom of the wall, with a much larger degree of yielding, the lateral earth pressure will be substantially lower than the Rankine active earth pressure. As a result, the distribution of lateral earth pressure will vary substantially in comparison to the linear distribution assumed in the case of retaining walls.

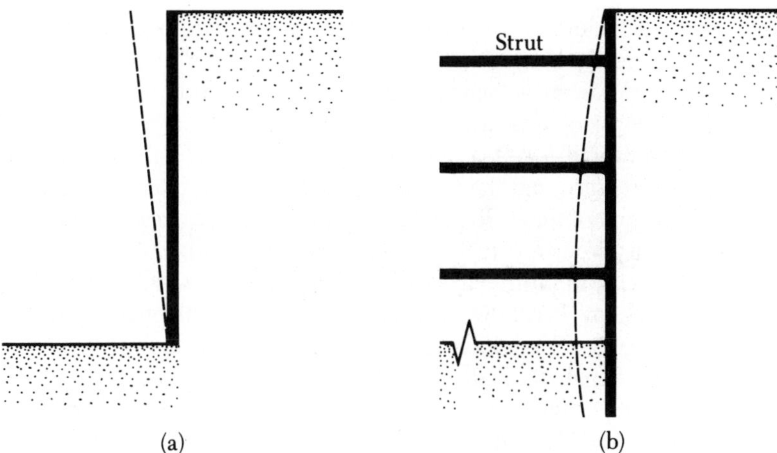

▼ **FIGURE 7.2** Nature of yielding of walls: (a) retaining wall; (b) braced cut

The total lateral force, P, imposed on a wall may be evaluated theoretically by using Terzaghi's (1943a) general wedge theory (Figure 7.3a). The failure surface is assumed to be the arc of a logarithmic spiral, defined as

$$r = r_o e^{\theta \tan \phi} \tag{7.1}$$

where ϕ = angle of friction of soil

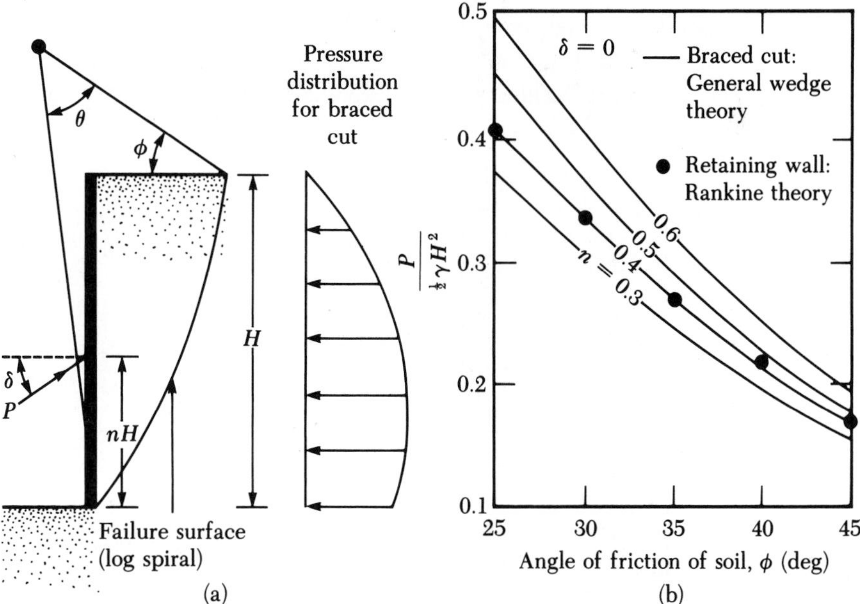

▼ **FIGURE 7.3** Comparison of lateral earth pressure for braced cuts and retaining walls in sand ($\delta = 0$)

A detailed outline for the evaluation of P is beyond the scope of this text; those interested should check a soil mechanics text for more information (for example, Das, 1994). However, a comparison of the lateral earth pressure for braced cuts in sand (with angle of wall friction $\delta = 0$) with that for a retaining wall ($\delta = 0$) is shown in Figure 7.3b. If $\delta = 0$, a retaining wall of height H will be subjected to a Rankine active earth pressure, and the resultant active force will intersect the wall at distance nH from the bottom of the wall. For this case, $n = 1/3$. In contrast, the value of n for a braced cut may vary from 0.33 to 0.5 or 0.6. The general wedge theory may also be used to analyze braced cuts in saturated clay (for example, see Das and Seeley, 1975).

In any event, when choosing a lateral soil pressure distribution for design of braced cuts, the engineer must keep in mind that the nature of failure in braced cuts is much different from that in retaining walls. After observation of several braced cuts, Peck (1969) suggested using *design pressure envelopes* for braced cuts in sand and clay. Figures 7.4, 7.5, and 7.6 show Peck's pressure envelopes, to which the following guidelines apply.

Cuts in Sand

Figure 7.4 shows the pressure envelope for cuts in sand. This pressure, p_a, may be expressed as

$$p_a = 0.65\gamma H K_a \tag{7.2}$$

where γ = unit weight
H = height of the cut
K_a = Rankine active pressure coefficient = $\tan^2(45 - \phi/2)$

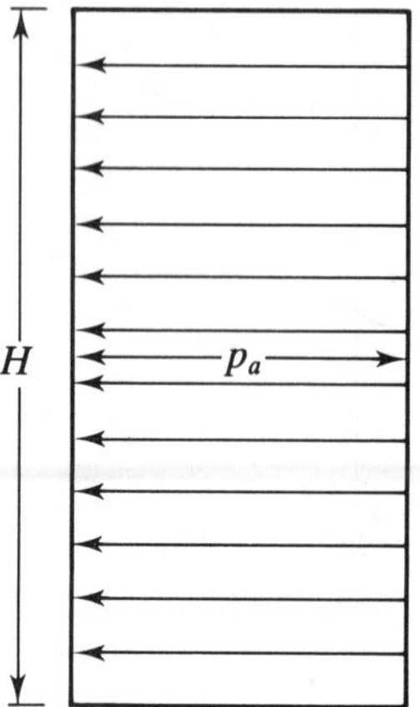

▼ **FIGURE 7.4** Peck's (1969) apparent pressure envelope for cuts in sand

Cuts in Soft and Medium Clay

The pressure envelope for soft to medium clay is shown in Figure 7.5. It is applicable for the condition

$$\frac{\gamma H}{c} > 4$$

where c = undrained cohesion ($\phi = 0$)

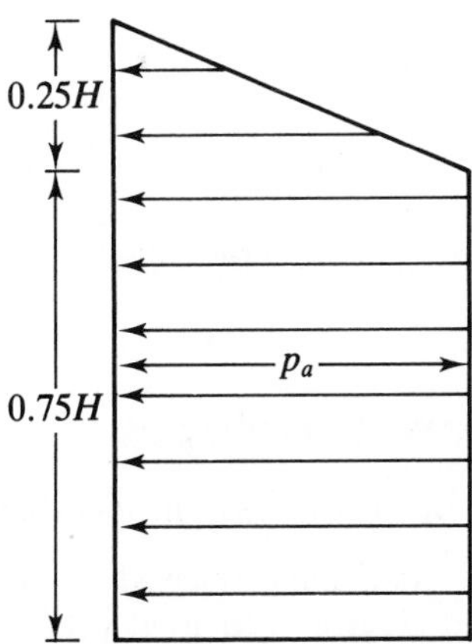

▼ **FIGURE 7.5** Peck's (1969) apparent pressure envelope for cuts in soft to medium clay

The pressure, p_a, is the larger of

$$p_a = \gamma H\left[1 - \left(\frac{4c}{\gamma H}\right)\right] \quad \text{or} \quad p = 0.3\gamma H \tag{7.3}$$

where γ = unit weight of clay

Cuts in Stiff Clay

The pressure envelope shown in Figure 7.6, in which

$$p_a = 0.2\gamma H \text{ to } 0.4\gamma H \qquad \text{(with an average of } 0.3\gamma H) \tag{7.4}$$

is applicable to the condition $\gamma H/c \leq 4$.

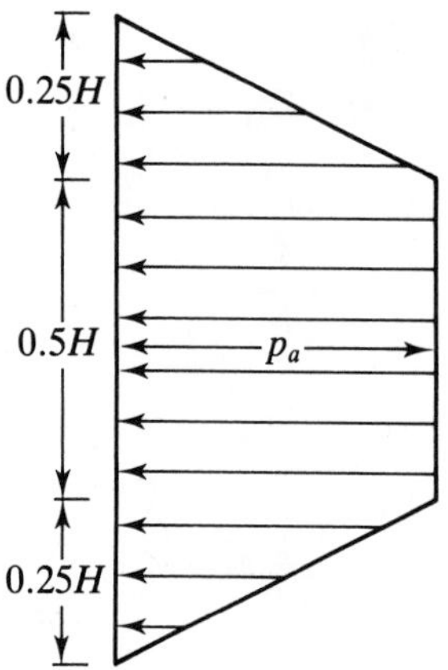

▼ **FIGURE 7.6** Peck's (1969) apparent pressure envelope for cuts in stiff clay

Limitations for the Pressure Envelopes

When using the pressure envelopes just described, keep the following points in mind.

1. The pressure envelopes are sometimes referred to as *apparent pressure envelopes*. However, the actual pressure distribution is a function of the construction sequence and the relative flexibility of the wall.
2. They apply to excavations having depths greater than about 20 ft ($\approx$6 m).
3. They are based on the assumption that the water table is below the bottom of the cut.
4. Sand is assumed to be drained with zero pore water pressure.
5. Clay is assumed to be undrained and pore water pressure is not considered.

Cuts in Layered Soil

Sometimes, layers of both sand and clay are encountered when a braced cut is being constructed. In this case, Peck (1943) proposed that an equivalent value of cohesion ($\phi = 0$ concept) should be determined in the following manner (refer to Figure 7.7a):

$$c_{av} = \frac{1}{2H}[\gamma_s K_s H_s^2 \tan \phi_s + (H - H_s)n' q_u] \tag{7.5}$$

where H = total height of the cut
γ_s = unit weight of sand
H_s = height of the sand layer
K_s = a lateral earth pressure coefficient for the sand layer ($\approx$1)

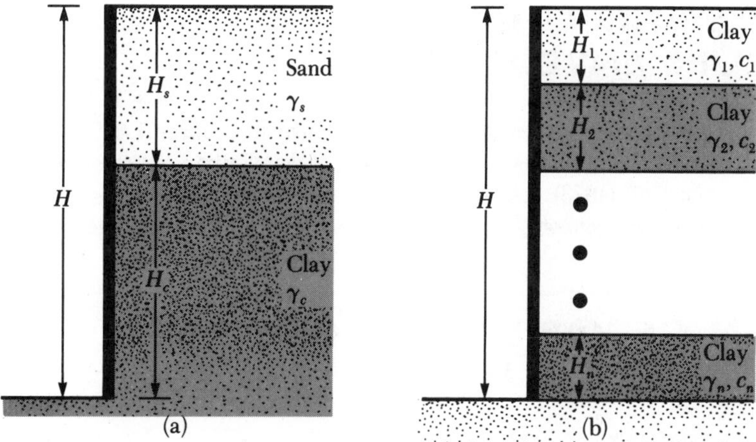

▼ **FIGURE 7.7** Layered soils in braced cuts

ϕ_s = angle of friction of sand
q_u = unconfined compression strength of clay
n' = a coefficient of progressive failure (ranges from 0.5 to 1.0; average value 0.75)

The average unit weight, γ_a, of the layers may be expressed as

$$\gamma_a = \frac{1}{H}[\gamma_s H_s + (H - H_s)\gamma_c] \tag{7.6}$$

where γ_c = saturated unit weight of clay layer

Once the average values of cohesion and unit weight are determined, the pressure envelopes in clay can be used to design the cuts.

Similarly, when several clay layers are encountered in the cut (Figure 7.7b), the average undrained cohesion becomes

$$c_{\text{av}} = \frac{1}{H}(c_1 H_1 + c_2 H_2 + \cdots + c_n H_n) \tag{7.7}$$

where $c_1, c_2, \ldots, c_n$ = undrained cohesion in layers 1, 2, ..., n
$H_1, H_2, \ldots, H_n$ = thickness of layers 1, 3, ..., n

The average unit weight, γ_a, is

$$\gamma_a = \frac{1}{H}(\gamma_1 H_1 + \gamma_2 H_2 + \gamma_3 H_3 + \cdots + \gamma_n H_n) \tag{7.8}$$

7.3 TSCHEBOTARIOFF'S PRESSURE ENVELOPES

Similar to the pressure envelopes shown in Figures 7.4, 7.5, and 7.6, which were suggested by Peck (1969), another form of distribution of pressure was suggested by Tschebotarioff (1973). It is shown in Figure 7.8 and is sometimes used for design. In this text, however, *Figures 7.4, 7.5, and 7.6 are used for all calculations and problems.*

7.4 DESIGN OF VARIOUS COMPONENTS OF A BRACED CUT

Struts

In construction work, struts should have a minimum vertical spacing of about 9 ft (2.75 m) or more. The struts are actually horizontal columns subject to bending. The load-carrying capacity of columns depends on the *slenderness ratio,* l/r. The slenderness ratio can be reduced by providing vertical and horizontal supports at intermediate points. For wide cuts, splicing the struts may be necessary. For braced cuts in clayey soils, the depth of the first strut below the ground surface should be less than the depth of tensile crack, z_c. From Eq. (5.13),

$$\sigma_a = \gamma z K_a - 2c\sqrt{K_a}$$

where K_a = coefficient of Rankine active pressure

For determining the depth of tensile crack,

$$\sigma_a = 0 = \gamma z_c K_a - 2c\sqrt{K_a}$$

or

$$z_c = \frac{2c}{\sqrt{K_a}\gamma}$$

With $\phi = 0$, $K_a = \tan^2(45 - \phi/2) = 1$. So

$$z_c = \frac{2c}{\gamma}$$

A simplified conservative procedure may be used to determine the strut loads. Although this procedure will vary, depending on the engineers involved in the project, the following is a step-by-step outline of the general procedure (refer to Figure 7.9).

1. Draw the pressure envelope for the braced cut (see Figures 7.4, 7.5, and 7.6). Also show the proposed strut levels. Figure 7.9a shows a pressure envelope for a sandy soil; however, it could also be for a clay. The strut levels are marked A, B, C, and D. The sheet piles (or soldier beams) are assumed to be hinged at the strut levels, except for the top and bottom ones. In Figure 7.9a, the hinges are at the level of struts B and C. (Many designers also assume the

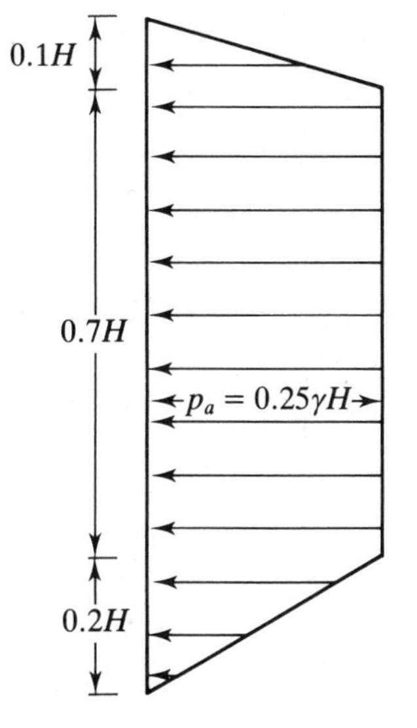

(a) Sand

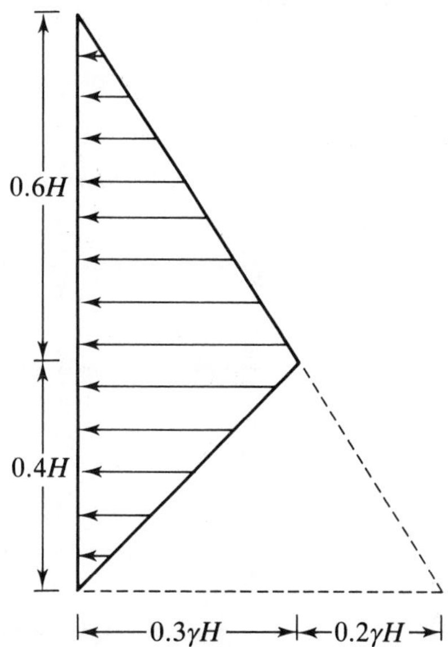

(b) Temporary support in stiff clay

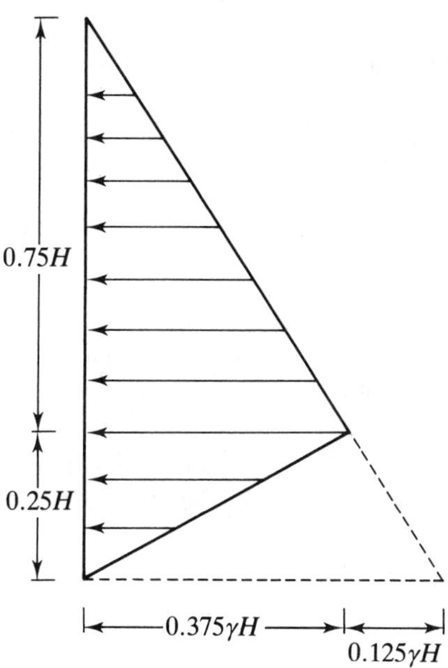

(c) Permanent support in medium clay

▼ **FIGURE 7.8** Tschebotarioff's pressure envelopes

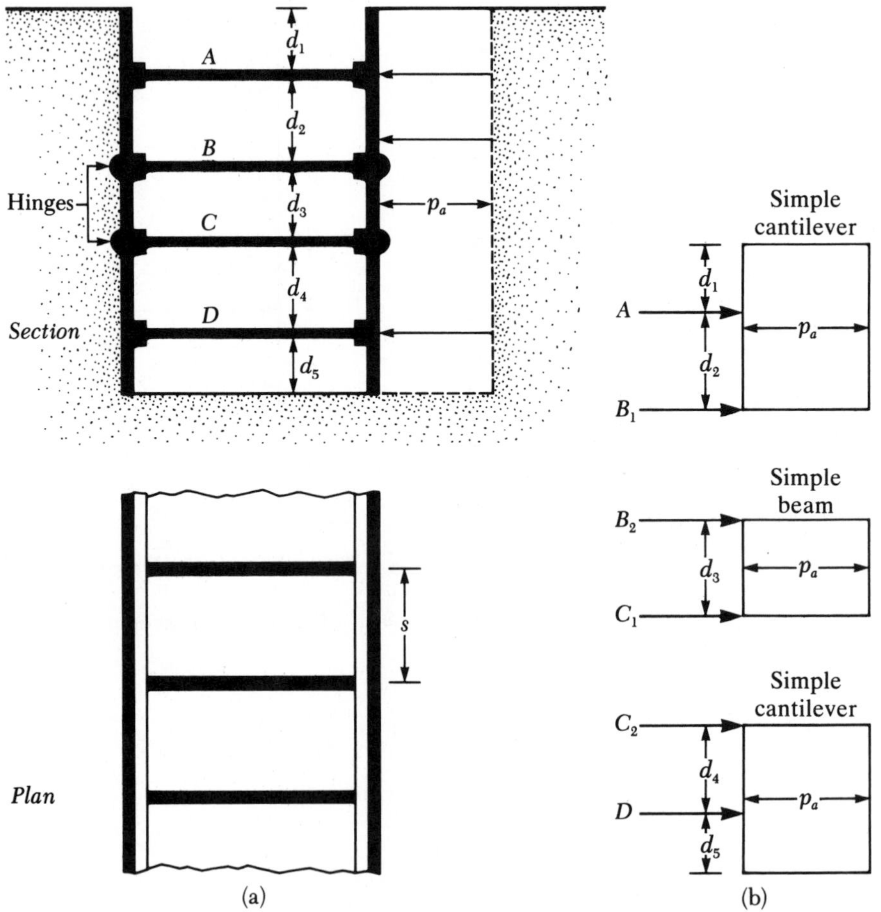

▼ **FIGURE 7.9** Determination of strut loads; (a) section and plan of the cut; (b) method for determining strut loads

sheet piles, or soldier beams, to be hinged at all strut levels, except for the top.)

2. Determine the reactions for the two simple cantilever beams (top and bottom) and all the simple beams between. In Figure 7.9b, these reactions are A, B_1, B_2, C_1, C_2, and D.
3. The strut loads in Figure 7.9 may be calculated as follows:

$$
\begin{aligned}
P_A &= (A)(s) \\
P_B &= (B_1 + B_2)(s) \\
P_C &= (C_1 + C_2)(s) \\
P_D &= (D)(s)
\end{aligned}
\tag{7.9}
$$

where P_A, P_B, P_C, P_D = loads to be taken by the individual struts at levels A, B, C, and D, respectively

A, B_1, B_2, C_1, C_2, D = reactions calculated in Step 2 (note unit: force/unit length of the braced cut)

s = horizontal spacing of the struts (see plan in Figure 7.9a)

4. Knowing the strut loads at each level and the intermediate bracing conditions allows selection of the proper sections from the steel construction manual.

Sheet Piles

The following steps are involved in designing the sheet piles.

1. For each of the sections shown in Figure 7.9b, determine the maximum bending moment.
2. Determine the maximum value of the maximum bending moments (M_{max}) obtained in step 1. Note that the unit of this moment will be, for example, lb-ft/ft (kN · m/m) length of the wall.
3. Obtain the required section modulus of the sheet piles:

$$S = \frac{M_{max}}{\sigma_{all}} \tag{7.10}$$

where σ_{all} = allowable flexural stress of the sheet pile material

4. Choose a sheet pile having a section modulus greater than or equal to the required section modulus from a table such as Table 6.1.

Wales

Wales may be treated as continuous horizontal members if they are spliced properly. Conservatively, they may also be treated as though they are pinned at the struts. For the section shown in Figure 7.9a, the maximum moments for the wales (assuming that they are pinned at the struts) are

$$\text{At level } A, \quad M_{max} = \frac{(A)(s^2)}{8}$$

$$\text{At level } B, \quad M_{max} = \frac{(B_1 + B_2)s^2}{8}$$

$$\text{At level } C, \quad M_{max} = \frac{(C_1 + C_2)s^2}{8}$$

$$\text{At level } D, \quad M_{max} = \frac{(D)(s^2)}{8}$$

where A, B_1, B_2, C_1, C_2, and D are the reactions under the struts per unit length of the wall (step 2 of strut design)

Determine the section modulus of the wales:

$$S = \frac{M_{\max}}{\sigma_{\text{all}}}$$

The wales are sometimes fastened to the sheet piles at points that satisfy the lateral support requirements.

▼ EXAMPLE 7.1

Figure 7.10 shows the cross section of a long braced cut.

a. Draw the pressure envelope.
b. Determine the strut loads at levels A, B, and C.
c. Determine the section modulus of the sheet pile required.
d. Determine the section modulus for the wales at level B.

The struts are placed 10 ft center-to-center.

Solution

Part a

$$\frac{\gamma H}{c} = \frac{(115)(22)}{750} = 3.37 < 4$$

So, the pressure envelope will be like the one in Figure 7.6. It is plotted in Figure 7.10 with a maximum pressure intensity, p_a, of $0.3\gamma H = 0.3(115)(22) =$ **759 lb/ft²**.

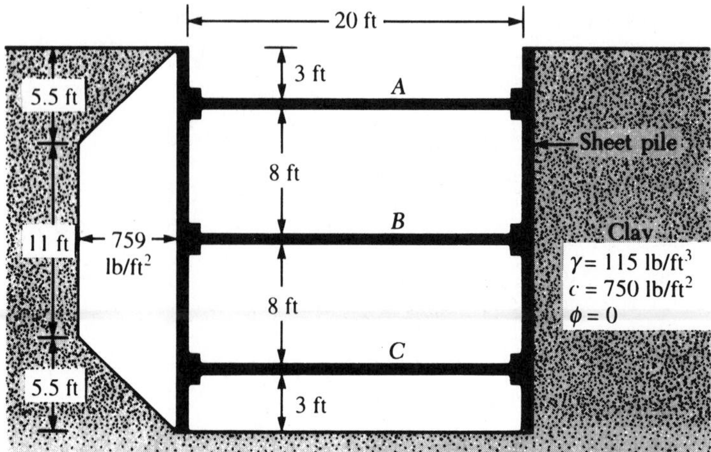

▼ **FIGURE 7.10**

Part b

To determine the strut loads, refer to Figure 7.11a. Taking the moment about B_1, $\Sigma M_{B_1} = 0$ and

$$A(8) - \frac{1}{2}(759)(5.5)\left(5.5 + \frac{5.5}{3}\right) - (5.5)(759)\left(\frac{5.5}{2}\right) = 0$$

$$8A - 15{,}306.5 - 11{,}479.9 = 0$$

$$A = 3348.3 \text{ lb}$$

Again, Σ vertical forces $= 0$ and

$$B_1 = \frac{1}{2}(5.5)(759) + (759)(5.5) - A$$

$$= 2913.5 \text{ lb}$$

Because of symmetry,

$$B_2 = 2913.5 \text{ lb}$$

$$C = 3348.3 \text{ lb}$$

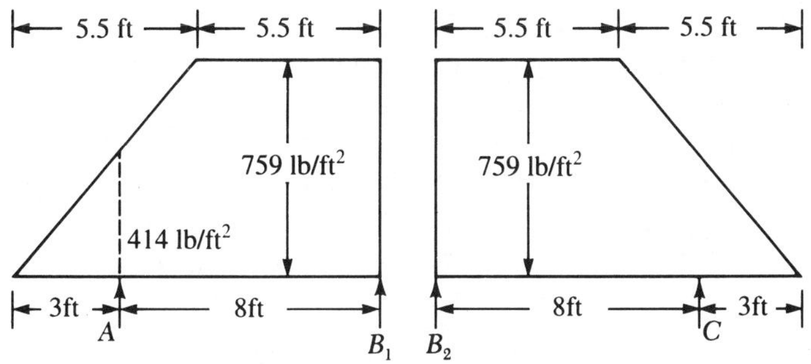

(a) Determination of reaction

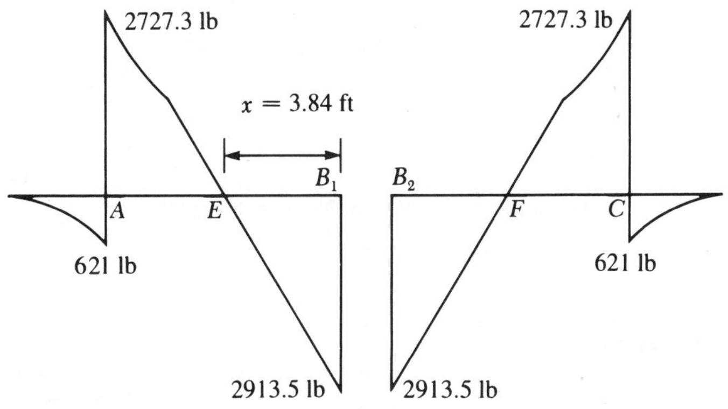

(b) Shear force diagram

▼ **FIGURE 7.11**

The strut loads at various levels are

$$P_A = (A)(\text{horizontal spacing of struts}) = (3348.3)(10) = 33{,}438 \text{ lb} \approx \mathbf{33.5 \text{ kip}}$$

$$P_B = (B_1 + B_2)(10) = (2913.5 + 2913.5)(10) = 58{,}270 \text{ lb} \approx \mathbf{58.3 \text{ kip}}$$

$$P_C = (3348.3)(10) \text{ lb} \approx \mathbf{33.5 \text{ kip}}$$

Part c

Refer to the left side of Figure 7.11a. For the maximum moment, the shear force should be zero. The nature of variation of the shear force is shown in Figure 7.11b, and the location of point E is

$$x = \frac{\text{reaction at } B_1}{759} = \frac{2913.5}{759} = 3.84 \text{ ft}$$

The magnitudes of the moments are

$$\text{At } A, \quad \frac{1}{2}(3)(414)\left(\frac{3}{3}\right) = 621 \text{ lb-ft/ft of wall}$$

$$\text{At } E, \quad \frac{1}{2}(3.84)(2913.5) \approx 5594 \text{ lb-ft/ft of wall}$$

Because the loading on the left and right sections of Figure 7.11a are the same, the magnitude of the moments at F and E (Figure 7.11b) will be the same as at C and A, respectively. Hence the maximum moment = 5594 lb-ft/ft of wall.

The section modulus of the sheet piles is

$$S = \frac{M_{max}}{\sigma_{all}} = \frac{(5594)(12) \text{ lb-in}}{25{,}000 \text{ lb/in}^2} = \mathbf{2.685 \text{ in}^3\text{/ft of wall}}$$

Part d

The reaction at level B was calculated in Part b. Hence

$$M_{max} = \frac{(B_1 + B_2)s^2}{8} = \frac{(2913.5 + 2913.5)(10)^2}{(8)(1000)} = 72.84 \text{ kip-ft}$$

The section modulus is

$$S = \frac{(72.84)(12) \text{ kip-in.}}{\sigma_{all}} = \frac{(72.84)(12)}{0.6F_y} = \frac{(72.84)(12)}{(0.6)(36)} = \mathbf{40.47 \text{ in}^3}. \quad ▼$$

▼ EXAMPLE 7.2

Refer to the braced cut shown in Figure 7.12, for which $\gamma = 112$ lb/ft³, $\phi = 32°$, and $c = 0$. The struts are located 12 ft on center in the plan. Draw the earth pressure envelope and determine the strut loads at levels A, B, and C.

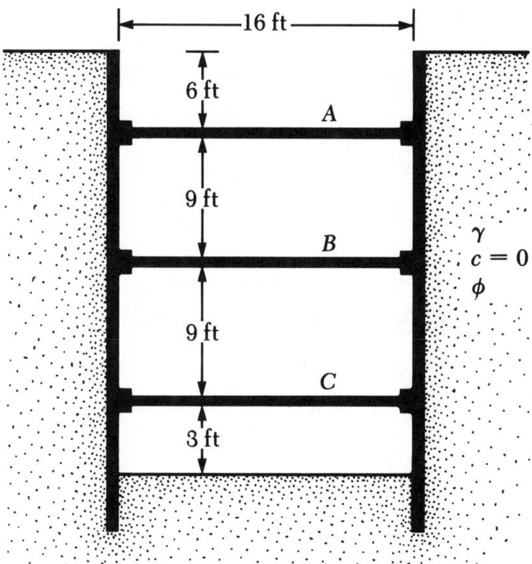

▼ **FIGURE 7.12**

Solution For this case, the earth pressure envelope shown in Figure 7.4 is applicable. Hence

$$K_a = \tan^2\left(45 - \frac{\phi}{2}\right) = \tan^2\left(45 - \frac{32}{2}\right) = 0.307$$

From Equation (7.2),

$$p_a = 0.65\gamma H K_a = (0.65)(112)(27)(0.307) = 603.44 \text{ lb/ft}^2$$

Figure 7.13a shows the pressure envelope. Refer to Figure 7.13b and calculate B_1:

$$\sum M_{B_1} = 0$$

$$A = \frac{(603.44)(15)\left(\frac{15}{2}\right)}{9} = 7543 \text{ lb/ft}$$

$$B_1 = (603.44)(15) - 7543 = 1508.6 \text{ lb/ft}$$

Now, refer to Figure 7.13c and calculate B_2:

$$\sum M_{B_2} = 0$$

$$C = \frac{(603.44)(12)\left(\frac{12}{2}\right)}{9} = 4827.5 \text{ lb/ft}$$

$$B_2 = (603.44)(12) - 4827.5 = 2413.7 \text{ lb/ft}$$

The strut loads are

At A, (7.543)(spacing) = (7.543)(12) = **90.52 kip**

At B, $(B_1 + B_2)$(spacing) = (1.509 + 2.414)(12) = **47.07 kip**

At C, (4.827) = (4.827)(12) = **57.93 kip.** ▼

▼ EXAMPLE 7.3

For the braced cut described in Example 7.2, determine:

a. The sheet pile section
b. The required section modulus of the wales at level A; assume that $\sigma_{all} =$ 24 kip/in^2

Solution

Part a

Refer to the load diagrams shown in Figure 7.13b and 7.13c. Figure 7.14 shows the shear force diagrams based on the load diagrams. First, determine x_1 and x_2:

$$x_1 = \frac{3.923}{0.603} = 6.5 \text{ ft}$$

$$x_2 = \frac{3.017}{0.603} = 5 \text{ ft}$$

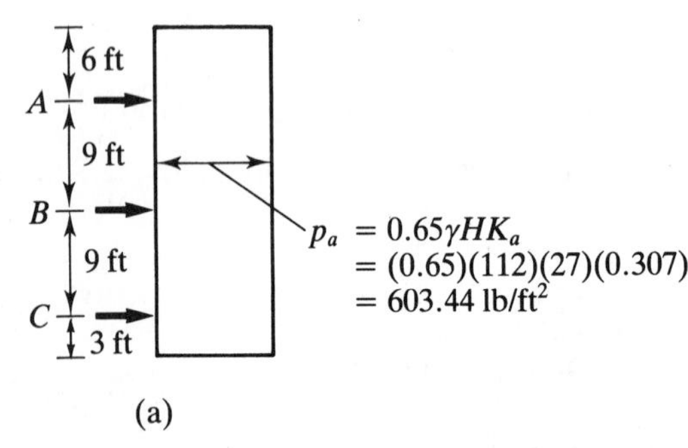

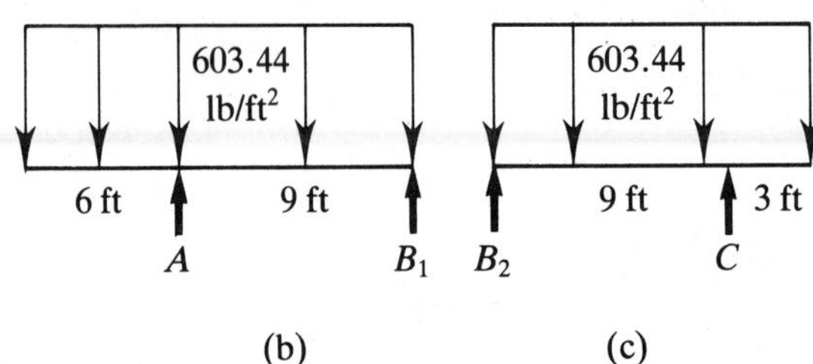

▼ FIGURE 7.13

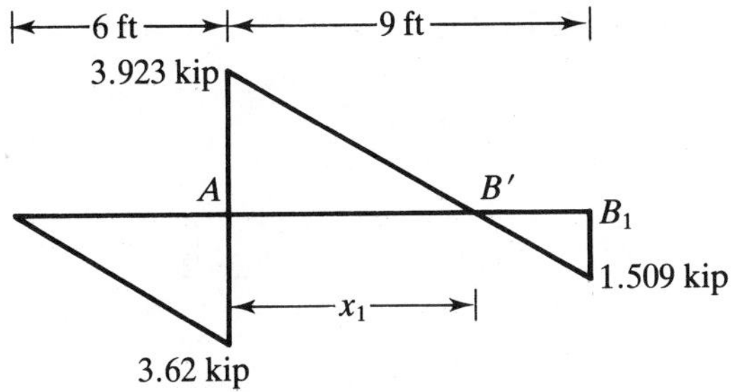

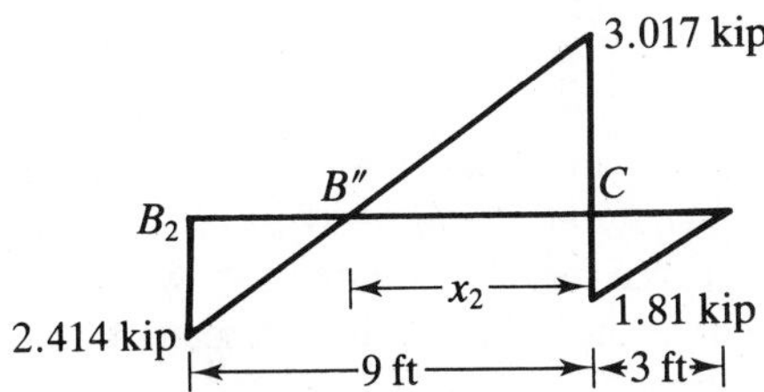

▼ **FIGURE 7.14**

Then the moments are

$$\text{At } A, \quad \frac{1}{2}(3.62)(6) = 10.86 \text{ kip-ft}$$

$$\text{At } C, \quad \frac{1}{2}(1.81)(3) = 2.715 \text{ kip-ft}$$

$$\text{At } B', \quad \frac{1}{2}(1.509)(2.5) = 1.89 \text{ kip-ft}$$

$$\text{At } B'', \quad \frac{1}{2}(2.414)(4) = 4.828 \text{ kip-ft}$$

M_A is maximum, so

$$S_x = \frac{M_{\max}}{\sigma_{\text{all}}} = \frac{(10.86 \text{ kip-ft})(12)}{24 \text{ kip/in}^2} = 5.43 \text{ in}^3$$

From Table 6.1,

Use PDA-27. S_x = 10.7 in^3/ft of wall.

(PMA-22 is just a little small.)

Part b

For the wale at level A,

$$M_{\max} = \frac{A(s^2)}{8}$$

$A = 7543$ lb/ft-(from Example 7.2). So

$$M_{\max} = \frac{(7.543)(12^2)}{8} = 135.77 \text{ kip-ft}$$

$$S_x = \frac{M_{\max}}{\sigma_{\text{all}}} = \frac{(135.77)(12)}{24 \text{ kip/in}^2} = \mathbf{67.9\ in^3/ft\ of\ wall}$$ ▼

7.5 HEAVE OF THE BOTTOM OF A CUT IN CLAY

Braced cuts in clay may become unstable as a result of heaving of the bottom of the excavation. Terzaghi (1943b) analyzed the factor of safety of braced excavations against bottom heave. The failure surface for such a case is shown in Figure 7.15. The vertical load per unit length of the cut at the bottom of the cut along line *bd* and *af* is

$$Q = \gamma H B_1 - cH \tag{7.11}$$

where $B_1 = 0.7B$
c = cohesion ($\phi = 0$ concept)

This load Q may be treated as a load per unit length on a continuous foundation at the level of *bd* (and *af*) and having a width of $B_1 = 0.7B$. Based on Terzaghi's bearing capacity theory, the net ultimate load-carrying capacity per unit length of this foundation (Chapter 3) is

$$Q_u = cN_c B_1 = 5.7cB_1$$

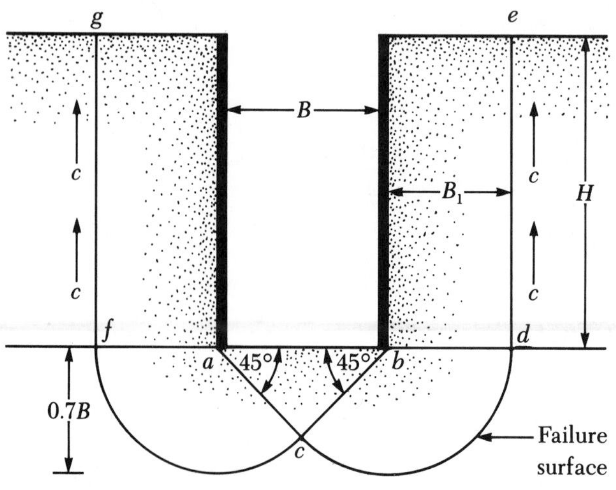

▼ **FIGURE 7.15** Factor of safety against bottom heave

Hence from Eq. (7.11), the factor of safety against bottom heave is

$$FS = \frac{Q_u}{Q} = \frac{5.7cB_1}{\gamma HB_1 - cH} = \frac{1}{H}\left(\frac{5.7c}{\gamma - \dfrac{c}{0.7B}}\right) \tag{7.12}$$

This factor of safety is based on the assumption that the clay layer is homogeneous, at least to a depth of $0.7B$ below the bottom of the cut. However, a *hard layer of rock or rocklike material at a depth of* $D < 0.7B$ will modify the failure surface to some extent. In such a case, the factor of safety becomes

$$FS = \frac{1}{H}\left(\frac{5.7c}{\gamma - c/D}\right) \tag{7.13}$$

Bjerrum and Eide (1956) also studied the problem of bottom heave for braced cuts in clay. For the factor of safety, they proposed:

$$FS = \frac{cN_c}{\gamma H} \tag{7.14}$$

The bearing capacity factor, N_c, varies with the ratios H/B and L/B (where L = length of the cut). For infinitely long cuts ($B/L = 0$), $N_c = 5.14$ at $H/B = 0$ and increases to $N_c = 7.6$ at $H/B = 4$. Beyond that—that is, for $H/B > 4$—the value of N_c remains constant. For cuts square in plan ($B/L = 1$), $N_c = 6.3$ at $H/B = 0$, and $N_c = 9$ for $H/B \geq 4$. In general, for any H/B,

$$N_{c(\text{rectangle})} = N_{c(\text{square})}\left(0.84 + 0.16\frac{B}{L}\right) \tag{7.15}$$

Figure 7.16 shows the variation of the value of N_c for $L/B = 1, 2, 3$, and ∞.

When Eqs. (7.14) and (7.15) are combined, the factor of safety against heave becomes

$$FS = \frac{cN_{c(\text{square})}\left(0.84 + 0.16\dfrac{B}{L}\right)}{\gamma H} \tag{7.16}$$

Equation (7.16) and the variation of the bearing capacity factor, N_c, as shown in Figure 7.16 are based on the assumptions that the clay layer below the bottom of the cut

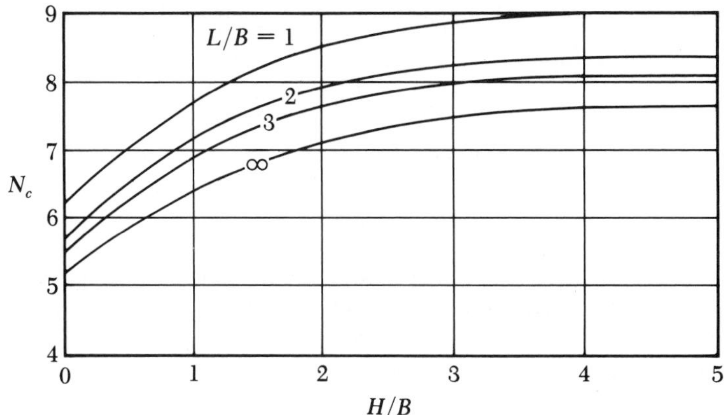

▼ **FIGURE 7.16** Variation of N_c with L/B and H/B [based on Bjerrum and Eide's equation, Eq. (7.15)]

is homogeneous and that the magnitude of the undrained cohesion in the soil that contains the failure surface is equal to c (Figure 7.17). However, if a stronger clay layer is encountered at a shallow depth, as shown in Figure 7.18a, the failure surface below the cut will be controlled by the undrained cohesions c_1 and c_2. For this type of condition, the factor of safety is

$$FS = \frac{c_1[N'_{c(\text{strip})}F_d]F_s}{\gamma H} \tag{7.17}$$

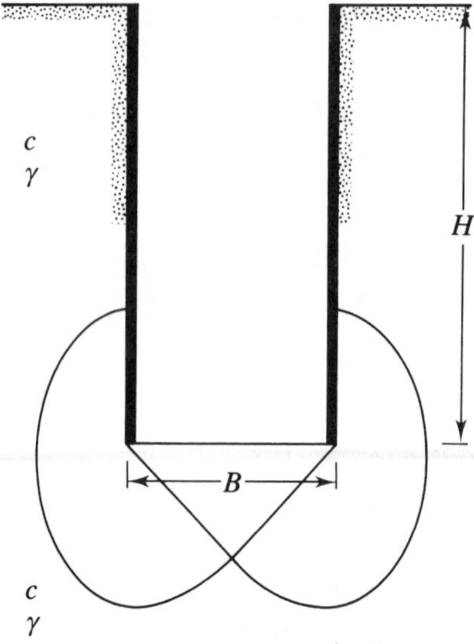

▼ **FIGURE 7.17** Derivation of Eq. (7.16)

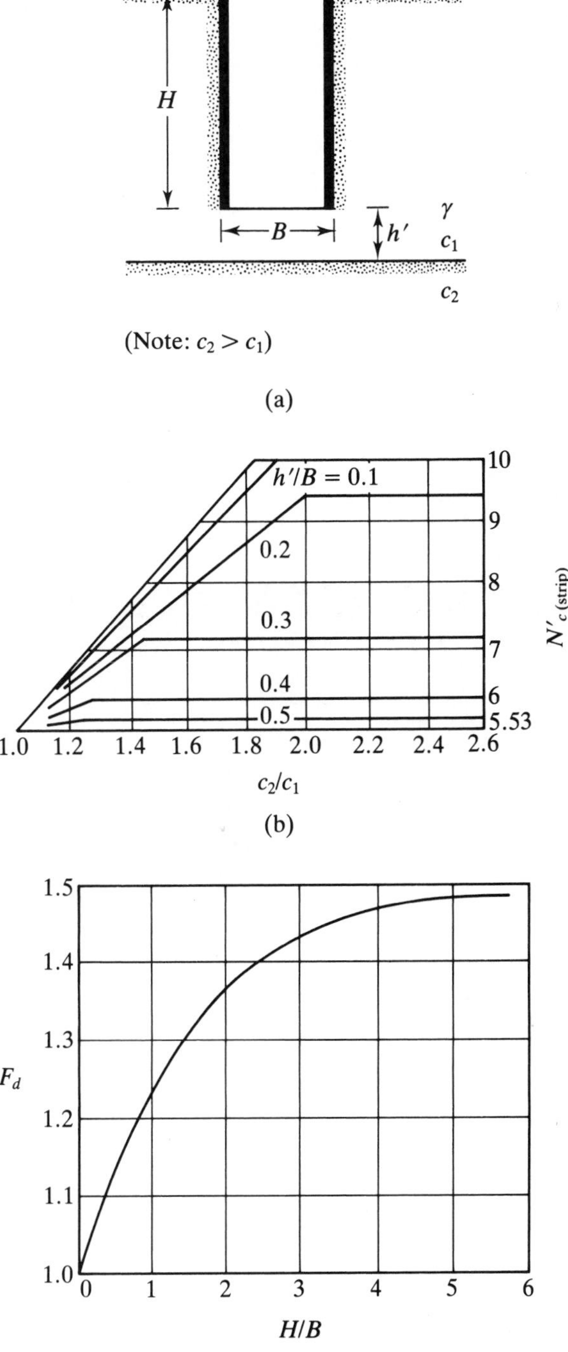

▼ **FIGURE 7.18** (a) Layered clay below the bottom of the cut; (b) variation of $N'_{c(\mathrm{strip})}$ with c_2/c_1 and h'/B (redrawn after Reddy and Srinivasan, 1967); and (c) variation of F_d with H/B

where $N'_{c(\text{strip})}$ = bearing capacity factor of an infinitely long cut ($B/L = 0$), which is a function of h'/B and c_2/c_1

F_d = depth factor, which is a function of H/B

F_s = shape factor

The variation of $N'_{c(\text{strip})}$ is shown in Figure 7.18b, and the variation of F_d as a function of H/B is given in Figure 7.18c. The shape factor, F_s, is

$$F_s = 1 + 0.2\frac{B}{L} \tag{7.18}$$

In most cases, a factor of safety of about 1.5 is generally recommended. If F_s becomes less than about 1.5, the sheet pile is driven deeper (Figure 7.19). Usually the depth, d is kept less than or equal to $B/2$. In that case, the force, P, per unit length of the buried sheet pile (aa' and bb') may be expressed as follows (U.S. Department of the Navy, 1971):

$$P = 0.7(\gamma HB - 1.4cH - \pi cB) \qquad \text{for } d > 0.47B \tag{7.19}$$

and

$$P = 1.5d\left(\gamma H - \frac{1.4cH}{B} - \pi c\right) \qquad \text{for } d < 0.47B \tag{7.20}$$

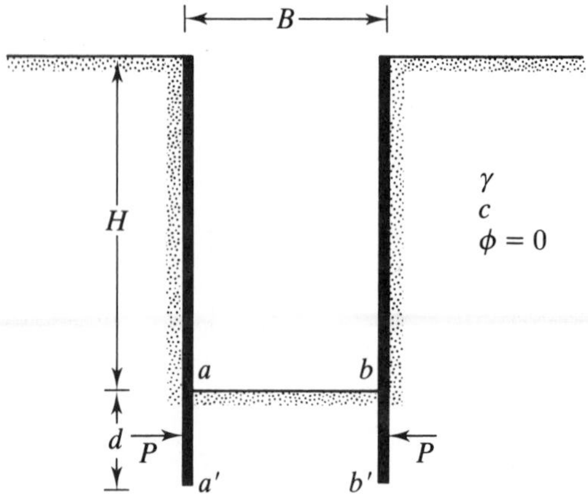

▼ **FIGURE 7.19** Force on the buried length of sheet pile

▼ EXAMPLE 7.4

A long braced cut in saturated clay has a width of cut, B, of 4.5 m and a depth of cut, H, of 8 m. For the clay, $\gamma = 17.2\ \text{kN/m}^3$ and $c = 42\ \text{kN/m}^2$. Determine the factor of safety against bottom heave by using

a. Eq. (7.12)
b. Eq. (7.14)

Assume that the clay extends to a great depth below the bottom of the cut.

Solution

Part a

$$FS = \frac{1}{H}\left(\frac{5.7c}{\gamma - \dfrac{c}{0.7B}}\right) = \frac{1}{8}\left(\frac{5.7 \times 42}{17.2 - \dfrac{42}{0.7 \times 4.5}}\right) = \mathbf{7.74}$$

Part b

$$FS = \frac{cN_c}{\gamma H}$$

From Figure 7.16 for $H/B = 8/4.5 = 1.78$ and $B/L \approx 0$, the magnitude of $N_c \approx 7$. So

$$FS = \frac{(42)(7)}{(17.2)(8)} = \mathbf{2.14}$$ ▼

▼ EXAMPLE 7.5

Refer to Example 7.4. If a stiffer clay layer ($c = 55\ \text{kN/m}^2$) is encountered 1.5 m below the bottom of the cut, what will be the factor of safety against bottom heave?

Solution For layered clay encountered below the bottom of the cut, use Eq. (7.17). Refer to Figure 7.18a. First,

$$\frac{c_2}{c_1} = \frac{55}{42} = 1.31$$

$$\frac{h'}{B} = \frac{1.5}{4.5} = 0.33$$

From Figure 7.18b for $c_2/c_1 = 1.31$ and $h'/B \approx 0.33$, the magnitude of $N_{c(\text{strip})} \approx 6.5$. Again,

$$\frac{H}{B} = \frac{8}{4.5} = 1.78$$

So, from Figure 7.18c, $F_d \approx 1.34$. Also,

$$F_s = 1 + 0.2\left(\frac{B}{L}\right) = 1 + 0.2\left(\frac{10}{\infty}\right) = 1.0$$

So

$$FS = \frac{c_1[N'_{c(\text{strip})} F_d] F_s}{\gamma H} = \frac{(42)[(6.5)(1.34)](1.0)}{(17.2)(8)} = \mathbf{2.66}$$ ▼

7.6 STABILITY OF THE BOTTOM OF A CUT IN SAND

The bottom of a cut in sand is generally stable. When the water table is encountered, the bottom of the cut is stable as long as the water level inside the excavation is higher than the groundwater level. In case dewatering is needed (Figure 7.20), the factor of safety against piping should be checked. [*Piping* is another term for failure by heave, as defined in Section 1.12; see Eq. (1.48)]. Piping may occur when a high hydraulic gradient is created by water flowing into the excavation. To check the factor of safety, draw flow nets and determine the maximum exit gradient [$i_{\max(\text{exit})}$] that will occur at points A and B. Figure 7.21 shows such a flow net, for which the maximum exit gradient is

$$i_{\max(\text{exit})} = \frac{\frac{h}{N_d}}{a} = \frac{h}{N_d a} \tag{7.21}$$

where a = length of the flow element at A (or B)
N_d = number of drops (*note:* in Figure 7.21, $N_d = 8$—also see Section 1.10)

The factor of safety against piping may be expressed as

$$FS = \frac{i_{\text{cr}}}{i_{\max(\text{exit})}} \tag{7.22}$$

where i_{cr} = critical hydraulic gradient

The relationship for i_{cr} was given in Chapter 1 as

$$i_{\text{cr}} = \frac{G_s - 1}{e + 1}$$

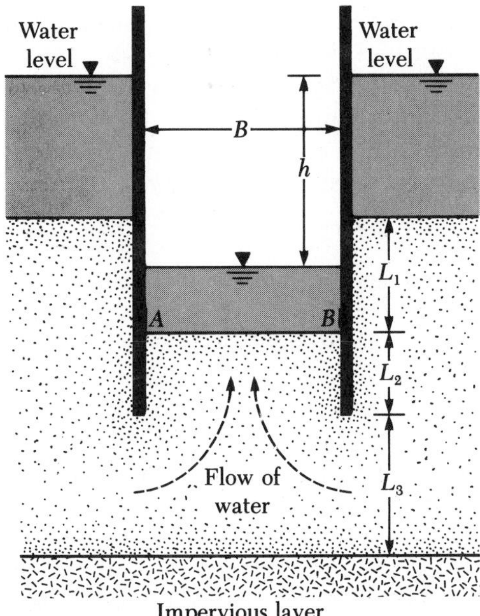

▼ **FIGURE 7.20**

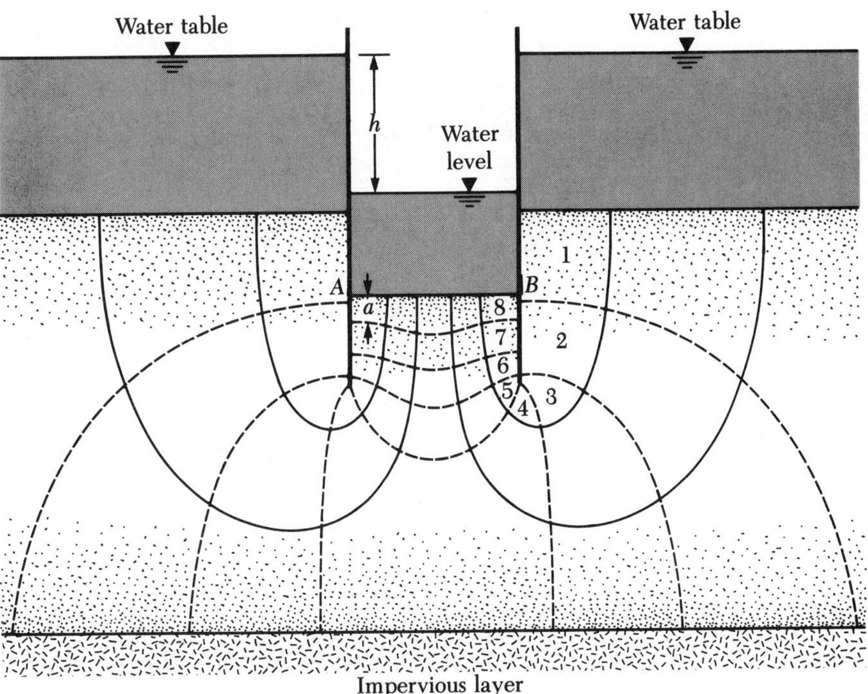

▼ **FIGURE 7.21** Determining the factor of safety against piping by drawing flow net

The magnitude of i_{cr} varies between 0.9 and 1.1 in most soils, with an average of about 1. A factor of safety of about 1.5 is desirable.

The maximum exit gradient for sheeted excavations in sands with $L_3 = \infty$ can also be evaluated theoretically (Harr, 1962). (Only the results of these mathematical derivations will be presented here. For further details, refer to the original work.) To calculate the maximum exit gradient, refer to Figures 7.22 and 7.23 and perform the following steps.

1. Determine the modulus, m, from Figure 7.22 by obtaining $2L_2/B$ (or $B/2L_2$) and $2L_1/B$.
2. With the known modulus and $2L_1/B$, refer to Figure 7.23 and determine $L_2 i_{\text{exit(max)}}/h$. Because L_2 and h will be known, $i_{\text{exit(max)}}$ can be calculated.
3. The factor of safety against piping can be evaluated by using Eq. (7.22).

Marsland (1958) presented the results of model tests conducted to study the influence of seepage on the stability of sheeted excavations in sand. They were summarized by the U.S. Department of the Navy (1971) in *NAVFAC DM-7* and are given in Figure 7.24a, b, and c (page 451). Note that Figure 7.24b is for the case of determining the sheet pile penetration (L_2) needed for the required factor of safety against piping when the sand layer extends to a great depth below the excavation. However, Figure 7.24c represents the case in which an impervious layer lies at depth $L_2 + L_3$ below the bottom of the excavation.

▼ EXAMPLE 7.6

Refer to Figure 7.20, for which $h = 4.5$ m, $L_1 = 5$ m, $L_2 = 4$ m, $B = 5$ m, and $L_3 = \infty$. Determine the factor of safety against piping.

Solution

$$\frac{2L_1}{B} = \frac{2(5)}{5} = 2$$

$$\frac{B}{2L_2} = \frac{5}{2(4)} = 0.625$$

According to Figure 7.22b for $2L_1/B = 2$ and $B/2L_2 = 0.625$, $m \approx 0.033$. From Figure 7.23a for $m = 0.033$ and $2L_1/B = 2$, $L_2 i_{\text{exit(max)}}/h = 0.55$. Hence

$$i_{\text{exit(max)}} = \frac{0.55(h)}{L_2} = 0.55(4.5)/4 = 0.619$$

$$FS = \frac{i_{cr}}{i_{\text{max(exit)}}} = \frac{1}{0.619} = \mathbf{1.616.}$$ ▼

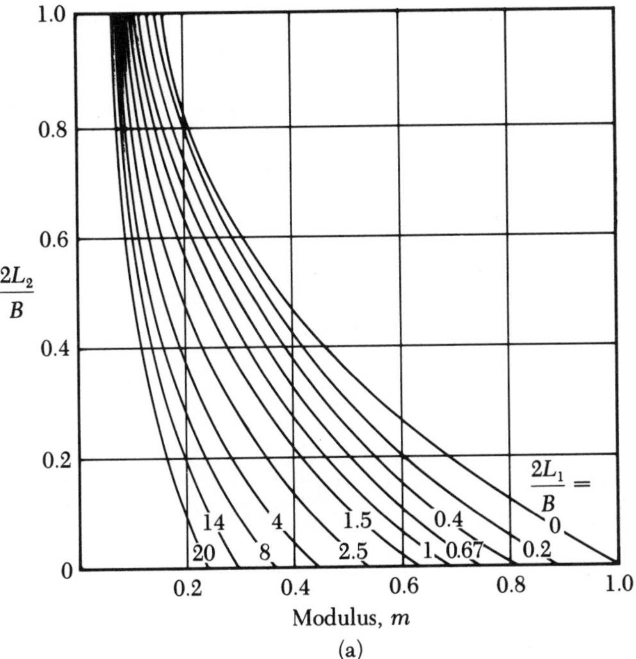

(a)

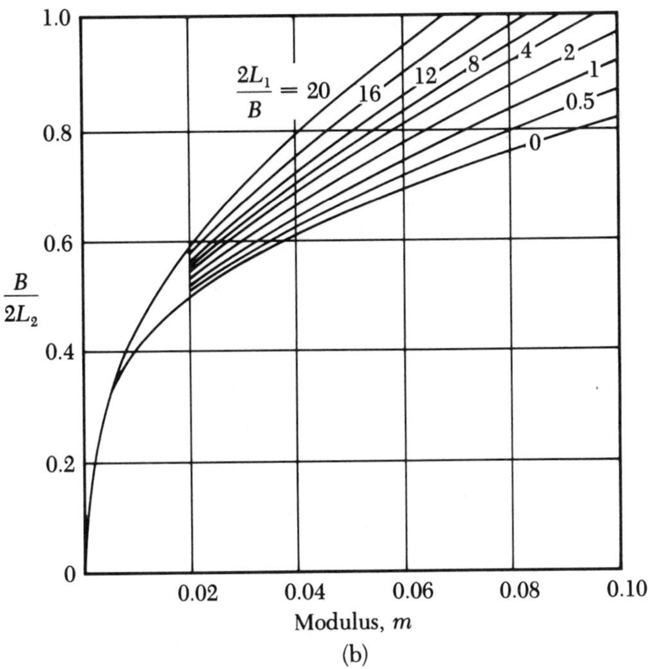

(b)

▼ **FIGURE 7.22** Variation of modulus (from *Groundwater and Seepage*, by M. E. Harr. Copyright © 1962 by McGraw-Hill. Used with permission.)

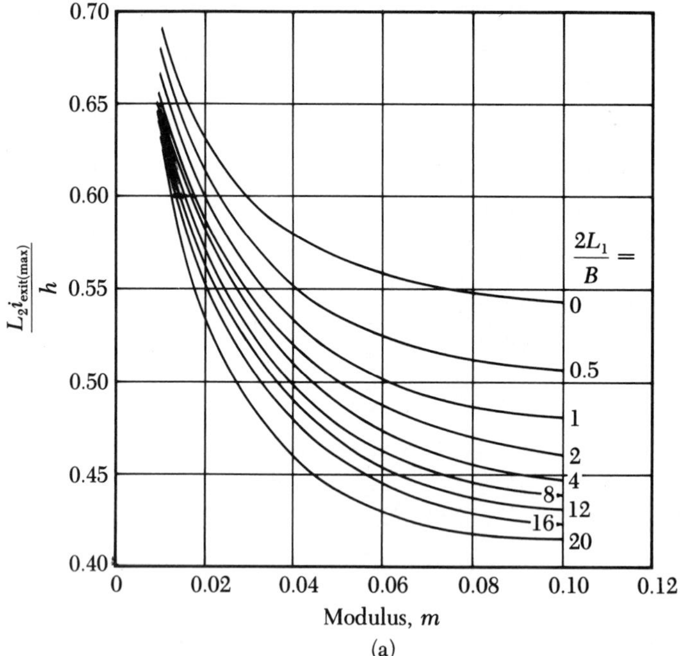

(a)

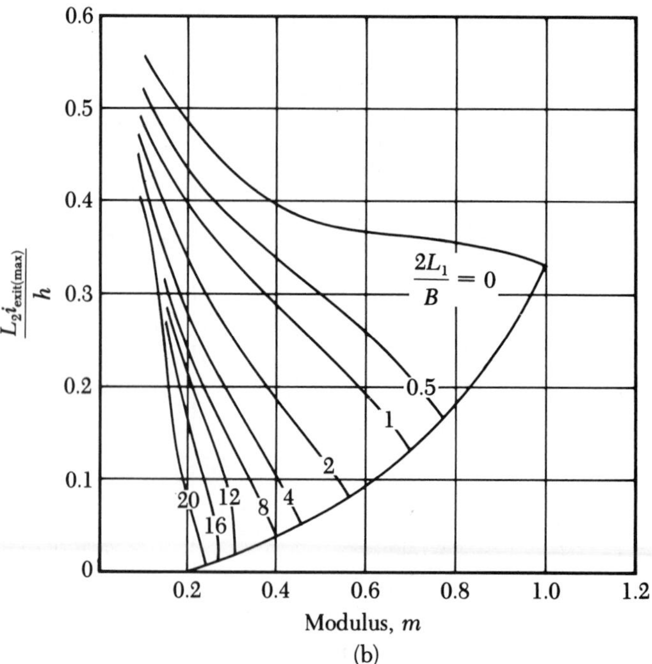

(b)

▼ **FIGURE 7.23** Variation of maximum exit gradient with modulus (from *Groundwater and Seepage*, by M. E. Harr. Copyright © 1962 by McGraw-Hill. Used with permission.)

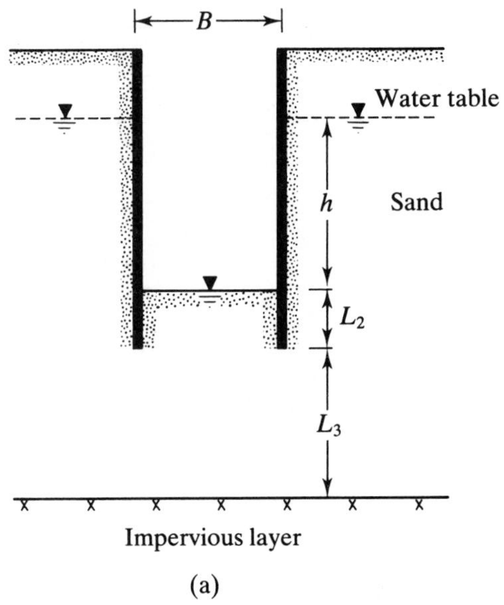

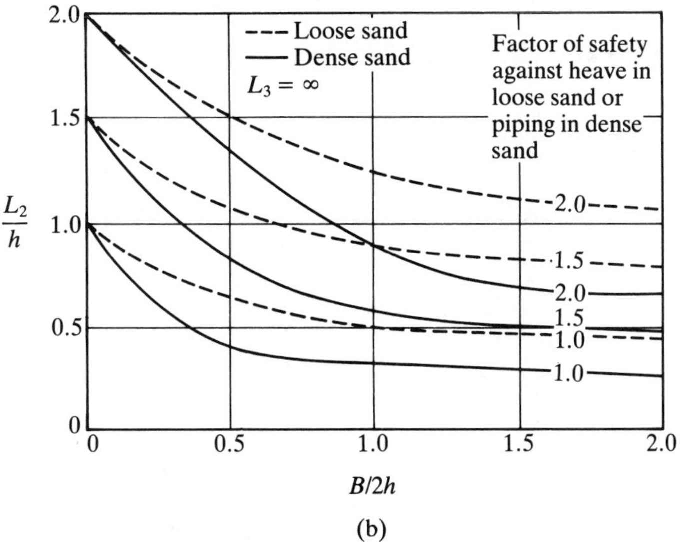

FIGURE 7.24 Influence of seepage on the stability of sheeted excavation (after U.S. Department of the Navy, 1971)

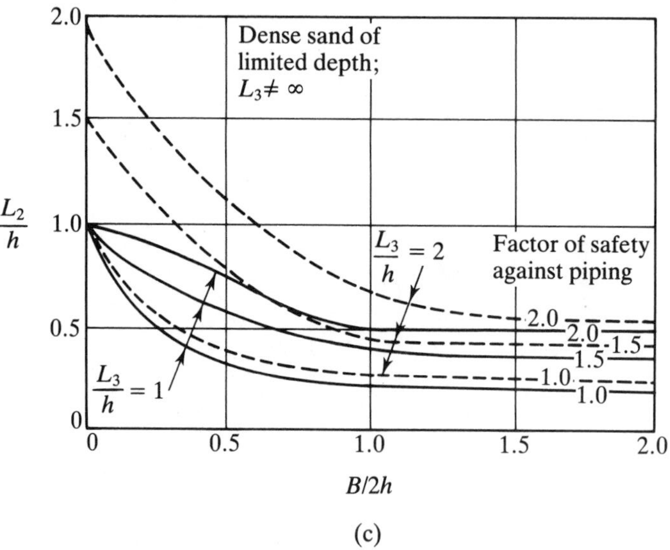

FIGURE 7.24 (CONTINUED)

7.7 LATERAL YIELDING OF SHEET PILES AND GROUND SETTLEMENT

In braced cuts, some lateral movement of sheet pile walls may be expected (Figure 7.25). The amount of lateral yield depends on several factors, the most important of which is the elapsed time between excavation and placement of wales and struts. Mana and Clough (1981) analyzed the field records of several braced cuts in clay from the San Francisco, Oslo (Norway), Boston, Chicago, and Bowline Point (New York) areas. Under ordinary construction conditions, they found that the maximum lateral wall yield, $\delta_{H(\max)}$, has a definite relationship with the factor of safety against heave, as shown in Figure 7.25. Note that the factor of safety against heave plotted in Figure 7.25 was calculated by using Eqs. (7.12) and (7.13).

As discussed before, in several instances the sheet piles (or the soldier piles, as the case may be) are driven to a certain depth below the bottom of the excavation. The reason is to reduce the lateral yielding of the walls during the last stages of excavation. Lateral yielding of the walls will cause the ground surface surrounding the cut to settle. The degree of lateral yielding, however, depends mostly on the soil type below the bottom of the cut. If clay below the cut extends to a great depth and $\gamma H/c$ is less than about 6, extension of the sheet piles or soldier piles below the bottom of the cut will help considerably in reducing the lateral yield of the walls.

However, under similar circumstances, if $\gamma H/c$ is about 8, the extension of sheet piles into the clay below the cut does not help greatly. In such circumstances, we may expect a great degree of wall yielding that may result in the total collapse of the bracing systems. If a hard soil layer lies below a clay layer at the bottom of the cut, the piles should be embedded in the stiffer layer. This action will greatly reduce lateral yield.

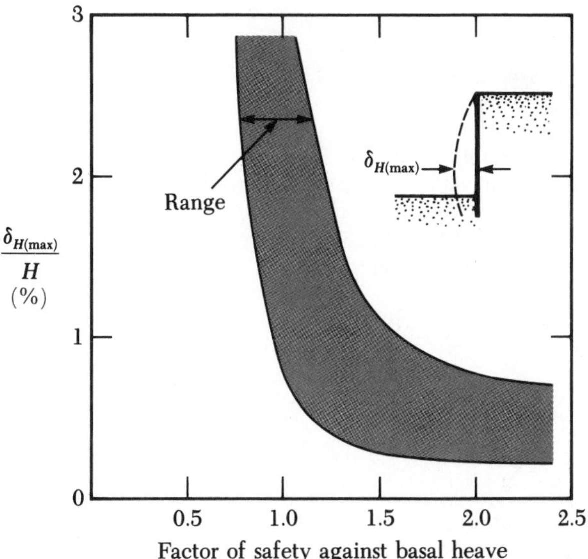

▼ **FIGURE 7.25** Range of variation of $\delta_{H(max)}/H$ with FS against basal heave from field observation (redrawn after Mana and Clough, 1981)

The lateral yielding of walls will generally induce ground settlement, δ_V, around a braced cut, which is generally referred to as *ground loss*. Based on several field observations, Peck (1969) provided curves for predicting ground setlement in various types of soil (see Figure 7.26). The magnitude of ground loss varies extensively; however, Figure 7.26 may be used as a general guide.

Based on the field data obtained from various cuts in the areas of San Francisco, Oslo, and Chicago, Mana and Clough (1981) provided a correlation between the maximum lateral yield of sheet piles, $\delta_{H(max)}$, and the maximum ground settlement, $\delta_{V(max)}$. It is shown in Figure 7.27. Note that

$$\delta_{V(max)} \approx 0.5\delta_{H(max)} \quad \text{to} \quad 1.0\delta_{H(max)} \tag{7.23}$$

7.8 CASE STUDIES OF BRACED CUTS

The procedure of determining strut loads and the design of sheet piles and wales presented in the preceding sections appears to be fairly straightforward. It is, however, only possible if a proper pressure envelope is chosen for the design, which is difficult. This section describes some case studies of braced cuts and highlights the difficulties and degree of judgment needed for successful completion of various projects.

Subway Extension of the Massachusetts Bay Transportation Authority (MBTA)

Lambe (1970) provided data on the performance of three excavations for the subway extension of the MBTA in Boston (test sections A, B, and D), all of which were well

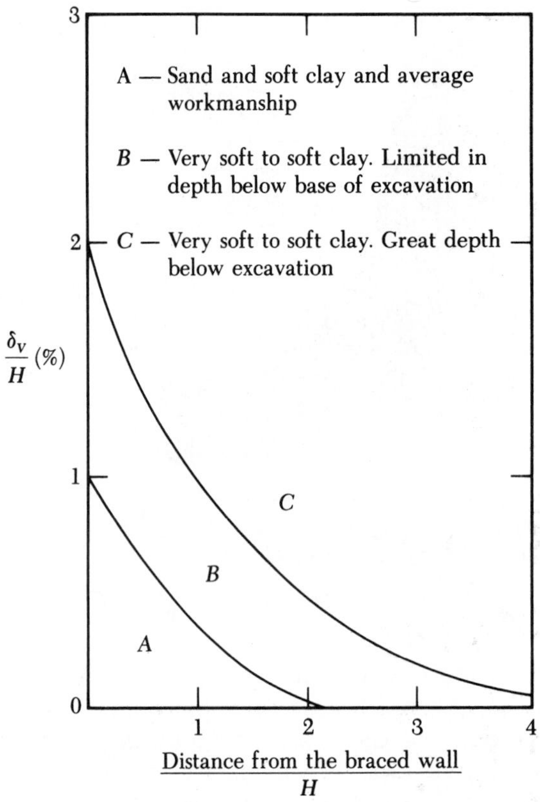

▼ **FIGURE 7.26** Variation of ground settlement with distance (after Peck, 1969)

instrumented. Figure 7.28 gives the details of test section B, where the cut was 58 ft ($\approx$18 m), including subsoil conditions. The subsoil consisted of gravel, sand, silt, and clay (fill) to a depth of about 26 ft (8 m), followed by a light gray, slightly organic silt to a depth of 46 ft (14 m). A layer of coarse sand and gravel with some clay was present from 46 ft to 54 ft (14 m to 16.5 m) below the ground surface. Rock was encountered below 54 ft (16.5 m). The details of the struts and wales are given below. The horizontal spacing of the struts was 12 ft (3.66 m) center-to-center.

Strut level	*Depth (ft)*	*Section of wales*	*Section of struts*
S1	4	14BP89	36WF150
S2	23	27WF160	14WF153
S3	36	27WF177	14WF167
S4	46	27WF160	14WF158
S5	52	27WF177	14WF167

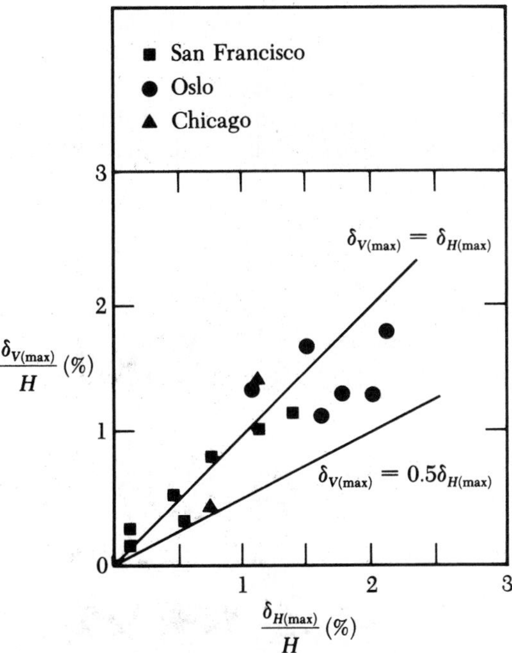

FIGURE 7.27 Variation of maximum lateral yield with maximum ground settlement (after Mana and Clough, 1981)

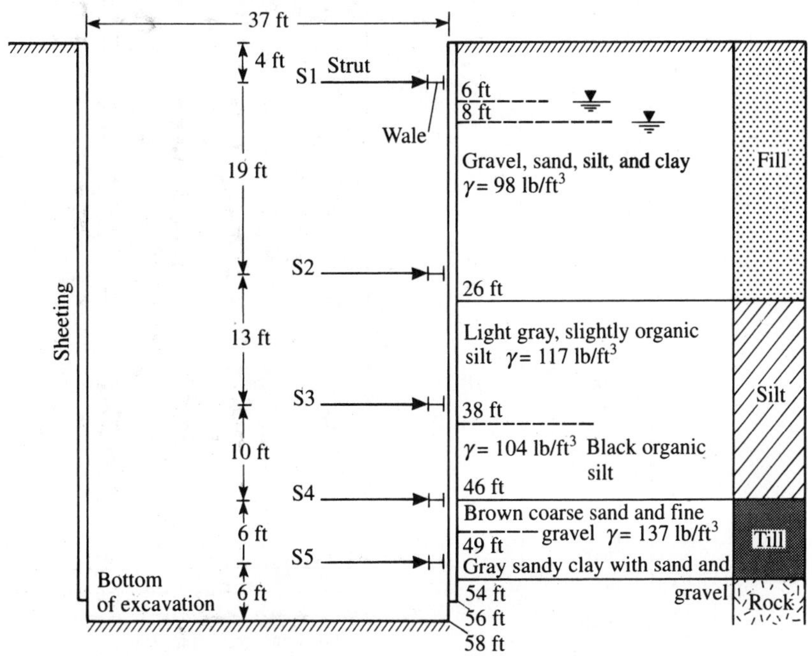

FIGURE 7.28 Test section B for subway extension, MBTA (after Lambe, 1970)

Because the apparent pressure envelopes available (Sections 7.2 and 7.3) are for *sand* and *clay* only, questions may arise about how to treat the fill, silt, and till. Figure 7.29 shows the apparent pressure envelopes proposed by Peck (1969), considering the soil as *sand* and also as *clay*, to overcome that problem. For the average soil parameters of the profile, the following values of p_a were used to develop the pressure envelopes shown in Figure 7.29.

Sand

$$p_a = 0.65\gamma H K_a \tag{7.2}$$

For $\gamma = 114\ \text{lb/ft}^3$, $H = 58$ ft, and $K_a = 0.26$,

$$p_a = (0.65)(114)(58)(0.26) = 1117\ \text{lb/ft}^2 \approx 1.12\ \text{kip/ft}^2$$

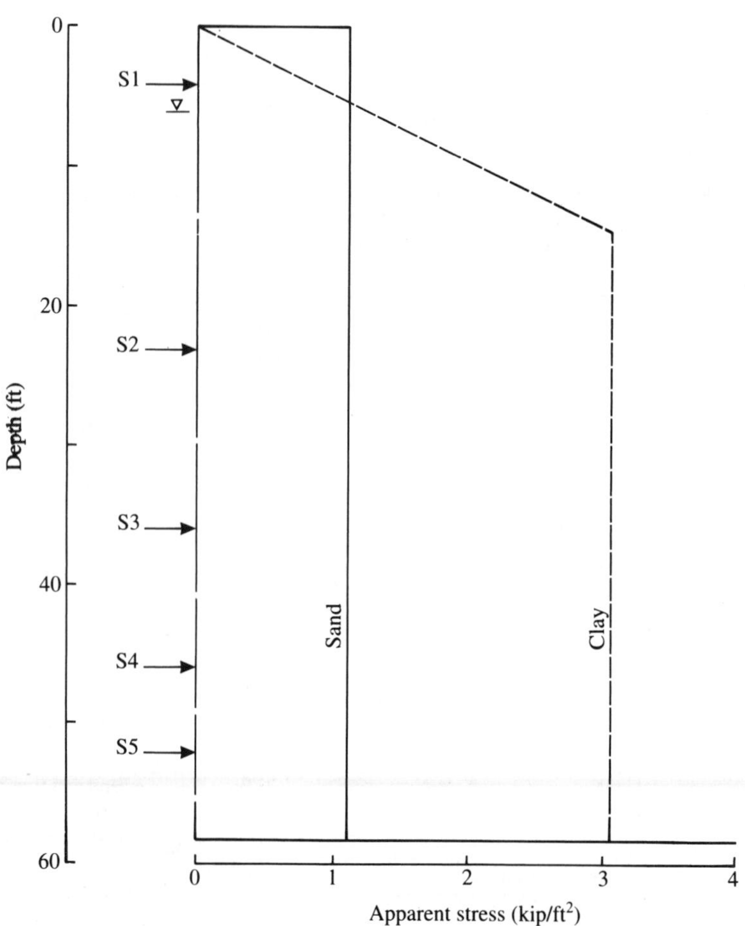

▼ **FIGURE 7.29** Apparent pressure envelopes for test section B, MBTA (after Lambe, 1970)

Clay

$$p_a = \gamma H\left[1 - \left(\frac{4c}{\gamma H}\right)\right] \tag{7.3}$$

For $c = 890\ \text{lb/ft}^2$,

$$p_a = (114)(58)\left[1 - \frac{(4)(890)}{(114)(58)}\right] = 3052\ \text{lb/ft}^2 \approx 3.05\ \text{kip/ft}^2$$

Figure 7.30 shows the variations of the strut load, based on the assumed pressure envelopes shown in Figure 7.29. Also shown in Figure 7.30 are the measured strut loads in the field and the design strut loads. This comparison indicates that:

1. In most cases the measured strut loads differed widely from those predicted. This result is due primarily to the uncertainties involved in the assumption of the soil parameters.
2. The actual design strut loads were substantially higher than those measured.

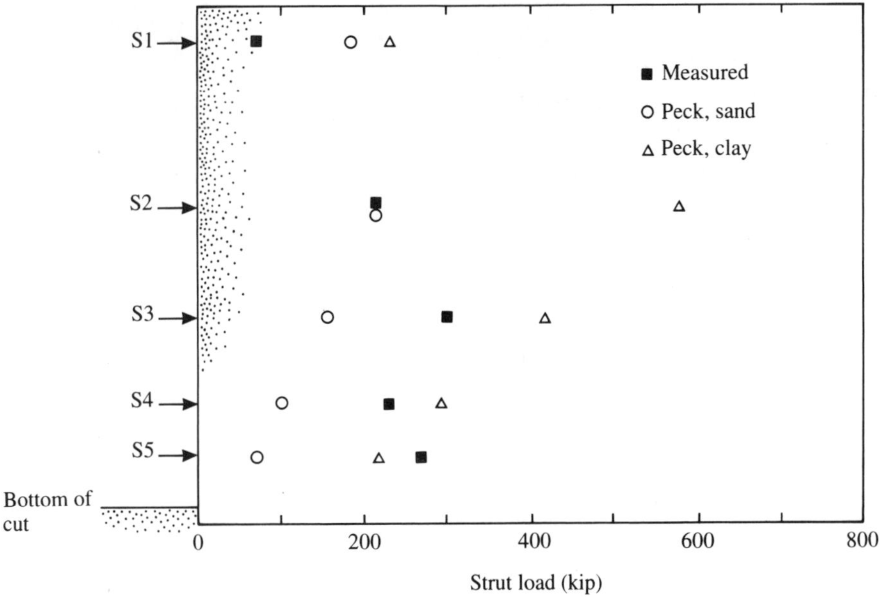

▼ **FIGURE 7.30** Measured and predicted strut loads, test section B, MBTA (after Lambe, 1970)

Figure 7.31 shows test section A for the subway extension along with the soil profile. The measured and predicted strut loads for this section (similar to Figure 7.30) are shown in Figure 7.32. Considering the uncertainties involved, the general agreement between the measured and predicted values is quite good.

Figure 7.33 shows soil movements in the vicinity of sections A and B in nondimensional form (δ_V/H and δ_H/H). They appear to be in general agreement with those presented in Section 7.7.

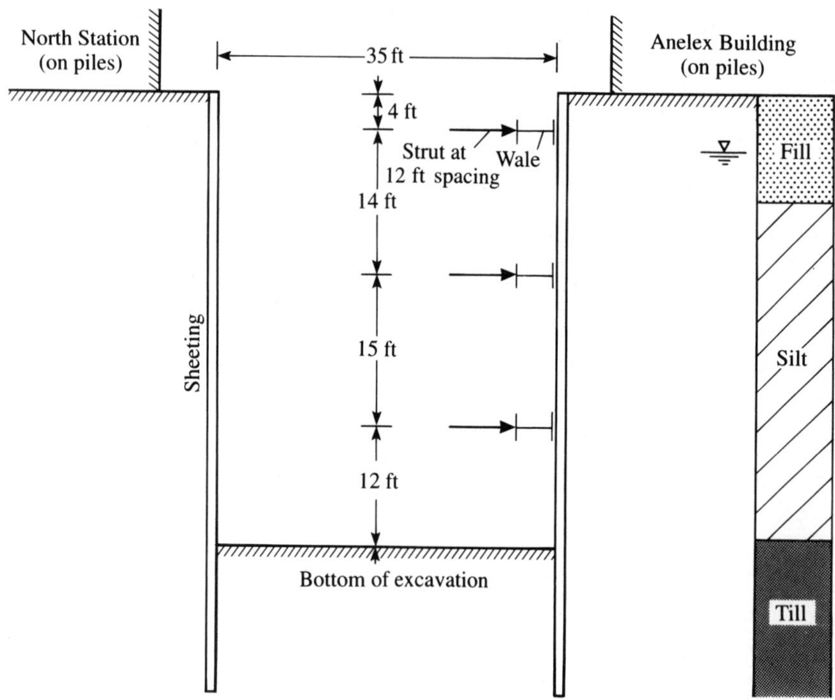

▼ **FIGURE 7.31** Test section A for subway extension, MBTA (after Lambe, 1970)

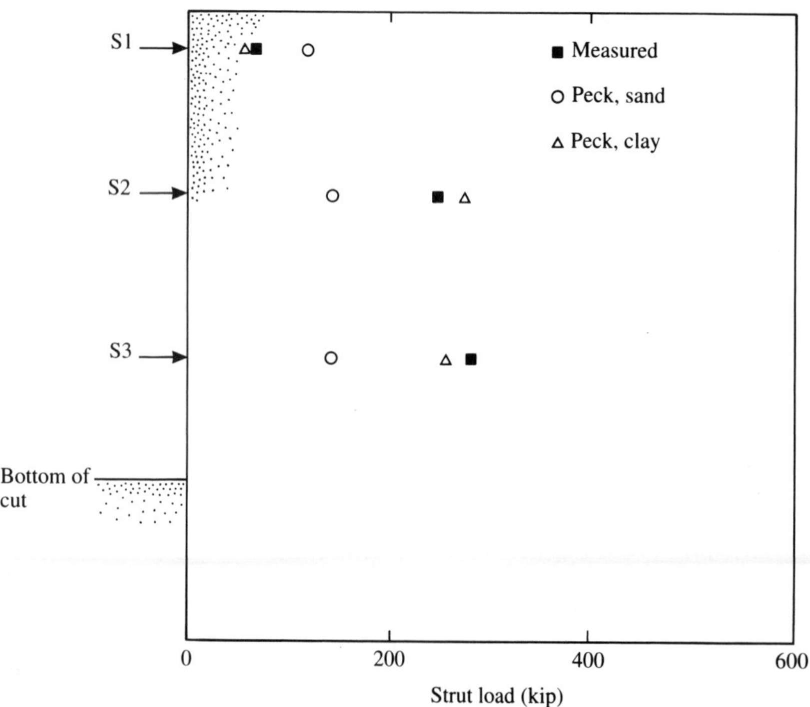

▼ **FIGURE 7.32** Measured and predicted strut loads, test section A, MBTA (after Lambe, 1970)

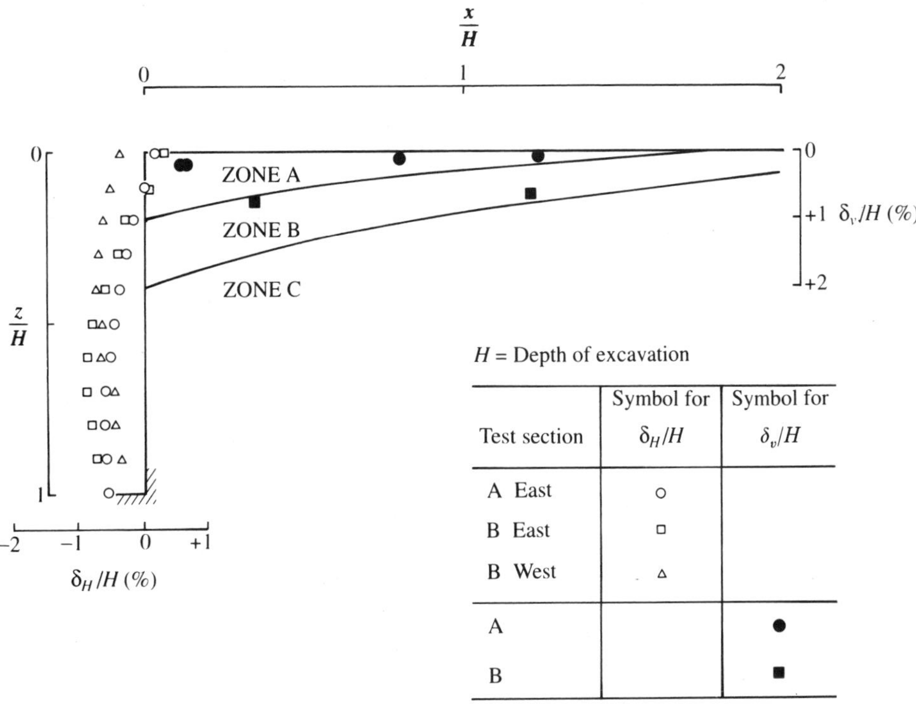

Test section	Symbol for δ_H/H	Symbol for δ_v/H
A East	○	
B East	□	
B West	△	
A		●
B		■

▼ **FIGURE 7.33** Variation of δ_H/H and δ_v/H in the vicinity of test sections A and B, MBTA (after Lambe, 1970)

Construction of National Plaza (South Half) in Chicago

The construction of the south half of the National Plaza in Chicago required a braced cut 70 ft ($\approx$21 m) deep. Swatek et al. (1972) reported the case history for this construction. Figure 7.34 shows a schematic diagram for the braced cut and the subsoil profile. There were six levels of struts. The following table gives the actual maximum wale and strut loads.

Strut level	*Elevation (ft)*	*Load measured (kip/ft)*
A	+3	16.0
B	−6	26.5
C	−15	29.0
D	−24.5	29.0
E	−34	29.0
F	−44.5	30.7
		Σ 160.2

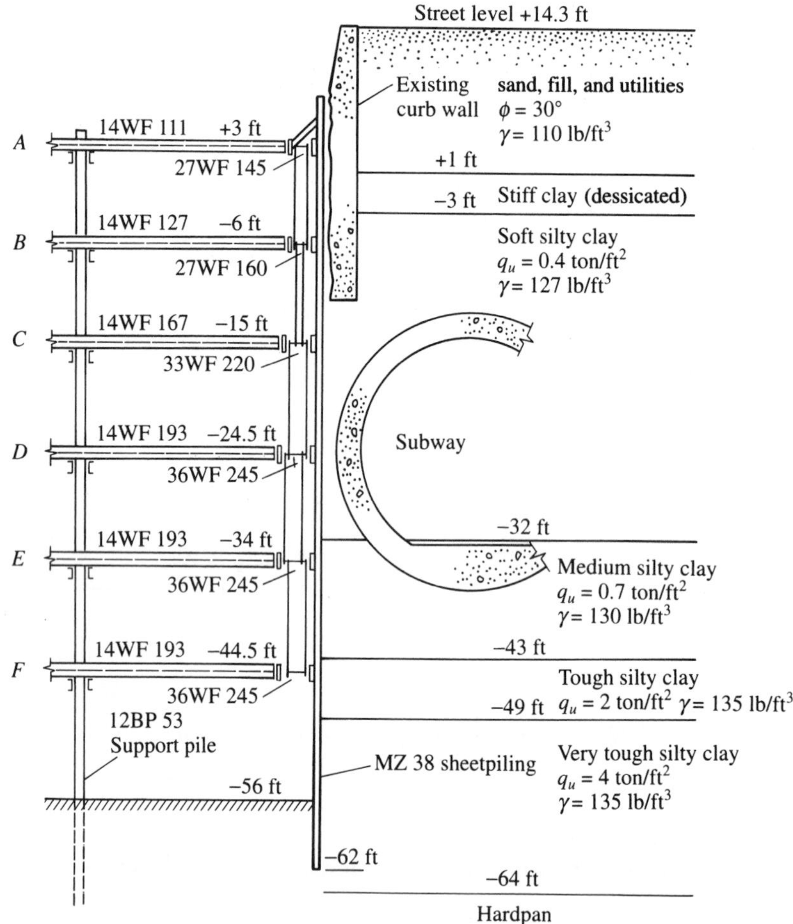

▼ **FIGURE 7.34** Schematic diagram of braced cut and subsoil profile, National Plaza of Chicago (after Swatek et al., 1972)

Figure 7.35 presents a lateral earth pressure envelope based on the maximum wale loads measured. To compare the theoretical prediction to the actual observation requires making an approximate calculation. To do so, we convert the clayey soil layers from Elevation +1 ft to −56 ft to a single equivalent layer by using Eq. (7.7).

Elevation (ft)	*Thickness, H_i (ft)*	*c (lb/ft²)*	*Equivalent c (lb/ft²)*
+1 to −32 ft	33	400	$c_{av} = \frac{1}{57}[(33)(400) + (11)(700) + (6)(2000) + (7)(4000)]$
−32 ft to −43 ft	11	700	
−43 ft to −49 ft	6	2000	$= 1068$ lb/ft²
−49 ft to −56 ft	7	4000	$q_u = 2136$ lb/ft²
	Σ 57		

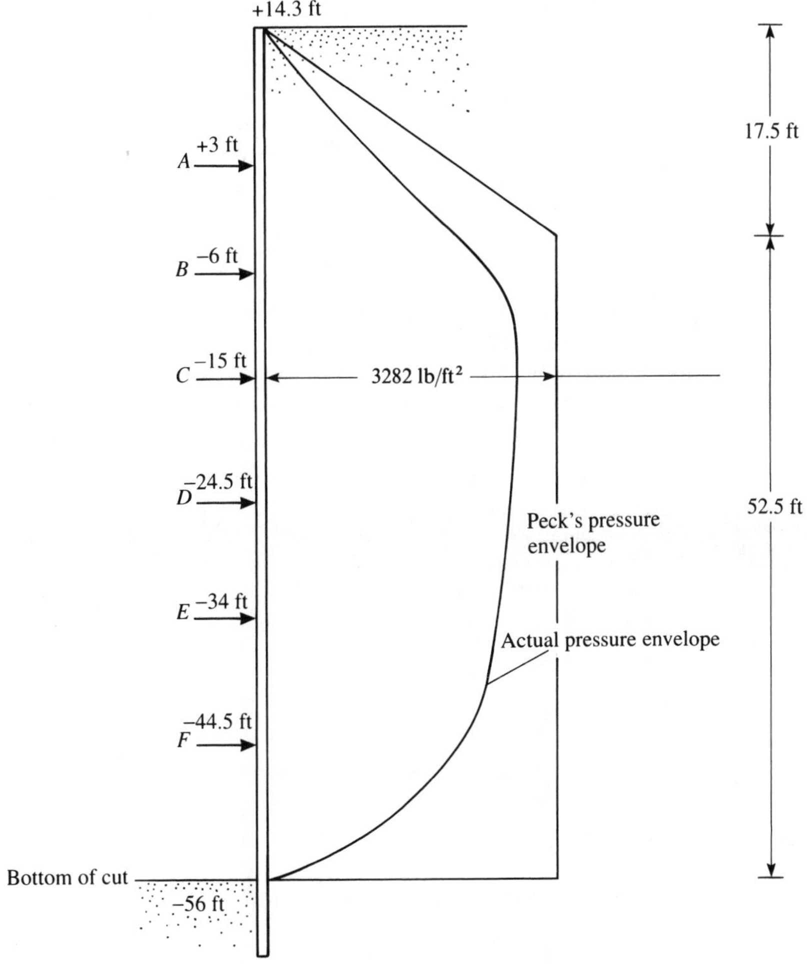

▼ **FIGURE 7.35** Comparison of actual and Peck's pressure envelopes

Now, using Eq. (7.5), we can convert the sand layer located between elevations +14 ft and +1 ft and the equivalent clay layer of 57 ft to one equivalent clay layer with a thickness of 70 ft:

$$c_{av} = \frac{1}{2H}[\gamma_s K_s H_s^2 \tan \phi_s + (H - H_s)n'q_u]$$

$$= \left[\frac{1}{(2)(70)}\right][(110)(1)(13)^2 \tan 30 + (57)(0.75)(2 \times 2136)] \approx 1381 \text{ lb/ft}^2$$

Equation (7.8) gives

$$\gamma_{av} = \frac{1}{H}(\gamma_1 H_1 + \gamma_2 H_2 + \cdots + \gamma_n H_n)$$

$$= \frac{1}{70}[(110)(13) + (127)(33) + (130)(11) + (135)(6) + (135)(7)] = 125.8 \text{ lb/ft}^3$$

For the equivalent clay layer of 70 ft,

$$\frac{\gamma_{av} H}{c_{av}} = \frac{(125.8)(70)}{1381} = 6.38 > 4$$

Hence the apparent pressure envelope will be of the type shown in Figure 7.5. From Eq. (7.3)

$$p_a = \gamma H\left[1 - \left(\frac{4c_{av}}{\gamma_{av} H}\right)\right] = (125.8)(70)\left[1 - \frac{(4)(1381)}{(125.8)(70)}\right] = 3282 \text{ lb/ft}^2$$

The pressure envelope is shown in Figure 7.35. The area of this pressure diagram is 201 kip/ft. Thus Peck's pressure envelope gives a lateral earth pressure of about 1.25 times that actually observed. This result is not surprising because the pressure envelope provided by Figure 7.5 is an envelope developed considering several cuts made at different locations. Under actual field conditions, past experience with the behavior of similar soils can help reduce overdesigning substantially.

PROBLEMS

7.1 Refer to the braced cut in Figure P7.1, for which $\gamma = 112$ lb/ft^3, $\phi = 32°$, and $c = 0$. The struts are located at 12 ft on center in the plan. Draw the earth pressure envelope and determine the strut loads at levels A, B, and C.

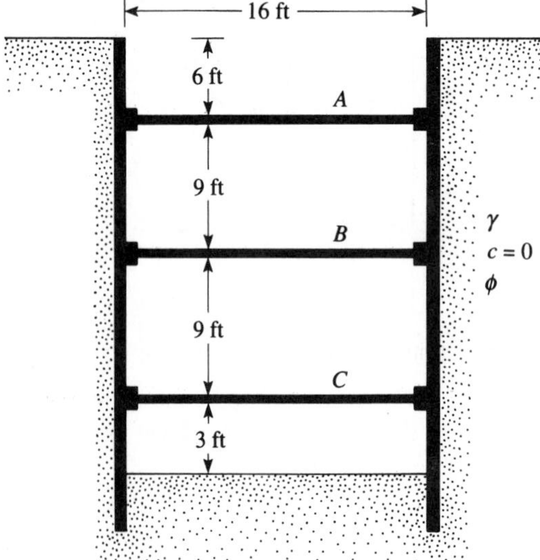

▼ **FIGURE P7.1**

7.2 For the braced cut described in Problem 7.1, assume that $\sigma_{all} = 25{,}000$ lb/in^2 and determine:

a. The sheet pile section

b. The section modulus of the wales at level A

7.3 Redo Problem 7.1 for $\gamma = 116$ lb/ft^3, $\phi = 35°$, $c = 0$, and center-to-center strut spacing in plan of 10 ft.

7.4 Determine the sheet pile section required for the braced cut described in Problem 7.3 for $\sigma_{all} = 25{,}000\ \text{lb/in}^2$.

7.5 Refer to Figure 7.7a. For the braced cut, $H = 6$ m, $H_s = 2$ m, $\gamma_s = 16.2\ \text{kN/m}^3$, angle of friction of sand, $\phi_s = 34°$, $H_c = 4$ m, $\gamma_c = 17.5\ \text{kN/m}^3$, and the unconfined compression strength of clay layer, $q_u = 68\ \text{kN/m}^2$.

a. Estimate the average cohesion, c_{av}, and average unit weight, γ_{av}, for development of the earth pressure envelope.

b. Plot the earth pressure envelope.

7.6 Refer to Figure 7.7b, which shows a braced cut in clay. Here, $H = 22$ ft, $H_1 = 6$ ft, $c_1 = 2125\ \text{lb/ft}^2$, $\gamma_1 = 111\ \text{lb/ft}^3$, $H_2 = 8$ ft, $c_2 = 1565\ \text{lb/ft}^2$, $\gamma_2 = 107\ \text{lb/ft}^3$, $H_3 = 8$ ft, $c_3 = 1670\ \text{lb/ft}^2$, and $\gamma_3 = 109\ \text{lb/ft}^3$.

a. Determine the average cohesion, c_{av}, and average unit weight, γ_{av}, for development of the earth pressure envelope.

b. Plot the earth pressure envelope.

7.7 Refer to Figure P7.7, for which $\gamma = 17.5\ \text{kN/m}^3$, $c = 30\ \text{kN/m}^2$, and center-to-center spacing of struts is 5 m. Draw the earth pressure envelope and determine the strut loads at levels A, B, and C.

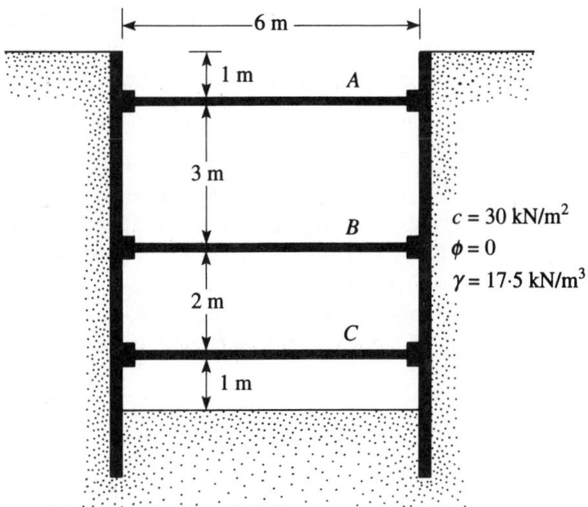

▼ **FIGURE P7.7**

7.8 For the braced cut described in Problem 7.7, determine the sheet pile section.

7.9 Redo Problem 7.7 for $c = 60\ \text{kN/m}^2$.

7.10 Determine the factor of safety against bottom heave for the braced cut described in Problem 7.7. Use Eqs. (7.12) and (7.16). For Eq. (7.16), assume the length of the cut, $L = 18$ m.

7.11 Refer to Figure 7.18a. For the braced cut, $H = 8$ m, $B = 4$ m, $L = 8$ m, $\gamma = 17.8\ \text{kN/m}^3$, $c_1 = 30\ \text{kN/m}^2$, $c_2 = 45\ \text{kN/m}^2$, and $h' = 2$ m. Determine the factor of safety against bottom heave.

7.12 Determine the factor of safety against bottom heave for the braced cut described in Problem 7.9. Use Eq. (7.16). The length of the cut is 12.5 m.

REFERENCES

Bjerrum, L., and Eide, O. (1956). "Stability of Strutted Excavation in Clay," *Geotechnique*, Vol. 6, No. 1, pp. 32–47.

Das, B. M. (1994). *Principles of Geotechnical Engineering*, 3rd ed., PWS, Boston.

Das, B. M., and Seeley, G. R. (1975). "Active Thrust on Braced Cut in Clay," *Journal of the Construction Division*, American Society of Civil Engineers, Vol. 101, No. CO4, pp. 945–949.

Harr, M. E. (1962). *Groundwater and Seepage*, McGraw-Hill, New York.

Lambe, T. W. (1970). "Braced Excavations," *Proceedings of the Specialty Conference on Lateral Stresses in the Ground and Design of Earth-Retaining Structures*, American Society of Civil Engineers, pp. 149–218.

Mana, A. I., and Clough, G. W. (1981). "Prediction of Movements for Braced Cuts in Clay," *Journal of the Geotechnical Engineering Division*, American Society of Civil Engineers, Vol. 107, No. GT8, pp. 759–777.

Marsland, A. (1958). "Model Experiments to Study the Influence of Seepage on the Stability of a Sheeted Excavation in Sand," *Geotechnique*, London, Vol. 3, p. 223.

Peck, R. B. (1943). "Earth Pressure Measurements in Open Cuts, Chicago (Ill.) Subway," *Transactions*, American Society of Civil Engineers, Vol. 108, pp. 1008–1058.

Peck, R. B. (1969). "Deep Excavation and Tunneling in Soft Ground," *Proceedings*, Seventh International Conference on Soil Mechanics and Foundation Engineering, Mexico City, State-of-the-Art Volume, pp. 225–290.

Reddy, A. S., and Srinivasan, R. J. (1967). "Bearing Capacity of Footing on Layered Clay," *Journal of the Soil Mechanics and Foundations Division*, American Society of Civil Engineers, Vol. 93, No. SM2, pp. 83–99.

Swatek, E. P., Jr., Asrow, S. P., and Seitz, A. (1972). "Performance of Bracing for Deep Chicago Excavation," *Proceeding of the Specialty Conference on Performance of Earth and Earth Supported Structures*, American Society of Civil Engineers, Vol. 1, Part 2, pp. 1303–1322.

Terzaghi, K. (1943a). "General Wedge Theory of Earth Pressure," *Transactions*, American Society of Civil Engineers, Vol. 106, pp. 69–97.

Terzaghi, K. (1943b). *Theoretical Soil Mechanics*, Wiley, New York.

Tschebotarioff, G. P. (1973). *Foundations, Retaining and Earth Structures*, 2nd ed., McGraw-Hill, New York.

U.S. Department of the Navy (1971). "Design Manual—Soil Mechanics, Foundations, and Earth Structures,"—NAVFAC DM-7, Washington, D.C.

CHAPTER EIGHT

PILE FOUNDATIONS

8.1 INTRODUCTION

Piles are structural members that are made of steel, concrete, and/or timber. They are used to build pile foundations, which are deep and which cost more than shallow foundations (Chapter 3). Despite the cost, the use of piles often is necessary to ensure structural safety. The following list identifies some of the conditions that require pile foundations.

1. When the upper soil layer(s) is (are) highly compressible and too weak to support the load transmitted by the superstructure, piles are used to transmit the load to underlying bedrock or a stronger soil layer, as shown in Figure 8.1a. When bedrock is not encountered at a reasonable depth below the ground surface, piles are used to transmit the structural load to the soil gradually. The resistance to the applied structural load is derived mainly from the frictional resistance developed at the soil–pile interface (Figure 8.1b).
2. When subjected to horizontal forces (see Figure 8.1c), pile foundations resist by bending while still supporting the vertical load transmitted by the superstructure. This type of situation is generally encountered in the design and construction of earth-retaining structures and foundations of tall structures that are subjected to high wind and/or earthquake forces.
3. In many cases, expansive and collapsible soils (Chapter 10) may be present at the site of a proposed structure. These soils may extend to a great depth below the ground surface. Expansive soils swell and shrink as the moisture content increases and decreases, and the swelling pressure of such soils can be considerable. If shallow foundations are used in such circumstances, the structure may suffer considerable damage. However, pile foundations may be considered as an alternative when piles are extended beyond the active zone, which swells and shrinks (Figure 8.1d).

   Soils such as loess are collapsible in nature. When the moisture content of these soils increases, their structures may break down. A sudden decrease in the void ratio of soil induces large settlements of structures supported by shallow foundations. In such cases, pile foundations may be

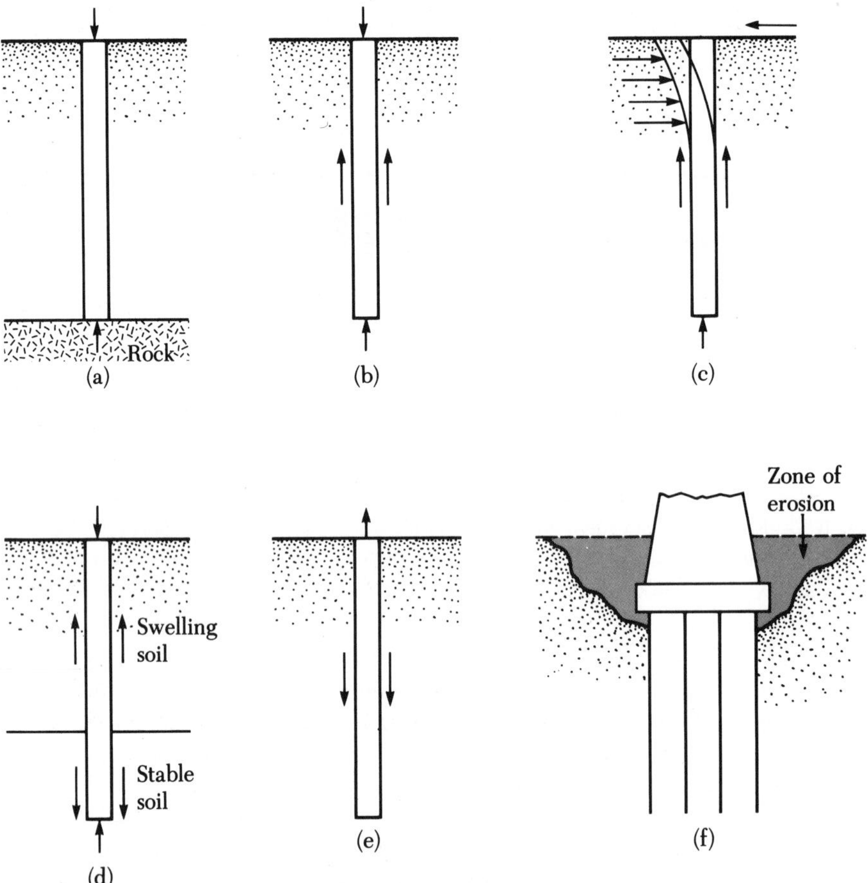

▼ **FIGURE 8.1** Conditions for use of pile foundations

used in which piles are extended into stable soil layers beyond the zone of possible moisture change.

4. Foundations of some structures, such as transmission towers, offshore platforms, and basement mats below the water table, are subjected to uplifting forces. Piles are sometimes used for these foundations to resist the uplifting force (Figure 8.1e).
5. Bridge abutments and piers are usually constructed over pile foundations to avoid the possible loss of bearing capacity that a shallow foundation might suffer because of soil erosion at the ground surface (Figure 8.1f).

Although numerous investigations, both theoretical and experimental, have been conducted in the past to predict the behavior and the load-bearing capacity of piles in granular and cohesive soils, the mechanisms are not yet entirely understood and may never be. The design of pile foundations may be considered somewhat of an "art" as a result of the uncertainties involved in working with some subsoil conditions. This chapter discusses the present state of the art for design and analysis of pile foundations.

8.2 TYPES OF PILES AND THEIR STRUCTURAL CHARACTERISTICS

Different types of piles are used in construction work, depending on the type of load to be carried, the subsoil conditions, and the water table. Piles can be divided into the following categories: (a) steel piles, (b) concrete piles, (c) wooden (timber) piles, and (d) composite piles.

Steel Piles

Steel piles generally are either *pipe piles* or *rolled steel H-section piles*. Pipe piles can be driven into the ground with their ends open or closed. Wide-flange and I-section steel beams can also be used as piles. However, H-section piles are usually preferred because their web and flange thicknesses are equal. In wide-flange and I-section beams, the web thicknesses are smaller than the thicknesses of the flange. Table 8.1 gives the dimensions of some standard H-section steel piles used in the United States. Table 8.2 shows selected pipe sections frequently used for piling purposes. In many cases, the pipe piles are filled with concrete after driving.

TABLE 8.1a Common H-Pile Sections Used in the United States (English Units)

Designation size (in.) × weight (lb/ft)	Depth d_1 (in.)	Section area (in^2)	Flange and web thickness w (in.)	Flange width d_2 (in.)	Moment of inertia (in^4)	
					I_{xx}	I_{yy}
HP 8 × 36	8.02	10.6	0.445	8.155	119	40.3
HP 10 × 57	9.99	16.8	0.565	10.225	294	101
× 42	9.70	12.4	0.420	10.075	210	71.7
HP 12 × 84	12.28	24.6	0.685	12.295	650	213
× 74	12.13	21.8	0.610	12.215	570	186
× 63	11.94	18.4	0.515	12.125	472	153
× 53	11.78	15.5	0.435	12.045	394	127
HP 13 × 100	13.15	29.4	0.766	13.21	886	294
× 87	12.95	25.5	0.665	13.11	755	250
× 73	12.74	21.6	0.565	13.01	630	207
× 60	12.54	17.5	0.460	12.90	503	165
HP 14 × 117	14.21	34.4	0.805	14.89	1220	443
× 102	14.01	30.0	0.705	14.78	1050	380
× 89	13.84	26.1	0.615	14.70	904	326
× 73	13.61	21.4	0.505	14.59	729	262

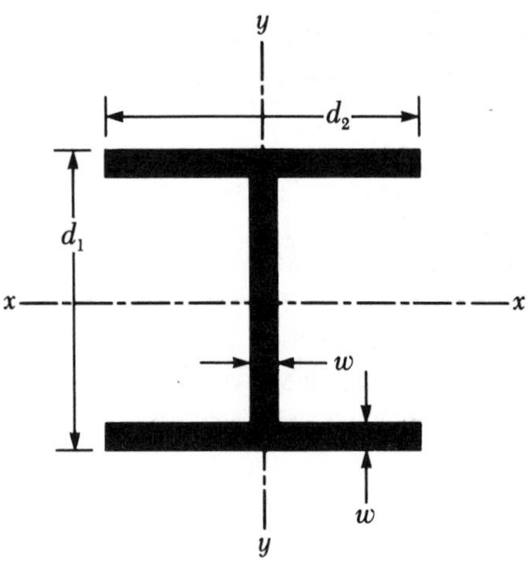

TABLE 8.1b Common H-Pile Sections Used in the United States (SI Units)

Designation, size (mm) × weight (kN/m)	Depth d_1 (mm)	Section area ($m^2 \times 10^{-3}$)	Flange and web thickness w (mm)	Flange width (mm)	Moment of inertia ($m^4 \times 10^{-6}$)	
					I_{xx}	I_{yy}
HP 200 × 0.52	204	6.84	11.3	207	49.4	16.8
HP 250 × 0.834	254	10.8	14.4	260	123	42
× 0.608	246	8.0	10.6	256	87.5	24
HP 310 × 1.226	312	15.9	17.5	312	271	89
× 1.079	308	14.1	15.49	310	237	77.5
× 0.912	303	11.9	13.1	308	197	63.7
× 0.775	299	10.0	11.05	306	164	62.9
HP 330 × 1.462	334	19.0	19.45	335	370	123
× 1.264	329	16.5	16.9	333	314	104
× 1.069	324	13.9	14.5	330	263	86
× 0.873	319	11.3	11.7	328	210	69
HP 360 × 1.707	361	22.2	20.45	378	508	184
× 1.491	356	19.4	17.91	376	437	158
× 1.295	351	16.8	15.62	373	374	136
× 1.060	346	13.8	12.82	371	303	109

The allowable structural capacity for steel piles is

$$Q_{all} = A_s f_s \tag{8.1}$$

where A_s = cross-sectional area of the steel
f_s = allowable stress of steel

Based on geotechnical considerations (once the design load for a pile is fixed) determining whether $Q_{(design)}$ is within the allowable range as defined by Eq. (8.1) is always advisable.

TABLE 8.2a Selected Pipe Pile Sections (English Units)

Outside diameter (in.)	Wall thickness (in.)	Area of steel (in^2)
$8\frac{5}{8}$	0.125	3.34
	0.188	4.98
	0.219	5.78
	0.312	8.17
10	0.188	5.81
	0.219	6.75
	0.250	7.66
12	0.188	6.96
	0.219	8.11
	0.250	9.25
16	0.188	9.34
	0.219	10.86
	0.250	12.37
18	0.219	12.23
	0.250	13.94
	0.312	17.34
20	0.219	13.62
	0.250	15.51
	0.312	19.30
24	0.250	18.7
	0.312	23.2
	0.375	27.8
	0.500	36.9

TABLE 8.2b Selected Pipe Pile Sections (SI Units)

Outside diameter (mm)	Wall thickness (mm)	Area of steel (cm^2)
219	3.17	21.5
	4.78	32.1
	5.56	37.3
	7.92	52.7
254	4.78	37.5
	5.56	43.6
	6.35	49.4
305	4.78	44.9
	5.56	52.3
	6.35	59.7
406	4.78	60.3
	5.56	70.1
	6.35	79.8
457	5.56	80
	6.35	90
	7.92	112
508	5.56	88
	6.35	100
	7.92	125
610	6.35	121
	7.92	150
	9.53	179
	12.70	238

When necessary, steel piles are spliced by welding or by riveting. Figure 8.2a shows a typical condition of splicing by welding for an H-pile. A typical case of splicing by welding for a pipe pile is shown in Figure 8.2b. Figure 8.2c shows a diagram of splicing an H-pile by rivets or bolts.

When hard driving conditions are expected, such as driving through dense gravel, shale, and soft rock, steel piles can be fitted with driving points or shoes. Figure 8.2d and 8.2e are diagrams of two types of shoe used for pipe piles.

Steel piles may be subject to corrosion. For example, swamps, peats, and other organic soils are corrosive. Soils that have a pH greater than 7 are not so corrosive. To offset the effect of corrosion, an additional thickness of steel (over the actual design cross-sectional area) is generally recommended. In many circumstances, factory-applied epoxy coatings on piles work satisfactorily against corrosion. These coatings are not easily damaged by pile driving. Concrete encasement of steel piles in most corrosive zones also protects against corrosion.

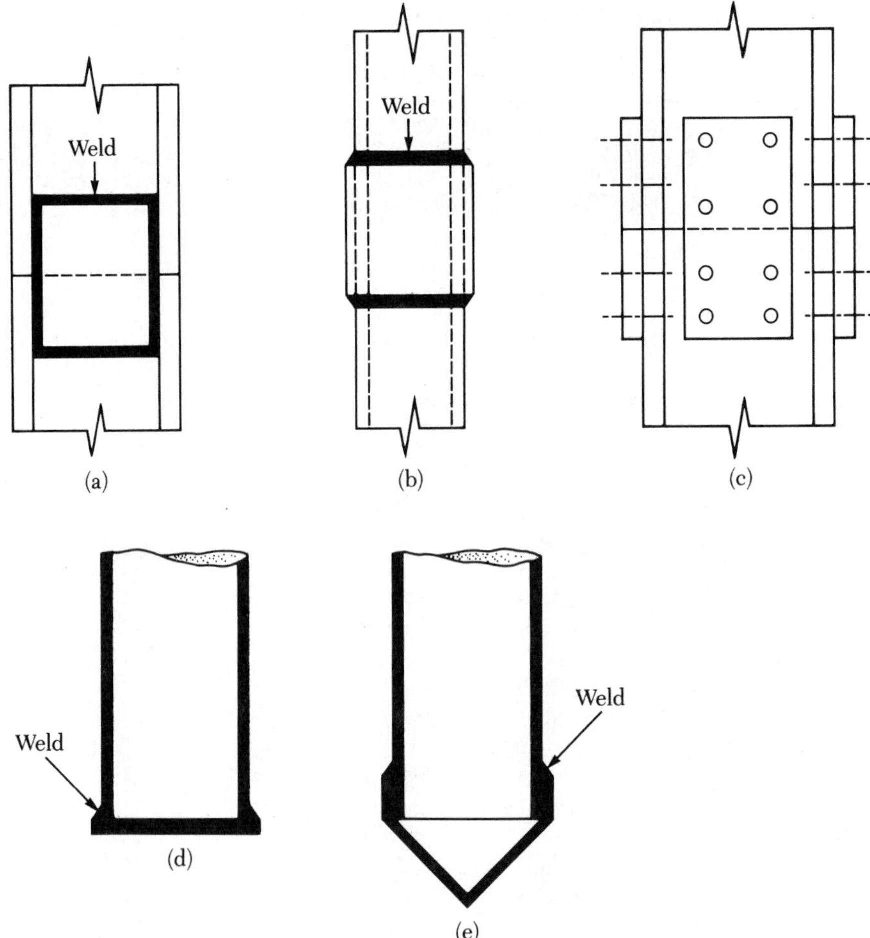

▼ **FIGURE 8.2** Steel piles: (a) splicing of H-pile by welding; (b) splicing of pipe pile by welding; (c) splicing of H-pile by rivets and bolts; (d) flat driving point of pipe pile; (e) conical driving point of pipe pile

Concrete Piles

Concrete piles may be divided into two basic categories: (a) precast piles and (b) cast-*in-situ* piles. *Precast piles* can be prepared by using ordinary reinforcement, and they can be square or octagonal in cross section (Figure 8.3). Reinforcement is provided to enable the pile to resist the bending moment developed during pickup and transportation, the vertical load, and the bending moment caused by lateral load. The piles are cast to desired lengths and cured before being transported to the work sites.

Precast piles can also be prestressed by the use of high-strength steel prestressing cables. The ultimate strength of these steel cables is about 260 ksi ($\approx$1800 MN/m^2). During casting of the piles, the cables are pretensioned to about 130–190 ksi ($\approx$900–1300 MN/m^2), and concrete is poured around them. After curing, the cables are cut, thus

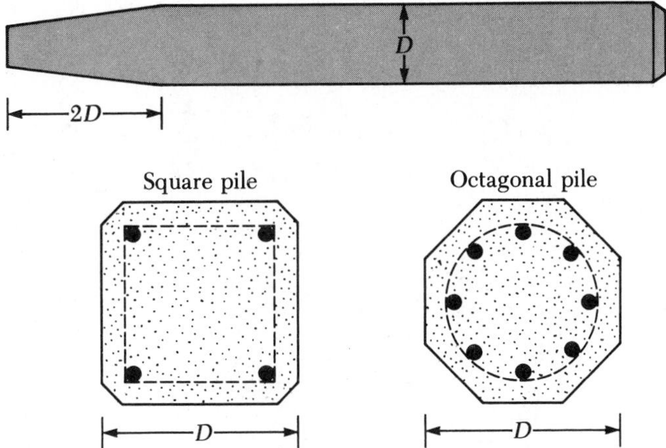

▼ **FIGURE 8.3** Precast piles with ordinary reinforcement

producing a compressive force on the pile section. Table 8.3 gives additional information about prestressed concrete piles with square and octagonal cross sections.

Cast-in-situ, or *cast-in-place, piles* are built by making a hole in the ground and then filling it with concrete. Various types of cast-in-place concrete pile are currently used in construction, and most of them have been patented by their manufacturers. These piles may be divided into two broad categories: (a) cased and (b) uncased. Both types may have a pedestal at the bottom.

Cased piles are made by driving a steel casing into the ground with the help of a mandrel placed inside the casing. When the pile reaches the proper depth, the mandrel is withdrawn and the casing is filled with concrete. Figure 8.4a, b, c, and d show some examples of cased piles without a pedestal. Table 8.4 (page 475) gives additional information about these cased piles. Figure 8.4e shows a cased pile with a pedestal. The pedestal is an expanded concrete bulb that is formed by dropping a hammer on fresh concrete.

Figure 8.4f and 8.4g are two types of uncased pile, one with a pedestal and the other without. The uncased piles are made by first driving the casing to the desired depth and then filling it with fresh concrete. The casing is then gradually withdrawn.

The allowable loads for cast-in-place concrete piles are given by the following equations.

Cased Pile

$$Q_{\text{all}} = A_s f_s + A_c f_c \tag{8.2a}$$

where A_s = area of cross section of steel
A_c = area of cross section of concrete
f_s = allowable stress of steel
f_c = allowable stress of concrete

Uncased Pile

$$Q_{\text{all}} = A_c f_c \tag{8.2b}$$

▼ **TABLE 8.3a** Typical Prestressed Concrete Pile in Use (English Units)

Pile shape[a]	D (in.)	Area of cross section (in²)	Perimeter (in.)	Number of strands		Minimum effective prestress force (kip)	Section modulus (in³)	Design bearing capacity (kip)	
								Concrete strength	
				½-in. diameter	$^7/_{16}$-in. diameter			5000 psi	6000 psi
S	10	100	40	4	4	70	167	125	175
O	10	83	33	4	4	58	109	104	125
S	12	144	48	5	6	101	288	180	216
O	12	119	40	4	5	83	189	149	178
S	14	196	56	6	8	137	457	245	295
O	14	162	46	5	7	113	300	203	243
S	16	256	64	8	11	179	683	320	385
O	16	212	53	7	9	148	448	265	318
S	18	324	72	10	13	227	972	405	486
O	18	268	60	8	11	188	638	336	402
S	20	400	80	12	16	280	1333	500	600
O	20	331	66	10	14	234	876	414	503
S	22	484	88	15	20	339	1775	605	727
O	22	401	73	12	16	281	1166	502	602
S	24	576	96	18	23	403	2304	710	851
O	24	477	80	15	19	334	2123	596	716

[a] S = square section; O = octagonal section

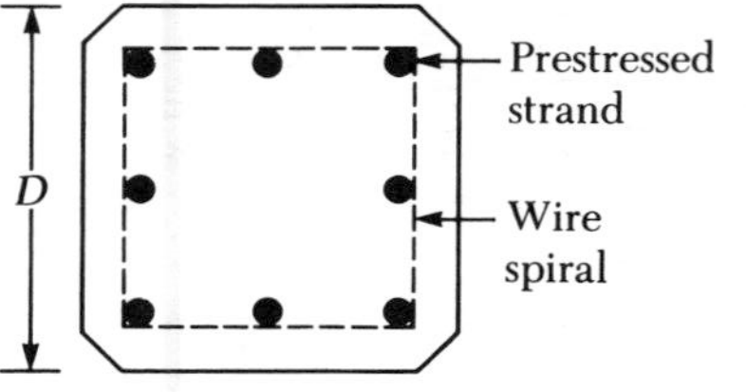

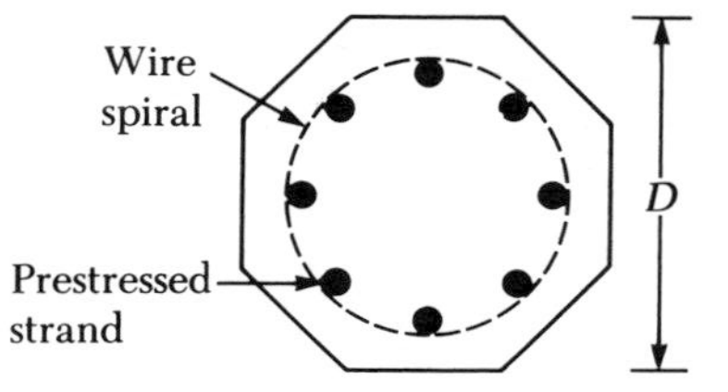

TABLE 8.3b Typical Prestressed Concrete Piles in Use (SI Units)

Pile shape[a]	D (mm)	Area of cross section (cm²)	Perimeter (mm)	Number of strands		Minimum effective prestress force (kN)	Section modulus (m³ × 10⁻³)	Design bearing capacity (kN)	
				12.7-mm diameter	*11.1-mm diameter*			Concrete strength (MN/m^2) 34.5	41.4
S	254	645	1016	4	4	312	2.737	556	778
O	254	536	838	4	4	258	1.786	462	555
S	305	929	1219	5	6	449	4.719	801	962
O	305	768	1016	4	5	369	3.097	662	795
S	356	1265	1422	6	8	610	7.489	1091	1310
O	356	1045	1168	5	7	503	4.916	901	1082
S	406	1652	1626	8	11	796	11.192	1425	1710
O	406	1368	1346	7	9	658	7.341	1180	1416
S	457	2090	1829	10	13	1010	15.928	1803	2163
O	457	1729	1524	8	11	836	10.455	1491	1790
S	508	2581	2032	12	16	1245	21.844	2226	2672
O	508	2136	1677	10	14	1032	14.355	1842	2239
S	559	3123	2235	15	20	1508	29.087	2694	3232
O	559	2587	1854	12	16	1250	19.107	2231	2678
S	610	3658	2438	18	23	1793	37.756	3155	3786
O	610	3078	2032	15	19	1486	34.794	2655	3186

[a] S = square section; O = octagonal section

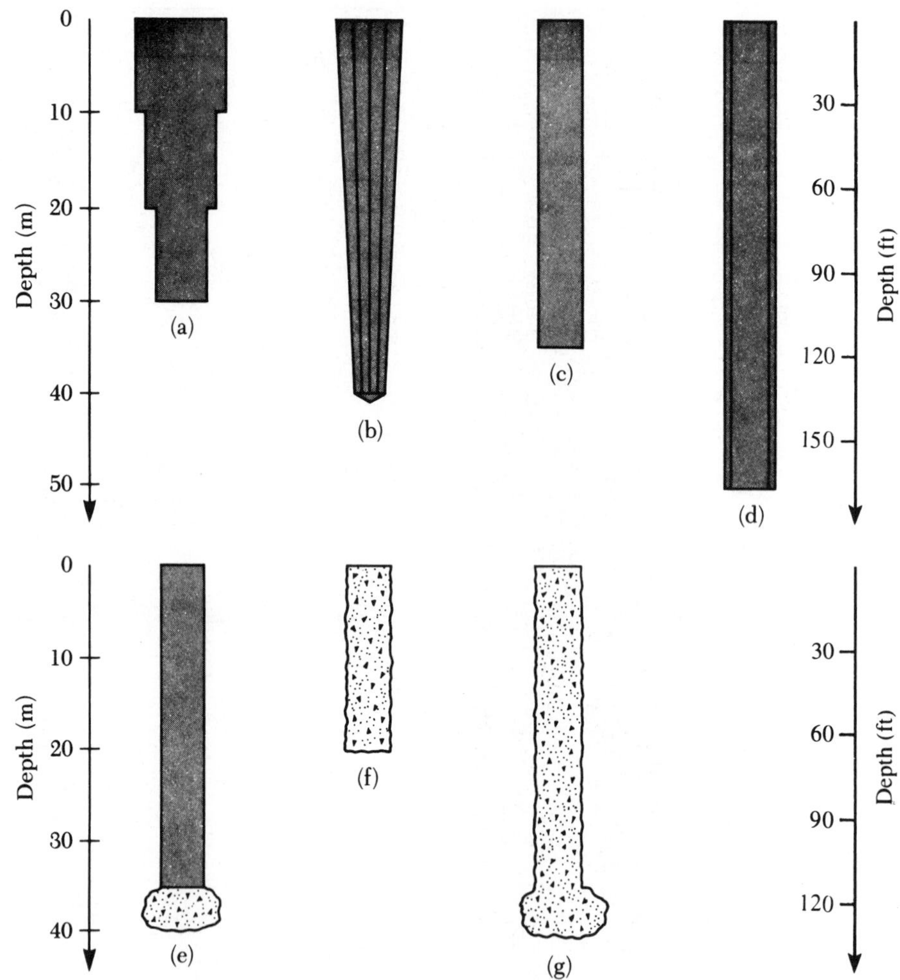

▼ **FIGURE 8.4** Cast-in-place concrete piles (see Table 8.4 for descriptions)

Timber Piles

Timber piles are tree trunks that have had their branches and bark carefully trimmed off. The maximum length of most timber piles is 30–65 ft (10–20 m). To qualify for use as a pile, the timber should be straight, sound, and without any defects. The American Society of Civil Engineers' *Manual of Practice*, No. 17 (1959), divided timber piles into three classifications:

1. *Class A piles* carry heavy loads. The minimum diameter of the butt should be 14 in. (356 mm).
2. *Class B piles* are used to carry medium loads. The minimum butt diameter should be 12–13 in. (305–330 mm).

TABLE 8.4 Descriptions of the Cast-in-Place Piles Shown in Figure 8.4

Part in Figure 8.4	Name of pile	Type of casing	Maximum usual depth of pile	
			(ft)	*(m)*
a	Raymond Step-Taper	Corrugated, thin cylindrical casing	100	30
b	Monotube or Union Metal	Thin fluted, taperd steel casing driven without mandrel	130	40
c	Western cased	Thin sheet casing	100–130	30–40
d	Seamless pipe or Armco	Straight steel pipe casing	160	50
e	Franki cased pedestal	Thin sheet casing	100–130	30–40
f	Western uncased without pedestal	—	50–65	15–20
g	Franki uncased pedestal	—	100–130	30–40

3. *Class C piles* are used in temporary construction work. They can be used permanently for structures when the entire pile is below the water table. The minimum butt diameter should be 12 in. (305 mm).

In any case, a pile tip should not have a diameter less than 6 in. (150 mm).

Timber piles cannot withstand hard driving stress; therefore, the pile capacity is generally limited to about 25–30 tons (220–270 kN). Steel shoes may be used to avoid damage at the pile tip (bottom). The tops of timber piles may also be damaged during the driving operation. The crushing of the wooden fibers caused by the impact of the hammer is referred to as *brooming*. To avoid damage to the pile top, a metal band or a cap may be used.

Splicing of timber piles should be avoided, particularly when they are expected to carry tensile load or lateral load. However, if splicing is necessary, it can be done by using *pipe sleeves* (Figure 8.5a) or *metal straps and bolts* (Figure 8.5b). The length of the pipe sleeve should be at least five times the diameter of the pile. The butting ends should be cut square so that full contact can be maintained. The spliced portions should be carefully trimmed so that they fit tightly to the inside of the pipe sleeve. In the case of metal straps and bolts, the butting ends should also be cut square. Also, the sides of the spliced portion should be trimmed plane for putting the straps on.

Timber piles can stay undamaged indefinitely if they are surrounded by saturated soil. However, in a marine environment timber piles are subject to attack by various organisms and can be damaged extensively in a few months. When located above the water table, the piles are subject to attack by insects. The life of the piles may be increased by treating them with preservatives such as creosote.

The allowable load-carrying capacity of wooden piles is

$$Q_{all} = A_p f_w \tag{8.3}$$

where A_p = average area of cross section of the pile
f_w = allowable stress for the timber

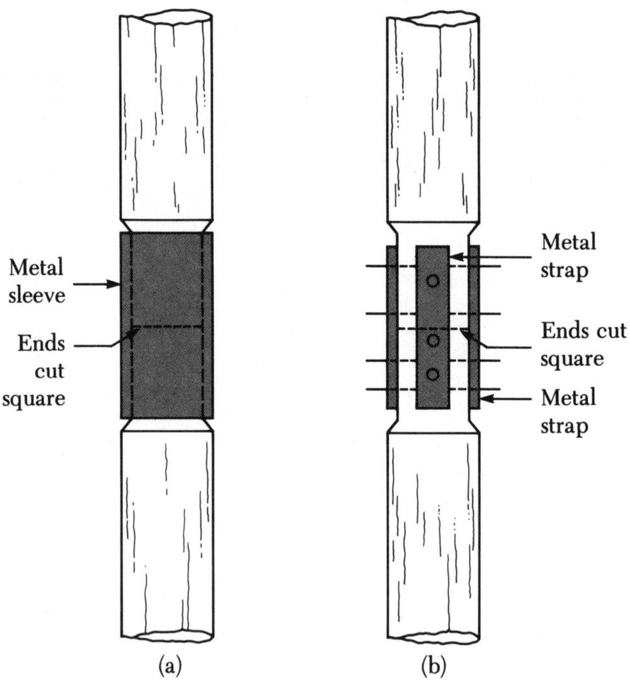

▼ **FIGURE 8.5** Splicing of timber piles: (a) use of pipe sleeves; (b) use of metal straps and bolts

The following allowable stresses are for pressure-treated round timber piles made from Pacific Coast Douglas fir and Southern pine, when used in hydraulic structures (ASCE, 1993).

Allowable stress	*Pacific Coast Douglas fir*	*Southern pine*
Compression parallel to grain	875 lb/in^2 (6.04 MN/m^2)	825 lb/in^2 (5.7 MN/m^2)
Bending	1700 lb/in^2 (11.7 MN/m^2)	1650 lb/in^2 (11.4 MN/m^2)
Horizontal shear	95 lb/in^2 (0.66 MN/m^2)	90 lb/in^2 (0.62 MN/m^2)
Compression perpendicular to grain	190 lb/in^2 (1.31 MN/m^2)	205 lb/in^2 (1.41 MN/m^2)

Composite Piles

The upper and lower portions of *composite piles* are made of different materials. For example, composite piles may be made of steel and concrete or timber and concrete. Steel and concrete piles consist of a lower portion of steel and an upper portion of cast-in-place concrete. This type of pile is the one used when the length of the pile required for adequate bearing exceeds the capacity of simple cast-in-place concrete piles. Timber and concrete piles usually consist of a lower portion of timber pile below the permanent water table and an upper portion of concrete. In any case, forming proper joints between two dissimilar materials is difficult, and, for that reason, composite piles are not widely used.

Comparison of Pile Types

Several factors affect the selection of piles for a particular structure at a specific site. Table 8.5 gives a brief comparison of the advantages and disadvantages of the various types of pile based on the pile material.

8.3 ESTIMATION OF PILE LENGTH

Selecting the type of pile to be used and estimating its necessary length are fairly difficult tasks that require good judgment. In addition to the classification given in Section 8.2, piles can be divided into three major categories, depending on their lengths and the mechanisms of load transfer to the soil: (a) point bearing piles, (b) friction piles, and (c) compaction piles.

Point Bearing Piles

If soil-bearing records establish the presence of bedrock or rocklike material at a site within a reasonable depth, piles can be extended to the rock surface (Figure 8.6a, page 480). In this case, the ultimate capacity of the piles depends entirely on the load-bearing capacity of the underlying material; thus the piles are called *point bearing piles*. In most of these cases, the necessary length of the pile can be fairly well established.

Instead of bedrock, if a fairly compact and hard stratum of soil is encountered at a reasonable depth, piles can be extended a few meters into the hard stratum (Figure 8.6b). Piles with pedestals can be constructed on the bed of the hard stratum, and the ultimate pile load may be expressed as

$$Q_u = Q_p + Q_s \tag{8.4}$$

where Q_p = load carried at the pile point

Q_s = load carried by skin friction developed at the side of the pile (caused by shearing resistance between the soil and the pile)

If Q_s is very small,

$$Q_u \approx Q_p \tag{8.5}$$

In this case, the required pile length may be estimated accurately if proper subsoil exploration records are available.

TABLE 8.5 Comparisons of Piles Made of Different Materials

Pile type	Usual length of piles	Maximum length of pile	Usual load	Approximate maximum load	Comments
Steel	50–200 ft (15–60 m)	Practically unlimited	67–270 kip (300–1200 KN)	Eq. (8.1)	*Advantages* a. Easy to handle with respect to cutoff and extension to the desired length b. Can stand high driving stresses c. Can penetrate hard layers such as dense gravel, soft rock d. High load-carrying capacity *Disadvantages* a. Relatively costly material b. High level of noise during pile driving c. Subject to corrosion d. H-piles may be damaged or deflected from the vertical during driving through hard layers or past major obstructions
Precast concrete	*Precast:* 30–50 ft (10–15 m) *Prestressed:* 30–150 ft (10–35 m)	*Precast:* 100 ft (30 m) *Prestressed:* 200 ft (60 m)	67–675 kip (300–3000 KN)	*Precast:* 180–200 kip (800–900 KN) *Prestressed:* 1700–1900 kip (7500–8500 KN)	*Advantages* a. Can be subjected to hard driving b. Corrosion resistant c. Can be easily combined with concrete superstructure *Disadvantages* a. Difficult to achieve proper cutoff b. Difficult to transport

▼ TABLE 8.5 (Continued)

Pile type	Usual length of piles	Maximum length of pile	Usual load	Approximate maximum load	Comments
Cased cast-in place concrete	15–50 ft (5–15 m)	15–130 ft (15–40 m)	45–115 kip (200–500 KN)	180 kip (800 KN)	*Advantages* a. Relatively cheap b. Possibility of inspection before pouring concrete c. Easy to extend *Disadvantages* a. Difficult to splice after concreting b. Thin casings may be damaged during driving
Uncased cast-in-place concrete	15–50 ft (5–15 m)	100–130 ft (30–40 m)	65–115 kip (300–500 KN)	160 kip (700 KN)	*Advantages* a. Initially economical b. Can be finished at any elevation *Disadvantages* a. Voids may be created if concrete is placed rapidly b. Difficult to splice after concreting c. In soft soils, the sides of the hole may cave in, thus squeezing the concrete
Wood	30–50 ft (10–15 m)	100 ft (30 m)	22–45 kip (100–200 KN)	60 kip (270 KN)	*Advantages* a. Economical b. Easy to handle c. Permanently submerged piles are fairly resistant to decay *Disadvantages* a. Decay above water table b. Can be damaged in hard driving c. Low load-bearing capacity d. Low resistance to tensile load when spliced

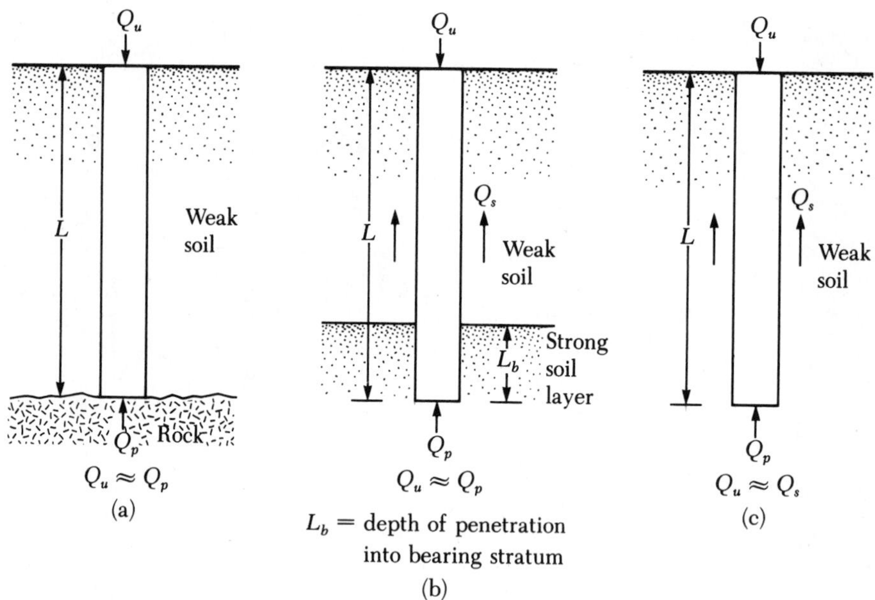

▼ **FIGURE 8.6** (a) and (b) Point bearing piles; (c) friction piles

Friction Piles

When no layer of rock or rocklike material is present at a reasonable depth at a site, point bearing piles become very long and uneconomical. For this type of subsoil condition, piles are driven through the softer material to specified depths (Figure 8.6c). The ultimate load of these piles may be expressed by Eq. (8.4). However, if the value of Q_p is relatively small,

$$Q_u \approx Q_s \tag{8.6}$$

These piles are called *friction piles* because most of the resistance is derived from skin friction. However, the term *friction pile,* although used often in literature, is a misnomer: in clayey soils, the resistance to applied load is also caused by *adhesion.*

The length of friction piles depends on the shear strength of the soil, the applied load, and the pile size. To determine the necessary lengths of these piles, an engineer needs a good understanding of soil–pile interaction, good judgment, and experience. Theoretical procedures for the calculation of load-bearing capacity of piles are presented in Section 8.6.

Compaction Piles

Under certain circumstances, piles are driven in granular soils to achieve proper compaction of soil close to the ground surface. These piles are called *compaction piles.* The length of compaction piles depends on factors such as (a) relative density of the soil before compaction, (b) desired relative density of the soil after compaction, and (c) required depth of compaction. These piles are generally short; however, some field tests are necessary to determine a reasonable length.

8.4 INSTALLATION OF PILES

Most piles are driven into the ground by means of *hammers* or *vibratory drivers*. In special circumstances, piles can also be inserted by *jetting* or *partial augering*. The types of hammer used for pile driving include the (a) drop hammer, (b) single-acting air or steam hammer, (c) double-acting and differential air or steam hammer, and (d) diesel hammer. In the driving operation, a cap is attached to the top of the pile. A cushion may be used between the pile and the cap. This cushion has the effect of reducing the impact force and spreading it over a longer time; however, its use is optional. A hammer cushion is placed on the pile cap. The hammer drops on the cushion.

Figure 8.7 illustrates various hammers. A drop hammer (Figure 8.7a) is raised by a winch and allowed to drop from a certain height H. It is the oldest type of hammer used for pile driving. The main disadvantage of the drop hammer is the slow rate of hammer blows. The principle of the single-acting air or steam hammer is shown in Figure 8.7b. In this case, the striking part, or ram, is raised by air or steam pressure and

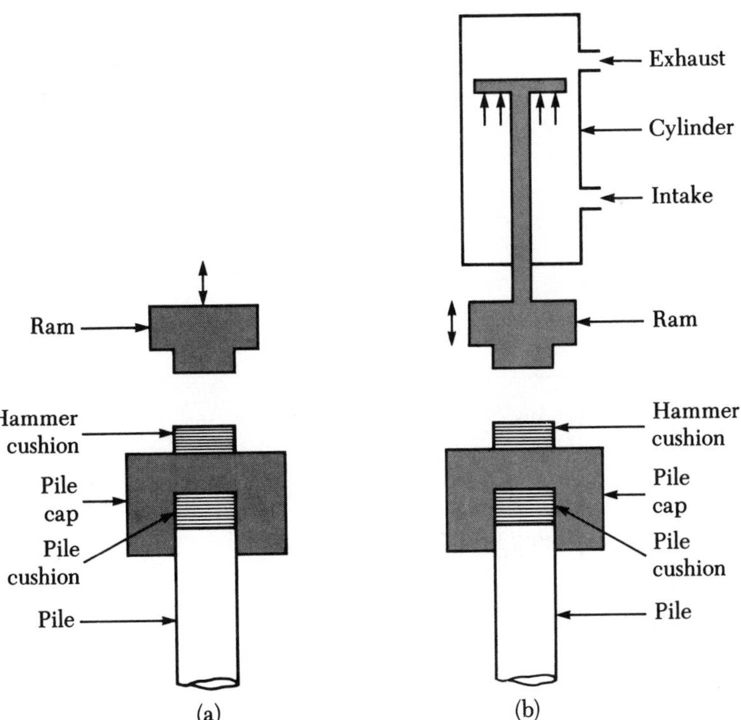

▼ **FIGURE 8.7** Pile-driving equipment: (a) drop hammer; (b) single-acting air or steam hammer; (c) double-acting and differential air or steam hammer; (d) diesel hammer; (e) vibratory pile driver

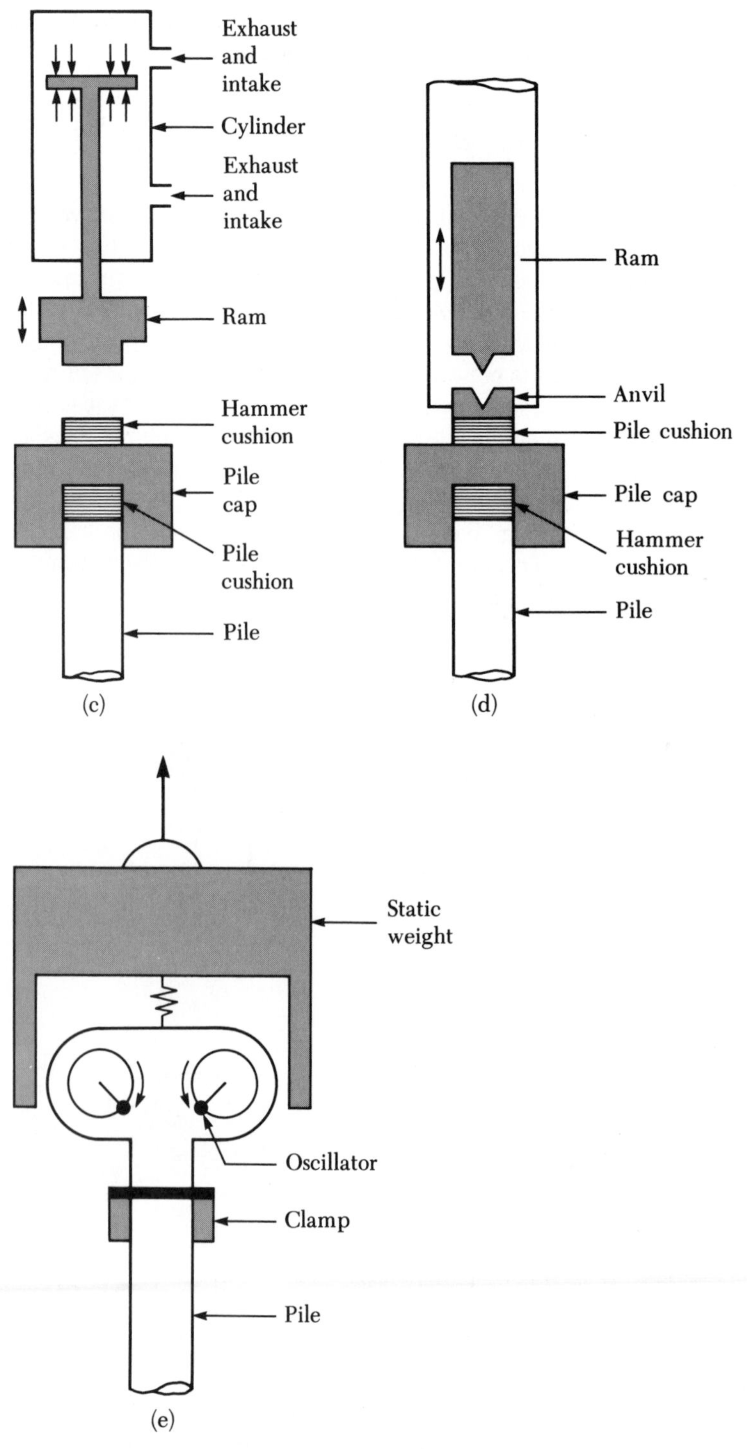

▼ **FIGURE 8.7** (Continued)

then drops by gravity. Figure 8.7c shows the operation of the double-acting and differential air or steam hammer. For these hammers, air or steam is used both to raise the ram and to push it downward. This increases the impact velocity of the ram. The diesel hammer (Figure 8.7d) essentially consists of a ram, an anvil block, and a fuel-injection system. During the operation, the ram is first raised and fuel is injected near the anvil. Then the ram is released. When the ram drops, it compresses the air–fuel mixture, which ignites it. This action, in effect, pushes the pile downward and raises the ram. Diesel hammers work well under hard driving conditions. In soft soils, the downward movement of the pile is rather large, and the upward movement of the ram is small. This differential may not be sufficient to ignite the air–fuel system, so the ram may have to be lifted manually. Tables 8.6 and 8.7 list some of the commercially available diesel, single-acting, double-acting, and differential hammers.

The principles of operation of a vibratory pile driver are shown in Figure 8.7e. This driver essentially consists of two counter-rotating weights. The horizontal components of the centrifugal force generated as a result of rotating masses cancel each other. As a result, a sinusoidal dynamic vertical force is produced on the pile and helps drive the pile downward.

Jetting is a technique sometimes used in pile driving, when the pile needs to penetrate a thin layer of hard soil (such as sand and gravel) overlying a softer soil

TABLE 8.6 Partial List of Typical Air and Steam Hammers

Maker of hammer[a]	Model no.	Type of hammer	Rated energy		Blows per minute	Ram weight	
			kip-ft	*kN · m*		*kip*	*kN*
V	3100	Single acting	300	406.8	58	100	448.8
V	540	Single acting	200	271.2	48	40.9	181.9
V	060	Single acting	180	244.1	62	60	266.9
MKT	OS-60	Single acting	180	244.1	55	60	266.9
V	040	Single acting	120	162.7	60	40	177.9
V	400C	Differential	113.5	153.9	100	40	177.9
R	8/0	Single acting	81.25	110.2	35	25	111.2
MKT	S-20	Single acting	60	81.4	60	20	89
R	5/0	Single acting	56.9	77.2	44	17.5	77.8
V	200-C	Differential	50.2	68.1	98	20	89
R	150-C	Differential	48.75	66.1	95–105	15	66.7
MKT	S-14	Single acting	37.5	50.9	60	14	62.3
V	140C	Differential	36	48.8	103	14	62.3
V	08	Single acting	26	35.3	50	8	35.6
MKT	S-8	Single acting	26	35.3	55	8	35.6
MKT	11B3	Double acting	19.2	26.1	95	5	22.2
MKT	C-5	Double acting	16.0	21.7	110	5	22.2
V	30-C	Double acting	7.3	9.9	133	3	13.3

[a] V—Vulcan Iron Works, Florida
MKT—McKiernan-Terry, New Jersey
R—Raymond International, Inc., Texas

TABLE 8.7 Partial List of Typical Diesel Hammers

Maker of hammer[a]	Model no.	Rated energy		Blows per minute	Piston weight	
		kip-ft	*kN · m*		*kN*	*kip*
K	K150	280	379.7	45–60	147.2	33.1
M	MB70	141–63.4	191.2–86	38–60	70.5	15.84
K	K-60	105.6	143.2	42–60	58.7	13.2
K	K-45	91.1	123.5	39–60	44.0	9.9
M	M-43	84–37.8	113.9–51.3	40–60	42.1	9.46
K	K-35	70.8	96	39–60	34.3	7.7
MKT	DE70B	63–42	85.4–57	40–50	31.1	7.0
K	K-25	50.7	68.8	39–60	24.5	5.51
V	N-46	32.55	44.1	50–60	17.6	3.96
L	520	26.3	35.7	80–84	22.6	5.07
M	M-14S	26–11.88	35.3–16.1	42–60	13.2	2.97
V	N-33	24.6	33.4	50–60	13.3	3.0
L	440	18.2	24.7	86–90	17.8	4.0
MKT	DE20	18.0–12.0	24.4–16.3	40–50	8.9	2.0
MKT	DE-10	8.8	11.9	40–50	4.9	1.1
L	180	8.1	11.0	90–95	7.7	1.73

[a] V—Vulcan Iron Works, Florida
M—Mitsubishi International Corporation
MKT—McKiernan-Terry, New Jersey
L—Link Belt, Cedar Rapids, Iowa
K—Kobe Diesel

layer. In this technique, water is discharged at the pile point by means of a pipe 2–3 in. (50–75 mm) in diameter to wash and loosen the sand and gravel.

Piles driven at an angle to the vertical, typically 14° to 20°, are referred to as *batter piles*. Batter piles are used in group piles when higher lateral load-bearing capacity is required. Piles also may be advanced by partial augering, with power augers (Chapter 2) being used to predrill holes part of the way. The piles can then be inserted into the holes and driven to the desired depth.

Based on the nature of their placement, piles may be divided into two categories: *displacement piles* and *nondisplacement piles*. Driven piles are displacement piles because they move some soil laterally; hence there is a tendency for densification of soil surrounding them. Concrete piles and closed-ended pipe piles are high-displacement piles. However, steel H-piles displace less soil laterally during driving, and so they are low-displacement piles. In contrast, bored piles are nondisplacement piles because their placement causes very little change in the state of stress in the soil.

8.5 LOAD TRANSFER MECHANISM

The load transfer mechanism from a pile to the soil is complicated. To understand it, consider a pile of length L, as shown in Figure 8.8a. The load on the pile is gradually increased from zero to $Q_{(z=0)}$ at the ground surface. Part of this load will be resisted by

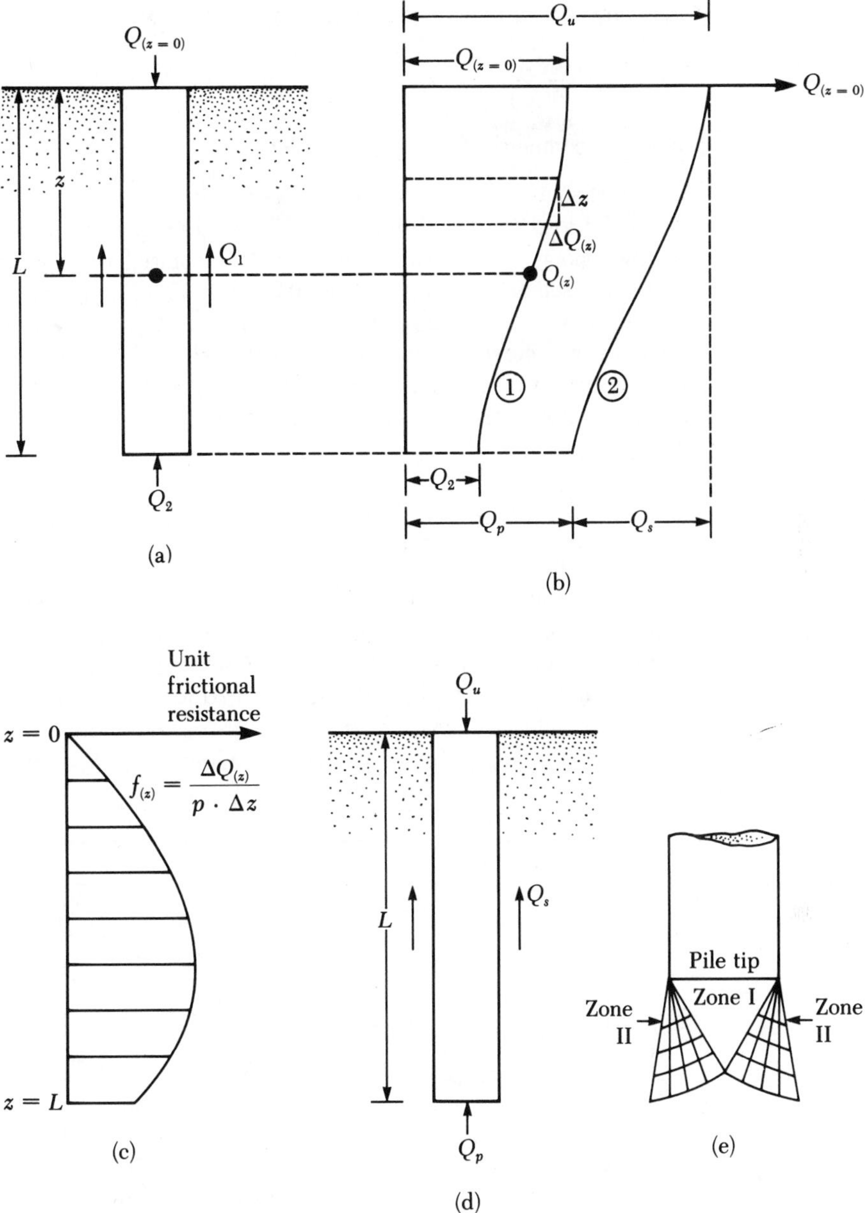

▼ **FIGURE 8.8** Load transfer mechanism for piles

the side friction developed along the shaft, Q_1, and part by the soil below the tip of the pile, Q_2. Now, how are Q_1 and Q_2 related to the total load? If measurements are made to obtain the load carried by the pile shaft $Q_{(z)}$, at any depth z, the nature of variation will be like that shown in curve 1 of Figure 8.8b. The *frictional resistance per unit area,*

$f_{(z)}$, at any depth z may be determined as

$$f_{(z)} = \frac{\Delta Q_{(z)}}{(p)(\Delta z)} \tag{8.7}$$

where p = perimeter of the pile cross section

Figure 8.8c shows the variation of $f_{(z)}$ with depth.

If the load Q at the ground surface is gradually increased, maximum frictional resistance along the pile shaft will be fully mobilized when the relative displacement between the soil and the pile is about 0.2–0.3 in. (5–10 mm) irrespective of pile size and length L. However, the maximum point resistance $Q_2 = Q_p$ will not be mobilized until the pile tip has moved about 10–25% of the pile width (or diameter). The lower limit applies to driven piles and the upper limit to bored piles. At ultimate load (Figure 8.8d and curve 2 in Figure 8.8b), $Q_{(z=0)} = Q_u$. Thus

$$Q_1 = Q_s$$

and

$$Q_2 = Q_p$$

The preceding explanation indicates that Q_s (or the unit skin friction, f, along the pile shaft) is developed at a *much smaller pile displacement compared to the point resistance*, Q_p. This condition can be seen in Vesic's (1970) pile load test results in granular soil, shown in Figure 8.9. Note that these results are for *pipe piles in dense sand.*

At ultimate load, the failure surface in the soil at the pile tip (bearing capacity failure caused by Q_p) is like that shown in Figure 8.8e. Note that pile foundations are

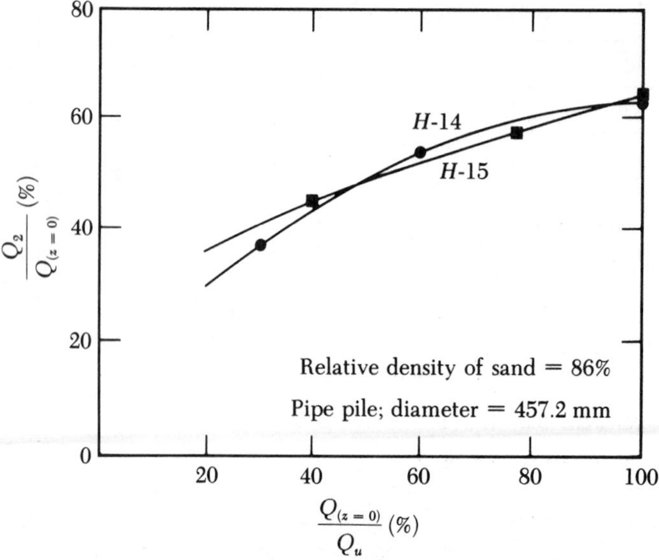

▼ **FIGURE 8.9** Relative magnitude of point load transferred at various stages of pile loading (redrawn after Vesic, 1970)

deep foundations and that the soil fails mostly in a *punching mode*, as illustrated previously in Figures 3.1c and 3.2. That is, a *triangular zone*, I, is developed at the pile tip, which is pushed downward without producing any other visible slip surface. In dense sands and stiff clayey soils, a *radial shear zone*, II, may partially develop. Hence the load displacement curves of piles will resemble those shown in Figure 3.1c.

8.6 EQUATIONS FOR ESTIMATION OF PILE CAPACITY

The ultimate load-carrying capacity of a pile is given by a simple equation as the sum of the load carried at the pile point plus the total frictional resistance (skin friction) derived from the soil–pile interface (Figure 8.10a), or

$$Q_u = Q_p + Q_s \tag{8.8}$$

where Q_u = ultimate pile capacity
Q_p = load-carrying capacity of the pile point
Q_s = frictional resistance

Numerous published studies cover the determination of the values of Q_p and Q_s. Excellent reviews of many of these investigations have been provided by Vesic (1977), Meyerhof (1976), and Coyle and Castello (1981). These studies provide insight into the problem of determining ultimate pile capacity.

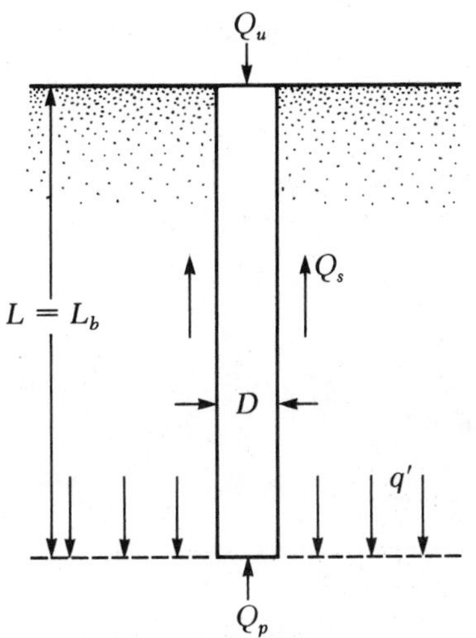

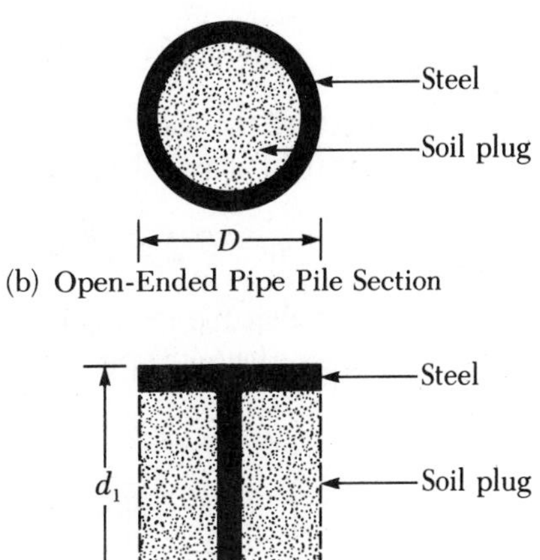

▼ **FIGURE 8.10**

Point Bearing Capacity, Q_p

The ultimate bearing capacity of shallow foundations was discussed in Chapter 3. According to Terzaghi's equations,

$$q_u = 1.3cN_c + qN_q + 0.4\gamma BN_\gamma \qquad \text{(for shallow square foundations)}$$

and

$$q_u = 1.3cN_c + qN_q + 0.3\gamma BN_\gamma \qquad \text{(for shallow circular foundations)}$$

Similarly, the general bearing capacity equation for shallow foundations was given in Chapter 3 (for vertical loading) as

$$q_u = cN_c F_{cs} F_{cd} + qN_q F_{qs} F_{qd} + \frac{1}{2}\gamma BN_\gamma F_{\gamma s} F_{\gamma d}$$

Hence, in general, the ultimate load-bearing capacity may be expressed as

$$q_u = cN_c^* + qN_q^* + \gamma BN_\gamma^* \tag{8.9a}$$

where N_c^*, N_q^*, and N_γ^* are the bearing capacity factors that include the necessary shape and depth factors

Pile foundations are deep. However, the ultimate resistance per unit area developed at the pile tip, q_p, may be expressed by an equation similar in form to that shown in Eq. (8.9a), although the values of N_c^*, N_q^*, and N_γ^* will change. The notation used in this chapter for the width of pile is D. Hence substituting D for B in Eq. (8.9a) gives

$$q_u = q_p = cN_c^* + qN_q^* + \gamma DN_\gamma^* \tag{8.9b}$$

Because the width D of a pile is relatively small, the term γDN_γ^* may be dropped from the right side of the preceding equation without introducing a serious error, or

$$q_p = cN_c^* + q'N_q^* \tag{8.10}$$

Note that the term q has been replaced by q' in Eq. (8.10) to signify effective vertical stress. Hence the point bearing of piles is

$$\boxed{Q_p = A_p q_p = A_p(cN_c^* + q'N_q^*)} \tag{8.11}$$

where
A_p = area of pile tip
c = cohesion of the soil supporting the pile tip
q_p = unit point resistance
q' = effective vertical stress at the level of the pile tip
N_c^*, N_q^* = the bearing capacity factors

There are several methods for determining the bearing capacity factors N_c^* and N_q^*, including Meyerhof's method, Vesic's method, and Janbu's method.

Meyerhof's Method The point bearing capacity, q_p, of a pile in sand generally increases with the depth of embedment in the bearing stratum and reaches a maximum value at an embedment ratio of $L_b/D = (L_b/D)_{cr}$. Note that in a homogeneous soil L_b is equal to the actual embedment length of the pile, L (see Figure 8.10a). However, in Figure 8.6b, where a pile has penetrated into a bearing stratum, $L_b < L$. Beyond the critical embedment ratio, $(L_b/D)_{cr}$, the value of q_p remains constant ($q_p = q_l$). That is, as shown in Figure 8.11 for the case of a homogeneous soil, $L = L_b$. The variation of $(L_b/D)_{cr}$ with the soil friction angle is shown in Figure 8.12. Note that the broken curve is for the determination of N_c^* and that the solid curve is for the determination of N_q^*. According to Meyerhof (1976), the bearing capacity factors increase with L_b/D and reach a maximum value at $L_b/D \approx 0.5(L_b/D)_{cr}$. Figure 8.12 indicates that $(L_b/D)_{cr}$ for $\phi = 45°$ is about 25 and that it decreases with the decrease of the friction angle, ϕ. In most cases, the magnitude of L_b/D for piles is greater than $0.5(L_b/D)_{cr}$. So the maximum values of N_c^* and N_q^* will apply for calculation of q_p for all piles. The variation of these maximum values of N_c^* and N_q^* with friction angle, ϕ, is shown in Figure 8.13.

For piles in sand, $c = 0$, and Eq. (8.11) simplifies to

$$Q_p = A_p q_p = A_p q' N_q^* \quad \text{(}N_q^* \uparrow \text{ Figure 8.13)} \tag{8.12}$$

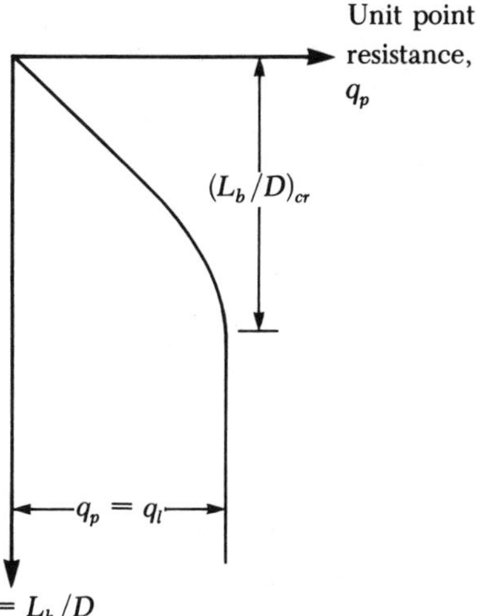

▼ **FIGURE 8.11** Nature of variation of unit point resistance in a homogeneous sand

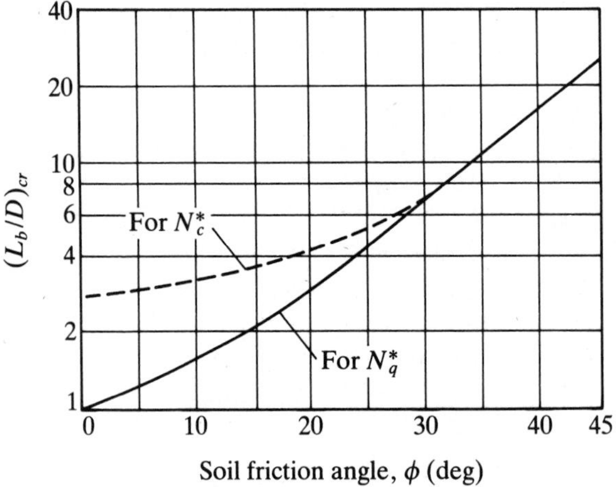

FIGURE 8.12 Variation of $(L_b/D)_{cr}$ with soil friction angle (after Meyerhof, 1976)

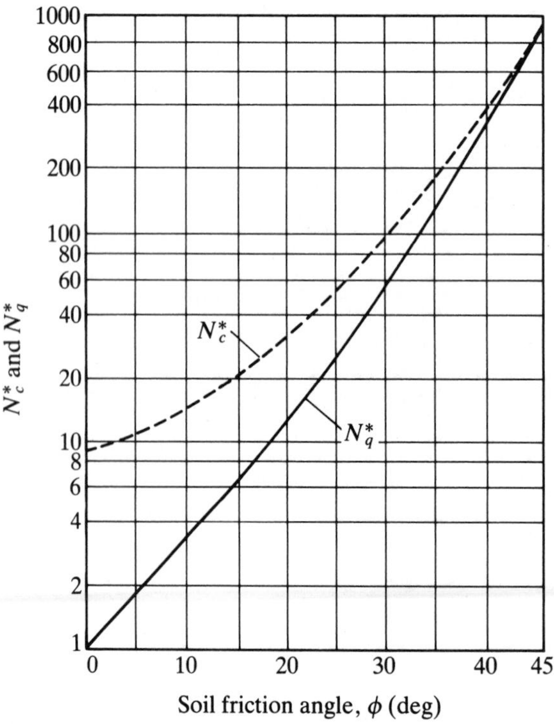

FIGURE 8.13 Variation of the maximum values of N_c^* and N_q^* with soil friction angle ϕ (after Meyerhof, 1976)

However, Q_p should not exceed the limiting value, or $A_p q_l$, so

$$Q_p = A_p q' N_q^* \leq A_p q_l \tag{8.13}$$

The limiting point resistance is

$$q_l(\text{kN/m}^2) = 50 N_q^* \tan \phi \tag{8.14}$$

where ϕ = soil friction angle in the bearing stratum

In English units, Eq. (8.14) becomes

$$q_l(\text{lb/ft}^2) = 1000 N_q^* \tan \phi \tag{8.15}$$

Based on field observations, Meyerhof (1976) also suggested that the ultimate point resistance, q_p, in a homogeneous granular soil ($L = L_b$) may be obtained from standard penetration numbers as

$$q_p(\text{kN/m}^2) = 40NL/D \leq 400N \tag{8.16a}$$

where N = average standard penetration number near the pile point (about $10D$ above and $4D$ below the pile point)

In English units

$$q_p(\text{lb/ft}^2) = 800NL/D \leq 8000N \tag{8.16b}$$

In many situations, a pile may initially penetrate a weak sand layer and then a dense layer, as shown in Figure 8.14. For such piles,

$$q_p = q_{(l)l} + \frac{[q_{l(d)} - q_{l(l)}]L_b}{10D} \leq q_{l(d)} \tag{8.17}$$

where $q_{l(l)}$ = limiting unit point resistance in the loose sand determined from Eq. (8.14) or (8.15) using the maximum value of N_q^* and ϕ value of the loose sand

$q_{l(d)}$ = limiting unit point resistance in the dense sand determined from Eq. (8.14) or (8.15) using the maximum value of N_q^* and ϕ value of the dense sand

L_b = depth of penetration into the dense sand layer

For piles in *saturated clays* in undrained conditions ($\phi = 0$),

$$Q_p = N_c^* c_u A_p = 9 c_u A_p \tag{8.18}$$

where c_u = undrained cohesion of the soil below the pile tip

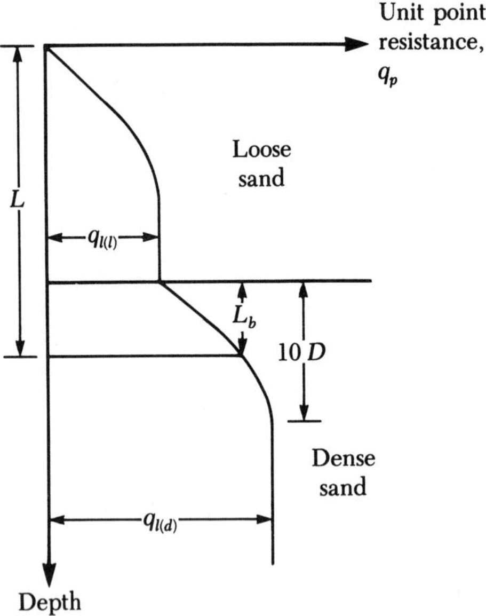

▼ **FIGURE 8.14** Variation of unit point resistance in layered soil

For clays with c and ϕ parameters present (effective stress basis), the ultimate point load is given by the relation presented in Eq. (8.11).

Vesic's Method Vesic (1977) proposed a method for estimating the pile point bearing capacity based on the theory of *expansion of cavities*. According to this theory, based on effective stress parameters,

$$Q_p = A_p q_p = A_p(cN_c^* + \sigma_o' N_\sigma^*) \tag{8.19}$$

where σ_o' = mean normal ground stress (effective) at the level of the pile point

$$= \left(\frac{1 + 2K_o}{3}\right)q' \tag{8.20}$$

K_o = earth pressure coefficient at rest $= 1 - \sin\phi$ (8.21)

N_c^*, N_σ^* = bearing capacity factors

Note that Eq. (8.19) is a modification of Eq. (8.11) with

$$N_\sigma^* = \frac{3N_q^*}{(1 + 2K_o)} \tag{8.22}$$

The relation for N_c^* given in Eq. (8.19) may be expressed as

$$N_c^* = (N_q^* - 1)\cot\phi \tag{8.23}$$

According to Vesic's theory,

$$N_\sigma^* = f(I_{rr}) \tag{8.24}$$

where I_{rr} = reduced rigidity index for the soil

However,

$$I_{rr} = \frac{I_r}{1 + I_r \Delta} \tag{8.25}$$

where I_r = rigidity index $= \dfrac{E_s}{2(1+\mu_s)(c + q' \tan\phi)} = \dfrac{G_s}{c + q' \tan\phi}$ (8.26)

E_s = modulus of elasticity of soil
μ_s = Poisson's ratio of soil
G_s = shear modulus of soil
Δ = average volumatic strain in the plastic zone below the pile point

For conditions of no volume change (dense sand or saturated clay), $\Delta = 0$. So

$$I_r = I_{rr} \tag{8.27}$$

Table 8.8 gives the values of N_c^* and N_σ^* for various values of the soil friction angle (ϕ) and I_{rr}. For $\phi = 0$ (undrained condition),

$$N_c^* = \frac{4}{3}(\ln I_{rr} + 1) + \frac{\pi}{2} + 1 \tag{8.28}$$

The values of I_r can be estimated from laboratory consolidation and triaxial tests corresponding to the proper stress levels. However, for preliminary use the following values are recommended.

Soil type	I_r
Sand	70–150
Silts and clays (drained condition)	50–100
Clays (undrained condition)	100–200

Janbu's Method Janbu (1976) proposed calculating Q_p as follows:

$$\boxed{Q_p = A_p(cN_c^* + q'N_q^*)} \tag{8.29}$$

▼ TABLE 8.8 Bearing Capacity Factors for Deep Foundations, N_c^* and N_σ^* (Eq. 8.19)

	I_{rr}									
ϕ	10	20	40	60	80	100	200	300	400	500
0	6.97	7.90	8.82	9.36	9.75	10.04	10.97	11.51	11.89	12.19
	1.00	1.00	1.00	1.00	1.00	1.00	1.00	1.00	1.00	1.00
1	7.34	8.37	9.42	10.04	10.49	10.83	11.92	12.57	13.03	13.39
	1.13	1.15	1.16	1.18	1.18	1.19	1.21	1.22	1.23	1.23
2	7.72	8.87	10.06	10.77	11.28	11.69	12.96	13.73	14.28	14.71
	1.27	1.31	1.35	1.38	1.39	1.41	1.45	1.48	1.50	1.51
3	8.12	9.40	10.74	11.55	12.14	12.61	14.10	15.00	15.66	16.18
	1.43	1.49	1.56	1.61	1.64	1.66	1.74	1.79	1.82	1.85
4	8.54	9.96	11.47	12.40	13.07	13.61	15.34	16.40	17.18	17.80
	1.60	1.70	1.80	1.87	1.91	1.95	2.07	2.15	2.20	2.24
5	8.99	10.56	12.25	13.30	14.07	14.69	16.69	17.94	18.86	19.59
	1.79	1.92	2.07	2.16	2.23	2.28	2.46	2.57	2.65	2.71
6	9.45	11.19	13.08	14.26	15.14	15.85	18.17	19.62	20.70	21.56
	1.99	2.18	2.37	2.50	2.59	2.67	2.91	3.06	3.18	3.27
7	9.94	11.85	13.96	15.30	16.30	17.10	19.77	12.46	22.71	23.73
	2.22	2.46	2.71	2.88	3.00	3.10	3.43	3.63	3.79	3.91
8	10.45	12.55	14.90	16.41	17.54	18.45	21.51	23.46	24.93	26.11
	2.47	2.76	3.09	3.31	3.46	3.59	4.02	4.30	4.50	4.67
9	10.99	13.29	15.91	17.59	18.87	19.90	23.39	25.64	27.35	28.73
	2.74	3.11	3.52	3.79	3.99	4.15	4.70	5.06	5.33	5.55
10	11.55	14.08	16.97	18.86	20.29	21.46	25.43	28.02	29.99	31.59
	3.04	3.48	3.99	4.32	4.58	4.78	5.48	5.94	6.29	6.57
11	12.14	14.90	18.10	20.20	21.81	23.13	27.64	30.61	32.87	34.73
	3.36	3.90	4.52	4.93	5.24	5.50	6.37	6.95	7.39	7.75
12	12.76	15.77	19.30	21.64	23.44	24.92	30.03	33.41	36.02	38.16
	3.71	4.35	5.10	5.60	5.98	6.30	7.38	8.10	8.66	9.11
13	13.41	16.69	20.57	23.17	25.18	26.84	32.60	36.46	39.44	41.89
	4.09	4.85	5.75	6.35	6.81	7.20	8.53	9.42	10.10	10.67
14	14.08	17.65	21.92	24.80	27.04	28.89	35.38	39.75	43.15	45.96
	4.51	5.40	6.47	7.18	7.74	8.20	9.82	10.91	11.76	12.46
15	14.79	18.66	23.35	26.53	29.02	31.08	38.37	43.32	47.18	50.39
	4.96	6.00	7.26	8.11	8.78	9.33	11.28	12.61	13.64	14.50
16	15.53	19.73	24.86	28.37	31.13	33.43	41.58	47.17	51.55	55.20
	5.45	6.66	8.13	9.14	9.93	10.58	12.92	14.53	15.78	16.83
17	16.30	20.85	26.46	30.33	33.37	35.92	45.04	51.32	56.27	60.42
	5.98	7.37	9.09	10.27	11.20	11.98	14.77	16.69	18.20	19.47
18	17.11	22.03	28.15	32.40	35.76	38.59	48.74	55.80	61.38	66.07
	6.56	8.16	10.15	11.53	12.62	13.54	16.84	19.13	20.94	22.47
19	17.95	23.26	29.93	34.59	38.30	41.42	52.71	60.61	66.89	72.18
	7.18	9.01	11.31	12.91	14.19	15.26	19.15	21.87	24.03	25.85
20	18.83	24.56	31.81	36.92	40.99	44.43	56.97	65.79	72.82	78.78
	7.85	9.94	12.58	14.44	15.92	17.17	21.73	24.94	27.51	29.67
21	19.75	25.92	33.80	39.38	43.85	47.64	61.51	71.34	79.22	85.90
	8.58	10.95	13.97	16.12	17.83	19.29	24.61	28.39	31.41	33.97

▼ **TABLE 8.8 (Continued)**

	I_{rr}									
ϕ	10	20	40	60	80	100	200	300	400	500
22	20.71	27.35	35.89	41.98	46.88	51.04	66.37	77.30	86.09	93.57
	9.37	12.05	15.50	17.96	19.94	21.62	27.82	32.23	35.78	38.81
23	21.71	28.84	38.09	44.73	50.08	54.66	71.56	83.68	93.47	101.83
	10.21	13.24	17.17	19.99	22.26	24.20	31.37	36.52	40.68	44.22
24	22.75	30.41	40.41	47.63	53.48	58.49	77.09	90.51	101.39	110.70
	11.13	14.54	18.99	22.21	24.81	27.04	35.32	41.30	46.14	50.29
25	23.84	32.05	42.85	50.69	57.07	62.54	82.98	97.81	109.88	120.23
	12.12	15.95	20.98	24.64	27.61	30.16	39.70	46.61	52.24	57.06
26	24.98	33.77	45.42	53.93	60.87	66.84	89.25	105.61	118.96	130.44
	13.18	17.47	23.15	27.30	30.69	33.60	44.53	52.51	59.02	64.62
27	26.16	35.57	48.13	57.34	64.88	71.39	95.02	113.92	128.67	141.39
	14.33	19.12	25.52	30.21	34.06	37.37	49.88	59.05	66.56	73.04
28	27.40	37.45	50.96	60.93	69.12	76.20	103.01	122.79	139.04	153.10
	15.57	20.91	28.10	33.40	37.75	41.51	55.77	66.29	74.93	82.40
29	28.69	39.42	53.95	64.71	73.58	81.28	110.54	132.23	150.11	165.61
	16.90	22.85	30.90	36.87	41.79	46.05	62.27	74.30	84.21	92.80
30	30.03	41.49	57.08	68.69	78.30	86.64	118.53	142.27	161.91	178.98
	18.24	24.95	33.95	40.66	46.21	51.02	69.43	83.14	94.48	104.33
31	31.43	43.64	60.37	72.88	83.27	92.31	126.99	152.95	174.49	193.23
	19.88	27.22	37.27	44.79	51.03	56.46	77.31	92.90	105.84	117.11
32	32.89	45.90	63.82	77.29	88.50	98.28	135.96	164.29	187.87	208.43
	21.55	29.68	40.88	49.30	56.30	62.41	85.96	103.66	118.39	131.24
33	34.41	48.26	67.44	81.92	94.01	104.58	145.46	176.33	202.09	224.62
	23.34	32.34	44.80	54.20	62.05	68.92	95.46	115.51	132.24	146.87
34	35.99	50.72	71.24	86.80	99.82	111.22	155.51	189.11	217.21	241.84
	25.28	35.21	49.05	59.54	68.33	76.02	105.90	128.55	147.51	164.12
35	37.65	53.30	75.22	91.91	105.92	118.22	166.14	202.64	233.27	260.15
	27.36	38.32	53.67	65.36	75.17	83.78	117.33	142.89	164.33	183.16
36	39.37	55.99	79.39	97.29	112.34	125.59	177.38	216.98	250.30	279.60
	29.60	41.68	58.68	71.69	82.62	92.24	129.87	158.65	182.85	204.14
37	41.17	58.81	83.77	102.94	119.10	133.34	189.25	232.17	268.36	300.26
	32.02	45.31	64.13	78.57	90.75	101.48	143.61	175.95	203.23	227.26
38	43.04	61.75	88.36	108.86	126.20	141.50	201.78	248.23	287.50	322.17
	34.63	49.24	70.03	86.05	99.60	111.56	158.65	194.94	225.62	252.71
39	44.99	64.83	93.17	115.09	133.66	150.09	215.01	265.23	307.78	345.41
	37.44	53.50	76.45	94.20	109.24	122.54	175.11	215.78	250.23	280.71
40	47.03	68.04	98.21	121.62	141.51	159.13	228.97	283.19	329.24	370.04
	40.47	58.10	83.40	103.05	119.74	134.52	193.13	238.62	277.26	311.50
41	49.16	71.41	103.49	128.48	149.75	168.63	243.69	302.17	351.95	396.12
	43.74	63.07	90.96	112.68	131.18	147.59	212.84	263.67	306.94	345.34
42	51.38	74.92	109.02	135.68	158.41	178.62	259.22	322.22	375.97	423.74
	47.27	68.46	99.16	123.16	143.64	161.83	234.40	291.13	339.52	382.53

▼ **TABLE 8.8 (Continued)**

	I_{rr}									
ϕ	10	20	40	60	80	100	200	300	400	500
43	53.70	78.60	114.82	143.23	167.51	189.13	275.59	343.40	401.36	452.96
	51.08	74.30	108.08	134.56	157.21	177.36	257.99	321.22	375.28	423.39
44	56.13	82.45	120.91	151.16	177.07	200.17	292.85	365.75	428.21	483.88
	55.20	80.62	117.76	146.97	172.00	194.31	283.80	354.20	414.51	468.28
45	58.66	86.48	127.28	159.48	187.12	211.79	311.04	389.35	456.57	516.58
	59.66	87.48	128.28	160.48	188.12	212.79	312.03	390.35	457.57	517.58
46	61.30	90.70	133.97	168.22	197.67	224.00	330.20	414.26	486.54	551.16
	64.48	94.92	139.73	175.20	205.70	232.96	342.94	429.98	504.82	571.74
47	64.07	95.12	140.99	177.40	208.77	236.85	350.41	440.54	518.20	587.72
	69.71	103.00	152.19	191.24	224.88	254.99	376.77	473.42	556.70	631.25
48	66.97	99.75	148.35	187.04	220.43	250.36	371.70	468.28	551.64	626.36
	75.38	111.78	165.76	208.73	245.81	279.06	413.82	521.08	613.65	696.64
49	70.01	104.60	156.09	197.17	232.70	264.58	394.15	497.56	586.96	667.21
	81.54	121.33	180.56	227.82	268.69	305.37	454.42	573.38	676.22	768.53
50	73.19	109.70	164.21	207.83	245.60	279.55	417.82	528.46	624.28	710.39
	88.23	131.73	196.70	248.68	293.70	334.15	498.94	630.80	744.99	847.61

From "Design of Pile Foundations," by A. S. Vesic, in NCHRP *Synthesis of Highway Practice 42,* Transportation Research Board, 1977. Reprinted by permission.
Note: Upper number N_c^*, lower number N_σ^*.

Note that Eq. (8.29) has the same form as Eq. (8.11). The bearing capacity factors N_c^* and N_q^* are calculated by assuming a failure surface in soil at the pile tip similar to that shown in the insert of Figure 8.15. The bearing capacity relationships then are

$$N_q^* = (\tan\phi + \sqrt{1 + \tan^2\phi})^2(e^{2\eta' \tan\phi}) \tag{8.30}$$

(The angle η' is defied in the insert of Figure 8.15.)

$$N_c^* = (N_q^* - 1)\cot\phi \tag{8.31}$$

$$\uparrow$$

$$\text{Eq. (8.30)}$$

Figure 8.15 shows the variation of N_q^* and N_c^* with ϕ and η'. The angle η' may vary from about 70° in soft clays to about 105° in dense sandy soils.

Regardless of the theoretical procedure used to calculate Q_p, its full magnitude cannot be realized until the pile tip has penetrated at least 10–25% of the width of the pile. This depth is critical in the case of sand.

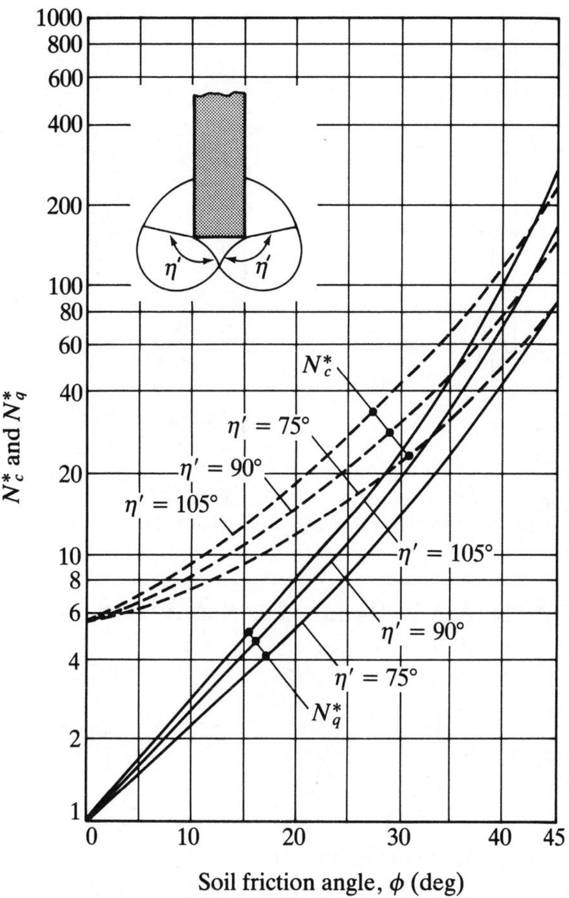

▼ **FIGURE 8.15** Janbu's bearing capacity factors

Frictional Resistance, Q_s

The frictional or skin resistance of a pile may be written as

$$Q_s = \sum p \, \Delta L \, f \tag{8.32}$$

where p = perimeter of the pile section

ΔL = incremental pile length over which p and f are taken constant (Figure 8.16a)

f = unit friction resistance at any depth z

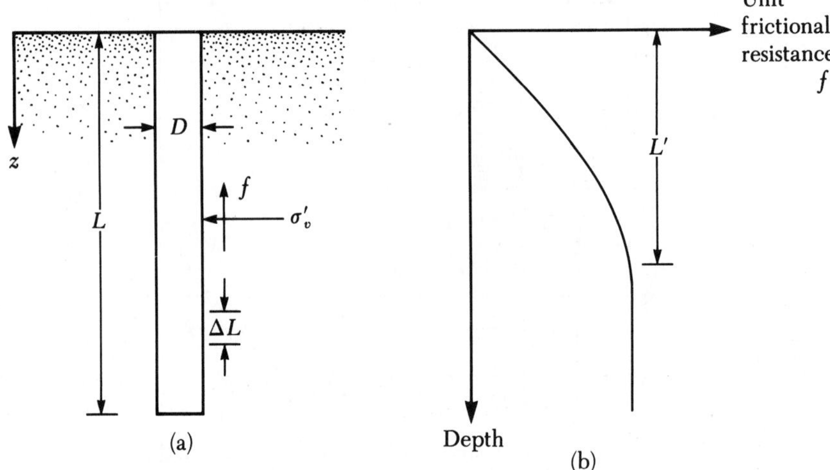

▼ **FIGURE 8.16** Unit frictional resistance for piles in sand

Frictional Resistance in Sand The unit frictional resistance at any depth for a pile is

$$f = K\sigma'_v \tan\delta \tag{8.33}$$

where K = earth pressure coefficient

σ'_v = effective vertical stress at the depth under consideration

δ = soil–pile friction angle

In reality, the magnitude of K varies with depth. It is approximately equal to the Rankine passive earth pressure coefficient, K_p, at the top of the pile and may be less than the at-rest earth pressure coefficient, K_o, at the pile tip. It also depends on the nature of pile installation. Based on presently available results, the following average values of K are recommended for use in Eq. (8.33).

Pile type	*K*
Bored or jetted	$\approx K_o = 1 - \sin\phi$
Low-displacement driven	$\approx K_o = 1 - \sin\phi$ to $1.4K_o = 1.4(1 - \sin\phi)$
High-displacement driven	$\approx K_o = 1 - \sin\phi$ to $1.8K_o = 1.8(1 - \sin\phi)$

For high-displacement driven piles, Bhusan (1982) recommended

$$K\tan\delta = 0.18 + 0.0065D_r \tag{8.34}$$

and

$$K = 0.5 + 0.008D_r \tag{8.35}$$

where D_r = relative density (%)

The effective vertical stress, σ'_v, for use in Eq. (8.33) increases with pile depth to a maximum limit at a depth of 15–20 pile diameters and remains constant thereafter, as shown in Figure 8.16b. This critical depth, L', depends on several factors, such as soil friction angle and compressibility and relative density. A conservative estimate would be to assume that

$$L' = 15D \tag{8.36}$$

The values of δ from various investigations appear to be in the range of 0.5ϕ to 0.8ϕ. Judgment must be used in choosing the value of δ.

Meyerhof (1976) also indicated that the average unit frictional resistance, f_{av}, for high-displacement driven piles may be obtained from average standard penetration resistance values as

$$f_{av}(\text{kN/m}^2) = 2\overline{N} \tag{8.37a}$$

where $\overline{N}$ = average value of standard penetration resistance

In English units, Eq. (8.37a) becomes

$$f_{av}(\text{lb/ft}^2) = 40\overline{N} \tag{8.37b}$$

For low-displacement driven piles

$$f_{av}(\text{kN/m}^2) = \overline{N} \tag{8.38a}$$

and

$$f_{av}(\text{lb/ft}^2) = 20\overline{N} \tag{8.38b}$$

Thus

$$Q_s = pLf_{av} \tag{8.39}$$

Frictional (or Skin) Resistance in Clay Several methods of obtaining unit frictional (or skin) resistance of piles in clay are available. Three of the presently accepted procedures are described briefly.

1. *λ Method:* This method was proposed by Vijayvergiya and Focht (1972). It is based on the assumption that the displacement of soil caused by pile driving results in a passive lateral pressure at any depth and that the average unit skin resistance is

$$\boxed{f_{av} = \lambda(\bar{\sigma}'_v + 2c_u)} \tag{8.40}$$

where $\bar{\sigma}'_v$ = mean effective vertical stress for the entire embedment length
c_u = mean undrained shear strength ($\phi = 0$ concept)

The value of λ changes with the depth of pile penetration (see Figure 8.17). Thus the total frictional resistance may be calculated as

$$Q_s = pLf_{av}$$

Care should be taken in obtaining the values of $\bar{\sigma}'_v$ and c_u in layered soil. Figure 8.18 helps explain the reason. According to Figure 8.18b, the mean value of c_u is $(c_{u(1)}L_1 + c_{u(2)}L_2 + \cdots)/L$. Similarly, Figure 8.18c shows the plot of the variation of effective stress with depth. The mean effective stress is

$$\bar{\sigma}'_v = \frac{A_1 + A_2 + A_3 + \cdots}{L} \tag{8.41}$$

where $A_1, A_2, A_3, \ldots$ = areas of the vertical effective stress diagrams

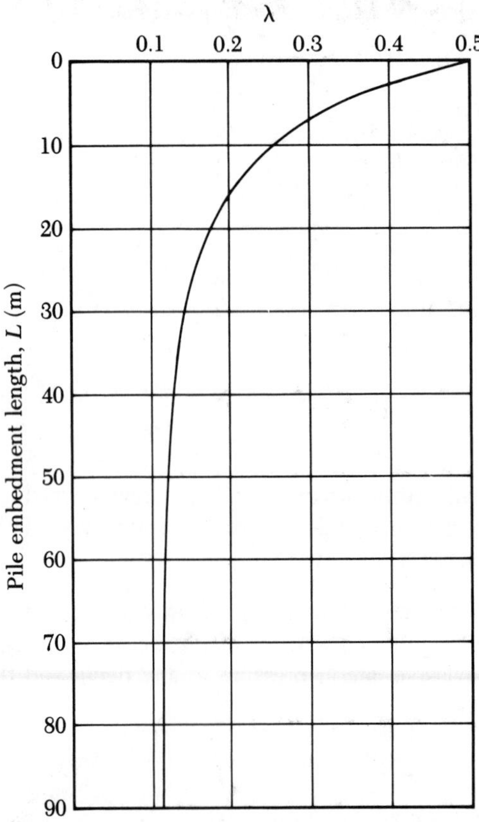

▼ **FIGURE 8.17** Variation of λ with pile embedment length (redrawn after McClelland, 1974)

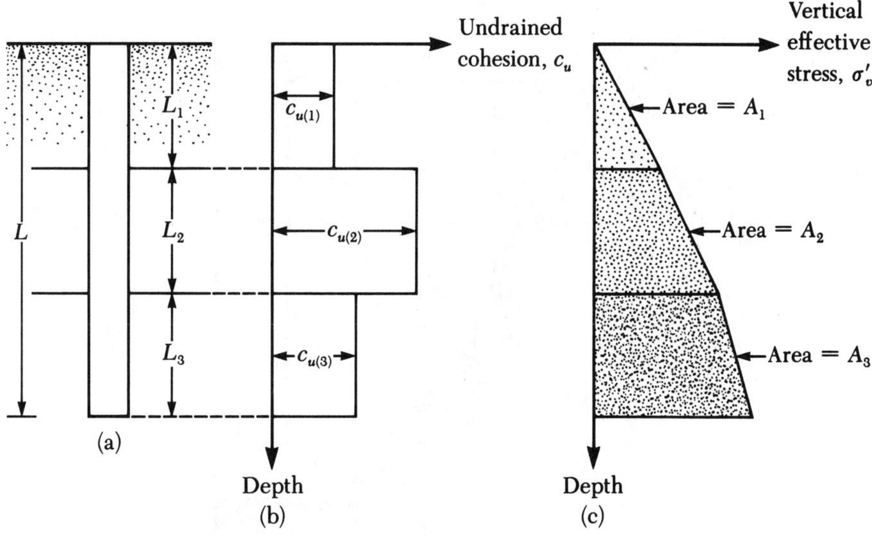

▼ **FIGURE 8.18** Application of λ method in layered soil

2. *α Method:* According to the α method, the unit skin resistance in clayey soils can be represented by the equation

$$f = \alpha c_u \tag{8.42}$$

where α = empirical adhesion factor

The approximate variation of the value of α is shown in Figure 8.19. Note that for normally consolidated clays with $c_u \leq$ about 1 kip/ft^2 (50 kN/m^2), $\alpha = 1$. Thus

$$Q_s = \sum fp \, \Delta L = \sum \alpha c_u p \, \Delta L \tag{8.43}$$

The American Petroleum Institute (1984) recommended a slightly different varition of α and c_u. It is shown in Figure 8.20.

3. *β Method:* When piles are driven into saturated clays, the pore water pressure in the soil around the piles increases. This excess pore water pressure in normally consolidated clays may be 4 to 6 times c_u. However, within a month or so, this pressure gradually dissipates. Hence the unit frictional resistance

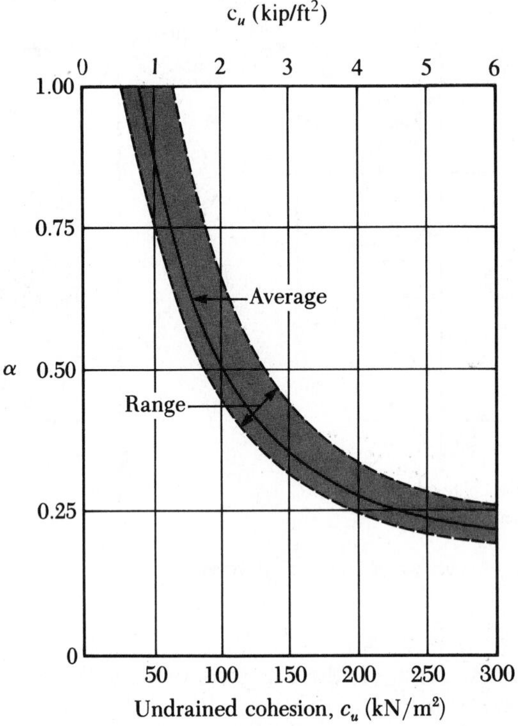

▼ **FIGURE 8.19** Variation of α with undrained cohesion of clay

for the pile can be determined on the basis of the effective stress parameters of the clay in a remolded state ($c = 0$). Thus at any depth

$$\boxed{f = \beta \sigma'_v} \tag{8.44}$$

where σ'_v = vertical effective stress
$\beta = K \tan \phi_R$
ϕ_R = drained friction angle of remolded clay (8.45)
K = earth pressure coefficient

Conservatively, the magnitude of K is the earth pressure coefficient at rest, or

$$K = 1 - \sin \phi_R \quad \text{(for normally consolidated clays)} \tag{8.46}$$

and

$$K = (1 - \sin \phi_R)\sqrt{OCR} \quad \text{(for overconsolidated clays)} \tag{8.47}$$

where OCR = overconsolidation ratio

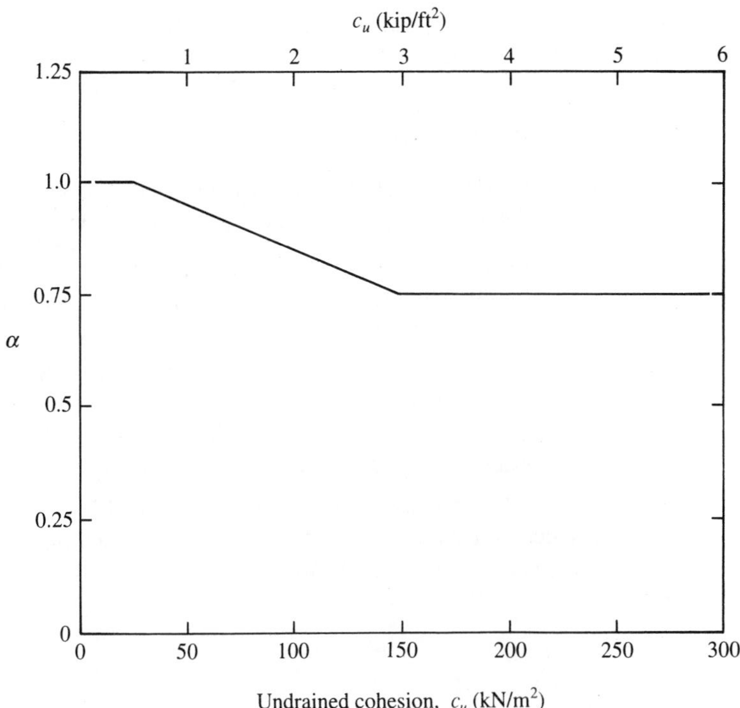

▼ **FIGURE 8.20** Variation of α, as recommended by the American Petroleum Institute (1984)

Combining Eqs. (8.44), (8.45), (8.46), and (8.47), for normally consolidated clays yields

$$f = (1 - \sin \phi_R) \tan \phi_R \, \sigma'_v \tag{8.48}$$

and for overconsolidated clays,

$$f = (1 - \sin \phi_R) \tan \phi_R \sqrt{OCR} \, \sigma'_v \tag{8.49}$$

With the value of f determined, the total frictional resistance may be evaluated as

$$Q_s = \Sigma \, fp \, \Delta L$$

Allowable Pile Capacity

After the total ultimate load-carrying capacity of a pile has been determined by summing the point bearing capacity and the frictional (or skin) resistance, a reasonable factor of safety should be used to obtain the total allowable load for each pile, or

$$Q_{\text{all}} = \frac{Q_u}{FS} \tag{8.50}$$

where Q_{all} = allowable load-carrying capacity for each pile
FS = factor of safety

The factor of safety generally used ranges from 2.5 to 4, depending on the uncertainties of ultimate load calculation.

General Comments

Although calculations for the ultimate load-carrying capacity of piles are made by using the preceding equations, an engineer needs to keep the following points in mind.

1. For an initial value of the soil friction angle, ϕ, driven piles in sand may show about 50–100% higher unit point resistance than bored piles do. This condition is a result of the densification of soil during pile driving.
2. In sandy soils, cast-in-place piles with pedestals may show about 50–100% higher unit point resistance than cast-in-place piles without pedestals do. The high-impact energy of the hammer building the pedestal causes substantial soil compaction and thus an increase of the soil friction angle.
3. In calculating the area of cross section, A_p, and the perimeter, p, of piles with developed profiles, such as H-piles and open-ended pipe piles, the effect of soil plug should be considered. According to Figure 8.10b and 8.10c, for pipe piles

$$A_p = \left(\frac{\pi}{4}\right)D^2$$

$$p = 2\pi D$$

Similarly, for H-piles

$$A_p = d_1 d_2$$

$$p = 2(d_1 + d_2)$$

Also, note that for H-piles, because $d_2 > d_1$, $D = d_1$.

4. The ultimate point load relations given in Eqs. (8.11), (8.19), and (8.29) are for the gross ultimate point load; that is, they include the weight of the pile. So, the net ultimate point load is approximately

$$Q_{p(\text{net})} = Q_{p(\text{gross})} - q'A_p$$

However, in practice, for soils with $\phi > 0$, the assumption is made that $Q_{p(\text{net})} = Q_{p(\text{gross})}$.

In cohesive soils with $\phi = 0$, $N_q^* = 1$ (Figure 8.13). Hence from Eq. (8.11),

$$Q_{p(\text{gross})} = (c_u N_c^* + q')A_p$$

So

$$Q_{p(\text{net})} = [(c_u N_c^* + q') - q']A_p = c_u N_c^* A_p = 9c_u A_p = Q_p$$

This relation is the one given in Eq. (8.18).

8.7 COYLE AND CASTELLO DESIGN CORRELATIONS

Coyle and Castello (1981) analyzed 24 large-scale field load tests of driven piles in sand. For sands, the ultimate load may be expressed as

$$Q_u = Q_p + Q_s = q'N_q^* A_p + f_{av} pL \tag{8.51}$$

where q' = effective vertical stress at the pile tip

f_{av} = average frictional resistance for the entire pile length and can be given by the relation

$$f_{av} = K\bar{\sigma}'_v \tan \delta \tag{8.52}$$

and

K = lateral earth pressure coefficient

$\bar{\sigma}'_v$ = average effective overburden pressure

δ = soil–pile friction angle

Based on that study, the calculated values of the bearing capacity factor (N_q^*) were correlated with the embedment ratio L/D. Figure 8.21 shows the values of N_q^* for

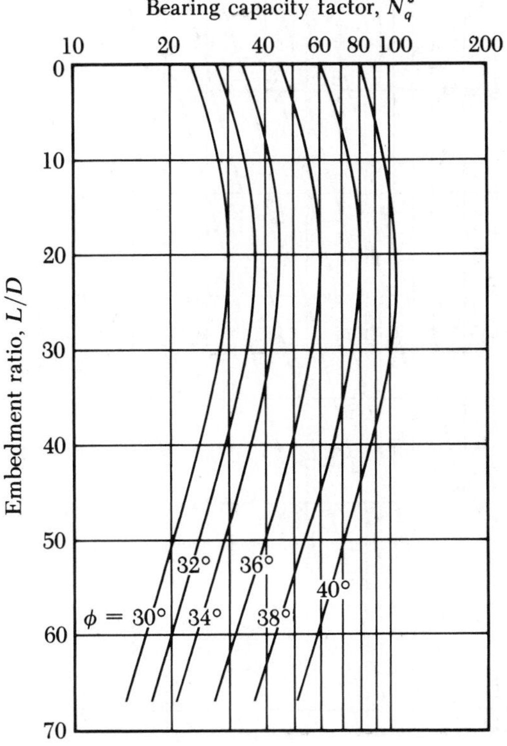

FIGURE 8.21 Variation of N_q^* with L/D (redrawn after Coyle and Castello, 1981)

various embedment ratios and soil friction angles. Note that N_q^* gradually increases with L/D to a maximum value and decreases thereafter.

Similarly the magnitudes of K deduced for various values of ϕ and L/D ratios are plotted in Figure 8.22. For any soil friction angle, K decreases linearly with embedment ratio. In Figure 8.22 the assumption is that

$$\delta = 0.8\phi \tag{8.53}$$

Hence combining Eqs. (8.51), (8.52), and (8.53) gives

$$Q_u = q'N_q^* A_p + pLK\bar{\sigma}_v' \tan(0.8\phi) \tag{8.54}$$

Using the results of 24 pile load tests, Coyle and Castello showed that Eq. (8.54) can predict the ultimate load with an error band of $\pm 30\%$, with a majority falling within an error band of $\pm 20\%$.

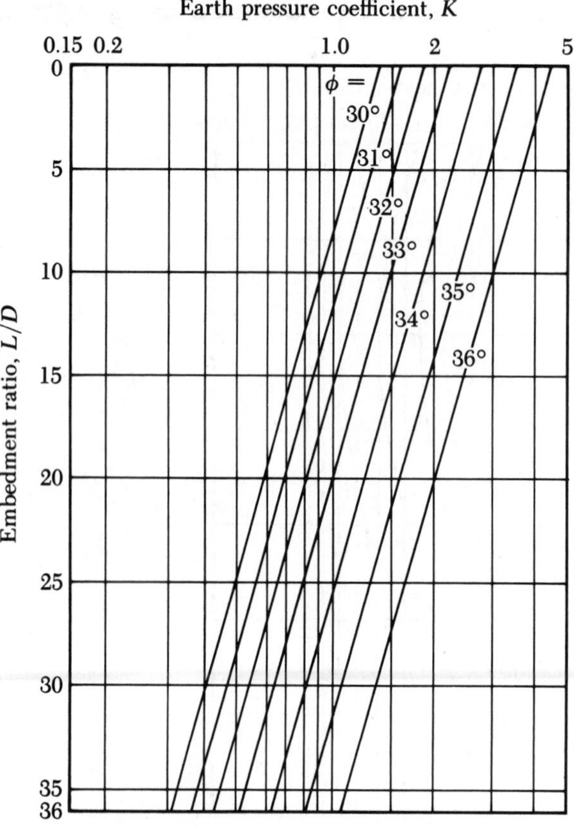

▼ **FIGURE 8.22** Variation of K with L/D (redrawn after Coyle and Castello, 1981)

▼ EXAMPLE 8.1

A fully embedded precast concrete pile 50 ft long is driven into a homogeneous sand layer ($c = 0$). The pile is square in cross section with sides measuring 12 in. The dry unit weight of sand, γ_d, is 110 lb/ft^3, the average soil friction angle is 35°, and the standard penetration resistance near the vicinity of the pile tip is 16. Calculate the ultimate point load on the pile by

a. Meyerhof's method using Eqs. (8.12) and (8.13)
b. Meyerhof's method using Eq. (8.16b)
c. Vesic's method using Eq. (8.19) and $I_r = I_{rr} = 90$
d. Coyle and Castello's method using Eq. (8.51) and Fig. 8.20

Solution

Part a: Meyerhof's Method [Eqs. (8.12) and (8.13)]

This soil is homogeneous, so $L_b = L$. For $\phi = 35°$, $N_q^* \approx 120$. Thus

$$q' = \gamma_d L = (110)(50) = 5500 \text{ lb/ft}^2$$

$$Q_p = A_p q' N_q^* = \left[\frac{(12)(12)}{144}\right](5500)(12) = 66 \times 10^6 \text{ lb} = 330 \text{ ton}$$

However, from Eq. (8.15),

$$q_l = 100 N_q^* \tan\phi = (1000)(120)(\tan 35°) = 84{,}025 \text{ lb/ft}^2 = 42 \text{ ton/ft}^2$$

$$Q_p = A_p q_l = \left[\frac{(12)(12)}{144}\right](42) = 42 \text{ ton}$$

So

$$Q_p = \mathbf{42\ ton}$$

Part b: Meyerhof's Method [Eq. (8.16b)]

From Eq. (8.16b),

$$q_p(\text{lb/ft}^2) = 800N\left(\frac{L}{D}\right) \le 8000N$$

$$\frac{L}{D} = \frac{50 \text{ ft}}{1 \text{ ft}} = 50$$

As $L/D > 10$,

$$q_p = 8000N = (8000)(16) = 128{,}000 \text{ lb/ft}^2$$

$$Q_p = A_p q_p = \left[\frac{(12)(12)}{144}\right](128{,}000) = 128{,}000 \text{ lb} = \mathbf{64\ ton}$$

Part c: Vesic's Method

Here, $I_{rr} \approx 90$. For $\phi = 35°$, Table 8.8 gives $N'_\sigma \approx 79.5$. From Eq. (8.19),

$$Q_p = A_p \sigma'_o N^*_\sigma$$

$$\sigma'_o = \frac{1 + 2K_o}{3} q'$$

$$K_o = 1 - \sin\phi = 1 - \sin 35° = 0.43$$

$$\sigma'_o = \left[\frac{1 + (2)(0.43)}{3}\right](5500) = 3410 \text{ lb/ft}^2$$

$$Q_p = \left[\frac{(12)(12)}{144}\right](3410)(79.5) = 271{,}095 \text{ lb} \approx \mathbf{135.5\ ton}$$

Part d: Coyle and Castello's Method

For $L/D = 50$ and $\phi = 35°$, Figure 8.21 gives $N^*_q = 33$. So

$$Q_p = q' N^*_q A_p = (5500)(33)\left[\frac{(12)(12)}{144}\right] = 181{,}500 \text{ lb} \approx \mathbf{91\ ton}$$

Note: For this problem, Vesic's equation gives a much higher value (135.5 ton). The next highest values are obtained from Coyle and Castello's equation (91 ton). A conservative estimation is

$$Q_p = \frac{42 + 64}{2} \approx \mathbf{53\ ton.}$$ ▼

▼ EXAMPLE 8.2

Consider a precast concrete pile 12 m long in a homogeneous soil layer. The pile cross section = 305 mm × 305 mm, the unit weight of sand, $\gamma_d = 16.8$ kN/m^3, and the soil friction angle, $\phi = 35°$. Determine the total frictional resistance.

a. Use Eqs. (8.32), (8.33), and (8.36). Also use $K = 1.4$ and $\delta = 0.6\phi$.
b. Use Coyle and Castello's method.

Solution

Part a

The unit skin friction at any depth is given by Eq. (8.33) as

$$f = K\sigma'_v \tan\delta$$

Also from Eq. (8.36),

$$L' = 15D$$

So, for depth $z = 0$–$15D$, $\sigma'_v = \gamma z = 16.8z$ (kN/m^2), and beyond $z \geq 15D$, $\sigma'_v = \gamma(15D) = (16.8)(15 \times 0.305) = 76.86$ kN/m^2. This result is shown in Figure 8.23.

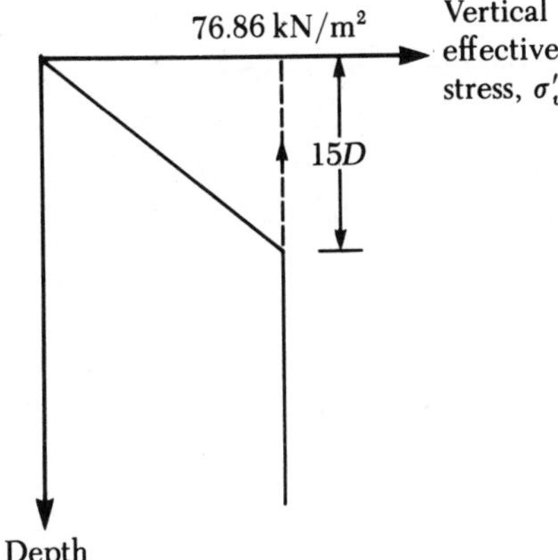

▼ **FIGURE 8.23**

The *frictional resistance from* $z = 0$ to $15D$ is

$$Q_s = pL'f_{av} = [(4)(0.305)][15D]\left[\frac{(1.4)(76.86)\tan(0.6 \times 35)}{2}\right]$$

$$= (1.22)(4.575)(20.65) = 115.26 \text{ kN}$$

The *frictional resistance from* $z = 15D$ to 12 m is

$$Q_s = p(L - L')f_{z=15D} = [(4)(0.305)][12 - 4.575][(1.4)(76.86)\tan(0.6 \times 35)]$$

$$= (1.22)(7.425)(41.3) = 374.1 \text{ kN}$$

So, the total frictional resistance equals $115.26 + 374.1 = 489.35$ kN ≈ **490 kN**

Part b: Coyle and Castello's Method

From Eqs. (8.52) and (8.53),

$$f_{av} = K\bar{\sigma}'_v \tan\delta$$

$$\delta = 0.8\phi$$

$$Q_s = f_{av}pL = [K\bar{\sigma}'_v \tan(0.8\phi)]pL$$

For this pile, $L/D = 39.34$. According to Figure 8.22 for determining K, this magnitude is out of the range of the graph. By interpolation, for $L/D = 39.34$ and $\phi = 35°$, $K \approx 0.7$. Now

$$\bar{\sigma}'_v = \frac{\gamma L}{2} = \frac{(16.8)(12)}{2} = 100.8 \text{ kN/m}^2$$

So

$$Q_s = [(0.7)(100.8)\tan(0.8 \times 35)](4 \times 0.305)(12) = 549.3 \text{ kN} \approx \mathbf{550 \text{ kN}}.$$ ▼

▼ EXAMPLE 8.3

A concrete pile embedded in sand has a cross section of 0.305 m × 0.305 m. The length of embedment of the pile is 15 m, the relative density of sand is 50%, and the unit weight of sand is 17 kN/m³. Use Eqs. (8.32), (8.33), (8.34), and (8.36) to determine the frictional resistance of the pile.

Solution

From Eq. (8.33),

$$f = K\sigma'_v \tan \delta$$

From Eq. (8.36),

$$L' = 15D = (15)(0.305) = 4.575 \text{ m}$$

From Eq. (8.34),

$$K \tan \delta = 0.18 + 0.0065D_r = 0.18 + (0.0065)(50) = 0.505$$

So

$$Q_s = pL'f_{\text{av}(z=0 \text{ to } 4.575 \text{ m})} + p(L - L')f_{z=4.575 \text{ m}}$$

$$= (4 \times 0.305)(4.575)\left[\frac{0 + (0.505)(17 \times 4.575)}{2}\right]$$

$$+ (4 \times 0.305)(15 - 4.575)[(0.505)(17 \times 4.575)]$$

$$= 109.6 + 499.5 \approx \mathbf{609\ kN}.$$ ▼

▼ EXAMPLE 8.4

An HP 310 × 1.079 steel pile is driven into sand, as shown in Figure 8.24a.

a. Calculate the ultimate point load (1) by Meyerhof's procedure, (2) by Vesic's procedure ($I_r = 150 = I_{rr}$), and (3) by using standard penetration resistance equations. (The average value of N in the vicinity of the pile point is 45.)
b. Estimate the value of the ultimate point load from the calculations in part (a).
c. Calculate the ultimate frictional resistance, Q_s. Use Eqs. (8.32), (8.33), and (8.36), $K = 1.4$, and $\delta = 0.6\phi$.
d. Calculate the allowable pile load. Use $FS = 4$.

Also check the allowable load-bearing capacity of the steel section of the pile. Use $f_s = 62{,}000$ kN/m² for steel.

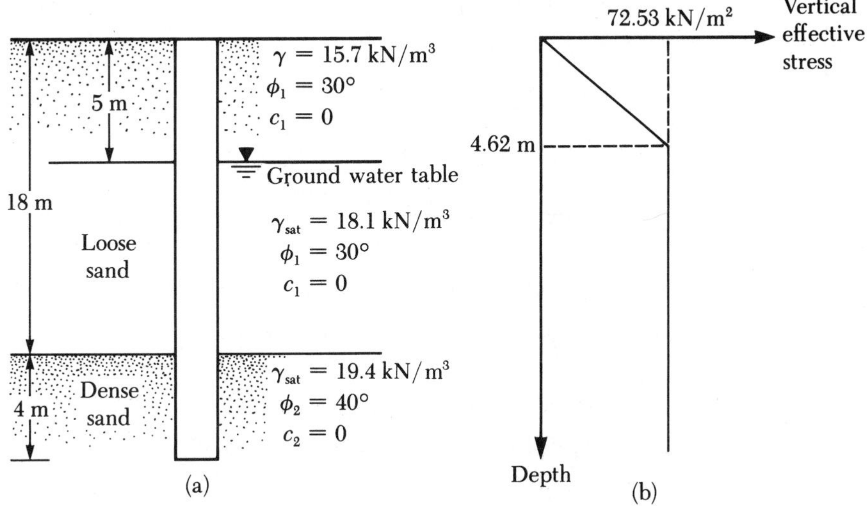

▼ **FIGURE 8.24**

Solution In Table 8.1b, the depth of the pile section, d_1 = 308 mm and the flange width = 310 mm. The area of the pile section, A_p, for capacity calculation = 0.308 × 0.310 = 0.0955 m².

Part a: Calculation of Ultimate Point Load

Meyerhof's Procedure

The variation of the unit point resistance will be like that in Figure 8.14. The depth of penetration of the lower dense sand layer, L_b, is 4 m. So $L_b/D = 4/0.308 = 12.99 > 10$. Hence from (8.17),

$$q_p = q_{l(d)} = 50N_q^* \tan \phi_2$$

For $\phi_2 = 40°$, $N_q^* \approx 350$ (Figure 8.13). Thus

$$q_p = (50)(350)(\tan 40°) \approx 14{,}684 \text{ kN/m}^2$$

So

$$Q_p = (14{,}684)(0.0955) = \mathbf{1402\ kN}$$

Also, check Eq. (8.12), from which $Q_p = A_p q' N_q^*$:

$$q' = 5(15.7) + 13(18.1 - 9.81) + 4(19.4 - 9.81)$$
$$= 78.5 + 107.77 + 38.36 = 224.63 \text{ kN/m}^2$$

So

$$Q_p = (0.0955)(224.63)(350) = 7508 \text{ kN}$$

Because Q_p = 1402 kN < 7508 kN, Eq. (8.17) controls. Thus Q_p = **1402 kN**

Vesic's Procedure

From Eq. (8.19),

$$Q_p = A_p \sigma'_o N^*_\sigma$$

$$K_o = 1 - \sin\phi = 1 - \sin 40° = 0.357$$

$$\sigma'_o = \frac{1 + 2K_o}{3} q' = \left[\frac{1 + (2)(0.357)}{3}\right](224.63) = 128.34 \text{ kN/m}^2$$

From Table 8.8 for $\phi = 40°$ and $I_{rr} = 150$, $N^*_\sigma \approx (134.52 + 193.13)/2 = 163.8$. So

$$Q_p = (0.0955)(128.34)(163.8) = \mathbf{2008\ kN}$$

Standard Penetration Resistance Equations

The average penetration resistance, N, near the pile point is about 45. From Eq. (8.16a),

$$q_p = 40N\frac{L}{D} \leq 400N$$

So

$$q_p = 40(45)\left(\frac{22}{0.308}\right) = 128{,}571 \text{ kN/m}^2$$

or

$$q_p = (400)(N) = (400)(45) = 18{,}000 \text{ kN/m}^2$$

Hence $q_p = 18{,}000$ kN/m^2 controls. So

$$Q_p = A_p q_p = (0.0955)(18{,}000) = \mathbf{1719\ kN}$$

Part b: Estimation of Value for Q_p

Considering all three results, we might use

$$Q_p = \frac{1402 + 2008 + 1719}{3} \approx \mathbf{1709\ kN}$$

Part c: Calculation of Ultimate Frictional Resistance

According to Eq. (8.36),

$$L' = 15D = 15(0.308) = 4.62 \text{ m}$$

For ultimate frictional resistance, σ'_v will remain constant for $z > 4.62$ m. The assumed variation of σ'_v with depth is shown in Figure 8.24b.

The frictional resistance from $z = 0$ to 4.62 m is

$$pLf_{av} = 2(0.308 + 0.310)(4.62)\left(\frac{K\sigma'_v \tan\delta}{2}\right)$$

$$= 5.71\left[\frac{(1.4)(72.53)\tan(0.6 \times 30)}{2}\right] = \mathbf{94.2\ kN}$$

The frictional resistance from $z = 4.62$ m to 22 m is

$$pLf_{(z=4.62\text{ m})} = 2(0.308 + 0.310)(22 - 4.62)(K\sigma'_v \tan \delta)$$
$$= 21.48[(1.4)(72.53)\tan \delta]$$

As an approximation, $\delta = 0.6\phi_1 = (0.6)(30) = 18°$ for the entire length. Thus

$$Q_{s(z=4.62-22\text{ m})} = (21.48)(1.4)(72.53)\tan 18° = 708.7 \text{ kN}$$

So the total frictional resistance is

$$Q_s = Q_{s(z=0-4.62\text{ m})} + Q_{s(z=4.62-22\text{ m})}$$
$$= 94.2 + 708.7 = 802.9 \text{ kN} \approx \mathbf{803\ kN}$$

Part d: Calculation of Allowable Load

To calculate $Q_u = Q_p + Q_s$, we use $Q_p = 1709$ kN from part (b) and $Q_s = 802.9$ kN from part (c). So $Q_u \approx 1709 + 803 = 2512$ kN. Thus

$$Q_{\text{all}} = \frac{Q_u}{FS} = \frac{2512}{4} = 628 \text{ kN}$$

We also need to check the allowable load-bearing capacity for the steel pile section. Table 8.1b shows that the area of steel section for the pile is 14.1×10^{-3} m^2, so

$$Q_{\text{all}} = (f_s)14.1 \times 10^{-3}$$
$$f_s = 62{,}000 \text{ kN/m}^2$$

and

$$Q_{\text{all}} = (62{,}000)(14.1 \times 10^{-3}) = 874.2 \text{ kN}$$

Hence the allowable pile load is **628 kN** (<874.2 kN). ▼

▼ EXAMPLE 8.5

A concrete pile 18 in. × 18 in. in cross section is embedded in a saturated clay. The length of embedment is 55 ft. The undrained cohesion, c_u, of clay is 1250 lb/ft^2, and the unit weight of clay is 118 lb/ft^3. Use a factor of safety of 5 to determine the allowable load the pile can carry.

a. Use the α method
b. Use the λ method

Solution

Part a: The α Method

From Eq. (8.18),

$$Q_p = A_p q_p = A_p c_u N_c^* = \frac{\left(\frac{18 \times 18}{144}\right)(1250)(9)}{1000} = 23.5 \text{ kip}$$

From Eqs. (8.42) and (8.43),

$$Q_s = \alpha c_u p L$$

From the average plot of Figure 8.19 for $c_u = 1250\ \text{lb/ft}^2$, $\alpha \approx 0.77$ and

$$Q_s = \frac{(0.77)(1250)\left(\frac{4 \times 18}{12}\right)(55)}{1000} = 317.6\ \text{kip}$$

$$Q_{\text{all}} = \frac{Q_p + Q_s}{F_s} = \frac{25.3 + 317.6}{5} \approx \mathbf{68.6\ kip}$$

Part b: The λ Method

From Eq. (8.40),

$$f_{\text{av}} = \lambda(\bar{\sigma}'_v + 2c_u)$$

Convert $L = 55$ ft to $L = 16.77$ m. From Figure 8.17 for $L = 16.77$ m, $\lambda \approx 0.2$, so

$$f_{\text{av}} = 0.2\left[\left(\frac{118 \times 55}{2}\right)\left(\frac{1}{1000}\right) + 2\left(\frac{1250}{1000}\right)\right] = 1.149\ \text{kip/ft}^2$$

$$Q_s = pLf_{\text{av}} = \left(4 \times \frac{18}{12}\right)(55)(1.149) = 379.2\ \text{kip}$$

As in part (a), $Q_p = 23.5$ kip. So

$$Q_{\text{all}} = \frac{Q_p + Q_s}{F_s} = \frac{25.3 + 379.2}{5} = \mathbf{80.9\ kip.}$$ ▼

▼ EXAMPLE 8.6

A driven pipe pile in clay is shown in Figure 8.25a. The pipe has an outside diameter of 406 mm and a wall thickness of 6.35 mm.

a. Calculate the net point bearing capacity. Use Eq. (8.18).
b. Calculate the skin resistance (1) by using Eqs. (8.42) and (8.43) (α method), (2) by using Eq. (8.40) (λ method), and (3) by using Eq. (8.44) (β method). For all clay layers, $\phi_R = 30°$. The top 10 m of clay is normally consolidated. The bottom clay layer has an *OCR* of 2.
c. Estimate the net allowable pile capacity. Use $FS = 4$.

Solution The area of cross section of the pile, including the soil inside the pile, is

$$A_p = \frac{\pi}{4}D^2 = \frac{\pi}{4}(0.406)^2 = 0.1295\ \text{m}^2$$

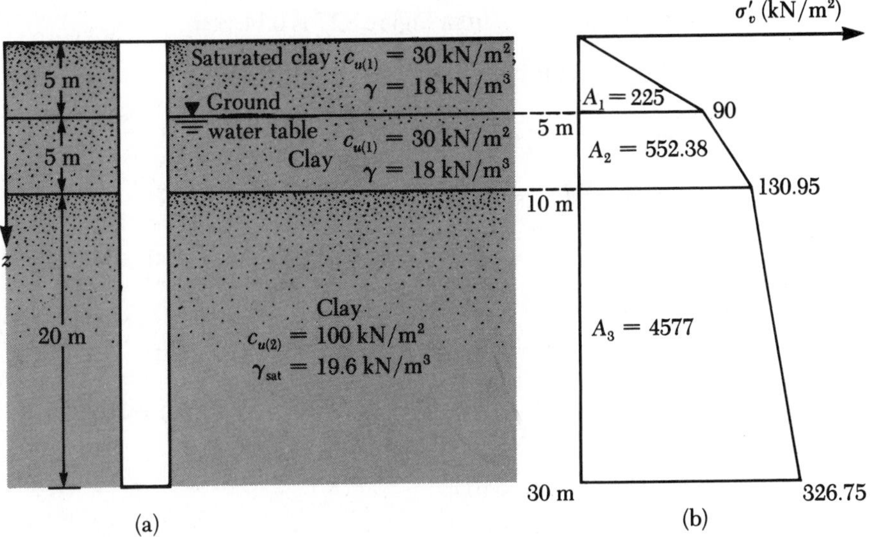

▼ **FIGURE 8.25**

Part a: Calculation of Net Point Bearing Capacity

From Eq. (8.18),

$$Q_p = A_p q_p = A_p N_c^* c_{u(2)} = (0.1295)(9)(100) = \mathbf{116.55\ kN}$$

Part b: Calculation of Skin Resistance

(1) Use of Eqs. (8.42) and (8.43): from Eq. (8.43),

$$Q_s = \Sigma\ \alpha c_u p\ \Delta L$$

For the top soil layer, $c_{u(1)} = 30$ kN/m². According to the average plot of Figure 8.19, $\alpha_1 = 1.0$. Similarly, for the bottom soil layer, $c_{u(2)} = 100$ kN/m²; $\alpha_2 = 0.5$. Thus

$$\begin{aligned} Q_s &= \alpha_1 c_{u(1)}[(\pi)(0.406)]10 + \alpha_2 c_{u(2)}[(\pi)(0.406)]20 \\ &= (1)(30)[(\pi)(0.406)]10 + (0.5)(100)[(\pi)(0.406)]20 \\ &= 382.7 + 1275.5 = \mathbf{1658.2\ kN} \end{aligned}$$

(2) Use of Eq. (8.40): $f_{av} = \lambda(\bar{\sigma}'_v + 2c_u)$. The average value of c_u is

$$\frac{c_{u(1)}(10) + c_{u(2)}(20)}{30} = \frac{(30)(10) + (100)(20)}{30} = 76.7 \text{ kN/m}^2$$

To obtain the average value of $\bar{\sigma}'_v$, the diagram for vertical effective stress variation with depth is plotted in Figure 8.25b. From Eq. (8.41),

$$\bar{\sigma}'_v = \frac{A_1 + A_2 + A_3}{L} = \frac{225 + 552.38 + 4577}{30} = 178.48 \text{ kN/m}^2$$

The magnitude of λ from Figure 8.17 is 0.14. So

$$f_{av} = 0.14[178.48 \times (2)(76.7)] = 46.46 \text{ kN/m}^2$$

Hence

$$Q_s = pLf_{av} = \pi(0.406)(30)(46.46) = \mathbf{1777.8\ kN}$$

(3) Use of Eq. (8.44): The top clay layer (10 m) is normally consolidated and $\phi_R = 30°$. For $z = 0$–5 m [Eq. (8.48)],

$$f_{av(1)} = (1 - \sin \phi_R) \tan \phi_R \, \sigma'_{v(av)}$$

$$= (1 - \sin 30°)(\tan 30°)\left(\frac{0 + 90}{2}\right) = 13.0 \text{ kN/m}^2$$

Similarly, for $z = 5$–10 m,

$$f_{av(2)} = (1 - \sin 30°)(\tan 30°)\left(\frac{90 + 130.95}{2}\right) = 31.9 \text{ kN/m}^2$$

For $z = 10$–30 m [Eq. (8.49)],

$$f_{av} = (1 - \sin \phi_R) \tan \phi_R \sqrt{OCR} \, \sigma'_{v(av)}$$

For $OCR = 2$,

$$f_{av(3)} = (1 - \sin 30°)(\tan 30°)\sqrt{2}\left(\frac{130.95 + 326.75}{2}\right) = 93.43 \text{ kN/m}^2$$

So

$$Q_s = p[f_{av(1)}(5) + f_{av(2)}(5) + f_{av(3)}(20)]$$
$$= (\pi)(0.406)[(13)(5) + (31.9)(5) + (93.43)(20)] = \mathbf{2669.7\ kN}$$

Part c: Calculation of Net Ultimate Capacity, Q_u

Comparing the three values shows that the α and λ methods give similar results. So we use

$$Q_s = \frac{1658.1 + 1777.8}{2} \approx 1718 \text{ kN}$$

Thus

$$Q_u = Q_p + Q_s = 116.46 + 1718 = 1834.46 \text{ kN}$$

$$Q_{all} = \frac{Q_u}{FS} = \frac{1834.46}{4} = \mathbf{458.6\ kN.}$$ ▼

8.8 CASE HISTORIES

Details of many field studies related to the estimation of the ultimate load-carrying capacity of various types of piles are available in the literature. In some cases the results generally agree with the theoretical predictions and in others they vary widely. The variations between theory and field test results may be attributed to factors such as improper interpretation of subsoil properties, incorrect theoretical assumptions, erroneous acquisition of field test results, and others. Following are summaries of two case histories of field load tests on piles and comparison of their results to existing theories.

Pile Load Test on New Lock and Dam No. 26, Mississippi River Near St. Louis

Briaud et al. (1989) reported the results of 28 axial load tests on impact driven H-piles and pipe piles in sand performed by the U.S. Army Engineering District (St. Louis) during the construction of the New Lock and Dam No. 26 on the Mississippi River. Figure 8.26 shows the grain-size distribution of the soil encountered at the site. Typical variations of field standard (uncorrected) penetration numbers with depth are shown in Figure 8.27.

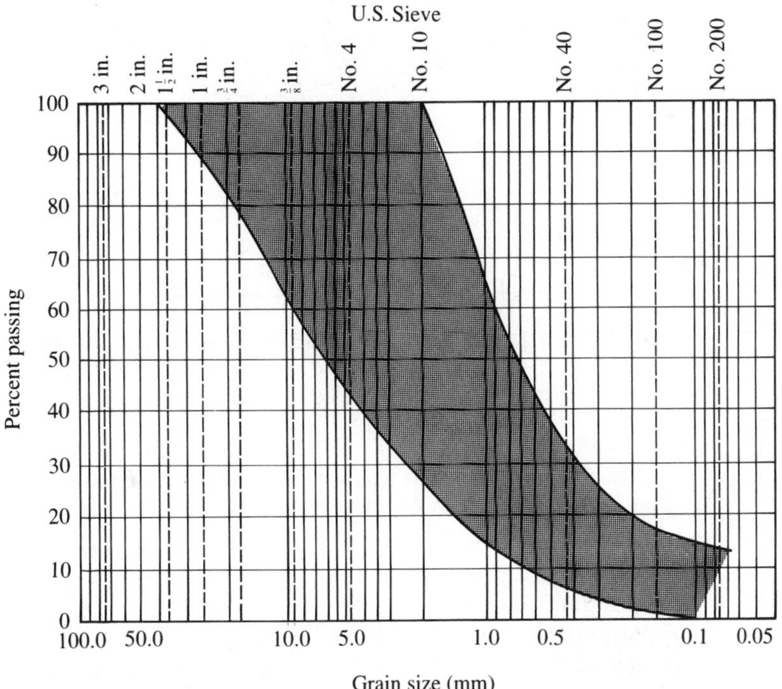

▼ **FIGURE 8.26** Grain-size distribution of the soil encountered (after Briaud et al., 1989)

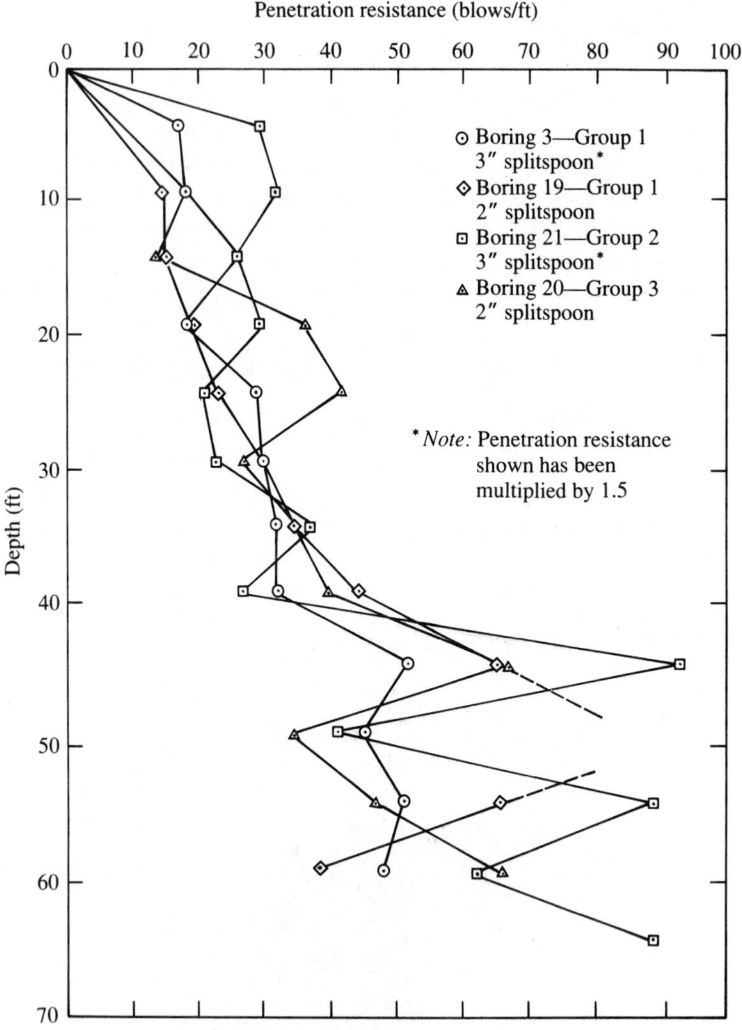

▼ **FIGURE 8.27** Results of the standard penetration test (after Briaud et al., 1989)

The results of the load tests on four H-piles obtained from this program are given in Figure 8.28. Details of the H-piles and the load test results for these four piles are summarized in Table 8.9. Figure 8.29 shows the load transfer curves for the piles obtained during the tests. Briaud et al. (1989) made a statistical analysis for the ratio of theoretical ultimate load to the measured ultimate load. The results of this analysis are summarized in Table 8.10 for the plugged case (Figure 8.10b). Note that a perfect prediction would have a mean = 1.0, standard deviation = 0, and a coefficient of variation = 0. Table 8.10 indicates that no method gave a perfect prediction; in general, Q_p was overestimated, and Q_s was underestimated.

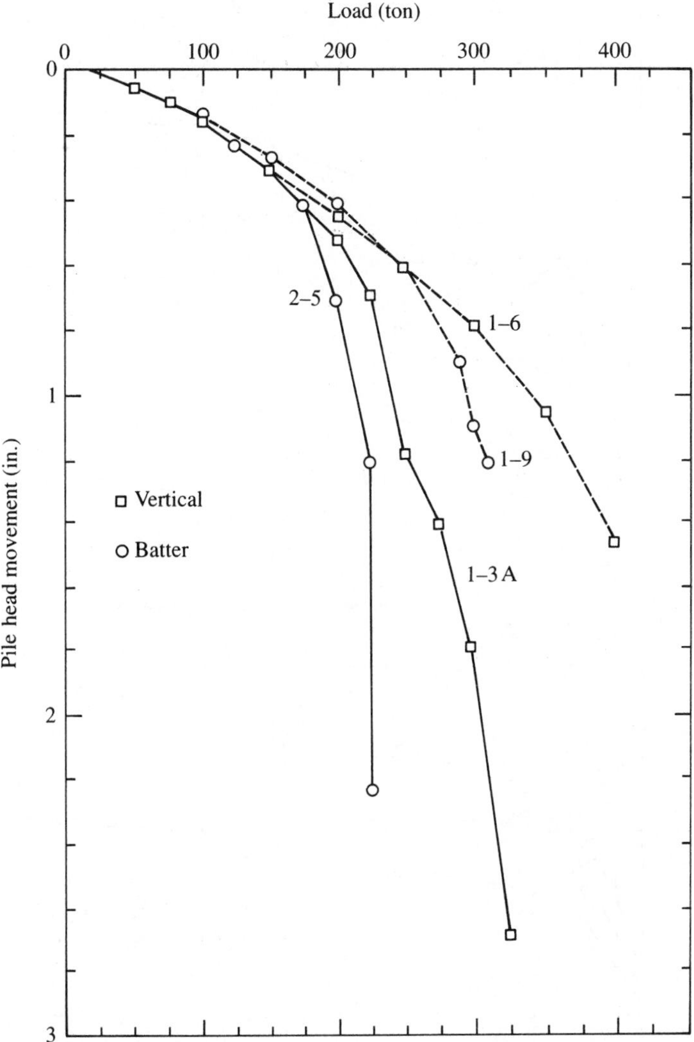

▼ **FIGURE 8.28** Load test results for H-piles in sand (after Briaud et al., 1989)

▼ **TABLE 8.9 Pile Load Test Results**

Pile no.	Pile type	Batter	Q_p (ton)	Q_s (ton)	Q_u (ton)	Pile length (ft)
1–3A	HP14 × 73	Vertical	152	161	313	54
1–6	HP14 × 73	Vertical	75	353	428	53
1–9	HP14 × 73	1 : 2.5	85	252	337	58
2–5	HP14 × 73	1 : 2.5	46	179	225	59

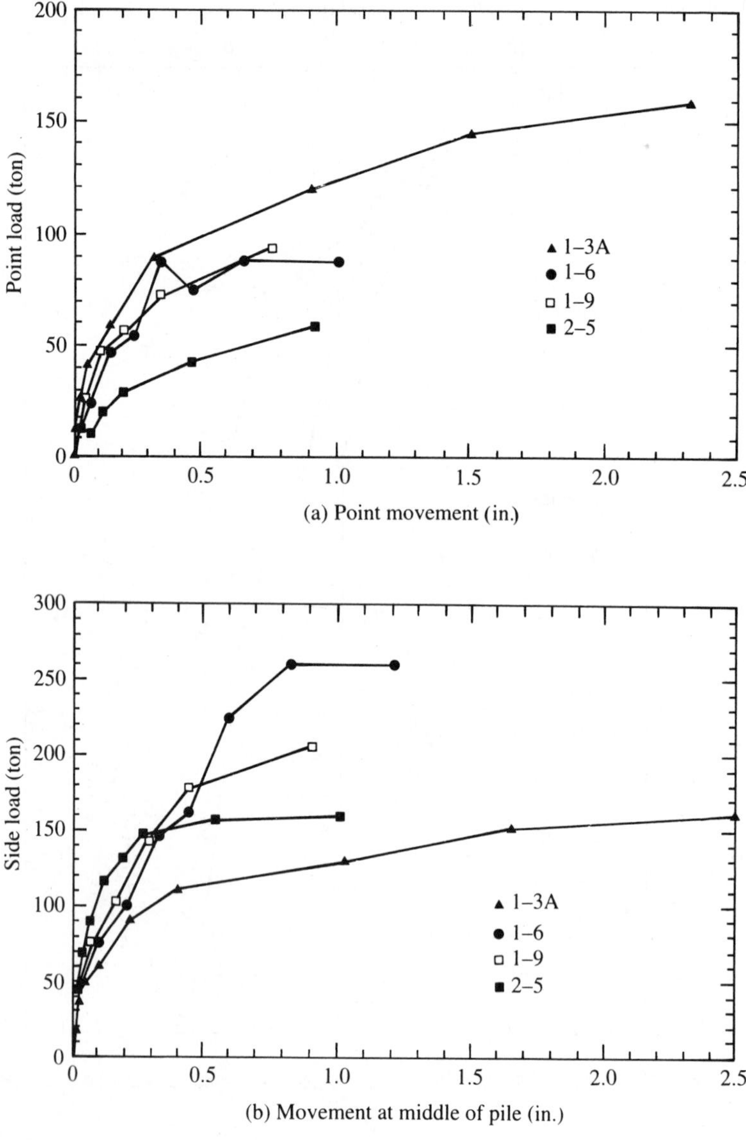

▼ **FIGURE 8.29** Load transfer curves for H-piles in sand (after Briaud et al., 1989)

Load Test on Two Drilled Piles in Sand in Alberta, Canada

Sharma and Joshi (1988) reported the results of field load tests on two cast-in-place concrete piles in a granular soil deposit. The length of these piles (TP-1 and TP-2) was about 12.3 m. Figure 8.30 shows the general soil conditions, pile dimensions, and load–

▼ **TABLE 8.10 Summary of Briaud et al.'s Statistical Analysis for H-Piles—Plugged Case**

Theoretical method	Q_p			Q_s			Q_u		
	Mean	*Standard deviation*	*Coefficient of variation*	*Mean*	*Standard deviation*	*Coefficient of variation*	*Mean*	*Standard deviation*	*Coefficient of variation*
Coyle and Castello (1981)	2.38	1.31	0.55	0.87	0.36	0.41	1.17	0.44	0.38
Briaud and Tucker (1984)	1.79	1.02	0.59	0.81	0.32	0.40	0.97	0.39	0.40
Meyerhof (1976)	4.37	2.76	0.63	0.92	0.43	0.46	1.68	0.76	0.45
API (1984)	1.62	1.00	0.62	0.59	0.25	0.43	0.79	0.34	0.43

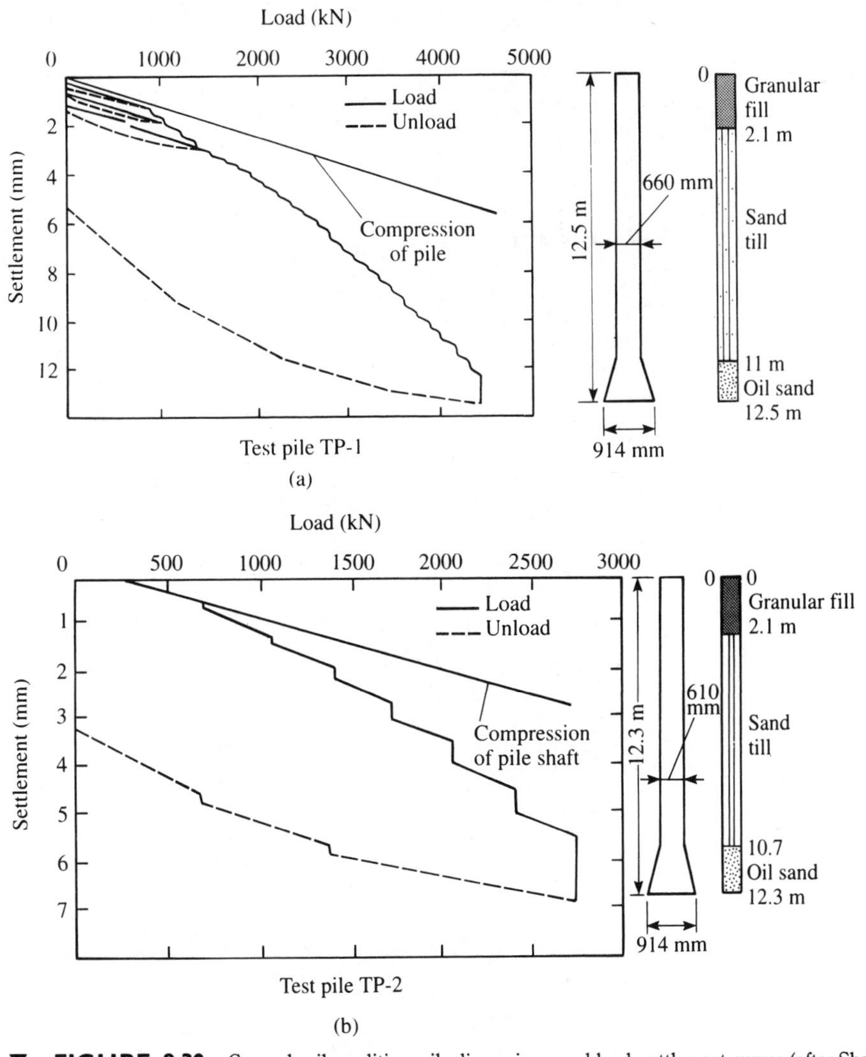

▼ **FIGURE 8.30** General soil condition, pile dimensions, and load–settlement curves (after Sharma and Joshi, 1988)

settlement curves. The load transfer mechanism (similar to Figure 8.8b) for the two test piles is shown in Figure 8.31. The average skin friction, f_{av}, is calculated as

$$f_{av} = \frac{Q_{top} - Q_{base}}{\pi D_s L} \tag{8.55}$$

where Q_{top} and Q_{base} = loads at the top and base of the pile, respectively
D_s = diameter of the pile shaft
L = pile length

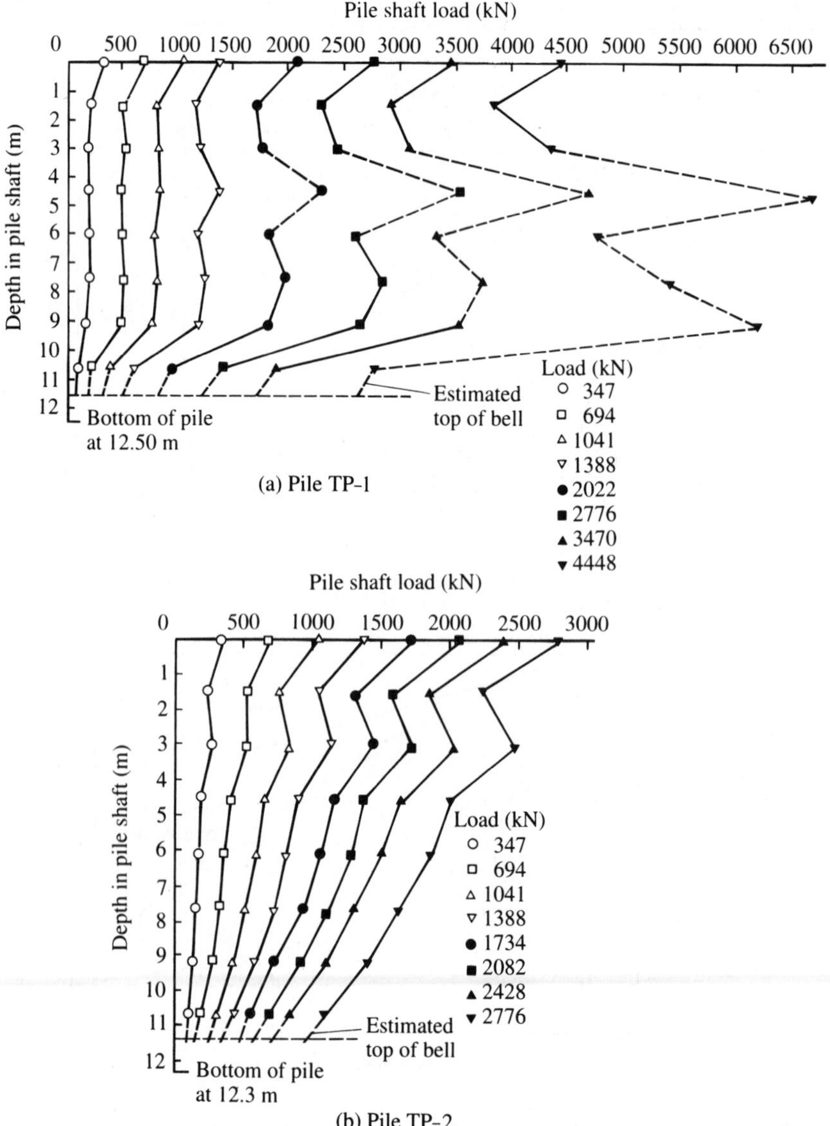

FIGURE 8.31 Load transfer mechanism for two test piles (after Sharma and Joshi, 1988)

The variations of f_{av} with load, Q, for the two piles are plotted in Figure 8.32. Note that, for test pile TP-1, the maximum value of f_{av} appears to be about 85 kN/m^2 at a load of about 4000 kN. In Figure 8.30a, it corresponds to a relative displacement of about 7 mm between the soil and the pile. This result confirms that frictional resistance between the pile and the shaft is fully mobilized in about 5–10 mm of pile head movement (Section 8.5). Again, referring to Eqs. (8.37a) and (8.38a), we can say that, in general,

$$f_{av}(\text{kN}/m^2) = m\overline{N} \tag{8.56}$$

where m = constant and varies between 1 and 2

For test pile TP-1, the shaft length (not including the bell) is about 11 m. Hence the following calculations may be made to determine f_{av}.

Soil	*Thickness (m)*	$\overline{N}$[a]	*Average* $\overline{N}$
Sand and gravel	2.1	15	$\dfrac{(15)(2.1) + (39)(8.9)}{11} = 34.4$
Sand till	8.9	39	

[a] From Sharma and Joshi (1988)

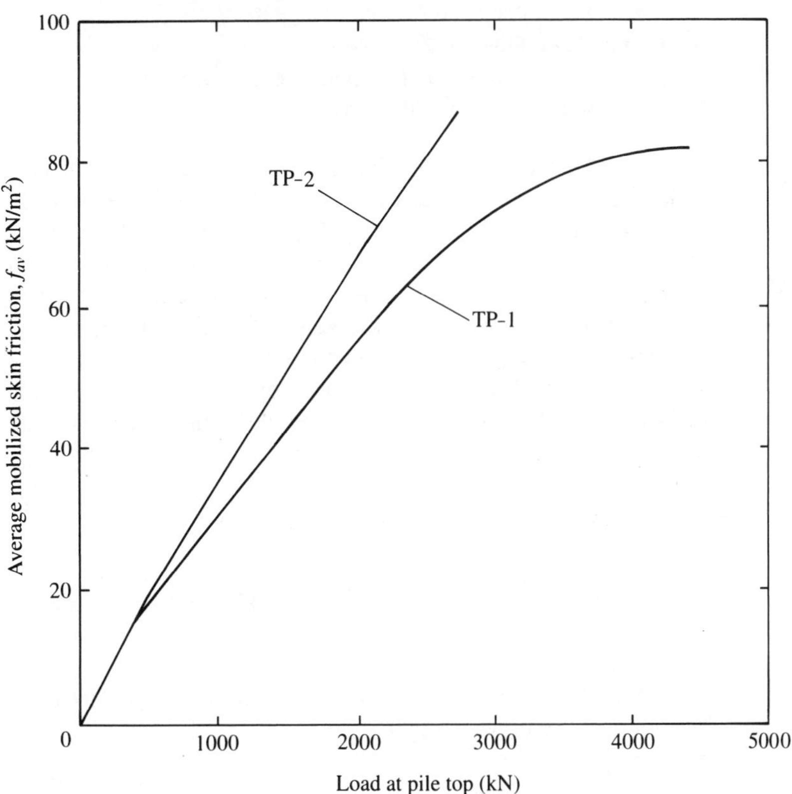

▼ **FIGURE 8.32** Variation of f_{av} with load, Q (after Sharma and Joshi, 1988)

The experimental value of f_{av} is about 85 kN/m^2, so from Eq. (8.56),

$$m = \frac{f_{av}}{\overline{\overline{N}}} = \frac{85}{34.4} = 2.47$$

This magnitude is somewhat higher than that given by either Eq. (8.37a) or (8.38a).

8.9 POINT BEARING CAPACITY OF PILES RESTING ON ROCK

Sometimes piles are driven to an underlying layer of rock. In such cases, the engineer must evaluate the bearing capacity of the rock. The ultimate unit point resistance in rock (Goodman, 1980) is approximately

$$\boxed{q_p = q_u(N_\phi + 1)} \tag{8.57}$$

where $N_\phi = \tan^2(45 + \phi/2)$
q_u = unconfined compression strength of rock
ϕ = drained angle of friction

The unconfined compression strength of rock can be determined by laboratory tests on rock specimens collected during field investigation. However, extreme caution should be used in obtaining the proper value of q_u because laboratory specimens usually are small in diameter. As the diameter of the specimen increases, the unconfined compression strength decreases, which is referred to as the *scale effect.* For specimens larger than about 3 ft (1 m) in diameter, the value of q_u remains approximately constant. There appears to be a fourfold to fivefold reduction of the magnitude of q_u in this process. The scale effect in rock is primarily caused by randomly distributed large and small fractures and also by progressive ruptures along the slip lines. Hence, we always recommend that

$$q_{u(\text{design})} = \frac{q_{u(\text{lab})}}{5} \tag{8.58}$$

Table 8.11 lists some representative values of (laboratory) unconfined compression strengths of rock. Representative values of the rock friction angle, ϕ, are given in Table 8.12.

A factor of safety of *at least 3* should be used to determine the allowable point bearing capacity of piles. Thus

$$Q_{p(\text{all})} = \frac{[q_u(N_\phi + 1)]A_p}{FS} \tag{8.59}$$

TABLE 8.11 Unconfined Compressive Strengths of Specimens of Representative Types of Rock

Description	q_u psi	q_u MPa
Berea sandstone	10,700	73.8
Navaje sandstone	31,030	214.0
Tensleep sandstone	10,500	72.4
Hackensack siltstone	17,800	122.7
Monticello Dam s.s. (greywacke)	11,500	79.3
Solenhofen limestone	35,500	245.0
Bedford limestone	7,400	51.0
Tavernalle limestone	14,200	97.9
Oneota dolomite	12,600	86.9
Lockport dolomite	13,100	90.3
Flaming Gorge shale	5,100	35.2
Micaceous shale	10,900	75.2
Dworshak Dam gneiss 45° to foliation	23,500	162.0
Quartz mica schist ⊥ schistocity	8,000	55.2
Baraboo quartzite	46,400	320.0
Taconic marble	8,990	62.0
Cherokee marble	9,700	66.9
Nevada Test Site granite	20,500	141.1
Pikes Peak granite	32,800	226.0
Cedar City tonalite	14,700	101.5
Palisades diabase	34,950	241.0
Nevada Test Site basalt	21,500	148.0
John Day basalt	51,500	355.0
Nevada Test Site tuff	1,639	11.3

From *Introduction to Rock Mechanics*, by R. E. Goodman. Copyright 1980 by John Wiley and Sons. Reprinted by permission.

TABLE 8.12 Representative Values for Angle of Internal Friction, ϕ, for Selected Types of Rock

Description	Porosity (%)	ϕ (deg)
Berea sandstone	18.2	27.8
Bartlesville sandstone		37.2
Pottsville sandstone	14.0	45.2
Repetto siltstone	5.6	32.1
Muddy shale	4.7	14.4
Stockton shale		22.0
Edmonton bentonitic shale (water content 30%)	44.0	7.5
Sioux quartzite		48.0
Texas slate; loaded		
30° to cleavage		21.0
90° to cleavage		26.9
Georgia marble	0.3	25.3
Wolf Camp limestone		34.8
Indiana limestone	19.4	42.0
Chalk	40.0	31.5
Hasmark dolomite	3.5	35.5
Blaine anhydrite		29.4
Inada biotite granite	0.4	47.7
Stone Mountain granite	0.2	51.0
Nevada Test Site basalt	4.6	31.0
Schistose gneiss		
90° to schistocity	0.5	28.0
30° to schistocity	1.9	27.6

From *Introduction to Rock Mechanics*, by R. E. Goodman. Copyright 1980 by John Wiley and Sons. Reprinted by permission.

EXAMPLE 8.7

An H-pile (size HP 310 × 1.226) having a length of embedment of 26 m is driven through a soft clay layer to rest on sandstone. The sandstone has a laboratory unconfined compression strength of 76 MN/m^2 and a friction angle of 28°. Use a factor of safety of 5 and estimate the allowable point bearing capacity.

Solution From Eqs. (8.58) and (8.59),

$$Q_{p(\text{all})} = \frac{\left\{\left[\frac{q_{u(\text{lab})}}{5}\right]\left[\tan^2\left(45 + \frac{\phi}{2}\right) + 1\right]\right\}A_p}{FS}$$

From Table 8.1b, for HP 310 × 1.226 piles, $A_p = 15.9 \times 10^{-3}\ \text{m}^2$. So

$$Q_{p(\text{all})} = \frac{\left\{\left[\frac{76 \times 10^3\ \text{kN/m}^2}{5}\right]\left[\tan^2\left(45 + \frac{28}{2}\right) + 1\right]\right\}(15.9 \times 10^{-3}\ \text{m}^2)}{5}$$

$$= \mathbf{182\ kN} \quad \blacktriangledown$$

8.10 SETTLEMENT OF PILES

The settlement of a pile under a vertical working load, Q_w, is caused by three factors:

$$s = s_1 + s_2 + s_3 \tag{8.60}$$

where s = total pile settlement
s_1 = settlement of pile shaft
s_2 = settlement of pile caused by the load at the pile point
s_3 = settlement of pile caused by the load transmitted along the pile shaft

Determination of s_1

If the pile material is assumed to be elastic, the deformation of the pile shaft can be evaluated using the fundamental principles of mechanics of materials:

$$s_1 = \frac{(Q_{wp} + \xi Q_{ws})L}{A_p E_p} \tag{8.61}$$

where Q_{wp} = load carried at the pile point under working load condition
Q_{ws} = load carried by frictional (skin) resistance under working load condition
A_p = area of pile cross section
L = length of pile
E_p = modulus of elasticity of the pile material

The magnitude of ξ will depend on the nature of unit friction (skin) resistance distribution along the pile shaft. If the distribution of f is uniform or parabolic, as shown in Figure 8.33a and 8.33b, $\xi = 0.5$. However, for triangular distribution of f (Figure 8.33c), the magnitude of ξ is about 0.67 (Vesic, 1977).

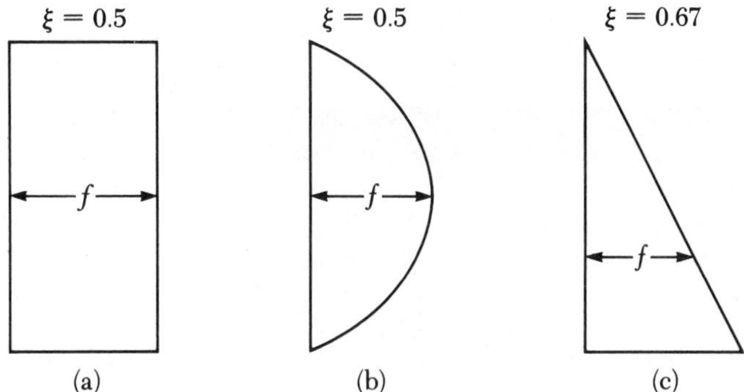

▼ **FIGURE 8.33** Various types of unit friction (skin) resistance distribution along the pile shaft

Determination of s_2

The settlement of a pile caused by the load carried at the pile point may be expressed in a form similar to that given for shallow foundations [Eq. (3.79)]:

$$s_2 = \frac{q_{wp} D}{E_s}(1 - \mu_s^2) I_{wp} \tag{8.62}$$

where D = width or diameter of pile
q_{wp} = point load per unit area at the pile point = Q_{wp}/A_p
E_s = modulus of elasticity of soil at or below the pile point
μ_s = Poisson's ratio of soil
I_{wp} = influence factor

For all practical purposes, I_{wp} equals α_r as given in Eq. (3.79) and may be evaluated from Figure 3.27. In the absence of any experimental results, representative values of Poisson's ratio may be obtained from Table 3.9.

Vesic (1977) also proposed a semiempirical method to obtain the magnitude of the settlement, s_2:

$$s_2 = \frac{Q_{wp} C_p}{D q_p} \tag{8.63}$$

where q_p = ultimate point resistance of the pile
C_p = an empirical coefficient

Representative values of C_p for various soils are given in Table 8.13.

▼ **TABLE 8.13 Typical Values of C_p [Eq. (8.63)]**

Soil type	Driven pile	Bored pile
Sand (dense to loose)	0.02–0.04	0.09–0.18
Clay (stiff to soft)	0.02–0.03	0.03–0.06
Silt (dense to loose)	0.03–0.05	0.09–0.12

From "Design of Pile Foundations," by A. S. Vesic, in NCHRB *Synthesis of Highway Practice 42*, Transportation Research Board, 1977. Reprinted by permission.

Determination of s_3

The settlement of a pile caused by the load carried by the pile shaft is given by a relation similar to Eq. (8.62), or

$$s_3 = \left(\frac{Q_{ws}}{pL}\right)\frac{D}{E_s}(1 - \mu_s^2)I_{ws} \tag{8.64}$$

where p = perimeter of the pile
L = embedded length of pile
I_{ws} = influence factor

Note that the term Q_{ws}/pL in Eq. (8.64) is the average value of f along the pile shaft. The influence factor, I_{ws}, has a simple empirical relation (Vesic, 1977):

$$I_{ws} = 2 + 0.35\sqrt{\frac{L}{D}} \tag{8.65}$$

Vesic (1977) also proposed a simple empirical relation similar to Eq. (8.63) for obtaining s_3:

$$s_3 = \frac{Q_{ws}C_s}{Lq_p} \tag{8.66}$$

where C_s = an empirical constant $= (0.93 + 0.16\sqrt{L/D})C_p$ (8.67)

The values of C_p for use in Eq. (8.66) may be estimated from Table 8.13.

Sharma and Joshi (1988) used Eqs. (8.60), (8.61), (8.63), and (8.66) to estimate the settlement of two concrete piles in sand, as shown previously in Figure 8.30, and compared them to observed values from the field. For these calculations, they used: $\xi = 0.5$ and 0.67, $C_p = 0.02$, and $C_s = 0.02$. Table 8.14 shows the comparison of s values. Note the fairly good agreement between estimated and observed values of settlement.

TABLE 8.14 Comparison of Observed and Estimated Values of Settlement of Two Concrete Piles (Figure 8.30)

Pile	Load on pile (kN)	Measured s (mm)	Calculated s	
			$\xi = 0.5$	$\xi = 0.67$
TP-1	694	1.08	1.456	1.571
	1388	2.91	3.350	3.55
	2776	6.67	7.195	7.535
	4448	13.41	11.67	13.651
TP-2	694	0.65	1.467	1.610
	1388	2.11	3.118	3.387
	2776	6.72	6.889	7.365

EXAMPLE 8.8

A 40-ft-long precast concrete pile is fully embedded in sand. The cross section of the pile measures 12 in. × 12 in. The allowable working load for the pile is 80 kip, of which 54 kip is contributed by skin friction. Determine the elastic settlement of the pile for $E_p = 3 \times 10^6$ lb/in², $E_s = 4500$ lb/in², and $\mu_s = 0.3$.

Solution From Eq. (8.61),

$$s_1 = \frac{(Q_{wp} + \xi Q_{ws})L}{A_p E_p}$$

Let $\xi = 0.6$, $E_p = 3 \times 10^6 \text{ lb/in}^2 = 3 \times 10^3 \text{ kip/in}^2$, $Q_{ws} = 54$ kip, $Q_{wp} = 26$ kip, and $A_p = 12 \times 12 = 144 \text{ in}^2$. Then

$$s_1 = \frac{[26 + (0.6)(54)](40 \times 12)}{(144)(3 \times 10^3)} = 0.065 \text{ in.}$$

From Eq. (8.62),

$$s_2 = \frac{q_{wp} D}{E_s}(1 - \mu_s^2) I_{wp}$$

From Figure 3.27, $I_{wp} = 0.82$. Also,

$$q_{wp} = \frac{Q_{wp}}{A_p} = \frac{26}{144} = 0.18 \text{ kip/in}^2$$

So

$$s_2 = \frac{0.18 \times 12}{\left(\frac{4500}{1000}\right)}(1 - 0.3^2)(0.82) = 0.358 \text{ in.}$$

Again, from Eq. (8.64),

$$s_3 = \left(\frac{Q_{ws}}{pL}\right)\frac{D}{E_s}(1 - \mu_s^2)I_{ws}$$

$$I_{ws} = 2 + 0.35\sqrt{\frac{L}{D}} = 2 + 0.35\sqrt{\frac{40}{1.0}} = 4.21$$

So

$$s_3 = \frac{54}{(4 \times 12)(40)}\frac{12}{\left(\frac{4500}{1000}\right)}(1 - 0.3^2)(4.21) = 0.287 \text{ in.}$$

Hence the total settlement is

$$s = 0.065 + 0.358 + 0.287 = \mathbf{0.71\ in.}$$ ▼

8.11 PULLOUT RESISTANCE OF PILES

In Section 8.1 we noted that, under certain construction conditions, piles are subjected to uplifting forces. The ultimate resistance of piles subjected to such force did not receive much attention among researchers until recently. The gross ultimate resistance of a pile subjected to uplifting force (Figure 8.34) is

$$T_{ug} = T_{un} + W \tag{8.68}$$

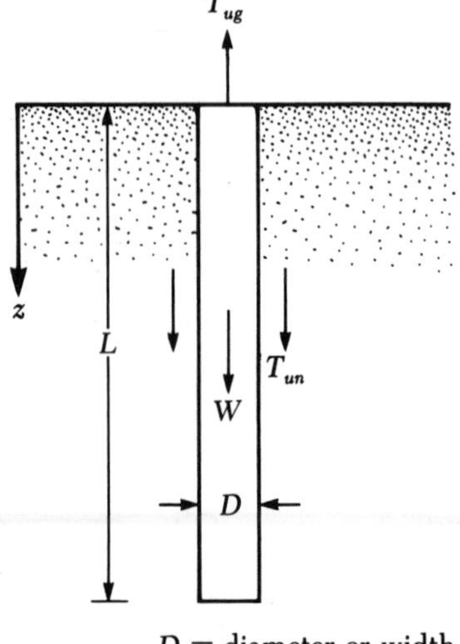

▼ **FIGURE 8.34** Uplift capacity of piles

where T_{ug} = gross uplift capacity
T_{un} = net uplift capacity
W = effective weight of the pile

Piles in Clay

The net ultimate uplift capacity of piles embedded in saturated clays was studied by Das and Seeley (1982). According to that study,

$$\boxed{T_{un} = Lp\alpha' c_u} \tag{8.69}$$

where L = length of the pile
p = perimeter of pile section
α' = adhesion coefficient at soil–pile interface
c_u = undrained cohesion of clay

For cast-*in-situ* concrete piles,

$$\alpha' = 0.9 - 0.00625c_u \qquad (\text{for } c_u \le 80 \text{ kN/m}^2) \tag{8.70}$$

and

$$\alpha' = 0.4 \qquad (\text{for } c_u > 80 \text{ kN/m}^2) \tag{8.71}$$

Similarly, for pipe piles,

$$\alpha' = 0.715 - 0.0191c_u \qquad (\text{for } c_u \le 27 \text{ kN/m}^2) \tag{8.72}$$

and

$$\alpha' = 0.2 \qquad (\text{for } c_u > 27 \text{ kN/m}^2) \tag{8.73}$$

Piles in Sand

When piles are embedded in granular soils ($c = 0$), the net ultimate uplift capacity (Das and Seeley, 1975) is

$$T_{un} = \int_0^L (f_u p)\, dz \tag{8.74}$$

where f_u = unit skin friction during uplift
p = perimeter of pile cross section

The unit skin friction during uplift, f_u, usually varies as shown in Figure 8.35a. It increases linearly to a depth of $z = L_{cr}$; beyond that it remains constant. For $z \le L_{cr}$,

$$f_u = K_u \sigma'_v \tan \delta \tag{8.75}$$

where K_u = uplift coefficient
σ'_v = effective vertical stress at a depth of z
δ = soil–pile friction angle

The variation of the uplift coefficient with soil friction angle ϕ is given in Figure 8.35b. Based on the author's experience, the values of L_{cr} and δ appear to depend on the relative density of soil. Figure 8.35c shows the approximate nature of these variations with the relative density of soil. For calculating the net ultimate uplift capacity of piles, the following procedure is suggested.

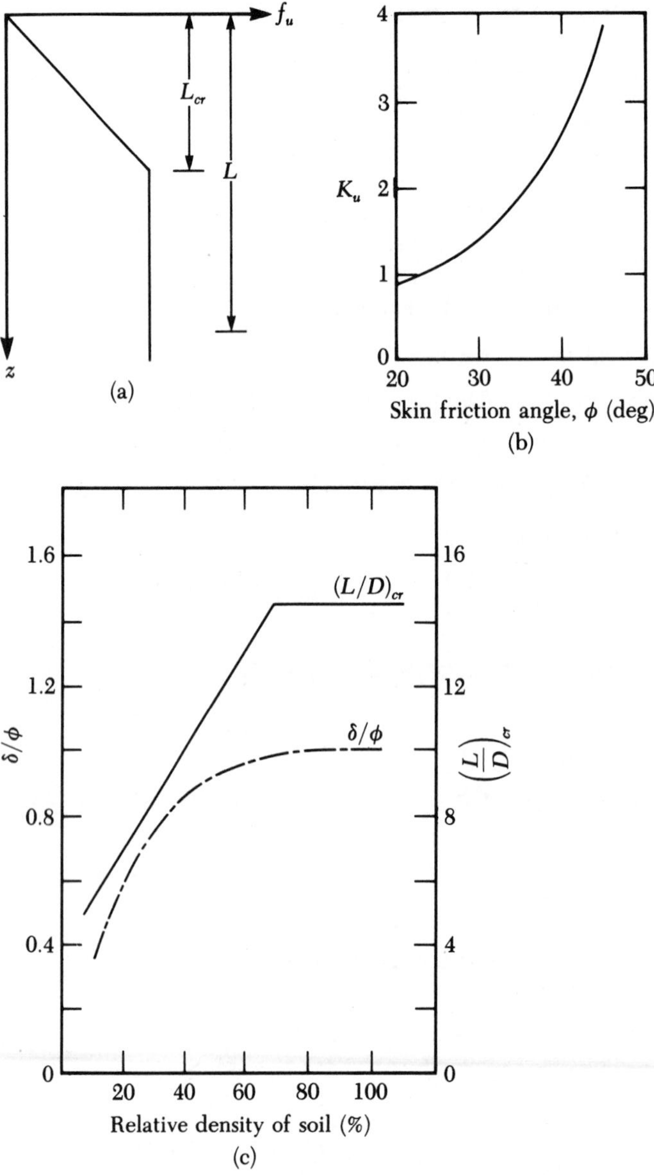

▼ **FIGURE 8.35** (a) Nature of variation of f_u; (b) uplift coefficient K_u; (c) variation of δ/ϕ and $(L/D)_{cr}$ with relative density of sand

1. Determine the relative density of the soil and, using Figure 8.35c, obtain the value of L_{cr}.
2. If the length of the pile, L, is less than or equal to L_{cr},

$$T_{un} = p \int_0^L f_u \, dz = p \int_0^L (\sigma'_v K_u \tan \delta) \, dz \tag{8.76}$$

In dry soils, $\sigma'_v = \gamma z$ (where γ = unit weight of soil). So

$$T_{un} = p \int_0^L (\sigma'_v K_u \tan \delta) \, dz = p \int_0^L \gamma z K_u \tan \delta \, dz$$

$$= \frac{1}{2} p \gamma L^2 K_u \tan \delta \tag{8.77}$$

Obtain the values of K_u and δ from Figure 8.35b and 8.35c.

3. For $L > L_{cr}$,

$$T_{un} = p \int_0^L f_u \, dz = p\left[\int_0^{L_{cr}} f_u \, dz + \int_{L_{cr}}^L f_u \, dz\right]$$

$$= p\left\{\int_0^{L_{cr}} [\sigma'_v K_u \tan \delta] \, dz + \int_{L_{cr}}^L \left[\sigma'_{v(\text{at } z = L_{cr})} K_u \tan \delta\right] dz\right\} \tag{8.78}$$

For dry soils, Eq. (8.78) simplifies to

$$T_{un} = \frac{1}{2} p \gamma L_{cr}^2 K_u \tan \delta + p \gamma L_{cr} K_u \tan \delta (L - L_{cr}) \tag{8.79}$$

Determine the values of K_u and δ from Figure 8.35b and 8.35c.

For estimating the net allowable uplift capacity, a factor of safety of 2–3 is recommended. Thus

$$T_{u(\text{all})} = \frac{T_{ug}}{FS}$$

where $T_{u(\text{all})}$ = allowable uplift capacity

▼ EXAMPLE 8.9

For the pipe pile given in Example 8.6, determine the net ultimate uplift capacity.

Solution We use Eq. (8.69) for this problem. Because the top and bottom layers have clays with $c_u > 27 \text{ kN/m}^2$, the value of α' for both layers is 0.2. So, from Eq. (8.69),

$$T_{un} = p\alpha' \sum c_u \, \Delta L = \pi(0.406)(0.2)[(30)(10) + (100)(20)] = \mathbf{586.7 \ kN}$$ ▼

▼ EXAMPLE 8.10

Refer to Example 8.1. For the concrete pile, determine the net ultimate pullout capacity. Assume the relative density of soil to be 60%.

Solution From Figure 8.35c for a relative density of 60%, $(L/D)_{cr} \approx 12.7$. So

$$L_{cr} = (12.7)(1) = 12.7 \text{ ft}$$

For this case, $L = 50 \text{ ft} > L_{cr}$, so Eq. (8.79) is to be used, or

$$T_{un} = \frac{1}{2} p\gamma L_{cr}^2 K_u \tan\delta + p\gamma L_{cr} K_u \tan\delta (L - L_{cr})$$

From Figure 8.35b for $\phi = 35°$, $K_u = 1.9$. Similarly, from Figure 8.35c for relative density = 60%, $(\delta/\phi) \approx 0.97$. So, $\delta = (0.97)(35) = 33.95°$. Substituting these values into Eq. (8.79) yields

$$T_{un} = \frac{1}{2}\left(4 \times \frac{12}{12}\right)(110)(12.7)^2(1.9)(\tan 33.95)$$

$$+ \left(4 \times \frac{12}{12}\right)(110)(12.7)(1.9)(\tan 33.95)(50 - 12.7)$$

$$= 312 \times 10^3 \text{ lb} = \mathbf{312\ kip}$$ ▼

8.12 LATERALLY LOADED VERTICAL PILES

Granular Soils

A general method for determining moments and displacements of a vertical pile subjected to lateral load and moment at the ground surface was given by Matlock and Reese (1960). Consider a pile of length L subjected to a lateral force Q_g and a moment M_g at the ground surface ($z = 0$), as shown in Figure 8.36a. Figure 8.36b shows the general deflected shape of the pile and the soil resistance caused by the applied load and the moment.

According to a simpler Winkler's model, an elastic medium (soil in this case) can be replaced by a series of infinitely close independent elastic springs. Based on this assumption,

$$k = \frac{p'(\text{kN/m or lb/ft})}{x(\text{m or ft})} \tag{8.80}$$

where k = modulus of subgrade reaction
p' = pressure on soil
x = deflection

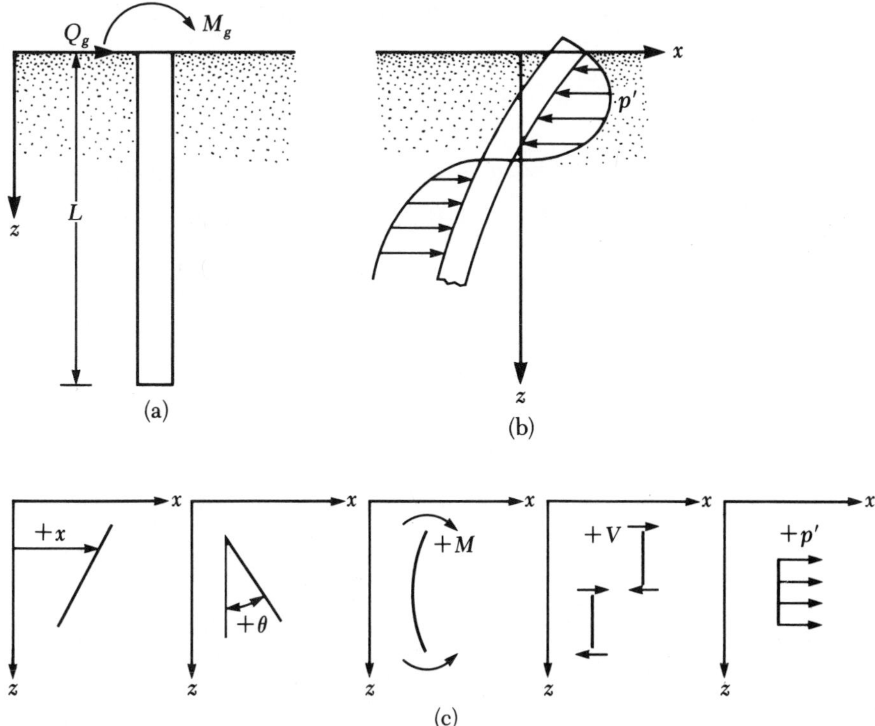

▼ **FIGURE 8.36** (a) Laterally loaded pile; (b) soil resistance on pile caused by lateral load; (c) sign conventions for displacement, slope, moment, shear, and soil reaction

The subgrade modulus for granular soils at a depth z is defined as

$$k_z = n_h z \tag{8.81}$$

where n_h = constant of modulus of horizontal subgrade reaction

Referring to Figure 8.36b and using the theory of beams on an elastic foundation, we can write

$$E_p I_p \frac{d^4 x}{dz^4} = p' \tag{8.82}$$

where E_p = modulus of elasticity of the pile material
I_p = moment of inertia of the pile section

Based on Winkler's model

$$p' = -kx \tag{8.83}$$

The sign in Eq. (8.83) is negative because the soil reaction is in the direction opposite to the pile deflection.

Combining Eqs. (8.82) and (8.83) gives

$$E_p I_p \frac{d^4x}{dz^4} + kx = 0 \tag{8.84}$$

The solution of Eq. (8.84) results in the following expressions.

Pile Deflection at Any Depth $[x_z(z)]$

$$x_z(z) = A_x \frac{Q_g T^3}{E_p I_p} + B_x \frac{M_g T^2}{E_p I_p} \tag{8.85}$$

Slope of Pile at Any Depth $[\theta_z(z)]$

$$\theta_z(z) = A_\theta \frac{Q_g T^2}{E_p I_p} + B_\theta \frac{M_g T}{E_p I_p} \tag{8.86}$$

Moment of Pile at Any Depth $[M_z(z)]$

$$M_z(z) = A_m Q_g T + B_m M_g \tag{8.87}$$

Shear Force on Pile at Any Depth $[V_z(z)]$

$$V_z(z) = A_v Q_g + B_v \frac{M_g}{T} \tag{8.88}$$

Soil Reaction at Any Depth $[p'_z(z)]$

$$p'_z(z) = A_{p'} \frac{Q_g}{T} + B_{p'} \frac{M_g}{T^2} \tag{8.89}$$

where A_x, B_x, A_θ, B_θ, A_m, B_m, A_v, B_v, $A_{p'}$, and $B_{p'}$ are coefficients

T = characteristic length of the soil–pile system

$$= \sqrt[5]{\frac{E_p I_p}{n_h}} \tag{8.90}$$

n_h has been defined in Eq. (8.81)

▼ **TABLE 8.15 Coefficients for Long Piles, $k_z = n_h z$**

Z	A_x	A_θ	A_m	A_v	A'_p	B_x	B_θ	B_m	B_v	B'_p
0.0	2.435	−1.623	0.000	1.000	0.000	1.623	−1.750	1.000	0.000	0.000
0.1	2.273	−1.618	0.100	0.989	−0.227	1.453	−1.650	1.000	−0.007	−0.145
0.2	2.112	−1.603	0.198	0.956	−0.422	1.293	−1.550	0.999	−0.028	−0.259
0.3	1.952	−1.578	0.291	0.906	−0.586	1.143	−1.450	0.994	−0.058	−0.343
0.4	1.796	−1.545	0.379	0.840	−0.718	1.003	−1.351	0.987	−0.095	−0.401
0.5	1.644	−1.503	0.459	0.764	−0.822	0.873	−1.253	0.976	−0.137	−0.436
0.6	1.496	−1.454	0.532	0.677	−0.897	0.752	−1.156	0.960	−0.181	−0.451
0.7	1.353	−1.397	0.595	0.585	−0.947	0.642	−1.061	0.939	−0.226	−0.449
0.8	1.216	−1.335	0.649	0.489	−0.973	0.540	−0.968	0.914	−0.270	−0.432
0.9	1.086	−1.268	0.693	0.392	−0.977	0.448	−0.878	0.885	−0.312	−0.403
1.0	0.962	−1.197	0.727	0.295	−0.962	0.364	−0.792	0.852	−0.350	−0.364
1.2	0.738	−1.047	0.767	0.109	−0.885	0.223	−0.629	0.775	−0.414	−0.268
1.4	0.544	−0.893	0.772	−0.056	−0.761	0.112	−0.482	0.688	−0.456	−0.157
1.6	0.381	−0.741	0.746	−0.193	−0.609	0.029	−0.354	0.594	−0.477	−0.047
1.8	0.247	−0.596	0.696	−0.298	−0.445	−0.030	−0.245	0.498	−0.476	0.054
2.0	0.142	−0.464	0.628	−0.371	−0.283	−0.070	−0.155	0.404	−0.456	0.140
3.0	−0.075	−0.040	0.225	−0.349	0.226	−0.089	0.057	0.059	−0.213	0.268
4.0	−0.050	0.052	0.000	−0.106	0.201	−0.028	0.049	−0.042	0.017	0.112
5.0	−0.009	0.025	−0.033	0.015	0.046	0.000	−0.011	−0.026	0.029	−0.002

When $L \geq 5T$, the pile is considered to be a *long pile*. For $L \leq 2T$, the pile is considered to be a *rigid pile*. Table 8.15 gives the values of the coefficients for long piles ($L/T \geq 5$) in Eqs. (8.85) to (8.89). Note that, in the first column of Table 8.15, Z is the nondimensional depth, or

$$Z = \frac{z}{T} \tag{8.91}$$

The positive sign conventions for $x_z(z)$, $\theta_z(z)$, $M_z(z)$, $V_z(z)$, and $p'_z(z)$ assumed in the derivations in Table 8.15 are shown in Figure 8.36c. Also, Figure 8.37 shows the variation of A_x, B_x, A_m, and B_m for various values of $L/T = Z_{max}$. It indicates that, when L/T is greater than about 5, the coefficients do not change, which is true of long piles only.

Calculating the characteristic length T for the pile requires assuming a proper value of n_h. Table 8.16 gives some representative values of n_h.

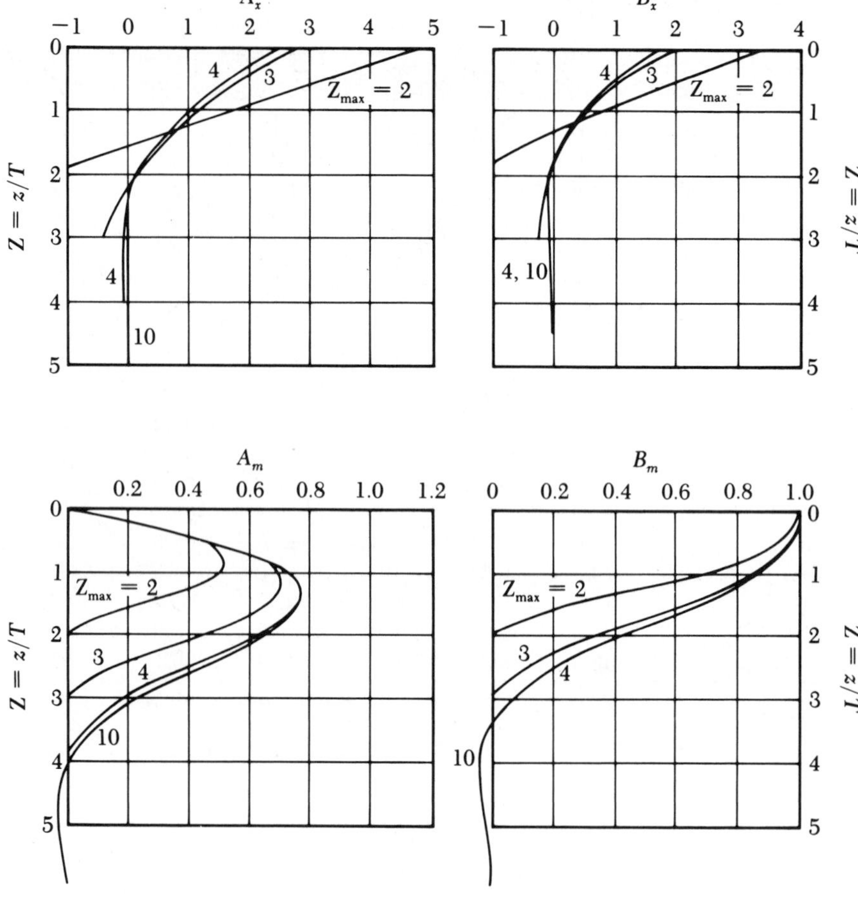

▼ **FIGURE 8.37** Variation of A_x, B_x, A_m, and B_m with Z (after Matlock and Reese, 1960)

▼ **TABLE 8.16 Representative Values of n_h**

Soil	n_h	
	lb/ft^3	kN/m^3
Dry or moist sand		
Loose	280–350	1800–2200
Medium	865–1100	5500–7000
Dense	2350–2850	15,000–18,000
Submerged sand		
Loose	160–220	1000–1400
Medium	550–700	3500–4500
Dense	1400–1900	9000–12,000

Cohesive Soils

Solutions similar to those given in Eqs. (8.85)–(8.89) were developed by Davisson and Gill (1963) for piles embedded in clay:

$$x_z(z) = A'_x \frac{Q_g R^3}{E_p I_p} + B'_x \frac{M_g R^2}{E_p I_p} \tag{8.92}$$

and

$$M_z(z) = A'_m Q_g R + B'_m M_g \tag{8.93}$$

where A'_x, B'_x, A'_m, and B'_m are coefficients

$$R = \sqrt[4]{\frac{E_p I_p}{k}} \tag{8.94}$$

The values of the A and B coefficients are given in Figure 8.38. Note that

$$Z = \frac{z}{R} \tag{8.95}$$

and

$$Z_{\max} = \frac{L}{R} \tag{8.96}$$

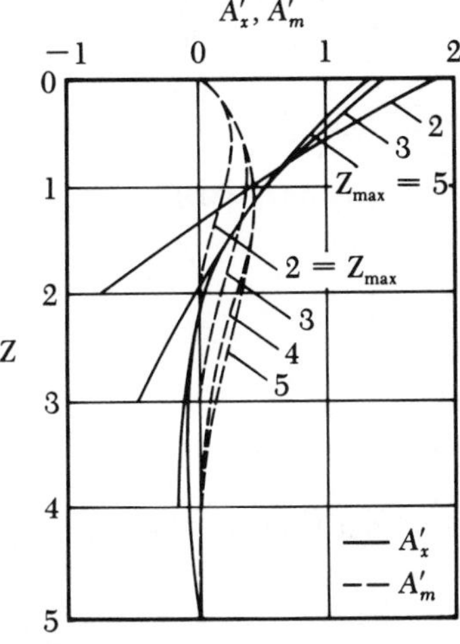

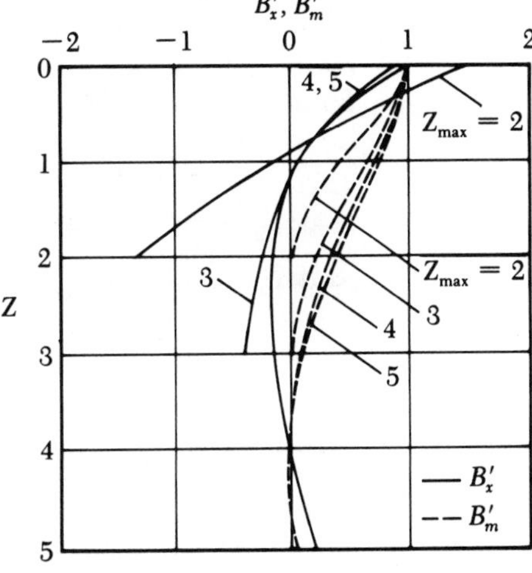

▼ **FIGURE 8.38** Variation of A'_x, B'_x, A'_m, and B'_m with Z (after Davisson and Gill, 1963)

The use of Eqs. (8.92) and (8.93) requires knowing the magnitude of the characteristic length, R. It can be calculated from Eq. (8.94), provided the coefficient of the subgrade reaction is known. For sands, the coefficient of subgrade reaction was given by Eq. (8.81), which showed a linear variation with depth. However, in cohesive soils, the subgrade reaction may be assumed to be approximately constant with depth. Vesic (1961) proposed the following equation to estimate the value of k:

$$k = 0.65 \sqrt[12]{\frac{E_s D^4}{E_p I_p}} \frac{E_s}{1 - \mu_s^2} \tag{8.97}$$

where E_s = modulus of elasticity of soil
D = pile width (or diameter)
μ_s = Poisson's ratio of the soil

The modulus of elasticity of clay, E_s, can be obtained from laboratory consolidation of the soil as

$$E_s = \frac{3(1 - \mu_s)}{m_v} \tag{8.98}$$

where m_v = volume coefficient of compressiblity (see Chapter 1)

$$m_v = \frac{\Delta e}{\Delta p(1 + e_{av})}$$

The value of μ_s is assumed to vary between 0.3 and 0.4.

▼ EXAMPLE 8.11

Consider a steel H-pile (HP 250 × 0.834) 25 m long embedded fully in a granular soil. Assume that n_h = 12,000 kN/m³. The allowable displacement at the top of the pile is 8 mm. Determine the allowable lateral load, Q_g. Assume that $M_g = 0$.

Solution From Table 8.1b for an HP 250 × 0.834 pile,

$$I_p = 123 \times 10^{-6}\ \text{m}^4 \qquad \text{(about the strong axis)}$$

$$E_p = 207 \times 10^6\ \text{kN/m}^2$$

From Eq. (8.90),

$$T = \sqrt[5]{\frac{E_p I_p}{n_h}} = \sqrt[5]{\frac{(207 \times 10^6)(123 \times 10^{-6})}{12{,}000}} = 1.16\ \text{m}$$

Here, $L/T = 25/1.16 = 21.55 > 5$, so it is a long pile. Because $M_g = 0$, Eq. (8.85) takes the form

$$x_z(z) = A_x \frac{Q_g T^3}{E_p I_p}$$

and

$$Q_g = \frac{x_z(z)E_p I_p}{A_x T^3}$$

At $z = 0$, $x_z = 8$ mm $= 0.008$ m, and $A_x = 2.435$ (Table 8.15). So

$$Q_g = \frac{(0.008)(207 \times 10^6)(123 \times 10^{-6})}{(2.435)(1.16^3)} = 53.59 \text{ kN}$$

This magnitude of Q_g is based on the *limiting displacement condition only.* However, the magnitude of Q_g based on the *moment capacity* of the pile also needs to be determined. For $M_g = 0$, Eq. (8.87) becomes

$$M_z(z) = A_m Q_g T$$

According to Table 8.15, the maximum value of A_m at any depth is 0.772. The maximum allowable moment that the pile can carry is

$$M_{z(\max)} = f_s \frac{I_p}{\frac{d_1}{2}}$$

Let $f_s = 125{,}000$ kN/m^2. From Table 8.1b, $I_p = 123 \times 10^{-6}$ m^4 and $d_1 = 0.254$ m. So

$$\frac{I_p}{\left(\frac{d_1}{2}\right)} = \frac{123 \times 10^{-6}}{\left(\frac{0.254}{2}\right)} = 968.5 \times 10^{-6} \text{ m}^3$$

Now

$$Q_g = \frac{M_{z(\max)}}{A_m T} = \frac{(968.5 \times 10^{-6})(125{,}000)}{(0.772)(1.16)} = 135.2 \text{ kN}$$

Because $Q_g = 135.2$ kN > 53.59 kN, the deflection criteria apply. Hence $Q_g =$ **53.59 kN**.

This result is only the first approximation. The validity of the assumption of $n_h = 12{,}000$ kN/m^3 may now be checked using $Q_g = 53.59$ kN. ▼

8.13 PILE-DRIVING FORMULAS

To develop the desired load-carrying capacity, a point bearing pile must penetrate the dense soil layer sufficiently or have sufficient contact with a layer of rock. This requirement cannot always be satisfied by driving a pile to a predetermined depth because soil profiles vary. For that reason, several equations have been developed to calculate the ultimate capacity of a pile during driving. Thee dynamic equations are widely used in the field to determine whether the pile has reached satisfactory bearing value at the predetermined depth. One of the earliest of these dynamic equations—commonly referred to as the *Engineering News Record* (*ENR*) *formula*—is derived from the work–energy theory. That is,

Energy imparted by the hammer per blow =

(pile resistance)(penetration per hammer blow)

According to the ENR formula, the pile resistance is the ultimate load Q_u, expressed as

$$Q_u = \frac{W_R h}{S + C} \tag{8.99}$$

where W_R = weight of the ram (for example, see Table 8.6)
h = height of fall of the ram
S = penetration of pile per hammer blow
C = a constant

The pile penetration, S, is usually based on the average value obtained from the last few driving blows. In the equation's original form, the following values of C were recommended.

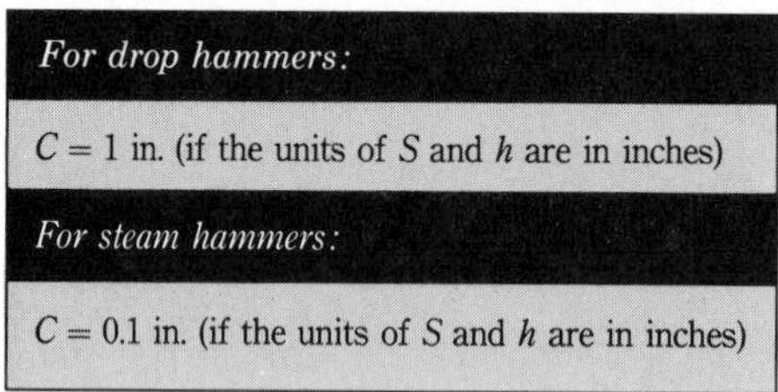

For drop hammers:

C = 1 in. (if the units of S and h are in inches)

For steam hammers:

C = 0.1 in. (if the units of S and h are in inches)

Also, a factor of safety, $FS = 6$, was recommended to estimate the allowable pile capacity. Note that, for single- and double-acting hammers, the term $W_R h$ can be replaced by EH_E (where E = hammer efficiency and H_E = rated energy of hammer). Thus

$$Q_u = \frac{EH_E}{S + C} \tag{8.100}$$

The ENR pile-driving formula has been revised several times over the years. A recent form—the *modified ENR formula*—is

$$Q_u = \frac{EW_R h}{S + C} \frac{W_R + n^2 W_p}{W_R + W_p} \tag{8.101}$$

where E = hammer efficiency
C = 0.1 in. if the units of S and h are in inches
W_p = weight of the pile
n = coefficient of restitution between the ram and the pile cap

The efficiencies of various pile driving hammers, E, are in the following ranges.

Hammer type	*Efficiency, E*
Single- and double-acting hammers	0.7–0.85
Diesel hammers	0.8–0.9
Drop hammers	0.7–0.9

Representative values of the coefficient of restitution, n, are given in the following table.

Pile material	*Coefficient of restitution, n*
Cast iron hammer and concrete piles (without cap)	0.4–0.5
Wood cushion on steel piles	0.3–0.4
Wooden piles	0.25–0.3

A factor of safety of 4 to 6 may be used in Eq. (8.101) to obtain the allowable load-bearing capacity of a pile.

The Michigan State Highway Commission (1965) undertook a study to obtain a rational pile-driving equation. At three diverse sites, a total of 88 piles were driven. Based on these tests, Michigan adopted a modified ENR formula:

$$Q_u = \frac{1.25 H_E}{S + C} \frac{W_R + n^2 W_p}{W_R + W_p} \tag{8.102}$$

where H_E = manufacturer's maximum rated hammer energy (lb-in.)
C = 0.1 in.

The unit of S is in inches in Eq. (8.102). A factor of safety of 6 is recommended.

Another equation referred to as the *Danish formula* also yields results as reliable as any other equation's:

$$Q_u = \frac{EH_E}{S + \sqrt{\dfrac{EH_E L}{2A_p E_p}}} \tag{8.103}$$

where E = hammer efficiency
H_E = rated hammer energy
E_p = modulus of elasticity of the pile material
L = length of pile
A_p = area of the pile cross section

(*Note:* The area of the soil plug, as shown in Figure 8.10b and 8.10c, should not be included.)

Consistent units must be used in Eq. (8.103). A factor of safety varying from 3 to 6 is recommended to estimate the allowable load-bearing capacity of piles.

Other frequently used equations for pile driving are those given by the Pacific Coast Uniform Building Code (International Conference of Building Officials, 1982) and by Janbu (1953).

Pacific Coast Uniform Building Code Formula

$$Q_u = \frac{(EH_E)\left(\dfrac{W_R + nW_p}{W_R + W_p}\right)}{S + \dfrac{Q_u L}{AE}} \tag{8.104}$$

The value of n in Eq. (8.104) should be 0.25 for steel piles and 0.1 for all other piles. A factor of safety of 4 is generally recommended.

Janbu's Formula

$$Q_u = \frac{EH_E}{K'_u S} \tag{8.105}$$

where $K'_u = C_d(1 + \sqrt{1 + \lambda/C_d})$ (8.106)

$$C_d = 0.75 + 0.15(W_p/W_R) \tag{8.107}$$

$$\lambda = (EH_E L/A_p E_p S^2) \tag{8.108}$$

A factor of safety of 4 to 5 is generally recommended.

▼ EXAMPLE 8.12

A precast concrete pile 12 in. × 12 in. in cross section is driven by a Vulcan hammer (model no. 08). The maximum rated hammer energy = 26 kip-ft (Table 8.6), the weight of ram = 8 kip, the total length of pile = 65 ft, hammer efficiency = 0.8, the coefficient of restitution = 0.45, the weight of pile cap = 0.72 kip, and the number of blows for the last 1 in. of penetration = 5. Estimate the allowable pile capacity by using

a. Equation (8.100), with $FS = 6$
b. Equation (8.101), with $FS = 4$
c. Equation (8.103), with $FS = 3$

Solution

Part a

Use of Eq. (8.100):

$$Q_u = \frac{EH_E}{S + C}$$

For

$$E = 0.8,\ H_E = 26 \text{ kip-ft}$$

$$S = \frac{1}{5} = 0.2 \text{ in.}$$

we obtain

$$Q_u = \frac{(0.8)\overbrace{(26)(12)}^{\text{kip-in.}}}{0.2 + 0.1} = 832 \text{ kip}$$

Hence

$$Q_{\text{all}} = \frac{Q_u}{FS} = \frac{832}{6} = \mathbf{138.7\ kip}$$

Part b

Use of Eq. (8.101):

$$Q_u = \frac{EW_R h}{S + C}\,\frac{W_R + n^2 W_p}{W_R + W_p}$$

$$\text{Weight of piles} = WA_p\gamma_c = (65 \text{ ft})(1 \text{ ft} \times 1 \text{ ft})(150 \text{ lb/ft}^3)$$
$$= 9750 \text{ lb} = 9.75 \text{ kip}$$

$$W_p = \text{weight of pile} + \text{weight of cap}$$
$$= 9.75 + 0.72 = 10.47 \text{ kip}$$

So

$$Q_u = \left[\frac{(0.8)(26)(12)}{0.2 + 0.1}\right]\left[\frac{8 + (0.45)^2(9.75)}{8 + 9.75}\right]$$

$$= (832)(0.562) = 467.6 \text{ kip}$$

$$Q_{all} = \frac{Q_u}{FS} = \frac{467.6}{4} = \mathbf{116.9\ kip}$$

Part c

Use of Eq. (8.103):

$$Q_u = \frac{EH_E}{S + \sqrt{\dfrac{EH_E L}{2A_p E_p}}}$$

Here, $E_p = 3 \times 10^6 \text{ lb/in}^2$, so

$$\sqrt{\frac{EH_E L}{2A_p E_p}} = \sqrt{\frac{(0.8)(26 \times 12)(65 \times 12)}{(2)(12 \times 12)\left(\underset{\substack{\uparrow \\ \text{kip/in}^2}}{\dfrac{3 \times 10^2}{1000}}\right)}} = 0.475 \text{ in.}$$

Hence

$$Q_u = \frac{(0.8)(26)(12)}{0.2 + 0.475} = 369.8 \text{ kip}$$

$$Q_{all} = \frac{Q_u}{FS} = \frac{369.8}{3} = \mathbf{123.3\ kip}$$ ▼

8.14 STRESS ON PILES DURING PILE DRIVING

The maximum stress developed on a pile during the driving operation can be estimated from the pile-driving formulas presented in the preceding section. To illustrate, we use the modified ENR formula given in Eq. (8.101):

$$Q_u = \frac{EW_R h}{S + C}\frac{W_R + n^2 W_p}{W_R + W_p}$$

In this equation, S equals the average penetration per hammer blow, which can also be expressed as

$$S = \frac{1}{N} \tag{8.109}$$

where S is in inches

N = number of hammer blows per inch of penetration

Thus

$$Q_u = \frac{EW_R h}{\dfrac{1}{N} + 0.1} \frac{W_R + n^2 W_p}{W_R + W_p} \tag{8.110}$$

Different values of N may be assumed for a given hammer and pile and Q_u calculated. The driving stress can then be calculated for each value of N and Q_u/A_p. This procedure can be demonstrated with a set of numerical values. Assume that a prestressed concrete pile 80 ft in length has to be driven by an 11B3 (MKT) hammer. The pile sides measure 10 in. From Table 8.3a for this pile,

$$A_p = 100 \text{ in}^2$$

The weight of the pile is

$$A_p L \gamma_c = \left(\frac{100 \text{ in}^2}{144}\right)(80 \text{ ft})(150 \text{ lb/ft}^3) = 8.33 \text{ kip}$$

If the weight of the cap is 0.67 kip,

$$W_p = 8.33 + 0.67 = 9 \text{ kip}$$

Again, from Table 8.6 for an 11B3 hammer,

$$\text{Rated energy} = 19.2 \text{ kip-ft} = H_E = W_R h$$

$$\text{Weight of ram} = 5 \text{ kip}$$

Assume that the hammer efficiency is 0.85 and that $n = 0.35$. Substituting these values in Eq. (8.110) yields

$$Q_u = \left[\frac{(0.85)(19.2 \times 12)}{\dfrac{1}{N} + 0.1}\right]\left[\frac{5 + (0.35)^2(9)}{5 + 9}\right] = \frac{85.37}{\dfrac{1}{N} + 0.2} \text{ kip}$$

Now the following table can be prepared.

N	Q_u (kip)	A_p (in²)	Q_u/A_p (kip/in²)
0	0	100	0
2	142.3	100	1.42
4	243.9	100	2.44
6	320.1	100	3.20
8	379.4	100	3.79
10	426.9	100	4.27
12	465.7	100	4.66
20	569.1	100	5.69

Both the number of hammer blows per inch and the stress can now be plotted in a graph, as shown in Figure 8.39. If such a curve is prepared, the number of blows per inch of pile penetration corresponding to the allowable pile-driving stress can be easily determined.

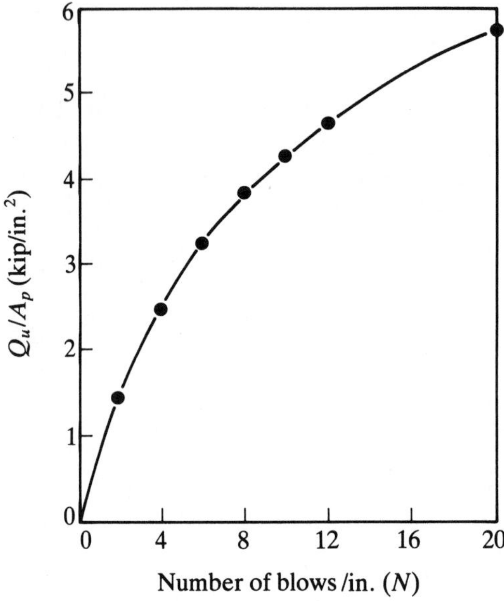

▼ **FIGURE 8.39**

Actual driving stresses in wooden piles are limited to about $0.7f_u$. Similarly, for concrete and steel piles, driving stresses are limited to about $0.6f_c'$ and $0.85f_y$, respectively.

In most cases, wooden piles are driven with a hammer energy of less than 45 kip-ft ($\approx$60 kN · m). Driving resistances are limited mostly to 4–5 blows per inch of pile penetration. For concrete and steel piles, the usual N values are 6–8 and 12–14, respectively.

8.15 PILE LOAD TESTS

In most large projects, a specific number of load tests must be conducted on piles. The primary reason is the unreliability of prediction methods. Vertical and lateral load-bearing capacity of a pile can be tested in the field. Figure 8.40a shows a schematic diagram of the pile load test arrangement for testing in *axial compression* in the field. The load is applied to the pile by a hydraulic jack. Step loads are applied to the pile, and sufficient time is allowed to elapse after each load so that a small amount of settlement occurs. The settlement of the pile is measured by dial gauges. The amount of load to be applied for each step will vary, depending on local building codes. Most building codes require that each step load be about one-fourth of the proposed working

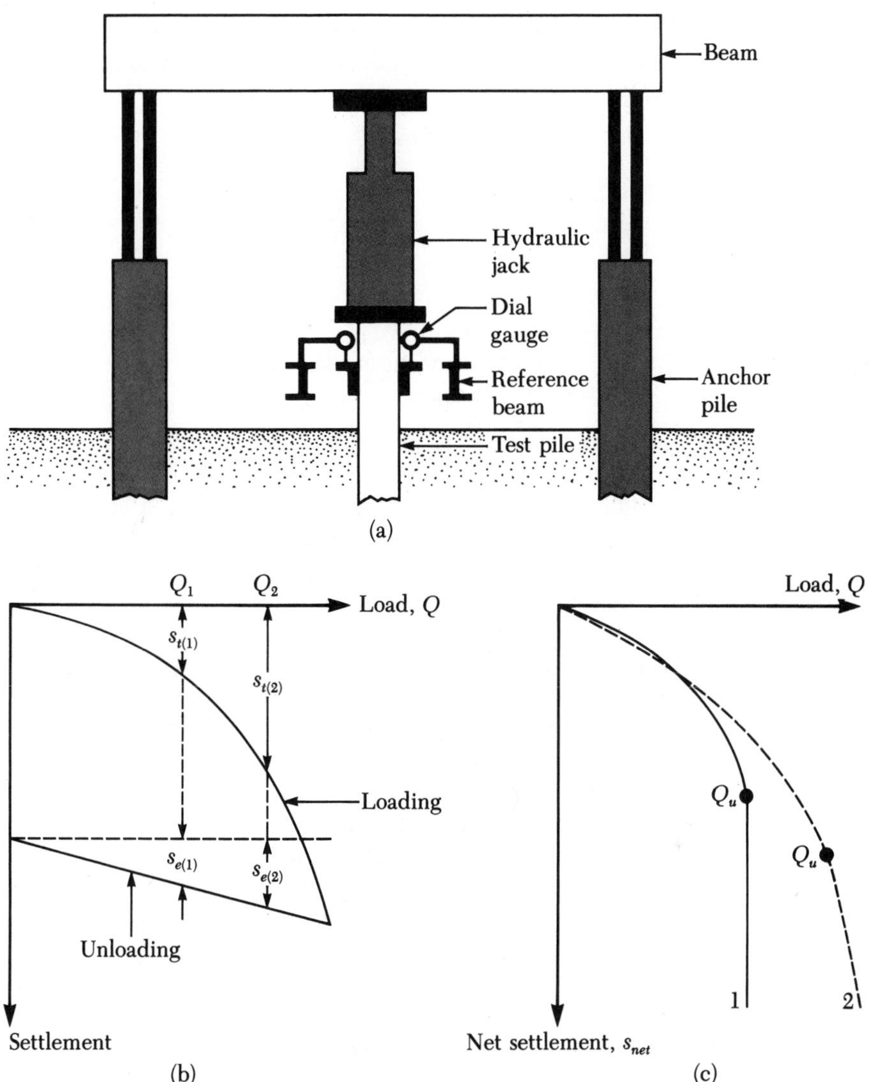

▼ **FIGURE 8.40** (a) Schematic diagram of pile load test arrangement; (b) plot of load against total settlement; (c) plot of load against net settlement

load. The load test should be carried out to at least a total load of two times the proposed working load. After reaching the desired pile load, the pile is gradually unloaded.

Load tests on piles in sand can be carried out immediately after the piles are driven. However, care should be taken in deciding the time lapse between driving and starting the load test when piles are embedded in clay. This time lapse can range from 30 to 60 days or more because the soil requires some time to gain its *thixotropic strength.*

Figure 8.40b shows a load settlement diagram obtained from field loading and unloading. For any load, Q, the net pile settlement can be calculated as follows. When $Q = Q_1$,

$$\text{Net settlement, } s_{\text{net}(1)} = s_{t(1)} - s_{e(1)}$$

When $Q = Q_2$,

$$\text{Net settlement, } s_{\text{net}(2)} = s_{t(2)} - s_{e(2)}$$

$$\vdots$$

where s_{net} = net settlement
s_e = elastic settlement of the pile itself
s_t = total settlement

These values of Q can be plotted in a graph against the corresponding net settlement, s_{net}, as shown in Figure 8.40c. The ultimate load of the pile can be determined from this graph. Pile settlement may increase with load to a certain point, beyond which the load–settlement curve becomes vertical. The load corresponding to the point where the Q–s_{net} curve becomes vertical is the ultimate load, Q_u, for the pile; it is shown by curve 1 in Figure 8.40c. In many cases, the latter stage of the load–settlement curve is almost linear, showing a large degree of settlement for a small increment of load; it is shown by curve 2 in Figure 8.40c. The ultimate load, Q_u, for such a case is determined from the point of the Q–s_{net} curve where this steep linear portion starts.

The load test procedure just described requires application of step loads on the piles and measurement of settlement and is called a *load-controlled* test. Another technique used for pile load test is the *constant-rate-of-penetration* test. In it, the load on the pile is continuously increased to maintain a constant rate of penetration, which can vary from 0.01 to 0.1 in./min (0.25 to 2.5 mm/min). This test gives a load–settlement plot similar to that obtained from the load-controlled test. Another type of pile load test is *cyclic loading*, in which an incremental load is repeatedly applied and removed.

8.16 GROUP PILES—EFFICIENCY

In most cases, piles are used in groups, as shown in Figure 8.41, to transmit the structural load to the soil. A *pile cap* is constructed over *group piles*. The pile cap can be in contact with the ground, as in most cases (Figure 8.41a), or well above the ground, as in the case of offshore platforms (Figure 8.41b).

Determination of the load-bearing capacity of group piles is extremely complicated and has not yet been fully resolved. When the piles are placed close to each other, a reasonable assumption is that the stresses transmitted by the piles to the soil will overlap (Figure 8.41c), reducing the load-bearing capacity of the piles. Ideally, the piles in a group should be spaced so that the load-bearing capacity of the group should not be less than the sum of the bearing capacity of the individual piles. In practice, the minimum center-to-center pile spacing, d, is $2.5D$, and in ordinary situations, is actually about 3–$3.5D$.

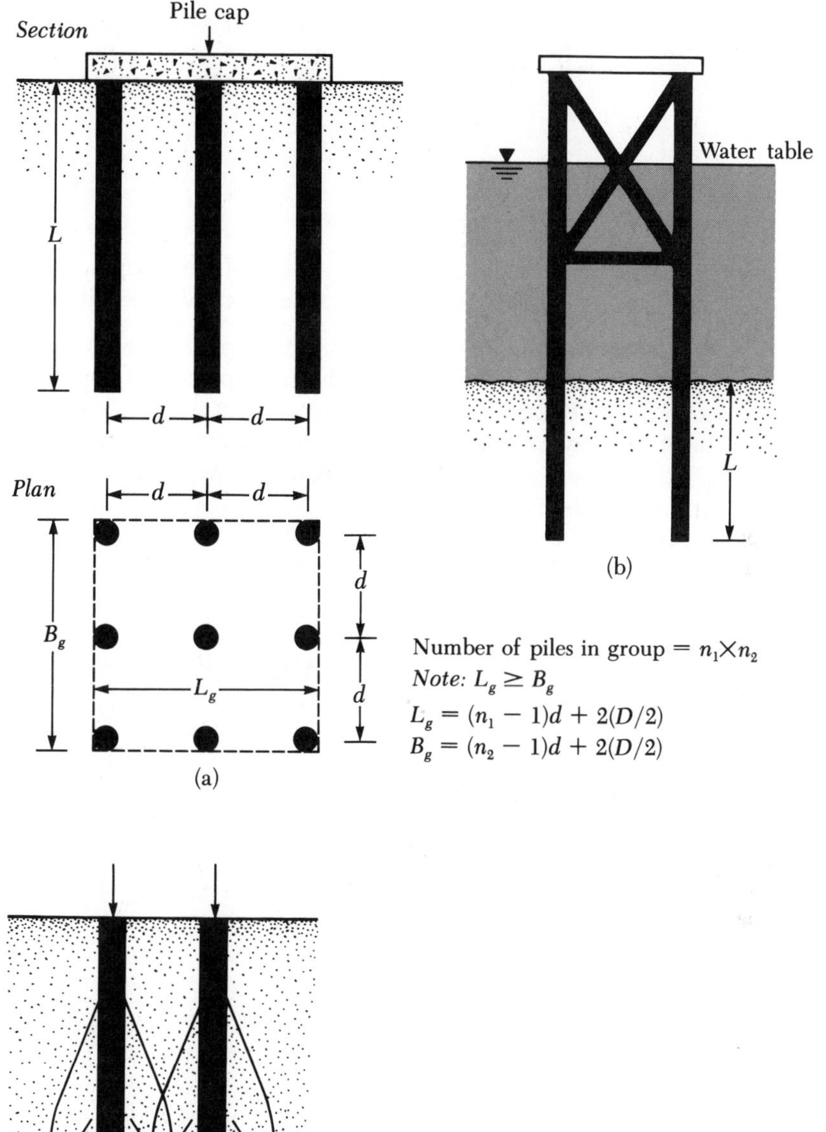

▼ **FIGURE 8.41** Pile groups

The efficiency of the load-bearing capacity of a group pile may be defined as

$$\eta = \frac{Q_{g(u)}}{\Sigma Q_u} \tag{8.111}$$

where η = group efficiency
$Q_{g(u)}$ = ultimate load-bearing capacity of the group pile
Q_u = ultimate load-bearing capacity of each pile without the group effect

Many structural engineers use a simplified analysis to obtain the group efficiency for friction piles, particularly in sand. This type of analysis can be explained with the aid of Figure 8.41a. Depending on their spacing within the group, the piles may act in one of two ways: (1) as a *block* with dimensions $L_g \times B_g \times L$, or (2) as *individual piles.* If the piles act as a block, the frictional capacity is $f_{av} p_g L \approx Q_{g(u)}$. [*Note:* p_g = perimeter of the cross section of block = $2(n_1 + n_2 - 2)d + 4D$, and f_{av} = average unit frictional resistance.] Similarly, for each pile acting individually, $Q_u \approx pLf_{av}$. (*Note:* p = perimeter of the cross section of each pile.) Thus

$$\eta = \frac{Q_{g(u)}}{\sum Q_u} = \frac{f_{av}[2(n_1 + n_2 - 2)d + 4D]L}{n_1 n_2 p L f_{av}} = \frac{2(n_1 + n_2 - 2)d + 4D}{p n_1 n_2} \tag{8.112}$$

Hence

$$Q_{g(u)} = \left[\frac{2(n_1 + n_2 - 2)d + 4D}{p n_1 n_2}\right] \sum Q_u \tag{8.113}$$

From Eq. (8.113), if the center-to-center spacing, d, is large enough, $\eta > 1$. In that case, the piles will behave as individual piles. Thus, in practice, if $\eta < 1$,

$$Q_{g(u)} = \eta \sum Q_u$$

and, if $\eta \geq 1$,

$$Q_{g(u)} = \sum Q_u$$

Another equation often referred to by design engineers is the *Converse–Labarre equation*:

$$\eta = 1 - \left[\frac{(n_1 - 1)n_2 + (n_2 - 1)n_1}{90 n_1 n_2}\right]\theta \tag{8.114}$$

where $\theta \text{ (deg)} = \tan^{-1}(D/d)$ (8.115)

Figure 8.42 shows a comparison of field test results in clay with the theoretical group efficiency calculated from Eq. (8.114). Reported by Brand et al. (1972), these tests were conducted in soil for which the details are given in Figure 3.5. Other test details included

Length of piles = 6 m

Diameter of piles = 150 mm

Pile groups tested = 2 × 2

Location of pile head = 1.5 m below the ground surface

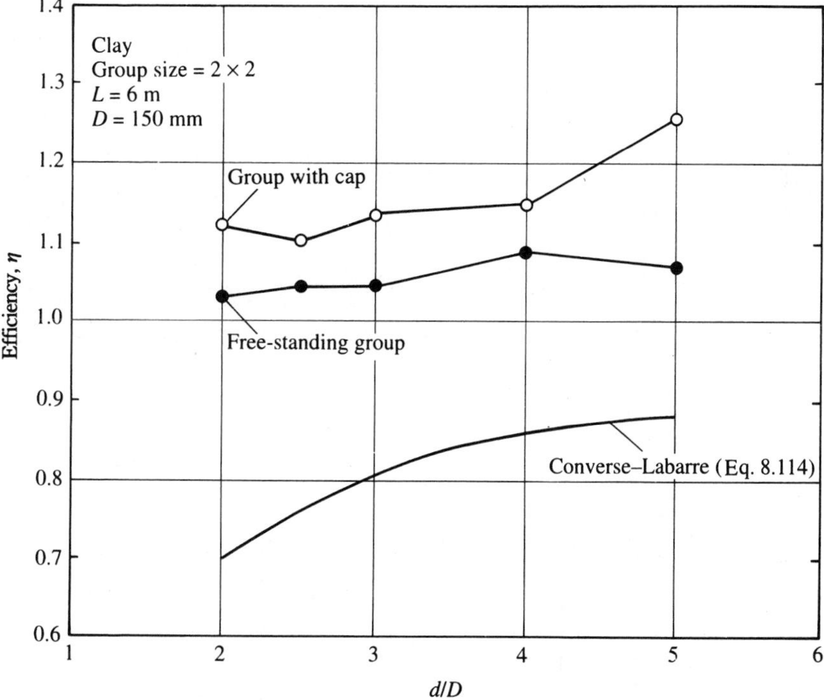

▼ **FIGURE 8.42** Variation of group efficiency with d/D (after Brand et al., 1972)

Pile tests were conducted with and without a cap (i.e. free-standing group). Note that for $d/D \geq 2$, the magnitude of η was greater than 1.0. Also for similar values of d/D the group efficiency was greater with the pile cap than without the cap. Figure 8.43 shows the pile group settlement at various stages of the load test.

Piles in Sand

Figure 8.44 shows a set of the author's laboratory model test results for round piles driven into dense sand. Note that the group efficiency, in reality, can be larger than 1. The reason is the soil compaction zones created around the piles during driving.

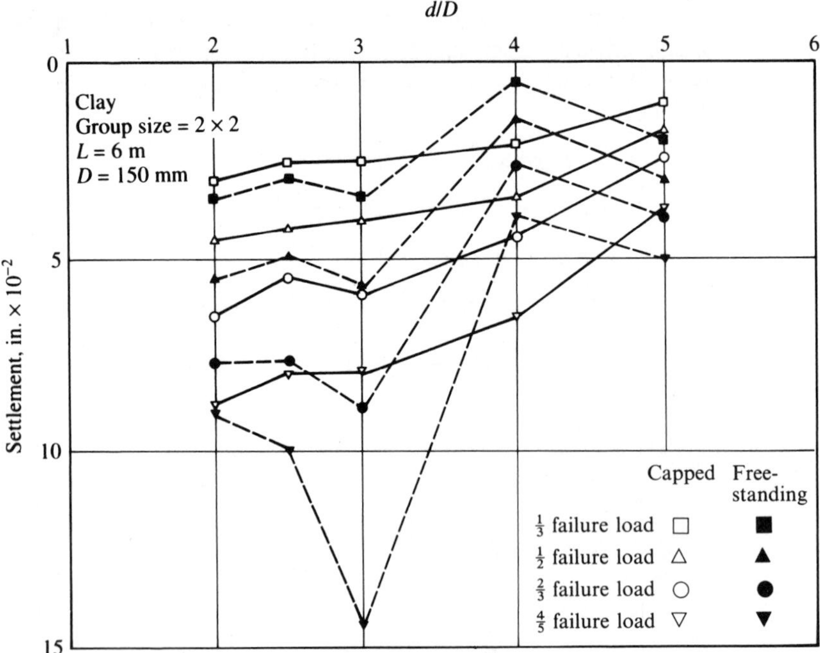

▼ **FIGURE 8.43** Variation of group pile settlement at various stages of load (after Brand et al., 1972)

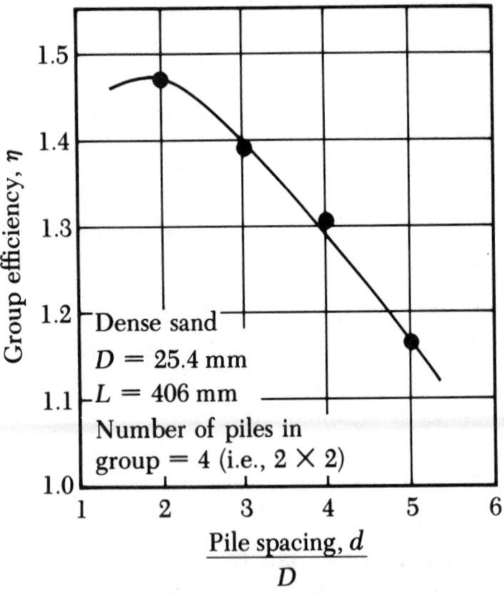

▼ **FIGURE 8.44** Results of a model test for group efficiency of piles in dense sand

Liu et al. (1985) reported the results of field tests on 58 pile groups and 23 single piles embedded in granular soil. Test details included

$$\text{Pile length, } L = 8D\text{–}23D$$

$$\text{Pile diameter, } D = 125 \text{ mm–}330 \text{ mm}$$

$$\text{Type of pile installation} = \text{bored}$$

$$\text{Spacing of piles in group, } d = 2D\text{–}6D$$

Figure 8.45 shows the behavior of 3 × 3 pile groups with low-set and high-set pile caps in terms of average skin friction, f_{av}. Figure 8.46 shows the variation of average skin friction based on the location of a pile in the group.

Based on the experimental observations of the behavior of group piles in sand to date, the following general conclusions may be drawn.

1. For *driven* group piles in *sand* with $d \geq 3D$, $Q_{g(u)}$ may be taken to be $\Sigma\, Q_u$, which includes the frictional and the point bearing capacities of individual piles.

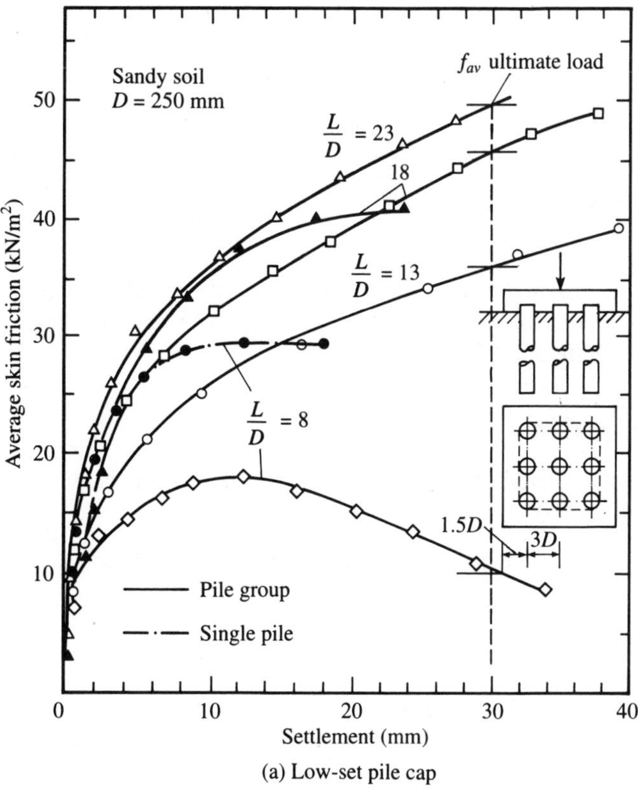

(a) Low-set pile cap

▼ **FIGURE 8.45** Behavior of low-set and high-set pile groups in terms of average skin friction (based on Liu et al., 1985)

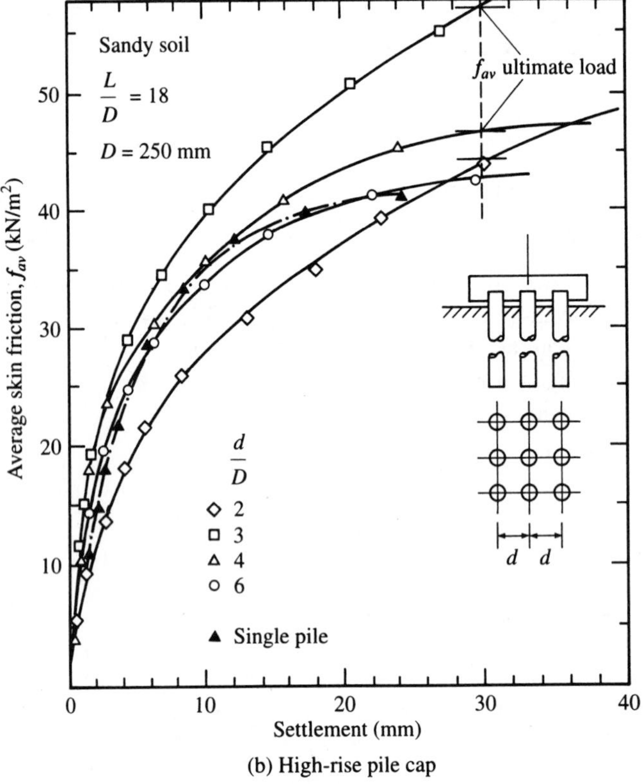

(b) High-rise pile cap

▼ **FIGURE 8.45** (Continued)

2. For *bored* group piles in *sand* at conventional spacings ($d \approx 3D$), $Q_{g(u)}$ may be taken to be 2/3 to 3/4 times $\Sigma\, Q_u$ (frictional and point bearing capacities of individual piles).

Piles in Clay

The ultimate load-bearing capacity of group piles in clay may be estimated in the following manner.

1. Determine $\Sigma\, Q_u = n_1 n_2 (Q_p + Q_s)$. From Eq. (8.18),

$$Q_p = A_p[9c_{u(p)}]$$

where $c_{u(p)}$ = undrained cohesion of the clay at the pile tip

Also, from Eq. (8.43),

$$Q_s = \sum \alpha p c_u \,\Delta L$$

So

$$\sum Q_u = n_1 n_2 [9A_p c_{u(p)} + \sum \alpha p c_u \,\Delta L] \tag{8.116}$$

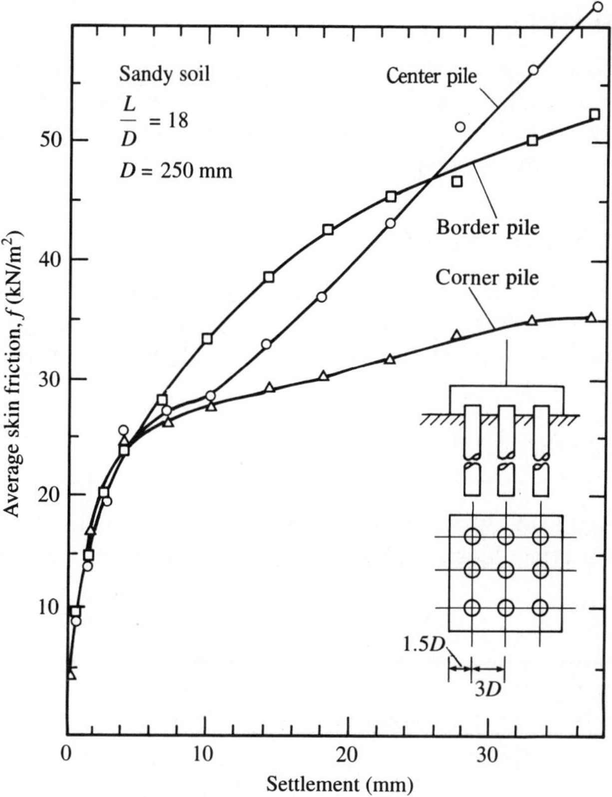

FIGURE 8.46 Average skin friction based on pile location (based on Liu et al., 1985)

2. Determine the ultimate capacity by assuming that the piles in the group act as a block with dimensions of $L_g \times B_g \times L$. The skin resistance of the block is

$$\sum p_g c_u \, \Delta L = \sum 2(L_g + B_g)c_u \, \Delta L$$

Calculate the point bearing capacity:

$$A_p q_p = A_p c_{u(p)} N_c^* = (L_g B_g) c_{u(p)} N_c^*$$

Obtain the value of the bearing capacity factor, N_c^*, from Figure 7.16. Note the change in notation: Along the abscissa, the term H/B in Figure 7.16 is equivalent to L/B_g for this problem; also, L/B in Figure 7.16 is equivalent to L_g/B_g. Thus the ultimate load is

$$\sum Q_u = L_g B_g c_{u(p)} N_c^* + \sum 2(L_g + B_g)c_u \, \Delta L \tag{8.117}$$

3. Compare the values obtained from Eqs. (8.116) and (8.117). The *lower* of the two values is $Q_{g(u)}$.

Piles in Rock

For point bearing piles resting on rock, most building codes specify that $Q_{g(u)} = \Sigma Q_u$, provided that the minimum center-to-center spacing of piles is $D + 300$ mm. For H-piles and piles with square cross sections, the magnitude of D is equal to the diagonal dimension of the pile cross section.

General Comments

A pile cap resting on soil, as shown in Figure 8.34a, will contribute to the load-bearing capacity of a pile group. However, this contribution may be neglected for design purposes because the support may be lost as a result of soil erosion or excavation during the life of the project.

▼ EXAMPLE 8.13

Refer to Figure 8.47 which shows the plan of a pile group. Each pile has a square cross section measuring 12 in. × 12 in. The center-to-center spacing of the piles is 30 in.

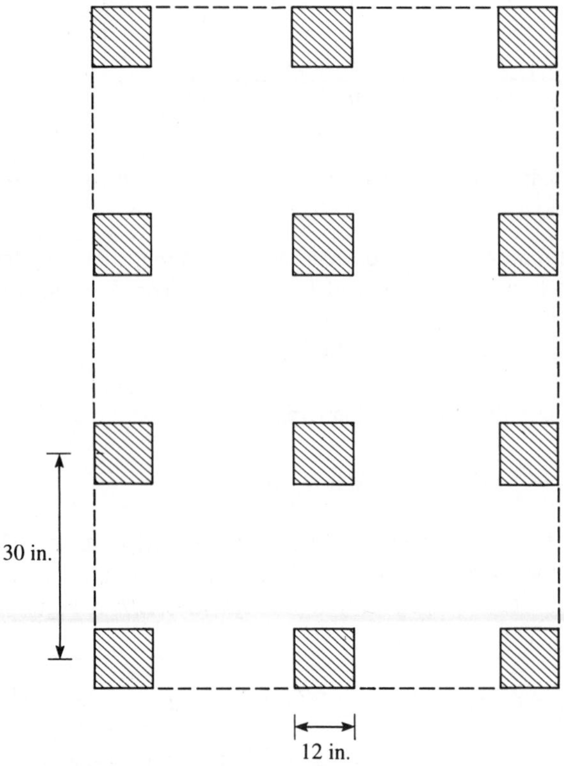

▼ **FIGURE 8.47**

Determine the group efficiency of the piles by using

a. Eq. (8.112)
b. Eq. (8.114)

Solution

Part a: Using Eq. (8.112)

$$\eta = \frac{2(n_1 + n_2 - 2)d + 4D}{pn_1n_2}$$

For $n_1 = 4$, $n_2 = 3$, $D = 12$ in., and $p = 4D = 48$ in.,

$$\eta = \frac{2(4 + 3 - 2)(30) + 48}{(48)(4)(3)} = 0.604 = \mathbf{60.4\%}$$

Part b: Using Eq. (8.114)

$$\eta = 1 - \left[\frac{(n_1 - 1)n_2 + (n_2 - 1)n_1}{90n_1n_2}\right]\tan^{-1}\left(\frac{D}{d}\right)$$

$$\tan^{-1}\left(\frac{D}{d}\right) = \tan^{-1}\left(\frac{12}{30}\right) = 21.8°$$

So

$$\eta = 1 - \left[\frac{(3)(3) + (2)(4)}{(90)(3)(4)}\right](21.8°) = 0.657 = \mathbf{65.7\%.}$$ ▼

▼ EXAMPLE 8.14

Refer to Figure 8.41a. For this group pile, $n_1 = 4$, $n_2 = 3$, $D = 305$ mm, $d = 1220$ mm, and $L = 15$ m. The piles are square in cross section and are embedded in a homogeneous clay with $c_u = 70$ kN/m^2. Use $FS = 4$ and determine the allowable load-bearing capacity of the group pile.

Solution From Eq. (8.116),

$$\sum Q_u = n_1n_2[9A_p c_{u(p)} + \sum \alpha p c_u \,\Delta L]$$

$$A_p = (0.305)(0.305) = 0.093 \text{ m}^2$$

$$p = (4)(0.305) = 1.22 \text{ m}$$

From Figure 8.19 for $c_u = 70$ kN/m^2, $\alpha = 0.63$. So

$$\sum Q_u = (4)(3)[(9)(0.093)(70) + (0.63)(1.22)(70)(15)]$$

$$= 12(58.59 + 807.03) \approx 10{,}387 \text{ kN}$$

Again, from Eq. (8.117), the ultimate block capacity is $L_g B_g c_{u(p)} N_c^* + \sum 2(L_g + B_g)c_u \Delta L$. So

$$L_g = (n_1 - 1)d + 2\left(\frac{D}{2}\right) = (4 - 1)(1.22) + 0.305 = 3.965 \text{ m}$$

$$B_g = (n_2 - 1)d + 2\left(\frac{D}{2}\right) = (3 - 1)(1.22) + 0.305 = 2.745 \text{ m}$$

$$\frac{L}{B_g} = \frac{15}{2.745} = 5.46$$

$$\frac{L_g}{B_g} = \frac{3.965}{2.745} = 1.44$$

From Figure 7.16, $N_c^* \approx 8.6$. Thus

$$\text{Block capacity} = (3.965)(2.745)(70)(8.6) + 2(3.965 + 2.745)(70)(15)$$

$$= 6552 + 14091 = 20{,}643 \text{ kN}$$

So

$$Q_{g(u)} = 10{,}387 \text{ kN} < 20{,}643 \text{ kN}$$

$$Q_{g(\text{all})} = \frac{Q_{g(u)}}{FS} = \frac{10{,}387}{4} \approx \mathbf{2597\ kN.}$$ ▼

8.17 CONSOLIDATION SETTLEMENT OF GROUP PILES

The consolidation settlement of a group pile in clay can be approximately estimated by using the 2 : 1 stress distribution method shown in Figure 3.38. The procedure of calculation involves the following steps (refer to Figure 8.48):

1. Let the depth of embedment of the piles be L. The group is subjected to a total load of Q_g. If the pile cap is below the original ground surface, Q_g equals the total load of the superstructure on the piles minus the effective weight of soil above the pile group removed by excavation.
2. Assume that the load Q_g is transmitted to the soil beginning at a depth of $2L/3$ from the top of the pile, as shown in Figure 8.48 ($z = 0$). The load Q_g spreads out along 2 vertical : 1 horizontal lines from this depth. Lines aa' and bb' are the two 2 : 1 lines.
3. Calculate the stress increase caused at the middle of each soil layer by the load Q_g:

$$\Delta p_i = \frac{Q_g}{(B_g + z_i)(L_g + z_i)} \tag{8.118}$$

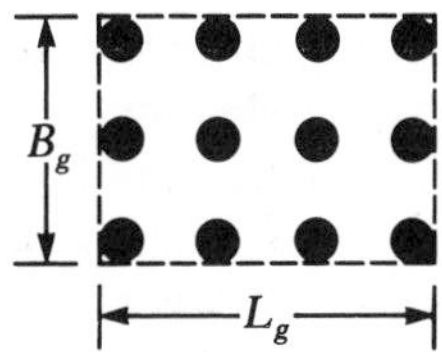

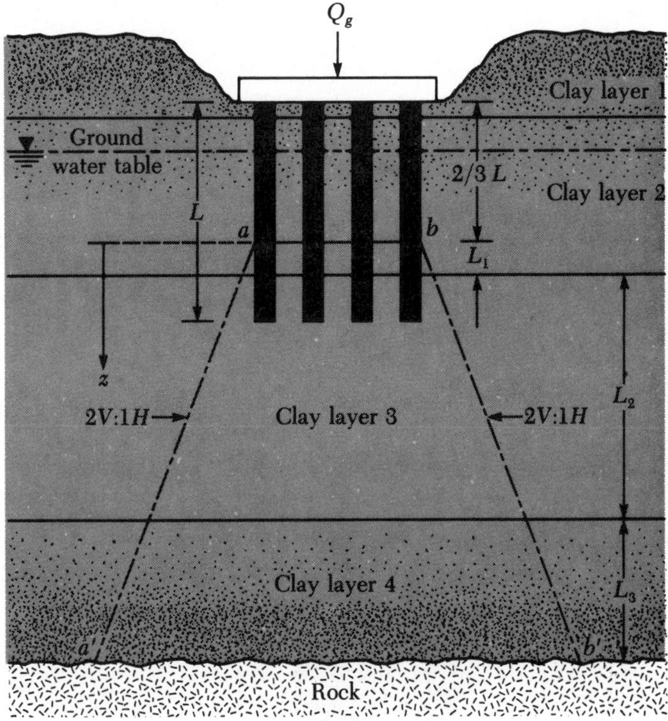

▼ **FIGURE 8.48** Consolidation settlement of group piles

where Δp_i = stress increase at the middle of layer i

L_g, B_g = length and width of the plan of pile group, respectively

z_i = distance from $z = 0$ to the middle of the clay layer, i

For example, in Figure 8.48 for layer 2, $z_i = L_1/2$, for layer 3, $z_i = L_1 + L_2/2$, and, for layer 4, $z_i = L_1 + L_2 + L_3/2$. Note, however, that there will be no stress increase in clay layer 1 because it is above the horizontal plane ($z = 0$) from which the stress distribution to the soil starts.

4. Calculate the settlement of each layer caused by the increased stress:

$$\Delta s_i = \left[\frac{\Delta e_{(i)}}{1 + e_{o(i)}}\right] H_i \tag{8.119}$$

where Δs_i = consolidation settlement of layer i
$\Delta e_{(i)}$ = change of void ratio caused by the stress increase in layer i
e_o = initial void ratio of layer i (before construction)
H_i = thickness of layer i (*Note:* In Figure 8.48, for layer 2 $H_i = L_1$, for layer 3, $H_i = L_2$, and for layer 4, $H_i = L_3$.)

Relations for $\Delta e_{(i)}$ are given in Chapter 1.

5. Total consolidation settlement of the pile group is then

$$\Delta s_{g(c)} = \sum \Delta s_i \tag{8.120}$$

Note that consolidation settlement of piles may be initiated by fills placed nearby, adjacent floor loads, and lowering of water tables.

▼ EXAMPLE 8.15

A group pile in clay is shown in Figure 8.49. Determine the consolidation settlement of the pile groups. All clays are normally consolidated.

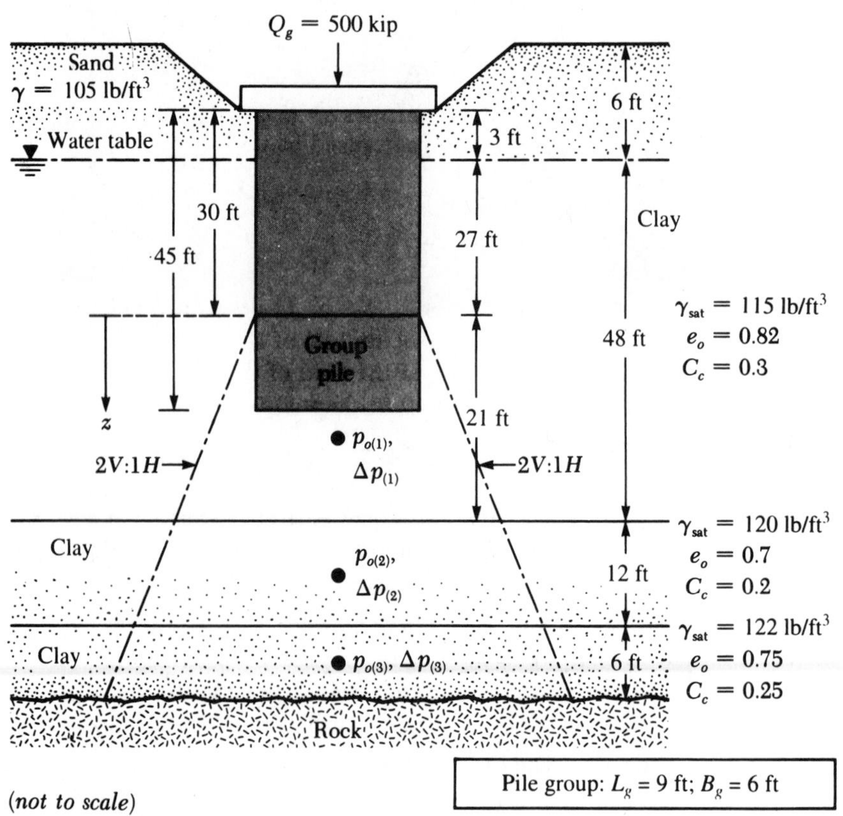

▼ **FIGURE 8.49**

Solution The stress distribution pattern is shown in Figure 8.49. Hence

$$\Delta p_{(1)} = \frac{Q_g}{(L_g + z_1)(B_g + z_1)} = \frac{(500)(1000)}{\left(9 + \frac{21}{2}\right)\left(6 + \frac{21}{2}\right)} = 1554 \text{ lb/ft}^2$$

$$\Delta p_{(2)} = \frac{(500)(1000)}{(9 + 27)(6 + 27)} = 421 \text{ lb/ft}^2$$

$$\Delta p_{(3)} = \frac{(500)(1000)}{(9 + 36)(6 + 36)} = 265 \text{ lb/ft}^2$$

$$\Delta s_1 = \frac{C_{c(1)} H_1}{1 + e_{o(1)}} \log\left[\frac{p_{o(1)} + \Delta p_{(1)}}{p_{o(1)}}\right]$$

$$p_{o(1)} = (6)(105) + \left(27 + \frac{21}{2}\right)(115 - 62.4) = 2603 \text{ lb/ft}^2$$

$$\Delta s_1 = \frac{(0.3)(21)}{1 + 0.82} \log\left(\frac{2603 + 1554}{2603}\right) = 0.7 \text{ ft} = 8.45 \text{ in.}$$

$$\Delta s_2 = \frac{C_{c(2)} H_2}{1 + e_{o(2)}} \log\left[\frac{p_{o(2)} + \Delta p_{(2)}}{p_{o(2)}}\right]$$

$$p_{o(2)} = (6)(105) + (27 + 21)(115 - 62.4) + (6)(120 - 62.4) = 3500 \text{ lb/ft}^2$$

$$\Delta s_2 = \frac{(0.2)(12)}{1 + 0.7} \log\left(\frac{3500 + 421}{3500}\right) = 0.07 \text{ ft} = 0.84 \text{ in.}$$

$$p_{o(3)} = (6)(105) + (48)(115 - 62.4) + (12)(120 - 62.4) + (3)(122 - 62.4) = 4025 \text{ lb/ft}^2$$

$$\Delta s_2 = \frac{(0.25)(6)}{1 + 0.75} \log\left(\frac{4025 + 265}{4025}\right) = 0.024 \text{ ft} \approx 0.29 \text{ in.}$$

Total settlement, $\Delta s_g = 8.45 + 0.84 + 0.29 =$ **9.58 in.** ▼

8.18 ELASTIC SETTLEMENT OF GROUP PILES

Several investigations relating to the settlement of group piles with widely varying results have been reported in the literature. The simplest relation for the settlement of group piles was given by Vesic (1969) as

$$\boxed{s_{g(e)} = \sqrt{\frac{B_g}{D}}\, s} \tag{8.121}$$

where $s_{g(e)}$ = elastic settlement of group piles
B_g = width of pile group section (see Figure 8.41a)
D = width or diameter of each pile in the group
s = elastic settlement of each pile at comparable working load (see Section 8.10)

For pile groups in sand and gravel, Meyerhof (1976) suggested the following empirical relation for elastic settlement:

$$s_{g(e)}(\text{mm}) = \frac{0.92q\sqrt{B_g}I}{N_{\text{cor}}} \tag{8.122}$$

where
$$q = Q_g/(L_g B_g) \tag{8.123}$$

L_g and B_g = length and width of the pile group section respectively
N_{cor} = average corrected standard penetration number within seat of settlement ($\approx B_g$ deep below the tip of the piles)
I = influence factor $= 1 - L/8B_g \geq 0.5$ (8.124)

L = length of embedment of piles

Similarly, the pile group settlement is related to the cone penetration resistance as

$$s_{g(e)} = \frac{qB_g I}{2q_c} \tag{8.125}$$

where q_c = average cone penetration resistance within the seat of settlement

In Eq. (8.125), all symbols are in consistent units.

8.19 UPLIFT CAPACITY OF GROUP PILES

The efficiency of group piles under compressive load was discussed in Section 8.16. However, under certain circumstances, group piles may be used for construction of foundations subjected to uplifting load (Figure 8.50). As in Eq. (8.111), the group efficiency under uplift may be expressed as

$$\eta_T = \frac{T_{un(g)}}{T_{un}} \tag{8.126}$$

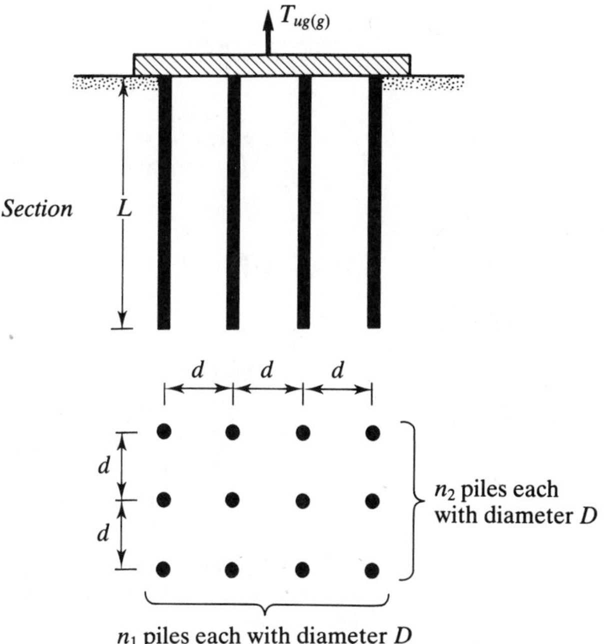

▼ **FIGURE 8.50** Group piles subjected to uplifting load

where η_T = group efficiency under uplift
$T_{un(g)}$ = net ultimate uplift capacity of pile group
T_{un} = net ultimate uplift capacity of single pile (Section 8.11)

Note that

$$T_{un(g)} = T_{ug(g)} - (n_1 \times n_2)W - W_{\text{cap}} \tag{8.127}$$

where $T_{ug(g)}$ = gross ultimate uplift capacity of group piles
W = effective self-weight of each pile
$n_1 \times n_2$ = number of piles in the group
W_{cap} = effective weight of pile cap

At present, few field and laboratory experimental results relating to the evaluation of η_T are available in the literature. Das and Azim (1985) conducted a limited number of model tests to determine the group efficiency, η_T, of rigid pile groups embedded in saturated clay. The results of this study are shown in Figure 8.51, from which the following general conclusions may be drawn.

1. For a pile group, η_T increases linearly with the d/D ratio until it reaches 100%. The d/D ratio at which η_T reaches a value of 100% is about $1/2(L/D)$.
2. For given d/D and L/D ratios, the magnitude of η_T decreases with the increase of the number of piles in a group.

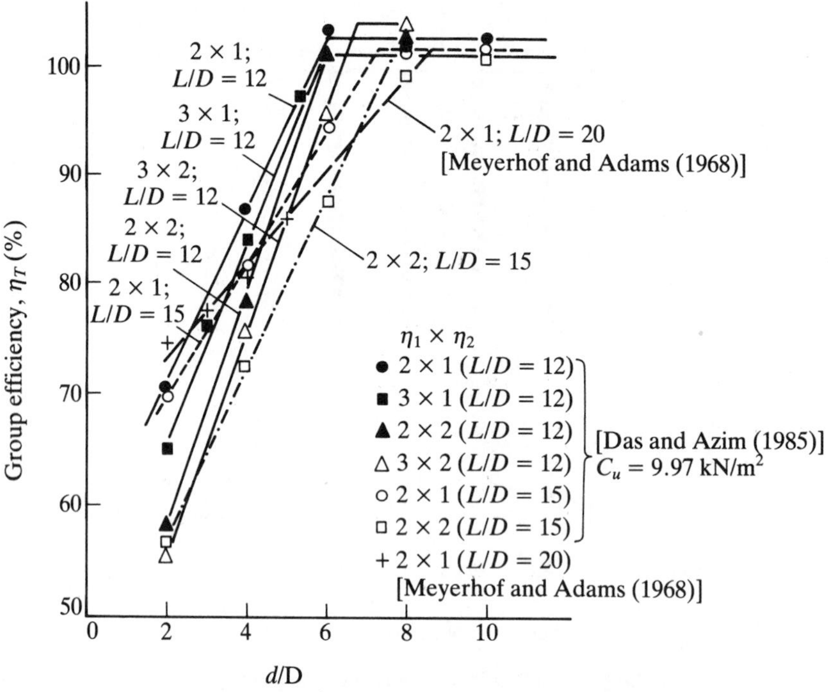

▼ **FIGURE 8.51** Efficiency of rigid pile groups embedded in saturated clay and subjected to uplifting force

3. For a given d/D ratio and number of piles in a group, the magnitude of η_T decreases with the increase of L/D.

Group efficiency, however, may be a function of the consistency of the clay.

Figure 8.52 shows the laboratory model test results for group efficiency of rough rigid piles embedded in loose and dense sand (Das, 1984). The group piles in this case had an L/D ratio of 15. Note that the magnitude of η_T is a function of L/D, d/D, the number of piles in the group, and the relative density of the sand.

More studies are required to define quantitatively the parameters controlling the group efficiency, η_T.

8.20 NEGATIVE SKIN FRICTION

Negative skin friction is a downward drag force exerted on the pile by the soil surrounding it. This action can occur under conditions such as the following.

1. If a fill of clay soil is placed over a granular soil layer into which a pile is driven, the fill will gradually consolidate. This consolidation process will exert a downward drag force on the pile (Figure 8.53a) during the period of consolidation.

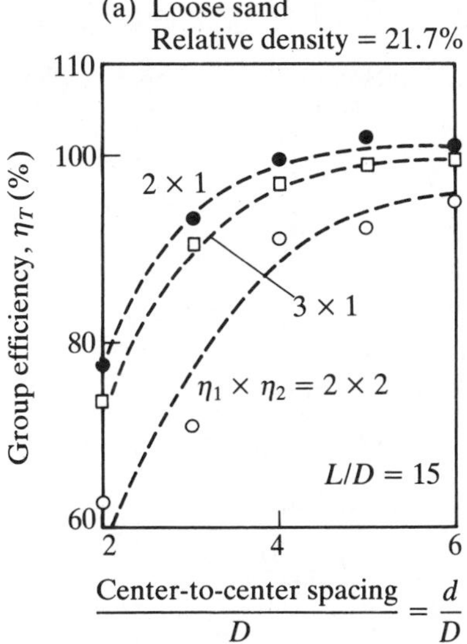

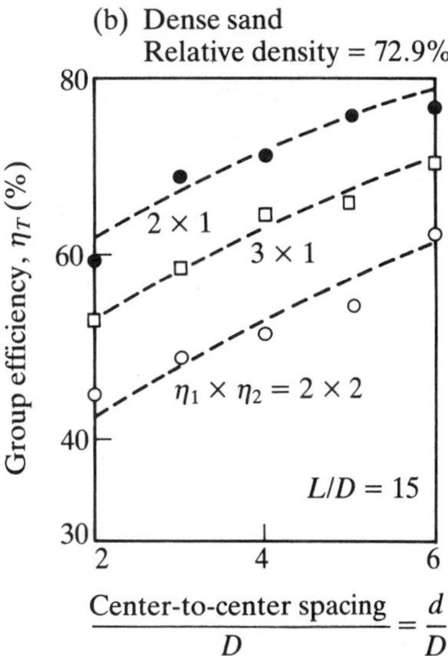

FIGURE 8.52 Efficiency of rigid pile groups embedded in sand and subjected to uplifting force (based on laboratory model test results of Das, 1984)

2. If a fill of granular soil is placed over a layer of soft clay, as shown in Figure 8.53b, it will induce the process of consolidation in the clay layer and thus exert a downward drag on the pile.
3. Lowering of the water table will increase the vertical effective stress on the soil at any depth, which will induce consolidation settlement in clay. If a pile is located in the clay layer, it will be subjected to a downward drag force.

In some cases, the downward drag force may be excessive and cause foundation failure. This section outlines two tentative methods for the calculation of negative skin friction.

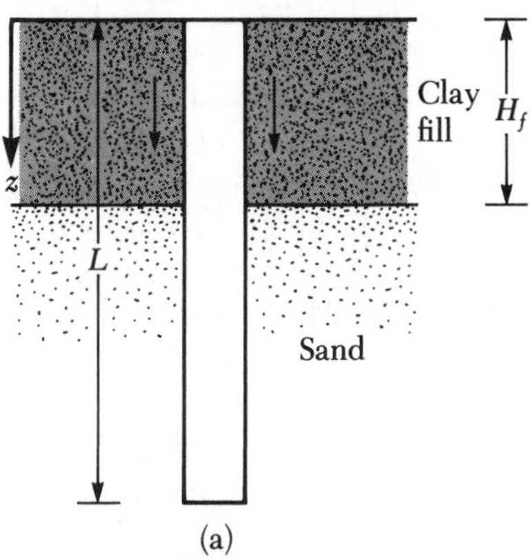

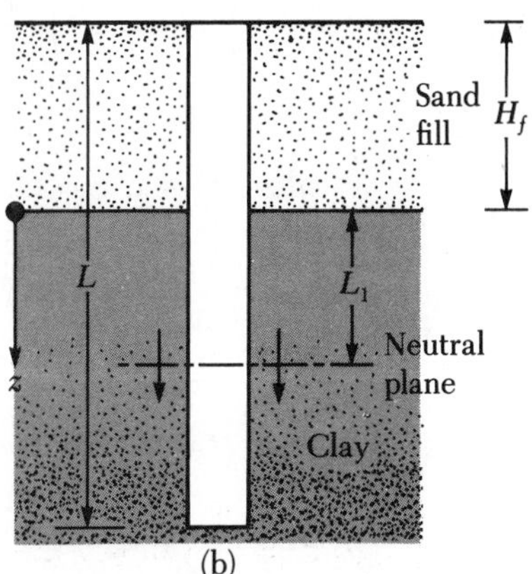

FIGURE 8.53 Negative skin friction

Clay Fill over Granular Soil (Figure 8.53a)

Similar to the β method presented in Section 8.6, the negative (downward) skin stress on the pile is

$$f_n = K'\sigma'_v \tan \delta \tag{8.128}$$

where K' = earth pressure coefficient = $K_o = 1 - \sin \phi$
σ'_v = vertical effective stress at any depth $z = \gamma'_f z$
γ'_f = effective unit weight of fill
δ = soil–pile friction angle $\approx$ 0.5–0.7ϕ

Hence the total downward drag foce, Q_n, on a pile is

$$Q_n = \int_0^{H_f} (pK'\gamma'_f \tan \delta)z \, dz = \frac{pK'\gamma'_f H_f^2 \tan \delta}{2} \tag{8.129}$$

where H_f = height of the fill

If the fill is above the water table, the effective unit weight, γ'_f, should be replaced by the moist unit weight.

Granular Soil Fill over Clay (Figure 8.53b)

In this case, the evidence indicates that the negative skin stress on the pile may exist from $z = 0$ to $z = L_1$, which is referred to as the *neutral depth* (see Vesic, 1977, pp. 25–26, for discussion). The neutral depth may be given as (Bowles, 1982):

$$L_1 = \frac{(L - H_f)}{L_1}\left[\frac{L - H_f}{2} + \frac{\gamma'_f H_f}{\gamma'}\right] - \frac{2\gamma'_f H_f}{\gamma'} \tag{8.130}$$

where γ'_f and γ' = effective unit weights of the fill and the underlying clay layer, respectively

Once the value of L_1 is determined, the downward drag force is obtained in the following manner. The unit negative skin friction at any depth from $z = 0$ to $z = L_1$ is

$$f_n = K'\sigma'_v \tan \delta \tag{8.131}$$

where $K' = K_o = 1 - \sin \phi$
$\sigma'_v = \gamma'_f H_f + \gamma' z$
δ = 0.5–0.7ϕ

Hence the total drag force is

$$Q_n = \int_0^{L_1} pf_n \, dz = \int_0^{L_1} pK'(\gamma'_f H_f \gamma' z) \tan \delta \, dz$$
$$= (pK'\gamma'_f H_f \tan \delta)L_1 + \frac{L_1^2 pK'\gamma' \tan \delta}{2} \quad (8.132)$$

If the soil and the fill are above the water table, the effective unit weights should be replaced by moist unit weights. In some cases, the piles can be coated with bitumen in the down-drag zone to avoid this problem. Baligh et al. (1978) summarized the results of several field tests that were conducted to evaluate the effectiveness of bitumen coating in reducing the negative skin friction. Their results are presented in Table 8.17.

▼ EXAMPLE 8.16

Refer to Figure 8.53a; $H_f = 2$ m. The pile is circular in cross section with a diameter of 0.305 m. For the fill that is above the water table, $\gamma_f = 16$ kN/m^3 and $\phi = 32°$. Determine the total drag force.

Solution From Eq. (8.129)

$$Q_n = \frac{pK'\gamma_f^2 \tan \delta}{2}$$

$$p = \pi(0.305) = 0.958 \text{ m}$$

$$K' = 1 - \sin \phi = 1 - \sin 32° = 0.47$$

$$\delta = (0.6)(32) = 19.2°$$

$$Q_n = \frac{(0.958)(0.47)(16)(2)^2 \tan 19.2°}{2} = \mathbf{5.02\ kN}$$ ▼

▼ EXAMPLE 8.17

Refer to Figure 8.53b. Here, $H_f = 2$ m, pile diameter = 0.305 m, $\gamma_f = 16.5$ kN/m^3, $\phi_{\text{clay}} = 34°$, $\gamma_{\text{sat(clay)}} = 17.2$ kN/m^3, and $L = 20$ m. The water table coincides with the top of the clay layer. Determine the downward drag force.

Solution The depth of the neutral plane is given in Eq. (8.130) as

$$L_1 = \frac{L - H_f}{L_1}\left(\frac{L - H_f}{2} + \frac{\gamma_f H_f}{\gamma'}\right) - \frac{2\gamma_f H_f}{\gamma'}$$

TABLE 8.17 Summary of Case Studies of Bitumen-Coated Piles[a]

	Downward drag				Test loadings		
Case number	1	2	3	4	5	6	7
Soil type	Fill, sand, and clay	Fill and silty clay	Fill and clay	Sand and silty clay	Silty clay	Silty clay	Sand fill, clay, and peat
Pile type	Cast-in-place concrete	Steel pipe	Steel pipe	Steel pipe	6 RC piles	6 RC piles	Precast concrete
Pile cross section (mm)	$D = 530$	$D = 300$	$D = 500$	$D = 760$	300 × 300	300 × 300	380 × 450
Length in contact with settling soil (m)	25	26	40	25	7–17	9–16	24
Installation method	Predriven casing	Enlarged tip and slurry	Enlarged tip and casing	Driving	Driving	Driving	Driving
Bitumen Coating							
Type (pen 25°C)	20/30	80/100	80/100	60/70	60/70	80–100 RC-0 cutback	43 special grade
Coating thickness (mm)	10	1.2	1.2	1.5	1.2	1.2	10
Measured Shaft Resistance							
Uncoated pile (ton)	70–80	120	300	180	31–40	31–40	160
Coated pile (ton)	5–7	10	15	3	10–33	20–42	
Coating effectiveness (%)	92	92	95	98	30–80	30–80	
Predicted Downdrag							
Coating pile (ton)	0.1	2–11	5	0–23			
Coating effectiveness (%)	100	91–98	98	87–100			

[a] After Baligh et al. (1978)

Note that γ'_f in Eq. (8.130) has been replaced by γ_f because the fill is above the water table. So

$$L_1 = \frac{(20-2)}{L_1}\left[\frac{(20-2)}{2} + \frac{(16.5)(2)}{(17.2-9.81)}\right] - \frac{(2)(16.5)(2)}{(17.2-9.81)}$$

$$= \frac{242.4}{L_1} - 8.93 = 11.75 \text{ m}$$

Now, referring to Eq. (8.132), we have

$$Q_n = (pK'\gamma_f H_f \tan\delta)L_1 + \frac{L_1^2 pK'\gamma' \tan\delta}{2}$$

$$p = \pi(0.305) = 0.958 \text{ m}$$

$$K' = 1 - \sin 34° = 0.44$$

$$Q_n = (0.958)(0.44)(16.5)(2)[\tan(0.6 \times 34)](11.75) + \frac{(11.75)^2(0.958)(0.44)(17.2-9.81)[\tan(0.6 \times 34)]}{2}$$

$$= 60.78 + 79.97 = \mathbf{40.75\ kN.}$$ ▼

PROBLEMS

8.1 A concrete pile is 50 ft long and 16 in. × 16 in. in cross section. The pile is fully embedded in sand, for which $\gamma = 110$ lb/ft^3 and $\phi = 30°$. Calculate:

a. The ultimate point load, Q_p, by Meyerhof's method [Eqs. (8.12), and (8.13)]

b. The total frictional resistance [Eqs. (8.32), (8.33), and (8.36)] for $K = 1.3$ and $\delta = 0.8\phi$.

8.2 Solve Problem 8.1 by Coyle ad Castello's method (Figures 8.21 and 8.22).

8.3 Solve Problem 8.1, part (a), by Vesic's method [Eq. (8.19)]. Use $I_r = I_{rr} = 50$.

8.4 Solve Problem 8.1, part (a), by Janbu's method [Eq. (8.29)]. Use $\eta' = 90°$.

8.5 Use the results of Problems 8.1–8.4 to estimate an allowable value for the point load. Use $FS = 4$.

8.6 Redo Problem 8.1 for $\gamma = 117$ lb/ft^3 and $\phi = 37°$.

8.7 Solve Problem 8.6 by Coyle and Castello's method (Figures 8.21 and 8.22).

8.8 A concrete pile fully embedded in sand has a cross section of 12 in. × 12 in. The length of embedment is 40 ft. The sand has an average relative density of 55% and a unit weight of 110 lb/ft^3. Use Eqs. (8.32), (8.33), (8.34), and (8.36) to determine the frictional resistance of the pile.

8.9 A driven closed ended pile is shown in Figure P8.9. Calculate:

a. The ultimate point load by Meyerhof's procedure

b. The ultimate point load by Vesic's procedure ($I_r = I_{rr} = 50$)

c. An approximate ultimate point load on the basis of parts (a) and (b)

d. The ultimate frictional resistance, Q_s; use Eqs. (8.32), (8.33), (8.36), $K = 1.4$ and $\delta = 0.6\phi$

e. The allowable load of the pile; use $FS = 4$

8.10 A concrete pile 20 m long having a cross section of 381 mm × 381 mm is fully embedded in a saturated clay layer. For the clay, $\gamma_{sat} = 18.5$ kN/m^3, $\phi = 0$, and $c_u = 70$ kN/m^2.

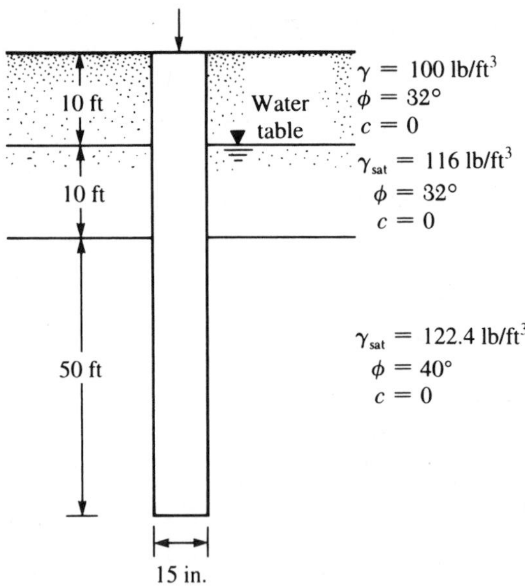

▼ **FIGURE P8.9**

Assume that the water table lies below the tip of the pile. Determine the allowable load that the pile can carry ($FS = 3$). Use the α method to estimate the skin resistance.

8.11 Redo Problem 8.10 using the λ method for estimating the skin resistance.

8.12 A concrete pile 405 mm × 405 mm in cross section is shown in Figure P8.12. Calculate the ultimate skin resistance by using the

a. α method

b. λ method

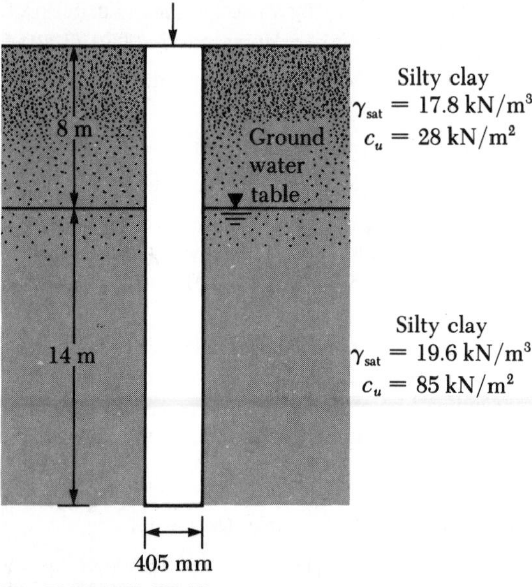

▼ **FIGURE P8.12**

c. β method
Use $\phi_R = 25°$ for all clays, which are normally consolidated.

8.13 A steel pile (H-section; HP 12 × 84; see Table 8.1a) is driven to a layer of sandstone. The length of the pile is 60 ft. For the sandstone, the unconfined compression strength is $q_{u(\text{lab})} = 13{,}600 \text{ lb/in}^2$, and the angle of friction is 34°. Use a factor of safety of 3 and estimate the allowable point load that can be carried by the pile.

8.14 The allowable working load on a prestressed concrete pile 21 m long that has been driven into sand is 502 kN. The pile is octagonal in shape with $D = 356$ mm (see Table 8.3b). Skin resistance carries 350 kN of the allowable load, and point bearing carries the rest. Use $E_p = 21 \times 10^6 \text{ kN/m}^2$, $E_s = 25 \times 10^3 \text{ kN/m}^2$, $\mu_s = 0.35$, and $\xi = 0.62$ [Eq. (8.61)]. Determine the elastic settlement of the pile. Use 0.8 for I_{wp} in Eq. (8.62).

8.15 A concrete pile is 60 ft long and has a cross section of 15 in. × 15 in. The pile is embedded in sand having $\gamma = 120 \text{ lb/ft}^3$ and $\phi = 38°$. The allowable working load is 170 kip. If 100 kip are contributed by the frictional resistance and 70 kip are from the point load, determine the elastic settlement of the pile. Here, $E_p = 3 \times 10^6 \text{ lb/in}^2$, $E_s = 5 \times 10^3 \text{ lb/in}^2$, $\mu_s = 0.35$, and $\xi = 0.62$.

8.16 A precast concrete pile with a cross section of 350 mm × 305 mm is embedded in sand. The length of the pile is 15 m. Assume that $\gamma_{\text{sand}} = 15.8 \text{ kN/m}^3$, $\phi_{\text{sand}} = 35°$, and the relative density of sand = 70%. Estimate the allowable pullout capacity of the pile ($FS = 4$).

8.17 A concrete pile 50 ft long is embedded in a saturated clay with $c_u = 850 \text{ lb/ft}^2$. The pile is 12 in. × 12 in. in cross section. Use $FS = 4$ and determine the allowable pullout capacity of the pile.

8.18 Redo Problem 8.17 with the following changes: for the top 10 ft of the clay, $c_u = 500 \text{ lb/ft}^2$, and below that $c_u = 1200 \text{ lb/ft}^2$.

8.19 A steel H-pile (Section: HP 14 × 117; see Table 8.1a) is driven by an MKT S-20 hammer (see Table 8.6). The length of the pile is 80 ft, the coefficient of restitution is 0.35, the weight of pile cap is 17.8 kip, hammer efficiency is 0.84, and the number of blows for the last inch of penetration is 10. Estimate the ultimate pile capacity by using Eq. (8.100). For the pile, $E_p = 30 \times 10^6 \text{ lb/in}^2$.

8.20 Redo Problem 8.19 using Eq. (8.101).

8.21 Redo Problem 8.19 using Eq. (8.103).

8.22 The plan of a group pile (friction pile) in sand is shown in Figure P8.22. The piles are

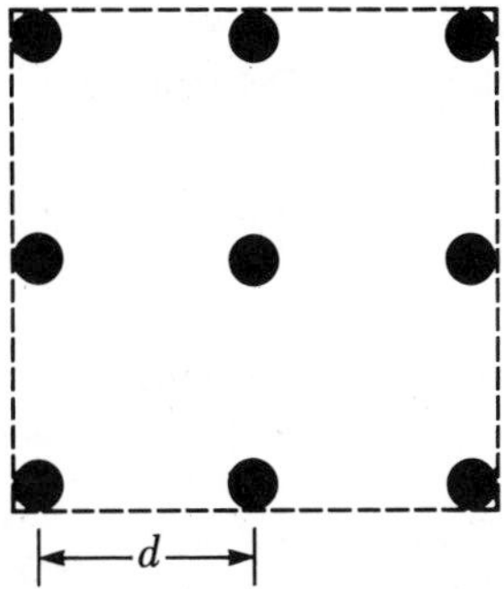

▼ **FIGURE P8.22**

circular in cross section and have an outside diameter of 18 in. The center-to-center spacing of the piles, *d*, is 36 in. Use Eq. (8.112) and find the efficiency of the pile group.

8.23 Solve Problem 8.22 using the Converse–Labarre equation.

8.24 Refer to Problem 8.22. If the center-to-center spacing is increased to 54 in., what will be the group efficiency?

8.25 Solve Problem 8.24 using the Converse–Labarre equation.

8.26 The plan of a group pile is shown in Figure P8.22. Asssume that the piles are embedded in a saturated homogeneous clay having a $c_u = 80\ \text{kN/m}^2$. For the piles, $D = 406$ mm, center-to-center spacing = 850 mm, and $L = 20$ m. Find the allowable load-carrying capacity of the pile group. Use $FS = 3$.

8.27 Redo Problem 8.26 for $d = 30$ in., $L = 50$ ft, $D = 15$ in., and $c_u = 1020\ \text{lb/ft}^2$.

8.28 The section of a 3 × 4 group pile in a layered saturation clay is shown in Figure P8.28. The piles are square in cross section (14 in. × 14 in.). The center-to-center spacing, *d*, of the piles is 35 in. Determine the allowable load-bearing capacity of the pile group. Use $FS = 4$.

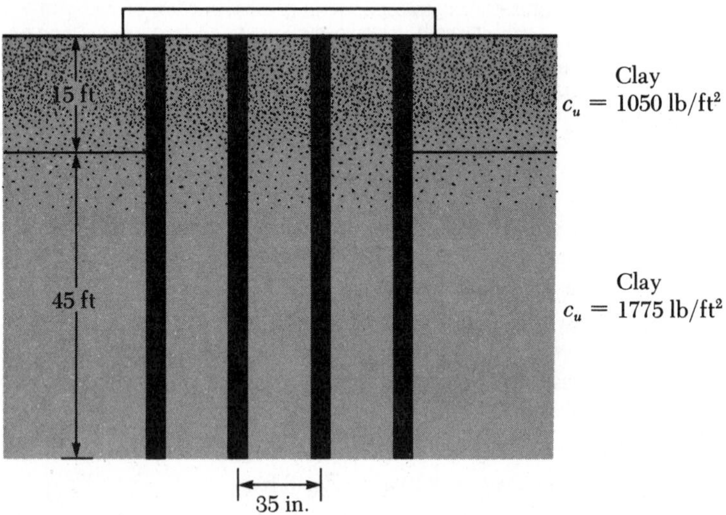

▼ **FIGURE P8.28**

8.29 Figure P8.29 shows a group pile in clay. Determine the consolidation settlement of the group.

8.30 Figure 8.53a shows a pile. Let $L = 50$ ft, $D = 18$ in., $H_f = 11.5$ ft, $\gamma_f = 112\ \text{lb/ft}^3$, and $\phi_{\text{fill}} = 28°$. Determine the total downward drag force on the pile. Assume that the fill is located above the water table and that $\delta = 0.6\phi_{\text{fill}}$.

8.31 Redo Problem 8.30 assuming that the water table coincides with the top of the fill and that $\gamma_{\text{sat(fill)}} = 124.5\ \text{lb/ft}^3$. If the other quantities remain the same, what would be the downward drag force on the pile? Assume that $\delta = 0.6\phi_{\text{fill}}$.

8.32 Refer to Figure 8.53b. Let $L = 19$ m, $\gamma_{\text{fill}} = 15.2\ \text{kN/m}^3$, $\gamma_{\text{sat(clay)}} = 19.5\ \text{kN/m}^3$, $\phi_{\text{clay}} = 30°$, $H_f = 3.2$ m, and $D = 0.46$ m. The water table coincides with the top of the clay layer. Determine the total downward drag on the pile. Assume that $\delta = 0.5\phi_{\text{clay}}$.

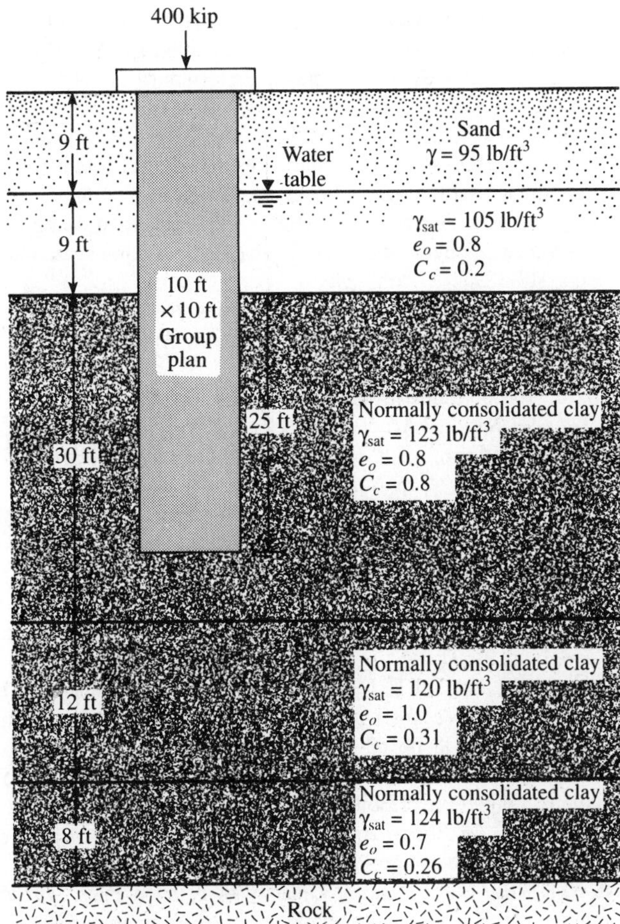

▼ **FIGURE P8.29**

REFERENCES

American Society of Civil Engineers (1959). "Timber Piles and Construction Timbers," *Manual of Practice*, No. 17, American Society of Civil Engineers, New York.

American Society of Civil Engineers (1993). *Design of Pile Foundations* (Technical Engineering and Design Guides as Adapted from the US Army Corps of Engineers, No. 1), American Society of Civil Engineers, New York.

American Petroleum Institute (1984). *Recommended Practice of Planning, Designing, and Construction of Fixed Offshore Platforms*, Report No. API-RF-2A, Dallas, 115 pp.

Baligh, M. M., Vivatrat, V., and Pigi, H. (1978). "Downdrag on Bitumen-Coated Piles," *Journal of the Geotechnical Engineering Division*, American Society of Civil Engineers, Vol. 104, No. GT11, pp. 1355–1370.

Bhusan, K. (1982). "Discussion: New Design Correlations for Piles in Sands," *Journal of the Geotechnical Engineering Division*, American Society of Civil Engineers, Vol. 108, No. GT11, pp. 1508–1510.

Bowles, J. E. (1982). *Foundation Design and Analysis*, McGraw-Hill, New York.

Brand, E. W., Muktabhant, C., and Taechathummarak, A. (1972). "Load Test on Small Foundations in Soft Clay," *Proceedings*, Performance of Earth and Earth-Supported Structures, American Society of Civil Engineers, Vol. 1, Part 2, pp. 903–928.

Briaud, J. L., Moore, B. H., and Mitchell, G. B. (1989). "Analysis of Pile Load Test at Lock and Dam 26," *Proceedings*, Foundation Engineering: Current Principles and Practices, American Sociey of Civil Engineers, Vol. 2, pp. 925–942.

Briaud, J. L., and Tucker, L. M. (1984). "Coefficient of Variation of *In-Situ* Tests in Sand," *Proceedings*, Symposium on Probabilistic Characterization of Soil Properties, Atlanta, pp. 119–139.

Coyle, H. M., and Castello, R. R. (1981). "New Design Correlations for Piles in Sand," *Journal of the Geotechnical Engineering Division*, American Society of Civil Engineers, Vol. 107, No. GT7, pp. 965–986.

Das, B. M. (1984). "Model Uplift Tests on Pile Groups in Sand," *Transportation Research Record No. 998*, National Academy of Sciences, Washington, D.C., pp. 25–28.

Das, B. M. and Azim, M. F. (1985). "Uplift Capacity of Rigid Pile Groups in Clay," *Soils and Foundations*, Vol. 25, No. 4, pp. 56–60.

Das, B. M., and Seeley, G. R. (1975). "Uplift Capacity of Buried Model Piles in Sand," *Journal of the Geotechnical Engineering Division*, American Society of Civil Engineers, Vol. 101, No. GT10, pp. 1091–1094.

Das, B. M., and Seeley, G. R. (1982). "Uplift Capacity of Pipe Piles in Saturated Clay," *Soils and Foundations*, The Japanese Society of Soil Mechanics and Foundation Engineering, Vol. 22, No. 1, pp. 91–94.

Davisson, M. T., and Gill, H. L. (1963). "Laterally Loaded Piles in a Layered Soil System," *Journal of the Soil Mechanics and Foundations Division*, American Society of Civil Engineers, Vol. 89, No. SM3, pp. 63–94.

Goodman, R. E. (1980). *Introduction to Rock Mechanics*, Wiley, New York.

International Conference of Building Officials (1982). "Uniform Building Code," Whittier, Calif.

Janbu, N. (1953). *An Energy Analysis of Pile Driving with the Use of Dimensionless Parameters*, Norwegian Geotechnical Institute, Oslo, Publication No. 3.

Janbu, N. (1976). "Static Bearing Capacity of Friction Piles," *Proceedings*, Sixth European Conference on Soil Mechanics and Foundation Engineering, Vol. 1.2, pp. 479–482.

Liu, J. L., Yuan, Z. L., and Zhang, K. P. (1985). "Cap-Pile-Soil Interaction of Bored Pile Groups," *Proceedings*, Eleventh International Conference on Soil Mechanics and Foundation Engineering, San Francisco, Vol. 3, pp. 1433–1436.

Matlock, H., and Reese, L. C. (1960). "Generalized Solution for Laterally Loaded Piles," *Journal of the Soil Mechanics and Foundations Division*, American Society of Civil Engineers, Vol. 86, No. SM5, Part I, pp. 63–91.

McClelland, B. (1974). "Design of Deep Penetration Piles for Ocean Structures," *Journal of the Geotechnical Engineering Division*, American Society of Civil Engineers, Vol. 100, No. GT7, pp. 709–747.

Meyerhof, G. G. (1976). "Bearing Capacity and Settlement of Pile Foundations," *Journal of the Geotechnical Engineering Division*, American Society of Civil Engineers, Vol. 102, No. GT3, pp. 197–228.

Meyerhof, G. G., and Adams, J. I. (1968). "The Ultimate Uplift Capacity of Foundations," *Canadian Geotechnical Journal*, Vol. 5, No. 4, pp. 225–244.

Michigan State Highway Commission (1965). *A Performance Investigation of Pile Driving Hammers and Piles*, Lansing, 338 pp.

Sharma, H. D., and Joshi, R. C. (1988). "Drilled Pile Behavior in Granular Deposit," *Canadian Geotechnical Journal*, Vol. 25, No. 2, pp. 222–232.

Vesic, A. S. (1961). "Bending of Beams Resting on Isotropic Elastic Solids," *Journal of the Engineering Mechanics Division*, American Society of Civil Engineers, Vol. 87, No. EM2, pp. 35–53.

Vesic, A. S. (1969). "Experiments with Instrumented Pile Groups in Sand," American Society for Testing and Materials; Special Technical Publication, No. 444, pp. 177–222.

Vesic, A. S. (1970). "Tests on Instrumented Piles—Ogeechee River Site," *Journal of the Soil Mechanics and Foundations Division*, American Society of Civil Engineers, Vol. 96, No. SM2, pp. 561–584.

Vesic, A. S. (1977). *Design of Pile Foundations*, National Cooperative Highway Research Program Synthesis of Practice No. 42, Transportation Research Board, Washington, D.C.

Vijayvergiya, V. N., and Focht, J. A. Jr. (1972). *A New Way to Predict Capacity of Piles in Clay*, Offshore Technology Conference Paper 1718, Fourth Offshore Technology Conference, Houston.

Woodward, R. J., Gardner, W. S., and Greer, D. M. (1972). *Drilled Pier Foundations*, McGraw-Hill, New York.

CHAPTER NINE

DRILLED-PIER AND CAISSON FOUNDATIONS

9.1 INTRODUCTION

The terms caisson, pier, drilled shaft, and drilled pier are often used interchangeably in foundation engineering; all refer to a *cast-in-place pile generally having a diameter of about* 2.5 ft ($\approx$750 mm) or more, with or without steel reinforcement and with or without an enlarged bottom. Sometimes the diameter can be as small as 1 ft ($\approx$305 mm).

To avoid confusion, we use the term *drilled pier* for a hole drilled or excavated to the bottom of a structure's foundation and then filled with concrete. Depending on the soil conditions, casings or *laggings* (boards or sheet piles) may be used to prevent the soil around the hole from caving in during construction. The diameter of the pier shaft is usually large enough for a person to enter for inspection.

The use of drilled-pier foundations has several advantages.

1. A single drilled pier may be used instead of a group of piles and the pile cap.
2. Constructing drilled piers in deposits of dense sand and gravel is easier than driving piles.
3. Drilled piers may be constructed before completion of grading operations.
4. When piles are driven by a hammer, the ground vibration may cause damage to nearby structures, which the use of drilled piers avoids.
5. Piles driven into clay soils may produce ground heaving and cause previously driven piles to move laterally, which do not occur during construction of drilled piers.
6. There is no hammer noise during the construction of drilled piers, as there is during pile driving.
7. Because the base of a drilled pier can be enlarged, it provides great resistance to the uplifting load.
8. The surface over which the base of the drilled pier is constructed can be visually inspected.
9. Construction of drilled piers generally utilizes mobile equipment, which,

under proper soil conditions, may prove to be more economical than methods of constructing pile foundations.
10. Drilled piers have high resistance to lateral loads.

There are also several drawbacks to the use of drilled-pier construction. The concreting operation may be delayed by bad weather and always needs close supervision. Also, as in the case of braced cuts, deep excavations for drilled piers may induce substantial ground loss and damage to nearby structures.

The term *caisson* refers to a substructure element used at wet construction sites, such as rivers, lakes, and docks. For the construction of caissons, a hollow shaft or a box is sunk into position to rest on firm ground. The lower part of the shaft or the box is provided with a cutting edge to help it penetrate the soft soil layers below the water level and come to rest on a load-bearing stratum. The material inside the shaft or box is dredged through the openings at the top, and then concrete is poured in. Bridge abutments, quay walls, and structures for shore protection can be built over caissons.

DRILLED PIERS

9.2 TYPES OF DRILLED PIERS

Drilled piers are classified according to the ways in which they are designed to transfer the structural load to the substratum. Figure 9.1a shows a drilled pier that has a *straight shaft*. It extends through the upper layer(s) of poor soil, and its tip rests on a strong load-bearing soil layer or rock. The shaft can be cased with steel shell or pipe

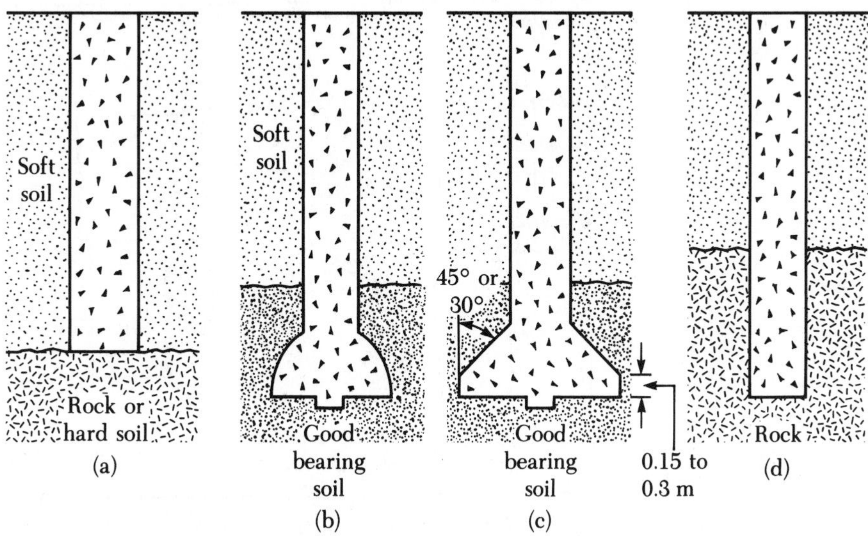

FIGURE 9.1 Types of drilled pier: (a) straight-shafted pier; (b) and (c) belled pier; (d) straight-shafted pier socketed into rock

when required (as in the case of cased, cast-in-place concrete piles; Figure 8.4). For such piers, the resistance to the applied load may develop from end bearing and also from side friction at the pier perimeter and soil interface.

A *belled pier* (Figure 9.1b and c) consists of a straight shaft with a bell at the bottom, which rests on good bearing soil. The bell can be constructed in the shape of a dome (Figure 9.1b), or it can be angled (Figure 9.1c). For angled bells, the underreaming tools commercially available can make 30° to 45° angles with the vertical. For the majority of drilled piers constructed in the United States, the entire load-carrying capacity is assigned to the end bearing only. However, under certain circumstances, the end-bearing capacity and the side friction are taken into account. In Europe, both the side frictional resistance and the end-bearing capacity are always taken into account.

Straight-shafted piers can also be extended into an underlying rock layer (Figure 9.1d). In the calculation of the load-bearing capacity of such piers, the end bearing and the shear stress developed along the pier perimeter and rock interface can be taken into account.

9.3 CONSTRUCTION PROCEDURES

One of the oldest methods of construction of drilled piers is the *Chicago* method (Figure 9.2a). In this method, circular holes with diameters of 3.5 ft (1.1 m) or more are excavated by hand for depths of 2–6 ft (0.6–1.8 m) at a time. The sides of the excavated hole are then lined with vertical boards, referred to as *laggings*. They are held tightly in place by two circular steel rings. After placement of the rings, the excavation is continued for another 2–6 ft (0.6–1.8 m). When the desired depth of excavation is

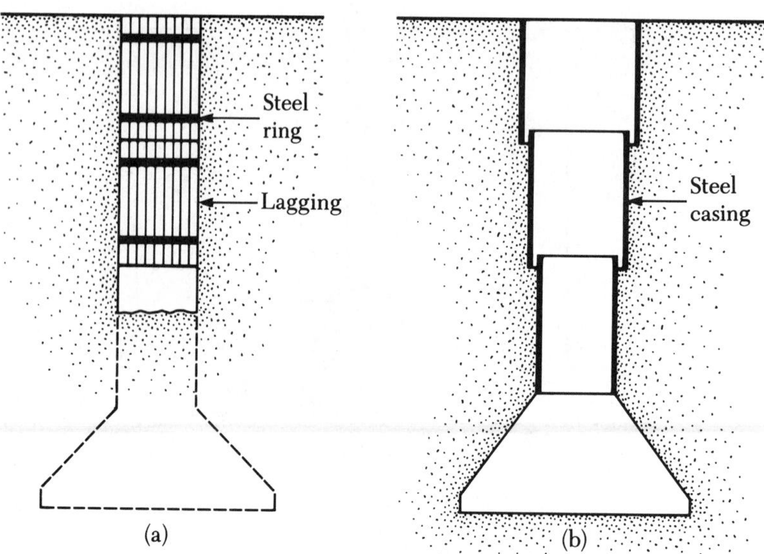

FIGURE 9.2 (a) Chicago method of pier construction; (b) Gow method of pier construction

reached, the bell of the pier is excavated. Following the completion of the excavation, the hole is filled with concrete.

In the *Gow* method of pier construction (Figure 9.2b), the hole is excavated by hand. Telescopic metal shells are used to maintain the shaft. The shells can be removed one section at a time as concreting progresses. The minimum diameter of a Gow drilled pier is about 4 ft (1.22 m). Any given section of the shell is about 2 in. (50 mm) less in diameter than the section immediately above it. Piers as deep as 100 ft (30 m) have been installed by this method.

Most pier shaft excavations are now done mechanically rather than by hand. Open helix augers (flight augers) are common excavation tools. These augers have cutting edges or cutting teeth. Those with cutting edges are used mostly for drilling in soft, homogeneous soil; those with cutting teeth are for drilling in hard soil and hard pan. The auger is attached to a square shaft referred to as the *Kelly* and pushed into the soil and rotated. When the flights are filled with soil, the auger is raised above the ground surface, and the soil is dumped into a pile by rotating the auger at high speed. These augers are available in various diameters; sometimes they may be as large as 10 ft (3 m) or more.

When the excavation is extended to the level of the load-bearing stratum, the auger is replaced by underreaming tools to shape the bell, if required. An underreamer essentially consists of a cylinder with two cutting blades hinged to the top of the cylinder (Figure 9.3). When the underreamer is lowered into the hole, the cutting blades stay folded inside the cylinder. When the bottom of the hole is reached, the blades are spread outward, and the underreamer is rotated. The loose soil falls inside the cylinder, which is raised periodically and emptied until the bell is completed. Most underreamers can cut bells with diameters as large as three times the diameter of the shaft.

Another common pier-drilling device is the *bucket type drill*. It is essentially a bucket with an opening and cutting edges at the bottom. The bucket is attached to the Kelly and rotated. The loose soil is collected in the bucket, which is periodically raised and emptied. Holes as large as 16–18 ft (5–5.5 m) in diameter can be drilled with this type of equipment.

When rock is encountered during drilling, *core barrels* with *tungsten carbide teeth* attached to the bottom of the barrels are used. *Shot barrels* are also used for drilling into very hard rock. The principle of rock coring by a shot barrel is shown in Figure 9.4.

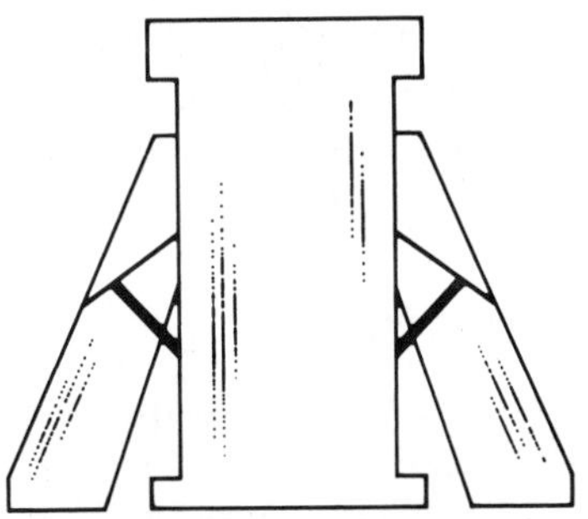

▼ **FIGURE 9.3** Underreamer

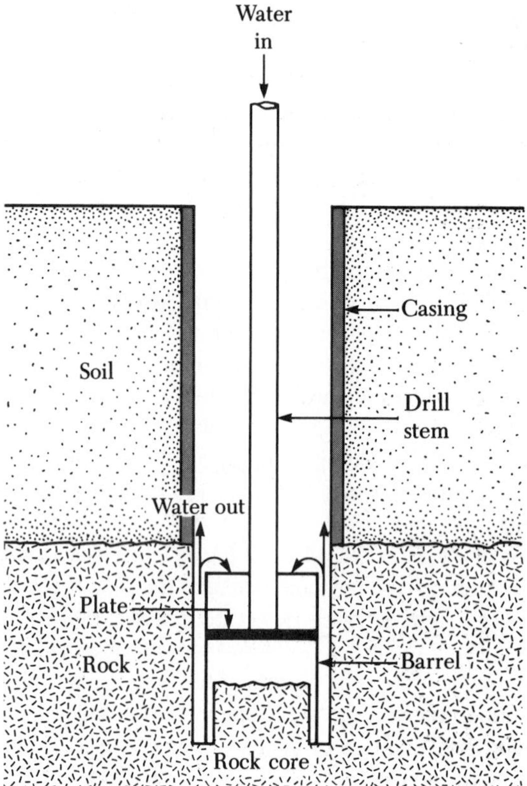

▼ **FIGURE 9.4** Schematic diagram of shot barrel

The drill stem is attached to the shot barrel's plate. The barrel has some feeder slots through which chilled steel shots are supplied to the bottom of the bore hole. The steel shots cut the rock when the barrel is rotated. Water is supplied to the drill hole through the drill stem. Fine rock and steel particles (produced by the grinding of the steel shots) are washed upward, and they settle on the upper portion of the barrel.

The *Benoto machine* is another type of pier-drilling equipment that is generally used when drilling conditions are difficult and many boulders are in the soil. It essentially consists of a steel tube that can be oscillated and pushed into the soil. A tool usually referred to as the *hammer grab*, which is fitted with cutting blades and jaws, is used to break up the soil and rock inside the tube and remove them.

Use of Casings and Drilling Mud

When holes for piers are driven in soft clays, the soil tends to squeeze in and close the hole. In such situations, casings may be used to keep the hole open and may have to be driven before excavation begins. Holes made in gravelly and sandy soils also tend to cave in. Excavation of pier holes in these soils can be continued either by casing as the hole progresses or by using *drilling mud.* As pointed out in Chapter 2, drilling mud is also used during field exploration.

Inspection of the Bottom of the Hole

In many instances, the bottom of the hole must be inspected to ensure that the load-bearing stratum is what was anticipated and that the bell is properly done. For these reasons, an inspector must descend to the bottom of the hole. Several safety precautions must be observed during this procedure.

1. If a casing is not already in the hole, one should be lowered by crane into it to prevent the hole and the bell from collapsing.
2. The hole should be tested for the presence of poisonous or explosive gases, which can be done by using a miner's safety lamp.
3. The inspector should wear a safety harness.
4. The inspector should also carry a safety lamp and an air tank.

9.4 OTHER DESIGN CONSIDERATIONS

For the design of ordinary drilled piers without casings, a minimum amount of vertical steel reinforcement is always desirable. Minimum reinforcement is 1% of the gross cross-sectional area of the shaft. In California, a reinforcing cage having a length of about 12 ft (3.65 m) is used in the top part of the caisson, and no reinforcement is provided at the bottom. This procedure helps in the construction process because the cage is placed after most of the concreting is complete.

For piers with nominal reinforcement, most building codes suggest using a design concrete strength, f_c, on the order of $f'_c/4$. Thus the minimum shaft diameter becomes

$$f_c = 0.25f'_c = \frac{Q_w}{A_{gs}} = \frac{Q_w}{\frac{\pi}{4}D_s^2}$$

or

$$D_s = \sqrt{\frac{Q_w}{\left(\frac{\pi}{4}\right)(0.25)f'_c}} = 2.257\sqrt{\frac{Q_w}{f'_c}} \tag{9.1}$$

where D_s = diameter of the pier shaft
f'_c = 28-day concrete strength
Q_w = working load of the pier
A_{gs} = gross cross-sectional area of the shaft

Depending on the loading conditions for a pier, the reinforcement percentage may sometimes be too high. In that case, use of a *single rolled-steel section* at the center of the pier (Figure 9.5b) may be considered. In that case,

$$Q_w = (A_{gs} - A_s)f_c + A_s f_s \tag{9.2}$$

where A_s = area of the steel section

f_s = allowable strength of steel $\approx 0.5\sigma_{\text{yield}}$

When a permanent steel casing is used for construction instead of a central rolled-steel section (Figure 9.5a), Eq. (9.2) may be used. However, f_s for steel should be on the order of $0.4f_s$.

If drilled piers are likely to be subjected to tensile loads, reinforcement should be continued for the entire length of the pier.

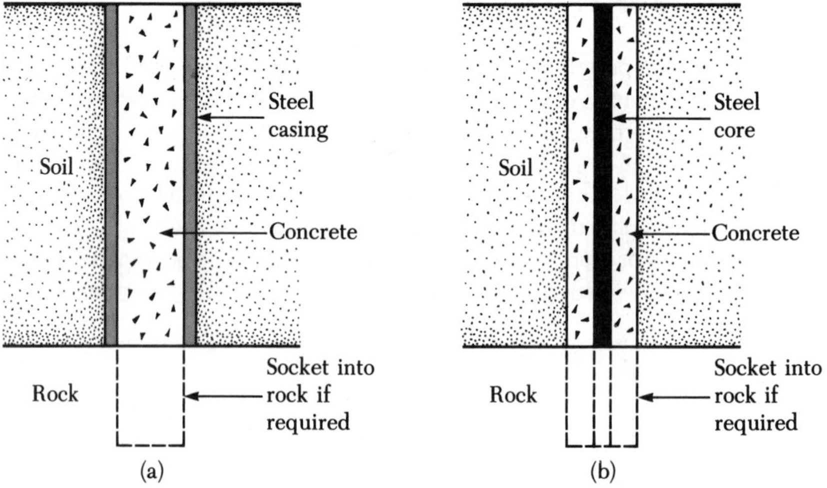

▼ **FIGURE 9.5** Drilled piers with (a) steel casing and (b) a central steel core

Concrete Mix Design

The concrete mix design for piers is not much different from that for any other concrete structure. When a reinforcing cage is used, consideration should be given to the ability of the concrete to flow through the reinforcement. In most cases, a concrete slump of about 6 in. (150 mm) is considered satisfactory. Also, the maximum size of the aggregate should be limited to about 0.75 in. (20 mm).

9.5 ESTIMATION OF LOAD-BEARING CAPACITY

The ultimate load-bearing capacity of a drilled pier (Figure 9.6) is

$$Q_u = Q_p + Q_s \tag{9.3}$$

where Q_u = ultimate load
Q_p = ultimate load-carrying capacity at the base
Q_s = frictional (skin) resistance

The equation for the ultimate base load is similar to that for shallow foundations:

$$Q_p = A_p(cN_c^* + q'N_q^* + 0.3\gamma D_b N_\gamma^*) \tag{9.4a}$$

where N_c^*, N_q^*, N_γ^* = the bearing capacity factors
q' = vertical effective stress at the level of the bottom of the pier
D_b = diameter of the base (see Figure 9.6a and b)
A_p = area of the base = $\pi/4D_b^2$

In most cases, the last term (containing N_γ^*) is neglected except for relatively short piers, so

$$Q_p = A_p(cN_c^* + q'N_q^*) \tag{9.4b}$$

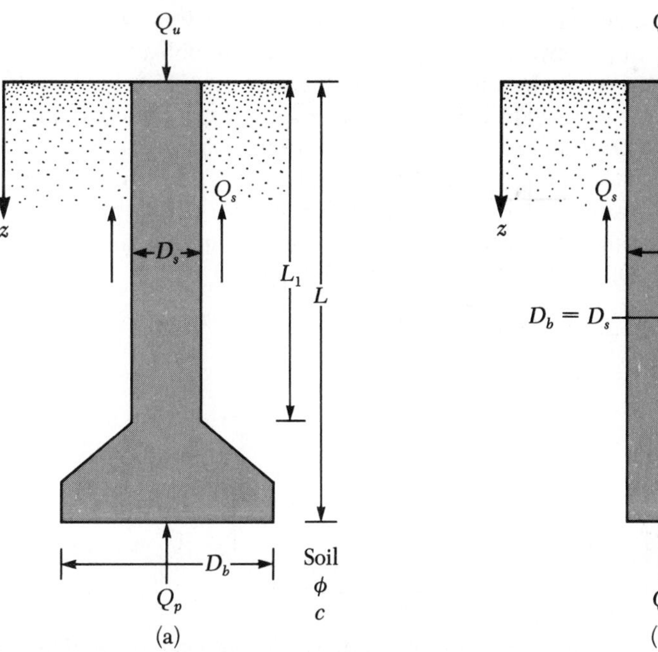

▼ **FIGURE 9.6** Ultimate bearing capacity of drilled piers: (a) with bell; (b) straight shaft

The net load-carrying capacity at the base (that is, the gross load minus the weight of the pier) may be approximated as

$$Q_{p(\text{net})} = A_p(cN_c^* + q'N_q^* - q') = A_p[cN_c^* + q'(N_q^* - 1)] \tag{9.5}$$

The expression for the frictional, or skin, resistance, Q_s, is similar to that for piles:

$$Q_s = \int_0^{L_1} pf\,dz \tag{9.6}$$

where p = shaft perimeter = πD_s
f = unit frictional (or skin) resistance

Piers in Sand

For piers in sand, $c = 0$ and, hence Eq. (9.5) simplifies to

$$Q_{p(\text{net})} = A_p q'(N_q^* - 1) \tag{9.7}$$

Determination of N_q^* is always a problem for deep foundations, as in the case of piles. Note, however, that all piers are *drilled*, unlike the majority of piles, which are *driven*. For similar initial soil conditions, the actual value of N_q^* may be substantially lower for objects drilled and placed *in situ* compared to that for objects that are driven. Vesic (1967) compared the theoretical results obtained by several investigators relating to the variation of N_q^* with soil friction angle. These investigators include DeBeer, Meyerhof, Hansen, Vesic, and Terzaghi. The values of N_q^* given by Vesic (1963) are approximately the lower bound, and hence are used in this text (see Figure 9.7). We also use Eq. (8.19) to calculate the ultimate point load, Q_p. Thus

$$Q_{p(\text{net})} = A_p(\sigma_o' N_\sigma^* - q')$$

where $\sigma_o' = [(1 + 2K_o)/3]q'$

or

$$Q_{p(\text{net})} = A_p\left[\frac{(1 + 2K_o)}{3}N_\sigma^* - 1\right]q' \tag{9.8}$$

Table 8.8 gave the values of N_σ^* for various magnitudes of I_{rr} and soil friction angles. For ease of calculation, those N_σ^* values are plotted in Figure 9.8.

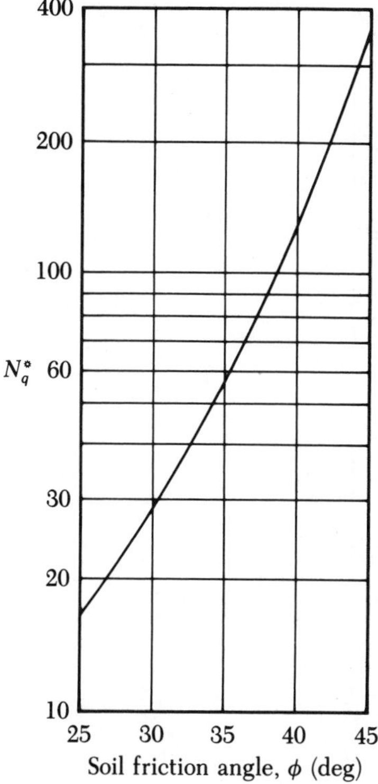

▼ **FIGURE 9.7** Vesic's bearing capacity factor, N_q^*, for deep foundations

The frictional resistance at ultimate load, Q_s, developed in a drilled pier may be calculated from the relation given in Eq. (9.6), in which

$$p = \text{shaft perimeter} = \pi D_s$$

$$f = \text{unit frictional (or skin) resistance} = K\sigma'_v \tan \delta \quad (9.9)$$

where K = earth pressure coefficient $\approx K_o = 1 - \sin \phi$
σ'_v = effective vertical stress at any depth z

Thus

$$Q_s = \int_0^{L_1} pf\,dz = \pi D_s(1 - \sin \phi) \int_0^{L_1} \sigma'_v \tan \delta\,dz \quad (9.10)$$

The value of σ'_v will increase to a depth of about $15D_s$ and will remain constant thereafter, as shown in Figure 8.16.

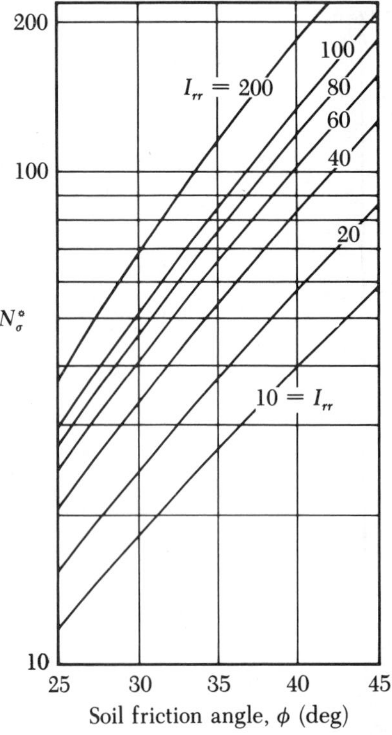

▼ **FIGURE 9.8** Plot of Vesic's bearing capacity factor, N_σ^* (see Table 8.8)

An appropriate factor of safety should be applied to the ultimate load to obtain the net allowable load, or

$$Q_{u(\text{net})} = \frac{Q_{p(\text{net})} + Q_s}{FS} \tag{9.11}$$

A reliable estimate of the soil friction angle, ϕ, must be made in obtaining the net base resistance, $Q_{p(\text{net})}$. Figure 9.9 shows a conservative correlation between the soil friction angle and the corresponding corrected standard penetration resistance numbers in granular soils. However, these friction angles are valid only for low confining pressures. At higher confining pressures, which occur in the case of deep foundations, ϕ can decrease substantially for medium to dense sands. This decrease affects the value of N_q^* or N_σ^* (and I_{rr}) to be used for estimating Q_p. For example, Vesic (1977) showed that, for Chattahoochee River sand at a relative density of about 80%, the triaxial angle of friction is about 45° at a confining pressure of 10 lb/in^2 (70 kN/m^2). However, at a confining pressure of 1500 lb/in^2 (10.35 MN/m^2), the friction angle is about 32.5°, which will ultimately result in a tenfold decrease of N_q^* or N_σ^*. Thus, for general working conditions of drilled piers, the estimated friction angle determined from Figure 9.9

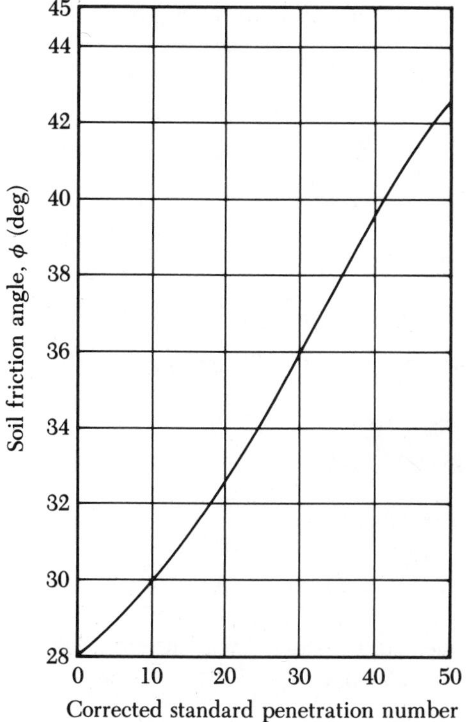

▼ **FIGURE 9.9** Correlation of corrected standard penetration number with the soil friction angle

should be reduced by about 10–15%. In general, the existing experimental values show the following range of N_q^* for standard drilled piers (or cast-in-place piles).

Sand type	*Relative density of sand*	*Range of N_q^**
Loose	40 or less	10–20
Medium	40–60	25–40
Dense	60–80	30–50
Very dense	>80	75–90

Based on the performance of bored piles in sand with an average diameter of 2.5 ft (750 mm), Touma and Reese (1974) suggested the following procedure for calculating the allowable load-carrying capacity. It is also applicable to drilled piers in sand.

For $L > 10D_b$ and a base movement of 1 in. (25.4 mm),

$$Q_{p(\text{net})} = \frac{0.508A_p}{D_b} q_p \tag{9.12}$$

where $Q_{p(\text{net})}$ is in kN, A_p is in m^2, D_b is in m, and q_p is the unit point resistance in kN/m^2

In English units,

$$Q_{p(\text{net})} = \frac{A_p}{0.6D_b} q_p \tag{9.13}$$

where $Q_{p(\text{net})}$ is in lb, A_p is in ft^2, D_b is in ft, and q_p is in lb/ft^2.

The values of q_p as recommended by Touma and Reese are

Sand type	q_p(kN/m^2)	q_p(lb/ft^2)
Loose	0	0
Medium	1530	32,000
Very dense	3830	80,000

For sands of intermediate densities, linear interpolation can be used. The shaft friction resistance can be calculated as

$$Q_s = \int_0^{L_1} (0.7)p\sigma_v' \tan\phi \, dz = 0.7(\pi D_s) \int_0^{L_1} \sigma_v' \tan\phi \, dz$$
$$= 2.2D_s \int_0^{L_1} \sigma_v' \tan\phi \, dz \tag{9.14}$$

where ϕ = soil friction angle
σ_v' = vertical effective stress at a depth z

With the base resistance and frictional resistance known, a suitable factor of safety (about 3) may be applied to determine the net allowable load.

Piers in Clay

From Eq. (9.5), for saturated clays with $\phi = 0$, $N_q^* = 1$; hence the net base resistance becomes

$$Q_{p(\text{net})} = A_p c_u N_c^* \tag{9.15}$$

where c_u = undrained cohesion

The bearing capacity factor N_c^* is usually taken to be 9. Figure 7.15 indicates that, when the L/D_b ratio is 4 or more, $N_c^* = 9$, which is the condition for most drilled piers. Experiments by Whitaker and Cooke (1966) showed that, for belled piers, the full value of $N_c^* = 9$ is realized with a base movement of about 10–15% of D_b. Similarly, for piers with straight shafts ($D_b = D_s$), the full value of $N_c^* = 9$ is obtained with a base movement of about 20% of D_b.

The expression for the skin resistance of piers in clay is similar to Eq. (8.43), or

$$Q_s = \sum_{L=0}^{L=L_1} \alpha^* c_u p \, \Delta L \tag{9.16}$$

where p = perimeter of the pier cross section

The value of α^* that can be used in Eq. (9.16) has not yet been fully established. However, the field test resuls available at this time indicate that α^* may vary between 1.0 to 0.3.

Kulhawy and Jackson (1989) reported the field test results of 106 straight-shafted piers—65 in uplift and 41 in compression. The magnitudes of α^* obtained from these tests are shown in Figure 9.10 (page 592). The best correlation obtained from these results is

$$\alpha^* = 0.21 + 0.25\left(\frac{P_a}{c_u}\right) \leq 1 \tag{9.17}$$

where p_a = atmospheric pressure = 1.058 ton/ft^2 (101.3 kN/m^2)

So, conservatively, we may assume that

$$\alpha^* = 0.4 \tag{9.18}$$

9.6 SETTLEMENT OF PIERS AT WORKING LOAD

The settlement of drilled piers at working load is calculated in a manner similar to the one outlined in Section 8.10. In many cases, the load carried by shaft resistance is small compared to the load carried at the base. In such cases, the contribution of s_3 may be ignored. Note that, in Eqs. (8.62) and (8.63), the term D should be replaced by D_b for piers.

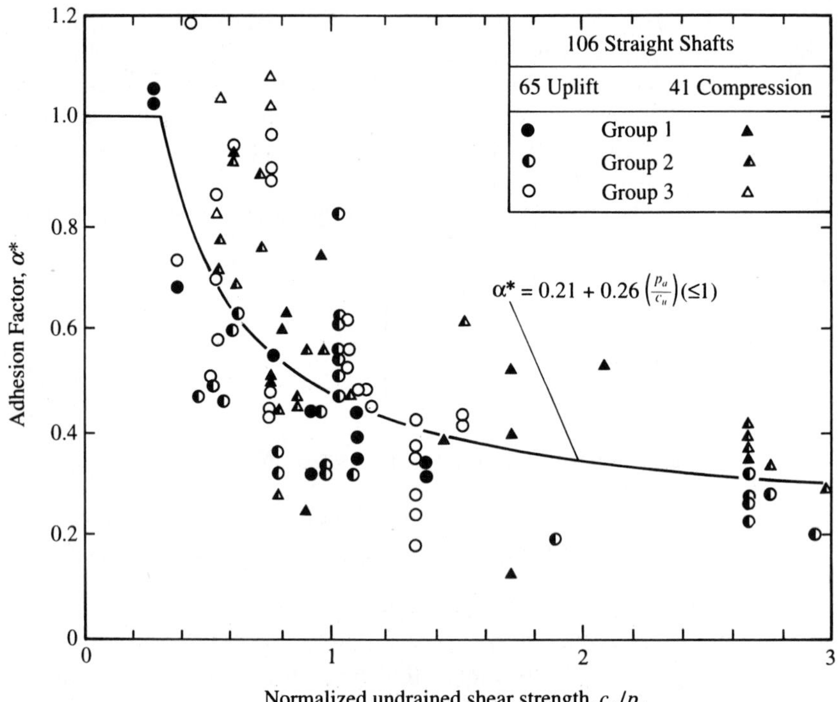

▼ **FIGURE 9.10** Variation of α^* with c_u/p_a (after Kulhawy and Jackson, 1989)

9.7 REESE AND O'NEILL'S METHOD FOR CALCULATING LOAD-BEARING CAPACITY

Based on a data base of 41 loading tests, Reese and O'Neill (1989) proposed a method to calculate the load-bearing capacity of drilled piers. The method is applicable to the following ranges.

1. Shaft diameter: $D_s = 1.7$ ft to 3.93 ft (0.52 m to 1.2 m)
2. Bell depth: $L = 15.4$ ft to 100 ft (4.7 m to 30.5 m)
3. $c_u = 600$ lb/ft^2 to 6000 lb/ft^2 (29 kN/m^2 to 287 kN/m^2)
4. Standard penetration resistance: $N = 5$ to 60
5. Overconsolidation ratio = 2 to 15
6. Concrete slump = 4 in. to 9 in. (100 mm to 225 mm)

Reese and O'Neill's procedure, with reference to Figure 9.11, gives

$$Q_u = \sum_{i=1}^{N} f_i p \, \Delta L_i + q_p A_b \tag{9.19}$$

where f_i = ultimate unit shearing resistance in layer i
p = perimeter of the shaft = πD_s
q_p = unit point resistance
A_b = area of the base = $(\pi/4)D_b^2$

Following are the relationships for determining Q_u in cohesive and granular soils.

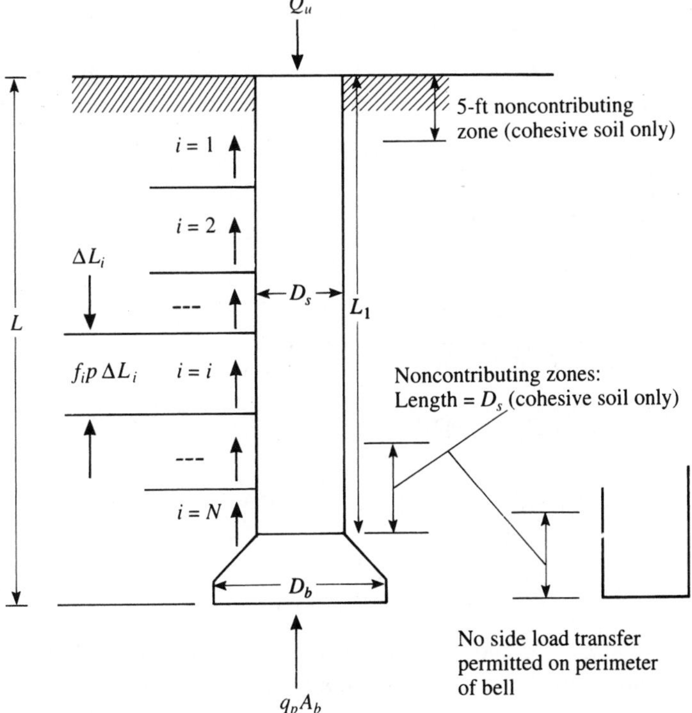

▼ **FIGURE 9.11** Development of Eq. (9.19)

Cohesive Soil

Based on Eq. (9.19),

$$f_i = \alpha_i^* c_{u(i)} \tag{9.20}$$

The following values are recommended for α_i^*:

> $\alpha_i^* = 0$ for the top 5 ft (1.5 m) and bottom 1 diameter, D_s, of the drilled pier. (*Note:* If $D_b > D_s$, then $\alpha^* = 0$ for 1 diameter above the top of the bell and for the peripheral area of the bell itself.)
>
> $\alpha_i^* = 0.55$ elsewhere

and

$$q_p = 6c_{ub}\left(1 + 0.2\frac{L}{D_b}\right) \leq 9c_{ub} \leq 80 \text{ kip/ft}^2 \text{ (3.83 MN/m}^2\text{)} \tag{9.21}$$

where c_{ub} = average undrained cohesion within $2D_b$ below the base

If D_b is large, excessive settlement will occur at the ultimate load per unit area, q_p, as given by Eq. (9.21). Thus, for $D_b > 75$ in. (1.91 m), q_p may be replaced by q_{pr}, or

$$q_{pr} = F_r q_{pr} \tag{9.22}$$

where
$$F_r = \frac{2.5}{\psi_1 D_b(\text{in.}) + \psi_2} \leq 1 \tag{9.23}$$

$$\psi_1 = 0.0071 + 0.0021\left(\frac{L}{D_b}\right) \leq 0.015 \tag{9.24}$$

$$\psi_2 = 1.125(\underset{\substack{\uparrow \\ \text{kip/ft}^2}}{c_{ub}})^{0.5} \qquad (0.5 \leq \psi_2 \leq 1.5) \tag{9.25}$$

Figures 9.12 and 9.13 may be used to evaluate short-term settlements. (Note that the ultimate bearing capacity in Figure 9.13 is q_p, not q_{pr}.) To do so

1. Select a value of settlement, s.
2. Calculate $\sum_{i=1}^{N} f_i p \,\Delta L_i$ and $q_p A_b$, as given in Eq. (9.18).
3. Using Figures 9.12 and 9.13 and the calculated values in step 2, determine the *side load* and the *end bearing load.*
4. The sum of the side load and the end bearing load gives the total applied load.

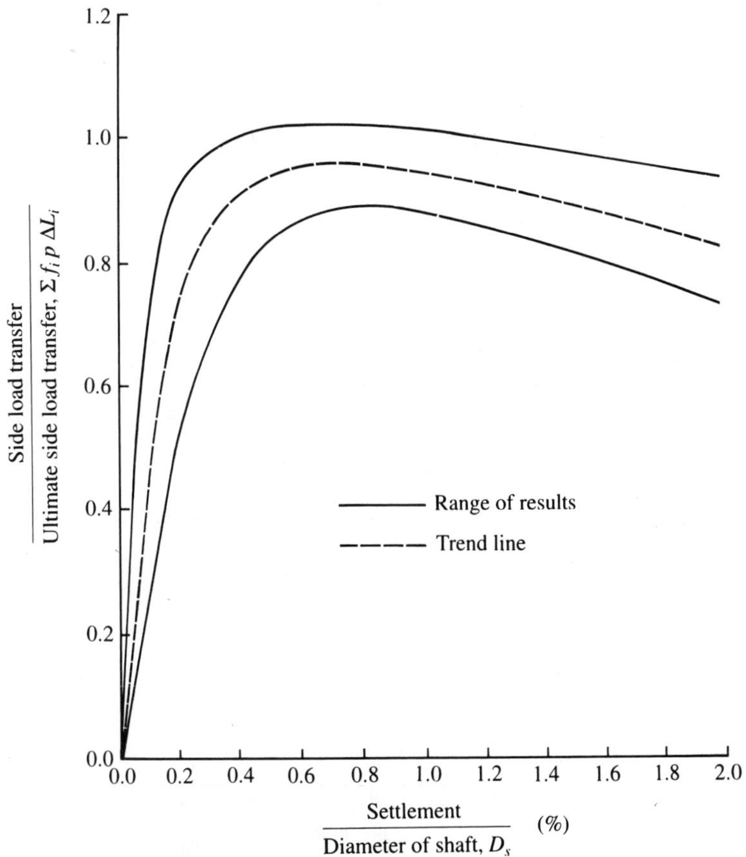

▼ **FIGURE 9.12** Normalized side load transfer vs. settlement for cohesive soil (after Reese and O'Neill, 1989)

Cohesionless Soil

Based on Eq. (9,19),

$$f_i = \beta \sigma'_{vzi} \tag{9.26}$$

where σ'_{vzi} = vertical effective stress at the middle of layer i

$$\beta = 1.5 - 0.135 z_i^{0.5} \qquad (0.25 \le \beta \le 1.2) \tag{9.27}$$

z_i = depth of the middle of layer i (ft)

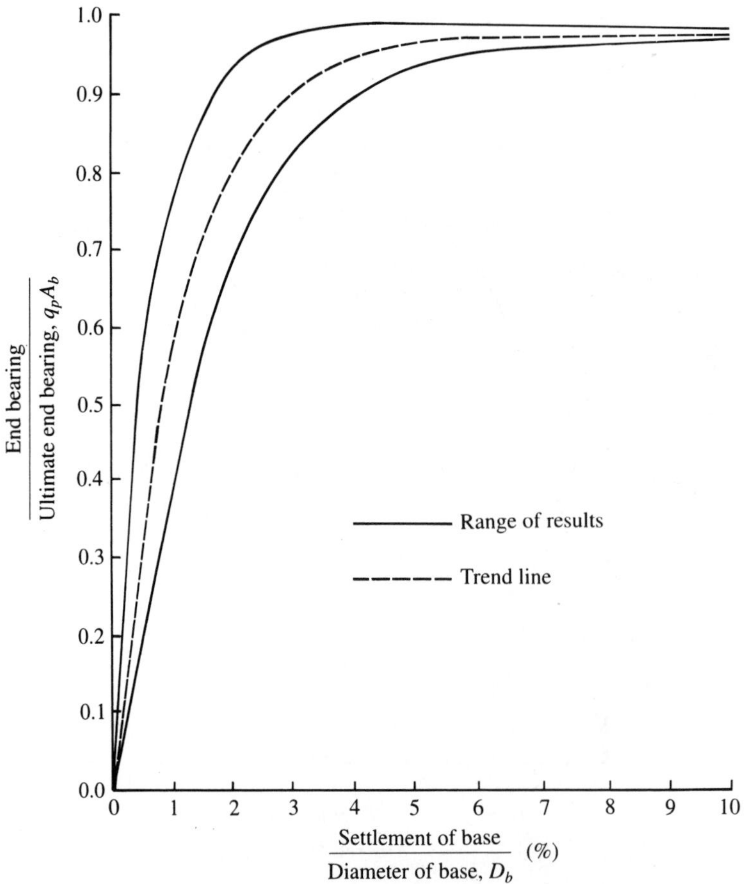

▼ **FIGURE 9.13** Normalized base load transfer vs. settlement for cohesive soil (after Reese and O'Neill, 1989)

The point bearing capacity is

$$q_p(\text{kip/ft}^2) = 1.2N \leq 90 \text{ kip/ft}^2 \tag{9.28}$$

where N = mean *uncorrected* standard penetration number within a distance of $2D_b$ below the base of the drilled pier

As in Eq. (9.22), to control excessive settlement, the magnitude of q_p may be modified as follows:

$$q_{pr} = \frac{50}{D_b(\text{in.})} q_p \qquad (\text{for } D_b \geq 50 \text{ in.}) \tag{9.29}$$

Figures 9.14 and 9.15 may be used to calculate short-term settlements. They are similar to Figures 9.12 and 9.13 for clay.

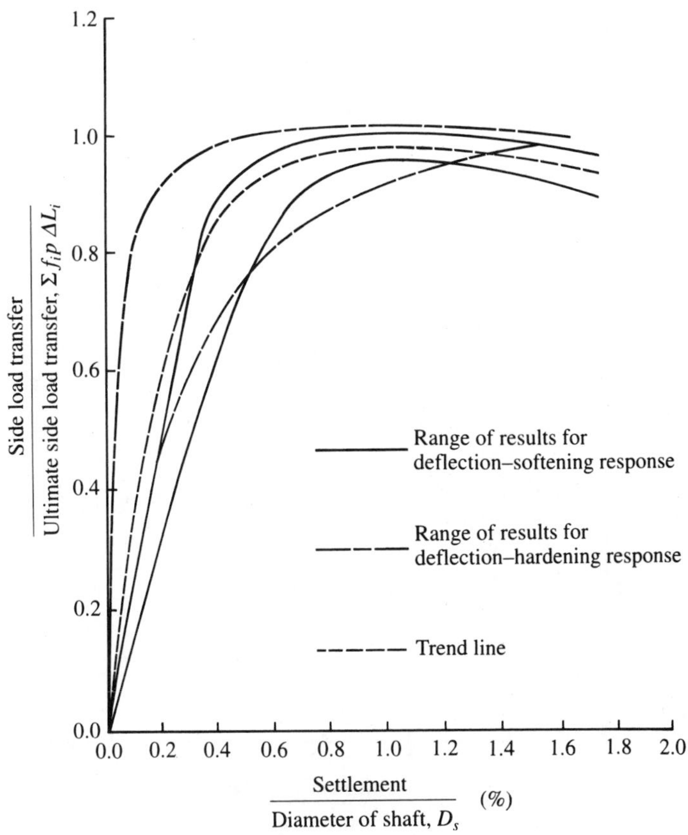

FIGURE 9.14 Normalized side load transfer vs. settlement for cohesionless soil (after Reese and O'Neill, 1989)

EXAMPLE 9.1

A soil profile is shown in Figure 9.16. A point bearing pier with a bell is to be placed in the dense sand and gravel layer. The working load, Q_w, is 2000 kN.

a. Determine the shaft diameter for $f'_c = 21{,}000$ kN/m^2.
b. Use Eq. (9.7) and a factor of safety of 4 to determine the bell diameter, D_b. Ignore the frictional resistance of the shaft.
c. Use Eq. (9.12) and obtain D_b for a settlement of 25.4 mm. Ignore the frictional resistance of the shaft. Use $q_p = 3000$ kN/m^2.
d. Discuss the differences in the results obtained from parts (b) and (c).
e. Choose a bell diameter for a settlement of 25.4 mm.
f. Estimate the modulus of elasticity for the dense sand layer.
g. Calculate the possible settlement of the pier from Eqs. (8.60), (8.61), and (8.62). [Assume s_3 in Eq. (8.60) to be zero.] Use D_s determined in part (a) and D_b in part (e); $\mu_s = 0.3$, $E_c = 21 \times 10^6$ kN/m^2.

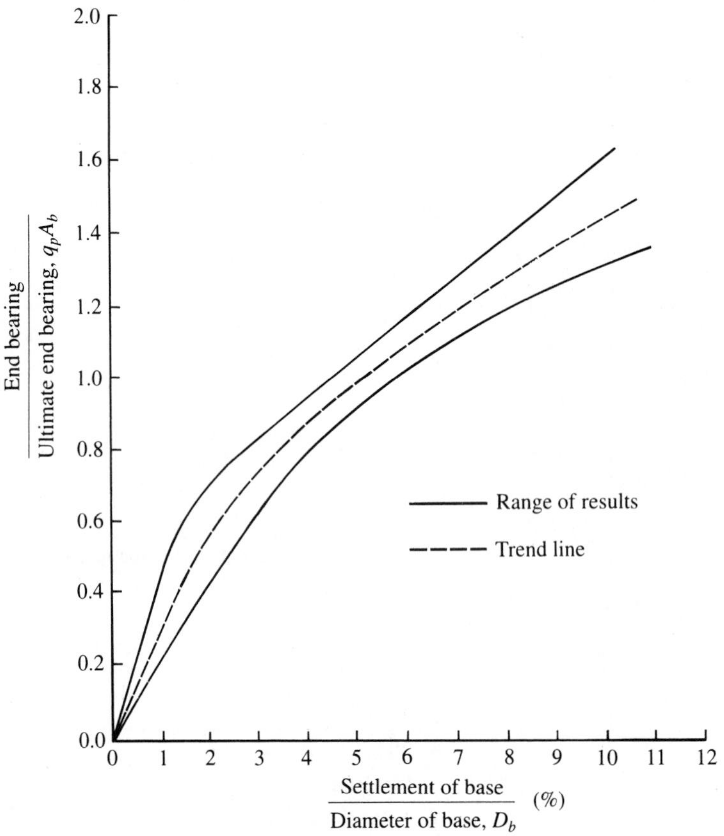

▼ **FIGURE 9.15** Normalized base load transfer vs. settlement for cohesionless soil (after Reese and O'Neill, 1989)

Solution

Part a: Determination of the Shaft Diameter, D_s

From Eq. (9.1),

$$D_s = 2.257\sqrt{\frac{Q_w}{f'_c}}$$

For $Q_w = 2000$ kN and $f'_c = 21{,}000$ kN/m^2,

$$D_s = 2.257\sqrt{\frac{2000}{21{,}000}} = 0.697 \text{ m}$$

Use $D_s = \mathbf{1\ m}$.

Part b: Determination of the Bell Diameter Using Eq. (9.7)

$$Q_{p(\text{net})} = A_p q'(N_q^* - 1)$$

For $N_{\text{cor}} = 40$, Figure 9.9 indicates that $\phi \approx 39.5°$. To be conservative, use a

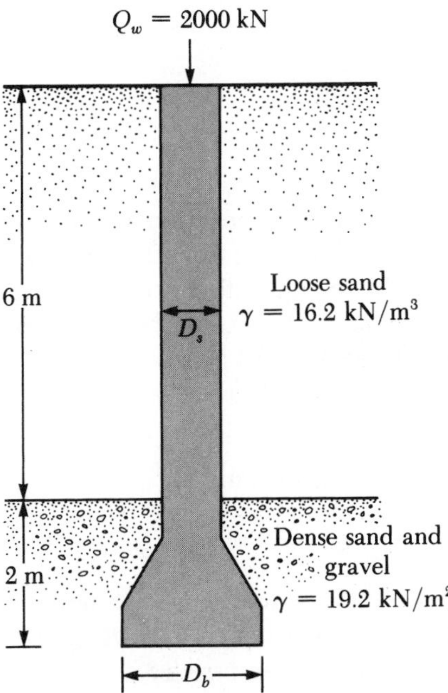

Average corrected standard penetration number $= 40 = N_{cor}$

▼ **FIGURE 9.16**

reduction of about 10%, or $\phi = 35.6$. From Figure 9.6, $N_q^* \approx 60$. So

$$q' = 6(16.2) + 2(19.2) = 135.6 \text{ kN/m}^2$$
$$Q_{p(\text{net})} = (Q_w)(FS) = (2000)(4) = 8000 \text{ kN}$$
$$8000 = (A_p)(135.6)(60 - 1)$$
$$A_p = 1.0 \text{ m}^2$$
$$D_b = \sqrt{\frac{1.0}{\frac{\pi}{4}}} = \mathbf{1.13\ m}$$

Part c: Determination of Bell Diameter Using Eq. (9.12)

$$Q_{p(\text{net})} = \frac{0.508A_p}{D_b}q_p$$

Because the limit of settlement is 25.4 mm and Eq. (9.12) is for the limiting settlement, a factor of safety over Q_w should not be used to obtain $Q_{p(\text{net})}$. So

$$Q_w = Q_{p(\text{net})}$$

Thus

$$Q_{p(\text{net})} = Q_w = 2000 = \frac{0.508A_p}{D_b}q_p = \frac{(0.508)(\pi/4)(D_b^2)q_p}{D_b}$$
$$= 0.399D_b q_p$$

or

$$D_b = \frac{2000}{(0.399)(3000)} = \mathbf{1.67\ m.}$$

Part d

The value of D_b determined in Part b corresponds to an allowable bearing capacity that is based on the ultimate bearing capacity. Settlement has not been taken into consideration at all, and the ultimate bearing capacity of drilled piers may occur at a settlement exceeding 10–15% of the bell diameter. The bell diameter in Part c corresponds to a settlement of 25.4 mm.

Part e

Use a bell diameter of 2 m to be conservative.

Part f

The effective overburden pressure at the surface of the dense sand gravel layer is 135.6 kN/m^2. Substituting this value of effective overburden pressure and N_{cor} = 40 in Eqs. (2.7) and (2.9) gives an uncorrected value for N of about 47. From Eq. (3.82), the modulus of elasticity is

$$E_s = 766N = 766(47) = \mathbf{36{,}002\ kN/m^2.}$$

Part g: Calculation of Settlement

From Eq. (8.61), with $\xi = 0$,

$$s_1 = \frac{Q_w L}{A_s E_p} = \frac{(2000)(6)}{(\pi/4)(1)^2(21 \times 10^6)} = 0.000728 \text{ m} = 0.728 \text{ mm}$$

From Eq. (8.62),

$$s_2 = \frac{q_{wp} D_b}{E_s}(1 - \mu_s^2) I_{wp}$$

$$I_{wp} = 0.88 \text{ (Figure 3.27)}$$

$$q_{wp} = \frac{2000}{(\pi/4)D_b^2} = \frac{2000}{(\pi/4)(2)^2} = 636.6 \text{ kN/m}^2$$

$$s_2 = \frac{(636.6)(2)}{36{,}002}(1 - 0.3^2)(0.88) = 0.0283 \text{ m} = 28.3 \text{ mm}$$

So, the total settlement is 28.3 + 0.728 = **29.03 mm.**

This settlement is higher than 25.4 mm. However, the assumption of E_s is approximate. ▼

▼ EXAMPLE 9.2

A drilled pier is shown in Figure 9.17. Assume that $Q_w = 2800$ kN.

a. For $f'_c = 28{,}000$ kN/m^2, determine whether the proposed diameter of the shaft is adequate.
b. Determine the net ultimate point load-carrying capacity.
c. Determine the ultimate skin resistance.
d. Calculate the factor of safety with respect to the working load, Q_w.
e. Estimate the total elastic settlement of the pier under the working load. Use Eqs. (8.61), (8.63), (8.66) and (8.67). $E_p = 22 \times 10^6$ kN/m^2.

Solution

Part a

From Eq. (9.1),

$$D_s = 2.257\sqrt{\frac{Q_w}{f'_c}} = 2.257\sqrt{\frac{2{,}800}{28{,}000}} = 0.714 \text{ m}$$

Proposed shaft diameter $D_s = \mathbf{1\ m > 0.714\ m}$**—OK.**

Part b

$$Q_{p(\text{net})} = c_u N_c^* A_p = (156)(9)\left[\left(\frac{\pi}{4}\right)(3)^2\right] = \mathbf{9924.4\ kN.}$$

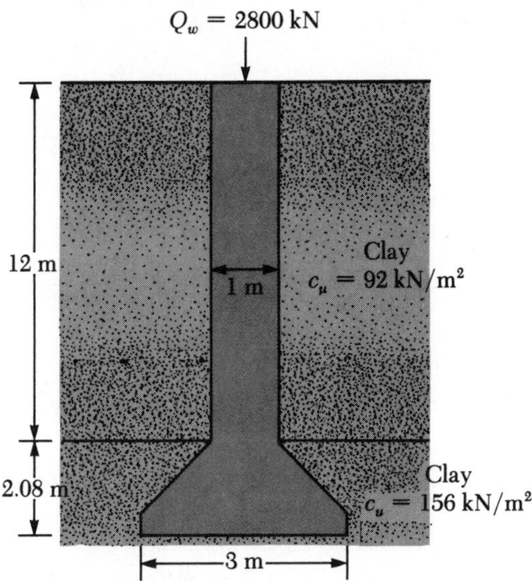

▼ **FIGURE 9.17**

Part c

According to Eq. (9.16),

$$Q_s = \pi D_s L_1 c_u \alpha^*$$

Assuming that $\alpha^* = 0.4$[Eq. (9.18)] yields

$$Q_s = (\pi)(1)(12)(92)(0.4) = \mathbf{1387.3\ kN.}$$

Part d

The factor of safety is

$$\frac{Q_u}{Q_w} = \frac{9924.3 + 1387.3}{2800} = \mathbf{4.04.}$$

Part e

From Eq. (8.61),

$$s_1 = \frac{(Q_{wp} + \xi Q_{ws})L}{A_p E_p}$$

Assume full mobilization of the skin resistance. Then $Q_{ws} = 1387.3$ kN and $Q_{wp} = 2800 - 1387.3 = 1412.7$ kN. Also, let $\xi = 0.6$. Substitute and solve for A_p:

$$A_p = \left(\frac{\pi}{4}\right)D_s^2 = \frac{\pi}{4}(1)^2 = 0.785\ \text{m}^2$$

So

$$s_1 = \frac{[1412.7 + (0.6)(1387.3)](14.08)}{(0.785)(22 \times 10^6)} = 0.00183\ \text{m} = \mathbf{1.83\ mm}$$

From Eq. (8.63),

$$s_2 = \frac{Q_{wp} C_p}{D_b q_p}$$

For stiff clay, C_p is about 0.04 (Table 8.13), so

$$q_p = cN_c^* = (156)(9) = 1404\ \text{kN/m}^2$$

and

$$s_2 = \frac{(1412.7)(0.04)}{(3)(1404)} = 0.01342\ \text{m} = \mathbf{13.42\ mm}$$

Again, from Eq. (8.66),

$$s_3 = \frac{Q_{ws} C_s}{L_1 q_p}$$

$$C_s = \left(0.93 + 0.16\sqrt{\frac{L_1}{D_s}}\right)C_p = \left(0.93 + 0.16\sqrt{\frac{12}{1}}\right)0.04 = 0.0594$$

Hence

$$s_3 = \frac{(1387.3)(0.0594)}{(12)(1404)} = 0.00489 \text{ m} = \mathbf{4.89 \text{ mm.}}$$

Total elastic settlement $s = s_1 + s_2 + s_3 = 1.83 + 13.42 + 4.89 = \mathbf{20.14 \text{ mm}}$ ▼

▼ EXAMPLE 9.3

A drilled pier in a cohesive soil is shown in Figure 9.18. Use the procedure outlined in Section 9.7 to determine:

a. The ultimate load-carrying capacity
b. The load-carrying capacity for an allowable settlement of 0.5 in.

Solution

Part a

From Eq. (9.20),

$$f_i = \alpha_i^* c_{u(i)}$$

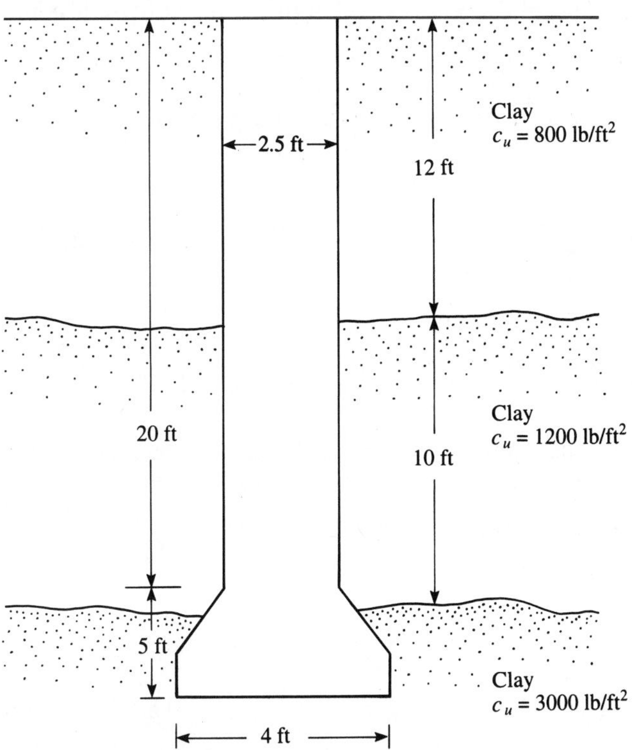

▼ **FIGURE 9.18**

From Figure 9.18,

$$\Delta L_1 = 12 - 5 = 7 \text{ ft}$$

$$\Delta L_2 = (20 - 12) - D_s = (20 - 12) - 2.5 = 5.5 \text{ ft}$$

$$c_{u(1)} = 800 \text{ lb/ft}^2$$

$$c_{u(2)} = 1200 \text{ lb/ft}^2$$

Hence

$$\sum f_i p \, \Delta L_i = \sum \alpha_i^* c_{u(i)} p \, \Delta L_i$$

$$= (0.55)(800)(\pi \times 2.5)(7) + (0.55)(1200)(\pi \times 2.5)(5.5)$$

$$= 52{,}700 \text{ lb} = 52.7 \text{ kip}$$

Again, from Eq. (9.21),

$$q_p = 6c_{ub}\left(1 + 0.2\frac{L}{D_b}\right) = (6)(3000)\left[1 + 0.2\left(\frac{20+5}{4}\right)\right] = 40{,}500 \text{ lb/ft}^2$$

$$= 40.5 \text{ kip/ft}^2$$

Check:

$$q_p = 9c_{ub} = (9)(3000) = 27{,}000 \text{ lb/ft}^2 = 27 \text{ kip/ft}^2 < 40.5 \text{ kip/ft}^2\text{—OK}$$

So, use $q_p = 27 \text{ kip/ft}^2$.

$$q_p A_b = q_p\left(\frac{\pi}{4}D_b^2\right) = (27)\left[\left(\frac{\pi}{4}\right)(4)^2\right] \approx 339.3 \text{ kip}$$

Hence

$$Q_u = \sum \alpha_i^* c_{u(i)} p \, \Delta L_i + q_p A_b = 52.7 + 339.3 = \mathbf{392 \text{ kip.}}$$

Part b

$$\frac{\text{Allowable settlement}}{D_s} = \frac{0.5}{(2.5)(12)} = 0.167 = 1.67\%$$

The trend line shown in Figure 9.12 indicates that, for a normalized settlement of 1.67%, the normalized side load is about 0.89. Thus the side load is

$$(0.89)\left(\sum f_i p \, \Delta L_i\right) = (0.89)(52.7) = 46.9 \text{ kip}$$

Again,

$$\frac{\text{Allowable settlement}}{D_b} = \frac{0.5}{(4)(12)} = 0.0104 = 1.04\%$$

The trend line shown in Figure 9.13 indicates that, for a normalized settlement of 1.04%, the normalized end bearing is about 0.57. So

$$\text{Base load} = (0.57)(q_p A_b) = (0.57)(339.3) = 193.4 \text{ kip}$$

Thus the total load is

$$Q = 46.9 + 193.4 = \mathbf{240.3\ kip.} \quad ▼$$

▼ EXAMPLE 9.4

A drilled pier is shown in Figure 9.19. The uncorrected average standard penetration number within a distance of $2D_b$ below the base of the pier is about 35. Determine:

a. The ultimate load-carrying capacity
b. The load-carrying capacity for a settlement of 0.5 in.

Solution

Part a

From Eqs. (9.26) and (9.27),

$$f_i = \beta\sigma'_{vzi}$$

$$\beta = 1.5 - 0.135z_i^{0.5}$$

For this problem, $z_i = 15/2 = 7.5$ ft. So

$$\beta = 1.5 - (0.135)(7.5)^{0.5} = 1.13$$

$$\sigma'_{vzi} = \gamma z_i = (112)(7.5) = 840 \text{ lb/ft}^2$$

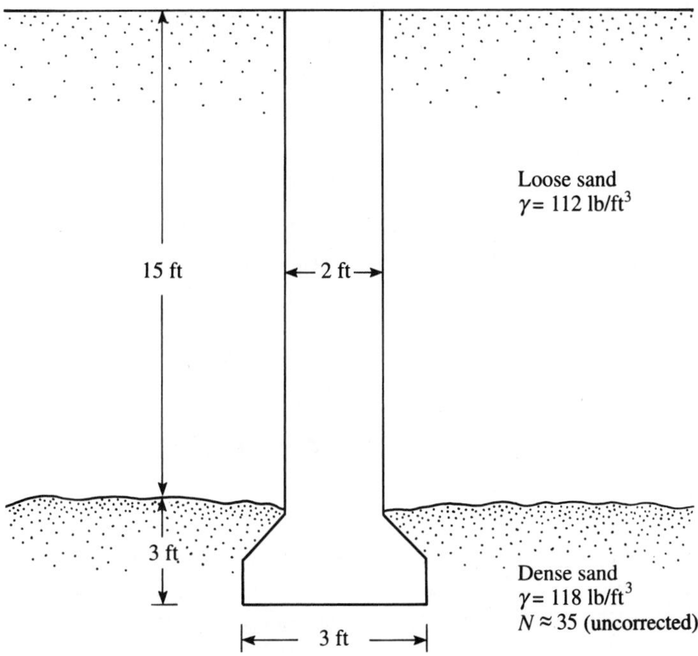

▼ **FIGURE 9.19**

Hence

$$f_i = (840)(1.13) = 949.2 \text{ lb/ft}^2$$

From Eq. (9.19),

$$\sum f_i p \, \Delta L_i = (949.2)(\pi \times 2)(15) = 89{,}460 \text{ lb} \approx 89.5 \text{ kip}$$

Again, from Eq. (9.28),

$$q_p = 1.2N = (1.2)(35) = 42 \text{ kip/ft}^2$$

From Eq. (9.19),

$$q_p A_b = (42)\left[\left(\frac{\pi}{4}\right)(3)^2\right] = 296.9 \text{ kip}$$

Thus

$$Q_u = \sum f_i p \, \Delta L_i + q_p A_b = 89.5 + 296.9 = \mathbf{386.4 \text{ kip.}}$$

Part b

$$\frac{\text{Allowable settlement}}{D_s} = \frac{0.5}{(2)(12)} = 0.021 = 2.1\%$$

The trend line shown in Figure 9.14 indicates that, for a normalized settlement of 2.1%, the normalized side load is about 0.9. Thus side load transfer is (0.9)(89.5) ≈ 88.7 kip. Similarly,

$$\frac{\text{Allowable settlement}}{D_b} = \frac{0.5}{(3)(12)} = 0.014 = 1.4\%$$

The trend line shown in Figure 9.15 indicates that, for a normalized settlement of 1.4%, the normalized base load is 0.312. So the base load is (0.312)(527.8) = 164.7 kip. Hence the total load is

$$Q = 88.7 + 164.7 \approx \mathbf{253 \text{ kip.}}$$ ▼

9.8 LOAD-BEARING CAPACITY OF PIERS EXTENDING INTO ROCK

In Section 9.1, we noted that drilled piers can be extended into rock. This section discusses the principles of analysis of the load-bearing capacity of such drilled piers. Figure 9.20 shows a drilled pier whose depth of embedment in rock equals L. Let the total load to be carried by the pier equal Q_w. Also, assume that (a) no load transfer takes place along the soil–pier interface and (b) under the pier loading condition, the

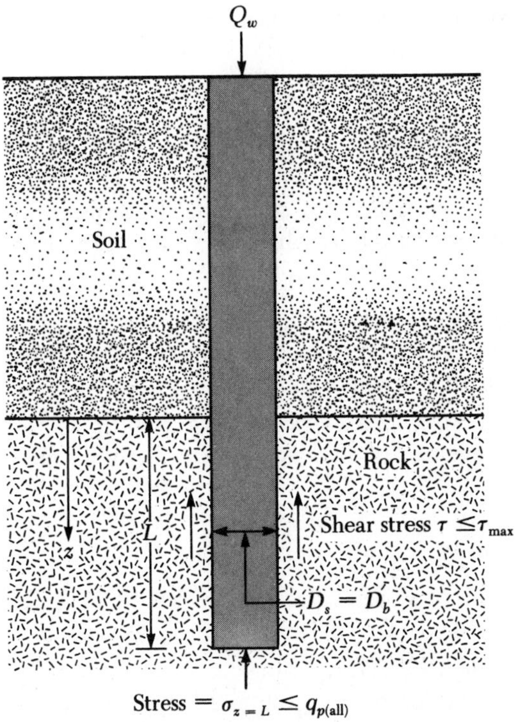

▼ **FIGURE 9.20** Drilled piers socketed into rock

bond between the concrete and the rock is broken. With these assumptions, the compressive stress along the cross section of the pier is

$$\sigma_z = \sigma_{max} \exp\left[-\frac{2\mu_c \tan \phi_{rc}}{1 - \mu_c + (1 + \mu_r)\dfrac{E_c}{E_r}} \frac{2z}{D_b} \right] \tag{9.30}$$

where $$\sigma_{max} = \frac{Q_{all}}{(\pi/4)D_b^2} \tag{9.31}$$

μ_c, μ_r = Poisson's ratio in concrete and rock, respectively
E_c, E_r = modulus of elasticity of concrete and rock, respectively
ϕ_{rc} = angle of friction along the rock–pier interface

The maximum shear stress developed along the rock and concrete pier perimeter, conservatively (Goodman, 1980), is

$$\tau_{max} = \frac{q_u}{20} \tag{9.32}$$

where q_u = unconfined compression strength of concrete or rock, whichever is lower

The allowable shear stress then becomes

$$\tau_{all} = \frac{\tau_{max}}{FS} \tag{9.33}$$

where FS = factor of safety

Once τ_{all} is known or assumed, the following step-by-step procedure should be utilized (Ladanyi, 1977) to determine the length, L, to which the pier should be embedded in rock.

1. Obtain the size of the shaft $D_s = D_b$ based on the load Q_w and the strength of the concrete. If a rolled-steel section core is used, the diameter D_s will depend on the strength of concrete and steel.
2. Assume that the load carried at the pier tip is zero and determine the maximum required length of embedment (L_1) of the pier:

$$L_1 = \frac{Q_w}{\pi D_s \tau_{all}} \tag{9.34}$$

3. Now, assume another value of the length of embedment $L_2 < L_1$. Use Eq. (9.30) and calculate σ_z at $z = L_2$. This value of $\sigma_{z=L_2}$ is the unit point resistance at the pier tip.
4. Compare the value of $\sigma_{z=L_2}$ obtained in step 3 with the allowable bearing capacity in rock, $q_{p(all)}$. To do so, use Eq. (8.57). If $\sigma_{z=L_2} > q_{p(all)}$, go back to step 3 and assume another value of L_2.
5. If $\sigma_{z=L_2} \leq q_{p(all)}$ in step 4, calculate τ developed along the perimeter of the pile as

$$\tau = \underbrace{\left[\left(1 - \frac{\sigma_{z=L_2}}{\sigma_{max}}\right) Q_w\right]}_{\text{load taken by shaft}} \frac{1}{\pi D_b L_2} \tag{9.35}$$

6. Compare the value of τ obtained from Eq. (9.35) to τ_{all} obtained from Eq. (9.33).
7. Repeat steps 3–6 to obtain the length L that is most desirable with $\sigma_{z=L_2} \leq q_{p(all)}$ and $\tau \leq \tau_{all}$. ▼

▼ EXAMPLE 9.5

Refer to Figure 9.20. The soil located above the rock is soft clay. Neglect the skin resistance developed at the pier perimeter–clay interface. Use $Q_w = 25{,}000$ kN, $E_r/E_c = 0.7$, $\mu_c = \mu_r = 0.3$, $\phi_{rc} = 38°$, $\tau_{all} = 490$ kN/m^2. For rock, $q_{p(all)} = 2500$ kN/m^2, and for concrete $f'_c = 21{,}000$ kN/m^2. Determine the required diameter and the length of embedment, L.

Solution

Calculation of $D_s = D_b$

Use $f_c = 0.25f'_c = (0.25)(21{,}000) = 5250\ \text{kN/m}^2$. So, from Eq. (9.1),

$$D_s = 2.257\sqrt{\frac{Q_w}{f'_c}} = 2.257\sqrt{\frac{25{,}000}{21{,}000}} = 2.46\ \text{m}$$

Use $\boldsymbol{D_s = 2.5}$ **m**.

Calculation of L_1

From Eq. (9.34),

$$L_1 = \frac{Q_w}{\pi D_s \tau_{\text{all}}} = \frac{25{,}000}{(\pi)(2.5)(490)} = 6.496 \approx \mathbf{6.5\ m}$$

Calculation of L

Assume an embedment length $= L_2 = 5$ m. From Eq. (9.30), with $z = 5$ m,

$$\frac{\sigma_{z=L_2}}{\sigma_{\max}} = \exp\left[-\frac{2\mu_c \tan\phi_{rc}}{1-\mu_c+(1+\mu_r)\dfrac{E_c}{E_r}}\frac{2z}{D_b}\right]$$

$$= \exp\left\{-\left[\frac{(2)(0.3)(\tan 38^\circ)}{1-0.3+(1+0.3)\left(\dfrac{1}{0.7}\right)}\right]\frac{(2)(5)}{2.5}\right\} = 0.48$$

So

$$\sigma_{z=L_2} = (\sigma_{\max})(0.48) = \left[\frac{Q_w}{(\pi/4)D_b^2}\right](0.48) = \frac{(25{,}000)(0.48)}{(0.785)(2.5^2)}$$

$$\approx 2446\ \text{kN/m}^2 < 2500\ \text{kN/m}^2 = q_{\text{all}}\text{—OK}$$

Now check the shear stress developed along the shaft–rock interface by using Eq. (9.35):

$$\tau = \left(1 - \frac{\sigma_{z=L_2}}{\sigma_{\max}}\right)\frac{Q_w}{\pi D_b L_2} = (1-0.48)\frac{25{,}000}{(\pi)(2.5)(5)}$$

$$= 331\ \text{kN/m}^2 \le \tau_{\text{all}} = 490\ \text{kN/m}^2$$

So, $L = L_2 =$ **5 m**.

Note that if the value of τ had been substantially lower than τ_{all}, the value of L_2 could have been reduced. That would require a new set of calculations of $(\sigma_{z=L_2})/\sigma_{\max}$, $\sigma_{z=L_2}$ and τ. However, if τ or $\sigma_{z=L_2}$ becomes less than τ_{all} and $q_{p(\text{all})}$, respectively, the length L_2 must be increased and checked again. ▼

9.9 UPLIFT CAPACITY OF PIERS

Sometimes drilled piers must resist uplifting loads. Field observations of drilled pier uplift capacity are relatively scarce. The procedure for determining the ultimate uplifting load for drilled piers without bells is similar to that for piles described in Chapter 8 (Section 8.11) and will not be repeated here. When a short drilled pier with a bell is subjected to an uplifting load, the nature of the failure surface in the soil will be like that shown in Figure 9.21. The net ultimate uplift capacity, T_{un}, is

$$T_{un} = T_{ug} - W \tag{9.36}$$

where T_{ug} = gross ultimate uplift capacity
W = effective weight of the pier

The magnitude of T_{un} for piers in sand can be estimated by the procedure outlined by Meyerhof and Adams (1968) and Das and Seeley (1975):

$$\boxed{T_{un} = B_q A_p \gamma L} \tag{9.37}$$

where B_q = breakout factor
$A_p = (\pi/4)D_b^2$
γ = unit weight of soil above the bell (*Note:* If the soil is submerged, the effective unit weight should be used.)

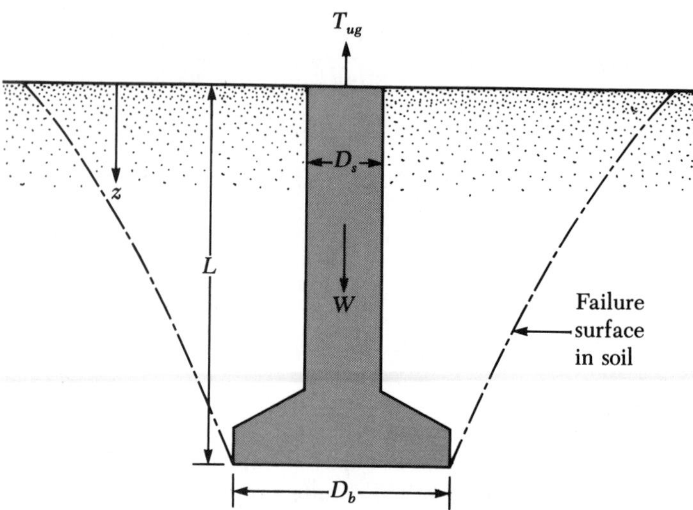

▼ **FIGURE 9.21** Nature of failure surface in soil caused by uplifting force on belled piers

The breakout factor may be expressed as

$$B_q = 2\frac{L}{D_b}K'_u \tan\phi\left(m\frac{L}{D_b} + 1\right) + 1 \tag{9.38}$$

where K'_u = nominal uplift coefficient
ϕ = soil friction angle
m = shape factor coefficient

The value of K'_u may be taken as 0.9 for all values of ϕ from 30–45°. Meyerhof and Adams (1968) gave the variation of m as

Soil friction angle, ϕ (deg)	m
30	0.15
35	0.25
40	0.35
45	0.50

Experiments have shown that the value of B_q increases with the L/D_b ratio to a critical value, $(L/D_b)_{cr}$, and remains constant thereafter. The critical embedment ratio, $(L/D_b)_{cr}$, increases with the soil friction angle. The approximate ranges are

Soil friction angle, ϕ (deg)	$(L/D_b)_{cr}$
30	4
35	5
40	7
45	9

Hence piers with $L/D_b \le (L/D_b)_{cr}$ are *shallow foundations*, and piers with $L/D_b > L/D_b)_{cr}$ are *deep foundations* with regard to the uplift. The failure surface in soil at failure as shown in Figure 9.21 is for shallow foundations. For deep foundations, local shear failure takes place, and the failure surface in soil *does not extend up to the ground surface*. Based on the preceding considerations, the variation of B_q with L/D_b is shown in Figure 9.22.

Following is a step-by-step procedure for the calculation of the net ultimate uplift capacity of drilled piers with bells in sand.

1. Determine L, D_b, and L/D_b.
2. Estimate $(L/D_b)_{cr}$ and hence L_{cr}.

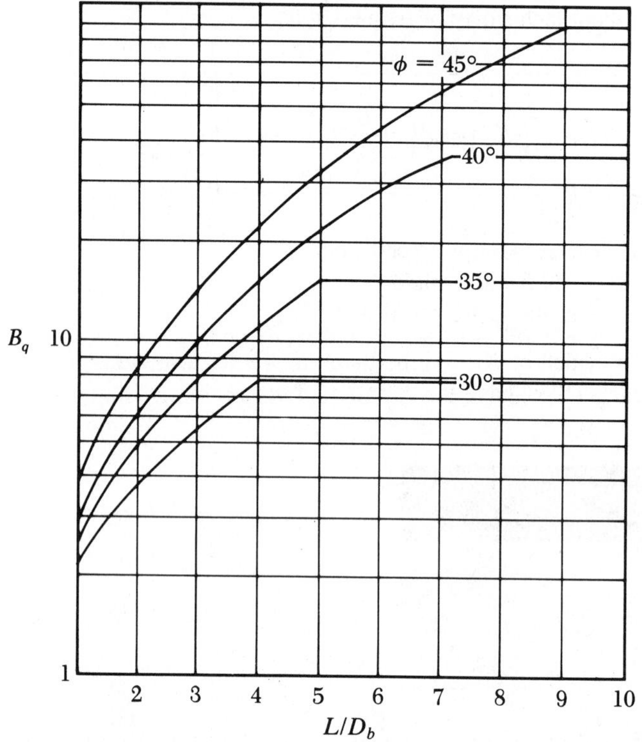

▼ **FIGURE 9.22** Variation of the breakout factor, B_q, with L/D_b and soil friction angle

3. If $(L/D_b) \leq (L/D_b)_{cr}$, obtain B_q from Figure 9.22. Now,

$$\boxed{T_{ug} = B_q A_p \gamma L + W}$$

4. If $(L/D_b) > (L/D_b)_{cr}$,

$$\boxed{T_{ug} = B_q A_p \gamma L + W + \int_0^{L-L_{cr}} (\pi D_s)\sigma'_v K'_u \tan \delta \, dz} \tag{9.39}$$

The last term of Eq. (9.39) is for the frictional resistance developed along the soil–shaft interface from $z = 0$ to $z = L - L_{cr}$ and is similar to Eqs. (8.76) and (8.77). The term σ'_v is the effective stress at any depth z, and K_u and δ are from Figure 8.35b and 8.35c, respectively.

The net ultimate uplift capacity of belled piers in clay can be estimated according to the procedure outlined by Das (1980):

$$T_{un} = \{c_u B_c + \gamma L\} A_p \tag{9.40}$$

where c_u = undrained cohesion
B_c = breakout factor
γ = unit weight of clay soil above the bell

As in the case of B_q, the value of B_c increases with the embedment ratio to a critical value of $L/D_b = (L/D_b)_{cr}$ and remains constant thereafter. Beyond the critical depth, $B_c \approx 9$. The critical embedment ratio is related to the undrained cohesion by

$$\left(\frac{L}{D_b}\right)_{cr} = 0.107c_u + 2.5 \leq 7 \tag{9.41}$$

where c_u is in kN/m^2

In English units,

$$\left(\frac{L}{D_b}\right)_{cr} = 0.738c_u + 2.5 \leq 7 \tag{9.42}$$

where c_u is in lb/in^2

Following is a step-by-step procedure for determining the net ultimate uplift capacity of belled piers in clay.

1. Determine c_u, L, D_b, and L/D_b.
2. Obtain $(L/D_b)_{cr}$ from Eq. (9.41) or Eq. (9.42) and obtain L_{cr}.
3. If $L/D < (L/D_b)_{cr}$, obtain the value of B_c from Figure 9.23.
4. Use Eq. (9.40) to obtain T_{un}.
5. If $L/D > (L/D_b)_{cr}$, $B_c = 9$. The magnitude of T_{un} may then be obtained from

$$T_{un} = (9c_u + \gamma L)A_p + \sum (\pi D_s)(L - L_{cr})\alpha' c_u \tag{9.43}$$

The last term of Eq. (9.43) is the skin resistance obtained from the adhesion along the soil–shaft interface and is similar to Eq. (8.69). The magnitude of α' can be obtained from Eqs. (8.71) and (8.72).

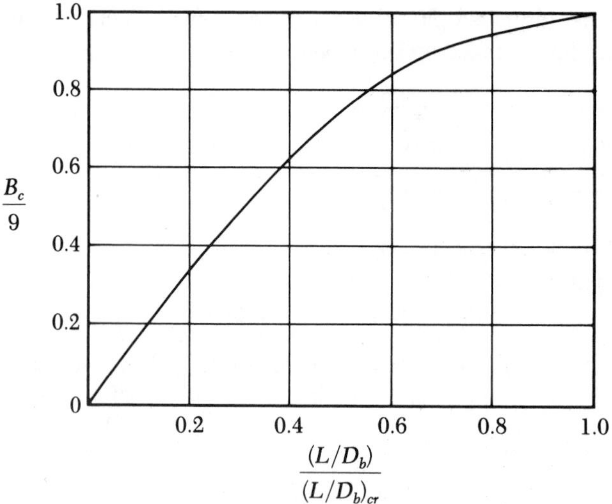

▼ **FIGURE 9.23** Nondimensional plot of the breakout factor, B_c

▼ EXAMPLE 9.6

Refer to Figure 9.21. A drilled pier with a bell has a shaft diameter of 0.76 m, a bell diameter of 1.85 m, and a length of 9.5 m. The bell is supported by a dense sand ($z > 9.5$ m) layer. However, a fine, loose sand layer exists above the bell ($z = 0$–9.5 m). For this sand, $\gamma = 16.4$ kN/m^3, $\phi = 32°$, and the approximate relative density is 30%. The entire pier is located above the water table. Determine the net allowable uplift capacity of the pier with a factor of safety of 3.

Solution We begin with $L = 9.5$ m, $D_b = 1.85$ m, and $L/D_b = 9.5/1.85 = 5.14$. For $\phi = 30°$, $(L/D_b)_{cr} = 4$; for $\phi = 35°$, $(L/D_b)_{cr} = 5$. By interpretation, $(L/D_b)_{cr} \approx 4.2$ for $\phi = 32°$. So $L_{cr} = (4.2)(D_b) = 7.77$. Because $L/D_b = 5.13 > (L/D_b)_{cr} = 4.2$, it is a deep foundation.

According to Eq. (9.38),

$$B_q = 2\left(\frac{L}{D_b}\right)_{cr} K_u' \tan\phi\left[m\left(\frac{L}{D_b}\right)_{cr} + 1\right] + 1$$

Note that $(L/D_b)_{cr}$ rather than L/D_b was used in the preceding equation because it is a deep foundation. For $\phi = 32°$, $m \approx 0.17$. Hence

$$B_q = (2)(4.2)(0.9)(\tan 32°)[(0.17)(4.2) + 1] + 1 = 9.09$$

From Eq. (9.39),

$$T_{un} = T_{ug} - W = B_q A_p \gamma L + \int_0^{L-L_{cr}} (\pi D_s)(\sigma_v' K_u' \tan\delta)\, dz$$

$$= B_q A_p \gamma L + \frac{\pi}{2}\gamma D_s K_u' \tan\delta (L - L_{cr})^2$$

$$A_p = \left(\frac{\pi}{4}\right)(D_b)^2 = \left(\frac{\pi}{4}\right)(1.85)^2 = 2.687 \text{ m}^2$$

$$L - L_{cr} = 9.5 - 7.77 = 1.73 \text{ m}$$

Also, from Figure 8.35b and 8.35c, for $\phi = 32°$ and relative density = 30%, $K'_u =$ 1.5 and $\delta/\phi \approx 0.73$. Hence

$$T_{un} = (9.09)(2.687)(16.4)(9.5) + \left(\frac{\pi}{2}\right)(16.4)(0.76)(1.5)$$

$$\times [\tan(0.73 \times 32)](1.73)^2$$

$$= 3805.4 + 37.96 = 3843.36 \approx 3843$$

So, the net allowable capacity $= 3843/FS = 3843/3 =$ **1281 kN.** ▼

▼ EXAMPLE 9.7

Consider the drilled pier described in Example 9.6. If the soil above the bell is clay with an average value of the undrained shear strength of 95 kN/m^2, calculate the net ultimate uplift capacity. For clay, $\gamma = 17.9$ kN/m^3.

Solution From Eq. (9.41),

$$\left(\frac{L}{D_b}\right)_{cr} = 0.107c_u + 2.5 = (0.107)(95) + 2.5 = 12.67$$

This quantity is more than 7, so use $(L/D_b)_{cr} = 7$. Hence $L_{cr} = (7)(1.85) = 12.95$ m. $L_{cr} = 12.95$ is greater than $L = 9.5$ m, so this pier is a shallow foundation for uplift consideration. For shallow foundations [Eq. (9.40)],

$$T_{un} = (c_u B_c + \gamma L)A_p$$

The magnitude of the breakout factor, B_c, is determined from Figure 9.23:

$$\frac{\left(\frac{L}{D_b}\right)}{\left(\frac{L}{D_b}\right)_{cr}} = \frac{\left(\frac{9.5}{1.85}\right)}{7} = 0.734$$

So, $B_c/9 = 0.92$, or $B_c = 8.28$, and $A_p = (\pi/4)D_b^2 = (\pi/4)(1.85)^2 = 2.687$ m^2. Thus

$$T_{un} = [(95)(8.28) + (17.9)(9.5)]2.687 = \mathbf{2570.5\ kN.}$$ ▼

9.10 LATERAL LOAD-CARRYING CAPACITY

The lateral load-carrying capacity of piers can be analyzed in a manner similar to that presented in Section 8.12 for piles. That method of analysis will not be repeated here.

CAISSONS

9.11 TYPES OF CAISSONS

Caissons are divided into three major types: (1) open caissons, (2) box caissons (or closed caissons), and (3) pneumatic caissons.

Open caissons (Figure 9.24) are concrete shafts that remain open at the top and bottom during construction. The bottom of the caisson has a cutting edge. The caisson is sunk into place, and soil from the inside of the shaft is removed by grab buckets until the bearing stratum is reached. The shafts may be circular, square, rectangular, or oval. Once the bearing stratum is reached, concrete is poured into the shaft (under water) to form a seal at its bottom. When the concrete seal hardens, the water inside the caisson shaft is pumped out. Concrete is then poured into the shaft to fill it. Open caissons can be extended to great depths, and the cost of construction is relatively low. However, one of their major disadvantages is the lack of quality control over the concrete poured into the shaft for the seal. Also, the bottom of the caisson cannot be thoroughly cleaned out. An alternative method of open-caisson construction is to drive some sheet piles to form an enclosed area, which is filled with sand and is generally referred to as a *sand island.*

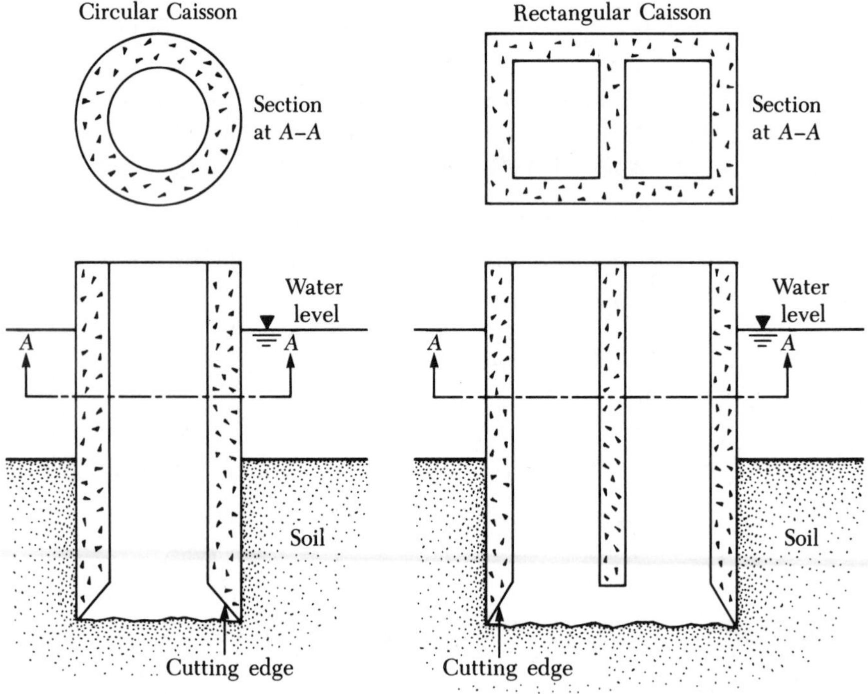

▼ **FIGURE 9.24** Open caisson

The caisson is then sunk through the sand to the desired bearing stratum. This procedure is somewhat analogous to sinking a caisson when the ground surface is above the water table.

Box caissons (Figure 9.25) are caissons with closed bottoms. They are constructed on land and then transported to the construction site. They are gradually sunk at the site by filling the inside with sand, ballast, water, or concrete. The cost for this type of construction is low. The bearing surface must be level, and if it is not, it must be leveled by excavation.

Pneumatic caissons (Figure 9.26) are generally used for depths of about 50–130 ft (15–40 m). This type of caisson is required when an excavation cannot be kept open because the soil flows into the excavated area faster than it can be removed. A pneumatic caisson has a work chamber at the bottom that is at least 10 ft ($\approx$3 m) high. In this chamber, the workers excavate the soil and place the concrete. The air pressure in the chamber is kept high enough to prevent water and soil from entering. Workers usually do not encounter severe discomfort when the chamber pressure is raised to about 15 lb/in^2 ($\approx$100 kN/m^2) above atmospheric pressure. Beyond this pressure, decompression periods are required when the workers leave the chamber. When chamber pressures of about 44 lb/in^2 ($\approx$300 kN/m^2) above atmospheric pressure are required, workers should not be kept inside the chamber for more than 1½–2 hours at a time. Workers enter and leave the chamber through a steel shaft by means of a ladder. This shaft is

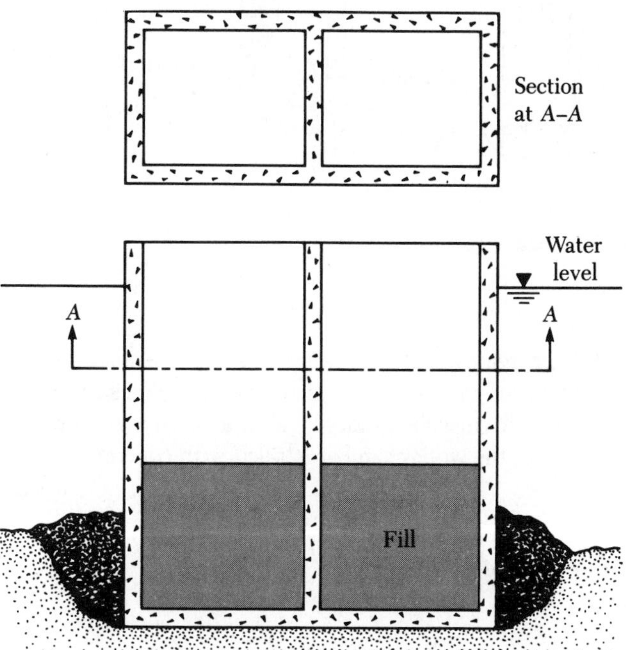

▼ **FIGURE 9.25** Box caisson

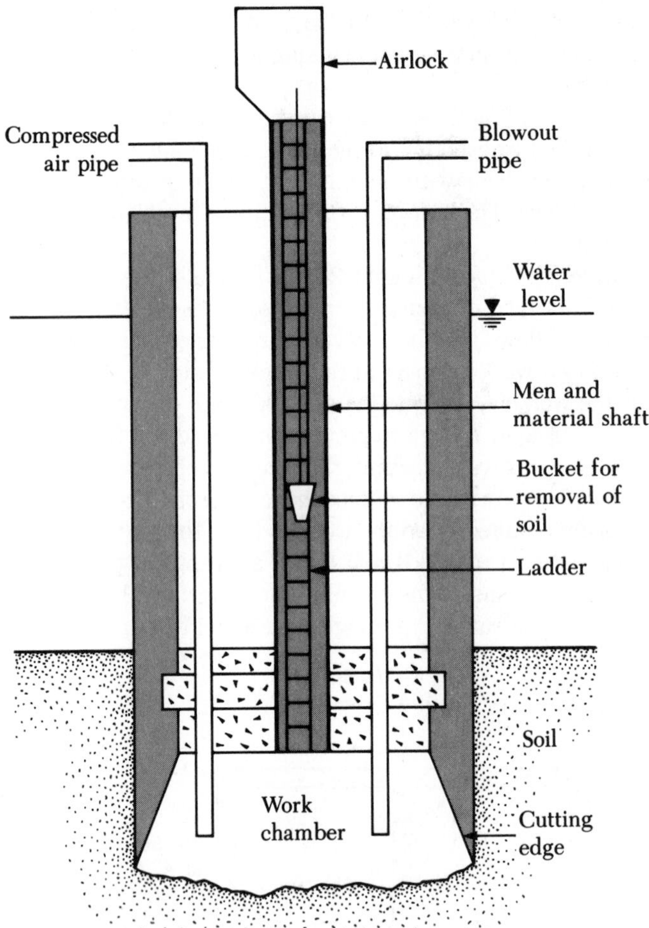

▼ **FIGURE 9.26** Pneumatic caisson

also used for the removal of excavated soil and the placement of concrete. For large caisson construction, more than one shaft may be necessary; an airlock is provided for each one. Pneumatic caissons gradually sink as excavation proceeds. When the bearing stratum is reached, the work chamber is filled with concrete.

9.12 LOAD-BEARING CAPACITY OF CAISSONS

Calculation of the load-bearing capacity of caissons is similar to that for drilled piers. Therefore it is not discussed further here.

9.13 THICKNESS OF CONCRETE SEAL IN OPEN CAISSONS

In Section 9.11, we mentioned that, before dewatering the caisson, a concrete seal is placed at the bottom of the shaft (Figure 9.27) and allowed to cure for some time. The concrete seal should be thick enough to withstand an upward hydrostatic force from its bottom after dewatering is complete and before concrete fills the shaft. Based on the theory of elasticity, the thickness, t, according to Teng (1962) is

$$t = 1.18R_i\sqrt{\frac{q}{f_c}} \quad \text{(circular caisson)} \tag{9.44}$$

and

$$t = 0.866B_i\sqrt{\frac{q}{f_c\left[1 + 1.61\left(\frac{L_i}{B_i}\right)\right]}} \quad \text{(rectangular caisson)} \tag{9.45}$$

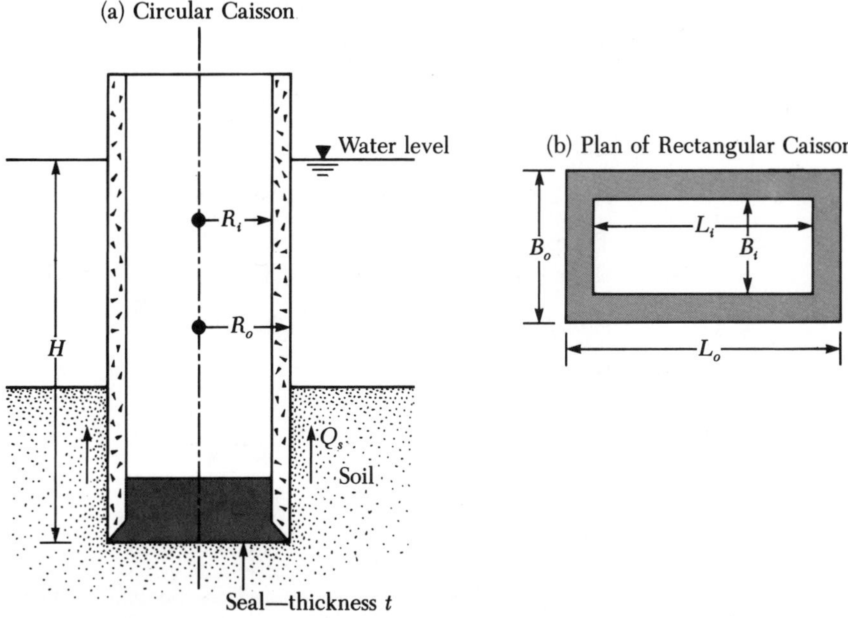

▼ **FIGURE 9.27** Calculation of the thickness of seal for an open caisson

where R_i = inside radius of a circular caisson
q = unit bearing pressure at the base of the caisson
f_c = allowable concrete flexural stress ($\approx$0.1–0.2 of f'_c, where f'_c is the 28-day compressive strength of concrete)
B_i, L_i = inside width and length, respectively, of rectangular caisson

According to Figure 9.27, the value of q in Eqs. (9.44) and (9.45) can be approximated as

$$q \approx H\gamma_w - t\gamma_c \tag{9.46}$$

where γ_c = unit weight of concrete

The thickness of the seal calculated by Eqs. (9.44) and (9.45) will be sufficient to protect it from cracking immediately after dewatering. However, two other conditions should also be checked for safety.

1. **Check for Perimeter Shear at Contact Face of Seal and Shaft**

   According to Figure 9.27, the net upward hydrostatic force from the bottom of the seal is $A_i H\gamma_w - A_i t\gamma_c$ (where $A_i = \pi R_i^2$ for circular caissons and $A_i = L_i B_i$ for rectangular caissons). So the perimeter shear developed is

$$v \approx \frac{A_i H\gamma_w - A_i t\gamma_c}{p_i t} \tag{9.47}$$

   where p_i = inside perimeter of the caisson

   Note that

$$p_i = 2\pi R_i \qquad \text{(for circular caissons)} \tag{9.48}$$

   and that

$$p_i = 2(L_i + B_i) \qquad \text{(for rectangular caissons)} \tag{9.49}$$

   The perimeter shear given by Eq. (9.47) should be less than the permissible shear stress, v_u, as given by Eq. (*A*.15a) (Appendix A), or

$$v(\text{MN/m}^2) \le v_u(\text{MN/m}^2) = 0.17\phi\sqrt{f'_c(\text{MN/m}^2)} \tag{9.50}$$

   where $\phi = 0.85$

   In English units,

$$v(\text{lb/in}^2) \le v_u(\text{lb/in}^2) = 2\phi\sqrt{f'_c(\text{lb/in}^2)} \tag{9.51}$$

   where $\phi = 0.85$

2. **Check for Buoyancy**

   If the shaft is completely dewatered, the buoyant upward force, F_u, is

$$F_u = (\pi R_o^2)H\gamma_w \qquad \text{(for circular caissons)} \tag{9.52}$$

and

$$F_u = (B_o L_o)H\gamma_w \qquad \text{(for rectangular caissons)} \tag{9.53}$$

The downward force, F_d, is caused by the weight of the caisson and the seal and by the skin friction at the caisson–soil interface, or

$$F_d = W_c + W_s + Q_s \tag{9.54}$$

where W_c = weight of caisson
W_s = weight of seal
Q_s = skin friction

If $F_d > F_u$, the caisson is safe from buoyancy. However, if $F_d < F_u$, dewatering the shaft completely will be unsafe. For that reason, the thickness of the seal should be increased by Δt [over the thickness calculated by using Eqs. (9.44) or (9.45)], or

$$\Delta t = \frac{F_u - F_d}{A_i \gamma_c} \tag{9.55}$$

▼ EXAMPLE 9.8

An open caisson (circular) is shown in Figure 9.28. Determine the thickness of the seal that will enable complete dewatering.

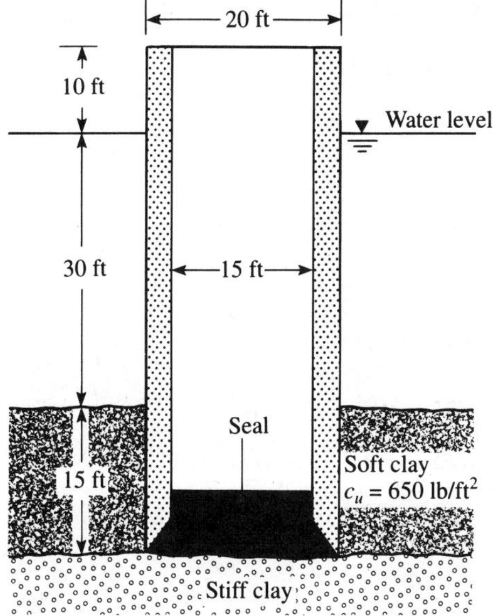

▼ **FIGURE 9.28**

Solution From Eq. (9.44),

$$t = 1.18R_i\sqrt{\frac{q}{f_c}}$$

For $R_i = 7.5$ ft,

$$q \approx (45)(62.4) - t\gamma_c$$

With $\gamma_c = 150$ lb/ft^3, $q = 2808 - 150t$ and

$$f_c = 0.1f'_c = 0.1 \times 3 \times 10^3 \text{ lb/in}^2 = 0.3 \times 10^3 \text{ lb/in}^2$$

So

$$t = (1.18)(7.5)\sqrt{\frac{2808 - 150t}{3000 \times 144}}$$

or

$$t^2 \times 0.027t - 0.509 = 0$$

$$t = 0.7 \text{ ft}$$

Use $t \approx 1$ ft.

Check for Perimeter Shear

According to Eq. (9.47),

$$v = \frac{\pi R_i^2 H\gamma_w - \pi R_i^2 t\gamma_c}{2\pi R_i t} = \frac{(\pi)(7.5)^2[(45)(62.4) - (1)(150)]}{(2)(\pi)(7.5)(1)} \approx 9968 \text{ lb/ft}^2 = 69 \text{ lb/in}^2$$

The allowable shear stress is

$$v_u = 2\phi\sqrt{f_c} = (2)(0.85)\sqrt{3000} = 93.1 \text{ lb/in}^2$$

$$v = 69 \text{ lb/in}^2 < v_u = \mathbf{93.1 \text{ lb/in}^2\text{—OK}}$$

Check Against Buoyancy

The buoyant upward force is

$$F_u = \pi R_o^2 H\gamma_w$$

For $R_o = 10$ ft,

$$F_u = \frac{(\pi)(10)^2(45)(62.4)}{1000} = 882.2 \text{ kip}$$

The downward force, $F_d = W_c + W_s + Q_s$ and

$$W_c = \pi(R_o^2 - R_i^2)(\gamma_c)(55) = \pi(10^2 - 7.5^2)(150)(55) = 1{,}133{,}919 \text{ lb} \approx 1134 \text{ kip}$$

$$W_s = (\pi R_i^2)t\gamma_c = (\pi)(7.5)^2(1)(150) = 26{,}507 \text{ lb} = 26.5 \text{ kip}$$

Assume that $Q_s \approx 0$. So

$$F_d = 1134 + 26.5 = 1160.5 \text{ kip}$$

Because $F_u < F_d$, it is safe. For design, **assume that $t = 1$ ft.** ▼

PROBLEMS

9.1 A drilled pier is shown in Figure P9.1. For the pier, $L_1 = 12$ ft, $L_2 = 7.5$ ft, $D_s = 3$ ft, and $D_b = 5.75$ ft. For the soil, $\gamma_c = 107$ lb/ft^3, $c_u = 550$ lb/ft^2, $\gamma_s = 118$ lb/ft^3, and $\phi = 37.5°$. Determine the net allowable point bearing capacity (factor of safety = 4). Do not reduce the friction angle of sand, ϕ (use Figure 9.7).

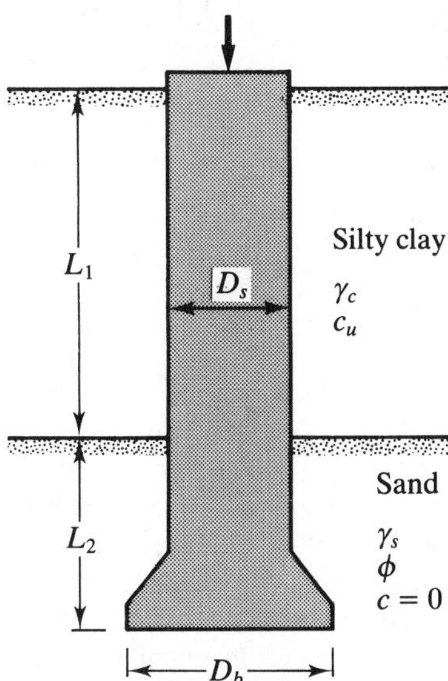

▼ **FIGURE P9.1**

9.2 For the drilled pier described in Problem 9.1, what skin resistance would develop for the top 12 ft, which is in clay?

9.3 Determine the net allowable point bearing capacity ($FS = 3$) of the pier described in Problem 9.1 by Vesic's method [Eq. (9.8)] for $I_{rr} = 130$. Reduce the friction angle by 10%.

9.4 Redo Problem 9.1 for $D_b = 1.75$ m, $D_s = 1$ m, $L_1 = 4$ m, and $L_2 = 2.5$ m; $c_u = 32$ kN/m^2, $\gamma_c = 17.8$ kN/m^3, $\gamma_s = 18.2$ kN/m^3, and $\phi = 32°$. Reduce the friction angle by 10%.

9.5 Solve Problem 9.4 by Vesic's method [Eq. (9.8)] for $I_{rr} = 80$.

9.6 For the drilled pier described in Problem 9.4, what skin resistance would develop in the top 4 m (the portion in clay soil)?

9.7 Figure P9.7 shows a drilled pier without a bell. Here, $L_1 = 27$ ft, $L_2 = 8.5$ ft, $D_s = 3.3$ ft, $c_{u(1)} = 1000$ lb/ft^2, and $c_{u(2)} = 2175$ lb/ft^2. Determine:

a. The net ultimate point bearing capacity
b. The ultimate skin resistance
c. The working load, Q_w ($FS = 3$)

Use the procedure outlined in Section 9.5.

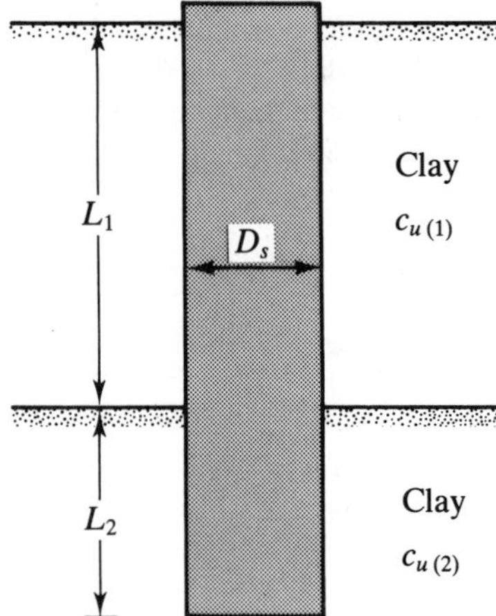

▼ **FIGURE P9.7**

9.8 For the drilled pier described in Problem 9.7, estimate the total elastic settlement at working load. Use Eqs. (8.61), (8.63), and (8.64). Assume that $E_p = 3 \times 10^6$ lb/in^2 and that $\xi = 0.65$. Make other assumptions as necessary.

9.9 For the drilled pier described in Problem 9.7, determine:

a. The ultimate load-carrying capacity;

b. The load-carrying capacity for a settlement of 0.5 in.

Use the procedure outlined in Section 9.7.

9.10 Refer to the soil profile shown in Figure P9.10. A drilled pier with a bell is to be constructed to support a working load, $Q_w = 900$ kN, with $f'_c = 21{,}000$ kN/m^2 and $FS = 3$.

a. Determine the minimum diameter of the pier shaft required [use Eq. (9.1)]. Make a reasonable assumption for the diameter to be used.

b. For the pier diameter obtained in part (a), determine the diameter of the bell needed. Skin friction and point bearing capacity are to be considered.

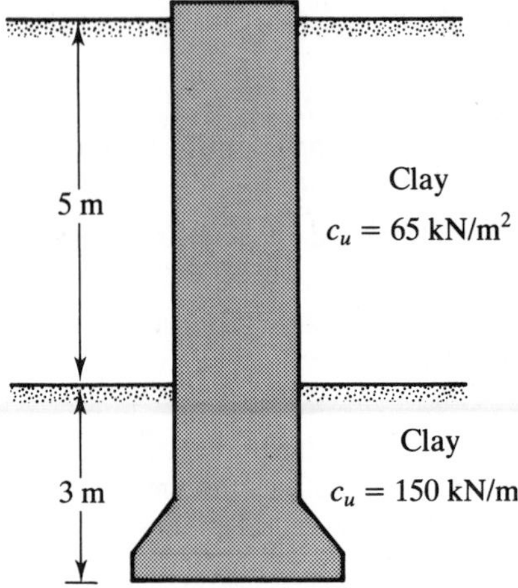

▼ **FIGURE P9.10**

9.11 A drilled pier in a medium sand is shown in Figure P9.11. For the pier, $L = 10$ m, $L_1 = 9.3$ m, $D_s = 0.7$ m, and $D_b = 1.4$ m. For the soil, $\gamma = 17.6$ kN/m^3, and $\phi = 35°$, and $D_\gamma = 60\%$. Use the method proposed by Touma and Reese to determine:

a. The net point resistance for a base movement of 25.4 mm

b. The shaft frictional resistance

c. The total load that can be carried by the pier for a total base movement of 25.4 mm

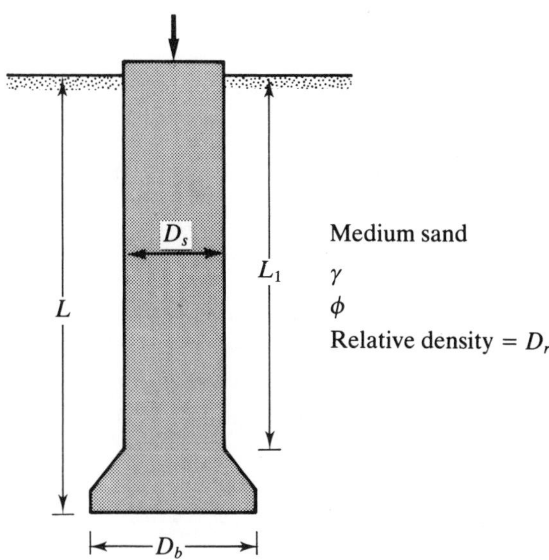

▼ **FIGURE P9.11**

9.12 Refer to Figure P9.11, for which $L = 20$ ft, $L_1 = 17$ ft, $D_s = 4$ ft, $D_b = 5.5$ ft, $\gamma = 100$ lb/ft^3, and $\phi = 33°$. The average uncorrected standard penetration number within $2D_b$ below the base is 32. Determine:

a. The ultimate load-carrying capacity;

b. The load-carrying capacity for a settlement of 1 in.

Use the procedure outlined in Section 9.7.

9.13 Assume the pier shown in Figure P9.13 to be a point bearing pier with a working load of 560 kip. Calculate the pier settlement from Eqs. (8.61) and (8.62) for $E_p = 3 \times 10^6$ lb/in^2, $\mu_s = 0.35$, and $E_s = 5070$ lb/in^2.

9.14 A drilled pier is socketed into rock, as shown in Figure 9.20. The design parameters are $Q_{all} = 18{,}000$ kN, $E_r/E_c = 0.6$, $\mu_c = \mu_r = 0.35$, $\phi_{rc} = 34°$, $\tau_{all} = 360$ kN/m^2, the allowable point bearing capacity of rock is 2200 kN/m^2, and f'_c for concrete is 28,000 kN/m^2. Determine the required length of embedment, L, of the pier in the rock.

9.15 Refer to the drilled pier in Problem 9.14. If the allowable bearing capacity of rock is 3000 kN/m^2 but all other quantities remain the same, what will be the required length of embedment of the pier in the rock?

9.16 Refer to Figure 9.21. For the pier, $D_s = 1$ m, $D_b = 1.8$ m, and $L = 8$ m. The drilled pier is in a homogeneous sand with $\phi = 38°$ and $\gamma = 18$ kN/m^3. Determine the net ultimate uplift capacity, T_{un}, of the pier.

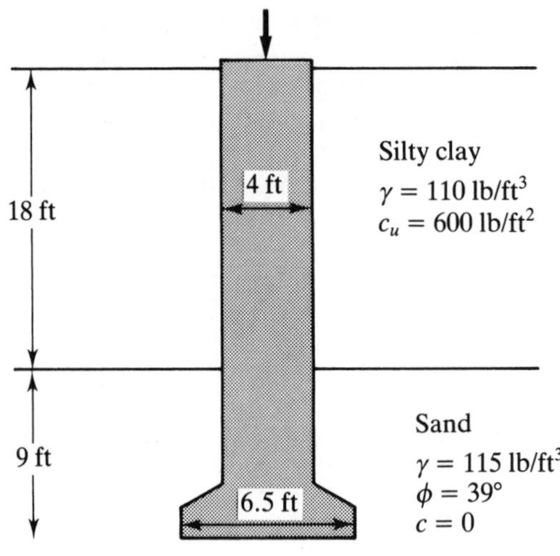

▼ **FIGURE P9.13**

9.17 Repeat Problem 9.16 for $L = 5$ m.

9.18 For the drilled pier in Figure 9.21, $D_s = 3$ ft, $D_b = 5$ ft, and $L = 20$ ft. The pier is in clay with $c_u = 1480$ lb/ft^2 and a unit weight of 115 lb/ft^3. Estimate the net ultimate uplift capacity.

9.19 Repeat Problem 9.18 for $c_u = 700$ lb/ft^2.

REFERENCES

Das, B. M. (1980). "A Procedure for Estimation of Ultimate Uplift Capacity of Foundations in Clay," *Soils and Foundations*, The Japanese Society of Soil Mechanics and Foundation Engineering, Vol. 20, No. 1, pp. 77–82.

Das, B. M., and Seeley, G. R. (1975). "Breakout Resistance of Shallow Vertical Anchors," *Journal of the Geotechnical Engineering Division*, Americal Society of Civil Engineers, Vol. 101, No. GT9, pp. 999–1003.

Goodman, R. E. (1980). *Introduction to Rock Mechanics*, Wiley, New York.

Kulhawy, F. H., and Jackson, C. S. (1989). "Some Observations on Undrained Side Resistance of Drilled Shafts," *Proceedings*, Foundation Engineering: Current Principles and Practices, American Society of Civil Engineers, Vol. 2, pp. 1011–1025.

Ladanyi, B. (1977). "Discussion on Friction and Endbearing Tests on Bedrock for High Capacity Socket Design," *Canadian Geotechnical Journal*, Vol. 14, No. 1, pp. 153–156.

Meyerhof, G. G., and Adams, J. I. (1968). "The Ultimate Uplift Capacity of Foundations," *Canadian Geotechnical Journal*, Vol. 5, No. 4, pp. 225–244.

Reese, L. C., and O'Neill, M. W. (1989). "New Design Method for Drilled Shafts from Common Soil and Rock Tests," *Proceedings*, Foundation Engineering: Current Principles and Practices, American Society of Civil Engineers, Vol. 2, pp. 1026–1039.

Teng, W. C. (1962). *Foundation Design*, Prentice-Hall, Englewood Cliffs, N.J.

Touma, F. T., and Reese, L. C. (1974). "Behavior of Bored Piles in Sand," *Journal of the Geotechnical Engineering Division*, American Society of Civil Engineers, Vol. 100, No. G17, pp. 749–761.

Vesic, A. S. (1963). "Bearing Capacity of Deep Foundations in Sand," *Highway Research Record*, No. 39, Highway Research Board, National Academy of Science, Washington, D.C., pp. 112–153.

Vesic, A. S. (1967). "Ultimate Load and Settlement of Deep Foundations in Sand," *Proceedings*, Symposium on Bearing Capacity and Settlement of Foundations, Duke University, Durham, N.C., p. 53.

Vesic, A. S. (1977). "Design of Pile Foundations," *NCHRP No. 42*, Transportation Research Board, National Research Council, Washington, D.C.

Whitaker, T., and Cooke, R. W. (1966). "An Investigation of the Shaft and Base Resistance of Large Bored Piles in London Clay," *Proceedings*, Conference on Large Bored Piles, Institute of Civil Engineers, London, pp. 7–49.

CHAPTER TEN

FOUNDATIONS ON DIFFICULT SOILS

10.1 INTRODUCTION

In many areas of the United States and other parts of the world, certain soils make construction of foundations extremely difficult. For example, expansive or collapsible soils may cause high differential movements in structures by excessive heave or settlement. Similar problems can also arise when foundations are constructed over sanitary landfills. Foundation engineers must be able to identify difficult soils when they are encountered in the field. Although not all the problems caused by all soils can be solved, preventive measures can be taken to reduce the possibility of damage to structures built on them. This chapter outlines the fundamental properties of three major soil conditions—collapsible soils, expansive soils, and sanitary landfills—and methods of careful foundation construction.

COLLAPSING SOIL

10.2 DEFINITION AND TYPES OF COLLAPSING SOIL

Collapsing soils, which are sometimes referred to as *metastable soils*, are unsaturated soils that undergo a large volume change upon saturation. This volume change may or may not be the result of the application of additional load. The behavior of collapsing soils under load is best explained by the typical void ratio–pressure plot (e against $\log p$) for a collapsing soil, as shown in Figure 10.1. Branch ab is determined from the consolidation test on a specimen at its natural moisture content. At a pressure level of p_w, the equilibrium void ratio is e_1. However, if water is introduced into the specimen for saturation, the soil structure will collapse. After saturation, the equilibrium void ratio at the same pressure level p_w is e_2; cd is the branch of $e \log p$ curve under additional load after saturation. Foundations that are constructed on such soils may undergo large and sudden settlement if and when the soil under them

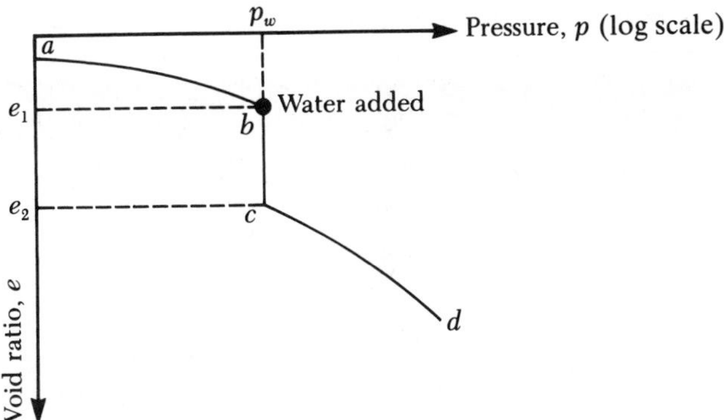

▼ **FIGURE 10.1** Nature of variation of void ratio with pressure for a collapsing soil

becomes saturated with an unanticipated supply of moisture. This moisture may come from several sources, such as (a) broken water pipelines, (b) leaky sewers, (c) drainage from reservoirs and swimming pools, (d) slow increase of groundwater, and so on. This type of settlement generally causes considerable structural damage. Hence identification of collapsing soils during field exploration is crucial.

The majority of naturally occurring collapsing soils are *aeolian*—that is, wind-deposited sand and/or silts, such as loess, aeolic beaches, and volcanic dust deposits. These deposits have high void ratios and low unit weights and are cohesionless or only slightly cohesive. *Loess* deposits have silt-sized particles. The cohesion in loess may be the result of the presence of clay coatings around the silt-size particles, which holds them in a rather stable condition in an unsaturated state. The cohesion may also be caused by the presence of chemical precipitates leached by rainwater. When the soil becomes saturated, the clay binders lose their strength and hence undergo a structural collapse. In the United States, large parts of the Midwest and arid West have such types of deposit. *Loess* deposits are also found over 15–20% of Europe and over large parts of China.

Many collapsing soils may be residual soils that are products of weathering of parent rocks. The weathering process produces soils with a large range of particle-size distribution. Soluble and colloidal materials are leached out by weathering, resulting in large void ratios and thus unstable structures. Many parts of South Africa and Rhodesia have residual soils that are decomposed granites. Sometimes collapsing soil deposits may be left by flash floods and mud flows. These deposits dry out and are poorly consolidated. An excellent review of collapsing soils is that of Clemence and Finbarr (1981).

10.3 PHYSICAL PARAMETERS FOR IDENTIFICATION

Several investigators have proposed various methods to evaluate the physical parameters of collapsing soils for identification. Some of these methods are discussed briefly in Table 10.1.

TABLE 10.1 Reported Criteria for Identification of Collapsing Soil[a]

Investigator	Year	Criteria
Denisov	1951	Coefficient of subsidence: $K = \frac{\text{void ratio at liquid limit}}{\text{natural void ratio}}$ $K = 0.5$–0.75: highly collapsible $K = 1.0$: noncollapsible loam $K = 1.5$–2.0: noncollapsible soils
Clevenger	1958	If dry unit weight is less than 80 lb/ft³ (≈ 12.6 kN/m³), settlement will be large; if dry unit weight is greater than 90 lb/ft³ (≈ 14.1 kN/m³), settlement will be small.
Priklonski	1952	$K_D = \frac{\text{natural moisture content} - \text{plastic limit}}{\text{plasticity index}}$ $K_D < 0$: highly collapsible soils $K_D > 0.5$: noncollapsible soils $K_D > 1.0$: swelling soils
Gibbs	1961	Collapse ratio, $R = \frac{\text{saturation moisture content}}{\text{liquid limit}}$ This was put into graph form.
Soviet Building Code	1962	$L = \frac{e_o - e_L}{1 + e_o}$ where e_o = natural void ratio and e_L = void ratio at liquid limit. For natural degree of saturation less than 60%, if $L > -0.1$, it is a collapsing soil.
Feda	1964	$K_L = \frac{w_o}{S_r} - \frac{PL}{PI}$ where w_o = natural water content, S_r = natural degree of saturation, PL = plastic limit, and PI = plasticity index. For $S_r < 100\%$, if $K_L > 0.85$, it is a subsident soil.
Benites	1968	A dispersion test in which 2 g of soil are dropped into 12 ml of distilled water and specimen is timed until dispersed; dispersion times of 20 to 30 s were obtained for collapsing Arizona soils.
Handy	1973	Iowa loess with clay (<0.002 mm) contents: <16%: high probability of collapse 16–24%: probability of collapse 24–32%: less than 50% probability of collapse >32%: usually safe from collapse

[a] Modified after Lutenegger and Saber (1988)

Jennings and Knight (1975) suggested a procedure to describe the *collapse potential* of a soil. It can be determined by taking an undisturbed soil specimen at natural moisture content in a consolidation ring. Step loads are applied to the specimen up to a pressure level of 29 lb/in^2 (≈ 200 kN/m^2). (In Figure 10.1, this is p_w.) At this pressure ($p_w = 29$ lb/in^2), the specimen is flooded for saturation and left for 24 hours. This test provides the void ratios (e_1 and e_2) before and after flooding. The collapse potential, C_p, may now be calculated as

$$C_p = \Delta\varepsilon = \frac{e_1 - e_2}{1 + e_o} \tag{10.1}$$

where e_o = natural void ratio of the soil
$\Delta\varepsilon$ = vertical strain

The severity of foundation problems associated with a collapsible soil have been correlated with the collapse potential, C_p, by Jennings and Knight (1975). They were summarized by Clemence and Finbarr (1981) and are given in Table 10.2.

Holtz and Hilf (1961) suggested that a loessial soil that has a void ratio large enough to allow its moisture content to exceed its liquid limit upon saturation is susceptible to collapse. So, for collapse

$$w_{(\text{saturated})} \geq LL \tag{10.2}$$

However, for saturated soils

$$e_o = wG_s \tag{10.3}$$

where LL = liquid limit
G_s = specific gravity of soil solids

Combining Eqs. (10.2) and (10.3), for collapsing soils, yields

$$e_o \geq (LL)(G_s) \tag{10.4}$$

The natural dry unit weight, γ_d, of the soil for collapse is

$$\gamma_d \leq \frac{G_s \gamma_w}{1 + e_o} = \frac{G_s \gamma_w}{1 + (LL)(G_s)} \tag{10.5}$$

TABLE 10.2 Relation of Collapse Potential to the Severity of Foundation Problems[a]

C_p(%)	Severity of problem
0–1	No problem
1–5	Moderate trouble
5–10	Trouble
10–20	Severe trouble
20	Very severe trouble

[a] After Clemence and Finbarr (1981)

For an average value of $G_s = 2.65$, the limiting values of γ_d for various liquid limits may now be calculated from Eq. (10.5):

Liquid limit (%)	Limiting values of γ_d (lb/ft^3)	Limiting values of γ_d (kN/m^3)
10	130.8	20.56
15	118.3	18.60
20	108.1	16.99
25	99.5	15.64
30	92.1	14.48
35	85.8	13.49
40	80.3	12.62
45	75.4	11.86

Figure 10.2 shows a plot of the preceding limiting dry unit weights against the corresponding liquid limits. For any soil, if the natural dry unit weight falls below the limiting line, the soil is likely to collapse.

Care should be taken to obtain undisturbed samples for determining the collapse potentials and dry unit weights, preferably block samples cut by hand. The reason is

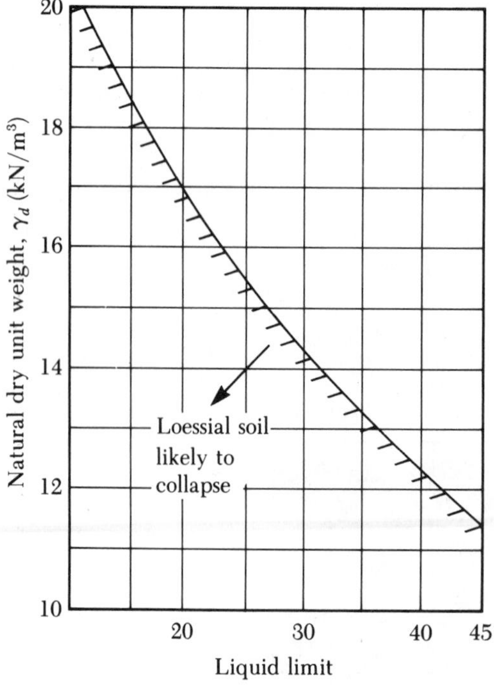

▼ **FIGURE 10.2** Loessial soil likely to collapse

that samples obtained by thin wall tubes may undergo some compression during the sampling process. However, if this procedure is used, the boreholes should be made *without water.*

10.4 PROCEDURE FOR CALCULATING COLLAPSE SETTLEMENT

Jennings and Knight (1975) proposed the following laboratory procedure to determine the collapse settlement of structures upon saturation of soil.

1. Obtain *two* undisturbed soil specimens for tests in a standard consolidation test apparatus (oedometer).
2. Place the two specimens under 0.15 lb/in^2 (1 kN/m^2) pressure for 24 hours.
3. After 24 hours, saturate one specimen by flooding. Keep the other specimen at natural moisture content.
4. After 24 hours of flooding, resume the consolidation test for both specimens by doubling the load (same procedure as the standard consolidation test) to the desired pressure level.
5. Plot the e–log p graphs for both specimens (Figure 10.3a and b).
6. Calculate the *in situ* effective pressure, p_o. Draw a vertical line corresponding to the pressure p_o.
7. From the e–log p curve of the soaked sample, determine the preconsolidation pressure, p_c. If $p_c/p_o = 0.8$–1.5, the soil is normally consolidated; however, if $p_c/p_o > 1.5$, it is preconsolidated.
8. Determine e'_o, corresponding to p_o from the e–log p curve of the soaked sample. (This procedure for normally consolidated and overconsolidated soils is shown in Figure 10.3a and b, respectively.)
9. Through point (p_o, e'_o) draw a curve that is similar to the e–log p curve obtained from the specimen tested at natural moisture content.
10. Determine the incremental pressure, Δp, on the soil caused by the construction of the foundation. Draw a vertical line corresponding to the pressure of $p_o + \Delta p$ in the e–log p curve.
11. Now, determine Δe_1 and Δe_2. The settlement of soil without change in the natural moisture content is

$$S_1 = \frac{\Delta e_1}{1 + e'_o}(H) \tag{10.6}$$

Also, the settlement caused by collapse in the soil structure is

$$S_2 = \frac{\Delta e_2}{1 + e'_o}(H) \tag{10.7}$$

where H = thickness of soil susceptible to collapse

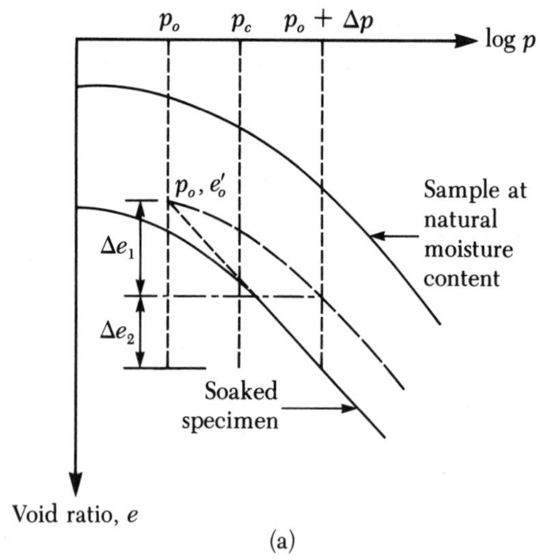

(a)

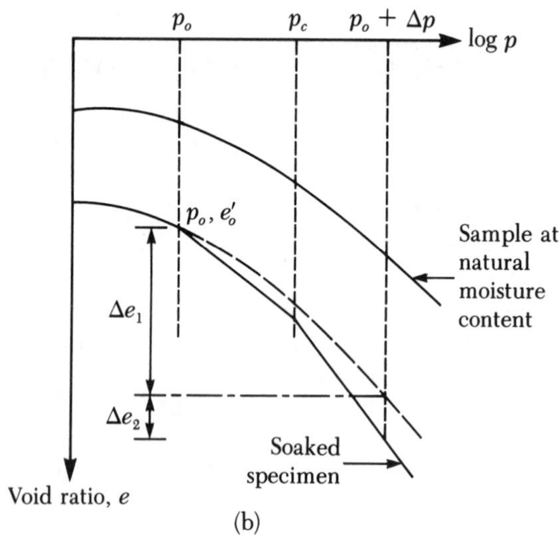

(b)

▼ **FIGURE 10.3** Settlement calculation from double oedometer test: (a) normally consolidated soil; (b) overconsolidated soil

10.5 FOUNDATION DESIGN IN SOILS NOT SUSCEPTIBLE TO WETTING

For actual foundation design purposes, some standard field load tests may also be conducted. Figure 10.4 shows the results of some field load tests in loess deposits in Nebraska and Iowa. Note that the load–settlement relationships are essentially linear up to a certain critical pressure, p_{cr}, at which there is a breakdown of the soil structure and

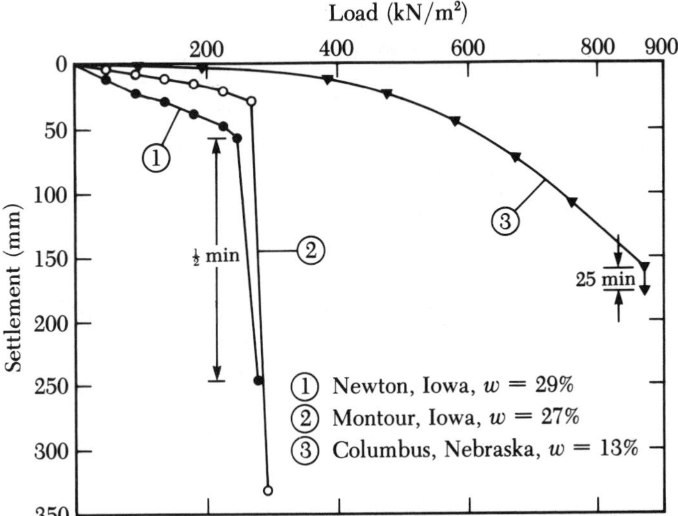

▼ **FIGURE 10.4** Results of standard load test on loess deposits in Iowa and Nebraska (adapted from *Foundation Engineering*, Second Edition, by R. B. Peck, W. E. Hanson, and T. H. Thornburn. Copyright 1974 by John Wiley and Sons. Reprinted by permission.)

hence a large settlement. Sudden breakdown of soil structure is more common with soils having a high natural moisture content than with normally dry soils.

If enough precautions are taken in the field to prevent moisture from increasing under structures, spread foundations and raft foundations may be built on potentially collapsible soils. However, the foundations must be proportioned so that the critical stresses (Figure 10.4) in the field are never exceeded. A factor of safety of about 2.5 to 3 should be used to calculate the allowable soil pressure, or

$$p_{\text{all}} = \frac{p_{\text{cr}}}{FS} \tag{10.8}$$

where p_{all} = allowable soil pressure
FS = factor of safety (about 2.5 to 3)

The differential and total settlements of these foundations should be similar to those of foundations designed for sandy soils.

Continuous foundations may be safer than isolated foundations over collapsible soils in that they can effectively minimize differential settlement. Figure 10.5 shows a typical procedure for construction of continuous foundations. This procedure uses footing beams and longitudinal load-bearing beams.

In the construction of heavy structures, such as grain elevators, over collapsible soils, settlements up to about 1 ft ($\approx$0.3 m) are sometimes allowed (Peck, Hanson, and Thornburn, 1974). In this case, tilting of the foundation is not likely to occur because there is no eccentric loading. The total expected settlement for such structures can be

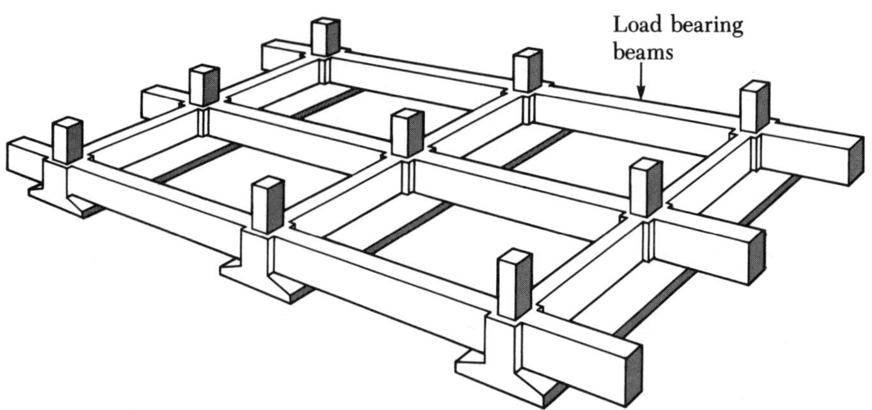

▼ **FIGURE 10.5** Continuous foundation with load-bearing beams (after Clemence and Finbarr, 1981)

estimated from standard consolidation tests on samples at field moisture contents. Without eccentric loading, the foundations will exhibit uniform settlement over loessial deposits; however, if the soil is of residual or colluvial nature, settlement may not be uniform. The reason is the nonuniformity generally encountered in residual soils.

Extreme caution must be used in building heavy structures over collapsible soils. If large settlements are expected, drilled-pier and pile foundations should be considered. These types of foundation can transfer the load to a stronger load-bearing stratum.

10.6 FOUNDATION DESIGN IN SOILS SUSCEPTIBLE TO WETTING

If the upper layer of soil is likely to get wet and collapse at some time after construction of the foundation, several design techniques to avoid foundation failure may be considered.

1. If the expected depth of wetting is about 5 to 6.5 ft ($\approx$1.5 to 2 m) from the ground surface, the soil may be moistened and recompacted by heavy rollers. Spread footings and rafts may be constructed over the compacted soil. An alternative to recompaction by heavy rollers is *heavy tamping*, which is sometimes referred to as *dynamic consolidation* (see Chapter 12). It consists primarily of dropping a heavy weight repeatedly on the ground. The height of the hammer drop can vary from 25 to 100 ft ($\approx$8 to 30 m). The stress waves generated by the hammer drop help in the densification of the soil.
2. If conditions are favorable, foundation trenches can be flooded with solutions of sodium silicate and calcium chloride to stabilize the soil chemically. The soil will behave like a soft sandstone and resist collapse upon saturation. This method is successful only if the solutions can penetrate to the desired depth; thus it is most applicable to fine sand deposits. Silicates are rather costly and are not generally used. However, in some parts of Denver, silicates have been used very successfully.

The injection of a sodium silicate solution for stabilization of collapsible soil deposits has been used extensively in the former Soviet Union and Bulgaria (Houston and Houston, 1989). This process is used for dry collapsible soils and for wet collapsible soils that are likely to compresss under the added weight of the structure to be built and consists of three steps:

Step 1. Injection of carbon dioxide for removal of any water present and preliminary activation of soil

Step 2. Injection of sodium silicate grout

Step 3. Injection of carbon dioxide for neutralization of alkali

3. When the soil layer is susceptible to wetting to a depth of about 10 m, several techniques may be used to cause collapse of the soil *before* foundation construction. Two of these are *vibroflotation* and *ponding* (also called *flooding*). Vibroflotation is used successfully in free-draining soil (see Chapter 12). The procedure of ponding—by constructing low dikes—is utilized at sites that have no impervious layers. However, even after saturation and collapse of the soil by ponding, some additional settlement of the soil may occur after foundation construction. Additional settlement may also be caused by incomplete saturation of the soil at the time of construction. Ponding may be used successfully in the construction of earth dams.
4. If precollapsing of soil is not practical, foundations may be extended beyond the zone of possible wetting, which may require drilled piers and piles. The design of drilled piers and piles must take into consideration the effect of negative skin friction resulting from the collapse of the soil structure and the associated settlement of the zone of subsequent wetting.

In some cases, a *rock column type of foundation* (*vibroreplacement*) may also be considered. Rock columns are built with large boulders that penetrate the potentially collapsible soil layer. They act as piles in transferring the load to a more stable soil layer (also see Chapter 12).

10.7 CASE HISTORIES OF STABILIZATION OF COLLAPSIBLE SOIL

Use of Dynamic Compaction

Lutenegger (1986) reported the use of dynamic compaction to stabilize a thick layer of friable loess before construction of a foundation in Russe, Bulgaria. During field exploration, the water table was not encountered to a depth of 33 ft (10 m), and the natural moisture content was below the plastic limit. Initial density measurements made on undisturbed soil specimens indicated that the moisture content at saturation would exceed the liquid limit, a property usually encountered in collapsible loess.

For dynamic compaction of the soil, the upper 5.6 ft (1.7 m) of crust material was excavated. A circular concrete weight of 15 ton ($\approx$133 kN) was used as a hammer. At each grid point, compaction was achieved by dropping the hammer 7 to 12 times through a vertical distance of 8.2 ft (2.5 m).

Figure 10.6a shows the dry density of the soil before and after compaction. Figure 10.6b shows the increase in standard penetration resistance before and after compaction. The increase in dry density of the soil and standard penetration resistance shows that dynamic compaction can be used effectively to stabilize collapsible soil.

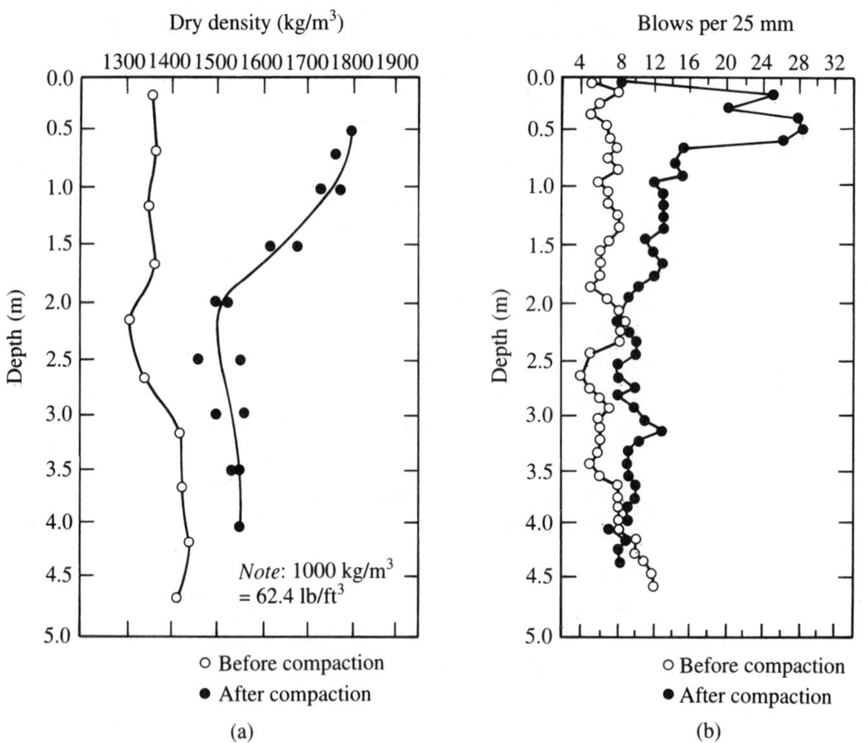

▼ **FIGURE 10.6** (a) Dry density before and after compaction; (b) penetration resistance before and after compaction (after Lutenegger, 1986)

Chemical Stabilization

Semkin et al. (1986) reported on chemical stabilization of a loessial soil deposit with a carbon dioxide, sodium silicate, and carbon dioxide injection scheme (also see Houston and Houston, 1989). The site is that of the Interregional Center in Tashkent, which consists of two buildings—one three stories high with strip foundations and the other one story high with spread foundations. The loessial soil deposit at the site was about 115 ft (35 m) thick, and the water table was at a depth of about 60 ft (18 m). The natural moisture content and porosity of the soil above the water table was 10–25% and 0.48, respectively.

The Interregional Center was constructed in 1973. Unanticipated leakage from conduits in the center caused differential settlement to occur in 1974. Without shutting down the center, chemical stabilization was used effectively, and the differential settlement was stopped.

EXPANSIVE SOILS

10.8 EXPANSIVE SOILS—GENERAL

Many plastic clays swell considerably when water is added to them and then shrink with the loss of water. Foundations constructed on these clays are subjected to large uplifting forces caused by the swelling. These forces will induce heaving, cracking, and breakup of both building foundations and slab-on-grade members. Expansive clays cover large parts of the United States, South America, Africa, Australia, and India. In the United States, these clays are predominant in Texas, Oklahoma, and the upper Missouri Valley. In general, potentially expansive clays have liquid limits and plasticity indices greater than about 40 and 15, respectively.

As noted, an increase in moisture content causes clay to swell. The depth in a soil to which periodic changes of moisture occur is usually referred to as the *active zone*. The depth of the active zone varies, depending on location. Some typical active-zone depths in American cities are given in Table 10.3. In some clays and clay shales in the western United States, the depth of the active zone can be as much as 50 ft ($\approx$15 m). The active-zone depth can be easily determined by plotting the liquidity index against the depth of the soil profile over several seasons. Figure 10.7 shows such a plot for the Beaumont formation in the Houston area.

An example of the effect of seasonal change in the active zone related to shrinking and swelling of an expansive soil deposit is shown in Figure 10.8. It is a typical record of vertical ground movement at an open-field test plot in Regina, Saskatchewan (Canada), for the depths below the ground surface indicated. The seasonal ground movement virtually ceases at a depth of about 10–12 ft (3–4 m).

TABLE 10.3 Typical Active-Zone Depths in Some U.S. Cities[a]

City	Depth of active zone (ft)	Depth of active zone (m)
Houston	5 to 10	1.5 to 3
Dallas	7 to 15	2.1 to 4.6
San Antonio	10 to 20	3 to 9
Denver	10 to 15	3 to 4.6

[a] After O'Neill and Poormoayed (1980)

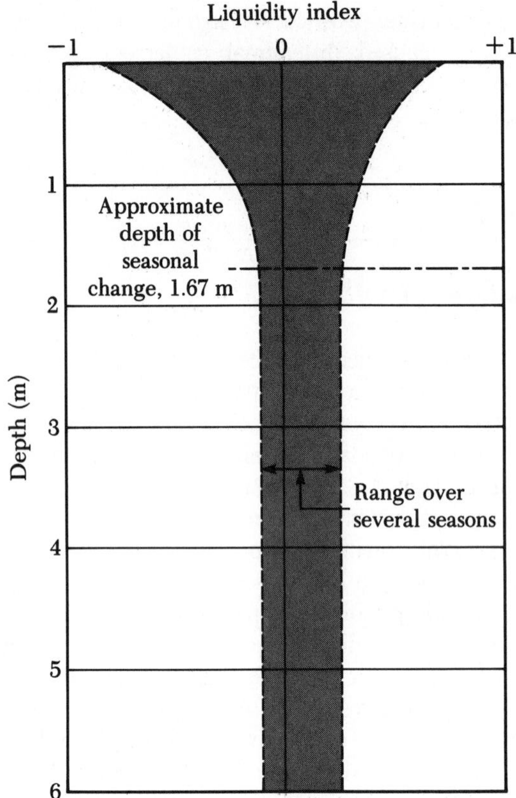

▼ **FIGURE 10.7** Active zone in Houston area—Beaumont formation (after O'Neill and Poormoayed, 1980)

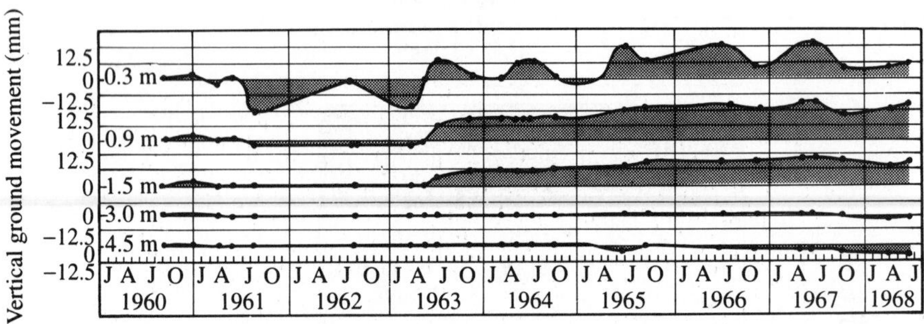

▼ **FIGURE 10.8** Vertical ground movements for an open-field test plot at Regina, Saskatchewan, as measured by Hamilton 1968 (after Sattler and Fredlund, 1991)

10.9 LABORATORY MEASUREMENT OF SWELL

To study the magnitude of possible swell in a clay, simple laboratory oedometer tests can be conducted on undisturbed specimens. Two common tests are the unrestrained swell test and swelling pressure test.

In the *unrestrained swell test*, the specimen is placed in an oedometer under a small surcharge of about 1 lb/in^2 (6.9 kN/m^2). Water is then added to the specimen, and the expansion of the volume of the specimen (i.e., height; the area of cross section is constant) is measured until equilibrium is reached. The percent of free swell may be expressed as a ratio:

$$s_{w(\text{free})}(\%) = \frac{\Delta H}{H}(100) \tag{10.9}$$

where $s_{w(\text{free})}$ = free swell
ΔH = height of swell due to saturation
H = original height of the specimen

Vijayvergiya and Ghazzaly (1973) analyzed various soil test results obtained in this manner and prepared a correlation chart of the free swell, liquid limit, and natural moisture content, as shown in Figure 10.9. O'Neill and Poormoayed (1980) developed a relationship for calculating the free surface swell from this chart:

$$\Delta S_F = 0.0033 Z s_{w(\text{free})} \tag{10.10}$$

where ΔS_F = free surface swell
Z = depth of active zone
$s_{w(\text{free})}$ = free swell, as a percent (Figure 10.9)

More recently, Sivapullaiah et al. (1987) suggested a new test method for obtaining a *modified free swell index* for clays, which appears to give a better indication for the swelling potential of clayey soils. This test begins with an oven-dried soil with a mass of about 10 g. The soil mass is well pulverized and transferred into a 100-ml graduated jar containing distilled water. Aftr 24 hours, the swollen sediment volume is measured. The *modified free swell index* is then calculated:

$$\text{Modified free swell index} = \frac{V - V_s}{V_s} \tag{10.11}$$

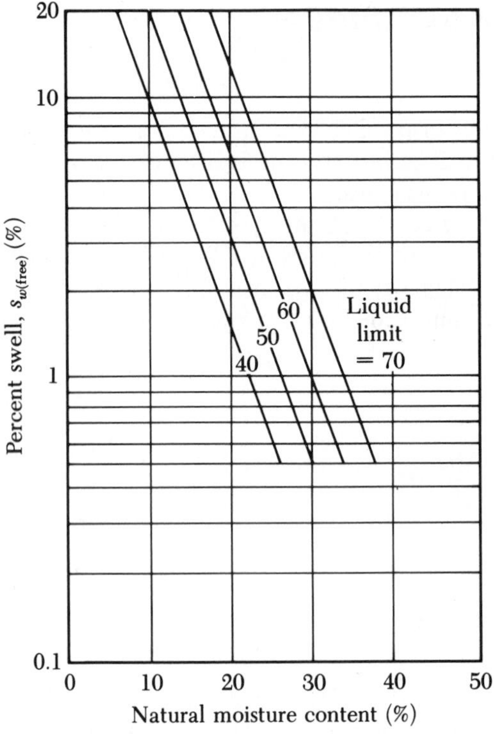

FIGURE 10.9 Relation between percent free swell, liquid limit, and natural moisture content (after Vijayvergiya and Ghazzaly, 1973)

where V = soil volume after swelling

V_s = volume of soil solid = $\dfrac{W_s}{G_s \gamma_w}$

W_s = weight of oven-dried soil

G_s = specific gravity of soil solids

γ_w = unit weight of water

Based on the modified free swell index, the swelling potential of a soil may be qualitatively classified as follows:

Modified free swell index	*Swelling potential*
<2.5	Negligible
2.5 to 10	Moderate
10 to 20	High
>20	Very high

Sikh (1993) reported the results of several free swell tests on undisturbed soil specimens obtained from Southern California. The tests were conducted by subjecting the soil specimens to the *actual effective overburden pressure*. The results of these tests are given in Figure 10.10. The upper bound curve indicates that, for an effective overburden pressure of about 1.4 kip/ft^2 or greater, the vertical free swell [Eq. (10.9)] generally decreases to less than 1%.

The *swelling pressure test* can be conducted by taking a specimen in a consolidation ring and applying a pressure equal to the effective overburden pressure, p_o, plus the approximate anticipated surcharge caused by the foundation, p_s. Water is then added to the specimen. As the specimen starts to swell, pressure is applied in small

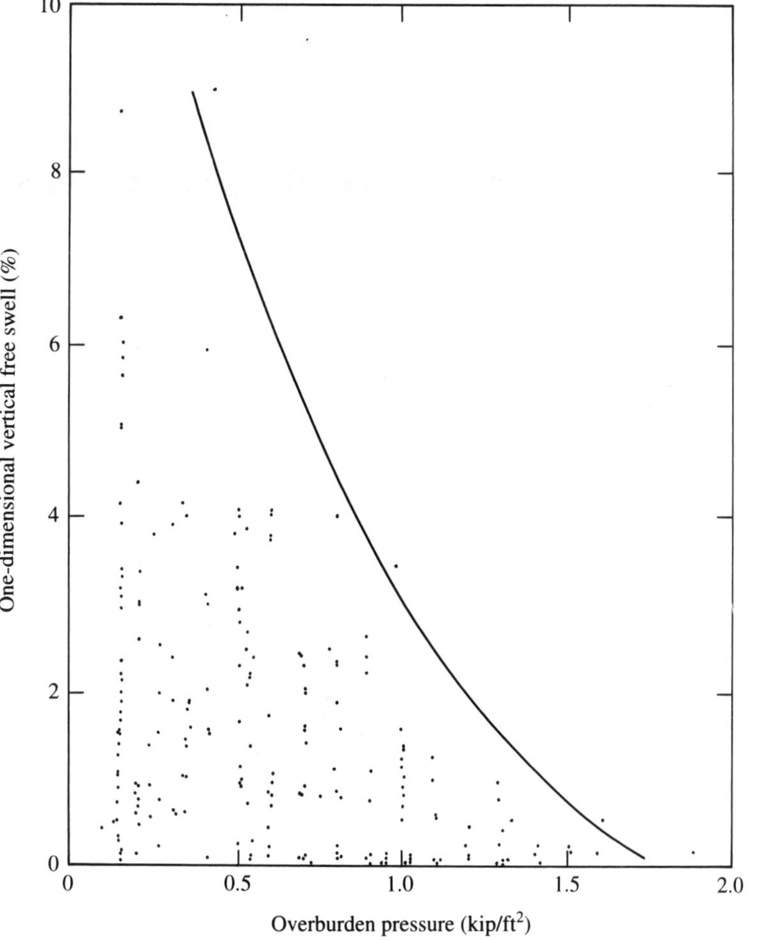

▼ **FIGURE 10.10** One-dimensional vertical free swell of some southern California soils (after Sikh, 1993)

increments to prevent swelling. It is continued until full swelling pressure is developed on the specimen. At that time, the total pressure is

$$p_T = p_o + p_s + p_1 \tag{10.12}$$

where p_T = total pressure to prevent swelling, or zero swell pressure
p_1 = additional pressure added to prevent swelling after addition of water

Figure 10.11 shows the variation of the percentage of swell against pressure during a swelling pressure test. For more information on this type of test, see Sridharan et al. (1986).

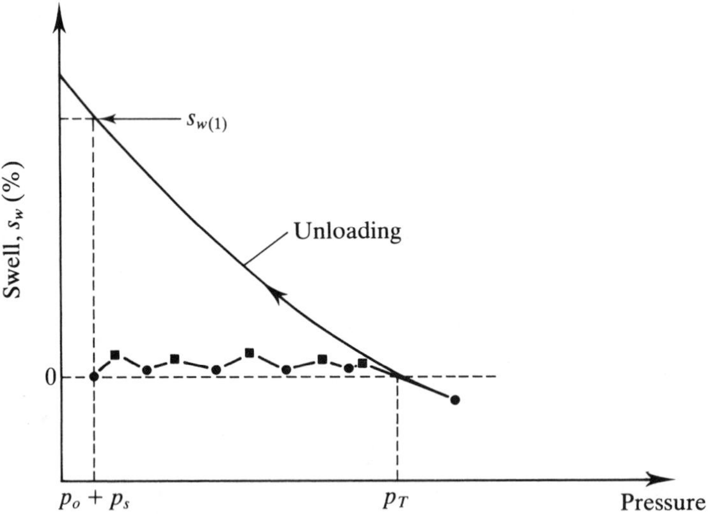

▼ **FIGURE 10.11** Swelling pressure test

A p_T of about 0.4–0.65 kip/ft² (20–30 kN/m²) is considered to be low, and a p_T of 30–40 kip/ft² (1500–2000 kN/m²) is considered to be high. After zero swell pressure is attained, the soil specimen can be unloaded in steps to the level of the overburden pressure, p_o. This unloading process will cause the specimen to swell. The equilibrium swell for each pressure level is also recorded. The variation of the swell, in percent, s_w%, and the applied pressure on the specimen will be like that shown in Figure 10.11.

The *swelling pressure test* can be used to determine the surface heave, ΔS, for a foundation (O'Neill and Poormoayed, 1980) as

$$\Delta S = \sum_{i=1}^{n} [s_{w(1)}\%](H_i)(0.01) \tag{10.13}$$

where $s_{w(1)}\% =$ swell, in percent, for layer i under a pressure of $p_o + p_s$ (see Figure 10.11)

$\Delta H_i =$ thickness of layer i

▼ EXAMPLE 10.1

A soil profile has an active zone of expansive soil of 6 ft. The liquid limit and the average natural moisture content during the construction season are 50% and 20%, respectively. Determine the free surface swell.

Solution From Figure 10.9 for $LL = 50\%$ and $w = 20\%$, $s_{w(\text{free})} = 3\%$. From Eq. (10.10),

$$\Delta S_F = 0.0033 Z s_{w(\text{free})}$$

Hence

$$\Delta S_F = 0.0033(6)(3)(12) = \mathbf{0.71\ in.}$$ ▼

▼ EXAMPLE 10.2

A soil profile's active-zone depth is 3.5 m. If a foundation is to be placed 0.5 m below the ground surface, what would be the estimated total swell? The following data were obtained from laboratory tests.

Depth (in.)	*Swell under overburden and estimated foundation surcharge pressure,* $s_{w(1)}(\%)$
0.5	2
1	1.5
2	0.75
3	0.25

Solution The values of $s_{w(1)}(\%)$ have been plotted with depth in Figure 10.12a. The area of this diagram will be the total swell. The trapezoidal rule provides

$$\Delta S = \frac{1}{100}\left[\frac{1}{2}(1)(0 + 0.5) + \frac{1}{2}(1)(0.5 + 1.1) + \frac{1}{2}(1)(1.1 + 2)\right]$$

$$= 0.026 \text{ m} = \mathbf{26\ mm.}$$ ▼

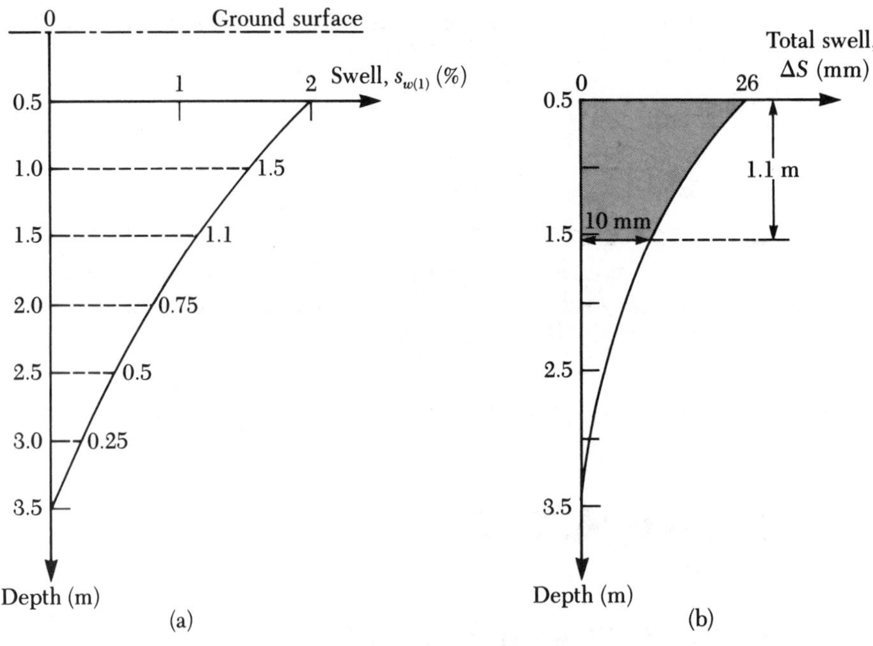

▼ **FIGURE 10.12**

▼ EXAMPLE 10.3

In Example 10.2, if the allowable total swell is 10 mm, what would be the undercut necessary to reduce the total swell?

Solution Using the procedure outlined in Example 10.2, we calculate the total swell at various depths below the foundation from Figure 10.12a as follows:

Depth (m)	*Total swell, ΔS(mm)*
3.5	0
3	$0 + \left[\frac{1}{2}(0.5)(0.25)\right]\frac{1}{100} = 0.000625 \text{ m} = 0.625 \text{ mm}$
2.5	$0.000625 + \frac{1}{100}\left[\frac{1}{2}(0.5)(0.25 + 0.5)\right] = 0.0025 \text{ m} = 2.5 \text{ mm}$
1.5	$0.0025 + \frac{1}{100}\left[\frac{1}{2}(1)(0.5 + 1.1)\right] = 0.0105 \text{ m} = 10.5 \text{ mm}$
0.5	26 mm

Plotted in Figure 10.12b, these total settlements show that a total swell of 10 mm corresponds to a depth of 1.6 m below the ground surface.

▶ Hence the uncercut below the foundation is **1.6 − 0.5 = 1.1 m.**

This soil should be excavated, replaced by nonswelling soil, and recompacted. ▼

10.10 CLASSIFICATION OF EXPANSIVE SOIL BASED ON INDEX TESTS

Classification systems for expansive soils are based on the problems they create in the construction of foundations (potential swell). Most of the classifications contained in the literature are summarized in Table 10.4 and Figure 10.13. However, the classification system developed by U.S. Army Waterways Experiment Station (Snethen et al., 1977) is the one most widely used in the United States. It has also been summarized by O'Neill and Poormoayed (1980); see Table 10.5.

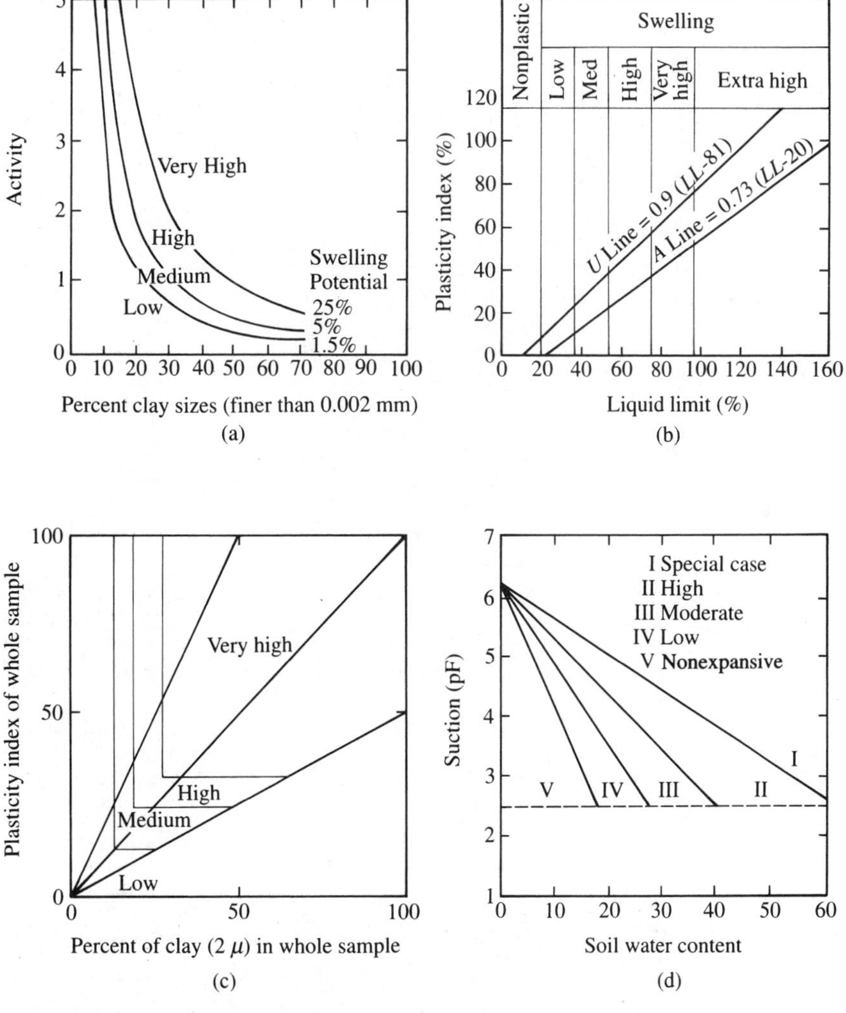

▼ **FIGURE 10.13** Commonly used criteria for determining swell potential (after Abduljauwad and Al-Sulaimani, 1993)

TABLE 10.4 Summary of Some Criteria for Identifying Swell Potential (after Abduljauwad and Al-Sulaimani, 1993)

Reference	Criteria	Remarks
Holtz (1959)	$CC > 28$, $PI > 35$, and $SL < 11$ (very high) $20 \le CC \le 31$, $25 \le PI \le 41$, and $7 \le SL \le 12$ (high) $13 \le CC \le 23$, $15 \le PI \le 28$, and $10 \le SL \le 16$ (medium) $CC \le 15$, $PI \le 18$, and $SL \ge 15$ (low)	Based on *CC*, *PI*, and *SL*
Seed et al. (1962)	See Figure 10.13a	Based on oedometer test using compacted specimen, percentage of clay < 2 μm and activity
Altmeyer (1955)	$LS < 5$, $SL > 12$, and $PS < 0.5$ (noncritical) $5 \le LS \le 8$, $10 \le SL \le 12$, and $0.5 \le PS \le 1.5$ (marginal) $LS > 8$, $SL < 10$, and $PS > 1.5$ (critical)	Based on *LS*, *SL*, and *PS* Remolded sample ($\rho_{d\,max}$ and w_{opt}) Soaked under 6.9 kPa surcharge
Dakshanamanthy and Raman (1973)	See Figure 10.13b	Based on plasticity chart
Raman (1967)	$PI > 32$ and $SI > 40$ (very high) $23 \le PI \le 32$ and $30 \le SI \le 40$ (high) $12 \le PI \le 23$ and $15 \le SI \le 30$ (medium) $PI < 12$ and $SI < 15$ (low)	Based on *PI* and *SI*
Sowers and Sowers (1970)	$SL < 10$ and $PI > 30$ (high) $10 \le SL \le 12$ and $15 \le PI \le 30$ (moderate) $SL > 12$ and $PI < 15$ (low)	Little swell will occur when w_0 results in *LI* of 0.25
Van Der Merwe (1964)	See Figure 10.13c	Based on *PI*, percentage of clay <2 μm, and activity
Uniform Building Code, 1968	$EI > 130$ (very high) and $91 \le EI \le 130$ (high) $51 \le EI \le 90$ (medium) and $21 \le EI \le 50$ (low) $0 \le EI \le 20$ (very low)	Based on oedometer test on compacted specimen with degree of saturation close to 50% and a surcharge of 6.9 kPa
Snethen (1984)	$LL > 60$, $PI > 35$, $\tau_{nat} > 4$, and $SP > 1.5$ (high) $30 \le LL \le 60$, $25 \le PI \le 35$, $1.5 \le \tau_{nat} \le 4$, and $0.5 \le SP \le 1.5$ (medium) $LL < 30$, $PI < 25$, $\tau_{nat} < 1.5$, and $SP < 0.5$ (low)	*PS* is representative for field condition, can be used without τ_{nat}, but accuracy will be reduced
Chen (1988)	$PI \ge 35$ (very high) and $20 \le PI \le 55$ (high) $10 \le PI \le 35$ (medium) and $PI \le 15$ (low)	Based on *PI*
McKeen (1992)	Figure 10.13d	Based on measurements of soft water content, suction, and volume change on drying
Vijayvergiya and Ghazzaly (1973)	$\text{Log } SP = (1/12)(0.44LL - w_0 + 5.5)$	Empirical equations
Nayak and Christensen (1974)	$SP = (0.00229PI)(1.45c)/w_0 + 6.38$	Empirical equations
Weston (1980)	$SP = 0.00411(LL_w)^{4.17} q^{-3.86} w_0^{-2.33}$	Empirical equations

Note: C = clay, %
CC = colloidal content, %
EI = Expansion index = 100 × percent swell × fraction passing No. 4 sieve
LI = liquidity index, %
LL = liquid limit, %
LL_w = weighted liquid limit, %
LS = linear shrinkage, %
PI = plasticity index, %
PS = probable swell, %
q = surcharge
SI = shrinkage index = $LL - SL$, %
SL = shrinkage limit, %
SP = swell potential, %
w_0 = natural soil moisture
w_{opt} = optimum moisture content, %
τ_{nat} = natural soil suction in tsf
$\rho_{d\,max}$ = max dry density

▼ **TABLE 10.5 Expansive Soil Classification System**[a]

Liquid limit	Plasticity index	Potential swell (%)	Potential swell classification
<50	<25	<0.5	Low
50–60	25–35	0.5–1.5	Marginal
>60	>35	>1.5	High

Potential swell = vertical swell under a pressure equal to overburden pressure

[a] Compiled from O'Neill and Poormoayed (1980)

10.11 FOUNDATION CONSIDERATIONS FOR EXPANSIVE SOILS

If a soil has a low swell potential, standard construction practices may be followed. However, if the soil possesses a marginal or high swell potential, precautions need to be taken, which may entail

1. Replacing the expansive soil under the foundation
2. Changing the nature of the expansive soil by compaction control, prewetting, installation of moisture barriers, and/or chemical stabilization
3. Strengthening the structures to withstand heave, constructing structures that are flexible enough to withstand the differential soil heave without failure, or constructing isolated deep foundations below the depth of the active zone

One particular method may not be sufficient in all situations. Combining several techniques may be necessary, and local construction experience should always be considered. Following are details of some of the commonly used techniques of dealing with expansive soils.

Replacement of Expansive Soil

When shallow, moderately expansive soils are present at the surface, they can be removed and replaced by less expansive soils and then compacted properly.

Changing the Nature of Expansive Soil

1. *Compaction:* Heave of expansive soils decreases substantially when the soil is compacted to a lower unit weight on the high side of the optimum moisture content (possibly 3–4% above the optimum moisture content). Even under such conditions, a slab-on-ground type of construction should not be considered where the total probable heave is expected to be about 1.5 in. (38 mm) or more. Figure 10.14a shows the recommended limits of soil compaction in

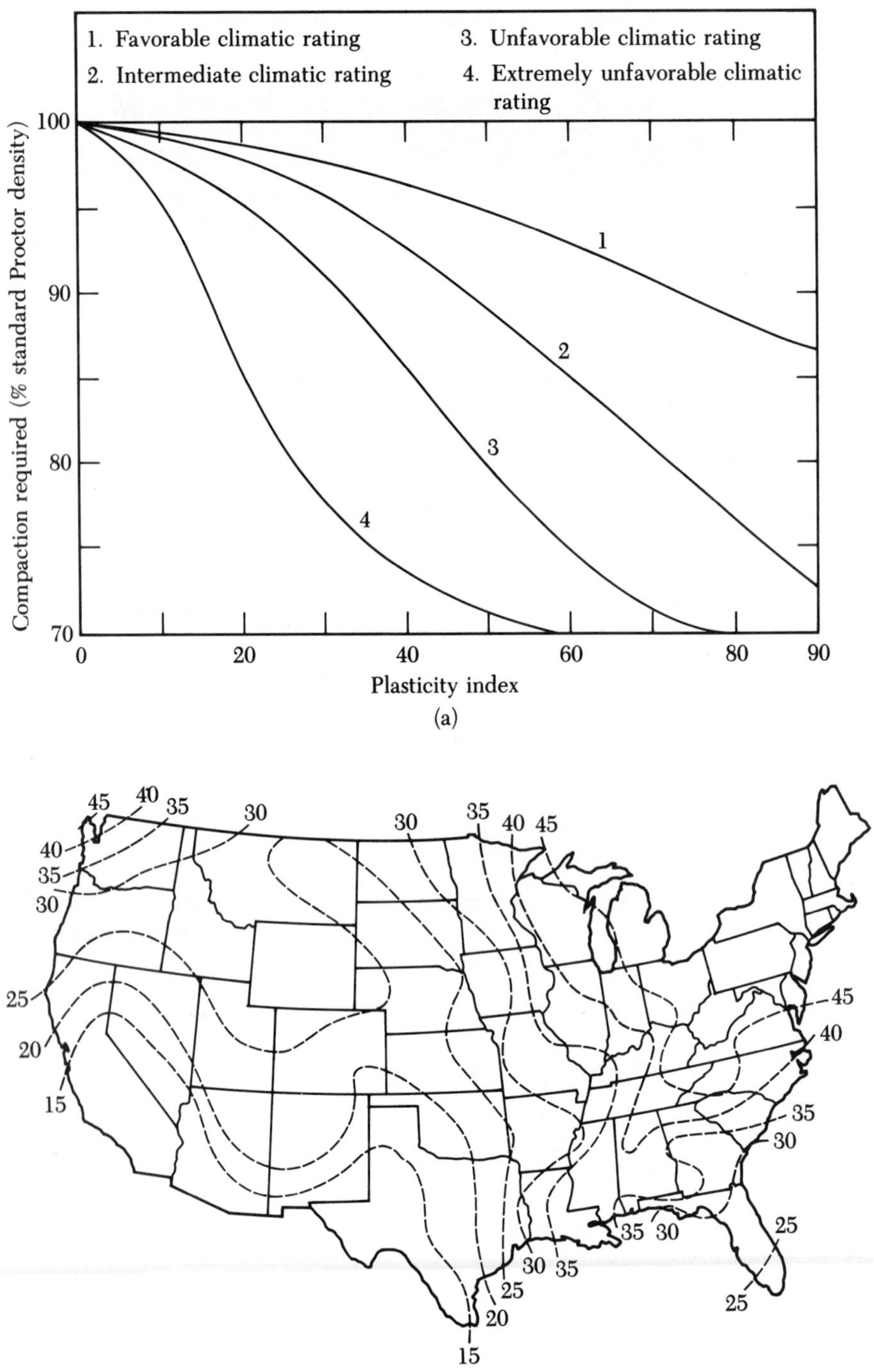

▼ **FIGURE 10.14** (a) Soil compaction requirement based on climatic rating; (b) equivalent climatic rating of the United States (after Gromko, 1974)

the field for reduction of heave. Note that the recommended dry unit weights are based on climatic ratings. According to U.S. Weather Bureau data, a climatic rating of 15 represents an extremely unfavorable climatic condition; a rating of 45 represents a favorable climatic condition. The isobars of climatic rating for the continental United States are shown in Figure 10.14b.

2. *Prewetting:* One technique for increasing the moisture content of the soil is by ponding and hence achieving most of the heave before construction. However, this technique may be time-consuming because the seepage of water through highly plastic clays is slow. After ponding, 4–5% of hydrated lime may be added to the top layer of the soil to make it less plastic and more workable (Gromko, 1974).
3. *Installation of moisture barriers:* The long-term effect of the differential heave can be reduced by controlling the moisture variation in the soil. It is achieved by providing vertical moisture barriers about 5 ft ($\approx$1.5 m) deep around the perimeter of slabs for the slab-on-grade type of construction. These moisture barriers may be constructed in trenches filled with gravel, lean concrete, or impervious membranes.
4. *Stabilization of soil:* Chemical stabilization with the aid of lime and cement has often proved useful. A mix containing about 5% lime is sufficient in most cases. Lime or cement and water are mixed with the top layer of soil and compacted. The addition of lime or cement will decrease the liquid limit, the plasticity index, and the swell characteristics of the soil. This type of stabilization work can be done to a depth of 3–5 ft ($\approx$1–1.5 m). Hydrated high-calcium lime and dolomite lime are generally used for lime stabilization.

Another method of stabilization of expansive soil is the *pressure injection* of lime slurry or lime–fly ash slurry into the soil, usually to a depth of 12–16 ft (4–5 m) and occasionally deeper to cover the active zone. Further details of the pressure injection technique are presented in Chapter 12. Depending on the soil conditions at a site, single or multiple injections can be planned, as shown in Figure 10.15. Figure 10.16 shows the slurry pressure injection work for a building pad. The stakes marked are the planned injection points. Figure 10.17 shows lime–fly ash stabilization by pressure injection of the bank of a canal that had experienced sloughs and slides.

10.12 CONSTRUCTION ON EXPANSIVE SOILS

Care must be exercised in choosing the type of foundation to be used on expansive soils. Table 10.6 shows some recommended construction procedures based on the total predicted heave, ΔS, and the length-to-height ratio of the wall panels.

For example, Table 10.6 proposes the use of waffle slabs as an alternative in designing rigid buildings capable of tolerating movement. Figure 10.18 (page 654) shows a schematic diagram of a waffle slab. In this type of construction, the ribs hold the structural load. The waffle voids allow the expansion of soil.

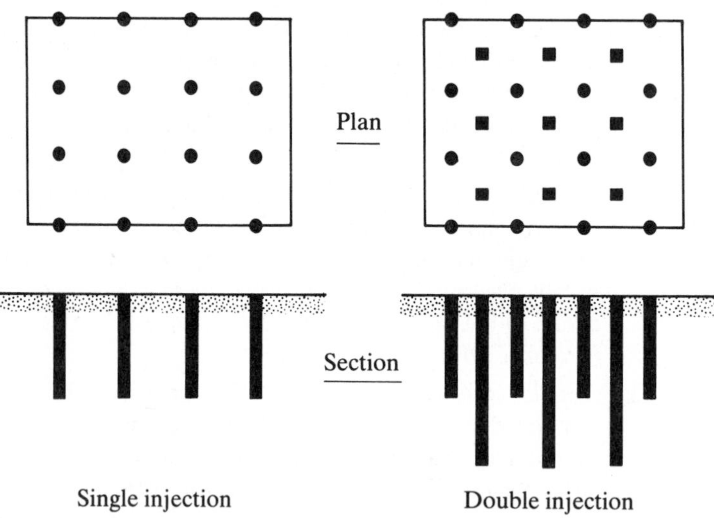

▼ **FIGURE 10.15** Multiple lime slurry injection planning for a building pad

Table 10.6 also suggests the use of foundation piers with a suspended floor slab for the construction of structures independent of movement. Figure 10.19a shows a schematic diagram of such an arrangement. The bottom of the piers should be placed below the active zone of the expansive soil. For the design of the piers, the uplifting force, U, may be estimated (Figure 10.19b) from the equation

$$U = \pi D_s Z p_T \tan \phi_{ps} \tag{10.14}$$

▼ **FIGURE 10.16** Pressure injection of lime slurry for a building pad (Courtesy of GKN Hayward Baker, Inc., Woodbine Division, Ft. Worth, Texas)

▼ TABLE 10.6 Construction Procedures for Expansive Clay Soils[a]

Total predicted heave (mm)				
$L/H = 1.25$	$L/H = 2.5$	Recommended construction	Method	Remarks
0 to 6.35	12.7	No precaution		
6.35 to 12.7	12.7 to 50.8	Rigid building tolerating movement (steel reinforcement as necessary)	*Foundations:* Pads, Strip footings, Raft (waffle)	Footings should be small and deep, consistent with the soil-bearing capacity. Rafts should resist bending.
			Floor slabs: Waffle, Tile	Slabs should be designed to resist bending and should be independent of grade beams.
			Walls:	Walls on a raft should be as flexible as the raft. No rigid connections vertically. Brick works should be strengthened with tie bars or bands.
12.7 to 50.8	50.8 to 101.6	Building damping movement	*Joints:* Clear, Flexible	Contacts between structural units should be avoided; or flexible, waterproof material may be inserted in the joints.
			Walls: Flexible, Unit construction, Steel frame	Walls or rectangular building units should heave as a unit.
			Foundations: Three point, Cellular, Jacks	Cellular foundations allow slight soil expansion to reduce swelling pressure. Adjustable jacks can be inconvenient to owners. Three-point loading allows motion without duress.
>50.8	>101.6	Building independent of movement	*Foundation piers:* Straight shaft, Bell bottom	Smallest-diameter and widely spaced piers compatible with load should be placed. Clearance should be allowed under grade beams.
			Suspended floor:	Floor should be suspended on grade beams 12 to 18 in. above the soil.

[a] After Gromko, 1974

▼ **FIGURE 10.17** Slope stabilization of a canal bank by pressure injection of lime–fly ash slurry (Courtesy of GKN Hayward Baker, Inc., Woodbine Division, Ft. Worth, Texas)

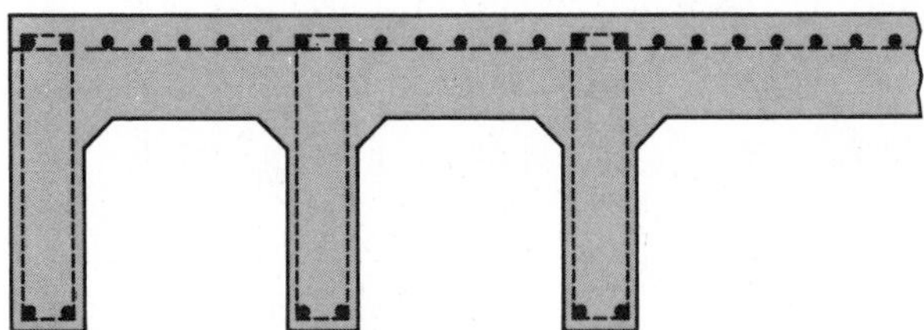

▼ **FIGURE 10.18** Waffle slab

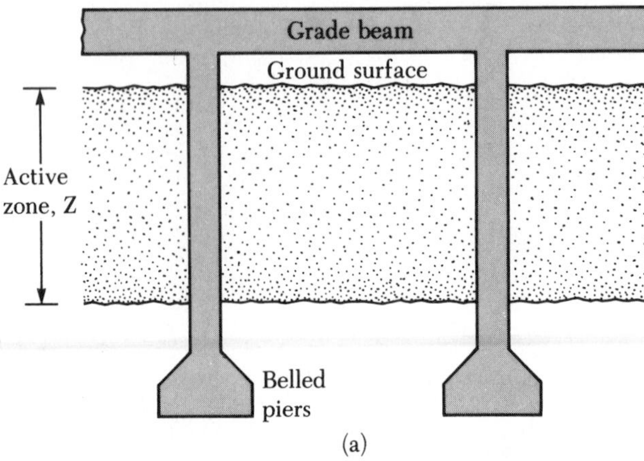

▼ **FIGURE 10.19** (a) Construction of belled piers and grade beam; (b) definition of parameters in Eq. (10.14)

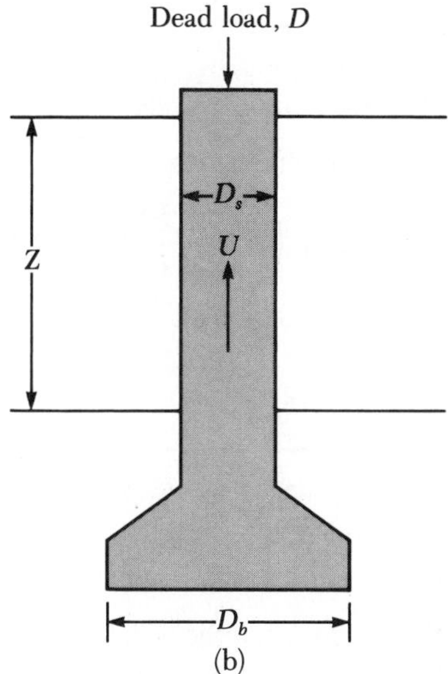

▼ **FIGURE 10.19** (Continued)

where D_s = diameter of the shaft of the pier
Z = depth of the active zone
ϕ_{ps} = effective angle of plinth–soil friction
p_T = pressure for zero horizontal swell (see Figure 10.11; $p_T = p_o + p_s + p_1$)

In most cases, the value of ϕ_{ps} varies between 10° and 20°. An average value of the zero horizontal swell pressure must be determined in the laboratory. In the absence of laboratory results, $p_T \tan \phi_{ps}$ may be considered equal to the undrained shear strength of clay, c_u, in the active zone.

The belled portion of the drilled pier will act as an anchor to resist the uplifting force. Ignoring the weight of the pier

$$Q_{net} = U - D \tag{10.15}$$

where Q_{net} = net uplift load
D = dead load

Now

$$Q_{net} \approx \frac{c_u N_c}{FS}\left(\frac{\pi}{4}\right)(D_b^2 - D_s^2) \tag{10.16}$$

where c_u = undrained cohesion of the clay in which the bell of the pier is located

Combining Eqs. (10.15) and (10.16) gives

$$U - D = \frac{c_u N_c}{FS}\left(\frac{\pi}{4}\right)(D_b^2 - D_s^2) \tag{10.17}$$

where N_c = bearing capacity factor
FS = factor of safety
D_b = diameter of the bell of the pier

Conservatively, N_c (Tables 3.4 and 3.5) is

$$N_c \approx N_{c(\text{strip})} F_{cs} = N_{c(\text{strip})}\left(1 + \frac{N_q B}{N_c L}\right) \approx 5.14\left(1 + \frac{1}{5.14}\right) = 6.14$$

An example of a drilled-pier design is given in Example 10.4.

▼ EXAMPLE 10.4

Figure 10.20 shows a drilled pier. The depth of the active zone is 15 ft. The zero swell pressure of the swelling clay (p_T) is 70 lb/in^2. For the pier the dead load is 135 kip and the live load is 68 kip.

a. Determine the diameter of the bell, D_b.
b. Determine the reinforcement required for the pier shaft.
c. Check the bearing capacity of the pier assuming zero uplift force.

Solution

Part a: Determining the Bell Diameter, D_b

The uplift force, Eq. (10.14), is

$$U = \pi D_s Z p_T \tan \phi_{ps}$$

Assume that $\phi_{ps} \approx 12°$, $Z = 15$ ft, and $p_T = 70$ lb/in^2. Then

$$U = \pi(2.5 \times 12)(15 \times 12)(70) \tan 12° = 252{,}416 \text{ lb} \approx 252.2 \text{ kip}$$

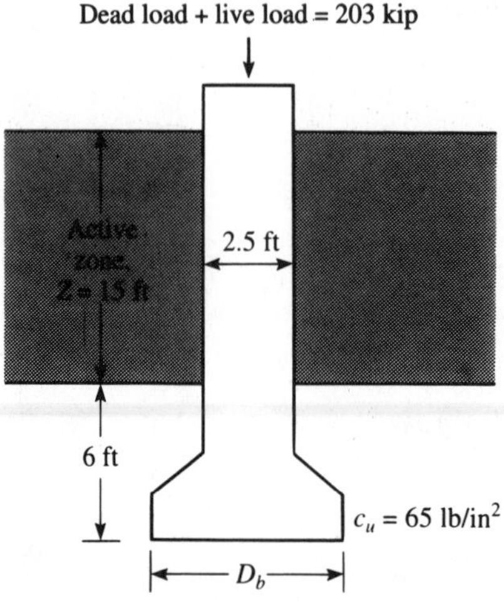

▼ **FIGURE 10.20**

Assume the dead load and live load to be zero, and FS in Eq. (10.17) to be 1.25. So, from Eq. (10.17),

$$U = \frac{c_u N_c}{FS}\left(\frac{\pi}{4}\right)(D_b^2 - D_s^2)$$

$$252.5 = \frac{\left(\dfrac{65}{1000}\right)(6.14)}{1.25}\left(\frac{\pi}{4}\right)(D_b^2 - 30^2)$$

$$D_b = 43.67 \text{ in.; use } \mathbf{45\ in.}$$

The factor of safety against uplift with the dead load also should be checked. A factor of safety of at least 3 is desirable. So, from Eq. (10.17),

$$FS = \frac{c_u N_c\left(\dfrac{\pi}{4}\right)(D_b^2 - D_s^2)}{U - D} = \frac{\left(\dfrac{65}{1000}\right)(6.14)\left(\dfrac{\pi}{4}\right)(45^2 - 30^2)}{135 - 68} = \mathbf{5.26 > 3\text{—}OK}$$

Part b: Reinforcement

Reinforcement should be provided for the total uplift load, or 252.5 kip (assuming that dead load and live load are zero). So the area of steel required is

$$A_s = \frac{U}{\left(\dfrac{\text{yield stress of steel}}{\text{factor of safety}}\right)}$$

An adequate FS is 1.25, and the yield stress of steel $\approx$ 40,000 lb/in². Hence

$$A_s = \frac{(252.5)(1.25)}{40} = 7.9 \text{ in}^2$$

Part c: Check for Bearing Capacity

Assume that $U = 0$. Then

$$\text{Dead load + live load} = 135 + 68 = 203 \text{ kip}$$

$$\text{Downward load per unit area} = \frac{203}{(\pi/4)(D_b^2)} = \frac{203}{(\pi/4)(45^2)}$$

$$= 0.128 \text{ kip/in}^2 = 128 \text{ lb/in}^2$$

$$\text{Net bearing capacity of the soil under the bell} = q_u = c_u N_c = (65)(6.14)$$

$$= 399 \text{ lb/in}^2$$

Hence the factor of safety against bearing capacity failure is $= \dfrac{399}{128} = \mathbf{3.12 > 3\text{—}OK}$

▼

SANITARY LANDFILLS

10.13 SANITARY LANDFILLS—GENERAL

Sanitary landfills provide a way to dispose of refuse on land without endangering public health. Sanitary landfills are used in almost all countries, with varying degrees of success. The refuse disposed of in sanitary landfills may contain organic, wood, paper, and fibrous wastes or demolition wastes such as bricks and stones. The refuse is dumped and compacted at frequent intervals and then covered with a layer of soil, as shown in Figure 10.21. In the compacted state, the average unit weight of the refuse may vary between 32–64 lb/ft^3 (5–10 kN/m^3). A typical city in the United States, with a population of one million, generates about 135×10^6 ft^3 ($\approx 3.8 \times 10^6$ m^3) of compacted landfill material per year.

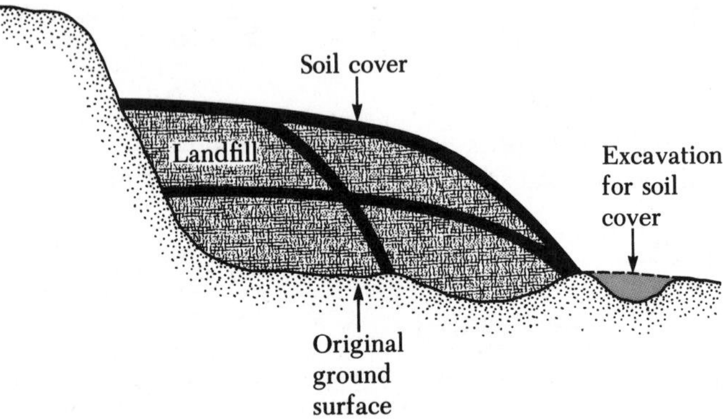

▼ **FIGURE 10.21** Schematic diagram of sanitary landfill in progress

As property values continue to increase in densely populated areas, constructing structures over sanitary landfills becomes more and more tempting. In some instances, a visual site inspection may not be enough to detect an old sanitary landfill. However, construction of foundations over sanitary landfills is generally problematic because of poisonous gases (e.g., methane); excessive settlement, and low inherent bearing capacity.

10.14 SETTLEMENT OF SANITARY LANDFILLS

Sanitary landfills undergo large continuous settlements over a long period of time. Yen and Scanlon (1975) documented the settlement of several landfill sites in California. The settlement rate after completion of the landfill (Figure 10.22) may be expressed as

$$m = \frac{\Delta H_f}{\Delta t} \tag{10.18}$$

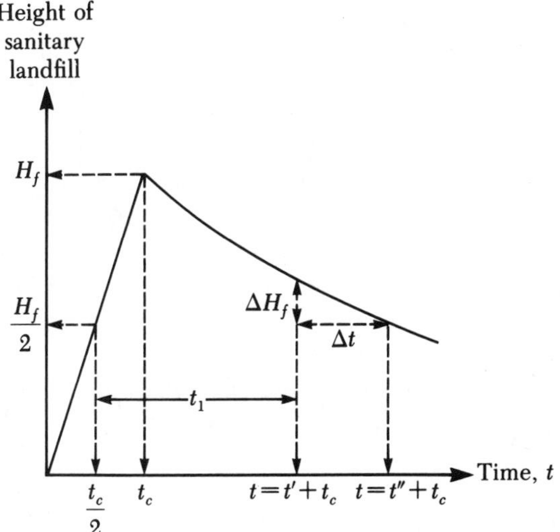

▼ **FIGURE 10.22** Settlement of sanitary landfills

where m = settlement rate
H_f = maximum height of the sanitary landfill

Based on several field observations, Yen and Scanlon (1975) determined the following empirical correlations for the settlement rate:

$$m = 0.0268 - 0.0116 \log t_1 \quad \text{(for fill heights ranging from 12–24 m)} \tag{10.19}$$

$$m = 0.038 - 0.0155 \log t_1 \quad \text{(for fill heights ranging from 24–30 m)} \tag{10.20}$$

$$m = 0.0433 - 0.0183 \log t_1 \quad \text{(for fill heights greater than 30 m)} \tag{10.21}$$

where m is in m/mo.
t_1 is the median fill age, in months

The medium fill age may be defined from Figure 10.22 as follows:

$$t_1 = t - \frac{t_c}{2} \tag{10.22}$$

where t = time from the beginning of landfill
t_c = time for completion of the landfill

Equations (10.19), (10.20), and (10.21) were based on field data from landfills for which t_c varied from 70 to 82 months. To get an idea of the approximate length of time required for a sanitary landfill to undergo complete settlement, consider Eq. (10.19). For a fill 12 m high and t_c = 72 months,

$$m = 0.0268 - 0.0116 \log t_1$$

$$\log t_1 = \frac{0.0268 - m}{0.0116}$$

If $m = 0$ (zero settlement rate), $\log t_1 = 2.31$, or $t_1 \approx 200$ months. Thus settlement will continue for $t_1 - t_c/2 = 200 - 36 = 164$ months (≈ 14 years) after completion of the fill—a fairly long time. This calculation emphasizes the need to pay close attention to the settlement of foundations constructed on sanitary landfills.

A comparison of Eqs. (10.19) to (10.21) for rates of settlement shows that the value of m increases with the height of the fill. However, for fill heights greater than about 30 m, the rate of settlement should not be much different from that obtained from Eq. (10.21). The reason is that decomposition of organic matter close to the surface is mainly the result of an anaerobic environment. For deeper fills, the decomposition is slower. Hence, for fill heights greater than about 30 m, the rate of settlement does not exceed those for fills that are about 30 m in height.

Sowers (1973) also proposed a relation for calculation of the settlement of a sanitary landfill:

$$\boxed{\Delta H = \frac{\alpha H_f}{1 + e} \log\left(\frac{t''}{t'}\right)} \tag{10.23}$$

where H_f = height of the fill
e = void ratio
α = a coefficient for settlement
t'', t' = times (see Figure 10.22)
ΔH = settlement between times t' and t''

The coefficients α fall between

$$\alpha = 0.09e \qquad \text{(for conditions favorable to decomposition)} \tag{10.24}$$

and

$$\alpha = 0.03e \qquad \text{(for conditions unfavorable to decomposition)} \tag{10.25}$$

Equation (10.23) is similar to the equation for secondary consolidation settlement.

10.15 BEARING CAPACITY OF FOUNDATIONS ON SANITARY LANDFILLS

Shallow foundations constructed on sanitary landfills with a compacted soil cover may fail in two ways: by punching shear or by rotational shear, as shown in Figure 10.23. Punching shear failure (Figure 10.23a) occurs when the width of the foundation, B, is relatively small compared to the thickness of the soil cover, D_C. However, when the thickness of the soil cover is relatively small compared to the foundation width and when the strength of the soil cover is low, rotational shear failure may occur (Figure 10.23b). The allowable bearing capacity of shallow foundations for light residential or

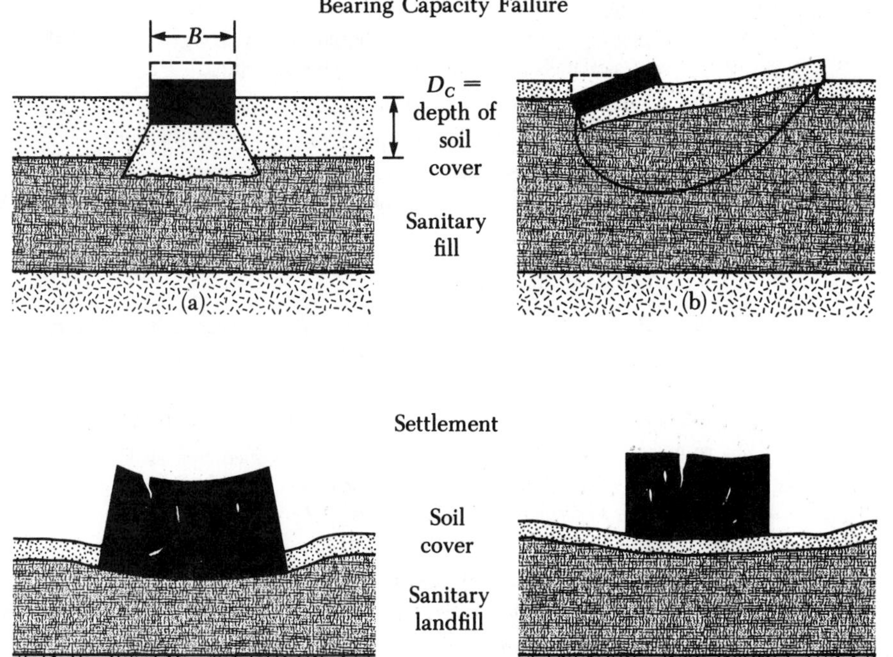

▼ **FIGURE 10.23** Nature of bearing capacity failure and settlement of shallow foundations on sanitary landfills (redrawn after Sowers, 1968)

office buildings over sanitary landfills should not be greater than about 400–800 lb/ft^2 ($\approx$20–40 kN/m^2).

Sometimes the allowable bearing capacity of shallow foundations can be increased by increasing the thickness of the compacted soil cover so that $D_C \geq 1.5\text{–}2B$. Note, however, that this excess weight of the fill and the compaction process may eventually increase the ultimate settlement of the structure.

When the fill is relatively homogeneous and light structures are constructed over it, the settlement pattern will be somewhat like that in Figure 10.23c. However, when the fill is nonhomogeneous with irregular hard zones, such as boulders, the settlement is nonuniform, as shown in Figure 10.23d. Serious damage to structures is usually caused by this type of settlement.

In several instances, the use of continuous foundations (such as that shown in Figure 10.5) may help reduce differential settlement. If the estimated settlement of a structure is not tolerable, or if heavier structures are to be built, pile or drilled-pier foundations are valid alternatives. In this case, noncorroding materials will have to be used because sanitary landfills with moisture may corrode metal piles and damage concrete. If pile or pier foundations are used, the floor slab should be poured independently of the grade beams to avoid cracking from differential settlement; otherwise, a structural slab will be necessary.

PROBLEMS

10.1 Refer to Figure 10.2, which is based on Eq. (10.5) and $G_s = 2.65$. Draw a similar curve, plotting γ_d (in lb/ft^3) against liquid limit with $G_s = 2.69$, and show the zone in which the loessial soils are likely to collapse on saturation.

10.2 A natural loessial soil deposit has a dry unit weight of 90 lb/ft^3, the liquid limit of the soil is 31, and $G_s = 2.64$. Is collapse likely to occur in this soil?

10.3 A collapsible soil layer is 10 ft thick. The average effective overburden pressure on the soil layer is 1200 lb/ft^2. An undisturbed specimen of this soil was subjected to a double oedometer test (refer to Figure 10.3). The preconsolidation pressure of the specimen as determined from the soaked specimen was 1800 lb/ft^2. Is this soil normally consolidated or preconsolidated?

10.4 An expansive soil has an active-zone thickness of 8 m. The natural moisture content of the soil is 20%, and its liquid limit is 50. Calculate the free surface swell of the expansive soil upon saturation.

10.5 Repeat Problem 10.4 for a liquid limit of the soil of 55. All other quantities are the same.

10.6 The following are the results of a modified free swell index test: mass of dry soil = 10 grams, $G_s = 2.71$, and volume of swollen sediment after 24 hours in water = 26.3 cm^3.

a. Determine the modified free swell index.

b. Describe the swell potential.

10.7 An expansive soil profile has an active-zone thickness of 5.2 m. A shallow foundation is to be constructed 1.2 m below the ground surface. A swelling pressure test provided the following data.

Depth below ground surface (m)	*Swell under overburden and estimated foundation surcharge pressure, $s_{w(1)}$(%)*
1.2	3.0
2.2	2.0
3.2	1.2
4.2	0.55
5.2	0.0

Estimate the total possible swell under the foundation.

10.8 Repeat Problem 10.7 for an active zone thickness of 25 ft, a shallow foundation depth of 2.5 ft, and the following data.

Depth below ground surface (ft)	*Swell under overburden and estimated foundation surcharge pressure, $s_{w(1)}$(%)*
2.5	4.7
5.0	3.85
10.0	2.45
15.0	1.3
20.0	0.4
25.0	0.0

10.9 Refer to Problem 10.7. If the allowable total swell is 15 mm, what would be the necessary undercut?

10.10 Refer to Problem 10.8. If the allowable total swell is 1.0 in., what would be the necessary undercut?

10.11 Refer to Figure 10.19b. For the drilled pier, the thickness of the active zone, $Z = 25$ ft, dead load = 250 kip, live load = 60 kip, diameter of pier shaft, $D_s = 3.5$ ft, zero swell pressure for the clay in the active zone = 6 ton/ft^2, average angle of plinth–soil friction, $\phi_{ps} = 15°$, and average undrained cohesion of the clay around the bell = 3020 lb/ft^2. Determine the diameter of the pier bell, D_b. A factor of safety of 2 against uplift is required, and the dead load plus live load is zero.

10.12 Refer to Problem 10.11. If an additional requirement is that the factor of safety against uplift be at least 3 with the dead load on (live-load = 0), what should be the diameter of the bell?

REFERENCES

Abduljauwad, S. N., and Al-Sulaimani, G. J. (1993). "Determination of Swell Potential of Al-Qatif Clay," *Geotechical Testing Journal*, American Society for Testing and Materials, Vol. 16, No. 4, pp. 469–484.

Altmeyer, W. T. (1955). "Discussion of Engineering Properties of Expansive Clays," *Journal of the Soil Mechanics and Foundations Division*, American Society of Civil Engineers, Vol. 81, No. SM2, pp. 17–19.

Benites, L. A. (1968). "Geotechnical Properties of the Soils Affected by Piping Near the Benson Area, Cochise County, Arizona," M.S. Thesis, University of Arizona, Tucson.

Chen, F. H. (1988). *Foundations on Expansive Soils*, Elsevier, Amsterdam.

Clemence, S. P., and Finbarr, A. O. (1981). "Design Considerations for Collapsible Soils," *Journal of the Geotechnical Engineering Division*, American Society of Civil Engineers, Vol. 107, No. GT3, pp. 305–317.

Clevenger, W. (1958). "Experience with Loess as Foundation Material," *Transactions*, American Society of Civil Engineers, Vol. 123, pp. 151–170.

Dakshanamanthy, V., and Raman, V. (1973). "A Simple Method of Identifying an Expansive Soil," *Soils and Foundations*, Vol. 13, No. 1, pp. 97–104.

Denisov, N. Y. (1951). *The Engineering Properties of Loess and Loess Loams*, Gosstroiizdat, Moscow.

Feda, J. (1964). "Colloidal Activity, Shrinking and Swelling of Some Clays," *Proceedings*, Soil Mechanics Seminar, Loda, Illinois, pp. 531–546.

Gibbs, H. J. (1961). "Properties Which Divide Loose and Dense Uncemented Soils," *Earth Laboratory Report EM-658*, Bureau of Reclamation, U.S. Department of the Interior, Washington, D.C.

Gromko, G. J. (1974). "Review of Expansive Soils," *Journal of the Geotechnical Engineering Division*, American Society of Civil Engineers, Vol. 100, No. GT6, pp. 667–687.

Hamilton, J. J. (1968). "Effect of Natural and Man-Made Environments on the Performance of Shallow Foundations," *Proceedings*, Twenty-First Annual Canadian Soil Mechanics Conference, Winnipeg, Manitoba.

Handy, R. L. (1973). "Collapsible Loess in Iowa," *Proceedings*, Soil Science Society of America, Vol. 37, pp. 281–284.

Holtz, W. G. (1959). "Expansive Clays—Properties and Problems," *Journal of the Colorado School of Mines*, Vol. 54, No. 4, pp. 89–125.

Holtz, W. G., and Hilf, J. W. (1961). "Settlement of Soil Foundations Due to Saturation," *Proceedings*, Fifth International Conference on Soil Mechanics and Foundation Engineering, Paris, Vol. 1, 1961, pp. 673–679.

Houston, W. N., and Houston, S. L. (1989). "State-of-the-Practice Mitigation Measures for Collapsible Soil Sites," *Proceedings*, Foundation Engineering: Current Principles and Practices, American Society of Civil Engineers, Vol. 1, pp. 161–175.

Jennings, J. E., and Knight, K. (1975). "A Guide to Construction on or with Materials Exhibiting Additional Settlements Due to 'Collapse' of Grain Structure," *Proceedings*, Sixth Regional Conference for Africa on Soil Mechanics and Foundation Engineering, Johannesburg, pp. 99–105.

Lutenegger, A. J. (1986). "Dynamic Compaction in Friable Loess," *Journal of Geotechnical Engineering*, American Society of Civil Engineers, Vol. 112, No. GT6, pp. 663–667.

Lutenegger, A. J., and Saber, R. T. (1988). "Determination of Collapse Potential of Soils," *Geotechnical Testing Journal*, American Society for Testing and Materials, Vol. 11, No. 3, pp. 173–178.

McKeen, R. G. (1992). "A Model for Predicting Expansive Soil Behavior," *Proceedings*, Seventh International Conference on Expansive Soils, Dallas, Vol. 1, pp. 1–6.

Nayak, N. V., and Christensen, R. W. (1974). "Swell Characteristics of Compacted Expansive Soils," *Clay and Clay Minerals*, Vol. 19, pp. 251–261.

O'Neill, M. W., and Poormoayed, N. (1980). "Methodology for Foundations on Expansive Clays," *Journal of the Geotechnical Engineering Division*, American Society of Civil Engineers, Vol. 106, No. GT12, p. 1345–1367.

Peck, R. B., Hanson, W. E., and Thornburn, T. B. (1974). *Foundation Engineering*, Wiley, New York.

Priklonski, V. A. (1952). *Gruntovedenia-Vtoraid Chast*, Gosgeolzdat, Moscow.

Raman, V. (1967). "Identification of Expansive Soils from the Plasticity Index and the Shrinkage Index Data," *The Indian Engineer*, Vol. 11, No. 1, pp. 17–22.

Sattler, P. J., and Fredlund, D. G. (1991). "Modelling Vertical Ground Movements Using Surface Climate Flux," *Proceedings*, Geotechnical Engineering Congress, American Society of Civil Engineers, Vol. II, pp. 1292–1306.

Seed, H. B., Woodward, R. J., Jr., and Lundgren, R. (1962). "Prediction of Swelling Potential for Compacted Clays," *Journal of the Soil Mechanics and Foundations Division*, American Society of Civil Engineers, Vol. 88, No. SM3, pp. 53–87.

Semkin, V. V., Ermoshin, V. M., and Okishev, N. D. (1986). "Chemical Stabilization of Loess Soils in Uzbekistan," *Soil Mechanics and Foundation Engineering* (trans. from Russian), Vol. 23, No. 5, pp. 196–199.

Sikh, T. S. (1993). "Swell Potential Versus Overburden Pressure," *Geotechnical Testing Journal*, American Society for Testing and Materials, Vol. 16, No. 3, pp. 393–396.

Sivapullaiah, P. V., Sitharam, T. G., and Rao, K. S. S. (1987). "Modified Free Swell Index for Clay," *Geotechnical Testing Journal*, American Society for Testing and Materials, Vol. 11, No. 2, pp. 80–85.

Snethen, D. R. (1984). "Evaluation of Expedient Methods for Identification and Classification of Potentially Expansive Soils," *Proceedings*, Fifth International Conference on Expansive Soils, Adelaide, Australia, pp. 22–26.

Snethen, D. R., Johnson, L. D., and Patrick, D. M. (1977). "An Evaluation of Expedient Methodology for Indentification of Potentially Expansive Soils," *Report No. FHWA-RD-77-94*, U.S. Army Engineers Waterways Experiment Station, Vicksburg, Miss.

Sowers, G. B., and Sowers, G. F. (1970). *Introductory Soil Mechanics and Foundations*, 3rd ed. Macmillan, New York.

Sowers, G. F. (1968). "Foundation Problems in Sanitary Landfills," *Journal of the Sanitary Engineering Division*, American Society of Civil Engineers, Vol. 94, No. SA1, pp. 103–116.

Sowers, G. F. (1973). "Settlement of Waste Disposal Fills," *Proceedings*, Eighth International Conference on Soil Mechanics and Foundation Engineering, Moscow, pp. 207–210.

Sridharan, A., Rao, A. S., and Sivapullaiah, P. V. (1986). "Swelling Pressure of Clays," *Geotechnical Testing Journal*, American Society for Testing and Materials, Vol. 9, No. 1, pp. 24–33.

Uniform Building Code (1968). *UBC Standard No. 29-2.*

Van Der Merwe, D. H. (1964). "The Prediction of Heave from the Plasticity Index and Percentage Clay Fraction of Soils," *Civil Engineer in South Africa*, Vol. 6, No. 6, pp. 103–106.

Vijayvergiya, V. N., and Ghazzaly, O. I. (1973). "Prediction of Swelling Potential of Natural Clays," *Proceedings*, Third International Research and Engineering Conference on Expansive Clays, pp. 227–234.

Weston, D. J. (1980). "Expansive Roadbed Treatment for Southern Africa," *Proceedings*, Fourth International Conference on Expansive Soils, Vol. 1, pp. 339–360.

Yen, B. C., and Scanlon, B. (1975). "Sanitary Landfill Settlement Rates," *Journal of the Geotechnical Engineering Division*, American Society of Civil Engineers, Vol. 101, No. GT5, pp. 475–487.

CHAPTER ELEVEN

REINFORCED EARTH STRUCTURES

11.1 INTRODUCTION

The use of reinforced earth is a recent development in the design and construction of foundations and earth-retaining structures. *Reinforced earth* is a construction material comprising soil that has been strengthened by tensile elements such as metal rods and/or strips, nonbiodegradable fabrics (geotextiles), geogrids, and the like. The fundamental idea of reinforcing soil is not new; in fact, it goes back to biblical times. However, the present concept of systematic analysis and design was developed by a French engineer, H. Vidal (1966). The French Road Research Laboratory has done extensive research on the applicability and the beneficial effects of the use of reinforced earth as a construction material. This research has been documented in detail by Darbin (1970), Schlosser and Long (1974), and Schlosser and Vidal (1969). The tests conducted involved the use of metallic strips as reinforcing material.

Retaining walls with reinforced earth have been constructed around the world since Vidal began his work. The first reinforced earth retaining wall with metal strips as reinforcement in the United States was constructed in 1972 in southern California.

The beneficial effects of soil reinforcement derive from (a) the soil's increased tensile strength and (b) the shear resistance developed from the friction at the soil–reinforcement interfaces. Such reinforcement is comparable to that of concrete structures. Currently, most reinforced earth design is done with *free-draining granular soil only*. Thus the effect of pore water development in cohesive soils, which, in turn, reduces the shear strength of the soil, is avoided.

11.2 GENERAL CONSIDERATIONS FOR SOIL REINFORCEMENT

Metal Strips

In most instances, galvanized steel strips are used as reinforcement in soil. However, galvanized steel is subject to corrosion. The rate of corrosion depends on several environmental factors. Binquet and Lee (1975b) suggested that the average rate of corrosion of galvanized steel strips varies between 0.025 and 0.050 mm/yr. So, in the actual design of reinforcement, allowance must be made for the rate of corrosion. Thus

$$t_c = t_{\text{design}} + r \text{ (life span of structure)}$$

where t_c = actual thickness of reinforcing strips to be used in construction
t_{design} = thickness of strips determined from design calculations
r = rate of corrosion

Further research needs to be done on corrosion-resistant materials such as fiberglass before they can be used as reinforcing strips.

Nonbiodegradable Fabrics

Nonbiodegradable fabrics are generally referred to as *geotextiles*. Since 1970, the use of geotextiles in construction has increased tremendously around the world. The fabrics are usually made from petroleum products—polyester, polyethylene, and polypropylene. They may also be made from fiberglass. Geotextiles are not prepared from natural fabrics because they decay too quickly. Geotextiles may be woven, knitted, or nonwoven.

Woven geotextiles are made of two sets of parallel filaments or strands of yarn systematically interlaced to form a planar structure. *Knitted geotextiles* are formed by interlocking a series of loops of one or more filaments or strands of yarn to form a planar structure. *Nonwoven geotextiles* are formed from filaments or short fibers arranged in an oriented or random pattern in a planar structure. These filaments or short fibers are, in the beginning, arranged into a loose web. They are then bonded by one or a combination of the following processes.

1. *Chemical bonding*—by glue, rubber, latex, cellulose derivative, and the like
2. *Thermal bonding*—by heat for partial melting of filaments
3. *Mechanical bonding*—by needle punching

Needle-punched nonwoven geotextiles are thick and have high in-plane permeability.

Geotextiles have four primary uses in foundation engineering.

1. *Drainage:* The fabrics can rapidly channel water from soil to various outlets, thereby providing a higher soil shear strength and hence stability.
2. *Filtration:* When placed between two soil layers, one coarse grained and the other fine grained, the fabric allows free seepage of water from one layer to the other. However, it protects the fine-grained soil from being washed into the coarse-grained soil.

3. *Separation:* Geotextiles help keep various soil layers separate after construction and during the projected service period of the structure. For example, in the construction of highways, a clayey subgrade can be kept separate from a granular base course.
4. *Reinforcement:* The tensile strength of geofabrics increases the load-bearing capacity of the soil.

Geogrids

Geogrids are high-modulus polymer materials, such as polypropylene and polyethylene, and are prepared by tensile drawing. Netlon Ltd. of the United Kingdom was the first producer of geogrids. In 1982, the Tensar Corporation, presently Tensar Earth Technologies, Inc., introduced geogrids in the United States.

The major function of geogrids is *reinforcement.* Geogrids are relatively stiff netlike materials with large openings called *apertures*. These apertures are large enough to allow interlocking with the surrounding soil and/or rock to perform the function(s) of reinforcement and/or segregation.

Geogrids generally are of two types: (a) biaxial geogrids and (b) uniaxial geogrids. Figure 11.1a and 11.1b show the two types of geogrids just described, which are produced by Tensar Earth Technologies, Inc. Uniaxial TENSAR grids are manufactured by stretching a punched sheet of extruded high-density polyethylene in one direction under carefully controlled conditions. This process aligns the polymer's long-chain molecules in the direction of draw and results in a product with high one-directional tensile strength and modulus. Biaxial TENSAR grids are manufactured by stretching the punched sheet of polypropylene in two orthogonal directions. This process results in a product with high tensile strength and modulus in two perpendicular directions. The resulting grid apertures are either square or rectangular.

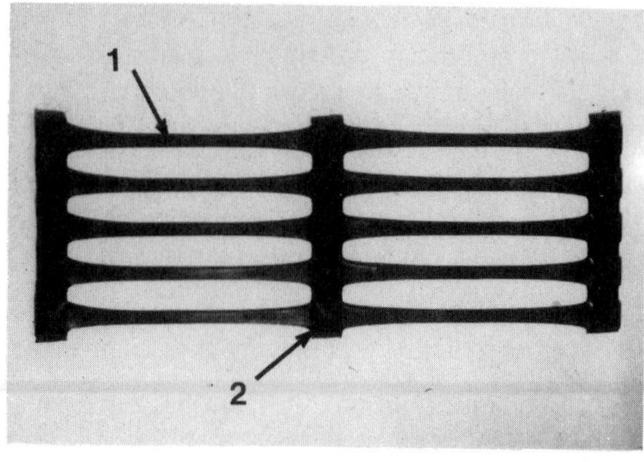

(a)

▼ **FIGURE 11.1** Geogrids: (a) uniaxial; (b) biaxial (*note:* 1—longitudinal rib; 2—transverse bar; 3—transverse rib; 4—junction)

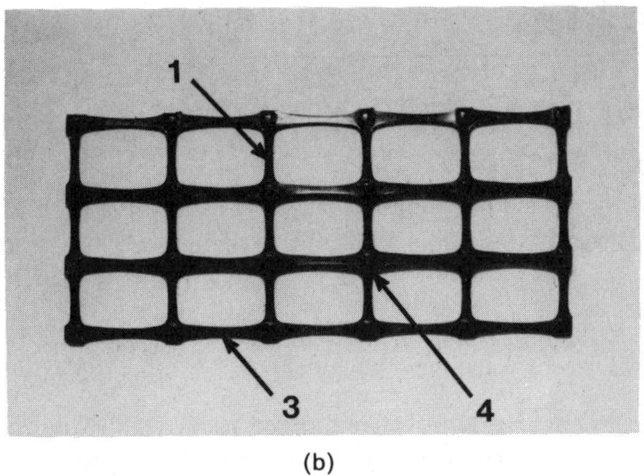

(b)

FIGURE 11.1 (Continued)

The commercial geogrids currently available for soil reinforcement have nominal rib thicknesses of about 0.02–0.06 in. (0.5–1.5 mm) and junctions of about 0.1–0.2 in. (2.5–5 mm). The grids used for soil reinforcement usually have apertures that are rectangular or elliptical in shape. The dimensions of the apertures vary from about 1–6 in. (25–150 mm). Geogrids are manufactured so that the open areas of the grids are greater than 50% of the total area. They develop reinforcing strength at low strain levels, such as 2% (Carroll, 1988). Table 11.1 gives some properties of the TENSAR biaxial geogrids currently available commercially.

TABLE 11.1 **Properties of TENSAR Biaxial Geogrids**

Property	Geogrid		
	BX100	*BX1100*	*BX1200*
Aperture size			
Machine direction	1 in. (nominal)	1 in. (nominal)	1 in. (nominal)
Cross-machine direction	1.3 in. (nominal)	1.3 in. (nominal)	1.3 in. (nominal)
Open area	70% (minimum)	74% (nominal)	77% (nominal)
Junction			
Thickness	0.09 in. (nominal)	0.11 in. (nominal)	0.16 in. (nominal)
Tensile modulus			
Machine direction	12,500 lb/ft (minimum)	14,000 lb/ft (minimum)	18,500 lb/ft (minimum)
Cross-machine direction	12,500 lb/ft (minimum)	20,000 lb/ft (minimum)	30,000 lb/ft (minimum)
Material			
Polypropylene	97% (minimum)	99% (nominal)	99% (nominal)
Carbon black	2% (minimum)	1% (nominal)	1% (nominal)

RETAINING WALLS

11.3 RETAINING WALLS WITH METALLIC STRIP REINFORCEMENT

Reinforced earth walls are flexible walls. Their main components are

1. *Backfill*, which is granular soil
2. *Reinforcing strips*, which are thin, wide strips placed at regular intervals
3. *A cover* on the front face, which is referred to as the *skin*

Figure 11.2 is a diagram of a reinforced earth wall. Note that, at any depth, the reinforcing strips or ties are placed with a horizontal spacing of S_H center-to-center; the vertical spacing of the strips or ties is S_V center-to-center. The skin can be constructed with sections of relatively flexible thin material. Lee et al. (1973) showed that, with a conservative design, a 0.2 in. ($\approx$5 mm) thick galvanized steel skin would be enough to hold a wall about 45–50 ft (14–15 m) high. In most cases, precast concrete slabs can also be used as skin. The slabs are grooved to fit into each other so that soil cannot flow out between the joints. When metal skins are used, they are bolted together, and reinforcing strips are placed between the skins.

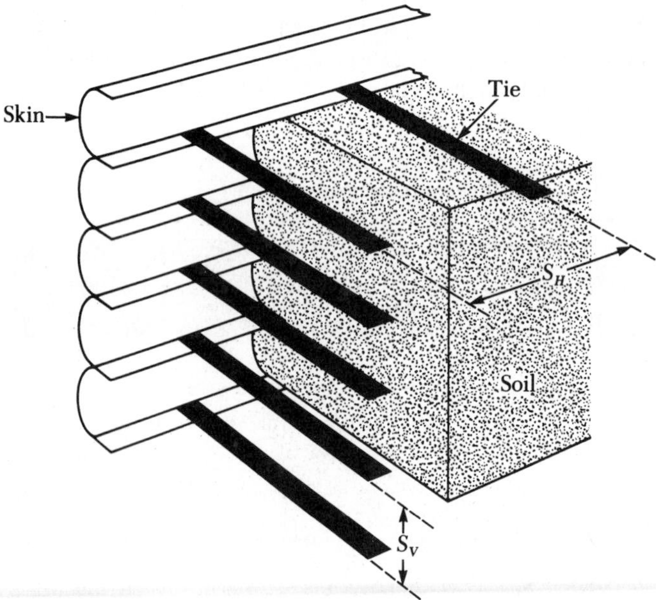

▼ **FIGURE 11.2** Reinforced earth retaining wall

Figures 11.3 and 11.4 show a reinforced earth retaining wall under construction; its skin (facing) is a precast concrete slab. Figure 11.5 shows a metallic reinforcement tie attached to the concrete slab.

▼ **FIGURE 11.3** Reinforced earth retaining wall (with metallic strip) under construction

The simplest and most common method for design of ties is the *Rankine method.* The following is a detailed discussion of this procedure.

Calculation of Active Horizontal and Vertical Pressure

Figure 11.6a shows a retaining wall with a granular backfill having a unit weight of γ_1 and a friction angle of ϕ_1. Below the base of the retaining wall, the *in situ* soil has been excavated and recompacted, with granular soil used as backfill. Below the backfill, the *in situ* soil has a unit weight of γ_2, a friction angle of ϕ_2, and cohesion of c_2. A surcharge having an intensity of q per unit area lies atop the retaining wall. The wall has reinforcement ties at depths $z = 0, S_V, 2S_V, \ldots, NS_V$. The height of the wall is $NS_V = H$.

▼ **FIGURE 11.4** Another view of the retaining wall shown in Figure 11.3

▼ **FIGURE 11.5** Metallic strip attachment to the precast concrete slab used as the skin

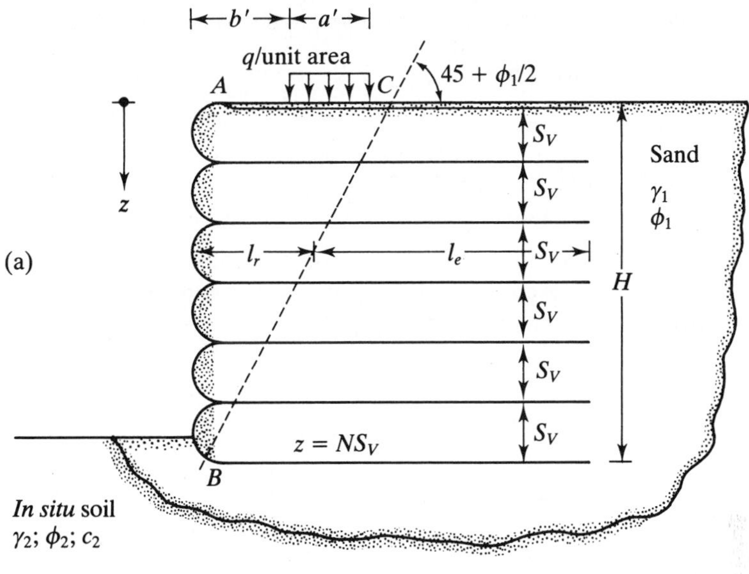

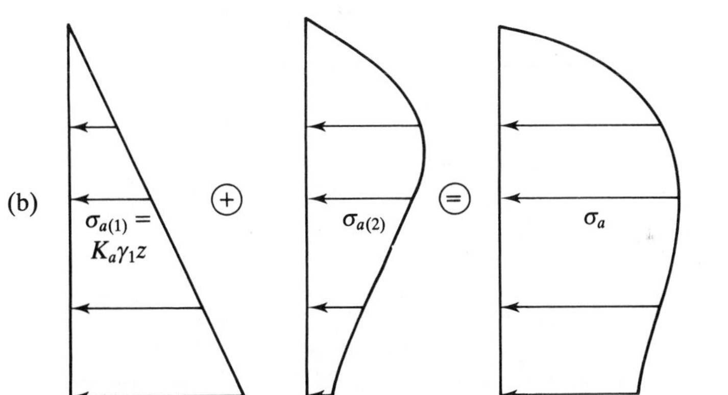

▼ **FIGURE 11.6** Analysis of a reinforced earth retaining wall

According to the Rankine active pressure theory (Section 5.3),

$$\sigma_a = \sigma_v K_a - 2c\sqrt{K_a}$$

where σ_a = Rankine active pressure at any depth z

For dry granular soils with no surcharge at the top, $c = 0$, $\sigma_v = \gamma_1 z$, and $K_a = \tan^2(45 - \phi_1/2)$. Thus

$$\boxed{\sigma_a = \gamma_1 z K_a} \tag{11.1}$$

When a surcharge is added at the top, as shown in Figure 11.6,

$$\sigma_v = \underset{\substack{\uparrow \\ = \gamma_1 z \\ \text{Due to} \\ \text{soil only}}}{\sigma_{v(1)}} + \underset{\substack{\uparrow \\ \text{Due to the} \\ \text{surcharge}}}{\sigma_{v(2)}} \tag{11.2}$$

The magnitude of $\sigma_{v(2)}$ can be calculated by using the 2 : 1 method of stress distribution described in Eq. (3.108) and Figure 3.42. It is shown in Figure 11.7a. According to Laba and Kennedy (1986),

$$\sigma_{v(2)} = \frac{qa'}{a' + z} \quad \text{(for } z \leq 2b'\text{)} \tag{11.3}$$

and

$$\sigma_{v(2)} = \frac{qa'}{a' + \frac{z}{2} + b'} \quad \text{(for } z > 2b'\text{)} \tag{11.4}$$

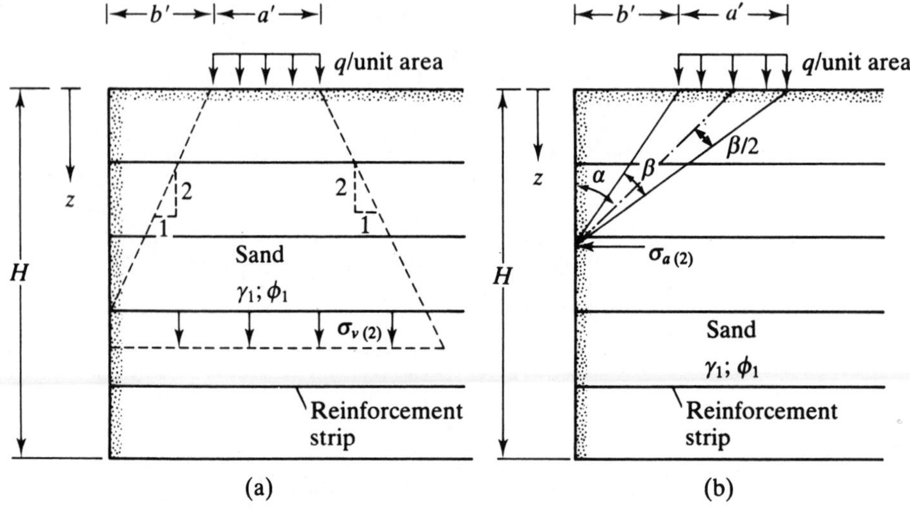

▼ **FIGURE 11.7** (a) Notation for the relationship of $\sigma_{v(2)}$—Eqs. (11.3) and (11.4); (b) notation for the relationship of $\sigma_{a(2)}$—Eqs. (11.6) and (11.7)

Also, when a surcharge is added at the top, the lateral pressure at any depth is

$$\sigma_a = \underset{\substack{\uparrow \\ = K_a \gamma_1 z \\ \text{Due to} \\ \text{soil only}}}{\sigma_{a(1)}} + \underset{\substack{\uparrow \\ \text{Due to the} \\ \text{surcharge}}}{\sigma_{a(2)}} \tag{11.5}$$

According to Laba and Kennedy (1986), $\sigma_{a(2)}$ may be expressed (Figure 11.7b) as

$$\sigma_{a(2)} = M\left[\frac{2q}{\pi}(\underset{\substack{\uparrow \\ \text{(in radians)}}}{\beta} - \sin\beta\cos 2\alpha)\right] \tag{11.6}$$

where

$$M = 1.4 - \frac{0.4b'}{0.14H} \geq 1 \tag{11.7}$$

The net active (lateral) pressure distribution on the retaining wall calculated by using Eqs. (11.5), (11.6), and (11.7) is shown in Figure 11.6b.

Tie Force

Refer again to Figure 11.6. The tie force per unit length of the wall developed at any depth z is

$$\begin{aligned} T &= \text{active earth pressure at depth } z \\ &\quad \times \text{ area of the wall to be supported by the tie} \\ &= (\sigma_a)(S_V S_H) \end{aligned} \tag{11.8}$$

Factor of Safety Against Tie Failure

The reinforcement ties at each level and thus the walls could fail by either (a) tie breaking or (b) tie pullout.

The factor of safety against *tie breaking* may be determined as

$$FS_{(B)} = \frac{\text{yield or breaking strength of each tie}}{\text{maximum tie force in any tie}} = \frac{wtf_y}{\sigma_a S_V S_H} \tag{11.9}$$

where w = width of each tie
t = thickness of each tie
f_y = yield or breaking strength of the tie material

A factor of safety of about 2.5–3 is generally recommended for ties at all levels.

Reinforcing ties at any depth, z, will fail by pullout if the frictional resistance developed along their surfaces is less than the force to which the ties are being subjected. The *effective length* of the ties along which the frictional resistance is developed may be conservatively taken as the length that extends *beyond the limits of the Rankine active failure zone*, which is the zone ABC in Figure 11.6. Line BC in Figure 11.6 makes an angle of $45 + \phi_1/2$ with the horizontal. Now, the maximum friction force F_R that can be realized for a tie at depth z is

$$F_R = 2l_e w\sigma_v \tan \phi_\mu \tag{11.10}$$

where l_e = effective length
σ_v = effective vertical pressure at a depth z
ϕ_μ = soil–tie friction angle

Thus the factor of safety against *tie pullout* at any depth z is

$$FS_{(P)} = \frac{F_R}{T} \tag{11.11}$$

where $FS_{(p)}$ = factor of safety against tie pullout

Substituting Eqs. (11.8) and (11.10) into Eq. (11.11) yields

$$FS_{(P)} = \frac{2l_e w\sigma_v \tan \phi_\mu}{\sigma_a S_V S_H} \tag{11.12}$$

Total Length of Tie

The total length of ties at any depth is

$$L = l_r + l_e \tag{11.13}$$

where l_r = length within the Rankine failure zone
l_e = effective length

For a given $FS_{(P)}$ from Eq. (11.12),

$$l_e = \frac{FS_{(P)} \sigma_a S_V S_H}{2w\sigma_v \tan \phi_\mu} \tag{11.14}$$

Again, at any depth z,

$$l_r = \frac{(H - z)}{\tan\left(45 + \frac{\phi_1}{2}\right)} \tag{11.15}$$

So, combining Eqs. (11.13), (11.14), and (11.15) gives

$$L = \frac{(H - z)}{\tan\left(45 + \frac{\phi_1}{2}\right)} + \frac{FS_{(P)} \sigma_a S_V S_H}{2w\sigma_v \tan \phi_\mu} \tag{11.16}$$

General Design Procedure

Following is a step-by-step procedure for the design of reinforced earth retaining walls.

1. Determine the height of the wall, H, and the properties of the granular backfill material, such as unit weight (γ_1) and angle of friction (ϕ_1).
2. Obtain the soil–tie friction angle, ϕ_μ, and the required values of $FS_{(B)}$ and $FS_{(P)}$.
3. Assume values for horizontal and vertical tie spacing. Also assume the width of reinforcing strip, w, to be used.
4. Calculate σ_a from Eqs. (11.5), (11.6), and (11.7).
5. Calculate the tie forces at various levels from Eq. (11.8).
6. For the known values of $FS_{(B)}$, calculate the thickness of ties, t, to resist the tie breakout:

$$T = \sigma_a S_V S_H = \frac{wtf_y}{FS_{(B)}}$$

or

$$t = \frac{(\sigma_a S_V S_H)[FS_{(B)}]}{wf_y} \tag{11.17}$$

Convention is to keep the magnitude of t the same at all levels. So σ_a in Eq. (11.17) should equal $\sigma_{a(\max)}$.

7. For the known values of ϕ_μ and $FS_{(P)}$, determine the length, L, of the ties at various levels from Eq. (11.16).

8. The magnitudes of S_V, S_H, t, w, and L may be changed to obtain the most economical design.
9. Once the reinforcements have been designed, check for the overall stability of the wall; that is, check for overturning, sliding, and bearing capacity failure. This check is similar to that done for retaining walls in Chapter 5 (see Figure 11.8).

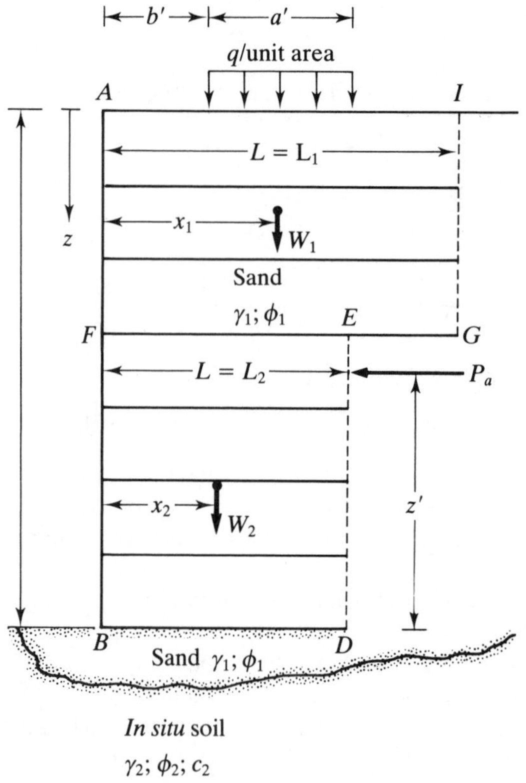

▼ **FIGURE 11.8** Stability check for the retaining wall

Check for Overturning

Taking the moment about B yields the overturning moment for the unit length of the wall:

$$M_O = P_a z' \tag{11.18}$$

where P_a = active force = $\int_0^H \sigma_a \, dz$

The resisting moment per unit length of the wall

$$M_R = W_1 x_1 + W_2 x_2 + \cdots + qa'\left(b' + \frac{a'}{2}\right) \tag{11.19}$$

where $W_1 = (\text{area } AFEGI)(1)(\gamma_1)$
$W_2 = (\text{area } FBDE)(1)(\gamma_1)$
$\vdots$

So

$$FS_{(\text{overturning})} = \frac{M_R}{M_O} = \frac{W_1 x_1 + W_2 x_2 + \cdots + qa'\left(b' + \frac{a'}{2}\right)}{\left(\int_0^H \sigma_a \, dz\right) z'} \tag{11.20}$$

Check for Sliding

As in Eq. (5.66), the factor of safety against sliding may be given as

$$FS_{(\text{sliding})} = \frac{(W_1 + W_2 + \cdots + qa')[\tan(k\phi_1)]}{P_a} \tag{11.21}$$

where $k \approx 2/3$.

Check for Bearing Capacity Failure

The ultimate bearing capacity of a shallow foundation (Chapter 3) is

$$q_{\text{ult}} = cN_c F_{cs} F_{cd} F_{ci} + qN_q F_{qs} F_{qd} F_{qi} + \frac{1}{2}\gamma B N_\gamma F_{\gamma s} F_{\gamma d} F_{\gamma i} \tag{3.17}$$

For the present case, all the shape, depth, and inclination factors equal 1. Also, $B = L_2$, $c = c_2$, $\gamma = \gamma_2$, and $q = 0$ because the depth of the foundation is zero. So

$$q_{\text{ult}} = c_2 N_c + \frac{1}{2}\gamma_2 L_2 N_\gamma \tag{11.22}$$

The bearing capacity factor N_c and N_γ correspond to the soil friction angle ϕ_2 (Table 3.4). The vertical stress at $z = H$, from Eq. (11.2), is

$$\sigma_{v(H)} = \gamma_1 H + \sigma_{v(2)} \tag{11.23}$$

So the factor of safety against bearing capacity failure is

$$FS_{(\text{bearing capacity})} = \frac{q_{\text{ult}}}{\sigma_{v(H)}} \tag{11.24}$$

Generally, minimum values of $FS_{(overturning)} = 3$, $FS_{(sliding)} = 3$, and $FS_{(bearing\ capacity\ failure)} = 3$ to 5 are recommended.

▼ EXAMPLE 11.1

A reinforced earth retaining wall is to be 8 m high. The properties of the backfill material are $\gamma_1 = 16.6$ kN/m^3 and $\phi_1 = 30°$. Galvanized steel ties are to be used for the construction of the wall. Design the reinforcements with $FS_{(B)} = 3$, $FS_{(P)} = 3$, $f_y = 2.4 \times 10^5$ kN/m^2, and $\phi_\mu = 20°$. The properties of the *in situ* soil below the retaining wall are $\gamma_2 = 18$ kN/m^3, $\phi_2 = 28°$, and $c_2 = 52$ kN/m^2.

Solution

Design of Tie Thickness

Let $S_V = 0.5$ m, $S_H = 1$ m, and $w = 75$ mm. For the soil friction angle $\phi_1 = 30°$, $K_a = \tan^2(45 - \phi_1/2) = \tan^2(45 - 30/2) = 1/3$. Hence from (11.8), the tie force is

$$T = \sigma_a S_V S_H$$

The maximum tie force will be where σ_a is maximum. For this case $\sigma_{a(max)} = \gamma H K_a$, so

$$T_{max} = \gamma H K_a S_V S_H = (16.6)(8)\left(\frac{1}{3}\right)(0.5)(1) = 22.14 \text{ kN}$$

From Eq. (11.17), the thickness of ties is

$$t = \frac{(T_{max})[FS_{(B)}]}{wf_y}$$

or

$$t = \frac{(22.14)(3)}{\left(\frac{75}{1000}\right)(2.4 \times 10^5)} = 0.00369 \text{ m} = 3.69 \text{ mm}$$

If the rate of corrosion is 0.025 mm/yr and the life span of the structure is 50 yr, then the actual thickness, t, of the ties will be

$$t = 3.69 + (0.025)50 = 4.94 \text{ mm}$$

So, a **tie thickness of 5 mm** would be enough.

Determination of Tie Length

Refer to Eq. (11.16). For this case $\sigma_a = \gamma_1 z K_a$ and $\sigma_v = \gamma_1 z$, so

$$L = \frac{(H - z)}{\tan\left(45 + \frac{\phi_1}{2}\right)} + \frac{FS_{(P)}\gamma_1 z K_a S_V S_H}{2w\gamma_1 z \tan\phi_\mu}$$

Now the following table can be prepared. (*Note:* $FS_{(P)} = 3$, $H = 8$ m, $w = 0.075$ m, and $\phi_\mu = 20°$.)

z	$\dfrac{(H-z)}{\tan\left(45+\dfrac{\phi_1}{2}\right)}$ (m)	$\dfrac{FS_{(P)}\gamma_1 z K_a S_V S_H}{2w\gamma_1 z \tan\phi_\mu}$ (m)	L (m)
1	2.34	9.16	12.0
2	2.0	9.16	11.16
3	1.67	9.16	10.83
4	1.34	9.16	10.50
5	1.0	9.16	10.16
6	0.67	9.16	9.83
7	0.33	9.16	9.49

So, **use $L = 12$ m for $z = 0$ to 5 m, and use $L = 10$ m below that** (see Figure 11.9).

Check for Overall Stability

For Overturning

From Eq. (11.20) and Figure (11.9),

$$FS_{(\text{overturning})} = \frac{W_1 x_1 + W_2 x_2}{\left[\int_0^H \sigma_a\, dz\right] z'}$$

$$W_1 = (12)(5)(1)(\gamma_1) = (12)(5)(1)(16.6) = 996 \text{ kN}$$

$$W_2 = (10)(3)(1)(\gamma_1) = (10)(3)(1)(16.6) = 498 \text{ kN}$$

Also, $x_1 = 6$ m, $x_2 = 5$ m, and

$$\int_0^H \sigma_a\, dz = P_a = \frac{1}{2}\gamma_1 K_a H^2 = \left(\frac{1}{2}\right)(16.6)\left(\frac{1}{3}\right)(8)^2 = 177 \text{ kN}$$

So

$$FS_{(\text{overturning})} = \frac{(996)(6) + (489)(5)}{(177)\left(\dfrac{8}{3}\right)} = \frac{8466}{472} = \mathbf{17.94 > 3\text{—OK}}$$

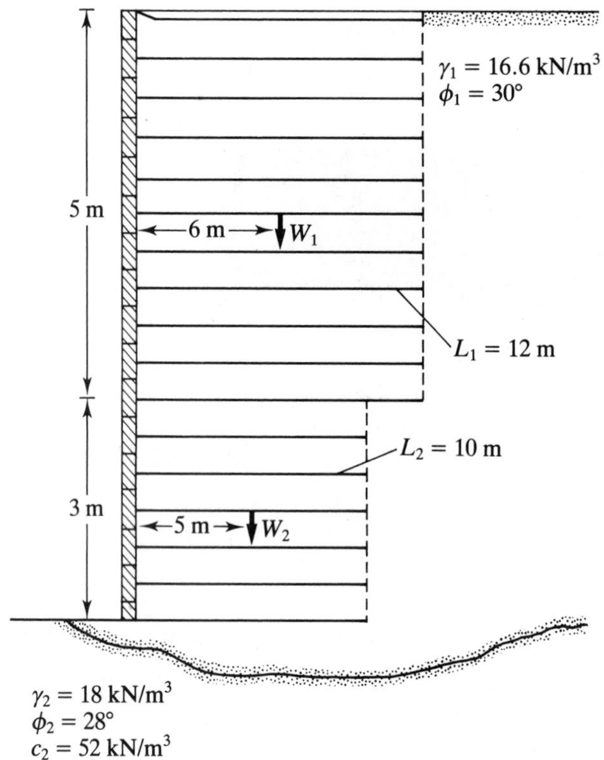

▼ **FIGURE 11.9**

For Sliding

From Eq. (11.21),

$$FS_{\text{(sliding)}} = \frac{(W_1 + W_2)\tan(k\phi)}{P_a}$$

$$= \frac{(996 + 498)\tan\left[\left(\frac{2}{3}\right)(30)\right]}{177} = \mathbf{3.07 > 3—OK}$$

For Bearing Capacity Failure

For $\phi_2 = 28°$, $N_c = 25.8$ and $N_\gamma = 16.72$ (Table 3.4). From Eq. (11.22),

$$q_{\text{ult}} = c_2 N_c + \frac{1}{2}\gamma_2 L_2 N_\gamma$$

$$= (52)(25.8) + (0.5)(18)(10)(16.72)$$

$$= 1341.6 + 1504.8 = 2846.4 \text{ kN/m}^2$$

From Eq. (11.23)

$$\sigma_{v(H)} = \gamma_1 H = (16.6)(8) = 132.8 \text{ kN/m}^2$$

So

$$FS_{\text{(bearing capacity failure)}} = \frac{q_{\text{ult}}}{\sigma_{v(H)}} = \frac{2846.4}{132.8} = \mathbf{21.43 > 5—OK.}$$ ▼

11.4 RETAINING WALLS WITH GEOTEXTILE REINFORCEMENT

Figure 11.10 shows a retaining wall in which layers of geotextile have been used as reinforcement. As in Figure 11.7, the backfill is a granular soil. In this type of retaining wall, the facing of the wall is formed by lapping the sheets as shown with a lap length of l_l. When construction of the wall is finished, the exposed face of the wall must be covered; otherwise, the geotextile will deteriorate from exposure to ultraviolet light. *Bitumen emulsion* or *Gunite* is sprayed on the wall face, and a wire mesh anchored to the geotextile facing may be necessary to keep the coating on the face of the wall.

The design of this type of retaining wall is similar to that presented in Section 11.3. Following is a step-by-step procedure for design based on the recommendations of Bell et al. (1975) and Koerner (1990).

1. Determine the active pressure distribution on the wall from

$$\sigma_a = K_a \sigma_v = K_a \gamma_1 z \tag{11.25}$$

where K_a = Rankine earth pressure coefficient
$= \tan^2 (45 - \phi_1/2)$
γ_1 = unit weight of the granular backfill
ϕ_1 = friction angle of the granular backfill

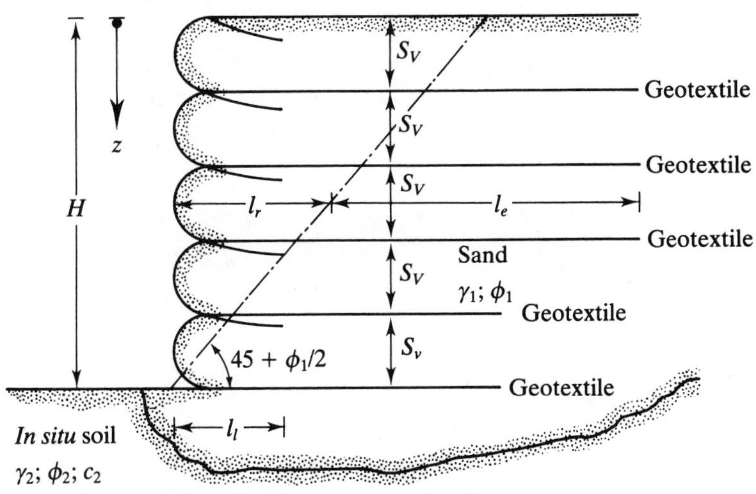

▼ **FIGURE 11.10** Retaining wall with geotextile reinforcement

2. Select a geotextile fabric that has an allowable strength of σ_G (lb/ft or kN/m).
3. Determine the vertical spacing of the layers at any depth z from

$$S_V = \frac{\sigma_G}{\sigma_a FS_{(B)}} = \frac{\sigma_G}{(\gamma_1 z K_a)[FS_{(B)}]} \tag{11.26}$$

Note that Eq. (11.26) is similar to Eq. (11.9). The magnitude of $FS_{(B)}$ is generally 1.3–1.5.

4. Determine the length of each layer of geotextile from

$$L = l_r + l_e \tag{11.27}$$

where

$$l_r = \frac{H - z}{\tan\left(45 + \frac{\phi_1}{2}\right)} \tag{11.28}$$

and

$$l_e = \frac{S_V \sigma_a [FS_{(P)}]}{2\sigma_v \tan \phi_F} \tag{11.29}$$

$$\sigma_a = \gamma_1 z K_a$$

$$\sigma_v = \gamma_1 z$$

$$FS_{(P)} = 1.3 \text{ to } 1.5$$

$$\phi_F = \text{friction angle at geotextile–soil interface} \approx \frac{2}{3}\phi_1$$

Note that Eqs. (11.27), (11.28), and (11.29) are similar to Eqs. (11.13), (11.15), and (11.14), respectively.

Based on the published results, the assumption of $\phi_F/\phi_1 \approx \frac{2}{3}$ is reasonable and appears to be conservative. Martin et al. (1984) presented the following laboratory test results for ϕ_F/ϕ_1 between various types of geotextiles and sand.

Type	ϕ_F/ϕ_1
Woven—monofilament/concrete sand	0.87
Woven—silt film/concrete sand	0.8
Woven—silt film/rounded sand	0.86
Woven—silt film/silty sand	0.92
Nonwoven—melt-bonded/concrete sand	0.87
Nonwoven—needle-punched/concrete sand	1.0
Nonwoven—needle-punched/rounded sand	0.93
Nonwoven—needle-punched/silty sand	0.91

5. Determine the lap length, l_l from

$$l_l = \frac{S_V \sigma_a FS_{(P)}}{4\sigma_v \tan \phi_F} \tag{11.30}$$

The minimum lap length should be 3 ft (1 m).

6. Check the overall stability and determine the factors of safety against overturning, sliding, and bearing capacity failure as described in item 9 of the design procedure in Section 11.3.

▼ EXAMPLE 11.2

A geotextile reinforced retaining wall 16 ft high is shown in Figure 11.11. For the granular backfill, $\gamma_1 = 110$ lb/ft^3 and $\phi_1 = 35°$. For the geotextile, $\sigma_G = 80$ lb/in. For the design of the wall, determine S_V, L, and l_l.

Solution

$$K_a = \tan^2\left(45 - \frac{\phi_1}{2}\right) = 0.26$$

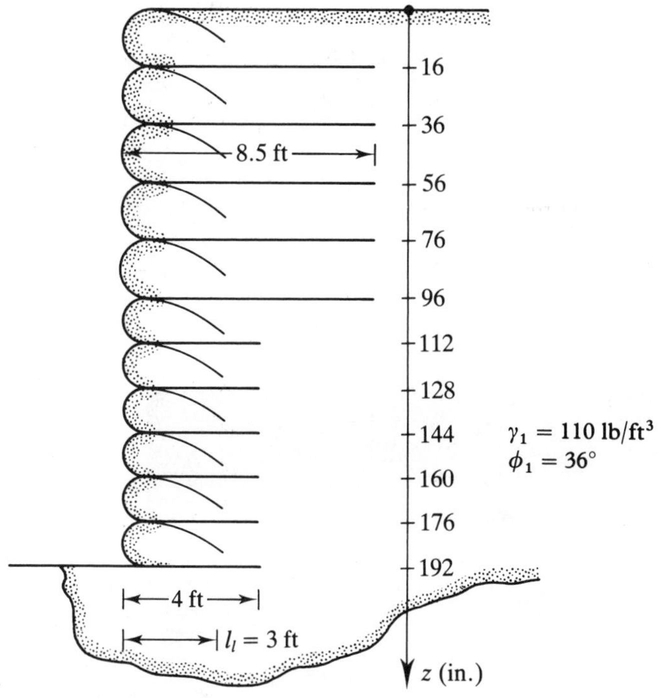

▼ **FIGURE 11.11**

Determination of S_V

To find S_V, we make a few trials. From Eq. (11.26),

$$S_V = \frac{\sigma_G}{(\gamma_1 z K_a)[FS_{(B)}]}$$

With $FS_{(B)} = 1.5$ at $z = 8$ ft,

$$S_V = \frac{(80 \times 12 \text{ lb/ft})}{(110)(8)(0.26)(1.5)} = 2.8 \text{ ft} \approx 33.6 \text{ in.}$$

At $z = 12$ ft,

$$S_V = \frac{(80 \times 12 \text{ lb/ft})}{(110)(12)(0.26)(1.5)} = 1.87 \text{ ft} \approx 22 \text{ in.}$$

At $z = 16$ ft,

$$S_V = \frac{(80 \times 12 \text{ lb/ft})}{(110)(16)(0.26)(1.5)} = 1.4 \text{ ft} \approx 16.8 \text{ in.}$$

So, **use $S_V = 20$ in. for $z = 0$ to $z = 8$ ft and $S_V = 16$ in. for $z > 8$ ft.** This is shown in Figure 11.10.

Determination of L

From Eqs. (11.27), (11.28), and (11.29),

$$L = \frac{(H - z)}{\tan\left(45 + \frac{\phi_1}{2}\right)} + \frac{S_V K_a [FS_{(P)}]}{2 \tan \phi_F}$$

For $FS_{(P)} = 1.5$, $\tan \phi_F = \tan\left[\left(\frac{2}{3}\right)(36)\right] = 0.445$ and

$$L = (0.51)(H - z) + 0.483 S_V$$

Now the following table can be prepared.

z (in.)	z (ft)	S_V (ft)	$(0.51)(H - z)$ (ft)	$0.483S_V$ (ft)	L (ft)
16	1.33	1.67	7.48	0.81	8.29
56	4.67	1.67	5.78	0.81	6.59
76	6.34	1.67	4.93	0.81	5.74
96	8.0	1.67	4.08	0.81	4.89
112	9.34	1.33	3.23	0.64	3.87
144	12.0	1.33	2.04	0.64	2.68
176	14.67	1.33	0.68	0.64	1.32

Based on the preceding calculations, **use $L = 8.5$ ft for $z \le 8$ ft and $L = 4$ ft for $z > 8$ ft.**

Determination of l_l

From Eq. (11.30),

$$l_l = \frac{S_V \sigma_a [FS_{(P)}]}{4\sigma_v \tan \phi_F}$$

With $\sigma_a = \gamma_1 z K_a$, $FS_{(P)} = 1.5$; with $\sigma_v = \gamma_1 z$, $\phi_F = \frac{2}{3}\phi_1$. So

$$l_l = \frac{S_V K_a [FS_{(P)}]}{4 \tan \phi_F} = \frac{S_V (0.26)(1.5)}{4 \tan\left[\left(\frac{2}{3}\right)(36)\right]} = 0.219 S_V$$

At $z = 16$ in.,

$$l_l = 0.219 S_V = (0.219)\left(\frac{20}{12}\right) = 0.365 \text{ ft} \le 3 \text{ ft}$$

So, use $l_l = 3$ ft. ▼

11.5 COMMENTS ON THE FAILURE SURFACE ASSUMPTION—RETAINING WALL WITH GEOTEXTILE REINFORCEMENT

Figure 11.10 showed that Rankine's active state failure surface in the backfill may be assumed in order to calculate the lateral earth pressure and l_e. Recent field and laboratory observations show that the actual failure surface may be closer to an arc of a logarithmic spiral. This result may be illustrated by reviewing the laboratory results of a load test of a large-scale geotextile reinforced retaining wall conducted by Billard and Wu (1991). The height of the retaining wall tested was 5 ft 1 in. ($\approx$1.55 m). The design of this wall was based on the assumptions of Rankine active pressure distribution and $FS_{(B)} = 1$ [Eq. (11.26)] for a surcharge, q, of 850 lb/ft^2 ($\approx$40.7 kN/m^2) on the surface of the backfill. The wall actually failed when the surcharge reached 2660 lb/ft^2 (127.5 kN/m^2).

Figure 11.12 shows a schematic diagram of the retaining wall tested. During the application of surcharge in the laboratory, strain measurements were made along various layers of geotextile. Figure 11.13 shows the strain variation along layer 1 at failure ($q = 2660$ lb/ft^2). The potential failure surface in the soil mass can be obtained by joining points on the geotextile layers at which peak strain occurred. That surface, along with the theoretical Rankine active failure surface, is shown in Figure 11.12. Measurements during the test also showed that the soil moved downward and outward during application of the surcharge, as shown in Figure 11.14.

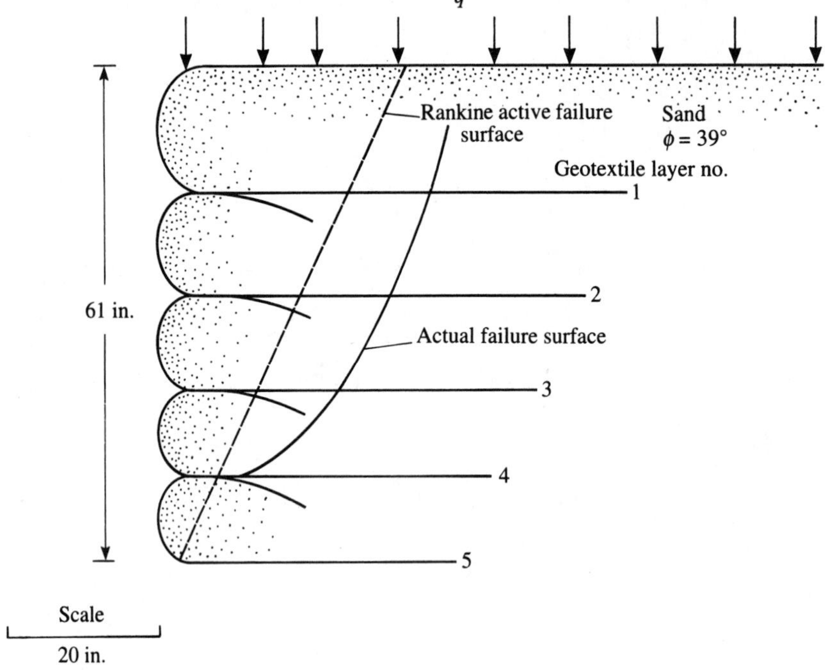

▼ **FIGURE 11.12** Comparison between actual and Rankine active failure surfaces in the backfill of retaining wall with geotextile reinforcement (based on the tests of Billard and Wu, 1991)

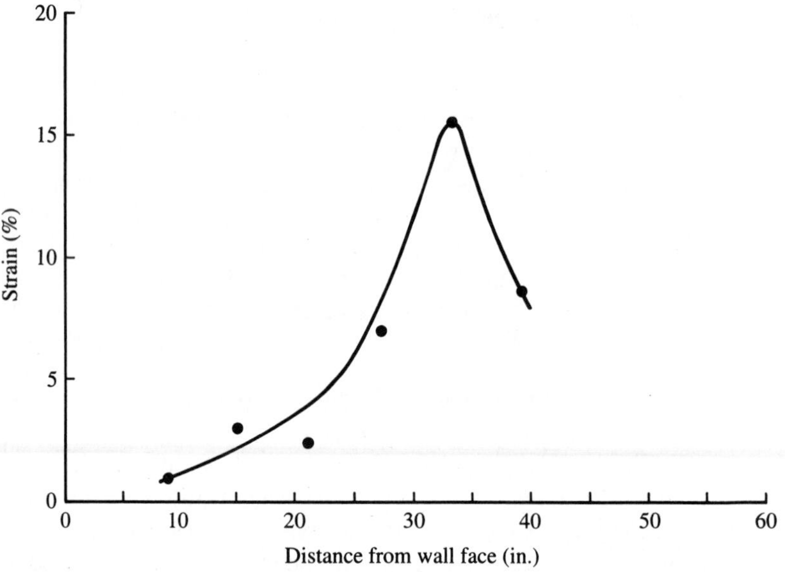

▼ **FIGURE 11.13** Variation of strain along geotextile layer no. 1, $q = 2660$ lb/ft^2 (based on the results of Billard and Wu, 1991)

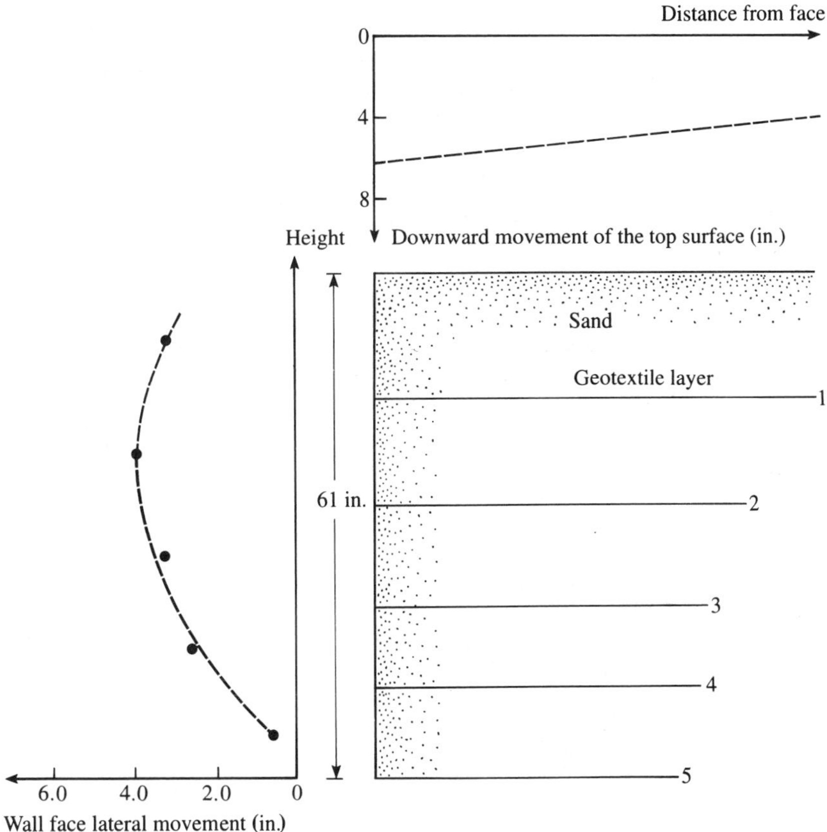

FIGURE 11.14 Movement of wall (based on the results of Billard and Wu, 1991)

11.6 RETAINING WALLS WITH GEOGRID REINFORCEMENT

Geogrids can also be used as reinforcement in granular backfill for the construction of retaining walls. Figure 11.15 shows typical schematic diagrams of retaining walls with geogrid reinforcement.

The design procedure for retaining walls with geogrid reinforcement is similar to that presented in Section 11.4 for geotextiles, so that procedure is not elaborated on here. However, for estimating active pressure [see Eq. (11.25) and Figure 11.10 in Section 11.4], the following relationships may be used (Jones, 1984; Koerner, 1990). For $H > 20$ ft (6 m),

$$\sigma_a = \tan^2\left(45 - \frac{\phi_1}{2}\right)\gamma_1 z \tag{11.31}$$

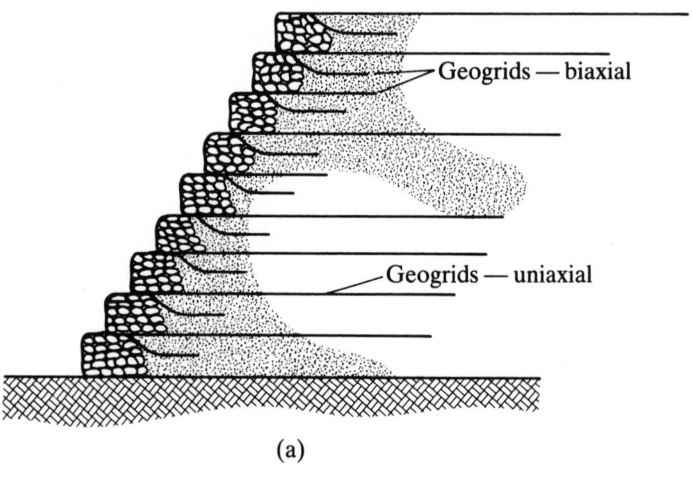

(a)

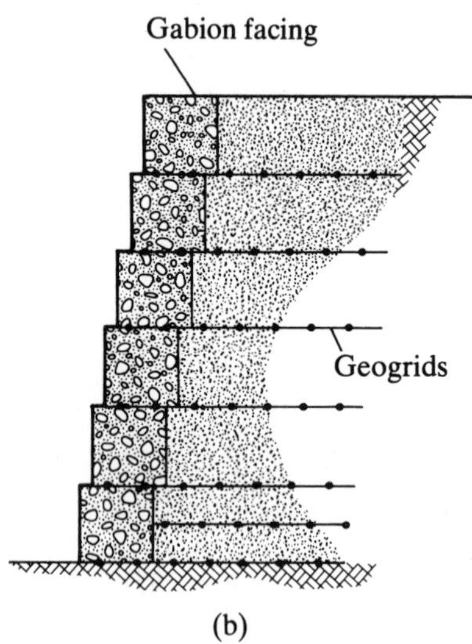

(b)

▼ **FIGURE 11.15** Typical schematic diagrams of retaining walls with geogrid reinforcement: (a) geogrid wraparound wall; (b) wall with gabion facing; (c) concrete panel– faced wall (after The Tensar Corporation, 1986)

and for $H \leq 20$ ft (6 m),

$$\sigma_a = \left[(1 - \sin\phi_1)\left(1 - \frac{z}{H}\right) + \tan^2\left(45 - \frac{\phi_1}{2}\right)\left(\frac{z}{H}\right)\right]\gamma_1 z \tag{11.32}$$

Relatively few field measurements are available for lateral earth pressure on retaining walls constructed with geogrid reinforcement. Figure 11.16 shows a compari-

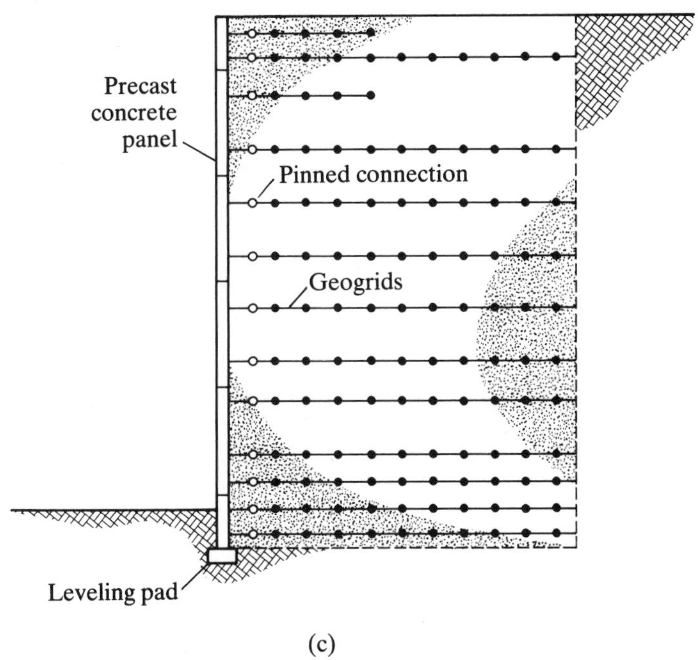

▼ **FIGURE 11.15** (Continued)

son of measured and design lateral pressures (Berg et al., 1986) for two retaining walls constructed with precast panel facing (see Figure 11.15c). It indicates that the measured earth pressures were substantially smaller than those calculated for the Rankine active case.

The results of another interesting full-scale test on a retaining wall with geogrid reinforcement, granular backfill, and a height of 3.6 m was reported by Thamm et al. (1990). The main reinforcement for the wall was TENSAR SR2 geogrid. Figure 11.17 shows a schematic diagram of the retaining wall. Failure in the wall was caused by applying load to a concrete slab measuring 2.4 m × 0.9 m. The wall failed when the vertical load, V, on the concrete slab reached 1065 kN. Figure 11.18 (page 694) shows the variation of the wall face displacement and the distribution of lateral pressure as the loading progressed, from which the following conclusions can be drawn.

1. The shape of the lateral earth pressure distribution on the wall face is similar to that shown in Figure 11.6b.
2. At failure load, the magnitude of $\Delta L/H$ (ΔL = facing displacement) at the top of the wall was about 1.7%, which is considerably higher than may be encountered for a rigid retaining wall.

Thamm et al. (1990) also observed the variation of strain in the geogrid layers. The potential failure surface observed from the locus of the peak strain appears to be similar to that shown in Figure 11.13.

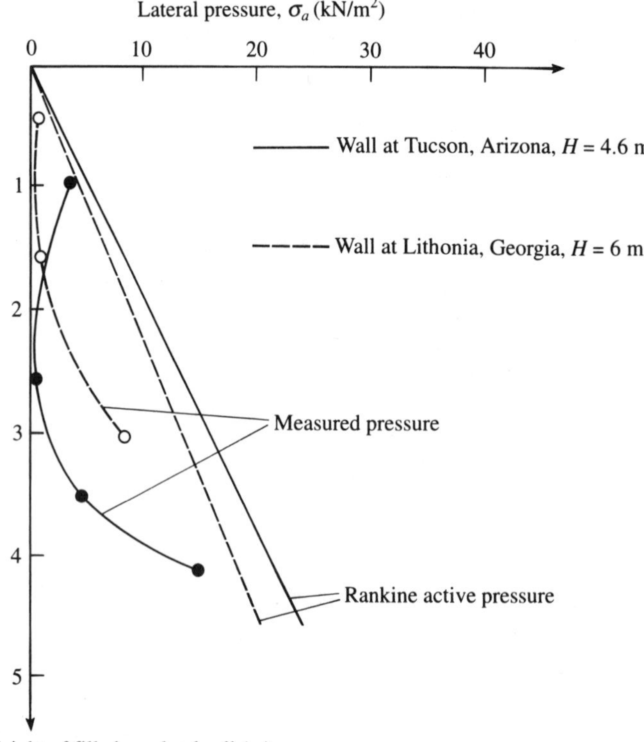

▼ **FIGURE 11.16** Comparison of theoretical and measured lateral pressures in geogrid reinforced retaining walls (based on Berg et al., 1986)

BEARING CAPACITY OF CONTINUOUS FOUNDATION ON GRANULAR SOIL REINFORCED BY METALLIC STRIPS

11.7 MODES OF FAILURE

The bearing capacity of shallow foundations resting on reinforced earth has been studied in detail by Binquet and Lee (1975a, b), who proposed the rational design method presented next.

The nature of bearing capacity failure of a shallow strip foundation resting on a compact and homogeneous soil mass was presented in Figure 3.1a. In contrast, if layers of reinforcing strips, or *ties*, are placed in the soil under a shallow strip foundation, the nature of failure in the soil mass will be like that shown in Figure 11.19a, b, and c.

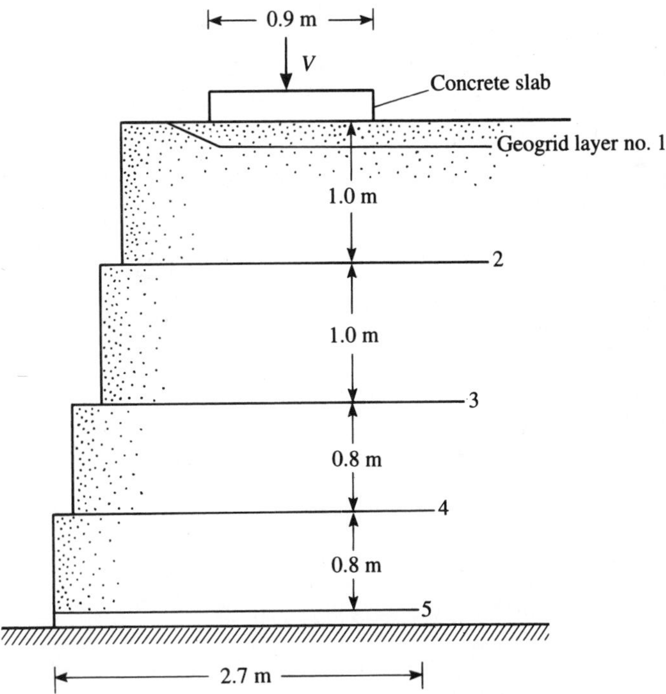

▼ **FIGURE 11.17** Schematic diagram of the retaining wall tested by Thamm et al. (1990)

The type of failure in the soil mass shown in Figure 11.19a generally occurs when the first layer of reinforcement is placed at a depth, d, greater than about $\frac{2}{3}B$ (B = width of the foundation). If the reinforcements in the first layer are strong and they are sufficiently concentrated, they may act as a rigid base at a limited depth. The bearing capacity of foundations in such cases can be evaluated by the theory presented by Mandel and Salencon (1972). Experimental laboratory results for the bearing capacity of shallow foundations resting on a sand layer with a rigid rough base at a limited depth have also been provided by Meyerhof (1974), Pfeifle and Das (1979), and Das (1981).

The type of failure shown in Figure 11.19b could occur if d/B is less than about $\frac{2}{3}$ and the number of layers of reinforcement, N, is less than about 2–3. In this type of failure, reinforcement tie pullout occurs.

The most beneficial effect of reinforced earth is obtained when d/B is less than about $\frac{2}{3}$ and the number of reinforcement layers is greater than 4 but no more than 6–7. (The ties must be sufficiently long; see Section 11.9 for length calculation.) In this case, the soil mass fails when the upper ties break (see Figure 11.19c).

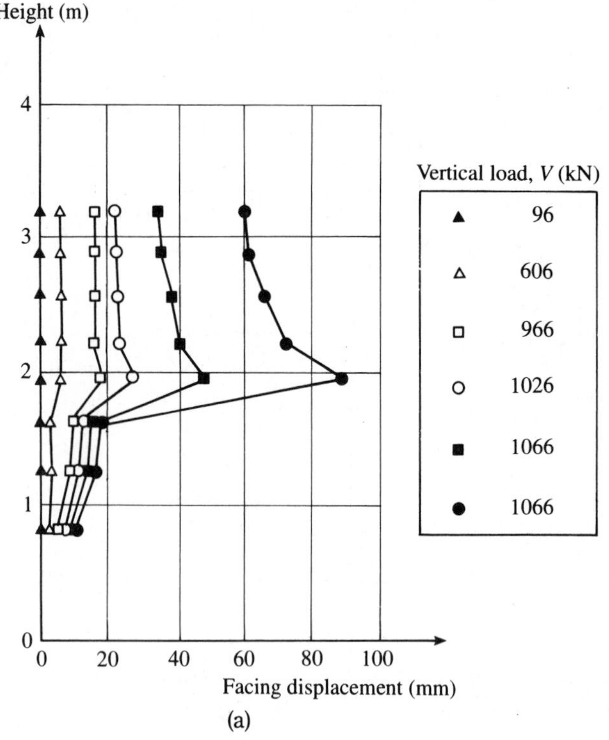

(a)

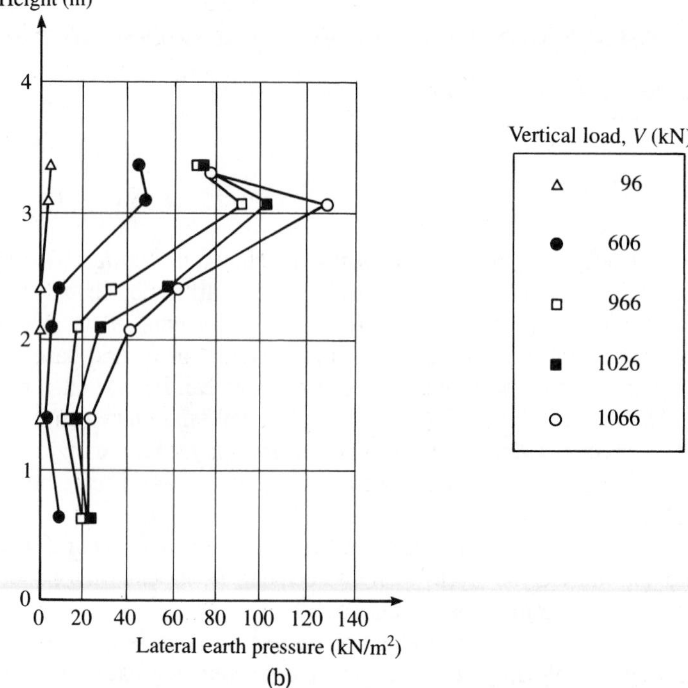

(b)

▼ **FIGURE 11.18** Observations from tests on the retaining wall shown in Figure 11.17: (a) facing displacement with loading; (b) lateral earth pressure with loading (based on Thamm et al., 1990)

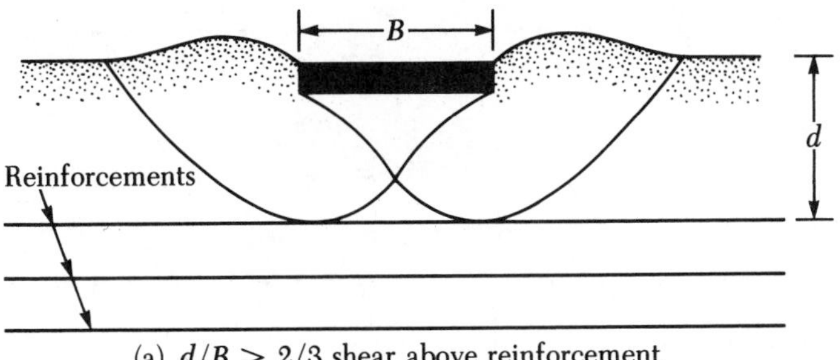

(a) $d/B > 2/3$ shear above reinforcement

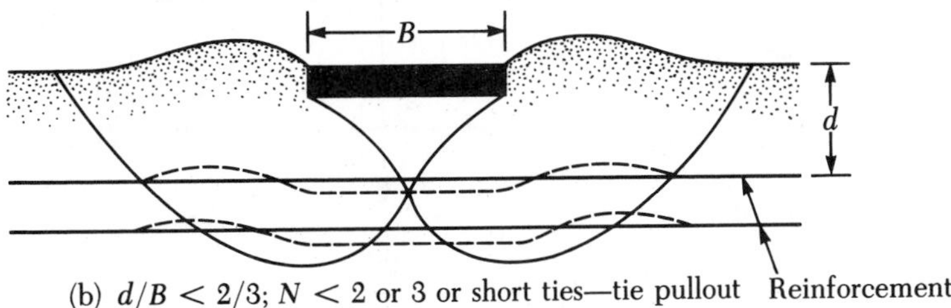

(b) $d/B < 2/3$; $N < 2$ or 3 or short ties—tie pullout Reinforcements

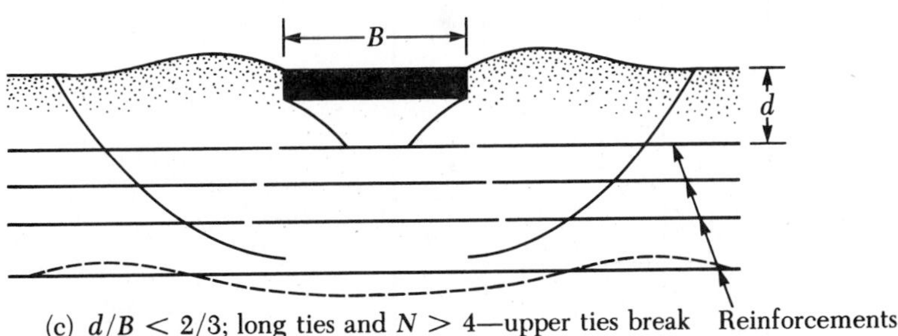

(c) $d/B < 2/3$; long ties and $N > 4$—upper ties break Reinforcements

▼ **FIGURE 11.19** Three modes of bearing capacity failure in reinforced earth (redrawn after Binquet and Lee, 1975b)

11.8 DETERMINATION OF THE FORCE INDUCED IN REINFORCEMENT TIES

Location of Failure Surface

When designing shallow strip foundations, an engineer must estimate the force that develops in the reinforcing ties as a result of the foundation load. This section presents the analytical procedure for estimation proposed by Binquet and Lee (1975b).

Figure 11.20 shows an idealized condition for development of the failure surface in soil for the condition shown in Figure 11.19c. It consists of a central zone—zone I—immediately below the foundation that settles along with the foundation with the application of load. On each side of zone I, the soil is pushed outward and upward—this is

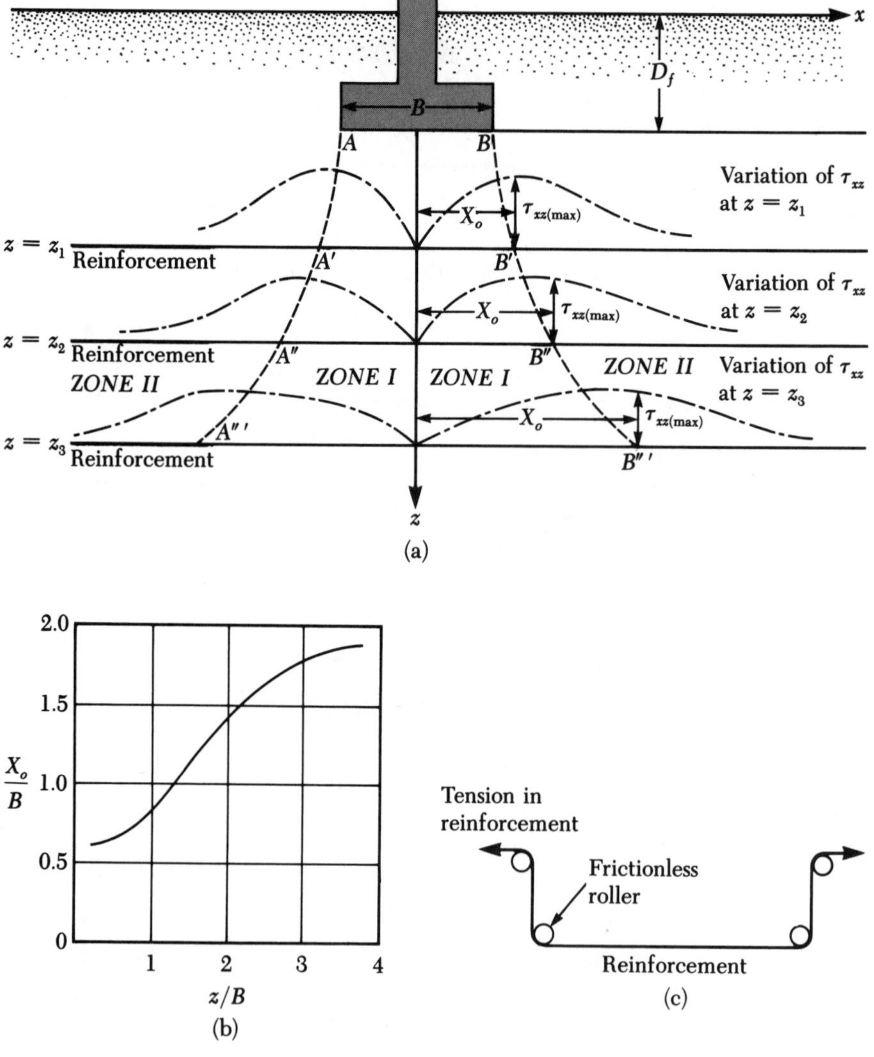

▼ **FIGURE 11.20** Failure mechanism under a foundation supported by reinforced earth [part (b) after Binquet and Lee, 1975b]

zone II. The points A', A'', A''', …, and B', B'', B''', …, which define the limiting lines between zones I and II, can be obtained by considering the shear stress distribution, τ_{xz}, in the soil caused by the foundation load. The term τ_{xz} refers to the shear stress developed at a depth z below the foundation at a distance x measured from the center line of the foundation. If integration of Boussinesq's equation is used, τ_{xz} is given by the relation

$$\tau_{xz} = \frac{4bq_R xz^2}{\pi[(x^2 + z^2 - b^2)^2 + 4b^2z^2]} \tag{11.33}$$

where b = half-width of the foundation = $B/2$
B = width of foundation
q_R = load per unit area on the foundation

The variation of τ_{xz} at any depth, z, is shown by the broken lines in Figure 11.20a. Points A' and B' refer to the points at which the value of τ_{xz} is maximum at $z = z_1$. Similarly, A'' and B'' refer to the points at which τ_{xz} is maximum at $z = z_2$. The distances $x = X_o$ at which the maximum value of τ_{xz} occurs take a nondimensional form and are shown in Figure 11.20b.

Other Assumptions

Other assumptions needed to obtain the tie force at any given depth are as follows:

1. Under the application of bearing pressure by the foundation, the reinforcing ties at points A', A'', A''', . . . , and B', B'', B''', . . . , take the shape shown in Figure 11.20c. That is, the ties take two right angle turns on each side of zone I around two frictionless rollers.
2. For N reinforcing layers, the ratio of the load per unit area on the foundation supported by reinforced earth, q_R, to the load per unit area on the foundation supported by unreinforced earth, q_o, is constant irrespective of the settlement level, s (see Figure 11.21). Binquet and Lee (1975a) proved this relation in laboratory experiments.

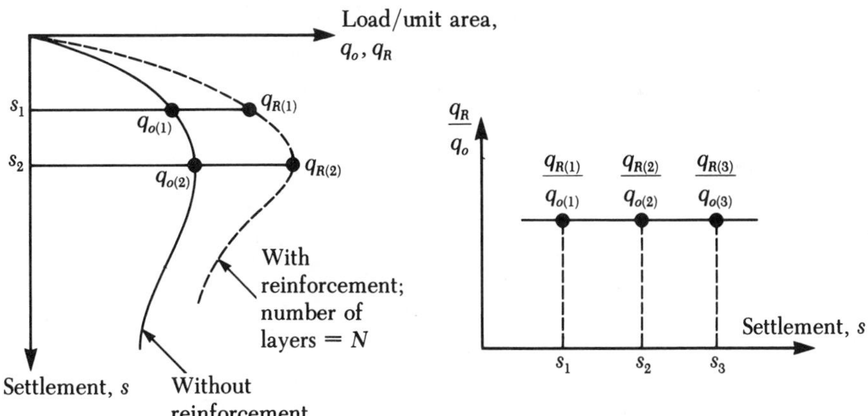

▼ **FIGURE 11.21** Relationship between load per unit area and settlement for foundations resting on reinforced and unreinforced soil

Derivation of Equation

Figure 11.22a shows a continuous foundation supported by unreinforced soil and subjected to a load of q_o per unit area. Similarly, Figure 11.22b shows a continuous foundation supported by a reinforced soil layer (one layer of reinforcement, or $N = 1$) and

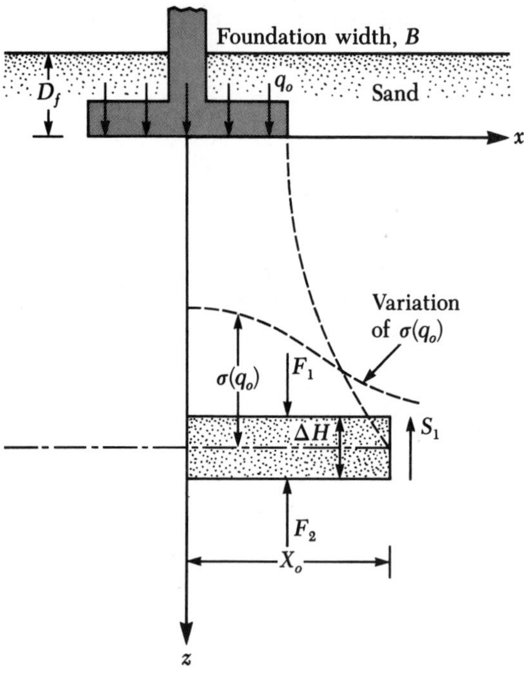

(a) Foundation of unreinforced soil

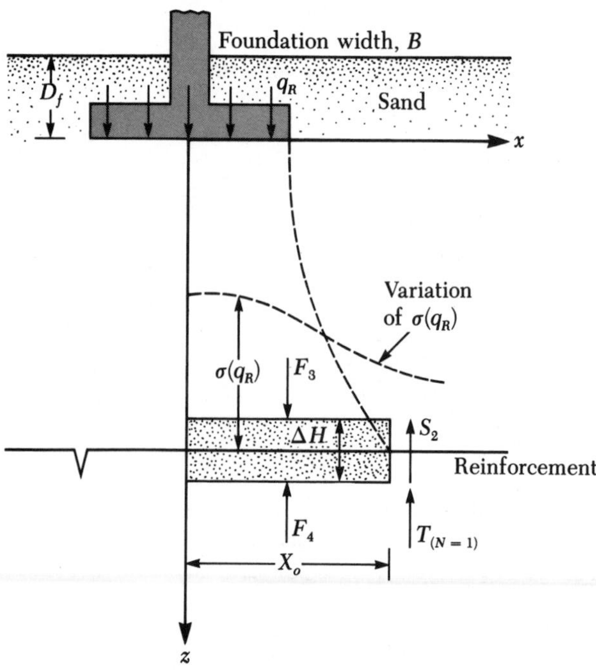

(b) Foundation of reinforced soil (one layer reinforcement)

▼ **FIGURE 11.22** Derivation of Eq. (11.52)

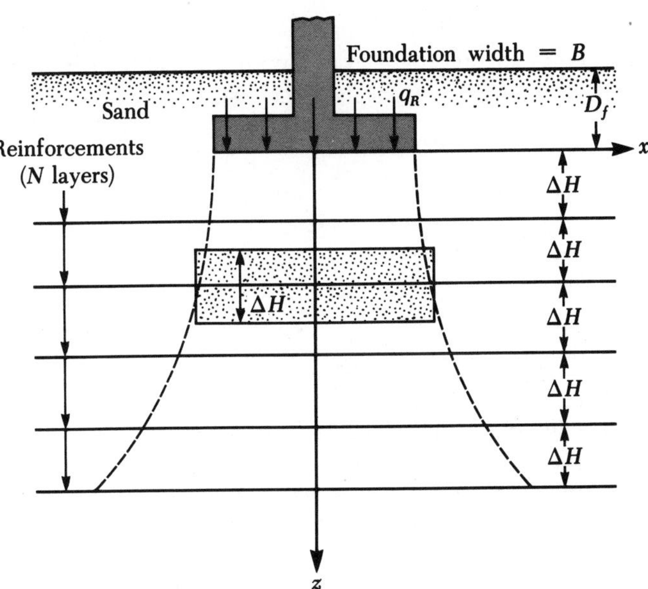

(c) Foundation on reinforced soil (*N* layers of reinforcement)

▼ **FIGURE 11.22** (Continued)

subjected to a load of q_R per unit area. (Due to symmetry only one-half of the foundation is shown in Figure 11.22). In both cases—that is, in Figures 11.22a and 11.22b—let the settlement equal *s*. For one-half of each foundation under consideration, the following are the forces per unit length on a soil element of thickness ΔH located at a depth *z*.

Unreinforced Case F_1 and F_2 are the vertical forces, and S_1 is the shear force. Hence, for equilibrium,

$$F_1 - F_2 - S_1 = 0 \tag{11.34}$$

Reinforced Case Here, F_3 and F_4 are the vertical forces, S_2 is the shear force, and $T_{(N=1)}$ is the tensile force developed in the reinforcement. The force $T_{(N=1)}$ is vertical because of the assumption made for the deformation of reinforcement as shown in Figure 11.20c. So

$$F_3 - F_4 - S_2 - T_{(N=1)} = 0 \tag{11.35}$$

If the foundation settlement, *s*, is the same in both cases,

$$F_2 = F_4 \tag{11.36}$$

Subtracting Eq. (11.34) from Eq. (11.35) and using the relationship given in Eq. (11.36), we obtain

$$T_{(N=1)} = F_3 - F_1 - S_2 + S_1 \tag{11.37}$$

Note that the force F_1 is caused by the vertical stress, σ, on the soil element under consideration as a result of the load q_o on the foundation. Similarly, F_3 is caused by the vertical stress imposed on the soil element as a result of the load q_R. Hence

$$F_1 = \int_0^{X_o} \sigma(q_o)\, dx \tag{11.38}$$

$$F_3 = \int_0^{X_o} \sigma(q_R)\, dx \tag{11.39}$$

$$S_1 = \tau_{xz}(q_o)\, \Delta H \tag{11.40}$$

$$S_2 = \tau_{xz}(q_R)\, \Delta H \tag{11.41}$$

where $\sigma(q_o)$ and $\sigma(q_R)$ are the vertical stresses at a depth z caused by the loads q_o and q_R on the foundation

$\tau_{xz}(q_o)$ and $\tau_{xz}(q_R)$ are the shear stresses at a depth z and at a distance X_o from the center line caused by the loads q_o and q_R

Integrating Boussinesq's solution yields

$$\sigma(q_o) = \frac{q_o}{\pi}\left[\tan^{-1}\frac{z}{x-b} - \tan^{-1}\frac{z}{x+b} - \frac{2bz(x^2 - z^2 - b^2)}{(x^2 + z^2 - b^2)^2 + 4b^2z^2}\right] \tag{11.42}$$

$$\sigma(q_R) = \frac{q_R}{\pi}\left[\tan^{-1}\frac{z}{x-b} - \tan^{-1}\frac{z}{x+b} - \frac{2bz(x^2 - z^2 - b^2)}{(x^2 + z^2 - b^2)^2 + 4b^2z^2}\right] \tag{11.43}$$

$$\tau_{xz}(q_o) = \frac{4bq_oX_oz^2}{\pi[X_o^2 + z^2 - b^2)^2 + 4b^2z^2]} \tag{11.44}$$

$$\tau_{xz}(q_R) = \frac{4bq_RX_oz^2}{\pi[(X_o^2 + z^2 - b^2)^2 + 4b^2z^2]} \tag{11.45}$$

where $b = B/2$

The procedure for derivation of Eqs. (11.42) to (11.45) is not presented here; for this information see a soil mechanics textbook (for example, Das, 1983). Proper substitution of Eqs. (11.42) to (11.45) into Eqs. (11.38) to (11.41) and simplification yields

$$F_1 = A_1 q_o B \tag{11.46}$$

$$F_3 = A_1 q_R B \tag{11.47}$$

$$S_1 = A_2 q_o\, \Delta H \tag{11.48}$$

$$S_2 = A_2 q_R\, \Delta H \tag{11.49}$$

where A_1 and $A_2 = f(z/B)$

The variations of A_1 and A_2 with nondimensional depth z are given in Figure 11.23.

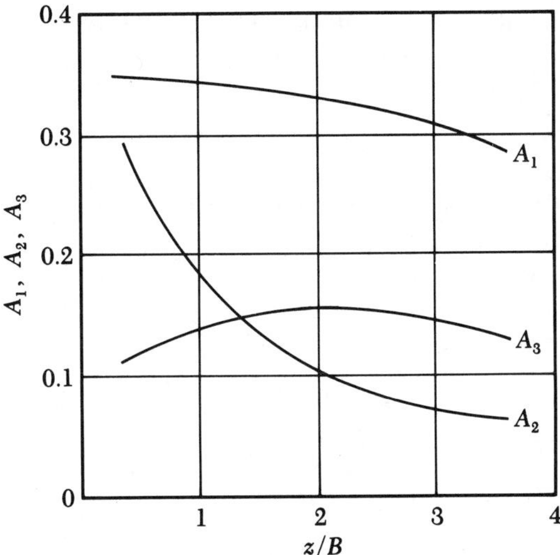

▼ **FIGURE 11.23** Variation of A_1, A_2, and A_3 with z/B (after Binquet and Lee, 1975b)

Substituting Eqs. (11.46)–(11.49) into Eq. (11.37) gives

$$\begin{aligned} T_{(N=1)} &= A_1 q_R B - A_1 q_o B - A_2 q_R\,\Delta H + A_2 q_o\,\Delta H \\ &= A_1 B(q_R - q_o) - A_2\,\Delta H(q_R - q_o) \\ &= q_o\left(\frac{q_R}{q_o} - 1\right)(A_1 B - A_2\,\Delta H) \end{aligned} \tag{11.50}$$

Note that the derivation of Eq. (11.50) was based on the assumption that there is only one layer of reinforcement under the foundation shown in Figure 11.22b. However, if there are N layers of reinforcement under the foundation with center-to-center spacing of ΔH, as shown in Figure 11.22c, the assumption can be made that

$$T_{(N)} = \frac{T_{(N=1)}}{N} \tag{11.51}$$

Combining Eqs. (11.50) and (11.51) gives

$$T_{(N)} = \frac{1}{N}\left[q_o\left(\frac{q_R}{q_o} - 1\right)(A_1 B - A_2\,\Delta H)\right] \tag{11.52}$$

The unit of $T_{(N)}$ in Eq. (11.52) is lb/ft (or kN/m) per unit length of foundation.

11.9 FACTOR OF SAFETY OF TIES AGAINST BREAKING AND PULLOUT

Once the tie forces that develop in each layer as the result of the foundation load are determined from Eq. (11.52), an engineer must determine whether the ties at any depth z

will fail either by *breaking* or by *pullout*. The factor of safety against tie breaking at any depth z below the foundation can be calculated as

$$FS_{(B)} = \frac{wtnf_y}{T_{(N)}} \tag{11.53}$$

where $FS_{(B)}$ = factor of safety against tie breaking
w = width of a single tie
t = thickness of each tie
n = number of ties per unit length of the foundation
f_y = yield or breaking strength of the tie material

The term wn may be defined as the *linear density ratio, LDR*, so

$$FS_{(B)} = \left[\frac{tf_y}{T_{(N)}}\right](LDR) \tag{11.54}$$

The resistance against the tie being pulled out derives from the frictional resistance between the soil and the ties at any depth. From the fundamental principles of statics, we know that the frictional force per unit length of the foundation resisting tie pullout at any depth z (Figure 11.24) is

$$F_B = 2\tan\phi_\mu[\text{normal force}]$$

$$= \underset{\substack{\uparrow \\ \text{Two sides of tie} \\ \text{(i.e., top and bottom)}}}{2\tan\phi_\mu}\left[\underbrace{(LDR)\int_{X_o}^{L_o}\sigma(q_R)\,dx}_{\text{Due to foundation load } = F_5} + \underbrace{(LDR)(\gamma)(L_o - X_o)(z + D_f)}_{\text{Due to effective overburden pressure } = F_6}\right] \tag{11.55}$$

where γ = unit weight of soil
D_f = depth of foundation
ϕ_μ = tie–soil friction angle

The relation for $\sigma(q_R)$ was defined in Eq. (11.43). The value of $x = L_o$ is generally assumed to be the distance at which $\sigma(q_R)$ equals $0.1q_R$. The value of L_o as a function of depth z is given in Figure 11.25. Equation (11.55) may be simplified as

$$F_B = 2\tan\phi_\mu(LDR)\left[A_3 Bq_o\left(\frac{q_R}{q_o}\right) + \gamma(L_o - X_o)(z + D_f)\right] \tag{11.56}$$

where A_3 is a nondimensional quantity that may be expressed as a function of depth (z/B) (see Figure 11.23)

The factor of safety against tie pullout, $FS_{(P)}$, is

$$FS_{(P)} = \frac{F_B}{T_{(N)}} \tag{11.57}$$

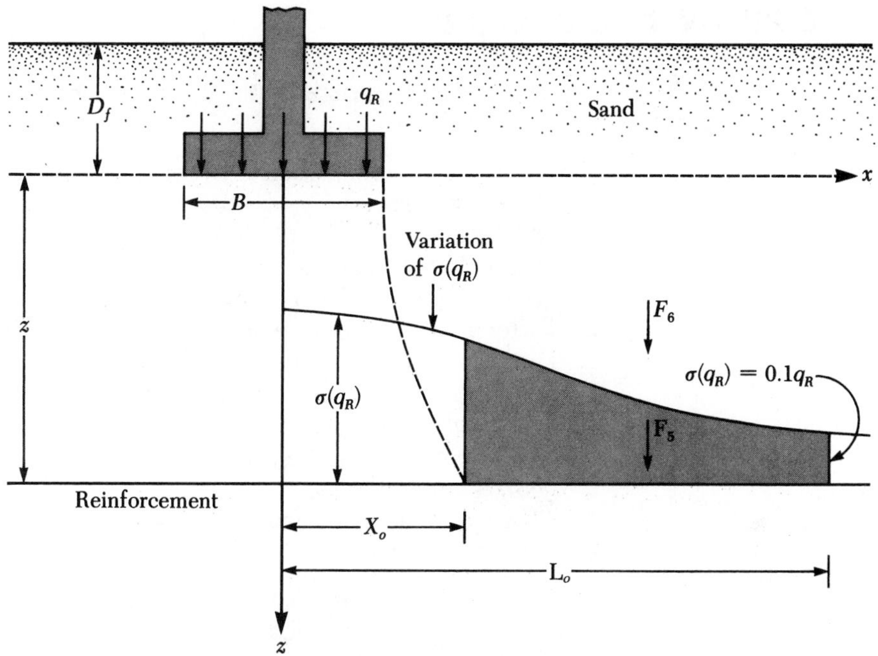

FIGURE 11.24 Derivation of Eq. (11.56)

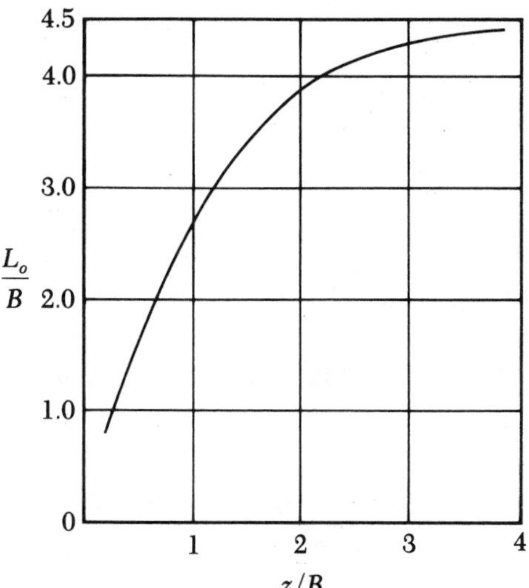

FIGURE 11.25 Variation of L_o/B with z/B (after Binquet and Lee, 1975b)

11.10 DESIGN PROCEDURE

Following is a step-by-step procedure for the design of a continuous foundation supported by reinforced earth.

1. Obtain the total load to be supported per unit length of the foundation. Also obtain the quantities
   a. Soil–friction angle, ϕ
   b. Soil–tie friction angle, ϕ_μ
   c. Factor of safety against bearing capacity failure
   d. Factor of safety against tie breaking, $FS_{(B)}$
   e. Factor of safety against tie pullout, $FS_{(P)}$
   f. Breaking strength of reinforcement ties, f_y
   g. Unit weight of soil, γ
   h. Modulus of elasticity of soil, E_s
   i. Poisson's ratio of soil, μ_s
   j. Allowable settlement of foundations, s
   k. Depth of foundation, D_f
2. Assume a width of foundation, B, and also d and N. The value of d should be less than $\frac{2}{3}B$. Also, the distance from the bottom of the foundation to the lowest layer of the reinforcement should be about $2B$ or less. Calculate ΔH.
3. Assume a value of LDR.
4. For width B (step 2) determine the ultimate bearing capacity, q_u, for unreinforced soil [Eq. (3.3); *note*: $c = 0$]. Determine $q_{\text{all}(1)}$:

$$q_{\text{all}(1)} = \frac{q_u}{FS \text{ against bearing capacity failure}} \tag{11.58}$$

5. Calculate the allowable load, $q_{\text{all}(2)}$, based on the tolerable settlement, s, assuming that the soil is not reinforced [Eq. (3.79)]:

$$s = \frac{Bq_{\text{all}(2)}}{E_s}(1 - \mu_s^2)\alpha_r$$

   For $L/B = \infty$, the value of α_r may be taken as 2, or

$$q_{\text{all}(2)} = \frac{E_s s}{B(1 - \mu_s^2)\alpha_r} \tag{11.59}$$

   (The allowable load for a given settlement, s, could have been determined from equations in Chapter 3 that relate to standard penetration resistances.)
6. Determine the lower of the two values of q_{all} obtained from steps 4 and 5. The lower value of q_{all} equals q_o.
7. Calculate the magnitude of q_R for the foundation supported by reinforced earth:

$$q_R = \frac{\text{load on foundation per unit length}}{B} \tag{11.60}$$

8. Calculate the tie force, $T_{(N)}$, in each layer of reinforcement by using Eq. (11.52) (*note*: unit of $T_{(N)}$ as kN/m of foundation).
9. Calculate the frictional resistance of ties for each layer per unit length of foundation, F_B, by using Eq. (11.56). For each layer, determine whether $F_B/T_{(N)} \geq FS_{(P)}$. If $F_B/T_{(N)} < FS_{(P)}$, the length of the reinforcing strips for a layer may be increased. That will increase the value of F_B and thus $FS_{(P)}$, and so Eq. (11.56) must be rewritten as

$$F_B = 2 \tan \phi_\mu (LDR)\left[A_3 B q_o\left(\frac{q_R}{q_o}\right) + \gamma(L - X_o)(z + D_f)\right] \tag{11.61}$$

where L = the required length to obtain the desired value of F_B

10. Use Eq. (11.54) to obtain the tie thickness for each layer. Some allowance should be made for the corrosion effect of the reinforcements during the life of the structure.
11. If the design is unsatisfactory, repeat steps 2–10.

The following example demonstrates the application of these steps.

▼ EXAMPLE 11.3

Design a continuous foundation that will carry a load of 1.8 MN/m. Use the following parameters.

- *Soil:* $\gamma = 17.3$ kN/m^3; $\phi = 35°$; $E_s = 3 \times 10^4$ kN/m^2; $\mu_s = 0.35$
- *Reinforcement ties:* $f_y = 2.5 \times 10^5$ kN/m^2; $\phi_\mu = 28°$; $FS_{(B)} = 3$; $FS_{(P)} = 2.5$
- *Foundation:* $D_f = 1$ m; factor of safety against bearing capacity failure = 3, tolerable settlement = s = 25 mm; desired life of structure = 50 years.

Solution Let

$B = 1$ m
d = depth from the bottom of the foundation to the first reinforcing layer = 0.5 m
$\Delta H = 0.5$ m
$N = 5$
$LDR = 65\%$

If the reinforcing strips used are 75 mm wide, then

$$wn = LDR$$

or

$$n = \frac{LDR}{w} = \frac{0.65}{0.075 \text{ m}} = \mathbf{8.67/m}$$

Hence each layer will contain 8.66 strips per meter length of the foundation.

Determination of q_o

For an unreinforced foundation

$$q_u = \gamma D_f N_q + \frac{1}{2}\gamma B N_\gamma$$

From Table 3.4 for $\phi = 35°$, $N_q = 33.30$ and $N_\gamma = 48.03$. Thus

$$q_u = (17.3)(1)(33.3) + \frac{1}{2}(17.3)(1)(48.03)$$

$$= 576.09 + 415.46 = 991.55 \approx 992 \text{ kN/m}^2$$

$$q_{\text{all}(1)} = \frac{q_u}{FS} = \frac{992}{3} = 330.7 \text{ kN/m}^2$$

From Eq. (11.59),

$$q_{\text{all}(2)} = \frac{(E_s)(s)}{B(1-\mu_s^2)\alpha_r} = \frac{(30{,}000 \text{ kN/m}^2)(0.025 \text{ m})}{(1 \text{ m})(1-0.35^2)(2)} = 427.35 \text{ kN/m}^2$$

As $q_{\text{all}(1)} < q_{\text{all}(2)}$, $q_o = q_{\text{all}(1)} = \mathbf{330.7\ kN/m^2}$

Determination of q_R

From Eq. (11.60),

$$q_R = \frac{1.8 \text{ MN/m}}{B} = \frac{1.8 \times 10^3}{1} = \mathbf{1.8 \times 10^3\ kN/m^2}.$$

Calculation of Tie Force

From Eq. (11.52),

$$T_{(N)} = \left(\frac{q_o}{N}\right)\left(\frac{q_R}{q_o} - 1\right)(A_1 B - A_2\,\Delta H)$$

The tie forces for each layer are given in the following table.

Layer no.	$\left(\frac{q_o}{N}\right)\left(\frac{q_R}{q_o}-1\right)$	z (m)	$\frac{z}{B}$	$A_1 B$	$A_2\,\Delta H$	$A_1 B - A_2\,\Delta H$	$T_{(N)}$ (kN/m)
1	293.7	0.5	0.5	0.35	0.125	0.225	66.08
2	293.7	1.0	1.0	0.34	0.09	0.25	73.43
3	293.7	1.5	1.5	0.34	0.065	0.275	80.77
4	293.7	2.0	2.0	0.33	0.05	0.28	82.24
5	293.7	2.5	2.5	0.32	0.04	0.28	82.24

Note: A_1 is from Figure 11.23; $B = 1$ m; $\Delta H = 0.5$ m; A_2 is from Figure 11.23; $q_R/q_o = 1.8 \times 10^3/330.7 \approx 5.45$

Calculation of Tie Resistance Due to Friction, F_B

Use Eq. (11.56):

$$F_B = 2 \tan \phi_\mu (LDR)\left[A_3 Bq_o\left(\frac{q_R}{q_o}\right) + \gamma(L_o - X_o)(z + D_f)\right]$$

The following table shows the magnitude of F_B for each layer.

Quantity	*Layer number* 1	2	3	4	5
$2 \tan \phi_\mu (LDR)$	0.691	0.691	0.691	0.691	0.691
A_3	0.125	0.14	0.15	0.15	0.15
$A_3 Bq_o(q_R/q_o)$	225.0	252.0	270.0	270.0	270.0
z (m)	0.5	1.0	1.5	2.0	2.5
z/B	0.5	1.0	1.5	2.0	2.5
L_o (m)	1.55	2.6	3.4	3.85	4.2
X_o (m)	0.55	0.8	1.1	1.4	1.65
$L_o - X_o$ (m)	1.0	1.8	2.3	2.45	2.55
$z + D_f$ (m)	1.5	2.0	2.5	3.0	3.5
$\gamma(L_o - X_o)(z + D_f)$	25.95	62.28	99.48	127.16	154.4
F_B (kN/m)	173.4	217.2	255.1	274.4	293.3
$FS_{(P)} = F_B/T_{(N)}$	2.62	2.96	3.16	3.34	3.57

Note: A_3 is from Figure 11.23; X_o is from Figure 11.20; L_o is from Figure 11.25; $T_{(N)}$ is from the preceding table

The minimum factor of safety is greater than the required value of $FS_{(P)}$, which is 2.5.

Calculation of Tie Thickness to Resist Tie Breaking

From Eq. (11.54),

$$FS_{(B)} = \frac{tf_y}{T_{(N)}}(LDR)$$

$$t = \frac{FS_{(B)} T_{(N)}}{(LDR)(f_y)}$$

Here, $f_y = 2.5 \times 10^5$ kN/m^2, $LDR = 0.65$, and $FS_{(B)} = 3$. So

$$t = \left[\frac{3}{(2.5 \times 10^5)(0.65)}\right] T_{(N)} = (1.846 \times 10^{-5}) T_{(N)}$$

So, for layer 1

$$t = (1.846 \times 10^{-5})(66.08) = 0.00122 \text{ m} = \mathbf{1.22 \text{ mm}}$$

For layer 2

$$t = (1.846 \times 10^{-5})(73.43) = 0.00136 \text{ m} = \mathbf{1.36 \text{ mm}}$$

Similarly, for layer 3

$$t = 0.00149 = \mathbf{1.49\ mm}$$

For layer 4

$$t = \mathbf{1.52\ mm}$$

For layer 5

$$t = \mathbf{1.52\ mm}$$

Thus in each layer ties with a thickness of 1.6 mm will be sufficient. However, if galvanized steel is used, the rate of corrosion is about 0.025 mm/yr. So, t should be $1.6 + (0.025)(50) = \mathbf{2.85\ mm}$.

Calculation of Minimum Length of Ties

The minimum length of ties in each layer should equal $2L_o$. Following is the length of ties in each layer.

Layer no.	*Minimum length of the tie, $2L_o$ (m)*
1	3.1
2	5.2
3	6.8
4	7.7
5	8.4

Figure 11.26 is a diagram of the foundation with the ties. The design could be changed by varying B, d, N, and ΔH to determine the most economical combination.

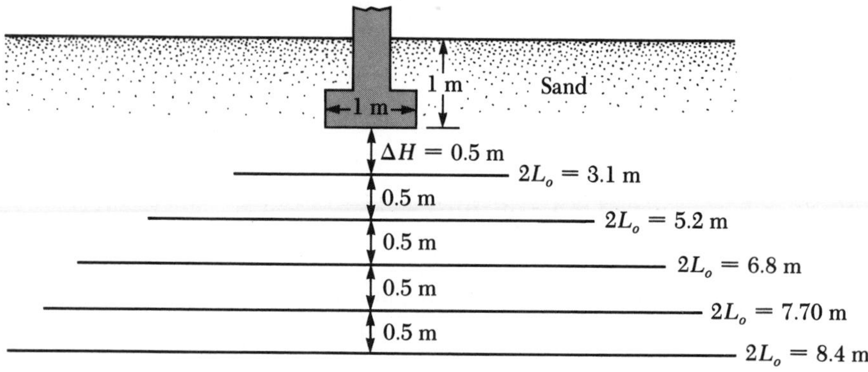

FIGURE 11.26

▼ EXAMPLE 11.4

Refer to Example 11.3. For the loading given, determine the width of the foundation that is needed for unreinforced earth. Note that the factor of safety against bearing capacity failure is 3 and that the tolerable settlement is 25 mm.

Solution

Bearing Capacity Consideration

For a continuous foundation,

$$q_u = \gamma D_f N_q + \frac{1}{2}\gamma B N_\gamma$$

For $\phi = 35°$, $N_q = 33.3$ and $N_\gamma = 48.03$. So

$$q_{\text{all}} = \frac{q_u}{FS} = \frac{1}{FS}\left[\gamma D_f N_q + \frac{1}{2}\gamma B N_\gamma\right]$$

or

$$q_{\text{all}} = \frac{1}{3}\left[(17.3)(1)(33.3) + \frac{1}{2}(17.3)(B)(48.03)\right] \tag{a}$$

$$= 192.03 + 138.5B$$

However,

$$q_{\text{all}} = \frac{1.8 \times 10^3 \text{ kN}}{(B)(1)} \tag{b}$$

Equating the right-hand sides of Eqs. (a) and (b) yields

$$\frac{1800}{(B)(1)} = 192.03 + 138.5B$$

Solving the preceding equation gives $B \approx 3$ m. So, with $B = 3$ m, $q_{\text{all}} =$ **600 kN/m²**.

Settlement Consideration

For a friction angle of $\phi = 35°$, the average standard penetration number is about 10–15 (Table 2.4). From Eq. (3.119b) for the higher value, $N = 15$,

$$q_{\text{all}} = 11.98N\left(\frac{3.28B + 1}{3.28}\right)^2\left(1 + \frac{0.33D_f}{B}\right)$$

for a settlement of about 25 mm. Now, we can make a few trials:

Assumed B (m) (1)	$q_{\text{all}} = 11.98N\left(\frac{3.28B+1}{3.28B}\right)^2\left(1+\frac{0.33D_f}{B}\right)$ (kN/m²) (2)	$Q = (B)(q_{\text{all}})$ = Col. 1 × Col. 2 (kN/m)
6	209	1254
9	199	1791[a]

Note: $D_f = 1$ m
[a] Required 1800 kN/m

For $N = 15$, the width of the foundation should be 9 m or more. Based on the consideration of bearing capacity failure and tolerable settlement, the latter settlement criteria will control. So, B is about **9 m.**

Note: At first, the results of this calculation may show the use of reinforced earth for foundation construction to be desirable. However, several factors must be considered before a final decision is made. For example, reinforced earth needs overexcavation and backfilling. Hence, under many circumstances, proper material selection and compaction may make the construction of foundations on *unreinforced* soils more economical.

▼

RECENT ADVANCES IN BEARING CAPACITY OF FOUNDATIONS ON REINFORCED SOIL

11.11 FOUNDATION ON SAND WITH GEOTEXTILE REINFORCEMENT

Laboratory model tests for determining the bearing capacity of a *square* foundation supported by loose sand (relative density = 50%) and reinforced by layers of nonwoven heat-bonded geotextiles have been reported by Guido et al. (1985). Some of their test results are shown in Figure 11.27b. For these tests, several parameters were varied: d, ΔH, and L_o (Figure 11.27a); number of layers of geotextile, N; and tensile strength of geotextile, σ_G. In general, results show that, when the geotextile layers are placed within a depth equal to the width of the foundation, they increase the load-bearing capacity of the foundation—but only after a measurable settlement has occurred. This result is logical because the geotextile layers have to deform before their reinforcing benefits can be realized.

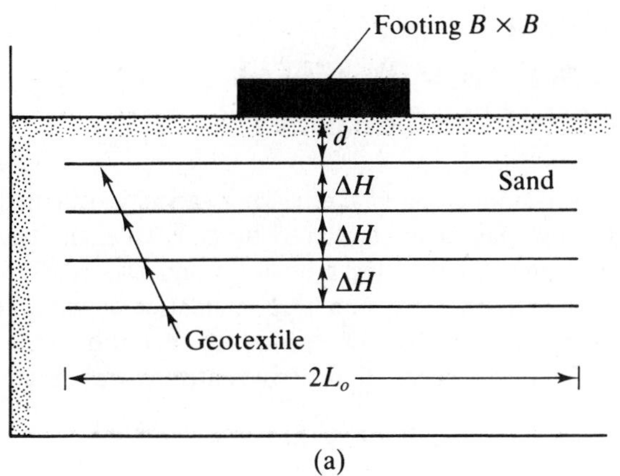

(a)

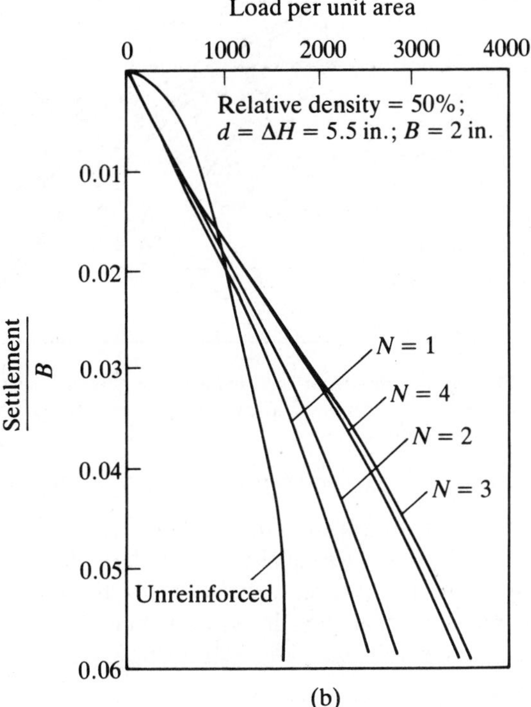

(b)

▼ **FIGURE 11.27** Bearing capacity test of square foundation on loose sand with geotextile reinforcement; N = number of layers of reinforcement (based on the model test results of Guido et al., 1985)

11.12 FOUNDATION ON SATURATED CLAY ($\phi = 0$) WITH GEOTEXTILE REINFORCEMENT

Studies relating to determination of the bearing capacity of a shallow foundation supported by a saturated clay layer reinforced by geotextile, similar to that described in Section 11.11, are rather limited. Recently, Sakti and Das (1987) reported some model test results on the bearing capacity of a *strip* foundation on saturated clay. They used a heat-bonded nonwoven geotextile for reinforcement (grab tensile strength = 534 N). Some of the load–settlement curves thus derived are shown in Figure 11.28.

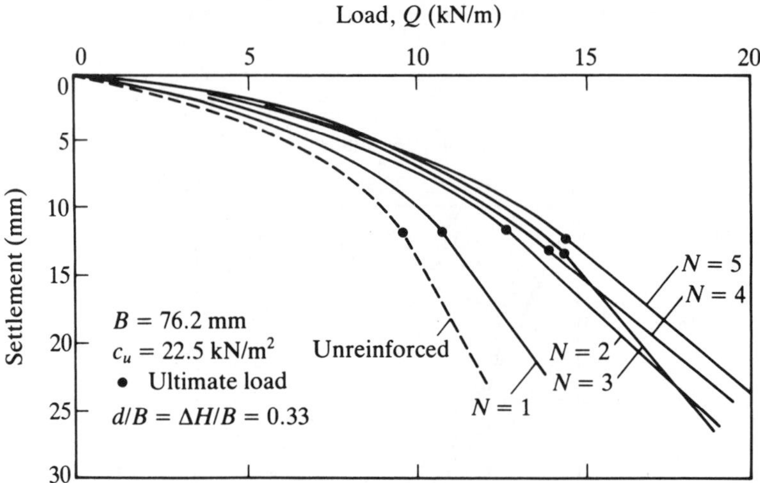

▼ **FIGURE 11.28** Bearing capacity test on strip footing on saturated clay with geotextile reinforcement; N = number of layers of reinforcement (based on the results of Sakti and Das, 1987)

From those tests, the following general conclusions may be drawn.

1. Beneficial effects of geotextile reinforcement are realized when reinforcement is placed within a distance equal to the width of the foundation.
2. The first layer of geotextile reinforcement should be placed at a distance $d = 0.35B$ (B = foundation width) for maximum benefit.
3. The most economical value of L_o/B is about 2. (See Figure 11.27a for a definition of L_o.)

11.13 FOUNDATIONS ON SAND WITH GEOGRID REINFORCEMENT

As pointed out in Sections 11.11 and 11.12, the ultimate bearing capacity of shallow foundations increases when geotextiles are used for soil reinforcement. Recall also (Chapter 3) that, when the width of a shallow foundation is greater than about 3 ft (1 m), the design is primarily controlled by settlement rather than the ultimate bearing capacity. Figure 11.27 indicates that the flexibility of geotextiles does not improve load-bearing capacity at limited levels of settlement. For that reason, several studies of the possible use of geogrid layers as reinforcement in sand to support shallow foundations have been made (e.g., Guido et al., 1986; Guido et al., 1987; Khing et al., 1993; Omar et al., 1993a and 1993b). All were conducted in the laboratory on small-scale models. The results are summarized in this section.

Figure 11.29 shows a rectangular foundation of width B and length L being supported on a sand layer with N layers of geogrid as reinforcement. Each layer of reinforcement had dimensions of $2L_o \times 2L_l$. The first layer of reinforcement is located at a depth d from the bottom of the foundation. The total depth of geogrid reinforcement from the bottom of the foundation may be given as

$$u = d + (N - 1)(\Delta H) \tag{11.62}$$

In general, for any d, N, ΔH, and L_o, the load–settlement curve for a foundation with and without geogrid reinforcement will be as shown in Figure 11.30. Based on this concept, the increase in the bearing capacity due to reinforcement may be expressed in nondimensional form as

$$BCR_u = \frac{q_{u(R)}}{q_u} \tag{11.63}$$

and

$$BCR_s = \frac{q_R}{q_o} \tag{11.64}$$

where BCR_u = bearing capacity ratio with respect to the ultimate bearing capacity
BCR_s = bearing capacity ratio at given settlement level, s, for the foundation
q_R, q_o = load per unit area of the foundation (at a settlement level $s \le s_u$) with and without geogrid reinforcement, respectively
$q_{u(R)}, q_u$ = ultimate bearing capacity with and without geogrid reinforcement, respectively

For a foundation on sand the magnitude of BCR_u generally varies with d/B as shown in Figure 11.31. Beyond a critical value of d/B $[d/B \ge (d/B)_{cr}]$, the magnitude of BCR_u will decrease. At $d/B = (d/B)_{max}$ the failure surface in soil below the foundation will be the type shown in Figure 11.19a. With other parameters remaining constant, if the number of geogrid layers, N, is increased (thus increasing u/B), the value of BCR_u will increase to a maximum at $u/B = (u/B)_{cr}$ and remain virtually constant thereafter (Figure 11.32). Similarly, there is a critical value of $L_o/B = (L_o/B)_{cr}$ and $L_l/B = (L_l/B)_{cr}$ at which the magnitudes of BCR_u will nearly reach a maximum. Figure 11.33 shows the variation of BCR_u with u/B for various magnitudes of the B/L ratio of the foundation.

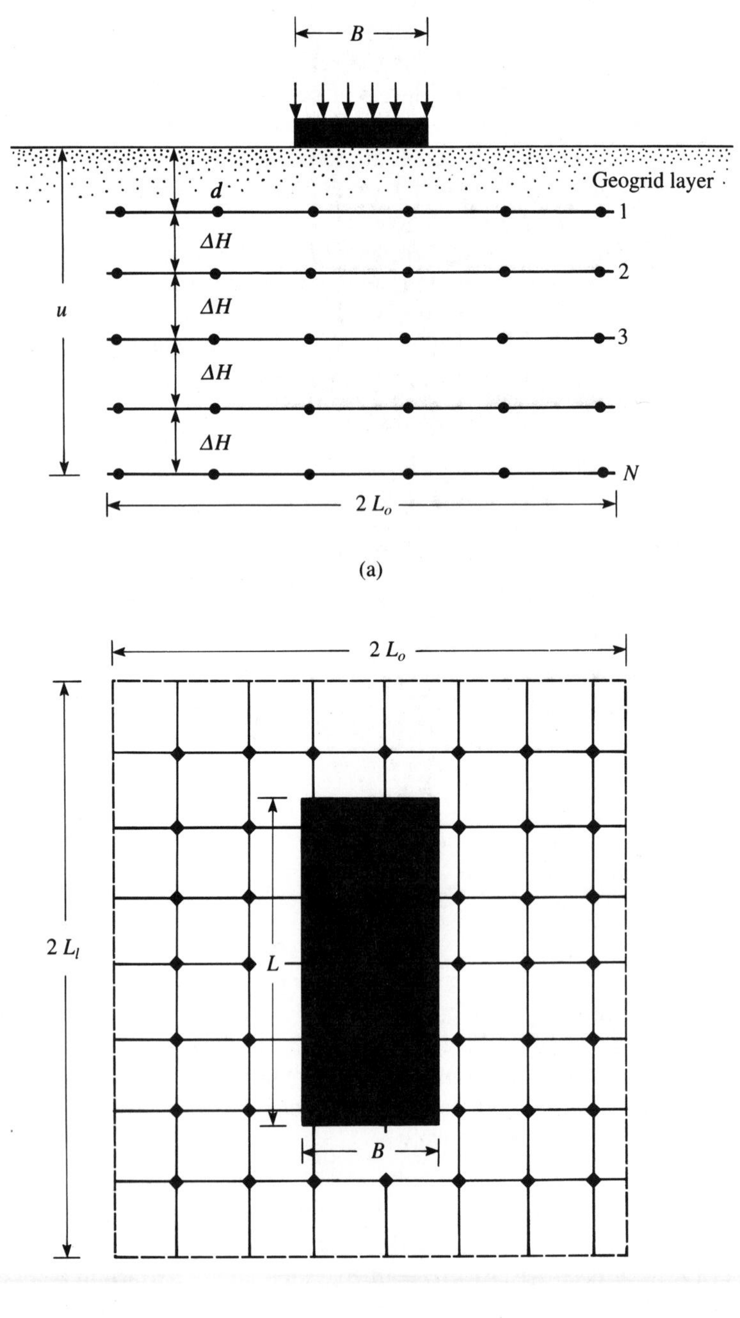

▼ **FIGURE 11.29** Rectangular foundation on sand with geogrid reinforcement

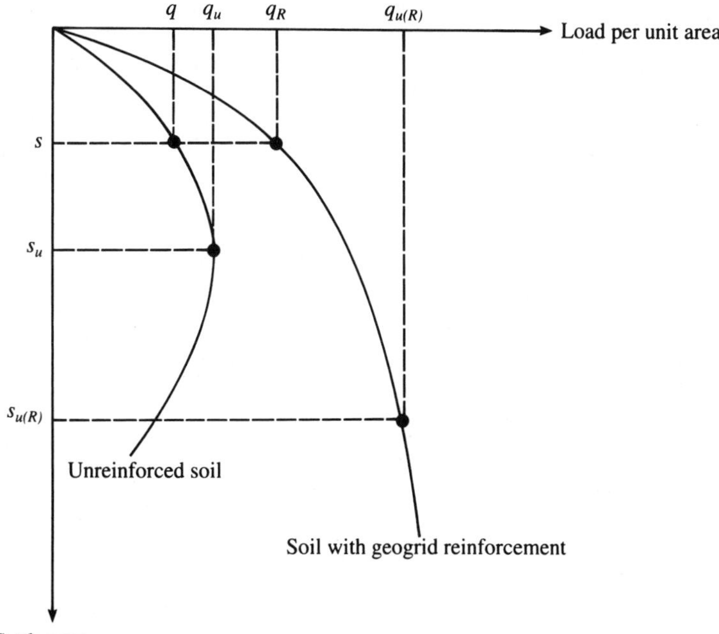

FIGURE 11.30 General form of load–settlement curves for unreinforced soil and soil with geogrid reinforcement supporting a foundation

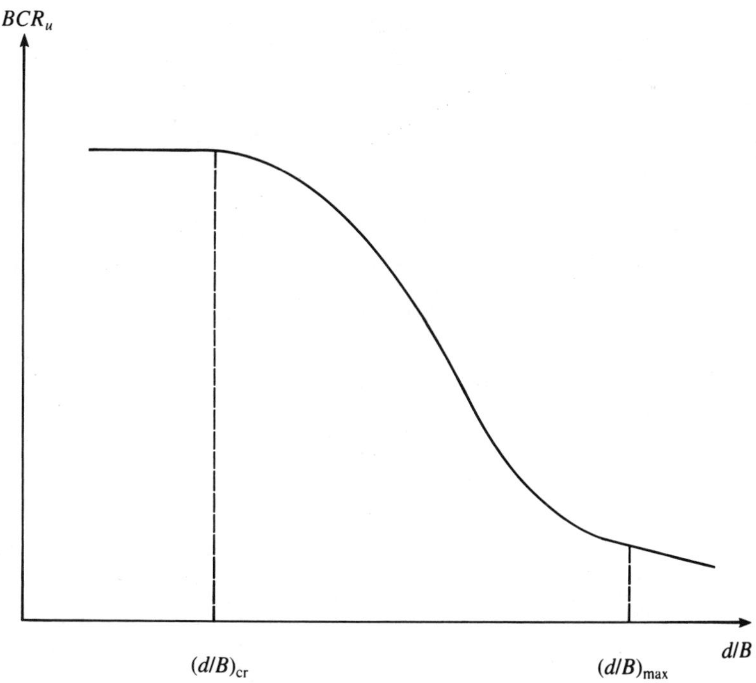

FIGURE 11.31 Nature of variation of BCR_u with d/B for given values of L_o/B, L_l/B, $\Delta H/B$, and N

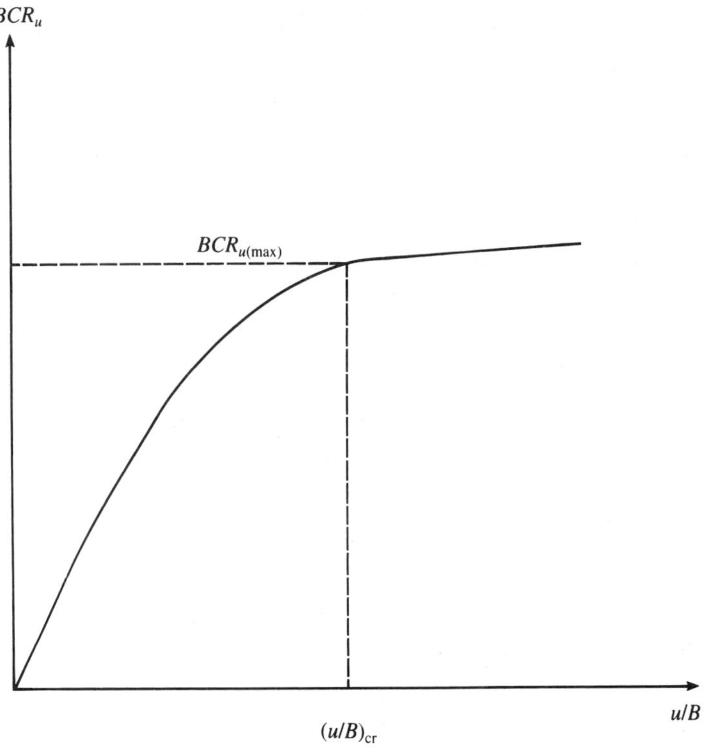

FIGURE 11.32 Variation of BCR_u with u/B

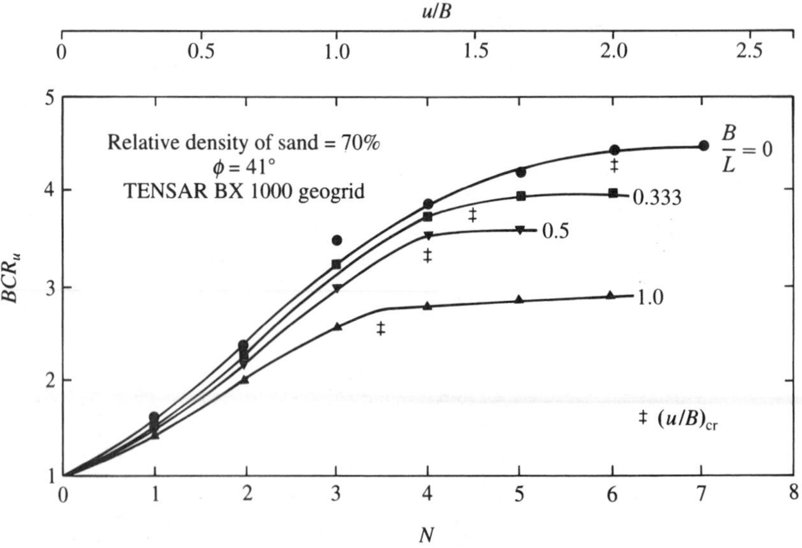

FIGURE 11.33 Variation of BCR_u with u/B for $d/B = \Delta H/B = 0.333$ (after Omar et al., 1993a)

Based on their experimental results, Omar et al. (1993a) provided the following empirical relationships:

$$\left(\frac{u}{B}\right)_{cr} = 2 - 1.4\left(\frac{B}{L}\right) \quad \left(\text{for } 0 \le \frac{B}{L} \le 0.5\right) \tag{11.65}$$

$$\left(\frac{u}{B}\right)_{cr} = 1.43 - 0.26\left(\frac{B}{L}\right) \quad \left(\text{for } 0.5 \le \frac{B}{L} \le 1.0\right) \tag{11.66}$$

$$\left(\frac{d}{B}\right)_{max} \approx 0.9 - 1.0 \tag{11.67}$$

$$\left(\frac{L_o}{B}\right)_{cr} = 4 - 1.75\left(\frac{B}{L}\right)^{0.51} \tag{11.68}$$

$$\left(\frac{L_l}{B}\right)_{cr} = 1.75\left(\frac{B}{L}\right) + \frac{L}{2B} \tag{11.69}$$

Omar et al. (1993b) also showed that, for similar soil and geogrid reinforcement systems, $d/B = 0.25$ to about 0.4:

$$BCR_u \approx 1.7 \text{ to } 1.8(BCR_s) \quad \left(\text{for } \frac{B}{L} = 0\right) \tag{11.70}$$

and

$$BCR_u \approx 1.4 \text{ to } 1.45(BCR_s) \quad \left(\text{for } \frac{B}{L} = 1\right) \tag{11.71}$$

Based on the preliminary model test results, geogrids apparently can be used as soil reinforcement to increase the ultimate and allowable bearing capacities of shallow foundations. Design methodologies are expected to be developed soon for field applications.

11.14 STRIP FOUNDATIONS ON SATURATED CLAY ($\phi = 0$) WITH GEOGRID REINFORCEMENT

Shin et al. (1993) reported laboratory model test results for the ultimate bearing capacity of a surface strip foundation on saturated clay ($\phi = 0$) with geogrid reinforcement. Unlike the results of the tests conducted in sand (Section 11.13),

$$BCR_u = BCR_s = BCR \tag{11.72}$$

Also, the ultimate bearing capacities with and without reinforcement, $q_{u(R)}$ and q_u, occurred at similar settlement levels (i.e., $s_u/B \approx s_{u(R)}/B$—see Figure 11.30). Figures 11.34, 11.35, and 11.36 show the variations of $BCR_u = BCR_s = BCR$ with d/B,

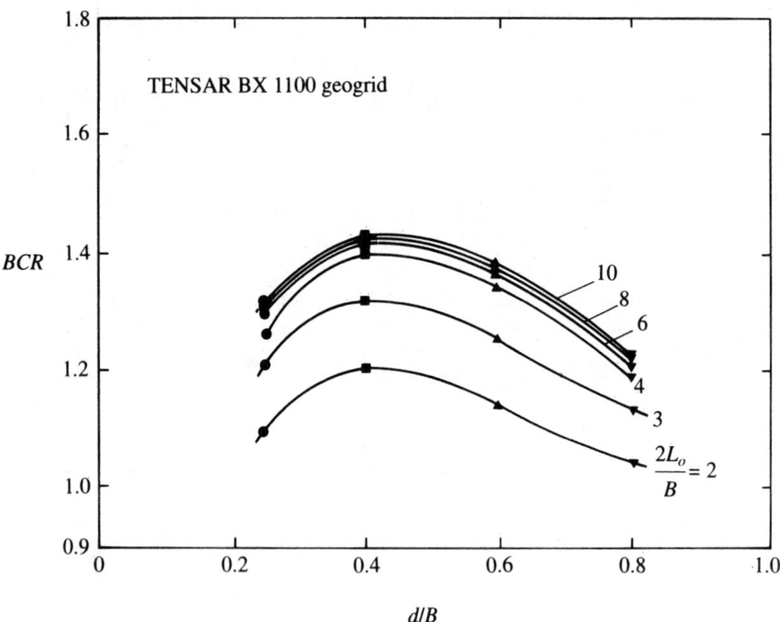

▼ **FIGURE 11.34** Variation of *BCR* with d/B for $c_u = 3.14$ kN/m^2, $\Delta H/B = 0.333$, and $N = 4$ (after Shin et al., 1993)

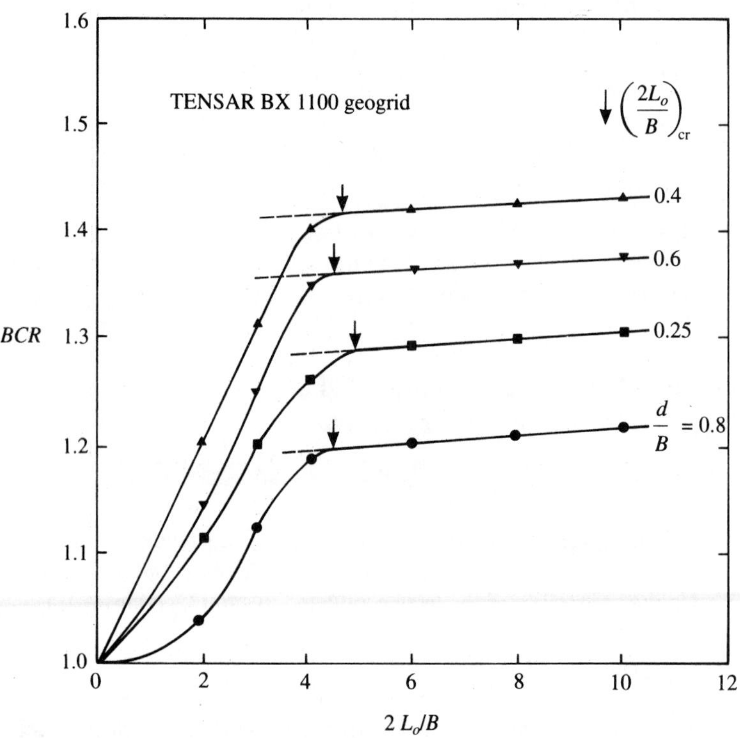

▼ **FIGURE 11.35** Variation of *BCR* with $2L_o/B$ for $c_u = 3.14$ kN/m^2, $\Delta H/B = 0.333$, and $N = 4$ (after Shin et al., 1993)

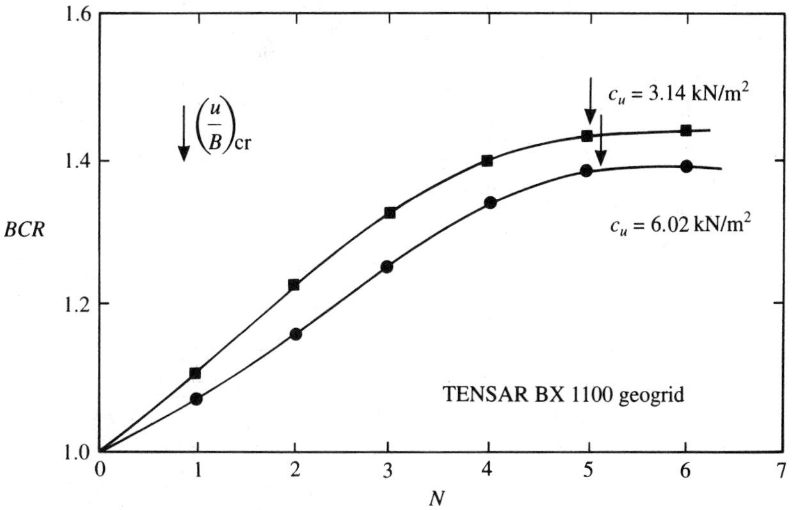

▼ **FIGURE 11.36** Variation of *BCR* with *N* (i.e., u/B) for $2L_o/B = 4$, $d/B = 0.4$, and $\Delta H/B = 0.333$ (after Shin et al., 1993)

$2L_o/B$, and N (or u/B). Based on these model test results, Shin et al. (1993) determined the following parameters:

$$\left(\frac{d}{B}\right)_{cr} \approx 0.4$$

$$\left(\frac{d}{B}\right)_{max} \approx 0.9 - 1.0$$

$$\left(\frac{2L_o}{B}\right)_{cr} \approx 4.0 \text{ to } 4.5$$

$$\left(\frac{u}{B}\right)_{cr} \approx 1.8$$

PROBLEMS

11.1 Refer to Figure 11.6. Use the following parameters.

- ▶ *Wall:* $H = 6$ m
- ▶ *Soil:* $\gamma_1 = 16.5\ \text{kN/m}^3$ and $\phi_1 = 35°$
- ▶ *Reinforcement:* $S_V = 1$ m and $S_H = 1.5$ m
- ▶ *Surcharge:* $q = 50\ \text{kN/m}^2$, $a' = 1.5$ m, and $b' = 2$ m

Calculate the vertical stress, σ_v [Eqs. (11.2), (11.3), and (11.4)] at $z = 1$ m, 2 m, 3 m, 4 m, 5 m, and 6 m.

11.2 For Problem 11.1, calculate the lateral pressure σ_a at $z = 1$ m, 2 m, 3 m, 4 m, 5 m, and 6 m. Use Eqs. (11.5), (11.6), and (11.7).

11.3 A reinforced earth retaining wall (Figure 11.6) is to be 30 ft high. Here,

- ▶ *Backfill:* unit weight, $\gamma_1 = 119\ \text{lb/ft}^3$, for the soil friction angle, $\phi_1 = 34°$
- ▶ *Reinforcement:* vertical spacing, $S_V = 3$ ft, horizontal spacing, $S_H = 4$ ft, width of reinforcement = 4.75 in., $f_y = 38{,}000\ \text{lb/in}^2$, $\phi_\mu = 25°$, factor of safety against tie pullout = 3, and factor of safety against tie breaking = 3

Determine:

a. The required thickness of ties

b. The required maximum length of ties

11.4 In Problem 11.3, assume that the ties at all depths are the length determined in part (b). For *in situ* soil, $\phi_2 = 25°$, $\gamma_2 = 116$ lb/ft^3, and $c_2 = 650$ lb/ft^2. Calculate the factor of safety against (a) overturning, (b) sliding, and (c) bearing capacity failure.

11.5 Redo Problem 11.3 for a retaining wall with a height of 24 ft.

11.6 In Problem 11.5, assume that the ties at all depths are the length determined in part (b). For the *in situ* soil, $\phi_2 = 28°$, $\gamma_2 = 121$ lb/ft^3, and $c_2 = 500$ lb/ft. Calculate the factor of safety against (a) overturning, (b) sliding, and (c) bearing capacity failure.

11.7 Redo Problem 11.3 and change S_V to 1.5 ft.

11.8 A retaining wall with geotextile reinforcement is 6 m high. For the granular backfill, $\gamma_1 = 15.9$ kN/m^3 and $\phi_1 = 30°$. For the geotextile, $\sigma_G = 16$ kN/m. For the design of the wall, determine S_V, L, and l_l. Use $FS_{(B)} = FS_{(P)} = 1.5$.

11.9 For the S_V, L, and l_l determined in Problem 11.8, check the overall stability (that is, factor of safety against overturning, sliding, and bearing capacity failure). For the *in situ* soil, $\gamma_2 = 16.8$ kN/m^3, $\phi_2 = 20°$, and $c_2 = 55$ kN/m^2.

11.10 Check the overall stability (that is, factor of safety against overturning, sliding, and bearing capacity failure) of the retaining wall with geotextile reinforcement given in Example 11.2. Use $\gamma_2 = 108$ lb/ft^3, $\phi_2 = 20°$, and $c_2 = 1200$ lb/ft^2.

11.11 Figure 11.22c shows a continuous foundation on reinforced soil. Here, $B = 0.9$ m, $D_f = 1$ m, number of layers of reinforcement, $N = 5$, $\Delta H = 0.4$ m. Make the necessary calculations and plot the lines on both sides of the foundation that define the point of maximum shear stress, $\tau_{xz(\max)}$, on the reinforcements.

11.12 The tie forces under a continuous foundation are given by Eq. (11.52). For the foundation described in Problem 11.11, $q_o = 200$ kN/m^2 and $q_R/q_o = 4.5$. Determine the tie forces, $T_{(N)}$, in kN/m for each layer of reinforcement.

11.13 Repeat Problem 11.12 with $q_o = 300$ kN/m^2 and $q_R/q_o = 6$.

11.14 A continuous foundation (see Figure 11.22c) is to be built on reinforced earth to carry a load of 82.3 kips/ft. Use the following parameters.

- *Foundation*: $B = 4$ ft, $D_f = 2.6$ ft, factor of safety against bearing capacity failure = 3, and tolerable settlement = 0.8 in.
- *Soil:* $\gamma = 116$ lb/ft^3, $\phi = 37°$, $E_s = 5200$ lb/in^2, and $\mu_s = 0.30$
- *Reinforcement:* $\Delta H = 1.3$ ft, $N = 5$, $LDR = 70\%$, and width of reinforcement strips = 0.23 ft

Calculate:

a. The number of reinforcement strips per foot length of the foundation

b. The allowable load per unit area of the foundation, q_o, without reinforcement

c. The ratio q_R/q_o

d. The tie forces for each layer of reinforcement under the foundation (kip/ft)

11.15 Refer to Problem 11.14. For the reinforcements, $f_y = 38{,}000$ lb/in^2, $\phi_\mu = 25°$, factor of safety against tie breaking = 2.5, and factor of safety againt tie pullout = 2.5. Calculate:

a. The minimum thickness of ties needed to resist tie breaking

b. The minimum length of ties necessary for each layer of reinforcement

REFERENCES

Bell, J. R., Stilley, A. N., and Vandre, B. (1975). "Fabric Retaining Earth Walls," *Proceedings*, Thirteenth Engineering Geology and Soils Engineering Symposium, Moscow, Idaho.

Berg, R. R., Bonaparte, R., Anderson, R. P., and Chouery, V. E. (1986). "Design Construction and Performance of Two Tensar Geogrid Reinforced Walls," *Proceedings*, Third International Conference on Geotextiles, Vienna, pp. 401–406.

Billard, J. W., and Wu, J. T. H. (1991). "Load Test of a Large Scale Geotextile-Reinforced Retaining Walls," *Proceedings*, Geosynthetics '91, Atlanta, Vol. 2, pp. 537–548.

Binquet, J., and Lee, K. L. (1975a). "Bearing Capacity Tests on Reinforced Earth Mass," *Journal of the Geotechnical Engineering Division*, American Society of Civil Engineers, Vol. 101, No. GT12, pp. 1241–1255.

Binquet, J., and Lee, K. L. (1975b). "Bearing Capacity Analysis of Reinforced Earth Slabs," *Journal of the Geotechnical Engineering Division*, American Society of Civil Engineers, Vol. 101, No. GT12, pp. 1257–1276.

Carroll, R., Jr. (1988). "Specifying Geogrids," *Geotechnical Fabric Report*, Industrial Fabric Association International, St. Paul, March/April.

Darbin, M. (1970). "Reinforced Earth for Construction of Freeways" (in French), *Revue Générale des Routes et Aerodromes*, No. 457, September.

Das, B. M. (1981). "Bearing Capacity of Eccentrically Loaded Surface Footings on Sand," *Soils and Foundations*, Vol. 21, No. 1, pp. 115–119.

Das, B. M. (1983). *Advanced Soil Mechanics*, McGraw-Hill, New York.

Guido, V. A., Biesiadecki, G. L., and Sullivan, M. J. (1985). "Bearing Capacity of a Geotextile Reinforced Foundation," *Proceedings*, Eleventh International Conference on Soil Mechanics and Foundation Engineering, San Francisco, Vol. 3, pp. 1777–1780.

Guido, V. A., Chang, D. K., and Sweeny, M. A. (1986). "Comparison of Geogrid and Geotextile Reinforced Slabs," *Canadian Geotechnical Journal*, Vol. 23, pp. 435–440.

Guido, V. A., Knueppel, J. D., and Sweeny, M. A. (1987). "Plate Load Tests on Geogrid-Reinforced Earth Slabs," *Proceedings*, Geosynthetics '87, pp. 216–225.

Jones, C. J. F. P. (1984). "Design and Construction Methods," *Proceedings*, Symposium on Polymer Grid Reinforcement, March 22–23, Institute of Engineers, London, Paper No. 6.1.

Khing, K. H., Das, B. M., Puri, V. K., Cook, E. E., and Yen, S. C. (1993). "The Bearing Capacity of a Strip Foundation on Geogrid-Reinforced Sand," *Geotextiles and Geomembranes*, Vol. 12, No. 4, pp. 351–361.

Koerner, R. B. (1990). *Design with Geosynthetics*, 2nd ed., Prentice-Hall, Englewood Cliffs, N.J.

Laba, J. T., and Kennedy, J. B. (1986). "Reinforced Earth Retaining Wall Analysis and Design," *Canadian Geotechnical Journal*, Vol. 23, No. 3, pp. 317–326.

Lee, K. L., Adams, B. D., and Vagneron, J. J. (1973). "Reinforced Earth Retaining Walls," *Journal of the Soil Mechanics and Foundations Division*, American Society of Civil Engineers, Vol. 99, No. SM10, pp. 745–763.

Mandel, J., and Salencon, J. (1972). "Force portante d'un sol sur une assise rigide (étude theorizué)," *Geotechnique*, Vol. 22, No. 1, pp. 79–93.

Martin, J. P., Koerner, R. M., and Whitty, J. E. (1984). "Experimental Friction Evaluation of Slippage Between Geomembranes, Geotextiles, and Soils," *Proceedings*, International Conference on Geomembranes, Denver, pp. 191–196.

Meyerhof, G. G. (1974). "Ultimate Bearing Capacity of Footings on Sand Layer Overlying Clay," *Canadian Geotechnical Journal*, Vol. 11, No. 2, pp. 223–229.

Omar, M. T., Das, B. M., Yen, S. C., Puri, V. K., and Cook, E. E. (1993a). "Ultimate Bearing Capacity of Rectangular Foundations on Geogrid-Reinforced Sand," *Geotechnical Testing Journal*, American Society for Testing and Materials, Vol. 16, No. 2, pp. 246–252.

Omar, M. T., Das, B. M., Yen, S. C., Puri, V. K., and Cook, E. E. (1993b). "Shallow Foundations on Geogrid-Reinforced Sand," *Transportation Research Record No. 1414*, National Academy of Sciences, National Research Council, pp. 59–64.

Pfeifle, T. W., and Das, B. M. (1979). "Bearing Capacity of Surface Footings on Sand Layer Resting on a Rigid Rough Base," *Soils and Foundations*, Vol. 19, No. 1, pp. 1–11.

Sakti, J., and Das, B. M. (1987). "Model Tests for Strip Foundation on Clay Reinforced with Geotextile Layers," *Transportation Research Record No. 1153,* National Academy of Sciences, Washington, D.C., pp. 40–45.

Schlosser, F., and Long, N. (1974). "Recent Results in French Research on Reinforced Earth," *Journal of the Construction Division*, American Society of Civil Engineers, Vol. 100, No. CO3, pp. 113–237.

Schlosser, F., and Vidal, H. (1969). "Reinforced Earth" (in French), *Bulletin de Liaison des Laboratories Routier*, Ponts et Chassées, Paris, France, November, pp. 101–144.

Shin, E. C., Das, B. M., Puri, V. K., Yen, S. C., and Cook, E. E. (1993). "Bearing Capacity of Strip Foundation on Geogrid-Reinforced Clay," *Geotechnical Testing Journal*, American Society for Testing and Materials, Vol. 17, No. 4, pp. 534–541.

Tensar Corporation (1986). *The Tensar Technical Note. No. TTN:RW1*, August.

Thamm, B. R., Krieger, B., and Krieger, J. (1990). "Full-Scale Test on a Geotextile-Reinforced Retaining Structure," *Proceedings*, Fourth International Conference on Geotextiles, Geomembranes, and Related Products, The Hague, Vol. 1, pp. 3–8.

Vidal, H. (1966). "La terre Armee," *Anales de l'Institut Technique du Bâtiment et des Travaux Publiques*, France, July–August, pp. 888–938.

CHAPTER TWELVE

SOIL IMPROVEMENT

12.1 INTRODUCTION

The existing soil at a construction site may not always be totally suitable for supporting structures such as buildings, bridges, highways, and dams. For example, in granular soil deposits the *in situ* soil may be very loose and indicate a large elastic settlement. In such a case, the soil needs to be densified to increase its unit weight and thus the shear strength.

Sometimes the top layers of soil are undesirable and must be removed and replaced with better soil, on which the structural foundation can be built. The soil used as fill should be well compacted to sustain the desired structural load. Compacted fills may also be required in low-lying areas to raise the ground elevation for foundation construction.

Soft saturated clay layers are often encountered at shallow depths below foundation(s). Depending on the structural load and the depth of the clay layer(s), unusually large consolidation settlement may occur. Special soil-improvement techniques are required to minimize settlement.

In Chapter 10 we mentioned that the properties of expansive soils could be altered substantially by adding stabilizing agents such as lime. Improving *in situ* soils by using additives is usually referred to as *stabilization.*

Various techniques for improving soil are used to

1. Reduce the settlement of structures
2. Improve the shear strength of soil and thus increase the bearing capacity of shallow foundations
3. Increase the factor of safety against possible slope failure of embankments and earth dams
4. Reduce the shrinkage and swelling of soils

The chapter is divided into six main parts: (1) compaction, (2) vibroflotation, (3) precompression, (4) sand drains, (5) soil stabilization by admixtures, and (6) use of stone columns and granular trenches in weak clays for foundation construction.

12.2 COMPACTION—GENERAL PRINCIPLES

If a small amount of water is added to a soil that is then compacted, the soil will have a certain unit weight. If the moisture content of the same soil is gradually increased and the compaction is the same, the dry unit weight of the soil will gradually increase. The reason is that water acts as a lubricant between the soil particles, and under compaction it helps rearrange the solid particles into a denser state. The increase in dry unit weight with increase of moisture content for a soil will reach a limiting value beyond which further addition of water to the soil will result in a *reduction* of dry unit weight. The moisture content at which the *maximum dry unit weight* is obtained is referred to as the *optimum moisture content.*

The standard laboratory tests used for evaluation of maximum dry unit weights and optimum moisture contents for various soils are (a) the *standard Proctor test* [ASTM designation D-698; Title: Moisture Density Relations and Soils and Soil–Aggregate Mixtures Using 5.5 lb (2.49 kg) Rammer and 12 in. (305 mm) Drop] and (b) the *modified Proctor test* [ASTM designation D-1557; Title: Moisture Density Relations of Soils and Soil-Aggregate Mixtures Using 10 lb (4.54 kg) Rammer and 18 in. (457 mm) Drop]. Both tests are conducted in a mold having a volume of 1/30 ft^3 ($0.944 \times 10^{-3}\ \text{m}^3$). The soil is compacted in several layers by a hammer. The moisture content of the soil, w, is changed, and the dry unit weight, γ_d, of compaction for each test is determined. The maximum dry unit weight of compaction and the corresponding optimum moisture content are determined by plotting a graph of γ_d against w (%). The standard specifications for the two types of Proctor test are given in Table 12.1.

Figure 12.1 shows the plot of γ_d against w (%) for a clayey silt obtained from standard and modified Proctor tests. The following conclusions may be drawn.

1. The maximum dry unit weight and the optimum moisture content depend on the amount of compaction.
2. The higher the energy of compaction, the higher is the maximum dry unit weight.
3. The higher the energy of compaction, the lower is the optimum moisture content.
4. No portion of the compaction curve can lie to the right of the zero-air-void line. The zero-air-void dry unit weight, γ_{zav}, at a given moisture content is the theoretical maximum value of γ_d, which means that all the void spaces of the compacted soil are filled with water, or

$$\gamma_{zav} = \frac{\gamma_w}{\dfrac{1}{G_s} + w} \tag{12.1}$$

where γ_w = unit weight of water
G_s = specific gravity of the soil solids
w = moisture content

5. The maximum dry unit weight of compaction and the corresponding optimum moisture content will vary from soil to soil.

TABLE 12.1 Specifications for the Standard and Modified Proctor Tests

No.	Item	Specifications: *Standard Proctor*	*Modified Proctor*
1	Volume of mold	1/30 ft^3 (0.944 × 10^{-3} m^3)	1/30 ft^3 (0.944 × 10^{-3} m^3)
2	Mass of hammer	5.5 lb (2.495 kg)	10 lb (4.536 kg)
3	Height of drop of the hammer	12 in. (304.8 mm)	18 in. (457 mm)
4	Number of hammer blows per layer of soil	25	25
5	Number of layers of compaction	3	5
6	Energy of compaction	12,375 ft-lb/ft^3 (593 kJ/m^3)	56,259 ft-lb/ft^3 (2695 kJ/m^3)

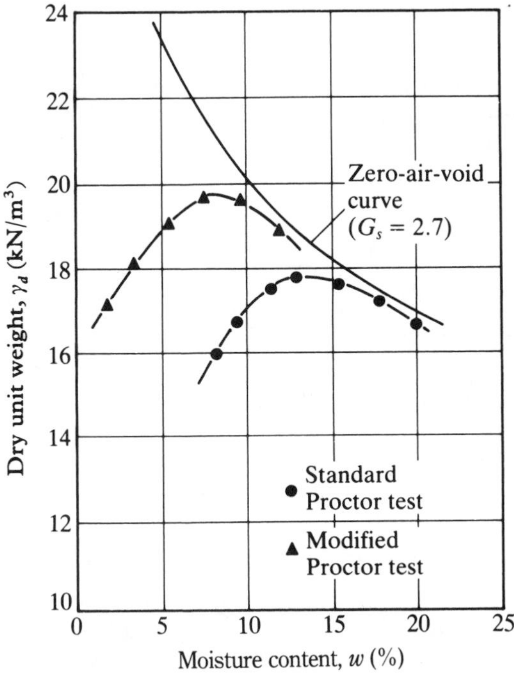

FIGURE 12.1 Standard and modified Proctor compaction curves for a clayey silt

Using the results of the laboratory compaction (γ_d against w), specifications may be written for the compaction of a given soil in the field. In most cases, the contractor is required to achieve a relative compaction of 90% or more on the basis of a specific laboratory test (either the standard or the modified Proctor compaction test). Relative compaction, RC, is defined as

$$RC = \frac{\gamma_{d(\text{field})}}{\gamma_{d(\text{max})}} \tag{12.2}$$

Chapter 1 introduced the concept of relative density (for compaction of granular soils). Relative density was defined as

$$D_r = \left[\frac{\gamma_d - \gamma_{d(\text{min})}}{\gamma_{d(\text{max})} - \gamma_{d(\text{min})}}\right]\frac{\gamma_{d(\text{max})}}{\gamma_d}$$

where D_r = relative density
γ_d = dry unit weight of compaction in the field
$\gamma_{d(\text{max})}$ = maximum dry unit weight of compaction as determined in the laboratory
$\gamma_{d(\text{min})}$ = minimum dry unit weight of compaction as determined in the laboratory

For granular soils in the field, the degree of compaction obtained is often measured in terms of relative density. Comparing the expressions for relative density and relative compaction reveals that

$$RC = \frac{A}{1 - D_r(1 - A)} \tag{12.3}$$

where $A = \dfrac{\gamma_{d(\text{min})}}{\gamma_{d(\text{max})}}$

Lee and Singh (1971) reviewed 47 different soils, and, based on their review, presented the correlation:

$$D_r(\%) = \frac{(RC - 80)}{0.2} \tag{12.4}$$

One-Point Method of Obtaining $\gamma_{d(\max)}$

The state highway department of Ohio has developed a family of standard curves for various soil types, as shown in Figure 12.2. Note that they are plots of *wet unit weight*, γ, against moisture content, w (%). These curves are used to obtain $\gamma_{d(\max)}$ in the field. This technique, referred to as the *one-point* method, serves as a rapid means of field compaction control. This method first involves a standard Proctor test with the soil in use and a determination of the moist unit weight of compaction and the corresponding moisture content. Then a plot of the values of γ and w identifies the compaction curve number (Figure 12.2) corresponding to the test results. Using this curve number with Table 12.2 gives the maximum dry unit weight and the corresponding optimum moisture content.

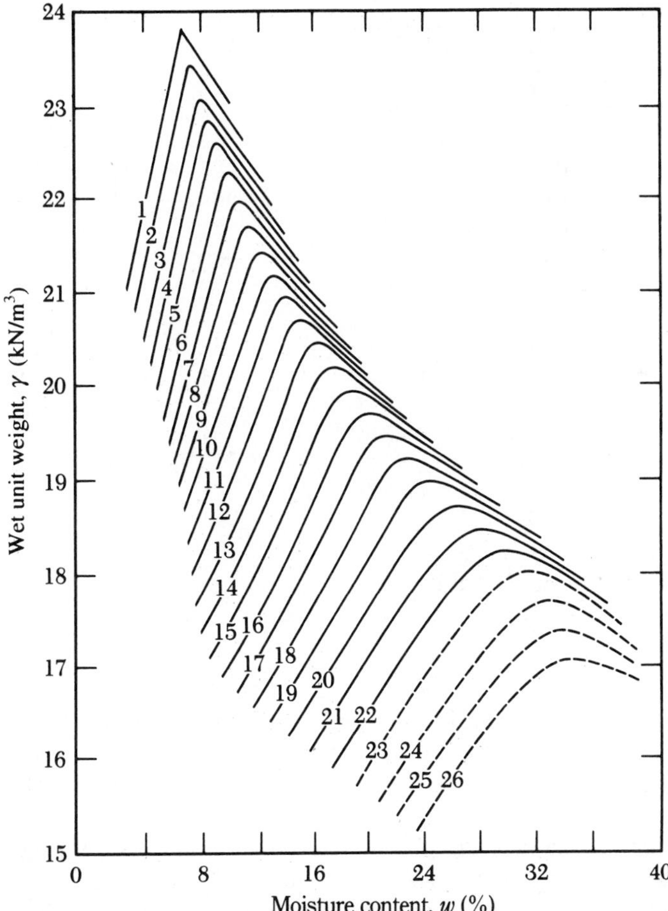

▼ **FIGURE 12.2** Ohio compaction curves (from "Factors That Influence Field Compaction of Soils," by A. W. Johnson and J. R. Sallberg, *Bulletin No. 262*, Highway Research Board, 1960. Reprinted by permission)

TABLE 12.2 Maximum Dry Unit Weight and Optimum Moisture Content for the Compaction Curves in Figure 12.2[a]

Curve number	Maximum dry unit weight		Optimum moisture content
	lb/ft^3	*kN/m*^{3}	(%)
1	142.8	22.29	6.6
2	139.1	21.87	7.2
3	136.3	21.43	7.9
4	134.1	21.08	8.5
5	132.0	20.75	9.0
6	129.3	20.33	9.7
7	126.6	19.90	10.5
8	124.2	19.53	11.2
9	121.7	19.13	11.9
10	119.3	18.76	12.7
11	117.0	18.39	13.5
12	114.6	18.02	14.6
13	112.0	17.61	15.8
14	109.6	17.23	16.9
15	107.1	16.84	18.1
16	104.7	16.46	19.2
17	102.4	16.10	20.3
18	99.9	15.71	21.5
19	97.4	15.31	22.7
20	94.6	14.87	24.4
21	92.1	14.48	25.8
22	89.9	14.13	27.4
23	87.5	13.76	29.5
24	85.0	13.36	30.5
25	83.0	13.05	31.5
26	81.1	12.75	32.5

[a] After Johnson and Sallberg (1960)

The one-point method appears to be simple and easy to use. However, that may not always be the case. Researchers have determined that not all soils yield the bell-shaped compaction curves shown in Figure 12.2. Lee and Suedkamp (1972) performed 700 compaction tests on 35 soil samples. Their results show that, depending on the property of the soil, the plot of γ_d against w (%) may exhibit one of four different shapes. These shapes are shown in Figure 12.3 and are marked Types I, II, III, and IV. Type I is a standard bell-shaped curve. Type II is a curve showing one and one-half peaks. Type III is a double-peak curve. Type IV is an oddly shaped curve that shows no distinct optimum moisture content. Lee and Suedkamp (1972) then developed the follow-

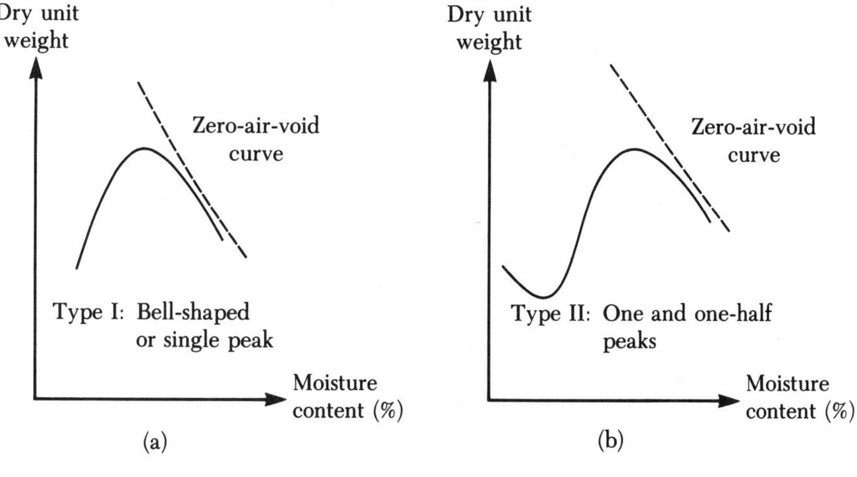

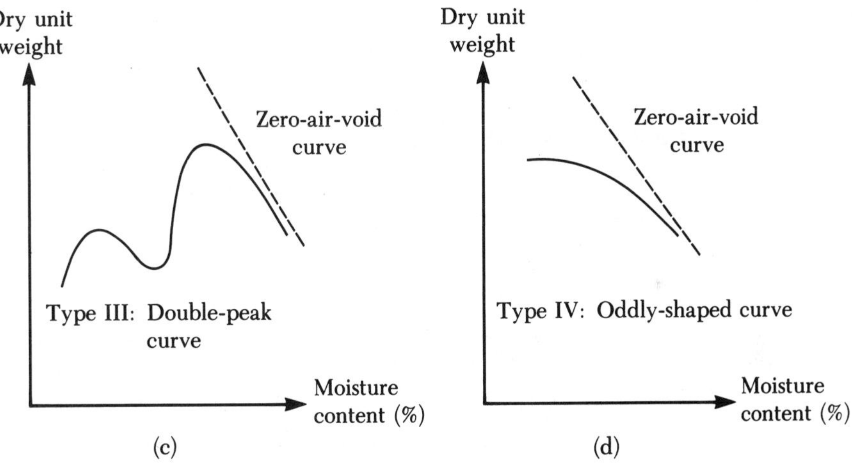

▼ **FIGURE 12.3** Various types of compaction curve

ing guidelines to help predict the nature of compaction curves that may be obtained from various soils.

Liquid limit of soil	*Nature of compaction curve to be expected*
30 to 70	Type I
Less than 30	Types II and III
Greater than 70	Types III and IV

▼ EXAMPLE 12.1

A soil was compacted in the field by the standard Proctor test procedure. The weight of compacted wet soil in the mold = 17.2 N, and the moisture content = 14%. Use Figure 12.2 to determine $\gamma_{d(\min)}$ and the optimum moisture content.

Solution The moist unit weight of compaction is

$$\gamma = \frac{17.2\ \text{N}}{\text{volume of Proctor mold}} = \frac{17.2}{0.944 \times 10^{-3}} = 18.22\ \text{kN/m}^3$$

According to Figure 12.2 (with $\gamma = 18.22$ kN/m^3 and $w = 14\%$), the soil appears to fall between curves 15 and 16. According to Table 12.2, $\gamma_{d(\max)}$ is between 16.84 kN/m^3 and 16.46 kN/m^3, and the optimum moisture content is between 18.1 and 19.2%. So, for this soil,

$$\gamma_{d(\max)} \approx \mathbf{16.6\ kN/m^3}$$

and

optimum moisture content ≈ **18.5%** ▼

Field Compaction

Ordinary compaction in the field is done by rollers. Of the several types of roller used, the most common are

1. Smooth wheel rollers (or smooth drum rollers)
2. Pneumatic rubber-tired rollers
3. Sheepsfoot rollers
4. Vibratory rollers

Figure 12.4 shows a *smooth wheel roller* that can also create vertical vibration during compaction. Smooth wheel rollers are suitable for proof-rolling subgrades and for finishing the construction of fills with sandy or clayey soils. They provide 100% coverage under the wheels, and the contact pressure can be as high as 45–60 lb/in^2 (≈300–400 kN/m^2). However, they do not produce uniform unit weight of compaction when used on thick layers.

Pneumatic rubber-tired rollers (Figure 12.5) are better in many respects than smooth wheel rollers. These rollers, which may weigh as much as 450 kip (2000 kN), consist of a heavily loaded wagon with several rows of tires. These tires are closely spaced—four to six in a row. The contact pressure under the tires may range up to 85–100 lb/in^2 (≈600–700 kN/m^2), and they produce about 70–80% coverage. Pneumatic rollers, which can be used for sandy and clayey soil compaction, produce a combination of pressure and kneading action.

Sheepsfoot rollers (Figure 12.6) consist basically of drums with large numbers of projections. The area of each of the projections may be 4–14 in^2 (25–90 cm^2). These rollers are *most effective in compacting cohesive soils*. The contact pressure under the projections may range from 215–1100 lb/in^2 (≈1500–7500 kN/m^2). During compaction

▼ **FIGURE 12.4** Vibratory smooth wheel rollers (courtesy of Tampo Manufacturing Co., Inc., San Antonio, Texas)

▼ **FIGURE 12.5** Pneumatic rubber-tired roller (courtesy of Tampo Manufacturing Co., Inc., San Antonio, Texas)

▼ **FIGURE 12.6** Vibratory sheepsfoot roller (courtesy of Tampo Manufacturing Co., Inc., San Antonio, Texas)

in the field, the initial passes compact the lower portion of a lift. Later, the middle and top of the lift are compacted.

Vibratory rollers are efficient in compacting granular soils. Vibrators can be attached to smooth wheel, pneumatic rubber-tired, or sheepsfoot rollers to send vibrations into the soil being compacted. Figure 12.4 and 12.6 show vibratory smooth wheel rollers and a vibratory sheepsfoot roller.

In general, compaction in the field depends on several factors, such as the type of compactor, soil type, moisture content, lift thickness, towing speed of the compactor, and the number of roller passes. Figure 12.7 shows the variation of the dry unit weight of a heavy clay with the number of passes of pneumatic-tired rollers. Table 12.3 gives the details of the variables for the three curves shown in Figure 12.7.

Figure 12.8 shows the variation of the unit weight of compaction with depth for a poorly graded dune sand compacted by a vibratory drum roller. Vibration was produced by mounting an eccentric weight on a single rotating shaft within the drum cylinder. The weight of the roller used for this compaction was 55.7 kN and the drum diameter was 1.19 m. The lifts were kept at 2.44 m. Note that, at any depth, the dry unit weight of compaction increases with the number of roller passes. However, the rate of increase of unit weight gradually decreases after about 15 passes. Note also the variation of dry unit weight with depth by number of roller passes. The dry unit weight and

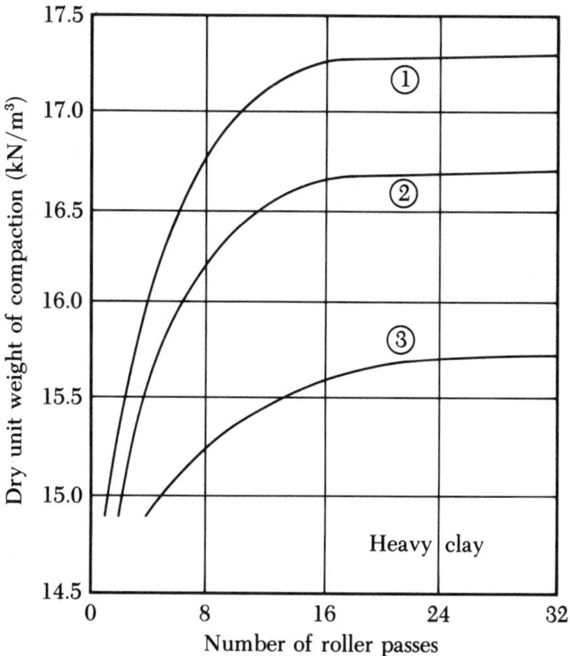

▼ **FIGURE 12.7** Relation between dry unit weight of compaction for the upper 150 mm of soil and the number of passes of pneumatic-tired roller (from "Factors That Influence Field Compaction of Soils," by A. W. Johnson and J. R. Sallberg, *Bulletin No. 262*, Highway Research Board, 1960. Reprinted by permission)

▼ **TABLE 12.3 Details of the Variables for the Three Curves Shown in Figure 12.7**[a]

Curve no.	1	2	3
Moist content as rolled (%)	19.0	20.0	24.0
Optimum moisture content—standard Proctor test (%)	22.8	22.8	22.8
Roller rating (kN)	416.0	416.0	120.0
Wheel load (kN)	99.6	49.8	13.3
Tire pressure (kN/m^2)	966.0	621.0	248.4
Loose lift thickness (mm)	305.0	305.0	229.0

[a] After Johnson and Sallberg (1960)

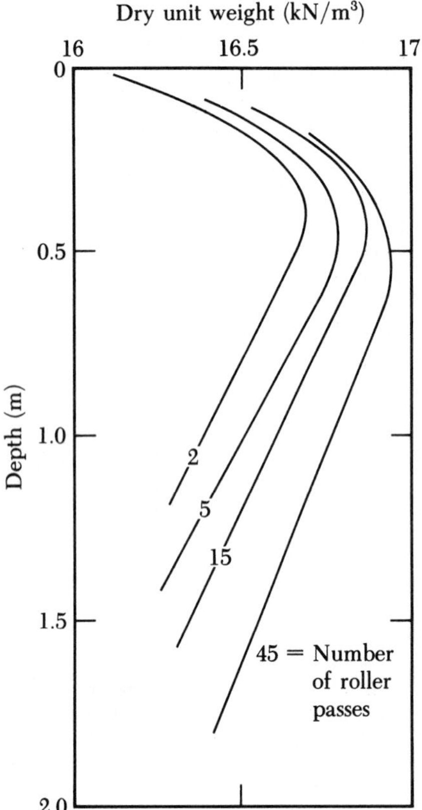

▼ **FIGURE 12.8** Vibratory compaction of a sand—variation of dry unit weight with depth and number of roller passes; lift thickness = 2.44 m (after D'Appolonia et al., 1969)

hence the relative density, D_r, reach maximum values at a depth of about 0.5 m and then gradually decrease as the depth decreases. The reason is the lack of confining pressure toward the surface. Once the depth against relative density (or dry unit weight) relation for a soil for a given number of roller passes is determined, estimating the approximate thickness of each lift is easy. This procedure is shown in Figure 12.9.

12.3 VIBROFLOTATION

Vibroflotation is a technique developed in Germany in the 1930s for *in situ* densification of thick layers of loose granular soil deposits. Vibroflotation was first used in the United States about 10 years later. The process involves the use of a *vibroflot* (called the *vibrating unit*), as shown in Figure 12.10, which is about 6 ft (2 m) in length. This vibrating unit has an eccentric weight inside it and can develop a centrifugal force. The weight enables the vibrating unit to vibrate horizontally. There are openings at the bottom and top of the vibrating unit for water jets. The vibrating unit is attached to a

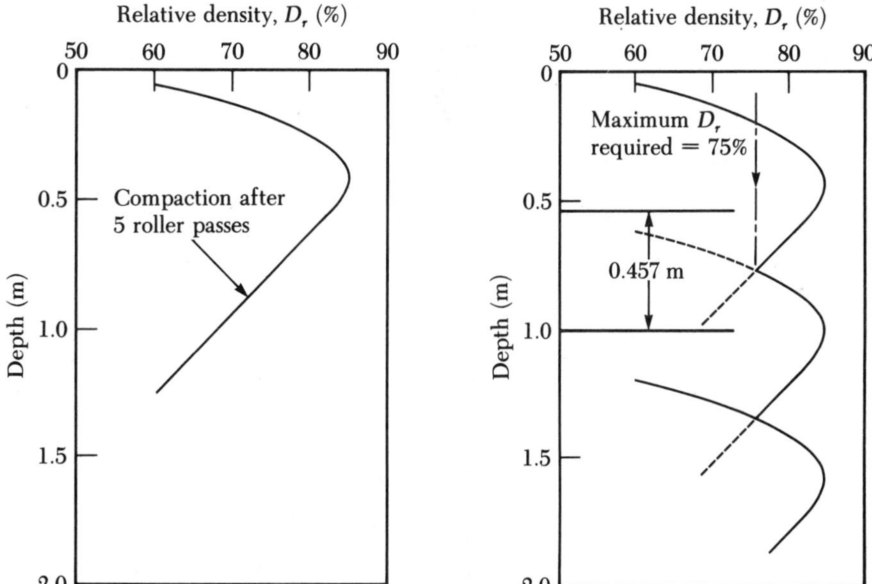

▼ **FIGURE 12.9** A method for estimating compaction lift thickness. Minimum relative density required is 75% after five roller passes (after D'Appolonia et al., 1969)

follow-up pipe. Figure 12.10 shows the vibroflotation equipment necessary for compaction in the field.

The entire compaction process can be divided into four stages (Figure 12.11, page 738):

Stage 1. The jet at the bottom of the vibroflot is turned on, and the vibroflot is lowered into the ground.

Stage 2. The water jet creates a quick condition in the soil, which allows the vibrating unit to sink.

Stage 3. Granular material is poured into the top of the hole. The water from the lower jet is transferred to the jet at the top of the vibrating unit. This water carries the granular material down the hole.

Stage 4. The vibrating unit is gradually raised in about 1 ft (0.3 m) lifts and held vibrating for about 30 seconds at a time. This process compacts the soil to the desired unit weight.

Table 12.4 gives the details of various types of vibroflot unit used in the United States. The 30-HP electric units have been used since the latter part of the 1940s. The 100-HP units were introduced in the early 1970s.

The zone of compaction around a single probe will vary according to the type of vibroflot used. The cylindrical zone of compaction will have a radius of about 6 ft (2 m) for a 30-HP unit. This radius may extend to about 10 ft (3 m) for a 100-HP unit. Compaction by vibroflotation involves various probe spacings, depending on the zone of compaction (see Figure 12.12, page 738). Mitchell (1970) and Brown (1977) reported several successful cases of foundation design using vibroflotation.

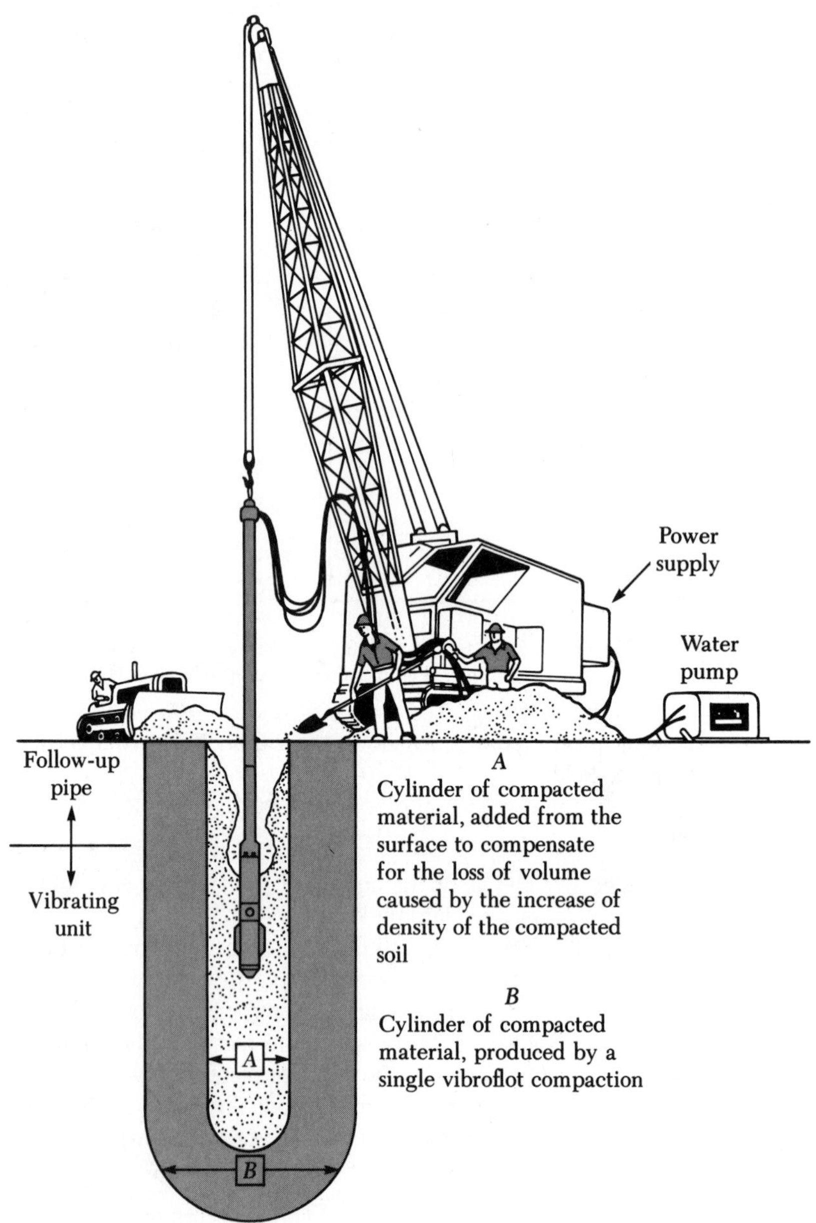

▼ **FIGURE 12.10** Vibroflotation unit (after Brown, 1977)

The capacity of successful densification of *in situ* soil depends on several factors, the most important of which is the grain-size distribution of the soil and also the nature of backfill used to fill the holes during the withdrawal period of the vibroflot. The range of the grain-size distribution of *in situ* soil marked Zone 1 in Figure 12.13 is most suitable for compaction by vibroflotation. Soils that contain excessive amounts of fine

TABLE 12.4 Types of Vibrating Units[a]

	100-HP electric and hydraulic motors	30-HP electric motors
(a) Vibrating tip		
Length	7 ft (2.1 m)	6.11 ft (1.86 m)
Diameter	16 in. (406.4 mm)	15 in. (381 mm)
Weight	4000 lb (17.8 kN)	4000 lb (17.8 kN)
Maximum movement when free	0.49 in. (12.45 mm)	0.3 in. (7.62 mm)
Centrifugal force	18 ton (160 kN)	10 ton (89 kN)
(b) Eccentric		
Weight	260 lb (1.16 kN)	170 lb (0.76 kN)
Offset	1.5 in. (38.1 mm)	1.25 in. (31.75 mm)
Length	24 in. (610 mm)	15.25 in. (387 mm)
Speed	1800 rpm	1800 rpm
(c) Pump		
Operating flow rate	0–400 gal/min (0–1.6 m^3/min)	0–150 gal/min (0–6 m^3/min)
Pressure	100–150 lb/in^2 (690–1035 kN/m^2)	100–150 lb/in^2 (690–1035 kN/m^2)
(d) Lower follow-up pipe and extensions		
Diameter	12 in. (305 mm)	12 in. (305 mm)
Weight	250 lb/ft (3.65 kN/m)	250 lb/ft (3.65 kN/m)

[a] After Brown (1977)

sand and silt-size particles are difficult to compact; for them, considerable effort is needed to reach proper relative density of compaction. Zone 2 in Figure 12.13 is the approximate lower limit of grain-size distribution for compaction by vibroflotation. Soil deposits whose grain-size distribution falls in Zone 3 contain appreciable amounts of gravel. For these soils, the rate of probe penetration may be rather slow, and so compaction by vibroflotation might prove to be uneconomical in the long run.

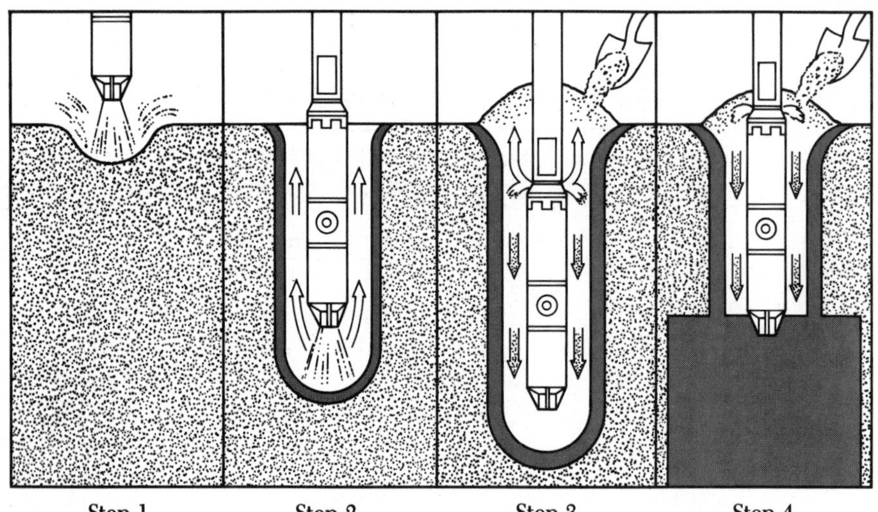

▼ **FIGURE 12.11** Compaction by the vibroflotation process (after Brown, 1977)

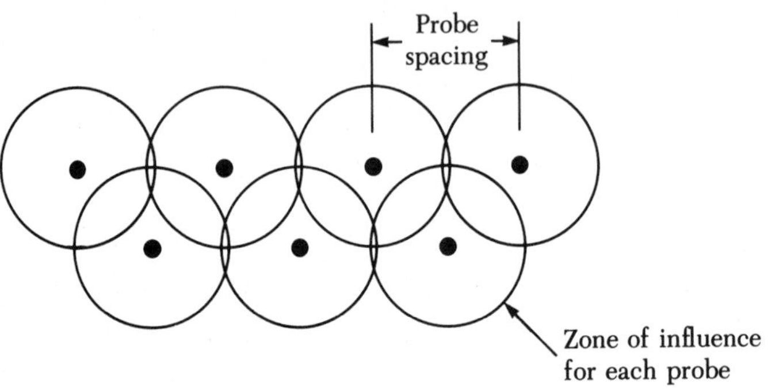

▼ **FIGURE 12.12** Nature of probe spacing for vibroflotation

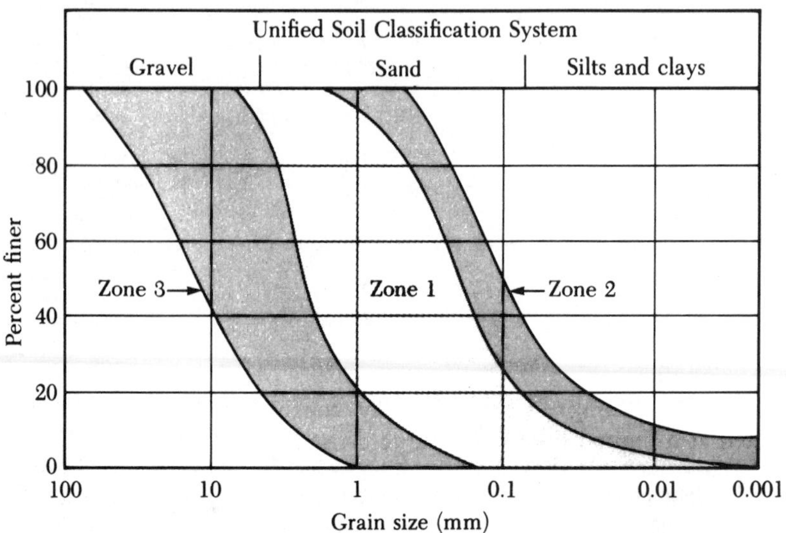

▼ **FIGURE 12.13** Effective range of grain-size distribution of soil for vibroflotation

The grain-size distribution of the backfill material is one of the factors that control the rate of densification. Brown (1977) defined a quantity called ***suitability number***, S_N, for rating a backfill material:

$$S_N = 1.7\sqrt{\frac{3}{(D_{50})^2} + \frac{1}{(D_{20})^2} + \frac{1}{(D_{10})^2}} \tag{12.5}$$

where D_{50}, D_{20}, and D_{10} are the diameters (in mm) through which 50%, 20%, and 10%, respectively, of the material is passing.

The smaller the value of S_N, the more desirable is the backfill material. Following is a backfill rating system as proposed by Brown (1977):

Range of S_N	*Rating as backfill*
0–10	Excellent
10–20	Good
20–30	Fair
30–50	Poor
>50	Unsuitable

12.4 CASE STUDY OF DENSIFICATION BY VIBROFLOTATION

An excellent case study that evaluated the benefits of vibroflotation was presented by Basore and Boitano (1969). Densification of granular subsoil was necessary for construction of a three-story office building at the Treasure Island Naval Station in San Francisco, California. The top 30 ft ($\approx$9 m) of soil at the site was loose to medium-dense sand fill that had to be compacted. Figure 12.14 shows the layout of the vibroflotation compaction points and the location of the test borings. Sixteen compaction points were arranged in groups of four, with 4-ft, 5-ft, 6-ft, 7-ft, and 8-ft spacing. Prior to compaction, standard penetration tests were conducted at the centers of groups of three compaction points. After completion of compaction by vibroflotation, the variation of the standard penetration resistance with depth was determined at the same points.

Figure 12.15 (page 741) shows the variation of the standard penetration resistance, N (blows/ft), with depth before and after compaction. The 4-ft spacing produced the greatest increase in density of the sand, whereas the 8-ft spacing had practically no effect. Figure 12.16 (page 742) shows the relationship between the standard penetration resistance before and after compaction, spacing between compaction points, and the depth below the ground surface. For any given spacing between compaction points, the standard penetration resistance decreased with an increase in depth. The increase in the standard penetration resistance at any depth indicates the increase in the relative

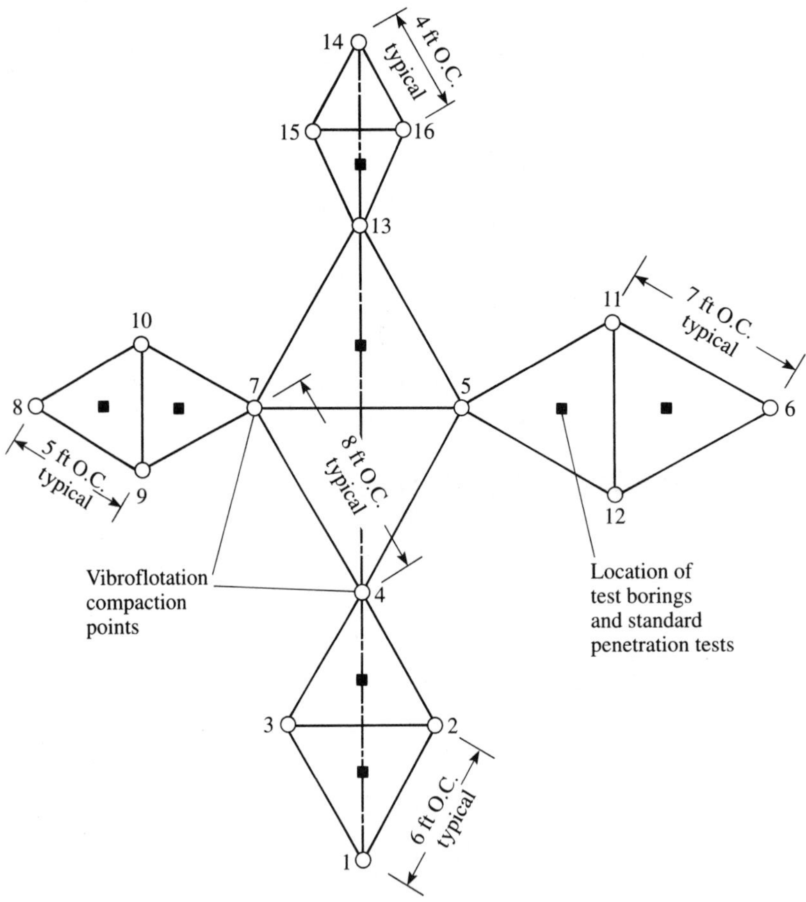

▼ **FIGURE 12.14** Layout of vibroflotation compaction points and test borings (after Basore and Boitano, 1969)

density of compaction, D_r, of sand. Figure 12.17 (page 743) shows the variation of D_r before and after compaction for depths up to 30 ft.

During the past 20 to 25 years, the vibroflotation technique has been used successfully on large projects to compact granular subsoils, thereby controlling structural settlement.

12.5 PRECOMPRESSION—GENERAL CONSIDERATIONS

When highly compressible, normally consolidated clayey soil layers lie at a limited depth and large consolidation settlements are expected as the result of the construction of large buildings, highway embankments, or earth dams, precompression of soil may be used to minimize postconstruction settlement. The principles of precompression are

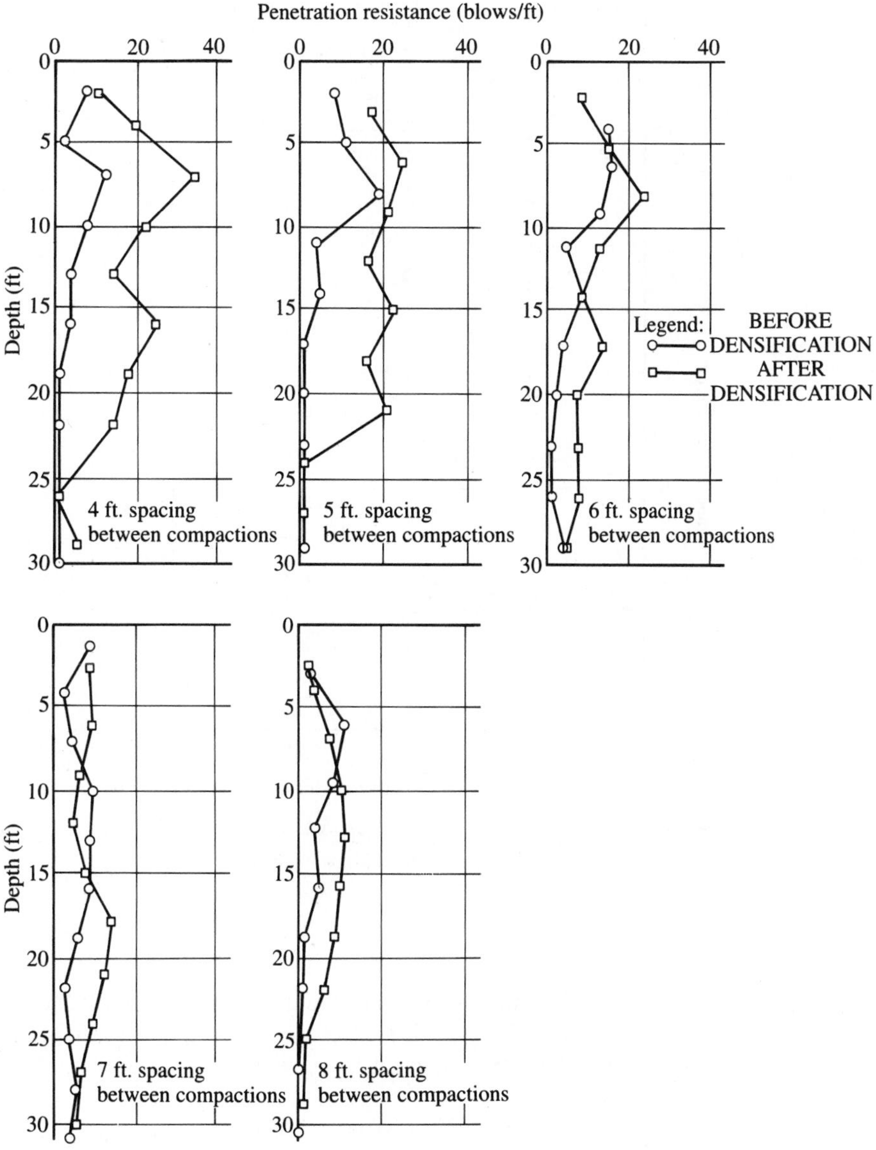

▼ **FIGURE 12.15** Variation of standard penetration resistance before and after compaction (after Basore and Boitano, 1969)

best explained by reference to Figure 12.18. Here, the proposed structural load per unit area is $\Delta p_{(p)}$ and the thickness of the clay layer undergoing consolidation is H_c. The maximum primary consolidation settlement caused by the structural load, $S_{(p)}$, then is

$$S_{(p)} = \frac{C_c H_c}{1 + e_o} \log \frac{p_o + \Delta p_{(p)}}{p_o} \tag{12.6}$$

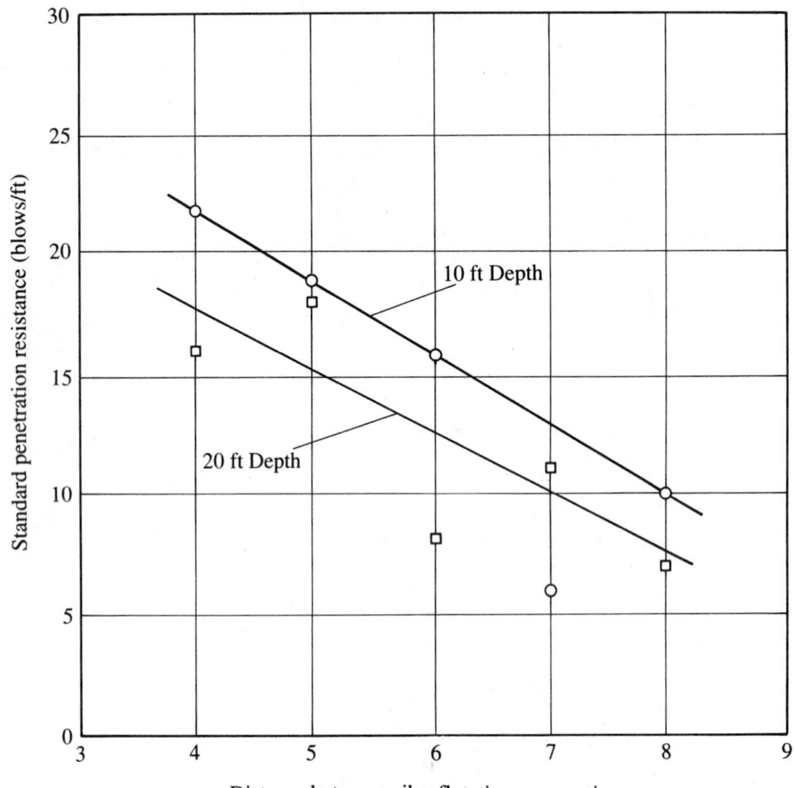

▼ **FIGURE 12.16** Variation of standard penetration resistance after compaction with spacing and depth (after Basore and Boitano, 1969)

The settlement–time relationship under the structural load will be like that shown in Figure 12.18b. However, if a surcharge of $\Delta p_{(p)} + \Delta p_{(f)}$ is placed on the ground, the primary consolidation settlement $S_{(p+f)}$ will be

$$S_{(p+f)} = \frac{C_c H_c}{1 + e_o} \log \frac{p_o + [\Delta p_{(p)} + \Delta p_{(f)}]}{p_o} \tag{12.7}$$

The settlement–time relationship under a surcharge of $\Delta p_{(p)} + \Delta p_{(f)}$ is also shown in Figure 12.18b. Note that a total settlement of $S_{(p)}$ would occur at a time t_2, which is much shorter than t_1. So, if a temporary total surcharge of $\Delta p_{(f)} + \Delta p_{(p)}$ is applied on the ground surface for time t_2, the settlement will equal $S_{(p)}$. At that time, if the surcharge is removed and a structure with a permanent load per unit area of $\Delta p_{(p)}$ is built, no appreciable settlement will occur. The procedure just described is *precompression*. The total surcharge $\Delta p_{(p)} + \Delta p_{(f)}$ can be applied by means of temporary fills.

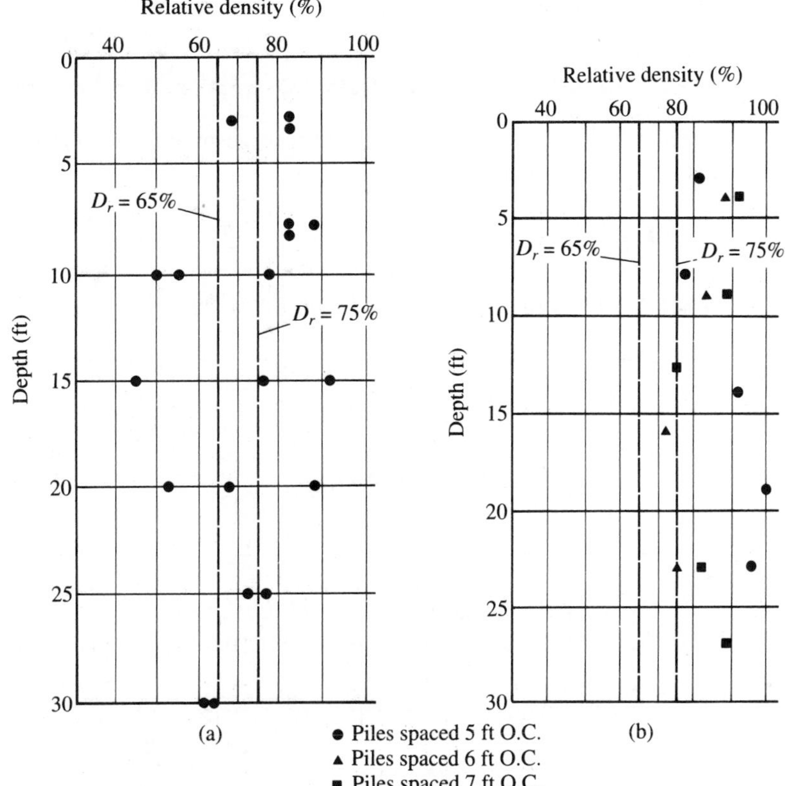

▼ **FIGURE 12.17** Variation of relative density: (a) before compaction; (b) after compaction (after Basore and Boitano, 1969)

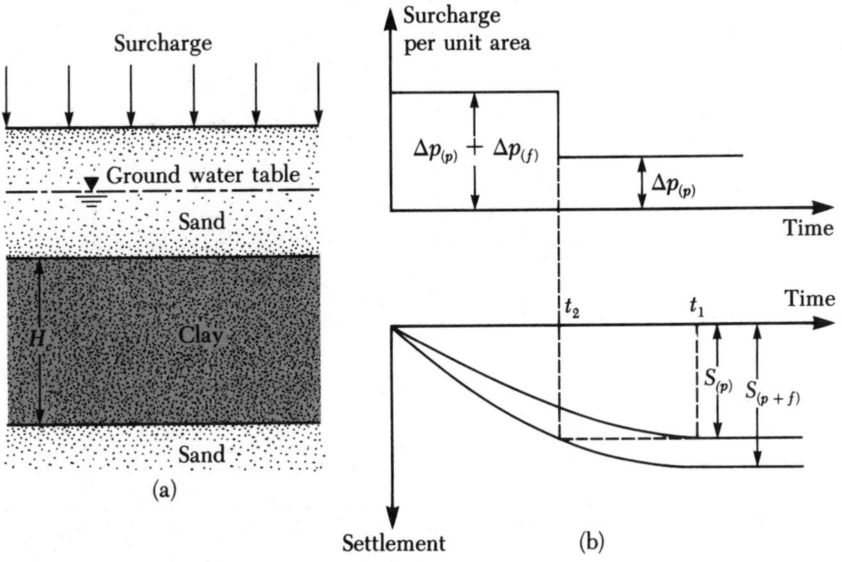

▼ **FIGURE 12.18** Principles of precompression

Derivation of Equations to Obtain Δp_f and t_2

Figure 12.18b shows that, under a surcharge of $\Delta p_{(p)} + \Delta p_{(f)}$, the degree of consolidation at time t_2 after load application is

$$U = \frac{S_{(p)}}{S_{(p+f)}} \tag{12.8}$$

Substitution of Eqs. (12.6) and (12.7) into Eq. (12.8) yields

$$U = \frac{\log\left[\dfrac{p_o + \Delta p_{(p)}}{p_o}\right]}{\log\left[\dfrac{p_o + \Delta p_{(p)} + \Delta p_{(f)}}{p_o}\right]} = \frac{\log\left[1 + \dfrac{\Delta p_{(p)}}{p_o}\right]}{\log\left\{1 + \dfrac{\Delta p_{(p)}}{p_o}\left[1 + \dfrac{\Delta p_{(f)}}{\Delta p_{(p)}}\right]\right\}} \tag{12.9}$$

Figure 12.19 gives magnitudes of U for various combinations of $\Delta p_{(p)}/p_o$ and $\Delta p_{(f)}/\Delta p_{(p)}$. The degree of consolidation referred to in Eq. (12.9) is actually the average

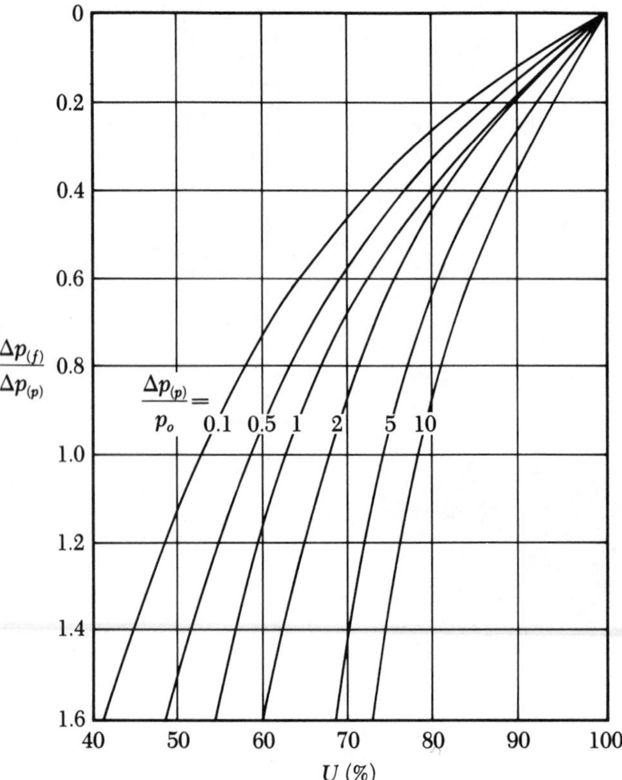

▼ **FIGURE 12.19** Plot of $\Delta p_{(f)}/\Delta p_{(p)}$ against U for various values of $\Delta p_{(p)}/p_o$—Eq. (12.9)

degree of consolidation at time t_2, as shown in Figure 12.18b. However, if the average degree of consolidation is used to determine time t_2, some construction problems might occur. The reason is that, after the removal of the surcharge and placement of the structural load, the portion of clay close to the drainage surface will continue to swell, and the soil close to the midplane will continue to settle (Figure 12.20). In some cases, net continuous settlement might result. A conservative approach may solve this problem—that is, assume that U in Eq. (12.9) is the midplane degree of consolidation (Johnson, 1970a). Now, from Eq. (1.72),

$$U = f(T_v) \tag{1.68}$$

where T_v = time factor = $C_v t_2/H^2$
C_v = coefficient of consolidation
t_2 = time
H = maximum drainage path ($=H_c/2$ for two-way drainage and equal to H_c for one-way drainage)

The variation of U (midplane degree of consolidation) with T_v is given in Figure 12.21.

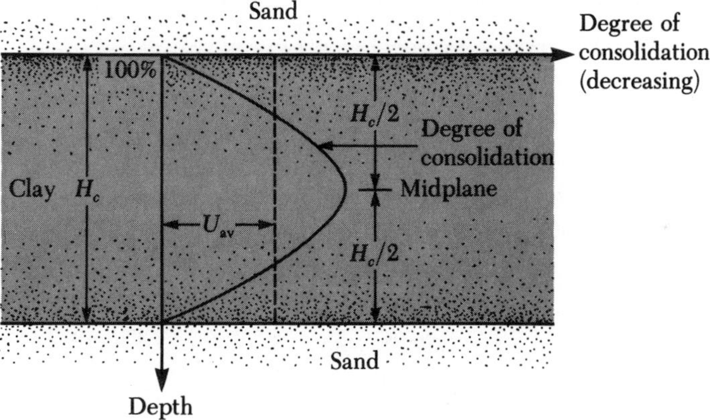

▼ **FIGURE 12.20**

Procedure for Obtaining Precompression Parameters

Two problems may be encountered by engineers during precompression work in the field:

1. The value of $\Delta p_{(f)}$ is known, but t_2 must be obtained. In such a case, obtain p_o, $\Delta p_{(p)}$, and solve for U using Eq. (12.9) or Figure 12.19. For this value of U, obtain T_v from Figure 12.21. Then

$$t_2 = \frac{T_v H^2}{C_v} \tag{12.10}$$

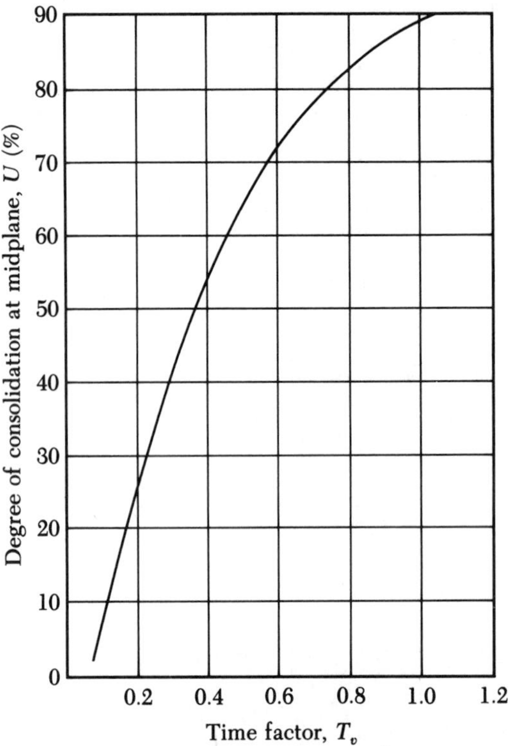

▼ **FIGURE 12.21** Plot of midplane degree of consolidation against T_v

2. For a specified value of t_2, $\Delta p_{(f)}$ must be obtained. In such a case, calculate T_v. Then refer to Figure 12.21 to obtain the midplane degree of consolidation, U. With the estimated value of U, go to Figure 12.19 to get the required $\Delta p_{(f)}/\Delta p_{(p)}$ and then calculate $\Delta p_{(f)}$.

Examples of Precompression and General Comments

Johnson (1970a) presented an excellent review of the use of precompression for improving foundation soils for several projects, including the Morganza Floodway Control Structure near Baton Rouge, Louisiana; the Old River Low-Sill Control Structure near Natchez, Mississippi; and the Old River Overbank Control Structure, Port Elizabeth Marine Terminal, New York. Figure 12.22 shows the subsoil conditions encountered near the Port Elizabeth Marine Terminal before the construction of warehouse buildings No. 131 and 132 located in the Jersey Meadows just west of New York City. Details of the precompression of the subsoil before the construction of the buildings are shown in Figure 12.23. Also shown is the theoretical variation of the settlement with time. In most cases, the predicted settlement exceeded the actual consolidation settlement. The reason is that several variables are involved in proper precompression design and performance.

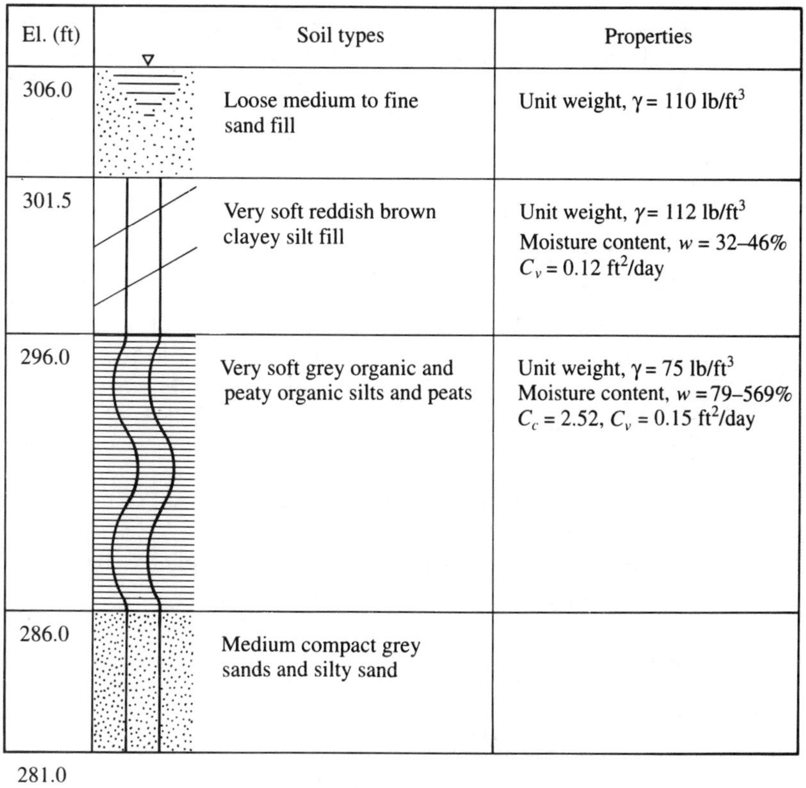

El. (ft)
Soil types
Properties
306.0
Loose medium to fine sand fill
Unit weight, γ = 110 lb/ft³
301.5
Very soft reddish brown clayey silt fill
Unit weight, γ = 112 lb/ft³
Moisture content, w = 32–46%
Cv = 0.12 ft²/day
296.0
Very soft grey organic and peaty organic silts and peats
Unit weight, γ = 75 lb/ft³
Moisture content, w = 79–569%
Cc = 2.52, Cv = 0.15 ft²/day
286.0
Medium compact grey sands and silty sand
281.0

FIGURE 12.22 Subsoil condition at Port Elizabeth Marine Terminal (after Johnson, 1970a)

Fill el. (ft)
335
325
315
305
Surcharge fill
Settlement (ft)
0
1
2
3
4
5
Plate 281
Plate 236
Plate 232
Plate 241
Theoretical
N D J F M A M J J A S O N D J F M A M J J A
1961
1962
1963
Time (months)

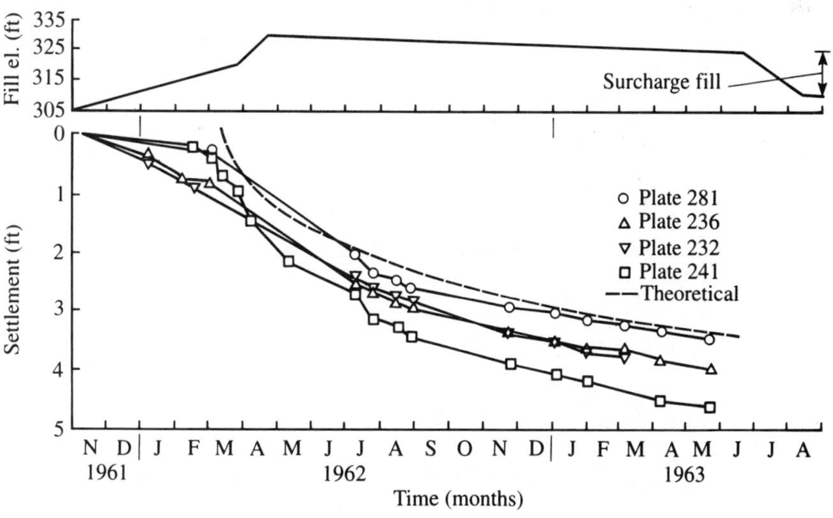

FIGURE 12.23 Precompression for support of warehouses No. 131 and 132, Port Elizabeth Marine Terminal (after Johnson, 1970a)

The information obtained from only a handful of borings is used in the calculation of both the surcharge load and the time necessary for removal of the surcharge. Hence precise numbers for precompression design may be difficult to obtain. Settlement observations should be continued during the period of surcharge application because they may dictate design changes.

▼ EXAMPLE 12.2

Refer to Figure 12.18. During the construction of a highway bridge, the average permanent load on the clay layer is expected to increase by about 115 kN/m². The average effective overburden pressure at the middle of the clay layer is 210 kN/m². Here, $H_c = 6$ m, $C_c = 0.28$, $e_o = 0.9$, and $C_v = 0.36$ m²/mo. The clay is normally consolidated. Determine:

a. The total primary consolidation settlement of the bridge without precompression
b. The surcharge, $\Delta p_{(f)}$, needed to eliminate by precompression the entire primary consolidation settlement in 9 mo.

Solution

Part a

The total primary consolidation settlement may be calculated from Eq. (12.6):

$$S_{(p)} = \frac{C_c H_c}{1 + e_o} \log\left[\frac{p_o + \Delta p_{(p)}}{p_o}\right] = \frac{(0.28)(6)}{1 + 0.9} \log\left[\frac{210 + 115}{210}\right]$$

$$= 0.1677 \text{ m} = \mathbf{167.7 \text{ mm}}$$

Part b

$$T_v = \frac{C_v t_2}{H^2}$$

$$C_v = 0.36 \text{ m}^2/\text{mo.}$$

$$H = 3 \text{ m (two-way drainage)}$$

$$t_2 = 9 \text{ mo.}$$

Hence

$$T_v = \frac{(0.36)(9)}{3^2} = 0.36$$

According to Figure 12.21 for $T_v = 0.36$, the value of U is 47%. Now

$$\Delta p_{(p)} = 115 \text{ kN/m}^2$$

$$p_o = 210 \text{ kN/m}^2$$

So

$$\frac{\Delta p_{(p)}}{p_o} = \frac{115}{210} = 0.548$$

According to Figure 12.19 for $U = 47\%$ and $\Delta p_{(p)}/p_o = 0.548$, $\Delta p_{(f)}/\Delta p_{(p)} \approx 1.8$. So

$$\Delta p_{(f)} = (1.8)(115) = \mathbf{207\ kN/m^2} \qquad \blacktriangledown$$

12.6 SAND DRAINS

The use of *sand drains* is another way to accelerate the consolidation settlement of soft, normally consolidated clay layers and achieve precompression before foundation construction. Sand drains are constructed by drilling holes through the clay layer(s) in the field at regular intervals. The holes are then backfilled with highly permeable sand (see Figure 12.24a). After backfilling the drill holes with sand, a surcharge is applied at the ground surface. This surcharge will increase the pore water pressure in the clay. The excess pore water pressure in the clay will be dissipated by drainage—both vertically and radially to the sand drains—which accelerates settlement of the clay layer.

Note that the radius of the sand drains is r_w (Figure 12.24a). Figure 12.24b shows the plan of the layout of the sand drains. The effective zone from which the radial drainage will be directed toward a given sand drain is approximately cylindrical, with a diameter of d_e.

To determine the surcharge that needs to be applied at the ground surface and the length of time that it has to be maintained, refer to Figure 12.18 and use the corresponding equation, Eq. (12.9):

$$U_{v,r} = \frac{\log\left[1 + \frac{\Delta p_{(p)}}{p_o}\right]}{\log\left\{1 + \frac{\Delta p_{(p)}}{p_o}\left[1 + \frac{\Delta p_{(f)}}{\Delta p_{(p)}}\right]\right\}} \tag{12.11}$$

The notations $\Delta p_{(p)}$, p_o, and $\Delta p_{(f)}$ are the same as those in Eq. (12.9). However, unlike Eq. (12.9), the left-hand side of Eq. (12.11) is the *average degree* of consolidation instead of the degree of consolidation at midplane. Both *radial* and *vertical* drainage contribute to the average degree of consolidation. If $U_{v,r}$ can be determined for any time t_2 (see Figure 12.18b), the total surcharge $\Delta p_{(f)} + \Delta p_{(p)}$ may be obtained easily from Figure 12.19. The procedure for determination of the average degree of consolidation ($U_{v,r}$) is given in the following sections.

The successful use of sand drains has been described in detail by Johnson (1970b). As for precompression, constant field settlement observations may be necessary during the period of surcharge application.

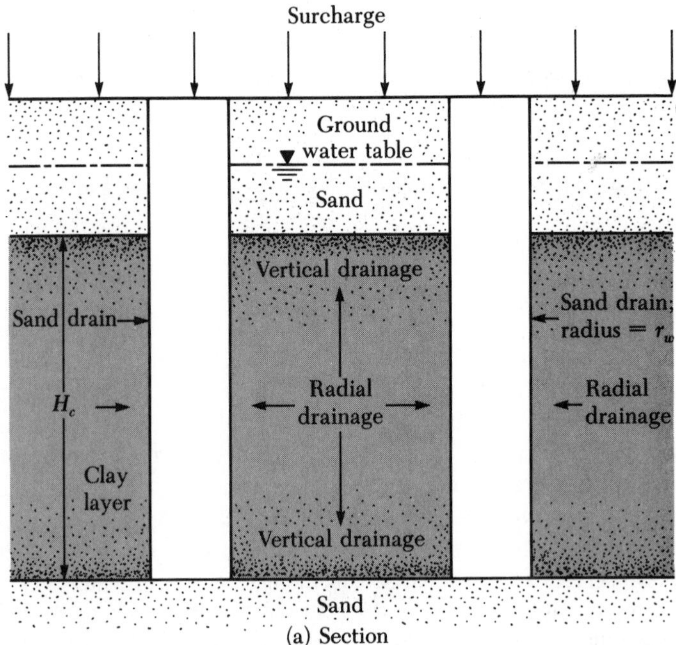

(a) Section

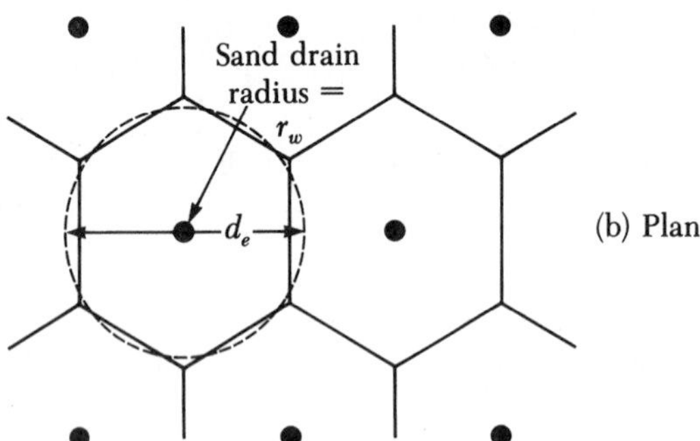

(b) Plan

▼ **FIGURE 12.24** Sand drains

Average Degree of Consolidation Due to Radial Drainage Only

The theory for equal-strain consolidation due to radial drainage only (with no smear) was developed by Barron (1948). It is based on the assumption that there is *no drainage in the vertical direction*. According to this theory,

$$U_r = 1 - \exp\left(\frac{-8T_r}{m}\right) \tag{12.12}$$

where U_r = average degree of consolidation due to radial drainage only

$$m = \left(\frac{n^2}{n^2 - 1}\right)\ln(n) - \frac{3n^2 - 1}{4n^2} \tag{12.13}$$

$$n = \frac{d_e}{2r_w} \tag{12.14}$$

T_r = nondimensional time factor for radial drainage only

$$= \frac{C_{vr}t_2}{d_e^2} \tag{12.15}$$

C_{vr} = coefficient of consolidation for radial drainage

$$= \frac{k_h}{\left[\dfrac{\Delta e}{\Delta p(1 + e_{av})}\right]\gamma_w} \tag{12.16}$$

Note that Eq. (12.16) is similar to Eq. (1.66). In Eq. (1.66), k was the coefficient of permeability in the vertical direction of the clay layer. In Eq. (12.16), k has to be replaced by k_h, the coefficient of permeability for flow in the horizontal direction. In some cases, k_h may be assumed to equal k; however, for soils like varved clay, $k_h > k$.

Figure 12.25 shows the plot of U_r against T_r for various values of n.

Average Degree of Consolidation Due to Vertical Drainage Only

The average degree of consolidation due to vertical drainage only may be obtained from Eqs. (1.73) and (1.74) (or Figure 1.25):

$$T_v = \frac{\pi}{4}\left[\frac{U_v(\%)}{100}\right] \qquad (\text{for } U_v = 0\text{–}60\%) \tag{1.73}$$

and

$$T_v = 1.781 - 0.933\log(100 - U_v\%) \qquad (\text{for } U_v > 60\%) \tag{1.74}$$

where U_v = average degree of consolidation due to vertical drainage only

$$T_v = \frac{C_v t_2}{H^2} \tag{1.68}$$

C_v = coefficient of consolidation for vertical drainage

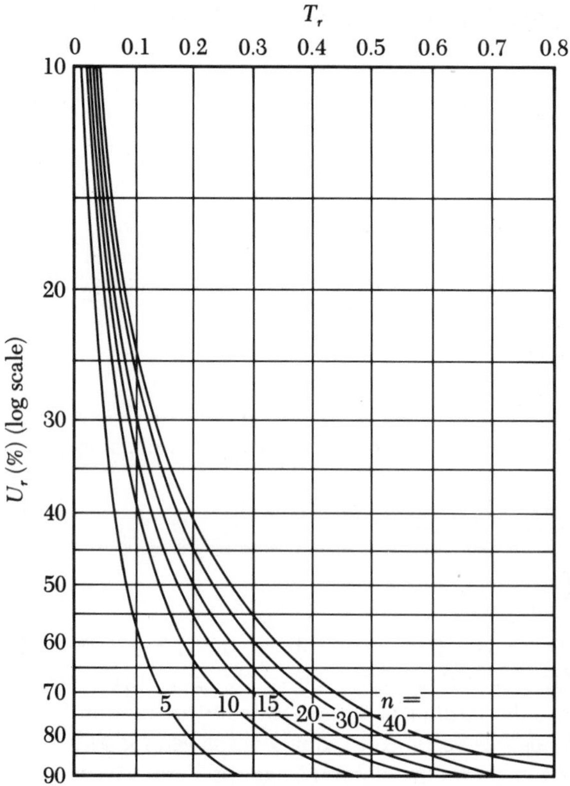

▼ **FIGURE 12.25** Average degree of consolidation for radial drainage only—Eq. (12.12)

Average Degree of Consolidation Due to Vertical and Radial Drainage

For a given surcharge and duration t_2, the average degree of consolidation due to drainage in the vertical and radial directions is

$$U_{v,r} = 1 - (1 - U_r)(1 - U_v) \tag{12.17}$$

Wick Drains

The *wick drain* was recently developed as an alternative to the sand drain for inducing veritcal drainage in saturated clay deposits. Wick drains appear to be better, faster, and cheaper. They essentially consist of paper or plastic strips that are held in a long tube. The tube is pushed into the soft clay deposit, then withdrawn, leaving behind the strips. These strips act as vertical drains and induce rapid consolidation. Wick drains can be placed at desired spacings like sand drains. The main advantage of wick drains over sand drains is that they do not require drilling, and thus installation is much faster.

▼ EXAMPLE 12.3

Redo Example 12.2 with the addition of some sand drains. Assume that $r_w = 0.1$ m, $d_e = 3$ m, and $C_v = C_{vr}$.

Solution

Part a

The total primary consolidation settlement will be 167.7 mm as before.

Part b

From Example 12.2, $T_v = 0.36$. The value of U_v, from Figure 1.21, is about 67%. From Eq. (12.14),

$$n = \frac{d_e}{2r_w} = \frac{3}{2 \times 0.1} = 15$$

Again,

$$T_r = \frac{C_{vr} t_2}{d_e^2} = \frac{(0.36)(9)}{(3)^2} = 0.36$$

From Figure 12.25 for $n = 15$ and $T_r = 0.36$, the value of U_r is about 77%. Hence

$$U_{v,r} = 1 - (1 - U_v)(1 - U_r) = 1 - (1 - 0.67)(1 - 0.77)$$
$$= 0.924 = 92.4\%$$

Now, from Figure 12.19 for $\Delta p_{(p)}/p_o = 0.548$ and $U_{v,r} = 92.4\%$, the value of $\Delta p_{(f)}/\Delta p_{(p)} \approx 0.12$. Hence

$$\Delta p_{(f)} = (115)(0.12) = \mathbf{13.8\ kN/m^2}$$ ▼

12.7 AN EXAMPLE OF A SAND DRAIN APPLICATION

Aboshi and Monden (1963) provided details on the field performance of 2700 sand drains used to construct the Toya Quay Wall on reclaimed land in Japan in a study that was summarized by Johnson (1970b). The location of the project site is shown in the insert of Figure 12.26. The soil at the site consisted of 30-m thick soft normally consolidated clayey silt. The following data are for the *in situ* soil and the sand drains.

▶ *In situ* soil: Liquid limit (*LL*) = 110
Plastic limit (*PL*) = 48
Natural moisture content, w = 74–65%

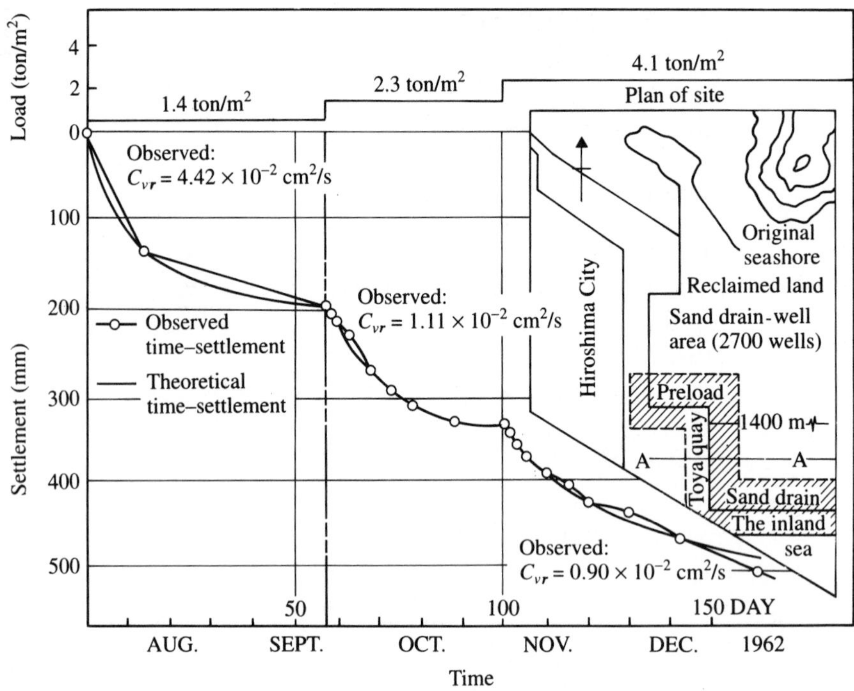

FIGURE 12.26 Comparison of observed and theoretical settlements due to sand drawn only for Toya Quay Wall Construction, Japan (after Johnson, 1970b)

- Sand drains: Total number used = 2700
  Length = 15 m
  $d_e = 3.15$ m
  $r_w = 0.225$ m
  $\left.\frac{C_{vr}}{C_v}\right\} \begin{matrix} = 2.7 & \text{(from consolidometer)} \\ = 1.7 & \text{(from triaxial device)} \end{matrix}$

The top portion of Figure 12.26 shows the variation of the surcharge load application with time. The bottom portion shows the observed and theoretical variation of settlement due to *sand drains only*. The agreement appears to be excellent.

12.8 SOIL STABILIZATION BY ADMIXTURES

As mentioned in Section 12.1, admixtures are occasionally used to stabilize soils in the field—particularly fine-grained soils. The most common admixtures are lime, cement and lime–fly ash. The main purposes of soil stabilization are to (a) modify the soil, (b) expedite construction, and (c) improve the strength and durability of the soil.

Lime Stabilization

The types of *lime* commonly used for stabilization of fine-grained soils are hydrated high-calcium lime [$Ca(OH)_2$], calcitic quick lime (CaO), monohydrated dolomitic lime [$Ca(OH)_2 \cdot MgO$], and dolomitic quick lime. The quantity of lime used for stabilization of most soils usually is in the range of 5–10%. When lime is added to clayey soils, several chemical reactions occur: *cation exchange* and *flocculation–agglomeration*, and they are also *pozzolanic*. In the cation exchange and flocculation–agglomeration reactions, the *monovalent* cations generally associated with clays are replaced by the *divalent* calcium ions. Based on their affinity for exchange, the cations can be arranged in a series:

$$Al^{3+} > Ca^{2+} > Mg^{2+} > NH_4^+ > K^+ > Na^+ > Li^+$$

Any cation can replace the ions to its right. For example, calcium ions can replace potassium and sodium ions from a clay. Flocculation and agglomeration produce a change in the texture of clay soils. The clay particles tend to clump together to form larger particles. These reactions tend to (a) decrease the liquid limit, (b) increase the plastic limit, (c) decrease the plasticity index, (d) increase the shrinkage limit, (e) increase the workability, and (f) improve the strength and deformation properties of a soil.

Pozzolanic reaction between soil and lime involves a reaction between lime and the silica and alumina of soil to form cementing material. For example,

$$Ca(OH)_2 + \underset{\substack{\uparrow \\ \text{Clay silica}}}{SiO_2} \rightarrow CSH$$

where $C = CaO$
$S = SiO_2$
$H = H_2O$

The pozzolanic reaction may continue for a long period of time.

Figure 12.27 shows the variation of the liquid limit, the plasticity index, and the shrinkage limit of a clay with percentage of lime admixture. The first 2–3% lime (on the dry weight basis) substantially influences the workability and the property (such as plasticity) of the soil. The addition of lime to clayey soils affects their compaction characteristics.

Figure 12.28a shows the results of standard Proctor tests for Vicksburg clay without any additives and also with 4% high-calcium hydrated lime additive (uncured). Note that the addition of lime helps reduce the maximum compacted dry unit weight and increase the optimum moisture content. Figure 12.28b also shows the change of the unconfined compressive strength, q_u, of uncured Vicksburg clay with the percentage of high-calcium hydrated lime. The value of q_u with 6% lime is about six times that obtained with no additive. Note that the specimens prepared for the determination of q_u were all at a moisture content of 29–29.5%. This is shown as the molding moisture content in Figure 12.28a.

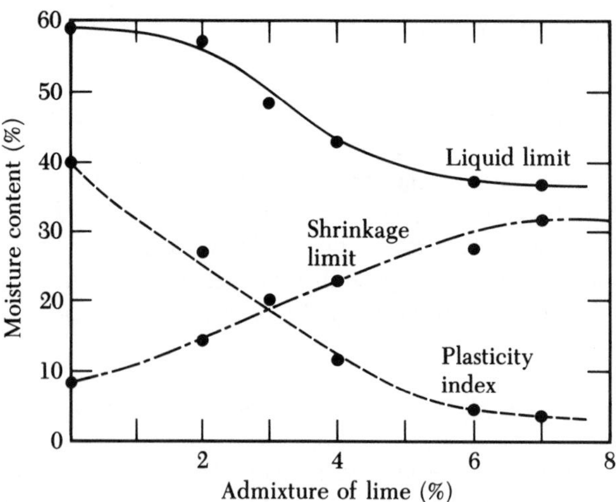

▼ **Figure 12.27** Variation of liquid limit, plasticity index, and shrinkage of a clay with lime additive

Arman and Munfakh (1972) evaluated the lime stabilization of organic clays found in Louisiana. Figure 12.29a shows the change of plasticity with $Ca(OH)_2$ content for an organic soil with 22% organic material. The curing time for these soil specimens was 48 hours. The effects of lime are generally similar to those shown in Figure 12.29. The change of the unconfined compression strength of the same soil with lime additives is shown in Figure 12.29b. Based on their study, Arman and Munfakh concluded that (a) the presence of organic matter does not block the pozzolanic reaction that helps change the fundamental soil properties and make the soil more workable and (b) about 2% of lime is sufficient to satisfy the base exchange capacity of organic matters.

Lime stabilization in the field can be done in three ways:

1. The *in situ* material and/or the borrowed material can be mixed with the proper amount of lime at the site and then compacted after the addition of moisture.
2. The soil can be mixed with the proper amount of lime and water at a plant and then hauled back to the site for compaction.
3. Lime slurry can be pressure injected into the soil to a depth of 12 to 16 ft (4–5 m). Figure 12.30 (page 759) shows a vehicle used for pressure injection of lime slurry. The slurry injection mechanical unit is mounted to the injection vehicle. A common injection unit is a hydraulic-lift mast with cross beams that contain the injection rods. The injection rods are pushed into the ground by the action of the lift mast beams. The slurry is generally mixed in a batching tank about 10 ft (3 m) in diameter and 36 ft (12 m) long and is pumped at high pressure to the injection rods. Figure 12.31 (page 760) is a photograph of the lime slurry pressure injection process. The ratio typically specified for preparation of lime slurry is 2.5 lb of dry lime to a gallon of water. For more information on this technique, see Blacklock and Pengelly (1988).

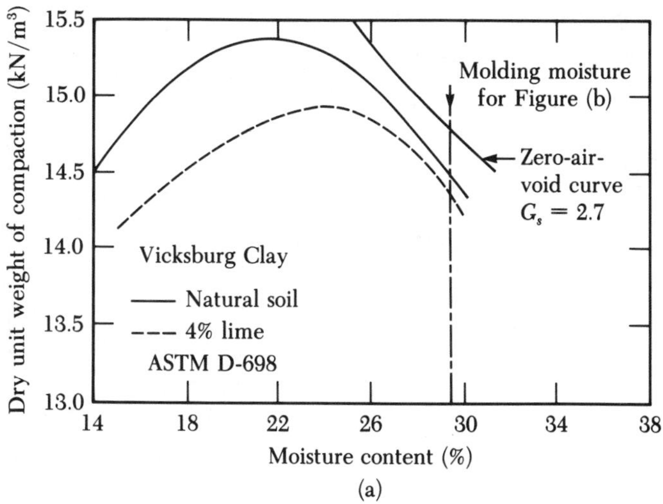

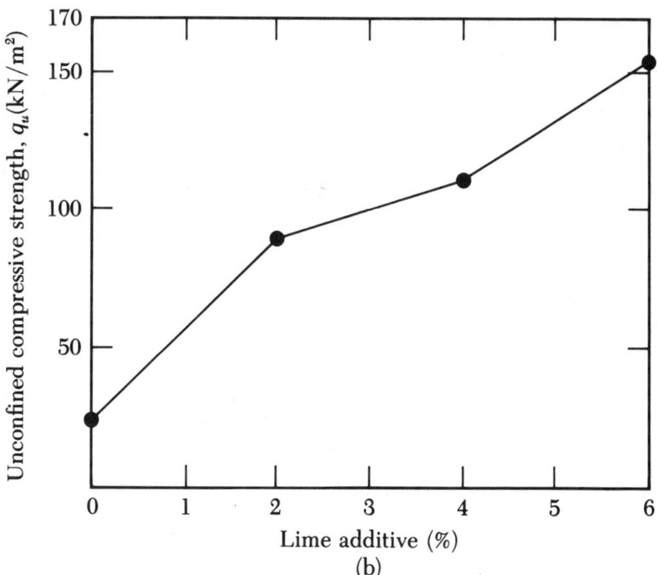

▼ **FIGURE 12.28** Lime stabilization of Vicksburg clay (% less than 2μ size = 46; liquid limit = 59, plasticity index = 30, A-7-6(20), pH = 6): (a) laboratory dry unit weight against moisture content curve; (b) change of unconfined compression strength with percent of lime. *Note:* The specimens for (b) were molded at a moisture content shown in (a) (from "Stability Properties of Uncured Lime-Treated Fine Grained Soil," by C. H. Neubauer and M. R. Thompson. In *Highway Research Record No. 381*, Highway Research Board, 1972, pp. 20–26. Reprinted by permission)

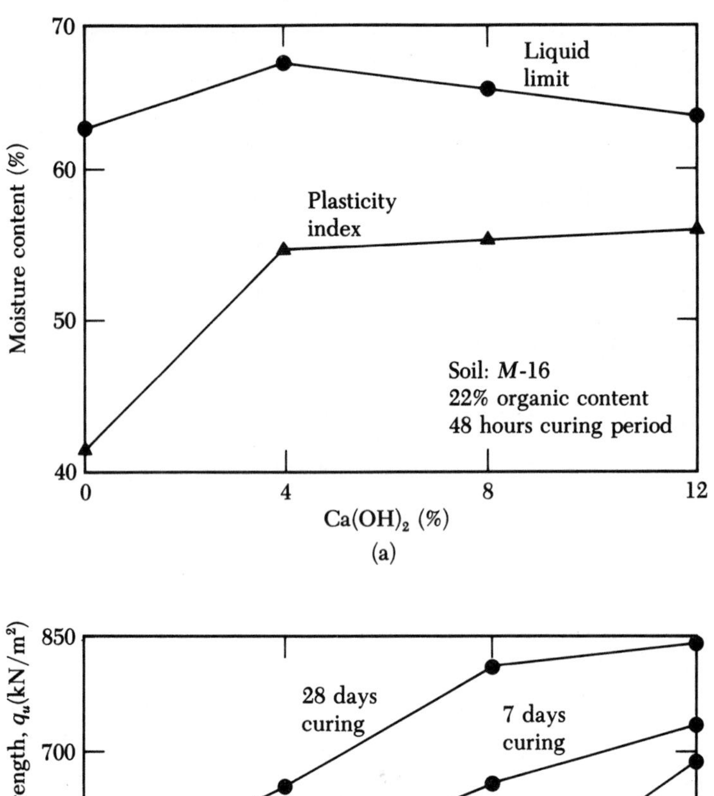

▼ **FIGURE 12.29** Lime stabilization of organic soil: (a) variation of liquid limit and plasticity index with 48 hours' curing; (b) variation of unconfined compression strength (from "Lime Stabilization of Organic Soil," by A. Arman and G. A. Munfakh. In *Highway Research Record No. 381*, Highway Research Board, 1972, pp. 37–45. Reprinted by permission)

Because the addition of hydrated lime to soft clayey soils immediately increases the plastic limit, thus changing the soil from plastic to solid and making it appear to "dry up," limited amounts of it can be thrown on muddy and troublesome construction sites. This action improves trafficability and may save money and time.

▼ **FIGURE 12.30** Equipment for pressure injection of lime slurry (courtesy of GKN Hayward Baker, Inc., Woodbine Division, Ft. Worth, Texas)

Quick limes have also been successfully used in drill holes having diameters of 4 in. to 6 in. (100 mm to 150 mm) for stabilization of subgrades and slopes. For this type of work, holes are drilled in a grid pattern and then filled with quick lime.

Cement Stabilization

Cement is increasingly used as a stabilizing material for soil, particularly for the construction of highways and earth dams. The first controlled soil–cement construction in the United States was carried out near Johnsonville, South Carolina, in 1935. Cement can be used to stabilize sandy and clayey soils. As in the case of lime, cement helps decrease the liquid limit and increase the plasticity index and workability of clayey soils. For clayey soils, cement stabilization is effective when the liquid limit is less than 45–50 and the plasticity index is less than about 25. The optimum requirements of cement by volume for effective stabilization of various types of soil are given in Table 12.5.

Like lime, cement helps increase the strength of soils, and strength increases with curing time. Table 12.6 presents some typical values of the unconfined compressive strength of various types of untreated soil and soil–cement mixture made with approximately 10% cement by weight.

Granular soils and clayey soils with low plasticity obviously are most suitable for cement stabilization. Calcium clays are more easily stabilized by the addition of cement, whereas sodium and hydrogen clays, which are expansive in nature, respond better to lime stabilization. For these reasons, proper care should be given in the selection of the stabilizing material.

▼ **FIGURE 12.31** Pressure injection of lime slurry (courtesy of GKN Hayward Baker, Inc., Woodbine Division, Ft. Worth, Texas)

For field compaction, the proper amount of cement can be mixed with soil either at the site or at a mixing plant and then carried to the site. The soil is compacted to the required unit weight with a predetermined amount of water.

Similar to lime injection, cement slurry made of Portland Cement and water (water–cement ratio = 0.5 : 5) can be used for pressure grouting of poor soils under foundations of buildings and other structures. Grouting decreases the permeability of soils and increases the strength and the load-bearing capacity. For design of low-frequency machine foundations subjected to vibrating forces, stiffening the foundation soil by grouting and thereby increasing the resonant frequency is sometimes necessary.

TABLE 12.5 Cement Requirement by Volume for Effective Stabilization of Various Soils[a]

Soil type		Percent cement by volume
AASHTO classification	*Unified classification*	
A-2 and A-3	GP, SP, and SW	6–10
A-4 and A-5	CL, ML, and MH	8–12
A-6 and A-7	CL, CH	10–14

[a] After Mitchell and Freitag (1959)

TABLE 12.6 Typical Compressive Strengths of Soils and Soil–Cement Mixtures[a]

Material	Unconfined compressive strength range	
	lb/in²	*(kN/m²)*[b]
Untreated soil:		
Clay, peat	Less than 50	Less than 350
Well-compacted sandy clay	10–40	70–280
Well-compacted gravel, sand, and clay mixtures	40–100	280–700
Soil–cement (10% cement by weight):		
Clay, organic soils	Less than 50	Less than 350
Silts, silty clays, very poorly graded sands, slightly organic soils	50–150	350–1050
Silty clays, sandy clays, very poorly graded sands, and gravels	100–250	700–1730
Silty sands, sandy clays, sands, and gravels	250–500	1730–3460
Well-graded sand–clay or gravel–sand–clay mixtures and sands and gravels	500–1500	3460–10,350

[a] After Mitchell and Freitag (1959)
[b] Rounded off

Fly Ash Stabilization

Fly ash is a by-product of the pulverized coal combustion process usually associated with electric power generating plants. It is a fine-grained dust and is primarily composed of silica, alumina, and various oxides and alkalies. It is pozzolanic in nature and can react with hydrated lime to produce cementitious products. For that reason, lime–fly ash mixtures can be used for stabilization of highway bases and subbases. Effective mixes can be prepared with 10–35% fly ash and 2–10% lime. Soil–lime–fly ash mixes are compacted under controlled conditions with proper amounts of moisture to obtain stabilized soil layers.

A certain type of fly ash is obtained from the burning of coal primarily from the western United States, and it is referred to as "Type C" fly ash. It contains a fairly large proportion (up to about 25%) of free lime that, with the addition of water, will react with other fly ash compounds to form cementitious products. Its use may eliminate the need to add manufactured lime.

12.9 STONE COLUMNS

A method now being used to increase the load-bearing capacity of shallow foundations on soft clay layers is the construction of *stone columns*. Construction of a stone column generally consists of water jetting a vibroflot (Section 12.3) into the soft clay layer to make a circular hole that extends through the clay to firmer soil. The hole is then filled with an imported gravel. The gravel in the hole is gradually compacted as the vibrator is withdrawn. The gravel used for the stone column has sizes ranging from 0.25–1.5 in. (6–40 mm). Stone columns usually have diameters of 1.6–2.5 ft (0.5–0.75 m) and are spaced at about 5–10 ft (1.5–3 m) center-to-center.

After the construction of stone columns, a fill material should always be placed over the ground surface and compacted before construction of the foundation. The stone columns tend to reduce the settlement of foundations at allowable loads. Several case histories of construction projects using stone columns are presented in Hughes and Withers (1974), Hughes et al. (1975), Mitchell and Huber (1985), and others.

At this time there is no standard way to estimate the settlement of foundations constructed over stone columns. However, based on the recommendation of Greenwood and Thompson (1984) and on observations of the author, a tentative chart for estimating settlement is given in Figure 12.32. To utilize 12.32, use the following procedure.

1. Determine the cross-sectional area of the stone column, A_S.
2. Determine the average area of the column foundation, A_F.
3. Calculate the ratio of A_F/A_S.
4. Estimate the undrained shear strength of the clay, c_u, and the probable settlement of a column foundation assuming that it was constructed without the stone columns, S_F.
5. With known values of A_F/A_S and c_u, determine the ratio of S_F/S_S (S_S = probable settlement of the foundation constructed over stone columns) from Figure 12.32b.
6. With known values of S_F and S_F/S_S, calculate S_S.

Stone columns work more effectively when used for stabilizing a large area where the undrained shear strength of the subsoil is in the range of 200–1000 lb/ft^2 (10–15 kN/m^2) than does improving the bearing capacity of structural foundations (Bachus and Barksdale, 1989). Subsoils weaker than that may not provide sufficient lateral support for the stone columns. For large-site improvement, stone columns are most effective to a depth of 20–30 ft (6–10 m). However, stone columns have been constructed to a depth of 100 ft (31 m). Bachus and Barksdale provided the following general guidelines for the design of stone columns for stabilizing large areas.

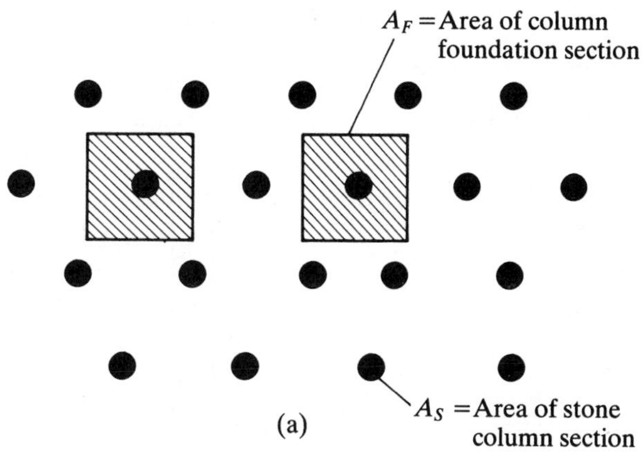

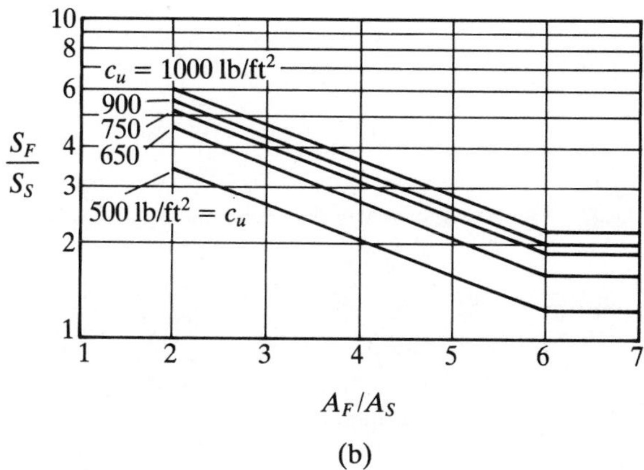

▼ **FIGURE 12.32** Settlement of foundation built on stone columns

Figure 12.33a shows the plan view of several stone columns, and Figure 12.33b depicts the unit cell idealization of a stone column. The area replacement ratio, a_s, for the stone columns may be expressed as

$$a_s = \frac{A_s}{A} \tag{12.18}$$

where A_s = area of the stone column
A = total area within the unit cell

For an *equilateral triangular pattern* of stone columns,

$$a_s = 0.907\left(\frac{D}{s}\right)^2 \tag{12.19}$$

where D = diameter of the stone column
s = spacing between the stone columns

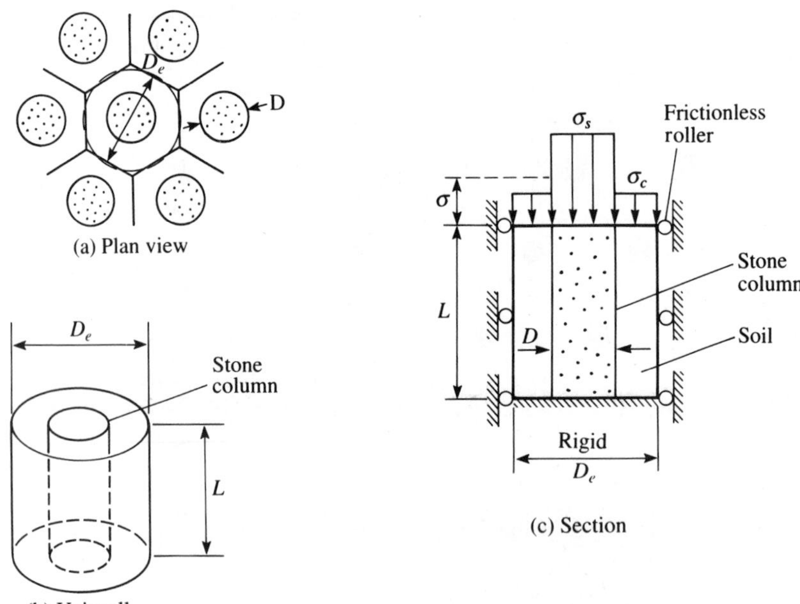

FIGURE 12.33 Unit cell idealization of stone column (after Bachus and Barksdale, 1989)

When a uniform stress by means of a fill operation is applied to an area with stone columns to induce consolidation, a stress concentration occurs due to the change in the stiffness between the stone columns and the surrounding soil (Figure 12.33c). The stress concentration factor, n', is defined as

$$n' = \frac{\sigma_s}{\sigma_c} \tag{12.20}$$

where σ_s = stress in the stone column
σ_c = stress in the subgrade soil

The relationships for σ_s and σ_c are

$$\sigma_s = \sigma\left[\frac{n'}{1 + (n' - 1)a_s}\right] = \mu_s \sigma \tag{12.21}$$

$$\sigma_c = \sigma\left[\frac{1}{1 + (n' - 1)a_s}\right] = \mu_c \sigma \tag{12.22}$$

where σ = average vertical stress
μ_s, μ_c = stress concentration factors

The variation of μ_c and a_s and n' is shown in Figure 12.34.

The improvement of the soil owing to the stone columns may be expressed as

$$\frac{S_t}{S} = \mu_c \tag{12.23}$$

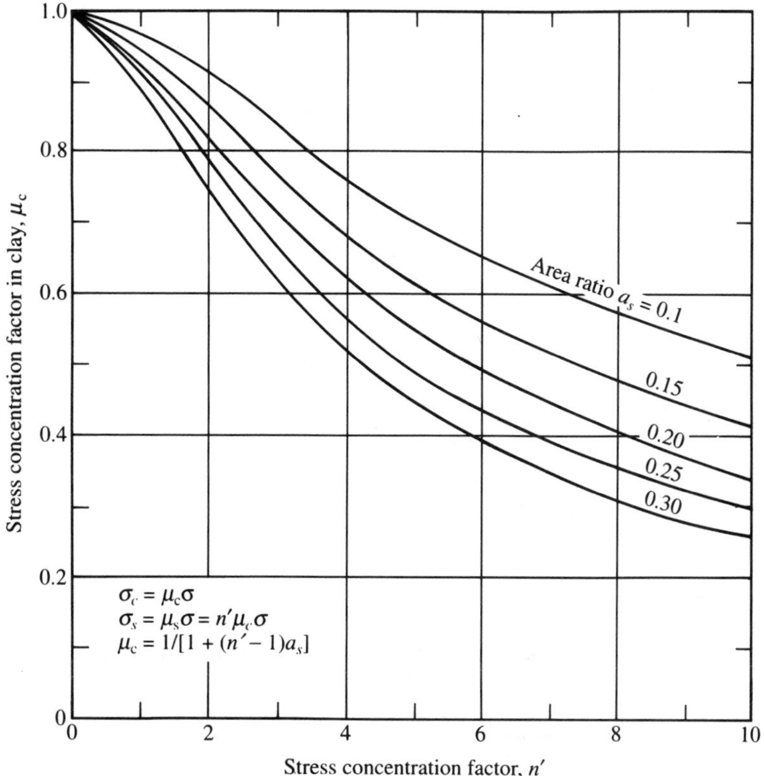

▼ **FIGURE 12.34** Variation of μ_s with a_s and n' (after Bachus and Barksdale, 1989)

where S_t = settlement of the treated soil
S = total settlement of the untreated soil

▼ EXAMPLE 12.4

Stone columns were constructed in a deposit of soft clay soil 20 ft thick.

- *Clay:* undrained cohesion, $c_u = 750\ \text{lb/ft}^2$
  modulus of elasticity, $E_s = 1400\ \text{lb/in}^2$
- *Stone column:* diameter of each column = 1.5 ft
  center-to-center spacing = 8 ft
- *Column foundation* (Figure 12.35): plan = 3 ft × 3 ft
  center-to-center spacing of columns = 10 ft
  depth of foundation, $D_f = 3$ ft
  load on columns = 8000 lb/ft²

Estimate the settlement of the column foundations.

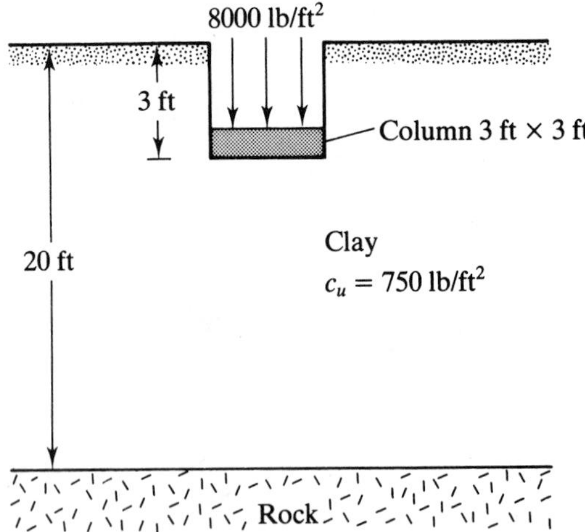

▼ **FIGURE 12.35**

Solution

Calculation of the Settlement of Columns without the Stone Columns

From Eq. (3.80),

$$S_F = A_1 A_2 \left(\frac{q_o B}{E_s}\right)$$

Here, $B = 3$ ft, $q_o = 8000$ lb/ft², and $E_s = 1400$ lb/in². Refer to Figure 3.28: $H/B = 17/3 = 5.67$ and $D_f/B = 1$. So $A_2 = 0.6$, $A_1 = 0.94$, and

$$S_F = (0.94)(0.6)\left[\frac{(8000)(3)}{(1400)(144)}\right] = 0.067 \text{ ft} \approx \mathbf{0.81\ in.}$$

Settlement with Stone Columns

$$A_s = \left(\frac{\pi}{4}\right)(1.5)^2 = 1.676 \text{ ft}^2$$

$$A_F = (3)^2 = 9 \text{ ft}^2$$

$$\frac{A_F}{A_s} = \frac{9}{1.767} \approx 5.1$$

From Figure 12.32 for $c_u = 750$ lb/ft² and $A_F/A_S = 5.1$, $S_F/S_S \approx 2$. So

$$S_S = \frac{S_F}{2} = \frac{0.81}{2} = \mathbf{0.405\ in.}$$ ▼

12.10 FOUNDATIONS ON GRANULAR TRENCHES

In Chapter 3 we pointed out that the allowable bearing capacity of a shallow foundation is controlled by two factors: (a) ultimate bearing capacity and (b) tolerable settlement. When the width of a foundation is relatively small, the ultimate bearing capacity is the controlling factor. Such foundations, when constructed over soft clay soil, will still undergo undesirable settlement. Their allowable load-bearing capacity can be substantially enhanced and settlement reduced by constructing them over granular (sand) trenches made in the soft clay, as shown in Figure 12.36. A foundation having dimensions of $B \times L$ is supported by a granular trench having dimensions of $B \times L \times H$. The parameters for the compacted sand in the trench are

- Dry unit weight: γ_s
- Angle of friction: ϕ_s

For the soft clay, the unit weight and the undrained shear strength are γ_c and c_u, respectively.

The ultimate bearing capacity of a foundation as shown in Figure 12.36 increases linearly with H/B to a maximum at $H/B = (H/B)_{cr}$ and remains constant thereafter

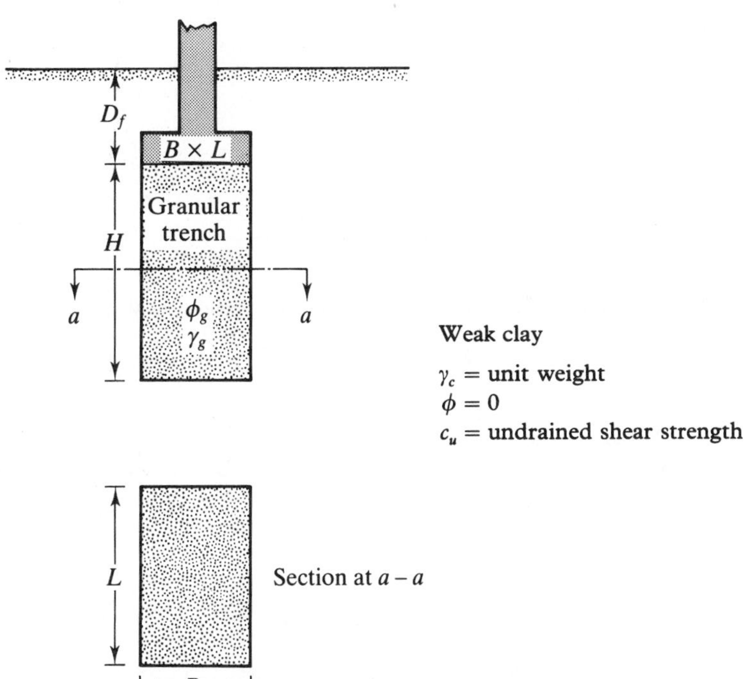

FIGURE 12.36 Foundation on granular trench made in weak clay

(Figure 12.37) (Das and Hanna, 1988; Das, 1989). The maximum value of the ultimate bearing capacity, $q_{u(\max)}$, may be expressed as

$$q_{u(\max)} = \left(\frac{1 + \sin \phi_s}{1 - \sin \phi_s}\right)(\gamma_c D_f + 2F_s c_u) \tag{12.24}$$

where F_s = shape factor $= 1 + B/L$ (12.25)

The magnitude of $(H/B)_{cr}$ is approximately 3. Laboratory model tests have shown that the settlement of a foundation at ultimate load with $H/B = 3$ is about one-third the settlement obtained at ultimate load without the granular trench.

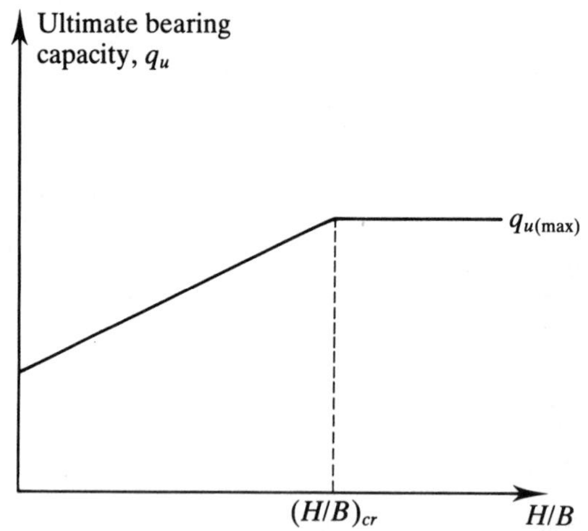

▼ **FIGURE 12.37** Variation of q_u with H/B for foundations on granular trenches

▼ EXAMPLE 12.5

Refer to Figure 12.36.

Foundation: $B = 2.5$ ft, $L = 5$ ft, $D_f = 3$ ft

Clay: $c_u = 480$ lb/ft², $\gamma_c = 120$ lb/ft³

Sand in granular trench: $\phi_s = 38°$, $\gamma_s = 115$ lb/ft³

Estimate the ultimate bearing capacity of the foundation.

Solution From Eqs. (12.24) and (12.25),

$$q_u = \left(\frac{1 + \sin \phi_s}{1 - \sin \phi_s}\right)\left[\gamma D_f + 2\left(1 + \frac{B}{L}\right)c_u\right]$$

$$= \left(\frac{1 + \sin 38}{1 - \sin 38}\right)\left[(120)(3) + (2)\left(1 + \frac{2.5}{5}\right)(480)\right]$$

$$= (4.2)(360 + 1440) = \mathbf{7560\ lb/ft^2}.$$ ▼

12.11 DYNAMIC COMPACTION

Dynamic compaction is a technique that is beginning to gain popularity in the United States for densification of granular soil deposits. This process primarily involves dropping a heavy weight repeatedly on the ground at regular intervals. The weight of the hammer used varies from 8 to 35 metric tons, and the height of the hammer drop varies between 25 and 100 ft ($\simeq$7.5 and 30.5 m). The stress waves generated by the hammer drops help in the densification. The degree of compaction achieved depends on the

a. Weight of the hammer
b. Height of hammer drop
c. Spacing of the locations at which the hammer is dropped

Leonards et al. (1980) suggested that the significant depth of influence for compaction is approximately

$$D \simeq \frac{1}{2}\sqrt{W_H h} \tag{12.26}$$

where D = significant depth of densification (m)
W_H = dropping weight (metric ton)
h = height of drop (in.)

In English units, Eq. (12.26) becomes

$$D = 0.61\sqrt{W_H h} \tag{12.27}$$

where D and h are in ft and W_H is in kip

Partos et al. (1989) provided several case histories of site improvement using dynamic compaction. Figure 12.38 shows the effect of dynamic compaction in improving the standard penetration resistance at the construction site of an office building in the Riverview Executive Park (Trenton, New Jersey). For this dynamic compaction,

Weight of the hammer, W_h = 18.5 ton (163 kN)

Height of drop, h = 85 ft (26 m)

Spacing between hammer drops = 10.6 ft (3.3 m)

Number of drops at each location = 7

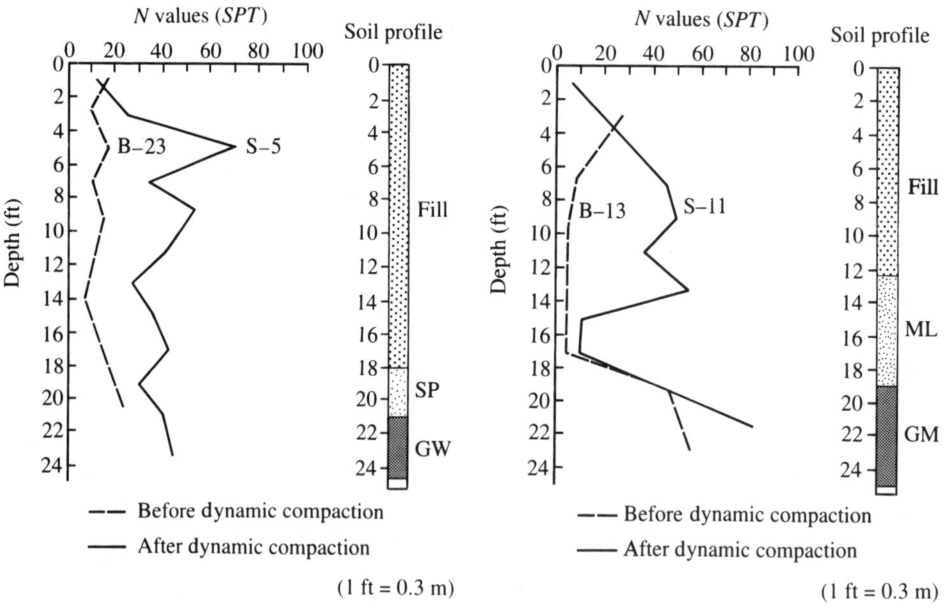

▼ **FIGURE 12.38** Standard penetration resistance before and after dynamic compaction, Riverview Executive Park, Trenton, New Jersey (after Partos et al., 1989)

PROBLEMS

12.1 Make the necessary calculations and prepare the zero-air-void unit weight (in lb/ft³) curves related to a Proctor compaction test for $G_s = 2.6$, 2.65, 2.7, and 2.75.

12.2 The maximum dry unit weight of a soil was determined by a Proctor compaction test to be 113.3 lb/ft³. If the same soil is used in the compaction of an embankment to a unit weight of 95.3 lb/ft³, what would be the relative compaction?

12.3 A sandy soil has a maximum dry unit weight of 109.5 lb/ft³ and a dry unit weight of compaction in the field of 99 lb/ft³. Use Eqs. (12.2), (12.3), and (12.4) and estimate the

a. Relative compaction in the field
b. Relative density in the field
c. Minimum dry unit weight of the soil

12.4 A soil was compacted in the field by the standard Proctor test procedure. The moist unit weight of compaction was 18 kN/m³ and the moisture content was 12%. Estimate $\gamma_{d(\max)}$ and the optimum moisture content for the soil according to the Ohio one-point method.

12.5 Repeat Problem 12.4 for a moist unit weight of compaction of 114 lb/ft³ and a moisture content of 12%.

12.6 According to the Ohio one-point method, a soil will have a maximum dry unit weight of 99.9 lb/ft³ at an optimum moisture content of 21.5%. Estimate the dry unit weight of the soil when it is compacted to a moisture content of 18%.

12.7 For a vibroflotation work, the backfill to be used has the following characteristics: $D_{50} = 1$ mm, $D_{20} = 0.5$ mm, and $D_{10} = 0.08$ mm. Determine the suitability number of the backfill. How would you rate the material?

12.8 Repeat Problem 12.7 for $D_{50} = 1.8$ mm, $D_{20} = 0.75$ mm, and $D_{10} = 0.12$ mm.

12.9 Refer to Figure 12.18. For the construction of an airport, a large fill operation is required. For the work, the average permanent load, $\Delta p_{(p)}$, on the clay layer will increase by about 1460 lb/ft^2. The average effective overburden pressure on the clay layer before the fill operation is 1985 lb/ft^2. For the clay layer, which is normally consolidated and drained at top and bottom, $H_c = 16.75$ ft, $C_c = 0.24$, $e_o = 0.81$, and $C_v = 4.73$ ft^2/mo. Determine:

a. The primary consolidation settlement of the clay layer caused by the additional permanent load, $\Delta p_{(p)}$

b. The time required for 90% of primary consolidation settlement under the additional permanent load only

c. The temporary surcharge, $\Delta p_{(f)}$, that will be required to eliminate the entire primary consolidation settlement in 6 months by the precompression technique

12.10 Redo part (c) of Problem 12.9 for a time of elimination of primary consolidation settlement of 7 months.

12.11 Repeat Problem 12.9 with $\Delta p_{(p)} = 1200$ lb/ft^2, the average effective overburden pressure on clay layer = 1000 lb/ft^2, $H_c = 15$ ft, $C_c = 0.3$, $e_o = 1.0$, and $C_v = 1.5 \times 10^{-2}$ in^2/min.

12.12 The diagram of a sand drain is shown in Figure 12.24. If $r_w = 0.25$ m, $d_e = 4$ m, $C_v = C_{vr} = 0.28$ m^2/mo, and $H = 8.4$ m, determine the degree of consolidation caused only by sand drain after 6 months of surcharge application.

12.13 Estimate the degree of consolidation for the clay layer described in Problem 12.12 that is caused by the combination of vertical drainage (drained on top and bottom) and radial drainage after 6 months of the application of surcharge.

12.14 A 12-ft thick clay layer is drained at top and bottom. Its characteristics are $C_{vr} = C_v$ (for vertical damage) = 0.042 ft^2/day, $r_w = 8$ in., and $d_e = 6$ ft. Estimate the degree of consolidation of the clay layer caused by the combination of vertical and radial drainage at $t = 0.2$, 0.4, 0.8 and 1 yr.

12.15 Repeat Example 12.4 with the following:

- *Clay*: thickness of clay layer = 10 ft
  undrained shear strength, $c_u = 580$ lb/ft^2
  modulus of elasticity = 1300 lb/in^2
- *Stone columns*: diameter of each column = 15 in.
  center-to-center spacing = 45 in.
- *Column foundations*: plan = 4 ft × 4 ft
  center-to-center spacing = 15 ft
  depth of foundation = 3.5 ft
  load on each column = 10,000 lb/ft^2

12.16 Estimate the ultimate bearing capacity of a foundation constructed on a granular trench. For the foundation, $B = 1.2$ m, $L = 2$ m, and $D_f = 1$ m. For the clay, $c_u = 21$ kN/m^2 and $\gamma = 18$ kN/m^3. For the sand in a granular trench, $\phi_s = 40°$ and $\gamma_s = 17$ kN/m^3. The height of the granular trench = 4 m.

REFERENCES

Aboshi, H., and Monden, H. (1963). "Determination of the Horizontal Coefficient of Consolidation of an Alluvial Clay," *Proceedings*, Fourth Australia–New Zealand Conference on Soil Mechanics and Foundation Engineering, pp. 159–164.

Arman, A., and Munfakh, G. A. (1972). "Lime Stabilization of Organic Soils," *Highway Research Record, No. 381*, National Academy of Sciences, pp. 37–45.

Bachus, R. C., and Barksdale, R. D. (1989). "Design Methodology for Foundations on Stone Columns," *Proceedings*, Foundation Engineering: Current Principles and Practices, American Society of Civil Engineers, Vol. 1, pp. 244–257.

Barron, R. A. (1948). "Consolidation of Fine-Grained Soils by Drain Wells," *Transactions*, American Society of Civil Engineers, Vol. 113, pp. 718–754.

Basore, C. E., and Boitano, J. D. (1969). "Sand Densification by Piles and Vibroflotation," *Journal of the Soil Mechanics and Foundations Division*, American Society of Civil Engineers, Vol. 95, No. SM6, pp. 1303–1323.

Blacklock, J. R., and Pengelly, A. D. (1988). "Soil Treatment for Foundations on Expansive Clay," *Special Topics in Foundations*, GSP No. 16 (ed. B. M. Das), American Society of Civil Engineers, pp. 73–92.

Brown, R. E. (1977). "Vibroflotation Compaction of Cohesionless Soils," *Journal of the Geotechnical Engineering Division*, American Society of Civil Engineers, Vol. 103, No. GT12, pp. 1437–1451.

D'Appolonia, D. J., Whitman, R. V., and D'Appolonia, E. (1969). "Sand Compaction with Vibratory Rollers," *Journal of the Soil Mechanics and Foundations Division*, American Society of Civil Engineers, Vol. 95, No. SM1, pp. 263–284.

Das, B. M. (1989). "Bearing Capacity of Shallow Foundation on Granular Column in Weak Clay," *Proceedings*, Geotechnical Engineering Congress, American Society of Civil Engineers, Vol. 2, pp. 1252–1263.

Das, B. M., and Hanna, A. M. (1988). "Model Tests for Shallow Strip Foundation on Granular Trench," *Special Topics in Foundations*, GSP No. 16 (ed. B. M. Das), American Society of Civil Engineers, pp. 110–124.

Greenwood, D. A., and Thompson, G. H. (1984). *Ground Stabilization: Deep Compaction and Grouting*, ICE Works Construction Guides, Thomas Telford Ltd., London.

Hughes, J. M. O., and Withers, N. J. (1974). "Reinforcing of Soft Cohesive Soil with Stone Columns," *Ground Engineering*, Vol. 7, pp. 42–49.

Hughes, J. M. O., Withers, N. J., and Greenwood, D. A. (1975). "A Field Trial of Reinforcing Effects of Stone Columns in Soil," *Geotechnique*, Vol. 25, No. 1, pp. 31–34.

Johnson, A. W., and Sallberg, J. R. (1960). "Factors That Influence Field Compaction of Soils," *Bulletin No. 272*, Highway Research Board, National Academy of Sciences, Washington, D.C.

Johnson, S. J. (1970a). "Precompression for Improving Foundation Soils," *Journal of the Soil Mechanics and Foundations Division*, American Society of Civil Engineers, Vol. 96, No. SM1, pp. 114–144.

Johnson, S. J. (1970b). "Foundation Precompression with Vertical Sand Drains," *Journal of the Soil Mechanics and Foundations Division*, American Society of Civil Engineers, Vol. 96, No. SM1, pp. 145–175.

Lee, K. L., and Singh, A. (1971). "Relative Density and Relative Compaction," *Journal of the Soil Mechanics and Foundations Division*, American Society of Civil Engineers, Vol. 97, No. SM7, pp. 1049–1052.

Lee, P. Y., and Suedkamp, R. J. (1972). "Characteristics of Irregularly Shaped Compaction Curves of Soils," *Highway Research Record No. 381*, National Academy of Sciences, Washington, D.C., pp. 1–9.

Leonards, G. A., Cutter, W. A., and Holtz, R. D. (1980). "Dynamic Compaction of Granular Soils," *Journal of Geotechnical Engineering Division*, ASCE, Vol. 96, No. GT1, pp. 73–110.

Mitchell, J. K. (1970). "In-Place Treatment of Foundation Soils," *Journal of the Soil Mechanics and Foundations Division*, American Society of Civil Engineers, Vol. 96, No. SM1, pp. 73–110.

Mitchell, J. K., and Freitag, D. R. (1959). "A Review and Evaluation of Soil-Cement Pavements," *Journal of the Soil Mechanics and Foundations Division*, American Society of Civil Engineers, Vol. 85, No. SM6, pp. 49–73.

Mitchell, J. K., and Huber, T. R. (1985). "Performance of a Stone Column Foundation," *Journal of Geotechnical Engineering*, American Society of Civil Engineers, Vol. 111, No. GT2, pp. 205–223.

Neubauer, C. H., Jr., and Thompson, M. R. (1972). "Stability Properties of Uncured Lime-Treated Fine-Grained Soils," *Highway Research Record No. 381*, National Academy of Sciences, pp. 20–26.

Partos, A., Welsh, J. P., Kazaniwsky, P. W., and Sander, E. (1989). "Case Histories of Shallow Foundation on Improved Soil," *Proceedings*, Foundation Engineering: Current Principles and Practices, American Society of Civil Engineers, Vol. 1, pp. 313–327.

APPENDIX

A

REINFORCED CONCRETE DESIGN

A.1 FUNDAMENTALS OF REINFORCED CONCRETE DESIGN

At the present time, most reinforced concrete designs are based on the recommendations of the building code prepared by the American Concrete Institute (1989)—that is, ACI 318-89. The basis for this code is the *ultimate strength design* or *strength design*. Some of the fundamental recommendations of the code are briefly summarized in the following sections.

Load Factors

According to ACI Code Section 9.2, the ultimate load-carrying capacity of a structural member should be

$$\boxed{U = 1.4D + 1.7L} \tag{A.1}$$

where U = ultimate load-carrying capacity of a member
D = dead load
L = live load

If the wind load is to be considered for design,

$$\boxed{U = 0.75(1.4D + 1.7L + 1.7W)} \tag{A.2}$$

where W = wind load

If there is no live load,

$$U = 0.9D + 1.3W \tag{A.3}$$

However, in no case should the magnitude of U be less than that given by Eq. (A.1).

Strength Reduction Factor

The design strength provided by a structural member is equal to the theoretical strength times a strength reduction factor, ϕ, or

Design strength = ϕ(theoretical strength)

The reduction factor, ϕ, takes into account the inaccuracies in the design assumptions, changes in property or strength of the construction materials, and so on. Following are some of the recommended values of ϕ (ACI Code Section 9.3).

Condition	ϕ
a. Axial tension; flexure with or without axial tension	0.9
b. Shear or torsion	0.85
c. Axial compression with or without flexure, spiral reinforcement	0.75
d. Axial compression with or without flexure, tied reinforcement	0.7
e. Bearing on concrete	0.7
f. Flexure in plain concrete	0.65

Design Concepts for a Rectangular Section in Bending

Figure A.1a shows a section of a concrete beam having a width b and a depth h. The assumed stress distribution across the section at ultimate load is shown in Figure A.1b. The following notation is used:

f'_c = compressive strength of concrete at 28 days

A_s = area of steel tension reinforcement

f_y = yield stress of reinforcement in tension

d = effective depth

l = location of the natural axis measured from the top of the compression face

$a = \beta l$

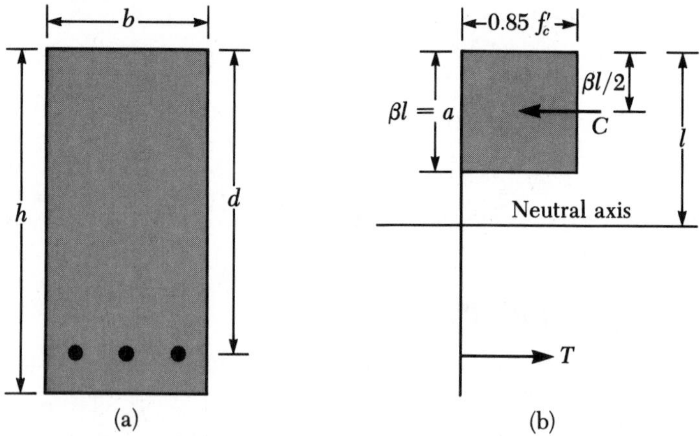

▼ **FIGURE A.1** Rectangular section in bending

$\beta = 0.85$ for f'_c of 4000 lb/ft² (28 MN/m²) or less and decreases at the rate of 0.05 for every 1000 lb/ft² (7 MN/m²) increase of f'_c. However, it cannot be less than 0.65 in any case (ACI Code Section 10.2.7).

From the principles of statics, for the section

Σ compressive force, $C = \Sigma$ tensile force, T

Thus

$$0.85f'_c ab = A_s f_y$$

or

$$a = \frac{A_s f_y}{0.85f'_c b} \tag{A.4}$$

Also, for the beam section, the nominal ultimate moment is

$$M_n = A_s f_y\left(d - \frac{a}{2}\right) \tag{A.5}$$

where M_n = theoretical ultimate moment

The design ultimate moment is

$$M_u = \phi A_s f_y\left(d - \frac{a}{2}\right) \tag{A.6}$$

Combining Eqs. (A.4) and (A.6) yields

$$M_u = \phi A_s f_y\left[d - \left(\frac{1}{2}\right)\frac{A_s f_y}{0.85f'_c b}\right] = \phi A_s f_y\left(d - \frac{0.59A_s f_y}{f'_c b}\right) \tag{A.7}$$

The steel percentage is defined by the equation

$$s = \frac{A_s}{bd} \tag{A.8a}$$

In a balanced beam, failure would occur by sudden simultaneous yielding of tensile steel and crushing of concrete. The balanced percentage of steel (for modulus of elasticity of steel, $E_s = 200$ MN/m^2) is

$$s_b = \frac{0.85 f'_c}{f_y}(\beta)\left(\frac{600}{600 + f_y}\right) \tag{A.8b}$$

where f'_c and f_y are in MN/m^2.

In conventional English units (with $E_s = 29 \times 10^6$ lb/in^2),

$$s_b = \frac{0.85 f'_c}{f_y}(\beta)\left(\frac{87{,}000}{87{,}000 + f_y}\right) \tag{A.8c}$$

where f'_c and f_y are in lb/in^2

To avoid sudden failure without warning, ACI Code Section 10.3.3 recommends that the maximum steel percentage be limited to $0.75 s_b$, or

$$s_{\max} = 0.75 s_b \tag{A.9}$$

Table A.1 gives the values of $s_{\max}$ for various values of f'_c and f_y.

▼ TABLE A.1 Values of $s_{\max}$ [Eq. (A.9)]

f_y		f'_c			
lb/in²	*MN/m²*	*3000 lb/in² (≈21 MN/m²)*	*4000 lb/in² (≈28 MN/m²)*	*5000 lb/in² (≈35 MN/m²)*	*6000 lb/in² (≈42 MN/m²)*
40,000	276	0.0284	0.0378	0.0445	0.0501
50,000	345	0.0209	0.0279	0.0329	0.0370
60,000	414	0.0163	0.0217	0.0255	0.0287
		$\beta = 0.85$	$\beta = 0.85$	$\beta = 0.80$	$\beta = 0.75$

The nominal or theoretical share strength of a section, V_n, may be given as

$$V_n = V_c + V_s \tag{A.10}$$

where V_c = nominal shear strength of concrete
V_s = nominal shear strength of reinforcement

The permissible shear strength, V_u, may be given by

$$V_u = \phi V_n = \phi(V_c + V_s) \tag{A.11}$$

The values of V_c may be given by the following equations (ACI Code Sections 11.3 and 11.11):

$$V_c = 0.17\sqrt{f'_c}\, bd \quad \text{(for member subjected to shear and flexure)} \tag{A.12a}$$

and

$$V_c = 0.34\sqrt{f'_c}\, bd \quad \text{(for member subjected to diagonal tension)} \tag{A.12b}$$

where f'_c is in MN/m^2, V_c is in MN, and b and d are in m

In conventional English units, Eqs. (A.12a) and (A.12b) become

$$V_c = 2\sqrt{f'_c}\, bd \tag{A.13a}$$

and

$$V_c = 4\sqrt{f'_c}\, bd \tag{A.13b}$$

where V_c is in lb, f'_c is in lb/in^2, and b and d are in inches

Note that

$$v_c = \frac{V_c}{bd} \tag{A.14}$$

where v_c is the shear stress

Now, combining Eqs. (A.11), (A.12a), and (A.14), we obtain

$$\text{Permissible shear stress} = v_u = \frac{V_u}{bd} = 0.17\phi\sqrt{f'_c} \tag{A.15a}$$

Similarly, from Eqs. (A.11), (A.12b), and (A.14),

$$v_u = 0.34\phi\sqrt{f'_c} \tag{A.15b}$$

Table A.2 gives the values of v_u/ϕ for various values of f'_c.

Similarly, combining Eqs. (A.11), (A.13a), (A.13b), and (A.14), we obtain

$$v_u = 2\phi\sqrt{f'_c} \quad \text{(A.16a)}$$

and

$$v_u = 4\phi\sqrt{f'_c} \quad \text{(A.16b)}$$

Table A.3 gives the values of v_u/ϕ for various values of f'_c.

TABLE A.2 Values of v_u/ϕ [Eqs. (A.15a) and (A.15b)]

Equation number	f'_c (MN/m²) 21	28	35	42
Eq. (A.15a)	0.78	0.90	1.0	1.1
Eq. (A.15b)	1.56	1.80	2.0	2.2

TABLE A.3 Values of v_u/ϕ [Eqs. (A.16a) and (A.16b)]

Equation number	f'_c (lb/in²) 3000	4000	5000	6000
Eq. (A.16a)	109.5	126.5	141.4	154.9
Eq. (A.16b)	219.0	253.0	282.8	309.8

A.2 REINFORCING BARS

The nominal sizes of reinforcing bars commonly used in the United States are given in Table A.4.

TABLE A.4 Nominal Sizes of Reinforcing Bars Used in the United States

Bar no.	Diameter (mm)	Diameter (in.)	Area of cross section (mm²)	Area of cross section (in²)
3	9.52	0.375	71	0.11
4	12.70	0.500	129	0.20
5	15.88	0.625	200	0.31
6	19.05	0.750	284	0.44
7	22.22	0.875	387	0.60
8	25.40	1.000	510	0.79
9	28.65	1.128	645	1.00
10	32.26	1.270	819	1.27
11	35.81	1.410	1006	1.56
14	43.00	1.693	1452	2.25
18	57.33	2.257	2580	4.00

The details regarding standard metric bars used in Canada are as follows:

Bar number	*Diameter (mm)*	*Area (mm²)*
10	11.3	100
15	16.0	200
20	19.5	300
25	25.2	500
30	29.9	700
35	35.7	1000
45	43.7	1500
55	56.4	2500

Reinforcing bar sizes in the metric system have been recommended by UNESCO (1971) as follows:

Bar diameter (mm)	*Area (mm²)*
6	28
8	50
10	79
12	113
14	154
16	201
18	254
20	314
22	380
25	491
30	707
32	804
40	1256
50	1963
60	2827

Sections A.6–A.8 use the standard bar diameters recommended by UNESCO.

A.3 DEVELOPMENT LENGTH

The development length, L_d, is the length of embedment required to develop the yield stress in the tension reinforcement for a section in flexure. ACI Code Section 12.2.2 lists the basic development lengths for tension reinforcement as

a. 35-mm bar and smaller $\quad 0.019A_b f_y/\sqrt{f'_c}$
but not less than $\quad 0.058d_b f_y$

b. 43-mm bar $26f_y/\sqrt{f'_c}$
c. 57-mm bar $34f_y/\sqrt{f'_c}$

where A_b = area of the individual bar (mm^2)
d_b = nominal diameter of the bar (mm)

The units of f_y and f'_c in the preceding expressions are in MN/m^2, and L_d is in millimeters.

In conventional English units, L_d is expressed in inches. The expressions for L_d are

a. No. 11 (U.S.) bar and smaller $0.04A_b f_y/\sqrt{f'_c}$
but not less than $0.0004d_b f_y$
b. No. 14 (U.S.) bar $0.085f_y/\sqrt{f'_c}$
c. No. 18 (U.S.) bar $0.11f_y/\sqrt{f'_c}$

The units of A_b and d_b are in in^2 and in., respectively. The values of f_y and f'_c are in lb/in^2.

The basic development length must be multiplied by appropriate factors given by ACI Code Sections 12.2.3 and 12.2.4:

a. Top reinforcement 1.4
b. Reinforcement with $f_y > 414$ MPa $2 - \dfrac{414}{f_y\ (MN/m^2)}$
In English units, for $f_y > 60{,}000\ lb/in^2$ $2 - \dfrac{60{,}000}{f_y\ (lb/in^2)}$
c. For lightweight concrete 1.33
d. Reinforcement spaced at least 152 mm on center and at least 76 mm in from all sides 0.8
e. Reinforcement in excess of that required $\left(\dfrac{\text{as required}}{\text{as provided}}\right)$

In any case, the basic development length should not be less than 12 in. (305 mm).

A.4 SUMMARY OF ACI 318-89 CODE REQUIREMENTS

For convenience, Table A.5 gives a summary of the strength design principles that apply to foundation design. The table has been divided into two parts: (1) general design principles that apply to strength design and (2) principles that are specifically applicable to foundation design.

TABLE A.5 Summary of ACI 318-89 Code Requirements

Principle	Design item	Code requirement	Code section
GENERAL	Load	$U = 1.4D + 1.7L$ $U = 0.75(1.4D + 1.7L + 1.7W)$ $U = 0.9D + 1.3W$ (See Article A.1.1 for explanations)	9.2
	Load factor, ϕ	Flexure: 0.9 Shear and torsion: 0.85 Bearing: 0.7 Flexure in plain concrete: 0.65 (See Article A.1.2)	9.3
	Maximum flexure reinforcement	$s_{max} = 0.75s_b$ [See Eqs. (A.8b), (A.8c), and (A.9)]	10.3.3
	Minimum flexure reinforcement—steel percentage	$s_{min} = \dfrac{1.4}{f_y \text{ (MN/m}^2)}$ $s_{min} = \dfrac{200}{f_y \text{ (lb/in}^2)}$ Uniform thickness: use steel percentage equal to that required for shrinkage and temperature	10.5
	Shrinkage and temperature reinforcement—steel percentage	For $f_y = 40$ ksi (275 MN/m²) or 50 ksi (345 MN/m²); $s_s = (0.002)$(gross concrete area) For $f_y = 60$ ksi (414 kN/m²) $s_s = (0.0018)$(gross concrete area)	7.12
	β factor (See Fig. A.1)	$\beta = 0.85$ for $f'_c \leq 4000$ lb/in² (28 MN/m²) and reduces by 0.05 for every 1000 lb/in² (7 MN/m² in excess of 28 MN/m²). *Minimum value* = 0.65	10.2.7
	Shear reinforcement	Refer to ACI Code	11.5
	Development length, L_d	See Section A.3	12.2
	Reinforcement spacing	Clear distance not less than diameter of bar or 1 in. (25.4 mm)	7.6.1
		Walls and slabs: not to be spaced farther apart than 3 times the wall or slab thickness or 18 in. (457 mm)	7.6.5
	Minimum reinforcement cover	3 in. (76 mm) for concrete cast against and permanently exposed to earth	7.7.1
	Modulus of elasticity of concrete, E_c	*SI system:* $E_c \text{ (MN/m}^2) = (W_c^{1.5})(0.043)\sqrt{f'_c} \text{ (MN/m}^2)$ W_c = density of concrete (for 1500 kg/m³ to 2500 kg/m³)	8.5

▼ **TABLE A.5 (Continued)**

Principle	Design item	Code requirement	Code section
		E_c (MN/m^2) $= 4700\sqrt{f'_c}$ (MN/m^2) (for normal weight concrete)	
		English system:	
		E_c (lb/in^2) $= (W_c^{1.5})(33)\sqrt{f'_c}$ (lb/in^2) for $W_c = 90$ to 155 lb/ft^3	
		E_c (lb/in^2) $= 57{,}000\sqrt{f'_c}$ (lb/in^2) (for normal weight concrete)	
	Shear strength	$v_n = \dfrac{V_n}{bd}$	
		Wide beam:	11.3
		v_c (MN/m^2) $= 0.17\sqrt{f'_c}$ (MN/m^2)	
		v_c (lb/in^2) $= 2\sqrt{f'_c}$ (lb/in^2)	
		Diagonal tension:	11.11
		v_c (MN/m^2) $= 0.34\sqrt{f'_c}$ (MN/m^2)	
		v_c (lb/in^2) $= 4\sqrt{f'_c}$ (lb/in^2)	
		[See Eqs. (A.12) and (A.13)]	
	Bearing strength	Bearing strength $= 0.85\phi f'_c A_1$	10.15
		$\phi = 0.7$	
		Exceptions: when supporting surface is wider on all sides than the loaded area, the bearing strength on the loaded area is equal to $0.85\phi f'_c A_1\sqrt{A_2/A_1}$. Limit of $\sqrt{A_2/A_1} \le 2$. A_1 = loaded area; A_2 = area of the portion of the supporting surface that is concentric and geometrically similar to the loaded area	
FOUNDATIONS			
Footings	General considerations	See ACI Code	15
	Maximum moment	See ACI Code	15.4
	Shear	v_c (MN/m^2) $= 0.083\left(2 + \dfrac{4}{\beta_c}\right)\sqrt{f'_c}$ (MN/m^2) $\le 0.34\sqrt{f'_c}$ (MN/m^2)	11.12.2.1, 15.5
		v_c (lb/in^2) $= \left(2 + \dfrac{4}{\beta_c}\right)\sqrt{f'_c}$ (lb/in^2) $\le 4\sqrt{f'_c}$ (lb/in^2)	
		β_c = ratio of long side to short side of concentrated load or reaction area	
	Minimum footing depth	Not less than 6 in. (152 mm) above the bottom of reinforcement for footing on soil. Not less than 12 in. (305 mm) for footing on piles	15.7

▼ TABLE A.5 (Continued)

Principle	Design item	Code requirement	Code section
	Transfer of force at base of column of reinforced pedestal	Area of reinforcement ≥ 0.005 gross area of supported member	15.8.2.1
	Round columns	Treat as square columns with same area for location of critical sections for moment, shear, and development of reinforcement in footings	15.3
WALLS	General considerations	Refer to ACI Code	14
	Minimum thickness	Not less than 1/25 the supported height or length, whichever is shorter; not less than 4 in. (102 mm)	14.5.3.1
		Exterior basement walls and foundation walls not less than 7.5 in. (191 mm)	14.5.3.2
	Grade beam	See ACI Code	14.7
	Reinforcement	Horizontal: $A_s \geq 0.002A_g$ of wall	14.3.3
		Vertical: $A_s \geq 0.0012A_g$ of wall A_s = area of reinforcement A_g = gross area of the wall	14.3.2

A.5 DESIGN EXAMPLE OF A CONTINUOUS WALL FOUNDATION

This section describes the design of a load-bearing wall with the following characteristics:

- Dead load = D = 3000 lb/ft
- Live load = L = 1200 lb/ft
- Gross allowable bearing capacity of soil = 2000 lb/ft^2
- Depth of the top of foundation from the ground surface = 4 ft
- $f_y = 60$ kip/in^2
- $f'_c = 3$ kip/in^2
- Unit weight of soil = $\gamma = 110$ lb/ft^3
- Unit weight of concrete = $\gamma_c = 150$ lb/ft^3

General Considerations

For this design, we assume that the foundation thickness is 12 in., the minimum cover over the steel reinforcement (ACI Code Section 7.7.1) is 3 in., and the steel bars to be used are U.S. No. 4 bars (diameter = 0.5 in.). From Figure A.2a,

$$d = 12 - 3 - \frac{0.5}{2} = 8.75 \text{ in.}$$

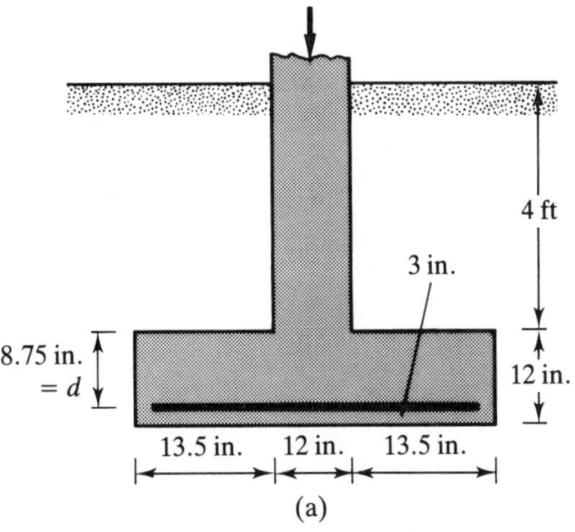

(a)

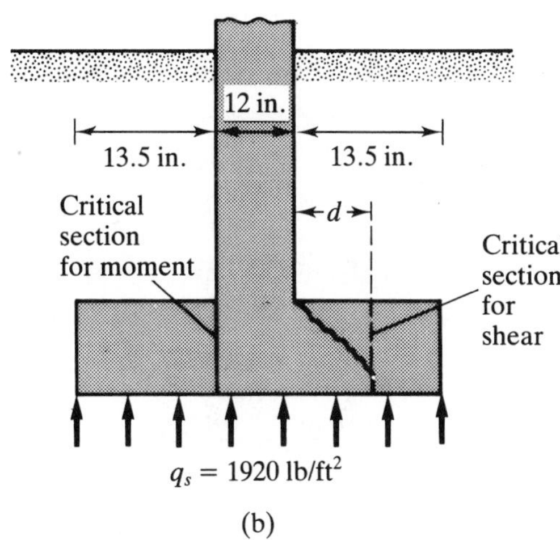

(b)

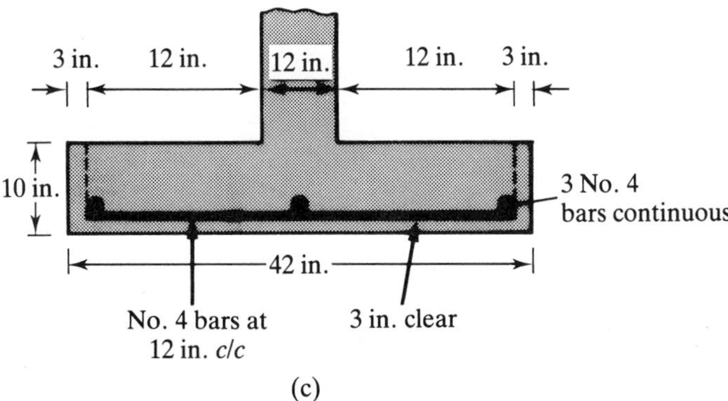

(c)

▼ **FIGURE A.2** Continuous wall foundation

Then we calculate:

$$\text{Weight of foundation per foot length} = \left(\frac{12\text{ in.}}{12}\right)\gamma_c = \left(\frac{12}{12}\right)(150) = 150\text{ lb/ft}^2$$

$$\text{Weight of soil above the foundation} = (4)(110) = 440\text{ lb/ft}^2$$

So, the net allowable soil-bearing capacity is

$$q_{\text{net(all)}} = 2000 - 150 - 400 = 1410\text{ lb/ft}^2$$

Hence the required width of the foundation is

$$B = \frac{D + L}{q_{\text{net(all)}}} = \frac{3000 + 1200}{1410} = 2.98\text{ ft}$$

So, we assume that $B = 3.25$ ft. According to ACI Code Section 9.2,

$$U = 1.4D + 1.7L = (1.4)(3000) + (1.7)(1200) = 6240\text{ lb/ft}$$

Converting the net allowable soil pressure to an ultimate (factored value) we get

$$q_s = \frac{U}{(B)(1\text{ ft})} = \frac{6240}{3.25} = 1920\text{ lb/ft}^2$$

Investigation of Shear Strength of the Foundation

The critical section for shear occurs at a distance d from the face of the wall (ACI Code Sections 15.5 and 11.11), as shown in Figure A.2b. So, the shear there is

$$V_u = \frac{(13.5\text{ in.} - d)}{12} q_s(1) = \frac{(13.5 - 8.75)}{12}(1920)(1\text{ ft})$$

$$= 760\text{ lb/ft}$$

From Eq. (A.13a),

$$V_c = 2\sqrt{f'_c}\,bd = 2\sqrt{3000}\,(12\text{ in.})(8.75\text{ in.}) = 11{,}502\text{ lb/ft}$$

Also, from Eq. (A.11),

$$\phi V_c = (0.85)(11{,}502) = 9777\text{ lb/ft} > V_u = 760\text{ lb/ft—OK}$$

Because $V_u < \phi V_c$, the total thickness of the foundations could be reduced to 10 in. to give

$$d = 10 - 3 - \frac{0.5}{2} = 6.75\text{ in.} > 6\text{ in.} = d_{\text{min}} \qquad \text{(ACI Code Section 15.7)}$$

If $d = 6.75$ in.,

$$\phi V_c = (0.85)(2)\sqrt{3000}\,(12\text{ in.})(6.75\text{ in.}) = 7542\text{ lb/ft} > V_u\text{—OK}$$

Flexural Reinforcement

For steel reinforcement, the factored moment at the face of the wall has to be determined (ACI Code Section 15.4). The bonding of the foundation will be in one direction only. So, according to Figure A.2b, the design ultimate moment is

$$M_u = \frac{q_s l^2}{2}$$

where $q_s = 1920\ \text{lb/ft}^3$

$l = 13.5$ in.

So

$$M_u = \frac{(1920)\left(\frac{13.5}{12}\right)^2}{2} = 1215\ \text{lb-ft/ft} = 14.58 \times 10^3\ \text{lb-in./ft}$$

From Eqs. (A.4) and (A.5),

$$M_n = A_s f_y\left(d - \frac{a}{2}\right)$$

$$a = \frac{A_s f_y}{0.85 f'_c b} = \frac{A_s(60{,}000)}{(0.85)(3000)(12\ \text{in.})} = 1.961 A_s$$

Thus

$$M_n = (A_s)(60{,}000)\left(6.75 - \frac{1.961}{2}A_s\right)$$

$$= 405 \times 10^3 A_s - 58.83 \times 10^3 A_s^2$$

Again, from Eq. (A.6),

$$M_u = \phi M_u$$

where $\phi = 0.9$

Thus

$$14.58 \times 10^3 = (0.9)(10^3)(405 A_s - 58.83 A_s^2)$$

From the preceding equation,

$$A_{s(1)} = 6.85\ \text{in}^2; \qquad A_{s(2)} = 0.04\ \text{in}^2$$

Hence the steel percentage with $A_{s(1)}$ is

$$s_1 = \frac{A_{s(1)}}{bd} = \frac{6.85\ \text{in}^2}{(12\ \text{in.})(6.75\ \text{in.})} = 0.0846$$

Similarly,

$$s_2 = \frac{A_{s(2)}}{bd} = \frac{0.04}{(12\ \text{in.})(6.75\ \text{in.})}$$

$$= 0.000494 < s_{\min} = 0.0018 \qquad \text{(ACI Code Section 7.12.2)}$$

The maximum steel percentage that can be provided is given in Eqs. (A.8c) and (A.9). Thus

$$s_{max} = (0.75)(0.85)\frac{f'_c}{f_y}\beta\left(\frac{87{,}000}{87{,}000 + f_y}\right)$$

Note that $\beta = 0.85$. Substituting the proper values of β, f'_c, and f_y into the preceding equation yields

$$s_{max} = 0.016$$

Note that $s_1 = 0.0846 > s_{max} = 0.016$. So use $s = s_{min} = 0.0018$. Then

$$A_s = (s_{min})(b)(d) = (0.0018)(12)(6.75) = 0.1458 \text{ in}^2$$

Use U.S. No. 4 bars (0.5-in. diameter) at 12 in. center-to-center. Hence

$$A_{s(\text{provided})} = \left[\frac{(1 \text{ ft})(12)}{(12 \text{ in.})}\right]\left(\frac{\pi}{4}\right)(0.5)^2 = 0.196 \text{ in}^2$$

Development Length of Reinforcement Bars

According to Section A.3, for No. 4 bars, $L_d = 0.04A_b(f_y/\sqrt{f'_c})$ but not less than $0.0004d_b f_y$ or 12 in. For this case, $A_b = 0.196$ in^2 and $d_b = 0.5$ in. So

$$L_d = 0.04A_b\left(\frac{f_y}{\sqrt{f'_c}}\right) = (0.04)(0.196)\left(\frac{60{,}000}{\sqrt{3000}}\right) = 8.59 \text{ in.}$$

$$L_d = 0.0004d_b f_y = (0.0004)(0.5)(60{,}000) = 12 \text{ in.}$$

Hence

$$L_d = 12 \text{ in.}$$

Now, for a 3-in. cover on the sides of the foundation, the development length would be 13.5 in. − 3 in. = 10.5 in. < 12 in. To achieve the proper development length, we increase the width of the foundation, B, to 42 in. This will give 15-in. cantilevers, as shown in Figure A.2c. This increase of B will not greatly affect the structural steel required. It will reduce the value of soil-bearing pressure, q_s, while the shear and moment capacities of the cross section remain constant.

Minimum reinforcement should be furnished in the long direction to offset shrinkage and temperature effects (ACI Code Section 7.12). Thus

$$A_s = (0.0018)(b)(d) = (0.0018)[(15)(2) + 12](6.75) = 0.51 \text{ in}^2$$

Provide three No. 4 bars ($A_s = 0.588$ in^2).

The final design sketch is shown in Figure A.2c.

A.6 DESIGN EXAMPLE OF A SQUARE FOUNDATION FOR A COLUMN

Figure A.3a shows a square column foundation with the following conditions:

- Live load = L = 675 kN
- Dead load = D = 1125 kN
- Allowable gross soil-bearing capacity = q_{all} = 145 kN/m^2
- Column size = 0.5 m × 0.5 m
- f'_c = 20.68 MN/m^2
- f_y = 413.7 MN/m^2

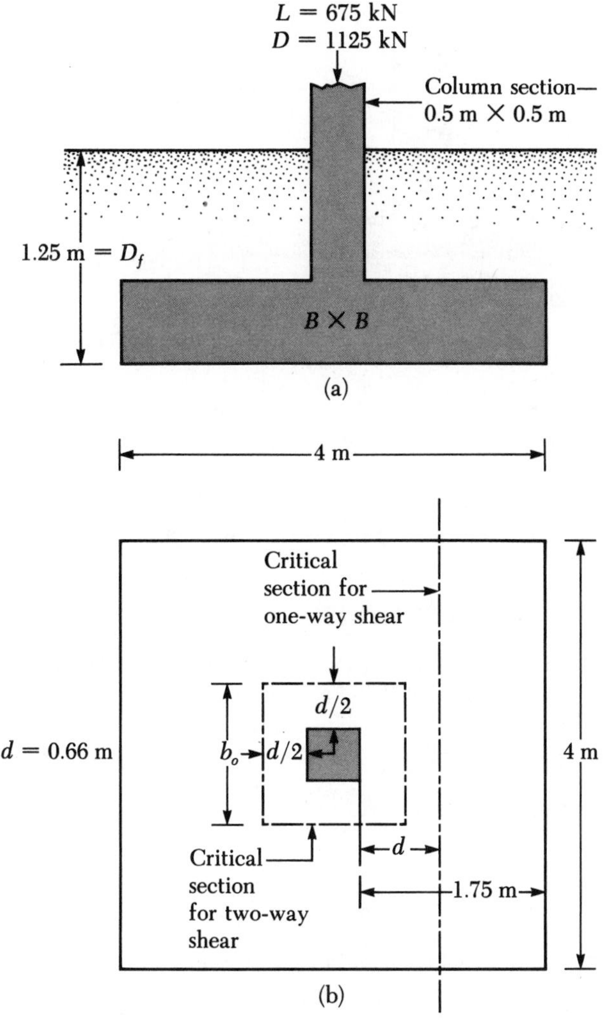

▼ **FIGURE A.3** Square foundation for a column

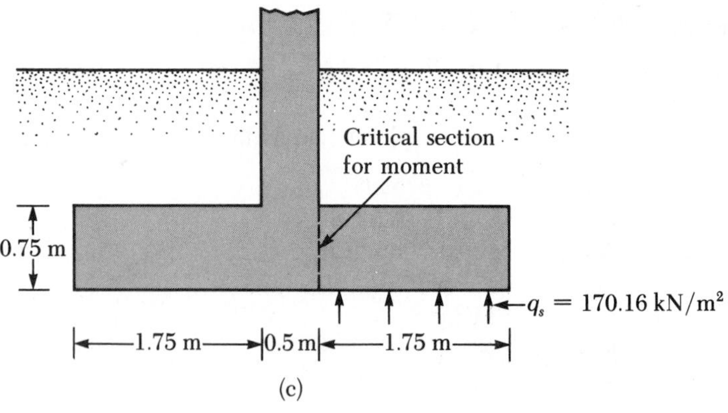

(c)

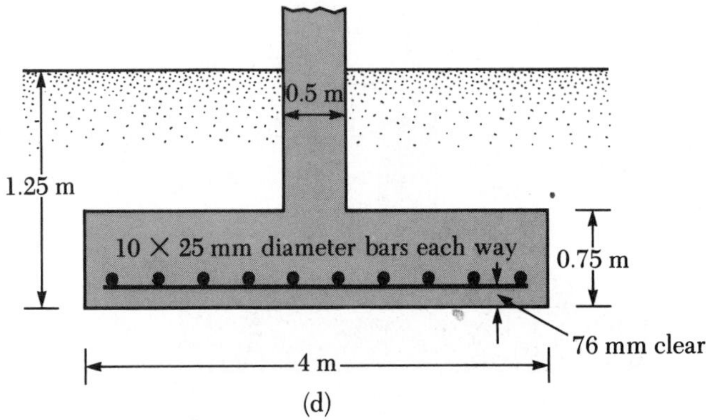

(d)

▼ **FIGURE A.3** (Continued)

The foundation can be designed in the following manner.

General Considerations

Let the average unit weight of concrete and soil above the base of the foundation be 21.97 kN/m³. So the net allowable soil-bearing capacity is

$$q_{\text{all(net)}} = 145 - (D_f)(21.97) = 145 - (1.25)(21.97) = 117.54 \text{ kN/m}^2$$

Hence the required foundation area is

$$A = B^2 = \frac{D + L}{q_{\text{all(net)}}} = \frac{675 + 1125}{117.54} = 15.31 \text{ m}^2$$

Use a foundation with dimensions, B, of 4 m × 4 m.

The factored load for the foundation is

$$U = 1.4D + 1.7L = (1.4)(1125) + (1.7)(675) = 2722.5 \text{ kN}$$

Hence the factored soil pressure is

$$q_s = \frac{U}{B^2} = \frac{2722.5}{16} = 170.16 \text{ kN/m}^2$$

Assume the thickness of the foundation to be equal to 0.75 m. With a clear cover of 76 mm under the steel bars and an assumed bar diameter of 25 mm,

$$d = 0.75 - 0.076 - \frac{0.025}{2} = 0.6615 \text{ m}$$

Check for Shear

As we showed in Section A.5, V_u should be equal to or less than ϕV_c. For one-way shear,

$$V_u \leq \phi(0.17)\sqrt{f'_c}\,bd$$

The critical section for one-way shear is distance d from the edge of the column (ACI Code Section 11.11.1.1), as shown in Figure A.3b. So

$$V_u = q_s \times \text{critical area} = (170.16)(4)(1.75 - 0.6615) = 740.9 \text{ kN}$$

Also

$$\phi V_c = (0.85)(0.17)(\sqrt{20.68})(4)(0.6615)(1000) = 1738.7 \text{ kN}$$

So,

$$V_u = 740.9 \text{ kN} \leq \phi V_c = 1738.7 \text{ kN—OK}$$

For two-way shear, the critical section is distance $d/2$ from the edge of the column (ACI Code Section 11.11.1.2), as shown in Figure A.3b. For this case,

$$\phi V_c = \phi(0.34)\sqrt{f'_c}\,b_o d$$

The term b_o is the perimeter of the critical section for two-way shear. Or, for this design,

$$b_o = 4[0.5 + 2(d/2)] = 4[0.5 + 2(0.3308)] = 4.65 \text{ m}$$

Hence

$$\phi V_c = (0.85)(0.34)(\sqrt{20.68})(4.65)(0.6615) = 4.042 \text{ MN} = 4042 \text{ kN}$$

Also

$$V_u = (q_s)(\text{critical area})$$

$$\text{Critical area} = (4 \times 4) - (0.5 + 0.6615)^2 = 14.65 \text{ m}^2$$

So

$$V_u = (170.16)(14.65) = 2492.84 \text{ kN}$$

$$V_u = 2492.84 \text{ kN} < \phi V_c = 4042 \text{ kN—OK}$$

The assumed depth of foundation is more than adequate.

Flexural Reinforcement

According to Figure A.3c, the moment at critical section (ACI Code Section 15.4.2) is

$$M_u = (q_s B)\left(\frac{1.75}{2}\right)^2 + \frac{[(170.16)(4)](1.75)^2}{2} = 1042.23 \text{ kN}\cdot\text{m}$$

From Eq. (A.4),

$$a = \frac{A_s f_y}{0.85 f'_c b} \qquad (note: b = B)$$

or

$$A_s = \frac{0.85 f'_c Ba}{f_y} = \frac{(0.85)(20.68)(4)a}{413.7} = 0.17a$$

From Eq. (A.6),

$$M_u \leq \phi A_s f_y\left(d - \frac{a}{2}\right)$$

With $\phi = 0.9$ and $A_s = 0.17$a,

$$M_u = 1042.23 = (0.9)(0.17a)(413700)\left(0.6615 - \frac{a}{2}\right)$$

Solution of the preceding equation gives $a = 0.0254$ m. Hence

$$A_s = 0.17a = (0.17)(0.0254) = 0.0043 \text{ m}^2$$

Percentage of steel

$$s = \frac{A_s}{bd} = \frac{A_s}{Bd} = \frac{0.0043}{(4)(0.6615)} = 0.00163 < s_{\text{min}}$$

$$= 0.0018 \text{ (ACI Code Section 7.12.2)}$$

So

$$A_{s(\text{min})} = (0.0018)(B)(d) = (0.0018)(4)(0.6615)$$

$$= 0.004762 \text{ m}^2 = 47.62 \text{ cm}^2$$

Provide 10 × 25-mm (≈ No. 8 U.S.) diameter bars each way [$A_s = (4.91)(10) = 49.1 \text{ cm}^2$].

Check for Development Length

From Section A.3, the development length is

$$L_d = 0.019 A_b \frac{f_y}{\sqrt{f'_c}} = (0.019)(491 \text{ mm}^2)\left(\frac{413.7}{\sqrt{20.68}}\right) = 848.68 \text{ mm}$$

Also

$$L_d \geq 0.058 d_b f_y = (0.058)(25)(413.7) = 599.87 \text{ mm}$$

So $L_d = 848.68$ mm controls. Actual L_d is $(4 - 0.5/2) - 0.076$ (cover) $= 1.674$ m > 599.87 mm—OK.

Check for Bearing Strength

Table A.5 indicates that the bearing strength should be at least $0.85\phi f'_c A_1\sqrt{A_2/A_1}$, with a limit of $\sqrt{A_2/A_1} \leq 2$. For this problem, $\sqrt{A_2/A_1} = \sqrt{(4 \times 4)/(0.5 \times 0.5)} = 8$, so use $\sqrt{A_2/A_1} = 2$. Also $\phi = 0.7$. Hence the design bearing strength $=$ $(0.85)(0.7)(20.68)(0.5 \times 0.5)(2) = 6.15$ MN $= 6150$ kN. However, the factored column load $U = 2722.5$ kN < 6150 kN—OK.

The final design section is shown in Figure A.3d.

A.7 DESIGN EXAMPLE OF A RECTANGULAR FOUNDATION FOR A COLUMN

This section describes the design of a rectangular foundation to support a column having dimensions of 0.4 m $\times$ 0.4 m in cross section. Other details are as follows:

- Dead load $= D = 290$ kN
- Live load $= L = 110$ kN
- Depth from the ground surface to the top of the foundation $= 1.2$ m
- Allowable gross soil-bearing capacity $= 120$ kN/m^2
- Maximum width of foundation $= B = 1.5$ m
- $f_y = 413.7$ MN/m^2
- $f'_c = 20.68$ MN/m^2
- Unit weight of soil $= \gamma = 17.27$ kN/m^3
- Unit weight of concrete $= \gamma_c = 22.97$ kN/m^3

General Considerations

For this design, we assume a foundation depth of 0.45 m (Figure A.4a). The weight of the foundation/m^2 $= 0.45\gamma_c = (0.45)(22.97) = 10.34$ kN/m^2, and the weight of the soil above the foundation/m^2 $= (1.2)\gamma = (1.2)(17.27) = 20.72$ kN/m^2. Hence the net allowable soil-bearing capacity, $q_{\text{net(all)}} = 120 - 10.34 - 20.72 = 88.94$ kN/m^2.

The required area of the foundation $= (D + L)/q_{\text{net(all)}} = (290 + 110)/88.94 =$ 4.5 m^2. Hence the length of the foundation is 4.5 m^2$/B = 4.5/1.5 = 3$ m.

The factored column load $= 1.4D + 1.7L = 1.4(290) + 1.7(110) = 593$ kN.

The factored soil-bearing capacity, $q_s =$ factored load/foundation area $=$ $593/4.5 = 131.78$ kN/m^2.

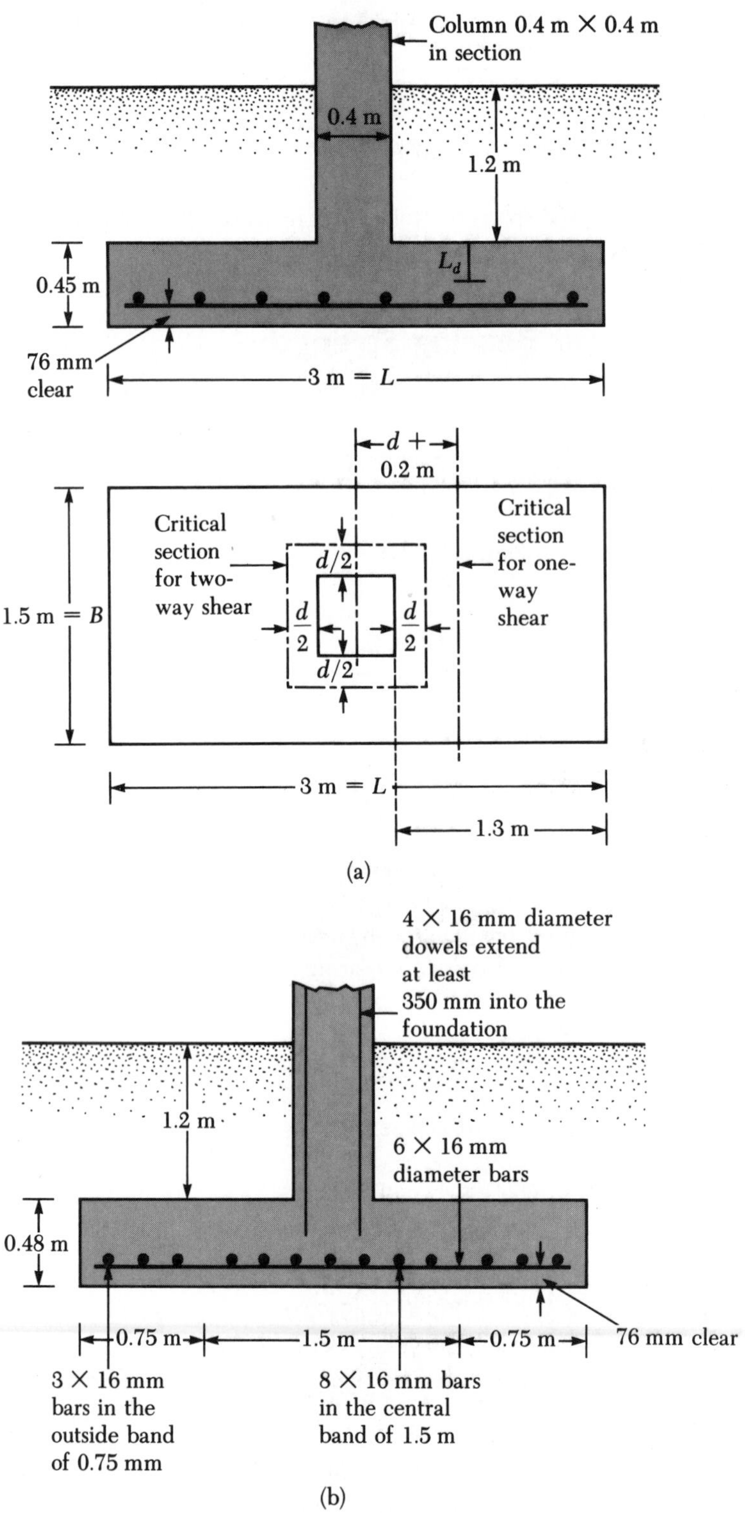

▼ **FIGURE A.4** Rectangular foundation for a column

Shear Strength of Foundation

We assume that the steel bars to be used have a diameter of 16 mm. So, the effective depth $d = 450 - 76 - 16 = 358$ mm. (Note that the assumed clear cover is 76 mm.)

Figure A.4a shows the critical section for one-way shear (ACI Code Section 11.11.1.1):

$$V_u = \left(1.5 - \frac{0.4}{2} - 0.358\right)Bq_s = (0.942)(1.5)(131.78) = 186.21 \text{ kN}$$

The nominal shear capacity of concrete for one-way beam action is

$$V_c = 0.17\sqrt{f'_c}Bd = 0.17(\sqrt{20.68})(1.5)(0.358) = 0.4152 \text{ MN} = 415.2 \text{ kN}$$

Now

$$V_u = 184.22 \leq \phi V_c = (0.85)(415.2) = 352.92 \text{ kN—OK}$$

The critical section for two-way shear is also shown in Figure A.4a. It is based on the recommendations of ACI Code Section 11.11.1.2. For this section,

$$V_u = q_s[(1.5)(3) - 0.758^2] = 517.3 \text{ kN}$$

The nominal shear capacity of the foundation (ACI Code Section 11.11.2.1; also see Table A.5 of the text) is

$$V_c = v_c b_o d = 0.083\left(2 + \frac{4}{\beta_c}\right)\sqrt{f'_c}\, b_o d$$

where b_o = perimeter of the critical section
β_c = length of foundation/width of foundation

or

$$V_c = 0.083\left[2 + \frac{4}{\frac{3}{1.5}}\right]\sqrt{20.68}(4 \times 0.758)(0.358) = 1.638 \text{ MN}$$

So, for the two-way shear condition,

$$V_u = 517.3 \text{ kN} < \phi V_c = (0.85)(1639) = 1393 \text{ kN}$$

Therefore the section is adequate.

Check for Bearing Capacity of Concrete Column at the Interface with Foundation

According to ACI Code Section 10.15 (also see Table A.5), bearing strength = $0.85\phi f'_c A_1 (\phi = 0.7)$. For this problem, $U = 593$ kN < bearing strength = $(0.85)(0.7)(20.68)(0.4)^2 = 1.969$ MN.

So, a minimum area of dowels should be provided across the interface of the column and the foundation. Based on ACI Code Section 15.8.2.1,

$$\text{Minimum area of steel} = (0.005)(\text{area of column})$$
$$= (0.005)(400^2) = 800 \text{ mm}^2$$

We use 4 × 16-mm (≈ No. 5 U.S.) diameter bars as dowels.

The minimum required length of development, L_d, of dowels into the foundation is $(0.24 f_y d_b)/\sqrt{f'_c}$, but not less than $0.044 f_y d_b$ (ACI Code Section 12.3.2). So

$$L_d = \frac{0.24 f_y d_b}{\sqrt{f'_c}} = \frac{(0.24)(413.7)(16)}{\sqrt{20.68}} = 349.33 \text{ mm}$$

Also

$$L_d = 0.044 f_y d_b = (0.044)(413.7)(16) = 291.25 \text{ mm}$$

Hence $L_d = 349.33$ mm controls.

Available depth for the dowels (Figure A.4a) is 450 − 76 − 16 − 16 = 342 mm. Hooks cannot be used, so the foundation depth must be increased. We let the new depth be 480 mm to accommodate the required $L_d = 349.33$ mm. Hence the new value of d is 480 − 76 − 16 = 388 mm.

Flexural Reinforcement in the Long Direction

According to Figure A.4a, the design moment about the column face is

$$M_u = \frac{(q_s B)1.3^2}{2} = \frac{(131.78)(1.5)(1.3)^2}{2} = 167.07 \text{ kN} \cdot \text{m}$$

From Eq. (A.4),

$$a = \frac{A_s f_y}{0.85 f'_c b} = \frac{(A_s)(413.7)}{(0.85)(20.68)(1.5)} = 15.69 A_s$$

From Eq. (A.6),

$$M_u = \phi M_n = \phi A_s f_y \left(d - \frac{a}{2}\right)$$

or

$$167.07 = (0.9)(A_s)(413.7 \times 10^3)\left[0.388 - \frac{15.69}{2}(A_s)\right]$$
$$= 144{,}464 A_s - 2{,}920{,}928 A_s^2$$

The solution of the preceding equation gives

$$A_{s(1)} = 0.0483 \text{ m}^2$$

That is, the steel percentage is

$$\frac{A_{s(1)}}{Bd} = \frac{0.0483}{(1.5)(0.388)} = 0.0829 = s_1$$

and

$$A_{s(2)} = 0.0012 \text{ m}^2$$

That is, the steel percentage is

$$\frac{A_{s(2)}}{Bd} = \frac{0.00120}{(1.5)(0.388)} = 0.00206 = s_2$$

Section A.5 (for similar values of f'_c and f_y) indicated that $s_{\text{max}} = 0.016$. Also, from ACI Code Section 7.12.2, $s_{\text{min}} = 0.0018$. Note that $s_1 > s_{\text{max}}$ and $s_2 > s_{\text{min}}$. So, $A_s = A_{s(2)}$ may be used. Hence we provide 6×16 mm diameter bars (A_s provided is 0.001206 m^2).

Flexural Reinforcement in the Short Direction

According to Figure A.4a, the moment at the face of the column is

$$M_u = \frac{(q_s L)(0.55)^2}{2} = \frac{(131.78)(3)(0.55)^2}{2} = 59.8 \text{ kN} \cdot \text{m}$$

From Eq. (A.4),

$$a = \frac{A_s f_y}{0.85 f'_c b} = \frac{(A_s)(413.7)}{(0.85)(20.68)(3)} = 7.845 A_s$$

From Eq. (A.6),

$$M_u = \phi A_s f_y \left(d - \frac{a}{2}\right)$$

or

$$59.8 = (0.9)(A_s)(413.7 \times 10^3)\left[0.388 - \frac{7.845}{2}(A_s)\right]$$

Solution of the preceding equation gives

$$A_{s(1)} = 0.0985 \text{ m}^2 \qquad (\text{thus } s_1 > s_{\text{max}})$$

$$A_{s(2)} = 0.0004 \text{ m}^2 \qquad (\text{thus } s_2 < s_{\text{min}})$$

Use $s = s_{\text{min}}$, or

$$A_s = s_{\text{min}} bd = (0.0018)(3)(0.388) \approx 0.0021 \text{ m}^2$$

Use 12×16-mm ($\approx$ No. 5 U.S.) diameter bars.

Final Design Sketch

According to ACI Code Section 15.4.4.2, a portion of the reinforcement in the short direction is to be distributed uniformly over a bandwidth equal to the smallest dimension of the foundation. The remainder of the reinforcement should be distributed uniformly outside the central band of the foundation. The reinforcement in the central band is $2/(\beta_c + 1)$ (where $\beta_c = L/B$). For this problem, $\beta_c = 2$. Hence ⅔ of the reinforcing bars (that is, 8 bars) should be placed in the center band of the foundation. The remaining 4 bars should be placed outside the central band. However, we need to check the steel percentage in the outside band, or

$$s = \frac{A_s}{bd} = \frac{(2)(201\ \text{mm}^2)}{\left(\dfrac{3000 - 1500}{2}\right)(388)} = 0.0014 < s_{\text{min}} = 0.0018$$

Use $A_s = (s_{\text{min}})(b)(d) = (0.0018)(750)(388) = 523.8\ \text{mm}^2$. Hence 3 × 16-mm (≈ No. 5 U.S.) diameter bars on each side of the central band will be sufficient.

The final design sketch is shown in Figure A.4b.

A.8 DESIGN EXAMPLE OF A CANTILEVER RETAINING WALL

The cross section of a cantilever retaining wall is shown in Figure A.5. The overall stability of the wall (i.e., factors of safety against overturning, sliding, and bearing capacity failure) will be checked first and will be followed by the design of the stem, heel, and toe. For this case, $f_y = 413.7\ \text{MN/m}^2$ and $f'_c = 20.68\ \text{MN/m}^2$.

General Considerations

From Figure A.5,

$$H' = H_1 + H_2 + H_3 = 2.6 \tan 10° + 6 + 0.7$$

$$= 0.458 + 6 + 0.7 = 7.158\ \text{m}$$

Rankine active force per unit length of wall $= P_p = \tfrac{1}{2}\gamma_1 H'^2 K_a$. For $\phi_1 = 30°$ and $\alpha = 10°$, $K_a = 0.350$ (Table 5.8). Thus

$$P_a = \frac{1}{2}(18)(7.158)^2(0.35) = 161.4\ \text{kN/m}$$

$$P_v = P_a \sin 10° = 161.4(\sin 10°) = 28.03\ \text{kN/m}$$

$$P_h = P_a \cos 10° = 161.4(\cos 10°) = 158.95\ \text{kN/m}$$

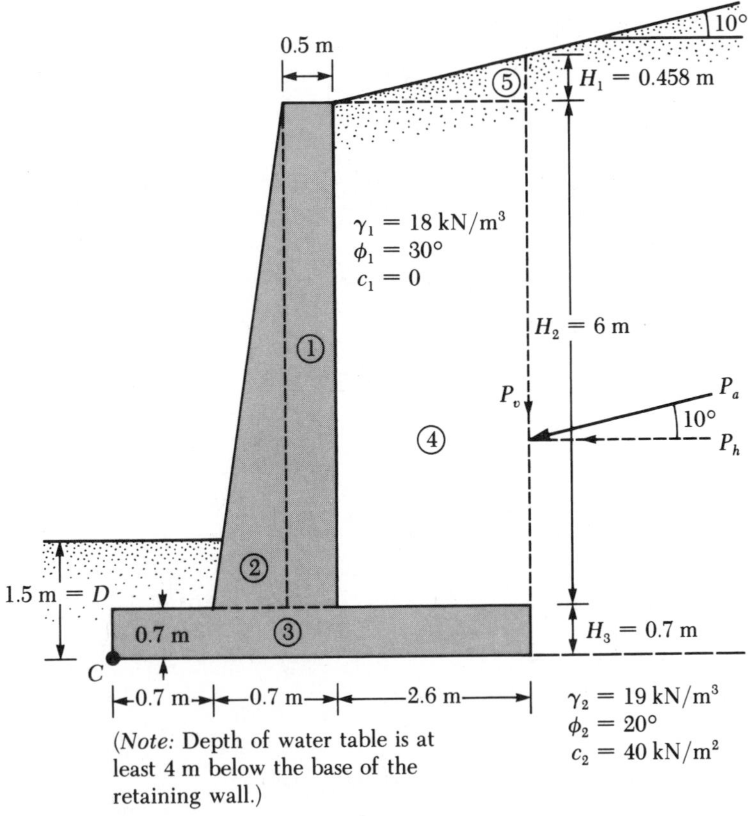

▼ **FIGURE A.5**

Factor of Safety Against Overturning

The following table can now be prepared for determination of the resisting moment.

Section no.[a]	*Area (m^2)*	*Weight/unit length (kN/m)*	*Moment arm from point C (m)*	*Moment (kN · m)*
1	6 × 0.5 = 3	70.74	1.15	81.35
2	½(0.2)6 = 0.6	15.15	0.833	11.79
3	4 × 0.7 = 2.8	66.02	2.0	132.04
4	6 × 2.6 = 15.6	280.80	2.7	758.16
5	½(2.6)(0.458) = 0.595	10.71	3.13	33.52
		$P_v = 28.03$	4.0	112.12
		$\sum V = 470.45$		$\sum 1128.98 = \sum M_R$

[a] For section numbers, refer to Figure A.5
$\gamma_{concrete} = 23.58$ kN/m³

The overturning moment, M_O, is

$$M_O = P_h\left(\frac{H'}{3}\right) = 158.95\left(\frac{7.158}{3}\right) = 379.25 \text{ kN} \cdot \text{m}$$

$$FS_{(\text{overturning})} = \frac{\sum M_R}{M_O} = \frac{1128.98}{379.25} = 2.98 > 2\text{—OK}$$

Factor of Safety Against Sliding

From Eq. (5.67),

$$FS_{(\text{sliding})} = \frac{(\sum V)\tan(k_1\phi_1) + Bk_2c_2 + P_p}{P_a \cos\alpha}$$

Let $k_1 = k_2 = 2/3$. Also

$$P_p = \frac{1}{2}K_p\gamma_2 D^2 + 2c_2\sqrt{K_p}D$$

$$K_p = \tan^2\left(45 + \frac{\phi_2}{2}\right) = \tan^2(45 + 10) = 2.04$$

$$D = 1.5 \text{ m}$$

So

$$P_p = \frac{1}{2}(2.04)(19)(1.5)^2 + 2(40)(\sqrt{204})(1.5)$$

$$= 43.61 + 171.39 = 215 \text{ kN/m}$$

Hence

$$FS_{(\text{sliding})} = \frac{(470.45)\tan\left(\frac{2 \times 20}{3}\right) + (4)\left(\frac{2}{3}\right)(40) + 215}{158.95}$$

$$= \frac{111.5 + 106.67 + 215}{158.95} = 2.73 > 1.5\text{—OK}$$

Note: For some designs, the depth D for passive pressure calculation may be taken to be *equal to the thickness of the base slab.*

Factor of Safety Against Bearing Capacity Failure

Combining Eqs. (5.62), (5.63), and (5.64) yields

$$e = \frac{B}{2} - \frac{\sum M_R - \sum M_O}{\sum V} = \frac{4}{2} - \frac{1128.98 - 379.25}{470.45}$$

$$= 0.406 \text{ m} < \frac{B}{6} = \frac{4}{6} = 0.666 \text{ m}$$

Again, from Eqs. (5.66) and (5.67)

$$q_{\substack{\text{toe}\\ \text{heel}}} = \frac{\sum V}{B}\left(1 \pm \frac{6e}{B}\right) = \frac{470.45}{4}\left(1 \pm \frac{6 \times 0.406}{4}\right) = 189.2 \text{ kN/m}^2 \text{ (toe)}$$
$$= 45.99 \text{ kN/m}^2 \text{ (heel)}$$

The ultimate bearing capacity of the soil can be determined from Eq. (5.68):

$$q_u = c_2 N_c F_{cd} F_{ci} + qN_q F_{qd} F_{qi} + \frac{1}{2}\gamma_2 B' N_\gamma F_{\gamma d} F_{\gamma i}$$

For $\phi_2 = 20°$ (Table 3.4), $N_c = 14.83$, $N_q = 6.4$, and $N_\gamma = 5.39$. Also

$$q = \gamma_2 D = (19)(1.5) = 28.5 \text{ kN/m}^2$$

$$B' = B - 2e = 4 - 2(0.406) = 3.188 \text{ m}$$

$$F_{cd} = 1 + 0.4\left(\frac{D}{B'}\right) = 1 + 0.4\left(\frac{1.5}{3.188}\right) = 1.188$$

$$F_{qd} = 1 + 2 \tan \phi_2(1 - \sin \phi_2)^2\left(\frac{D}{B'}\right) = 1 + 0.315\left(\frac{1.5}{3.188}\right) = 1.148$$

$$F_{\gamma d} = 1$$

$$F_{ci} = F_{qi} = \left(1 - \frac{\psi°}{90°}\right)^2$$

$$\psi = \tan^{-1}\left(\frac{P_a \cos \alpha}{\sum V}\right) = \tan^{-1}\left(\frac{158.95}{470.45}\right) = 18.67°$$

So

$$F_{ci} = F_{qi} = \left(1 - \frac{18.67}{90}\right)^2 = 0.628$$

$$F_{\gamma i} = \left(1 - \frac{\psi}{\phi}\right)^2 = \left(1 - \frac{18.67}{20}\right)^2 \approx 0$$

Hence

$$q_u = (40)(14.83)(1.188)(0.628) + (28.5)(6.4)(1.148)(0.628)$$
$$+ \frac{1}{2}(19)(5.93)(3.188)(1)(0)$$
$$= 442.57 + 131.50 + 0 = 574.07 \text{ kN/m}^2$$

$$FS_{\text{(bearing capacity)}} = \frac{q_u}{q_{\text{toe}}} = \frac{574.07}{189.2} = 3.03 > 3\text{—OK}$$

Stem Design

The lateral earth pressure distribution behind the stem of the wall given in Figure A.5 is shown in Figure A.6a. Note that, at any depth z from the top of the wall,

$$\sigma_a = \gamma_1 z K_a$$

The horizontal component of the lateral pressure is

$$\sigma_{a(H)} = \gamma_1 z K_a \cos \alpha \tag{A.17}$$

Hence the moment at any depth z is

$$M = \frac{1}{6}\gamma_1 z^3 K_a \cos \alpha \tag{A.18}$$

The ultimate design moment (ACI Code Section 9.2.4) is

$$M_u = 1.7M = \frac{1.7}{6}\gamma_1 z^3 K_a \cos \alpha \tag{A.19}$$

The variations of M_u at $z = 0$, 2, 4, and 6 m have been calculated by using Eq. (A.19) and are tabulated in Table A.6. From Eq. (A.4),

$$A_s = \frac{0.85af'_c b}{f_y} = \frac{(0.85)(a)(20.68)(1)}{413.7} = 0.0425a \tag{A.20}$$

From Eq. (A.6),

$$M_u = \phi A_s f_y\left(d - \frac{a}{2}\right)$$

With $\phi = 0.9$ and $A_s = 0.0425a$,

$$M_u = (0.9)(0.0425a)(413.7 \times 10^3 \text{ kN/m}^2)\left(d - \frac{a}{2}\right)$$

or

$$M_u = 15{,}824.03ad - 7912.01a^2 \tag{A.21}$$

▼ **TABLE A.6** **Stem Design of a Retaining Wall**

z (m)	Thickness of stem (m)	d (m)	M_u (kN · m/m)	a (m)	A_s (cm²)
0	0.5	0.42	0	0	0[a]
2	0.57	0.49	14.06	0.0018	0.77[a]
4	0.64	0.56	112.5	0.0128	5.44[a]
6	0.7	0.62	379.7	0.0400	17.00

Note: d = thickness of stem − 0.08 m; M_u from Eq. (A.19); a from Eq. (A.21); A_s from Eq. (A.20)

[a] $A_s < A_{s(\min)}$; so use $A_{s(\min)} = 10.5$ cm²

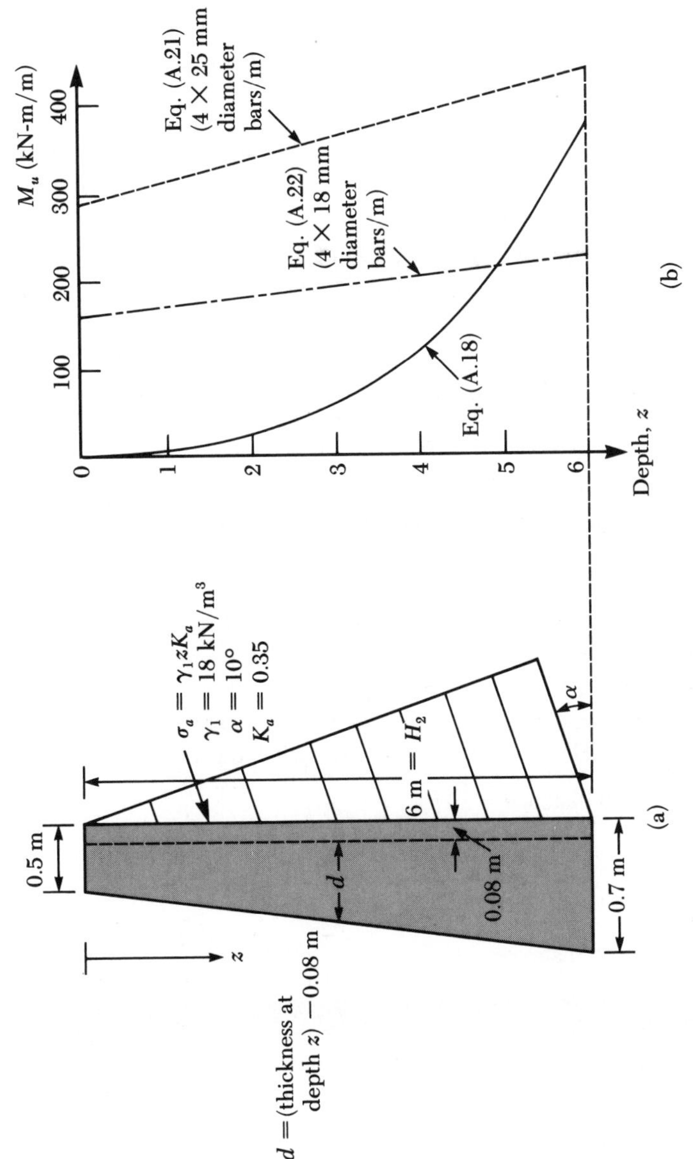

FIGURE A.6 Stem design of a retaining wall

Assume that the value of d at any depth z is equal to the thickness of the stem at that depth minus a cover of 80 mm. These values of d at $z = 0$, 2, 4, and 6 m are shown in Table A.6. Now, with known values of d and M_u at any depth, the magnitude of a can be obtained from Eq. (A.21) and thus A_s from Eq. (A.20), shown in Table A.6. Note that at $z = 0$, 2, and 4 m, A_s is less than $A_{s(\min)}$. Therefore use (ACI Code Section 14.3.2):

$$A_s = A_{s(\min)} = (0.0015)(\text{gross wall area}) = (0.0015)(1)(0.7)$$

$$= 0.00105 \text{ m}^2 = 10.5 \text{ cm}^2$$

To select reinforcement bars, try 4 × 25-mm (≈ No. 8 U.S.) diameter bars per meter for the entire height of the stem. Thus $A_s = (4)(\pi/4)(2.5)^2 = 19.63 \text{ cm}^2$. For this reinforcement, from Eq. (A.20),

$$a = \frac{A_s}{0.0425} = \frac{19.64 \times 10^{-4} \text{ m}^2}{0.0425} = 0.0462 \text{ m}$$

From Eq. (A.21),

$$M_u = 15{,}824.03ad - 7912.01a^2 = (15{,}824.03)(0.0462)d - (7912.01)(0.0462)^2$$

$$= 731.07d - 16.888 \tag{A.22}$$

Similarly, 4 × 18-mm (≈ No. 6 U.S.) diameter bars $[A_s = 10.15 \text{ cm}^2 \approx A_{s(\min)}]$ can be tried for the entire height of the wall. Next obtain

$$M_u = 378.19d - 4.52 \tag{A.23}$$

Figure A.6b shows the variation of actual M_u from Table A.6 and also the variation of M_u from the relations given by Eqs. (A.22) and (A.23). Figure A.6b shows that, for economy, the 25-mm bars should be cut off close to the base of the stem. To lap the 18-mm diameter bars to the 25-mm diameter bars, refer to ACI Code Section 12.15. Because 100% of the bars are to be lapped, the lap splice class is *C*. Thus

$$\text{Lap distance} = 1.7L_d \tag{A.24}$$

where L_d = tensile development length (see Section A.3)
$= 0.019A_b f_y/\sqrt{f'_c}$

So, the lap distance $= (1.7)(0.019)\left(\frac{\pi}{4} \cdot 25^2\right)\frac{413.7}{\sqrt{20.68}} = 1440 \text{ mm} = 1.44 \text{ m}$.

Therefore the 25-mm diameter bars must be extended beyond the cutoff point by 1.44 m. The cutoff point can be determined by combining Eqs. (A.19) and (A.23), or

$$\frac{1.7}{6}\gamma_1 z^3 K_a \cos\alpha = 378.19d - 4.52 \tag{A.25}$$

where $d = 0.42 + 0.0333z$ (A.26)

Substituting $\gamma_1 = 18 \text{ kN/m}^3$, $K_a = 0.35$, and $\alpha = 10°$ in Eq. (A.25) and combining Eqs. (A.25) and (A.26) gives $z = 4.98$ m. So extend the 25-mm bars to a height of $6 - 4.98 + 1.44 = 2.46$ m above the base of the stem.

The cutting off of bars in the tension zone (ACI Code Section 12.10.5.1) also needs to be checked. According to the ACI Code, in that section V_u should be less than or equal to ⅔ of the shear capacity of the section. The shear capacity at distance $z = 3.54$ m above the base of the stem is

$$0.17\phi\sqrt{f'_c}\,bd = 0.17(0.85)(\sqrt{20.68})(1)(0.538) = 0.3535 \text{ MN/m} = 353.5 \text{ kN/m}$$

Also, at that depth

$$V_u = (1.7)\left(\frac{1}{2}\right)\gamma_1 z^2 K_a \cos\alpha = (1.7)\left(\frac{1}{2}\right)(18)(3.54)^2(0.35)(\cos 10°)$$

$$= 66.08 \text{ kN} < \left(\frac{2}{3}\right)353.5 \text{ kN—OK}$$

Determining the Development Length of the Main Reinforcement Bars into the Foundation According to ACI Code Section 12.2.2, the development length is

$$L_d = 0.019A_b\frac{f_y}{\sqrt{f'_c}}$$

For the 25-mm diameter bars,

$$L_d = (0.019)\left(\frac{\pi}{4}25^2\right)\frac{413.7}{\sqrt{20.68}} = 848.7 \text{ mm}$$

The $L_d = 848.7$ mm calculated is more than the thickness of the base slab, which is 700 mm (Figure A.5). To obtain the proper development length in tension, use standard hooks. A standard hook develops a tensile stress that may be given as

$$f_h = \chi\sqrt{f'_c} \tag{A.27}$$

For a 25-mm diameter bar, $\chi = 30$, so

$$f_h = 30\sqrt{20.68} = 136.43 \text{ MN/m}^2$$

Hence the remaining stress to be developed is $f_y - 136.43 = 413.7 - 136.43 = 277.27$ MN/m^2. The extra embedment length required to develop the stress of 277.27 MN/m^2 is $(277.27/f_y)L_d = (277.27/413.7)(848.7) = 569$ mm ≈ 0.57 m. Figure A.7a shows a sketch of the hook and the embedded length of a bar. Note that the distance from the top of the base slab to the bottom of the hook is 0.645 m. If a cover of 76 mm is to be provided, the minimum thickness of the base slab should be $0.645 + 0.076 = 0.721$ m. So, for final design purposes, the thickness of the base slab should be increased to 0.75 m (from 0.7 m, as shown in Figure A.5).

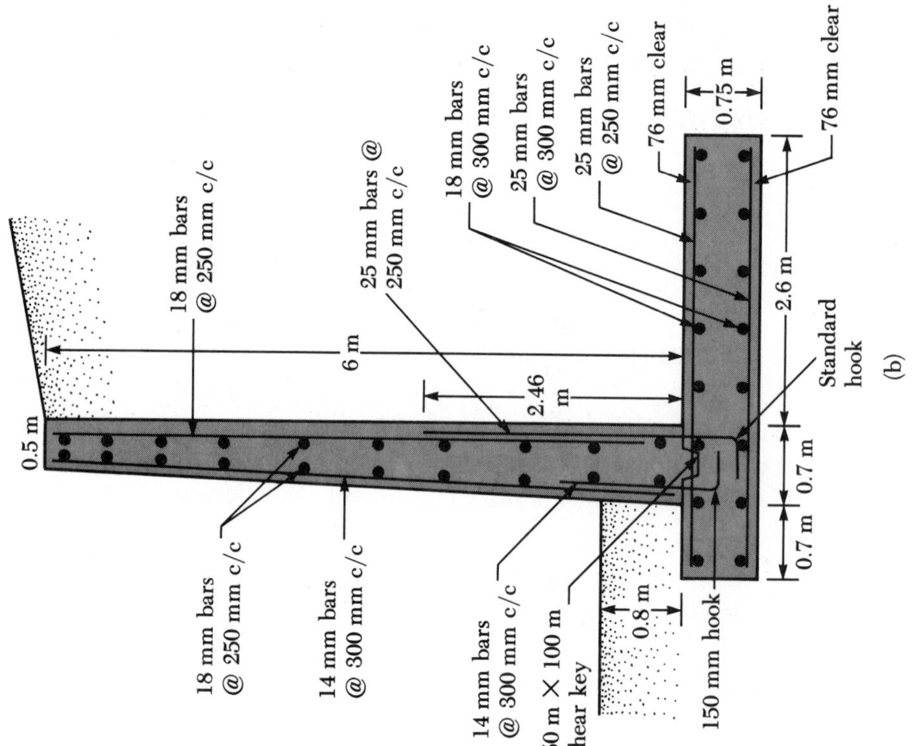

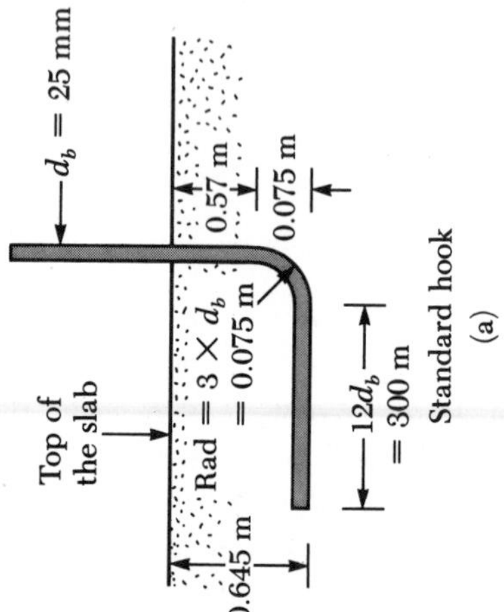

FIGURE A.7 Final design sketch of the retaining wall

Check for Shear Strength at the Base of the Wall From Eq. (A.17), the shear at the base of the wall is

$$V_u = (1.7)(V) = (1.7)\left(\frac{1}{2}\gamma_1 H_2^2 K_a \cos\alpha\right)$$

$$= (1.7)\left(\frac{1}{2}\right)(18)(6)^2(0.35)(\cos 10°) = 189.9 \text{ kN/m}$$

A shear key, usually 50 mm × 100 mm, is provided at the base of the stem. The shear stress in the key should not exceed a nominal stress of $0.2f'_c$, or 5.52 MN/m². So

$$\frac{V_u}{A_{\text{key}}} = \frac{189.9 \text{ kN}}{(10 \times 10^{-2} \text{ m})(1)} = 1899 \text{ kN/m}^2 < 0.2\phi f'_c$$

$$= (0.2)(0.85)20.68 = 3.52 \text{ MN/m}^2\text{—OK}$$

Provide a 50-mm × 100-mm shear key at the base of the stem.

Temperature and Shrinkage Steel Horizontal temperature and shrinkage steel must be provided in the wall; according to ACI Code Section 14.3.3,

$$A_s = (0.0025)(\text{gross area of the wall})$$

$$= (0.0025)(1)(0.7) = 0.00175 \text{ m}^2/\text{m} = 1750 \text{ mm}^2/\text{m of wall}$$

Hence provide 18-mm diameter bars at 250 mm center-to-center at each face of the wall ($A_s = 2032$ cm²). Also provide 14-mm diameter bars at 300 mm center-to-center at the outside face of the wall.

Heel Design

For the design of the heel, refer to Figure A.8. Note that the thickness of the base slab has been increased to 0.75 m, per the findings from the stem design. (In Figure A.5, it is 0.7 m.) The equations for load, shear, and moment for the heel of the retaining wall are as follows:

$$q = q_1 + q_2 - q_3 \tag{A.28}$$

where q_1 = load caused by the soil above the heel = γH_{av}
= 18(6 + 6.458)/2 = 112.12 kN/m²
q_2 = load caused by the concrete slab = $\gamma_c(0.75)$ = (23.58)(0.75)
= 17.69 kN/m²
q_3 = soil reaction = $q_{\text{heel}} + mx$
= $45.99 + 35.8x$

Substitution of the proper values of q_1, q_2, and q_3 into Eq. (A.28) gives the load:

$$q = 112.12 + 17.69 - 45.99 - 35.8x = 83.82 - 35.8x \tag{A.29}$$

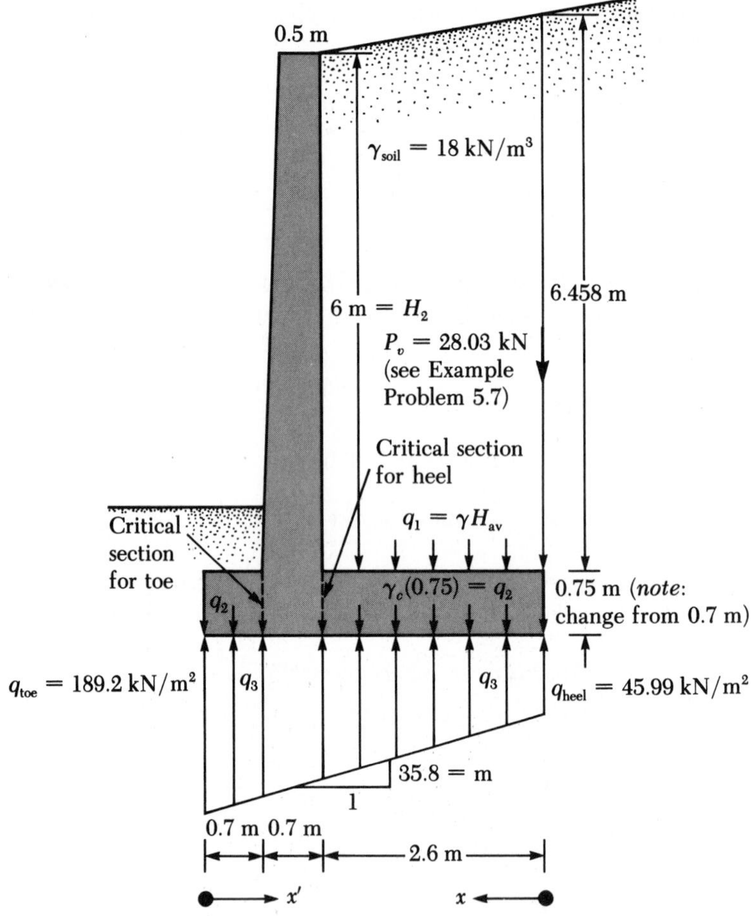

▼ **FIGURE A.8** Design of heel and toe of a retaining wall

For the shear,

$$V = \int q\, dx = 83.82x - \frac{35.8x^2}{2} + C_1$$

where C_1 = a constant

At $x = 0$, $V = P_v$ (see Figure A.8) = 28.03 kN/m, so

$$V = 83.82x - \frac{35.8x^2}{2} + 28.03 \tag{A.30}$$

For the moment,

$$M = \int V\, dx = \frac{83.82x^2}{2} - \frac{35.8x^3}{6} + 28.03x \tag{A.31}$$

The critical section for shear and moment is at $x = 2.6$ m. At the critical section, from Eqs. (A.30) and (A.31),

$$V = 124.96 \text{ kN/m}$$

and

$$M = 251.32 \text{ kN} \cdot \text{m/m}$$

Hence

$$V_u = (1.7)V = (1.7)(124.96) = 212.43 \text{ kN/m}$$

and

$$M_u = (1.7)M = (1.7)(251.32) = 427.24 \text{ kN} \cdot \text{m/m}$$

Check for Shear From Eq. (A.12a),

$$V_c = 0.17\sqrt{f'_c}\,bd$$

With $b = 1$ m, $d = 0.75 - 0.076 - 0.025/2 \approx 0.662$ m

$$V_c = (0.17)(\sqrt{20.68})(1)(0.662) = 0.5118 \text{ MN/m} = 511.8 \text{ kN/m}$$

Also

$$\phi V_c = (0.85)(511.8 \text{ kN/m}) = 435.03 \text{ kN/m} > V_u = 212.43 \text{ kN/m}$$

Hence the section is adequate for shear.

Flexural Reinforcement From Eq. (A.6),

$$M_u = \phi A_s f_y\left(d - \frac{a}{2}\right)$$

For this design, $M_u = 427.24$ kN · m/m and $a = [(A_s)(413.7)]/[(0.85)(20.68)(1)]$, or

$$A_s = 0.0425a$$

Thus

$$427.24 = (0.9)(0.0425a)(413.7 \times 10^3)\left(0.662 - \frac{a}{2}\right)$$

Solution of the preceding equation gives $a = 0.0461$ m. Hence $A_s = (0.0425)a = (0.0425)(0.0421) = 0.00178 \text{ m}^2$. This result gives a steel percentage that is higher than $s_{\min}$. So provide 25-mm diameter bars at 250 mm center-to-center, which gives $A_s = 1000/250 \times (\pi/4)(2.5)^2 = 19.63 \text{ cm}^2$.

Toe Design

As in the case of the heel design, refer to Figure A.8. The equation for load, shear, and moment at any point of toe may be written

$$q = -q_2 + q_3 \tag{A.32}$$

where q_2 = load caused by the concrete slab = $\gamma_c(0.75) = (23.58)(0.75) = 17.69 \text{ kN/m}^2$

q_3 = soil reaction = $189.2 - mx' = 189.2 - 35.8x'$

Note that in Eq. (A.32) the weight of the soil above the toe has been ignored; thus

$$q = 189.2 - 35.8x' - 17.69 = 171.51 - 35.8x' \tag{A.33}$$

$$V = \int q\, dx' = 171.51x' - \frac{35.8x'^2}{2} \tag{A.34}$$

$$M = \int V\, dx' = \frac{171.51x'^2}{2} - \frac{35.8x'^3}{6} \tag{A.35}$$

For the critical section, $x' = 0.7$ m, so

$$V = 111.29 \text{ kN/m}$$

Then

$$V_u = 1.7V = 189.2 \text{ kN/m}$$

$$M = 39.98 \text{ kN} \cdot \text{m/m}$$

and

$$M_u = 1.7M = 67.97 \text{ kN} \cdot \text{m/m}$$

Check for Shear Because V_u at the critical section of the toe is less than V_u at the critical section of the heel, the section is adequate for shear.

Flexural Reinforcement Design of the heel showed that

$$A_s = 0.0425a$$

and

$$M_u = (0.9)(0.0425a)(413.7 \times 10^3)\left(0.6 - \frac{a}{2}\right)$$

Solution of the preceding equation gives

$$a = 0.0072 \text{ m}$$

So

$$A_s = 0.0425a = (0.0425)(0.0072) = 0.000306 \text{ m}^2$$

Hence the steel percentage is

$$s = \frac{A_s}{bd} = \frac{0.000306}{(1)(0.662)} = 0.000462 < s_{\min}$$

Use $A_{s(\min)} = s_{\min} bd = (0.0018)(1)(0.75) \approx 0.00135 \text{ m}^2 = 13.5 \text{ cm}^2$. Hence provide 25-mm diameter bars at 300 mm center-to-center, which gives $A_s = 16.35 \text{ cm}^2$.

Shrinkage and Temperature Reinforcement for Heel and Toe For shrinkage and temperature, minimum steel should be used. Thus

$$A_s = s_{\text{min}}\, bd = (0.0018)(1)(0.75) = 0.00135 \text{ m}^2$$

Provide 18-mm diameter bars at 300 mm center-to-center.

The final design sketch of a retaining wall is shown in Fig. A.7.

REFERENCES

American Concrete Institute (1989). *ACI Standard—Building Code Requirements for Reinforced Concrete, ACI 318-89* Detroit.

UNESCO (1971). *Reinforced Concrete: An International Manual*, Butterworth, London.

APPENDIX

B

CONVERSION FACTORS

B.1 CONVERSION FACTORS FROM ENGLISH TO SI UNITS

▶ Length:	1 ft	= 0.3048 m
	1 ft	= 30.48 cm
	1 ft	= 304.8 mm
	1 in.	= 0.0254 m
	1 in.	= 2.54 cm
	1 in.	= 25.4 mm
▶ Area:	1 ft^2	= 929.03×10^{-4} m^2
	1 ft^2	= 929.03 cm^2
	1 ft^2	= 929.03×10^2 mm^2
	1 in^2	= 6.452×10^{-4} m^2
	1 in^2	= 6.452 cm^2
	1 in^2	= 645.16 mm^2
▶ Volume:	1 ft^3	= 28.317×10^{-3} m^3
	1 ft^3	= 28.317 cm^3
	1 in^3	= 16.387×10^{-6} m^3
	1 in^3	= 16.387 cm^3
▶ Section Modulus:	1 in^3	= 0.16387×10^5 mm^3
	1 in^3	= 0.16387×10^{-4} m^3
▶ Coefficient of Permeability:	1 ft/min	= 0.3048 m/min
	1 ft/min	= 30.48 cm/min
	1 ft/min	= 304.8 mm/min
	1 ft/sec	= 0.3048 m/s
	1 ft/sec	= 304.8 mm/s
	1 in./min	= 0.0254 m/min
	1 in./sec	= 2.54 cm/s
	1 in./sec	= 25.4 mm/s
▶ Coefficient of Consolidation:	1 in^2/sec	= 6.452 cm^2/s
	1 in^2/sec	= 20.346×10^3 m^2/yr
	1 ft^2/sec	= 929.03 cm^2/s

▶ Force:	1 lb	= 4.448 N
	1 lb	= 4.448×10^{-3} kN
	1 lb	= 0.4536 kgf
	1 kip	= 4.448 kN
	1 U.S. ton	= 8.896 kN
	1 lb	= 0.4536×10^{-3} metric ton
	1 lb/ft	= 14.593 N/m
▶ Stress:	1 lb/ft^2	= 47.88 N/m^2
	1 lb/ft^2	= 0.04788 kN/m^2
	1 U.S. ton/ft^2	= 95.76 kN/m^2
	1 kip/ft^2	= 47.88 kN/m^2
	1 lb/in^2	= 6.895 kN/m^2
▶ Unit Weight:	1 lb/ft^3	= 0.1572 kN/m^3
	1 lb/in^3	= 271.43 kN/m^3
▶ Moment:	1 lb-ft	= 1.3558 N · m
	1 lb-in.	= 0.11298 N · m
▶ Energy:	1 ft-lb	= 1.3558 J
▶ Moment of Inertia:	1 in^4	= 0.4162×10^{6} mm^4
	1 in^4	= 0.4162×10^{-6} m^4

B.2 CONVERSION FACTORS FROM SI TO ENGLISH UNITS

▶ Length:	1 m	= 3.281 ft
	1 cm	= 3.281×10^{-2} ft
	1 mm	= 3.281×10^{-3} ft
	1 m	= 39.37 in.
	1 cm	= 0.3937 in.
	1 mm	= 0.03937 in.
▶ Area:	1 m^2	= 10.764 ft^2
	1 cm^2	= 10.764×10^{-4} ft^2
	1 mm^2	= 10.764×10^{-6} ft^2
	1 m^2	= 1550 in^2
	1 cm^2	= 0.155 in^2
	1 mm^2	= 0.155×10^{-2} in^2
▶ Volume:	1 m^3	= 35.32 ft^3
	1 cm^3	= 35.32×10^{-4} ft^3
	1 m^3	= 61,023.4 in^3
	1 cm^3	= 0.061023 in^3
▶ Section Modulus:	1 mm^3	= 6.102×10^{-5} in^3
	1 m^3	= 6.102×10^{4} in^3

▶ Coefficient of Permeability:	1 m/min	= 3.281 ft/min
	1 cm/min	= 0.03281 ft/min
	1 mm/min	= 0.003281 ft/min
	1 m/s	= 3.281 ft/sec
	1 mm/s	= 0.03281 ft/sec
	1 m/min	= 39.37 in./min
	1 cm/s	= 0.3937 in./sec
	1 mm/s	= 0.03937 in./sec
▶ Coefficient of Consolidation:	1 cm^2/s	= 0.155 in^2/sec
	1 m^2/yr	= 4.915×10^{-5} in^2/sec
	1 cm^2/s	= 1.0764×10^{-3} ft^2/sec
▶ Force:	1 N	= 0.2248 lb
	1 kN	= 224.8 lb
	1 kgf	= 2.2046 lb
	1 kN	= 0.2248 kip
	1 kN	= 0.1124 U.S. ton
	1 metric ton	= 2204.6 lb
	1 N/m	= 0.0685 lb/ft
▶ Stress:	1 N/m^2	= 20.885×10^{-3} lb/ft^2
	1 kN/m^2	= 20.885 lb/ft^2
	1 kN/m^2	= 0.01044 U.S. ton/ft^2
	1 kN/m^2	= 20.885×10^{-3} kip/ft^2
	1 kN/m^2	= 0.145 lb/in^2
▶ Unit Weight:	1 kN/m^3	= 6.361 lb/ft^3
	1 kN/m^3	= 0.003682 lb/in^3
▶ Moment:	1 N · m	= 0.7375 lb-ft
	1 N · m	= 8.851 lb-in.
▶ Energy:	1 J	= 0.7375 ft-lb
▶ Moment of Inertia:	1 mm^4	= 2.402×10^{-6} in^4
	1 m^4	= 2.402×10^{6} in^4

ANSWERS TO EVEN-NUMBERED PROBLEMS

Chapter 1

1.2 a. 0.39; b. 58%; c. 16.05 kN/m^3

1.4 a. 0.55; b. 0.355; c. 57.8%; d. 106.7 lb/ft^3

1.6 a. 0.97; b. 0.49; c. 2.69; d. 115.9 lb/ft^3

1.8 $\gamma_d = 16.07$ kN/m^3; $\gamma = 17.68$ kN/m^3

1.10

Soil	*Classification*
A	SM, silty sand
B	SM, silty sand
C	MH, elastic silt with sand
D	ML, sandy silt
E	SM, silty sand
F	CL, sandy lean clay

1.12 0.5

1.14

Location	σ *(kN/m^2)*	*u (kN/m^2)*	σ' *(kN/m^2)*
A	0	0	0
B	32.48	0	32.48
C	74.36	19.62	54.74
D	133.91	50	83.91

1.16 38.8 lb/in.^{2}
1.18 1.47 in.
1.20 234.77 days
1.22 32°
1.24 $\phi = 28°$; $c = 30$ kN/m^2
1.26 8.87 kN/m^2
1.28 23.29 kN/m^2

Chapter 2

2.2 7.54%
2.4

	N_{cor}	
Depth (ft)	*Part a*	*Part b*
5	11	10
10	11	10
15	10	10
20	9	9
25	13	13
30	11	10

c. The values are approximately the same.
2.6

	N_{cor}		
Depth (ft)	*Part a*	*Part b*	*Part c*
10	9	9	9
15	10	10	10
20	11	11	11
25	14	14	15
30	14	13	15
35	14	13	16
40	14	13	16

2.8 8.07 m
2.10 44.8 kN/m^2
2.12 a. 738 lb/ft^2; b. 627 lb/ft^2
2.14 53%
2.16 56%
2.18 2154 kN/m^2
2.20 $v_1 = 678.4$ ft/sec; $v_2 = 1748.25$ ft/sec; $Z_1 = 32.87$ ft

Chapter 3

3.2 1805 kN
3.4 2.6 m
3.6 2400 kN
3.8 4.1 ft
3.10 2.75 ft
3.12 442 kN

3.14 1447 kN
3.16 435 kN
3.18 a. 39°; b. 2086 kN/m^2; c. 908 kN/m^2
3.20 579 kN
3.22 623 kN
3.24 0.54 in.
3.26 0.34 in.
3.28 88.8 lb/ft^2
3.30 157.5 lb/ft^2
3.32 a. 993 lb/ft^2; b. 788 lb/ft^2
3.34 556 lb/ft^2
3.36 1.13 in.
3.38 4.31 kip/ft^2

Chapter 4

4.2 632 kN/m^2
4.4 168 kN/m^2
4.6 19.6 ft
4.8 0.233 m
4.10

Point	*Pressure* (*kip*/*ft*^{2})
A	0.486
B	0.468
C	0.451
D	0.521
E	0.451
F	0.607
G	0.624
H	0.555

4.12 25-mm diameter bars at 175 mm center-to-center for positive reinforcement; 25-mm diameter bars at 250 mm center-to-center for negative reinforcement
4.14 15.18 lb/in.^{2}

Chapter 5

5.2 $P_0 = 84.6$ kN/m; $\bar{z} = 1.48$ m
5.4 $P_0 = 98.05$ kN/m; $\bar{z} = 1.34$ m
5.6 $P_0 = 18{,}957$ lb/ft; $\bar{z} = 6.0$ ft
5.8 17.97 kN/m
5.10 14.48 kip/ft
5.12 71.21 kip/ft
5.14 87.75 kN/m at 1.67 m from the bottom of the wall
5.16 47.08 kip/ft
5.18 a. 915.2 lb/ft; b. 6.75 ft
5.20 $FS_{(\text{overturning})} = 3.78$; $FS_{(\text{sliding})} = 1.78$; $FS_{(\text{bearing})} = 4.86$
5.22 $FS_{(\text{overturning})} = 3.38$; $FS_{(\text{sliding})} = 1.94$; $FS_{(\text{bearing})} = 4.16$
5.24 2.41 m

Chapter 6

6.2 a. 10.43 m; c. 13.56 m
6.4 $M_{max} = 1424.11$ kN-m/m; $S = 8.26 \times 10^{-3}$ m^3/m

6.6 $M_{max} = 173$ kip-ft/ft; $S = 69.17$ in.^{3}/ft
6.8 3.25 m; 59.8 kN-m/m **6.10** a. 7 m; c. 9.8 m
6.12 $M_{max} = 367.04$ kN-m/m; $S = 2.13 \times 10^{-3}$ m^3/m
6.14 $D = 5$ ft; $M_{max} = 6108$ lb-ft/ft
6.16 a. 4.1 m; c. 115 kN/m **6.18** a. 11.23 ft; c. 8.07 kip/ft
6.20 a. 2.8 m; b. 582.2 kN/m **6.22** $D = 2.73$ m; $F = 92$ kN/m
6.24 $D = 15.3$ ft; $F = 8825$ lb/ft; $M_{max} = 88{,}248$ lb-ft/ft
6.26 28 kip
6.28

Part	Δu *(m)*	*P (kN)*
a	0.084	7.91
b	0.072	12.55
c	0.063	17.51

Chapter 7

7.2 a. 5.43 in.^{3}/ft; b. 65.17 in.^{3}/ft **7.4** 4.75 in.^{3}/ft
7.6 a. 1756 lb/ft^2; 108.8 lb/ft^3; b. 718 lb/ft^2
7.8 22.94×10^{-5} m^3/m **7.10** 1.75
7.12 3.6

Chapter 8

8.2 a. 244.3 kip; b. 326.4 kip **8.4** 185.7 kip
8.6 a. 201 kip; b. 368.5 kip **8.8** 115 kip
8.10 514 kN
8.12 a. 1423 kN; b. 1645 kN; c. 1536 kN
8.14 18.87 mm **8.16** 490 kN
8.18 29.7 kip **8.20** 2177 kip
8.22 70.7% **8.24** 99%
8.26 3831 kN **8.28** 926 kip
8.30 5584 lb **8.32** 30.8 kN

Chapter 9

9.2 24.88 kip **9.4** 1758 kN
9.6 161 kN **9.8** 0.29 in.
9.10 a. 0.5 m; b. 1.5 m **9.12** a. 1113 kip; b. 599 kip
9.14 6.5 m **9.16** 4031 kN
9.18 254 kip

Chapter 10

10.2 Yes

10.4 79 mm

10.6 a. 6.1; b. moderate

10.8 0.41 ft

10.10 10.9 ft

10.12 12 ft

Chapter 11

11.2

Depth (m)	σ_a *(kN/m²)*
1	14.68
2	19.61
3	21.10
4	22.97
5	25.7
6	29.08

11.4 a. 22.33; b. 4.29; c.11.47

11.6 a. 29.97; b. 4.96; c. 18.8

11.8 $S_v = 0.336$ m; $L = 3.7$ m; $l_l = 1$ m

11.10 $FS_{(\text{overturning})} = 1.99$; $FS_{(\text{sliding})} = 1.3$; $FS_{(\text{bearing})} = 10.84$

11.12

z (m)	$T_{(N)}$ *(kN/m)*
0.4	29.1
0.8	32.9
1.2	35.6
1.6	36.4
2.0	38.2

11.14 a. 3.04/ft; b. 6857 lb/ft²; c. 3;
d.

Layer No.	*z (ft)*	$T_{(N)}$ *(kip/ft)*
1	1.3	2.83
2	2.6	3.06
3	3.9	3.09
4	5.2	3.23
5	6.5	3.32

Chapter 12

12.2 84%

12.4 $\gamma_{d(max)} = 16.84$ kN/m^3; $w_{(optimum)} = 18.1\%$

12.6 15.3 kN/m^3

12.8 $S_N = 25.48$; Rating: Fair

12.10 1606 lb/ft^2

12.12 46%

12.14

t (yr)	$u_{v,r}$
0.2	0.75
0.4	0.9
0.8	0.98
1.0	0.99

12.16 392 kN/m^2

INDEX